MAKERS OF MODERN CULTURE

edited by Justin Wintle and Richard Kenin
The Dictionary of Biographical Quotation

MAKERS OF MODERN CULTURE

Edited by
Justin Wintle

Facts On File, Inc.
119 West 57th Street
New York, N.Y. 10019

Makers
of
Modern
Culture

First published in the United Kingdom in 1981 by
Routledge & Kegan Paul Ltd., London

Published in the United States of America in 1981 by
Facts On File, Inc.

Library of Congress Cataloging in Publication Data

Wintle, Justin.

Makers of modern culture.

Bibliography: p.
Includes index.
1. Biography—20th century. I. Title.
CT120.W56   920'.009'04   80–20199
ISBN 0–87196–493–7

Printed in USA

for Peter Hopkins

Contents

Contributors

Dr E. A. Abramson
Michael Alexander
Nigel Algar
Susan Allen
Dr Roy Armes
Alison Armstrong
Dr Stephen Arnold
William Ash
Chris Auty
Professor Lawrence Badash
Dr Ninette Bailey
Paul Bailey
Joseph Bain
Malcolm Barry
Harold Beaver
Christopher Bettinson
Professor Michael Biddiss
Lewis Biggs
C. W. E. Bigsby
Marianne Boelscher
Alan Bold
David Bradby
Robin Briggs
Celia Britton
Vincent Brome
John Brooke
Geoff Brown
Professor John Russell Brown
Janice Bumstead
Dr T. E. Burke
Dr John Butt
R. P. Calcraft
Léonie Caldecott
Peter Calvocoressi
Roger Cardinal
Anthony W. Clare
Patrick Conner
Dr David Corker
Neil Cornwell
Dr John Cottingham
David Cox

Michael Cox
Professor Bernard Crick
Joyce Crick
Valentine Cunningham
Robert Cushman
Dr John Daniel
Howell Daniels
Professor Margaret Davies
Dr Jon Dorling
Philip Drummond
Paul Edwards
Dr Michel Elias
Martin Esslin
Gavin Ewart
Dr Adam Fairclough
Duncan Fallowell
Dr Stephen Fender
Dr Alison Finch
Professor Antony Flew
Professor J. E. Flower
Dr Peter France
Dr John Frazer
Professor Richard Freeborn
Ted Freeman
R. B. D. French
Professor Dennis Fry
John Furse
Peter Gathercole
Norman Geras
Andrew Gibson
Peter Gidal
Dr Ranulph Glanville
John A. Gledson
Dr Anthony Glees
Mike Gonzalez
Philip Gooden
Keith Gore
Richard Percival Graves
Dr John N. Green
Professor Charles Gregory
Paul Griffiths

Dr John Haffenden
Dr Alan Hagger
Professor Peter Hallberg
Jonathan Harvey
Nicholas Hern
Robert Hewison
Annemarie Heywood
Stephen Hinton
Dilip Hiro
Professor Matthew Hodgart
Michael Holroyd
William Horsley
Sylvester Houédard
Maggie Humm
Richard Humphreys
Dr Roger Huss
Dr Athar Hussain
G. M. Hyde
Timothy Hyman
Dr Hisao Inagaki
Dr S. J. Ingle
Adrian Jack
Dr Douglas Jarman
Alan Jefferson
Ann Jefferson
Dr Miriam Jelinek
Steve Jenkins
Professor Frederic J. Jones
Peter Jones
Verina Jones
Dr Paul Jorion
Jonathan Keates
Dr Michael Kenny
Clare Kitson
Ronald Knowles
Dr P. F. Kornicki
Dr Kim H. Kowalke
Professor Adam Kuper
John Lahr
Professor Lester C. Lamon
Philip Larkin
Robert Layton
Bobbie Lederman
A. Robert Lee
Professor Donald N. Levine
David J. Levy
David H. Lewis
Ian Littlewood

Dr Bernard Lombart
Ronald Lumsden
Peter Lund
Professor William Lyell
Rita McAlister
W. J. McCormack
Malcolm MacDonald
Professor Norman MacKenzie
Peter Mackridge
Dr Duncan MacLeod
Dr Roger McLure
Helen McNeil
Conroy Maddox
Pierre Manent
Dr R. H. P. Mason
Dr Ann Massa
Elizabeth Matthews
Dr Wolfe Mays
David Meakin
Professor Volker Meja
Wilfrid Mellers
Dr K. S. Menzies
J. G. Merquior
Linda Miles
Tom Milne
Dr John Milner
Robin Milner-Gulland
Professor Brian Moloney
Janet Montefiore
Professor Geoffrey Moore
Stuart Morgan
Blake Morrison
Eric Mottram
Chantal Mouffe
Dr D. R. Murdoch
Professor A. B. Murphy
W. H. Newton-Smith
Paul Nicholls
Robert Nowell
Geoffrey Nowell-Smith
Michael O'Brien
Kaori O'Connor
Terence O'Keeffe
Dr Robert Olby
Roger Opie
Christopher Ormell
David Osmond-Smith
Timothy O'Sullivan

Professor Ian Parrott
Christopher Petit
Pierluigi Petrobelli
Monica Petzal
Michael Pick
Dr W. S. F. Pickering
John Porter
Stephen Pruslin
Dr M. L. G. Redhead
Professor John Rex
Dr Dieter Rexroth
Professor James Richmond
Professor Peter Rickard
Mark Ridley
Dr Neil Roberts
Michael Rosenthal
Francis Routh
Michael Rubinstein
Dr Charles Rycroft
Dr Geoffrey Sampson
Dr Christopher Schaefer
Michael Schmidt
Fred Scott
Edward Seidensticker
Professor D. L. Shaw
Dr Chris Shorley
Paul Sidey
Phil Slater
Keith Smith
Penny Sparke
Jon Stallworthy
Frank G. Steele
Professor Nico Stehr
Professor Sam Stevens

Corbet Stewart
Anthony Storr
Dr David Sturgeon
Professor A. V. Subiotto
Dr Slavka Sverakova
David Sweet
Gary Thompson
Dr J. E. Tiles
Dr Mary Tiles
David Trotter
Pat Turner
Wilfried van der Will
Professor Robert G. Vaughn
Dr Shirley Vinall
Christopher Wagstaff
Helen Waites
James Faure Walker
Ronald G. Walker
Chris Wallace-Crabbe
Giles Waterfield
Gray Watson
Margaret Whitford
Dr Arnold Whittall
Dr John Whitworth
Brian Wicker
Annwyl Williams
Karel Williams
Jason Wilson
Richard Wilson
Simon Wilson
Dr J. M. Winter
Christopher Wintle
Dr Hilary Wise
Gayle Graham Yates

Acknowledgments

My thanks to all the contributors. Special thanks to Dr John Cottingham, Professor Bernard Crick, Dr Ann Jefferson, Professor José Merquior, Annwyl Williams, Karel Williams and Christopher Wintle, who each gave much advice and help during the compilation. Further thanks to Dr John Carroll, Dr Brian Powell and Dr Charles Webster; and to Clare Alexander, Carol Stevens and Eileen Wood at Routledge & Kegan Paul. Final thanks to Mrs Jennifer Martin, who typed the entire manuscript, and to Carol Gardiner who prepared it for the printer.

J. W.

Introduction

This book is simply intended to be useful. In a world of many teachers, many styles, many philosophies even, a world in which new orthodoxies dissolve before they can harden, accounts of modern culture must be as sympathetically diverse as needs to know vary. Each entry is concerned with the cultural achievement (not always positive) of a particular individual; but each entry is also written by an individual, and unlike many dictionary-makers, I have not tried to disguise the fact. Deliberately I encouraged the contributors to be interpretative, within certain limits. Why? Because culture itself (and by culture I mean *how we see ourselves*) is interpretative, and it is that, above all else, which I wished to be conveyed. To pretend that culture, or any part of culture, can be neatly packaged in an objective summary, in an authorized version, is directly antithetical to the business of culture.

Perhaps any attempt to put a subject as enormous and diffuse as culture, even of a particular period, within the confines of a reference-book is questionable. But set against that is the need to know. The commonest shorthand for referring to a group of ideas or system of thought is to use the name of its progenitor. (But not the only shorthand, and so the Index supplies reference to such terms as Cubism, Logical Positivism and Frankfurt School.) Vast complexes of attitude and behaviour, of interpretation, are denoted by words like Platonic, Christian, Buddhist, Cartesian, Newtonian, Kantian, Darwinian, Marxist and Freudian. On a lesser scale too, when we discuss divisions within the great systems, we still tend to employ eponymous labels: Lutheran and Calvinist, for example, Trotskyite and Leninist. We also use the names of established figures within a particular field to characterize its newcomers. A poet is described as Wordsworthian or Audenesque; a painter is 'like Matisse' or 'like Jackson Pollock'. But unless we are already familiar with the work of Wordsworth and Auden, of Matisse and Jackson Pollock, the meanings of these terms are lost.

But what is also lost, what becomes buried beneath the shorthand, even when it does effectively communicate a meaning, is that the work of a Buddha, a Christ, a Darwin or a Marx is the product of a particular intelligence interacting with particular societies at a particular stage in their development.

In treating culture through its originating individuals it is the particularity of individual intelligence that is emphasized, that is given pride of place. This will annoy all strict determinists, but I believe there are solid grounds for the course adopted. While it would be senseless to deny that each individual is largely the outcome of other individuals, just as one set of conditions is the offspring of its predecessors, the principle of individual originality should also be allowed. No twins, by the time they are adult, remain identical; no two white middle-class male novelists, raised in the same street, will write quite the same novel – and the differences are often not trivial. There is in everyone the germ of difference, and it is this germ that is responsible for the achievements of the past, of whatever sort, and will be responsible for the achievements of the future.

Why, therefore, anatomize those achievements into schools and movements, into -isms and -ologies? If we wish to understand them we should begin where they begin: with the individuals who created them.

Such an approach has two immediate advantages: it disposes of the need to present what is not fact as fact; and it goes some way to seeing off the need to employ dictionaryese, the crabbed and clipped prose-style that, in many reference-books, only ossifies its subject-matter.

Rather, I have sought to impose as little uniformity of style as possible on each entry. In this respect, *Makers of Modern Culture* is the expression of its contributors, not of its editor; a collective enterprise without, I hope, a collective face. And this, in my view, given its subject, is exactly how it should be.

There have been editorial biases, however, and these should be declared. Chief among them of course has been my working definition of culture, which has inevitably provided the overall framework. Here I endeavoured to steer a middle course between the old sense of 'relating exclusively to the fine arts' and the newest application (total culture) 'referring to every goddam item, thought and disposition'. Originally I was concerned with the notion of *ideas*, and it was only when I considered what *kind* of ideas I wished to be represented that the word *culture* came gradually to seem appropriate. For I wanted to combine the ideas of philosophers, sociologists, anthropologists, theologians and political theorists with the ideas of the arts, of music, cinema, painting, fiction and poetry, fields in which ideas are overtly expressed as much in·form as in content.

But what was the precise link between the arts and the disciplines enumerated above? What conjoins the humanities? Scattered across so many fields, do the ideas of each have anything in common? The answer was a functional yes: each idea or group of ideas could be seen as an act of understanding and interpretation: of ourselves, of our relations between ourselves and each other and to the world around us: essentially of *how we see ourselves*. And the only single term available for that formula was the word *culture*.

What I mean by culture, therefore, is rooted in a broad response to the word *ideas*, and in the ways we seek to articulate our perceptions in a wide spectrum of activities. *How we see ourselves* also had the advantage of seeming to offer hospitality to the principle of individual originality.

By far the hardest task confronting me was the selection of people to be included, partly because I had already decided that their number would have to be limited in order to give each entry proper space. Three groups whom one might have expected to find had to be excluded. These are, with certain exceptions, politicians, performing artists and those scientists who are remembered more for research than for conceptualization. Constraint of space was the major determining factor here, but not the only one. Simply I felt, since I was looking for excuses, that the majority of politicians and inventors can be seen to work within established paradigms; although where a politician or scientist has made a significant theoretical contribution, or has substantially altered the paradigm, then he or she has been included. Similarly with performers. Actors, dancers, singers, orchestral conductors achieve prominence and influence by interpreting the ideas of others. This is not to belittle their contribution, which not only breathes life into culture itself but plays a crucial role in shaping a society's cultural institutions. In some cases however, where they have been responsible for new idioms (an obvious example is in jazz), performers or groups of performers have been admitted.

Those whom I have included are people who have initiated cultural change in the period covered, whose names occur most frequently in the critical press, and whose achievements seem the most significant. The period covered extends from about 1914. I say 'from about', because in practice it was impossible to be rigid, and necessary to operate what amounts to a two-tier system: those who produced important work before as well as after 1914 are included, unless they were also significantly productive before 1900, in which case they must await their turn until the compilation of *Makers of Nineteenth-Century Culture*. Some important turn-of-the-century figures, omitted here, are not therefore being ignored. Several (the most notable perhaps being Hardy and Gaudier-Brzeska) had claims to be in both volumes.

But let me not evade the real issue, the judgment of merit as regards who is and who is not included. To set out with the modern period may seem almost cavalier: for whereas there can with hindsight exist something akin to a consensus as to who was most important in earlier periods, to draw up a short-list of outstanding contemporaries and near-contemporaries can only be to offer hostages to fortune. In making the selection I tried to be as open-minded as possible, while seeing to the needs of each specific field within the context of the whole and pursuing a hybrid sense of balance. In doing this it deserves to be said here, and not in the generally unread Acknowledgments, that I was constantly indebted to many contributors who offered criticisms of the list I circulated, and made suggestions for its improvement. The final roll-call, therefore, represents a consensus to a degree the original did not; but because I did not accept every suggestion that was made, responsibility for absentees lies entirely at my door.

Finally, the articles themselves. It will be noticed that there is a considerable difference in length from one entry to the next. Such discrepancy does not always or necessarily reflect a judgment of the relative stature of the figures concerned. Different writers required different lengths not just because of conventional importance, but because of different degrees in complexity and output. In addition it should be said that there has been a deliberate bias, both in the matter of length and in the number of subjects chosen, towards writers over artists. A regard for language as the life-blood of culture also explains the preponderance of English-writing subjects over others. This book, compiled in, say, Uruguay, would obviously have contained a somewhat different pantheon of culture-makers. Simply, consolidating existing boundaries has been seen to be at least as important as extending new horizons.

But that said, and because the enterprise is in itself inter-disciplinary, I am confident that every reader will find new horizons within these pages – mainly because I found so many myself. At least, I hope that some readers will be led into the complexities of modern culture as practised in Britain and the United States: to this end brief bibliographies are provided.

Justin Wintle
London 1980

A

1

AALTO, Hugo Alvar Henrik 1898–1976

Finnish architect and designer

Some eleven years younger than Le Corbusier*, Alvar Aalto belonged to the second generation of architects in the International Modern movement, the architecture dominant in the twentieth century in much the same way that baroque was dominant in the seventeenth. To it Aalto brought an informality and sensitivity, deriving ultimately from the crudely charming but usable vernacular of his nature country, that most commentators would agree had previously been lacking. Partly because he eschewed theorizing and polemics, and partly because of the enormous variety of his invention over a period of more than fifty years, he qualifies more than any other as the architect's architect, among both his contemporaries and his successors.

Aalto was born into a family with strong rural traditions. While his mother's father was a Swedish-speaking forester, his own was a land surveyor concerned chiefly with the construction of railroads through forests. For most of his childhood he lived in Jyväskylä, in a house shared by a Russian countess and an alcoholic confectioner. Admonished 'always to remain a gentleman' by his father, he left home at eighteen to study architecture at what is now the Helsinki Technical University, but returned to Jyväskylä after he had qualified five years later. There he set up his first office (1923–7) and began the career that was to make him famous. Broadly this can be divided into three periods (although elements characteristic to each tended to reappear in the others): an early white period of the /International style; a red, or brick period; and a marble period, beginning *c.* 1960. His earliest works, however, were in a neo-classical idiom. These include the Jyväskylä Workers' Club (1923–5) and the rather delicate church at Muurame (1926–9). It was not until he moved his office to the old Finnish capital, Turku, in 1927, that his originality began to assert itself. Probably the decisive inspiration came from his first wife, the architect Aino Marsio, a designer of considerable imagination whom he married in 1925, and with whom he worked in closest collaboration until her death in 1949. The changes in his style can be most clearly observed in the development of his designs for the town library at Viipuri (now Vyborg in the USSR). This project began in 1928 along neo-classical lines, but by the time of its completion in 1935 it had been transformed into an obviously modernist building. With its sunken reading-well, its cylindrical skylights, and the wavy form of its lecture-hall ceiling, it also served as a test-bed for many of Aalto's prototypes. Concurrently he worked on a number of other projects in the same idiom, of which the most important are the newspaper offices of Turun Sanomat in Turku (1927–9), and the remarkable Tuberculosis Sanatorium at Paimo (1927–33), one of the outstanding buildings of the International style.

In 1933 he again moved offices, this time to Helsinki. This coincided with the creation of Artek, a firm he set up to produce the furnishing, light-fittings and vases which he had also begun to design for his interiors. Aalto's furniture, made inexpensively from bent-wooden laminates that gave him the fluidity of form he so liked, while straightforwardly satisfying the obvious functional requirements, has had considerable impact and, unlike the furniture designed by most other eminent architects, is still in production. To finance this operation he sought the patronage of Harry and Maire Gullischen, for whom he later built the Villa Mairea (1938–9), one of the great modern houses, referred to by Siegfried Giedeion as 'architectural chamber music'.

It was towards the end of the 1930s that Aalto evolved his second, 'red' phase – although such a soubriquet does little justice to the variety of either materials or designs employed. The most important constructions here were the expressionistic Cellulose Sulphate Factory at Sunila (1936–9); the Baker House Dormitory for MIT in Chicago (where he was Professor of Architecture 1945–9), his first foreign commission; the Iron Federation Building in Helsinki (1951–5); the complicatedly sited National Pensions Institute (1952–6); the Jyväskylä Pedagogical University (1950–7); the Communist Party Headquarters and Culture House (1955–8), with its curvy walls built out of a specially designed reinforced brick; and Louis Carré's private villa at Bazoches in France. But of all his buildings in this style the Town Hall and Civic Centre for the small community at Säynätsalo (1950–2) in the centre of Finland was the masterpiece, where he achieved a dignified harmony between his materials (brick, wood and copper) and the surrounding forest.

Aalto's last period was altogether more mannerist in its approach, and is characterized by the use of white marble and blue ceramic tiles. Although even his earliest buildings showed an unusual interest in fragmented forms, curves and non-right-angles, these themes now became particularly prominent, perhaps encouraged by the nature of the commissions he received, often for churches and auditoria, buildings that demand unusual forms and precise foci. Amongst these he seems to have considered Finlandia Hall, with its added Conference Centre (1967–75), his testament, realizing the main generative element of his partially executed and slightly Italianate Central Helsinki plan (1959–64). The Cultural Centre at Wolfsburg, West Germany (1953–63), the suite of public buildings at Seinäjoki (1959–65), and the lonely Scandinavian House in Reykjavik, Iceland (1965–8) are also outstanding. These projects were carried out in partnership with his second wife, Elissa Mäkiniemi, whom he married in 1952 and who still maintains their office.

As is the case with most architects Aalto's reputation rests on his larger, public buildings, and yet he was also involved with work of a humbler kind. After the Second World War, when Finland was in need of massive reconstruction, Aalto played a major role in the re-planning of Lapland, an area particularly devastated by the German withdrawal. As a part of this responsibility he designed a series of self-help, minimal space, expansible timber houses of remarkable ingenuity.

Dr Ranulph Glanville

Aalto's relatively scant literary output has been collected in *Alvar Aalto*, ed. Karl Fleig (3 vols, Zürich 1963). See also: George Baird, *Alvar Aalto* (1971); *Architectural Association Quarterly*, vol. 10, no. 3 (1978); and Paul David Pearson, *Alvar Aalto and the International Style* (1978).

2
ABE KŌBŌ 1924–

Japanese writer

Much of his youth was spent in Manchuria due to his father's position at the Medical College in Mukden. Exposed to the incongruity of a traditional Japanese upbringing and ideology implanted against an alien cultural background, Abe Kōbō was subsequently deeply affected by the social and spiritual disintegration which accompanied the downfall of the Japanese empire in Manchuria as well as in Japan. Already before completing his medical studies at Tokyo University he had begun to write poetry and short stories and by the end of the 1960s was, alongside Mishima*, the most widely translated post-war Japanese author.

Unlike Mishima and in striking contrast to the tradition prevailing even amongst contemporary Japanese writers and artists in general, Abe's writing did not stem from an attachment to an established writer or group; as a whole it is strikingly individualistic, without distinct links to any current, traditional or foreign literary trend or creed. In this respect, too, he is said to personify the rift created in Japan by the post-war experience, as well as the final emergence of Japanese literature as part of a modern universal, world culture.

Early enthusiasm for Rilke* and Poe, a period of affinity with leftist movements and surrealist groups, and a lasting admiration for Kafka* are amongst the known aesthetic and philosophical influences, reflected in the author's preoccupation with matter, concept and meaning, the real and unreal, in his black humour and frequent surrealistic motifs, such as metamorphosis, which are particularly prominent in his earlier works. However, despite their wide popularity and high critical appraisal, his later novels and dramas completely elude categorization as well as serious literary analysis. The critic, like the reader, has his established precepts and attitudes one by one thrown into doubt, while becoming increasingly disorientated, irritated and at the same time drawn further into the story, searching for its apparent yet obscure hidden meaning. The open-ended series of events, often unlikely or bizarre, is narrated in detail usually by the protagonist himself with convincing immediacy. The resulting impression is that of a possibly allegorical but certainly plausible mystery which brings into focus the alienation and virtual displacement of the contemporary urban man and the absurdity of his quest for something tangible in the tenebrous, confusing world that surrounds him.

This background theme permeates all of Abe Kōbō's prolific work, irrespective of genre or immediate subject-matter – more explicit in his essays and travel sketches, yet equally present in the radio, stage and screen adaptations of his fiction as well as in original dramatic works. The latter's continuing success since the mid-1950s is no doubt due to the prominent features of all his writing: the ingenious tight plotting, the dramatic quality of each episode as well as the meticulous and dynamic descriptions of the phenomena of the physical world, which bring a uniquely poetic element into the blank, harsh atmosphere created by the otherwise detached, documentary, and often derisively objective style of narration.

Dr Miriam Jelinek

Abe Kōbō's novels include: *The Woman in the Dunes* (*Suna no onna*, 1962, trans. 1964); *The Face of Another* (*Tanin no kao*, 1964, trans. 1966); *The Ruined Map* (*Moetsukita chizu*, 1969, trans. 1963); *The Box Man* (*Hako otoko*, 1975, trans. 1977).

3

ADAMOV, Arthur 1908–70

Russo-Armenian/French dramatist

Adamov was brought up in Baku on the Caspian Sea, where his family owned a number of oil wells. He was looked after by an Armenian nanny, a French demoiselle and an overbearing sister. His father had a Dostoevskian passion for gambling and some of his most unhappy childhood memories were associated with the family's travels from one European gambling centre to another. In this way most of the family wealth had been lost by 1917, when the remainder was expropriated by the Revolution. The family passed rapidly from riches to rags, moving first to Germany, then to Paris where, as a young man, Adamov frequented the fringes of the Surrealist circle and made friends with Bataille, Blin, Giacometti*, Gilbert-Lecomte, Artaud*. He wrote a number of Surrealist texts and translated Rilke* and Jung* into French. This period was marked by a life of loneliness, obsession and a variety of neurotic practices described in searing detail in his two major autobiographical works, *The Confession (L'Aveu,* 1946) and *Man and Child (L'Homme et l'Enfant*, 1968).

After the war he began writing plays, completing seven in the years 1947–53. They depict a world of terror and persecution, in which isolated individuals suffer inexplicable tortures, often associated with figures of authority within the family. Adamov found that writing about his obsessions afforded him a measure of liberation from them and, although his name had become associated with the avant-garde theatre of Ionesco* and Beckett*, his play *Ping-Pong* (1955) heralded a move away from fatalism towards the political plays of the next ten years, which were broadly Marxist in inspiration.

His next play *Paolo Paoli* was produced by Roger Planchon at Lyon in 1957. It was hailed as the first 'Brechtian' play to be written in France and was the only one of Adamov's plays to enjoy a long run. After this he wrote a massively researched play on the Commune, *Spring '71 (Le Printemps '71*, 1960), followed by three radio plays and more stage plays on political themes. But he was forced into a period of relative inactivity by poor health and a disintoxication cure. In the late 1960s, however, he wrote two of his best plays, *Off Limits* (1968) and *If Summer came again (Si l'été revenait*, 1969).

For a time, it was common to think of his career as dividing sharply into Absurdist and Political, but this view has given way to an understanding of how all his work is marked by a complex interplay of private neurosis and public, political forces. Everything he wrote is characterized by extreme candour, considerable stylistic originality and a determination to question received opinions. His late plays show a complex awareness of the problems of ideology in communications and were an attempt to combine the demystifying function of Brecht's* drama with the powerful characterization of Chekhov and Strindberg. At their best, as in *Off Limits*, they can be pithy, powerful, imaginative. At other times they are dogged by wordiness. Combining characteristics of Naturalism, Symbolism and Expressionism, they require a director with a fertile imagination and a sure touch. Planchon's production of *AA, Théâtres d'Adamov*, an amalgam of Adamov's work put on in 1974, showed how successful it can be in the theatre. Planchon considers that his work resembles that of Büchner (whom Adamov also translated into French) – plays that will never have a large popular success, but that will be a constant source of interest and inspiration to future dramatists.

David Bradby

Théâtre (from 1953); *Ici et Maintenant* (1964). See also René Gaudy, *Arthur Adamov, Essai et Document* (1971).

4

ADLER, Alfred 1870–1937

Austrian psychiatrist

Alfred Adler was born on 7 February 1870, the second of six children in the family of a merchant named Leopold Adler. He was brought up in a suburb of Vienna, and suffered so severely from rickets in early childhood that he did not walk until he was four years old. This early infirmity not only dictated his choice of medicine as a career, but also convinced him of the importance of organic, physical defects as determinants of personality. Since he was unable to join other boys in sport, he read extensively, and, in later life, became an eloquent speaker who could quote the Bible and who drew upon an extensive knowledge of Schopenhauer, Nietzsche and Kant. His favourite authors were Homer, Goethe and Shakespeare. He studied medicine at the University of Vienna, obtaining his degree in 1895. After three years working in hospital, he launched into private practice as an eye specialist, but soon turned to general practice. Finally, as a consequence of attending lectures by the neuropsychiatrist Krafft-Ebing, whose writings had steered Jung* in the direction of psychiatry, Adler decided to specialize in the study and treatment of nervous disorders. During his early years in practice, Adler developed a passionate concern with social problems, became a socialist, and published a pamphlet on the health of tailors, who often had to work in deplorable conditions, and who seemed particularly prone to develop eye complaints. Adler's interest in the problems of society remained with him all his life, and shaped his later psychological concepts. In 1909 he wrote a paper on the psychology of Marxism which, unfortunately, has disappeared. His Russian wife was a friend of Trotsky* and other revolutionaries.

In 1902, Adler's early advocacy of Freud* brought him an invitation to join Freud's discussion group; and, in 1910, he was made president of the Vienna Psychoanalytic Society into which that group had developed. However, Adler's ideas became increasingly at variance with what were then the fundamental tenets of psychoanalysis, and, in 1911, Adler and a few followers parted company with Freud and his disciples. Adler was the first major dissenter amongst the early psychoanalysts. In 1912, he founded his own 'Society for Individual Psychology', and, after the First World War, started a large number of child guidance clinics in Vienna. Adler's 'Individual Psychology' reached its peak of popularity during the 1920s and early 1930s. At one time there were thirty-four local associations promoting Adlerian ideas, the majority of which were in central Europe, but others of which were founded in the USA and Great Britain. Adler himself edited a journal in German; and there were also journals in English on both sides of the Atlantic which served to promulgate the Adlerian point of view. However, the advent of Hitler* caused the disappearance of most of the associations in Europe, and the majority of Adler's followers were compelled to emigrate. Adler himself died of a heart attack on 28 May 1937 in Aberdeen. With his death the German and American journals ceased publication, and the English journal was also discontinued at a later date. For a time, Adler's ideas and even his name faded from sight; but, in recent years, it has been increasingly recognized that he did make important contributions to psychological medicine, and that he was the originator of ideas which have been appropriated or taken over by others.

Adler's original point of view was first made manifest in 1907 when he wrote a paper on 'The Inferiority of Organs' and the way in which individuals compensated or over-compensated for such defects. This was clearly based upon his own experience of rickets in childhood. Adler's insistence upon the psychological importance of birth order was as clearly derived from the fact that he himself was a second child. Adler believed that second children tended to be particularly ambitious because they were always striving to surpass their elder sibling. He considered that Freud's resentment of his own divergence from psychoanalysis was typical of an eldest son who felt threatened by dethronement by younger siblings.

In Adler's view, 'aggression', in the sense of self-assertion and the will to power, took precedence over sex as the prime mover of human conduct. Adler pictured the child as feeling itself to be weak and inferior, and therefore motivated towards achievement in order to overcome such feelings. Since, in Western society, men have more power than women, the feminine pos-

ition is one of weakness; and both sexes exhibit a 'masculine protest' in so far as they strive to overcome a sense of inferiority to those they envy and try to emulate.

Very early in life, the child develops a particular 'style of life' in accordance with his genetic endowment, position within the family, and type of upbringing. Thus, the clever child tries to achieve superiority through his intellect, whilst his physically more agile brother develops his muscles. Adler used often to ask his patients to recall their earliest childhood memory, alleging, with some justification, that such memories often revealed what 'style of life' the individual had adopted from the beginning. If this point of view is adopted, it follows that personality is more determined by the goals toward which the individual is striving than by what had happened to him in the past, as Freud supposed. Adler freely acknowledged a teleological viewpoint; and with it linked the notion of fictional goals, based upon misconceptions, which he derived from Hans Vaihinger's book *The Psychology of 'as if'*. Vaihinger advanced the notion that men lived by a number of fictional ideas which had no basis in fact, but which nevertheless provided guides toward living or goals at which to aim. If one believes in hell and heaven, for example, such a belief is bound to have a profound effect upon one's conduct. Neurotics are often motivated by fictional goals, of which the desire to gain power over others rather than the wish to achieve co-operative relations on equal terms is the most important.

As Adler grew older, his concept of striving for superiority became modified into something analogous to self-actualization or self-realization; a goal of completion which was always sought, but never quite achieved. However, this ideal was never a matter of the perfection of the individual in isolation, but was always firmly anchored within a social context. Freud regarded society as a limitation upon the individual, restraining him from the uninhibited expression of his instincts. Adler, true to his socialist principles, thought of social interaction and co-operation as essential to mental health. Adler's later work repeatedly refers to *Gemeinschaftsgefühl* or 'social interest' as it has been rather lamely translated. No one could be healthy unless he had replaced the goal of dominating his fellow men with the goal of an ideal community. As Adler himself wrote: 'Individual Psychology has uncovered the fact that the deviations and failures of the human character – neurosis, psychosis, crime, drug addiction etc. – are nothing but forms of expression and symptoms of the striving for superiority directed against fellowmanship. . . . Never can the individual be the goal of the ideal of perfection, but only mankind as a *co-operating community*. A *partial community* of any kind – perhaps groups that are associated through certain political, religious, or other ideals – is also not sufficient. Neither do we mean the *existing* society, but an *ideal* society yet to be developed, which comprises *all* men, all filled by the common striving for perfection. This is how the Individual Psychology concept of social interest (*Gemeinschaftsgefühl*) is to be understood.'

Adler was essentially a teacher and publicist rather than a theoretician. His books, which are generally written in a popular style, are often repetitive, because they nearly all took origin from lectures. Many of Adler's ideas, like the famous 'inferiority complex', have been incorporated into the teaching of school-children and the counselling of adults without recognition being given to their originator. Adler was a man with considerable force of character and charm of personality. The virtual eclipse of his school of Individual Psychology after his death bears witness not only to his persuasive powers as an individual, but also to his failure to present his ideas in other than a popular form. Whilst Jung and Freud are both represented by Collected Works in many volumes of varying degrees of profundity and erudition, Adler has left no such corpus of scholarly work behind him. In spite of this, his influence has probably been underestimated. His early insistence upon the importance of aggression has been fully vindicated. His recognition of 'organ inferiority' and its consequences provided a springboard for the development of psychosomatic medicine. He founded the first child guidance clinic; and his theories have provided inspiration to several generations of teachers. In addition, his emphasis upon the individual's need to be a part of, and play a part in, society was a valuable antithesis to Freud's negative view of altruism and Jung's concentration upon the development of the individual in isolation.

Anthony Storr

Translations of Adler's works include: *The Neurotic Constitution* (1921); *The Practice and Theory of Individual Psychology* (1925); *Understanding Human Nature* (1928); *What Life should mean to you* (1932). See also: Phyllis Bottome, *Alfred Adler: a Biography* (1939); H. L. and Rowena R. Ansbacher, *The Individual Psychology of Alfred Adler: a Systematic Presentation and Selection from his Writings* (1956); H. L. and Rowena R. Ansbacher, *Superiority and Social Interest: A Collection of Later Writings* (1965); Hertha Orgler, *Alfred Adler; the Man and his Work* (1973).

5
ADORNO, Theodor Wiesengrund 1903–69

German social theorist

One of the century's most complex thinkers, Theodor W. Adorno was born into the wealthy half-Jewish Wiesengrund family in Frankfurt. While still at school, he was befriended by the journalist and critic, Siegfried Kracauer, who opened up problems ranging from Kant's *Critique of Pure Reason* to the mass media. At the age of twenty-one, under the illustrious neo-Kantian, Hans Cornelius, Adorno received his doctorate from Frankfurt University for a thesis on Husserl's* phenomenology. Meanwhile this brilliant scholar had acquired from his half-Corsican ex-opera-singer mother not only the surname of Adorno, but also an inextinguishable interest in music. With his doctorate secured, Adorno joined Alban Berg* in Vienna to undertake an intensive study of piano technique in the circle around Arnold Schoenberg*, the originator of atonal music. But Adorno never abandoned his theoretical pursuits, and after leaving Vienna he became increasingly involved with the Frankfurt Institute of Social Research, particularly after the appointment of his friend Max Horkheimer* as Director in 1930 ushered in the Institute's 'Frankfurt School' era.

Adorno's Marxism owed most to Georg Lukács's* *History and Class Consciousness* of 1923, with its key concept of 'reification' showing how social relations of production come to appear as qualities of *things*; this, what Marx called 'commodity fetishism', proved the cornerstone of Adorno's entire work. In the first volume (1932) of the Institute's *Zeitschrift für Sozialforschung* (Journal of Social Research), he located the socially critical function of music in its refusal to 'represent', that is, be *equivalent to* anything, even the political struggle against capitalism; this isolation was painful, but to do 'more' meant reification, musical hara-kiri.

Although Adorno was able, perhaps due to a combination of his Italian surname and idiosyncratic style, to visit Germany as late as 1936, the revocation of his right to teach in 1933 had driven him to try and establish himself at Oxford. This was apparently unsuccessful, and in 1938 he crossed the Atlantic to work as musical director in Paul Lazarsfeld's Princeton Radio Research Office. Adorno's crusade against reification hardly equipped him for what Americans understood by 'media research', however, and he took refuge in Horkheimer's newly established Institute in New York, contributing to its journal, which eventually appeared in English as *Studies in Philosophy and Social Science*. When the latter was discontinued in 1941, Adorno moved to California, to find himself in a community of distinguished exiles, including Thomas Mann*, who drew on his musical expertise heavily (plagiaristically, in Adorno's estimation) for the technical details of *Doctor Faustus*. Greatly influenced by Husserl's *Crisis of European Science*, Adorno now devoted himself to a joint undertaking with Horkheimer, the *Dialectic of Enlightenment* (trans. 1972): the 'Light of Reason' (symbolized by Bacon, but prefigured in Greek philosophy) had stopped short of a critique of its own structure, thereby becoming a new and dangerous mythology, subjecting the world to the totalitarian command of technological domination. For Horkheimer, this book seems to have been a farewell to Marx, who was indicted as a spell-bound accomplice of this tradition; Adorno, on the other hand, though equally critical of Marx's techno-centrism, was in many ways only extending to philosophy and science the never-to-be-forgotten message of 'commodity fetishism' that he had learned (via Lukács) precisely from Marx.

Adorno also worked on Horkheimer's *Studies in Prejudice*, contributing to the volume on *The Authoritarian Personality*. But by the time this appeared in 1950, Adorno had followed Horkheimer back to Frankfurt, to teach at the University, help re-establish the Institute for Social Research, and still engage in a prolific output of theoretical writings. As the *enfant terrible* of the German Sociological Society, he even found time to provoke the 'Positivism Dispute' at its 1961 Conference. Karl Popper*, himself a critic of positivism, argued that knowledge advanced by rejecting accepted theories as incompatible with the facts and advancing new theories capable of subsuming these facts. Adorno in turn rejected this 'critical rationalism' of Popper's as itself a variant of positivism: the incompatibility of theories with 'facts' was the necessary expression of an objectively antagonistic social reality, and it was the latter, rather than isolated theories, that had to be criticized and overturned.

This, as Adorno rightly stressed, constitutes the project of a 'critical theory of society' as formulated by Horkheimer in the 1930s. Ironically, however, as this theory (now dubbed 'Frankfurt School') assumed concrete political force in the student anti-authoritarian movement, Adorno found himself in the position of seeing his genuine reservations *vis-à-vis* that movement used by the authorities to justify an armed repression that was even more distasteful to him. He collapsed and died in the tumultuous days of 1969. By then, however, 'Frankfurt School' theory was making its mark on Anglo-Saxon intellectual life via Herbert Marcuse*, and this brought in its wake a string of translations of Adorno's works. These have left their mark in many forms: in a generalized antipathy to 'disciplines' such as sociology; in institutions like the Centre for Contemporary Cultural Study at Birmingham; in American journals such as *Telos* and *New German Critique*; and in a growing understanding that Marx's value theory is not a question of 'economics', but a critique of capitalist relations of production.

Phil Slater

Adorno's *Collected Works* (Frankfurt 1970 onwards) will fill over twenty volumes. The English reader is best advised to start with the selected essays entitled *Prisms* (1967), and then tackle the joint work with Horkheimer, *Dialectic of Enlightenment* (1972; German original 1947). The most difficult but logically constitutive book is *Negative Dialectics* (1973; German

original Frankfurt 1966). See also: *Philosophy of Modern Music* (1973; German original 1949) and *The Positivism Dispute in German Sociology* (1976; German original Darmstadt 1969). A partial intellectual autobiography is available in the uncharacteristically readable 'Scientific Experiences of a European Scholar in America' in D. Fleming (ed.), *The Intellectual Migration: Europe and America, 1930–1960* (1969). Gillian Rose, *The Melancholy Science* (1978), provides a tightly structured survey and level-headed critique of Adorno's vast intellectual production.

6

AIKEN, Conrad Potter 1889–1973

US poet

Conrad Aiken was born on 5 August 1889 at Savannah, Georgia, where his father practised as a doctor and took an amateur interest in writing and painting. When Conrad was eleven his father killed his mother, then committed suicide. As Aiken recalled in his stream-of-consciousness autobiographical essay *Ushant* (1952), this traumatic event haunted him for the rest of his life: 'After the desultory early-morning quarrel, came the half-stifled scream, and then the sound of his father's voice counting three, and the two loud pistol-shots; and he had tiptoed into the dark room, where the two bodies lay motionless, and apart, and, finding them dead, found himself possessed of them forever.' Much later Aiken re-created the nightmare in the nursery-idiom of his poem 'Obituary in Bitcherell':

> Then all went sour: all went mad:
> the kitchen was sullen: the house was bad . . .
> And the morning quarrel, and shots, and then
> four orphaned children taken north again.

After the tragedy Aiken was taken to live with relatives in Massachusetts and in 1911 he was at Harvard where his fellow students included T. S. Eliot*, Robert Benchley and Walter Lippman. Unlike Eliot Aiken was not passionately attracted to experimental verse and his first collection, *Earth Triumphant* (1914), comprised narrative tales in the manner of Masefield though, in a foreword, Aiken claimed that 'before I ever heard of Masefield I was experimenting with narrative poems of modern daily life'. His next collection, *Turns and Movies* (1916), substituted the influence of Masefield for that of Edgar Lee Masters. Aiken's early reputation as an incorrigibly derivative writer was confirmed when he published *Blue Voyage* (1927), a novel modelled on Joyce's* *Ulysses*.

Up to then Aiken had been an evasive writer and man – avoiding the literary challenge of his childhood and, surprisingly, gaining exemption from military service during the First World War by successfully insisting that his pursuit of poetry constituted an essential industry. With *Preludes for Memnon* (1931) he claimed his own poetic territory by exploring with technical precision and subjective delicacy the destruction of innocence by the inevitability of death. His majestic lines reached out to examine the decay implicit in all organic growth and this theme was extended in a subsequent collection of Preludes, *Time in the Rock* (1936), on which his position as a major poet rests. Displaying a wide variety of poetic forms Aiken faced his memories of tragedy with dignity and, occasionally, grim humour:

> Give us this day our daily death, that we
> may learn to live.

Aiken's greatest influences were Shakespeare, Blake, Poe, the French Symbolists, and Emily Dickinson (whose poems he edited in 1924). He had none of the precocity of Eliot and Pound* and his stature was only gradually appreciated by the reading public. However, he was showered with honours after the publication of his *Collected Poems* (1953): the Pulitzer Prize and the National Book Award in 1954; the Bollingen Prize in 1956; the Fellowship of the Academy of American Poets in 1957; the Gold Medal for Poetry in 1958. His best poetry and prose habitually used the eternal theme of the voyage from birth to death and it took all Aiken's metrical dexterity to avoid the monotony implicit in the subject. In his masterly Preludes and his finest novels – for example the psychologically intense *Great Circle* (1933) – he proved a powerful writer who created a modern myth of personal martyrdom.

Alan Bold

Aiken's *Collected Poems* (1970) are complemented by *The Collected Short Stories* (1966); Aiken's work is the subject of a critical study *Conrad Aiken* (1962) by Frederick J. Hoffman.

7
ALBEE, Edward Franklin 1928–

US dramatist

The adopted son of a millionaire, Albee was quickly promoted as a natural successor to Arthur Miller* and Tennessee Williams*, both of whose careers seemed in decline in the late 1950s. But when he refused to capitalize on his early success by obligingly abandoning what many critics regarded as a wilful experimentalism his reputation suffered an ill-deserved decline.

His first one-act play, which received its premiere in Berlin in 1959, was *The Zoo Story*. Not the absurdist play which it was taken to be, it was in fact a powerful plea for the centrality of human relationships and a rejection of what is presented as a destructive materialism. Much the same could be said of his first Broadway production, *Who's Afraid of Virginia Woolf?* (1962). Ostensibly a Strindbergian drama of sexual conflict, it was also a Catonian warning against the erosion of human values and the consequence of a failure to engage the real. Set in the ironically named New Carthage, it combines a brilliantly witty drama of personal relations with an articulate assault on the collapse of private and public values. In his early works, indeed, he is something of a social critic, insisting that while 'we are no longer looking for panaceas against all evils or solutions manufactured abroad', his concern was 'to prevent our political system from being denatured by too much facile conformism', asserting that this 'is already a programme in itself'. But, if *Who's Afraid of Virginia Woolf?* advocated a confrontation with social and sexual realities, it evaded the question of definition. Reality was taken to be substantial and immediate. In his subsequent plays he pressed his enquiry further. *Tiny Alice* (1965), for example, examines the nature of religious conviction in a play whose symbols many found baffling and whose characters have begun a slide towards abstraction which strengthened with his subsequent plays. In *A Delicate Balance* (1966), awarded the Pulitzer Prize denied to his earlier and more worthy *Who's Afraid of Virginia Woolf?*, he dramatized his sense of an absurdity which could no longer be neutralized by a quixotic gesture or even a determined effort to reestablish communal values.

And so the confidence of his early plays slowly erodes until, in *Quotations from Chairman Mao Tse-tung* (1968), words become found-objects and character little more than social role, a series of contingent acts. The play combines literal quotations from Mao's* work with a poem by the nineteenth-century American sentimental poet Will Carleton. Only one character speaks lines actually written by Albee and each narrative is broken into fragments, these being juxtaposed to one another. The effect is to create occasional moments of consonance, as passages seem to comment on one another. But for the most part any coherent meaning must be the product of individual members of the audience as they struggle to create totality out of fragments – a process which is offered as an accurate account of the process whereby experience is reduced to meaning.

Albee's experiments in recent years have tended in this direction. The world, which in his early plays he still believed could be saved with compassion and a liberal respect for reality and a language which, if wilfully deceptive, could still offer hints for the restoration of harmony, collapses. In *Counting the Ways* and *Listening*, rather as in Pinter's* and Beckett's* more recent work, the word 'reality' has lost all meaning. We are left with a present which is no more than the recalling of a past which may never have happened.

Even the substance of the physical surroundings has shrivelled into a space which offers no clue as to meaning or time.

For a time Albee tended to alternate original plays with adaptations. But the latter were almost invariably disappointing. Either he set himself to dramatize the undramatizable – in the form of Carson McCullers's southern grotesques in *The Ballad of the Sad Cafe* (1963), or James Purdy's surreal characters in *Malcolm* (1966) – or he simply adapted a work, like Giles Cooper's *Everything in the Garden* (1968) which benefited little from transposition from an English to an American environment. His real talent lay in the consummate skill with which he dissected private and public deceptions and articulated first his liberal convictions and subsequently his deepening scepticism about life and art.

Albee's work is characterized by a coruscating wit, an articulateness which at times became his subject as well as his method, a fascination with language and a sensitive control over rhythm and tone, which gives his works at times a musical structure. He has remained unafraid to experiment. Never allowing himself to become trapped in the simple repetition of his early success, he has paid for his sustained experimentation with a decline of critical and popular reputation. But he remains a powerful playwright, without doubt the American dramatist most completely dedicated to examining the essence of theatricality and dissecting the nature of his own language and art.

C. W. E. Bigsby

Albee's other works include: the one-act plays, *The American Dream* (1962), *The Sandbox* (1960), and *The Death of Bessie Smith* (1960); and three other full-length dramas, *All Over* (1971), *Seascape* (1975) and *The Lady from Dubuque* (1980). Critical works include: C. W. E. Bigsby, *Albee* (1969) and *Edward Albee* (1975); Michael Rutenberg, *Edward Albee: Playwright in Protest* (1969); and Anne Paolucci, *From Tension to Panic: The Plays of Edward Albee* (1972).

8
ALBERS, Josef 1888–1976

German/US teacher, painter

Born in Bottrop in 1888 Josef Albers prepared himself early for what was to be a long career in education. He gained his teaching certificate in 1908 and began teaching in his home town. He became more interested in art and in 1920, after studies in Essen and Munich, he began, as a student, his thirteen-year association with the influential school of Art and Design, the Bauhaus, founded by Walter Gropius* in 1919. As a teacher first at Weimar then at Dessau, where the school

transferred in 1925, Albers became a major figure, running the famous Preliminary Course which all students took before opting for later specialization.

When the school was forced to close in 1933 he left for America, continuing his advocacy of Bauhaus concepts for sixteen years at Black Mountain College, North Carolina, and later at Yale University where he was head of the Design Department from 1950 to 1958. Between his retirement and his death at the age of eighty-eight he was much honoured by art institutions and universities in the USA and Germany.

In America his influence as an art educator has been particularly extensive and the course he established at the Bauhaus, which attempted to instil a discriminating respect for the singular physical properties of a wide range of art and craft materials, was much imitated. He extended this idea to include colour, treating it too as a material from which structures could be made. In his publication *The Interaction of Colour* (1963) he charts at great length the different perceptual effects caused by modifying the area, proximity and chromatic intensity of several flat colours within a simple abstract format.

Much of Albers's graphic work is weakened by a didactic desire to trap the unwary viewer. A typical series of drawings of 1964, *Structural Constellations*, for instance, consists of linear structures which at first sight suggest an interlocking pattern of isometric cubes. However on closer examination it becomes clear that because of deliberate anomalies the pattern cannot be consistently interpreted as a three-dimensional construct and so the casual response to 'see' volumes on a flat surface is intentionally penalized. However, pedagogy is largely absent from his famous series of geometric colour paintings, started in 1949, entitled *Homage to the Square*. With only minor variations all these paintings use the same simple centred schema of four squares of diminishing size, one inside the other, flatly painted in different colours which are adjusted to associate or disassociate visually in many subtle chromatic exchanges.

In particular these works have had a marked influence on painters in the 1960s, such as Frank Stella* and Kenneth Noland*, and in general though Albers does not approach the rigour of comparable Europeans like Max Bill, his procedural discipline and the uncompromising nature of his abstraction have made him a useful counterbalance to the emotional and imagist excesses of other American artists.

David Sweet

Other writings: *Search Versus Research, Three Lectures* (1969); *Despite Straight Lines* (1977). See also *Poems and Drawings* (1958). About Albers: François Bucher, *Josef Albers: An Analysis of his Graphic Constructions* (1961); Eugen Gomringer, *Josef Albers* (1968).

9

ALTHUSSER, Louis 1918–

French Marxist philosopher

Born in Birmandreis, near Algiers, Althusser studied philosophy at the École Normale Supérieure in Paris, where he has remained a teacher ever since. As a young man he was active in Catholic youth organizations, but a few years after the Second World War he joined the Parti Communiste Français. In the late 1960s his attempt to redefine Marx's historical materialism made him the star of the moment within left-wing intellectual circles. Already, however, the most significant outcome of Althusserianism would seem to be *Marx's Capital and Capitalism Today* (1977, ed. Antony Cutler), a collection of essays in post-Marxist economic theory by ex-Althusserians.

In *For Marx* (*Pour Marx*, 1965, trans. 1969) and *Reading Capital* (*Lire le Capitale*, 1965, trans. 1969), Althusser tried to legislate on the distinction between sciences and ideologies. Earlier positivist philosophers of science, like Carnap* or Popper*, had similar legislative pretensions, but Althusser's position in 1965, when these texts were first published, was different in a number of respects.

Althusser developed an anti-empiricist epistemology. He criticized a conception of knowledge as abstraction; 'empiricism' supposed that a knowing subject abstracted the essence of a real object. This established a problem of knowledge which was insoluble because possible knowledge was circumscribed by the predicates of the subject. Althusser proposed an alternative conception of knowledge as production; this 'theory of theoretical practice' described how knowledge of the real was produced inside theory by applying theoretical means of production to specific raw materials. The empiricist problem of knowledge was displaced because a knowing subject did not foreclose the Althusserian knowledge process.

On the basis of this anti-empiricist epistemology, Althusser was able to propose new criteria of scientificity. The corollary of the theory of theoretical practice was a new technical practice of reading, 'symptomatic reading', which disclosed the theoretical means of production in different discourses. These means of production were systems of concepts which Althusser termed 'problematics'. Ideologies and sciences, the vicious and virtuous forms of knowledge, were separated by a difference in the systematic form of their problematics. This difference provided a criterion of scientificity which was then applied to the specific task of defining Marxist scientific theory and demarcating that discourse from its ideological competitors. Unlike earlier positivist philosophers of science, Althusser was not preoccupied with rationalizing the success of the natural sciences.

Marxist theory, or 'historical materialism', interrelated a regional theory of economy and a global theory of society or 'the social formation'. Marx theorized the economy as the sphere of dominance of a mode of production which was a historically variable combination of invariant elements. Engels and Mao* theorized the social formation as so many practices (economic, political, ideological and theoretical) which made up a complex totality irreducible to one level. The theoretical systems of the regional and global theories were complex and exemplary. Marx's theory of the economy established 'structural causality' whereby phenomena were subject to determination by structural relations. Marxist theory of the social formation established 'overdetermined contradiction' whereby phenomena developed according to their conditions of existence in a complex whole. This complexity of articulation justified Althusser's claim that historical materialism was the science of history.

Various bourgeois theories of society and of the economy competed with historical materialism. All bourgeois theories of society were 'historicist' in that they presumed society was reducible to one essential level. All bourgeois theories of the economy were 'humanist' in that they departed from the assumption of economic man. The theoretical systems of historicism and humanism were simple and vicious. Bourgeois theories of society established an 'expressive causality' whereby the phenomena of an historical epoch were reducible to the inner essence of that epoch. Bourgeois theories of the economy established a 'mechanical causality' whereby economic phenomena were the effects of the existence of economic man. This simplicity of articulation justified Althusser's claim that all bourgeois theories of society and of the economy were ideological.

Althusserian legislation required a first difference between the theory of theoretical practice and empiricism and a second difference between historical materialism and its competitor discourses. The problem was that both these differences were unsustainable.

The theory of theoretical practice did not avoid what Althusser had criticized in empiricism. According to Althusser's epistemology, a 'knowledge effect' was produced inside scientific theory by theoretical practice, but the produced knowledge referred to and 'appropriated' the real. As Glucksmann argued, this presupposed that there was some kind of mysterious correspondence between the categories of (theoretical) reason and the structure of reality. In this respect, Althusser's new epistemology was like old Kantianism or Spinozism. Althusser had not evicted or demoted the subject but only changed the identity of the subject by substituting a rationalist reason for the empiricist's experience. The theory of theoretical practice only reposed the problem of knowledge in a variant form using many neologisms.

As for the difference between the complexity of historical materialism and the simplicity of its competitor discourses, this difference was a surface effect which was compatible with similarity of organization at an underlying level. Economic man acted as a substantial essence in bourgeois theories of the economy. The relations of production, established by a determinate mode of production, acted as a kind of relational essence in Marx's theory of the economy. Even if the structures of Marxist theory established a complex system of relations, there was still a theoretical essence. When analysis disclosed the same complexity of organization at every point inside the Marxist theory of the social formation, complexity itself acted as a kind of theoretical essence. A theoretical essence is defined not by substantial identity or simplicity, but by the relation of expression from essence to theoretical epiphenomena. By this criterion, there is no difference of form between historical materialism and its competitor discourses.

Althusser's characterization of historical materialism and its competitor discourses was also thoroughly uninformative. It encouraged dismissive criticism of ideological discourses like Hegelian philosophy or classical political economy. Everything which came before Marx and Freud* could be written off as humanist and historicist. Althusser's praise of Marx's scientificity was equally unfortunate because it promoted a discussion of Marx's achievement and development in comparative static terms. His analysis simply antithesized the young humanist Marx of the 1844 *Economic and Philosophical Manuscripts* and the old historical materialist Marx of *Capital*.

If Althusser has never accepted the necessity for rereading Marx and redefining historical materialism, since 1967 he has accepted that his earlier texts are complicit in the philosophy which they criticize. In *Lenin and Philosophy* (various essays, trans. 1971) and *Essays in Self-Criticism* (various essays, trans. 1976) he reacted by jettisoning the theory of theoretical practice and proposing a second definition of philosophy as a double intervention in political practice and theoretical practice. The Marxist's 'materialist philosophy' is no more scientific than idealist philosophy, but it can and must be used to defend historical materialism. Thus, materialist philosophy is 'in the last instance, class struggle in the field of theory'. Althusser's erstwhile epistemological legislation is now transformed into theoretical opportunism for the good of the cause; the existing resources of Western philosophy can be used to help everything come right (that is, left) in the end. This post-1967 position neither resolves nor transcends the problems posed by the failure of the earlier differentiations.

Karel Williams

Other works: *Politics and History* (various essays, 1972); *Positions 1964–75* (1976). See: A. Glucksmann,

'A Ventriloquist Structuralism' in *New Left Review* (issue 72, 1968); N. Poulantzas, *Political Power and Social Classes* (1973).

10
AMIS, Kingsley 1922–

British novelist and poet

Kingsley Amis was born in London and educated at the City of London School and St John's College, Oxford. After military service during the war he combined writing with lectureships in English at Swansea, in America and at Peterhouse, Cambridge. His first novel was *Lucky Jim* (1954). The rancorous tone, the brashness and the protests of its central character Jim Dixon against a vaguely conceived establishment of tradition and authority allied Amis in the public mind with writers like John Braine and John Osborne*. Over the years Amis, like the other 'Angry Young Men', has changed, at least politically: 'Why Lucky Jim Turned Right' is the title of one of his essays. This would be insignificant were it not that one of Amis's traits as a novelist is his capacity to be easily irritated and irritating; he has always enjoyed baiting his enemies, left and right. The rich and socialist composer-conductor who figures in *Girl, 20* (1971) makes himself ridiculous, though only in the eyes of the narrator and reader, by his middle-aged pursuit of the dubious property of youth, the politically and culturally fashionable. In a typical Amis come-uppance he is assaulted and his Stradivarius smashed after he has performed at a pop concert. Characters with the names of people on the left of British politics appear as members of the Catholic hierarchy in *The Alteration* (1976), an 'alternative world' science fiction novel which posits that the Reformation never took place and that the curiously lopsided England which results is subject to an authoritarian religious rule from Rome. Amis mistrusts the doctrinaire, whether political, religious or social. He is aided in his satire on everything progressive and permissive by an acute eye and ear, the ability to 'place' a character by his possessions or his idiom.

The moral aspect of Amis's novels, the complement of the satire, is less assured. In an early book like *That Uncertain Feeling* (1955) the hero settles for his own concepts of decency and moderation; in others, such as *One Fat Englishman* (1963) or *I Want It Now* (1968), the awfulness of the central characters is partly mitigated by the greater awfulness of others surrounding them or a tentative improvement towards the end – 'Helping each other not to be as bad as we would be on our own' as the girl puts it in *I Want It Now*. Increasingly Amis has been preoccupied with death and ageing: *The Anti-Death League* (1966), his most ambitious and least comic novel, describes an army establishment set up to develop a germ-warfare project. Military routine, which also forms the background to some of Amis's short stories (*My Enemy's Enemy*, 1962), is disrupted by a kind of saboteur of convention who protests not merely against the army's activities but against the conditions of life, particularly those that entail premature or unreasonable death. The novel is an impressively systematic presentation of 'a bit of life it's death to enter'. In *Ending Up* (1974) Amis describes with cold precision the antics of a group of old people; the book culminates in a multiple death-scene. *Jake's Thing* (1978) combines misanthrophy and misogyny as a menopausal don (male) embraces a well-wined solitude in preference to the miseries of sexual rejuvenation.

'The genres . . . have been fascinating me for over thirty years,' Amis has written. In the last decade he has produced, interspersed with more overtly comic novels, versions of the ghost story (*The Green Man*, 1969), a period detective story (*The Riverside Villas Murder*, 1973), as well as a thriller and a piece of science fiction. The interest of these novels comes not only from their narrative strengths and the quality of the writing as well as Amis's respectful but not reverential treatment of each genre but also from the way in which the concerns of his comic fiction are carried over into other forms. In siding with the taste of the 'ordinary chap' Amis administers a snub to the pretentious and pseudo-intellectual. Some of his later poetry ('Ode to Me'; 'Crisis Song') illustrates well this no-nonsense public stance.

Philip Gooden

Amis's other books include: *I Like it Here* (1958); *Take a Girl Like You* (1960); the 'James Bond' novel, *Colonel Sun* (under the pseudonym Robert Markham, 1968); a critical work on science fiction, *New Maps of Hell* (1960); *Collected Poems 1944–79* (1979).

11
ANDERSON, Sherwood 1876–1941

US writer

As Irving Howe points out in his study of Sherwood Anderson, the educated American reader of the 1920s admired Anderson's work almost as much as his counterpart of today admires Faulkner's*. It took twenty years for some of the excitement to wear off and even in the early 1940s, when Lionel Trilling* dared to attack Anderson's reputation (in the *Kenyon Review*, 1941), it created a minor literary sensation. Anderson, in fact, is one of those writers whose stories have an especial validity for Americans because of some area of peculiarly American experience which they lay bare – in this case the hidden longings of small-town Middle Westerners. Judged by less parochial standards, however, Anderson's work leaves something to be desired. Only in, perhaps, half a dozen of his short stories, among them 'I Want to Know Why', 'I'm a Fool', 'The Egg' and 'Death in the Woods', does he achieve the very highest quality.

Anderson was a mystic in the Lawrentian mould, although he lacked Lawrence's* intellectual grasp and moral strength. He reacted against the narrowness and religious bigotry of the Middle West, as a number of late-nineteenth-century writers (Edgar Watson Howe, for example, and Hamlin Garland) had done before him. But, unlike them, Anderson had the benefit of Freud*, and he used him unmercifully. He joined the band of rather selfconscious 'bohemians' (Carl Sandburg*, Floyd Dell, Ben Hecht) who flaunted their differentness in the face of materialistic Chicago in the 1920s.

His career both before and after this decisive event in his life was colourful. He was born in Camden, and brought up in Clyde, Ohio, one of seven children of an itinerant sign-painter and harness-maker. In a childhood without much schooling he grew up to know the farm-hands, the local printers and the race-meeting touts about whom he writes in his stories. When he was nineteen his mother died, and Anderson worked in Chicago and various parts of the Middle West. In 1898, he joined the National Guard and was sent to Cuba at the end of the Spanish-American War. On his return, at the age of twenty-three, he spent a year at a high school in Springfield, Ohio, then became a successful writer of advertising copy in Chicago. In 1907, he formed the Anderson Manufacturing Company in Elyria, Ohio, but, although he made a very successful living manufacturing paint for five years, he suddenly, in the middle of dictating a letter to his secretary, walked out of his factory. He was discovered some days afterwards in a hospital in Cleveland. The nervous breakdown which followed this event afforded him, according to his own account, a means of escaping, at the age of thirty-six, from middle-class respectability into the world of 'art'. He went to Chicago to become a writer, leaving his wife and three children behind. The marriage did not break up until four years later, but Anderson was to be married three times after that.

Windy McPherson's Son (1916) is the story of a poor country boy who became a successful manufacturer and then gave up his business in order to seek the 'truth'. This was followed in 1917 by *Marching Men*, a novel about the Pennsylvania coalfield, in 1918 by a book of verse, *Mid-American Chants*, and in 1919 by the 'novel' which made his reputation, *Winesburg, Ohio*. *Winesburg, Ohio* is a series of psychological studies of small-town life, some of them, like 'Hands', delicately and poetically told, but others marred by that sense of grievance which runs through Anderson's work. Like his fellow 'bohemians', he believed that organized society stood in the way of human fulfilment. In the Anderson view of existence an individual will be awakened and try to break out, but for the most part he and his fellow human beings wander frustrated and lonely through a life from which they extract no joy.

In 1921, after the appearance of his novel *Poor White*, Anderson went to Europe and met Joyce*, then to New Orleans, where he 'discovered' William Faulkner. *The Triumph of the Egg* and *Horses and Men*, two of his best books of stories, appeared in 1921 and 1923. He continued writing novels, stories and autobiographical accounts but he became increasingly interested in politics in his later years, and in the end settled down in Marion, Virginia, where he edited both the Democratic and Republican newspapers.

Anderson's contribution to American literature lies in the skill of his story-telling. 'Story-teller' in fact is what he called himself in his autobiography. Like the men and boys of his youth in Ohio, he liked to spin tales, and he developed the raconteur's art into a literary method. This method is diametrically opposed to that of such subtle and sophisticated literary artists as Hemingway* and Faulkner, for where they imply, Anderson 'talks about' in the traditional manner. There is no colourful evocation, no 'sensuous immediacy' through the use of carefully selected physical details, yet, as in 'The Egg', he manages to convey a sense of tension and of the sadness of the human predicament. He is equally good in his first-person stories, of which 'I Want to Know Why' is one of the most powerful. This device for conveying verisimilitude, used first in a great way by Mark Twain in *Huckleberry Finn*, is in fact the triumph of American short-story writers. Here they seem to feel most at home. The slang may be dated, but the sense of sincerity is powerful. Out of a small human incident a parable of human life is created. There are few more poignant stories than 'I Want to Know Why' about a boy's loss of innocence and initiation into the world's corruption.

Geoffrey Moore

See: Irving Howe, *Sherwood Anderson* (1951); James Schevill, *Sherwood Anderson: His Life and Work* (1951); C. B. Chase, *Sherwood Anderson* (1977); W. D. Taylor, *Sherwood Anderson* (1977); R. L. White, *Sherwood Anderson* (1977).

12
ANOUILH, Jean 1910–

French dramatist

Despite being dismissed as 'played out' by one critic as early as 1946, Anouilh has been one of the most successful and prolific dramatists this century. None of his plays is universally considered to be great, but several of them are studied and performed in schools all over the Western world and in this way, if in no other, his work has had a pervasive influence.

His career is a long one; his first play was composed in 1929 and he is still writing. As well as plays, he has written a great many film scripts, and this work has given him financial independence since about 1935. His early life was spent in Bordeaux, where his father was a tailor and his mother played in a local orchestra. At the age of nine he moved with his family to Paris, where he went to school, then worked briefly as a secretary to Louis Jouvet and later as a copy writer in an advertising agency. He has always lived a retiring life, refusing to give interviews. He has survived successive movements in the French theatre, even being championed by Sartre* as an Existentialist playwright; but he has not become identified with any one movement and has continued to produce work that is idiosyncratic.

His plays depict a wide variety of periods and subjects but his style bears the imprint of the inter-war period when he was beginning to write; both Pirandello* and Giraudoux exerted a strong influence upon him. The characters in his plays suggest the inter-war preoccupation with finding a non-realistic style rather like commedia dell'arte: they usually lack depth, being reduced to a single social or psychological governing principle. But they are brought face to face in a series of conflicts which, though sometimes simplistic, are generally well managed. In Anouilh's best plays, they are placed in a frankly theatrical context which, paradoxically, can sometimes increase the sympathetic involvement of an audience.

Anouilh's main themes are the damaging effects of past experience and the idealist's hopeless dream of innocence. Despite his frequent use of religious subjects (e.g. Antigone, St Joan, Becket), his plays make little appeal to transcendental values. Tiresias is significantly absent from his *Antigone* and Antigone herself is just one of a series of heroines who accept death not for the sake of a positive belief, but because they cannot bear the thought of growing up. Few of his plays have any pretensions to social relevance. Though they vary from the light and humorous to the bitterly ironic, they all belong to a theatre of types, providing social satire of only the most generalized kind. This kind of play can seem very relevant at times of social crisis, as *Antigone* did at the time of its first performance in 1944, but will not bear the weight of consistent interpretation along social or political lines.

Some have seen Anouilh's repeated refusal of realism as refreshing; others have criticized it as escapism. His most recent plays revolve around what appear to be autobiographical problems of the writer for whom imaginary characters take on a greater reality than the people he meets in everyday life. His influence on modern culture is more as a popularizer of the techniques and ideas of others, such as Pirandello, than as an original thinker.

David Bradby

Anouilh's plays are published by La Table Ronde in a collected edition beginning with *Pièces Noires* and *Pièces Roses* (from 1958). See also Philip Thody, *Anouilh* (1968).

13
APOLLINAIRE, Guillaume (Wilhelm Apollinaris de Kostrowitzky) 1880–1918

French poet

Illegitimate and of mixed parentage – his mother Polish, his father Swiss – Apollinaire's education took place mainly in the south of France. After short periods in Paris and Belgium, he spent the year 1901–2 as a private tutor in Germany, before launching himself into the literary and artistic life of Paris. He made the acquaintance of many of the major artists of the time and, over the years, established himself firmly as an influential figure in the avant-garde. Although not of French nationality (his naturalization was granted only in 1916) he joined up at the outbreak of war, and saw active service until 1916, when he was wounded in the head by a shell fragment. In the remaining two years of his life he returned to his former existence in Paris. He died on 9 November 1918, a victim of the Spanish 'flu epidemic.

Apollinaire's lasting reputation is based mainly on his work as a poet, but his importance during his own lifetime owed much to his activity as an art critic who, between 1902 and 1918, a particularly fertile period for painting in Paris, defended and promoted new tendencies as well as the work of individual artists (Fauves, Cubists, Futurists; Picasso*, Matisse*, Derain, Braque* . . .). In 1913, he published *Cubist Painters* (*Les peintres cubistes, méditations esthétiques*, 1913, trans. 1976). As evidence of the position he occupied, it is worth noting that he wrote the programme note for the ballet *Parade* (1917), written by Cocteau*, setting and costumes by Picasso, music by Satie*, choreography by Léonide Massine, performed by Diaghilev's* Ballets Russes.

Apart from his critical writing, his prose works include *L'Enchanteur pourrissant* ('The rotting charmer', 1909), with characters such as Merlin, Helen of Troy, the Sphinx; *L'Hérésiarque et Cⁱᵉ* ('Heresiarch & Co.', 1910), a collection of strange, fantastic stories; *The Poet Assassinated* (*Le Poète assassiné*, 1916, trans. 1968), a further collection of stories; and the best-known of his three excursions into the theatre: *Les Mamelles de Tirésias* ('Tiresias's breasts') produced in 1917, and celebrated,

amongst other reasons, for its sub-title, *drame surréaliste* – one of the earliest uses of this epithet.

He began publishing poetry as early as 1898, but his main period of activity dates from 1902, when he settled in Paris and came into contact with men like Alfred Jarry, Max Jacob, André Salmon, and Picasso. The poems of his earlier years were collected in *Alcools* ('Alcohol', 1913); in a lecture on 'La Phalange nouvelle', delivered the same year, he defined his poetry as 'the search for a lyricism at once humanist and new' ('la recherche d'un lyrisme neuf et humaniste à la fois'). The summary is apt in that his revolutionary aspirations (partly under the influence, at this time, of Blaise Cendrars, and involving startling juxtapositions of images, the use of free verse and the suppression of punctuation) are tempered by a lyricism of a traditional nature (inspired, for example, by unrequited love). His second collection of poems, *Caligrammes* (1918), as its name suggests, is noteworthy for the attempt to manipulate the text of the poem in order to produce the visual representation of an object.

Views have differed on the question of Apollinaire's originality, and precedents can indeed be found for many of the techniques he exploited. But he remains a figure of importance: by bringing together within his work the diverse notions and practices of his day, he succeeded in focusing the poetic movement of his time; the more so, perhaps, since he was sensitive to established poetic qualities, and therefore set his innovations in the context of a tradition.

Keith Gore

See: P. Pia, *Apollinaire* (1974); R. Little, *Guillaume Apollinaire* (1976); D. Oster, *Guillaume Apollinaire* (1978).

14
ARENDT, Hannah 1906–75

German/US philosopher and political theorist

Hannah Arendt was one of that generation of German-Jewish refugees who did so much, perhaps no one more than she, to rescue American intellectuals from an excessive parochiality. She was born in Hanover and studied philosophy together with theology and Greek at Heidelberg, completing her doctoral dissertation at the age of 22 years on St Augustine's concept of love, studying under Jaspers* and Heidegger*, whose existentialism had a lasting influence. After being arrested briefly by the Gestapo, she fled to Paris in 1933 and worked for Zionist bodies sending Jewish orphans to Palestine, though she hoped that an unnationalistic Arab-Jewish state would emerge. She fled to the United States in 1940, gladly becoming a citizen but living mainly among émigrés in New York. She worked for

Jewish organizations and for publishers until a remarkable series of articles on the basic issues of modern politics led to her first great book, *The Origins of Totalitarianism* (1951). Thereafter she moved in the university world until she was able to devote her time entirely to writing. She was a wholly serious and modest private person but died a controversial and famous public figure.

It is disputable whether her central concern was political theory or pure philosophy. Some see *The Origins of Totalitarianism* as her main achievement. She was the first to argue, on such a scale, that there were common elements in Nazism and in Stalinism such as created a wholly new kind of government based upon the systematic use of terror for the purposes of comprehensive and world-changing ideologies, those of race and of economics, both of which enjoyed genuine mass support. Their origins lay deep in the breakdown of European political tradition which followed the French Revolution, in the discrediting of liberalism by the irrationality of the First World War, and specifically in anti-semitism, European imperialism, and the vulnerability of nationalism to racialism. Her later books can all be seen as attempting either to extend these empirical arguments or to resolve difficulties in them. *The Human Condition* (1958) is then seen as tracing the decay of the Greek ideal which links thinking to political action and as pointing out that liberals quite as much as Marxists view *labour* (what we need to stay alive and what we consume) as an end in itself, a restless and self-defeating cycle, debasing *work*. Work is the distinctively human world of created objects made to last. The worship of labour also debases *action*, all things that are newly done, individual and spontaneous. To her the essence of the human condition is the public *vita activa* where men interact, neither the *vita contemplativa* of the philosophers nor the view of man as *animal laborans*, the creature of necessity. She attacks modern liberalism for valuing the realm of privacy above that of public action. She is often thought of as a modern Aristotelian, but in fact she argues that Aristotle's view of political action is teleological and purely instrumental, whereas to her political action, debate and decisions made freely and spontaneously among equals are ends in themselves to be valued irrespective of consequences.

Eichmann in Jerusalem, A Report on the Banality of Evil (1961) is then a case study of what happens in the most extreme conditions when there is no political tradition in a persecuted people and when resistance, pragmatically speaking, is hopeless. *On Revolution* (1963) tries to sustain hope, by pointing to the original ideal of free political action in both the French and the American Revolutions, before that became debased by the imposition of attempted equality in Russia. Both *On Revolution* and subsequent editions of the *Origins* put great stress on the emergence, however briefly, of self-governing workers' councils in the Hungarian revolt of 1956, like the short-lived soviets of 1917. Many critics found her scepticism of egalitarian socialism and her enthusiasm for anarchist-like councils a pair of strange bedfellows. And in her unusually terse *On Violence* (1970) she argued that *power* must always be 'acting in concert' and that *violence* is a mere instrumentality, never something, like her view of *action*, good in itself. Violence can only be justified, when at all, for limited ends, never as the vehicle of general ideas like social transformation.

However, if Arendt is viewed as a pure philosopher (in the German manner) then *The Human Condition* becomes her central book. Her preoccupations are then seen as primarily ontological. Mankind make their own world out of nature by work, capable of emancipating themselves from mere labour but also, and above all else, capable of memorable actions, whether in speculative thinking or in politics. Pragmatic judgments are replaced by aesthetic. In her last years, she turned to Kant's theory of aesthetics, not of practical reason, to try to develop a theory of judgment that might have formed a volume of her posthumous 'The Life of the Mind', of which only *Thinking* and *Willing* (1978) were completed. Ultimately it is judgment that mediates between thought and action.

Philosophy and politics came closest together in her controversial and much misunderstood *Eichmann in Jerusalem*. Some fellow Jews, especially, objected to her account of Eichmann as not a monster of irrational evil, but a rational, pragmatic bureaucrat, a typically modern figure accepting evil commands in a banal and routine manner. Many challenged her assumption that there was little organized resistance among the Jewish communities in Europe, still more her claim (or her right to claim) that some should have resisted even if hopelessly. But the real issue for Arendt was to show the dangers of judging even good politics by results: we must judge the worthiness of actions in themselves, like aesthetic not practical judgments.

Perhaps she was not primarily a political philosopher, but from her philosophy she judged politics and society. Her moves from ontology to commentary on current affairs were at times bewildering. She saw Watergate and Vietnam as 'banal' applications of practical reason, and more horrible for that reason than when dismissing them from normality as simply abhorrent evils. She could move from, at times, overprecise definitions and philological excursions (as if early meanings are true meanings) into broad generalizations about cultural history. She was not always careful on points of fact. Famously she attacked Brecht* for his 'Hymns to Stalin', republishing the essay even when their existence was disproved: to her his authorship was 'symbolically true'. It was ungenerous but understandable for Sir Isaiah Berlin to dismiss her work as 'metaphysical free-association'. She is as bewilderingly eclectic as she is stimulatingly bold and original. Perhaps she will finally be judged like Rousseau and Nietzsche for her fruitfulness rather than for her coherence. She interpreted rather than created systems. She forces us to think about the nature of the world, not simply about problems in disciplines.

Professor Bernard Crick

Her main books are mentioned above except for her *Rahel Varnhagen: the Life of a Jewess* (1958, written in the early 1930s). Her key essays are found in: *Between Past and Future* (1961); *Men in Dark Times* (1968); and *Crises of the Republic* (1972). See: Margaret Canovan, *The Political Thought of Hannah Arendt* (1974); Melvyn A. Hill (ed.), *Hannah Arendt: Recovery of the Public World* (1979).

15
ARMSTRONG, Daniel Louis (Satchmo) 1900–71

US jazz cornetist, trumpeter, singer, actor

Louis rose from a poor New Orleans background to become one of the greatest of all jazz musicians. At the age of twenty-two he was in Chicago, second cornetist in King Oliver's Creole Jazz Band, and even at this stage the younger man's advanced conception of improvisation in comparison with the sobre, classic New Orleans style of Oliver is apparent. He moved on to New York in 1924, to small group recordings with Clarence Williams and Sidney Bechet, to backing blues singers like Bessie Smith, and to big band work with Fletcher Henderson in 1924–5.

Back in Chicago in 1925, he formed a small pick-up group and called it the Hot Five. This group revolutionized jazz. It contained New Orleans musicians with the standard instrumentation. The New Orleans style had the three front-line wind players improvising a collective polyphony, interspersed with solos. Louis broke with tradition, increased the domination of the cornet lead and the proportion of soloing to ensemble playing, and organized the three minutes permitted by the 10-inch, 78-r.p.m. disc into a slowly developing climax of intensity and virtuosity. The pianist Earl Hines then joined the fluid personnel of the Hot Fives and Hot Sevens, and from 1927 to 1929 Louis produced, one after another, about fifty of the greatest jazz recordings ever made.

Typical of Louis's soloing during these years are the use of the 'break', when the rhythm section stops playing for a few bars and the soloist continues alone, and the solo against stop-chords in the accompaniment (the other players sound only the first beat in each, or in every other, bar). Both these devices are used by Louis to enable him to rise away from the implied beat and superimpose on it complex rhythmical patterns of his own, full of syncopation and of triplets. In a stop-chord solo he tends to build his lines in two-bar phrases, leaping and winding through the chords, each phrase expanded by the next, with the solo fitting together as a whole both on the rhetorical level, as a gradual crescendo of emotional tension, and on the melodic level, as a developing variation on the melody of the song. A fine example of his style is *Basin Street Blues* of 1928, in which can be found twelve-bar blues soloing where he gradually increases the density of notes and rhythmical complexity after the fourth bar, a scat-sung (i.e. wordless) chorus, four solo choruses where he builds to a climax and then winds down, and an example of his restraint where three choruses are played quietly around one low-register note.

In 1929 he was featured in a Broadway show, *Hot Chocolates*. By now he was on the one hand the model for every jazz trumpeter, and on the other the happy entertainer and singer for mainly white audiences. If Louis distinguished between the two, it was to give precedence to the art of communicating with the greatest number of people through his music. From 1930 onwards he led a succession of big bands, with which he recorded a large number of popular songs of the day in a fairly constant format: he would play the melody once with the band, sing it, and then take one or more solo choruses, leading the band out at the end – often soaring into the upper register. In nearly all of these performances he transcended the material, and in many of them he played magnificent solos. He toured widely in Europe, and acted in Hollywood films – throughout his life he appeared in about fifty in all. His singing gradually began to dominate his performances, and it may be for this that his influence has been widest. His gravelly, laughing voice had immense charm, but more importantly, he was able to dismantle a song into short, rhythmically strong phrases which he sang slightly behind the beat, mingled with scat-sung interjections and 'fills'. In this way he took the art of the crooner and gave it swing and vitality by tempering his melodies with the speech-rhythms characteristic of Southern black folk-song.

In the 1940s he formed a small group (the All-Stars) of first-rate musicians (including the trombonist Jack Teagarden), and rode the crest of the New Orleans revivalist wave. But he was always reaching towards the biggest audiences as well. There is no reason to believe that Louis saw his record *Hello Dolly*, which pushed the Beatles* from the top of the lists of best-selling records in 1964, as being a lesser achievement than his magnificent 1927 *Potato Head Blues*. Not only was he indisputably superior to any other jazz musician of his time between 1924 and 1932, but the magnitude of his achievement during that period, in establishing standards of musicianship and a vocabulary of improvisation, is unsurpassed.

Christopher Wagstaff

Most of Louis's original 78-r.p.m. records have been reissued on long-playing discs, notably on World Records – EMI, CBS, RCA, MCA. Books by Armstrong: *Swing That Music* (1936); *Satchmo: My Life in New Orleans* (1955). Books about him and his music: Max Jones and John Chilton, *Louis* (1971); Albert McCarthy, *Louis Armstrong* (1961); Richard Meryman, *Louis Armstrong – A Self-Portrait* (1971); Hugues Panassié, *Louis Armstrong* (1971). Studies of his solos are to be found in: André Hodier, *Jazz: Its Evolution and Essence* (1956); Richard Hadlock, *Jazz Masters of the Twenties* (1965); Gunther Schuller, *Early Jazz: Its Roots and Musical Development* (1968). Louis's solos transcribed can be found in: *44 Trumpet Solos & 125 Jazz Breaks* (published by Charles Hansen, New York); and *Louis Armstrong, A Jazz Master* (20 solos, published by MCA, New York).

16

ARON, Raymond 1905–

French philosopher, sociologist and journalist

Identified in Soviet propaganda as 'the main ideologist of the French bourgeoisie', a fairer portrait of Raymond Aron would show a man striving for an accurate understanding of modern – communist as well as liberal – societies. While his attacks on Stalinism* during the 1950s and the student revolt of 1968 reflect an essentially anti-Marxist position, his early advocacy of Algerian independence, and his opposition to Charles de Gaulle throughout the 1960s, chiefly over the issue of foreign policy were direct criticisms of the Establishment and its interests. A realist and a meliorist, a liberal thinker *in partibus infidelium*, Aron stands for a school of thinking, emergent during the late 1970s, that sees democratic order and democratic disorders not as dispensable impediments, but as a desirable part of life itself.

After studying at the École Normale Supérieure (1924–8), where he met and befriended Sartre*, he went to Germany where he studied and taught in Cologne and Berlin (1930–3). But whereas Sartre discovered Husserl* and Heidegger*, Aron turned his attention to German sociology and philosophy of history. Returning to France he composed his doctoral thesis, published as *Introduction à la philosophie de l'histoire* ('An Introduction to the Philosophy of History') in 1938. Through a detailed and comprehensive analysis of man's historical condition, from knowledge of himself to knowledge of the many wholes in which the self finds its place, Aron elaborated a convincing criticism of determinist philosophies of history. Supporting the claim of philosophy not to be deduced from anything else, by any kind of conditioning (history is *not* to be a substitute for philosophy), he proposed that 'ultimately the possibility of a philosophy of history is at one with the possibility of a philosophy in spite of history' – thus also disposing of the Hegelian possibility, that the achievement of history and the achievement of philosophy are one and the same thing.

The *Introduction* suggests a conflict of loyalties, of loyalty to history and loyalty to philosophy, of loyalty to the *is* and of loyalty to the *ought*; it expresses and analyses the perplexities of a Kantian mind in a post-Hegelian world. Its effect was to supply its author with a philosophy that set him free to forget philosophy. Events, institutions and societies were henceforward to be faced on their own terms, and not on those of an elusive philosophy; and Aron's subsequent career as a polemicist, sociologist and political commentator can be seen to stem directly from his early conclusions. After the war (he had joined the Free French Forces in London and edited its *La France libre*) he became a fertile, pungent and formidably argumentative journalist, contributing to the left-wing *Combat* (1946–7), then to the centrist newspaper *Le Figaro* (1947–77). In 1946 his friendly relations with Sartre were abruptly severed as the two men took diametrically opposed views on the Soviet regime. The main target of *The Opium of the Intellectuals* (*L'opium des intellectuels*, 1955, trans. 1957), however, was not so much the Communists – the ironclad brains – as the Progressivists, whose severity in criticizing every defect of Western democracies left them blind to the crimes of an allegedly Marxist state. In a way sharing many of the ideals of the left, it was the perversion of their spirit that Aron mourned, the more so as the culprits, principally Sartre and Merleau-Ponty*, were admitted to be highly gifted.

Other eloquent broadsides followed, in particular *Democracy and Totalitarianism* (*Démocratie et totalitarisme*, 1965, trans. 1968) and *The Elusive Revolution* (*La Révolution introuvable*, 1968, trans. 1969), *D'une sainte famille à l'autre* ('From one holy family to another', 1969 – directed largely against Althusser*) and *In Defence of Decadent Europe* (*Plaidoyer pour l'Europe décadente*, 1977, trans. 1979). In 1955 he also resumed his academic career, becoming a professor of sociology at the Sorbonne, and making the problems of strategy his special study. Two books, *Peace and War* (*Paix et guerre entre les nations*, 1961, trans. 1967) and *Penser la guerre, Clausewitz* (1976), are perhaps unrivalled in the contemporary literature on the subject. War is what is most opposed to the moral imperative of the Kantian philosopher, and equally what cannot be laid aside by the political thinker. And nowhere are the *is* and the *ought* more sharply distinguished. As Aron shows, the comprehension of the phenomena of war requires an understanding of things as they are; but it also requires at the same time reference to the unrealized ideal of peace: together, a forgetting of and a longing for philosophy.

Elsewhere, in his sociology (see *Dix-huit leçons sur la*

société industrielle, 18 Lectures on Industrial Society, 1963, trans. 1967, and *Les Étapes de la pensée sociologique, Main Currents in Sociological Thought*, 1965, trans. 1968, for example), Aron displays a similar concern for the antinomies of the human condition. He has been reproached, often fiercely, for being essentially critical, for failing to provide programmes for the improvement or reconstruction of society, for not offering a blueprint of *the* good society. His point of departure, however, is what our societies say of themselves, and the ideals to which they are dedicated. It is the conflict and interplay between those ideals (for example, liberty and equality) which he explores, not their ultimate values: indeed such values cannot be reached, for Aron's philosophy precludes any standard of judgment outside history – unless it is to be found in the moral consciousness of the individual, and then only in a given situation.

Pierre Manent

See also: *The Imperial* (*République Impériale*, 1973, trans. 1979).

17
ARP, Jean (Hans) 1887–1966

French sculptor, painter and poet

Arp's nationality can perhaps be best defined as Dadaist for he, more than other members of that group, remained true to its original principles his entire life. He was born in Strasbourg. In addition to Alsatian, he spoke fluent French and German and is the author of a considerable body of poetry in both languages as well as being an important sculptor and pioneer of a particular sort of abstract art. The supposed 'split' in his character between his allegiances to the French (as Jean) and German (as Hans), to literature and to plastic arts, to nature and to art, is a mistaken notion. Perhaps due to his mixed nationality he was better able to integrate his various artistic activities and share a fundamental concern of early European modernists: to break down what were seen as artificial barriers between the art media.

In 1904, Arp was excited by his first exposure to modernist art in Paris. He attended the Academy of Fine Arts in Weimar from 1905 to 1907. In 1908 he studied at Académie Julian in Paris. Dissatisfied there, he retired to Weggis in Switzerland to spend two years working quietly to rejuvenate art by means of direct contact between his unconscious perceptions and nature – to preserve innocence through art. He called his first innovations 'concrete art'. In 1947 he would write: 'We want to create as the plant creates its fruit, and not re-create. . . . As there is no trace of abstraction to be seen in this kind of art, we call it concrete art.'

His early artistic commitment led to a series of important contacts. In 1909 he met Klee*. In 1911 the Moderner Bund held its first exhibition at Lucerne where Arp showed along with Matisse* and Picasso*. In 1912 he went to Berlin, called on Kandinsky* and took part in a famous Blaue Reiter exhibition. In 1913, again in Berlin, he joined leading German Expressionists in the Erste Herbstsalon show organized by Walden who, in his magazine *Der Sturm*, had published drawings by Arp – human figures sketched in undulating lines – as well as the first version of the prose poem 'Kokoschka sketch-book'. In 1914 Arp caught the last train into Paris (according to Max Ernst*) before the First World War commenced. There he met Max Jacob, Modigliani*, Apollinaire* and Delaunay. When war broke out he returned to Switzerland and, in December 1915, exhibited his first 'abstract' works at the Tanner Gallery, Zürich. Here, he met the artist and teacher Sophie Taeuber with whom he collaborated on experimental art in various media. They were married in 1922 and continued their work together until her death in 1943 from asphyxiation on a trip to Zürich from Grasse where they had taken refuge from the Second World War.

Arp's 'abstraction' had nothing to do with description and, unlike works of abstract painters such as Mondrian*, involved (after 1915) a conscious rejection of rectilinear, 'logical' forms, giving preference to objects 'arranged according to the law of chance – rudimentary, irrational, mutilated'. This preference was to make Arp sympathetic to the aims of Dadaism which was born in the Cabaret Voltaire early in 1916 when Hugo Ball invited Arp to work with him in Zürich. Dada set out to counteract creatively the machine-age mentality and national egoism which led to wars, and bourgeois values that confined artistic expression. Unlike Tzara*, Janco, Huelsenbeck, *et al.*, Arp was less interested in shocking the bourgeoisie than in creation and 'the satisfaction of his sense of fun'.

Arp also collaborated with Max Ernst in 1920, met Kurt Schwitters in 1923 and contributed to his review *Merz*, and, with El Lissitsky, published *The Isms of Art* (1925). In sculpture and reliefs, Arp is best known for his 'neutral forms' and 'navels' or undulating ovals symbolic of natural growth and metamorphosis. He often juxtaposes unlikely objects, for example, *Egg Board* (relief, 1917), *Shirt Front and Fork* (relief, 1924), and the deceptively simple reliefs *Fork and Navel* (1927) and *Infinite Amphora* (1929), or combines playfulness with purity of form, as in *Head with Two Annoying Objects* (sculpture, 1930) and *Three-navel Fruit* (sculpture, 1960).

In 1926, Arp and Sophie moved to Meudon near Paris and joined the Surrealist group until 1930; in this year their *papiers déchirés* appeared. Their activities were not confined to Paris, for, in collaboration with S. T. and Theo van Doesburg, they decorated the *café dansant*

L'Aubette in Strasbourg. As a member of the Circle and Square group, Arp took part in its international exhibition in April 1930. The following year he joined the Abstraction-Creation group and concentrated on 'pictures' in twine and torn paper and produced his first full relief.

His poetry of this period includes *the bird plus one* into which he incorporated an early verse, 'Kaspar is tot'; his poetic technique might be called *déchirés*, developing imagery in language in conjunction with collage experiments. His major poetic collections, however, appeared late in life: *Moonsand* (1960); *Pensive Flames* (1961); *The Dream Captain's Log Book* (1965). In the prose work *Jalons* (1950) he wrote about his increasing interest in genetic force and how he had developed this fascination since 1916: 'The wood relief *Formes terrestres*, reproduced by Picabia in his review *391* . . . is the first of a long series on which I have not ceased to work.' His aim for fusion of man, nature and object is manifest in all his work.

Arp made three important trips to the USA: in 1949 for the Curt Valentin Gallery, in 1950 when he was invited by Gropius* to execute the Harvard Graduate Center wall relief, and in 1958 for the MOMA retrospective in New York. In 1959, Arp married an old friend Marguerite Hagenbach who had collaborated with him and Sophie in Zürich.

Arp's plastic art falls into four distinct categories: (1) reliefs in media other than stone; (2) sculpture (both stone carvings and casts in bronze, silver, etc.); (3) collages, *papiers déchirés*, embroideries and 'architectural formations'; (4) graphic work (woodcuts, engravings, drawings). Arp also formulated five types of his verse. His 'sophisticated schizophrenic dialect', though shared by other Dadaists such as Schwitters, is distinguished by its clarity and serenity, even when apparently unintelligible due to surreal imagery:

> the lips rise out of the words
> like beauty out of the billows of the sky
> beauty is shut in by light
> as the bell is by kisses
> ('The Skeleton of the Day', 1937).

Arp's creations embody his freshness of vision, his freedom from overly theoretical reservations (despite his involvements with various groups and movements); they are 'anonymous like clouds, mountains, animals, men', as he described them in his 1947 essay 'Concrete Art'. His oeuvre is a blossoming, a rounding out of his experience and integrity.

Alison Armstrong

Arp's earlier writings are collected in *On My Way; Poetry and Essays 1912–1947* (1948). See: L. Forster, *The Poetry of Significant Nonsense* (1962); C. Giedion-Welcker, *Jean Arp* (1957) and *Modern Plastic Art:*

Elements of Reality, Volume and Disintegration (1937); R. W. Last, *Hans Arp: The Poet of Dadaism* (1969); G. Marchiori, *Arp* (1964); Herbert Read, *Arp* (1968); H. Richter, *Dada* (1965); Eduard Trier, *Jean Arp: Sculpture 1957–1966* (1968).

18

ARRABAL, Fernando 1932–

Spanish/French dramatist

Arrabal's life and work are dominated by the traumas of childhood. His father, a career officer in the Spanish army, was known for his Republican sympathies and was therefore an early casualty of Franco's rebellion in 1936. He was arrested, sentenced to death but had his sentence commuted to a thirty-year prison term. His mother, a good Catholic, bombarded the unfortunate father with letters accusing him of having compromised his children's future and cut his head out of all the family photographs.

From an early age therefore Fernando Arrabal's loyalties were torn in different directions. In the end the influence of his father's memory was strongest: he left his mother and Spain to write subversive plays in Paris. His plays are all more or less dream works. They present characters who, shorn of the normal constraints of everyday life, behave according to basic Freudian* drives. Capable of extreme childlike naivety, but also of extreme cruelty, they pass through situations of warfare, torture or exile which they fail to comprehend. Being incapable of understanding or articulating, they resort to magic and ceremonial.

The first performance of a play by Arrabal in France was in 1959. Critics were casting around for a writer who would breathe new life into the Theatre of the Absurd. Arrabal's work seemed even more daring than that of Ionesco* *et alia*, and he became a figure of some notoriety during the 1960s, particularly after some strikingly imaginative productions of his work by Jorge Lavelli and Victor García.

Since the early 1960s he has grouped his numerous new plays under the general heading of Panic Theatre, designed to produce a disordering of the senses by administering shocks to the potential roots of neurosis in the audience's minds. Sadism and blasphemy are presented as a response to the repressive world of Spanish Catholicism and in this his work is sometimes reminiscent of Buñuel's*. But it is also self-indulgent and lacks Buñuel's incisive grasp of social and political realities.

Together with his friend the film director Jodorowski, he may be said to have exerted some influence on forms of sexual and psychological anarchism. A recent structuralist study by Angel Berenguer argues that the shape if not the content of the early plays portrays the fate of the Spanish *petite bourgeoisie* under Franco, but this has not been perceived by audiences, who have mostly reacted to the sensationalist aspects of the plays.

David Bradby

Théâtre (from 1958); *L'Enterrement de la Sardine* (1961); *Fêtes et Rites de la Confusion* (1967). See also Angel Berenguer, *L'Exil et la Cérémonie* (1977).

19
ARTAUD, Antonin (Marie Joseph) 1896–1948

French actor, writer and man of the theatre

Antonin Artaud displays a peculiar merging of life and art so that it is almost impossible to say where one ends and the other begins. From an early age he suffered from a variety of nervous diseases perhaps occasioned by an attack of meningitis when he was five. These were to lead to prolonged stays in sanatoria and mental institutions, the first of which came in his late teens, when he also began the habit of drug dependency that was to cause him extreme agony and hardship in later life.

In 1920 he moved from Marseilles to Paris, where he began to engage in the literary and theatrical life. He acted for Lugné-Poe, Dullin and Pitoëff, scoring a particular success as Tiresias in Cocteau's* *Antigone* (1922), as well as publishing poems and articles on various subjects. In 1923 he submitted some poems to the *Nouvelle Revue Française*, which were turned down by Jacques Rivière, but led to a correspondence in which Artaud developed the idea that his own failure to find satisfactory self-expression might constitute a paradigm for the problem of artistic creation in the twentieth century. In 1923 he joined the Surrealist group, only to be expelled again in 1926 when Breton*, Eluard and others joined the Communist Party.

During this period he published further poems and laid plans for his own theatre. These were partially realized in 1928 when, with the collaboration of Roger Vitrac, he produced a number of isolated and fragmentary performances under the umbrella name of The Alfred Jarry Theatre. The most notable productions were of Strindberg's *Dream Play* and Vitrac's *Victor*. Bankruptcy and depression followed, but in 1931 Artaud felt he had experienced a new revelation while watching a performance by the Balinese dancers at the Colonial Exhibition. Over the next three years he wrote the texts later published as *The Theatre and its Double* (1938, trans. 1970), adapted work by Seneca and Shelley (*The Cenci*) and wrote a scenario entitled *The Conquest of Mexico*. His last full-scale theatrical venture was the Theatre of Cruelty, which lasted for just seventeen performances of *The Cenci* in 1935. Its failure was followed by a period of travelling (to Mexico and Ireland)

and disintegration, during which he published the apocalyptic *New Revelations of Being* (*Les Nouvelles Révélations de l'Être*, 1937). The travels came to an end when he was deported from Ireland and locked up in a French institution as a dangerous lunatic. He spent the war years in a variety of asylums, subject to all kinds of privation and to electro-convulsive ·therapy (ECT), which he particularly dreaded. He was released in 1946 and spent the last two years of his life in a spate of literary activity, publishing letters, poems, an essay on Van Gogh, and producing a radio programme of his own work, which was banned at the last minute.

Artaud made a powerful impact on his contemporaries by his acting style which had a passionate, spiritual quality that can still be glimpsed in some of his film performances – the young monk in Dreyer's *Passion of Joan of Arc* (1927) or Marat in Gance's *Napoléon* (1927). His scenario *The Seashell and the Clergyman* (*La Coquille et le Clergyman*, filmed by Germaine Dulac in 1928) shows him to have been a master of Surrealist film. But most of his energies were devoted to the theatre and this is where his influence has been greatest – something of a paradox, since all his own productions failed and he left so little in the way of production plans. His influence has passed through two main channels: the playwrights, directors and actors who knew him personally, and the essays grouped under the title *The Theatre and its Double*. Although the expression of his thought is sometimes deliberately antilogical and difficult to follow, the idea of this work can be summarized as follows. The theatre is like the plague: it attacks a whole community and produces a paroxysm which may be destructive but can also perform a cathartic function. Western theatre has been killed by excessive attention to logical, verbal, grammatical language. A text is not something that exists prior to performance, but is written by the actor, who becomes a moving hieroglyph. The use of sounds, lights, movements, gestures, etc., takes on primary importance because 'the domain of the theatre is not psychological but plastic and physical'.

In place of the literary theatre of his time, Artaud was proposing a conception that was almost primeval – an all-engulfing experience in which metaphysics would be translated into violent physical realities. The failure of his own attempts was largely because of his own unwillingness to think about the audience: primeval theatre did not harmonize with sophisticated Parisian theatre-going. It has been left to other directors to put his ideas into practice. The most notable have been Roger Blin, Peter Brook* and Jerzy Grotowski*. But Artaud has also influenced thinking about madness, especially in its relationship to language, as can be seen in the work of R. D. Laing*, Michel Foucault* or Jacques Derrida*.

David Bradby

Oeuvres Complètes (from 1956). See also: Alain Virmaux, *Antonin Artaud et le Théâtre* (1970); Martin Esslin, *Artaud* (1976).

20
ASHBY, William Ross 1903–72

British neurologist, psychiatrist and cybernetician

W. Ross Ashby was born in London and educated at the Edinburgh Academy, Sidney Sussex College, Cambridge, where he took a degree in natural sciences, and at St Bartholomew's Hospital, London, qualifying as a psychiatrist. Following this he worked as a research pathologist at St Andrew's Hospital, Northampton, concentrating on neurology, until the beginning of the Second World War, when he became an officer in the Royal Medical Corps. When hostilities ended he became director of research at Barnwood House, a psychological institute in Gloucestershire. The publication of *Cybernetics* by Norbert Wiener* in 1948 provided Ashby with a discipline which could unite his interests in neurology and psychiatry, and the field in which his most important work was subsequently accomplished.

Cybernetics, in Wiener's words, purports to study 'communication and control in man and machine', and as such grew out of a series of discussions between Wiener and the physiologist Arturo Rosenbleuth at MIT concerning the workings of feedback and servo-mechanisms. While it is not clear to what extent Ashby worked independently of Wiener, his *Design for a Brain* (1952) immediately established him as a leading exponent of the new science. In it Ashby reaffirmed the simulative and descriptive nature of scientific knowledge in a manner that has been of general use in, for instance, computer modelling studies. His purpose, he insisted, was not to imitate the detailed action of the (human) brain, but rather to build descriptions which, while as a theoretical computer producing the same behavioural patterns as (a part of) the brain, would not necessarily function in the same manner.

This simulative approach was made even more explicit in Ashby's following book, *An Introduction to Cybernetics* (1956). Here he states that the reality of our knowledge of reality is made up of a collection of 'black boxes', which provide simulations of the performance of an entity, and through which we make descriptions that allow us to predict behaviours. Such description-building corresponds to what Wiener referred to as 'making a black-box white', and which he, in turn, had derived from the Scottish physicist J. C. Maxwell (1831–79). The particular value of *An Introduction*, however, is the bringing together of three separate phenomena within a common theoretical structure. First the cybernetic concept of 'state' is refined and elaborated

as a precise and powerful tool. Then state and state change are used as a basis for the modelling of behaviours. Not surprisingly, in view of his background in neurology, the demonstrations Ashby provides are applied to organisms as they function *in vivo* (and not *in vitrio*, as a dead brain does not of course 'behave'). One of the most significant characteristics of living systems is their stability in different circumstances and environments, known as homeostasis, of which, using his concept of state, Ashby produced a working description and then an electro-mechanical device with a similar performance. This allowed the concept to be understood much better than it had been previously. The third phenomenon was the invention of the measure 'variety'. Variety is a measure of the states – and their interconnectedness – that a system may have. A generalization of Claude Shannon's measure 'information', it also relates to the concept of entropy as used in Information Theory, which was developed contemporaneously with cybernetics. The particular power of variety is embodied in the Law of Requisite Variety, which requires that a control system has as much variety as the system it is to control if it is to be effective.

Although the generality and profundity of the Law of Requisite Variety is still being discovered, it may be said to represent Ashby's special contribution to cybernetics. After the publication of his two books, first as director of the Burden Neurological Institute, then as Professor of Electrical Engineering at the University of Illinois, Ashby continued his theoretical work, applying his conclusions and techniques in a way that has increased our understanding of theoretical computers.

Dr Ranulph Glanville

A list of publications and a representative selection of Ashby's papers may be found in Heinz von Foerster, *Cybernetics of Cybernetics* (1974).

21
ASIMOV, Isaac 1920–

US writer

How does one categorize a writer who has published over 200 books? Isaac Asimov is perhaps best known as a science fiction writer and a general science popularizer. He has also written mysteries (some with a robot detective), edited magazines and anthologies, written innumerable columns for various magazines, and hosted the TV science show 'Nova'. In his autobiography (1979) he claims to have published *thus far* only 15 million words.

Born in Russia, he was taken to America in 1923 and became an American citizen in 1928. His Brooklyn boyhood was hardly typical since his accelerated education enabled him to graduate from Columbia University at the age of nineteen. Still, his father's corner store was filled with pulp magazines and the lure of the gaudy. His undimmed love of that most statistically oriented of sports, baseball, also dates from those times. Graduate school at Columbia proved equally easy as Asimov earned an MA in 1941 and a PhD in 1948; 1939 was also the year of his first publication, a short story in *Amazing Stories* called 'Marooned off Vesta'. After taking his PhD Asimov accepted a position on the faculty of the Boston University School of Medicine, eventually becoming a full professor at that institution.

Although he published frequently in magazines and journals during the 1940s, Asimov did not publish his first book (a novel called *Pebble in the Sky*) until he was thirty. He then speeded up incredibly, publishing 100 books in the next two decades and then doubling his output in the 1970s so that he could publish an anthology entitled *Opus 200* in 1979, a selection of material from his second hundred books.

Asimov's major contribution to science fiction was certainly first felt in the 1940s in *Astounding Science Fiction* under the guidance of editor John W. Campbell, Jr, where he published most of his early stories about robots (formulating his still monumental 'Three Laws of Robotics') and the stories that would eventually provide the basis for his *Foundation* trilogy. Before Asimov, robots were mostly mechanical monsters beyond the control of men and often aligned against them in a 'war between species'. Asimov humanized them and provided the built-in 'laws' that have resulted in the current glut of lovable beeping and clanking robotic media stars. The Three Laws of Robotics are: (1) a robot may not injure a human being, or, through inaction, allow a human being to come to harm; (2) a robot must obey the orders given it by human beings except where such orders would conflict with the First Law; (3) a robot must protect its own existence, as long as such protection does not conflict with the First or Second Law. The *Foundation* trilogy, *Foundation* (1951), *Foundation and Empire* (1952), and *Second Foundation* (1953), has proved even more important as one of the first and most influential efforts to turn the trend in the field away from the technological sciences and toward the social sciences. Since this was done by a practising biochemist writing for a magazine (*ASF*) that always sold out at newstands at Los Alamos and other technological centres, the achievement is even more astonishing. Asimov's concept of 'Psychohistory' in the trilogy seems firmly based on the writings of Karl Marx and his belief in the 'patterns' of history. Psychohistorians can predict future patterns for the Galactic Empire, its fall, the aftermath, and the establishment of new empire. Knowing these patterns means that such historians can interfere at the correct moment

to assure the continuation of the right patterns. Such a concept must be plotted over thousands of years and many solar systems; yet Asimov finds the right combination of concrete human conflict in specific situations to match against his grander pattern. Brian Aldiss in his history of science fiction credits Asimov (and Heinlein) with establishing a hitherto lacking 'literary law and order' in the field in that Asimov not only posited patterns by which robots must behave but civilizations as well. And indeed some historians of the science fiction field do insist that Asimov at this point in his career provides the symbolic BA/AA dividing line (Before Asimov/After Asimov). Modern science fiction begins thus with the stories collected in *I, Robot* and the *Foundation* trilogy.

Asimov has continued to write distinguished science fiction, including a series of teenage novels under the pseudonym of Paul French, until the present time. His output has lessened in the 1970s, however, and perhaps only *The Gods Themselves* (1972) has drawn particular notice, despite the general high quality of his work.

His popular anthologies of his own work, general collections in the field, European SF, and his own recently established magazine suggest that his name alone provides a stamp of approval for a large audience. Even those who do not read science fiction have probably read such general science popularizations as *The Intelligent Man's Guide to Science* (1961) or watched him explain in lucid and urbane tones new speculations and discoveries on TV. His influence thus extends far beyond that of even the finest current SF writers (inheritors of the tradition he helped establish) due to his endless curiosity, facility with words and concepts, and willingness to lend his name to new explorations of fiction and fact.

Professor Charles Gregory

See also: *The Autobiography of Isaac Asimov 1920–1954* (1979).

22
AUDEN, Wystan Hugh 1907–73

English/US poet, dramatist, librettist and essayist

W. H. Auden was born in York, the youngest son of a doctor (all his life, Auden was to take an interest in sickness and healing, though defining neither in orthodox medical terms). His childhood, spent in Solihull, then a village just outside Birmingham, was a happy one, apart from the crucial absence of his father during the war years 1914–19. The atmosphere of the Auden home combined affectionate family life with a lively interest in the arts, especially music, a penchant for intellectual pursuits, and High Anglican Christianity. Auden's interests as a child included Icelandic sagas and the construction of an imaginary world whose main features were a northern limestone landscape and a lead-mining industry.

Auden was educated at St Edmund's Preparatory School, where he first met his future collaborator and lifelong friend, Christopher Isherwood*, and at Gresham's School, Holt, where Benjamin Britten* was a much younger pupil. Auden's interests as a schoolboy were mainly scientific (he intended to become a mining engineer), though he also profited greatly from the music teaching. By his own account, he did not then think of himself as a writer, and only when a friend asked him if he wrote poetry did he suddenly realize his vocation. By the time Auden went up to Oxford, he was already a technically highly accomplished poet in the Georgian mode, Hardy being his first poetic master. In 1925, he entered Christ Church College, Oxford, as a scholar in Natural Sciences. He soon, however, changed his course, first to P.P.E. and then to English Language and Literature in which he was tutored by Nevill Coghill, later the translator of Chaucer. Auden was particularly fascinated by Old English poetry (then as now compulsory at Oxford), echoes, phrases and rhythms from which haunt his early work.

Auden, as an undergraduate who had read Freud* and Jung* during his schooldays, was far more intellectually sophisticated than most of his Oxford contemporaries. He became something of a legendary figure, dispensing psychological and aesthetic wisdom (he had by now been converted to 'modernist' writing) in his artificially darkened college rooms. He was a central figure in a group of talented young men, including Stephen Spender*. During this time Auden was also reintroduced to Isherwood and their friendship reopened. Via Isherwood, he met the writer Edward Upward and was initiated into 'Mortmere', the surreal imaginary world whose grotesqueness parodies English conventionality, which Upward and Isherwood had invented during their Cambridge undergraduate days. Although the direct influence of 'Mortmere' on Auden's work seems comparatively slight except in *The Orators* (1932), it certainly contributed to the making of the imaginary worlds which both stand apart from and explain or criticize 'reality', which are such a marked feature of Auden's work both during the 1930s and after.

In 1928 Auden spent a year in Berlin, where he was fascinated by the cultural and political milieu of Weimar Germany, enjoyed the homosexual night life, and began writing some of his finest poems. In Berlin he also met and was much influenced by John Layard, a disciple of the recently dead Homer Lane, a psychologist who taught that all disease was psychosomatic, the result of psychic conflicts or repressions. This doctrine provided the framework of many poems, although it is not quite certain how literally Auden took it. All his life he had a love of totalizing intellectual models

in which to systematize human experience and make it intelligible and coherent. (Like W. B. Yeats*, Auden had a penchant for tabular exposition.) The systems might be psychoanalytic, philosophical or theological; Auden used all but retained a permanent allegiance to none. He would employ such models in poetry (or conversation) with a dogmatism which contained a discernible element of camp.

In 1930 Auden made his public début with the appearance of the charade *Paid on Both Sides* in the *Criterion* and then of *Poems*, his first full-scale collection, which includes the justly famous 'Consider this and in our time', '1929', and 'Sir, no man's enemy'. The date of this collection's publication is appropriate, for Auden was to be regarded as the 'poet of the 1930s' *par excellence*. That is, not only was Auden generally acknowledged, then and now, as the central figure of the 'thirties group' of young writers (usually identified as Auden, MacNeice, Day Lewis, Spender and Upward) who were left-wing in their politics and 'modified modernist' in their technique, but also Auden's poems set the tone of the public poetry that was to dominate the decade. The intellectual structure of these poems owes much to Marx and Freud (the latter definitely predominating in *Poems*, 1930); their tone is, characteristically, didactic diagnosis, and their technique combines the sophisticated exploitation of, usually, traditional verse-forms with casually witty language and with vivid images or vignettes (which are frequently small allegories in themselves). Also immensely influential (and often copied) were the landscapes of Auden's early poetry: desolate frontier regions marked by a derelict industrialism, whose compelling power not only had an obvious contemporary relevance to the economic Depression, but also, in a more subterranean way, evoked folk-memories of the devastated no-man's land of the trenches in the First World War.

Poems was succeeded by *The Orators*, a parodic mélange of discourses both public (the joke Litany, the Odes) and private (the 'Journal of an Airman'). All the speakers in the book insist that England is 'a country where nobody is well'; the difficulty for the reader is that all the speakers appear to be at least as sick as their subjects.

Auden supported himself during the early and mid-1930s by various schoolmastering jobs. In 1935 he spent six months working with Grierson's GPO film unit, for which he wrote the words for the documentaries *Coal Face*, *Night Mail* and *The Road to the Sea*. In this work he met Britten, who was in charge of composing the music and sound effects. The two became friends, and Britten set many of Auden's lyric poems to music, as well as composing the music for the Group Theatre productions of the Auden and Isherwood plays. Many of the poems Britten set to music (including the song cycle *On this Island*, 1938) were published in *Look, Stranger!* (1936), which contains, as well as many beautiful lyric poems, the superb public poems 'A bride in the thirties', 'A Summer Night', 'The Malverns' and 'To a writer on his birthday'.

In the summer of 1936 Auden went to Iceland with Louis MacNeice for a long holiday, which produced the collaborative *Letters from Iceland* (1937), a delight-fully unsystematic travel book which contains the brilliantly entertaining autobiographical 'Letter to Lord Byron'. While Auden was in Iceland, the Spanish Civil War broke out. Auden went to Spain, intending first to fight on the Republican side and then to work as an ambulance-driver. In the event, he took no active part in the war, but wrote his finest political poem 'Spain 1937' (collected in *Another Time*, 1940). In this poem, the political/military conflict is presented as a point of momentous choice between a past stretching back to prehistory and forward to a possible future of human justice. The choice, it is insisted, is urgent: 'the time is short, and/History to the defeated/May say alas but cannot help or pardon.' (A conclusion which the poet was later to repudiate as immoral.)

Auden returned from Spain in 1937. The following year he and Isherwood set off for China to write a book about the Sino-Japanese war. *Journey to a War* (1939) offers the reader an odd contrast between a mainly comic travel diary ascribed to Isherwood and 'In Time of War', a very serious, ambitious and successful sonnet sequence.

The 1930s was also the period of Auden's plays. His first publicly performed play, *The Dance of Death* (1933), is an allegory of the decline of the bourgeoisie, which though it has some fine songs was too frivolous and unstructured to be successful. This was succeeded by *The Dog beneath the Skin* (with Isherwood, 1935), in which a Candide-like public school hero wanders around two imaginary European countries, reactionary royalist (Ostnia) and fascist (Westland), in search of the missing heir of Pressan Ambo (a parodic imaginary English village). The play, owing much to Brecht*, is episodic and non-naturalistic in form, cut up by superb poetic choruses and songs. *The Ascent of F 6* (1936), Auden and Isherwood's most ambitious play, followed; here, Michael Ransom, a hero recalling T. E. Lawrence*, attempts to climb the inaccessible mountain F 6. His action is determined partly by the manipulation of reactionary capitalist politicians, and partly by Ransom's own neurotic Oedipal compulsions. Ransom, in fact, is the Truly Weak Man, a mythical/parabolic figure invented by Isherwood, whose 'heroic' deeds are really attempts to escape his own inner weakness (as opposed to the Truly Strong Man, a less interesting character who has no private fears and consequently doesn't do heroic things because he doesn't need to prove himself). The last play that the two friends collaborated on was *On the Frontier* (1938), a much more directly political play than its predecessors, in which

Ostnia and Westland slide towards a disastrous war that neither site really wants.

The last of what Auden's bibliographer has styled the 'English Auden' collections, *Another Time*, which contains 'September 1939', 'Spain' and the elegies on Yeats and Freud as well as the famous lyric 'Lullaby', came out in 1940. By this time, however, Auden, together with Isherwood, had left for America in 1939, an act for which both were heavily criticized and for which some of Auden's English readers never forgave him. He had been celebrated for years as the admired poet of the left (a position which in fact had increasingly irked him), and his leaving England just before the war against the fascism he had been condemning for years seemed to his admirers a betrayal of what he had been thought to stand for. It is certainly clear that 1939–40 was a turning point in Auden's life and works. Several important events in his life occurred then; he met Chester Kallman, his lover and lifelong companion; he returned to the Church, becoming an existentialist Kierkegaardian Anglican; and his mother died in 1941. A very marked change also came over Auden's poetry at this point, both in style and content. Auden had always been much concerned as a poet with what art was *for*. In the 1930s, he tended to state or imply that art has a social or humane value, as in his much-quoted formulation of the two kinds of art: 'escape-art, for man needs escape as he needs food or deep sleep, and parable-art, that art which shall teach man to unlearn hatred and learn love' (*Psychology and Art*, 1932). This stance ('We must love one another or die') changed, partly under the pressure of political events (poetry had demonstrably failed to stop Hitler*) and partly through personal Christian conviction. Already in his elegy on Yeats (1939) Auden had asserted that 'Poetry makes nothing happen'; to this was added the conviction that poetry is a purely aesthetic, not an ethical or religious practice. His own art, in its exploitation of pastiche and parody, had always partially depended on raising a game of nuances between poem and reader; this now became the basis of his aesthetic. From this time on, Auden insisted that poetry was 'only' a game (which did not prevent him from writing religious didactic poems). He was thus in the paradoxical role of being a magician who did not approve of magic.

The first fruit of Auden's conversion to Christianity and America was a series of long poems. *New Year Letter* (1941; entitled *The Double Man* in America) is a discursive philosophical poem in octosyllabic couplets accompanied by a long commentary and a sonnet sequence, 'The Quest'. It attempts, first through 'conversational' argumentative verse, and then through the metaphor of the 'Quest', to question what the human condition in 1940 is, and to give a Christian answer. It was followed by *For the Time Being* (1944), a 'Christmas oratorio' which dramatizes states of mind and dilemmas both Christian and humanist. It was published together with *The Sea and the Mirror*, a verse commentary on *The Tempest*, which is the most brilliant of Auden's longer poems. The Shakespearean reference point gives the poem a strong and flexible structure both dramatically and intellectually, while the overcoming of technical difficulties (it is an expertly fertile *tour de force* of verse forms) is accompanied by a remarkable verbal richness and vitality. The last of these long poems is *The Age of Anxiety* (1947), a 'baroque eclogue' of four persons written in alliterative accentual metre which although it is not easy to read contains some of the richest of the 'middle Auden' poetry.

By the end of the war, Auden had made New York his permanent home, although until the end of his life he usually summered in Europe. Partly under the influence of Kallman, Auden became an opera-lover. He and Kallman collaborated on the libretto for Stravinsky's* score of *The Rake's Progress* (1951), and other librettos followed, including a translation of *The Magic Flute* (1957). He was also a reviewer and lecturer of distinction. From 1955 to 1958 he was Professor of Poetry at the University of Oxford. His lectures were collected in the brilliant book of criticism *The Dyer's Hand* (1962), and he gave a generous amount of time and help to students interested in poetry. His poetic output also remained prolific and impressive. *Nones* (1950) was his first post-war collection, whose lyric poems are especially fine; it also contains the beautiful 'In Praise of Limestone'. It is followed by *The Shield of Achilles* (1955), Auden's most impressive post-war collection. The title poem is one of his greatest; the book also contains the brilliant allegorical landscape poems 'Bucolics' and 'Horae Canonicae'. *Homage to Clio* (1960) has some fine pieces, particularly the title poem, and is the first collection in which Auden included a large proportion of his light verse 'shorts'. *About the House* (1965) is mainly a sequence of discursive syllabic poems, each of which starts off from some aspect of domesticity. *City Without Walls* (1969) is darker in tone and more nostalgic. It contains more translations and occasional verse than previous collections, including the short poem 'August 1968', about the invasion of Czechoslovakia. *Epistle to a Godson* (1972) has poems of enormous skill, wit, learning and technical accomplishment. Auden's last collection, *Thank you, Fog* (1974), seems the work of a poet still possessed of his powers but increasingly weary of the world. Its last poem 'Lullaby' has an apparent cosiness and real cold detachment which make it one of the most haunting Auden ever wrote.

All of Auden's later poems, while they exhibit plenty of change and development, have a discernibly similar tone. Technically, they are often virtuoso performances; they are humane and conversational in style, and they carry with ease and grace a load of quirky learning (and often outlandish words; they send the reader to the dictionary more often than to Freud or Kierkegaard). This later work, while some readers find it less exciting than the shifting rhythms and obscure challenge of Auden's early poems, certainly adds up to much more of a whole man's life, embracing work, love, play, learning, religion and pleasure. 'Late Audenesque' is a style in reading and appreciating as much as writing; it ranges from theology to cookery books, from biology to opera. Auden certainly regarded his work from 1940 on as the most important. He repudiated most of his best-known political poems of the 1930s, ommiting many of them from *Collected Shorter Poems 1927–1957* (1966), and others were radically revised. With or without the political poems, Auden's poetic achievement remains the richest, most wide-ranging, ambitious, impressive and influential of any English poet of the twentieth century.

Janet Montefiore

See: *Collected Poems* (1976) and *The English Auden: Poems, Essays and Dramatic Writings 1927–1939* (1977), both ed. Edward Mendelson; *Forewords and Afterwords* (1970). See also Bloomfield and Mendelson (eds), *W. H. Auden: a Bibliography* (1970). About Auden: John Bayley, *The Romantic Survival* (1957); Monroe Spears, *The Poetry of W. H. Auden* (1963); John Fuller, *A Reader's Guide to W. H. Auden* (1970); Samuel Hynes, *The Auden Generation* (1976); Charles Osborne, *W. H. Auden: The Life of a Poet* (1980).

23

AUSTIN, John Langshaw 1911–60

British philosopher

The father of this 'implacable professor' was an architect who, after service in the First World War, became Secretary of St Leonard's School in the ancient Fifeshire university town of St Andrew's. The son went to Shrewsbury School (where Charles Darwin had been a pupil), proceeding from there on an open scholarship to Balliol College, Oxford. Except for a wartime interlude of outstandingly valuable service in the Intelligence Corps, and two short visiting appointments at Harvard and the University of California, Austin's entire working life was spent at Oxford, where he became successively Fellow of All Souls, Fellow of Magdalen, and White's Professor of Moral Philosophy.

Austin's influence on and through his colleagues and pupils was far greater than the small extent of his publications would suggest. His main mission – pursued with a formidable combination of intensity, intellectual force, and wit – was to apply the methods and standards of a scholar of the Greco-Roman classical texts to various, usually non-technical areas of contemporary English discourse. For how else are concepts to be elucidated if not by meticulous attention to the usage of the words through which these concepts are expressed?

The nature of this mission, and the philosophical profit to be won from it, is perhaps best seen in the articles 'Other Minds' (1946) and 'A Plea for Excuses' (1956), reprinted in the posthumous *Philosophical Papers* (1961). The former contains Austin's first account of performatory utterances: speech-acts which are in themselves the performance of an action. Thus to say 'I promise' in the appropriate conditions is in itself the making of a promise, not a mere statement about a promise. The latter article brings out the great richness and some of the detailed characteristics of our everyday vocabulary of extenuation and excuse. It also contains, on one and the same page, Austin's most incisive repudiations of two views often but falsely attributed to him by those hostile to his philosophical methods: first, that any such map-work is the be-all and end-all of philosophy (as opposed to the begin-all); and second, that our untechnical vocabulary never needs to be revised or supplemented. His true thesis was that the resources of any vernacular, as the naturally selected product of generations of practical experience, are likely to be greater than those of some hastily and uncritically contrived professional jargon: here as everywhere the reform which is to be improvement must wait on an understanding of the *status quo*.

In his again posthumous lectures on *Sense and Sensibilia* (1962) Austin dissected, and some would say demolished, the entire tradition, dating back through Descartes to the Greek Sceptics, which denied that we can be immediately aware of anything but our own most private sense data.

In his last years – represented by the 1955 William James Lectures, published as *How To Do Things With Words* (1962) – Austin sophisticated upon the notion of performative utterances. He distinguished, for instance, the illocutionary force of a speech-act (what is done *in* saying something) from its locutionary force (what it is the act *of* saying), and its perlocutionary force (what is effected in others by the saying). Because Austin always somehow 'failed to leave enough time in which to say why what I have said is interesting' his later work has often been thought to be philosophically irrelevant linguistics.

Professor Antony Flew

See also: K. T. Fann (ed.), *Symposium on J. L. Austin* (1969); Isaiah Berlin (ed.), *Essays on J. L. Austin* (1973).

24
AYER, Sir Alfred Jules 1910–

British philosopher

A. J. Ayer's career is a paradigm of academic success. A King's scholar at Eton, he went on to become a classical scholar and later lecturer in philosophy at Christ Church, Oxford. From 1946 to 1959 he was Professor of Philosophy at University College, London, and from 1959 to 1979 he held the Wykam Professorship of Logic at Oxford. He was knighted in 1970.

From the philosophical point of view the most important event of Ayer's life was his visit to Vienna as a young graduate in 1933. Armed with a letter of introduction from Gilbert Ryle*, Ayer was able to attend the discussions of the celebrated Vienna Circle (Wiener Kreis) of philosophers, containing such brilliant figures as Moritz Schlick* and Rudolf Carnap*. Ayer was deeply impressed by the philosophical approach of the circle, which came to be known as Logical Positivism. Soon after his return to England he published his first and easily best-known book, *Language, Truth and Logic* (1936). This rapidly became, for the English-speaking world, the manifesto of the Logical Positivist movement, and it remains in many ways the definitive exposition of positivist philosophy.

The central demand of Ayer's treatise was for the 'elimination of metaphysics' (the title of Chapter 1): 'No statement which refers to a reality transcending the limits of all possible sense experience can possibly have any literal significance; from which it must follow that the labours of those who have striven to describe such a reality have all been devoted to the production of nonsense.' The tool for the removal of metaphysics was the famous Principle of Verification: 'A sentence is factually significant to a given person if, and only if, he knows how to verify the proposition it purports to express.' The results of applying this criterion were devastating: apart from the tautologies of logic and mathematics, no statement was to be accepted as meaningful which could not be checked by empirical observation. Thus the whole of substantive ethics, and the entire body of religious claims are discarded as a collection of meaningless pseudo-propositions. The only statements to survive the holocaust turn out to be those of science: 'Philosophy is virtually empty without science'; there is no future for philosophy except as the Logic of Science.

The details of Ayer's argument are of an extraordinary rigour and clarity, and the catch-words of *Language, Truth and Logic* – 'empirical', 'criterion', 'factual significance', 'observation-statement' – were to dominate the philosophical scene for the next quarter-century. What led to the eventual decline of Positivism was that it slowly became clear that its own darling, natural science, could not pass the test of strict verifiability. The highly generalized statements of scientific theory just cannot be reduced to observation statements; and if the verification test is made less rigorous so as to accommodate scientific theory, then religion and metaphysics will be able to creep back in as well. This is a problem with which Ayer wrestles in the long Introduction to the second edition of *Language, Truth and Logic* (1946); but he was later forced to admit that it could not be solved.

It would be wrong to say that Ayer's reputation rests on *Language, Truth and Logic* alone. But his prolific subsequent writings have never achieved the pivotal importance of the first book. It is often asserted that its central ideas are now dead and buried, but this is seriously misleading. Although it is true that most philosophers (including Ayer himself) had, by the late 1960s, abandoned strict verificationism, much subsequent philosophy has developed as a response to Ayer's radical empiricist challenge. As for 'metaphysics', this is once again a respectable term; but the kind of metaphysics practised in academic departments is of a highly analytical kind, and is very largely conducted within the strictly logical and linguistic philosophical framework which Ayer helped create.

Dr John Cottingham

Ayer's other work includes: *Philosophical Essays* (1954); *The Problem of Knowledge* (1956); *The Concept of a Person* (1964); *Metaphysics and Common Sense* (1967); *The Central Questions of Philosophy* (1973); *The Origins of Pragmatism* (1968); and *Russell and Moore, The Analytic Heritage* (1971). He is also the editor of *Logical Positivism* (1959), a collection of expository and critical materials.

B

BABBITT, Milton Byron 1916–

US composer

Babbitt was born in Philadelphia and brought up in Jackson, Mississippi. As a child he took a lively interest in mathematics and music (studying the violin and clarinet) and continued these interests as an undergraduate at the Universities of North Carolina, Pennsylvania and New York City. During his student days in the 1930s he followed a brief career as a Tin Pan Alley musician, composing a number of pop songs and, somewhat later, in 1946, the score for the musical *Fabulous Voyager*. He has an encyclopedic knowledge of older pop music and an abiding affection for it which manifested itself in 1977 in his recorded selection of forgotten songs from Broadway, Hollywood and Tin Pan Alley, *Where Have We Met Before?* But it was also in the early 1930s that Babbitt became familiar with the music of the members of the Second Viennese School and, under this crucial influence, chose to concentrate his studies on music which became his major subject at NYU. His awareness of the European avant-garde of the day was intensified not only by Schoenberg's* arrival in New York in 1933, but also by his teacher, Marion Bauer, who was unusual in the breadth and detail of her knowledge of twentieth-century music. Between 1935 and 1938 Babbitt was a private student of the distinguished American composer, Roger Sessions, and continued to study with him after 1938 as a graduate student of Princeton University, where he became a junior member of the faculty and where he received his Master of Fine Arts degree in 1942. During the Second World War Babbitt continued teaching, but was also engaged in intelligence work in Washington. His association with Princeton University has continued to the present day and he currently holds the Conant Professorship in Music (in succession to Sessions).

Babbitt is celebrated for his unashamed intellectualism in general and for his virtuoso handling of twelve-tone musical technique in particular. He strongly maintains that musical composition need concede nothing in terms of intellectual rigour to any other of the intellectual disciplines, and that his own compositions are an attempt to 'utilize the inter-related and non-separable dimensions of music to the full of their perceptual susceptibility to musical structuring'. He has inherited from Schoenberg and his pupils the concern to make each aspect, small or large, of a composition relate on many levels to every other aspect; but, while the musical relationships between Schoenberg and Babbitt are crucially important in understanding the latter, it is just as important to realize that Babbitt's extensions of Schoenbergian technique and their integration with his extensions of techniques associated with Webern*, Berg* and Stravinsky* represent the foundations of a new grammar of music whose implications are both radical and far-reaching.

Since 1947 (the date of his earliest published composition) Babbitt has written upwards of forty works for nearly all genres including electronically synthesized tape. All of them are manifestations of the twelve-tone language, but so to describe them gives no idea of the great variety of their technical invention.

Many of the earlier works (e.g. the *Compositions* for four instruments, 1947–8, twelve instruments, rev. 1954, viola and piano, 1950, and piano solo, 1947–8) integrate extensions of Schoenbergian combinatoriality with extensions of Webernian set derivation, but employ varied approaches to the organization of the rhythmic domain. One of the most entertaining of this group of works recalls the composer's earlier excursions into the realm of popular music: *All Set* (1957) is for jazz ensemble, and its timbral organization causes each of the 'melody' instruments to deliver the typical solo 'break'.

Following an exploratory period (*c.* 1957–64), when he sought to develop his existing technique into a still more flexible means of musical expression and when he first had access to the revolutionary RCA synthesizer (on which instrument all his 'electronic' compositions have been realized), Babbitt arrived at two new concepts – the 'generalized aggregate' and the 'time-point' system of rhythmic organization – which have provided the technical foundation for all his subsequent compositions. Among the more important of these are *Ensembles* (1964), *Relata I and II* (1965 and 1968), *String Quartets Nos 3 and 4* (1969–70 and 1970), *Tableaux* (1972), *Arie da Capo* (1973–4), *Reflections* (1974), *Concerti* (1975–6) and *Images* (1979).

Babbitt's titles frequently have layers of meaning: *Post-Partitions* for solo piano (1966), for example, refers to (i) an earlier piano work, *Partitions* (1957), (ii) partitioning of the piano range into six separate registers,

(iii) partitioning into *legato* and *staccato* modes of articulation, (iv) various partitionings of the twelve-tone aggregate into layers of different dimensions, and (v) the name of the mathematician Emil Post who made notable contributions to the field of multiple-valued logic.

The later group of works presents extraordinary difficulties for performers, yet their subtle interplay of correspondence and contrast, symmetry and asymmetry, repetition and variation, afford the listener a musical experience of rare poise and distinction. Whereas so much of contemporary musical composition seems neo-Romantic in its extra-musical and expressive concerns, Babbitt's musical concerns, although *not* his surface style, seem almost to justify the epithet 'neo-Classical'.

Babbitt's influence on contemporary American musical life has been enormous. Not only have many younger American composers (Howe, Lansky, Martino, Melby, Westergaard *et al.*) been his students, but many who have not, both young and old, acknowledge the value for them of his brilliant, and brilliantly articulate, contributions to music theory. In addition, his pioneering work in electronic music and musical perception has encouraged new levels of refinement and precision in many kinds of synthetically realized music, while his challenging musical style has impelled performers to scale new heights of virtuosity.

Stephen Arnold

A comprehensive list of Babbitt's compositions to 1977 and articles to 1976 is given in *Perspectives of New Music*, vol. 14, no. 2, and vol. 15, no. 1.

26
BACHELARD, Gaston 1884–1962

French philosopher

Bachelard took a degree in mathematics and science before beginning his academic career as a teacher in his home town. He was appointed professor of philosophy in the University of Dijon in 1930, and from 1940 to 1954 he held the chair of the history and philosophy of science in the University of Paris.

Reflection on the developments of modern science led Bachelard to reject the Cartesian assumption that science operates within an immutable framework of first principles discoverable by pure reason. His major claims concerning the structure of scientific thought flow from his view of the creative interplay between reason and experience: reason enables experiment, which in turn produces data that force reason to reform itself in the radical and creative way illustrated by the replacement, in modern physics, of substantival by mathematical notions. However, since old conceptual frameworks are not jettisoned, but given a fresh although equally provisional meaning, the creative leaps by which science moves forward consolidate what is superseded, a process which Bachelard describes as 'the philosophy of saying no'. This 'open rationalism' leads to an 'applied rationalism', in that according to Bachelard science progresses by multiplying regional models which resist integration into a master scheme. This pluralistic view is offered as a truer account of the activity of scientific reason than that given by Meyerson and Brunschvicg, who claimed to see manifested in science the allegedly fundamental impulse of the mind to pursue unification. Bachelard remains unclear, however, about what he himself understands the *telos* of reason to be.

This style of epistemology, with its emphasis on creative discontinuity and the dependence of fact on thought, echoes in a rationalist key the existentialists' ethical concern with 'open morality'. But whereas some existentialist thinkers invoke the fictional character of scientific conceptions in order to affirm the intrinsic meaninglessness of the world, Bachelard sees in the success of empirical testing a guarantee that the external world takes our fictions seriously, and that its intelligibility is therefore not purely imposed by the mind. Although reason constantly re-creates the world, the promptings and feedback it receives from the world discredit existentialist talk of absurdity.

The latter half of Bachelard's writings is devoted mainly to the study of the creative imagination. The impetus for this new departure came from a fresh way of looking at the 'material imagination', which sustains alchemy and which Bachelard had blamed for the persistent difficulty the scientific mind experiences in sloughing off outmoded naturalistic habits of thought. Later, however, he comes to view the hold which the material elements have on the imagination as a psychological phenomenon worth studying in its own right, rather than as a source of error in science. His theory of the psychological significance of the four elements claims to show that the vision of material objects expressed in some poetry is a creative generalization of the poet's unconscious obsession with a single elemental (archetypal) image.

Bachelard denies that the freedom of the imagination is limited by the particular archetypical image which 'dynamizes' it. For the archetype is an *idée-force* whose meaning (a universal unconscious complex) is not determined by the primitive meaning of the complex, since it is evolved by the creative verbal expressions it gives rise to through the medium of reverie focused on a given element. Poetic images are not mere symbols, for they transfigure the 'deep instincts' which they symbolize in the act of evoking and expressing them. The unconscious is for Bachelard a power-house generating imagery, rather than a storehouse for past perceptions. Hence, the task of the psychoanalysis of art is not to 'explain the flower by the fertilizer', as in traditional Freudian* approaches, but to retrace phenomenologically the creative processes by which the imagination develops the potency of the archetype to produce aesthetic meanings transcending the biological meanings of which archetypes are primary transfigurations.

Attempts have been made to show that there is a unity between the two sides of Bachelard's philosophy, despite his own opinion that conceptual and imaginative thinking are 'opposed poles which repel one another'. It is possible to see unity in the creative role he assigns to the mind in both scientific reason and art, but to take this view is to pose the problem of understanding how the same creative function can espouse dialectically opposed forms.

Dr Roger McLure

Bachelard's works include: *L'intuition de l'instant* (1932); *Le nouvel esprit scientifique* (1934); *La Formation de l'esprit scientifique* (1938); *La Psychanalyse du feu* (1938); *La Philosophie du non* (1940); *Le Rationalisme appliqué* (1949); *La Poétique de l'espace* (1957); *La Poétique de la rêverie* (1960). See also: F. Dagognet, *Gaston Bachelard. Sa vie, son oeuvre, avec un exposé de sa philosophie* (1956); P. Quillet, *Gaston Bachelard* (1964); F. Pire, *De l'imagination poétique dans l'oeuvre de Gaston Bachelard* (1967). For a complete bibliography of Bachelard's works and for articles on him, see the *Revue Internationale de Philosophie*, vol. 19 (1964).

27
BACON, Francis 1909–

British artist

Francis Bacon was born in Dublin, the son of a successful English horse-trainer, and spent an unsettled childhood in Ireland and England. At the age of twenty he achieved some celebrity as a designer of fabrics and steel-framed furniture. At about this time he began to paint in oils, exhibiting occasionally, but very few of his works of the years 1930–44 survive. His artistic endeavour began in earnest just before the end of the war, when *Three studies for figures at the Base of a Crucifixion* was shown in April 1945 at the Lefèvre Gallery in London. This triptych of contorted monsters, grimacing against a strident orange background, was unacceptable to many who sought distraction from the genocide and unprecedented destruction which that year revealed.

Dictatorial, enthroned figures and dismembered carcasses were themes which dominated Bacon's paintings of the following years. In 1951 he executed the first series of 'Popes', shown staring intently or screaming with rage, within a rectangular framework reminiscent of his earlier furniture designs. In particular he adapted Velázquez's *Pope Innocent X* to achieve a formidable expression of savagery and naked power. He made use of Van Gogh's paintings, the cinematic stills of Eadweard Muybridge, and photographs discovered in newspapers, to produce an effect quite different from that of the initial inspiration. Many of Bacon's images gain force from the ambiguity of their reference: the associations of butcher's meat with the Crucifixion, of a hypodermic syringe with the nailing of Christ, and of wrestlers with lovers are repeatedly exploited. Bacon has often emphasized the role of chance in his work; fortuitous juxtapositions are developed and semi-accidental blobs and smears of paint are allowed to remain on the canvas.

After a period in the 1950s in which his work was characterized by dark tones and blurred forms, Bacon returned to sharper contours and more vivid colours, not only in his backgrounds but in limbs, nose and lips, accentuating the powerful effect of his brushstrokes. In 1962 he painted his second triptych, a format which he was to employ many times subsequently. In the same year a retrospective exhibition of his work was held at the Tate Gallery, before being circulated in Europe, where his reputation was consolidated. Neither the product nor the initiator of an artistic 'movement', he has won international respect through the unabated ferocity of his personal vision.

Some of Bacon's most arresting works are portraits, and in the traditionally respectful genre of portraiture he has overthrown convention. In the 1960s his portraits became increasingly violent, with facial features obscured or blurred in parabolic swathes of pigment. His figures sit or lie in a space defined only by a grid of intersecting lines, or in a stark room supplied with one or two characteristic items – an unshaded light bulb, a swivel chair or bar stool, cigarette butts, a window blind, a washbasin or lavatory. The tendency of Bacon's work is to expose his subjects, alone and often naked, without the support of the setting in which they are customarily seen; all that is homely or comforting is stripped away in his relentless pursuit of the individual in isolation.

Patrick Conner

The illustrated catalogue of Bacon's work exhibited at the Grand Palais, Paris, in 1971–2 contains a full bibliography and an introduction by Michael Leiris. The outstanding critical study is John Russell, *Francis Bacon* (1979). See also David Sylvester, *Interviews with Francis Bacon* (1975).

28

BALDWIN, James Arthur 1924–

US writer

America's foremost living black writer, James Baldwin has attempted in nearly all his work to portray frankly the dehumanizing effects of racism upon both blacks and whites. Much of his writing is set in the Harlem of his youth. His first and most respected novel, *Go Tell It On The Mountain* (1953), told of the religious conversion of a fourteen-year-old boy, and drew, as did his play *The Amen Corner* (1953), upon the author's own adolescent experience as a store-front preacher. Many of his essays also evoke, autobiographically, the pressures of the Harlem ghetto, pressures which Baldwin attempted to escape in 1948 when, like his mentor Richard Wright, he chose to live in France.

In other novels Baldwin explored the problem of achieving honest sexual and personal relationships in an immoral and guilt-ridden world. *Giovanni's Room* (1956) described an affair in Paris between two homosexuals and the tragedy that occurred when one had to choose between homosexual and heterosexual love. *Another Country* (1962) examined chaotic sexual entanglements among a group of blacks and whites in New York's Greenwich Village. Attacked by some as obscene and nihilistic, it was praised by many as a candid and accurate indictment of American values. *Tell Me How Long The Train's Been Gone* (1968) and *If Beale Street Could Talk* (1974) treated more directly the racial dilemma of black Americans and the personal tragedies that so often accompany it.

Baldwin the essayist is an outspoken social critic. His viewpoint is usually intensely personal, recounting his own experiences of racism in America and Europe and his quest for identity in a society that is hostile to dark-skinned peoples (*Notes of a Native Son*, 1956; *Nobody Knows My Name*, 1961; and *No Name In The Street*, 1972). A friend of both Martin Luther King* and Malcolm X*, Baldwin supported the civil rights movement and became an active member of the Congress of Racial Equality. Although in no sense a civil rights leader, Baldwin claimed to speak for and embody the feelings of all black Americans. *The Fire Next Time* (1963) predicted widespread violence unless whites ended racial injustice, and it brought Baldwin to the apogee of his fame. Many whites heeded his voice as an authentic expression of black grievances and aspirations. Like King, Baldwin designed his message to awaken their consciences, although he was far more insistent than King on depicting black anger and white guilt. Baldwin's didactic, accusatory style, however, proved less successful on the stage: his play *Blues for Mister Charlie* (1964) was criticized for being too polemical.

King's assassination and the inconclusive outcome of the civil rights movement produced a profound sense of despair in Baldwin, a mood which accentuated his preference for emotionalism to logic and his fondness for hyperbolic condemnations of whites and the Western world. These faults marred his discussion with Margaret Mead* in *A Rap On Race* (1971). But, although often bitter and emotive, Baldwin's strictures are rarely unjust. When most whites are trying to ignore the problem of racism, Baldwin insists on confronting it. His voice may be moralistic, but his words are eloquent and uncompromisingly honest. As an essayist he has few peers in America today.

Dr Adam Fairclough

Baldwin's other writings include: *Going To Meet the Man* (1965), short stories; *One Day, When I Was Lost* (1973), a screenplay; *The Devil Finds Work* (1976), film criticism; *Little Man, Little Man* (1977), a children's story; and *Just Above My Head* (1979), a novel. See also: Fern M. Eckman, *The Furious Passage of James Baldwin* (1967); Edward Margolies, *Native Son* (1968); and Stanley Macebuh, *James Baldwin: A Critical Study* (1973).

29

BALTHUS, Count Balthazar Klossowski de Rola 1908–

Polish/French painter

Le Comte Balthazar Klossowski de Rola, as he styles himself, has claimed Lord Byron as an ancestor, and although part of his celebrity rests upon a romantic and historical appreciation of his position as a figurative painter in an age when most artists have moved in other directions, his work has attracted an audience also for the power of its technique and imagery.

Since both parents were painters, Balthus did not have to go far for instruction and inspiration: their friends included Bonnard*, Derain, Marquet, Roussel and Denis among others. R. M. Rilke*, however, was probably the greatest influence on the young Balthus, and in 1921 published a series of drawings by him with a preface by himself. Balthus left Geneva and Berlin to live in Paris in 1924. Here he trained himself by copying Poussin, made the acquaintance of Gide* and Cocteau*, and, like them, used the theme of childhood in his work from the very beginning.

His earliest Impressionist works gave way to the powerful style based on Masaccio and Piero della Francesca which can be seen in *La Rue* of 1934. It was this work which gave Balthus an overnight celebrity among the Surrealists, who appreciated the mysterious and noble figures in an everyday street. Like the Surrealists, Balthus was in revolt against the abstract academicism of late Cubism; he shared their interest in the poetry of the subject, especially the themes of mystery, violence and sexuality. At the same time he rejected (and here we should take account of his Swiss upbringing) the hedonism of Impressionism, replacing it with a moral vision of humanity which has elements in common with both Rilke's and Artaud's*.

Balthus lays great emphasis on the craft of painting, and has taken as his models the fresco painters of the Quattrocento, the art of China and Japan, and, nearer to home, Courbet. From them he derives his mathematically clear compositions, and his delight in the 'matière' of paint and in the play of light. Two of Balthus's largest and most compelling works date from 1952–4: *Le Passage du Commerce Saint-André* is another street scene which might be an allegory of the 'three ages of man'; *La Chambre* shows a dwarfish woman drawing a curtain, while a naked girl on a divan lies ecstatic in the flood of light. At this time, Balthus left Paris to work on landscapes in the country for six years, until his appointment by André Malraux* to the directorship of the Académie Française, in the Villa Medici in Rome. *La Chambre Turque* (collection of the Centre National d'Art Contemporain in Paris) shows a room in the Villa. In this work, he combines a Japanese model with an oriental use of perspective.

Part of Balthus's reputation lies in his ability in technique and composition, part in the subject matter which has of late become increasingly inscrutable beneath the flatness of the composition and the encrusted paint surface. His subject is always the same: while some see it as relating to Nabokov's* *Lolita*, others recognize in his obsession with childhood Rilke's spiritual urgency. The best guides of all are the writings of Georges Bataille and the artist's brother, Pierre Klossowski.

Balthus's continued artistic practice is one assurance that the history of art in Europe between the wars will eventually be rewritten, and that the Parisian 'Indépendants' – Modigliani*, Chagall*, Soutine*, Tchelitchew, Berman, Giacometti* – will be seen to cohere as a humanist counterpart to their more polemical and extremist contemporaries.

Lewis Biggs

Two exhibition catalogues have been published in English, one by the Museum of Modern Art, New York (1956), the other by the Tate Gallery, London (1968). See also Jean Leymarie, *Balthus* (1979).

30

BARTH, Karl 1886–1968

Swiss reformed theologian

Son of a Swiss New Testament scholar, Barth was born in Basel, and educated in the theological faculties of the universities of Bern, Berlin, Tübingen and Mar-

burg. In Berlin and Marburg his teachers were renowned representatives of the school of German Liberal Protestantism, and Barth's first employment was as an associate editor of the popular and influential liberal-protestant periodical *Die Christliche Welt* (1908–9). After a short period (1909–11) as assistant pastor of the German-speaking reformed church in Geneva, Barth became parish pastor of Safenwil (Canton Aargau) in 1911, where he included amongst his activities sympathetic encouragement for industrial workers agitating for higher wages and improved working conditions, a leftist political stance which he maintained and consolidated for the remainder of his life, and which involved him in a temporary alliance with the South German and Swiss Christian Socialists led by Leonhard Ragaz and Hermann Kutter.

The outbreak of the war in 1914, and the ensuing appalling suffering, were quite crucial for Barth's epoch-making theological 'change of mind'. German war-aims had been vigorously defended in 1914 by many German intellectuals (including certain liberal theologians, several of Barth's former teachers among them), and this led him publicly to dissociate himself from what he described as their optimistic, humanistic, utopianistic, progressivistic, and superficial ethico-religious doctrines, which he characterized as anthropocentric rather than theocentric. Under the realization that Christian theology urgently needed a 'new beginning', he turned to a systematic re-examination of Scripture in the light of a thorough study of the sixteenth-century Reformers (particularly Calvin), the Danish father of Existentialism Kierkegaard, and the novels of Dostoievski, the concrete result of which was the publication in 1919 of Barth's *Commentary on Romans* (*Der Römerbrief*, trans. 1933, described by a Catholic theologian as 'the bombshell tossed on to the playground of the theologians'). Under the form of a commentary on the Pauline text, Barth's *Romans* is in reality an attack on the presuppositions and content of nineteenth-century German protestant liberalism, which is compared most unfavourably with Barth's own neo-orthodoxy, which described God as the 'Wholly Other' (Kierkegaard), as absolutely discontinuous with human reason, ideals, experience and expectations, as 'infinitely qualitatively distinct' from everything finite. All human achievements and institutions, within which Barth pointedly included religion itself, are under the Judgment of and exposed to the Wrath of God. Mankind is living in a time of *KRISIS* (judgment, turning point): hence one of the earliest titles of Barth's new thinking, 'Crisis Theology'. There is no genuine knowledge of God whatsoever apart from God's Word to man in Jesus Christ, who is simultaneously God's 'Yes' and 'No' to sinful, fallen man, a 'Yes' and 'No' corresponding to certain dialectical opposites which lie at the heart of the Christian faith, Grace and Wrath, Sin and Righteousness, Gospel and

Law – hence the other title of Barth's revolutionary work, 'Dialectical Theology'.

There followed for Barth theological professorships in Germany – at Göttingen (1921), Münster (1925) and Bonn (1930), and the years 1921–35 saw the laying of the foundations of his main life's work, the multivolumed *Church Dogmatics* (*Kirchliche Dogmatik*, trans. 1961), in which Barth both extended and corrected the basic ideas set forth in his *Romans* – the exclusive centrality of Christ in all of God's dealings with men, the defunctness of human reason as a source of divine truth (the attack on 'natural theology'), the priority of the Word of God over Church and world; the humble, presuppositionless and obedient attitude required of all readers and hearers of God's Word, the repudiation of religious and moral experience as presuppositions of coming into the situation of faith which is absolutely and exclusively created by Christian preaching, and the referral of all human and historical issues to the final judgment of God. During the period Barth's principal adherents were Eduard Thurneysen and Emil Brunner; and the young Bonhoeffer* was strongly influenced by his revolutionary thinking. Barth's teaching received heavy practical development by his deep involvement in the German Church Struggle of 1933–45. A profound crisis was produced for German Christianity after the advent of the Nazis by the proposal of the 'German Christians' that positive collaboration between the Church and the Nazi state was both possible and desirable on the basis of that 'revelation' of the divine purpose and destiny in history, politics and race – especially in the ineradicable 'Orders of Creation', such as ethnic differentiation, the state and natural reason. Barth responded by categorically denying the existence and authority of any such revelation, and at the Synod of Barmen in May 1934 was deeply involved in the foundation of the Confessing Church which was opposed to all adulteration of Christianity with National Socialist ideology, and the constitutive document of this Church, the Declaration of Barmen, which explicitly denied the existence of all revelations secondary to and apart from Christ ('Christomonism') was largely the work of Barth himself. Further opposition to Nazism by Barth culminated in his refusal to sign in 1935 the oath of loyalty to Hitler* required of all German professors; Barth was dismissed from his professorship at Bonn by the state and returned to his native Switzerland, where he became Professor of Dogmatics in Basel until his retirement in 1962.

During the years 1935–45, Barth, as teacher, writer and broadcaster, became a focus of Christian opposition to the Nazi regime and ideology, and addressed 'open letters' to the Christians of Britain, France and the USA. In the post-war years, he continued as a theological teacher and writer, and controversially extended sympathy, by writing and visiting, to the regimes of Eastern Europe. He appeared to qualify his extreme position on divine–human discontinuity in his essay *The Humanity of God* (*Die Menschlichkeit Gottes*, 1957, trans. 1961) by suggesting that a certain continuity did exist through the existence of humanity in God (although he denied divinity to man), but his critics have judged that this late concession does not amount to much. His work is still being evaluated; despite his greatness, many interpreters have judged that the extreme and inflexible Christomonism of his system has bequeathed to modern theology many acute problems in the areas of the relation of faith to reason, theology to philosophy, and religion to culture.

Professor James Richmond

Other works include: *Dogmatics in Outline* (*Dogmatik in Grundriss*, 1947, trans. 1949); *Protestant Theology in the Nineteenth Century* (*Die Protestantische Theologie*, 1952, trans. 1972). See: T. F. Torrance, *Karl Barth: An Introduction to his Early Theology 1910–1931* (1962); Eberhard Busch, *Karl Barth* (1976), the standard biography, contains a complete bibliography.

31
BARTHES, Roland 1915–80

French writer-critic and teacher

The writing of Roland Barthes embraces literature and the arts, as well as a much wider range of cultural phenomena: he wrote, for example, on women's fashion, on advertising, food and the Citroën D. S. His interest was in cultural phenomena as language systems, and to this extent he may be thought of as a structuralist, although he is not a structuralist in the orthodox sense. Broadly speaking his work belongs within an anti-positivist, anti-empiricist tradition whose basic references are Marx, Nietzsche, Saussure* and Freud*.

Barthes published some fifteen books and a sizeable body of articles and prefaces. Chronologically two major shifts of emphasis, and therefore three phases, may be distinguished. In the first phase the emphasis is twofold: (1) on demystifying the stereotypes of bourgeois culture, and (2) on studying culture as form. Barthes is concerned with literature and the history of French literature in *Writing Degree Zero* (*Le Degré Zéro de l'Écriture*, 1953, trans. 1967), with the link between writing and biography in *Michelet par lui-même* (1954) and with so-called mass culture as a sub-product of bourgeois culture in *Mythologies* (1957, trans. 1972) and *The Eiffel Tower and Other Mythologies* (1979–80). His early work is much influenced by Sartre* and Brecht*.

The second phase may be labelled the semiotic phase. It begins with Barthes's reading of Saussure in 1956, and the methodological appendix to *Mythologies*. In this phase Barthes takes over Saussure's concept of the sign and analysis of language as a sign system. 'Elements of Semiology' ('Éléments de sémiologie', *Communications* 4, 1964, trans. 1967) is a theoretical work in which Barthes considers the adaptation of Saussure's model to the study of cultural phenomena other than language. *Système de la Mode* ('The System of Fashion', 1967) applies the methods of semiology to a corpus of fashion articles from *Elle* and *Jardin des Modes*.

The third phase is established with the publication of *S/Z* (1970, trans. 1974). At this point Barthes moves away from Saussurean semiology towards a theory of 'the text', defined as the field of play of the signifier and of the symbolic (Lacan*). *S/Z* is a reading of Balzac's *Sarrasine* which plots the migrations of five 'codes', understood as open groupings of signifieds and as the points of crossing with other texts. The distinction between 'le scriptible' (the writeable) and 'le lisible' (the readable), between what can be written/ rewritten today, i.e. actively produced by the reader, and what can no longer be written, but only read, i.e. passively consumed, provides a new basis for evaluation, and is extended in *The Pleasure of the Text* (*Le Plaisir du Texte*, 1973, trans. 1975) via the metaphor of the body as text and language as an object of desire.

S/Z, *The Pleasure of the Text*, as well as all the other books published by Barthes in the 1970s, have in common the fact that they are written in the form of fragments. This represents for Barthes a conscious retreat from what he sees as the discourse of domination and power, caught in the subject/object relationship and the habits of rhetoric. He distinguishes now between 'the ideological' and 'the aesthetic', between the language of science, which deals in stable meanings and is identified with the sign, and the language of writing and criticism, which aims at displacement, denaturalization, dispersion. Barthes offered 'textual' readings of Japan in *L'Empire des Signes* ('The Empire of Signs', 1970), of the founders of new languages in *Sade-Fourier-Loyola* (1971, trans. 1976), of himself in *Roland Barthes by Roland Barthes* (*Roland Barthes par Roland Barthes*, 1975, trans. 1977) and of the outdated, discredited discourse of love in *A Lover's Discourse* (*Fragments d'un Discours Amoureux*, 1977, trans. 1978).

Barthes's mode of progress is itself characterized by displacement. Apart from the major shifts of emphasis already described, shifts and turns can occur from one work to the next, and even from one sentence to the next and within single words. 'Semiology' for instance is used quite differently in the 1970s, in association with art, aesthetics and theories of the subject.

Barthes was from 1960–2 Chef de travaux and from 1962–76 Directeur d'études at the École Pratique des Hautes Études, Paris; in 1976 he became Professor of literary semiology at the Collège de France, Paris. Teaching was for him an important activity, closely related to writing. He was interested especially in the forms through which knowledge and culture are conveyed, speaking latterly of the digression, the equivalent of the fragment in writing, as a means whereby teaching might be freed from didacticism.

Barthes's recent work is undoubtedly problematical in its insistence that the essential struggle is against the sign. On the other hand there can be no return to the positions which, indirectly, he has done so much to help us criticize; he leaves for us the pleasure of his texts.

Annwyl Williams

Other works include: *On Racine* (*Sur Racine*, 1963, trans. 1964); *Critical Essays* (*Essais Critiques*, 1964, trans. 1972); *Critique et Vérité* ('Criticism and Truth', 1966); 'L'ancienne rhétorique (Aide-mémoire)' ('Classical rhetoric, working notes', *Communications* 16, 1970); *Lecture Leçon* (1978 trans. 1979) and *La Chambre claire. Note sur la photographie* (1980). *Image-Music-Text* (1977) contains essays selected and translated by Stephen Heath. On Barthes: G. de Mallac and M. Eberbach, *Barthes* (1971); L.-J. Calvet, *Roland Barthes. Un regard politique sur le signe* (1973); S. Heath, *Vertige du déplacement* (1974); P. Thody, *Roland Barthes: a conservative estimate* (1977); and J.-B. Fages, *Comprendre Roland Barthes* (1979). Parody of Barthes: M.-A. Burnier and P. Rambaud, *Le Roland-Barthes sans peine* (1978).

32
BARTÓK, Béla 1881–1945

Hungarian composer

A fervent nationalist, Bartók relinquished the opportunity of studying in Vienna in favour of the Budapest Royal Academy of Music where he became known less as a composer than as a brilliant pianist. From 1907 his own teaching there was influential and, with concert tours, provided the means by which he sustained his folk-music research until becoming a member of the Hungarian Academy of Science in 1934. By then, too, the radical individuality of his music was established abroad. With the increasing Nazification of Hungary he departed for the United States in 1940 and was awarded an Honorary Doctorate at Columbia University where he continued his research until 1942. During the remaining three years, despite recurring illness, he composed the Concerto for Orchestra (1943), Sonata for Solo Violin (1944) and the 3rd Piano Concerto (1945).

With Schoenberg* and Stravinsky*, Bartók is one of the great innovators of his epoch. The image of him as 'folklorist', while true, can be deceptively facile. His individuality arises from the rare concurrence in one intelligence of elements both scrupulously scientific enough to seek out, analyse and classify a forgotten language, and powerfully creative enough to evolve a new one.

His output falls broadly into two periods: the first (c. 1903–23) is involved with the assimilation of folk-music and the development of his style; a second period (from 1924) is dominated by the synthesis of large-scale forms. He subscribed to none of the accepted contemporary musical tendencies but, being eclectic, aimed for a measured balance of these elements. His music, lyrical and dramatic in expression, depends on sonata-type forms for its fulfilment and is characterized by the intensely organic way in which these are evolved and interrelated (thematically, through a process derived from Franz Liszt).

The monumental set of six String Quartets (No. 1, Op. 7, 1909; No. 2, Op. 17, 1915–17; No. 3, 1927; No. 4, 1928; No. 5, 1934; No. 6, 1939), long regarded as the core of his work, display such formal preoccupations. Of the First it could be said that its main theme only emerges in the third (last) movement, whereas in the Second everything is contained in the opening. The Third, based on some two or three motives, is reduced to one movement of four sections whose first and third have related material: the nascent arch-form. The Fourth and Fifth show elaborated arch-forms of five movements (schematically ABCBA), while the Sixth forsakes them for an introductory motto-theme which introduces each movement and is developed in the last.

Up to 1905 Bartók's style was compounded of popular Hungarian and teutonic elements (Brahms, Wagner, Strauss*), but a basic change took place then because of the ethnomusicology begun with Kodály*. Revealed to him was the spirit of a 'new Hungarian art-music' and melodies of 'unsurpassable beauty and perfection'. They were the spontaneous expression of the rural peasantry, completely unknown and distinct from the gypsy music of urban civilization. Unlike Kodály, Bartók extended his interest to Slovak, Romanian, Arabic and Turkish music. The hours spent collecting this music were the happiest of his life, his identification with rural life and art complete. The allegorical *Cantata Profana* (1930) is the quintessence of this spirit.

But the most direct interaction with folk-music can be traced in the numerous song-settings and piano transcriptions. Bartók's vitality of rhythm is greatly influenced by improvisatory speech-rhythm (*parlando rubato*), dance-rhythm (*tempo giusto*, mainly duple pulse except for the pliancy of Bulgarian rhythms), and the 'dotted' rhythm derived from the Hungarian language. Moreover these melodies were based on pentatonic, modal and oriental scales, not the diatonic ones of Western classical music. Harmonies derived from the first led to a more free use of 2nds, 4ths and 7ths, traditionally considered dissonant. If these were applied (chromatically) to modal tunes the increased pos-

sibilities resulted in a mixture of modes, hence bi- and poly-modality. However Bartók retained, at any given moment, the authority of a fundamental tone, unlike the claims of 'atonality' and 'polytonality'. Although one of various principles, modality identifies some of Bartók's characteristics: the gravitation of his (own) melodies around specific tones, the variation of otherwise strict contrapuntal forms (canon, fugue, inversion) and the rich diversification of his harmonic palette generally. The last of the *Eight Improvisations on Hungarian Peasant Songs*, Op. 20 (1920) was admitted to be the extreme limit reached by him in adding daring accompaniments to simple folk-tunes. So complete was his absorption that the creation of original works in imitation of folk-music followed naturally, of which the *Piano Suite*, Op. 14 (1916) and orchestral *Dance Suite* (1923) are fine examples.

From the speculative *Fourteen Bagatelles*, Op. 6 (1908) which mark the beginning of his personal style, up to the *Two Violin and Piano Sonatas* (1921/2) there is a swing from the simpler to the more complex, from romanticism to expressionism, from the opera *Duke Bluebeard's Castle*, Op. 11 (1911), through *The Wooden Prince* ballet (1914–16) and *Songs*, Opp. 15 and 16 (1915–16) to *The Wonderful Mandarin* pantomime, Op. 19 (1918–19). The piano music alone affords a varied panorama of this period and sees the beginning of his overtly pedagogical music which, from *Ten Easy Pieces* (1908) to the *153 Mikrokosmos* (1926–39) and *Forty-four Duos* (1931) for two violins, is without equal this century. Liberally endowed with folk material and stylistic innovations, their often graphic qualities enhance the musical points made. Instrumental technique was highly developed in Bartók but never exaggerated. His treatment of percussion instruments was actually refined while his exploitation of stringed instruments was little short of miraculous.

Coinciding with editions of baroque keyboard music, the three works of 1926 are marked by economy of line and propulsive rhythm (Piano Sonata, First Piano Concerto, *Out of Doors*). While the Second Piano Concerto (1930–1) might be termed 'neo-classic' in its interlocking patterns and confessed aim to be more pleasing, this music indicates a more raw awareness of the reality in the ethnic experience and its alignment to art-music. Stripped of the inessential except in the pursuit of sonority, an unyielding force flows through it which yet contains the delicacy of 'Musiques Nocturnes' (*Out of Doors*).

The elucidation of golden sections and tonal axes of symmetry confirm what is already felt in the dynamic equilibrium of the succeeding works. All kinds of scale-segments are drawn upon for the compression and expansion of pitch (and rhythm) that transforms one idea over a span of four movements in *Music for Strings, Percussion and Celesta* (1936), whose fugal first movement is itself a unique structuring of musical space. A constant regeneration of invention promotes a form as large as the first movement of the *Sonata for Two Pianos and Percussion* (1937). A vision which can seem to question the very substance of musical material in the Fourth Quartet can later embrace the variational exuberance of the Violin Concerto (No. 2, 1937–8). With these achievements comes a rejuvenation of classical proportions which *Contrasts* (1938) and the *Divertimento* (1939) share with the works of the American period, granting Bartók a wide appeal and understanding which has not diminished. His influence on post-war composers has been selective, as witness Stockhausen's* early dissertation on the rhythmic aspects (alone) of the *1937 Sonata*; or the fascination, particularly for serially-minded commentators, of the Fourth Quartet's integration. Others have emulated subtleties of sound and texture or his pedagogical style. The humane integrity of Bartók's utterly musical art remains invincible.

Ronald Lumsden

An unfinished Viola Concerto (1945) was reconstructed and orchestrated by Tibor Serly. See: Serge Moreux, *Béla Bartók* (trans. London 1953); Halsey Stevens, *The Life and Music of Béla Bartók* (1953, revised 1964); Ernö Lendvai, *Béla Bartók* (1971); *Béla Bartók Essays*, ed. Benjamin Suchoff (London 1976).

33
BEATLES, The 1962–70

British pop group

Teenage culture which emerged so suddenly with Elvis Presley* as its figurehead was widened and deepened by the Beatles, the biggest phenomenon in the history of pop music. The group, which consisted of John Lennon (b. 1940), George Harrison (b. 1943), Paul McCartney (b. 1942) and Ringo Starr (b. 1940), all came from Liverpool. Their first phase, that of spontaneous and hysterical idolatry known as Beatlemania, began in 1963 with the release of their second single 'Please Please Me'. It gathered momentum throughout that year with the release of 'From Me To You', 'She Loves You', 'I Wanna Hold Your Hand', all number one singles, by which time they had passed from obscurity, through commercial success, to the point at which they were generating the most extravagant fanaticism ever accorded popular entertainers. Like Presley, the Beatles focused adolescent energy quite abruptly, and caused a similarly radical alteration in the behaviour and appearance of young people. Unlike Presley, they wrote their own songs which was the underlying factor in their freshness and richer sense of freedom. The self-reliant group (in the Beatles' case:

Lennon – rhythm guitar, McCartney – bass guitar, Harrison – lead guitar, Starr – drums) replaced the dependent performer as the essential outlet for pop music. But the Beatles' intelligent and disarming individuality, the skill and beauty of Lennon and McCartney's songs, plus the aggressive simplicity with which they were originally performed, gave them a unique status and they rose to the occasion so well that in the liberal mood of the 1960s they won over those establishment and parental figures who had been discomfited by the appearance of a generation which seemed to be running wild. That the Beatles were able to navigate this unprecedented adulation and continue to develop as individuals was as remarkable as Beatlemania itself. They toured the world; they made two films (*A Hard Day's Night* and *Help!*) with Dick Lester which represent as well as anything else the exuberant weirdness characteristic of 'Swinging London'; and they were awarded the MBE.

Beatlemania came to an end at the beginning of 1967 with the release of the single 'Penny Lane/Strawberry Fields'. It failed to reach number one. The group began serious experimentation on the album *Revolver* the previous year, introducing chamber music into 'Eleanor Rigby' and avant-garde electronic music into 'Tomorrow Never Knows', a song marking their public association with the LSD 'Flower Power' movement whose prime mover was Timothy Leary*. After the initial surprise they recaptured their audience in a far more adult fashion. With the release of the album *Sergeant Pepper's Lonely Hearts Club Band* in the summer of 1967, the traditional straightforward melodiousness of popular songs meshed with intellectual ideas and strangely alluring tonal and structural inventions. Pop music ostentatiously announced itself as a modern art form which it has remained ever since. However raw it may sometimes be, pop music is now considered as a wholly legitimate vehicle for ideas.

It was during this 'Summer of Love' that the Beatles were involved with the Indian mystic, the Maharishi Mahesh Yogi – it was a symptom of the growing interest in Eastern thought being taken by non-specialists. Unlike many of their contemporaries the Beatles never committed themselves to drugs or (with the exception of George Harrison) to oriental philosophies. After *Sergeant Pepper* the albums illustrate the disintegration of their collective identity (brilliantly turned to account with the album *Abbey Road* and less brilliantly with *Let It Be*) and it was no surprise when they disbanded in 1970.

The Beatles are important for the function they performed as providing the integrating soundtracks, or points of cross-reference on a global scale, for a decade which saw an astonishing development of ideas. They hastened popular interest in many subjects previously esoteric and were the most important 'bonding' input of the social evolution one associates with the 1960s, since when their songs have become classics of the popular repertoire. Paul McCartney, whose subsequent career was more prosperous than that of the others, has been formally acknowledged in *The Guinness Book of Records* as the world's most commercially successful composer.

Duncan Fallowell

See Hunter Davies, *The Beatles* (1968).

34

BEATON, Sir Cecil Walter Hardy 1904–80

British photographer and designer

With his interest in the glamour of the Edwardian stage fired by his 'Bolivian Aunt' (she was married to a South American diplomat), Beaton early developed an eye for the minutiae of design surrounding a beautiful woman. He was educated at St Cyprians in Hampstead (fellow-pupils included Cyril Connolly* and Evelyn Waugh*), at Harrow, and at St John's College, Cambridge. His designs for the Marlowe Society's 1923 production of *Volpone* attracted wide attention: while clearly derived from Léon Bakst, they also provided the first showing of Beaton's ability to eliminate superfluous detail, a touch that characterized most of his pursuits to come, as photographer, costume and set designer, illustrator, portraitist and even actor. In 1924 photographs of his sisters Nancy and Baba, posed as angels in medieval costumes, were published in *Vogue*, and marked the beginning of a long association with that magazine. At the same time he enjoyed the patronage of the Sitwells, which led to his classic portrait of Edith Sitwell*, recumbent on squared linoleum and flanked by *putti*, a mingling of the Baroque and Gothic. The unorthodox lighting employed in this photograph, accentuating the sitter's hands and facial bone structure, was quickly assimilated into Beaton's style; by 1929 he was shown at the Düsseldorf exhibition and had an international reputation. His other distinctive ploy was the use of unlikely and eye-catching props, as comments on the character of the subject: polka-dotted cloth (Nancy Cunard), foil paper (Lady Lavery), even a surreal glass-bell-shaped cover over a head (Lady Loughborough). During the 1930s his technique was augmented by increasingly sophisticated backdrops, ranging from the deliberately Romantic to stark card cut-outs with surreal images, so that, with his innate gift for composition, much of his work achieved qualities more often associated with painting: texture, a sense of colour (even in monochrome), and a feeling of space and time, which his 1939 photographs of Queen Elizabeth best capture.

From 1939 to 1945 Beaton was an official war photographer, attached to the Ministry of Information.

Separated from his accustomed world of high fashion and high society, his talent triumphed. More poignant and terrible than his earlier surreal fantasies, his war images – of the Near and Far Eastern Fronts, of the aftermath of Tobruk, of St Paul's Cathedral amid the smoking waste of the City of London – are generally regarded as the peak of Beaton's photographic genius.

Never abandoning his gift for portraiture, Beaton became a celebrated designer in the post-war years, his strength lying in the re-creation of nineteenth-century and Edwardian decoration. In 1945 he designed John Gielgud's productions of Wilde's *Lady Windermere's Fan*, and acted in the subsequent productions in San Francisco and New York, where he was commissioned by the Metropolitan Opera to create the sets for a number of operas and ballets, including *Taras* and *Camille* (both 1946). He was equally, if not more, at home with the film. While early successes included *Major Barbara* (1941), *Anna Karenina* (1948) and *An Ideal Husband* (1948), his skill in capturing the colours, fabrics and movements of a period was ideally utilized in the musicals *Gigi* (1958) and *My Fair Lady* (1963, from the stage show of 1956, also designed by Beaton).

Michael Pick

Beaton's *Glass of Fashion* (1954) remains one of the best accounts of fashion and design in the first half of the century, while his *Diaries* (6 vols, 1961–77) are important both as autobiography and social history. Most of his photographs have been published with accompanying texts as books, of which there are more than thirty volumes. See also: Francis Rose, *Saying Life* (1961); and Charles Spencer, *Cecil Beaton: Stage and Film Designs* (1975).

35

BEAUVOIR, Simone de 1908–

French writer

Simone de Beauvoir has given a full account of her own origins, upbringing, and evolution in her three large volumes of autobiography: *Memoirs of a Dutiful Daughter* (*Mémoires d'une fille rangée*, 1958, trans. 1959); *The Prime of Life* (*La Force de l'âge*, 1960, trans. 1962); *The Force of Circumstance* (*La Force des choses*, 1963, trans. 1965). She was born into a solid middle-class Paris environment, and, although her early education took place in private institutions, her family was liberal enough to allow a daughter to follow her wish and undertake a course of university study. It was in 1929, during her preparation for the *agrégation* in philosophy, that she met Jean-Paul Sartre*, with whom she has been closely associated ever since. Like him she became a teacher, like him retired from that profession during the war – in her case in 1943, after the publication of her novel *She came to Stay* (*L'Invitée*, 1943, trans. 1949).

One of the main differences between her thinking and that of Sartre is that, whereas he fails to produce his promised Ethics, Simone de Beauvoir has concentrated much of her attention on the personal and the moral. In the novels of the 1940s she seeks to work out the implications of the Existentialist view of freedom and choice, action and commitment, life and death. This is true of *She came to Stay* as well as of *The Blood of Others* (*Le Sang des autres*, 1944, trans. 1948) and of *All Men are Mortal* (*Tous les hommes sont mortels*, 1946, trans. 1955). With her one play, she comes to the critical ethico-social problem of the relative value of individual existences, in terms both of each other and of their social usefulness: in *Les Bouches inutiles* ('Useless mouths', 1945) decisions have to be made about which individuals should be sacrificed first to ensure the survival of the group in a town under siege.

It is not, therefore, surprising that she should at this time have produced a sequence of essays of an ethical nature; *Pyrrhus et Cinéas* (1944), *Pour une morale de l'ambiguïté* ('Towards an ethics of ambiguity', 1947), and *L'Existentialisme et la sagesse des nations* ('Existentialism and popular wisdom', 1948) spell out the attitudes towards personal relationships underlying some of Sartre's work, underline the weaknesses of conventional moral 'values', and demonstrate the essentially pessimistic view of mankind implied in popular judgment of human behaviour. These texts, along with her work on *Les Temps modernes* (with which, like Sartre, she had been involved since it was launched in 1945), prepared the way for her most important publications in this period. *The Second Sex* (*Le deuxième sexe*, 1949, trans. 1953), like the later study of *Old Age* (*La Vieillesse*, 1970, trans. 1972), is a massive and sometimes indigestible compilation of evidence intended not only to document the history of attitudes to women (or old people) but also to demonstrate the way in which such groups are victims of the society in which they are assigned an inferior status. *The Mandarins* (*Les Mandarins*, 1954, trans. 1957), although a novel and winner of the Prix Goncourt, is not far removed from the same set of preoccupations, partly because its main characters are women, but also because they and the whole of the essentially Parisian intellectual society to which they belong are frustrated in their aspirations, whether they be intellectual, political, or personal.

This is no doubt to some extent true of Simone de Beauvoir herself. Intellectually, she may have been too close to Sartre to be able to produce anything of great philosophical originality; in politics, despite an active and continuing commitment, despite what her autobiography suggests that she herself believes, and despite the number of declarations she has signed or the number of marches in which she has taken part, she still looks very much the middle-class intellectual; at

the personal level, her sense of fulfilment may well be greater, though even there the approach of old age seriously modifies the self-confident euphoria of *The Prime of Life*. Ultimately (and she would no doubt not complain about that) it may be as a woman that she leaves her deepest mark: both through her example and by the things she was prepared to write as early as *The Second Sex* she has pointed out the way to be followed by her juniors of more than one generation.

Keith Gore

Other works: *The Woman Destroyed* (*La Femme rompue*, 1967, trans. 1969); *A Very Easy Death* (*Une Mort très douce*, 1964, trans. 1966); *All Said and Done* (*Tout compte fait*, 1972, trans. 1974); *Simone de Beauvoir* (the transcript of Josée Dayan's film, Paris, 1979). See: M. Descubes, *Connaître Simone de Beauvoir* (1974); F. Jeanson, *Simone de Beauvoir, ou l'entreprise de vivre* (1966); A.-M. Lasocki, *Simone de Beauvoir, ou l'entreprise d'écrire* (1971).

36

BECKETT, Samuel 1906–

Irish writer

Irish (born in Dublin of a Protestant, originally French Huguenot, family) poet (though his poems count for little), playwright and fictionist, the greater part of whose work has been done in a self-imposed exile in Paris. So the verbal self-consciousness of the Irish and Anglo-Irish tradition – Beckett's work has affinities with e.g. Sterne, Joyce* and Flann O'Brien (Brian O'Nolan) – has been reinforced by a lively bilingualism (Beckett has written now in French, now in English, and does his own translations into the other language) and by first-hand contact with the modernist European 'revolution of the Word' early associated with the linguistics of Ferdinand de Saussure* and the experiments of the Dadaists and Surrealists. Beckett only came to general notice in 1952 with his play *En attendant Godot* (*Waiting for Godot*, 1955), by which time much of his most substantial work (he appeared first in 1929 as one of Joyce's twelve disciples chosen to explain what became *Finnegans Wake* in *Our Exagmination Round his Factification for Incamination of Work in Progress*) had been done: the book on *Proust* (1931), the stories of *More Pricks than Kicks* (1934), *Murphy* (1938), *Watt* (written 1942; published Paris 1953); the great Trilogy (*Molloy, Malone Meurt* (*Malone Dies*), *L'Innommable* (*The Unnameable*), all written, like *Godot*, 1948–9), and the extremely important quartet of post-war *nouvelles* written in 1946, *Premier Amour* (*First Love*), *L'Expulsé* (*The Expelled*), *La Fin* (*The End*), *Le Calmant* (*The Calmative*).

From the beginning, Beckett's fictions (and there is a close correspondence between his plays, his novels and his shorter fictions) have with startling jocularity inhabited heavily depressing locales – Dublin in *More Pricks*, London in *Murphy*, and after that an increasingly abstracted Paris. They have plunged their people into ever grimmer varieties of physical disability; Beckett so loves deficiencies of limb, especially deformities of the feet, diabetes, skin disorders (eczema of the sacrum, for instance), and the like, that his people compose an almost Biblical crowd of the halt, the maimed and the blind. Action, from ironic epicure Belacqua relishing his blackened toast and stinking cheese ('What he wanted was a good green stenching rotten lump of Gorgonzola cheese, alive, and by God he would have it') to, say, Molloy's rutting like a dog in a rubbish dump with a person of indeterminate sex suffering from rheumatism and lumbago, is conducted at an animaline level of bare human survival in the ditch, the gutter, the loony-bin, the derelict's shake-down. And these seedy existences (far seedier than the renowned seediness of Graham Greene's* fictions) imprison. Murphy is an early 'seedy solipsist', locked into a welcomed series of solipsistic enclosures – rooms, wombs, a padded cell, a lunatic asylum. It is a set of 'closed systems' that Beckett's work keenly expands into a zesty catalogue of tomb- and womb-like places: beds, lavatories, motor vehicles, sheds, bags, bottles, jars, boats, and so on. Imprisoning too are the routines that fill up otherwise empty interstices of fictional space: repetitive plays with hats or with stage-patter that recall music-hall comics and silent-film stars – particularly Charlie Chaplin*, of whom Joyce too was fond, and Buster Keaton* (star of Beckett's film, *Film*, 1964). And above all there is a steady stylistic progression away from fictions like *More Pricks* and *Murphy* which 'tell a story' to writing which exists to a large extent for its own sake, a hypnotic litany of verbal rigmaroles increasingly composing a classic case of what modern French criticism knows as *une écriture*, a mere dance or *jeu* of signifiers to be enjoyed 'for its own sake' and not for some other signified meaning.

It is too easy, though, to read Beckett merely as a central instance of 'the Absurd'. To be sure, he does present a sick-joke world and a world of sick jokes, a universe whose increasingly clamant negativity is announced in a procession of negating titles like *L'Innommable, Textes pour Rien* and *Imagination Morte, Imaginez* (both in *No's Knife*), *Actes sans Paroles, Sans, Not I*. He is a determined minimalist, more and more resolutely cutting down and hemming in his characters, just as he fiercely cuts back the lengths of his *nouvelles* and plays with an almost suicidal asceticism of form: so that eventually *Breath* (1969) enacts only the briefest of brief lives – a cry of parturition and 'inspiration' elided into an exhalation of death, an 'expiration' – in a stage performance lasting fifteen seconds. And he does deconstruct language not just into 'a play of signifiers' but into what gets very close in texts like

How It Is (*Comment c'est*, 1961; trans. 1964) and particularly in *Watt* to nonsense. But there is nothing lifeless or gloomy about the way in which Beckett's texts and his characters keep up their 'obligation to express' even whilst there is 'nothing to express': Beckett's textual practice – not least the tremendously zestful passage between the French and English versions that he presides over, and the constant detonation of the jokes and puns his language is explosively packed with – makes a continual tonal counterpoint to the gloom of much of his fiction's pronouncements about the crisis of language and epistemology. What is more, the persistent deconstruction of conventional discourse, Beckett's undermining of the sentence and the conventional novel (in which he stands clearly as the inheritor of *Tristram Shandy* and *Finnegans Wake*), is not randomly aimed. A main target is Judaeo-Christianity. The de-creation of language in *Watt*, for example, is conducted explicitly in terms of a parody and reversal of God's seven-day creativeness in *Genesis*: it is a descent into a post-theological non-significance. As they do in the fictions of Joyce, undoing allusions to the Bible and Christian theology abound in Beckett's work. His people, afflicted in their feet, confined to wheel-chairs, deprived of their bicycles, are anti-pilgrims, on a 'headlong tardigrade' that gets slower and slower, consigned as they are to an ever-increasing stationariness. And as they make their ever tinier progress they not only endure the Biblical mortifications of their disabilities, but their torments are put in a specifically Christian light. They are harried by policeman (the Law: seen in almost Pauline terms as an oppression which pushes people 'to Christ'); they are nailed into a round of Gethsemanes, Golgothas, crucifixions: a 'Christian' plight whose Pauline 'pricks' are the ones against which they 'kick' (or would kick if their feet were in better shape).

Their most despondent response – a response many readers believe to be Beckett's own – would be to assume the fixity of despair in the immobility of their journey between womb and tomb – caught between *mère* and *mort* – a suspension insisted on in Beckett's repeated use of his own name *Sam* for his characters: a name that refuses to resolve the tension between the *m* at its end ('one syllable M at the end all that matters') and *S* at its beginning (a Greek Capital *S* is an *M* on its side, Σ: Beckett likes playing with M-shapes; many of his places and people have names beginning and ending with *M* or *W*). Despondency is the response of Belacqua in Dante's *Divine Comedy* (hence the name Belacqua for the hero of *More Pricks than Kicks*), a failed penitent, immobilized on the mount of Purgatory, his head between his knees in the foetal or lavatorial position Beckett is fond of putting his people in. But having imposed on his characters the philosophically immobilizing situation of the Biblical Two Thieves (suspended between the 'presumption' of salvation and the 'despair' of damnation, discerned there by St Augustine: one of Beckett's favourite bits of theology), and having used his sequences of closed systems to prove the circularity of life's awfulness ('The syndrome known as life is too diffuse to admit of palliation. For every symptom that is eased, another is made worse'), Beckett won't allow this plight to be seen, Dantesquely, as failure. He describes this negative condition, in fact, in the vocabulary of Epicurean negative capability: *apathia, ataraxia, athambia*, the abilities required to endure suffering without excitement or complaint. And these qualities are put as divine ones, explicitly by Lucky in his long rant about 'God' (certainly not the Judaeo-Christian God) in *Waiting for Godot*: 'divine apathia, divine athambia', even, and apt to the deconstruction of language going on in Beckett's work, 'divine aphasia' (aphasics have suffered loss of speech, due to cerebral damage). But Beckett will not allow even this meagre degree of positiveness to be softly consoling: settling for this way of Greek endurance notably fails to produce any end of suffering. The hero of *La Fin*, suffering as usual Christianly (settled into a boathouse he makes a lid for his chosen coffin-like boat, with a *cross-bar* and *spikes for the hands*), yearns to sail on to the adjacent lake and sink calmly (*galenismos*, another Epicurean technical term, signified the desired philosophic calm: the calm of a smooth sea). But this escape is only a fantasy: he remains marooned between present Christian torments and the Greek end he craves. It is a refusal of easy solutions by Beckett, amounting to a staunch and even cheering acceptance of humanity in the middle of the modern end-less, God-less, linguistically deprived misery that his writing depicts so strongly. It is an undespondent endlessness characteristic of one of twentieth-century literature's most unblinkingly resolute of didactic humanists.

Valentine Cunningham

Other works include: Poetry: *Poems in English* (1961); Plays: *All that Fall* (radio, 1957); *Endgame* (*Fin de partie*, 1957, English version 1958); *Krapp's Last Tape* and *Embers* (1959); *Happy Days* (1961; *Oh les beaux jours*, 1962; dual language edition ed. James Knowlson, 1978); *Play* (1964); *Eh Joe* (television, 1967). See: Hugh Kenner, *Samuel Beckett: a Critical Study* (1961); Ruby Cohn, *Samuel Beckett: The Comic Gamut* (1962); Ludovic Janvier, *Beckett par lui-même* (1969); A. Alvarez, *Beckett* (1973); John Fletcher *et al.*, *A Student's Guide to the Plays of Samuel Beckett* (1978).

37
BECKMANN, Max 1884–1950

German painter

The son of a miller, brought up in Leipzig and Bruns-

wick, Beckmann showed early promise and after three years' training in Weimar moved to Berlin in 1904, where he exhibited in the Sezession. A series of vast creaking machines brought him fame – *The Sinking of the Titanic, The Battle of the Amazons* – as well as the doubtful soubriquet of 'The German Delacroix'. In 1914 he entered the trenches as a medical orderly; within a few months he had suffered a terrible breakdown and by 1916 both his marriage and his career in Berlin as the white hope of the academic cause were broken. Henceforth he would speak in the rougher accents of the outsider. *The Night* (1918–19) shows him responding to the years of famine and civil war; the meaningless violence of the gang who break into the family, who rape the mother and hang the father. At this point he comes closest to the 'Neue Sachlichkeit' of Brecht*, the 'Return to Objectivity' which reacted against the subjectivity of Expressionism and attempted to harness its emotional force towards social participation. 'Just now,' wrote Beckmann in the 1920s, 'I feel the need to be in the cities among my fellow-men. This is where our place is. We must take part in the whole misery that is to come. . . . We must give them a picture of their fate.'

The language of *The Night* was inherited from the crowded bony scenes of northern altarpieces; from 1925 however Beckmann and his second wife began to oscillate between Frankfurt and Paris, and his art broadened, taking on something of the monumentality of Léger*, the hedonism of Matisse*. His themes were now café, party and street, as well as a superb group of self-portraits, aggressive presences often facing us head-on, as in the *Self-portrait in Tuxedo* (1927). When in 1933 Beckmann was dismissed from his professorship in Frankfurt, he returned to Berlin, where his art entered its decisive phase in *Departure*, the first of the nine triptychs on which his reputation is centred. In 1937, just before the Degenerate Art campaign began, Beckmann emigrated to Holland; and by 1939 (after a trip to London where he admired Blake's work and delivered his lecture *On My Art*) he was in effect a prisoner, cut off in occupied Amsterdam, but completing such masterpieces as *Blindman's Buff* (1944–5) and his drawings to Goethe's *Faust*. When the war ended he was sixty-two; he never returned to Germany but spent his last years teaching in St Louis and New York.

For many artists who have grown up since the 1960s, in reaction against the formal emphasis of the post-war avant-garde, Beckmann has come to seem a central figure. His works are often tangles of myth, allegory, and dream with obvious parallels to Hesse* and Jung*, but Beckmann is less portentous, more astringent. His triptychs have been seen as 'post-Christian Altarpieces', and in them Beckmann makes explicit his attempt to bring together Nietzsche's 'Apollonian' and 'Dionysian'. The general scheme of *Departure* is clear enough; between two panels depicting suffering, the middle opens into a calm sea. The form of the triptych has allowed Beckmann to bring together both the urgent horror of *The Night* and the sensual pleasures of his Parisian works, and to place them in a dialectical relation. In transcending both Expressionism and Neue Sachlichkeit – the confessional and the societal, fantasy and critique – Beckmann created a visionary synthesis unique in our time.

Timothy Hyman

Beckmann's lecture *On My Art* is included in *Modern Artists on Art*, ed. R. L. Herbert (1964). Other writings have been published by the Max Beckmann Bund in Munich. For reproductions of his work see: F. Fischer, *Max Beckmann* (1973); and Max Beckmann, *Aquarelle und Zeichnungen* (1978). See also: C. Kessler, *Max Beckmann's Triptychs* (1970); and S. Lackner, *Beckmann* (1978).

38

BEERBOHM, Sir Henry Maximilian (Max)
1872–1956

British caricaturist, parodist and essayist

G. B. Shaw* called him 'the incomparable Max', Wilde observed that 'The gods bestowed on Max the gift of perpetual old age'; however, the subject of these comments was a man so various that he defied neat labels and the public were never sure how seriously to take him. Max Beerbohm was born in London on 24 August 1872, and was educated at Charterhouse School, then Merton College, Oxford, where he claimed to have read only three books: Thackeray's *Four Georges*, Wilde's *Intentions* and Edward Lear's *Book of Nonsense*. Of that unholy trinity of influences it was Wilde who most appealed to Max, who first came to prominence with a Wildean essay 'A Defence of Cosmetics' in the first number of the *Yellow Book* (April 1894). Confronted by this paradoxical celebration of 'the era of rouge', the public were outraged at what seemed to them the nadir of decadence. The controversy did Max no harm at all and he was rapidly established as a witty and dandified personality.

Max recalled in 1920, 'When I started writing I delighted in being rude to eminent elder men. And oh, my delight when (as frequently happened) I "drew" them.' His targets included figures like Arthur Conan Doyle ('I never regard him as anything but a medical man') and Whistler ('I doubt whether Mr Whistler has ever suffered greatly in the pursuit of his art'). Soon his verbal attacks on pomposity found a visual counterpart in the drawings that made up *Caricatures of Twenty-Five Gentlemen* (1896, revised 1920). He portrayed Kipling* as hopelessly awkward, Shaw (whom he succeeded as drama critic on the *Saturday Review* in

1898) as impossibly slight. He also chose to infuriate his enemies by publishing his essays, at the age of twenty-four, under the portentous title *The Works of Max Beerbohm* (1896); the sequels were simply called *More* (1899), *Yet Again* (1909) and *And Even Now* (1920).

However wickedly pointed his work was, Max never failed to entertain his public and he was always willing to respond creatively to criticism. After his grotesque caricatures of the traditional figure of John Bull had appeared in the *Daily Mail* in 1901, Max unkindly caricatured himself in the paper over the caption 'Regretting that I live in this self-advertising age, I respond to the invitation to portray myself'. Perhaps his most astute antagonist was Henry James, whose ornately formal style supplied enough material to keep Max busy for some sixty years. Max's 'The Mote in the Middle Distance by H*nry J*m*s' was such a brilliant parody that when James was asked about his future plans he gestured to Max and said, 'Ask that young man. He knows me better than I know myself.'

In 1910 Max married the actress Florence Kahn and the couple settled in Rapallo in the Italian Riviera (though he visited London in 1936 and spent the Second World War in England). A year after the marriage Max's literary skill was magnificently demonstrated in his novel *Zuleika Dobson* (1911) which told of the devastating (and disastrous) impact of a beautiful woman on the exclusively masculine company at Oxford. As the book built up to its suicidal climax Max produced an exquisite parody of aesthetic writing: 'Yes, certainly, it is this mild miasmal air, not less than the grey beauty and gravity of the buildings, that has helped Oxford to produce, and foster eternally, her peculiar race of artist-scholars, scholar-artists.'

Max outlived his early reputation as an *enfant terrible* and became a much-respected figure who was duly knighted in 1939. His wartime broadcasts for the BBC, collected as *Mainly on the Air* (1946), revealed him as a man who was content to look back with nostalgia on his great days in the 1890s. He was, with Wilde and Aubrey Beardsley, one of the outstanding figures of a glittering period he could never really recapture. As early as 1896, after all, he had reflected: 'Already I feel myself to be a trifle outmoded. I belong to the Beardsley period.'

Alan Bold

The outstanding biography is *Max* (1964) by Lord David Cecil who also edited a comprehensive selection of Max's writing in *The Bodley Head Beerbohm* (1970); the best early caricatures can be seen in *Max's Nineties: Drawings 1892–1899*, eds Rupert Hart-Davis and Allan Wade (1913); John Felstiner's illustrated *The Lies of Art* (1973) is an appraisal of Max as parodist and caricaturist.

39
BEHAN, Brendan 1923–64

Irish playwright

Behan was born in Dublin in a working-class household. He joined the Irish Republican Army's junior corps aged eight, and was jailed twice in England (1939–41, 1947) and once in Ireland (1942–6) for his political/military operations. But after the Second World War he had begun to establish himself in Dublin's bourgeois bohemia as a writer and raconteur. His real success came with *The Quare Fellow* (1954) which anticipated the kitchen-sink and absurd movements. Joan Littlewood took it to the Theatre Workshop, Stratford East, in 1956 and it successfully moved to London's West End later. Beyond this Behan's life is really the failure to accept success. Himself the son of a house painter, he married in 1955 Beatrice Salkeld, the daughter of an artist. Caught between these vocations and ambitions, he came to rely heavily on drink, travel, outrage and a deeply compassionate anger for protection. He died in March 1964: the IRA funeral he insisted on was a final rejection of his own ambitions.

His reputation rests on his drama, one of the prose works (*Borstal Boy*, 1958), and fading recollections of his conversation and song. Imprisonment is the recurring theme, not simply for biographical reasons, but because it encapsulates the paradox of man's urge towards institutional violence and his individual sense of love and fellowship. In *The Quare Fellow* the prison's atmosphere on the eve of an execution is subtly and humorously maintained. In *The Hostage* (1958), on the other hand, sentiment saps Behan's genuine talents as a writer of dialogue. The earlier play also benefits from its very specific assault on respectable hypocrisy and abstract law, whereas *The Hostage* really attempts an abstract objective – the underlying humanity of differing cultures and nationalities.

In part invented by the media as a successor to Dylan Thomas*, Behan fits in uneasily in the 1960s, compelled to be a scourge of complacency. The terrorist 1970s and 1980s are the world he foresaw and strove to avoid. None who wish to assess Behan can ignore his casual songs and his Spoken Arts record: he was, perhaps in essence, the flower of an oral, urban culture rather than a man of the commercial theatre.

W. J. McCormack

See: *The Complete Plays* (1978); Ulick O'Connor, *Brendan Behan* (1970); Anthony Cronin, *Dead as Doornails* (1976); Colbert Kearney, *The Writings of Brendan Behan* (1977).

40
BELLOW, Saul 1915–

US novelist

Born in Quebec, Canada, of Jewish immigrant parents who moved to Chicago when he was nine, Saul Bellow attended Chicago, Northwestern and Wisconsin Universities. He has been acclaimed as an exponent of the Jewish comic story tradition and his characters seen as schlemiels; as a liberal-humanist; and as a follower of the Naturalist tradition, exploring the social forces impinging on the individual. Undoubtedly, all these are influences, plus the example of Existentialist writers, such as Sartre*, especially upon his first novel, *Dangling Man* (1944). In his hands, however, the central theme is not nihilism versus commitment, but the need to recognize one's continuity with others and one's era. His protagonists all believe themselves to be privileged to inhabit a sphere of intellectual and spiritual freedom and regard those who occupy roles or defend boundaries with bewilderment, fascination and contempt. The comedy of Bellow's writing stems from the ironic contrast between their personalities, usually childish, sulky, ingenuous, and their pretensions to the cherished values of the Western intellectual tradition, that is: detachment from self-interest or worldly ambitions, the pursuit of self-knowledge by introspection, and aesthetic contemplation of the products of both nature and culture.

Bellow's novels raise no significant epistemological problems and break no new ground stylistically, being first-person narratives shifting between conversation, narration, journal or letter-writing and inner monologue. It is the juxtaposition of these varying perspectives which reveals the persona of the narrator, his defences and pretences. Usually the protagonists confront, not only the conventional, but also 'reality-instructors', people whose beliefs or behaviour point to those areas forbidden to common sense and rational scepticism. Thus, Allbee in *The Victim* (1947) confronts Leventhal with the consequences, albeit unintended, of his past actions, by blaming him for his being sacked and made unemployable. This not only challenges Leventhal's sense of superiority and his innocence, but makes him question the boundaries we normally establish between people and between our motives and our actions. Bellow's conclusion seems to be that we draw the lines arbitrarily but must take full responsibility for our choice as to where to draw them.

Henderson of *Henderson the Rain King* (1959), driven by a craving for fulfilment and significance, voyages through a surreal Africa to find a version of himself as saviour, symbol or hero. He wins the title of Rain King with the Wariri, but only slowly realizes what King Dahfu tries to tell him, that, although we choose our roles, we do so totally, for they remake our bodies and our lives. The title carries with it a function and a destiny, to be king and to be slaughtered, and from this fate Henderson flees, but not unchanged by his awareness of the reality of symbols. Similarly, Moses E. Herzog of *Herzog* (1964) blames his wife, her lover, his producer, the whole twentieth century for the dissatisfactions he feels. He wants to put himself in the position of knowing why our situation is as it is, but such a contemplative, detached awareness, brilliant though it may be, cannot solve the problems of how to act, as he finds out when he tries to murder his wife's lover. Again, the gulf to be bridged is that between ideas and their embodiment, for in isolation, the mind breeds only the delusions of pride, megalomania and embittered impatience.

Whereas Herzog's answers centred around Romanticism and Existentialism, Sammler of *Mr Sammler's Planet* (1970) has the rational humanism and elitism of H. G. Wells* and the Bloomsbury Group. Against his experience of Auschwitz or New York in the 1960s such a perspective can only act as a defence until he can be drawn to see the same valuable human reasoning powers operating through the seemingly irrational modes of aggression, display, sexuality and even obsession and impulsiveness. The lesson here is that each intellectual or rational mode of thought must be seen as part of a historical and cultural setting rather than some timeless Platonic realm. Charley Citrine of *Humboldt's Gift* (1975) takes up this train of thought for, as a dramatist, he is offended by Humboldt's fascination with money, politics, power and historical trends, preferring the serene world of Steinerian spirituality. However, it is Humboldt, with all his quirks and failings, who provides the inspiration for Citrine's art, and he is eventually forced to accept the common origins between art and history.

Besides his novels, Bellow has written short stories and two plays. As perhaps the greatest mid-century American novelist, his consistent thrust has been against the atomic individualism of most Western sociological and psychological thought, and to assert the continuity between mind and body, individuals and their forms of expression, whether social, aesthetic or intellectual, and between people themselves, sharing a common condition.

Dr David Corker

Bellow's other works include: *The Adventures of Augie March* (1953); *Seize the Day* (1956); a play, *The Last Analysis* (1965); and *To Jerusalem and Back: A Personal Account* (1976). See also: Marcus Klein, *After Alienation* (1964); Tony Tanner, *Saul Bellow* (1965); John J. Clayton, *Saul Bellow: In Defense of Man* (1968).

41
BENJAMIN, Walter 1892–1940

German literary critic and philosopher

Walter Benjamin, now considered by many to be the foremost German literary critic of the first half of the century, was born in Berlin, the son of a well-to-do Jewish art-dealer. A sickly child, he was schooled at a humanistic Gymnasium and then studied philosophy and literature in Freiburg-im-Breisgau as well as in his native city, soon becoming an eloquent student leader. During the First World War he made friends with Gershom Scholem, a young Zionist intellectual with anarchist sympathies who interested him in Judaism and the Kabbala; went to study in Munich, where he met Rilke* and read Mallarmé; and, having married a former university friend, eventually settled in Bern and became close to Ernst Bloch*, the apologist of utopian thought. In the early 1920s he made half-hearted attempts to establish himself as a critic and academic. His first major essay, on Goethe's *Elective Affinities*, was welcomed by a leading literary figure, Hugo von Hofmannsthal, into his magazine; but his unconventional scholarly work on literary history, *The Origin of German Tragic Drama* (published in book form in 1928, trans. 1977), was rejected by the University of Frankfurt. In the mid-1920s Benjamin, whose family was impoverished by the German inflation of 1923, had to earn his living as a reviewer and translator (notably of Proust*), a literary reporter and scriptwriter for radio. Under the influence of Lukács's* *History and Class Consciousness*, and encouraged by his Latvian mistress, Asja Lacis, an assistant of Brecht* (to whom she introduced Benjamin), he moved towards Marxism. The coming of Nazism drove him into exile and put an end to his journalistic activities. Living in Paris, he received a modest scholarship from the Frankfurt Institute for Social Research, then transferred to Columbia University and contributed to its review, the *Zeitschrift für Sozialforschung*. The invasion of France finally convinced him to try to escape to America through Spain. However, when he reached the border at Port Bou he was refused a pass. Told that he would be delivered to the Gestapo he took his own life. Suicide, he had written previously, was 'the achievement of modernity in the field of passions'.

A prolific writer, Benjamin was pre-eminently a master of the essay form. His lucid German brought literary criticism to an unheard-of level of thoughtfulness; yet the denser it is, the lighter it becomes to the reader. But the originality of his approach as an essayist was constantly energized by a peculiar pathos, a unique mixture of social criticism and historical nostalgia. Although he very much opposed the dominant gloomy aesthetic and philosophical trends of his lifetime, Expressionism and Existentialism, he may be reckoned himself as one of the greatest (if, by then, quite uninfluential) examples of *Kulturpessimismus* in most of the inter-war period. He had a keen eye for all that which was thwarted, repressed and frustrated in the course of cultural evolution, for 'the image of history . . . in its rejects' – the victims of progress.

Of his neo-Kantian training Benjamin retained an outright distrust of philosophical systems. Unlike the neo-Kantians, however, he also questioned every idealistic standpoint. His Bern dissertation, *Der Begriff der Kunstkritik in der deutschen Romantik* ('The Concept of Art Criticism in German Romanticism', 1919), still accepted the Romantic notion of art as a privileged grasp of being, and of criticism as a 'fulfilment' of the artwork; but he suspected concepts such as consciousness and self-reflection of postulating an improbable harmony between subject and object, or spiritual intention and historical reality. Therefore, instead of a new idealism, he tried to devise 'a science of the origin', a search for truth as 'the death of intention'. He transposed Goethe's vision of an *Urphänomenon* from nature into history, and came to speak of an *Urgeschichte*, a primeval archetypal history.

At bottom, Benjamin's ideas belong to his Kabbalistic metaphysics of the noun, to his mystical postulate of an uncanny, primeval link between the word and the world (he thought that meaning was communicated '*in* language, not just through it'). Yet only in *epochal* moments of time does language recover Adam's godlike power to create by naming. Thus the quest for *Urgeschichte* proved to be a kind of secularized hermeneutics of the Holy Writ, a laicization of the idea of the Torah (the Jewish Revelation); and Benjamin's profound respect for language as ontology also explains his life-long love (shared by the otherwise dissimilar Karl Kraus*) for quoting. The ideal piece of criticism was in his eyes a mosaic of quotations. Surprisingly, for all its being steeped in medieval theology and mysticism, this essayism of exegesis by montage ended up in remarkable similarity to the techniques of modern art, from cubism to surrealism and the film. The masterpiece of the genre was published by Benjamin in 1928, under the title *One-Way Street* (trans. 1979).

The dismal temper of Benjamin found an altogether congenial subject-matter in the baroque *Trauerspiel*, or 'mourning play', an intensely saturnine brand of poetical drama. He opposes tragedy, grounded in myth, to the Christian sorrow-play, rooted in history experienced as fate. Instead of the tragic hero, who is ethically superior to the gods, the *Trauerspiel* gives pride of place to the tyrant and the martyr, often merged into the same person. It sings the mortification of the flesh by presenting characters who on their way to damnation desperately cling to the world, with a passionate sense of both *carpe diem* and *memento mori*.

Furthermore, baroque drama is the realm of the allegoric, and *allegory* is the key concept of Benjaminian aesthetics. 'Allegories are amidst ideas what ruins are amidst things': hidden signs of the past, which always say something *else* in regard to what was meant. As such, baroque allegories connote the alienation of intentional meaning, the sad primacy of things over consciousness. The melancholy hero of the *Trauerspiel* 'betrays the world for knowledge', entangled among objects turned enigmatic and hostile to man. *Modern* allegory, on the other hand, defines itself by its concentration on the inmost aspects of alienation and dehumanization. It is the emblem of the decay of genuine experience. Its birth dates from the poetry of Baudelaire, which first embodied the 'fencing' of lyrics against the repressiveness of urban life. But the allegorical is also the pith and marrow of twentieth-century modernism, as in Proust, Kafka* or surrealism. The latter was to Benjamin the epitome of the poetics of allegory in our time, a style made up of 'profane illuminations', that is to say, of arcane epiphanies, at once fascinated by and deeply at odds with urban life within mass society.

Benjamin's concern with Baudelaire was just a part of a planned *Urgeschichte* of modernity, centred in Second Empire Paris as 'the capital of the nineteenth century'. The greater bulk of this unfinished *opus magnum* is known as the *Passagenarbeit*, a study of the arcades of Paris, a focus of city life and hence of its most telling 'phantasmagoriae', i.e., the social-grounded self-delusions of the bourgeois mind. Benjamin's image of Haussmann's Paris is a highly ambivalent one, torn between the protest against modernization and the loving delight in the humane qualities of the only truly walkable big city in the West, the natural home of the *flâneur* and the bohemian.

However, some six years before his death, and much under the spell of Brecht's dealienation theatre, he came to envisage an aesthetic utopia starkly unlike the spiritual martyrdom expressed by modern allegories. In the essay 'The work of art in the age of its mechanical reproduction', the Chaplin*-like film is endowed with a liberating effect and entrusted with the task of voicing a healthy total denial of the 'aura' of traditional artistic contemplation. *Aura* is 'the unique, unrepeatable experience of distance'. Originally a religious attitude, it dominated the enjoyment of art before the age of widespread reproduction, falling into abeyance since then. Yet most of Benjamin's criticism of modern letters bespeaks a quite different mood: the mood that led him to celebrate (while writing on Kafka) 'the purity and beauty of a failure'. Then, he reserves his praise for those who silently rise against 'myth' (i.e. power as meaning) by making their works into secret codes of revolt.

J. G. Merquior

The complete works of Benjamin are being published by Suhrkamp, in Frankfurt, since 1972. English translations include: *Charles Baudelaire: a Lyric Poet in the Era of High Capitalism* (1973, with excerpts from the *Passagenarbeit*); and *Illuminations* (1968). See also: Hannah Arendt, *Men in Dark Times* (1968); Rolf Tiedemann, *Studien zur Philosophie W. Benjamins* (1965); Bernd Witte, *Walter Benjamins – der Intellektuelle als Kritiker* (1976). See also the volume *Aesthetics and Politics* (debates between Bloch, Lukács, Brecht, Benjamin and Adorno), ed. Ronald Taylor (1977).

42

BENNETT, Enoch Arnold 1867–1931

English writer

Some writers undergo a miraculous resuscitation long after their deaths, and such has been the case with Arnold Bennett. His first name, Enoch, though never used in reference to the author, is none the less instructive, for its popularity belongs archetypally to the industrial Staffordshire in which the boy grew up. Despite the fact that he left the county at a comparatively early age and practically never returned to it, the world of the Staffordshire 'pottery' towns forms the background to all his major work.

He was never wholly able to shake off his provincial past, though there must have been moments when he heartily wished to do so. An extraordinary application to hard work, combined with the flowering of an unquestionable talent, brought its inevitable rewards of literary and social success. Bennett's gift for friendship and his well-known generosity (though allied to equally legendary meanness) made him widely popular, and the role of the clubman and the *bon viveur* came very easily to him. The latter aspect of his life was brought agreeably into play in the novel *Grand Babylon Hotel* (1902). His love of France and French culture found its inevitable echo (though little real fufilment) in his marriage to Marguerite Soulié. Separating from her in 1922, he pursued a liaison with an actress, Dorothy Cheston, becoming, in the final years of his life, one of the more judiciously admired survivors from the generation of Edwardian novelists which included Galsworthy* and Wells*.

Bennett's gifts, modest as he was about them, were considerable and amply justify the reappraisal of his work which has taken place in recent years. Like Trollope, whom he resembled both in character and interests, he was concerned to portray modest, reticent, 'ordinary' people in essentially humdrum provincial settings. The short story 'Clarice of the Autumn Concerts', in which the heroine renounces the drama of a professional musical career and settles instead for a marriage to a local teacher, encapsulates the some-times rather chilly compromise reached at the end of most Bennett novels.

Like several other English writers of the period, most notably Galsworthy, Bennett attempted a series of linked novels in the *Clayhanger* trilogy (1910–15), the story of the relationship between Edwin Clayhanger and Hilda Lessways, who have both striven to break free from the restraints of a narrow and conventional background. His best work, however, is to be found in the early *Anna of the Five Towns* (1902), with its appropriately bleak close, and in *The Old Wives' Tale* (1908), a magnificent account of the efforts of two Staffordshire girls to escape from a life of provincial dreariness in the Five Towns of the Pottery district. A rich vein of comedy, found in *Clayhanger* and *The Old Wives' Tale* in characters such as Auntie Hamps and Mr Povey, receives its fullest release in *Riceyman Steps* (1923) and *Grand Babylon Hotel; Buried Alive* (1908) is less successful as a venture into the grotesque.

Bennett's weakness was principally in his too-willing submission to the notional superiorities of French realism. His humility and sense of proportion may well have saved him from taking too particular a view of his achievement – thus indirectly guaranteeing its enduring appeal. His influence can be felt diffusing itself throughout the English provincial novel for the entire inter-war period.

Jonathan Keates

See: *The Journals of Arnold Bennett 1896–1928* (3 vols, 1932–3); see also John Lucas, *Arnold Bennett, a Study of his Fiction* (1974); Margaret Drabble, *Arnold Bennett* (1974).

43

BERG, Alban 1885–1935

Austrian composer

Born in Vienna, Berg began to compose while still a teenager. From 1904 to 1910 he studied composition with Arnold Schoenberg* and his earliest published works date from this period of his life. These early works demonstrate the gradual development of Berg's musical style from the Schumann, Wolf and, occasionally, Debussy* inspired idiom of the *Seven Early Songs* (1905–8) to the post-Wagnerian *Piano Sonata* Op. 1 (1907–8) and thence to the highly chromatic expressionism of the *Four Songs* Op. 2 (1909–10) and the *String Quartet* Op. 3 (1910).

By the early 1910s Berg's music, like that of his teacher Schoenberg and of his fellow pupil and lifelong friend Anton Webern*, had reached a point at which traditional tonal criteria no longer operated. The disappearance of the tonal relationships upon which the formal designs of eighteenth- and nineteenth-century music had depended inevitably created acute structural problems. For a period both Schoenberg and Webern attempted to overcome these problems by devoting themselves, almost exclusively, to the composition of short pieces and something of the influence of his two colleagues can be seen in the miniature forms of Berg's *Altenberg Lieder* Op. 4 (1912) and the *Four Pieces* for clarinet and piano Op. 5 (1913). Berg, however, was never really attracted to the miniature as a form of expression. His greatest and most individual achievements lie in his organizing of large-scale structure and the *Three Orchestral Pieces* Op. 6 (1914–15), which are Mahlerian in both size and emotional atmosphere, are more characteristic of his work.

In May 1914 Berg attended a performance of Büchner's *Woyzeck* and immediately began work on an opera based on the play. First performed under Erich Kleiber in Berlin in December 1925, *Wozzeck* established Berg as one of the foremost composers of his generation. A 'free' atonal work, completed before Schoenberg had evolved his twelve-note system, *Wozzeck* exhibits the intricate, labyrinthine formal design and that fusion of traditional and radical elements that characterize all Berg's mature music. Each of the three acts of *Wozzeck*, and each scene within each act, is designed as a self-contained unit based upon a traditional musical form, usually a form associated with 'absolute' instrumental music. Thus Act I sc. 4 is a Passacaglia, Act II sc. 1 a strict Sonata form movement, Act II sc. 2 a Fantasia and Fugue and so on. Within this structure operate both a complex leitmotiv system and a variety of intricate, predetermined compositional schemes. In *Wozzeck*, as in all Berg's music, the rigorous and highly calculated compositional techniques give rise to a work of overwhelming, and apparently spontaneous, emotional and dramatic effect. With *Wozzeck* and his subsequent works Berg, alone amongst the three composers of the so-called 'Second Viennese School', achieved critical and popular success, and from 1926 until 1933, when his music was banned in Germany by the Nazi party, he was able to live on his royalties.

In the last song of the *Altenberg Lieder* and in sections of *Wozzeck* Berg had employed a twelve-note theme as the basic structural element. A number of twelve-note themes also appear in the *Chamber Concerto* (1923–5). It was not until 1925 when writing the *Lyric Suite* for string quartet, however, that Berg deliberately employed (albeit in only a few of the work's six movements) Schoenberg's method of composition with twelve notes for the first time.

Berg's handling of the twelve-note technique differs radically from that of his colleagues. In the music of Schoenberg and Webern the twelve-note row is defined by interval succession; in Berg's music the note row is assumed to have other characteristics (such as melodic contour and quasi-tonal connotations) which are regarded as being as important as – and, sometimes, more important than – the interval sequence. Thus, for example, Berg frequently employs within a single work a number of different rows which are related through the common harmonic content of their various segments. Similarly, the interval succession may be modified in order to enhance the melodic or tonal relationship between different row forms.

In 1928 Berg began work on an opera based on Frank Wedekind's two *Lulu* plays, *Erdgeist* (1895) and *Die Büchse der Pandora* (1904). Work on *Lulu* was interrupted by the composition of the concert aria *Der Wein* (1929) and the *Violin Concerto* (1935) and Berg died having completed the opera in short score but without having finished the orchestration of Act III. The first performance of the work as a three-act opera, with the orchestration of Act III completed by Friedrich Cerha, took place in Paris in February 1979.

More complicated even than *Wozzeck* in its structural design, *Lulu* combines the vocal forms of the traditional 'number opera' with both a large-scale formal plan, in which each of the three acts is dominated by a single self-contained musical form, and an intricate network of musical, dramatic and textual cross-references. The leitmotiv system of the opera affects not only melodic and harmonic elements but is extended in such a way that it embraces twelve-note rows, rhythms, metres, instrumental colours, production details (such as the casting of performers in specific double and triple roles) and almost every other aspect of the work.

At a time when music was undergoing one of the most profound changes in its history Berg seems to have felt the need to assert the relationship between the new musical language that he and his colleagues were evolving and the great eighteenth- and nineteenth-century tradition of Austro-German music. His natural lyricism, his traditional conception of thematic structure and development, his feeling for large-scale theatrical and dramatic gesture and the intense emotional atmosphere of his music all look back to the world of the late Romantics and the Mahlerian symphonic tradition. For many years Berg's critical standing rested upon the response to these apparently traditional elements and, consequently, fluctuated wildly as critical fashions changed. Thus, for example, the fact that Berg's twelve-note works employed note rows designed to give rise to melodic and harmonic formations reminiscent of those of tonal music was initially hailed by many commentators as an indication of Berg's 'innate musicality' and his lack of dogma; the same features were subsequently condemned by composers such as Boulez* as indicating Berg's failure to understand, or at least his refusal to accept, the true structural implications of the twelve-note method.

It is now possible to appreciate that Berg's attitude to the procedures and designs of earlier music was far more ambivalent than is generally recognized and that, alongside its more obviously traditional aspects, Berg's music demonstrates a number of radical, and, indeed, revolutionary, features. While some of these features – such as his almost obsessional interest in palindromic and other complicated symmetrical structures – seem to have had a deeply personal significance, many are peculiarly relevant to more recent musical developments. Thus one can find in Berg's music constructive note rows some ten years before Schoenberg developed the twelve-note system, symmetrical arch-forms which predate those of Bartók*, systematically applied rhythmic and durational patterns of a kind later associated with Messiaen*, metric modulations (Elliot Carter*), schematic metronome marks (Stockhausen*), superimposed tempi (Stockhausen and Ligeti) and the use of elaborate numerological and other precompositional determinants that look forward to the work of Maxwell Davies* and many other contemporary composers.

Dr Douglas Jarman

Berg's published output amounts to a mere eighteen works (although over eighty early songs remain, as yet, unpublished), the most important of which are mentioned above. All Berg's music is published by Universal Edition. About Berg: H. F. Redlich, *Alban Berg* (1957); W. Reich, *Alban Berg* (1957); Mosco Carner, *Alban Berg* (1975); and Douglas Jarman, *The Music of Alban Berg* (1979). See also: George Perle, *Serial Composition and Atonality* (1962); and *Alban Berg: Letters to his Wife*, edited and translated by Bernard Grün (1971).

44

BERGMAN, Ingmar 1918–

Swedish film and theatre director

Ingmar Bergman was the son of a Lutheran clergyman and all his work is marked far more by spiritual anguish than by social or political concern. As a child he was fascinated by the mysterious imaginary worlds opened up by his magic lantern and toy theatre, and later he left the University of Stockholm without completing his degree to become a theatre director, first in Halsingborg, then in Gothenburg.

His work in the cinema began with the script, *Frenzy*, in 1944 and he made his début as a film director with *Crisis*, released in 1946. In these early films the themes of youthful despair and impotent revolt are already apparent. Bergman has always been a prolific director and he had made nine feature films and scripted five others by the time his first major work, *Summer Interlude*, appeared in 1951. From the start he shared many of the metaphysical and existentialist concerns of the new writers and artists who emerged in Sweden during the 1940s.

In the early 1950s, while simultaneously working as a stage director in Malmö, Bergman began to attract a wider audience with films like *Summer with Monica* (1952) and *Sawdust and Tinsel* (1953). The contrast of these two works – the first a simple, directly told story of a short-lived love affair, the second a complex intermixing of a circus troupe's hopes, inadequacies and humiliations shot in a totally expressionist style – points to the breadth and versatility of Bergman's style at this period. His international career began with the award-winning *Smiles of a Summer Night* (1955), an uncharacteristically light work, reminiscent of Renoir's* *La Règle du jeu*, which remains his most satisfying comedy. This opened the way to an uneven period of intense creativity, marked by a number of striking and ambitious works of which *The Seventh Seal* (1956), with its portentous symbolism, and the complexly structured *Wild Strawberries* (1957) are perhaps the most successful.

In 1961 he embarked on what was to become a major trilogy – *Through a Glass Darkly* (1961), *Winter Light* (1962), *The Silence* (1963) – which gave fresh expression to the themes of solitude, suffering, religious doubt and anxiety which had haunted his work up to this point. Bergman's developing relationships with his players have always been crucial to his work and, in both theatre and film, he has constantly used the same small group of performers in leading roles. In the 1950s and early 1960s his style continually changed so as to capture the specific qualities of his actors, Gunnar Bjornstrand and Max von Sydow, and, more especially, his actresses: Harriet Anderson, Eva Dahlbeck, Bibi Andersson and Ingrid Thulin. From 1963 to 1966 he deepened his theatrical involvement by taking on the post of head of the Royal Dramatic Theatre in Stockholm. Then, with *Persona* in 1966, he began a deeply personal exploration of the problems of human communication which, through *Hour of the Wolf* (1966), *The Shame* (1967), and *A Passion* (1969) to *Cries and Whispers* (1972), featured the Norwegian-born actress Liv Ullman. Subsequently Bergman has turned away to some extent from the mainstream of Swedish cinema, making two television series (both subsequently edited down as feature films), *Scenes from a Marriage* (1973) and *Face to Face* (1975), a version of his production of the opera *The Magic Flute* (1974) and two German-made features, *The Serpent's Egg* (1977) and *Autumn Sonata* (1978).

Bergman's career has been one of the most significant in modern European cinema. Until the 1970s he resisted the lure of international co-production and rooted his work firmly in the context of Swedish life and culture. His career of over thirty-five years shows both constant thematic innovation and an ever-increasing directness of expression. In the 1950s he established the concept of the film-maker as a self-conscious artist in quite a new way for a whole generation of critics and film directors. His own work has always been deeply personal – reflecting the joys and contradictions of an emotional life marked by no less than six marriages. In the 1960s and early 1970s he pioneered a form of intensely, even painfully, direct expression of these themes in a pared-down, brilliantly controlled style which confirmed his status as a film-maker of the very first rank.

Dr Roy Armes

Bergman's other films are: *It Rains on our Love* (1946); *A Ship to India* (1947); *Night is My Future* (1948); *Port of Call* (1948); *Prison/The Devil's Wanton* (1949); *Thirst* (1949); *To Joy* (1950); *This Can't Happen Here* (1950); *Waiting Women* (1952); *A Lesson in Love* (1954); *Journey into Autumn* (1955); *So Close to Life* (1958); *The Face/ The Magician* (1958); *The Virgin Spring* (1960); *The Devil's Eye* (1960); *Now About These Women* (1964); one episode in *Stimulantia* (1967); *The Rite* (1969); *Faro Document* (1970); *The Touch* (1970). See also: *Bergman on Bergman* (1973); Jörn Donner, *The Personal Vision of Ingmar Bergman* (1964); Robin Wood, *Ingmar Bergman* (1969); John Simon, *Ingmar Bergman Directs* (1972); Stuart M. Kaminsky (ed.), *Ingmar Bergman: Essays in Criticism.*

45
BERGSON, Henri Louis 1859–1941

French philosopher

Bergson was born in Paris, the second son of a gifted Polish Jewish musician. Although his mother was English, and although he spoke English fluently, his education and the whole of his career took place in France. In 1878 he was admitted to the École Normale Supérieure to study philosophy, and returned there as a lecturer in 1897 before being appointed Professor of Greek and Latin Philosophy at the Collège de France in 1900 – a post he retained until ill-health forced him to retire in 1924. After the First World War, during which he served on diplomatic missions to Spain and the USA, he was appointed chairman of the League of Nations Committee on International Co-operation. In 1928 he was awarded the Nobel Prize for Literature. Although toward the end of his life his thought became increasingly religious in a Catholic direction, when the Second World War broke out he chose not to dissociate himself from his co-religionists and declined exemption from the Nazi Jewish laws. He died in Paris during the darkest hour of the German occupation.

While Bergson described his early thinking as 'wholly imbued' with purely mechanistic theories of change, largely derived from a reading of Herbert Spencer, the philosophy of his maturity represents a complete break with the scientific materialism and determinism which prevailed in his youth. Although he did not set out to build a new system of the universe, his treatment of a number of philosophical problems amounted, in the end, to a more or less comprehensive world-view. The most important of these problems were the nature of time and freedom, mind, memory and matter, evolution and morality.

Of these, Bergson insisted that the understanding of time was the key. His first major work, *Time and Free Will* (*Essai sur les données immédiates de la conscience*, 1889, trans. 1910), revealed a sceptical attitude towards the primacy of the intellect as a mode of understanding reality. Our immediate awareness is one of existing in time and space, but time as we perceive it internally, and not as measured by a clock. What he calls real time, or duration, is personal, not abstract; qualitative, not quantitative. States of mind or consciousness are not separated in space like external objects, but merge and interpenetrate. Clock time, though needful for our practical, external purposes, is but a symbolic abstraction borrowed from spatial measurement and, by analysing that which flows into discrete instants, is false to reality.

From this distinction between time and duration flows another between intellect and intuition. Just as duration is grasped not by the analysing intellect but by a direct awareness of the inner self freed from the tyranny of abstraction, so intuition is the apprehension of reality as change and flow. There are no substances to which change happens; simply, reality is becoming. Intuition is the mode of the internal self, intellect the mode of the external and superficial self. And from this view of reality stems Bergson's notion of freedom. Once we cease regarding 'character', 'feelings' and 'motives' deterministically, as blocks or entities exerting influence on succeeding separate blocks, the actions which are expressive of the whole personality are undetermined and free. While he does not dispute that some actions are mere responses to physical and social conditions, he says that in order to be free we should pay heed to the inner self, and not to the world of action and convention. To define this freedom further, however, would be impossible without resorting to falsifying analysis.

In his next work, *Matter and Memory* (*Matière et mémoire*, 1896, trans. 1911), Bergson considers the relation between mind and body. While the brain is an organ of the material body, *esprit* (mind or spirit) is not. This distinction is abetted by the identification of two kinds of memory: habit-memory, and pure memory. Habit-memory, exemplified by rote learning, is a form of physical action which depends on the brain, and can thus be impaired. Pure memory, or the persisting, integral retention of past experience, is non-functional, independent of the brain, and cannot be destroyed. The past is always present to this psychical state, and the brain filters these riches when actions are performed. Pathological conditions of the brain may impede memory's outward expression, but cannot destroy it.

The book of Bergson's that most captured the public's imagination was *Creative Evolution* (*L'Évolution créatrice*, 1907, trans. 1911). Again attacking scientific materialism, he seeks alternatives to both the mechanistic and teleological views of evolution. Here his dualism operates between matter and life. In evolutionary change he identifies a creative, organizing, self-realizing aspect which is analogous to the creative aspect of the human mind as we experience it intuitively. Just as the mind is free to initiate novelty, so life is a creative drive toward novel forms, and not the random response to existing forms recognized by Darwin and Spencer. Living beings, individually as well as collectively within their species, transcend mere adaptation to their environment and develop forms expressive of their own individuality. Life requires matter in order to manifest its existence, and in living forms there is an 'élan vital' or impulse toward perfectibility. However, that there is no final term in this process Bergson illustrates through his comparison of evolution with an exploding shell whose fragments in turn explode.

All this was apprehended by the intuition rather than comprehended by the intellect. Since the life impulse was constantly creative, Bergson did not posit a creator. However, in a much later work, *Two Sources of Morality and Religion* (*Les deux sources de la morale et de la religion*, 1932, trans. 1935), he did discuss the universe as being the visible and tangible aspect of a divine need to love. Once again a dualism between the static and the dynamic is discerned, and is used to distinguish between two forms of morality and two forms of religion. Static morality is a mechanical obedience to rules, while dynamic morality is aspirational, relating man to mankind and not just to the closed society of his tribe. Similarly static religion responds to ritual, while dynamic religion is essentially mystical.

Since the 1920s Bergson's vitalistic doctrines have found scant shelter within any major philosophical movement, either in Europe or in the English-speaking world. While they were overshadowed by the rise of phenomenology and existentialism, they were directly antithetical to the tenets of logical positivism, and of no interest to the school of linguistic philosophy nurtured by Wittgenstein*. It has been argued that there is a link between his anti-determinist assertion of man's fundamental freedom and the personal, creative aspect of moral choice that Sartre* and others relate to the notion of authenticity, but the link is at best tenuous. In retrospect the reputation he enjoyed seems almost inexplicable. And yet it is evidenced not only in the work of Santayana* and A. N. Whitehead*, but far outside the limits of philosophy proper as well: in the work of Gertrude Stein* for example, or Shaw's* 'Life Force' as exemplified in *Man and Superman* and *Back to Methuselah*. In France Bergsonism entered literature

through the Catholic poet and mystic Charles Péguy, and to a lesser extent in the work of Valéry* and Proust*. Some explanation may be found in his prose, which was largely free of technicalities, and, though often rhetorical, is still dazzling in its illustrative imagery. For those intimidated by the harshness of scientific materialism he provided a sense of optimism, even exaltation. If his philosophy led Bergson himself towards belief, it had the power to lead others with him.

Dr Alan Hagger

Other translations include: *Laughter: An Essay on the Meaning of the Comic* (*Le rire*, 1900, trans. 1910); *An Introduction to Metaphysics* (*Introduction à la métaphysique*, 1903, trans. 1912). See also: Bertrand Russell, *The Philosophy of Bergson* (1914); F. C. Coppleston, *Bergson and Morality* (*Proceedings of the British Academy*, vol. 41, 1955); F. Meyer, *La Pensée de Bergson* (4th edn, 1964); A. E. Pilkington, *Bergson and his Influence: A Reassessment* (1976).

46

BERIO, Luciano 1925–

Italian composer

Born in Oneglia, a small coastal town near the Italian – French border, Luciano Berio was of that generation of Italian artists and intellectuals who emerged from apprenticeship – provided in Berio's case by his choirmaster father, Ghedini, at the Milan Conservatory, and Dallapiccola's* composition course at Tanglewood, USA – to confront the cultural vacuum left in the wake of Mussolini's* regime. Their response, typified by the work of Berio's close associates, the semiotician Umberto Eco and the poet Eduardo Sanguinetti, was an ebullient exploration of the more radical intellectual and technical innovations that Europe and America had to offer, coupled – albeit obliquely in Berio's case – with a vivid concern for the ideological confrontations that rapid post-war industrialization had brought in its wake. Although Berio was subsequently to spend substantial periods of time outside Italy, due primarily to his teaching commitments in a number of American institutions, notably the Juilliard School in New York (1965–71), and to his subsequent work as head of the electro-acoustic section of IRCAM in Paris, he has never lost the omnivorous cultural curiosity and delight in intellectual adventure characteristic of his background. So that although the musical substance of his works rests upon a comparatively conservative vision of musical craftsmanship, evidenced both in the meticulous handling of instrumentation and texture learnt from such mentors as Stravinsky* and Dallapiccola, and in a traditional fascination with engendering extensive and complex musical statements from parsimonious resources, they also incorporate a wide range of external stimuli – notably structural phonetics, folk-song and experimental literature in the Joyce*/Pound* tradition, but also extending to structural anthropology (*Sinfonia*, 1968) and fictional phonologies (*Visage*, 1961).

Berio's exploration of electronic resources has provided an opportunity for combining his enthusiasm for innovation and his respect for technique. His involvement with electronic music dates from the 1950s when, having returned from Tanglewood, he took up work with the Italian Radio in Milan. There, with Bruno Maderna, he founded the Studio di Fonologia Musicale, of which he became Director in 1959. Although the resultant tape pieces form only a small part of his oeuvre, their influence extends into many of his works for large instrumental and vocal groups, where multiple superimpositions produce internally complex, multi-faceted blocks of sound. Electronic resources were only occasionally used in his works of the mid-1960s and early 1970s, but he has since reaffirmed his commitment to the medium through his work on computer-aided techniques at IRCAM.

The same ready appreciation for the innovatory potential of a specific medium is apparent in his works involving the human voice. Not only is the vocal performer's repertoire extended to include all possible forms of emission – a feature which, though shared with composers such as Kagel and Schnebel, is developed to an unprecedented degree of virtuosity in those works written for his long-term collaborator, Cathy Berberian, such as *Sequenza III* (1965) or *Visage* – but semantic coherence itself becomes moulded into an extraordinarily rich compositional parameter. This is effected by two principle means. First, the phonetic components of his text are accorded an autonomous status. This possibility was first explored in the tape-piece, *Omaggio a Joyce* (1958), where Berberian's reading of a text from *Ulysses* dissolves into an exploration of its acoustic features, and also appeared briefly, but centrally in *Circles* (1960). But its most systematic use was in *Sequenza III* and *O King* (1967), where articulatory features of the phonetic material – the position of the mouth in producing them – became manipulated as structural features in their own right.

In his works for multiple voices, the resultant ebb and flow of coherent language is compounded by the superimposition of disparate verbal fragments. This technique owes much to his collaboration, in *Passaggio* (1962) and *Laborintus II* (1965), with Sanguinetti, of whose multi-layered – indeed multilingual – style this is but a logical extension. The extraction and juxtaposition of significant fragments that Sanguinetti applies to Dante in *Laborintus II* is then applied by Berio to Lévi-Strauss* in *Sinfonia*. The third movement of the latter work also provides a musical analogue to this process, using a wide array of quotations from works by other composers as material for a commentary upon the third movement of Mahler's 2nd Symphony.

Musical commentary – upon Berio's own pre-existent works in all save the above example – is another consistent feature, most clearly seen in his *Chemins* series. Each of these works takes one of the virtuoso *Sequenzas* for solo instrument, and preserving it intact, superimposes upon it a simultaneous commentary from other instruments. This may conserve the large-scale contours of the work as a frame for a more complex and variegated textural dialogue – as in *Chemins I* (1965) for Harp and Orchestra, or *Chemins IV* (1975) for Oboe and Strings – or, more radically, may partially submerge the original formal characteristics, leaving the accretions to establish their own structural balance, as in *Chemins II* (1967) and *III* (1968), for Viola and Chamber Ensemble, plus, in *III*, Orchestra, or the Mahler commentary from *Sinfonia*. The second movement of this latter work provides a more subtle example, enriching *O King* of the previous year by extending the process of harmonic derivation from a pitch series.

This harmonic commentary upon a recurring linear figuration has itself become an important feature in recent works, such as *Bewegung* (1971), *Points on the Curve to Find* (1973), *Calmo* (1974) and *Ritorno degli snovidenie* (1975) – indeed, it underlines a shift in emphasis within Berio's work from the linear, rhetorically 'gestural' writing of the 1950s and 1960s to a rich, flexible harmonic palette, employed either in rotational or permutational form, as in *Bewegung*, or the Neruda* settings from *Coro* (1976), or else as a process of slow development, as in the middle section of the *Concerto for Two Pianos and Orchestra* (1972). This recuperation of harmonic gratification – albeit at the cost of the almost virulent cutting edge that many of his earlier works possessed – marks a further evolution in his most consistent and perennial preoccupation: an intense and delighted exploration of the sensual impact of his sound materials.

David Osmond-Smith

Other major works include: *Allelujah II* (1956/8); *Tempi Concertati* (1958/9); *Epifanie* (1961); *Opera* (1970); *Ora* and *Amores* (1971); *Eindrücke* and *A-ronne* (1974).

47

BERRYMAN, John 1914–72

US poet

Born in Oklahoma, Berryman attended Columbia College, New York, and Clare College, Cambridge, and subsequently taught at a number of American universities, including Wayne, Harvard, Princeton, and finally Minnesota, where he committed suicide.

'All the way through my work is a tendency to regard the individual human soul under stress,' Berryman said. 'I have tried, therefore, to study two souls in my long poems.' The souls in question are those of Anne Bradstreet in *Homage to Mistress Bradstreet* (1956) and the persona 'Henry' (a version of the poet himself) in *The Dream Songs* (1969), first published as *77 Dream Songs* (1964) and *His Toy, His Dream, His Rest* (1968). *Homage to Mistress Bradstreet*, which the critic Edmund Wilson considered 'the most distinguished long poem by an American since *The Waste Land*' (*vide* T. S. Eliot), is a taut narrative in which the disembodied voice of the poet engages in a drama of temptation and rebellion with the first woman poet of the New World. Much critical commentary has assumed that Berryman tried to recover the personality and community of the historical Anne Bradstreet, and has regretted that he deliberately distorted the historical record, even to the point of calumniating his heroine. While the work is certainly freighted with a great deal of historical information, it must be properly estimated as both a personal lyric and a dramatic subterfuge: as the recapitulation and literary purgation of Berryman's own experiences of adultery. The poem figures Anne Bradstreet as alienated from her culture and personal relationships and provoked to fulfil herself in an adultery with the poet: it deliberately reinterprets Berryman's personal liaisons, with all their psychological tensions and distress, as a form of metaphysics.

The essential personalism of the poem is prefigured in *Berryman's Sonnets* (1967), a sequence of 115 poems mostly written in 1947 (shortly before the poet began work on the fifty-seven tightly and efficiently structured stanzas of *Homage to Mistress Bradstreet*), in which Berryman's procedure may be properly described as being to annex the incidents and responses of his own life to a creative pattern. Since the life and writing unfolded in tandem, the moral scheme of the sonnets (which begins in reciprocal passion and ecstasy and leads on to reproach and remorse) was fortuitous, and not a preconceived plot. While suffering and assessing his own emotions and thoughts, the poet does more than record them as a diarist, he formulates them – fabricating a myth of self – in an arrangement of striking attitudes. Although the sequence is doubtlessly a *tour de force*, it seems likely to prove a lost leader, both for its strained technique and for chance of circumstances. *Homage to Mistress Bradstreet* is by so much more successful a poem than *Berryman's Sonnets* to the degree in which Berryman directs his attention beyond the random application of self-consciousness to a specific location, a conceptual design, and a semi-dramatic use of dialogue.

Composed over a period of thirteen years, *The Dream Songs*, which is arguably Berryman's greatest achievement, is a formal sequence of 385 poems, each of three six-line stanzas. In spite of its vaunted difficulties of syntax, idiom, and allusive density, the poem may be happily read as one long poem, if not strictly an epic, which Berryman once whimsically termed the 'Tragical History of Henry'. It derives its character from the poet's habit of studying and treating selectively his life, attitudes, reading and concerns (which centrally include Freud*, theology, and the concepts of death and dread), as a developing and changing pattern of sometimes dire but often funny complexity. The emergence of whatever structure the poem possesses, which is much mooted by the critics, was dependent on Berryman's own growing ability to define his relationship to his persona.

Love & Fame (1971), a collection of lyrics, is at first blush more accessibly autobiographical, since it largely deploys anecdotes and reflections of the poet's earlier life. Although the final section of the book contains a sequence which professes an idiosyncratic belief in God and provides the volume with an ironic structure (since it seems to refute the values of earlier poems), the book as a whole does engage fascinating problems of internal irony as well as moral and idiomatic risks.

While Berryman is often associated with other so-called 'confessional' poets such as Robert Lowell* and Sylvia Plath*, and has accordingly been rather facilely placed within the tradition of what the poet Douglas Dunn has called the 'crazed exposure of the American ego', the term 'confessional' is singularly inadequate to describe his work, which – even when it draws on the poet's personal life for subject-matter – is at all times concerned not with expressive outpourings but with composing and crafting works of sustained imagination.

Dr John Haffenden

Other works include: *Delusions, Etc.* (1972); *Henry's Fate & Other Poems 1967–1972* (1978); *The Freedom of the Poet* (1977); and *Recovery* (1973). See also: J. M. Linebarger, *John Berryman* (1974); Joel Conarroe, *John Berryman: An Introduction to the Poetry* (1977); and John Haffenden, *John Berryman: A Critical Commentary* (1980).

48

BETJEMAN, Sir John 1906–

English poet

When Betjeman's first books appeared in the early 1930s, he was known only to a small group of friends as an admirer of unfashionable architecture and the author of eccentric poems about nonconformist chapels and suburban manners. Twenty-five years later, the publication of his *Collected Poems* (1958) suddenly made him one of the most popular poets of the century, after which his appointment to the Laureateship in 1972 caused no surprise. Yet he had not changed: simply (in Wordsworth's phrase) created the taste by which he was relished.

As a poet he was completely opposed to his time. His poems owed nothing to the Pound* – Eliot* revolution; they rhymed and scanned, and were not obscure. Nor were they about the working class or the unconscious; his subjects were children's parties, handsome tennis-girls, the arrest of Oscar Wilde and church furnishing, mingled with snatches of autobiography and personal statements about death and lust and remorse, with the occasional flight into farce or fantasy. What made them perplexing was their ambivalence (both funny and serious); what made them memorable was the utter sincerity of their feeling and the precise vivacity of their language.

Betjeman's lifelong interest was not literature but architecture, but for him architecture meant more than antiquarian detail or even fashions in building; it was the record of how people had lived and behaved, and so was instinct with humanity. From this conviction he made what was really a new kind of poetry that dealt with people in terms of places and places in terms of people: Myfanwy and North Oxford, the Anglican nun and Felixstowe, the elderly Oxford dons and their memories of 'the long-dead generations coming in from Eights' are all inseparable vignettes of remarkable human and historical clarity, sometimes (as in 'The Metropolitan Railway') reaching a conclusion of extreme poignancy:

Cancer has killed him. Heart is killing her.
The trees are down. An Odeon flashes fire
Where stood their villa by the murmuring fir.

The other side of this vision is Betjeman's constant warfare with the present. Poems beginning 'Come, friendly bombs, and fall on Slough'; 'We plough the fields and scatter The poison on the ground'; or 'I am a young executive. No cuffs than mine are cleaner' are all arraignments of an age in which insensitivity and greed destroy inherited beauty and proportion. If Betjeman seems at times to take up these attitudes too easily, what he is saying has begun increasingly to be echoed by those concerned with the environment and the quality of our life in it.

Betjeman has long been accepted as a writer of original and amusing light verse who is able at times to touch deeper emotions, but the description hardly does justice to the range of his poetry, that takes in uproarious comedy, delicate pathos and brutal honesty with an equally sure touch. Nor does it make clear his crucial position as an alternative to modernist poetry, who by maintaining the older tradition of direct communication in unambiguous language showed that a vast public still exists for it.

Philip Larkin

Betjeman's *Collected Poems* (1958) has been revised and enlarged over the years, and contains the main body of his verse. Principal prose works include *Ghastly Good Taste* (1933, revised 1970), *An Oxford University Chest* (1938), *Collins Guide to English Parish Churches* (1958), and a selection of essays, *First and Last Loves* (1952). *Summoned by Bells* (1960) is a verse autobiography to the age of twenty-one. See also: Margaret L. Stapleton, *Sir John Betjeman: a Bibliography of Writings By and About Him* (1974); Derek Stanford, *Sir John Betjeman: a Study* (1961); and John Press, *John Betjeman* (1974).

49

BEUYS, Joseph 1921–

German sculptor

Like Warhol*, Beuys constructed his own legend as his career took shape. Before the 1960s, therefore, the facts of his life are hotly debated. As promulgated by the artist himself, they can be summarized as follows. At the age of seven he moved from Kleve to Rindern but ran away to join a travelling circus, performing as an escapologist. In the Second World War he served first as a radio operator, then a combat pilot, was injured five times and nearly died in 1943 when his plane crashed in the Crimea and he was rescued in a snowstorm after German search parties had given up hope. Tartars took him to their tents, covered his body in fat and wrapped him in felt. Three years later he returned to Kleve and throughout the 1950s worked on a farm there, in a state of profound mental disturbance caused by the war. After working on a zoological film with the naturalist Heinz Sielmann, he enrolled at the Düsseldorf Academy under Ewald Mataré, who passed on to him a commission for a church door for Cologne Cathedral.

In 1961 Beuys was appointed Professor of Monumental Sculpture at the Academy, and between 1962 and 1965 was closely involved with Fluxus, a group of international neo-Dadaists dedicated to collective activity. Gradually his work became more overtly political. Teaching and forming groups was important: the German Student Party (1967), the Organization for Direct Democracy (1970), the Organization for Non-Voters and Free Referendum (1970) and the Free University (1977). In 1972, however, he was sacked from his teaching position. A six-year lawsuit followed. At last Beuys won his case for wrongful dismissal against Johannes Rau, Minister for Science and Research for Northern Westphalia. By the end of the 1970s his political aspirations had intensified; in 1979, the year of his great retrospective at the Guggenheim Museum, New York, Beuys stood for election to the European Community Parliament.

Despite the fiasco at Düsseldorf Beuys's title of 'monumental sculptor' describes his achievement well; the balance between 'public' issues and more private 'artistic' concerns, maintained for twenty years, has served to sketch a theory of sculpture as activity, demonstration and social comment, with no sacrifice of aesthetic power. His art arises naturally from the testing of his world view and the fictionalization of incidents in his life. Operating in every conceivable mode, he employs an unsystematic personal mythology – rooted in the folkloristic and scientific strains of German Romantic thought – to redress failure of intuition and spiritual awareness in an era of disintegrating capitalist values. If topics of world importance are tackled, they are dealt with obliquely. A felt-covered piano is devised for pieces composed by thalidomide children. He suggests that the Berlin wall be raised five centimetres 'for aesthetic reasons'. Beuys's technique may resemble a more obviously political version of Duchamp's* ready-mades; he creates a bone radio or an earth telephone, or constructs his *Fond* series, as batteries which do not work. And, like Duchamp, he rises to levels of precarious, perhaps confused, allegory. Invited to design sets for *Iphigenie* and *Titus Andronicus* at the Frankfurt Theatre Festival in 1969 Beuys offered to perform them simultaneously instead. On a stage with chalk diagrams and scores for the performance, Beuys, dressed at first in a white fur coat, recited *Iphigenie* while behind him a white horse stood on a sheet of iron. Over loudspeakers actors recited a montage of both plays, while Beuys repeated a set of gestures, reading lines and moving away, making flying movements, feeding sugar to the horse, crouching, measuring his head in both hands, making animal noises and spitting margarine into an empty area of the stage. In *I Like America and America Likes Me* Beuys was blindfolded, flown to New York, taken in an ambulance to the gallery and locked in a cage for a week with a wild coyote, armed only with a felt blanket, a stick and a triangle, gloves and, every day, fifty copies of the *Wall Street Journal*. The coyote, revered by the Red Indian as a shape-changer, was despised by the White Man and reduced to the level of a trickster. By making friends with the coyote and adopting his way of life temporarily Beuys attempted to make contact with what he regarded as an American trauma. In both *Aktionen* the physical manifestation meshed with Beuys's own complex theories – explained more directly by the artist in his *Energy Plan for Western Man* lectures – yet the visual impact was undiminished. Remembering *Iphigenie*, wrote the playwright Peter Handke*, 'an excited state of stillness comes over me

. . . it activates me; it is so painfully beautiful that it becomes Utopian, and that means political.'

Even without his physical presence Beuys's sculpture speaks eloquently of the social significance of the act of its making. *Tallow*, created for an outdoor site in Münster, resulted from filling a huge useless area in a badly designed concrete underpass. A plywood mould was made and twenty tons of mutton fat – plus a little beef fat for firmness – was melted and poured in. It took three months to cool and was cut into five great sections, like icebergs. *Honey-Pump* at Documenta 6 in Kassel in 1977 was in action for the hundred days of the Free University. Two ships' engines pumped two tons of honey through plastic pipes connecting every room in the building. Honey, fat, felt . . . however unfamiliar his strategies, Beuys's compulsive repetition of materials, his desire to inject significance into every aspect of the surrounding world – even his clothes – are reminiscent of the story of the airman who returned to life. Beuys became a survival artist, intent on showing others how to go on living.

Stuart Morgan

See: G. Adriani, W. Konnertz and K. Thomas, *Joseph Beuys* (1970); Caroline Tisdall, *Joseph Beuys* (Solomon R. Guggenheim Museum, 1979).

50

BISHOP, Elizabeth 1911–79

US poet

It has taken a long time for Elizabeth Bishop to be given her due. The New Criticism of the late 1940s and the 1950s found it hard to assimilate her, admiring the 'observant eye', but accusing her of randomness and lack of finish; and the 1960s' esteem for 'confessional' poetry meant that she was sometimes written off as being too impersonal. There is also the problem of locating Bishop within the modern tradition: she has no obvious antecedents, comparisons occasionally made between her work and that of American near-contemporaries (Marianne Moore*, Robert Lowell* and more recently John Ashbery) rarely look convincing, and there have been no followers. To this extent, Bishop's independence has worked against her. For many years she had the gratifying but unglamorous reputation of being a poet's poet, admired by a few fellow practitioners but neglected by critics; and to this day no good critical assessment exists. Only in the last few years of her life did the climate alter, and Bishop receive some of the acclaim she deserves. What was once dismissed as arbitrariness and irresolution – 'Everything only connected by "and" and "and" ', as one of her poems puts it – now seems a refreshingly honest coming to terms with the 'untidy activity' of living. And her refusal to enter into either the particulars of her private life or the public realm of politics has begun to seem, not reprehensible, but a consequence of her rootlessness and restlessness – something more than compensated for, in any case, by her powerful evocations of place.

Bishop's life began tragically: shortly after her birth her father died and her mother was admitted to a mental home. The childhood that followed seems to have been – to adopt one of her own phrases – 'awful but cheerful'. She grew up partly in Nova Scotia, with grandparents, and partly with an aunt in Boston. She was educated at Vassar College, New York, and by the time of her graduation, in 1934, had begun to write seriously: in the 1933 poem 'Some Dreams They Forgot', the unmistakable tone of voice has already been struck and some of the favourite imagery (weather, birds, flowers) is present. But it was not until the publication of *North and South* (1946) that she officially 'arrived'. Subsequent collections have followed at the rate of one per decade: like that of the English poet Philip Larkin*, Bishop's output is sparse. *The Complete Poems* (1969) and *Geography III* (1976) contain most of the poems she wished to preserve.

Bishop's poetry is delicately balanced between freedom and formality. She speaks in a casual, conversational voice, but is capable of resonance and even grandiloquence; she prefers free verse, often of very uneven line length yet controlled by internal rhyme. The most striking feature of all is perhaps her bold and at times outrageous use of metaphor: as a phrase from 'The Bight' has it, her work is 'littered with old correspondences'. Analogies taken from the workaday world are especially common and have the knack of making the natural world seem cosy, intimate, on close terms with humanity. A beach 'hisses like fat', the sea has 'the colour of the gas flame turned as low as possible', mist is 'like a first coat of whitewash when it's wet', a rooster's cry 'grates like a wet match', fireflies are (more decoratively) 'exactly like the bubbles in champagne'. At times this method becomes reductive, over-confidently domesticating and anthropomorphizing. The greater successes come when she moves in the other direction, discerning organic patterns in the ordinary or mechanical:

the water wagon comes

throwing its hissing, snowy fan across
peelings and newspapers. The water dries
light-dry, dark-wet, the pattern
of the cool watermelon.

Bishop's description of familiar objects as strange and beautiful has led her to be called 'surrealist': her posture is one of 'sleeping standing up', dreaming and yet wide-awake. Ultimately, however, the term 'surrealist'

seems inappropriate: it is not that she *transforms* the real world (her devotion to it is too deep for that), but that she finds the strangeness that is already there. Even a map, straightforwardly described, can become a place of 'excitement': 'The names of seashore towns run out to sea,/The names of cities cross the neighbouring mountains.'

The methods of mapmakers are very much Bishop's own: faithful representation of topography doesn't prevent some curious displacements. And as 'The Map' also suggests, she has a special fascination with coastlines, the meeting of land and sea. In many of her best poems – 'The Bight', 'At the Fish-houses', 'Sandpiper', 'Florida', 'Cape Breton', 'Crusoe in England' – she watches from the shore and discovers meaning in the sea: 'It is like what we imagine knowledge to be:/dark, salt, clear, moving, utterly free.' Lush vegetation, whether that of Brazil (where she lived for many years) or Florida, is something else which draws her, and seems a symbol of what she would like her poetry to be – colourful, exotic, but deeply rooted in its immediate environment. In a post-war Anglo-American tradition fond of half-lights and the grey areas of doubt, Bishop cuts an oddly garish figure; but she is one of the few certain to increase her reputation.

Blake Morrison

51

BLOCH, Ernst 1885–1977

German philosopher

Ernst Bloch is a paradoxical figure in twentieth-century culture. A Marxist atheist, his main influence has been in the field of Christian theology where men like Jürgen Moltmann and Harvey Cox have drawn on Bloch's ideas in formulating a socially radical theology of hope and revolution. Bloch was born in the Rhineland industrial town of Ludwigshaven. He studied philosophy in Würzburg, Berlin and Heidelberg, withdrawing to Switzerland on the outbreak of war in 1914. There he composed his first book *Geist der Utopie* ('The Spirit of Utopia', 1918), which was followed by his powerful study of the leader of the German peasant revolt crushed in 1525 *Thomas Munzer als Theologe der Revolution* ('Thomas Munzer as Theologian of Revolution', 1921). A friend of Bertolt Brecht*, Kurt Weill* and Walter Benjamin*, Bloch worked as a free-lance writer in Munich and Berlin during the 1920s. He left Germany in 1933 for the United States where he began to compose his major work *Das Prinzip Hoffnung* ('The Principle of Hope', 3 vols, 1954–9). After the war he returned, like Brecht, to East Germany where, from 1949 until 1957, he taught philosophy at the University of Leipzig. However, Bloch's relations with the Communist regime were uneasy and, in 1961, he asked for political asylum in the Federal Republic. Appointed a visiting professor at the University of Tübingen, he played an active role in the student unrest of the late 1960s.

Asked once to sum up his thought in a single sentence, Bloch replied, 'S is not yet P.' Subject is not yet predicate, nothing is yet the self that it will become. With this contention Bloch attempts to encapsulate the central premise of his utopian ontology. Though anchored in the tradition of revolutionary Marxism, Bloch's thought draws deeply on the German idealist philosophy of nature found in the work of Hegel and Schelling, on Christian and Jewish mysticism and on neo-Platonism. Every current of thought that tends to undermine our conception of reality as fixed or stable is grist to Bloch's mill, for he conceives reality as essentially dynamic, an open process culminating in 'Utopia', a state of affairs in which such fundamental distinctions as those between heaven and earth, subject and object will be overcome. Man is defined, if the notion of 'definition' can be applied to a being as undetermined as the human, by his hope for a future perfection. Religious expectation is the ancient form of hope, the expression of man's furthest possibilities in a context that denies them, but today, Bloch writes, 'Whatever is non-illusionary and really possible in images of hope will tend towards Marx, affecting (however varied and rationed out according to the current situation it may be) the socialist transformation of the world.' Bloch develops the old Marxist theme that religion is the mystified expression of earthly hopes but goes far beyond most Marxists in believing that the image of the community of saints literally prefigures an attainable future.

In Bloch's thought Marxism is presented openly as the utopianism its critics have always accused it of being. This is of no concern to Bloch for whom 'Utopia' is neither more nor less than the fulfilment of the immanent possibilities of the process of reality, but it disturbs other more sober thinkers in the revolutionary tradition. Even Herbert Marcuse* has criticized Bloch's effort to undermine the subject/object distinction in his heady identification of the object of hope with the substance of the future. Radical theologians, on the other hand, find in Bloch one of the main sources for their contention that, in the not unrepresentative formulation of Harvey Cox, God is not above, nor below, nor even within, but ahead.

David J. Levy

English translations include: *Man on his Own* (1970); *On Karl Marx* (1971); and *A Philosophy of the Future* (1970). See also Fredric Jameson, *Marxism and Form* (1971).

52
BOAS, Franz 1858–1942

US anthropologist

Although born and educated in Germany, Franz Boas is considered the founding father of American anthropology. His contributions, ranging from vast collections of ethnographic data, statistical studies in physical anthropology and descriptive studies of American Indian languages, to treatises on the aims and methods in the study of the subject, shaped anthropological research into a science and had an immense impact on future generations of anthropologists.

The son of a prosperous businessman, Boas was born in Minden, Westphalia, and was educated at the universities of Heidelberg, Bonn and Kiel. Majoring in physics with geography as a minor, he received his doctorate in 1881 with a thesis called *Beiträge zur Erkenntnis der Farbe des Wassers* ('Contributions towards the understanding of the colour of water', 1881). His interest, however, soon turned to cultural geography, influenced by his teacher Theobald Fischer and the writings of Friedrich Ratzel and Wilhelm Wundt. His growing interest in the relationship between environment and culture took him on a research expedition to the Arctic in 1883–4 which resulted in a number of geographical and ethnographic articles on the Eskimo as well as his monograph *The Central Eskimo* (1888). It was this trip that also established the basis for the dominant aspect of his anthropological thinking: the awareness of the infinite complexity of human culture and how it came into being.

While he was assistant at the Berlin Völkerkunde Museum under A. Bastian in 1885, a group of Indians from the north-west coast of America were 'exhibited' there, which inspired him to do field research among the Kwakiutl Indians of British Columbia, whose study was to become his lifelong occupation.

Upon his return from the field he decided to emigrate to America and subsequently settled and married in New York. After holding a number of poorly remunerated positions as assistant editor of the journal *Science*, docent in anthropology at Clark University and curator at the Chicago Field Museum, he became curator of the American Museum of Natural History, and then professor in anthropology at Columbia University, where he stayed until his retirement in 1936. In addition, Boas played an instrumental role in the establishment of professional organizations and was the editor of the *American Anthropologist* and the *Journal of American Folklore*, as well as founding and editing the *International Journal of American Linguistics*.

The large bulk of Boas's publications consists of his ethnographic material on the Indians of the Pacific coast. Over a period of almost six decades, he published more than ten thousand pages on the natives of this area. While these writings include such synthesized accounts as *The Social Organization and Secret Societies of the Kwakiutl Indians* (Report of the US National Museum for 1895, 1897) and the posthumously published *Kwakiutl Ethnography* (1966), it is characteristic of his approach that the remainder of the materials are collections of texts recorded in the native language. With the help of a native informant, George Hunt, he transcribed, translated and edited thousands of pages of texts, including myths, family histories, customs, dreams, accounts of religious ceremonies and even recipes. Only texts collected in this manner, he believed, were undistorted and presented the view from within the culture. Moreover, he had little regard for the description of informal behaviour: with the American Indian way of life quickly disappearing under the impact of the white man, his preoccupation was with the symbolic and ceremonial aspects of native mentality.

It is difficult to label Boas's contribution to anthropological theory, since he usually presented his views as critiques of what he took to be others' reductionist assumptions. In a number of essays reprinted in *Race, Language and Culture* (1940), he incessantly points out the immense complexity of cultural growth, employing the concept of historicity: the particular shape individual cultures take is due to multiplex processes of adaptation and borrowing from other cultures. With the time factor introduced, there is a dynamic relationship between single cultures, between culture and environment, between individual and society. He thus argued both against the evolutionists' assumption of universal laws governing the development of civilization and against theories of environmental determination: culture itself emerged as a factor shaping human civilization.

His investigations in physical anthropology ultimately point in the same direction: in *The Mind of Primitive Man* (1911, revised 1938) – a book on the purge list of the Nazi German book-burning in 1933 – he demystified the concept of race, heretofore dominated by Eurocentric notions of superiority; his statistical studies on growth, heredity and modification of bodily form among descendants of immigrants pointed out the impact of cultural environment on physical growth. Interestingly, these studies had some practical significance, being utilized, for example, in the administration of American orphanages. Last, and not least, he used the results of his studies on race in his outspoken opposition against the racism of the German Nazi regime.

In linguistics, Boas was completely self-taught, although he was influenced by the humanistic language theories of W. von Humboldt, J. G. Herder and H. Steinthal. His study of Indian languages taught him that these operate with categories not assumed by Indo-European linguistics. These categories, however, must be analysed and described in their own terms, undistorted by the categories of Indo-European languages. Examples of such linguistic analysis are his short grammars of Chinook, Tsimshian and Kwakiutl in the *Handbook of American Indian Languages* (1911), which he also edited, and his extensive, posthumously published *Kwakiutl Grammar* (1947). Linguistic analysis, however, to him was not an aim in itself, but was part of ethnographic analysis. In fact, as he pointed out in his famous introduction to the *Handbook*, language, as a manifestation of the human mind which is yet empirically observable, helps us to gain a clearer understanding of ethnological phenomena, precisely because of its unconscious nature: the very nature of other languages' lexical and grammatical categories points to different ways of categorizing experience. These notions opened the way to more radical hypotheses on the relationship between language and world view brought forth by his student Sapir* and by Whorf*.

Finally, one concept emerges from all of Boas's investigations into race, language and culture: the study of different and strange ways of behaviour enables us to free ourselves from the 'shackles of our own civilization' and to view it more objectively (*The Aims of Ethnology*, 1889). Boas trained a whole generation of American anthropologists and linguists, who in turn spread his legacy. Among them are, to name only a few: A. L. Kroeber, Ruth Benedict, R. H. Lowie, Margaret Mead*, Sapir, M. J. Herskovits and P. Radin.

Marianne Boelscher

Other works include: *Tsimshian Mythology* (Bureau of American Ethnology, 31st Annual Report, 1916); *Primitive Art* (1927); *Anthropology and Modern Life* (1928); and editorship and contributions to *General Anthropology* (1938). See also: Melville Herskovits (ed.), *Franz Boas, The Science of Man in the Making* (no. 61 of the Memoir Series of the American Anthropological Association, 1943); Walter Goldschmidt (ed.), *The Anthropology of Franz Boas* (Memoir No. 89, 1959); Leslie A. White, *The Ethnography and Ethnology of Franz Boas* (1963).

53

BOHR, Niels Henrik David 1885–1962

Danish physicist

One of the greatest figures in twentieth-century physics, Niels Bohr was born and brought up in Copenhagen. His family was well-to-do and distinguished for its intellect, culture and humanity. After gaining his doctorate in 1911 for a dissertation on the Lorentz – Thomson electron theory of metals Bohr went to Cambridge to pursue research under Sir J. J. Thomson, going on after several months to Manchester to study under Ernest Rutherford*. He married Margarethe Nørlund in 1912. One of his six sons, Aage Bohr, was, like his father, to win the Nobel Prize for physics.

While in Britain Bohr turned his attention to Rutherford's model of atomic structure, according to which the simplest atom, hydrogen, consists of a comparatively heavy, positively charged particle, the proton, orbited by a much lighter, negatively charged particle, the electron. According to classical electrodynamics, however, such a system ought rapidly to collapse, the electron spiralling down into the nucleus and giving off radiation of a frequency equal to its orbital period. Bohr saw that the obvious stability of the atom could not be explained by classical electrodynamics and that what was required was a nonclassical theory of atomic structure. Employing Planck's* notion of the quantization of energy, he constructed just such a theory, postulating that the atom can exist only in a finite number of discrete energy states and can emit and absorb radiation only during transitions between two different states, when the electrons 'jump' from one discrete orbit to another, emitting or absorbing radiation of a frequency proportional to the difference in energy between the two states in question.

Bohr's quantum theory of the atom, published in the *Philosophical Magazine* in 1913, was remarkably bold and novel (flatly contradicting classical electrodynamics) and of considerable explanatory and predictive power. Elaborated by Bohr and others during the next ten years, this theory was one of the mainsprings in the development of the Quantum Theory. Particularly important in this respect was Bohr's *correspondence principle* to the effect that the results of the Quantum Theory should agree approximately with those of classical physics in the limited field in which the latter is approximately valid.

Bohr became Professor of Theoretical Physics at Copenhagen in 1916, and his institute, founded in 1920, rapidly became one of the world centres for physics, attracting like a magnet many of the most gifted young physicists, such as Werner Heisenberg*, Wolfgang Pauli, and P. A. M. Dirac. Bohr was awarded the Nobel Prize in 1922.

In 1927 Bohr proposed his conception of *complementarity* as a solution to the pressing problem of the physical interpretation of the new quantum mechanics and to the paradoxes of wave-particle duality, i.e. the fact that radiation and matter appear in some experimental situations to behave like particles and in others like waves. Bohr argued that the wave and particle conceptions are complementary in the sense that they are equally indispensable for a complete interpretation of quantum mechanics and of experimental evidence concerning matter and radiation, yet mutually exclusive in that they cannot be applied in the same context, in one and the same experimental situation. Heisenberg's

uncertainty principle (discovered at Bohr's institute) is, Bohr argued, a special case of complementarity: the position and momentum of a microphysical object can each be measured exactly, though they cannot both be measured exactly at the same time, since the different measurements require mutually exclusive experimental arrangements. Consequently there can be no deterministic description of the behaviour of microphysical objects, since that requires exact knowledge of simultaneous position and momentum.

Bohr's interpretation of quantum mechanics was to form the basis of the 'Copenhagen interpretation', which was accepted by all but a small minority of physicists, which included such prominent figures as Schrödinger* and Einstein*. Einstein could not accept that the indeterminability implied by complementarity is, as Bohr held, ultimate and irrevocable, and that no non-complementary realist description of microphysical objects is possible. Again and again he tried to refute Bohr's position. The outcome of the great debate between these two intellectual giants is generally held to be in Bohr's favour, though the decision is not uncontroversial, since there is no general agreement among philosophers of physics about exactly how Bohr's theory of complementarity is to be understood.

During the 1930s Bohr elaborated and refined his doctrine of complementarity, convinced that it had important applications not only in physics but also in biology, psychology and the social sciences. He suggested, for example, that a deterministic, physiological account of human action and an indeterministic, psychological account are complementary. In the 1930s Bohr also made an important contribution to nuclear physics, his liquid drop model of the atomic nucleus providing an explanation of the process of fission of the uranium atom.

Working tirelessly to help physicist victims of Nazi oppression, Bohr was forced to flee with his family from Nazi-occupied Denmark in 1943, spending the remainder of the war in Britain and the USA. Alarmed at the tremendous dangers of nuclear weapons, he strove to alert Roosevelt and Churchill to the perils and the urgent necessity for the international control of these, arguing that this required free exchange of information and complete co-operation between the super-powers. He saw here a unique opportunity for securing international trust as a basis for continuing peace.

Bohr's thinking made a great impact on twentieth-century physics: he is important not only for his physical theories and philosophy of physics, as one of the principal creators of the twentieth-century world picture, but also for the inspiration which he gave to others, such as Heisenberg and Einstein.

Dr D. R. Murdoch

For biographical information, see S. Rozental (ed.),

Niels Bohr (1968). The standard edition of his works is *Niels Bohr: Collected Works*, ed. L. Rosenfeld (1971). For his philosophical writings, see *Atomic Theory and the Description of Nature* (Cambridge 1934); *Atomic Physics and Human Knowledge* (New York 1958), which contains his classic account of his long debate with Einstein, 'Discussion with Einstein on Epistemological Problems in Atomic Physics', one of the best accounts of his philosophy; and *Essays 1958–1962 on Atomic Physics and Human Knowledge* (New York 1963). For a more technical analysis of his ideas, see Erhard Scheibe, *The Logical Analysis of Quantum Mechanics* (1973), ch. 1; C. A. Hooker, 'The Nature of Quantum Mechanical Reality: Einstein versus Bohr', in *Paradoxes and Paradigms*, ed. R. G. Colodny (1972). See also: Max Jammer, *The Conceptual Development of Quantum Mechanics* (1966).

54
BÖLL, Heinrich 1917–

German novelist and essayist

Böll was born in the Catholic city of Cologne, and a major theme in his work has always been the conflict between the unquestioning faith of a devout Catholic and the rejection of the Church as an entrenched temporal power supporting the establishment. Böll embarked on an apprenticeship in a bookshop and engaged in some literary studies at University before being called up in 1939. He served throughout the war in different parts of Europe and spent a brief period as a prisoner-of-war of the Western Allies. After his release Böll began to publish short stories in newspapers and magazines and soon came into prominence for his accurate reflections of the life and mood of post-war Germany. His novels in particular voiced strong social criticism and unease about the political development of West Germany, especially the covert resurgence of fascistoid attitudes. During the 1960s he became more and more involved in public controversies, campaigning vigorously for different causes (e.g. against the Emergency Laws of 1968). In 1969 Böll was elected President of the German PEN Club, and of the International PEN club in 1971. He also helped to set up the German Writers' Union. The 1970s were dominated by the effects of his outspoken criticism in 1972 of the official handling of terrorism in Germany. In the same year he joined Günter Grass* and other prominent writers campaigning for Willy Brandt and the SPD in the national elections and was awarded the Nobel Prize for Literature. Two years later Böll was instrumental in helping Solzhenitsyn* settle in the West, but despite his denunciation of the harassment of 'dissidents' in Eastern Europe he has been branded in many quarters at home as a subversive sympathizer and virtual terrorist himself.

Though not of a polemical nature Böll has found that the conscience he clearly does not mask as a novelist and his growing fame throughout the world have turned him into a 'moral authority', an influential commentator on public questions, as three substantial volumes of essays and lectures since 1967 demonstrate. Yet Böll is still primarily a novelist who has the ability to capture in imaginative form and persuasive situations the problems and preoccupations besetting Germany since 1945: first emerging as a country exhausted by defeat and guilt, then re-establishing itself industrially, trying to forget the past or pretend it never happened, and finally finding its society a generation later once again prone to violence, paranoia, intimidation and the curtailment of individual freedom.

From the time when he first wrote in *The Train was on Time* (*Der Zug war pünktlich*, 1949, trans. 1956) and *And where were you, Adam?* (*Wo warst du, Adam?*, 1951, trans. 1955) of the filth, elemental fear and bewilderment of unheroic soldiers, and the apathy shared by the numbed civilians they returned to in the shattered cities, Böll has never forgotten that the hopes offered by meretricious ideologies are illusory. He spoke for the 'middle' generation, those old enough in the Nazi years to be deceived and sacrificed in 'the almost total senselessness of military life', but too young to have a voice in determining their country's destiny. This is the generation that after 1945 refused to accept their elders' facile 'overcoming of the burden of the past' ('Bewältigung der Vergangenheit'); instead Böll probed the mentality of the Adenauer period in Germany with its powerful tendencies to restoration when the tacit watchword was to shrug off a past which had led to the holocaust. In the successive generations of the idiosyncratic Fähmel family in *Billiards at half-past nine* (*Billard um halbzehn*, 1959, trans. 1961) Böll incorporates the dissonant conscience of Germans who did not share and refused to conform to the assertive ideology, nationalism and aggressiveness of their rulers. In the light of the sharpened awareness generated by the students' revolt in the late 1960s this theme is even more trenchantly explored in the life of Leni, the heroine of *Group Portrait with Lady* (*Gruppenbild mit Dame*, 1971, trans. 1973).

The protests of the younger generation that erupted in the 1960s were a vociferous counterpart to the more restrained attacks of non-conforming intellectuals like Böll. The acts of protest of the Fähmels, of Hans Schnier in *The Clown* (*Ansichten eines Clowns*, 1963, trans. 1965), of Schmölder in *Absent without Leave* (*Entfernung von der Truppe*, 1964, trans. 1965), of the Gruhls in *The End of a Mission* (*Ende einer Dienstfahrt*, 1966, trans. 1968) all articulate Böll's opposition to the reactionary complexion of West Germany's political development since the war and his rejection of the dominant and all-pervasive ethos of success – productivity, consumerism, materialist values and disparagement of the disadvantaged. Böll wants his books to 'spark off critical thoughts' since 'the artist belongs by nature to the extra-parliamentary opposition'. In this respect, therefore, Böll makes 'the great refusal' that Herbert Marcuse* argued was the function of artists in every society, bringing critical bite to the affirmation of a far from perfect state. But Böll's brief political support for the SPD was, unlike that of Grass, only brought about by a diffuse awareness that this party offered a less evil alternative than the Christian Democrats; without being a conservative he wishes to preserve liberal humane values, above all the overriding respect for the single citizen, since 'the dignity of the individual is sacred'.

It is on this point that Böll has become the standard-bearer of civil liberty in Germany, taking up the cudgels for democratic principles in a looming police state. His most influential novel to date, *The Lost Honour of Katharina Blum* (*Die verlorene Ehre der Katharina Blum*, 1974, trans. 1975), is a bitterly satirical exposure of the techniques systematically employed by the media to distort and manipulate the truth in order to defame an individual. This, for Böll, is far more dangerous than any overt terrorism, for it is insidious violence with permanently damaging social effects, albeit without guns and bombs. In *Fürsorgliche Belagerung* ('Protective Siege', 1979) Böll turns his irony to the paradoxical situation of important public figures who are virtual prisoners of the measures taken to protect them from possible terrorist attack. Böll's courage in taking on almost single-handed powerful sectors of the German establishment has earned him much vilification, but also an honoured place as an intellectual accurately assessing and commenting on the state and temper of his country's moral culture.

Professor A. V. Subiotto

Other translations include: *Traveller, if you come to Spa* (*Wanderer, kommst du nach Spa . . .* , 1950, trans. 1956); *Acquainted with the Night* (*Und sagte kein einziges Wort*, 1953, trans. 1954); *The Unguarded House* or *Tomorrow and Yesterday* (*Haus ohne Hüter*, 1954, trans. 1957); *Missing Persons and Other Essays* (trans. Leila Vennewitz 1977). See also: J. H. Reid, *Heinrich Böll. Withdrawal and Re-emergence* (1973); Christian Linder, *Böll* (Hamburg 1978); J. Vogt, *Heinrich Böll* (Munich 1978).

55

BOND, Edward 1934–

English dramatist

Edward Bond is a self-made dramatist. Early in his career he was helped by Bill Gaskill and other young directors of the English Stage Company at the Royal Court Theatre, London, but by this time he had already completed numerous unperformed plays. His stubborn ambition to write for the theatre had been fired by visits to music halls – where one of his sisters was, for some time, sawn in half twice-nightly by a magician – and by the experience of seeing Donald Wolfit play Macbeth: 'It was the first thing that made sense of my life for me; the first time I'd found something beautiful and exciting and alive.'

Edward Bond was born in Holloway, London, the son of a farm labourer. In 1940 he was evacuated to Cornwall, and later to his grandparents in the small village of Shippea Hill in the Fenland countryside. At school he was not considered fit to take the eleven-plus examinations, and he left at the age of fifteen. After numerous dead-end jobs, he had two years of National Service, mostly spent in office work with the Allied Army of Occupation in Austria. Here he started to write. Back in London, Bond set himself to learn theatre-craft. For two years he visited almost all the plays in London and late in 1958, on the strength of two scripts submitted to the Royal Court, he joined the 'Writers' Group' at that theatre. Here Gaskill directed his *The Pope's Wedding* (1962), *Saved* (1965) and *Early Morning* (1968). The first was a 'Sunday Night production without décor'; the other two ran foul of the official censor, the Lord Chamberlain, for blasphemy, violence and portrayal of royal personages, so that they too had few performances, and a great deal of litigation and unhelpful press coverage.

But now Bond was already on course. *Saved* had been performed in Vienna in 1966 and the Munich production of 1967 was voted by *Theater Heute* the best play of the year. Theatre censorship was abolished in Britain, as if the powers-that-be agreed with Bond that 'it would be immoral not to write about violence' in the last decades of the twentieth century. From the early 1960s onwards Bond has worked steadily for the theatre, taking time for film scripts (including Antonioni's *Blow-up*) only to make enough money to live. He has written short political plays, such as *Black Mass* (1970) and *The Swing: A Documentary* (1976), and a libretto, *We Come to the River*, for an opera by Hans Werner Henze* at Covent Garden in 1976. He has set himself to learn practically from other writers by adapting Middleton's *A Chaste Maid in Cheapside* and Webster's *The White Devil* and translating Chekhov's *Three Sisters* and Wedekind's *Spring Awakening*. In Brecht*, he found encouragement to deal with 'the whole world', and not 'write about little things anymore'. His own major plays present a steadily progressing command of stage and language, and a restless and crafty pursuit of what he has called a 'rational' theatre – plays that show what life is in a godless, technological, repressive society.

The Pope's Wedding and *Saved* are set in the Fens and London which Bond knew at first hand, but *Early Morning* brings Queen Victoria, Florence Nightingale, the Prince Consort and many other mythical figures on stage as the play shows one of a pair of Siamese twins seeking freedom. This was to be Bond's way forward; the reshaping of old myths to highlight contemporary life, revealing the cruelty of power, the stupidity of privilege, the insufficiency of intelligence without action, the strength of goodness. He is a prodigal inventor of stories that reveal right and wrong, the switching of almost every label and the fetters of inherited corruption. In *Bingo* (1973), Shakespeare commits suicide, hopeless in his life. In *Lear* (1971), the King is hunted down by Cordelia and comforted by a ghost. In *The Woman* (1978) – the first new play to be produced in the Olivier Theatre on the South Bank in London and the first of Bond's plays to open directed by its author – Hecuba survives the sack of Troy and kills Heros, leader of the new Athens, in order to protect the islanders among whom she has found refuge.

Edward Bond views the past and its great authors without fear or fawning, and uses them to sharpen his picture of the present world in almost desperate need of revolution. He is a master of concision, yet his plays are unhurried and sometimes lengthy, taking their numerous characters through complicated events and ever closer to ultimate judgment. His plays are unambiguous and passionate, and yet deft, and often delicate; their author is in cool command and challenges an audience at every turn. Unmistakable heroes tell all in soliloquy, and yet emphasis is on relationships between characters: these men and women are judged by their humanity, not by the intensity, originality or complexity of their interior life.

Professor John Russell Brown

Two volumes of Bond's *Plays* have already appeared in The Master Playwrights series, published by Eyre Methuen, London (1977, 1978). These include: *Narrow Road to the Deep North* (1968); *The Sea* (1973), *The Fool* (1974). A volume of *Theatre Poems and Songs* was published in 1978 and, in the same year, *Edward Bond: a Companion to the Plays*, compiled by Malcolm Hay and Philip Roberts. The fullest critical study is *Bond: A Study of his Plays* by M. Hay and P. Roberts (1980).

56
BONHOEFFER, Dietrich 1906–45

German Lutheran pastor and theologian

Bonhoeffer was the son of a psychiatrist who was brought up in Germany in the last days of liberal-protestant orthodoxy. Educated at the universities of Tübingen and Berlin, by the end of the 1920s he was an enthusiastic supporter of the neo-orthodox Christian theology of the Barthian* school. For a short period assistant pastor of the German congregation in Barcelona, he was during 1929–30 a graduate student at Union Theological Seminary in New York. In 1931 he was appointed lecturer (*Dozent*) at Berlin, a post he occupied in conjunction with a pastorate. In 1934 he signed the Barmen Declaration, the constitutive document of the German Confessing Church, which was set up in opposition to the Nazi-oriented 'German Christian Church'. After further pastoral experience in London (1933–5), he became head of the Confessing Church's theological seminary at Finkenwalde, which was closed by the Nazi government in 1937. The Second World War broke out while he was once more resident in New York, and he immediately returned home, in spite of the dangers involved in continuing his work and resistance in wartime Germany. From the beginning of the war he was associated with an anti-Nazi resistance circle (whose members included Karl Goerdeler, Hans von Dohnanyi, James Count von Moltke, Admiral Canaris and General Beck), and it was as an emissary of this group that he travelled to Stockholm in 1942 in order to put its case to George Bell, Bishop of Chichester. He was arrested by the Gestapo in April 1943, on account of this suspected association; after imprisonment for eighteen months in Berlin, he was moved to Buchenwald and then to Flossenbürg, where he was hanged by the Gestapo on 9 April 1945, just prior to its liberation by the American Army.

Bonhoeffer's books have been highly influential in both ecclesiastical and academic circles, and it is worth mentioning two of them here. In his *The Cost of Discipleship* (*Nachfolge*, 1937, trans. 1948, rev. 1959) he explained and attacked the notion of 'cheap grace', which is involved in a type of Christianity which costs its followers nothing in the way of suffering, discomfort and sacrifice. In contradistinction, genuinely Christian grace is 'costly' precisely because it involves active, real and exclusive discipleship with Christ with all of its concomitant hardships, unpopularity and self-abnegation. But, according to Bonhoeffer, the grace involved in such a relationship confers newness and authenticity of life. Bonhoeffer's best-known book is undoubtedly his *Letters and Papers from Prison* (*Widerstand und Ergebung*, 1951, trans. 1955, enlarged 1971), consisting largely of letters smuggled out of his prison-cell to his brother-in-law and post-war editor, Eberhard Bethge, in which Bonhoeffer discussed some of the most burning issues of the age. One of its most controversial themes is Bonhoeffer's plea for a 'religionless' or 'worldly' Christianity. He radicalized Barth's attack on 'religion' as a pre-requisite for Christian commitment and existence. By 'religion' he seems to have meant three things – individualism (lacking in concern for the world of men), inwardness (pietistic, mystical, etc.) and metaphysics. By this latter term he denoted the attempt to fill in gaps in our secular-scientific knowledge with the 'God' of speculation. In the book, he also shows hostility towards 'psychotherapeutic' and 'existentialist' versions of Christianity, by which he seems to mean Christian preaching directed towards man in his weakness, in his sin, in his uncertain and anxious vulnerability. In contradistinction to all such Christianity built upon 'religious a prioris' (upon the 'religious premise') he pleaded for a 'secular' Christianity directed towards 'man come of age', towards modern mature man whose being has been unaffected by out-of-date 'religious' predispositions; similarly, he pleaded for a 'non-religious interpretation' of theological concepts; he wanted a version of Christianity which appealed to men where they are strong, not where they are weak, which would be of relevance in the central 'market-place' of life rather than on or beyond its boundaries.

Literally world-wide responses to these pleas have constituted an enormous corpus of 'Bonhoeffer-literature', aided and encouraged by the international Bonhoeffer Society (which holds regular congresses), with which Bethge has close connections. At the same time, those who are less enthusiastic about Bonhoeffer's rather fragmentary and enigmatic remarks have argued that he has become something of a cult-figure, and that his untimely heroic death as a Christian martyr has tended not merely to 'canonize' him but to make the task of criticizing his writings an embarrassing if not unpopular task. Amongst those influenced by these writings was Dr J. A. T. Robinson, the author of *Honest to God* (1963), and the British *Honest to God* controversy of the 1960s was largely, if partly uncomprehendingly, about certain Bonhoefferian concepts popularized by Robinson.

Professor James Richmond

Other works include: *Act and Being* (*Akt und Sein*, 1931, trans. 1962); *No Rusty Swords* (1965), *Christology* (1966) and *The Way to Freedom* (1966) are selections from *Gesammelte Schriften*, the collected shorter writings (5 vols, 1965–9). See: Eberhard Bethge, *Dietrich Bonhoeffer* (1967, trans. 1970); Ronald Gregor Smith (ed.), *World Come of Age: A Symposium* (1967); John A. Phillips, *The Form of Christ in the World: A Study of Bonhoeffer's Christology* (1966).

57

BONNARD, Pierre 1867–1947

French painter

Bonnard died in 1947 having lived through thirty years of post-Cubist abstraction seemingly unaffected by it.

His art, like the man himself, is emotionally tied to the nineteenth century. Born into the amiable atmosphere of the quiet Paris suburb of Fontenay aux Roses, his life was typically bourgeois – comfortable and uneventful. This peaceful way of life is reflected in the early work which deals with unspectacular events in an unspectacular way. The more pleasant aspects of Parisian street life are observed with a keen eye for the hustle and bustle of city life without ever drawing attention to the stresses and strains of modern living. He is careful not to disturb our acceptance of a way of life he finds perfectly agreeable. Quiet in tone and gentle in mood, his is an art of the intimate gesture and sunlit rooms full of flowers and bowls of fruit. Outside there is a garden and a shady terrace.

Mild he might be but there is nothing naive or primitive about Bonnard. Well read and widely travelled, he simply preferred his art to show the brighter side of life.

Originally intended for a legal career, he felt his years at the École des Beaux Arts to have been wasted but willingly accepted the importance of friendships made at the less austere Académie Julian with the group of painters later to be known as the 'Nabis' (Prophets), among whom were Édouard Vuillard and Maurice Denis. Through Denis he became acquainted with the ideas of Paul Gauguin and though it is difficult to pin-point with any certainty how Gauguin's influence filtered into his work there are hints here and there of a 'Symbolist' attitude to the meaning of colour. The influence of Japanese prints is more obvious, particularly in the graphic work. Bonnard was an illustrator of some subtlety and his lithographic drawings for Verlaine's *Parallèlement* published by Vollard in 1900 are delightfully apt.

Throughout his life Bonnard maintained that he belonged to no specific school and it is important not to see him as the direct descendant of the French Impressionists who made little impact on him. Unlike his French predecessors he was essentially a decorator and after the move south to Le Cannet near Cannes in 1925 colour became all important. Above all he was a painter of sunlight and warm air and this is echoed in the sheer sensual delight with which he applies his paint. Towards the end of his life there is even a hint of the twentieth-century tendency to rely on pure painterly effects and *The Studio at Le Cannet with Mimosa* completed in 1946 well shows the importance he placed on surface pattern. Indeed he often said that he wanted every square inch of his canvases to look 'pretty'. He painted with loving care for both subject and spectator.

Love was important to Bonnard whether it was the presumed illicit love of *L'Indolente* painted in 1899 and almost Munch*-like in its frankness, or the love expressed in the countless nudes of his wife painted between 1925 and 1937 where he delights as the water reflects the palest colours of her skin off the shimmering tiles that surround her bath or the sunlight from the open window flickers across her breasts as she looks thoughtfully at herself in the mirror.

Bonnard understood love and he understood the pleasure it can give and though he might well have been a man of the nineteenth century he well understood the need for such sentiments in the new machine age.

John Furse

Denys Sutton, *Bonnard* (1957); *Bonnard and His Environment*, Exhibition Catalogue with texts by J. T. Soby, J. Elliott and M. Wheeler, The Museum of Modern Art, New York 1964.

58
BORGES, Jorge Luis 1899–

Argentine short-story writer, essayist and poet

With Pablo Neruda* one of the two most distinguished contemporary Latin American men of letters. Of mixed British and Argentine stock, he has published both in Spanish and English. After a private education in Geneva, he moved to Spain and came under the influence of the innovatory poetic movement *ultraismo* whose aim was to break away from formal constraints and express complex and beautiful patterns of rhythms and images in free verse. He introduced the movement to Argentina, with momentarily striking success, in 1921. Between 1921 and 1930 he published numerous essays and three collections of poetry including *Fervor de Buenos Aires* (1923), moving away from experimentalism towards more meditative verse. In his later poetry (for example, *El otro, el mismo*, 1969), after a long gap, increasing blindness – and maturity – led him back to traditional metres and added new themes drawn from his study of old Germanic languages, his obsession with time, his philosophical interests, dominated by Schopenhauer and Berkeley, and his cult of his forebears. His latest poetry shows almost classical restraint and depth.

In 1938 he came close to death from septicaemia. On his recovery, fearing that his creative abilities might have been affected, he wrote a spoof learned article to test them. This became one of the stories of *Ficciones* (1944; trans. A. Kerrigan, 1962) which, with *El Aleph* (1949) (trans. Borges and Di Giovanni, 1970) established him as the most influential prose writer in Spanish since Unamuno*. Later collections include *El informe de Brodie* (1970) and *El libro de arena* (1975). His most characteristic tales can be described as fantastic fables which illustrate the collapse of man's comforting certainties and the bewildering possibilities which thus emerge. Borges holds that belief in the meaningfulness of existence is hard to maintain, that confidence in our ability to understand reality is probably an illusion, and that we ourselves are a mystery. All combinations of experience are theoretically possible; anything, logical or illogical, can happen; any explanation, credible or incredible, may be true.

Many of his best short stories examine existence and reality as if they formed part of some strange and bewildering puzzle. Among his favourite themes are: the impossible quest (for some ultimate certainty); the ironic fulfilment of man's greatest dreams (of immortality, of changing the past, of total knowledge); the implications of philosophical idealism; the nonexistence of the individual personality; the chaos and futility of existence; the circularity of time; and the defeat of reason. His attitude, however, is not one of spiritual stress but rather one of gentle humour, the expression of a detached, playful awareness of the absurdity of the human condition. For a long time his favourite symbol of this last was that of a circular labyrinth without a centre, since an endless maze perfectly conveys the combination of apparently significant regularity and total bafflement. But occasionally in his work men by acts of courage reach the centre of their own private existential labyrinths and discover their real identities.

Borges writes extremely slowly and meticulously. Each 'inlaid detail' of the meaning can be seen to fit, each feature of the narrative technique performs a conscious function. This produces a Kafka*-like density of texture (though Borges prefers to describe the Argentine Macedonio Fernández, along with Hawthorne, R. L. Stevenson and G. K. Chesterton*, as major influences). Borges's impact on Latin American literature, where he has led an entire generation of younger writers towards a new conception of the ambiguity of reality and the role of the creative imagination, has been immense. It has also been attested by writers in North America and France especially.

D. L. Shaw

Borges's Complete Works, *Obras completas* (Emecé, Buenos Aires), is in progress. For poetry in translation: *Selected Poems 1923–67* (bilingual edition, 1972) and *In Praise of Darkness* (1974). For stories and essays other than those mentioned: *Labyrinths* (1961); *Dreamtigers* (1964); *Other Inquisitions* (1964); *A Personal Anthology* (1967); *The Book of Imaginary Beings* (1969); *A Universal History of Infamy* (1972); and *Doctor Brodie's Report* (1972). The most useful critical works in English are A. M. Barrenechea, *Borges, The Labyrinth Maker* (1965); R. J. Christ, *The Narrow Act: Borges' Art of Allusion* (1969); and for beginners M. S. Stabb, *Jorge Luis Borges* (1970). The best biographical introduction is Borges's own 'Autobiographical Notes' in *The Aleph and other stories* mentioned above.

59
BOULEZ, Pierre 1925–

French composer

The son of an industrialist, he studied with Oliver Messiaen* at the Paris Conservatoire in 1944–5 and also had lessons in serial technique from René Leibowitz, a pupil of Schoenberg* and Webern*. At once he recognized serialism as the necessary basis for a new musical language, to be joined by the rhythmic procedures he found in Stravinsky* and Messiaen. His first published works, the *Sonatina for Flute and Piano* and the *First Piano Sonata* (both 1946), show his Webern-inspired use of serialism to develop small patterns of notes, but the Schoenbergian frenzy of his piano writing, the restless rhythms and the rapidity of the musical thought announce a quite individual style, one of impatient vehemence. The cantata *Le Visage nuptial* (1946–7), originally scored for two female voices and instrumental quartet but later revised for soprano, contralto, women's chorus and large orchestra (1951–2), gives this forceful rhetoric a focus in the response to the highly charged poetry of René Char.

Boulez's early style reached a climax of complexity and violent passion in his *Second Piano Sonata* (1947–8), where he subjects his small musical cells to elaborate development in dense contrapuntal textures; the work remains one of the most fearsome – and rewarding – tests of a pianist's intellectual stamina. It was followed by the *Livre pour quatuor* for string quartet (1948–9), where the new medium imposes a certain reticence, but where too the development of cells is carried still further in a quest for perpetual variety.

Influenced by Messiaen's *Mode de valeurs et d'intensités* (1949) Boulez appears to have recognized that his music was leading him towards total serialism, i.e. the application of serial methods to the non-pitch parameters of music: duration, loudness and timbre. This he put into practice in *Polyphonie X* for eighteen instruments (1951), in two *Études* composed on tape (1951–2) and in the first book of *Structures* for two pianos (1951–2). *Structures Ia* is the *locus classicus* of total serialism, a piece of rigorous construction whose discipline Boulez felt necessary to liberate him from the burden of the past and to open the way towards a richer serial grammar, towards the more flexible manner of *Structures Ib*.

Even more importantly, it was the experience of *Structures Ia* which made possible *Le Marteau sans maître* (1953–5). This work gained an immediate success, thanks partly to its unusual instrumentation: the nine movements use various combinations from an ensemble of alto flute, viola, guitar, vibraphone, xylorimba and untuned percussion, with a contralto voice singing short poems by Char in four of them. As Boulez has pointed out, the ensemble can allude to the sounds of Balinese (vibraphone) or of black African (xylorimba) music, though in style *Le Marteau* is not at all exotic. Indeed, it shows Boulez's serial proliferations working at high pressure along routes of allusive connection, and it draws together threads from Schoenberg, Webern, Messiaen and Debussy*.

Boulez's next objective was to find a more general way of balancing free invention with strict technique; his solution was to include a role for chance within the composition itself. His *Third Piano Sonata* (1956–7) is in five movements, or 'formants' as he prefers to call them, which may be arranged in various possible orders and which contain other opportunities for the performer to exercise choice: passages which may be omitted, alternative routes through given material, variable tempos and so on. In the second book of *Structures* for two pianos (1956–61) he adds further mobility in the relationship between the players, and in *Pli selon pli* (1957–62) he deploys his recent innovations on a grander scale to create a portrait of Mallarmé, the literary source of his aleatory thinking.

Since this period Boulez's works have tended to appear piecemeal. Only two formants of the *Third Sonata* have been published, and *Pli selon pli* grew gradually from a pair of pieces for soprano and resonant percussion ensemble to an hour-long composition for soprano and orchestra. Similarly, the short *Éclat* for fifteen instruments (1965) has been greatly extended to form *Éclat/multiples* for orchestra (begun 1966), and various other projects – including *Figures – Doubles – Prismes* for orchestra (begun 1957–8), *Domaines* for clarinet and six instrumental groups (begun 1961) and '. . . explosante-fixe . . .' for eight instruments and electronics (begun 1971) – remain to be completed.

To some degree Boulez's slower pace of creative activity since 1960 may be attributed to his growing activity as a conductor. In 1954 he established a Paris concert series, eventually known as the Domaine Musical, for furthering modern music, and since 1957 he has appeared widely as a conductor, at first specializing in twentieth-century music but later ranging into the standard repertory, particularly while he held appointments with the New York Philharmonic (1971–7) and the BBC Symphony Orchestra (1971–5). But his reluctance to bring works to completion also has less mundane causes. His musical world is one of constant variation, and ideas, as in the case of *Éclat*, will suggest almost limitless extension. Furthermore, his assumption of a duty to establish a general framework for musical discourse – a duty which he is now fulfilling as director of the Institut de Recherche et de Coordination Acoustique/Musique in Paris – makes his an onerous task in an age of such stylistic diversity.

Paul Griffiths

Other works: *Le Soleil des eaux* (1948, revised 1958, further revised 1965), cantata to poems by Char;

Poésie pour pouvoir (1958, withdrawn) for tape and orchestra, after Michaux; *'Cummings ist der Dichter . . .'* (1970) for chamber chorus and small orchestra; *Rituel* (1974–5) for orchestra; *Messagesquisse* (1970) for solo cello and six other cellos. Writings: *Penser la musique aujourd'hui* (1963, trans. Susan Bradshaw and Richard Rodney Bennett, *Boulez on Music Today*, 1971); *Relevés d'apprenti* (1966, trans., *Notes of an Apprenticeship*, 1968); *Werkstatt-Texte* (Frankfurt and Berlin 1972); *Anhaltspunkte* (Stuttgart and Zürich 1975); *Par Volonté et par hasard: entretiens avec Célestin Deliège* (1975, trans., *Conversations with Célestin Deliège*, 1977). About Boulez: Antoine Goléa, *Rencontres avec Pierre Boulez* (1958); Joan Peyser, *Boulez: Composer, Conductor, Enigma* (1976); Paul Griffiths, *Boulez* (1978).

60

BRAKHAGE, Stan 1933–

US independent film-maker

Stan Brakhage is the most prolific and celebrated of North American post-war independent film-makers, whose oeuvre, encompassing more than 130 films by 1979, richly illustrates the evolution of the entire American avant-garde film tradition over the last thirty years. Born Robert Sanders in Kansas City, Missouri, in 1933, the adopted Stan Brakhage spent his teens in Denver, Colorado, before completing his first short film, *Interim*, in 1952 at the age of nineteen. Afer high school, Brakhage studied at Dartmouth College and at the San Francisco Institute of Fine Art. In this period he drew influences from his work in amateur theatre as actor and director, and from encounters with a range of American avant-gardists – the poets Duncan, Zukofsky, Rexroth, Patchen, McClure, the musicians Cage* and Varèse*, the film-makers Maas and Menken.

This was the period of Brakhage's four main early 'trance' films or psychodramas – *The Way to Shadow Garden* (1955), *Reflections on Black* (1955), *Flesh of Morning* (1956), and *Daybreak* and *Whiteye* (1957), which confirm Brakhage's preoccupation with the dramatization of 'visionary' experience in film through surrealist/expressionist narrative structures. Combining commercial and experimental film work, Brakhage moved with *The Wonder Ring* (1955) towards more abstract colour forms involving a greater degree of formal experiment with montage, and a new role for the film-maker as visionary protagonist rather than observer, marked by a sensuous handling of the camera. This is the period of the so-called 'lyrical' film, which achieved maturity in *Anticipation of the Night* (1958) and in Brakhage's main lyrical films through until the mid-1960s: *Window Water Baby Moving* (1959), *Cat's Cradle* (1959), *Sirius Remembered* (1959), *The Dead* (1960), *Thigh Line Lyre Triangular* (1961), *Mothlight* (1963), *Vein* (1964), *Fire* (1965), and *Pasht* (1965). His marriage to Jane Collom at the end of 1957 provided his film-making with a domestic context from which it was to draw much of the subject-matter for the lyric mode – the births of children (*Window Water Baby Moving* and *Thigh Line Lyre Triangular*), a dead pet (*Sirius Remembered*), the marriage relationship itself (*Wedlock House: an Intercourse*, 1959).

By the early 1960s Brakhage had achieved national and international recognition for his work, following the unofficial prize for the ensemble of his work awarded by the Selection Jury at the 1958 Knokke International Experimental Film Festival. In 1962 he received *Film Culture* magazine's fourth Independent Film Award for *Prelude: Dog Star Man* (1961) and *The Dead*, and *Film Culture* no. 30, for Autumn 1963, was devoted to a volume of theoretical and working texts by Brakhage, 'Metaphors on Vision', resolutely championing the importance of personal and visionary film practice.

The year 1963 also marked the end of Brakhage's reliance on income from commercial film work and the beginnings of a career relying on independent film work alone – lectures, teaching, film-rentals, and grants. The following year, after several years of moving, Brakhage settled permanently with his family in Colorado. The period was also characterized by two new directions in his work. The lyric form gave way to the epic and mythopoeic strain in Brakhage's imagination, in the form of the five-part *Dog Star Man* (1961–4), reworked as the four-and-a-half-hour *Art of Vision* (1964). But the theft of his 16mm equipment led Brakhage to explore the possibility of 8mm film-making, resulting in the cycle of thirty lyric *Songs* (1964–9), all extremely brief with the exception of the feature-length *23rd Psalm Branch* (1967).

At the end of the 1960s Brakhage embarked upon his autobiographical 'Book of the Film' project, seen as a film of some twenty hours' duration, commencing with the four-part *Scenes from Under Childhood* (1968–70). His most recent work on this project includes *Sincerity* (1973–8) and *Duplicity* (1978), but the sixty-odd films completed by Brakhage during the 1970s also naturally belong to other categories. They include the six-film *Sexual Meditation* cycle (1970–2); the documentary series *Eyes* (1970), *Deus Ex* (1971), *The Act of Seeing with One's Own Eyes* (1971) and *The Governor* (1977) – on the police, hospital life, mortuary work, and politics respectively – and his feature-length study in abstraction, *The Text of Light* (1974).

One of Brakhage's primary claims to importance is his radical alteration of the social base of cinema. His work represents the supreme reversion from industrial to artisanal modes of film production, with the film-maker the total author of his/her work, producing a new kind of 'personal cinema'. This stress on the artisanal also includes Brakhage's radical reintegration of film practice within everyday experience, notably within the domestic sphere of family life. Made as a natural feature of the domestic continuum, the films emerge from a different social space, and with different social purposes, than those of traditional 'mass' cinema. These changes are also marked at the level of film distribution. Several of the films, notably the suite of 8mm *Songs*, can be purchased from the Brakhages at their home address, while the general distribution of the films through the international co-operative movement also marks Brakhage's adherence to new collective forms of social practice in the independent cinema.

The artisanal and domestic qualities of Brakhage's work, however, by no means predicate a simplified relation to technology or to production 'values'. The 'barefoot' author of *Mothlight* (1963), a film made without a camera by pasting moths' wings between clear tape and printing from this 'master', is also the technical virtuoso of *The Art of Vision* with its complex multi-layering of material from *Dog Star Man*, and the dazzling editor of *Cat's Cradle* with its shimmering array of 700 shots in just five minutes' screen-time. Rather, he finds new purposes for that technology, bearing a camera 'as economical, as flexible and intimate as the pen' (Field).

Brakhage was thus led to shape new structural and new generic models for film. These range from the extremely dense and compressed films of the 1960s through to the extended forms of the 'major mythopoeia' of *Dog Star Man* and *The Art of Vision*. This difference in 'volume' goes hand in hand with an interest in simultaneity, and the reversibility/repeatability of temporal relations and in altering notions of duration. Frequently achieved through complex and accelerated editing procedures, these concerns extend the temporal innovations of the Soviet montage directors to a new degree of poetic and musical intensity early symbolized in the *Songs*, with their explicit dedication to the musical poetics of Pound's* *Cantos*.

Brakhage's contribution to the liberation of film-structure, and his movement towards poetic and musical models, also involves him in a re-examination of film 'material' itself. His interest in the relation between film and music, for example, soon led him, in a radical gesture, to abandon work with sound in order to return to the potential of early cinema in an exploration of the 'musicality' of visual emphasis and rhythm in silent film. The picture-track was to undergo similarly radical revision. Largely rejecting the 'transparency' of realist cinema, Brakhage foregrounds the materiality and textuality of film material itself, exploring not only processes of abstraction in general, but at times engaging in painterly work upon the stock itself in a manner reminiscent of the Abstract Expressionist painters who were his contemporaries in the early period of the lyrical film. These stylistic and expressive features correspond to Brakhage's commitment not only to a new liberated mobility for 'open-eye' vision, but to the rarer, more intimate, and frequently more opaque discoveries of 'closed eye' and subjective vision.

For new generations of film-makers and critics Brakhage's enormous influence presents a complex heritage. It represents the fusion of particularly potent Romantic and idealist traditions of 'personal' and transcendental experience – postulated on the primacy of 'vision' and buttressed by the ideology of domesticity and the family – with materialist preoccupations to do with film language and film substance, an anti-illusionistic view of cinema as a complex and material semiotic system. It is amongst the differing and even contradictory strands of this legacy that film-makers of a younger generation are now choosing in their quest not only for new textual practices in film, but for new forms of social practice and of ideology for the cinema as a whole.

Philip Drummond

Other writings include: *A Moving Picture Giving and Taking Book* (1971); *The Brakhage Lectures* (1972). See: Simon Field, *Stan Brakhage: An American Independent Film-maker* (1979); P. Adams Sitney, *Visionary Film: the American Avant-Garde 1943–1978* (2nd edn 1979).

61

BRANCUSI, Constantin 1876–1957

Romanian sculptor

Hailed as the pioneer of modern sculpture by some, and blamed for its degeneration by others, Constantin Brancusi can without doubt be placed at the forefront of those who created an abstract idiom to replace figurative representation for the art in its Western form. Born in Hobitza, a hamlet of Pestisani in southern Romania, he received no formal schooling, but worked first as a shepherd, then at a variety of menial jobs in nearby towns. With the help of a local industrialist, who was impressed by Brancusi's skill at carving domestic artefacts in wood (a traditional peasant craft), he attended the School of Arts in Craiova (1895–8), and then the National School of Fine Arts in Bucharest (1898–1902), where he trained as a sculptor, simultaneously teaching himself to read and write. Drawn to Paris by the reputation of Auguste Rodin, he arrived there in 1904, having spent some months in Munich, and making most of his journey on foot. In 1905 he enrolled at the École des Beaux Arts, and in 1907 received his first important commission, a statue for the tomb of Peter Stanescu, in Buzau cemetery, Romania. This work, *The Prayer*, depicts a young girl kneeling, and, although recognizably classical, already suggests the artist's move towards apparent simplicity of form. During the next twelve years he worked on many of his most important themes: *The Kiss, Sleeping Muse, Torso, Narciss, The Wisdom of the Earth, Prometheus, Maiastra, Mlle Pogany, Penguins, The Newborn, Princess X, Endless Column,* and *Bird in Space.* During the 1920s, while continuing to develop most of these, he added *Adam and Eve, The Fish, Leda, The White Negress,* and the *Cock.* The high abstraction he attained at this period is attested by an attempt made by the US Customs Department to have Brancusi arraigned for secretly importing industrial parts into America, following their unwillingness to believe that a bronze *Bird in Space* was a sculpture. The main addition to his work in the 1930s was the sculptural programme for the Public Park in Tirgu Jiu (Romania): *The Table of Silence,* two benches, *The Gate of the Kiss,* and the 100 ft high *Endless Column,* constructed from steel (all 1937–8). At the same time he travelled to India, where the Maharajah of Indore had asked him to create a temple, but the Maharajah's death prevented the project's fruition.

Unlike some other modern artists and sculptors, Brancusi's style did not suddenly emerge, or come into its own as an all-of-a-piece affair, but developed gradually over a period of twenty-five years. His achievement therefore has the advantage of being self-documented; while the full force of it can only be experienced by contrasting 'early' and 'mature' pieces. Thus, while the bronze *Torment* of 1907 presents the notion of mimesis of a natural form, full of details to convey deep emotion, subsequent works (the marble *Prometheus* of 1911, through the bronze *Prometheus* of the same year, the bronze *Newborn* of 1915, to the bronze, egg-like *Beginning of the World* of 1924, also known as the *Sculpture for the Blind*) exhibit a progressive refinement, or as some would say reduction, towards the essence of the sculpted object, achieved by a fusion of the internal substructure and sculptural detail in the plane of a skin-deep surface. Increasingly, as the plane rotates, the unessential details (neck, nose, lips, eyes, hair) decrease. The essential form then enters into a reflective relationship with its base, be it a plate or a cushion. The abstracting force of this creative process, however, is, in Brancusi, balanced by his deep, often sensual, response to the particular materials used, from the direct rough carving in wood to the highly polished metals. From this he also developed a sophisticated spatiotemporal idea. Traditionally the space of a sculpture was understood to be underneath, or contained within, its surface. But Brancusi activated the space between the surface and the beholder, making that space subjective, to be experienced and lived through in time. His larger works have the power to enclose the viewer at a distance – hence their 'closed' form, and the 'silence' that envelops them. His final images, clear, exact and precise, become mysteries.

Brancusi claimed that 'a well made sculpture should have the power to heal the beholder', and that 'it must be lovely to touch, friendly to live with'. His work, whose idiom has to a large extent become the *lingua franca* of modern sculpture, was an extraordinary marriage of distinct backgrounds. His attitude towards materials and craftsmanship, his repetitiveness, and the rejection of haste and willingness to work on a piece over a number of years, together with a personal self-effacement, were as Romanian as his themes: the pagan myths of rebirth (egg, cock, bird), the sky – earth axis (endless column), so important in the lives of Romanian farmers, and the solar motifs (love, birth, growth). While it has been suggested that these aspects may have been further cultivated by Brancusi's reading of a treatise by the eleventh-century Tibetan monk Milarepa, the impact of French culture was the other important determinant. It furnished Brancusi on the one hand, through the later works of Rodin, with the idea that the meaning of a sculpture was located on its surface; and on the other, with the neo-platonic view, advanced by Charles Blanc in 1880, that the role of sculpture 'is to create a life of images analogous to real life'.

Although the full catalogue of Brancusi's oeuvre is relatively small, individual works have found their way into museums throughout Europe and America. This, together with the considerable critical attention he has received, has ensured Brancusi a high place in modern sculpture. If the ambiguous interfusion between the primitive and high art was neither inevitable nor peculiar to Brancusi, its continuation has in turn been abetted by the ambivalence of his reputation.

Dr Slavka Sverakova

See: D. Lewis, *Brancusi* (1957); C. Giedion Welcker, *Constantin Brancusi* (1959); H. Read, *A Concise History of Modern Sculpture* (1964); S. Geist, *Brancusi* (1968); A. T. Spear, *Brancusi's Birds* (1969).

62
BRAQUE, Georges 1882–1963

French painter

It was as a decorator that Braque arrived in Paris in 1900 to attend evening courses in painting and design at the Cours Municipal des Batignolles. In later life, even in his severest works, there survived a decorative sense of great beauty. Only after military service in 1901–2 did Braque enrol at the Académie Humbert in Paris, and begin to execute oil paintings of his family.

During 1902 his involvement with painting grew and developed through visits to the Louvre, through an increasing circle of friends amongst practising painters, including Marie Laurencin and Francis Picabia, but also through the experience of Impressionist and Post-

Impressionist paintings seen at the commercial galleries of Vollard and Durand-Ruel. By 1903 Braque was committed to painting. He entered the École des Beaux-Arts under Bonnat but subsequently returned to the Académie Humbert. In 1904 he was working independently and the following year was overwhelmed by the ferocity and vitality of the Fauve painters at the Salon d'Automne. From this moment forward, a moment of insight into possibilities within his reach, Braque never ceased to explore and consolidate his achievements. Never reaching beyond the lucid tracing of his tactile and sensual experience, Braque became a connoisseur of visual sensation, committed at once to freshness of colour and touch, an explorer of visual experience. Within such a development the particular blend of rigid discipline and sensual delight that distinguishes a brilliant decorative painter was never absent.

His links with the Fauve painters flourished through his personal friendships with Othon Friesz and Raoul Dufy. For Braque the bright explosion of Fauve paintings by Derain, Matisse* and Vlaminck in particular signalled the final and decisive acceptance of brilliant Post-Impressionist colour and the lively articulation of individual brushmarks. Pointillisme in particular had emphasized both of these qualities, and Signac had communicated their principles directly to Matisse. The fresh *tache*, recording the touch of the brush, was given new force and vitality. Into so rhythmic and colourful an effusion of paint Braque saw room for the extension of his own abilities. He painted Fauve paintings throughout 1906 and exhibited the following year at both the Salon des Indépendants and at the Salon d'Automne, making his aesthetic allegiance clear. *The Port at Antwerp* (1906) reveals Braque's debt to the Fauves. The calligraphic qualities of this painting, where balcony ironwork is depicted in a singular curling line and the reflections of boats in the harbour are loose dashes of colour, combine a natural painterliness with the freshness and immediacy of the Fauves. Yet Braque's colour in 1906 is not fully recognizable as Fauve unless it is comparable with that of his friend, Othon Friesz, whose vibrant but dense and slow-moving mauves do find a response in Braque's 1906 sea- and river-scapes. They lack the fiery crackling of wilder Fauve brushwork. Braque retains a strength of compositional structure comparable to that which Matisse had only briefly abandoned. Fauve painting was, however, for Braque a vital initiation into a new range of painterly techniques and priorities.

In 1908 Guillaume Apollinaire* wrote an introduction for Braque's one-man exhibition at Kahnweiler's gallery in Paris. By this time his work had undergone dramatic modification. During the intervening years two major artistic experiences followed upon the impact of Fauvism. First, Braque was overwhelmingly impressed by a memorial retrospective of Cézanne's work, and second Braque became friendly with Pablo Picasso* whose *Demoiselles d'Avignon*, an unresolved and violently new work, was glimpsed by Braque in Picasso's studio. Both events encouraged a fierce disciplining of the energy let loose by Fauve painters, and until the First World War when Braque was called up for military service, the colour-range of his palette was severely limited to black, earth browns and ochres. Through their creative repartee, through innovations in aim and technique, exchanged and extended continuously, Braque and Picasso during this period evolved the central core of Cubism, perhaps the single most influential development in twentieth-century art in Europe and America. From the monumental and Cézannesque strength of paintings executed at L'Estaque in 1908, Braque, in collaboration with Picasso, evolved a more crystalline and rhythmic style in which forms resembled fragmented geometrical solids; single viewpoint perspective was abandoned and contradictory light sources were employed. This complex faceting of forms locked objects into the context of their immediate surroundings. Their forms were recorded as much in intellectual as in visual terms, reducing a guitar to a few recognizable elements of shape and detail, an approach that was analytical and devoid of accidental effects of light, weather or application. As the subject became more difficult to recognize, except through hints and clues left within the crystalline framework by the painter, this analytical phase of Cubism came more and more to rely upon identifiable signs. In effect analytical Cubism radically altered the painter's visual language, whilst remaining firmly committed to depiction: the very means of painting and the nature of representation were brought into consideration by the Cubist works of Braque and Picasso. As the means and techniques employed for such references were extended, Cubism increasingly played off against each other differing forms of representation. The viewer, alerted by recognizable clues, was encouraged to interpret further images within the painting. For example, the crystalline and vigorously modelled planes of Braque's *Violin and Palette* (1910) emphasize an implied depth within the picture space, yet the *trompe l'oeil* nail at top centre of the painting appears to fasten the canvas to a wall, and the viewer is forcefully reminded of the flat surface of the canvas. Such a painting as the equally vigorous *Still Life with Playing Card* (1913) reveals much of the subsequent development of Cubism. Colour remains restrained and certain images are at once recognizable: the drawing of a cluster of grapes and the imagery of playing cards are an example. Beyond this, Braque is more suggestive and less explicit, and in these areas more recent Cubist techniques are clearly evident. Lettering, introduced by Braque to Cubism in 1911 with his painting *Le Portugais*, inhabits the flat canvas surface and recalls printed text, perhaps a newspaper. Elsewhere Braque has imitated decorators' woodgraining techniques to suggest material qualities. Furthermore, the shapes of these woodgrained sections are such as to suggest that they have been cut from a printed woodgrain wall covering and stuck on to the canvas, a technique employed from 1912 by both Picasso and Braque in Cubist collages. This slowing down of interpretation led to a more intimate examination of the techniques, concerns and methods of representation open to the painter and employed by him. These means, more than any specific style or technique, were to spread throughout the world. Georges Braque's contribution before 1914 was inextricable from that of his close friend and collaborator Pablo Picasso. Indeed, after the war, Braque retained Cubist devices and constructions in his paintings, adding an intellectual delight to the sensually ravishing surfaces of many of his later paintings. The Tate Gallery's *Still Life with Mandolin, Glass, Pot and Fruit* (1927) exemplifies this. Sombre, resonant colour inhabits the most liquid of lines, yet the division of the pot into areas of light and shade is effected decisively with a single zigzag line. Into so severe and intellectual a system of painting Braque has reintroduced a different form of exploration that rivals Matisse as readily as Picasso, for in the manipulation of colours Braque became a great explorer and an epicurean sensualist. The hints he gives of succulence, or rigidity, of translucency or weight, all testify to an almost tactile immediacy of sensation. His complexity and his confidence in this achievement made of his later still-lives an orchestration of sensual associations in which perception and articulation appear to flow one from the other completely without hindrance. *The Shower of Rain* (1952) shows no loss of this succinctness: the suddenness and transparency of a shower are caught in a group of descending lines: the perception, astutely edited, is presented by means entirely appropriate to painting.

Braque's contribution to Cubism and to later painting was increasingly recognized. He was invited to present a special exhibition at the Salon d'Automne in 1922, and major exhibitions followed at the Galérie Paul Rosenberg, Paris, from 1924, the Basle Kunsthalle in 1933, the San Francisco Museum of Art in 1940, the Museum of Modern Art in New York in 1948, the Kunsthalle at Berne in 1953, and the Basle Kunsthalle again in 1960.

Dr John Milner

See: Georges Braque, *Le Jour et la nuit* (1952). See also: Guillaume Apollinaire, *Les Peintres cubistes* (1913); P. Heron, *Braque* (1958); John Golding, *Cubism: A History and Analysis 1907–1914* (1959); John Russell, *Georges Braque* (1959); Edwin Mullins, *Braque* (1968).

63
BRAUDEL, Fernand 1902–

French historian

Born in a small village on the Lorraine–Champagne border, Fernand Braudel was educated at the Lycée Voltaire in Paris and at the Sorbonne. Until 1932 he taught at a lycée in Algiers, and at the University of São Paulo from 1935 to 1937, returning to the École des Hautes Études in Paris in 1937 with the intention of writing up the doctoral thesis he had begun in 1927. Captured in 1940, he spent the war in captivity at Mainz and Lübeck. Although deprived of his notes, it was during these years that he wrote his thesis on *The Mediterranean and the Mediterranean World in the Age of Philip II* (1949, trans. 1972–3). In 1948 Braudel became director of the Centre de Recherches Historiques within the VIe section of the École des Hautes Études, and in 1950 was appointed a professor at the Collège de France. From 1956 to his retirement in 1972 he was President of the VIe section, and from 1957 to 1968 editorial director of the periodical *Annales*. Since 1972 he has been administrator of the Maison des Sciences de l'Homme in Paris.

Braudel has been the great second-generation leader of the '*Annales* school', named after the journal founded by Lucien Febvre and Marc Bloch in 1929. He was deeply influenced by Febvre, and by the older Henri Berr, in his rejection of the 'histoire événementielle' practised by the historical establishment of his youth – the detailed study of diplomacy and politics. Braudel's great work on the Mediterranean is a triumphant vindication of his belief that historical development can only be understood in terms of impersonal long-term forces. The human geography, trading patterns, demographic fluctuations, and other elements of the sixteenth-century world are brought together to form a complex and dynamic whole. The military and commercial efforts of governments and merchants, shackled by the cost and difficulty of travel, and slender financial resources, appear puny beside the long-term movements of the 'conjoncture'. Working on the grand scale helps Braudel to show how both ordinary men and statesmen were carried along by the logic of factors and events they could neither control nor understand.

Braudel has since been engaged on a study of *Capitalism and Material Life, 1400–1800* (vol. 1, 1967, trans. 1973), which is again remarkable for its geographical range – global this time – and for its highly sophisticated approach to historical explanation. His work has been widely admired, but not precisely imitated. This partly reflects the skill with which he chose his subjects; the Mediterranean offered a unique opportunity for integrated historical study. His greatest influence has probably come through the institutional power of the VIe section and the *Annales*, which together have become the dominant force in French historical studies. The brilliant pioneer work of the founders has been succeeded by a broad-front offensive of research teams, collecting and analysing statistical data, and by a series of admirable local studies, far narrower than Braudel's own work. The academic and intellectual success of a movement which began as a repudiation of traditional historical styles has naturally given rise to some internal tensions, and to a kind of mutation. The *Annales* tradition, under Braudel's sympathetic guidance, has been expanded, rendered more eclectic, until it has few definable characteristics beyond a particular concern with causal links, and a quantitative bias. It does seem probable that this has led to a relative decline of political and administrative history in France; elsewhere the influence has also been very great, although less overpowering. As the man who has presided over this triumphal march, Braudel has been perhaps the most influental living historian.

Robin Briggs

A full bibliography of Braudel's writings to 1971 will be found in *Mélanges en l'honneur de Fernand Braudel* (1973). Apart from the two major works, there is a collection of shorter essays, *Écrits sur l'histoire* (1969).

64

BRECHT, Bertolt 1898–1956

German poet, playwright and director

Brecht, one of the most influential playwrights of the twentieth century, was the son of the manager of a paper mill in the Bavarian city of Augsburg. When he left grammar school (*Gymnasium*) at the age of eighteen, he decided to study medicine, largely in order to avoid combat duty in the First World War, then at its height. He succeeded in being assigned to a military hospital in his native city as a medical orderly and it is said that the suffering of the wounded he saw there instilled in him the passionate hatred of war, and the bourgeois society that had instigated it, which determined his later political development.

During his pre-medical studies at the University of Munich after the war he drifted gradually into theatrical circles, wrote ballads he himself sang to the guitar and published poems, stories and theatre reviews. His first play to be performed, *Drums in the Night* (*Trommeln in der Nacht*, written 1920; first performed Munich 1922), won the coveted Kleist Prize and established him as one of the most promising playwrights of the new post-war generation. From 1922 onwards he spent more and more time in Berlin, where he settled in 1924. From 1926 onwards he became increasingly interested in Marxism which he came to regard as a strictly scientific doctrine that alone would be

capable of eradicating war and poverty from the earth. Brecht's first major theatrical success was the *Threepenny Opera* (*Dreigroschenoper*, Berlin 1928). After Hitler's* accession to power in Germany Brecht went into exile and settled in Denmark (1933–9) but, after brief interludes in Sweden (1939–40) and Finland (1940–1), decided to go to America. Not only is it significant that he did not want to stay in the Soviet Union, where Stalin* was conducting a vigorous campaign against avant-garde art, but that, to get to the United States in June 1941, he had to cross the entire Soviet Union to reach Vladivostok where he embarked on a boat going to California a few days before the Germans invaded Russia. In Hollywood he tried to make a living as a film script writer. Although he sold a few ideas, only one of his scripts ever reached the screen: *Hangmen also die* (directed by Fritz Lang*, 1942). In 1947, having been subpoenaed as a witness by the House Un-American Activities Committee investigating Communist subversion in the film industry, and having skilfully avoided implicating any of his friends, he returned to Europe. After some time spent in Switzerland, devoted to a cautious exploration of the possibilities for creating a theatre of his own, he decided to accept an East German offer to start his own company in East Berlin. This company, the Berliner Ensemble, was formally inaugurated in 1949. But before he returned to East Berlin Brecht had laid the foundations for freedom of movement and independence in publishing his work by applying for Austrian citizenship and by vesting the copyright of his writings in a West German publisher.

Brecht's massive oeuvre can be divided into a number of fairly clearly distinct phases: a wildly anarchic period of exuberantly poetic plays, reflecting an intense sensual enjoyment of life coupled with a deeply pessimistic conviction that all is futile and must end in a senseless death – 1918 to *c*. 1928; among the plays of this period are *Baal* (1918); *Drums in the Night* (1920); *In the Jungle of the Cities* (*Im Dickicht der Staedte*, 1922/3); *Edward II* (a free adaptation of Marlowe's Elizabethan tragedy, first performed in Munich, 1924) and *Man equals Man* (*Mann ist Mann*, 1926). Brecht's greatest success, the *Threepenny Opera* (1928), marks his transition from this exuberantly anarchic phase to the period of his austerely didactic *Lehrstuecke* (didactic plays, teaching plays): 1929 to *c*. 1934. These concise, pared-down, almost diagrammatically schematic works, relying often so heavily on music that they become operas or oratorios rather than plays in the usual sense, were designed not so much for the instruction of an audience as for that of the actors and other participants, to whom they would give an opportunity of learning, by actually experiencing it, what it was like to be oppressor and oppressed, or an individual sacrificed for the benefit of society and the beneficiary of that sacrifice. As this implies, Brecht insisted that the actors in the didactic plays should play all parts in turn. Outstanding among these didactic plays are the 'school operas', *The Yes-Sayer* (*Der Jasager*, 1930) and *The No-Sayer* (*Der Neinsager*, 1930); the oratorio *The Measures Taken* (*Die Massnahme*, music by Hanns Eisler*, 1930); *The Exception and the Rule* (*Die Ausnahme und die Regel*, 1930, first performance, Paris 1947); *The Mother* (*Die Mutter*, after a novel by Gorky*, 1932). In a less austere style but with equally didactic intentions, Brecht wrote, in the same period, the opera *Mahagonny* (*Aufstieg und Fall der Stadt Mahagonny*, 1930, music by Kurt Weill*, who had also largely contributed to the phenomenal success of the *Threepenny Opera*) and the play *St Joan of the Stockyards* (*Die Heilige Johanna der Schlachthoefe*, 1931, first performed in Hamburg, 1959).

In the years of his exile Brecht at first (1934–8) tried to make an active contribution to the overthrow of Hitler by writing what amounted to topical propaganda material of small artistic merit. When it became clear, after Hitler's occupation of Austria in March 1938, that such contributions had become futile, Brecht could return to more ambitious projects. He thus entered on the most fruitful period of his playwriting career: 1938 to 1947, the period of his great parable plays: *The Life of Galileo* (*Leben des Galilei*, 1938, first performance, Zürich 1943); *The Good Woman of Setzuan* (*Der Gute Mensch von Setzuan*, 1938–40, first performance, Zürich 1943); *Mother Courage* (*Mutter Courage und ihre Kinder*, 1939, first performance, Zürich 1941); *Mr Puntila and his Man Matti* (*Herr Puntila und sein Knecht Matti*, 1940–1, first performance, Zürich 1948); and *The Caucasian Chalk Circle* (*Der Kaukasische Kreidekreis*, 1944–5, first performance, Northfields, Minnesota, 1948).

After his return to East Berlin Brecht devoted himself mainly to the production of these plays and of adaptations of the classics he had made for the Berliner Ensemble.

Much of Brecht's immense world-wide impact on modern drama derives from his attempts, after his conversion to Marxism, to develop what he regarded as the only possible aesthetic theory for a Marxist theatre, his theory of 'epic theatre' and the *Verfremdungseffekt* (strange-making effect, distancing or 'alienation' effect). Brecht was convinced that the traditional theory of drama (which he called 'Aristotelian' but actually derived from the German eighteenth-century classics Goethe and Schiller) is based on the assumption that in the theatre the audience should be made to believe that they are witnessing an event actually taking place before their eyes in an 'eternal present' and that therefore the actors should identify themselves as much as possible with the characters they are portraying, so that the audience in turn can identify with the action of the play and feel what the characters are experiencing. These assumptions, Brecht maintained, imply that throughout the ages human emotions have always been the same, that, in fact, there is such a thing as a permanent, unchangeable 'human nature'. But Marxism, Brecht asserted, is based on the opposite assumption, namely that human nature, human consciousness, human values, are constantly changing, in accordance with changes in the economic and social basis of material conditions. If, therefore, a spectator, as the Aristotelian theory postulates, could really say, 'Yes, I felt exactly what Oedipus or Lear or Macbeth must have felt', that would imply that the Marxist view of human nature was invalid. What was needed, therefore, was a truly Marxist theory of drama, which would not only show that human nature has radically changed throughout the ages, but also that it would still further have to be transformed by changing the organization of society. Hence the devices, usually called 'dramatic', of breathless suspense, high emotional intensity, total identification of actor and character, maximum involvement in an action happening 'here and now', must be rejected and replaced by devices, such as obtain in narrative literature, epic poetry: reflective detachment, critical and relaxed observation of events which are experienced as happening in a distanced past tense, 'there and then'. In other words the theatre must cease to be 'dramatic' in the traditional sense and become 'epic'. The spectator should now see Oedipus or Lear or Macbeth as specimens of humanity determined by different social conditions, as useful examples of changes in human development upon which he could sharpen his critical perception of present social conditions as a preliminary to changing those for the better. In recognizing that Oedipus, for example, was the victim of taboos which have now become senseless, the spectator should realize that similar taboos of his own time might be equally ripe for rejection. Thus, by *historicizing* the dramatic performance, the audience could be induced to think critically about their own society.

The means by which Brecht wanted to bring about this *epic* theatre were what he called his *distancing effects* (*V-Effekte*): chief among these are an avoidance of relentless climaxes in the writing of the play and the avoidance of suspense by announcing the outcome of the action beforehand (so that the audience should direct their attention not on what is going to happen next, but on *how* it is happening); a detached and cooled-down acting style; the avoidance of anything designed to make the audience forget that they are in a theatre, i.e. non-illusionistic scenery; unconcealed lighting apparatus and brilliant, unchanging lighting throughout to inhibit the production of moods and emotions through sentimental lighting effects; the independence of music and design from the words, so that rather than reinforcing them, these elements would act as a contrapuntal critical commentary on the action, i.e. harsh music would expose the false sentimentality of a love song, projections of rotting corpses would comment on a patriotic speech; to show that they are not identifying with their characters, the actors will talk directly to the audience, etc., etc.

Brecht discussed these ideas in voluminous theoretical writings, the most important among which is his *Little Organon for the Theatre* (*Kleines Organon fuer das Theater*, 1948).

Whether the philosophical and psychological basis of these theories is correct or not, their use results in an immensely interesting poetic style of theatre. Brecht's own practice as a director with the Berliner Ensemble in the last years of his life produced performances of an elegance, lightness of touch and grace unusual in the German theatre which had always tended to rely on heavily emotional effects and an intensity which often resulted in screaming and grandiloquent bombast. What is far more questionable is the political impact of the Brechtian theatre. It has been argued that Brecht was too good a dramatist, by instinct, ever to have been able to produce work which would be biased enough to achieve the intended effect of converting audiences to his own political views. Indeed, in his plays, the characters he intended to have a negative impact often arouse more sympathies than the positive heroes, where, in fact, there are any; most of Brecht's later plays heavily rely on irony, in showing what *not* to do rather than trying to influence the public by positive precept. In practice his plays, therefore, often achieve a different effect from the one he intended: Mother Courage, who is supposed to show that being a trader (hence a capitalist) in a war must inevitably lead to the death of her children, is often felt by the public to be a rousing example of selfless devotion and mother love. Brecht was distressed by this, but refused to alter the play to comply with the demands of the Communist authorities who wanted a more direct impact for their cause.

What was even more galling to Brecht was the fact that in his lifetime the aesthetics of drama officially prescribed in the Soviet Union were based on the ideas of Stanislavsky*, which are in direct contradiction to what Brecht regarded as the truly Marxist aesthetics of drama, the Brechtian epic theatre. Brecht's theories and his plays were long rejected and suppressed in the Soviet sphere of influence as smacking of formalism and avant-garde experimentation. It was only in East Germany that Brecht was tolerated in his lifetime, because the presence of Germany's foremost playwright within its borders shed lustre on a regime struggling for international recognition. But even here Brecht's plays and his productions often met official disapproval and had more than once to be withdrawn. Only after his death was he canonized into a great national classic.

Brecht was, above all, a supreme master of the German language and a very great poet. Even his plays, ultimately, owe their greatness to the sheer brilliance of their language rather than any other, purely dramatic, qualities. Hence it is difficult for non-German audiences to experience their full impact, as all translations must of necessity be imperfect. His theory, although put forward in a highly contemporary Marxist idiom, owes a great deal to his acknowledged models and forerunners, above all the Elizabethan theatre, the classical drama of China and Japan, and the Austro-Bavarian folk-theatre. Seen in its historical context, Brecht's theory emerges as an attempt to reject the bourgeois respectability and academic pretensions of the nineteenth-century theatre and the dominance of the photographic illusionism of the naturalistic stage, and to return to a barnstorming, crudely vital popular proletarian theatre which has its roots in the music hall and the fairground. To achieve this end Brecht forged a splendid idiom of earthy speech, in striking contrast to the highly artificial traditional stage-German. In his poetry Brecht acknowledged the influence of poets as diverse as Villon, Rimbaud, Rudyard Kipling*; of Luther's Bible as well as obscene folk ballads. He also made frequent use of other poets' work through parody; many scenes in his plays are savage parodies of Shakespeare, Schiller and Goethe. In this and in his many adaptations of acknowledged classics Brecht expressed his convictions that the literature of the past was useful only as 'raw material' for quarrying.

Martin Esslin

Collected editions of Brecht's plays in English translation are in the course of publication in Britain (Eyre Methuen) and the United States (Random House). For Brecht's principal theoretical writings, see John Willett, *Brecht on Theatre* (1964). See also: Klaus Voelker, *Brecht, a Biography* (1976); and an excellent pictorial survey of Brecht's life, *Bertolt Brecht. Sein Leben in Bildern und Texten*, ed. W. Hecht (1978). Critical overviews of Brecht's life and work can be found in John Willett, *The Theatre of Bertolt Brecht* (1959); and Martin Esslin, *Brecht – A Choice of Evils* (1959, revised 1980).

65

BRETON, André 1896–1966

French writer

During the four decades he spent at the centre of that tumult of debate and agitation which was French Surrealism, André Breton aroused many passions. He was always a man whose temperament required him to define and defend with total intensity certain ideas which mattered to him. If at times this cost him the pain of broken friendships, as witness his quarrels with Antonin Artaud* and Louis Aragon, it also gained him the lifelong support of the poet Benjamin Péret and the allegiance of a stream of younger Surrealists eager to further the Surrealist project. As mentor, spokesman and animator of the Surrealist movement – never its bigoted, infallible Pope, as his enemies have charged – Breton exerted enormous influence over the French cultural scene from the 1920s onwards. In many ways he was a most self-concerned writer, fascinated by his personal intellectual co-ordinates and his private responses; and yet he became a voice for the modern artistic sensibility at large, a cultural exemplar of a rare kind.

Drawn to poetry at an early age, Breton first published sonnets in the Symbolist style of Paul Valéry*. But during the First World War he came upon the hallucinatory writings of Arthur Rimbaud and this discovery, along with his brief friendship with the sardonic·iconoclast Jacques Vaché, led Breton to envisage a purely literary career as narrow and artificial. His work as an orderly in a military hospital had put him in direct contact with the strange utterances of the mentally deranged on whom he had (as one of the first to do so in France) essayed the techniques of Freudian analysis. By 1919 he had produced, in collaboration with Philippe Soupault, the texts of *Les Champs magnétiques* ('Magnetic Fields', 1920), the first sample of Surrealist automatism or trance-writing. After the wild interlude of Paris Dada, the nascent Surrealist group found its charter in Breton's *Manifeste du surréalisme* of 1924, which not only codified automatic practice as a prospection, in the light of Freud's* researches, of the raw material of the unconscious made available in the form of non-directed language, but defined poetry as a purposeful activity which must lead the poet out of the closed space of literature and into the real world.

The scandalous 'secret society' of Surrealism manifested itself in various acts of revolt against the status quo, with virulent attacks on the Catholic church or establishment writers like Anatole France, and in the publication of a journal, *La Révolution surréaliste* ('The Surrealist Revolution', 1924–9), of which Breton became editor. Following his enthusiastic reading of Trotsky's* *Lenin*, Breton was converted to dialectical materialism and led the group into protracted negotiations with the French Communists in an effort to conciliate the Surrealist quest with the militant aims of the Party. The latter was, predictably, reluctant to envisage avant-garde experimentation as an integral part of the proletarian struggle. Breton's patchwork book *Les Vases communicants* ('Communicating Vessels', 1932) reflects his efforts to reconcile the idea of the poet as dreamer with that of the poet as revolutionary: but his enquiries into his personal sleeping and waking experiences, in the manner of Freud's auto-analyses, sit ill beside political passages laced with quotations from Engels, Marx and other like authorities.

The break with official Communism was sealed with the news of the Moscow Trials in 1936 when Breton showed himself one of the fiercest European critics of the Stalinist* betrayal of the great idea of the Russian Revolution; his political sympathies now lay with Trotsky, whom he visited in Mexico in 1938. Following the Second World War and his own exile in the USA, Breton shifted his ground somewhat, propounding the central relevance to the Surrealist cause of the writings of the utopian socialist Fourier (*Ode à Charles Fourier*, 1947). The Paris group, reconstituted after Breton's return in 1946, moved eventually towards a libertarian position, collaborating with the *Fédération anarchiste* during the early 1950s. Unfortunately Breton did not live to witness the brief realization of many aspects of the Surrealist poetico-political vision in the May Events of 1968 in Paris.

Breton's writings range from the dreamy suggestiveness of the fantastic worlds evoked in the automatic prose of *Poisson soluble* ('Soluble Fish', 1924) to the persistent argument of programmatic texts like the three Surrealist manifestos (1924, 1930, 1942) or the hard-edged political articles he wrote for the 1930s magazine *Le Surréalisme au service de la révolution*. A genre in which he excels is the personal memoir in which the record of private experiences – dreams, love affairs, visits to such distant places as Tenerife in *L'Amour fou* ('Mad Love', 1937) or the Gaspé peninsula in *Arcane 17* (*Arcanum XVII*, New York 1945) – forms the raw material on which his associative imagination can work, eliciting from particular facts whole chains of analogies and new meanings such that the accidents of an individual life are transcended in a series of propositions about the collective perspectives of Surrealism. In this sense, all Breton's works hover between being confessions and proclamations: his most public statements (such as *Position politique du surréalisme*, 1935) contain passages of intimate reflection, while his most lyrical writings, including a poetry of cascading images (*Poèmes*, 1948), bear the imprint of a mind intent on universal resonances. The mode of Breton's thinking is resolutely analogical: no idea or image emerges in one domain which is not immediately tested for its appropriateness to other, wider domains.

Throughout the history of the political and artistic experiments of Surrealism, Breton pursued knowledge with the passion of one whose final purpose was the delineation of an entirely new mentality, liberated from the orthodoxies of reason and habit. Scornful of the cultural moulds he had inherited, Breton took as his measure the Surrealist commitment to the future and the discipline of spontaneity, of loyalty to the secret self, as evinced in the experiments of automatism and in the wider-ranging adventures of falling in love or, eventually, of taking part in an insurrection.

Reinstating what he saw as a primary faculty shared by children and primitive peoples, Breton sought to define an approach to experience which would reconcile dream-life with actual perceptions and exploit the creative interpenetration of inner and outer reality. Surreality is nothing less than the passionately witnessed coincidence of individual and world, of representation and perception, the imaginary and the tangible, the pleasure principle and the reality principle.

A host of associated values – the marvellous, the enigmatic, the delirious, the convulsive – echo throughout Breton's work. Books such as *Nadja* (1928), in which he relates his affair with an inspired mad girl, point to the emergence of an attitude of delightful susceptibility to the invitations of chance and love: in describing his wanderings through the Paris streets, Breton effectively elaborates a method of intellectual enquiry into the correspondences between mental and material phenomena, and, extrapolating from an essentially Romantic vision of the universe mediated through the imagination, points toward a revolutionary thesis: that the overthrow of repressive political systems is inseparable from poetic revolution within the individual consciousness. Breton's watchword 'the imaginary is that which tends to become real' is the corollary of the premise that allegiance to one's total being – in both its irrational and rational aspects – is the sole guarantee of a fully satisfying implementation of desire at the level of material existence.

As a thinker receptive to many out-of-the-way ideas, Breton followed a zigzag intellectual path, fervently admiring by turns such figures as the Decadent writer Huysmans, the neurologist Babinski, the poets Apollinaire* and Tzara*, the psychoanalyst Freud, the revolutionaries Lenin* and Trotsky, the erotic novelist Sade, the social theorist Fourier. The intellectual system which he evolved owes its richness and fluency to his capacity for synthesizing such diversely stimulating influences. Breton's synthesis has in turn exercised its own influence. In the political sphere, his ideas find an echo in the writings of Herbert Marcuse* and anticipate many theses of the Situationists. Many of his insights into the nature of language have filtered through into the thinking of such recent post-Freudian theorists as Jacques Lacan* and Roland Barthes*. In literary terms, Breton did much to help rewrite nineteenth-century literary history, rescuing neglected figures like Nerval, Lautréamont and Jarry. In the field of the visual arts, he contributed, through such authoritative texts as *Le Surréalisme et la Peinture* ('Surrealism and Painting', 1928), to the evolution in perception that has led to the public recognition of De Chirico*, Duchamp*, Ernst* and Picasso* as major artists of the age.

Breton was equally alert to a host of other art forms, including naive painting, mediumistic and psychotic art, and tribal art: he owned a considerable personal collection of Polynesian and Red Indian artefacts. In this, as in his other seemingly eccentric enthusiasms – for Gothic novels or rare texts on alchemy, for agate stones or butterflies – Breton displayed the virtues of a sensibility at one with itself and thus able to commit itself unhesitatingly to any and every genuinely felt attraction.

A system of thought which encompasses incredible disparities within an overall unity; a prose style in which explosive images are marshalled by a concern for lucid theoretical formulation; a moral rigour in relationships which none the less allowed for a well-attested capacity for loyalty even beyond the limits of the 'reasonable' – these are just a few of the paradoxes which emerge from a consideration of Breton's complex career. They are factors of confusion in an exact portrayal of where he stood and what he was: yet there is no denying that Breton occupied a central position in French cultural life during his lifetime and that his example remains a powerful, if often occulted, force in contemporary France. If for nothing else he will be remembered for his unswerving commitment to the theme of prospecting man's hidden potentialities.

Roger Cardinal

Other works: *L'Immaculée Conception* (with Paul Eluard, 1930); *Anthologie de l'humour noir* (1941); *Entretiens* (1952); *L'Art magique* (1957). See also: J. Gracq, *André Breton: quelques aspects de l'écrivain* (1948); M. Carrouges, *André Breton et les données fondamentales du surréalisme* (1950); C. Browder, *André Breton: Arbiter of Surrealism* (1967); S. Alexandrian, *André Breton par lui-même* (1971); M. Bonnet, *André Breton: naissance de l'aventure surréaliste* (1975); G. Legrand, *André Breton en son temps* (1976).

66

BRITTEN, Benjamin, Lord 1913–76

English composer

Benjamin Britten was born in Suffolk, an area of England to which he remained devoted, and where he lived for most of his life. Yet he was in certain significant respects an outsider. He was a homosexual, without the bohemian flair which would have enabled him to live in places where conventional morality could be more easily discounted. His contacts with the Auden* – Isherwood* circle in the 1930s encouraged a move to America at the start of the war, but the establishment of a permanent relationship with the singer Peter Pears combined with a longing for Suffolk to bring him home in 1942. He was also a pacifist, but after the war this naturally affected the character of his work more than that of his everyday life.

As composer, conductor, pianist, and director of the Aldeburgh Festival, Britten was for thirty years after the war a central figure in British musical life. This period saw substantial changes in taste and style, so it was inevitable that Britten should, at the end, seem old-fashioned alongside Harrison Birtwistle or Peter Maxwell Davies*. Even after his first major success, the opera *Peter Grimes* (1945), he was still regarded by some as a clever but superficial composer, and this reaction was one result of his earlier rejection (with the encouragement of his principal teacher Frank Bridge) of much that was most insular in the British music of the 1920s. His early taste was for Mahler, Stravinsky*, some Berg* and Schoenberg*, and various popular idioms, and his style soon cast off any trace of British pastoralisms in favour of an expanded tonal harmony relating to Bartók* and Stravinsky, and a technique of thematic integration comparable to Bartók or even Schoenberg. Britten was always a remarkably economical composer, a supreme miniaturist, as the song cycles prove. Yet he was also highly skilled at sustaining tensions over the largest scale available to a composer, opera, where the conflicts of the plot could be mirrored in purely musical tensions and interactions.

With the exception of a rather sprawling *String Quartet* (1931), Britten's early works – for example, the *Sinfonietta* Op. 1, and the choral variations *A Boy Was Born* Op. 3 – are notable for tight formal control, textural inventiveness and a remarkably mature technique of thematic manipulation. Between 1933 and 1939, he spent much time working on various radio, film and theatre projects, but during the late 1930s and early 1940s he composed several fine song cycles, including the *Seven Sonnets of Michelangelo* (1940), and some important orchestral works, including the Violin Concerto (1939) and the *Sinfonia da Requiem* (1940). With the first performance of *Peter Grimes* the foundation was laid for a contribution to opera which embraced works for children (*Let's Make an Opera*, 1949), chamber opera (*Rape of Lucretia*, 1946; *Albert Herring*, 1947; and *The Turn of the Screw*, 1954) and grand opera (*Billy Budd*, 1951; *Gloriana*, 1953; *A Midsummer Night's Dream*, 1960; and *Death in Venice*, 1973), as well as three 'parables for church performance' (*Curlew River*, 1964; *The Burning Fiery Furnace*, 1966; and *The Prodigal Son*, 1968) and one opera specifically for television, *Owen Wingrave* (1970). Opera was the genre in which Britten worked most consistently, though he also composed a wide variety of other vocal works, from song cycles to the *War Requiem* (1962), and in the field of instrumental music particular artists stimulated the creation of some important compositions: for example, a sonata with piano, three solo suites and a symphony with orchestra were all written for the cellist Mstislav Rostropovich.

It is not in itself remarkable that Britten's preferred texts for his songs dealt with various forms of vulnerability, nor that his operatic subject-matter returned obsessively to the outsider, the alienated, the lonely. Serious poetry and drama, especially of the more Romantic variety, deals constantly with these issues. But it is remarkable that, given the recurrences of these ideas and images, Britten's music evolved so distinctively, while remaining essentially concerned with the purely musical techniques for exploring fundamental tonal relationships and the forces capable of undermining them.

Britten was never a teacher, and although his style, like any distinctive form of expression, lends itself to mimicry, his influence has been most fruitful on composers who have preserved his concern for communicating through lyric melody in which goal-directed linear processes project the essence of a firm harmonic logic, even when that logic is no longer governed by traditional triadic progressions.

Arnold Whittall

Britten's many other works include: *Our Hunting Fathers* (1936, text devised by Auden); *Variations on a Theme of Frank Bridge* (1937); *Les Illuminations* (1939); *The Young Person's Guide to the Orchestra* (1945); *Spring Symphony* (1949); *Cantata Misericordium* (1963); *Songs and Proverbs of William Blake* (1965). Britten's principal publishers are Boosey and Hawkes and Faber Music. The definitive study of his music is Peter Evans, *The Music of Benjamin Britten* (1979). See also: Donald Mitchell and John Evans (eds), *Benjamin Britten. Pictures from a Life* (1978).

67
BROOK, Peter Stephen Paul 1925–

British theatre director

Of Russian descent, Peter Brook was educated at Westminster, Gresham's School, and Magdalen College, Oxford; at seventeen, he was one of the youngest undergraduates ever accepted by the college. Brook was soon an active participant in university drama, and his first work as a director, a production of Marlowe's *Doctor Faustus*, was seen in London at the Torch Theatre in 1943. That same year, as president of the University Film Society, he directed a precocious adaptation of Sterne's *A Sentimental Journey*. In 1944 Brook joined a London-based film company, but left the following year to direct Cocteau's* *The Infernal Machine*. He went on to join the then prestigious Birmingham Repertory Company, where he directed works by, amongst others, Shaw*, Ibsen and Shakespeare. His production of *King John* marked the beginning of Brook's interest in some of the more neglected of Shakespeare's plays. In 1947 he worked for the first time at Stratford-upon-Avon. His interpretation of *Romeo and Juliet* was disliked by most of the national critics, who seemed to see it as a battle in which the Bard lost out to Peter Brook. But at the age of twenty-two Brook was already very much his own man, unwilling to satisfy other people's expectations of classic texts. From 1947 to 1950 he was also Director of Productions at the Royal Opera House, Covent Garden, where he staged a memorable version of *Salome*, with designs by Salvador Dali*.

During the 1950s Brook worked prodigiously, both at home and abroad, in the United States and on the Continent. He worked in French for the first time on a production of *Death of a Salesman* at the Belgian National Theatre in 1951. In 1953 he brought Otway's tragedy *Venice Preserv'd* back into the public eye, with John Gielgud and Paul Scofield in central roles. In 1962 Brook was invited by Peter Hall to join the recently established Royal Shakespeare Company; he did so, on the understanding that he be allowed to experiment outside the company's normal field. He went on to direct a now legendary production of *King Lear*, again with Paul Scofield. Influenced by the Polish scholar Jan Kott, Brook saw *Lear* as 'the epic unfolding of the nature of the human condition', a black Beckettian* farce.

During the 1960s Brook became increasingly influenced by the ideas of Antonin Artaud* on the 'Theatre of Cruelty', which title he gave to a four-week experimental season with the RSC in 1964. With the same basic group of actors he went on to direct the *Marat/ Sade*, a play by the European Marxist Peter Weiss. In 1966, still with the RSC, he co-ordinated a 'group-happening-collective spectacle' entitled *US*. Dealing with public reaction to the Vietnam war, *US* was the subject of attempted, though unsuccessful, political censorship; the Lord Chamberlain described it as 'bestial, anti-American, and communist'. Controversial *US* may have been, but Brook's most successful collaboration with the RSC was in his 1970 production of *A Midsummer Night's Dream*, which he himself described as 'a celebration of the arts of the theatre'.

During the making of *US* Brook had worked briefly with the Polish director Jerzy Grotowski*, founder of the Theatre-Laboratory of Warsaw, whom he admired for his relentless and committed investigation of the nature of acting. Aware of the value of research such as was being carried out by Grotowski, Brook helped to form, in 1970, the International Centre for Theatre Research, based in Paris. It was with this organization that he did most of his work during the 1970s. Their first major production was *Orghast*, a spectacle performed at the ruined palace of Darius the Great in Persepolis, in a language invented by the poet Ted Hughes*. Brook went on to travel widely in Africa and Asia with the ICTR, though he returned once again to Stratford in 1978 to direct a long-awaited production of *Antony and Cleopatra*.

In his book *The Empty Space* (1968), Brook defined theatre as a search for form. 'The destruction of old forms, the experimenting with new ones: new words, new relationships, new places, new buildings.' Peter Brook's entire oeuvre, and especially the work since

1962, has revealed him engaging in this process of discovery. The demands made upon his actors are great. But, as one who believes that the 'theatre has one precise social function – to disturb the spectator', neither is he prepared to allow his audience the easy option. Since *Romeo and Juliet* in 1947 Brook has been trying to make his audiences see 'the hidden play behind the text'. It is scarcely his fault if they often do not like what they see.

Paul Nicholls

Brook's films include: *The Beggar's Opera* (1953); *Lord of the Flies* (1963); *Marat/Sade* (1967); *Tell Me Lies* (1968, based on *US*); *King Lear* (1971); and *Meetings with Remarkable Men* (1979). See also: J. C. Trewin, *Peter Brook – A Biography* (1971); A. C. H. Smith, *Orghast at Persepolis* (1972); John Heilpern, *Conference of the Birds: the Story of Peter Brook in Africa* (1977).

68
BROOKE, Rupert Chawner 1887–1915

English poet

Rupert Brooke was born on 3 August 1887 in Rugby and was educated at Rugby School where his father was a housemaster. While a student at King's College, Cambridge, he specialized in Elizabethan drama and after university settled at The Old Vicarage, Grantchester, which he celebrated in the famous poem of that name:

> Stands the Church clock at ten to three?
> And is there honey still for tea?

He had many famous friends – such as the Asquiths and Walter de la Mare – all of whom were convinced that Brooke had a brilliant future in whatever field he chose to dominate. His schoolboyish good looks and aesthetic manner made him the darling of the privileged social circles he frequented.

In 1911 Brooke published *Poems* (1911) and, on the strength of his dissertation 'John Webster and the Elizabethan Drama' (1916), was elected a Fellow of King's College, Cambridge. His poems, with their rich euphony and Tennysonian imagery, were highly praised and Brooke planned, with Harold Monro, to influence literary taste through the anthology *Georgian Poetry* (edited by Edward Marsh from 1912 to 1922). He travelled to America, Hawaii, Samoa, Fiji, New Zealand and Tahiti in 1913 but the outbreak of war brought him back to England. After some initial hesitation about enlisting, he joined the Artists' Rifles in 1914, then in September accepted a commission in the Royal Naval Division from the First Lord of the Admiralty himself, Winston Churchill. Brooke sailed to

Antwerp on 4 October to assist in the relief of the Belgians and saw enough action to convince him that he should provide the fighting man with a poetic voice.

On Christmas leave the poet went home to Rugby and there he wrote five sonnets on war which were published in December 1914 in the fourth and final issue of *New Numbers*. These five sonnets (collectively known as '1914') were unashamedly romantic; one of them, 'The Soldier', seemed to many to epitomize the quiet heroism of the Englishman:

> If I should die, think only this of me:
>   That there's some corner of a foreign field
> That is for ever England.

On Easter Sunday, 4 April 1915, the Dean of St Paul's preached a sermon which, as *The Times* reported, quoted 'The Soldier' as 'a beautiful little poem . . . a sonnet by a young soldier who would, he ventured to think, take rank with our great poets'.

As Dean Inge was preaching his sermon Brooke was in Lemnos while his division prepared to go to Gallipoli as part of Churchill's Dardanelles operation. On 17 April 1915 they landed at Skyros (the island of Achilles) where Brooke, suffering from blood poisoning, was transferred to a French hospital ship. He died on 23 April. Though he had not died in action his death was sufficiently tragic for Churchill to use it as a propagandist weapon. In *The Times* of 26 April Churchill wrote an obituary whose prose was as purple as Brooke's own poetry: 'He expected to die; he was willing to die for the dear England whose beauty and majesty he knew; and he advanced towards the brink in perfect serenity, with absolute conviction of the rightness of his country's cause and a heart devoid of hate for fellow-men.' England had an official martyr, blessed by the Dean of St Paul's and consecrated by the First Lord of the Admiralty. Because Brooke's war sonnets were written without any experience of trench warfare they seem excessively sentimental in comparison with the realistic war poems of Wilfred Owen*. However, Brooke deserves to be remembered as a talented poet who died before he could fulfil his promise and not only as a symbol of what Owen called 'doomed youth'.

Alan Bold

The Poetical Works of Rupert Brooke (1946) was edited by Geoffrey Keynes; the romantic legend is examined in Timothy Rogers, *Rupert Brooke* (1971).

69
BUBER, Martin 1878–1965

Jewish religious thinker

Born in Vienna, Buber spent his childhood in Lvov with his grandfather. After studies in Vienna, Leipzig, Berlin and Zürich, he became active in the Zionist movement. As editor of the Zionist *Die Welt* in 1901, he opposed Theodore Herzl at the Fifth Zionist Conference and formed the Zionist Democratic Faction. He founded the German Jewish monthly *Der Jude* in 1916 which did much to bring about a Jewish intellectual renaissance in Central Europe. He was active in the Zionist socialist movement, advocating a form of utopian socialism based on personal transformation. Along with Franz Rosenzweig and others, he started the *Freies Jüdisches Lehrhaus* (Free Jewish House of Learning) in Frankfurt where from 1923 he lectured in the University on Jewish religion and ethics. He became Professor of Religion at the University of Frankfurt in 1930 and was dismissed from his post in 1933. He left Germany for Palestine in 1938 where he became Professor of Social Philosophy at the Hebrew University of Jerusalem. Along with Y. L. Magnes, he became a leader in the Ihud movement, devoted to Arab – Jewish understanding and advocating the establishment of a joint Arab – Jewish state in Palestine. He died in Jerusalem.

The philosophical influences on Buber's thought may be found in Kant, Nietzsche and Kierkegaard. From Kant Buber took the insight that time and space are not something alien to the human person but are bound up with our way of perceiving the world. From Kant also comes Buber's acceptance that objective knowledge of the world in itself is impossible since we know it only through the categories we impose upon it. The strongly personalist note in Buber's anthropology owes much to Nietzsche and Kierkegaard but Buber was at pains to correct the solitariness of the Nietzschean and Kierkegaardian individual by stressing that personal relationships are not accidental but essential and constitutive of the human person. A profound influence on Buber's thought which makes his work specifically Jewish was Hasidism, a religious and social movement within Judaism in eighteenth-century central Europe. Though having a strong mystical element (based on the Kabbala), the features of the Hasidic tradition which attracted Buber were its doctrine that God is to be found in everything and everything in God, that the created world is to be redeemed rather than escaped from, and that God is to be worshipped by the whole human physical dimension.

Like Heidegger's* *Being and Time*, Buber's best-known work *I and Thou* (*Ich und Du*, 1923, trans. 1937) can be read as an attempt to present a way of looking at the world that overcomes the Cartesian split between knowing subject and objective world. It presents a theory of knowledge, in elusive and poetical terms, that is based on encounter. Buber refers to two primary words, 'I-Thou' and 'I-It' – roughly the way we relate to persons and to things. 'I-Thou' can only be spoken with the whole being, in a total openness to the other.

'I-It' on the contrary can never be spoken with the whole being; as a way of relating objectively to the world, it is always partial. It is Buber's contention that I-Thou relations frequently are supplanted by I-It relations where persons are treated as less than personal. Thus *dialogue* (a key term in Buber's anthropology) in order to be genuine must be characterized by an openness and a willingness to listen and receive as well as to speak and to give. The I of such personal relations is a different I from that of the I-It: for Buber, the I is never independent of such relations.

I-Thou relations carry more risk than I-It relations since in the former the entire I must be offered and nothing withheld. The Thou so encountered also poses risks since as personal it is met not in the context of determinism but in its full freedom and unpredictability. Such a 'dialogic' theory of knowledge is linked by Buber to time. I-It relations are always of the past, never of the present. Objective knowledge of a person is about his past actions. Since what he is or could be is never totally calculable, on the basis of his past, only I-Thou relations are genuinely in the present, open to any response in dialogue.

Buber does not wish to insist that all relations with persons must be intensely emotional, rather that they are significantly different from our relations with non-personal objects. Nor does he wish to set up two worlds, of persons and of objects. He wishes to pinpoint a possibility for human beings that must be grasped and yet is at stake. 'I become through my relations with the *Thou*; as *I* become *I*, I say *Thou*' (*I and Thou*). Between individualism and collectivism there is another possibility. 'Only when the individual knows the other in all his otherness as himself, as man, and from there breaks through to the other, has he broken through his solitude in a strict and transforming meeting' (*Between Man and Man*, 1947).

Buber's religious outlook takes its roots from Biblical personalism. He rejects the Greek philosophical tradition in which God is seen as an object of thought or belief. God is the subject, the Eternal Thou, one term in an I – Thou relation. Deeply influenced by the Hasidic tradition of the holiness of the secular, Buber insists that God is not known through propositions or speculation but through every particular I – Thou relation. 'In each Thou we address the Eternal Thou' (*I and Thou*). (Buber asserts that I – Thou relations are possible not only with persons but in a derived sense with nature and with what he obscurely calls 'spiritual existences'.) 'God may properly only be addressed, not expressed' (*I and Thou*) and revelation is just this encounter, not a record of the past only but present in one's life. Biblical revelations are not qualitatively different from the personal revelations of everyday life. In stressing that the Bible is not a dead book but living speech, Buber undertook (with Rosenzweig) a German translation of the Bible, completed in 1961, that sought to preserve the original character of Hebrew speech. Religion must therefore be considered not as the affirmation of certain religious beliefs but as the way in which one responds to the struggles of everyday life.

In his ethics Buber does not offer the security of a system. At the heart of moral decision is a risk. 'The risk does not ensure the truth for us; but it, and it alone, leads us to where the breath of truth is to be felt' (*Between Man and Man*). Though Buber stressed that moral values must be absolute, following a Kantian distinction of moral duty from expediency or prudential choice, yet every moral situation is unique and every decision involves the risk of being mistaken. As well as this tension between absolute values and individual situation, there is also a tension in Buber's ethics between a concept of 'authentic existence' as the source of the moral ought and the willingness to trace back moral obligation to the command and will of God. His concept of encounter with God as encounter with the Eternal Thou attempts to bring together his religious outlook and his self-realization ethic.

Buber's anthropology based on I – Thou relations, as well as his stress that all public life is redeemable, involves a social principle which has political consequences. Beginning from a distinction between society (*Gesellschaft*) as an artificial order of people living in common with shared interests, and community (*Gemeinschaft*) as a natural group of people bound together with a personal life in common, Buber's social thought is directed towards the realization of community among men and among nations. Early in his life he was involved with groups of religious socialists in Germany and was a friend of the socialist Gustav Landauer. Though influenced by Marxism, Buber insists that the transformation of society is first and foremost a transformation of man from within rather than a change in the state. This accounts for his strongly moral and religious outlook in politics with a consequent distance from concrete socialist action. His socialism is religious and utopian and, as expressed in his *Paths in Utopia* (*Pfade in Utopie*, 1950, trans. 1950), he is resigned to seeing his ideals unrealized. He had considerable influence on 'Labour Zionism' though he constantly warned against a crude identification of politics with religion or morality, and against the dangers of assuming that political aims override moral considerations. He was fascinated by (though critical of) Gandhi's* blending of religion and politics and saw a danger of secularized Messianism in some Zionist thought. 'Religion means goal and way; politics implies ends and means. . . . The religious goal remains . . . that which simply provides direction; it never enters into historical consummation' (*Pointing the Way*, 1957). Only in the socialist life of some early kibbutzim in Israel did Buber see some fragmentary realization of community among men.

Buber's views of personal relations have had far-reaching effects in theology (particularly with Paul Tillich*), in philosophy (in the thought of Gabriel Marcel), in a concentration on the role of the therapist in psychotherapy (through a concept of 'genuine listening') and in new models of educational theory. Though showing certain affinities with existentialism (due to a common source in Kierkegaard), Buber cannot be simply seen as an existentialist philosopher or theologian. He is rather in the prophetic tradition of Judaism, seeing man in his relation to God and concerned that modern man is 'at the edge', needing salvation from mass depersonalization and dehumanization. His writings seek to bring the Hebraic tradition to as central a position in Western culture as the Greek.

Terence O'Keeffe

Publication of the collected works of Buber in German began in Munich in 1962. Other English translations include: *The Prophetic Faith* (1949); *Two Types of Faith* (1951); *The Eclipse of God* (1953); *Good and Evil: Two Interpretations* (1953); *Tales of the Hasidim* (2 vols, 1961); *The Ways of Man according to the Teachings of Hasidism* (1951); and *The Legend of the Baal-Shem* (1956). On Buber, see M. Friedman, *Martin Buber: The Life of Dialogue* (1955); R. G. Smith, *Martin Buber* (1967); and P. Schlipp and M. Friedman, *The Philosophy of Martin Buber* (1967).

70
BUKHARIN, Nikolay Ivanovich 1888–1938

Russian revolutionary, economist and politician

Nikolay Bukharin was a major figure in the Bolshevik Party until the late 1920s. Though he never held a major administrative post, his impact – as a theoretician, as editor of *Pravda*, as a senior member of the Politburo, as head of the Comintern – on affairs in the Soviet Union was in many respects second only to Lenin's*. After the death of Lenin he was a contender for the highest positions in the Soviet party and state; the influence of his ideas is far from exhausted in the modern Soviet Union.

Even before entering university in 1907 Bukharin was an experienced revolutionary. Sentenced to internal exile in 1911 he subsequently escaped to Western Europe. Leading the life of an intellectual/political émigré he began a serious study of philosophy, sociology and economics, attending – in Vienna – the lectures of Eugen Böhm-Bawerk, and coming into contact with such Austro-Marxists as Otto Bauer and Rudolf Hilferding. These influences resulted in two books, *The Economic Theory of the Leisure Class* (1914, trans. 1970) – a critique of Austrian marginalist economics – and *Imperialism and World Economy* (1915, trans. 1972). The

latter text advanced an original argument to the effect that imperialism was a necessary concomitant of the consolidation of capitalist production into monopolies and trusts organized and co-ordinated by large banks; the influence of Hilferding's *Finanzkapital* is clear, and Bukharin's work in turn influenced Lenin's *Imperialism, the Highest Stage of Capitalism*.

During the revolution Bukharin was an important figure in the complex struggles within the Moscow region and the Moscow Party Committee. The following years were marked by the serious economic difficulties of early Soviet society; there was more or less complete disagreement within the party on appropriate economic policy for the entire twelve years between 1917 and late 1928. The economic problems to a large extent underlay the internal political struggles of the period, and certainly structured Bukharin's life and work. During the civil war which followed the revolution the economy was organized on the basis of 'War Communism', that is as a directly administered, moneyless economy with virtually all production and distribution nationalized. In his important work *The Politics and Economics of the Transition Period* (1920, trans. 1979) Bukharin produced a theory of socialist construction which was so heavily based on the experience of this time that it has been called, rightly, 'the theoretical manifesto of War Communism'; but although the programmatic recommendations of the text were soon abandoned, the work contained themes which were to reappear in Bukharin's later, apparently very different, work. These themes involved a conception of socioeconomic development in terms of the construction, dissolution and reconstruction of 'equilibrium' between social classes and branches of production. After 1921 Bukharin shifted his ground, enthusiastically supporting the New Economic Policy (NEP) – essentially a restoration of market relations and the formation of a 'state capitalism' in the USSR – eventually becoming, after the death of Lenin, its principal theorist and spokesman in the Politburo. In alliance with Stalin*, Bukharin led the mid-1920s Politburo majority which rejected the economic programme of the Left Opposition and destroyed Trotsky* and his followers as a political force.

During these years the crucial policy questions in the Soviet economy revolved around the problem of grain supply and the role of the agrarian sector in industrial construction. The Left Opposition – particularly Evgeny Preobrazhensky – argued for a rapid industrialization programme financed by turning agricultural-industrial terms of trade against the peasantry; Bukharin successfully countered this with the argument that it would constrict agricultural supply, close off the peasant market for industrial goods, and generate a peasant opposition which would threaten the stability of the Soviet State. His own policy involved industrialization on the basis of NEP: slow growth, expansion of the rural market by a growth in peasant incomes, securing of food supplies by high grain prices and the orienting of industrial production to goods demanded by the peasantry; in a word, 'equilibrium', between workers and peasants, between agriculture and industry.

Bukharin's critics argued, with some justification, that such policies would – in the first place – fail to achieve industrial growth rates high enough either to secure the Soviet Union against the long-term strategic threat from the West, or to provide any sort of industrial basis for socialism, and – in the second place – would engender a ramifying peasant capitalism, with political consequences at least as serious as those of Preobrazhensky's policy of exactions. These critics came to include Stalin in their number; the consequences for Bukharin proved fatal.

Quite abruptly, in 1928, Stalin adopted a new economic strategy which had been worked out by planners in the State Planning Commission and the Supreme Council of the National Economy between 1926 and 1928; this involved rapid industrialization, with investment priority for the capital goods sector and unprecedentedly high rates of growth. He proposed a simultaneous collectivization of agriculture, and succeeded in consolidating the support of upper echelon members of the party behind the policy. Bukharin's last major work, the famous 'Notes of an Economist' (published in *Pravda*, 30 September 1928), was a trenchant critique of these measures; but the struggle was over almost before it had begun, and Bukharin's removal from the Politburo a year later was a mere formality. From 1930 to 1933 he was director of research in the Commissariat of Heavy Industry, playing an active role in the Academy of Sciences. During this period he visited London, and on another occasion – according to Robert Jungk – stunned the German physicist Gamow and caused a flurry of concern in scientific circles in the West by asking whether it would be possible to reproduce the thermonuclear reactions of the sun on earth (i.e. develop nuclear power sources and weapons).

Following one of the most grotesque of the show trials Bukharin was executed in March 1938; he conducted himself throughout with great courage and, almost alone among Stalin's victims, offered a determined and mocking defence. He was not rehabilitated in Khrushchev's post-1956 attack on Stalin; but, as his biographer Stephen Cohen remarks, this critique 'produced an outburst of what may be termed pseudonymous Bukharinism – a rebirth of Bukharinist ideas that could not be, and were not, identified with his name'. There is occurring, at the present time, a major debate among Soviet economists on efficiency problems in socialist economies in which Bukharin's ideas – on rates and proportions of economic development, on the role of the market in economic decentralization – are

playing a significant part. Moshe Lewin's important study concludes that: 'It was astonishing to discover how many ideas of Bukharin's anti-Stalinist programme of 1928–1929 were adopted by current reformers as their own and how much of their critique of past practices followed his strictures and prophecies even in their expression.' There are many weaknesses in the Bukharinist economic programme, and one may be sceptical about the possibility of such a programme ever being implemented in the USSR; but any examination of his ideas must also bring to light his civilized and humane ideas on the construction of a democratic socialism, and this can only have positive effects in the Soviet Union and elsewhere.

Keith Smith

See Bukharin's 'Notes of an Economist', *Economy and Society*, vol. 8, no. 4, November 1979. See also: Stephen F. Cohen, *Bukharin and the Bolshevik Revolution. A Political Biography 1888–1938* (1975); Moshe Lewin, *Political Undercurrents in Soviet Economic Debates. From Bukharin to the Modern Reformers* (1975); Gary Littlejohn, 'State, Plan and Market in the Transition to Socialism: the Legacy of Bukharin', *Economy and Society*, vol. 8, no. 2, May 1979; Keith Smith, 'Introduction to Bukharin: Economic Theory and the Closure of the Soviet Industrialization Debate', *Economy and Society,* vol. 8, no. 4, November 1979.

71
BULTMANN, Rudolf 1884–1976

German Lutheran New Testament scholar and theologian

Born in Wiefelstede, Bultmann received his theological education in Tübingen, Berlin and Marburg. After a short period (1912–16) as instructor in Marburg, he was from 1916 to 1920 an assistant professor of the New Testament at Breslau, from 1920 to 1921 a professor at Giessen, and from 1921 to 1951 Professor of New Testament at Marburg. From 1951 until his death he was an emeritus professor at Marburg.

Generally considered to be one of the greatest New Testament scholars of the twentieth century, Bultmann has contributed to many branches of New Testament scholarship. With Karl Ludwig Schmidt and Martin Dibelius Bultmann is considered one of the founders of Form Criticism, and his book *The History of the Synoptic Tradition* (*Die Geschichte der synoptischen Tradition*, 1921, trans. 1963) has been dubbed 'The Bible of Form Criticism'. The standpoint of this school was that the three synoptic gospels (Mark, Matthew and Luke) give us *primarily* a glimpse into the period after Jesus' death when the primitive church was defining its standpoints, settling controversies, opposing criticisms and slanders, and relating itself to its cultural setting. Anecdotes about Jesus and sayings of Jesus were in this period *edited* by the evangelists into a *form* which reflects the cultrual *milieu* of the evangelists themselves. The Form Critics attempted, in a highly technical and scholarly way, to classify the various items (each of which they called a 'Pericope') according to the life-situations which occasioned them. Thus in Bultmann we find groups such as miracle-stories, controversial pronouncements, scenic descriptions and the like. By analysing the *form* of each of these Bultmann and his collaborators reached judgments about the probable *date* of each item and therefore about its trustworthiness as reliable history of the actual Jesus. Their publications (especially Bultmann's) evoked considerable theological controversy and the accusation that their techniques had cast grave scepticism upon the historicity of the Gospel narratives, an accusation that was reiterated upon the publication of Bultmann's little book *Jesus and the Word* (*Jesus*, 1926, trans. 1958). But Bultmann had already in the early 1920s associated himself somewhat with the school of dialectical theologians under Karl Barth*, which enabled him to say that the truth of Christianity does not in the last analysis depend upon historical criticism of the synoptic gospels but upon that faith evoked and created by the preaching of Jesus Christ.

But the association between Bultmann and Barth could not and did not survive for long. By 1928–9 Bultmann had begun to express disillusionment with Barth's account of God's communication with man, which in Bultmann's view grotesquely over-emphasized the invincible triumph of revelatory grace, which produced in man the appropriate response of faith, without any need for human presuppositions or co-operation. To be more precise, Bultmann began to deplore the absence in Barth's account of the place of human *understanding* within this process, and it is noteworthy that two of the most significant volumes published by Bultmann were entitled 'Faith and Understanding' (*Glauben und Verstehen*, I and II) and were brought out in 1933 (trans. *Faith and Understanding*, trans. 1966) and 1952 (trans. *Essays: Philosophical and Theological*, trans. 1955). In exploring the difficulties from human understanding inherent in the New Testament message Bultmann came to categorize these as *myth*. But during the same period (from about 1926 at the latest) Bultmann developed a lively interest in modern existentialist philosophy, mainly because of the work of one of his Marburger colleagues, the philosopher Martin Heidegger*, whose extremely important book *Being and Time* was first published in 1927.

These two themes, the problems inherent in understanding New Testament mythology and the teachings of existentialism coalesced in Bultmann's mind, and their fusion was first brought to the notice of the theological public by the publication in 1941 of Bultmann's epoch-making *New Testament and Mythology* (*Neues Testament und Mythologie*, trans. 1953). In the late 1940s, the dissemination of this and similar essays by Bultmann sparked off the famous *demythologizing* controversy, which had literally a world-wide impact, and which by the early 1950s had generated a quite enormous corpus of theological literature, of which the most important was published in a series of volumes entitled *Kerygma and Myth*. Within this debate, Bultmann's initial thesis was that much of the New Testament is beyond modern man's understanding because it is expressed in myth – which Bultmann derives from Jewish Apocalyptic Gnosticism and from an Aristotelian-Ptolemaic cosmology. Notions such as Christ's descent into hell and heavenly ascension, for example, presuppose the acceptability of the latter. In order to render Christianity intelligible for modernity, Bultmann proposed that its mythological statements should be translated completely and exhaustively into the language of human existence, and in putting this proposal into practice he utilized the existential terminology of the existentialist Heidegger. In doing so, Bultmann claimed that there was a basic affinity between the notion of being presupposed by religious existentialism and that presupposed by the biblical writers. Bultmann's detailed proposals evoked quite enormous controversy, not all of it well-informed. In the main, the attacks of his critics proceeded along two lines. First, in insisting that all God-language should be located within existential discourse, Bultmann, it was argued, was 'existentializing' God to an extent that completely overlooked that there are ontological (or metaphysical) aspects of the notion of God. Bultmann's replies to the criticism that he was completely humanizing God retain considerable perennial interest and importance. Second, in his account of Christianity, Bultmann insisted that genuine Christian faith is concerned overwhelmingly with the present, kerygmatic Christ who is present in his word, challenging, enriching, forgiving, and freeing: talk like this, retorted his critics, amounted to a rejection of Christianity as a *historical* religion, firmly rooted in the historical Jesus, a criticism which generated a debate of great intrinsic interest. These two criticisms, that Bultmann's 'existentializing' of Christianity both 'de-ontologized' and 'de-historicized' it, were thoroughly debated on a world-wide scale, a debate which called into being a vast amount of literature which will find a permanent place in the history of Western theology.

Bultmann also contributed during his long lifetime to the philosophy of historiography, to research into Christian origins, to the science of hermeneutics, to the understanding of secularization, to the debate on the relation between science and religion, and to Johannine studies. Amongst those said to have influenced his work are his teacher at Marburg Wilhelm Herrmann, the philosopher Wilhelm Dilthey, the historiographer

Count Yorck von Wartenburg, members of the existentialist tradition from Kierkegaard to Heidegger, the nineteenth-century biblical critic D. F. Strauss, Martin Buber*, the literary critic Erich Auerbach, and the German Lutheran theologians of the nineteenth century. Those influenced by Bultmann in more than a dozen countries are literally innumerable.

Professor James Richmond

Other works include: *Jesus Christ and Mythology* (1958). See: Walter Schmithals, *An Introduction to the Theology of Rudolf Bultmann* (1968); Ian Henderson, *Rudolf Bultmann* (1965); John Macquarrie, *An Existentialist Theology* (1955) and *The Scope of Demythologizing* (1960); Hans-Werner Bartsch (ed.), *Kerygma and Myth*, I and II (1953 and 1962).

72
BUÑUEL, Luis 1900–

Spanish film director

A man (Buñuel himself) stands by a window sharpening a razor. Outside a cloud passes across a full moon. A woman stares in impassive close-up towards the camera. The razor is drawn across her eyeball.

After over half a century this opening sequence from Buñuel's first film has lost none of its power to shock. *Un Chien andalou* (1928), made in collaboration with Salvador Dali*, was a Surrealist *succès de scandale*.

Buñuel described his second independent feature, *L'Age d'or* (1930s, with Dali), as a 'desperate and passionate appeal to murder'. In Paris, where it was first shown, the police had to be called in to clear the cinema. To convict Buñuel of the charge of anarchy, blasphemy, pornography or even high seriousness would be to reduce his obsessions to the literal banality of moral and aesthetic terrorism. His genius is to combine the unnatural, the incongruous, the outrageous with an unblinking matter-of-factness that not only subverts the narrative preconceptions of his audience, but which also dramatizes an emotional collage of images and associations that haunt the mind.

In Buñuel's words, 'Neo-realist reality is incomplete, official, and altogether reasonable; but the poetry, the mystery, everything which enlarges tangible reality is missing.' However, Buñuel's next venture was an uncompromising documentary, *Land Without Bread* (1932). With cool, almost surgical precision, scenes of appalling poverty, sickness and despair in a small Spanish village are contrasted with the rich and remote trappings of the Church. It was too much for the Republican authorities. The film was banned.

For seventeen years Buñuel's career went into eclipse. He did a dubbing stint for Paramount in Paris, produced for Warners in Spain, and was even invited to Hollywood to make anti-Nazi propaganda. But an accusation from his old friend Dali that he was an atheist, communist, or both, forced his resignation. He emigrated to Mexico – directed a musical box-office flop, then a comedy hit which permitted him to make the award-winning *Los Olvidados* (1950). After Vittorio de Sica's sentimental social indictment of slum life, *Bicycle Thieves* (1948), Buñuel's underworld of beggars, assassins, the blind, the drunken and the innocent strikes with the iconoclastic force of hallucinatory vision.

'I am against all conventional morals, traditional fantasies, sentimentality, and all that moral filth,' he says. 'Bourgeois morality is for me anti-morality, because it is based on three unjust institutions – religion, family and country.'

Shock tactics had scored Buñuel high critical ratings. But for almost the next ten years he was to concentrate on more obviously popular and commercial cinema. It is a prolific and varied interlude – ranging from 'B' feature potboilers, picaresque melodramas, quirky interpretations of classic novels like *Robinson Crusoe* (1952) and *Wuthering Heights* (1953), to the morbid paranoia of *El* (1952), revolutionary thrillers, and the deliriously erotic black comedy of *The Criminal Life of Archibaldo de la Cruz* (1955).

Just in case there was any danger of his audience being lulled into a false sense of security, Buñuel responded first with the stark ferocity of *Nazarin* (1958), and two years later with *Viridiana* (1960). In both films a character who is religiously committed to a concept of goodness and charity is forced into dramatic confrontation with its physical, mental and social antithesis. In both cases the moral code disintegrates. *Viridiana* caused a sensation. It won the Palme d'Or at Cannes, but was immediately banned by the Spanish authorities who had felt safe to make the picture their official entry at the festival. The beggars' banquet which freezes into a 'Last Supper' tableau ensured that once more Buñuel was firmly back on the Catholic Church's blacklist.

But Mexico was not so squeamish. Buñuel returned there to make *The Exterminating Angel* (1962), a *Huis Clos* surreal drama, where a group of bored, wealthy socialites, mysteriously confined in an elegant house, are slowly but surely stripped of their protective, civilized layers.

'Surrealism taught me that life had a moral meaning that man cannot ignore. Through surrealism I discovered that man is not free. I used to believe that man's freedom was unlimited, but in surrealism I saw a discipline to be followed. It was one of the great lessons of my life; a marvellous, poetic step forward.'

Buñuel can create images with the emotional resonance of depth-charges. In *Diary of a Chambermaid* (1965), a snail slowly crawls up the exposed thigh of a young girl who has been sexually assaulted and murdered.

Buñuel's world is anything but black and white, but working with colour and Catherine Deneuve, *Belle de Jour* (1968) made bourgeois sado-masochistic fantasy chic for a whole new audience. But Buñuel has not sold out. The limpid elegance of his later films does not reflect a sudden slump towards fashionable cynicism, erotica, and style for style's sake. The shocking and the startling are still viewed with the same unblinking gaze. Perhaps the old anarchic anger has been tempered into a more humorous compassion in films like *The Discreet Charm of the Bourgeoisie* (1972) and *The Phantom of Liberty* (1974). However, at the age of seventy-seven, partially deaf, but claiming, 'I'm still an atheist, thank God!' Buñuel can still make magic with his profound, sensual and ironic study of *l'amour fou*, *That Obscure Object of Desire* (1977).

Paul Sidey

See: Ado Kyrou, *Luis Buñuel* (1963); Freddy Buache, *Luis Buñuel* (1964); Raymond Durgnat, *Luis Buñuel* (1967).

73

BURGESS, Anthony 1917–

British novelist and critic

John Anthony Burgess Wilson was born in Manchester in 1917 and educated at the Xavierian College and Manchester University. After military service during the war he taught in England and worked as an education officer in the colonial civil service in Malaya. In 1959 he was invalided home with a suspected brain tumour; given one year to live, he produced five novels. Although he had written fiction earlier, this was the beginning of Burgess's career as a full-time novelist, critic, script-writer and reviewer. His long-standing love of music (he has had a symphony performed in America), linguistics and phonetics has always informed his work.

Burgess's prolific output, the range of his subject-matter, his responsiveness and invention mark him out from most other authors. In his biography *Shakespeare* (1970) he comments: ' "A snapper-up of unconsidered trifles" – that is Autolycus in *The Winter's Tale*; it is also Shakespeare and, indeed, any writer of drama or narrative fiction.' Living by his own dictum, Burgess ransacks in an original fashion any cache of history and information, especially those stored up by other artists. *1985* (1978) is an ingenious variant on *1984* by George Orwell*; *Nothing Like the Sun* (1964) is a fictional recreation of Shakespeare's early life; *ABBA ABBA* (1977) describes Keats's dying days in Rome; *Tremor of Intent* (1966) is partly a parody of Ian Fleming's spy

stories; the structure of *Napoleon Symphony* (1974) is based on the pattern provided by Beethoven's Eroica Symphony; the anthropological jokes and riddles of *MF* (1971) are a nod in the direction of Lévi-Strauss*. Linguistically the chief influence on Burgess is James Joyce*, although the attractions that Shakespeare and the Jesuit poet Gerard Manley Hopkins provide are also significant, while the puzzle-playing of some of his novels is reminiscent of Nabokov*. *The Malayan Trilogy* (*Time for a Tiger*, *The Enemy in the Blanket* and *Beds in the East*, 1956, 1958 and 1959) and *Devil of a State* (1961) describe the uneasy shoulder-rubbing of different cultures in Asia and Africa during the waning of colonialism. Burgess does not much regret the withdrawal of the white rulers nor does he expect much of the new regimes. He exploits the farcical discomforts of racial and religious collision and dives enthusiastically into a linguistic mélange, using to the full his talent for mimicry. The return to England is without illusions: the anaemic tellyland of, for example, *The Right to an Answer* (1960) is projected into the future in the anti-utopian novels, *A Clockwork Orange* (1962), *The Wanting Seed* (1962) and *1985*, with their visions of a half-hearted totalitarianism and individual protest.

The fiction dealing with famous historical figures, the sequence of novels about the poet Enderby (who composes best in the lavatory), the gloomy prospects of the future show Burgess's distrust of the state and all its organizations. There is a complementary emphasis on the individual although the heroism of his central characters is based often on quirkiness and a lack of allegiances rather than any positive acts of defiance. The jaunty hero of *A Clockwork Orange*, a book for which Burgess created a special argot derived from Russian, is a teenage hooligan who robs, rapes and kills for pleasure. Forcibly and chemically rehabilitated by the state he can choose only to be good; simultaneously he loses his love of classical music, as the hero of *Inside Mr Enderby* (1963) loses his poetic faculty after psychiatric treatment. Burgess prefers voluntary damnation to enforced social salvation. His Catholic background has coloured his fiction not just in its pessimistic view of human progress but in its conviction of human evil and corruption.

'All art springs from delight in raw material,' Burgess claims in *Language Made Plain* (1964). His preference for exotic locations in his novels comes from a well-conveyed feeling that countries less temperate, in both senses, than England provide a rawer, more confused material on which to work – even the inertness of the East is made verbally energetic. The delight Burgess communicates to the reader springs from his comedy, the headlong brilliance of his language and the restlessness of his books.

Philip Gooden

Burgess's other books include: *The Doctor is Sick*

(1960); *Urgent Copy* (1968); See Bernard Bergonzi, *The Situation of the Novel* (1970).

74

BURROUGHS, William Seward 1914–

US novelist

William Burroughs's grandfather invented the adding machine, and it is said the Depression scotched what would have been a considerable family fortune. Burroughs himself has written: 'As a young child I wanted to be a writer because writers were rich and famous. They lounged around Singapore and Rangoon smoking opium in a yellow pongee silk suit. They sniffed cocaine in Mayfair and they penetrated forbidden swamps with a faithful native boy and lived in the native quarter of Tangier smoking hashish and languidly caressing a pet gazelle.' Drugs, travel, homosexuality, exoticism, the contemplation of unusual wealth – the most striking aspects of his life and work are present in this recollection.

After attending Harvard, Burroughs travelled to Vienna where in 1936 he studied medicine at the university for one term. Later, on a GI grant, he investigated Pre-Columbian civilizations in Mexico City (where he accidentally killed his wife with a revolver), and has since lived in New York, Tangier, Paris and London. He was associated with the Beat Movement but his books have deliberate epistemological ambitions which set him apart.

His first major novel, *Naked Lunch*, published by Maurice Girodias at the Olympia Press in Paris (1959), adumbrates those essential preoccupations which have made him one of the most impressively exploratory and also least accessible of modern novelists. Wilfully encompassing philosophy, poetry, psychology, journalism, cybernetics, sociology and politics, as well as sheer fantasy, and having many of the features associated with speculative physics (viz. probability, indeterminacy, synchronicity, acausality), *Naked Lunch* replaces linear narrative and enclosed characterization with a new model which resembles montage. Burroughs pursued these formal experiments in *The Soft Machine* (1961) and *The Ticket That Exploded* (1962), introducing his famous 'cut-up/fold-in' method, a technique developed from the ideas of Brion Gysin. 'Cut-up' refers to the practice of randomizing his own or borrowed texts with the help of scissors; while 'fold-in' involves folding a page down its middle and typing out the resulting interpenetration of words. This recourse to chance in the preparation of a final surface was a violent attempt to release language from its role as manipulation, but it is difficult to see what is really achieved other than an intransigent affectation of style.

In it one detects the misappropriation of mechanical devices by a non-mechanical medium.

Burroughs's use of such external devices is paralleled by his involvement with drugs, particularly by his heroin addiction whose tragic mystique he created by representing it as both repulsive and seminal to his mentation. He was cured by a treatment based on apomorphine, a drug which acts upon the hypothalamus to reduce anxiety and reschedule the metabolism but provoking severe vomiting. This purgation, described as 'medieval' by some other addicts, would appeal however to a man with so pronounced a sado-masochistic psyche as Burroughs. The characters who flicker through his lurid pages are either masters or slaves or both. In his work one is never far from an elaborate and brutal symbolism centred on the concept of control of the individual by, or submission of the individual to, exterior factors that are explicitly malign. In his own words, a paranoiac is 'a man in possession of all the facts'.

Only love may briefly break this vicious circle, or in Burroughs's case, homosexuality – although here he is still pessimistic, quite the opposite of Genet*. Burroughs's books ache with a homosexual passion staunched by Midwestern reserve. Whereas Genet's love moves outward in a clear intoxication, Burroughs's emotion is erratic and hyperobsessive (viz, the endless recurrences produced by cut-up/fold-in) which makes the vehemence with which he constructs homosexuality into a bio-evolutionary command understandably suspect and illustrates the danger a novelist runs when his fiction enters the territory of naked polemic. What is true or plausible is confused with what, in the writer's opinion, is desirable, and one is left holding a manifesto of his frustrations. On the other hand, viewed from a slightly differing angle, the previous sentence describes the strategy of every creative imagination and so Burroughs's homosexuality becomes another sensational tactic for animating his universe at the very moment when he is perforce suspending it in the fixative of a novel. His books become the playground of forces which the reader is obliged to stabilize for himself. In this respect the reader–text relationship approximates to the universe of the Quantum physicist who in himself represents a mathematical co-ordinate of its identification.

However wanton it may sometimes appear, Burroughs's writing is conventionally redeemed by the quality of its satire, and like most satirists his outlook is moralistic and gloomy. His finest literary passages are whimsical and peculiar: the master of high camp collides with the prophet of doom in bursts of outrageous comedy, gruesome perversions, and theatrical speculation. The stylistic refrigeration which came with his exploitation of cut-ups, after the exhilarating freedom of *Naked Lunch*, has been moderated in the later work as Burroughs acknowledges that he had simply been putting one crude limitation in the place of another (i.e. narrative form), and himself falling into 'the dogmatic mind' which it had been his intention to ridicule as self-righteous and bestial in others. Thus *The Wild Boys* (1971) is almost agreeably comprehensible as a straightforward futuristic fantasy. Unfortunately this reduces sharply the pressure of emotional danger and psychological adventure so crucial to his effects.

Burroughs has said that it is possible to write a book which can kill people, but that no one has yet managed it. However questionable this proposition, it reveals him as an intensely serious writer whose faith in his art as a living, developing organism has the power to trivialize the work of most of his contemporaries. By abandoning so many of the novel's conventions, he has risked being dismissed as a peripheral eccentric. But his determination to make of fiction more than passive entertainment, to involve the reader in a questing experience in which the reader himself is the central figure and consciously so, has turned Burroughs into a solitary intelligence, isolated by his courage, and perhaps the only novelist in English currently capable of communicating the awesome excitement of an art form that for him is still expanding.

Duncan Fallowell

Burroughs's other books include: *Junkie* (1953); *Dead Fingers Talk* (1963); *The Yage Letters* (with Allen Ginsberg, 1963); *Nova Express* (1964); *Exterminator!* (1974); *The Third Mind* (with Brian Gysin, 1978); *Ah Pook Is Here* (1979). *The Job* (1969) is a book of interviews with Burroughs conducted by Daniel Odier. The best critical study is Eric Mottram, *William Burroughs: The Algebra of Need* (1977).

75
BUSONI, Ferruccio Benvenuto 1866–1924

Italian composer

Son of an itinerant clarinet virtuoso and a pianist, in his own words Busoni 'never had a childhood'. He was thrown into a career as a touring pianistic *Wunderkind* at the age of seven; his flair for composition was marked from an equally early age, but he was practically self-taught except for a year in Graz with Wilhelm Meyer-Remy. In 1888 he left his parents' home in Trieste, but the pressure to support them drove him through a succession of teaching posts: he was Professor of Piano at Helsingfors (1888–90, where he formed a lifelong friendship with Sibelius*), Moscow (1890, where he married the Swedish pianist Gerda Sjöstrand), and finally Boston (1891–4). He returned to Europe in 1894 and settled in Berlin; his activities broadened from those of simply a great virtuoso, and his master classes

in Weimar (1901–2) were as much for the benefit of composers as pianists. From 1902 to 1909 he financed and conducted a series of modern music concerts in Berlin including premières of music by Bartók*, Delius*, Debussy*, Elgar*, Nielsen and Sibelius. In 1913 he was appointed Director of the Bologna Liceo Rossini, but his hopes for a revival of Italian musical culture were dashed by the Great War, during which he refused to reside in any of the belligerent nations and settled in Zürich until 1920. In the latter year he returned to Berlin as head of the Masterclass in Composition at the Prussian Academy of Arts (where his pupils included Kurt Weill*, Wladimir Vogel and Stefan Wolpe). His health was in decline and he concentrated his efforts on completing his opera *Doktor Faust*, which was, however, still unfinished at his death.

Busoni is still better known as an arranger of Bach for the piano than as a composer in his own right, but his music and thinking have been a seminal influence. His life-work shows a heroic will to balance plurality in a personal imaginative world riven by dichotomies. His earliest influences were Italian *bel canto* (his father's repertoire chiefly consisted of operatic fantasies) and the massive Germanic formal and contrapuntal logic of Bach (whom his father forced him to study unremittingly); he soon combined these with Brahmsian romanticism and the revolutionary harmonic thinking of the late works of Liszt. His early music culminated in the gigantic *Piano Concerto* (Op. 39, 1904), Germanic-Romantic in overall form but with two disruptive Italianate scherzos, a progressively less bravura piano part, and a final Lisztian 'chorus mysticus' for male voices. After this his *6 Elegies* for piano (1907) and the opera *Die Brautwahl* (Op. 45, 1908–11) saw him moving towards a more personal, speculative style: major and minor tonalities coalesce in highly chromatic harmony, suggestive of an eerily disembodied world. The *Sonatina Seconda* for piano (1912) is extreme in this respect – it is also freed from regular rhythmic pulse, and introduces a modern notational technique which dispenses with natural signs. Meanwhile the huge *Fantasia Contrappuntistica* (three versions for solo piano, 1910–12; later for two pianos, for organ and for orchestra), based on the unfinished fugue from Bach's *Art of Fugue*, demonstrated both a highly creative reverence for tradition and an unrivalled polyphonic mastery. The *Indian Diary* (1915), fruit of an interest in American Indian music sparked off on a tour of the USA in 1910–11, anticipates Bartók in its rhythms and treatment of 'primitive' folk elements; the opera *Turandot* (1917) introduces exotic scales such as he had already advocated in *Sketch for a New Aesthetic of Music* (1906), an essay which forecasts microtonal systems and electronic instruments (he also proposed the 12-note chromatic scale as the basic unit of tonality, with the abolition of 'consonance' and 'dissonance'); his orchestration led the way to a more 'chamber-musical' approach to scoring; and *Doktor Faust* incorporates old instrumental forms into a dramatic context in a similar manner to Berg's* *Wozzeck*. However, a parallel concern with 're-newed classicality' (*junge Klassizität*) – by no means identical with Stravinsky's* 'neo-classicism' – to recapture the Mozartian spirit is manifest in the 'theatrical capriccio' *Arlecchino* (1916–17) and later instrumental and orchestral pieces. He was an inveterate champion of the younger generation, and both Schoenberg* and Varèse* profited by his encouragement; Egon Petri, Percy Grainger and Harriet Cohen were among his piano pupils.

Superficial estimates (there have been many) portray Busoni as a haphazard harbinger of others' greater achievements, rather than the unique and potent phenomenon he was. He radically extended the fron-tiers of musical language, but refused at any point to be a mere systematizer, preferring fluidity and spon-taneity and an unashamed 'impurity' of style wherever resources could be usefully combined. An ironic hu-morist and a romantic humanist, he was also at heart a mystic – but not the type of passive, orientalist mystic to which twentieth-century thought is comfortably ac-customed. *Doktor Faust*, his masterpiece, based not on Goethe but on the ancient puppet-plays, is a profound-ly, even achingly spiritual work, unsettlingly unat-tached to any conventional religious purpose. With seeming familiarity it expresses the extremes of mortal terror and spiritual radiance – a religious ardour di-rected, like that of the Renaissance alchemists, towards a new and magical world symbolized by the naked youth born from the body of the dead magus, Faust. Its message of psychic struggle is one that still inter-mittently haunts the music of later generations.

Malcolm MacDonald

Other works include: *Violin Concerto* (1897), and other concerted works for piano (*Konzertstück*, 1890; *Indian Fantasy*, 1914; *Romanza e scherzoso*, 1921), clarinet (*Concertino*, 1919) and flute (*Divertimento*, 1920); *Berceuse élégiaque* (1909), *Nocturne symphonique* (1912) and *Tanzwalzer* (1920) for orchestra; two *Violin Sonatas* (1890, 1898); five *Goethe-Lieder* (1919–24); six *Sonatinas* (1910–20) and many other works for piano; transcriptions and editions of other composers' music, notably Bach, Liszt, Mozart and Schoenberg. Writings: *Sketch for a New Aesthetic of Music* (trans. 1911); *The Essence of Music and Other Papers* (trans. 1957). See: E. J. Dent, *Ferruccio Busoni* (1933); H. H. Stuckenschmidt, *Ferruccio Busoni* (1970).

76
BUTOR, Michel Marie François 1926–

French writer

Michel Butor is an erudite and much-travelled writer whose work over the last twenty-five years covers a wide range of subjects; his doctoral thesis, supervised by Bachelard*, was on mathematics and the idea of necessity, he worked with Lucien Goldmann on a translation of Lukács*, and dedicated an early poem to Charlie Parker*. In 1971 he was made associate professor at Nice. He is best known for his four novels, which represent an important contribution to the Nou-veau Roman. These, however, were all produced with-in a comparatively short period (1954–60), after which he parted company with the Nouveau Roman group, largely because they were working *against* existing cul-ture and he was working *through* it. His later writings are more diffuse. Three strands can be distinguished: literary and aesthetic criticism in the four volumes of *Répertoire* (1960, 1964, 1968, 1974); writings about places, firstly the Mediterranean, especially Egypt, in *Le Génie du lieu* (1958) and continuing with *Où – Le Génie du lieu II* (1971) and *Boomerang – Le Génie du lieu III* (1979); and pieces stimulated by visual images (paintings, photographs, etc.) in the four volumes of *Illustrations* (1964, 1969, 1973, 1976).

Underlying this diversity is the continuing pursuit of an understanding of *culture*, defined as a collective and mainly unconscious world view, an attempt to situate modern Western European culture in relation both to its historical roots in Christian, Graeco-Roman and Egyptian traditions, and to the rest of the world. Butor is fascinated by the *otherness* of non-European societies, because in offering different possible articu-lations of reality they illuminate the boundaries of our own.

His first response to this otherness is *Mobile* (1962), written after a visit to the USA and sub-titled 'Étude pour une représentation des États-Unis'. America is a contrast to Europe, and also a projection of European contradictions on a larger scale. Moreover, the domi-nant American culture contains its own otherness in the form of black people and the Amerindians; i.e. America is not a unity, but is profoundly split, or 'fissured'. So is Europe: the theme of the fissure was first explored in *La Modification* (1957), with its hero's discovery of the irremediable fragmentation of the post-imperial world. (In fact, most of the concerns of the later works can be traced back to the novels – e.g. *L'Emploi du Temps*, 1956, has the alien African immi-grant in Britain, *Degrés*, 1960, is based on a geography lesson about the discovery of the New World, etc.) Western man, Butor says, tends to assume that he is universal Man; he lives with a nostalgic illusion of centrality, as though the great empires still existed.

Mobile also constitutes a formal break. Butor's novels already display a very complex, subtle sense of urban space: the block of flats in *Passage de Milan* (1954), the labyrinth of Bleston, the correspondences between Paris and Rome. But with *Mobile* this 'spatiality' is materialized in the text itself, which is a kind of collage

– he calls it a patchwork quilt like the early settlers made, constructing an intricate pattern out of odd bits of rag – but a 'mobile' collage, exploiting ambiguities of reference (e.g. different towns have the same name) and shifting time-scales as he moves across the continent. Typographical experiments bring into play the spatial resources of the page, and the elaborate, well-defined structuring of the novels becomes an equally complex but more fluid juxtaposition of fragments.

This view of the text evolves through subsequent works. Many of these explore the contrast between liquidity and solidity (the 'monumental') – e.g. in *Description de San Marco* (1963) the tourists' chatter 'laps against' the façade of the cathedral, while Niagara Falls is, paradoxically, a liquid monument (*6 810 000 litres d'eau par seconde*, 1965). It also allows him to integrate writing with the visual arts – already in *L'Emploi du Temps* the novel is likened to a cathedral, and the *Illustrations* series creates similar connections. More abstractly, *textual* and *geographical* space are linked through his view of culture: if culture is representation, the mapping-out of its forms necessarily invokes dimensions in space.

Thus all his excursions into architecture, typography (*Illustrations* is dedicated to the type-setter), ethnography, alchemy (in *Portrait de l'artiste en jeune singe*, 1967), etc., are rooted in the theory of culture. This also accounts for another key emphasis – on the unconscious. Dreams and myths are means whereby the individual enters into communication with that collective, ancestral unconscious that forms the substratum of culture. Hence Butor's interest in them, already evident in the novels and pursued through *Histoire extraordinaire* (1961) and *Matière de rêves* (1975), among other works.

Correlatively, *writing* is seen almost as a form of psychoanalysis, elucidating the structures in which our individual and collective existence is grounded, by reflecting them in its own structures; for Butor, structure is the means whereby thought reflects upon itself. Writing is the effort towards enlightenment; it is a struggle against repression.

Celia Britton

Other works include: *Réseau aérien* (1962); *Essais sur les Modernes* (1964); *Les Mots dans la peinture* (1969); *Dialogue avec 33 variations de Ludwig van Beethoven sur une valse de Diabelli* (1971); *L'Oeil des Sargasses* (1972). Three of the novels have been translated as: *A Change of Heart* (in the US) or *Second Thoughts* (in Britain) (*La Modification*, 1958); *Passing Time* (*L'Emploi du Temps*, 1961); *Degrees* (*Degrés*, 1962). See also: *L'Arc*, no. 39 (1969); F. Aubral, *Michel Butor: choix de textes* (1973); G. Charbonnier, *Entretiens avec Michel Butor* (1967); L. Dällenbach, *Le Livre et ses miroirs dans l'oeuvre romanesque de Michel Butor* (1972); J. Roudaut, *Michel Butor ou le livre futur* (1964); L. Roudiez, *Michel Butor* (1965); M. Spencer, *Michel Butor* (1974).

C

77

CAGE, John 1912–

US composer

'I have nothing to say and I am saying it and that is poetry' sums up Cage's assessment of his contribution to twentieth-century art. Such a dictum is intentionally paradoxical, for most of his musico-philosophical statements over the past thirty years reflect not only his adherence to the tenets of Zen Buddhism but also his unique approach to the world of sound. The son of an inventor, Cage was born in Los Angeles and received instruction from Henry Cowell and Arnold Schoenberg*, two of the most influential composer-teachers in America during the 1930s. His early chamber works and songs are generally chromatic, dissonant and confined to ranges of twenty-five notes arranged in contrapuntal textures. Study under the guidance of Cowell at the New School for Social Research, New York, enabled him to survey developments in contemporary, oriental and folk musics with the result that he formed a percussion group which specialized in the use of unusual instruments such as tin cans, brake drums, water gongs and flower pots creating totally new sonorities. Representative works of this period are three pieces entitled *Construction in Metal* and *Amores* which includes a part for Cage's own invention, the 'prepared piano' whose sound is modified with the addition of screws, bolts, pieces of wood and rubber placed between the strings: later pieces using this medium were the *Sonatas and Interludes* (1946–8), a host of works written in collaboration with the Merce Cunningham Dance Company, and the *Concerto for Prepared Piano and Chamber Orchestra* (1951). A continuing interest in the musical potential of unusual sounds promoted experiments with electronic sources such as variable speed turntables and radio signals (*Imaginary Landscape*, Nos 1 and 4 of 1939 and 1951); later gramophone cartridges, contact microphones and amplifiers were used.

Soon after the war Cage made a study of the music of Satie* and Webern* at a time when neither composer's work was yet acknowledged as musically significant. He prophesied that their attitudes towards and treatment of musical form via proportional time lengths would point the way to future methods of composition, and as a result silence could only be perceived in terms of time duration and not as an opposition to melody and harmony. Demonstrations of such theories found shape in the *String Quartet in 4 Parts* of 1950 and the silent piece *4'33"* of the following year, a work which depended on audience and environmental response for its effect. It was also at this time that Cage took studies in Zen Buddhism under D. T. Suzuki* at Columbia University and came under the influence of the *I Ching*, the Chinese method of throwing coins or marked sticks for chance numbers. By employing this method in his ensuing compositions he could ensure that they were free of individual taste and memory in their order of events. From now on the concept of Indeterminacy would be used as a guide towards the placing of tempi, durations, sound and dynamics in most of his new compositions. *Music of Changes* for piano solo (1951) was the first work to employ such a system and very soon was followed by similarly inspired compositions from Cage's close associates Earle Brown, Morton Feldman and Christian Wolff.

From an early age John Cage had been interested in a synthesis of the creative arts but the opportunity to hold such a mixed-media event did not arise until the summer schools at Black Mountain College, North Carolina, where between 1948 and 1952 he was encouraged to work with Charles Olson*, Robert Rauschenberg*, Merce Cunningham (dancer) and David Tudor (pianist) to produce the first 'Happening' which incorporated music, dance, painting, poetry reading, actions, recordings, films and slides. Such a collaboration was to herald a host of similar events in the 1950s and 1960s which were put on tour around the country and abroad. Recent works in this genre include *Theatre Piece* (1960), *Musicircus* (1967), *HPSCHD* (1969), *Apartment House 1776* and *Renga* (1976). Besides the promotion of intermedia events Cage continues to construct scores for traditional instrumental forces even though at times these are for unusual combinations and often call for additional electronic sound sources. His most recent preoccupation is with the use of amplified plant materials, a concept appropriately entitled 'Biomusic'.

The example and encouragement of John Cage, life-long musical inventor, experimenter and revolutionary, continues. His innovations over the past forty-five years in the realm of new sound sources, indeterminacy, graphic notation and artistic integration have influenced most of the post-war avant-garde and contemporary experimental composers.

Michael Alexander

Principal writings: *Silence* (1968); *A Year from Monday* (1968); *M-Writings '67-'72* (1973); *Notations* (1969); *Empty Words* (1980). See also: C. Tomkins, *Bride and the Bachelors* (USA)/ *Ahead of the Game* (UK) (1965); *John Cage*, ed. R. Kostelanetz (1971); H. Wiley Hitchcock, *Music in the United States* (2nd edn 1974); P. Yates, *Twentieth-Century Music* (1967); W. Mellers, *Music in a New Found Land* (1965).

78

CALDER, Alexander 1898–1976

US sculptor

Famous as the man who invented the 'mobile', who introduced motion into sculpture, it was not until his mid-twenties that Alexander Calder purposively turned his attention to art, despite the fact that both his father and grandfather were sculptors. In 1919 he graduated from the Stevens Institute of Technology in Hoboken, New Jersey, with a degree in mechanical engineering. A gifted draughtsman, his initial ambition was to become a successful commercial artist, and with this in mind signed up as an illustrator for the *National Police Gazette* in 1924. The drawings, which Calder dubbed 'man-made approximations', revealed a rapid observation and abstracting power. His experiments with the use of wire as a means of lifting line off the page resulted in *Josephine Baker 1,* which, with a number of other 'wire portraits', was exhibited in a one-man show at the Weyhe Gallery in New York (1927). At the same time he made his first journey to Paris (in 1926), and devoted much of his time and energy to making the small figures that together composed his *Circus* (1924–31), which he loved to 'perform' for small invited audiences to the sound of the record 'Ramona'. These pieces were constructed from corks, pieces of felt, wood and whatever other scraps of material came to hand. They were anthropomorphic, capable of transformation into 'live' creatures with magic immediacy. In the sense that it tackled the problems of balance and of space, the *Circus* was the prototype mobile.

Calder's childhood memories, recollected in *An Autobiography with Pictures* (1966), dictated to his son-in-law, were full of the observation of mechanical movement, of trains, bicycles and coasters. Also warmly remembered were the toys he made for his sister Peggy. 'I have always been delighted by the way things are hooked together,' he said – a delight which was transmitted later through the delicate spins of his sculptures. As a student he was similarly drawn to the 'discussion of the laws governing the plane motions of rigid bodies, with applications to machines, compound and torsion

pendulum, translating and rotating bodies'; and he was inculcated with a picture of the universe as a mechanical structure of moving parts.

Except for a brief flirtation with Abstraction-Creation (1932–4) Calder never attached himself to any artistic school. On the other hand Paris, which he made his second home after his marriage to Louisa James in 1931, brought him in contact with the newest ideas and many of their exponents, including Léger*, Mondrian*, Miró* and Duchamp*. It was in fact Duchamp who provided his moving figures with the label 'Mobiles', and Arp* who termed the frozen mobiles 'Stabiles'. According to their construction, the mobiles divide into two types: standing and hanging. Both were collapsible, and could therefore be transported easily. The earlier ones incorporated 'found objects', while the later ones were made from designed metal pieces painted either black or in primary colours. Finally, the mobiles of the 1970s used steel. But while his work can be seen to develop towards increasingly larger structures (*The Four Elements*, 1962, and *Hello Girls*, 1964, both standing mobiles) sometimes serving a directly representational purpose (*The Circle*, 1935, or *Spirale*, 1958), most of Calder's work is underlined by a basic sense of play, which on occasion manifested itself as a pure, abstracted humour (*Performing Seal*, 1950). This was reflected in his choice of titles. Behind their whimsicality there was usually a perfectly matter-of-fact explanation. Either they referred to the natural phenomena that had prompted the piece in question (*Snow Flurry*, 1948), or to the thickness of the material employed (*.125*, 1958), to the person who had commissioned it (*Gwenfritz*, 1969 = Gwendolyn Cafritz), or simply to the place of installation (*La Défense*, 1975). But such betrayal of sophistication was indicative of Calder's attitude: he would never, for example, refer to himself as an artist.

Calder's output extended to motorized mobiles, tapestries, stage designs, oil paintings, woodcarvings, bronzes, toys, magazine covers, etchings, lithographs, household utensils, jewellery, two fountains, an acoustic ceiling and the decoration of two aeroplanes and a BMW car. In addition he was a gifted illustrator of children's books. But it was his hanging mobiles that captured the public's imagination and accounted for a world-wide reputation that began in the 1950s, after taking the First Prize for sculpture at the Venice Biennale (1952). People simply enjoyed watching them without feeling a need for explanation. As Pierre Restany put it, 'He was Francis of Assisi turned lay engineer.' Some of the later mobiles (e.g. the series *Gongs*) had polished bronze elements, which produced a resonant ring when struck by other parts. If this draws attention to a range of artefacts produced in the Orient from time immemorial, in the context of contemporary Western sculpture Calder has, almost playfully, inserted a new dimension. A mobile 'spins out its tale of achieved volume' (Kraus).

Dr Slavka Sverakova

Several films portraying Calder's work include: *Works of Calder* (1951); *Mobiles* (1966); *Calder un portrait* (1972). See: J. J. Sweeney, *Alexander Calder* (1951); H. H. Arnason, *Calder* (1966); J. Lipman, *Calder's Universe* (1976). See also R. E. Kraus, *Passages in Modern Sculpture* (1977).

79
CAMPBELL, Ignatius Roy 1901–57

South African poet

Roy Campbell was born in Durban; his mother came from a Scottish Highland family and his father Samuel had qualified as a doctor in Edinburgh. Dr Campbell, a Major with the Durban Light Infantry, combined his equestrian interests with a love of literature and corresponded with friends like Mark Twain. Campbell inherited the two passions from his father and later wrote in his autobiography *Light on a Dark Horse* (1951): 'It was through my father's sharing and cherishing my literary ambitions that I was able to get a start as a writer. . . . Above all, from a utilitarian point of view, I owe to my father my mastery of horses which has been my passport through every frontier.'

In 1918 Campbell left Durban and came to Oxford where he spent a year reading Elizabethan drama and French symbolist poetry before abandoning any idea of an academic career. He moved to London where he met T. S. Eliot*, the Sitwells, and fell under the influence of Wyndham Lewis*, whose argumentative style and provocative manner he adopted. In Campbell's case the aggression was not confined to books and he became known as a hell-raiser who was as quick with his fists as he was with his wits. Campbell, who fancied himself as a skilled boxer, played the tough-guy role to perfection. He also flaunted his reactionary views before the left-wing London intellectuals who were naturally overwhelmed by his reputation for physical belligerence. When his long poem *The Flaming Terrapin* (1924) appeared its energetic and self-consciously virile symbolism was acclaimed in England; Campbell decided it was time to return, with his wife Mary, to his native land.

He edited the South African magazine *Voorslag* from 1926 to 1927 before being frozen out by an establishment so reactionary they found even his views dangerously liberal. He took his revenge on his South African opponents in the satirical *Wayzgoose* (1928) published on his return to England. Campbell's extraordinary life as a man of action led him to earn his living as a Provençal jouster and bullfighter; his literary targets were the more easily wounded members of the Bloomsbury Group, who were attacked in the pointed couplets of *The Georgiad* (1931). By this time Campbell had made himself thoroughly unpopular with the leading lights of the London literati and his artistic ostracism was completed after his political stance in Spain.

Campbell went to Spain with the proofs of his memoir *Broken Record* (1934) and hoped to support himself by his writing. He became a Roman Catholic and, when the Spanish Civil War broke out in 1936, allied himself to Franco's fascists. Subsequently Campbell boasted of his military heroism but he probably exaggerated his own role in the fighting for, according to Hugh D. Ford's *A Poet's War* (1965), 'He left Spain in August 1936 . . . and returned sometime later as a "well-protected war correspondent".' Campbell's authorized version of his part in the war was described in the poem *Flowering Rifle* (1939), in which the Reds are ruthlessly cut down by Campbell on the warpath:

> So where you thought to slash the bulging nape
> It is a face you widen in its gape

Such sentiments made him seem like a mindless thug but Campbell was always at pains to conceal his artistic temperament.

In the Second World War, Campbell joined the British army, sustained a broken hip while training in Burma, and was discharged with a life pension as being permanently disabled. He returned to England, then to Spain, and died in a car crash in Portugal. Campbell's satirical poetry has dated and his lyrics, as in *Mithraic Emblems* (1936), often seem mechanical. He is remembered, though, as a colourful character and a brilliant translator of poets as diverse as Baudelaire and St John of the Cross.

Alan Bold

Roy Campbell, *Collected Poems* (3 vols, 1949, 1957, 1960).

80
CAMUS, Albert 1913–60

French writer

One of the most significant, and redeeming, features of cultural life in France is its willingness to welcome a major intellectual who has emerged from a humble background and whose work remains accessible to a wide reading public. Such a writer is Albert Camus, whose origins as a *pied noir* from the working-class district of Algiers were as obscure as those of any of the eight French winners of the Nobel Prize for Literature who preceded him. He first became known in metropolitan France towards the end of the Second World War through his work on the Resistance newspaper *Combat*. In the years immediately following the war he was rapidly established, together with his contemporary Jean-Paul Sartre* and the latter's mistress Simone de Beauvoir*, as one of the leaders of the new generation of committed French writers, philosophers and critics. Their common concern was the struggle for the freedom, justice and dignity of man in an age of successive and conflicting tyrannies which could be fought only in circumstances of considerable moral ambiguity.

Camus had in fact been active as early as 1935, while a student at Algiers University, in the propaganda warfare against international fascism, and had also taken on the conservative French establishment in defending the rights of the Arab population. From the middle 1930s onwards Camus's career reflects both in his creative works and his journalism a quarter century of intense debate of the great issues of the times: fascism, genocide, the savage post-war purges of French collaborators, repressive colonialism (e.g. the French in Madagascar and the British in Cyprus), the death penalty, torture, racialism and conscientious objection amongst others. All of these drew from Camus a clear moral response. So too did Stalinism* and revolutionary terrorism from the late 1940s onwards. The widening gulf between Camus and the French left as a result of the latter reached unbridgeable dimensions after the outbreak of the Algerian War in 1954, when Camus refused to support the FLN, *grosso modo*, in their struggle for Algerian, i.e. Arab, independence from France. He was killed in a car crash in January 1960. Although only forty-six he was considered by his critics to be a spent force; the Nobel Prize award in 1957 had been regarded as the consecration of his passage to the ranks of the *bien-pensants*.

Like many French intellectuals of his time Camus expressed himself creatively in the two major literary genres, prose fiction and the theatre, as well as in philosophical essays and copious journalism. Camus's reputation was made very quickly while he was still young in the five years immediately following the Second World War (sometimes on the strength of work first published or performed earlier). His four original plays, *Caligula* (1944), *Cross Purposes* (*Le Malentendu*, 1944), *State of Siege* (*L'État de Siège*, 1948), *The Just Assassins* (*Les Justes*, 1950, all four trans. 1958); his two major philosophical essays, *The Myth of Sisyphus* (*Le Mythe de Sisyphe*, 1942, trans. 1955), *The Rebel* (*L'Homme révolté*, 1951, trans. 1953); and particularly his novels, *The Outsider* (*L'Étranger*, 1942, trans. 1946, as *The Stranger* in the US) and *The Plague* (*La Peste*, 1947, trans. 1948), brought him a considerable degree of material ease and fame. Camus's early popularity was enhanced by his personal image and life-style: the 'Mediterranean' type (of mixed French – Spanish origins),

handsome, athletic, a lover of football, swimming, dancing and womanizing. This is particularly the vestigial Camus of the Algerian period, the 'Philosopher of the Absurd' who wrote *The Outsider*, *The Myth of Sisyphus* and short essays such as *Nuptials* (*Noces*, 1939, trans. in *Lyrical and Critical* 1967): 'In Algiers whoever is young and alive finds sanctuary and occasion for triumphs everywhere: in the sun, the bay . . . the flowers and sports stadiums, the cool-legged girls. But for whoever has lost his youth there is nothing to cling to and nowhere for melancholy to escape itself' ('Summer in Algiers'). In these early works Camus is stressing certain *essences* such as what we would now recognize as the machismo of the *pied noir* and southern Europeans generally, a continuity of pagan Greek values and, less credibly, a symbiosis of European and Arab cultures. Life is short; the simple, sensual pleasures of Mediterranean man, swimming, sun-bathing, making love, are to be enjoyed while one is young, as they are by Meursault, the enigmatic hero of *The Outsider*. The more keenly man enjoys these pleasures, the more scandalous is the fact of his mortality. For Camus the crime, on discovery of this mortality and of the limitations on man's ability to comprehend and order the universe, is to do one of three things: (a) to commit suicide literally, (b) to commit intellectual suicide by looking to a life after death, or (c) to do what Caligula does in Camus's play, rush headlong into a destructive rebellion against a world which can offer man the most intense physical joys only to mock him and cast him off irrevocably at the cruellest moment: a sort of metaphysical coitus interruptus. The stoic but life-enhancing course to adopt, as expounded in *The Myth of Sisyphus*, is not to attempt to defeat the absurd (or, to be precise, destroy the absurd *relationship* between man and the resistant external world) but to maintain it with courage and lucidity. Man must take up the challenge of the absurd and live in a state of spiritual tension to which Camus gave the name *revolt*.

The great divide in Camus's work occurs in the early 1940s in the face of the harsh realities of the German occupation. The exalted, solipsistic world of *The Myth of Sisyphus* was soon left behind as Camus came to feel increasingly during the 1940s, especially as Nazism was succeeded by Stalinism, that revolt degenerated all too easily into what he considered to be a nihilistic and cynically pursued absolute, *revolution*. The result was that Camus waged an increasingly shrill campaign towards the end of the decade not just against revolutionary violence and the ethic of ideological expediency but specifically against communism and its Marxist philosophy of history. *State of Siege* and *The Just Assassins* were skirmishes before the full-scale battle provoked by *The Rebel* in 1951 and the consequent break with Sartre and friends. Many readers, particularly in the United States, prefer (or know only) this Camus, the Cold Warrior of the middle period. But with the passage of time it will surely be recognized that his masterpiece is not *The Plague*, with its botched allegory of the Occupation and its cosy, up-beat conclusion ('what one learns in time of pestilence is that there are more things to admire in man than to despise'), but rather *The Fall* (*La Chute*, 1956, trans. 1957). This last major piece of prose fiction, produced during the relatively barren last decade of Camus's life, is a brilliantly ironic, mock-cynical *tour de force* in confessional form. The confession, in this work rich in puns and sly cultural allusions, is that of Jean-Baptiste Clamence, a man who, like Camus and many of his fellow intellectuals, has spent his life in the liberal conscience industry. The captain of such an industry should go down with his ship; Clamence failed even to attempt to rescue a girl who plunged into the Seine. The ship that Camus declined to go down with was that of justice in Algeria. *The Fall* is Camus's best work: his most deeply personal, his most tragic, and at the same time – an effect he sought unsuccessfully to capture previously – his most comic.

Ted Freeman

Gallimard's 2-volume Pléiade edition of Camus's works is comprehensive and scholarly: *Théâtre, Récits, Nouvelles* (vol. 1); *Essais* (vol. 2). See also: *Exile and the Kingdom* (*L'Exil et le Royaume*, stories, 1957, trans. 1958). See: J.-C. Brisville, *Camus* (1960); J. Cruickshank, *Albert Camus and the literature of Revolt* (1960); C. C. O'Brien, *Camus* (1970); R. Quilliot, *La Mer et les prisons* (1956); Herbert R. Lottman, *Albert Camus* (1979).

81
ČAPEK, Karel 1890–1938

Czech writer

Karel Čapek was born in Malé Svatoňovice, a small Bohemian town where his father worked as a doctor. His brother Josef (1887–1945), as well as being Karel's literary collaborator for almost twenty years from 1907, was a distinguished painter. Karel himself read philosophy at Charles University in Prague, and subsequently travelled to Paris and Berlin to continue his studies. In 1915 he was awarded a doctorate for a thesis on 'Objective Methods in Aesthetics' (unpublished). A brief flirtation with pragmatism gave way to an abiding interest in relativism and pluralism, largely as a result of his reading of Karl Mannheim* and Ortega y Gasset*. The other important philosophical influence was the vitalism of Henri Bergson*.

Čapek's prolific output included plays, novels, short stories, journalism and children's books. The appeal of his work is a combination of a brilliant, though sometimes uneven, handling of philosophical materials in a profusion of forms (ranging from the detective story to collage and interior monologue, often deployed in rapid succession), with a style that drew resourcefully on colloquial Czech. While the issuing incongruity frequently generates an immediate humour, always underlying is a search for the truth of man's (not Čapek's) identity, a search embodied in three recurring themes: total destruction (war, plague, death); siege and isolation (the individual surrounded by apparently stronger forces); and the substitution of man by both natural and artificial entities (newts and insects, puppets and robots).

As a journalist working for the prestigious Brno people's paper *Lidové Noviny* (from 1921) Čapek perfected the *sloupek* ('little column'), defined as 'something actual like a leader, but lighter, livelier and witty', a form whose appeal was that 'it is not long enough to be boring and it is not boring enough to be an article'. Beginning with *O Věcech nejbližších* ('On the Things Nearest', 1925), several selections of his contributions to this genre were published. But it is with the short stories that Čapek first emerges as a writer of stature. The early *Boží Muka* ('Wayside Crosses', 1917) uses the detective format to discern spiritual values in ambiguous signs and symbols, a technique expanded in *Money and Other Stories* (*Trapné Povídky*, 1921, trans. 1929) and the later, highly popular *Povídky z jedné kapsy* and *Povídky z druhé kapsy* ('Tales from One Pocket' and 'Tales from the Other Pocket', both 1929, translated as *Tales from Two Pockets*, 1932). In all these the boundaries between reason and language, between truth and imagination, and the problems of imprisonment within a world of relative values, emerge as Čapek's particular territory. The same may be said of the plays, including the early *Loupežník* ('The Outlaw'), a comedy of youth and love written in three versions between 1911 and 1920. In each the outlaw assumes a different guise – of an American pioneer, of a primitive deity, and finally of a self-reliant, fearless tramp. The modernism of Čapek's approach to drama, however, only becomes apparent in the last version, in its sudden alternations between prose and poetry, in its juxtapositioning of the bookish and the folk, and its abrupt eruptions of farce. But it was *R.U.R.* (Rossum's Universal Robots, 1920, trans. 1923) that won him international acclaim, being soon performed in many countries, including the USA and Japan. Rossum refers to the Czech word *rozum*, meaning brain or intellect. Old Rossum invents a robot (a term coined by Josef Čapek), his nephew mass-produces robots, and Helena incites their revolt. Everyone is killed except Alquist, who is respected by the robots because he works with his hands, and who is privileged to witness Primus and Helena, his robotic servants, fall in love. In an otherwise merciless satire man is redeemed only because, through the miracle of love, the machines are transformed into human beings.

In the last play, *The Mother* (*Matka*, 1938, trans. 1940), the action is taken up mainly with a conversation between a woman and her last surviving son and apparitions of his father and four brothers who have each died serving a cause, and now Toni himself is called on to fight for his country. Overcoming her conviction that life is more important than honour, the mother at last gives him his rifle. Written at a time when Czechoslovakia was threatened by Hitler*, the play is visionary. A possible interpretation would be that all the mother's other men died for lesser causes, and not the one that mattered.

Of eight novels, *Hordubal* (1933, trans. 1934), *Meteor* (*Povĕtroň*, 1934, trans. 1935) and *An Ordinary Life* (*Obyčejný život*, 1934, trans. 1936) – a trilogy loosely connected by their common philosophical analysis of individual life – are outstanding. *Hordubal* contrasts the pastoral with the nomadic, resignation with romantic involvement, and the impossibilities of communication with the desire to reach out. *Meteor*, an exercise in epistemological perspectivism, presents, through a nun, a clairvoyant and a writer, three understandings of a man who lies dying in hospital after his plane has crashed; and through these understandings (ethical, noetical and aesthetic), the ambiguities of chance and order. *An Ordinary Life* pursues the trivial and banal in the person of a retired official, whose identity is perpetuated by his habits until the memory of an erotic incident reveals him to have been a poet, a dreamer, a hero, a beggar, a perverted sensualist, a hypochondriac, an ambitious and a ruthless man. His quest for self-knowledge leads him through all the paradoxes of the simple and the complex, until at last he dies of over-excitement.

Čapek's later works – notably the novel *The War with the Newts* (*Valka s mloky*, 1936, trans. 1937) and the play *Power and Glory* (*Bílá nemoc*, 1937, trans. 1938) – manifest his growing apprehensions of the coming armed conflict, and adopt at times urgent moral positions. His natural response to life, however, was away from any dogma, as the choice of endings provided for *The Insect Play* (*Ze Života Hmyzu*, with Josef, 1920, trans. 1923) demonstrates. It is left to the director to decide whether to end the production with an expression of existentialism, or with an interpretation of death as a dream and work as a joyful gift.

Dr Slavka Sverakova

Other novels include: *The Absolute at Large* (*Tovarna na absolutno*, 1922, trans. 1944); *An Atomic Phantasy* (*Krakatit*, 1924, trans. 1948); *The First Rescue Party* (*První Parta*, 1937, trans. 1940). See also: W. E. Harkins, *Karel Čapek* (1962).

82

CAPOTE, Truman 1924–

US novelist

Born Truman Streckfus Persons in New Orleans in 1924, Capote has described his early years as 'the most insecure childhood I know of' – a statement which reveals his tendency towards self-dramatization as well as how he felt about his childhood. He had little formal schooling and claims to be unable to recite the alphabet to this day. His parents divorced when he was four years old and his mother later married a Cuban textile manufacturer named Capote. Until he was ten he lived mainly in Monroeville, Alabama, with three maiden cousins and one man. 'I used up some of my loneliness by writing', he said later. He was taken to Millbrook, Connecticut, where he spent a year at Greenwich High School, running away repeatedly, once, he reports, with an older girl who later achieved notoriety as the 'Lonely Hearts murderer'. By the age of seventeen he was in New York, employed on the staff of the *New Yorker*. After the publication of a short story, 'Miriam', in *Mademoiselle* he signed a publisher's contract and moved back to New Orleans where he wrote his first novel, *Other Voices, Other Rooms* (1948). Since then he has kept a home in New York but has travelled extensively, often as a guest of the wealthy and the internationally famous.

Capote has a reputation as a short-story writer, as the author of *Breakfast at Tiffany's* (1958), and as the inventor of the 'non-fiction novel' exemplified by *In Cold Blood* (1966). In all his work he is known as a meticulous, rather ornate stylist. He is not immediately thought of as a writer from the deep South, perhaps because his two most famous books are set in New York and Kansas, but his chosen themes are connected with the South: Gothic horror, breakdown and a claustrophobic society in which the individual is hopelessly yearning for an elegant past or a glittering future. His literary ancestors include Edgar Allan Poe and William Faulkner* as well as Flaubert and Turgenev; his near contemporaries are Flannery O'Connor, Eudora Welty and Tennessee Williams*.

Other Voices, Other Rooms is a superb evocation of the Old South, especially in its descriptions of natural scenery where Capote has few equals. Although less well-known than his later books and less valued by the author, it has a texture and density which his subsequent work lacks. The self-conscious aestheticism matches the subject-matter which deals with a small boy, Joel Knox, trapped in a decaying mansion surrounded by distant, eccentric adults. There is a fine, unique portrait of the tomboy Idabel beside whom the more celebrated Holly Golightly in *Breakfast at Tiffany's* now seems rather dated and sentimental, although she made an electric effect when the book was published and in the film (1961) where she was played by Audrey Hepburn. Holly too is a waif from the poor South, longing for brilliance (Tiffany's) but only disappearing into blankless and probable death. In both these works homosexuality appears as a major theme but is presented with a certain evasion and coyness.

Capote spent five years researching *In Cold Blood*, carrying out exhaustive interviews with two murderers, Dick Hickcock and Perry Smith, as with everyone else connected with the murder of the Clutter family in their Kansas farmhouse. He became intensely involved in this case, particularly with Perry Smith who resembles the orphan-like protagonists in his earlier stories. The result is compulsive reading: the riveting attention that every macabre murder story commands, but in spite of the careful arrangement of chapters it lacks the inwardness of a novel. It owes its genesis, as does much of Capote's reporting and interviewing, to the long feature in the *New Yorker*. Like them, Capote's articles are beautifully crafted, precisely observed and somewhat long-winded.

John Daniel

Capote's other books include: *A Tree of Night and Other Stories* (1949); *The Grass Harp* (1952); and *The Dogs Bark* (1974). He has also written plays, *The Grass Harp* and *House of Flowers*, and film scenarios, *Beat the Devil* and *The Innocents*. See also: William L. Nance, *The Worlds of Truman Capote* (1973).

83

CARNAP, Rudolf 1891–1970

German/US philosopher

Having been a member of the Vienna Circle, Carnap is one of the father figures of the 'scientific' approach to philosophy. Born near Barmen, Germany, he studied physics, philosophy and mathematics at the Universities of Freiburg and Jena from 1910 to 1914. At Jena he was taught and greatly influenced by Gottlob Frege and he returned to Jena after First World War service to complete a doctorate, obtained in 1921.

The invitation to the University of Vienna came from Moritz Schlick* in 1926, when Carnap went there as Privatdozent. He soon became a leading figure in the Vienna Circle discussions and he saw his first major work, *Der logische Aufbau der Welt* (1928), as an expression of the philosophic spirit of these discussions. This almost emotional reaction against the German Idealists and the Nature Philosophie of Goethe and Schelling saw as its goal the elimination of all speculative and poetic work from philosophy. The Logical Positivists, as they came to be called, sought clarity of concepts, precision of methods and responsible theses. The guideline in philosophic work was to be the strict and responsible orientation of the scientific investigator. The belief was that by slow and careful construction, insight after insight could be won by co-operative effort, each philosopher playing his small, specialized part in the progress of unified science. The *Aufbau* was the first meticulous step on this road.

Carnap's aim was the construction of a system of concepts in which each concept would, in virtue of its manner of construction, have a genealogy showing how it is reducible to a selected number of basic concepts, ones which relate immediately to the items of experience (sense data) so making clear its empirical content. Both this aim and the logical techniques employed were derived from Bertrand Russell*. His supreme maxim of scientific philosophizing – 'Wherever possible, logical constructions are to be substituted for inferred entities' – is the maxim according to which the *Aufbau* was undertaken and the logical techniques used are drawn from Russell and Whitehead's* *Principia Mathematica*. But the actual analysis of reality was taken from Ernst Mach's *The Analysis of Sensations*. Carnap applied precise logical techniques to attempt the informal reduction suggested by Mach.

However, the aim was not fully achieved and Carnap came to realize that it is impossible to construct all the concepts required by science out of a few basic ones, hence reducing all such concepts to simple sensory ones. In 'Testability and Meaning' (1936) he abandoned the idea that all statements about things can be translated into statements about sense data. Instead he introduced 'reduction sentences', which, without effecting a full translation, show how experience bears on the truth or falsity of a statement so indicating how it might be tested. Sentences which can neither be confirmed nor refuted in the light of experience are to be regarded as without empirical significance and hence as worthless for science.

This paper was written soon after Carnap's arrival in America. He left Vienna in 1931 to take up the chair of Natural Philosophy in the Division of Natural Science at the German University in Prague. In 1935 the spread of Nazi influence forced him to leave Prague. He became a Professor of Philosophy at the University of Chicago, where he remained until 1952, when he spent two years at the Institute of Advanced Studies at Princeton. In 1954 he was appointed to the chair of Philosophy at the University of California at Los Angeles, where he stayed until his retirement in 1961.

Throughout his career Carnap remained faithful to the ideals of the Vienna Circle – the logical empiricism and the use of formal methods for the analysis of scientific discourse – but in detail his view of the nature of that discourse and of the sorts of methods to be employed in its analysis became increasingly flexible. This included admitting the methods of formal semantics (developed by Tarski) as well as the purely syntactical techniques of *Principia Mathematica* into the analysis of concepts, and the development of a logic of confirmation to articulate the link that could no longer be made by constructive definition, between statements about objects and the experiences used as evidence for or against them. Although few would now subscribe to the goal of constructing a fully analysed language for unified science, the immense contemporary interest in formal semantics, especially in America, where the scientific approach to the philosophy of science flourished, is a mark of Carnap's influence.

Dr Mary Tiles

Der logische Aufbau der Welt (1928, trans. Rolf A. George, *The Logical Structure of the World*, 1967). 'Testability and Meaning' originally appeared in *Philosophy of Science*, vol. 3 (1936) and vol. 4 (1937). It was reprinted as an appendix to an enlarged edition of *Meaning and Necessity* (Chicago 1956, original edition Chicago 1947) along with other important papers, including 'Empiricism, Semantics and Ontology'. Other major works are: *Logische Syntax der Sprache* (1934, trans. Amethe Smeaton, *The Logical Syntax of Language*, 1937) and *The Logical Foundations of Probability* (Chicago 1950, second edition 1962). See also: P. A. Schilpp (ed.), *The Philosophy of Rudolf Carnap*; Nelson Goodman, *The Structure of Appearance* (1951), which contains a detailed analysis of *Der logische Aufbau*.

84

CARTER, Elliott 1908–

US composer

Elliott Carter was born in New York on 11 December 1908 and received early encouragement from Charles Ives*, who recommended him to Harvard University. There, Carter studied literature until his final year, when he began composition study with Walter Piston. He subsequently studied with Nadia Boulanger in Paris.

His early music, in common with that of many of his colleagues, bears the imprints of Stravinskian* neo-classicism, which he had imbibed during his time in Paris. With the *Piano Sonata* of 1945–6, however, a powerful individual voice makes itself unmistakably felt. In this and in the succeeding works, the cogent *Cello Sonata* (1948), the *First String Quartet* (1951), which brought him to international prominence, and the exquisite *Sonata for flute, oboe, cello and harpsichord* (1952), the neo-classic element is at once paid tribute to, brought to a head and exorcized, as the mature musical personality comes more and more to the fore.

Since then Carter has slowly but inexorably amassed an impressive series of masterpieces which collectively have established his position as one of the most significant figures at work in the world today. Although the surface of his music has grown steadily more complex for composers and performers alike, this is an inseparable part of his own growth process and is accepted as such by his steadily increasing admirers in both groups, who also recognize that Carter's refusal to write down to them is the sign of his taking them seriously.

But even more than an act of faith on the part of his devotees, what has allowed Carter steadily to consolidate his position while maintaining an absolutely single-minded attitude to his own linguistic growth is the presence of certain constant attitudes through the entire oeuvre. He seems to have inherited from his mentor Ives not only a specific interest in the musical representation of simultaneity, but also a general measure of American transcendentalist common sense. With unerring instinct he balances his technical and conceptual flights by keeping several feet firmly on the ground.

When asked after a public lecture why instrumental difficulty seemed an essential ingredient of his music, Carter replied, 'These people spend years practising all of these beautiful instruments, and I feel it's my job to give them something to do on them.' The charming pragmatism of this remark bears fruit time and time again as we sense that here is someone who is literally writing for instruments and not against them – who positively delights in the things instruments can do. And every performer of Carter's music who has gone through all the rigour of learning one of his works for the first time must subsequently have had a feeling of surprise and gratification at how much has remained in the fingers and brain. For all of its difficulty, Carter's music feels right to a performer – the difficulty is justified, exhilarating and intrinsically related to the music's message.

And what helps get the message across is that every work is based on a powerful image that allows Carter to proliferate a density of event and a complexity of form without losing touch with the work's root experience. Very often this image concerns the use of the instruments themselves as the personae of an unstated but unmistakable drama: the unforgettable confrontation of darkness and light represented by the separation of high and low instruments in the slow movement of the *First Quartet*, the 'personalizing' of each instrument within a cadenza and an individual repertory of intervals in the *Second Quartet* (1959), reinforced by a wide spatial positioning on stage, and the confrontation in the *Third Quartet* (1971) of two duos (violin/viola and violin/cello) who play in a 'strict non-relation' to each other throughout the work – in all these cases, the listener's initial impression of linguistic complexity is immediately tempered by the recognition of a tangible intellectual and physical drama which is the more articulate for not being expressed in any overt programme.

Other works depend not on inbuilt dramas, but on the recognition of fundamental images from other areas of experience: the gritty, demanding surface of the *Duo for Violin and Piano* (1974) eventually yields, to reveal a purely instrumental version of a classical *pas de deux*, with the piano and violin taking on the respective qualities of the male and female dancers to an astonishing degree – while the large-scale wave motions of the *Double Concerto* for harpsichord, piano and two chamber orchestras (1961) suggest cosmic rhythms expressive of the formation, flourishing and destruction of the physical universe. And these are aurally and viscerally palpable even without reference to Carter's literary analogue with Lucretius.

All of the music so far discussed is 'absolute' and without text. No one else in our own century has so individually reinterpreted known genres (e.g. *String Quartet, Piano Concerto*, 1965, *Concerto for Orchestra*, 1969, *Symphony of Three Orchestras*, 1976) yet succeeded in restoring so much of their archetypal meaning. To one who has so purposefully achieved this, words come as a well-earned luxury in *A Mirror on which to Dwell* (1975). But Carter would never be content to rest even at this stage of his journey: in *Syringa* (1978) the baritone soloist sings ancient Greek texts about Orpheus while the mezzo-soprano retells the myth in the verse of the American poet John Ashbery, the result being one of Carter's most absorbing studies in simultaneity to date. With *Night Fantasies* (1980) he returns to the medium of solo piano, with which his mature music had begun thirty-five years before.

Stephen Pruslin

Other works include: *The Minotaur* (ballet, 1947); *Wind Quintet* (1950); *Eight Etudes and a Fantasy* (for woodwind quartet, 1950); *Eight Pieces for Four Timpani* (1950, 1966); *Variations for Orchestra* (1955); *Brass Quintet* (1974).

85

CASTANEDA, Carlos 1935–

Brazilian/US anthropologist

Carlos Castaneda was born, by his own account, to a well-known family in Brazil in 1935, his father a professor of literature. After his mother's death, left with the father, his behaviour caused him to be sent to a foster family in Los Angeles. By 1959 he had changed his name to Castaneda. But other evidence states that a Carlos Castaneda entered the US at San Francisco in 1951, that he was Peruvian, born in 1925. He enrolled at Los Angeles City College 1951–9, and gained a doctorate in anthropology at UCLA, based on his

alleged experiences with Don Juan Matus. This is as far as 'Don Juan and the Sorcerer's Apprentice', a pioneer article in *Time*, 5 March 1973, managed to reach, and there it more or less remains. Castaneda's five books – highly influential in America, where by 1973 the first one had sold 300,000 copies in paperback alone, and only to a slightly lesser extent elsewhere – seem now to be a version of the ancient quest for a spiritual or true father, a fiction of considerable renewed significance in an America whose younger generations in the 1970s revolted against the parental establishment. The books delineate the possibilities of white cultural and personal rejuvenation through ancient Indian procedures and beliefs surviving through the isolated Yaqui *brujo* (a term Castaneda translated as 'sorcerer'): *The Teachings of Don Juan: A Yaqui Way of Knowledge* (1968); *A Separate Reality* (1971); *Journey to Ixtlan* (1972); *Tales of Power* (1974); and *The Second Ring of Power* (1978). In 1961, at a time when many young American whites, blacks and Indians were investigating potential changes in both social action and personal consciousness, Castaneda travelled to New Mexico to research Indian medicinal plants. The anthropological student encountered Don Juan, old but active, in his Indian terms 'a man of knowledge'. There followed a first two years of intermittent apprenticeship to 'nonordinary reality', governed by three hallucinogenic plants – peyote, Jimson weed and psilocybe mushrooms. Castaneda's curiosity and rudimentary sense of 'a separate reality' from day-to-day contingency encouraged the old medicine man to train him to states and powers controlled by a combination of plant knowledge, intense awareness of geological environment, and advanced ability to concentrate consciousness with penetration and courage against unknown forces which might possibly become 'allies'. This was, of course, a highly traditional religious practice – the breaking of confidence in the rationally educated life. In the Yaqui reality, men may change into crows; an iridescent coyote talks and moves as both trickster and agent of power; hundred-foot gnats become huge guardians; men cross waterfalls unaided by technology and vanish. The white narrator's strength is to be willing to enter this reality and crumble at least some of his urban sceptical empiricism. Don Juan is not a tribal Indian, however. His survival is a lonely development of perception and 'impeccable will'. The tension in the first four books arises between his belief in a single world of visible and invisible controls, and the white American's divided belief in body and spirit, reality and unreality. Castaneda's narrator is a sceptical Cartesian surprised in the deserts of the South West, and training within an older science vestigial in the heads of Don Juan and his friend Don Gennaro, a Mazatec *brujo*, a training in responsibility for living 'in this marvellous desert, at this marvellous time' (*Journey to Ixtlan*) for the short term of human experience. Perhaps Castaneda's Peruvian ancestry enabled him in part to overcome his education, although this rationalism remains, and it is this kind of possible transformation which appealed to the young and made the first book an underground best-seller. 'A man of knowledge' has to proceed through fear to clarity and power. Fear leaves a man a bully or scared, a defeated entity. Clarity dispels fear but forces a man to doubt himself. He is courageous because he is clear, but he can stop at nothing. He may turn into a buoyant warrior but a clown, or a man who no longer yearns or learns, and 'he cannot tell when or how to use his power' (*The Teachings*). In the final stage, the man of knowledge's action embodies moments of clarity, power and knowledge which remain invisible. Castaneda's apprenticeship is a practice in watching, listening, controlled movement and careful scrutiny of environment. Psychedelic plants give some access to a synthesis of these procedures and to the 'allies'. Experience of flying, passing into and through matter, and loss of the sense of separate identity become parts of a semantic exploration of some seriousness, considering the risks to the body-mind might be severe. Radical changes in the self's boundaries are frightening rather than comforting, as a new fiction emerges to define reality under the aegis of what has been called 'technicians of the sacred'. And the training is less verbal than directly sensuous and psychic (but not erotic until *The Second Ring of Power*): a matter of participatory confrontations rather than textual study.

Matus himself resists personal enquiry but according to Castaneda it roughly emerges that he was born in 1891 and experienced the enforced dispersal of the Yaqui between 1890 and the 1910 revolution in Mexico, during which his parents were murdered by soldiers. He became a nomad, to derive his virtuosic *brujo* resources from several tribal vestiges. Part of his attraction as a hero for young Americans living in a period of interventionist wars and domestic chaos, in a culture reluctant to grant full civil rights to blacks and full tribal rights to Indians, in a society dominated by materialist competition, was Matus's ideal of a man of knowledge as a warrior of aristocratic assurance in leadership, commanding respect through outstanding practical and occult ability. Castaneda, the narrator, is modest about his own learning from Matus, but it is his books that provided an alternative action of confidence for some Americans, offering the image of a man who could really 'see', 'capable of knowledge that the world as we look at it everyday is only a description' (*Ixtlan*). Don Juan, as a character, is presented from notes taken between 1960 and 1962, and between 1968 and 1969. Don Juan himself observes in *Ixtlan*: 'Nobody knows who I am or what I do. Not even I . . . we take everything for sure and real, or we don't. If we follow the first path we get bored to death with ourselves and the world. If we follow the second and erase personal

history, we create a fog around us, a very exciting and mysterious state.' And in the second book: 'One should never reveal the name or whereabouts of a sorcerer. I believe you understand that you should never reveal my name, nor the place where my body is.' In traditional European terms, Matus is a white magician, a Faust without ambitions for political and sexual conquest, and an agent of a world increasingly offered in physics as fields of relatively unknown energy, a world which may require the revaluation of magic, consciousness and religious states. Matus is 'the master of choices' who knows 'how to live strategically'. Such advice is highly suited to the times, especially since it required no allegiance to fixed textual ideologies.

In 1976 appeared *Castaneda's Journey: The Power and the Allegory* by Richard DeMille, claiming that Castaneda's books were (proven) fiction – by which he meant a highly simplified version of that term. While believing that they 'contributed something of value to society', and that Castaneda 'has widely popularized certain metaphysical propositions some people think, including me, are both important and defensible', DeMille finds the first three books inconsistent and indicating that the experience did not 'happen' to Castaneda. This conclusion is broadly supported by Richard Gordon Wasson in *Soma: Divine Mushroom of Immortality* (1968), and by other Indian and drug-mysticism experts. In *Don Juan, Mescalito and Modern Magic* (1978) Nevill Drury takes up DeMille's analysis, compares the world view proposed by Don Juan with others in contemporary western magic, finds parallels, and concludes that 'in view of the doubts raised about Castaneda's originality these parallels might now assume an even greater significance'. But Castaneda's imaginative writing, whether record or fiction, certainly declined with *The Second Ring of Power* in which the narrator remains obstinately half-hearted in his convictions compared with the compelling allegiances of the first three volumes.

Eric Mottram

See also: David Silverman, *Reading Castaneda: A Prologue to the Social Sciences* (1975).

86
CASTRO, Fidel 1926–

Cuban politician

In 1953, a group of young revolutionaries attacked the Moncada Barracks in Santiago de Cuba. The attack failed. One of the participants, a young lawyer named Fidel Castro, was put on trial and delivered in his own defence a long speech, ending with the now famous slogan 'History will absolve me'. He was later to found a movement whose name commemorated Moncada – the 26 July Movement.

The background to that attack provides the key to Castro's own political biography. By the mid-1940s the Cuban Communist Party (PSP) was largely discredited. Its collaboration with the dictator Batista had brought it two ministries, and official control of the trade union movement which it retained under the presidencies of Prio Socarras and Grau (1944–52). For some sections of workers, this had brought considerable economic benefit; but the price had been a depoliticized working-class movement. Political opposition, therefore, was largely limited to student and petit-bourgeois sectors ranged around the student Directorio and Eduardo Chibas's Ortodoxo group. It was there that Castro received his political education. As a young man he had participated in the Directorio's abortive attempted invasion of the Dominican Republic (in 1947). In 1952, he was an Ortodoxo candidate for the elections, which were pre-empted by Batista's military coup.

For Castro, that experience demonstrated the futility of parliamentary politics. It convinced him that social change could only occur through the dedicated action of professional, armed revolutionaries. The political alterrative of a mass oppositional movement led by the working class was not on the agenda for Castro's generation.

In his 1953 speech, Fidel presented a programme for radical reform and economic development within a capitalist mould; the same policy was reiterated in his 'Sierra Maestra Declaration' of 1957. Both speeches revealed a deep suspicion of the Communists, and he did not invite them to join the united opposition formed in Miami in 1957.

Released from prison in 1955, Castro went to Mexico where he organized a guerilla group. In 1956 the group of eighty landed from the *Granma* and was met by an army ambush from which only twenty escaped. These twenty then launched the guerilla war against Batista from the Sierra Maestra mountains. By late 1957 a second front was formed by Raul Castro.

The 26 July Movement was a rural guerilla; its urban support came from Directorio members, who launched two partially successful general strikes in 1956 and April 1958, the latter with (reluctant) PSP support. Castro's main base, however, lay with the peasantry. He was aided by the internal collapse of Batista's regime and the US refusal to give it active support. By January 1959 the dictator had fled and Castro controlled Cuba.

The political ambiguity of the Movement now clearly had to be resolved. Throughout 1959, Castro responded to the immediate needs of the Revolution with a series of shifts in position that followed the balance of political forces. His own politics were still undefined, though the first trade union conference of the Move-ment purged the more right-wing, anti-Communist elements. This obvious attempt to conciliate the PSP stemmed from Castro's recognition that working-class and trade union support would be critical in the process of reconstruction.

Yet, at this stage, Castro was not a Communist. He remained suspicious of the PSP, and many American liberals hastened to point this out to the US government, urging reconciliation. None the less, the first expropriations brought official hostility and, in February 1960, relations were severed. Russian aid thus became a necessity; by 1961 it was running at one million dollars a day.

Henceforth, and especially after his declaration of 1961 that Cuba's was a 'Marxist-Leninist' revolution, relations with Russia were the key to Castro's political behaviour. After the 1962 Missile Crisis, Castro became critical of Soviet policy and moved closer to Guevara's* alternative strategy for economic growth and the extension of the Revolution into Latin America. After 1963, the rejection of the Russian model led Castro to enthusiastic support for OLAS, the Tricontinental Conference of 1965, the Cultural Congress and the Revolutionary Offensive, 1968. These were clear indications of a shift away from Russia (and the PSP) and towards the Guevarist alternative.

Two main considerations underlay Castro's political decisions: first, Cuba's economic survival; and second, its political independence. This has led him to adopt contradictory and changing positions. For while the second entails a high level of popular involvement in the revolutionary process, the first – especially after the failure of the Latin American guerillas – brought an increasingly close relationship with the Soviet Union. As a consequence, the Cuban Communist Party's role grew in significance. Castro's spirited defence of Russia at the Algiers Conference of 1970 and his support for the Soviet invasion of Czechoslovakia were responses to a perceived political reality.

In the Second Declaration of Havana, Castro stressed the need for mass participation in the Revolution; yet in the twenty years since 1959 there has been an increasing concentration of power and control in Cuba. By 1979, Castro was Secretary of the CCP, President and Chief of the Armed Forces. The organs of popular involvement, in their turn, have become organs of the State.

There is no evidence that Castro is anything other than a sincere revolutionary; his personal life-style is Spartan, his popularity undisputed. Yet his characteristic political pragmatism has led him to adopt widely differing positions and finally to compromise Cuban political independent in pursuit of economic growth. The 1979 Conference of Non-Aligned Nations and Cuban intervention in Africa show how far Cuba has been absorbed into the Russian ambit, both economically and politically.

Undoubtedly, Castro has led Cuba to a higher standard of living; yet Cuba remains dependent. Ironically, the Cuban Communist Party, with Castro at its head, governs Cuba now. Its political perspectives offer little promise of realizing that self-emancipation of the Cuban people that Castro promised in his earlier, less pragmatic, days.

Mike Gonzalez

See: *History will absolve me* (1967); *Fidel Castro Speaks* (1970); also H. Matthews, *Castro, a Political Biography* (1969).

87
CAVAFY, Constantine Peter 1863–1933

Greek poet

Cavafy was born into a Greek mercantile family in Alexandria, the city in which he lived most of his life and which he developed into a mythical universe in his poetry. After his father's death his mother took him to England, where they lived from 1872 until about 1877. After a spell in Istanbul (1882–5), he settled permanently in Alexandria, working as a clerk in the Irrigation Office, a job which allowed him plenty of free time.

A highly individual poet, Cavafy is known for his 'historical' and 'erotic' (homosexual) poems; a collection of 154 short poems appeared soon after his death.

Cavafy worked on his poetry without the help of a tradition; in Alexandria there was little Greek literary life in his early years, and he was not suited temperamentally to the folksy lyricism of his Athenian contemporaries. Thus he was a late developer. Some of his early verses are in English; his early Greek poems, influenced by Parnassianism, have Homeric or classical subjects. Though some of his earlier poems are among his most famous ('*I Polis*', 'The City'; '*Perimenondas tous Varvarous*', 'Waiting for the Barbarians'), he wrote consistently good poems only after finally crystallizing his style around 1911. From then on his 'historical' poems find the setting which he most favoured: Alexandria and the Greek world in general during the Hellenistic period. From then on, too, his 'erotic' poems become explicitly homosexual.

These two categories are, however, not mutually exclusive; some of his 'historical' poems contain a clear erotic element. In his historical poems Cavafy's world is one in which the Hellenistic kings and queens of Egypt and Syria try to come to terms with Roman domination; but it is also full of fictitious youths who are usually scholarly as well as handsome and who are either described with affectionate admiration by a contemporary or made to speak proudly for themselves about their hedonistic attitude to life. By contrast, the modern youths of the 'erotic' poems are shown going furtively about their amorous activities, of which the prudish society of the day disapproves.

The influences on his historical poems range from the epigrams of the Greek Anthology to more modern poets such as Browning; in his erotic poems he was one of the first writers of modern times to write of homosexual love, and in this again he was influenced by Hellenistic poetry. Cavafy has a tragic view of life: the individual is the victim of an inexorable fate, which brings failure and subjugation to his historical characters and enforced parting to the modern lovers. The irony of fate, however, brings with it a measure of humour, especially when Cavafy is deflating some pompous figure who is blissfully unaware of his impending doom. In the erotic poems, the tragic view is tempered by a belief in the power of art to complete what in life is fleeting and fragmentary.

Cavafy has been a major influence on Greek poetry, and he is the best known modern Greek poet abroad, where his influence has spread not only to literature (the *Alexandria Quartet* by Lawrence Durrell is a case in point), but to the work of David Hockney*.

Peter Mackridge

Poems: C. P. Cavafy, *Collected Poems*, trans. Edmund Keeley and Philip Sherrard (1975); *Passions and Ancient Days*, trans. Edmund Keeley and George Savidis (1971). Biography: Robert Liddell, *Cavafy: A Critical Biography* (1974). Critical studies: Peter Bien, *Constantine Cavafy* (1964); Edmund Keeley, *Cavafy's Alexandria* (1976).

88
CELAN, Paul (Paul Anczel) 1920–70

Austrian poet

Celan was born of Jewish parents in Czernovitz, Rumania. On leaving school he went to study medicine in Tours, France, but returned home some six months later to study Romance languages and literature at the University there. In 1941 Czernovitz, which had in the previous year become part of the Soviet Union, was occupied by German and Rumanian troops. Celan was confined to a ghetto and his parents sent to a concentration camp, from which they never returned. After escaping from the ghetto Celan spent some time in a work-camp in Rumania, but returned to Czernovitz in December 1943 to resume his studies. In 1945 he moved to Bucharest where he worked as a translator and publisher's reader and where his first poems appeared in the Rumanian periodical *Agora*. Celan moved to Vienna in December 1947, but in July of the following year decided to settle in Paris, where he lived for the rest of his life. Here he studied German Literature and Linguistics, gaining his L. ès L. in 1950, and then working for a time as a language assistant in German at the École Normale Supérieure. Also in 1950 he married the graphic artist Gisèle Lestrange, by whom he had one son. His first volume of poems, *Mohn und Gedächtnis* ('Poppy and Memory'), incorporating much material from an earlier, inaccurately printed and withdrawn volume, *Der Sand aus den Urnen* ('The Sand from the Urns', 1948), appeared in Germany in 1952 and was followed three years later by *Von Schwelle zu Schwelle* ('From Threshold to Threshold'). Further volumes (whose titles, the reader should be warned, are often very difficult to translate) are *Sprachgitter* ('Language grid' or 'grille', 1959); *Die Niemandsrose* ('The No-one's Rose', 1963); *Atemwende* ('Breath-solstice', 1967); *Fadensonnen* ('Thread-Suns', 1968); *Lichtzwang* ('Light-compulsion', 1970); and, posthumously, *Schneepart* ('Snow-part', 1971) and *Zeitgehöft* ('Time-farmyard', 1976). Celan also published many translations of poems by, among others, Shakespeare (Sonnets), Valéry* (*La Jeune Parque*), Supervielle, Michaux, André du Bouchet, Blok, Mandelstam* and Essenin. He committed suicide in 1970 by drowning in the Seine.

Celan's earlier work, especially in his first volume, contains a strong musical element: there is a predilection for flowing, dactylic rhythms and a certain psalm-like, incantatory quality: so that one has the impression of a voice singing out of a dream-world in which racial memories, memories of the dead and the difficulties of love endlessly preoccupy the dreamer and where, in a neo-Surrealistic manner, there are no barriers between the real and the imagined, the concrete and the abstract. Each poem exists within the world of a few land-marking images, but those images are frequently recurrent: simple, archetypal images – eye, water, stone, sister, king, almond, etc., recurring in ever-differing combinations which give the poems a certain obsessive quality. A transition occurs in Celan's third volume, *Sprachgitter*. A year after the publication of this, Celan received the coveted Georg Büchner Prize and delivered at the ceremony the speech entitled *Der Meridian*, one of his few quasi-theoretical utterances on the nature of his poetry. Starting out from the final scene of Büchner's play *Danton's Death*, Celan considers the role of what he calls 'das Gegenwort': the counter-word, that affirmation of the absurd, of what is contrary to living experience – absence, non-being, death – which is central to poetry. But death implies silence; and any poet who sets out, as Celan so often does, to explore the realm of the dead must inevitably arrive at a point where language and silence meet. But silence can also be arrived at by another route familiar to the modern poet – the feeling that language is no longer adequate to master the complexities of experience. Hence Celan expresses his conviction that the modern poem shows, as he puts it, 'eine starke Neigung zum Verstummen' ('a strong tendency to fall mute'); that it only just subsists at the very verge of its own extinction: 'It constantly calls and recalls itself from no-longer-existing into only-just-existing.' And yet, perhaps paradoxically, it is this only-just-existing which testifies to its humanity: for the poem, Celan insists, is not a self-sufficient entity, but an encounter, 'a conversation – often a desperate conversation'. At the same time, it is an exploration, itself precarious, like a boat which may at any moment be overwhelmed by the storm.

With these points in mind, one may perhaps see why Celan, from his third volume onwards, rejects the overt virtuosity of his earlier work in favour of an extremely tentative mode of utterance where the reader is almost as conscious of the spaces around the words as of the words themselves, which in turn are often cryptic or fragmented. Enjambement is frequent, but suggests not so much an energy striving against the poem's metrical constraints as the fact that the very act of utterance must proceed with extreme caution.

Celan's work has sometimes been described as hermetic and few would disagree that many of his poems – especially those of the later volumes – seem reluctant to release their secrets, or that Celan may fairly claim to be the most difficult European poet since Mallarmé. Yet his is a poetry springing from a concrete historical situation, that of the persecution of the Jews by the Nazis and, by natural extension, from Jewish – particularly Hasidic – legend and thought. As motto to one of his poems, Celan uses a phrase from the Russian poetess, Marina Zwetajewa: 'All poets are Jews.' This may have a number of implications: that all poets are outcasts, critics of the civilization in which they live, practitioners of legend or forgers of links between actuality and myth. The difficulties of Celan's work – the allusions and ambiguities, the often *recherché* terminology and the deliberate contradictions – are inherent in the very nature of his enterprise: for, from a position which might very roughly be described as *engagé*, Celan moves to the much deeper commitment of probing the nature of the expressive power both of language and of its opposite, silence.

Corbet Stewart

See: *Gedichte* (2 vols, Suhrkamp Verlag, Frankfurt, 1976); in English: *Selected Poems*, trans. Michael Hamburger and Christopher Middleton (1972).

89
CÉLINE, Louis-Ferdinand (L.-F. Destouches)
1894–1961

French novelist

One of the most controversial figures in modern literature, Céline was almost forty before he adopted his pseudonym and burst on to the literary scene with his *Journey to the End of the Night* (*Voyage au bout de la nuit*, 1932, trans. 1934). Born into the relative poverty of a struggling petit-bourgeois family, he left school early but determinedly continued to study in his spare time. In 1912 he enlisted in the army, was wounded in 1914 and invalided out. By 1924 he qualified as a doctor and during the following years travelled widely, transposing his experiences into that first novel, which caused a major stir on its appearance. A second novel, *Death on the Instalment Plan* (*Mort à crédit*, 1936, trans. 1938), was followed by the virulently racialist pamphlets *Bagatelles pour un massacre* ('Mere trifles for a massacre', 1937) and *L'École des cadavres* ('School for corpses', 1938). Regarded as an out-and-out collaborator, Céline fled Paris in 1944 and acted as official doctor to the French Vichyite colony in Sigmaringen. Subsequently he lived in exile in Denmark until, amnestied in 1951, he returned to France where he carried on his double life as doctor and writer until his death. Three major works, *Castle to Castle* (*D'un château à autre*, 1957, trans. 1968), *North* (*Nord*, 1960, trans. 1972) and *Rigodon* (1969, trans. 1975), date from these final years.

Céline's reputation has suffered from the violently expressed anti-semitism of his pre-war pamphlets, and debate still rages over the extent of his racialism. Until recently, only the novels written before the pamphlets were highly regarded; a current critical revaluation is, however, placing greater emphasis on the later writing. Nevertheless, in many respects that first *Journey* remains his finest achievement: none of the later narratives can match the breadth of experience it covers – a black, all-but-nihilistic, picaresque quest for total lucidity fictively reworking Céline's experiences in the absurdity of war, in the disease-and-exploitation-ridden tropics, in the barely more subtle alienation of the United States, and finally as a doctor amidst poverty in France. The novel turns around the two poles of human existence, war and sickness; the omnipresent music of death is evoked with paradoxical vitality by Céline's remarkable, innovatory style, borrowing the rhythms, structures and slang of popular speech but artistically heightening them to intense literary effect. The result – to be extended and radicalized in subsequent works – is a highly original language of Rabelaisian vigour, admirably fitted to the expression of extreme subjectivity, yet countering the grimness of the vision with a resilient humour reminiscent of Villon.

Whilst the novels, from *Journey* to *Rigodon*, use the material of the author's life, it would be misleading to take them as directly autobiographical: his avowed method was to 'blacken everything, oneself included', producing 'not slices of life, but delirium'. As a result, the novels slide hauntingly between unflinching realism and hallucination. The sense of persecution that underlies the *Journey* is heightened in *Death on the Instalment Plan*, where the style becomes correspondingly more exclamatory and vehement. It is doubtless this sense of persecution that drove Céline to the inexcusable folly of his own racialist mythology. And the tendency to write within a global myth of persecution acts as a limitation in the later narrative works, whose subject is chiefly the wanderings of Céline on his flight from France, the obsessive exposition of 'a certain way of existing, neither wholly fictive nor wholly real' for which his visionary method and style are admirably suited. There is a dehumanization in the final works, despite the sledgehammer power of certain passages and the ever-inventive language.

Céline remains an enigma: a man who could pour scorn on both writing and medicine and yet devote all his life to practising both; who professed cynicism and racialism but often betrayed pity for the defenceless; who saw the world as a place of sickness, cruelty and death, but delighted in the grace and beauty of dance (and wrote ballets as well as black novels); who was obsessed by persecution but seemed to court it single-mindedly. And who, finally, wrote untiringly to exorcize man's inhumanity by telling it all, going to the end of night and forging a new language to express what he found there, yet fell into the trap of contributing to that very inhumanity. His work shows how disturbingly narrow is the dividing-line between vision and paranoia.

David Meakin

Other works: *Guignol's Band, I* (1944); *Guignol's Band, II* (1963); *Féerie pour une autre fois* ('Fairyland for some other Time', 1952); *Normance* (1954); See: E. Ostrovsky, *Céline and his Vision* (1967); A. Thiher, *Céline: The Novel as Delirium* (1972); P. McCarthy, *Céline* (1975).

90
CHAGALL, Marc 1887–

Russian/French painter

Born at Vitebsk in western Russian, Chagall inherited the myths and traditions of folk legends, Jewish lore and the imagery of Russian orthodox churches. To this vital source, Chagall has brought the sophisticated practices of Parisian art. Chagall's paintings have evoked emotion and a poetic sense of beauty that they have drawn from direct experience: for Chagall painting has, of necessity, been an autobiographic activity, even when his themes as such are not directly observed. He has made of narrative paintings so succinct a vehicle for his emotional and spiritual life that their density and brilliance of colour, and even their supernatural or fantastic subjects, appear mischievous, rapturous or even epic. It is, however, for all his originality, a mistake to see Chagall out of context. He was first a student under Jehuda Pen in Vitebsk, and the Jewish community at Vitebsk, with which Chagall was closely associated, provided themes, such as the fiddler on the roof, to which Chagall was to return many times. In 1907 Chagall entered the Imperial School for the Encouragement of the Arts in St Petersburg where the love of decoration and of lavish colour characteristic of his tutor, Léon Bakst, served to confirm this tendency in Chagall's work although the elegance of Bakst found no reflection in the fierce individuality of Chagall's early works. Bakst also encouraged a lasting love of the theatre in Chagall, an outlet that has provided a regular activity for Russian painters. In this respect Chagall seems to have approached the *World of Art* circle whose cosmopolitan outlook did much to make Chagall more aware of French Post-Impressionist painting. On the other hand the ostensibly natural primitivism of Chagall's early work, its roughness and directness of expression, places him closer to the cultivated primitivism of such Russian contemporaries as Larionov, Goncharova and Malevich*. In this respect Chagall's fantastic themes appear less the products of an extraordinary and isolated imagination and more a lively contribution to a current vogue. The apparently unconventional qualities of his paintings frequently obscure the intellectual as well as emotional effort that has produced them. When Chagall travelled to Paris in 1910, living in the studio complex known as La Ruche, he found himself at the centre of a changing group of Russian artists and writers who had the most intimate links with French literary and artistic pioneers, among them Apollinaire*, Delaunay, Cendrars, Picasso*. Chagall's *Self Portrait with Seven Fingers* painted in Paris sums up his union of dreams of Russia with urban Paris, and of primitive painting with the devices of Cubism.

Upon the outbreak of war in 1914 Chagall returned to Russia, where particularly after the Revolutions of 1917, his achievement was recognized and his talents employed. He designed murals, sets and costumes for Granowsky's Moscow Jewish Theatre and was placed in control of the art-activities, teaching and exhibitions of Vitebsk. His paintings of this Russian period are exquisite evocations of Vitebsk, of rural Russian-Jewish life and of the elation of his relationship with Bella, his wife.

Chagall returned to Paris in 1922, retaining his extraordinary individuality and increasing his vocabulary of themes, potent images, some Jewish, some Christian and all suggestively powerful, that he characteristically isolated as being of importance to his expression. Their autobiographical sources were developed into more broadly applicable human themes. The breadth of Chagall's humanity in this sense is a central feature of his achievement. In 1933 he published the autobiographical *Ma Vie* in French (trans. *My Life*, 1965). He had seen his first retrospective exhibition in Paris in 1924 and his French links became extremely strong, alongside the Russian and Jewish elements of his identity and cultural life. Despite the fantastic features of his painting, Chagall remained unaffected by the Surrealist movement whose founding manifesto was published in Paris in 1924. Yet during the later 1930s his work reflected political developments and in particular the suffering of the Jews. In 1939 he was invited to New York by the Museum of Modern Art there and did not return to France until 1944.

If there are elements of his work that recall the grotesque fantasy of Nikolai Gogol's stories, there are elements also that recall Apollinaire or Cendrars. Chagall has become an international public figure whose ability to raise personal experience to a broadly human expression has made him brilliant in the execution of public works devoid of the ballast of affectation. His book designed for Vollard, his stained glass windows, his theatrical design and his colossal ceiling painting for the Paris Opera, unveiled in 1964, testify to his broadening scope and his indefatigable vitality.

Dr John Milner

See: J. J. Sweeney, *Marc Chagall* (1946); F. Meyer, *Marc Chagall* (1961); Jean Cassou, *Chagall* (1965).

91

CHANDLER, Raymond Thornton 1888–1959

US thriller writer

Raymond Chandler was born in Chicago but educated largely in England, at Dulwich College. After a period in London and service during the First World War in France he returned to America and worked at a variety of jobs (including the vice-presidency of a group of oil companies) before becoming a full-time writer in early middle age. Chandler did not create the detective story format but adapted it from the 'pulp' magazines of the 1930s, in particular the *Black Mask*, to which he contributed. His most notable predecessor is Dashiell Hammett, author of *The Maltese Falcon* (1930). The private eye, the lone and usually lonely individual who battles against a society and solves a mystery which springs from its corruption, can be traced back in some form at least as far as Edgar Allan Poe's amateur detective Auguste Dupin. Chandler found insulting and distasteful the sterile contrivance and lack of realism that characterized the so-called Gold Age of detective fiction, the early twentieth century. In his essay 'The Simple Art of Murder' (*Atlantic Monthy*, 1944) he claims that Hammett 'took murder out of the Venetian vase and dropped it into the alley'. In preferring the squalid-glamorous to the genteel Chandler was following an increasingly confident American tradition.

For his locale Chandler used Los Angeles, as far away in spirit as it was possible to get from murder in the English vicarage. Mystification rather than the neat, logical problems set by an Agatha Christie; a range of social types rather than the upper middle-class inhabitants of the drawing-room; a laconic and witty style, and a certain disconnectedness in narrative, instead of the pedestrian parade of suspects and motives – these were some of the ways in which Chandler broke from the standard English and American whodunnit. In California he found an atmosphere as much as a setting, one that appealed to the strong elements of romanticism and exoticism in him. Philip Marlowe, his hero, appears in seven novels; having found a satisfactory vehicle for his and his readers' fantasies, Chandler developed Marlowe little. 'Down these mean streets a man must go who is not himself mean, who is neither tarnished nor afraid': the famous rhapsody to the private-eye-as-hero describes a figure who is recognizable from the first novel, *The Big Sleep* (1939), to the last, *Playback* (1958). The format too hardly varies. Marlowe is approached by a client, accepts the case with weary charity, and pursues his quest, usually in search of a missing person, over dead bodies, through the estates and dubious private clinics of the rich, in the interrogation rooms of corrupt police forces, in the bars and boulevards of Los Angeles and its environs. Throughout Marlowe retains his independence, signified by his obstinacy in upholding his client's interests in the face of threats, bribes and sexual temptation. This quixoticism – it is significant that one of Marlowe's earlier incarnations in the pulp magazine period was named Mallory, recalling the author of *Morte d'Arthur* – reaches its peak in Chandler's most ambitious and substantial novel, *The Long Goodbye* (1953), the plot of which turns on Marlowe's irrational and unrewarded loyalty to a male friend. In the sexually ambiguous nature of their friendship, in the lengthy portrait of another character, an alcoholic writer whose survival and eventual death are in some way dependent on the hero, we see the closest approach between the author and his creation. In the later novels, apart from the atypical *Playback*, Marlowe also becomes more sententious, more invulnerable to temptation and perhaps less plausible. The direct and laconic style which owes something to Hemingway*, the wisecracking, the startling similes for which Chandler is noted are to be found in their most unalloyed forms in the earlier novels. It becomes clear in retrospect that the claims of realism Chandler made for the genre are only partially valid; that the Philip Marlowe novels are as stylized, ordered and remote from everyday experience as the classical detective stories of which Chandler was so disdainful. But his books skilfully embody certain heroic fantasies, being witty, tough and compassionate while remaining always loyal, to an inner unstated conception of integrity, being able to move easily in any level of a tainted society.

Philip Gooden

Chandler's other novels include: *Farewell, My Lovely* (1940); *The High Window* (1942); *The Lady in the Lake* (1943); *The Little Sister* (1949). See also: Frank MacShane, *The Life of Raymond Chandler* (1976); and *The World of Raymond Chandler*, ed. Miriam Gross (1977).

92
CHANEL, Gabrielle ('Coco') 1883–1971

French fashion designer

If modern fashion has a source, that source is indisputably Coco Chanel. More than any other designer she was responsible for relating looks to the new social attitudes which evolved during the first decades of the century, in particular the demands of women for greater social and economic independence.

Up until the First World War 'fashion' was generally restricted to the upper classes, where male values were dominant and ladies were not expected to work. Clothes were designed to exaggerate the female figure, making use of corsets, bones, basques, décolletages, hobble skirts and delicate fabrics which inhibited easy movement as well as comfort. However, those women who had participated in the war effort, were afterwards reluctant to resume their passive roles in society. This both reflected and reinforced the women's movement.

It was against this background that Chanel introduced her 'little boy look', *la mode garçonne*, a style that has intermittently controlled women's clothing ever since. A statement of sexual equality, it was a curiously ambiguous revolution since many of the individual designs were adapted from menswear. Breasts and hips disappeared and were replaced by simple lines in 'masculine' fabrics, such as flannel and tweed, that were easy to wear, easy to care for, and hardwearing. Equally Chanel popularized round-toed shoes, cloth coats and the colour black, each previously associated with peasant dress – another new look which Paul Poiret* characterized as 'poverty de luxe'.

Chanel's aim was always to provide practical clothes for living and working in, claiming, 'I care more about the city street than the drawing room.' Her styles were widely copied at every social level, and thus mass fashion was born. For the old snobbery of class and wealth she had substituted a new snobbery of youth, the 'young look', a bias that is still pervasive among contemporary designers.

In her own life Chanel epitomized the New Woman, free and independent in every sense. The daughter of an itinerant pedlar, she was raised in an orphanage, but later attracted the attention of several wealthy patrons. Despite a series of much-publicized liaisons she never married. When questioned about her rejection of a famous suitor, she once explained: 'There have been many Duchesses of Westminster, but there is only one Coco Chanel.'

Kaori O'Connor

Pierre Galant, *Mademoiselle Chanel* (1953); Marcel Haedrich, *Coco Chanel* (1972); Edmonde Charles-Roux, *L'Irrégulière* (1974, trans. as *Chanel* by Nancy Amphoux, 1975).

93

CHAPLIN, Charles Spencer 1889–1977

British/US film actor and director

Born into a family of struggling music hall entertainers, Chaplin experienced the ugly, poverty-stricken side of Victorian London in his childhood which undoubtedly contributed greatly to his 'little tramp' and his narrative settings. By the time he was approached by Mack Sennett in 1913, Chaplin had finished a long apprenticeship in the English music halls and was the star of Fred Karno's vaudeville 'Mumming Birds company'. Chaplin made thirty-five shorts for Sennett and as early as the second had evolved the costume for which he is famous: little bowler, tiny coat, baggy pants, and cane. 'Tillie's Punctured Romance' made him a star in 1914 and he left Sennett shortly after to work for Essenay, then Mutual, and First National. Chaplin quickly became one of the richest and most popular stars in Hollywood, and perhaps the only one to gain any prestige for the infant art form among intellectuals, earning praise from critics as diverse as T. S. Eliot* and Gilbert Seldes. In 1920 Chaplin directed his first feature-length film, *The Kid*. In 1923 he joined United Artists which he had helped Douglas Fairbanks, Mary Pickford, and D. W. Griffith* to form in 1919. Although he made his first sound films in 1931 (*City Lights*) and 1936 (*Modern Times*), Chaplin refused to allow any dialogue. Sound seems to discourage Chaplin, perhaps as representative of the modern technology and values that seemed so far away from his Victorian youth. His films became fewer and fewer. In 1940 he made *The Great Dictator*, a satire on Hitler* that probably earned him that unusual label from the American right of 'premature fascist'. His blackest comedy *Monsieur Verdoux*, a story about a Bluebeard-type murderer with a pacifist subtheme, was released in 1947. The overly sentimental *Limelight* (1952) was set in the London of his childhood and featured a guest appearance by his great comedic rival Buster Keaton*. His last two films, *A King in New York* (1957) and *A Countess from Hong Kong* (1967), were kindly ignored by the majority of critics and audiences.

Throughout his career in the United States Chaplin was pursued by controversy and court cases, first in his sensational marriage and divorce to teenage co-star Lita Grey (resulting in an underground best-seller called *Complaints of Lita Grey* based on the divorce proceedings); then his 1944 indictment under the Mann Act for which a jury eventually acquitted him on the fourth vote; and finally a September 1952 order from the Attorney General's office to refuse Chaplin re-admittance to the country under the undesirable aliens clause Section 137, Paragraph (c) of Title 8 of the US Code. Chaplin had been named many times as a 'commie' or left-winger by witnesses in the notorious Hollywood purge by the House Committee on Un-American Activities. *Limelight* was picketed by the American Legion and Chaplin did not return from his 1952 European vacation until the end of the 1970s when Hollywood offered him a belated award. Chaplin's bitterness at this ludicrous political purge deprived Americans of any chance to see his major features for the better part of two decades since he owned the rights to them (except *The Gold Rush*) and refused to allow them to be shown in America. Slowly he relented and the films became more available in the 1970s.

Chaplin's genius can best be compared with that of the great nineteenth-century stage producer/star who knew exactly how best to mount a production to show-case his particular talents. From the very beginning Chaplin somehow understood that the 'Keystone style' was too frenetic and he played against this prevailing mode with an infinitely more graceful and restrained style that quickly separated him from his cohorts who mugged and jumped their way into history in the homogeneous and anonymous Keystone style. Chaplin's Victorian roots became more and more evident as he moved from shorts into feature films. He offered himself as Everyman, an innocent victim, unconquerable idealist, and sentimental unrequited lover. His scripts were almost always episodic, absurdly sentimental, and outrageously simplistic. Yet his physical grace, his pantomime, his impregnable optimism, and irresistible wistfulness always seemed to overcome the dated vehicles in the minds of his audiences.

His career as a director, however, emphasizes his limitation as a film-maker while continuing to enhance his reputation as a performer. *The Kid* made a star out of child actor Jackie Coogan and wrung tears from every child-loving American and hardly anyone noticed that the situations and characters seemed ludicrous in the beginnings of the Jazz Age and the Angst following the slaughter in the just-ended war. *The Gold Rush* (1925) underlined his habit of worshipping young women without reason or realism while demonstrating how little he had noticed the technical and visual advances in cinema since his career began twelve years earlier. One has only to look at Keaton's *The General*, made in the same year, to see how Chaplin was falling behind as a director. Yet no one will ever forget Charlie sitting down to eat his boot with shoestrings as spaghetti or the parody of Robert Service in the saloon scenes. *City Lights* emphasizes his essentially Victorian sentimentalism with its street-ballad plot of the poor blind girl who befriends the little tramp and deserts him in the end. Chaplin's dramatic structure rarely escapes the obvious excesses of nineteenth-century melodrama even thirty or forty years into the twentieth century. *Modern Times* is perhaps his richest attempt to deal with contemporary issues although he stubbornly refuses to use dialogue. The early sequences of the Chaplin tramp caught up in the super-modern factory machinery and eventually leading – by accident – a radical demonstration were superseded by concentration on the gamine figure that obsesses Chaplin throughout his career. Thus Chaplin's social observations are overwhelmed by the female entanglements that ensnare the tramp far more totally than any technology can do. Even Chaplin's most tightly organized script, *Monsieur Verdoux*, suffers from a few gratuitous episodes and lacklustre camera movement and editing. Verdoux himself, however, is that much more moving as a man out of place in his own time, a gentleman murderer in an age of mass murderers. Verdoux's last moments before execution are a fitting epitaph for Chaplin's own career. After dismissing the priest with the words, 'I am at peace with God, my conflict is with man,' he decides to accept the offer of a glass of rum because he has never tried rum before. Then he takes the long walk to the prison courtyard, the last road the little tramp will ever walk because the horizon has become a stone wall.

Professor Charles Gregory

See: *Charlie Chaplin's Own Story* (1916); *My Autobiography* (1964). See also: Louis Delluc, *Charlie Chaplin* (1922); Theodore Huff, *Charlie Chaplin* (1951); Robert Payne, *The Great God Pan: A Biography of the Tramp played by Charles Chaplin* (1952); Isabel Quigley, *Charlie Chaplin: Early Comedies* (1968); Donald W. McCaffrey, *Focus on Chaplin* 9 (1971).

94
CHESTERTON, Gilbert Keith 1874–1936

English writer

G. K. Chesterton was born into a middle-class suburban family, sufficiently well off to pay for his education at St Paul's, then among the more liberal English public schools, and at London University. A career in journalism gave Chesterton mastery over one of his favourite literary forms, the essay, whether as a reviewer, parliamentary commentator or *feuilletoniste*,

and he soon became the most popular essayist of his day, upheld as a model to the generations of English schoolchildren between the death of Queen Victoria and the end of the Second World War. During the early days of broadcasting his piping voice became as well-known as the high-pitched tones of Wells*, the urbanities of Beerbohm* or Shaw's* carefully nurtured brogue, and he enjoyed comparable status as a 'literary man', enhanced by his obesity and eccentric touches of dress.

Despite several attempts to resuscitate his reputation, Chesterton has become something of a choice curiosity, to be savoured either as an exercise in nostalgia by those loyal to the English public school tradition, or by English and American Catholics in their more defensive moods. His lifelong friend was Hilaire Belloc, and the two (often identified by the public as the singular 'Chesterbelloc') not only shared a profound dislike of the Wellsian socialism they saw as threatening to engulf national life, but emphasized their Catholic allegiance as part of a notional 'Englishness' based on a distinctly partial view of vanished rural life centred in the sort of romantically envisaged Sussex Arcadia described by their contemporary Kipling*.

Unlike Belloc, whose viewpoint was essentially that of the late nineteenth-century French right, Chesterton advocated a kind of liberal reaction springing from the energies of the working class who, freed from synthetic socialism, would return to their cottage gardens – a vision reflected in the famous line 'We are the people of England and we have not spoken yet.' Catholic sentimentality, allied with a vivid, unforced handling of language and a considerable talent for characterization in a few deft strokes, are the outstanding features of *The Man who was Thursday* (1905), Chesterton's finest novel, and the five collections of short stories devoted to *Father Brown*, priest and amateur detective (1911–35). Apart from providing another link in the intriguing connection of Catholic writers with the whodunnit (e.g. Arthur Conan Doyle, Agatha Christie and Graham Greene*), the stories take a typically 'Chesterbelloc' stance in emphasizing intuition over logical deduction.

The cynical may perhaps decide that Chesterton's reputation depends too heavily on the loyalty of his co-religionists, such as Graham Greene, over whom he may be thought to have exerted an influence. He does deserve to be read, however, as a trenchant literary critic (his short book on *Robert Browning*, 1903, remains the best yet written on the poet), a pithy and wide-ranging essayist, a passable poet in the Kipling – Masefield – Drinkwater vein, and the writer of a handful of good novels and short stories.

Jonathan Keates

Other fiction: *The Napoleon of Notting Hill Gate* (1904); *The Club of Queer Trades* (1905). See also: *Charles*

Dickens (1906); *George Bernard Shaw* (1909); *William Cobbett* (1925) – monographs; *Autobiography* (1936); Christopher Hollis, *The Mind of Chesterton* (1970); John Sullivan (ed.), *G. K. Chesterton, a Centenary Appraisal* (1974).

95

CHILDE, Vere Gordon 1892–1957

Australian prehistorian

Gordon Childe graduated brilliantly in Latin, Greek and Philosophy at Sydney University in 1913. At Oxford he took a B.Litt. in archaeology in 1916 and obtained First Class Honours in Literae Humaniores in 1917. Back in Sydney he joined the Australian Union of Democratic Control, became deeply involved in the anti-conscription movement, and was eventually barred from university employment because of his left-wing views. He was employed as a civil servant in Sydney and London by the first Labour Government of New South Wales, but its fall left him virtually jobless. Disillusioned with the state of politics in Australia, Childe returned to England in 1922, determined to pursue an archaeological career, and travelled widely in Europe, visiting museums and archaeological sites. His first book, *How Labour Governs*, a scathing indictment of Labour politics in Australia, was published in 1923.

In 1925 Childe became Assistant Librarian at the Royal Anthropological Institute, London. Two years later he was appointed the first Professor of Prehistoric Archaeology at Edinburgh University. He remained there until 1946 when he became Professor of Prehistoric European Archaeology and Director of London University's Institute of Archaeology. He retired in 1956 and died in Australia.

In 1925 Childe published *The Dawn of European Civilization* which immediately placed him in the front rank of European prehistorians. Taking the concept of an archaeological culture as a recurrent assemblage of archaeological types, Childe proposed a series of culture sequences for the European Neolithic and earlier Bronze Ages which linked specific areas together and related them to the archaeology of the South West Orient. This interpretation was extended in a remarkable sequence of books in the next five years. *The Aryans* (1926), *The Most Ancient East* (1928), *The Danube in Prehistory* (1929) and *The Bronze Age* (1930). Childe saw the origin of human progress in the Neolithic Revolution, i.e. the process of transition from food gathering to food production characterized by the domestication of plants and animals, and the concomitant growth of new forms of settlement, social organization and ideology. In the South West Orient the economic surplus created laid the basis of a further major change, the

Urban Revolution, with 'ordered government, urban life, writing and conscious art'. The unique character of European prehistory he attributed to the emergence of independent metal workers and traders in the Bronze Age. Childe's analogy for these revolutions was technological, the Industrial Revolution of the eighteenth century, the argument being first set out in *Man Makes Himself* (1936). This argument, which also expressed Childe's belief in rational enquiry in archaeology as against certain racist arguments current at the time, was restated more powerfully in *What Happened in History* (1942), conceived in 1938 but given extra significance by the reverses experienced in the first half of the Second World War.

Profoundly influenced by Marx, Childe increasingly stressed the role of productive forces in determining the productive relations of prehistoric societies, and so, in the last analysis, their whole social and ideological superstructure. He also emphasized that archaeology should use scientific methods to show processes of change while at the same time demonstrating the historical factors involved. Increasingly after 1945 he saw the study of history as a creative process which freed him from the economic determinism implicit in *Man Makes Himself*, but led to philosophical difficulties which he did not entirely resolve. Thus in *Social Evolution* (1951), where he re-examined the Morgan–Engels argument of unilinear evolution, he concluded that the evidence vindicated 'the concept of cultural evolution as a rational and intelligible process'. On the other hand, although he laid great stress on defining the forces of production directly from the surviving evidence, he accepted that the relations of production could only be inferred. This meant that it was only possible to comprehend prehistoric thoughts in so far as they had been successfully embodied in archaeological evidence. 'Unsuccessful' thoughts (which he considered similar to Marx's concept of 'false consciousness') did not pass into archaeology and were therefore irrelevant. This argument tended to minimize the relevance of archaeology to the definition of prehistoric social institutions and to link it very closely to the study of the idea of progress. On the other hand, when writing on these topics Childe brought the study of the sociology of knowledge into archaeology by discussing in a number of papers after 1945 the effects of the historically perceived environment on social behaviour.

Many of these ideas were incorporated into *Piecing together the Past* (1956), Childe's only book on archaeological method. To a degree this anticipated later applications of statistics, ethnography and demography to the study of prehistory. Out of his desire to make archaeology both scientific and historical Childe broadened the discipline where it became, as he had long hoped, a social science, not, as he had found it, a 'postage stamp' subject. Criticized by some, notably after his death, as a synthesizer with strong diffusionist views, his *Society and Knowledge* (1956), which explained the philosophical underpinning of many of his ideas, was almost totally ignored until the 1970s, when there was a revival of interest in the man and his work.

Peter Gathercole

See: Isobel Smith in *Proc. Prehistoric Society* (*N.S.*) Vol. XXI (1955) for a bibliography.

96
CHIRICO, Giorgio de 1888–1977

Italian artist

Giorgio de Chirico was born in Greece of Italian parents and first studied art in Athens. In 1907 he went to Munich, where he experienced what he called 'severe crises of melancholy', becoming a devotee of the poetic gloom he found in certain writings of Schopenhauer and Nietzsche. On moving to Italy in 1909, he began painting in an unnatural, sepulchral manner derived from Arnold Böcklin. *The Enigma of the Oracle* (1910) shows the mysterious rear view of a dark figure gazing out to sea, balanced by a white figure (a statue?) practically hidden by a black drape. Already De Chirico was fascinated by the principle of simultaneously revealing and hiding his subject-matter. When in 1911 he moved to Paris and got to know Apollinaire*, he began to produce his so-called metaphysical paintings, commonly seen as the first manifestations of Surrealist art.

De Chirico's metaphysical work combined Mediterranean sunniness with a distinctly Nordic chill, opening on to dream spaces that relate uneasily to the world of straightforward perception. 'One must picture everything in the world as an enigma,' he wrote, 'and live in the world as if in a vast museum of strangeness.' *Mystery and Melancholy of a Street* (1914), in which a girl with a hoop runs past a parked removal van towards an unseen figure whose shadow, cast by the late afternoon sun, creeps menacingly forth from behind a building, introduces us to a city in the grip of invisible forces and conveys a sense of queer foreboding.

De Chirico's city contains gaping piazzas framed by Italianate buildings with sharply angled façades, spectral arcades and narrow towers and chimneys. These look as if they were cut from cardboard with fanatic care and are painted in dry neutral colours that lend an air of feigned innocence. Architectural incident is often cramped into the corners of the canvas, and the multiplication of vanishing points produces an effect of dizziness: 'Who can deny the troubling connection between perspective and metaphysics?' the artist once asked. Almost the only inhabitants of the city are clas-

sical statues (*Ariadne*, 1913) or faceless mannequins (*The Fatal Light*, 1915).

Often small objects are portentously arrayed in the foreground of the paintings – artichokes, gloves, biscuits, cotton-reels. 'He could only paint when he was *surprised* by certain dispositions of objects which presented to him a flagrant particularity,' observed André Breton*. In *The Uncertainty of the Poet* (1913), De Chirico shows an instinctive grasp of the Surrealist principle that visual surprise springs from violently illogical juxtapositions: a nude female torso in stone and a sheaf of bananas meet on an empty piazza, with a locomotive passing at the skyline (this last apparently in homage to the artist's father, a railway engineer).

The effect of such works is to instil a mood which has been variously categorized as nostalgic, fateful or melancholic. In detailing for us what he called 'the signs of the metaphysical alphabet', the artist developed a captivating idiom of cryptic allusion. *Self-Portrait* (1913) depicts a plaster cast of a left foot, a right foot which might be reality or replica, a rolled map, an egg and two chimneys. On a wall is inscribed a large letter X which both 'marks the spot' and masks the identity of the sitter. If this *is* a self-portrait, it seems the artist is either unwilling or unable to reveal who or what he really is. Other works, such as *The Song of Love* (1914) or *The Enigma of Fatality* (1914), use the motif of the glove or gauntlet to stage a gesture of urgent but unspecified pointing. The typical De Chirico effect is one of oracular profundity, the sensation of an impending revelation whose proper articulation is, however, always deferred. The viewer is kept hovering between puzzlement and understanding.

After a wartime association with the Futurist Carlo Carrá (who founded a short-lived *scuola metafisica*), De Chirico returned to Rome in 1918 to study the techniques of the Old Masters. 'It was in the museum of the Villa Borghese one morning, standing before a Titian, that I received the revelation of what great painting is: in the gallery I beheld tongues of flame. . . .' Almost from that moment on, De Chirico's career moved in a resolutely reactionary direction. Through the 1920s he distanced himself from the modern movement in general and Surrealism in particular. Though he produced a few sporadic pictures in a more or less Surrealist vein and even wrote a Surrealist novel, *Hebdomeros* (Paris 1929), De Chirico effectively spurned the Surrealists at the very time his influence over them was at its height. Painters like Ernst*, Tanguy, Magritte* and Dali* ignored the artist and concentrated on adjusting to their individual preoccupations the key formula offered by his work, namely the poetic suggestion of unconscious states in terms of the relations of objects in space.

Over the half-century of his post-metaphysical career, De Chirico produced academic canvases in a neoclassical or baroque manner which are, in the view of most critics, disappointingly derivative if not downright trashy, and certainly bereft of the hallucinatory magic of the metaphysical style. It may be surmised that he had come to see in his early work the symbolic record of feelings which he could not consciously tolerate. One senses an undercurrent of panic. The 'revealing symptom of the *inhabited depth*' which the artist saw as typifying the metaphysical perception of reality may have become for him the revealing symptom of personal insecurity; perhaps he eventually read the 'metaphysical alphabet' as registering an absurd lack of meaning in the world, emptiness rather than plenitude, paralysis rather than vibration. But whatever the meaning of these works for De Chirico (who repeatedly argued from the late 1920s on that 'nobody has ever understood them, either then or now'), there is no denying that the few brief years (c.1911–c.1919) of his metaphysical inspiration constitute a distinctive landmark on the map of modern art.

Roger Cardinal

De Chirico's metaphysical period is fully documented in J. T. Soby, *Giorgio de Chirico* (1966). See also *Catalogo general Giorgio de Chirico*, ed. C. Bruni (3 vols, 1971–3). Other writings by the artist: *The Memoirs of Giorgio de Chirico* (*Memorie della mia vita*, trans. 1971); selected texts in M. Carrá, *Metaphysical Art* (1971). See also: R. Vitrac, *Giorgio de Chirico et son oeuvre* (1927); I. Faldi, *Il Primo De Chirico* (1949); M. Jean, *The History of Surrealist Painting* (1960).

97

CHOMSKY, Avram Noam 1928–

US linguist and philosopher

Son of an eminent Hebrew scholar, Noam Chomsky became interested in radical politics at an early age, and has succeeded in combining an active political life with a brilliant academic career. He studied mathematics and philosophy at the University of Pennsylvania where he was drawn to the study of linguistics by Zellig Harris, whose political thinking had much in common with his own. His early work on Modern Hebrew attracted the interest of philosophers rather than linguists; it was as a research fellow at Harvard and later at the Massachusetts Institute of Technology that he developed the theory of generative grammar which was to earn him an international reputation by the age of forty.

It is common to talk of Chomsky's 'revolution' in linguistic theory, and certainly in the context of American structural linguistics his ideas represent a dramatic break with tradition. The structuralist method consists essentially in segmenting a large corpus of utterances into recurring sequences of sounds, which

are then classified into units according to their function and distribution. Impressive results were obtained at the levels of phonology and morphology, but structural techniques were less effective in revealing the syntactic structure of a language.

It is this latter weakness that is the focal point of Chomsky's attack, in *Syntactic Structures* (1957), on the methods, goals and assumptions of the structuralist school. He demonstrates clearly that a taxonomic approach can reveal no more than the most superficial syntactic relationships. Moreover, no body of data, however extensive, will contain all possible syntactic constructions; the resulting description is bound to be incomplete.

Chomsky proposed a radically different model in which the rules underlying the construction of all possible sentences in a language must be specified; structurally ambiguous sentences are assigned descriptions which reflect their different semantic interpretations and formal relationships are established between superficially differing structures. Rather than applying mechanical discovery procedures of segmentation and classification the linguist must try to formalize the 'competence' or intuitive knowledge which enables the native speaker to relate sequences of sounds to their semantic interpretation. The broader goal of linguistic theory is to 'discover the general properties of any system of rules that may serve as a basis for a human language, that is, to elaborate . . . the general *form of language* that underlies each particular realization, each particular natural language'. Descriptions of natural languages are therefore primarily of interest for the light they throw on the general theory of language, which in turn provides insights into the nature of mental processes, and in particular the mechanisms by which knowledge is acquired and stored. For Chomsky, linguistics is not an autonomous discipline but a major branch of cognitive psychology.

The impact of *Syntactic Structures*, first in the United States and later in Europe, was dramatic. It engendered bitter hostility on the part of scholars committed to the behaviourist-empiricist position, who accused Chomsky of being 'mentalistic' and 'unscientific'. At the same time his ideas aroused considerable interest among psychologists and philosophers, who had hitherto found little stimulus in the work of contemporary linguists. Chomsky rapidly attracted an impressive circle of graduate students to MIT, where he now holds the Ferrari P. Ward Chair of Modern Languages and Linguistics.

By the late 1960s Chomsky's ideas had engaged the younger generation of linguists in Europe and the United States, although many disagreed on the precise formulation of the theory. The basic distinction between a speaker's 'competence' and his 'performance' (the actual manifestation of his internalized system of rules) is now widely accepted (though many query whether the line between them has been drawn in the right place). Performance is the indirect reflection of competence, which may be affected by a wide range of extra-linguistic factors, such as memory span, the physical and emotional state of the speaker, and so on. Chomsky claims that a model of linguistic performance can only be seriously attempted once the facts of competence have been established. Underlying the competence–performance distinction is the rejection of psychology as a behavioural science; the observable facts of human behaviour are clues to the innate principles of mental organization, but their description is not in itself the ultimate goal.

Although there was little dialogue in the 1940s and 1950s between linguists and psychologists it had been generally assumed that the facts of language acquisition and use could be accounted for within the then accepted framework of behaviourist psychology. In 1959, in his scathing review (in *Language*, 35) of Skinner's* *Verbal Behaviour*, Chomsky exposed the inadequacies of reinforcement theory when applied to the complexities of linguistic behaviour. He stressed the creative aspect of language – our ability to produce and understand sentences we have never heard before – and the unpredictable nature of linguistic 'responses', which renders the notion of 'stimulus' in this context vague to the point of vacuity. Neither intelligence nor motivation appear to be vital factors in the acquisition of language, as every normal child can acquire his mother tongue on the basis of patchy and often imperfect data, with little direct reward. Chomsky concludes that genetic endowment must play a major role in the acquisition process: a child must be born with a knowledge of the basic principles of linguistic structure. Whether this knowledge takes the form of a specific set of rules governing the possible form of sentences in any human language, or whether the child is endowed with learning strategies which enable him to deduce the rules of the language to which he is exposed is still largely a matter for conjecture; some would claim that no genuine distinction exists between the two views.

Structural linguistics had tended to stress the differences between languages, partly because taxonomic techniques could be most successfully applied at levels where differences are most marked. Chomsky's insistence on the need to explore the more abstract levels of linguistic structure made possible the investigation of the common properties of natural languages. The existence of certain substantive universals, such as the distinction between nouns and verbs, had been recognized, but these had generally been explained in terms of universal features of the external world. Chomsky and his colleagues have suggested that *formal* universals, for which no such explanation can be invoked, closely constrain the structures and processes to be found in every language. The precise formulation

and testing of such hypotheses has proved to be one of the most fruitful areas of recent research.

Chomsky has related his view of language to the seventeenth-century Rationalist tradition of the continental Cartesians and the British Neo-Platonists, while rejecting any sharp distinction between body and mind: the acquisition and use of language must ultimately be explained in terms of neural structures, of which we have as yet an only rudimentary knowledge. The idea that universal structures underlie superficially diverse forms is to be found, for example, in the *Port-Royal* grammar of 1660. But in the absence of precise techniques for investigating the structure of language it had not been possible to develop the notion of a 'universal grammar'. In a sense, Chomsky's work can be seen as a synthesis of the insights of the Rationalist tradition and the rigorously objective methodology developed initially by the structuralists.

The essence of Chomsky's mature theory is contained in his *Aspects of a Theory of Syntax* (1965), in which the model proposed in *Syntactic Structures* is extended to account for the relationships between sound, syntactic structure and meaning. The abstruseness of the style makes it difficult of access for the non-specialist, who would be well advised to approach it via one of the more readable introductions to the subject. The model can be seen as a device capable of generating all (and only) the grammatical sentences of a language. The central component is a set of ordered syntactic rules which expand the basic element 'sentence' until the level of individual lexical and grammatical categories is reached. These 'phrase structure rules' produce tree-like 'deep structures' in which each branch is assigned a label in the course of the derivation. At this point the device has access to a lexical or dictionary component, from which words of the appropriate category are selected to substitute for the terminal elements in the tree. The semantic component operates on the deep structure of a sentence, combining an interpretation of the syntactic configuration with the interpretation of its individual elements.

As Chomsky points out in *Syntactic Structures*, phrase structure rules are implicit in many structuralist models, but are by themselves inadequate to account for all the syntactic structures of a language, and the semantic relations between them. He therefore proposes a second set of syntactic rules which operate on the output of the phrase structure rules, deleting and reordering elements in the underlying tree. An essential feature of these 'transformational rules', as proposed in the *Aspects* model, is that they should not affect the meaning of a sentence, only its 'surface structure'. A structurally ambiguous sentence, like 'flying planes can be dangerous' would therefore be assigned two quite different deep structures; it is the operation of the transformational rules which produces a common surface structure. When a sentence has been processed by the syntactic component the surface structure is converted into a sequence of speech sounds by a series of phonological rules. The syntactic component is central to Chomsky's model, with the semantic and phonological components playing interpretative roles. The precise relationship between the various components has given rise to much controversy, even within the 'generativist' camp. Chomsky himself has conceded that the surface structure of a sentence can partly determine its meaning, while some have argued that surface structures can be assigned semantic interpretations without the need for an intervening level of deep structure. Yet another breakaway group have proposed a theory of 'generative semantics' in which there is no clear boundary between syntax and semantics. Despite the disagreement surrounding the correct formulation of the theory, generative linguistics share the same basic assumptions about language and have succeeded in demonstrating beyond doubt the innateness and complexity of the language faculty.

Chomsky recognizes a connection between his philosophical position and his political views, powerfully expressed in works such as *For Reasons of State* (1973), *At War With Asia* (1970), *American Power and the New Mandarins* (1969), and *Reflections on Justice and Nationhood* (1974), and numerous articles in left-wing journals. In general he warns against the dangers of assuming that human beings can be manipulated by techniques which have proved successful with animals or machines; more specifically he charges the US government with applying a pseudo-scientific gloss to many of its methods, both to inhibit the participation of the ordinary citizen in decision-making, and to remove political questions from the moral to the purely pragmatic sphere. He has consistently opposed US commitment to the Zionist cause, and became one of the most outspoken critics of US involvement in South-East Asia. US foreign policies, he claims, are largely designed to protect and promote American economic interests, without regard to the legality or morality of the methods employed. His arguments are supported by the fact that distribution of a highly critical book on the Vietnam war, of which Chomsky was co-author, was banned after publication. On the domestic scene he alleges that repressive and brutal measures have been taken by US government agencies against vocal minorities and movements for social change. Declaring himself to be 'a kind of anarchist socialist', he opposes the concentration of power in the hands of groups of individuals or of the state, under either a capitalist or totalitarian system of government. In the face of doctrines which tend to deal with human beings in a mechanistic manner, Chomsky's contribution has been to reassert the dignity and uniqueness of the individual.

Hilary Wise

Other important works: *Cartesian Linguistics: A Chapter in the History of Rationalist Thought* (1966); *Language and Mind* (1968). C. F. Hockett, *The State of the Art* (1967) and P. H. Matthews in his review of *Aspects* in *Journal of Linguistics*, vol. 3 (1967) provide critical assessments of Chomsky's work. See also John Lyons, *Chomsky* (1970).

98
CLEAVER, Larry Eldridge 1935–

US radical, author

'We shall have our manhood. We shall have it or the earth will be leveled by our attempts to gain it' – in that kind of assertion, made on hearing of Malcolm X's* assassination in 1965, Eldridge Cleaver gave notice from his cell in Folsom Prison, California, of the spectacular, intransigent revolutionary spirit which made him, throughout the Civil Rights decade and the Lyndon Johnson/Richard Nixon Presidencies, a black ghetto and West Coast prison legend and a presence truly held in fear and loathing by white middle America. Born in Arkansas, he was raised in the Los Angeles black slums, an inmate of Juvenile Hall at twelve, then Whittier Reform School and the Preston School of Industries ('outlaw years, full of vandalism and petty crime'), and by his teens a veteran of robberies, rape and the gamut of street and ghetto hustle. Under different sentences, from sixteen onwards, he spent the next two decades in and out of prison, before an unbroken nine-year stint in San Quentin, Folsom and Soledad from 1957–66 earned him parole. During that time he became radicalized, an autodidact who began a reading programme which would take him to Mark, Lenin*, Che Guevara*, Castro*, Ho Chi Minh*, Frantz Fanon, W. E. B. DuBois and Richard Wright, who became briefly a Black Muslim before breaking with Elijah Muhammad* over Malcolm X and who, through the intervention of his white lawyer, Beverley Axelrod, smuggled out of prison the writings which eventually became his first book, *Soul On Ice* (1968), an immediate international best-seller. While on parole, he married his wife Katherine, became a *Ramparts* magazine editor and, most crucially, took up with the Oakland chapter of the Black Panthers, under its joint leadership of Huey Newton and Bobby Seale. A fiery, urgent orator, he quickly assumed the role of Panther Minister of Information; acted as Presidential candidate for the Peace and Freedom Party in 1968; sought alliances with kindred radical groups like SDS and the Spanish-speaking Young Lords and Brown Berets; became a campus celebrity at Berkeley and a much sought-after speaker; and served as a living provocation to almost every American law enforcement agency. When he was to have his parole revoked, over the shooting by the Oakland police of 'Little Bobby' Hutton in 1968, and with the prospect before him of unrelieved further incarceration, he went underground, surfacing first in Cuba where he met a disillusioning refusal to grant him 'political' status, then in Algeria. He travelled widely in the Third World before, in the late 1970s, ostensibly a born-again Christian, making his muted return from France to America and the prospect of a fresh round of legal fights.

Three publications mark out the central intellectual strands in Cleaver's evolution, each an impressive act of self-articulation. *Soul On Ice* gathers together the 'notes of an ofay-watcher', a convict existentialist taking measure of his own life and demanding an end to all manifestations of racist inequalities. Writing itself becomes a way to 'save myself', a means of sloughing off the Cleaver who 'came to prison', but 'no longer exists'. He argues his status as an imprisoned dissident, a black victim of American detestation in the line of slaves like Nat Turner and Denmark Vesey, anxious to strike back at his tormentors through his newly discovered powers of literary expression. In his opening piece, 'On Becoming', he sets out his essential goals – to stand full face against what he identifies as a racist power system, the American racial order of things which permits a Watts, or a Mississippi, or a George Wallace, or Lyndon Johnson's Asian war policies. From there he develops analyses of prison life in Folsom; his reaction to Malcolm X's death; the role of sports and other mythologies in the American racial psyche; his dismay at James Baldwin's* writing ('There is in James Baldwin's work the most grueling, agonizing, total hatred of blacks, particularly himself. . .'); the Johnson White House's Vietnam strategy and its implications for black Americans; 'Law and Order' in America; and in 'The Primeval Mitosis', a typology of black and white American sexual behaviour (the sexuality of power has long exercised Cleaver). For a first book, *Soul on Ice* stands up remarkably, the shrewd, stylish, honed witness of an 'underground' black American living almost always at the legal margins.

Post-Prison Essays and Speeches (1969), Cleaver's second collection, deals largely with his parole years; the open letters which carry his disgust with and taunts to Ronald Reagan, then Governor of California; his Black Panther involvement and allegiance to Newton, Seale, and figures like Stokely Carmichael and Rap Brown. Always he insists on the dividing line between the assimilationist politics of Martin Luther King* (see 'The Death of Martin Luther King: Requiem for Nonviolence') and the position espoused by the Panthers and other radical forces in America. His evolving socialism is hinted at in his hope of taking up the fallen revolutionary standard of Malcolm X. As he observes, in an interview with Nat Hentoff reprinted from *Playboy*, 'most of my life has been involved in conflicts with authority, and now that I've politicized that conflict,

I'm content to be working for black liberation.' *Conversation with Eldridge Cleaver* (ed. Lee Lockwood, 1970) offers Cleaver's thoughts in his Algerian exile, at this stage a committed Marxist-Leninist, aware of impending splits in the Panther cadre, and his further notations on the workings of capitalist economics and racism. He also recognizes other emerging black radicals, LeRoi Jones* and Ron Karenga notably.

Though first encountered as a quintessentially 1960s American voice, Cleaver has been more enduring. *Soul On Ice*, especially, has rightly become a landmark, taking its place with the essential radical literature of post-war Afro-America in company with Malcolm X's *Autobiography* (1964), Claude Brown's *Manchild in the Promised Land* (1965), H. Rap Brown's *Die Nigger Die!* (1969), George Jackson's *Soledad Brother* (1970), Bobby Seale's *Seize the Time* (1970), Huey Newton's *To Die for the People* (1974), and Angela Davis's *Autobiography* (1974). Cleaver cites with approval Che Guevara's dictum about 'revolutionary love'. His own life, especially its later phases, has been given precisely to that kind of 'love', a defiant and articulate political life whose shaping contours derive from the lovelessness of the ghetto, and, in Cleaver's scheme of things, America's racist State and Federal systems of police, law and prison. Cleaver has not been free of contradiction, or some fudging of history and rhetorical overkill. Nor has he been immune from the aura of revolutionary martyr. But even in his latterday political limbo, his name remains synonymous with the search for black American redress, a search maintained with no small bravery against punitive odds.

A. Robert Lee

See: Gene Marine, *The Black Panthers* (1969); Philip S. Foner (ed.), *The Black Panthers Speak* (1970); Stephen Butterfield, *Black Autobiography in America* (1974).

99
COCTEAU, Jean 1889–1963

French poet, painter, writer, film-maker, performer

Jean Cocteau liked to call all his work poetry, labelling it poetry of the novel, poetry of criticism, poetry of cinema, etc. He also liked to say that 'poetry is the same as morality', and both his life and work exhibit a total confusion of ethics with aesthetics. This confusion often found expression in Cocteau's love of the lapidary paradox, e.g. 'I am a lie that always tells the truth.'

His family circumstances influenced him strongly. His parents were rich, owning houses at Maisons-Laffitte and in Paris, but his secure childhood was shattered when his father committed suicide in 1898; his mother had a long life and Cocteau was always very dependent on her. As a child, he was an unwilling scholar and failed his baccalaureate; his real education was provided later by his high society friends in the Paris of *la belle époque*. He experienced the excitement of the Ballets Russes' first performances, made friends with Diaghilev* and got to know Stravinsky*, Picasso* and many others.

During the First World War he served for a while in the Red Cross and visited front-line trenches; out of this experience came *Thomas l'Imposteur* (1923), one of his best novels. He then returned to Paris, where he frequented a circle of painters, poets, musicians, aristocrats and dress-designers. In 1917 he produced his first ballet, *Parade*, with music by Satie* and designs by Picasso. This caused a fashionable 'scandale' and was followed by two more ballets in 1920 and 1921, by which time Cocteau had become the leader and acknowledged spokesman of the group of composers known as Les Six.

He formed a close friendship with the young novelist Raymond Radiguet. When Radiguet died of typhoid in 1923, Cocteau was deeply affected and took refuge in opium – an experience about which he later wrote.

His writing style was always characterized by clarity and concision, qualities that he claimed to have learned from the classics, and it was from the classics that he took much of his subject-matter, writing adaptations of the Antigone, Orpheus and Oedipus stories. In 1929, he published his best known novel, *Les Enfants terribles*, and in 1930 made his first film, a short surrealist sequence of images entitled *The Blood of a Poet* (*Le Sang d'un poète*). In 1932 he returned to classical subject-matter with *The Infernal Machine* (*La Machine infernale*), a meditation on the incomprehensibility and cruelty of fate constructed around the figure of Oedipus. *Les Parents terribles* in 1938 was his last big success in the theatre, though he wrote several more plays during and after the war.

In 1945, with *La Belle et la bête*, Cocteau made his first full-length film and this was followed by others including *Orphée* (1950) and *Le Testament d'Orphée* (1960). During the last ten years of his life, he achieved an academic respectability that had previously eluded him: he was elected to the Académie Française and awarded an honorary doctorate by Oxford University.

Cocteau's work covers an astonishing range of expressive forms, but through it all his preoccupations remain very similar; they are the difficulty of being true to oneself, the fascination of a small, incestuous world of self-consciously beautiful people, the fear of death and the problems of art. His favourite characters were Oedipus, who defied a cruel fate, and Orpheus, whose poetry could bring the dead to life.

But there was a marked lack of profundity in his work, a tendency to sacrifice all for the brilliant effect. Perhaps the most surprising thing about him was that despite his fashionable eccentricities he was such an able organizer of the talents of others. He managed to head a school of composers without ever writing music and to put on ballets with little knowledge of dance. Much of his best work was done in the cinema – essentially a collaborative art.

David Bradby

The collected Theatre and Poetry are published by Gallimard; there is an authoritative biography by Francis Steegmuller, *Cocteau, a Biography* (1970).

100
CONNOLLY, Cyril 1903–74

British critic, editor and essayist

Educated privately, his contemporaries included: at St Cyprian's Preparatory School, Cecil Beaton* and George Orwell*; at Eton, Harold Acton, Henry Green*, John Lehmann and Anthony Powell*; and at Balliol College, Oxford, where he was a Brackenbury Scholar, Kenneth Clark, Peter Quennell and Evelyn Waugh*. Few people can have grown up amid such diversified talent. It gave Connolly a first-hand insight into the making of a creative writer; but when this insight turned into an obsession, it perhaps prevented him from fully expanding his own gifts. His most important book, *Enemies of Promise* (1938, revised edition 1949), is successful as a discussion of the reasons for failure. In it he sets out the difficulties thrown in the way of anyone wanting to write a book that would 'last' ten years. These include drink, conversation, daydreaming, journalism, worldly success, duty, domesticity and sex. Such essential negativity repeats itself in Connolly's characterization of his own career, in his survey *The Modern Movement: One Hundred Key Books from England, France and America 1880-1950* (1965). The 1920s, he wrote, were the age of the 'Intellectual Mannerists', when 'it was joy to be alive'. His one novel, *The Rock Pool* (1936), belongs stylistically to this period, even though it was written in 1934. The 1930s he summarized as the 'disastrous decade', followed by the 'frustrated Forties, five years of total war and five more of recrimination and exhaustion'. For Connolly the creative writer the time was never right. In other capacities, however, as an editor and critic, hard times were less stunting. In 1940, with backing from Peter Watson and editorial assistance from Stephen Spender*, he launched *Horizon*, a magazine devoted to demonstrating that the arts could survive the war. 'Our standards are aesthetic, and our politics are in abeyance,' he announced in the first issue. While maintaining an often guilty sense of commitment to the Allied cause, he succeeded in securing a forum for new prose, poetry and criticism, as well as an outlet for new writers. But despite *Horizon*'s professed a-politicism, in spirit it drifted to the Left. Certainly Connolly welcomed the Labour government in 1945. Disappointment and disillusionment followed, and from 1948 he diagnosed 'cultural melancholia', induced in his own case by the strains of editing over too long a period. It was as a result of his growing loss of interest that *Horizon* folded in 1949, even though it still had a circulation of almost nine thousand.

His other wartime achievement was the publication of *The Unquiet Grave* (1944), initially under the pseudonym of 'Palinurus'. A collection of *pensées* in the form of a journal or commonplace book, its purpose was to show that 'the true function of a writer is to produce a masterpiece and that no other task is of any consequence.' From 1950 until his death his time was spent contributing reviews and occasional pieces to a host of publications. He was for many years principal critic on the London *Sunday Times*. His collected articles reflect his skills as a parodist, and as a writer of witty and well-ordered prose, as well as his peculiar knowledge of nineteenth-century French literature. His excellence as a critic, or, as he would have preferred to call himself, a Man of Letters, was by his own standards a symptom of a grander failure.

Robert Hewison

Connolly's other books include: *The Condemned Playground – Essays 1927–44* (1945); *Ideas and Places* (1953); *Previous Convictions* (1963); *The Evening Colonnade* (1973). See also: *A Romantic Friendship, The Letters of Cyril Connolly to Noel Blakiston* (1976); Ian Hamilton, *The Little Magazines* (1976); Robert Hewison, *Under Siege: Literary Life in London 1939–45* (1977); and *Adam*, nos 385–90 (1974–5).

101
CONRAD, Joseph 1857–1924

Polish/English writer

Conrad's work is marked by the overriding paradox of a Pole whose second language was French fervently desiring to become an Englishman. Jozef Konrad Korzeniowski was the son of a Polish revolutionary poet, with the bitter experience of having seen his country thoroughly cowed under Russian imperial domination. The boy's reading of English authors during his Cracow schooldays may have encouraged a wish to assume British nationality, but it was not until 1884, after ten years of seafaring and painstaking study of the English language, that he was able to realize his ambition and become a naturalized subject.

He was a capable sailor and had already gained his Board of Trade certificate as a Master. His travels took him all over the world during the last great era of sail as opposed to steam, and he was clearly alive to the romance of a fully rigged ship, just as he was conscious of the essentially prosaic image of the steamer (for his views on this, see *An Outcast of the Islands*, 1896). One area in particular has been associated with him. The 'Conrad world' is that of the East Indian islands around Java, Malaya, Sumatra and the Philippines, and especially the islands of the Molucca archipelago which provide the backgrounds of *Lord Jim* (1900), *Victory* (1915) and *An Outcast of the Islands*. Other exotic settings are an imaginary South American republic in *Nostromo* (1904) and the river Congo in the short story 'Heart of Darkness' (1902).

His first novel, *Almayer's Folly* (1895), was written during his last years at sea. Imperfect as it is, it shows an astonishing stylistic maturity in a first book whose author was writing in, essentially, a foreign language. A year after its appearance Conrad married and settled down quietly in Kent. He was admired and befriended by such disparate figures as Henry James, Ford Madox Ford* (with whom he also collaborated) and H. G. Wells*, and came increasingly to be seen, in the company of writers like Kipling* and Stevenson, and the eccentric adventurer Cunninghame-Graham, as the visionary analyst of British colonial experience.

Not all his novels, however, encompass a common subject-matter. Two of the finest, *The Secret Agent* (1907) and *Under Western Eyes* (1911), deal with the activities of anarchists and revolutionaries in England and Russia, and are undeniably coloured with recollections drawn from his family's own revolutionary tradition. *The Secret Agent* shows Conrad's astonishing ability to absorb and transmit the atmosphere of his adopted country and is as near perfect in its overall achievement as anything written during the immensely fertile period of English letters between the death of Queen Victoria and the First World War. Its single serious flaw is the outrage which the author chooses to place at the centre of the action. The destruction of Greenwich Observatory by a bomb seems altogether too abstract a process to engage our interest.

Conrad's increasing mastery of English is the first thing which strikes anyone who studies him seriously. Cautious, halting, and occasionally inexact in the earlier novels and stories, his style flowers, in *Lord Jim* and 'Heart of Darkness', into something of great richness, sonority and weight, moderated continually by his evident respect for this, his third language. His narrative technique too acquires a corresponding complexity, adding to *Nostromo*, with its contrasted time-shifts and varied character perspectives, a degree of experimental skill hitherto unknown in the European novel, with the possible exception of Sterne's *Tristram Shandy*.

His main concern, however, is not with style, technique, the evocation of atmosphere or the expression of socio-political criticism, so much as with the idea of a single man, or group of men, in a situation which will test human endurance to breaking point. Faced with danger and distress, his characters are summoned to proclaim their moral toughness. We think, for example, of Kurtz in 'Heart of Darkness', who is found 'hollow at the core', or the slow destruction of Willems in *An Outcast of the Islands*. The conclusions of his books are thus bleak, fatalistic, often, by implication, terrifying in their visions of darkness and disorder. The positive occupies a restricted domain and Conrad takes the true traveller's delight in exploiting the simple antithesis between the savage and the civilized.

Beginning with *Chance* (1913), and with the notable exception of *Victory* (1915), his later novels saw a decline into the sort of romantic yarn-spinning his public best liked. He is often verbose and tumid in his narrative, and his 'man is a man' world's view of women as either generally time-wasting or purely destructive (but not so Mrs Gould in *Nostromo*) has sometimes a dire effect on credibility. But his influence on later novelists, especially in America, has been immense, and he has been deservedly rescued from a role as a mere writer of adventure stories by the intensive reappraisal of the post-war decades.

Jonathan Keates

Conrad's other work includes: *The Nigger of the 'Narcissus'* (1897); *The Inheritors* (with Ford Madox Ford, 1901); *Youth: A Narrative and Two Other Stories* (1902); *Typhoon and Other Stories* (1903); *The Rescue* (1920); *The Rover* (1920). See also: F. M. Ford, *Joseph Conrad: A Personal Remembrance* (1924); F. R. Karl, *A Reader's Guide to Joseph Conrad* (1960); F. R. Leavis, *The Great Tradition* (1948); Leo Gurko, *Joseph Conrad: Giant in Exile* (1962); Jocelyn Baines, *Joseph Conrad, a Critical Biography* (1960); Edward Crankshaw, *Joseph Conrad* (1976); Frederick Karl, *Joseph Conrad: The Three Lives* (1979); Norman Sherry, *Conrad's Western World* (1971).

102
COPLAND, Aaron 1900–

US composer

The son of Lithuanian Jewish immigrants, he studied with Rubin Goldmark in New York and then with Nadia Boulanger in Paris (1921–5). Under Boulanger he came to admire the neo-classical Stravinsky*, whose influence is evident in such spare, driving works as the Symphony for organ and orchestra (1924) and the Dance Symphony (1925), but after his return to New York he decided that his music must be more American in character. He first tried to achieve this by using jazz idioms, most abundantly in his Piano Concerto (1926). The jazz phase, however, was shortlived, and in his next group of works, including the Piano Variations

(1930) and the Short Symphony (1933), he developed an imposing but austere style in which the thorough motivic working shows some connections with serialism.

Copland's continuing concern for a specifically American music, coupled with his feeling that composers were drawing apart from their audiences, led him next to simplify his manner and look for local colour. The first result was *El salón Mexico* (1936), a vibrant orchestral impression, and this was followed by three American ballets drawing on indigenous hymns, folk-songs and popular music: *Billy the Kid* (1938), *Rodeo* (1942) and *Appalachian Spring* (1944). The fresh colours and the clear, widespread harmonies of these scores seemed to conjure the virginal open spaces of America, and provided composers of film scores with the perfect style for Westerns. Yet at the same time Copland was pursuing his more abstract style, notably in his Piano Sonata (1941), and in his ambitious, public Third Symphony (1946) he brought together the two currents in his music of the previous decade.

In 1950, with his Piano Quartet, he began to use serial methods while retaining, like Stravinsky, his own distinctive feeling for chord placement and his own voice. The Piano Variations now gained added importance as the herald of this later style, and in 1957 Copland orchestrated the work. His other major serial compositions include the Piano Fantasy (1955–7) and two orchestral scores, *Connotations* (1961–2) and *Inscape* (1967), of which the second has remained his last undertaking on a large scale.

Throughout his career Copland has been active in various fields beyond composition. His pride in America, musically expressed not only in the cowboy ballets but also in the *Lincoln Portrait* for narrator and orchestra (1942), has caused him to work tirelessly on behalf of native composers: he founded the American Composers Alliance in 1937 and has served on various other boards. Similarly his democratic spirit, which has a musical emblem in his *Fanfare for the Common Man* (1942), has stimulated his work in popular musical education besides affecting the direction of his own music.

Paul Griffiths

Other works: *Music for the Theatre* for orchestra (1925); Symphony no. 1 (1928); Symphonic Ode (1928, revised 1955); *Vitebsk* for piano trio (1929); *Statements* for orchestra (1934); Sextet for clarinet, piano and string quartet (1937); *Quiet City* for orchestra (1940); *Danzón cubano* for orchestra (1942–4); Violin Sonata (1943); Clarinet Concerto (1948); Twelve Poems of Emily Dickinson for voice and piano (1950); Old American Songs for voice and piano (1950–2); *The Tender Land*, opera (1954); *Dance Panels* for orchestra (1959, revised 1962); Nonet for strings (1960); *Emblems* for band (1964); *Music for a*

Great City for orchestra (1964); Duo for flute and piano (1970–1). Writings: *What to Listen for in Music* (1938); *Our New Music* (1941, revised as *The New Music*, 1968); *Music and Imagination* (1952); *Copland on Music* (1960). About Copland: Arthur Berger, *Aaron Copland* (1953).

CORBUSIER, Le *see* Le Corbusier

103
COWARD, Sir Noël Pierce 1899–1973

English dramatist, actor, composer

Noël Coward was born and spent the first five years of his life in Teddington, Middlesex, where his father Arthur sold pianos and – with his wife Violet – sang in the local choir to the organ accompaniment of Noël's Uncle Jim. The whole family was musical and Coward remembered how 'The lyrics and melodies of Gilbert and Sullivan were hummed and strummed into my consciousness at an early age'; though he never learned any advanced musical technique he retained a remarkable ear for melody. Noël was educated at the Chapel Royal School, Clapham; in 1910, after auditioning for a part as a 'talented boy with attractive appearance', he began his career as a boy-actor in a children's play. The following year he was cast in a play starring Charles Hawtrey under whose influence he learned the rudiments of stagecraft. In 1913 he played Slightly in *Peter Pan* and subsequently began to build a reputation as an actor and dancer.

In 1917 Coward's first play, *Ida Collaborates* (written with Esmé Wynne who took the leading role), was presented in Aldershot; later that year he made his first film appearance as an extra in D. W. Griffith's* *Hearts of the World*. Coward's progress was interrupted by a nine-month spell in the Artists' Rifles in 1918 but he was found unfit for active service and discharged. After the war Coward attracted some attention with light comedies he had written, but his spectacular breakthrough as a dramatist came in 1924 with the production of *The Vortex* at the Everyman Theatre in London. In this play Coward's usual levity gradually darkened to explore the problem of drug addiction; audiences were not amused but scandalized at what seemed to them excessive realism. As a result *The Vortex* was a sensational triumph and Coward the actor-dramatist was transformed to Coward the wickedly witty personality, an image he carefully cultivated for the rest of his life.

Coward basked in his own success and in 1925 could enjoy the spectacle of three of his plays – *The Vortex, Hay Fever, Fallen Angels* – and a revue, *On with the Dance*, running in London's West End. In 1930 his promise

as the finest comic dramatist since Wilde was fulfilled by his production of *Private Lives* in which he starred (as Elyot) along with Gertrude Lawrence (Amanda) and Laurence Olivier (Victor). In this play, and many others, Coward exploited his gift for writing parts that fitted his own histrionic range to perfection. He was able to create roles, or songs (like 'Mad Dogs and Englishmen'), he could then perform in his own inimitable manner. He became a household word – a 'highly publicized and irritatingly successful figure', as he put it – and a synonym for sophistication. At the same time he could show more serious intentions and did so most memorably in his epic patriotic pageant *Cavalcade* (1931).

In the Second World War, Coward built up his patriotic persona by putting his many talents at the disposal of the war effort. He wrote, acted in, co-directed (with David Lean) and composed the music for *In Which We Serve* (1942), a naval propaganda film of considerable artistic merit. He also scripted and co-produced David Lean's sentimental romance *Brief Encounter* (1945). Coward's position as an *enfant terrible* of the English stage declined in the post-war period and, in contrast to the harshly realistic drama of the 1950s, he seemed a symbol of escapism. He consoled himself with his commercial success as an international cabaret performer and was delighted when his musical *Sail Away* (1962) initiated what he immodestly called 'the Noël Coward Renaissance'. *Hay Fever* was revived by Laurence Olivier at the National Theatre in 1964 and this was followed by other revivals and television celebrations of 'The Master' as he was now affectionately known. He was knighted in 1970 and was very much the distinguished Grand Old Man of the theatre when he died at his home in Jamaica.

Alan Bold

Noël Coward's dramatic work is contained in *Play Parade* (6 vols, 1934–62) and *Suite Three Keys* (1966), his lyrics in *The Lyrics of Noël Coward* (1965); his life is examined in Sheridan Morley's *A Talent to Amuse* (1969).

104
CRANE, Harold Hart 1899–1932

US poet

Few modern American poets have been as headily affected by late-nineteenth-century French Symbolism as Hart Crane. Wallace Stevens* is perhaps the only comparable example, others who were influenced, such as Eliot* and Pound*, being only mildly marked by the exposure. Where Eliot, for example, walked warily and 'discovered' with elaborate casualness the then little-known Laforgue, Crane was like a small boy at a County fair. Yet, despite his fascination with the exotic, Crane was saddled with the nagging conscience of the Middle West. Like Whitman, he entertained a poetic vision of his country, and proposed for his muse a grand design. If the stature of poets were to be reckoned by the ambitiousness of their plans, Crane would be a candidate for greatness.

He was born in Garretsville, Ohio, although he grew up in Cleveland. A boy given to day-dreams and dressing-up, he fell foul at an early age of his father, a prosperous sweet manufacturer, who was disturbed at how little his talented son conformed to his idea of the all-American boy. A separation between his parents increased Crane's sense of rootlessness. On his own or with his mother, he went to Cuba, to Paris, and to New York. While he was still in his teens, he took various jobs, working for a time for his father, and, briefly, as a reporter. In the early 1920s he settled in New York, where he began to write advertising copy to support him while he read and wrote the poetry for which he lived.

For a poet who produced so little, Crane had a great deal to say about himself. He disliked, he wrote in 1921, Elizabeth Barrett Browning, Tennyson, Thompson, Chatterton, Byron, Moore, but 'ran joyfully towards Messrs Poe, Whitman, Shakespeare, Keats, Shelley, Coleridge, John Donne, John Webster, Marlowe, Baudelaire, . . . Dante'. He also read Eliot with respect. He proposed, however, to take Eliot 'as a point of departure toward an almost complete reversal of direction'. He would, he said, 'apply as much of his erudition and technique as I can absorb and assemble toward a more positive, or (if I may put it so in a sceptical age) ecstatic goal.' In his first book, *White Buildings* (1926), Crane revealed his captivation with Symbolism by taking the poem out of the world in which words are treated as public and recognizable property into one in which connotations and private references make patterns which are at once fascinating and baffling. The mode was communication far removed from logical discourse, having to do with apprehending more than with comprehending.

Before the publication of *White Buildings* Crane had approached the philanthropist Otto Kahn for help in carrying out his project for an American epic. This was to be a myth of America from earliest times to the present, and it appeared in 1930 and was entitled *The Bridge*. Brooklyn Bridge, with an invocation to which the poem begins, is the symbol which binds the parts together. In Crane's imagination it became more than a triumph of engineering, or even a thing of beauty in itself, but a symbol of the heights to which man in the modern world might aspire. ('Unto us lowliest sometime sweep, descend/And of the curveship lend a myth to God.') He intended his poem to be a counterblast to *The Waste Land*, not a cry of despair for a world which had lost the values of the past, but a paean of praise for a world of undreamt-of possibilities. It was a noble ambition.

However, *The Bridge* succeeds only in parts. Metaphor mingles with slang; the scene shifts as in a film: Columbus, Cortez, 'Powhattan's daughter', Rip Van Winkle and Priscilla Alden dissolve into a landscape which takes in the span of the continent. About 'The River', for example, Crane wrote to Otto Kahn: 'The subway is simply a figurative, psychological "vehicle" for transporting the reader to the Middle West. He lands on the railroad tracks in the company of several tramps in the twilight. The extravagance of the first twenty-three lines of this section is an intentional burlesque on the cultural confusion of the present – a great conglomeration of noises analogous to the strident impression of a fast express rushing by. The rhythm is jazz. Thenceforward, the rhythm settles down to a steady pedestrian gait, like that of wanderers plodding along. My tramps are psychological vehicles, also. Their wanderings, as you notice, carry the reader into interior after interior, all of it funnelled by the Mississippi. They are the left-overs of the pioneers in at least this respect – that abstractedly their wanderings carry the reader through certain experiences roughly parallel to that of traders, adventurers, Boone and others.' When one reads *The Bridge* one is struck, not, as might have been expected from the over-planned synopsis, by the lamentable failure of the final version, but by the degree to which Crane managed to make the whole cumbersome machinery work. Only an American poet in modern times, one feels, would have had the eccentricity to propose such a grand design – and possess the combination of nerve and naïveté needed to tackle it. It was Crane's tragedy that, having worked hard and long at his 'epic', he had the intelligence to realize that he had failed. He did not have it in him to write a contemporary *Divine Comedy*. Yet much of the poetry of *The Bridge* has an impact which all but the best of lyrics lack. It is as if the realities of American life gave point to Crane's dreams and helped disperse some of the fog of self-conscious 'Symbolism' which makes his lyric verse so difficult.

Geoffrey Moore

See: Brom Weber, *Hart Crane* (1948); Vincent Quinn, *Hart Crane* (1963); Monroe K. Spears, *Hart Crane* (1965); Robert L. Perry, *The Shared Vision of Waldo Frank and Hart Crane* (1966); R. W. B. Lewis, *The Poetry of Hart Crane: A Critical Study* (1967); Herbert A. Leibowitz, *Hart Crane: An Introduction to the Poetry* (1968); R. W. Butterfield, *The Broken Arc: A Study of Hart Crane* (1969); P. Horton, *Hart Crane* (1976); and S. J. Hazo, *Smithereened Apart: A Critique of Hart Crane* (1977).

105

CROCE, Benedetto 1966–1952

Italian philosopher

Croce was born five years after the unification of Italy and died nine years after the fall of Mussolini*. For much of his life he exercised a virtual intellectual dictatorship over Italian culture. Born into a rich land-owning family, he left the University of Rome without taking a degree and spent his life in Naples as a scholar of private means. He published over seventy volumes of philosophy, history, politics and literary criticism. For some forty years he edited his own review *La Critica*, and was a dominant influence on the Laterza publishing house. He extended his influence through membership of the Italian Senate, and was Minister of Education in 1920–1. After an initial sympathy for Mussolini's government he became an opponent of Fascism and in 1925 drafted a public reply to the *Manifesto of Fascist Intellectuals*. He was elected President of the right-of-centre Italian Liberal Party in 1943 and held office in the post-war Constituent Assembly.

Croce was not purely a philosopher: his work revealed the constant interaction of research on concrete topics and philosophical theorizing. His early studies exposed him to nineteenth-century German theories of history and aesthetics. Other major influences which shaped his thought were Marxism, the seventeenth-century philosopher Giambattista Vico, the nineteenth-century Hegelian-inspired literary critic Francesco De Sanctis, his contemporary the philosopher Giovanni Gentile, and, in a sense, Hegel. The question of Croce's 'Hegelianism' is far from settled. He referred to himself in 1902 as a 'follower of idealism' since 'philosophy can only be idealism', but hastened to qualify that statement by redefining his philosophy as 'critical idealism', 'anti-metaphysical idealism', and even 'idealistic realism'. He feared in the term 'Idealism' the association with Hegelian Idealism, which he considered to be vitiated by a residual dualistic view of reality, by 'a sort of mythology of the Idea'. In an effort to eliminate all suspicion of dualism from his philosophy, he came to prefer the formulae 'absolute spiritualism' or 'absolute historicism'. There is no doubt, however, as to his rejection of Positivism: much of his cultural battle can be read as part of the European-wide movement of reaction against Positivist domination.

Croce takes for granted a view of reality as development ('history') of a 'spirit' (or 'Spirit'), which is articulated into certain 'forms' or 'categories' according to a precise internal rhythm. The Spirit is one, but its unity is a dialectical unity, composed of four distinct 'forms': the Beautiful, the True, the Useful, and the Good. The Beautiful and the True are the objects of the theoretical activity of the Spirit: cognition of the particular, i.e. Art, in the case of the Beautiful, cognition of the universal, i.e. Logic, or Philosophy, in the case of the True. The Useful and the Good, on the other hand, belong to the practical activity of the Spirit: volition of the particular, i.e. Economics, and volition of the universal, i.e. Ethics, respectively. Each of these categories, Art, Logic, Economics, and Ethics, presupposes the previous one, in that precise order, which is not however hierarchical: they are all equally necessary, they all have equal validity, none is either the absolute beginning or the absolute end. Croce chooses the symbol of the circle to signify their mutual relationship: the Spirit moves perpetually around a circular trajectory, forever enriched by the previous circulation. If philosophy can only be philosophy of the Spirit, which is the only reality, and if the Spirit is constant development, then the meaning of Croce's own formula 'absolute historicism' becomes clear: the only true knowledge is historical knowledge. This identity of philosophy and history was stated by Croce quite categorically: 'Philosophy of the Spirit in its concrete aspect can only be, and has actually always been, historical thought or historiography; in the historiographical process philosophy represents the aspect of methodological reflection' (*Il carattere della filosofia moderna*, 1941). If only historiography gives true knowledge, what of the sciences? These, according to Croce, do not produce knowledge, simply because they do not belong to theoretical activity: their concepts are not concepts at all (the 'pure concept' only belongs to philosophical judgment), but simply generalizations ('pseudo-concepts'), which are useful for practical purposes. The sciences then only retain their validity as long as they are assigned to their proper place, which is the economic category of the Spirit. The Spirit is, by definition, liberty, and one may note that it could hardly be otherwise, since it is the only reality. From this it follows that all philosophy, and all history, is the philosophy and history of liberty: value judgments on events belong to the ethical category of the Spirit, but from a philosophical, and therefore historical, point of view, no historical period is more or less progressive than any other. History 'never judges, but always justifies'. This serene, optimistic and essentially pacifying view of reality was hardly an adequate tool for the analysis of the tragic events of 1939–45. Croce himself seems to have been aware of the limitations of his theory in this respect. In a famous speech on 'The End of Civilization', delivered in Turin in 1946, he significantly, if ambivalently, shifted the emphasis from the theoretical to the practical realm of the Spirit, from the historical to the ethical judgment: 'History finds its meaning in ethics' (published in *Filosofia e Storiografia*, 1949).

Croce's reputation outside Italy perhaps rests mainly on his aesthetic theories. Art is a form of knowledge, but, unlike philosophy, it apprehends not the universal but the particular. It does so not through concepts, but through images and, again unlike philosophy, it is in no way concerned with the reality or unreality of its objects of cognition. Croce's strict categorizing of art within one specific form of the Spirit allows him to establish its autonomy from both utilitarian considerations and moral judgments, since these belong to the Economic and the Ethical categories respectively. 'Intuition' is the term that Croce uses to identify the particular form of cognition that constitutes art. Intuition, in order to be artistic, indeed in order to be intuition at all, must be expressed – art is 'unity of intuition and expression'. Croce's aesthetic theories are meant to apply to all art forms, but in practice he focused his attention on literature. His literary criticism aimed at identifying the writer's world of images, independent of conceptual or moral contents; it aimed, in fact, at deciding whether a work of art is indeed a work of Art. This position led Croce to disregard those writers, or parts of a writer's work, which give priority to the communication of specific content. The basic outline of Croce's aesthetic theories was laid down in the first edition of his *Estetica* (1902), and only received minor subsequent alterations and additions. In 1908 he redefined intuition as 'lyrical intuition'. That which is intuited, and expressed, in a work of Art is essentially a feeling, a state of mind, which must nevertheless be transcended rather than expressed in the immediacy of raw emotionalism. This was modified into the concept of 'cosmic intuition' in 1918, with the emphasis no longer on the individual aspect of art, but on its 'cosmic afflatus'. With *La poesia* ('Poetry', 1936) Croce introduced the theory of 'literature'. This concept applied to those writings, or parts of writings, that are pleasing or desirable but are not included within his category of artistic intuition.

Croce undoubtedly contributed to a profound renewal of Italian historiography and literary criticism. But the mark he made on Italian culture extends well beyond the range of any specific field of scholarship. *La Critica* moulded attitudes and events for half a century. Through his direction of two widely popular series of the Laterza publishing house ('Writers of Italy' and 'Classics of Modern Philosophy'), he was able to tell Italians what to read and what not to read – indeed to impose his own view of the development of Italian culture and its links with the rest of Europe. What is perhaps unique about Croce is the fact that his cultural hegemony was not confined to an intellectual elite. He succeeded as well in moulding the outlook of school teachers and journalists, placed in the best position to influence the Italian public, both at national and local level. Whilst during the years of Fascism Croce fulfilled a very important role by acting as a focus for cultural resistance to the regime, his overt influence declined rapidly after the war, when literary criticism began to embrace new methods, philosophers discovered new

schools of thought, and intellectuals generally felt the need for a new, and more militant, culture. And yet the Italian mind is still not free from its Crocean heritage. Turns of phrase, evaluations and assumptions that are taken for granted form a diffuse Croceanism that is all the more powerful for being unconsciously accepted.

Verina Jones

All Croce's major works have been published by Laterza of Bari, classified by himself into four sections: *Filosofia dello Spirito*, *Saggi filosofici* ('Philosophical Essays'), *Scritti di storia letteraria e politica* ('Writings on political and literary history'), and *Scritti vari* ('Miscellaneous'). English translations include: the four volumes of the *Philosophy of the Spirit* (*Aesthetic as Science of Expression and General Linguistic*, 1909, revised 1922 and 1953; *Philosophy of the Practical*, 1913; *Logic as the Science of the Pure Concept*, 1917; *Theory and History of Historiography*, 1921); *An Autobiography* (1927); *History as the Story of Liberty* (1941); *History of Europe in the nineteenth century* (1933); *European Literature in the Nineteenth Century* (1924); also the anthology *Philosophy, Poetry, History* (1966). See also: G. N. G. Orsini, *Benedetto Croce, Philosopher of Art and Literary Critic* (1961); G. Sasso, *Benedetto Croce. La ricerca della dialettica* (1975); M. Abbate, *La filosofia di Benedetto Croce e la crisi della società italiana* (1955).

106
CUKOR, George 1899–

US film director

The key to Cukor's work lies in his concept of 'performance' and in the subtle shading that he brings to the delineation of role-playing within the explicit theatricality of the stage as well as the implicit theatricality of everyday life. His own direction of acting performances from Garbo, Ingrid Bergman and, most notably, Katharine Hepburn won deserved acclaim, but it has required the more flexible critical ideology of the 1970s, open to notions of performance and anxious to evaluate representations of women in Hollywood cinema, to exhume Cukor's reputation from the shallow graves dug by earlier critics, prepared only to see him as a 'woman's director' or as a compliant, if high-grade, contract director.

In the 1920s Cukor rose to prominence on the Broadway stage with interpretative productions of such plays as *The Great Gatsby* and *The Constant Wife*. The Depression crash of Broadway theatre and the arrival of sound pictures hastened him westwards and he was initially engaged by Paramount as a dialogue director, later to direct his first film after working on the hugely successful *All Quiet on the Western Front* (1930). Cukor was one of the first sound-only directors to gain recognition for his skill in directing film adaptations of precisely those witty and literate salon plays that had resisted silent film treatment. His longevity as a director, more than fifty films in fewer years, is tribute to his ability to work within the parameters of Hollywood studio production and contrasts with the fate allotted such self-proclaimed auteurs as Von Sternberg* and Welles*.

From *What Price Hollywood?* (1932) to its virtual re-make *A Star is Born* (1945) and beyond, via *Dinner at Eight* (1933), *A Double Life* (1948), *The Actress* (1953) and others, Cukor's films have often taken place within the worlds of theatres, movies or showbusiness and equally frequently presented characters, especially women, who are obliged to assume a particular deliberate role. In her swan song, *Two-Faced Woman* (1941), Garbo plays a wife who decides to impersonate an imaginary loose-living twin sister to regain her husband's affections. Hepburn's ambiguous sexual appeal is used to advantage in *Sylvia Scarlett* (1935), in which she masquerades as a boy. Unlike the major genres which traditionally assign a limited range of stereotypes to women, Cukor's work is peopled with emotionally resilient heroines who, while acknowledging patriarchal might, none the less challenge the male's authority and frequently outflank him by the use of his own most cherished weapons of wit and intelligence. The bright and innovative series of Garson Kanin and Ruth Gordon scripted films, in particular the Hepburn/Tracy vehicles of *Adam's Rib* (1949) and *Pat and Mike* (1952), lay out the terrain on which the sexes engage, but the hostilities are less than grim and lead less to victories than to shared emotional growth. The presentation of the courtroom drama in *Adam's Rib* as a series of carefully constructed performances conveys Cukor's view of role-playing: he is no moralist, concerned to expose 'artifice' or 'deceit' in the name of Truth, but a benign explorer of all the discourses that make up a multiplicity of truths.

The literary and stage antecedents to much of Cukor's earlier work obscured the view of his discreet but effective style, that none the less took unobtrusive risks with lengthy takes or hand-held camera, and could assume more highly inflected characteristics when required for melodrama, as in *A Woman's Face* (1941) or *Gaslight* (1944). Rejecting the option of 'opening out' stage plays in a supposedly 'cinematic' way, Cukor preferred to concentrate his direction on the management of performances through the cinematic means of pacing, composition and camera placement. With *A Star is Born*, his first venture in Cinemascope and colour, Cukor however discovered a new stylistic richness and chromatic complexity in a project that yoked together the disparate genres of musical comedy, Hollywood chronicle and domestic drama to provide Judy Garland with a quasi-confessional role and Cukor

with a new boost of critical life. The musicals that followed were generally more uneven works, despite the massive popular success of *My Fair Lady* (1964) and his career now seems beached after the wreck of an attempted American – Russian co-production of *The Bluebird* (1976).

Nigel Algar

Other films include: *A Bill of Divorcement* (1932); *David Copperfield* (1934); *Camille* (1936); *Gone with the Wind* (1939) (Cukor worked on pre-production for a year and shot some material); *The Women* (1939); *The Philadelphia Story* (1940); *Born Yesterday* (1950); *It should happen to you* (1954); *Bhowani Junction* (1956); *Les Girls* (1957); *Heller in Pink Tights* (1959); *Let's Make Love* (1960); *The Chapman Report* (1962); *Travels with My Aunt* (1972). See: Carlos Clarens, *Cukor* (1976).

107
CUMMINGS, Edward Estlin 1894–1962

US poet

E. E. Cummings (or e. e. cummings as 'Mr Lowercase Highbrow' preferred) was born on 14 October 1894 at Cambridge, Massachusetts; his father taught at Harvard and subsequently became minister of Old South Church, a celebrated Unitarian institution in Boston. Cummings's background was thus eminently respectable and he gravitated naturally to the academic life. In 1911 he enrolled at Harvard where he contributed lush Keatsian verse to the college magazine and played a prominent part in establishing the Harvard Poetry Society. In 1915 he received his BA in English and Classics and the next year took his MA. Then, unpredictably, he quit academic life and went to New York to work for a mail order firm. It was an early assertion of his refusal to be typecast in a given social role.

In 1917, before the USA had entered the hostilities of the First World War, Cummings enlisted in the Norton-Harjes Ambulance Corps and was sent to France on active service. Because of his association with a friend – whose letters criticizing the French war effort were discovered by the censor – Cummings was classified as a suspicious person and detained for three months at the French prison camp of La Ferté Macé. There sixty men were kept under surveillance in an oblong room 'about 80 feet by 40, unmistakably ecclesiastical in feeling' – *The Enormous Room* (1922) of his first book. To Cummings the indignities so stoically endured by the inmates proved emphatically that the gifted individual could always transcend the hostile conditions inflicted by society; his personal credo of individualism was embodied in the Delectable Mountains, four supremely human beings. The shape of the book was suggested by Bunyan's *Pilgrim's Progress* (hence the Delectable Mountains) and the style was visionary: 'In the course of the next ten thousand years it may be possible to find Delectable Mountains without going to prison . . . it may be possible, I dare say, to encounter Delectable Mountains who are not in prison.'

After the war Cummings remained in Paris to study painting which, as is evident from his pictorial collection *CIOPW* (1931), remained a passion with him. He was impressed by the textural experiments of the French painters who used the anti-illusionistic method of Cubism to restore the subjective element to figurative art: the artist's vision was to transcend the objects that inspired it. Cummings applied this textural approach to poetry and discovered that he could revitalize traditional literary themes by presenting them in a typographically novel format. He had already published poems in the *Dial* magazine and his first collection *Tulips and Chimneys* (1923) brought him to the notice of a puzzled public. In the section 'Chansons Innocentes' Cummings evoked childhood with his visually attractive metrics:

> In Just-
> spring   when the world is mud-
> luscious the little
> lame balloonman
>
> whistles far   and wee.

Cummings also showed, by the inclusion of sixty-one sonnets in his first collection, that he was no destructive enemy of formal poetry; his method was (and remained) a means of shocking readers out of their complacent familiarity with the world.

Cummings had found in France, as he put it in his Charles Eliot Norton lectures *i: six nonlectures* (1953), 'an immediate reconciling of spirit and flesh, forever and now, heaven and earth. Paris was for me precisely and complexly this homogeneous duality: this accepting transcendence; this living and dying more than death or life.' In 1924 he returned to New York where he published *&* (1925) and received the *Dial* prize for poetry. Cummings then made a dramatic theatrical entrance with his play *Him* (1927) which was first performed by the Provincetown Players in 1927. In a programme note he warned the audience 'DON'T TRY TO UNDERSTAND IT, LET IT TRY TO UNDERSTAND YOU' and confronted them with the conflict between Him (an artist unable to function because of his denial of love) and Me (a pregnant woman frustrated by Him's resistance to domesticity). By rotating the theatrical room in which Him and Me performed Cummings deliberately denied the audience the reassurance of a fixed viewpoint.

In 1931 Cummings spent a month in the USSR; his vivid journal of this visit was published as *Eimi* (1933). With his transcendental belief in the sanctity of the individual, Cummings was appalled at the regimentation he saw in Russia: 'Russia, I felt, was more deadly than war; when nationalists hate, they hate by merely killing and maiming human beings; when internationalists hate, they hate by categorying and pigeonholing human beings.' Some of this political indignation entered his collection *No Thanks* (1935), so called because the manuscript was rejected by fourteen publishers whose names Cummings catalogued on his dedication page. However, the positive aspect of the poet was expressed in typographically extreme poems which juxtaposed images inside and outside parentheses:

> swi(
>   across! gold's
>
> rouNdly
>   )ftblac
> kl(ness)y.

Cummings was now a poetic law unto himself though his roots in the radical individualism of Blake, Emerson and Thoreau were obvious enough. He resisted Grand Old Man status by remaining true to his initial insights and in his fifth Charles Eliot Norton 'nonlecture' defined his abiding transcendental vision: 'We should go hugely astray in assuming that art was the only selftranscendence. Art is a mystery; all mysteries have their source in a mystery-of-mysteries who is love; and if lovers may reach eternity through love herself, their mystery remains essentially that of the loving artist whose way must lie through his art, and of the loving worshipper whose aim is oneness with his god.' He continued to make this philosophy startling by his technical vivacity, and his poetry – right up to the posthumous collection *73 Poems* (1963) – revealed, rather than concealed, a touching belief in humanity and a dazzling lyric gift.

Alan Bold

Cummings's poetry is collected in *Complete Poems* (2 vols, 1968; 1972); useful critical studies include Norman Friedman's *E. E. Cummings: The Growth of a Writer* (1964) and Charles Norman's *The Magic Maker: E. E. Cummings* (1969).

D

108

DALI, Salvador 1904–

Spanish painter

'With the coming of Dali,' wrote André Breton* in his introduction to the first Paris exhibition of 1929, 'it is perhaps the first time that the mental windows have been opened really wide, so that one can feel oneself gliding up towards the wild sky's trap.' For Surrealism it was a year of crisis and redirection. Since the movement's inception in 1924 the emphasis had been on automatism and the advantage of chance discovery as a contribution in artistic and literary creation. The Surrealists were to draw their inspiration not from reality but from a 'purely interior model'. But it was becoming increasingly apparent that the process had inherent weaknesses. The essentially passive role in which the writer and painter became instruments no longer had any validity. That 'state of effervescence' had degenerated into repetition, monotony and disillusionment. It did not mean a lack of faith in the process, but rather a recognition that it no longer constituted for Surrealism an end in itself. Dali fully shared the Surrealists' commitment to the automatic processes, which he had read about in various reviews and catalogues. In 1927, according to his own *The Secret Life of Salvador Dali* (1942), when he was still living in his home town of Figueras, near Barcelona, he 'spent the whole day seated before my easel, my eyes staring fixedly, trying to "see", like a medium, the images that would spring up in my imagination.' Two paintings date from this period, *Apparatus and Hand* and *Blood is Sweeter than Honey*, which not only reveal Surrealist influences but also show that, for the involuntary images inspired by a dream state to achieve their full potential, they had to be developed in a fully conscious manner. By 1929, using his technical dexterity as a 'means of forcing inspiration', he had produced some of the most genuinely Surrealist paintings of the time. For the next four years, according to Breton, Dali 'incarnated the Surrealist spirit and his genius made it shine as could only have been done by one who had in no way participated in the often ungrateful episodes of its birth.' There is little argument that he became the movement's most spectacular exponent, bringing to Surrealist art a new objectivity, painting like a madman rather than an occasional somnambulist. From the time when he had been a student at the Madrid School of Fine Arts he had expressed a preference for those artists who used a precise technique, and his own convincingly illusionist realism was now put to the use of painting as an illustrative medium and to revive a return to anecdotal art. A group of small works of hallucinatory intensity crystallized Dali's mature style: *The Lugubrious Game, Illumined Pleasures* and *Accommodations of Desire* (all 1929) combined photographic realism (at this time he even called his paintings 'handmade photography') with bits of collaged colour engravings and photographs to establish an all-over pattern of exactitude. Painted replicas of the collage elements were so carefully executed as to be indistinguishable.

Dali's intervention was ceaseless and on all levels, including revolutionary critical interpretation of familiar works of art. Millet's *Angelus* he saw as a monument to sexual repression, while in *The Legend of William Tell* he discovered not filial devotion but incestuous mutilation. In his own *The Enigma of William Tell* a kneeling figure with the face of Lenin* appears trouserless with an extended buttock supported by a crutch. Along with his fascination of all aspects of aberration, the provocative scatology of his subject-matter and his understanding of Freud's* psychology on which he based much of his early work led to the development of his theory of 'paranoiac-critical activity', which he describes as 'a spontaneous method of irrational knowledge based upon the critical and systematic objectification of delirious associations and interpretations'. It is, in fact, a form of image interpretation, in which the spectator sees in a picture or object a different image depending upon his or her own imaginative ability. Not unrelated to this method is one of his most lyrical paintings, *The Phantom Cart* of 1933, in which a horse-drawn cart is going towards a distant Eastern city. The two seated figures, we realize, are also the buildings in the city, suggesting that the cart has already reached its destination. Another influence on Dali was Art Nouveau architecture and decoration, which he called the 'undulant-convulsive' style. Many of the ectoplasmic forms in his paintings during the years 1930–4 are based on the decorative busts in that style or the wrought-iron vegetation of the Paris Métro.

Dali has always refused to explain the meaning of his paintings, adding that he is as astonished as anyone by the images that appear on his canvases. Yet we know from his account of his childhood in *The Secret Life*, from his interpretative studies of Millet, the Pre-Raphaelites and William Tell, that there is evidence of a meaning behind many of his fetish symbols. One obsessional image is watches, which first made their appearance in *The Persistence of Memory* (1931). He makes them limp, soft and pliable, hanging over ledges and tree trunks to express eternity and the flexibility of time. Equally dominant is the crutch which he uses to prop up fantastic forms. He sees in the bifurcated shape the whole concept of life and death but the emphasis he places on them in his autobiography suggests homosexual meaning and the need for masculinity. As a substitute for his father he uses the grasshopper. It is an image of fear, of discipline. Dali has called these objects 'a tangible, objective, and symbolic materialization of desire by sublimation, a wish or a prayer'.

More purely aesthetic influences became noticeable in a number of works between 1934 and 1936, in particular a growing interest in the nineteenth-century Romantic tradition. More serious perhaps were his political tendencies and the interest he began to show in Nazism, which gave rise to heated discussions within the Surrealist group, some of whom saw no reason to sponsor any of his private obsessions. Although an attempt to exclude him was not unanimous, he ceased to attend group meetings. Nevertheless he was still invited to contribute to the exhibitions.

Prior to the outbreak of the Second World War (which he spent in America) Dali made three visits to Italy. The works of Botticelli, Piero di Cosimo and Caravaggio, as well as Vermeer and Velázquez, began to play an important part in the iconography of his paintings. This return to classicism demanded a more conscious objectivity and a close study of the pictorial science of the Renaissance. For Dali it meant 'integration, synthesis, cosmogony, faith'. Not surprisingly this shift was accompanied by an increased belief in the Catholic hierarchy.

No longer a Surrealist, he has over the years become so identified with the movement, kept alive largely by his own provocative exhibitionism, that in the public mind Surrealism is Salvador Dali. Considering his mental gymnastics there is some excuse for the prevailing error.

Conroy Maddox

Dali's writings include: *Hidden Faces* (a novel, 1944); *Diary of a Genius* (1966); and *Dali by Dali* (1970). See: David Gascoyne, *A Short Survey of Surrealism* (1936); Fleur Cowles, *The Case of Salvador Dali* (1959); Marcel Jean, *The History of Surrealist Painting* (1960); Patrick Waldberg, *Surrealism* (1965); Roger Cardinal and Robert Short, *Surrealism - Permanent Revelation* (1970); R. Descharnes, *World of Salvador Dali* (1972); Conroy Maddox, *Dali* (1979).

109
DALLAPICCOLA, Luigi 1904–75

Italian composer

Born on the borders between the Latin and Slav worlds, from the beginning Dallapiccola's life was marked by the simultaneous presence of different cultural trends. His father, professor of classics at and director of the Italian Gymnasium in Pisino (then under Austrian rule), introduced him to Homer, the Greek lyric poets and Dante. In 1917 the family was forced, for political reasons, to move to Graz, where frequent visits to the opera house exposed the young student to Mozart and Wagner. Of particular importance was a performance of *The Flying Dutchman*, after which Dallapiccola decided to devote himself to music.

Music lessons had begun as early as 1914, in Pisino, and continued after the war at Trieste. In May 1922 he moved to Florence, where he enrolled at the Conservatorio Luigi Cherubini, obtaining a piano diploma in 1924. It was at this time that his personal interests and curiosity led him to discover the music of Debussy*, as well as Gesualdo and Monteverdi, whom he considered the masters of Italian polyphony. Then, in April 1924, a performance of Schoenberg's* *Pierrot Lunaire*, conducted by the composer, revealed yet another musical horizon. This and similar musical experiences were stored by Dallapiccola's exceptional memory, becoming models of expression for the present and for the future. Another case was the production of Verdi's *Simon Boccanegra* at the Vienna Opera House in 1930, which made Dallapiccola look at the music of the Italian composer in an altogether new way, and to discover in it powerful models of dramatic expression.

A career as a concert pianist soon gave way to a career as a composer, supported by a piano teaching post at the Conservatorio which he retained until 1967. Of the early compositions the *Divertimento in quattro esercizi* for voice and five instruments (published in 1936 together with the *Partita* for orchestra and *Inni*, 'Hymns', for three pianos) is most representative: a completely polyphonic texture is organized in forms derived from both instrumental (e.g. *bourrée*) and vocal (e.g. *arietta*) models. The movement of the parts over a spectrum that exceeds the purely diatonic reveals the influence of Busoni*, a composer whom Dallapiccola revered throughout his life. A meeting with Berg* in Venice in 1934, and performances of Schoenberg's *Variations* Op. 31 and Webern's* *Concerto* Op. 24 during the 1935 SIMC Festival in Prague introduced him to the twelve-note techniques of the Vienna School, then totally unknown in Italy, but soon to be defined as 'degenerate' by the fascist regime. But this would not deter Dallapiccola, who already had a strong concept of his activities as a musician: music being the means to express his position as a man in the face of historical events. And indeed this morally engaged attitude, which influenced his musical language at every level, accounts for the coherence of Dallapiccola's output as a whole. Thus, whether he is using serial principles or the older canonic techniques, first and foremost the method of composition is an act of intellectual discipline, *the* way for the musician to be engaged in his profession. Even Dallapiccola's choice of texts to be set to music, or of plots for his operas, usually reflects the same austere standards.

The years immediately before the Second World War saw the composition of *Volo di notte* ('Night Flight'), a one-act opera based on the novel by Saint-Exupéry, in which serialism is applied sparingly, followed by *Canti di prigionia* ('Songs of Imprisonment', 1938–42), where it plays a much larger and more functional role. A setting of texts by Mary Stuart, Boethius and Savonarola, the *Canti* were Dallapiccola's protest against the violence of the times. Complete serialism was applied for the first time in *Sex carmina Alcaei* ('Six songs of Alcaeus'), which, together with *Cinque frammenti di Saffo* ('Five Sappho fragments') and *Due liriche di Anacreonte* ('Two poems of Anachreon'), form the cycle *Liriche greche* ('Greek lyrics', 1942–5). Here Dallapiccola looks to the world of the Greek poets as an ideal means to assert the cathartic power of beauty, as opposed to suffering and cruelty. In his second opera, *Il prigioniero* ('The Prisoner', 1946), he returned to the problems of freedom, albeit in a deliberately enigmatic way, while in *Job* (a 'sacra rappresentazione', 1950) he is concerned with the confrontation between man and his creator. Meanwhile his interest at the purely contrapuntal level, outside serial techniques, was developed using materials of past composers, leading to his *Sonatina canonica* on themes by Paganini for piano (1946), *Tartiniana* (1951) and *Tartiniana seconda* (1956) for violin and orchestra. However, the mainstream of his composition remained twelve-note, and he used serial techniques in an increasingly complex and sophisticated way in such works as *Tre poemi* (1949), *Quaderno musicale di Annalibera* (a 'musical notebook' for his daughter, piano, 1951), *An Mathilde* (cantata on a text by Heine, 1955) and *Dialoghi* for cello and orchestra (1960). During the period of these compositions he also began work on what he rightly considered to be the sum of his musical, as well as his human, experience, the two-act opera *Ulisse*, premiered in Berlin in 1968. For Dallapiccola the myth of Ulysses, of his perennial travelling and questioning, both reflected the destiny of man and provided him with the opportunity to express, at the very end of the work, his mystical belief in a God who appeases and offers rest to life's torment. The last works, *Sicut umbra . . .* ('Like a shadow . . .', 1970) and *Commiato* ('Farewell', 1972), scored for voice and chamber group, are moved by the same spirit.

Although Dallapiccola never held a post in Italy as a teacher of composition, his influence has been considerable, particularly among American composers. He not only travelled to the United States as a visiting professor, but received several Americans privately at his home in Florence. His lectures, also delivered throughout Europe, and other writings are of equal importance, especially as he did not always confine himself to purely musical matters. *Appunti, incontri, meditazioni* ('Notes, meetings, meditations', 1970) deals with the events and ideas that prompted several of his own compositions, as well as with moments in music of the past in which, by detecting seminal ideas for his own work, Dallapiccola discovered some basic structural principles of the genre concerned. And it was at this level that he integrated serialism with the Italian tradition to which he belonged, bringing that tradition into the European mainstream. After their only meeting, in Vienna in 1942, Webern wrote to him: 'Your way of presentation (*Art der Darstellung*) may be quite different from mine, yet our way of thinking moves in circles which I feel are very close.'

Pierluigi Petrobelli

Other works include: *Sei cori di Michelangelo Buonarroti il Giovane* (1933–6); the one-act ballet *Marsia* (1942–3); *Ciaccona Intermezzo e Adagio* for solo cello (1945); *Quattro liriche di Antonio Machado* for soprano and piano (1948); *Goethe-Lieder* for mezzo and three clarinets (1953); *Canti di liberazione* for chorus and orchestra (1951–3); *Requiescant* for mixed choir and orchestra (1957–8); *Preghiere* for baritone and chamber orchestra (1962); *Parole di San Paolo* (1964); *Tempus destruendi – tempus aedificandi* for a capella choir (1970–1). See: R. Vlad, *Luigi Dallapiccola* (1957); and F. Nicolodi, *Luigi Dallapiccola: saggi, testimonianze, carteggio, biografia e bibliografia* (1975).

110
D'ANNUNZIO, Gabriele 1863–1938

Italian poet

No less an authority than Eugenio Montale* has declared that D'Annunzio influenced all subsequent Italian poets, yet even by 1910 younger writers had felt the need to react against his work. Factors which may explain this paradox include D'Annunzio's all-pervading presence, the variety of his experimentation, and the particular confusion of art and life which made much of his work highly rhetorical and led to his flamboyant political gestures. The social and political implications of his work and his involvement with nascent fascism were responsible for the total rejection of D'Annunzio immediately after the Second World War.

D'Annunzio was born at Pescara in the isolated

Abruzzi region, but was educated from 1874 to 1881 in Tuscany, at the well-known Collegio Cicognini in Prato. Literary fame came early, when his first collection of poetry, *Primo vere*, was published in 1879. This subsequently won him entry into literary circles in Rome, where he married a duke's daughter, Maria Hardouin di Gallese, in 1883. Many much-publicized affairs with other women followed.

His early poetry and prose followed prevailing Italian currents: *Canto novo* (1882) and the short stories of *Terra vergine* (1882) echoed respectively Carducci's classicism and Verga's realism. The moral convictions of these writers, however, were lacking, and instead D'Annunzio stressed the vitality of sensory experience, a feature which, in various forms, was to permeate his work.

During the later 1880s, worldly elegance and refinement, formal beauty and sophisticated sensuality eclipsed the elemental natural world in D'Annunzio's poetry: influenced particularly by Gautier and the French Parnassians, he pictured the poet as a goldsmith fashioning beautiful jewellery. The cult of Art pervades his first novel, *Il piacere* (1889, trans. as *The Child of Pleasure*, 1898), but the criticism of its protagonist, the decadent aesthete Andrea Sperelli, for his lack of will-power and his submission to sensuality foreshadows future developments.

From 1892 onwards, D'Annunzio's somewhat distorted understanding of Nietzsche's conception of the superman contributed to the evolution of his ideology: instead of rejecting banal reality for Art, several heroes of later novels and plays try to reshape the world by imposing their powerful wills, through violent, ruthless action or through their imagination. The idea that history is made by the superior few, whose happiness is all-important, found overt political expression in *Le vergini delle rocce* (1895, trans. as *The Virgins of the Rocks*, 1899), where strong government is envisaged as the means of favouring a privileged class and fostering imagination and beauty. Such anti-democratic and anti-egalitarian views, together with the novel's celebration of Latinity, appealed to many intellectuals of the post-Unification generation who feared the advance of socialism and cherished impractical dreams of Italian imperialism.

After a brief, ineffectual parliamentary career (1897–1900), D'Annunzio found in the First World War a more congenial theatre for his cult of action as a self-sufficient value: he became a powerful propagandist for the cause of Italian intervention in May 1915, and later performed several daring naval and aerial exploits. In 1919–20, he led the illegal occupation of Fiume, a territory claimed for Italy by nationalist groups: several features of his political style were later adopted by Mussolini*.

Alcyone (1904), the third of a poetic sequence called the *Laudi*, is generally considered D'Annunzio's masterpiece. Its theme is the superman's re-acquisition of a primitive, Dionysiac communion with nature through his senses, and the penetration and transfiguration of reality by his expressive power. Thus the rhetoric which was to be rejected by younger poets is still present, but many poems are outstanding for their re-creation of fleeting moments through an incantatory web of sounds and rhythms. The importance of musicality in *Alcyone* and its extensive metrical experimentation, the most far-reaching results of D'Annunzio's contacts with European symbolism, make this collection a crucial milestone in the development of modern Italian poetry.

Dr Shirley Vinall

D'Annunzio's many works are available in the series *Tutte le Opere di Gabriele D'Annunzio* (from 1939). G. Gatti, *Vita di Gabriele D'Annunzio* (1956) is the standard biography. See also: E. Mariano, *L'Arte di Gabriele D'Annunzio* (1968) and *D'Annunzio e il simbolismo europeo*; on the novels, J. Goudet, *D'Annunzio romanziere* (1975); and on D'Annunzio's politics, C. Salinari, *Miti e coscienza del decadentismo italiano* (1960), and R. De Felice, *D'Annunzio politico 1918–1938* (1978).

111
DAVIES, Peter Maxwell 1934–

British composer

Peter Maxwell Davies was born in Salford, Lancashire, and developed a consuming interest in music from a very early age. He was educated at Leigh Grammar School and the University of Manchester. While at the university he attended classes at the Royal Manchester College of Music where Richard Hall taught composition, and it was there that he became a member of a group of student composers and performers dedicated to the advancement of new music. The other members of the Manchester Group, as it became known, included Harrison Birtwistle, Alexander Goehr, Elgar Howarth and John Ogden. Following a period of study with the composer Goffredo Petrassi at the Accademia S. Cecilia in Rome, Davies was in 1959 appointed Director of Music at Cirencester Grammar School, and as a result of his work there acquired a considerable reputation as a music educator. In 1962 he spent eighteen months at Princeton University, USA, where he attended postgraduate classes by Milton Babbitt*, Earl Kim and James K. Randall. During the mid-1960s Davies and Birtwistle felt that their works were not receiving a sufficient number of good performances, and, to remedy this, they founded in 1967 a virtuoso chamber ensemble called the Pierrot Players. After a few years the collaboration came to an end, but Davies re-formed the group as the Fires of London. He has since travelled throughout the world directing them in performances of his works to great public and critical acclaim.

Davies is an artist who, more than most, needs solitude to bring his compositions to completion. In 1970 he moved from the south of England to Orkney, and eventually rebuilt a derelict croft on the remote island of Hoy. He has since identified himself and his music with Orkney, its culture, history and natural surroundings: in 1976 he founded, and has since helped to direct, the St Magnus Festival which takes place every midsummer in Orkney.

Davies's earliest compositions, written for himself to perform on the piano, date from his schoolboy days and reveal a structural strength and surface polish rare in teenage efforts: the principal influence is that of Bartók*. The works he wrote as a student and member of the Manchester Group, the *Sonata for Trumpet and Piano* (1955) and the *Five Piano Pieces* (1956), show a move towards a more 'advanced' idiom influenced by Messiaen* and Schoenberg*. Schoenberg was an important influence, not only from the strictly musical point of view, but also with regard to his attitude to the activity of composition and to the function of an artist in society: he has inherited Schoenberg's deep concern, on the one hand, to structure his musical arguments as meticulously as he is able, and, on the other, to communicate a personal vision with as great an intensity as possible. It is this Schoenbergian commitment to 'heart and brain' that has won him an enthusiastic international following.

Davies has long been interested in the medieval and renaissance periods, particularly because of the integration of the arts with daily religious and social life. In his composition he frequently utilizes early-music sources and techniques to aid, as if by sympathetic magic, the achievement of a parallel integration of his artistic vision into the everyday awareness of his audiences. The influence of early music is already apparent, at least to the analyst, in his earliest published compositions – *Alma Redemptoris Mater* (1957), *St Michael* (1957), *Prolation* (1959) and *Ricecar and Doubles* (1959). Although the direct relationship with the medieval models is in such works marked by Davies's own musical style, the link over subsequent years became ever clearer. The opera *Taverner* (1962–70), for instance, as well as being loosely based on the life of the Tudor composer, derives musically almost entirely from aspects of his compositions, and includes direct quotations from the *Gloria Tibi Trinitas* mass; while *Antechrist* (1967) and *L'Homme armé* (1968) unfold arguments based on initial, explicit statements of their source works.

But Davies is concerned with far more than mere quotation: the very fabric of his musical thought and technique is derived as much from the masters of the medieval and renaissance periods as from those of the earlier twentieth century. It is a process which at times can be precisely identified, yet which always retains a mystical quality: the acquisition of *auctoritas* through the inheriting of the mantle of tradition lies at the heart of Davies's artistic character. That this is not simply a question of musical language can be seen from his choice of subject for his music-theatre works, which all relate to historical, religious or even folkloristic traditions: e.g., *Eight Songs for a Mad King* (1968) concerns George III's mental derangement; *Vesalii Icones* (1968), the fourteen stations of the cross; and *The Martyrdom of St Magnus* (1976), the life and death of the Orcadian patron saint – a story which embraces all three kinds of tradition.

Since the move to Orkney, Orcadian texts and topics have come to dominate Davies's output. In the light of the received view of Davies as an avant-garde composer, it seems extraordinary to describe him as a 'nature composer' or a 'folk composer'; but, while he has continued to expand the technical resources of his compositions and to require new heights of virtuosity from his performers ('traditional' concerns of the avant-garde), such important works as *Stone Litany* (1973), *Hymn to St Magnus* (1972), *The Blind Fiddler* (1976), *Symphony* (1976), the chamber opera *The Martyrdom of St Magnus*, *A Mirror of Whitening Light* (1977), the children's opera *The Two Fiddlers* (1978), and *Solstice of Light* (1979) draw deeply for their inspiration on the composer's fascination with the sights, and especially the sounds, of the wild sea-and stark land-scapes of the extreme north and on the Scandinavian-influenced lore and legend of Orkney. The major literary influence is the outstanding Orcadian poet, George Mackay Brown, on whose work Davies has frequently drawn (*From Stone to Thorn*, 1971; *Fiddler at the Wedding*, 1973–4; *Dark Angels*, 1974; *The Blind Fiddler*, and *The Martyrdom*).

What concerns do such diverse interests and influences as Davies's articulate? They are at their most explicit in his music-theatre and operatic works, but are also at least implicit in most of his other substantial compositions. These might be characterized as the hypocrisy of institutionalized belief (*Taverner*, *Vesalii Icones* and *Le Jongleur de Notre Dame*, 1978), the betrayal and persecution of innocence (*Taverner*, *Eight Songs for a Mad King*, *Miss Donnithorne's Maggot*, 1974) and above all (in *The Two Fiddlers* and *Le Jongleur de Notre Dame*) the dedicated artist's power to create, thereby nourishing the soul and giving intimations of a spiritual reality which contrasts starkly with the mundane materialism of daily human affairs.

Stephen Arnold

A comprehensive list of Davies's compositions to 1978 is given in *Peter Maxwell Davies*, Tempo Booklet No. 2, which is devoted to a selection of the many contributions on Davies and his music which have appeared in the periodical *Tempo* since 1962.

112
DAVIS, Miles Dewey, Jr 1926–

US jazz trumpeter, composer, bandleader

Miles Davis has played a major role in the development of jazz from the mid-1940s to the mid-1970s. His contributions have been a personal and influential style of trumpet playing and improvisation, the leadership of innovative bands and recording sessions, and the ability to sense the potential in new forms of music and exploit them.

He was born into a well-to-do Illinois family and was destined for college when he chose music instead. He sought out and attached himself to Charlie Parker* in New York, becoming the trumpeter in his quintet from 1945–8, and playing on most of Parker's famous Savoy and Dial recordings. His tone is weaker and his articulation less sure than those of other bop trumpeters, but his mastery of the idiom and his improvisation are impressive for a nineteen-year-old.

In 1949 nine musicians gathered for a short engagement at the Royal Roost, and were recorded by Capitol. They made a sound quite unlike swing or bop music hitherto. The arrangements were relaxed, reflective and intimate, and caused the recordings to be titled 'The Birth of the Cool'. Even though he was not perhaps the originator of its ideas, Davis led the band, which was one of the sources of the 'cool jazz' of the 1950s. Most of the players were to be prominent in important bands of their own. Davis himself went on, after a fight with heroin, to lead a series of quintets through the 1950s, through which passed many major jazz musicians of the period, and whose recordings are considered classics of the post-war era. Davis made a virtue out of necessity where his trumpet playing was concerned, and further refined the small-scale, intimate sound, often playing through a Harmon mute with the stem removed. Whereas bop musicians used flurries of notes, Davis used few, well-chosen, and uttered with emotional intensity, as if to express a restrained passion. Young musicians everywhere began imitating his lack of vibrato, his cracked grace notes, his way of half-valving to make a note droop at the end, his way of giving a new flavour to what seemed unpromising material (e.g. *Bye Bye Blackbird*). In live performances, his personality also added to the aura: he was without consideration for the audience, would play with his back to them, leave the stage when he had finished soloing, and generally maintain that his music was all that he owed the listener. Davis's style was complemented by the very different style of his most important

saxophonist, John Coltrane, an improviser of awesome energy.

At the end of the 1950s Davis began playing numbers that, instead of having a sequence of rapidly changing chords, were based on a mode which lasted for a number of bars, and on which the player had more time to improvise melodies (the LP *Kind of Blue*). In this same period the arranger Gil Evans wrote orchestrations that highlighted Davis's soloing on trumpet or fluegel horn (*Miles Ahead*). The record *Sketches of Spain* (in which Rodrigo's *Concierto de Aranjuez* is played with Evans's arrangement and Davis's trumpet replacing the guitar) belongs in a category of music which has been called 'third stream', attempting to bring classical music and jazz together.

Towards the end of the 1960s, many jazzmen were moving in one of two directions: towards 'free jazz' (in which improvisers were no longer bound to harmonic structures), or towards a 'fusion' with rock music (intenser and more repetitive rhythms, simpler melodies, more use of electronic instruments and effects, less emphasis on solo improvising). Davis experimented with rock, and using a tenor saxophonist, guitarist, rhythm section augmented with assorted percussion, and various players at electronic keyboards, began a series of recordings and live performances which led to his being credited with the innovation of jazz-rock or electro-jazz (*In a Silent Way*, 1968). Certainly, once Miles Davis moved towards rock, many other jazzmen followed.

Davis has always managed to see how jazz could be brought closer and made more accessible to a large public. When bop seemed to be growing stale and repetitive, his quintets of the 1950s transformed it. His move towards rock has had the same effect, bringing thousands of young people into contact with a jazz music (diluted, perhaps) they would otherwise have ignored.

Christopher Wagstaff

Selected recordings: 1940s on Spotlite and Savoy, Capitol (*Birth of the Cool*); his 1950s recordings reissued by Prestige, and for CBS: *Milestones* (1958), *Kind of Blue* (1959), *Porgy and Bess* (1958), *Sketches of Spain* (1960), *My Funny Valentine* (1964), *E.S.P.* (1969), *Bitches Brew* (1970), *Live-Evil* (1972). Biography: Bill Cole, *Miles Davis* (1974); Joe Goldberg, *Jazz Masters of the Fifties* (1965); Michael James, *Miles Davis* (1961). See also: Mark Gridley, *Jazz Styles* (1978).

113
DEBUSSY, (Achille-) Claude 1862–1918

French composer

The composer who liked to sign himself 'musicien

français' was born of a line of farmers and artisans, and nothing in his heritage appears to have predisposed him to a musical career. In fact, his parents envisaged for him a career as a sailor. What may well have been a decisive influence came when he was eight years old – a meeting with Madame Mauté de Fleurville, a pupil of Chopin and mother-in-law of the poet Verlaine; and for three years he studied piano with her prior to entering the Paris Conservatoire. This early link with Chopin and Verlaine is indeed peculiarly significant: Chopin was perhaps the most important single musical influence in the formation of Debussy's highly individual style of composition; while Verlaine and other poets and writers of the time were part of an immensely influential literary ambience into which Debussy entered completely. At the Conservatoire he showed a mixture of brilliance and waywardness which led (not without difficulties) to his being awarded the coveted Prix de Rome. In Rome, however, he disliked intensely his stay at the Villa Medici, and fled from it twice, back to Paris, the second time for good.

His first work of lasting interest from about this time is *La Damoiselle élue* (written in 1887–8), a setting of a French version of Rossetti's 'Blessed Damozel' for solo voices, chorus and orchestra – a work which struck the academic judges as 'vague', with its fluctuating harmonies and rhythms. Wagner at the time was the idol of the Paris artistic world. Debussy greatly admired his *Tristan and Isolde*, and had the opportunity to hear Wagner operas at Bayreuth in 1888 and 1889. It was a strong influence against which he was later to react. Meanwhile, a Wagnerian richness pervaded some of his earlier compositions. Then he became acquainted with the score of Mussorgsky's opera *Boris Godunov*, and immediately he was an ardent admirer of that composer's original and very personal form of expression. This and other Russian influences, the fascination of the Javanese gamelan (heard at the Paris Exposition Universelle), and contact with the economical style of the composer Erik Satie* – all these elements were reflected in Debussy's work; in the String Quartet (1893), and above all in the *Prélude à l'Après-midi d'un Faune* (1892–4) which was his first fully personal expression. In this work he conveyed the spirit of the poem *L'Après-midi d'un Faune*, by his close friend Mallarmé, in a style which was closely related to the Symbolist movement in the arts – a style in which ideas and states of mind are *suggested* by symbols, and these symbols become more significant, in the inner world of reflection, than any external reality. Herein lies the essence of Debussy's mature style – and comparisons with Impressionism can be quite misleading. Some of Debussy's most fully characteristic work is found in his songs – his settings of Symbolist poets such as Verlaine, Baudelaire, Mallarmé: the *Fêtes galantes* (Verlaine) of 1903 which range from the brilliantly imaginative 'Fantoches' to the quiet intimacy of the 'Colloque

sentimental'; the passionate hope and despair of the *Cinq Poèmes de Baudelaire* (1887–9); the mixture of depth of expression and preciosity in his Mallarmé settings. The *Chansons de Bilitis* (1897) captured perfectly the simple, clear, erotic character of the prose-poems (supposed to be the work of a girl of Ancient Greece) by his friend Pierre Louÿs, for whose writings Debussy felt a particular sympathy. And there is a stark dramatic quality in the *Trois Ballades de François Villon*, a striking impression of the past seen through modern eyes. For the set of *Proses lyriques* (1892–3) Debussy wrote his own poems, with mixed results.

His freedom from conventional formulae is clearly shown in his opera *Pelléas et Mélisande* (composed between 1892 and 1902), which reflects the elusive, legendary atmosphere of Maeterlinck's play, all half-lights and suggestion. Revolutionary in its unemphatic recitative-like style, the opera was ridiculed by the critics, but it was nevertheless a success with the public and had a number of performances, later becoming part of the standard operatic repertoire. He tried other operatic ideas, but they were not brought to satisfactory completion. The elaborate incidental music which Debussy wrote for Gabriele D'Annunzio's* spectacular mystery play *Le Martyre de Saint-Sébastien* contains much of importance; but performances are rare, and without the dramatic context the music loses much of its point.

In the *Prélude à l'Après-midi d'un Faune* Debussy was translating sensual and emotional impressions into the symbolic language of music, and was departing from traditional and fixed forms, 'liquidating' tonality and tonal procedures in ways that were as significant and far-reaching as the processes which Schoenberg* was carrying out at about the same time. Important to Debussy also was tone-colour and rhythmic subtlety as ingredients in his style – a style which profoundly affected the work of practically every twentieth-century composer.

It is mostly through the earlier orchestral works that Debussy's full development as a composer is seen: the *Nocturnes* (1887–9), *La Mer* (1903–5), and *Images* (1906–12). The three *Nocturnes* may well have been suggested directly by the series of paintings with the same title by Whistler, whom Debussy admired – and the composer himself said that the movements were intended to convey 'all the various impressions and special effects of light that the word suggests'. With *La Mer* (a work in three closely linked movements, like a symphony) the first impulse may have been pictorial also – Turner's sea pictures, which made a deep impression on the composer. Form and content are both strong in this work, but we see it against a many-sided background, a fusion of the arts, a fusion of nature and art. It is far more than a purely musical impact. In the scherzo movement ('Jeux de vagues') Debussy showed that he was able to unify, to bind together consistently, extremely diverse textures and timbres on a background of ever-changing tonalities. This technique was further explored in the ballet *Jeux* (1912) – a technique (or style) which has been described by Pierre Boulez* as follows: 'A component section of a theme is defined as another is suggested; another phrase is added and we have the beginnings of a form. More material is added and we have a structure.' On the face of it, *Jeux* is not sensational (its thunder was stolen by Stravinsky's* *Rite of Spring*, which appeared at the same time and was more obviously revolutionary); the advance was a logical stage in Debussy's evolution – a greater degree of clarity in the freedom of form and the attitude to thematic material, structure, orchestral textures, timbres, rhythm. It was an outlook and technique which immediately foreshadowed later 'avant-garde' procedures.

The orchestral *Images* are three separate compositions – not a unified structure as *La Mer* was. Each is an extremely personal expression of a composer at the height of his powers. The first section, 'Gigues' (originally 'Gigues tristes'), was probably suggested by a poem of Verlaine, 'Streets', written in London (which city Debussy visited on more than one occasion), and the work incorporates treatments of 'The Keel Row', a dance-song associated with England's Tyneside district. In the second movement, 'Ibéria', the atmosphere and rhythms of Spain are brilliantly conveyed. With the third movement, 'Rondes de Printemps', we are back in France: a complex and subjective evocation of the reawakening of nature, introducing some very unobvious treatments of folk-song material.

The important piano compositions of Debussy belong to the later part of his life: the two series of *Images* (1905 and 1907), and in particular the twenty-four *Préludes* (in two books, 1910 and 1910–13), which sensitively explore an enormous range of mood, character and feeling, within the expressive and technical range of the piano as opened out by Chopin. We know that Debussy was a fine pianist. Those who heard him play have told of his remarkable quality of touch and an entirely personal way of using the sustaining pedal. A further development in his piano style was the remarkable *Douze Études* (1915), in a sense a homage to Chopin, but also a personal technical accomplishment of vital importance.

In the early years of the century, Debussy wrote: 'Every sound you hear around you can be reproduced. Everything that a keen ear perceives in the rhythm of the surrounding world can be represented musically.' The result was a richly imaginative world of elusive harmonies and rhythms; melodies and chords drawn from the whole-tone scale and other unusual scales; chords regarded as colour, often with 'dissonances' unresolved, and colour many times as an end in itself; the placing of an unusual chord (related to overtones) on every note of a melodic phrase; oriental flavour and design in ornamental passages; abrupt, unprepared modulations, 'false' relations, and tonally rapidly-shifting focal points. As Verlaine had suggested that the poetic image should be '*plus vague et plus soluble dans l'air*' – so too with music, more indefinite and more fluid in the air, with nothing to weigh it down.

Although Debussy, through this kind of freedom, loosened classical tonality, he did not destroy it, as Schoenberg had felt obliged to do. Focal points remained, however flexible. A richer, freer, and essentially positive attitude towards tonality was the result of Debussy's innovations. His sensual and picturesque imagination created a new, instinctive, dreamlike world of music, lyrical and pantheistic, contemplative and objective.

David Cox

The most important works of Debussy are all mentioned above. They are mostly published by Durand, Paris. About Debussy: Léon Vallas, *Debussy, sa vie et ses oeuvres* (1926, trans. 1933); Edward Lockspeiser, *Debussy, his life and mind* (2 vols, 1962 and 1965); Stefan Jarocinski, trans. Rollo Myers, *Debussy – Impressionism and Symbolism* (1976); David Cox, *Debussy's Orchestral Music* (1974); Roger Nichols, *Debussy* (1972); Alfred Cortot, *The Piano Music of Debussy* (London 1922).

DE KOONING, William *see* KOONING, William de.

114
DELIUS, Frederick (Fritz Theodore Albert)
1862–1934

English composer

Delius was born in Bradford, Yorkshire, of German parents who had emigrated from Bielefeld in about 1850 during the English wool boom. He was one of twelve surviving children, brought up strictly though comfortably in surroundings where wool was the chief topic of conversation. But Fritz taught himself to play the piano at an early age and resisted his father's intentions to put him into the family business. At school locally, then near London, then back in Bradford he always managed to hear and think about music at the expense of other work. His father grew desperate and sent him abroad, but this only made his truancies easier and he was always called back. At last Delius was packed off to become joint-caretaker of an orange grove in Florida – in 1884 when he was twenty-two – where he was enchanted by the Negroes' singing and their songs, which he carefully noted down. After only six months he accidentally met a professional musician,

Thomas Ward, in Jacksonville, persuaded him to return to the plantation with him and to give him the kind of musical tuition in theory and composition that he needed. For another six months (oranges forgotten) Delius applied himself willingly and industriously and this was the most useful musical education he ever received. By 1887 he persuaded his father to let him take the course at Leipzig Conservatoire – the most famous in the world – but he was soon disenchanted by the outdated methods. He went to Norway, met Grieg and Sinding, and began composing. His *Florida Suite* was performed in Leipzig (1888) to an audience of two and for the price of a barrel of beer. In 1889, with Grieg's support, Delius again overcame his father's objections and went to live in France, to compose. There his friendship with Gauguin and other artists in Paris set him in the right creative atmosphere, and he started to fill his shelves with unperformed scores. In 1896 he first met the painter, Jelka Rosen, and often visited her at the house which she rented at Grez-sur-Loing, 64 km from Paris near Fontainebleau. Two years later, Jelka bought the house and Delius moved in with her. He would sometimes return to Paris for a resumption of old *affaires*, and this behaviour did not cease until an emotional crisis in his life led him to marry Jelka in 1903. In 1899 he had given a concert of his own works in London, paid for with a legacy from his uncle, but lost a lot of money. Nor was his music comprehended. The German conductor, Julius Buths, began to take up some of Delius's works in Elberfeld, but only a fraction of his output had yet been heard and he was still composing. His greatest opera, *A Village Romeo and Juliet*, was first given in Berlin in 1907 with limited success, and Delius went on to London to look for an orchestra to give another concert. The turning point in his life came when he met Thomas Beecham, whose New Symphony Orchestra, Delius decided, was the best in London. Beecham and Delius took to one another and thereafter Beecham became his editor, promoter and publicist, playing Delius as often as possible for the next fifty years. In 1910, Beecham gave *A Village Romeo and Juliet* at Covent Garden and began to include Delius compositions, old and new, in his concert programmes.

After contracting syphilis at the turn of the century, Delius's health began to deteriorate and he had to spend much of his royalties on temporary 'cures'. He and Jelka left Grez at the beginning of the war in 1914, and from 1915 they stayed in England with either Beecham, Henry Wood or Norman O'Neill. When the Germans considered Delius to be an enemy alien and refused to allow his music to be heard, he changed his forename Fritz to Frederick; but he was in poor health and finances and was having trouble with his eyes.

By 1922 he had lost the use of both hands and was in a wheel-chair; but in 1924 he went to London to supervise the playing of his incidental music for James Elroy Flecker's play *Hassan*. His finances eased, due to incoming royalties, but his inability to set down his thoughts coupled with the conviction that nobody wanted to hear them caused him immense frustration until the arrival in Grez of a young Yorkshireman. This was Eric Fenby, who from 1928 became Delius's amanuensis. By this time Delius was completely blind and helpless, relying on a succession of German male nurses to look after and read to him daily, under a strict regime. Only musical visitors were welcome: Beecham, Percy Grainger and his wife, Peter Warlock and a few others. Otherwise Delius was brusque and totally self-centred because all his energy was spent in staving off the agonies which racked his body.

In 1929 Beecham organized and presented a Festival of all Delius's important works, and the ailing composer managed with difficulty to go to London and to appear at all of them. The result assured him that the English had at last begun to understand him, and he expressed the unexpected wish to be buried in England. He was created a C.H. and received other honours before his death and burial at Grez (in unhallowed ground) in 1934. His body was subsequently exhumed and reburied at Limpsfield Churchyard, Surrey, in 1935, when Beecham made a remarkable valedictory speech over the grave.

Delius expresses himself best through the orchestra, when he explores and gives a deeper account of nature and natural beauty in music than any other composer. His musical voice appears to come from no previous compositional source, nor did it found a new school. Its unique feature is its block-harmonic construction, so unusual and contrary to established practice that in the early days it was sometimes changed out of ignorance and disbelief, with disastrous results. Beecham was the unchallenged master of interpreting Delius's music which, in less understanding hands, fails to achieve its full intentions and can even sound mawkish. Hence the sharply divided factions for and against Delius.

Alan Jefferson

Other operas: *Koanga* (Elberfeld 1904); *Fennimore and Gerda* (Frankfurt-am-Main 1919); *Irmelin* (Oxford 1953); *The Magic Fountain* (BBC 1978). For soloist(s), chorus and orchestra: *Appalachia* (1904); *Sea Drift* (1906); *A Mass of Life* (1909); *Songs of Sunset* (1911); *Arabesk* (1920); *Song of the High Hills* (1920); *Requiem* (1922). Orchestral works: *Paris, A Nocturne* (1901); *Over the Hills and Far Away* (1899); *Brigg Fair* (1908); *In a Summer Garden* (1909); *Dance Rhapsody* (1909); *North Country Sketches* (1915); *Eventyr* (1919). Smaller orchestral pieces: *Summer Night on the River* (1914); *On Hearing the First Cuckoo in Spring* (1914). Concertos: Piano (1907); Violin (1919); Violin and Cello (1920); Cello (1921). Four Violin Sonatas (1892–1930). Sixty-nine Songs (orchestra or piano accompaniment,

1888–1919). See: P. Heseltine, *Frederick Delius* (1923 and 1952); Eric Fenby, *Delius as I Knew Him* (1936); Sir Thomas Beecham, *Frederick Delius* (1959); A. Jefferson, *Delius* (1972).

115

DeMILLE, Cecil Blount 1881–1959

US film director

Claudette Colbert bathing in ass's milk in *The Sign of the Cross* (1932) is an image which encapsulates a commonly held view of Cecil B. DeMille's work. He is often associated only with vulgar Hollywood versions of Biblical and Roman history, Christian moralizing sold with sex and spectacle in films like *The Ten Commandments* (1923, remade in 1959), *King of Kings* (1927), *Cleopatra* (1934), and *Samson and Delilah* (1949). However, such a view hardly does justice to the interest of the director's forty-two-year Hollywood career, and the seventy-six films he made between 1914 and 1956.

From 1900 DeMille was involved with theatre, as actor and playwright, and also opera, as singer and director, until, in 1913, together with Samuel Goldwyn and Jesse Lasky, he established the Lasky Feature Play Company, which would later form part of Paramount. DeMille directed *The Squaw Man* (which he would remake twice) in 1914 – the company's first production and the first-ever feature to be made in Hollywood. It was a huge success, costing $25,450 and grossing $255,000. DeMille's subsequent silent films, fifty-one in all, are extraordinarily diverse in character. They include Westerns, supernatural and psychological dramas, and range from the historical spectacle of *Joan the Woman* (1916), through powerful, exotic melodramas like *The Cheat* (1915), to social comedies such as *Male and Female* (1919) and *Why Change Your Wife* (1920). The latter are particularly interesting as worthy forerunners of Ernst Lubitsch's later, similar, and more celebrated work within the genre.

DeMille formed his own production company in 1925, which was responsible for five films, including *King of Kings*. Then, after a brief period with MGM, for whom he made *Dynamite* (1929), his first sound movie, he returned to Paramount in 1932. His association with the latter company continued until the end of his career. DeMille's best work from the 1930s and 1940s is his series of big-budget adventure films, dealing with events, and semi-legendary characters, from eighteenth- and nineteenth-century American history. *The Plainsman* (1936) starred Gary Cooper as Wild Bill Hickok, whilst Fredric March played Jean Lafitte in *The Buccaneer* (1938). *Union Pacific* (1939) dealt, in a spectacular fashion, with the building of the famous railroad, and was followed by *North West Mounted Police* (1939), *Reap The Wild Wind* (1942), and *Unconquered*

(1947). DeMille's achievement in these films was to combine pleasing spectacle (they are all to a degree 'epics') with a very sure sense of narrative construction and pace. Perhaps the most useful point of comparison, in terms of locating the films within American culture, is Fenimore Cooper's *Leatherstocking Tales*. As a group they clearly contrast strikingly with the 'sophisticated' comedy and musicals with which Paramount is usually associated at this time.

The director's last three films tie in squarely with his 'public image'. *Samson and Delilah* and *The Ten Commandments* featured, respectively, Victor Mature as Samson and Charlton Heston as Moses, whilst *The Greatest Show On Earth* (1952) was an all-star circus drama. They were all massive financial successes, aided by DeMille's customary vigorous promotion campaigns, but certainly compare unfavourably with his earlier sound work.

DeMille is one of the comparatively few film-makers who might justifiably be described as a 'household name'. But whereas the name Hitchcock* is associated with an identifiable body of work, 'DeMille', rather like 'Walt Disney'*, has the strong connotation of Hollywood as institution – its supposed values, its cynicism, excess and success. This is deceptive, as regards both the man and the oeuvre. Many of his early films failed in financial terms. He regarded himself as a thwarted 'serious' artist, whose later success was the result of consciously conceding to Hollywood's commercial demands – he gave them the product they required whilst believing that he was, to some extent, compromising himself. And his oft-proclaimed belief in the moral worth of his epics ('Who else – except the missionaries of God – has had our opportunity to make the brotherhood of man not a phrase but a reality?') may well have been as sincere as his passionate post-Second World War campaign against communism. In terms of the films themselves, DeMille's considerable achievements in the silent era have been overshadowed by the critical attention paid to D. W. Griffith*. The former should be recognized as an equally crucial figure in the early history and development of the American cinema. And the solid virtues of the previously mentioned adventure films should not be overlooked – DeMille is too easily and often dismissed as signifying only Bible and box-office.

Steve Jenkins

See: *The Autobiography of Cecil B. DeMille*, ed. Donald Hayne (1960); Gene Ringgold and DeWitt Bodeen, *The Films of Cecil B. DeMille* (1969).

116

DEMUTH, Charles Henry Buckius 1883–1935

US painter

Born in Lancaster, Pennsylvania, Demuth studied at the Drexel Institute in Philadelphia (1901–5), at the Pennsylvania Academy of the Fine Arts (1905–10) under Thomas Anschutz, Hugh Breckenridge and Henry McCarter, and in Paris at the Académies Colarossi, Moderne and Julian (1912–14). His first visit to France was in 1904. On his second (1907–8) he met Matisse* and other Fauve painters and during his third, two-year stay Gertrude Stein*, Picasso*, Duchamp*, Picabia, Juan Gris* and Delaunay. His first one-man exhibition at a commercial gallery was at the Daniels Gallery, New York, in 1914, a business relationship which lasted nine years. Later, after Alfred Stieglitz included his work in an exhibition called *Seven Americans* – with Arthur Dove, John Marin, Marsden Hartley, Georgia O'Keeffe and Paul Strand – Demuth showed at two Stieglitz galleries, the Intimate and An American Place.

Demuth's worst traits – cynicism, snobbery and preciosity – can be explained by circumstances; he was disabled and rich enough not to have to work to live. Permanently lame from the age of four because of a hip injury, he began to suffer from diabetes in 1920 and was treated with insulin, the new 'miracle drug'. In his *Autobiography* William Carlos Williams*, a close friend and practising doctor, maintained that Demuth's death was caused by his decision not to give himself the drug. Future biographers have other puzzles to solve, notably what Duchamp called a 'Freudian' relationship with his mother and the details of his homosexuality.

Demuth's habit was to turn what could be thought weakness into an undoubted strength. Too frail to carry an easel when young, he devoted himself instead to water-colours, a medium in which his only living American equal was Marin. His lameness he disguised with a special walk. The homosexuality which may have explained his near-alcoholism as a young man was celebrated in joyful sketches at the Lafayette Turkish Baths and the later, pornographic water-colours of sailors.

The key to his work is not easily located. Early still-lives of flowers and fruit and illustrations of texts by Henry James, Wedekind and Zola suggest introspection while stressing surfaces by means of virtuous draughtsmanship. 'Lightness is seldom understood,' he wrote. Hectic cabaret and circus scenes recall Toulouse Lautrec. During a stay in Bermuda (1916–17) he developed a blend of Cubism and Cézanne. Hardened and applied to industrial subject-matter, it became the Precisionist style most commonly associated with Demuth, who used it to emphasize the native elegance of grain-elevators (*My Egypt*, 1927), office windows (*Business*, 1929?) or painted signs (*Buildings, Lancaster*, 1930). His most mysterious works are the 'poster-portraits' of the 1920s, of Charles Duncan, Bert Savoy, Eugene O'Neill*, Arthur Dove, John Marin, Georgia O'Keeffe and William Carlos Williams. In these pictures Demuth found a way to combine his abstract and representational tendencies in an art both blatant and enigmatic, crude and elegant prefiguring some of the concerns of American photographers such as Walker Evans and 1960s painters like Indiana and Dine. It is no accident that Demuth's uninflected façades of paint barely conceal a certain nervous excitement. The man who idolized Watteau also wrote, 'I love Broadway and – well, and vulgarity, and gin. In fact, I love my country.'

Stuart Morgan

See: Emily Farnham, *Charles Demuth: Behind a Laughing Mask* (1971); Kermit Champa, 'Charlie Was Like That . . .', *Artforum*, March 1974.

117

DERRIDA, Jacques 1930–

French philosopher

Derrida was born in El Biar, Algiers, and came to France for his military service, staying on to work at the École Normale in Paris with the Hegel scholar, Jean Hyppolite. He spent a year in Harvard on a scholarship in 1956–7. From 1960 to 1964, he taught at the Sorbonne, and since 1965, has been teaching the history of philosophy at the École Normale Supérieure. He has also been a visiting professor at the American universities of Johns Hopkins and Yale. He is currently associated with GREPH: *Groupe de recherches sur l'enseignement philosophique*, a group concerned with the role and problems of philosophy teaching in France. In 1962, he won the Prix Cavaillès with his first book, a translation of Husserl's* *Origin of Geometry* (1962), with a lengthy and original introduction. His analysis of Husserl's phenomenology became the starting-point for the critique of Western philosophy which he developed in the three books which made him well-known: a study of Husserl, *Speech and Phenomena* (*La Voix et le phénomène*, 1967, trans. 1973) and two collections of essays, *Writing and Difference* (*L'Écriture et la différence*, 1967, trans. 1978) and *Of Grammatology* (*De la Grammatologie*, 1967, trans. 1976). His work is characterized by a systematic mistrust of all forms of metaphysical thought, coupled with the recognition that our language is riddled with the philosophical assumptions he is questioning. Describing the dominant current of philosophy since Plato as a metaphysics of *presence* – by which he means that perennial desire for some guarantee of certainty, some ultimate epistemological foundation or source of meaning, a desire displayed in such philosophical concepts as substance, essence, origin, identity, truth and so forth – he elaborates a way of reading texts, a strategy of *déconstruction* (he prefers to call it a strategy rather than a method) which enables him to identify metaphysical assumptions even in those philosophers who are apparently most critical of metaphysics (such as Nietzsche or Heidegger*). Claiming that it is an illusion to suppose that one can escape altogether from the pervasive metaphysics of presence, since to put oneself 'outside' metaphysics is an indirect way of affirming it, he suggests that one has to think in terms which neither affirm nor oppose but *resist* metaphysical concepts.

His later works are examples of the deconstructive strategy applied to a variety of texts, both literary and philosophical. Major essays are devoted to a wide range of thinkers and writers, from Plato to the twentieth century. The deconstructive strategy is controversial, partly because it is not entirely clear whether, despite his precautions, Derrida has altogether avoided implicit *a priori* arguments, partly because it tends to focus on what is apparently marginal or peripheral in the texts of the writers under discussion. However, his readings do operate a radical and salutary transformation of perspective, while at the same time they are designed to prevent his readers from attributing to him any philosophical doctrine, or seeing him as an 'authority': one of the central purposes of his work is to question the very notion of a philosophical 'thesis' and his own texts call for deconstruction in turn. His work is reminiscent of Nietzsche in its refusal to accept clear-cut distinctions between the philosophical and literary uses of language and invites comparison with Wittgenstein* in its reappraisal of traditional conceptions of language.

Although Derrida already has a considerable reputation in France and America, he is still relatively unfamiliar in Britain. It is probably too early yet to make any predictions about his future development or influence. What is clear is that he aims to disrupt and subvert, and he pursues this aim with a tantalizing brilliance which raises puzzling problems of assessment. His challenge to the institutionalization of thought has still to be fully explored.

Margaret Whitford

See: *La Dissémination* ('Dissemination', 1972); *Marges de la philosophie* ('Margins of philosophy', 1972); *Positions* (1972); *L'Archéologie du frivole* ('Archaeology of the frivolous', an essay on Condillac, 1973); *Glas* ('Knell', 1974); *Spurs* (*Éperons*, an essay on Nietzsche, 1976, trans. 1979); *La Vérité en peinture* ('Truth in painting', 1978); *La Carte postale* ('The postcard', 1980).

118

DEWEY, John 1859–1952

US philosopher, educator and social critic

Dewey left his deepest mark on educational theory, particularly in the USA. He was not the first to reject the authoritarian methods and emphasis on rote learning which characterized the nineteenth century, but he was the first to provide reformist impulses with a theoretical foundation in a philosophy of knowledge and to build on that foundation a clear account of the goals of progressive education. Dewey's philosophy, with that of C. S. Peirce and William James, is labelled 'pragmatism'. In both his pragmatism and progressive approach to education Dewey is often censored for the excesses of those who share these labels. Bertrand Russell*, a severe critic of pragmatism, took no notice of Dewey's explicit disassociation with certain of James's crucial doctrines. The accusation that Dewey aimed only at a well adjusted child whose intellectual abilities atrophy while he 'learns by doing' and 'discovers for himself' is also based on a misreading of Dewey.

The key to Dewey's thinking lies in the emphasis he placed on action in experience and the derivative role assigned to knowledge in his theory. As an undergraduate at the University of Vermont he was impressed by T. H. Huxley's text on physiology; as a graduate student at Johns Hopkins University he came under the spell of Hegelianism for some years. These influences left on Dewey a marked tendency to seek for and emphasize the organic interrelatedness of things. The relation of action to experience illustrates this. Philosophers from Plato to the empiricists have treated the human being as passive in experience, a piece of wax receiving an 'impression' from something outside of it. Experience could occur even if the subject of the experience were incapable of responding to it. Dewey insisted that, 'Disconnected doing and disconnected suffering are neither of them experience'; experience is 'the close connection between doing and suffering' (*Reconstruction in Philosophy*, 1920).

The attempt to provide a foundation for knowledge built upon the discrete 'givens' or 'data' of experience was, thus, for Dewey completely misconceived. What was required was to approach knowledge, which is but one kind of experience, through the activity which gives rise to it. Although Dewey was influenced toward pragmatism by reading James, his position developed closer to Peirce. He rejected James's doctrine that the truth of an idea consists in having consequences which satisfy desire (in *Essays in Experimental Logic*, 1916) and followed Peirce in seeking to understand knowledge through the activity of inquiry.

Inquiry is initiated in conditions of doubt and consists in 'the controlled or directed transformation of an indeterminate situation into one that is so determinate in its constituent distinctions and relations as to convert the elements of the original situation into a unified whole' (*Logic: The Theory of Inquiry*, 1938). What distinguishes theoretical activity from other productive activity which would fit this description is not made clear, but it is clear that for Dewey inquiry into *what is to be done* does fall under this definition and that he was more than content with the resulting subversion of the belief that values are not amenable to rational determination.

Knowledge is the product of inquiry and is better if produced by critically aware inquirers in touch with the stored-up results of human experience. Contact with this 'funded capital of civilization' is required because inquiry is not a series of independent activities but an organically unified whole. Following Peirce, Dewey made truth the ideal limit of inquiry, 'the opinion fated to be ultimately agreed to by all who investigate'. Education, then, is not the transmission of fixed pieces of knowledge, but of the methods of inquiry and 'the funded capital of civilization'. Because Dewey believed the human child to be already active, neither enticement nor coercion was needed to learn; existing interests should be neither repressed nor humoured, but rather guided into new attitudes and interests.

In 1894 Dewey was appointed chairman of the department of philosophy, psychology and education at the University of Chicago, where he helped to found the famous laboratory school. In 1904 he moved to Columbia University where he was able to exercise enormous influence over educational thinking. He continued his contributions to debates on wider social and political issues long after his retirement in 1930.

Dr J. E. Tiles

Other works: *How We Think* (1910); *Human Nature and Conduct* (1922); *Experience and Nature* (1925); *Art as Experience* (1934). On Dewey: S. Hook, *John Dewey, An Intellectual Portrait* (1939); R. J. Bernstein, *John Dewey* (1966); *The Philosophy of John Dewey*, ed. P. A. Schlipp (1939), contains a biographical sketch, seventeen critical essays, replies by Dewey and an extensive bibliography.

119
DIAGHILEV, Serge (Sergei Pavlovich Diaghilev)
1872–1929

Russian impresario

No more vital figure than Diaghilev was instrumental in introducing an awareness of Russian cultural vigour into the West. His role was catalytic: he provided for Russians a link with the West, and for the West his exhibitions and subsequently his brilliant Ballets Russes came as a revelation of the latest Russian developments in stage design, choreography, dancing and music. The impact of the Ballets Russes was sufficient to ensure for it as much a place in the history of French culture as of Russian culture.

Diaghilev was born of a noble family in the Novgorod region. His interest in music and fine art were early developments and his family had close contact with both Tchaikovsky and Mussorgsky. Studying in St Petersburg, Diaghilev met the painters Alexandre Benois and Léon Bakst with both of whom he collaborated on his periodical *Mir Iskusstva (The World of Art)* from its inception in 1898; subsequently Diaghilev, Benois and Bakst were to collaborate too upon the productions of the Ballets Russes.

Diaghilev's brilliant eye for talent, his thirst for astonishment and the force of his will in the increasingly complex area of his activities made him a significant contributor to the history of the theatre, of music, of art, and, above all, of ballet. Directly active in none of these spheres, Diaghilev's indirect achievement was to influence each of them enormously. His ruthless determination to elicit the best from his designers, composers, choreographers and dancers is well documented. As a result his ballets were never apologetic but were emphatically assertive in their modernism. His designers, dancers and choreographers worked so closely together that it is not possible to revive a Ballets Russes production without attempting to revive the union of these three. Diaghilev made maximum use of the designers, employing many remarkable painters. By the time of the Exhibition of Russian Art at the 1906 Salon d'Automne in Paris, Diaghilev's links with painters extended from the florid languor of Bakst to the fierce primitivism of Larionov. Through the Ballets Russes he was to work with very many French as well as Russian artists.

Diaghilev's initial theatrical season in Paris, 1908–9, at once relied heavily upon designers. Chaliapine sang *Boris Godunov* at the Paris Opera in 1908 clad in a densely jewelled costume designed by the painter Golovin and redolent of barbaric splendour. In the production of Borodin's *Prince Igor* which followed, the balletic explosion of the Polovtsian dances was equally un-European, with sets and costumes by Nikolai Roerich as tribal and wild as the frenzied music, a blend of wildness and sophistication, of barbaric vigour with a leap of the imagination, that electrified Parisian audiences and assured Diaghilev of fame, with a measure of infamy, from the very beginning of his musical and theatrical career in Paris.

A second phase of productions followed in which the urbane and cultivated luxury of Bakst alternated with the lightness and eighteenth-century freshness of Benois's *Pavillon d'Armide* (music Tchérépnine, choreography Fokine* and design by Benois). *Les Sylphides*, which was orchestrated by Stravinsky* from Mozart, choreographed by Fokine and danced by Karsavina, Pavlova and Nijinsky, confirmed that during 1909, in one brilliant year, Diaghilev had established a complex, vital and innovatory company that was strong in every part of its creative work. Diaghilev astonished his audiences with the combined talents of Fokine, Stravinsky, Bakst, Nijinsky and Karsavina. Contrast followed contrast as the other worldly luxury of *Schéhérazade* (1910), *Le Spectre de la Rose* (1911) and the infamous *L'Après-midi d'un Faune* (1912) gave way to Stravinsky's *Petrouchka* (1911) and *Rite of Spring* (1913), where the vigorous ferocity of folk and peasant themes returned. Increasingly the lavishness of Bakst gave way to the more angular but equally spectacular designs of Larionov, Goncharova, and eventually to French cubist and Italian futurist designs. *Parade* (1917), choreography by Massine, music by Satie*, theme by Cocteau* and design by Picasso*, was again revolutionary and of an originality that Diaghilev maintained until the end of his life. He continued to employ Russian designers after the Revolution in Russia but remained based in the West. The year 1927 saw Gabo* and Pevsner design *La Chatte*, Yakulov design *Pas d'Acier* and Tchelichev design *Ode*. George Balanchine became the prominent new choreographer of the closing years of Diaghilev's Ballets Russes. The final production *Le Fils Prodigue*, opened in Paris in May 1929, bringing sets by Rouault* to music by Prokofiev*: Diaghilev's unique ability to unite diverse talents had continued to the end of his career.

Dr John Milner

See: Richard Buckle, *Nijinsky* (1975), W. MacDonald, *Diaghilev Observed* (1976); Serge Lifar, *Serge Diaghilev: His Life, His Work, His Legend* (1977); *Diaghilev et les Ballets Russes* (Bibliothèque Nationale, 1979).

120
DISNEY, Walt 1901–66

US film-maker

In 1964 Walt Disney was awarded the President's Medal of Freedom, with the citation 'artist and impresario, in the course of entertaining an age Walt Disney has created on American folklore'. Had the world stopped when he died it would have been found to contain more reproductions – in films, books, toys, clothes, even wrist-watches – of the most famous of his creations, Mickey Mouse, than any other image, with the possible exceptions of the Crucifix and the Buddha. The first universal icon that expressed a sense of fun, the Mouse symbolized nothing so much as his creator's talent. That talent was somewhat more complex than any of its products. It grasped three things: line, business and technology. More importantly it grasped the potential of the relations between them.

Though born in Chicago, Disney spent his early childhood on a farm in rural Missouri, which left a small-town mid-American stamp on the boy for life. His father Elias was a carpenter and failed entrepreneur, forever moving house and veering from one money-making project to another, pushing the young Walt (and his brothers) out to work at a very early age. Thus imbued with a recognition of the need to make money from the start, Disney had his first taste of success when he was seventeen: having volunteered for driving service in France in 1918, he earned considerable sums painting fake medals and German helmets to sell to returning soldiers.

An early interest in cartoons (he did not invent animation, but simply became its by-word) led him to work for a number of commercial art firms, including the Kansas City Film Ad Company. Then, with his brother Roy Disney as the business manager, he opened his own company, Laugh-O-Grams, to make freelance advertisements for the Newman Theatre in Kansas. At the age of twenty he had already acquired a team of collaborators – including Ub Iwerks, Hugh Harman and Rudolph Ising – whom he recognized as superior draughtsmen to himself, but who were none the less prepared to defer to him. At the same time his skill for adapting technology began to assert itself. A team called the Fleischers had made their animated Koko pop out of an inkwell into the live-action world. Disney made his live-action Alice jump back into Cartoonland. The success of this was modest, but Disney was sufficiently inspired to set up a studio in Hollywood. There it was not until the release of *Steamboat Willie* in 1928 that Disney's pre-eminence in the cartoon world was established, for it was *Steamboat* that introduced Mickey Mouse to the public. But it was not the small-town, resourceful entrepreneurialism of the character that seized the imagination: it was the combination of sound and animation. This was the first sound cartoon, and from that day close synchronization of sound and picture was known as 'Mickey-mousing'. The technique was used to greater effect in *Skeleton Dance* (1928), and reached its first apogee in *The Band Concert* (1935), in which Mickey conducts the William Tell Overture while a tornado, in line with the music, wreaks havoc with his orchestra.

Other technological breakthroughs succeeded throughout the 1930s. *Flowers and Trees* (1932) was the first-ever colour cartoon; and Disney in fact negotiated a deal with Technicolor that gave him an exclusive franchise for the three-colour process, so that other studios had to make do with two-colour systems. Then came the multiplane camera, which set artwork at different levels, thereby giving the illusion of a third dimension in a two-dimensional medium, used most effectively in *Pinocchio* (1940). *Pinocchio* was also an example of another frontier that Disney crossed: from shorts to full-length features, beginning in 1937 with *Snow White and the Seven Dwarfs*, and continuing with *Fantasia* (1940), *Dumbo* (1941) and *Bambi* (1942). But if the shorts gradually became the bread-and-butter of his company, it is among them that the essential Disney is to be found. Mickey Mouse was joined by Donald Duck (1931), Goofy (1932) and Pluto (1933), each of them 'created' by Disney himself, as well as the *Silly Symphony* series. *Three Little Pigs* (1933), released at the height of the Depression, became a rallying point for popular audiences, while *Who Killed Cock Robin?* (1935), satirizing the stars of the day (Mae West, Bing Crosby and Harpo Marx among them), marked a change from simple slapstick towards a form of sit-com related to contemporary live-action comedies.

The 1930s were the golden era of Disney films, and all his productions of that period are immediately recognizable as Disney products. They are characterized by two aspects: a certain narrowness in the range of their plots and emotions (though this impression owes much to the fact that there were just so many Disney cartoons), and superb craftsmanship. They also bore the name of Disney, to the exclusion of those of his collaborators. In 1941 this led to a crisis from which Disney never fully recovered. Having opened a new studio, streamlined and rationalized, his animators went on strike. Disney, they felt, had not only monopolized the credit for their work, but had established an aesthetic dictatorship. They were the most talented draughtsmen in the business, but they were restricted, by and large, to actualizing Disney's conceptions. Harmony was eventually restored, but only after the strike leaders had seceded to set up their own studio, UPA; and it was the new UPA style, angular and determinedly two-dimensional, that dominated the post-war period. More and more Disney himself turned to live-action filming, or a mixture of live-action and animation, as in *Make Mine Music* (1946), *Song of the South* (1946) and *Melody Time* (1948). By the 1950s Disney Productions, while continuing to produce full-length animated features, was becoming less distinguishable from other Hollywood studios. In particular it devoted itself to live-action adventures, many of them specifically for children. With his unflagging instinct for good business, Disney brought to the family entertainment feature high technical standards (viz. *Davy Crockett*, 1955, or *Swiss Family Robinson*, 1960); but increasingly his films became recognizable as assembly-line products. A truer expression of the man was Disneyland, opened in 1954, an adventure park that combines all that is 'safe' with high spirits and precise technological organization.

Perhaps the most interesting feature of Disneyland is a series of figures, most notably Abraham Lincoln, animated by sound impulses activating pneumatic and hydraulic valves. Looked upon by many as monstros-

ities of bad taste, they embody perfectly Disney's vision of immediate entertainment supported by technological sophistication. His success was commercial because his products exuded inventiveness in an age that had an appetite for invention, and aestheticians seeking to find in him an aspect of primitivism are misguided.

Clare Kitson

See: Richard Schickel, *The Disney Version* (1968); Arseni, Bosi and Marconi, *Walt Disney – Magic Moments* (1973); Bob Thomas, *Walt Disney: An American Original* (1976); Christopher Finch, *The Art of Walt Disney* (1975).

121
DORN, Edward 1929–

US poet

Certain 'locations' have provided the context for much of Dorn's writing: his parents' farm in Illinois, which figures in early collections such as *The Newly Fallen* (1961) and *Hands Up!* (1964); the American northwest, traversed by the narrative poem 'Idaho Out', published in *Geography* (1965); central England, contemplated with a somewhat vengeful eye in *The North Atlantic Turbine* (1967). Attendance at Black Mountain College, where he studied with Charles Olson*, stimulated a more conceptual interest in environments, and especially in the work of the geographer Carl Sauer. Dorn, indeed, has generally been gathered with Olson and Robert Creeley into a group of poets named after a place (Black Mountain) and said to be crucially preoccupied with 'a grasp of *locality*' (Donald Davie, 'The Black Mountain Poets', in *The Survival of Poetry*, ed. Martin Dodsworth, 1970).

But whereas Olson resides, Dorn passes through. His landscapes are in the mind, not sifted historically and geographically but interrogated by means of a jaunty and compelling projection of ideas, a 'general tendency to conceptualize the world'. As he remarks in the preface to *Collected Poems 1956–1974* (1975), his writing is 'theoretic by nature and poetic by virtue of its inherent tone'. It can be characterized more accurately by the range of inherent tones that it includes than by any thematic preoccupation. Within that range two main tendencies can be distinguished: towards statement, and towards irony. The first tendency would include various tones (declamatory, lyric, reflective) out of which the bulk of his poetry up to and including *The North Atlantic Turbine* is composed. Above all, these tones *assert*: they embody the identity of a speaker, of a particular voice, and the poetic form they take follows as closely as possible the contours of that speaking. The preoccupation with place can then be seen as one expression of a larger desire to assert identity, to know where one stands. The poems written in this mode achieve at best an extraordinary natural eloquence, at worst shrill egotism.

Some of them, however, reveal a different interest, an interest not so much in speaking as in reprocessing what has already been spoken. In 1977, Dorn suggested that his function was not to write poetry but to 'compose the poetry that's constantly written on the air. What I've read and what I hear merge to make the field in which I compose' (see below, Fredman). The poet articulates (joins together, serializes) the articulated (the already spoken). 'My attitude toward writing is that I handle the language everyday like a material, and I keep it in *interesting* repair. I don't really care about *good* repair.' This ironic reprocessing of what has been written on the air provides the thrust of Dorn's masterpiece, *Slinger* (1975). *Slinger* is the only great *comic* epic in American poetry, a journey by stage-coach across the American south-west, but more importantly across myths and across multiple conventions of speech – a supremely dexterous repair job.

The interplay between statement and irony in Dorn's writing, between self-assertion and attention to what others say, has kept it responsive – perhaps uniquely responsive – to the dilemmas and absurdities of modern society; and holds it continually open, now, for further initiatives.

David Trotter

Dorn's other books include: *The Shoshoneans* (1966); *By the Sound* (1971); *Some Business Recently Transacted in the White World* (1971); *Recollections of Gran Apacheria* (1974); *Manchester Square* (with Jennifer Dunbar, 1975); *Hello, La Jolla* (1978). See also: Stephen Fredman, *Roadtesting the Language: An Interview with Edward Dorn* (1978).

122

DOS PASSOS, John Rodrigo 1896–1970

US novelist

If the reader believes that, to be satisfying, a novel must be of the genre of Jane Austen, Thackeray or Trollope and portray well-rounded characters in a realistic social setting, then by this standard Dos Passos's novels are not satisfying. However, between *The Scarlet Letter* and *Moby-Dick* on the one hand, and *To the Lighthouse*, *Ulysses*, and *The Sound and the Fury* on the other, it has been demonstrated that the novel form is large enough to contain a variety of types. The fact that Dos Passos has broken his narratives into sections, interpolated fragments of 'newsreels', and presented life as a series of changing patterns does not, in itself, afford a criterion for judgment. All this is perfectly acceptable (the devices themselves are, indeed, provoking and often enlightening) provided the reader feels that the picture of mankind thereby presented is both valid and convincing. It is on this issue that Dos Passos's stature as a novelist must be debated.

John Dos Passos was born in Chicago in 1896, the son of a wealthy New York lawyer, himself the son of a Portuguese immigrant. He travelled with his family before going to the prestigious Choate School, entered Harvard in 1912, and graduated *cum laude* in 1916. Like E. E. Cummings*, he contributed to *Eight Harvard Poets* in 1917, and, like him also, joined the Norton – Harjes Ambulance Corps in France. At that time he was already in Europe, having gone over in 1916, while the United States was still neutral, to study architecture in Spain. After the war, Dos Passos spent several years as a journalist and foreign correspondent, during which time he wrote three novels: *One Man's Initiation . . . 1917* (1920), *Three Soldiers* (1921) and *Streets of Night* (1923). The first two are concerned with the war, the third with precocious adolescents. Of the three, *Three Soldiers* is the best, but, like *One Man's Initiation*, it reveals an attitude to life which was to mar almost all Dos Passos's later work. This is an attitude of grievance. Against his main protagonists the dice are always loaded; in a brutal world, the men of sensitivity go down like ninepins. However graphically presented or even true this may be, the resultant work has an air of exaggeration, almost of propaganda. There is no balance of forces in Dos Passos's world.

With *Manhattan Transfer* (1925) – which presents a kaleidoscopic picture of New York between the 1890s and the mid-1920s – Dos Passos developed a technique of dealing with American social life which he was to exploit to the full in later novels. What interested him was not primarily an individual's spiritual problems or emotional entanglements, but the overall social pattern. He chose a variety of characters from various walks of life, caused them to meet or pass in the street, to live out their briefly tragic or sordid lives, but rarely to become involved with each other in anything approaching significant action. It is a sociological approach to literature which achieves its fullest expression in the *U.S.A.* trilogy.

These three novels were first published separately, as *The 42nd Parallel* (1930), *1919* (1932) and *The Big Money* (1936), and cover the period from 1900 to about 1930. Each is complete in itself, but since the technique is the same, and some of the characters are to be found in more than one book, they are almost always considered as parts of one large novel. Communication is attempted at four levels. The basic 'story' is carried in the accounts of the lives of such characters as 'Mac', 'Vag' or 'J. Ward Moorehouse', men and women from different walks of American life. Interspersed with these accounts are staccato 'biographies' of famous, or infamous, Americans: big business-men like Henry Ford* or John Pierpoint Morgan, labour leaders, radical thinkers like Eugene Debs or Thorstein Veblen*, or moving-picture idols like Rudolph Valentino. Then there are the 'News Reel' and, finally, the 'Camera Eye' sections. The former provide a scrap-book collection of headlines and snatches of popular song which evoke the mood of the period; the latter carry the 'inner' story, the reflections of the author either on his own life or on the events described in the book. Some of the 'Camera Eye' sections, especially those which are inspired by actual events like the Sacco – Vanzetti trial, are moving and successful. Far too often, however, they indulge that (for the 1920s) 'modernistic' device of 'stream of consciousness' in such a way as to make one regret that Dos Passos should ever think fit to drop the iron mask of social objectivity. This is a pity – and perhaps a critical straw in the wind – since the 'Camera Eye' sections seem to be very important to him.

In 1941, Dos Passos defined what he felt to be the American spirit in a series of essays on great Americans published under the title of *The Ground We Stand On*. The emphasis was on the independents and individualists from Roger Williams to modern times. At that time, however, he turned from a radical to a conservative point of view, as was evidenced in *District of Columbia*, his second trilogy, published in 1952, comprising *Adventures of a Young Man* (1939), *Number One* (1943) and *The Grand Design* (1949). No doubt this change was caused partly by the disillusionment with radical political action which many intellectuals felt in the late 1940s, and partly by the impact of the Second World War. With increasing conservatism of subject-matter, there also went an accompanying conservatism of technique.

Does this fact provide some foundation on which to attempt an evaluation of Dos Passos's contribution to the novel? As in the case of Virginia Woolf's* experiments, the famous technique of *Manhattan Transfer* and *U.S.A.* is now something of a museum piece. At least, that is how it seems now, when the pendulum has swung away from 'modernism'. Perhaps in time this technique will be revived, although there does not seem to be any immediate prospect of that in the era of the 'fabulists', as Robert Scholes calls the contemporary American novelists. Yet experiments like Dos Passos's are always valuable in mapping new areas of literary experience, even if those areas are not subsequently colonized. What, fundamentally, was Dos Passos trying to do? He was attempting, say those critics who understand him best, to make history itself the 'hero' of his work. Although at first this seems an odd approach to novel-writing, there is really no reason why we should object in principle to the method. Dos Passos's 'thèmes et structures' represent a merging of several disciplines: sociology, history and literature. His technique was forged out of a sense of anguish at the spiritual and social crises of the late twenties and early

thirties. The innovation is daring, the result impressive. Why, then, do many readers feel the need to express some reservation? Is it because they are relatively unsophisticated in their approach to the novel form and cannot 'get interested' in such an intellectual presentation? Some might put it this way. However, there is a more radical objection which even the most avant-garde admirer of the technique cannot explain away, and that is the relatively shallow view of life which Dos Passos's treatment of human nature implies. Here was a sensitive, privileged, romantic idealist who turned from aestheticism to social action through literature. Righteous indignation provided the spur. The labour and dedication were enormous. But Dos Passos was too concerned with the process of history to be much interested in people for their own sake. Massive as his contribution is, one can hardly avoid the impression that it is hollow at the centre.

Geoffrey Moore

See: Malcolm Cowley, *After the Genteel Tradition* (1937); Alfred Kazin, *On Native Grounds* (1942); W. M. Frohock, *The Novel of Violence in America* (1950); B. H. Gelfant, *The American City Novel* (1954); Charles Child Walcutt, *American Literary Naturalism; A Divided Stream* (1956); John H. Wrenn, *John Dos Passos* (1961).

123
DOVZHENKO, Alexander 1894–1956

Russian film director

Born into a large farming family in the Chernihiv region of the Ukraine, Dovzhenko began professional life as a teacher. After 1917 and a move from the provinces to Kiev, where he attended both the Commercial Institute and the Academy of Fine Art, he was active in student politics and organized local government facilities in the spheres of culture and education. A further move to Kharkov saw him employed as a diplomat with the People's Commissariat of Foreign Affairs, involving stays in Warsaw and Berlin. On his return to Kharkov in 1923 he became an illustrator on a local newspaper, and produced political cartoons, book illustrations, and film posters. Mixing in Ukrainian literary circles he became a founding member of VAPLITE, the Free Academy of Proletarian Literature, and came under the influence of the firebrand nationalism and romantic vitalism of its leader, Mykola Khylovy.

It was not until the age of thirty-two, in 1926, that, leaving Kharkov overnight for Odessa, Dovzhenko broke away from his literary and artistic background to enter the film industry. Here, within four years, he went from total inexperience to major stature as the director of what were to be his three most famous films: *Zvenigora* (1928), a political family drama with wide-ranging and fantastical historical flashbacks ('a catalogue of all my creative possibilities' according to its maker in 1939); *Arsenal* (1929), a poem about the Ukraine from the First World War through to the bloody suppression of workers barricaded in a Kiev munitions factory in 1918; and *Earth* (1930), a lyrical account of Soviet village life in the period of collectivization.

But Dovzhenko's leadership of the new cinema of the Ukraine was quickly quashed by Stalin's* aggression against the Ukraine and the erosion of its emerging cultural identity. *Earth*, already overtaken by the harsher realities of social and economic transformation, was attacked, shortened, and lost some of its distribution. *Ivan* (1932), Dovzhenko's first sound film, tackled these issues more centrally, focusing on the Dnieper hydro-electric project and a peasant boy's move from farm to construction site, but it was also attacked and dropped.

Dovzhenko took refuge in Moscow itself, throwing himself upon Stalin's mercy. He was assigned to make a film about the Far East, *Aerograd* (1935), on the building of an 'Air City' on the border with Japanese Manchuria, returning to the Kiev Studio, and the Ukrainian Civil War, for his only other film of the 1930s, *Shchors* (1939), on the Red Army Commander of the same name. In 1940 Dovzhenko became Artistic Supervisor of the Kiev Studio, but was evacuated when the Soviet film industry was placed on a war footing, and apart from involvement in a handful of newsreel and documentary projects – notably *The Battle for our Soviet Ukraine* (1943) and *Victory in the Right-Bank Ukraine and the Expulsion of the German Aggressors from the Boundaries of the Ukrainian Soviet Earth* (1945) – devoted much of his time to writing – as a war correspondent, as a propagandist, and as a scenarist. In 1944 Dovzhenko was castigated by Stalin for the nationalist bias of one of his two major scenarios of the period, *Ukraine in Flames*. His only completed project in the post-war period was *Michurin* (1949), his first colour film, about the famous naturalist, which itself was forced to undergo revision in the context of controversies emerging around the figure of Michurin's most conspicuous follower, Trofim Lysenko. Dovzhenko died in 1956, leaving behind a succession of uncompleted projects, including the preparations for an epic novel, *The Golden Gate*. His planned trilogy on the Ukraine was subsequently completed by his wife, Yulia Solntseva, his collaborator since *Earth* – *Poem of the Sea* (1958), *The Flaming Years* (1961), and *The Enchanted Desna* (1965); Kiev Studio, aptly, became Dovzhenko Studio.

For the French historian Georges Sadoul, Dovzhenko was 'the cinema's greatest living poet', taking as the central theme of his continuing epic the place of the Ukrainian peasantry in the development of Social-

ism. He is therefore best remembered for his seminal contribution to the emergence of a native cinema of the Ukraine with his early feature films of the late 1920s. *Zvenigora* and *Arsenal* are noted for the simplicity of their revolutionary romanticism coupled with their formal poetry and experiment; *Earth* for its lyrical and sensuous treatment of the natural landscape. Other overarching themes in his work – themes of patriotism and innocence, of the mythical and the poetic, the recurrent symbolic figures of grandfathers and young men, the concern with reconstruction and reform – also indicate the more general emotionalism and humanism of Dovzhenko's sensibility.

Philip Drummond

Dovzhenko, *Tvory v Pyaty Tomakh* ('Works in Five Volumes', 1964–6); *Sobraniye Sochineniy* ('Collected Works', 1966–9); Barthélémy Amengual, *Alexandre Dovjenko* (1970); Marco Carynnyk (ed.), *Alexander Dovzhenko: the Poet as Filmmaker* (1973); Marcel Oms, *Alexandre Dovjenko* (1968); Luda and Jean Schnitzer, *Alexandre Dovjenko* (1966); see also: Jay Leyda, *Kino: A History of the Russian and Soviet Film* (2nd edn, 1973).

124
DREISER, Herman Theodore 1871–1945

US novelist

Despite a rarely employed, strict Roman Catholic father and a doting, superstitious mother, the Indiana-born Dreiser (their ninth child) managed to struggle through a succession of parochial and public schools to earn a high school degree. He spent a year at the University of Indiana in 1889. Leaving the university, Dreiser found work in various cities as a journalist. In New York he was introduced to the glamorous world of Broadway by his brother Paul, an extremely popular songwriter. In 1900 Dreiser's first attempt at a novel was read by Frank Norris at Doubleday and he urged acceptance of the book. *Sister Carrie*, however, did not meet the puritanical standards of the publisher who abhorred the unpunished amoral heroine. Adhering to the letter of the contract Norris had given Dreiser, Doubleday published only one thousand copies which were never advertised or distributed. Norris tried desperately to convince reviewers about the novel's quality, but they agreed with the publishers. Dreiser, receiving only $68.40 in royalties, became quickly embittered and contemplated suicide. Brother Paul provided both the influence and the encouragement that helped Dreiser through this period until he finally published *Jennie Gerhardt* (1911). Despite Jennie being as 'sinful' as Carrie, the novel was received more favourably and Dreiser churned out the first novel of his 'Trilogy of Desire', *The Financier*, in 1912 with the help of advances from Harper's and the unusually sweet-tongued encouragement of a new-found friend, H. L. Mencken. Two more novels followed, swiftly establishing Dreiser as the reigning figure of 'Naturalism', *The Titan* (1914) and *The Genius* (1915). During the next decade he published several books expounding his philosophy based on the works of Herbert Spencer, Charles Darwin, Thomas Huxley and other major influences. Also at this time, like Frank Cowperwood of *The Titan* and Eugene Witla of *The Genius*, Dreiser was divorcing his first wife, marrying his mistress and conducting numerous other affairs. In 1925 he published in two volumes one of the great unread classics of American fiction, *An American Tragedy*. This relentless documentation of American banality and spiritual poverty was the lower-class other-side-of-the-coin of *The Great Gatsby* published in the same year. *An American Tragedy* emphasized the new political strain in Dreiser's personal philosophy. Perhaps social reform could, after all, cope with the naturalistic forces of the earlier novels. Ironically, in the 1930s Dreiser published no novels, but he was active in exposing the situation of the miners in Harlan County and other liberal causes. When he died in 1945 Theodore Dreiser was an awkward, almost embarrassing figure to American critics. His 'elephantine' prose offended the New Critics' sense of style while his themes were thought to be irrelevant in the coming existential age of 'the end of ideology'. Thus his two posthumous novels *The Bulwark* (1946) and *The Stoic* (1947) were ignored in the optimism and smugness of the post-war years.

With Eugene O'Neill*, Dreiser offended the fastidious with his sprawling narratives and clumsy prose; but the more open-minded are always moved by the sheer power of their stories and characters. They succeed as the observers of the American tragedy despite their own worst efforts. The outstanding novelist between Twain and Fitzgerald*, Dreiser records the period (1890–1920) of the great disruption of the American community, the move away from the farms and small towns to the sprawling industrialized centres as exemplified in the stories of Carrie Meeber and Clyde Griffiths. Dreiser really knows the boarding houses, cheap hotels, and flop houses, identifying with the people who drift from one to the other. But he also knows – or rather learned – the world of the Frank Cowperwoods, 'the captains of industry' who ruthlessly exploited people and resources for their own profit and – as a by-product – created cities like Dreiser's Chicago. Dreiser may fear that he is more Clyde Griffiths ('I was one of those who did the gulping; and indeed I was one of the worst') than Frank Cowperwood, but he records both as fully as possible. In *Sister Carrie* he describes not only the effortless rise of Carrie, but also the fall of her second lover, Hurstwood, the restaurateur brought low by his passion for the naive Carrie. Hurstwood's inevitable slide down the class ladder dramatizes how disastrous it can be to step out of one's place in the American class structure. Hurstwood is lost once he loses his rung, tumbling into flop-house oblivion, while Clyde's dream of moving up through marriage is also doomed from the beginning.

The successful Dreiser characters stand somehow apart from their society. Carrie's origins do not prevent her rise as mistress and actress since these professions are somehow outside 'class'. Frank Cowperwood also remains isolated throughout the monumental trilogy that follows his successes and set-backs in finance, society and sex. Based on the exploits of Charles T. Yerkes, Cowperwood is a milestone in American literature as perhaps the only successful attempt to portray the multifaceted dimensions of the great American robber barons both from their own 'survival of the fittest' philosophy and the point of view of the 'scientifically detached' Spencerian. Nothing else comes close to analysing critically these heroic modern pirates who believed that the business of America is Profit. In this way Dreiser forms an interesting link between the crusading muck-rakers and the cynical hard-boiled writers.

Professor Charles Gregory

Other works: *Twelve Men* (1919) contains biographical sketches including one of his brother Paul; *A Traveller at Forty* (1913), *A Book About Myself* (1922), *Dreiser Looks at Russia* (1928), *Tragic America* (1931), and *Hey-Rub-aDub-Dub: A Book of the Mystery of Life* (1919) are autobiographical and philosophical. About Dreiser: W. A. Swanberg, *Dreiser* (1965); *Forgotten Frontiers: Dreiser and the Land of the Free* by Dorothy Dudley (1932); F. O. Mathiessen, *Theodore Dreiser* (1951); Alfred Kazin and Charles Shapire, *The Stature of Theodore Dreiser* (1955); Robert Penn Warren, *An Homage* (1971).

125
DRUMMOND DE ANDRADE, Carlos 1902–

Brazilian poet

Born in the interior state of Minas Gerais, expelled from a Jesuit boarding-school in 1918 for 'mental insubordination', Drummond became the leader of the avant-garde modernist movement in his native state during the 1920s, moving to Rio in 1934. He has lived there, hardly leaving the city, since then, working as a civil servant. His reputation as Brazil's greatest poet is unchallenged.

'The poet of the finite and the material', he called himself in his exuberant central collection *A Rosa de Povo* ('The People's Rose', 1945), and the phrase serves to define him as well as any other. Unable to commit himself to any ideology or religion, Drummond begins from the simple and insistent assertion of the existence of objects. His most celebrated poem, from his earliest collection, *Alguma Poesia* ('Some Poetry', 1930), consists largely of the repeated phrase, 'In the middle of the road there was a stone.' From this point he builds up a complex picture of the struggle to make sense and order of a chaotic and senseless world: finally, he is sustained by a precarious faith that we – and the artist is privileged in this sense – are able to understand and communicate with one another, and thus do share a common humanity.

A much less optimistic and politically committed figure than Neruda* was in later years (though he was close to the Communist Party during the Second World War), one of his most sympathetic qualities is the ability to show internal conflict – 'to set fire to everything, including myself'. The bourgeois intellectual who would like to commit himself, but is held back by his past, his class background, or simple cowardice; the middle-aged lover torn between blinding passion and a sense of his own absurdity; the man genuinely nostalgic for a past which is lost and was by no means ideal – these are all roles he assumes at one time or another. His very down-to-earth Utopia remains Itabira, where he was born and lived until he was twenty. Drummond's Latin-Americanness can be found in his identification with the loss and exploitation of his native town, now the centre of a huge iron-mining complex. His evocation of this lost world is reminiscent in its detail, comedy and brutality of the fiction of writers like the Colombian García Márquez*.

Although one of the heirs of the symbolist generation, he is one of those who most intelligently question its more extreme presuppositions – in this sense, his central position in the general movement of poetry in the twentieth century cannot be denied. Language is not purifiable; poems are not perfect structures, but more or less perfect resolutions of conflicts; poetry both abstracts us from the world and helps us to understand it and even act within it.

John A. Gledson

The most extensive volume of English translations is *In the Middle of the Road* (1965); the best, those of Elizabeth Bishop, can be found in *An Anthology of Twentieth-Century Brazilian Poetry* (1972). For the originals, see *Obra Completa* (1973) and *Reunião* (1969, etc.). Criticism: Affonso Romano de Sant'anna, *Drummond: O Gauche no Tempo* (1972); José Guilherme Merquior, *Verso Universo em Drummond* (1975); and Antonio Candido, 'Inquietudes na poesia de Drummond', *Vários Escritos* (1970).

126
DUBUFFET, Jean-Philippe-Arthur 1901–

French artist

A former wine merchant, Jean Dubuffet has pursued a highly successful artistic career on the premise that originality stems from calculated acts of dissociation from the habits of perception and cultural conditioning. In the lecture 'Anticultural Positions' (1951), he announced that 'our culture is a garment which no longer fits. It is more and more estranged from our true life. I aspire to an art plugged directly in to everyday living.' His early paintings of ordinary people – a man on a bike, a girl milking a cow – combine the awkwardness of child art with the anonymity of graffiti, and reflect the artist's flair for making what seems least 'beautiful' become seductive. The scandalous *Corps de dames* series (1950), in which that touchstone of traditional aesthetics, the female nude, is caricatured as a horrendous hag, jaggedly incised into messy impasto, led to Dubuffet's installation as the *peintre maudit* of post-war international art.

Dubuffet's concern has been systematically to break the rules of orthodox representation and painterly technique; in so doing he has spawned a number of varied styles in a wide range of media, some of them suggesting (perhaps superficially) analogies with artists like Grosz, Klee*, Pollock*, Fautrier or Tapiès. In the late 1950s he celebrated the amorphous textures of non-human surfaces in resin-based pictures like *Exemplary Life of the Soil* (1958), which offers the spectator the equivalent, hung on the gallery wall, of a section of earth underfoot.

In 1962, Dubuffet arrived at his *ne plus ultra*, the *Hourloupe* style (allegedly inspired by a telephone-pad doodle), an idiom of interlocking irregular shapes grossly hatched in anti-natural colours (bold reds, blues, blacks) which flatten any object depicted and create an eerie continuum of busy segments without depth or differentiation. Over the next twelve years the *Hourloupe* cycle progressed in scale, with three-dimensional objects of painted polystyrene, then larger ones in epoxy such as the monumental *Group of Four Trees* (1969), set outside the Chase Manhattan Bank in New York. The cycle culminates in the *Closerie Falbala* (1969–76), an immense environmental work of white polyester striated in black, covering some 1,600 square metres, inside which the visitor may well experience a final sense of estrangement not only from culture but even from natural sensation. This unearthly edifice has been erected outside Paris as the centre-piece of the Dubuffet Foundation.

Of constant inspiration to the artist has been his collection of *Art brut* or 'raw art' – the work of madmen, mediums, hermits and other marginals who, in Dubuffet's view, create inventive art by virtue of their imperviousness to established culture. It is largely thanks to his sponsorship that the psychotic artists Adolf Wölfli and Aloïse Corbaz have lately achieved international recognition.

Roger Cardinal

Dubuffet's work is exhaustively detailed in the multi-volumed *Catalogue intégral des travaux de Jean Dubuffet*, ed. M. Loreau (1964–). His writings include *Prospectus et tous écrits suivants* (2 vols, 1967) and *Asphyxiante culture* (1968). See also: P. Selz, *The Work of Jean Dubuffet* (1962); *L'Herne*, no. 22, ed. J. Berne (1973); M. Loreau, *Jean Dubuffet: Stratégie de la création* (1973).

127
DUCHAMP, Marcel 1887–1968

French artist

Even if his reputation has passed its zenith, it remains true that no figure of his generation has influenced avant-garde art since about 1955 more than Duchamp. Whereas Picasso* directly revolutionized the mainstream of painting, Duchamp's subtle questioning took far longer to undermine existing preconceptions but when it did the revolution was more profound – not so much on account of what he produced as of what he thought.

Born in Blainville, Normandy, Marcel joined his elder artist brothers Jacques Villon and Raymond Duchamp-Villon in Paris in 1904. It was in their studios that the *Section d'Or* (Golden Section) circle of artists met in 1910 and 1911: this included most of the Cubists except for the two most important and advanced, Picasso and Braque*. Nevertheless, Duchamp's *Nude Descending a Staircase No. 2* (1912), which earned him fame and notoriety at the New York Armory Show of 1913, went beyond Cubism by its treatment of the human figure as an erotic machine, pre-figuring Duchamp's most famous work, possibly the greatest icon of modern art, *The Bride Stripped Bare by Her Bachelors, Even* (the *Large Glass*, 1915–23). Interpretations of this work are as legion as it is enigmatic. It is divided into two equal halves, the bride's domain above and the bachelors' apparatus beneath. At one level a mechanistic depiction of (failed) human love, it can also be seen in mystical, alchemical or kabbalistic terms, or as a historical myth about our culture. The most basic assumptions of art and science are subjected to a deeply serious but playful irony.

In 1913 Duchamp mounted a bicycle-wheel on a stool and next year bought and signed a bottle-rack. Thus began his series of 'readymades'. Eliminating all considerations of craftsmanship, the readymades were proposed as works of art purely on the basis of their being *chosen* by an artist. For Duchamp, art in the sense of skill and concern with *matière* was no longer relevant. Nor was the aesthetic attitude towards objects: the readymades were chosen for the aesthetic indifference which they inspired.

From 1920 Duchamp lived mostly in New York. Together with Man Ray*, he was the principal figure in New York Dada. Later, he was closely associated with the Surrealists as well as being friendly with, for example, Brancusi*, exerting considerable behind-the-scenes influence on the art world. He did not himself, however, create much art in the inter-war years after stopping work on the *Large Glass*; instead, he played chess and experimented with various optical devices. After the Second World War he worked secretly for twenty years (1946 to 1966) on his last masterpiece, *Given: 1. The Waterfall, 2. The Illuminating Gas*. Installed in Philadelphia, it consists of a rough wooden door containing two peep-holes through which can be glimpsed a shockingly realistic female nude holding up a gas lamp in front of a landscape with a simulated waterfall. Full of references to the elements and to the culture/nature dichotomy, it continues Duchamp's use of erotic imagery to tackle fundamental principles.

The rise in Duchamp's reputation in the late 1950s coincided with a renewed interest in chance, indifference and the relationship of art to life. Later developments like Pop, Minimal, Conceptual and Performance Art not only all owe him a vast debt but help to reveal the extent of his prophetic vision.

Gray Watson

For Duchamp's own writings, see: *The Essential Writings of Marcel Duchamp* (1973). See also: Pierre Cabanne, *Dialogues with Marcel Duchamp* (1971). Books about Duchamp: Walter Hopps, Ulf Linde and Arturo Schwarz, *Marcel Duchamp: Readymades, etc.* (1964); Calvin Tomkins and *Time-Life* editors, *The World of Marcel Duchamp* (1966); Arturo Schwarz, *Complete Works of Marcel Duchamp*; Octavio Paz, *Marcel Duchamp or the Castle of Purity* (1970); John Golding, *Duchamp's 'Bride Stripped Bare by Her Bachelors, Even'* (1972); Anne d'Harnoncourt and Kynaston McShine, *Marcel Duchamp* (1973). Duchamp appeared in the films *Entr'acte* (dir. René Clair, 1924) and *Dreams That Money Can Buy* (dir. Hans Richter, 1944–6).

128
DURAS, Marguerite 1914–

French writer

Born in what is now a southern province of Vietnam, Marguerite Donnadieu adopted the pen-name of Duras. Such a name, free from the religious connotation conveyed by Donnadieu (Donne-à-Dieu) fits this writer's fictional world, devoid as it is of spiritual concern. On the other hand Duras has literary associations, with a woman novelist in the eighteenth century, and with one of Proust's* main characters. But Marguerite Duras has developed a technique which has gradually separated her from this background. After her early conventional writings in the field of theatre, cinema and novels she emerged as an exponent of 'modernism' with the publication of *The Rapture of Lol. V. Stein* (*Le Ravissement de Lol. V. Stein*, 1964, trans. 1967), *The Vice-Consul* (*Le Vice-consul*, 1966, trans. 1968), *L'Amour* (1971), *La Femme du Gange* (1973) and *India Song* (1973). She has however shunned the excessive theorizing typical of the French neo-novelists. To the extent that she does not engage in critical reflection of her own or others' modes of writing, Duras is probably on the fringe of the modernistic movement. But at the level of literary production her contribution is considerable.

Its striking feature is the blurring of frontiers. Between genres in the first instance: *India Song* is (un)classified by the author as simultaneously *texte*, *théâtre*, *film*. Each of these terms is a pointer to modernistic stances: *texte*, instead of *roman*, *récit*, implies the rejection of the constraints of the realistic model; *théâtre* is a misnomer. *India Song* has no plot, no dramatic action. The characters the spectator sees do not speak, whereas those he hears are not seen. The relevance to modernism of this experimental device ('les voix extérieures au récit') lies in its being a *formal* innovation, proclaiming an interest in the signifier rather than in the signified. The third description given to *India Song* relates Duras to modernism if only because she, like Robbe-Grillet*, gives a literary status to cinematic activity. Second, the blurring of frontiers is between Duras's own works of fiction: here it is the intertextual dynamics relating one novel with another which proclaims a modernistic stance. Between the five 'texts' mentioned above there is a fluid interpenetration at the anecdotal and verbal levels, not to be confused with the recurrence of characters and their temporal evolution which Balzac's and indeed Proust's readers have been trained to expect.

Literary modernism involves of course structural organization, new narrative conventions, the development of symbolic patterns, all of which feature in Duras's writings. But it is principally the bold experimentation with disembodied voices and silent actors, the multiple rewriting of the same text to form a kind of fictional constellation, which marks her idiosyncratic and yet representative contribution to modern culture.

Dr Ninette Bailey

Other works include: *A Sea of Troubles* (*Un Barrage contre le Pacifique*, 1950, trans. 1953); *Days in the Trees* (*Des Journées entières dans les arbres*, 1953, trans. 1967); *Moderato Cantabile* (1958, trans. 1966); *Hiroshima mon amour* (filmscript, 1960); *The Afternoon of Monsieur Andesmas* (*L'Après-midi de Monsieur Andesmas*, 1962, trans. 1964); *Destroy* . . . (*Détruire, dit-elle*, 1969, trans. 1970). See John Fletcher, *New Directions in Literature* (1968); J.-L. Seylax, *Les Romans de Duras* (Archives des Lettres modernes no. 47, 1963); Ninette Bailey, 'Discours social: lecture socio-critique du *Vice-consul* du Marguerite Duras', in C. A. Burns (ed.), *Literature and Society* (1981).

129
DURKHEIM, Émile 1858–1917

French sociologist

Durkheim is generally regarded as one of the founders of sociology. More than any other single figure he is responsible for the branch of sociology that approaches social phenomena from the scientific standpoint. The notion that society is susceptible to scientific investigation is, however, only derivatively his. It is rather a systematic rationale for this conviction, together with his application of it in practice, which elevated Durkheim to a position of eminence unsurpassed within the discipline.

Of Jewish parentage, Durkheim was born in Épinal, Lorraine. He gained entry to the École Normale Supérieure in 1879 and later took one year's leave of absence (1885–6) to study in Germany. In the course of these formative years he was influenced by figures prominent in the French intellectual tradition, most notably Saint-Simon, Comte, Fustel de Coulanges and Émile Boutroux. Significant also were the neo-Kantian Renouvier and the German psychologist Wilhelm Wundt. He held a combined chair of sociology and education at Bordeaux from 1887 to 1902, and one at the Sorbonne from that time until his death. During this latter period he was instrumental in founding an influential journal for the yearly review of literature pertaining to the social sciences, *L'Année sociologique*. His own authorship in the field was considerable, the major works being *The Division of Labour in Society* (*De la Division du travail social: étude sur l'organisation des sociétés supérieures*, 1893); *The Rules of Sociological Method* (*Les Règles de la méthode sociologique*, 1895); *Suicide* (*Le Suicide: étude de sociologie*, 1897); and *The Elementary Forms of Religious Life* (*Les Formes élémentaires de la vie religieuse*, 1912).

Durkheim was the beneficiary of two streams of thought which gathered force towards the end of the nineteenth century. The first was a fervent optimism in the capacities of science; the second, a new conception of society based on considering it as an entity in its own right rather than a simple conglomerate of individual lives. Applying the first to the second of these ideas, Durkheim sought to establish a science of society. Early in his career he defined the distinctive character of the discipline he envisaged and clarified the ways in which it differed from psychology and biology, sciences which had already embarked upon the task of unravelling the mysteries of human behaviour. Society, he argued in *The Rules*, warrants its own scientific enterprise because the interaction of individuals generates customs, traditions and codes of conduct which themselves constitute an original and irreducible body of data. Although they exist in and through the minds of men, these phenomena are external to the individual in that they await him at birth and continue after his death. They are not products of his own creation but are received by him as part of his cultural heritage. Furthermore, they impose upon his will. Constraining the basic self-seeking impulses of his psyche, they regulate his conduct to conform with community standards. Hence they are not accurately classified as psychological. Yet neither are they biological in character. Social phenomena are not physical but ideational. They are 'ways of acting, thinking and feeling' (*RSM*, 3), which are, nevertheless, 'real' in the sense that they are objects of perception conceived from data drawn from outside the mind. Awareness of them comes from observation; it is through experience that we learn of their existence. To these phenomena Durkheim gave the name 'social facts'. For the sociologist: 'A social fact is recognized by the power of external coercion which it exercises or is capable of exercising over individuals, and the presence of this power may be recognized in its turn either by the existence of some specific sanction or by the resistance offered against every individual effort that tends to violate it. (*RSM*, 10.)

Having thus specified his subject-matter Durkheim set out the method by which it was to be investigated. Since the founding of an empirical science was his aim, the model he advocated was, in all fundamental respects, that of the natural sciences. Causal analysis was the keystone. Sociology was to determine the causal connections operating between human associations (as cause) and states of the 'conscious collective' (as effect). By the former Durkheim understood 'the ways in which the constituent parts of society (individuals) are grouped' (*RSM*, 112); by the latter, the set of beliefs and sentiments, duties and obligations commonly held within a given society (*DLS*, 79), which renders its individual members solidary. In *The Division of Labour in Society* he identified two such organizational aspects of the social milieu: '(1) the number of social units, or . . . the *size of a society*; and (2) the degree of concentration of the group . . . the *dynamic density*' (*DLS*, 113). These, he found, were correlated with states of the *conscience collective* as it changed over time. Durkheim endeavoured to show that, due to the division of labour, the *conscience collective* of modern Western society had been transformed. Whilst in the past the form of association had been segmental (all units identical) and communal solidarity based on similarity ('mechanical solidarity'), modern society was evolving a co-operative form (units differentiated) and a solidarity based on interdependence ('organic solidarity'). In the social aggregates of primitive peoples uniformity was undisturbed by factors of diversity. Daily existence was the same for all, each man being himself responsible for all items of sustenance. The division of labour brought diversity of occupation and with it individual variability. But even though social solidarity has thus been lessened, the weakness is only temporary. The emergent individuation of the species carries with it the seed of a new organic form of solidarity wherein each unit exists in a network of interdependent social relations.

There is, for the sociologist, an important lesson to be learned from this work. Here, Durkheim exemplifies his point (elaborated in *The Rules*) that the sociologist must beware of taking a lay definition of his subject of investigation as his starting-point. Dealing with that most familiar of phenomena, the social world, we must be constantly critical of the unconsidered assumptions upon which we order our daily lives. In Durkheim's time, the division of labour was commonly regarded as an obnoxious development which would corrupt or restrict the natural unfolding of human nature. His analysis exposed the latent prejudice in this assumption, a prejudice carried over from the layman's fear of the novel. Far from being an undesirable feature of the evolution of the species, the division of labour was, in Durkheim's view, destined to produce a tighter and more resilient social bonding than that which had existed previously. Again, the common-sense assumption that crime and deviance are social evils and disruptive of community will be shown false when subjected to dispassionate examination. According to Durkheim, moral sentiments are inculcated in the young and sustained in society at large, mainly through the witnessing of socially expressed disapproval: the application of sanctions. Hence it follows that society must have the opportunity to punish which only crime and deviance provide, and that therefore these elements are a functional necessity of social life.

This introduces another important aspect of Durkheim's sociology, viz. his functionalism. The aim of sociology is, he holds, to determine not only the causes of social phenomena but also their social function. It is through functional analysis that sociology will benefit mankind. Stripped of prejudice the sociologist's analyses would discriminate between 'normal' and 'pathological' developments. For instance, whilst the division of labour was found to be a normal development, suicide (in particular its increasing incidence in the Western world) is, Durkheim maintained, pathological. In *Suicide* he utilized the 'comparative method', this being his one methodological concession to the difference between the natural and social sciences. Due to the lack of experimental opportunity and the complexity of the causal networks operating in the social world, the sociologist must compare sets of social facts drawn from different societies, or different segments of the one society, in order to arrive at his generalizations. By comparing statistics of suicide rates, Durkheim was able to pinpoint specifically social causes for what appears to be a psychological or biological phenomenon. Finding the suicide rate to be correlated with religious affiliation, the divorce rate and severe disruptions in the social order – and this to be true of different societies – he exposed the integrative function of religion, marriage and family, and politico-economic stability. The obligations and duties imposed by the institutions of religion and family bind the individual to fellow members of these social groupings. And on a more general level, that individual is bound to his society as a whole by the moral order which establishes an equilibrium between, on the one hand, his situation in society and the purposes, ambitions and desires appropriate to it, and on the other, the social means and natural talents which render the attainment of these a real possibility. In modern society, both the political and economic spheres are in constant fluctuation and hence the individual's position and expectations are abruptly and frequently altered. He no longer knows what society expects of him or thinks proper to apportion to him, with the result that he himself has no notion of what he may reasonably desire or, in justice, be asked to give. He thus falls prey to discontent and uncertainty. In principle, everything is possible, for society fails to perform its delimiting and defining role. In practice, the inequality of human talent and ability determine that it is not. Society has cast him loose in a sea of infinite desires with no directions for selecting those possible of fulfilment.

Implicit in this is a view of human nature and a conception of the essence and role of morality. For all that Durkheim wants to establish sociology as a discipline independent of psychology, his social theory is founded on the assumption that men have a vital psychological need of morality. Far from being a mere social contrivance to oil the wheels of social intercourse, morality is essential to psychological well-being for it not only constrains but actually defines the purposes and desires of human existence. Unlike those of other animal species, human desires are boundless. Once the conditions necessary for his physical maintenance are supplied, man craves a higher standard of comfort. And once that is attained, he wants still more. Without the external regulating force of the moral order his passions are insatiable. The ungoverned imagination cannot escape 'the futility of an endless pursuit' that ends finally in consummate weariness and disillusionment (*Suicide*). This condition, a pathology of the modern world, Durkheim called 'anomie'. He saw it, however, as a transitory phase. Society being now an organic entity, the dysfunction of one component will, in time, be compensated by adjustment. For example, the decline in religious observance, seen by Durkheim as a concomitant of the progress of science, heralds the emergence of new secular religious forms which will, ultimately, fulfil the same integrative function as the religions of the past. This prediction follows from the main line of his argument in *The Elementary Forms of Religious Life*.

As in all his substantive work, Durkheim begins his study of religion by questioning the validity of the received conception of the phenomenon under investigation. The notion that the defining characteristic of religion is a belief in the supernatural does not, he found, stand up to examination. Some religions (an instance is Buddhism) do not hold this belief. What is common to all is a conceptual division of the world into the two domains of the sacred and the profane. Unlike profane objects which men deal with intellectually and practically, sacred objects elicit the religious feelings of awe and reverence. The true referent of these feelings is not, however, any supernatural being but is society. The gods, according to Durkheim, are the symbols which represent community. The religious conviction that there exists a transcendent entity is in fact man's awareness of his relation to society. Hence, although science will bring about the demise of particular religions founded in earlier centuries by rendering their particular symbols inappropriate, new forms will inevitably arise as men seek to restore their communion with the social milieu.

For Durkheim, all ideas issue from the collectivity and their emergence and decline reflect the changing character of society as it moves through time. It is this notion that underlies the sociology of knowledge, a field upon which he has had considerable impact. Durkheim holds that it is social organization that generates ideas. Even the most fundamental have this origin. Our ideas of space derive from the spatial organization of primitive community life. Likewise our organization of time into calendar units once corresponded to cyclical community celebrations and ritual observances. The *tabula rasa* is writ upon not by experience *per se* but by social experience. The very categories of thought are produced – not merely influenced – by the social environment.

In this extreme form Durkheim's conception of the societal input to knowledge has not found adherents. It is now regarded as an overstatement of the more modest yet indubitable truth that ideas are in large part shaped by the social context in which they arise. Nevertheless, it was with these arguments that Durkheim, together with Marx and Mannheim*, initiated the study of correlations between systems of thought and forms of social structure. He has been particularly influential in this and also one other development within the discipline. Both are forms of 'structuralism', but the other, through the Parsonian* synthesis, is less concerned with thought systems and places more emphasis on the organizational aspects of the social order and the structural relations among their elements. But Durkheim's greatest contribution to sociology has been the general one of setting the example for rigorous and innovative research guided by a clear conception of subject-matter and a systematic methodology.

Bobbie Lederman

T. Parsons, *The Structure of Social Actions* (1937); R. K. Merton, *Social Theory and Social Structure* (1957); A. Giddens, *Émile Durkheim: Selected Writings*, Introduction (1972); S. Lukes, *Émile Durkheim: His Life and Work* (1973); R. A. Nisbet, *The Sociology of Émile Durkheim* (1975).

130
DYLAN, Bob (Robert Allen Zimmerman) 1941–

US rock 'n' roll musician

Even his disclaimers ('I'm just an entertainer . . . a song and dance man . . . a trapeze artist') are part of the picture of Dylan as the articulate consciousness of his generation in the mid-1960s, the 'Angelic Dylan singing across the nation' of Allen Ginsberg's* 1966 *Wichita Vortex Sutra*. As a focus first for radical dissent, then for psychic revolution, he altered sensibilities and political attitudes; as a performer in the traditions of blues, rock and country music his influence is huge; as a poet and songwriter he is *the* major artist of rock 'n' roll.

Born in Duluth, Minnesota, and brought up in the nearby iron-ore mining town of Hibbing, he learnt piano, guitar and harmonica as a child, experiencing America's musical richness through radio. In his teens he played in high-school rock bands, and after a brief spell at the University of Minnesota in Minneapolis (1959–60) he left for New York, impassioned by the discovery of Woody Guthrie, the source of his early vocal style and political awareness, which he began to channel through the current vogue for folk-lyricism.

The first record, *Bob Dylan* (1962), presents arrangements of traditional songs and blues, delivered in a harsh nasal voice already showing the control, intensity and immaculate timing of a brilliant talent, suggesting depths of experience and suffering, as well as humour and sincerity. *The Freewheelin' Bob Dylan* (1963) is a variety of his own compositions: castigations of the war machine, dream-framework songs of nuclear insanity, wit and candour in love relationships, all with a chary clear-eyed wisdom. He transcends the folk idiom by refusing its nostalgia and by confronting current issues with imaginative breadth.

The label 'protest singer' was a commercial tag too narrow to define the visionary tone of *The Times They Are A-Changin'* (1974). The disgrace of a supposedly impartial justice when dealing with crimes against the Negro, the divisive tactics of a class society in fostering such crimes, are paired with vignettes of poor-white despair under the neglect and inhuman fluctuation of capitalist economics. An optimistic counterpart is in the album's title track, whose image of revolutionary flood under a new consciousness is extended in 'When The Ship Comes In', when 'The chains of the sea/Will have busted in the night/And will be buried at the bottom of the ocean.'

While such anthems were making him the spokesman for activism, Dylan was already claiming greater freedom of expression. 'Restless Farewell' is his goodbye to 'The dirt of gossip. . . . And the dust of rumours', and heralds the change from objective to subjective which is begun in *Another Side of Bob Dylan* (1964), and completed in *Bringing It All Back Home* (1965). Under the influence of Kennedy's* assassination, drugs, the reading of poets like Ginsberg and Rimbaud, confidence in his own artistic power, and the rock revival launched from England, he returned to the native traditions of Chicago, Memphis and the Mississippi Delta.

In 1964 he said, 'I don't want to write *for* people anymore. . . . I want to write from inside me', and this desire emerges in the Blakean visions and personal venom of *Another Side*, as well as in the generally more emphatic syncopation. The transition to a fuller musical sound is made with Side 1 of *Bringing It All Back Home*, when studio musicians are first used to accompany his guitar and harmonica. Zany, surreal, nihilistic fantasies full of tumbling images and transcendent juxtapositions complete this major statement. His ideas were now couched in an entirely different perceptual mould, the songs capable of simultaneously rewarding and evading intense scrutiny. The American Nightmare is indicted through invitation to enter a nightmare condition in which the promise of any security in known points of contact is withheld. Millions in the West were prepared to follow.

The final break with, or, in his own terms, the re-synthesis of American folk music, was made at the Newport Folk Festival in 1965, when Dylan performed with full electric blues-rock accompaniment. In the same year he worked with The Hawks, later known as The Band. Tuneful organ punctuations, percussive piano and tambourine, whining harmonica and wailing guitars achieve 'that thin, that wild mercury sound . . . metallic and bright gold' of his stated ideal on the two definitive rock albums of the 1960s, *Highway 61 Revisited* (1965) and *Blonde On Blonde* (1966). Here a painful, violent rage overspills through a weird swirl of imagined characters and situations, unresolved mysteries, the sense of confusion and alienation hurled in bitter accusations of which Dylan himself is the target as much as the disoriented victims of the songs. In this whirlwind period the pressure is towards reliance on imagination, creativity and self, rather than facts, culture and the other.

In August 1966 Dylan broke his neck in a motorcycle crash. The enforced rest was followed by several years of uncertain experiment in his music and attitudes, some of which is reflected in informal sessions with The Band, recorded in 1967 and released in 1975 as *The Basement Tapes*. The tone of his work in the next five years is predominantly low-key, even mellow. The simple melodies of *John Wesley Harding* (1968), using only bass and drum backing, deal in pity, guilt, remorse and loneliness, with a sense of order and morality replacing chaotic vision. *Nashville Skyline* (1969) is a happy country-style collection, and *Self-Portrait* (1970) an accomplished double album, mostly of other people's songs. *New Morning* (1970) begins a revival fully achieved in *Planet Waves* (1973), consisting largely of romantic love songs in which at least some of the productive ambiguity of the 1960s is apparent. The style is fresh, the voice strong, The Band's music a subtly beautiful counterpoint to the dominant themes of security in rural family seclusion and religious fundamentalism.

The year 1971 saw the publication of his book, *Tarantula*, 'a series of thoughts as they came to me . . . not judgments but comments'. His triumphal return to major public performance with The Band is recorded on *Before The Flood* (1974). *Blood On The Tracks* (1974) treats the theme of dissolution through powerful lyrics in which security is again lost in uneasy quest. *Desire* (1975) brings his continued re-invention of himself as artist to a new peak, 'treading on the heels of Rimbaud moving like a dancing bullet thru the secret streets of a hot New Jersey night filled with venom and wonder, meeting the Queen Angel in the reeds of Babylon and then to the fountain of sorrow to drift away in the hot mass of the deluge' (cover notes). More successful touring with The Rolling Thunder Review (*Hard Rain*, 1976, and *Bob Dylan at Budokan*, 1978) was combined with the production of his film, *Renaldo and Clara* (1978). The complex metaphor of *Street Legal* (1978) leads to what seems to be the start of a new period with *Slow Train Coming* (1979), in which the musical and vocal skills are now at the service of Christian dogma and petty nationalism.

John Porter

See: Bob Dylan, *Writings and Drawings* (1973); Michael Gray, *Song and Dance Man* (1972); Toby Thompson, *Positively Main Street* (1969); Anthony Scaduto, *Bob Dylan* (1972); *Bob Dylan: A Retrospective*, ed. Craig McGregor (1972); Sam Shepard, *Rolling Thunder Logbook* (1977); Robert Alexander, *Bob Dylan* (1968); Alan Rinzler, *Bob Dylan* (1978).

131

EAMES, Charles 1907–78

US designer

Charles Eames, together with his wife Ray, was involved in a wide range of artistic activity in this century. Best known as a chair designer, he also produced architecture, toys and films, adopting the same creative approach in all these diverse media.

Born in St Louis in 1907, Eames studied architecture and opened his own architectural office in 1930. In 1936 he accepted a fellowship and later a teaching post at Cranbrook Academy of Art where he met Eero Saarinen (the son of Eliel Saarinen), with whom he was to collaborate on some furniture designs. Other fellow-students included Florence Knoll and Harry Bertoia who also went on to become notable 'contemporary' furniture designers in the post-war years. The first designs he did with Saarinen were for some furniture for an exhibition at the Museum of Modern Art in New York, entitled 'Organic Design in Home Furnishings'. The furniture they exhibited owed much to contemporary Scandinavian ideas rather than to the popular functionalist ideas of immigrant German designers. The chairs were made of plywood shells, moulded in two directions, supported by thin metal rod legs. They were innovatory on both technical and aesthetic fronts simultaneously. Eames went on to develop his experiments in moulded plywood, working on stretchers and leg splints during the war and producing a new series of chairs in 1946, a polyester moulded chair in 1950 and a moulded plywood and leather padded chair in 1956 – produced initially as a TV chair for Billy Wilder. These were followed by aluminium-framed lounge chairs which exploited the visual combination of leather and metal – an idiom which has become a familiar appendage of many late twentieth-century public waiting areas.

Eames's chair designs all pursue the idea of visual juxtaposition, whether of wood and metal or leather and metal, and he had to evolve the technical expertise to be able to combine these different materials. The same aesthetic approach is applied to all his creations. The house he built for himself and his wife in Santa Monica in 1949 displays the same lightness as his furniture, this time through the juxtaposition of metal and glass. The house was built entirely of mass-produced materials and is an early example of prefabrication in architecture.

The films he produced through the 1950s and 1960s – early ones include *Parade*, *Blacktop* and *Communications Primer* – are short exercises in the pure juxtaposition of sound and vision. Several short films were produced for IBM exhibits in World Fairs through the period, including some multi-media productions. From 1967-71 the Eames office worked on the programme for the proposed National Aquarium in Washington, in association with the architectural firm of Kevin Roche and John Dinkeloo.

Penny Sparke

See: E. Noyes, 'Charles Eames', in *Arts and Architecture*, September 1946; A. Drexler, *Charles Eames – Furniture from the Design Collection*, Museum of Modern Art, New York 1973.

132

EDDINGTON, Sir Arthur 1882–1944

English astronomer

Educated at Owens College, Manchester, and Trinity College, Cambridge, Eddington worked at the Royal Observatory, Greenwich, from 1906 until 1913 when he was appointed Plumian Professor of Astronomy at Cambridge. Shortly thereafter he became the Director of Cambridge University Observatory, a post which he held with the professorship until his death. Eddington, a Quaker who never married, was knighted in 1930.

Eddington made significant contributions to astronomy and cosmology. His early work created the subject of stellar dynamics. As secretary of the Royal Astronomical Society he brought Einstein's* General Theory of Relativity to the attention of the English-speaking world by inviting de Sitter to produce an account of the theory for the Society's *Monthly Notices*. His own *The Mathematical Theory of Relativity* (1923) contributed to the understanding of relativity. As leader of the British expedition to the Gulf of Guinea which photographed stars in the vicinity of the sun during the eclipse of 1919, he obtained the first empirical confirmation of Einstein's General Theory by detecting the bending of light by the sun's gravitational field. His most significant contribution to theoretical astronomy came in 1924 when as a result of his study of the internal constitution of stars he derived the law relating the mass of a star to its luminosity. In 1930 he showed that Edwin Hubble's recent discovery of the recession of distant galaxies supported Georges Le Maître's expanding model of the universe, a model now known as the Eddington–Le Maître model.

Eddington devoted considerable attention to questions concerning the philosophical presuppositions and implications of modern physics. An entertaining, indeed exciting writer, he was guided more by analogy and metaphor than by argument. His resulting idealist metaphysics, which is a veritable labyrinth of confusion, received a hostile reaction both from philosophers and from physicists. Eddington assumed that as well as knowing the contents of his own mind, he knew of the existence of other minds with whom he was in partial communication. The external world is constructed from the elements common to this collectivity of minds on which it depends for its existence. This idealist metaphysics served to support his doctrine that the laws of physics can be discovered by a priori reflection. For on his account the laws are imposed by the mind on its own creation. The central tension in Eddington's metaphysics arises from the fact that he also held a causal theory of perception which implies the existence of non-mental causes of perceptions. According to Eddington, physical knowledge is a matter of understanding structures which are to be characterized by the mathematics of group theory. This highly abstract mathematical approach, when taken with his currents of mysticism, produced a quite unique perspective. Eddington argued for the existence of God and claimed that indeterminacy in quantum mechanics established the freedom of the will. His philosophical writings, unlike his scientific work, are unlikely to have a lasting influence. However, they had a major impact at the time through stimulating interest in the philosophical questions surrounding contemporary physics.

W. H. Newton-Smith

Eddington's works include: *Space, Time and Gravitation* (1920); *The Internal Constitution of the Stars* (1926); *Nature of the Physical World* (1926); *Stars and Atoms* (1927); *The Expanding Universe* (1933); *New Pathways in Science* (1935).

133
EINSTEIN, Albert 1879–1955

German/Swiss/US physicist

Albert Einstein was born in Ulm of middle-class Jewish parentage. His early academic career was not particularly brilliant. He disliked the rigid discipline of the Luitpold Gymnasium in Munich and later succeeded in entering the prestigious Swiss Federal Polytechnic School at Zürich only at the second attempt. Here he studied mathematics and physics, but on graduating in 1900 failed to obtain an academic appointment. Instead in 1902 he secured the post of Technical Expert (Third Class) in the Swiss Patent Office at Berne. (He had renounced his German nationality in 1896 and become a Swiss citizen in 1900.) It was while working at the Patent Office that Einstein in his spare time wrote his epoch-making papers of 1905 including his announcement of the special theory of relativity. His genius in theoretical physics was soon recognized. In 1908 he was appointed *Privatdozent* in the University of Berne and then in 1909 was made associate professor of theoretical physics in the University of Zürich. In 1911 he was appointed professor at the German University in Prague (temporarily acquiring Austro-Hungarian nationality), but returned to a chair in mathematical physics at the Polytechnic in Zürich in 1912. Then in 1914 he was appointed director of the new Kaiser Wilhelm Institute for Physics in Berlin, was made a member of the Prussian Academy of Sciences and was also given a professorship in the University of Berlin. It was here that Einstein produced the final version of his general theory of relativity. However, Einstein was awarded the 1921 Nobel Prize in Physics for his work on the photoelectric effect rather than the more speculative relativity. In 1933 he left Germany due to the Nazi persecution and became a member of the new Institute for Advanced Study at Princeton in the USA. Here he remained until his death, becoming a naturalized American in 1940.

Apart from his scientific work Einstein was a passionate advocate in the causes of pacificism and Zionism. Indeed in 1952 he was offered, but declined, the Presidency of Israel. His pacifist views were profoundly affected by Hitler's* rise to power in Germany and in 1939 he wrote a famous letter to Roosevelt warning him of the danger of atomic weapons and recommending a US programme of research in this field.

In the popular imagination Einstein is regarded as a mathematician who invented an impossibly recondite theory, relativity, according to which time is relative, space is curved, light does not travel in straight lines and so on. In fact Einstein's early work, prior to general relativity, used quite simple mathematics and was distinguished rather by an amazingly clear physical insight. In the case of general relativity Einstein did not himself invent new mathematical tools, but applied ideas on non-Euclidean geometry developed by Riemann, Ricci, Levi-Civita and others. As a mathematician Einstein was not particularly outstanding and in this respect must be regarded as the inferior of Newton. Indeed his later work on generalizations of relativity, unified theories designed to accommodate both electromagnetism and gravitation, was largely mathematical in character and showed a considerable falling off as compared with the quality of his earlier work.

It should be stressed that much of Einstein's most original work had nothing to do with relativity. His first research interest was in thermodynamics and statistical mechanics. He virtually invented the latter discipline for himself in papers published between 1902 and 1904, independently of the more widely known work of J. Willard Gibbs (1839–1903). Stressing the importance of fluctuations in statistical theories Einstein applied his ideas to the quantitative elucidation of the Brownian motion of suspended particles in a liquid. This was one of his three famous 1905 papers, all published in the Germany monthly journal, *Annalen der Physik*. It had a profound significance in demonstrating the essential correctness of the kinetic-atomic theory of matter.

The next field in which Einstein made a major contribution was the newly discovered Quantum theory in which Planck* in 1900 had introduced an element of fundamental discontinuity into the physics of black-body radiation. In 1905 Einstein boldly applied this idea to the radiation field itself so that light and other forms of electromagnetic radiation were to be regarded as exhibiting a corpuscular aspect in addition to their wave-like properties. He applied the new theory to explain among other things the detailed quantitative laws of the photoelectric effect, which were later to be brilliantly confirmed by the experiments of Robert A. Millikan. During the next twenty years Einstein continued to develop a number of significant aspects of the Quantum theory, in particular the theory of specific heats dating from 1907, and culminating in 1924 with his theory of gas degeneration, a phenomenon wherein he anticipated a wave aspect for material particles, which, together with the independent work of Louis de Broglie, led directly to Schrödinger's* development of wave mechanics. But Einstein was not in sympathy with the later interpretations of this theory and the closely associated Quantum mechanics of Heisenberg*. At this point Einstein fell out of line with the orthodox development of physics as reflected particularly in the views of Niels Bohr* and refused to accept a statistical instrumentalism as an ultimate account of happenings in the world of atoms and electrons. Einstein regarded the new Quantum theory as 'incomplete' and alien to the realistic interpretation of physical theories he had espoused since his early work on kinetic theory. It is fair to say that Einstein's sustained critique of the new micro-physics served to sharpen the at times rather unclear formulation of the orthodox Copenhagen school, but in combination with his long and unsuccessful attempts at extending general relativity it left Einstein for the last thirty years of his life almost completely isolated from the mainstream developments in theoretical physics.

It was Einstein's third 1905 paper which introduced the special theory of relativity. This was not unconnected with his light-quantum hypothesis in the theory of radiation. Since Einstein believed that Maxwell's equations of the electromagnetic field could not be an exact description, he wanted to distil from these equations a principle which would survive in any more accurate future theory of light. This led him to his formulation of a new relativity principle. In classical mechanics there was already incorporated the principle of Galilean relativity according to which the laws of mechanics were unchanged in form when referred to any so-called inertial reference frame, any two such frames being in uniform relative motion with respect to each other. As a result no purely mechanical phenomena could distinguish a state of absolute rest or motion, only the relative motion of bodies could be established – hence the term 'relativity'. Although motion was relative according to the Galilean principle, spatial extensions and temporal intervals were considered to be 'absolute' in the sense of being the same when measured with respect to any of the inertial reference frames. However the equations of electromagnetism, namely Maxwell's equations, failed to satisfy the relativity principle and suggested the possibility of identifying 'absolute' states of motion. Experiments designed to test the predicted failure of the principle in respect of electromagnetic phenomena, such as the propagation of light, showed apparently that the principle did hold here as well. Einstein was not really influenced in his work by these experimental findings (there is some doubt as to whether he even knew of them). Instead he proposed as a new principle of physics to extend relativity to cover all physical phenomena. In order to comprehend electromagnetism this meant revising the kinematic relationships between moving reference frames embodied in the Galilean principle. Since these in turn were based on the notion of absolute space and time the new Einstein principle resulted in a frame-dependence or 'relativity' of spatial and temporal interval measurements. (The Einstein transformations were formally identical with, although conceptually quite distinct from, earlier results of H. A. Lorentz.) Velocity was still in general 'relativized' with the exception of the unique velocity accorded by the Maxwell equations to the propagation of light in a vacuum. The velocity of light became the new 'absolute' element in the kinematic relationship between moving frames. The new Einstein relativity principle while designed specifically to accommodate electromagnetic phenomena as described by Maxwell's equations now failed in respect of the laws of classical mechanics. So Einstein proceeded to modify Newton's laws of mechanics in such a way as to conform to his new principle. In particular the mass of an object ceased to be an 'absolute' quantity but now varied in a characteristic manner with velocity. One consequence of this was the famous $E = mc^2$ relation between energy and mass where c is the velocity of light. (Incidentally this equation is often erroneously claimed to identify a new source of energy, namely mass, which is then said to be the origin of 'atomic energy' – in fact it applies to *all* forms of energy.) Einstein's special theory of relativity was a rather complicated blend of conventional or definitional components associated with his analysis of the relativity of simultaneity and a direct physical component which explained, for example, the null results of optical experiments designed to measure absolute motion. The unravelling of these two components has only been cleared up satisfactorily in the recent work of J. A. Winnie (1970). Einstein seems to have been influenced psychologically by the writings of the positivist philosopher of science Ernst Mach, in particular in his approach to the analysis of the time concept in physics, but the resulting theory with its continuing but revised blend of 'relative' and 'absolute' elements is far removed from Mach's crude sensationalism.

Although with special relativity Einstein had abolished the notion of absolute rest the question of absolute acceleration, as, for example, in rotational motion, remained. Under transformations to arbitrary reference frames the laws of physics would change their form even when they were adjusted to be invariant under transformations to uniformly moving reference frames as required by the special theory. However, Einstein proposed that this change in form could be compensated by a change in the gravitational field experienced by the physical system described by the law in question. In this way the relativity principle could be generalized from uniformly moving reference frames to arbitrarily moving reference frames. In order to implement this programme Einstein first invoked a principle of equivalence according to which the effect of an accelerated reference frame was 'equivalent' to an appropriate gravitational field in the unaccelerated frame. Extending this idea to the case of 'permanent' gravitational fields which could not be globally but only locally eliminated by a change of reference system Einstein arrived at his theory of general relativity which he thought would provide a solution to the absolute acceleration problem and also give a geometrical theory of gravitation in which the metrical properties of a non-Euclidean space-time continuum would be determined by the local distribution of matter and radiation. Considered as a theory of gravitation general relativity made three immediate predictions: a small correction to the motion of the planet Mercury which was already known to be required for agreement with observation; an effect of a gravitational field on the frequency of spectral lines; and, most striking of all, the bending of light in a gravitational field. This latter effect was strikingly confirmed in 1919 by observation of the shift in apparent direction of stars near the eclipsed sun. It was this successful novel prediction

that made Einstein famous overnight to an amazed but almost totally uncomprehending public. In 1917 Einstein applied this new theory to the cosmological problem of the universe as a whole and showed by a slight and later rejected modification of his field equations the possibility of a static, spatially closed, but unbounded universe. This was the starting point of the great explosion of interest in theoretical cosmology of the past sixty years.

Paradoxically it turned out that one of the guiding principles that led Einstein to general relativity, Mach's principle or the elimination of absolute acceleration, was not exemplified in the final theory. Exactly how one should attempt to incorporate Mach's principle into a physical theory has been one of the most debated issues of modern cosmology. Furthermore a second guiding principle of general covariance, according to which one should eliminate in all respects the frame-dependence of the laws of physics, turned out to be vacuous. Unlike the relativity principle of the special theory, it actually placed no constraint on possible physical theories as was pointed out by Kretschmann in 1917. Nevertheless, as a theory of gravitation general relativity has acquired an increasingly secure reputation, although it was in fact only after Einstein's death that it began to rival the special theory in scientific respectability due to a number of sophisticated experimental tests making use, for example, of satellite and radar technology. (The unequivocal detection of predicted gravitational waves remains however a major challenge to the experimentalists.) Furthermore the theoretical implications of the theory in respect of the intense gravitational fields associated with space-time singularities and 'black holes' have only come to be properly understood during the past fifteen years. General relativity has become the working tool of modern astrophysics and cosmology just as surely as special relativity has become second nature to the elementary particle physicist.

It is on the basis of detailed quantitative predictions, i.e. considered as a precise physical theory, that relativity is judged by physicists. Einstein, however, never paid much attention to the experimental tests of his theories. For him they were 'free inventions of the human intellect', discovered quite independently of anomalous observational data, guided by considerations of mathematical elegance and conceptual unity, and their very success has counterpointed the narrow positivistic and operationalist philosophy espoused by many contemporary physicists. Einstein was by far the greatest theoretical physicist of his age, and arguably in this field must rival even Newton whose work in so many respects he was to overthrow.

Dr M. L. G. Redhead

Einstein's major papers on relativity are included in the collection translated by W. Perrett and G. B.

Jeffrey, *The Principle of Relativity* (1923). Einstein's own autobiography is contained in P. A. Schilpp (ed.), *Albert Einstein: Philosopher-Scientist* (1949). See also: R. W. Clark, *Einstein: The Life and Times* (1973). Other useful biographies are: P. Frank, *Einstein: His Life and Times* (1947); and J. Bernstein, *Einstein* (1973). The best popular exposition of relativity remains Einstein's own book *Relativity, The Special and the General Theory* (1920). The best of the more technical accounts is C. Møller, *The Theory of Relativity* (1952). For an up-to-date assessment of general relativity, see S. W. Hawking and W. Israel (eds), *General Relativity: An Einstein Centenary Survey* (1979).

134

EISENSTEIN, Sergei Mikhailovitch 1898–1948

Russian film director

Eisenstein was born into the family of a city architect in Riga, and spent his childhood there and in St Petersburg before studying architecture and engineering at the Petrograd School of Public Works. In 1918 he enlisted in the Red Army, where he produced posters and theatre designs. After the Civil War, he moved to Moscow to study Japanese, but was diverted into the theatre after a chance encounter with a childhood friend, Maxim Strauch. It was in his theatrical work between 1920 and 1924 that Eisenstein was exposed to a range of Modernist experiments in dramaturgy that were to lead him in the direction of the cinema.

In the theatre he worked on a number of productions for the Proletcult between 1920 and 1921, then enrolled in Meyerhold's* State School for Stage Direction, where he made the acquaintance of Sergei Yutkevitch, with whom he was to produce a number of stage-pieces after leaving Meyerhold. Further encounters with Foregger's Workshop Theatre and the Factory of the Eccentric Actor led back to an assistantship with Meyerhold and then to the directorship of a branch of Proletcult, where Eisenstein's first production (Ostrovsky's *Even a Wise Man Stumbles*) included his first short film, *Glumov's Diary*, and triggered his first theoretical article, linking theatre and film, 'The Montage of Attractions', published by Mayakovsky* in *LEF* in 1923. The period as a whole is marked by Eisenstein's rejection of the psychological realism of the Moscow Art Theatre tradition and his search for new dramatic models in the general field of Constructivist aesthetics.

While with Proletcult, Eisenstein moved fully into film production with his exuberant and dynamic first feature, *Strike* (1925), the story of the bloody suppression of a factory strike in pre-Revolutionary Russian. By the end of the same year he had completed his second film, the stern five-act drama of *Battleship Potemkin* (1925), recounting the mutiny aboard the battleship in June 1905. Work on *October* (1927), a poetic chronicle for the tenth birthday of the Revolution, displaced the preparations for *Old and New* (formerly *The General Line*), a film dealing with the co-operativization of agriculture and the acquisition of new farming technologies, eventually premiered in 1928. These films and the theoretical writing that accompanies them established Eisenstein as the major new talent in Soviet cinema in the 1920s, and quickly led to international acclaim.

With this clutch of silent masterpieces behind him, Eisenstein set out in mid-1929 to tour Europe and to visit the United States. In Hollywood he and his collaborators Tisse and Alexandrov were hired by Paramount but were unable during 1930 to bring any projects to fruition. As a result the next three years were spent in vexed attempts, far from Hollywood, to produce *Que Viva Mexico!* independently for Upton Sinclair, an experience which brought Eisenstein into close proximity with the religious mysticism and eroticism of Mexico, its history and mythology. *Time in the Sun*, compiled by Eisenstein's biographer-to-be Marie Seton in 1939, is the best generally available record of this fraught endeavour.

The experience of surrendering his footage to Sinclair as the project failed was a severe blow to Eisenstein, who returned to the USSR and only gradually made his way back into the mainstream of Soviet film production, in a climate much less sympathetic than before. Between 1935 and 1937 his new film on agriculture, *Bezhin Meadow*, was halted first by Eisenstein's smallpox and then by State edict; remaining material being destroyed in the war, it survived only as a half-hour montage of stills and music compiled by Sergei Yutkevitch in 1966. Eisenstein's only finished project of the 1930s is his contribution to the anti-Fascist programme, *Alexander Nevsky* (1938), which dramatizes the defence of Novgorod and Pskov against the Teutonic Knights in 1242, although his theoretical and academic work continued and in 1939 he became the artistic head of Mosfilm.

Eisenstein's final film was *Ivan the Terrible*, an unfinished trilogy about the sixteenth-century Tsar who destroyed the autonomy of the nobles and created a united Russia. Part 1 was released in 1944, Part 2 in 1946, with Eisenstein now using colour for the first time for part of the film. In 1946 Eisenstein suffered a coronary; the second part of the trilogy was denounced by the Central Committee on Cinema and Theatre, sensitive to the unflattering parallels between Stalin* and Tsar Ivan; in 1947, working on Part 3 of *Ivan* he was heartbroken by his first sight of the American versions of his early 1930s Mexican material; early in 1948 he died of a further heart attack.

The work of Eisenstein has spheres of influence too

numerous to catalogue. The cinema has not ceased to absorb his ideas and his examples, or to acknowledge their importance by contesting them. He is invariably invoked in discussions of the cinema and the politics of socialism, both at the level of ideologies in general and also in terms of the ideology of film form. His films, with their constant return to history, form part of those central debates over the cinema and ideas of realism, with particular reference to the question of historical representation. His theories of film editing, and film style, are central to discussions of film 'language', while his interest and involvement in other media (theatre, literature, music, opera) also gives his work keen purchase on more general questions about artistic media and aesthetics.

Fundamental to these questions was Eisenstein's approach to problems of film form. The task of creating a new Soviet cinema led Eisenstein to dismantle the continuum of realist fiction, and to concentrate attention upon its constituent units, in particular the role of individual frames and shots and the system of connection, editing, that organized their flow. Editing then became a compositional principle, became the activity of 'montage', for which Eisenstein began to elaborate a possible typology of functions: metric, rhythmic, tonal, overtonal, and intellectual. For Eisenstein, drawing upon such diverse influences as dialectical materialism, ideogrammatic writing, Pavlov's work on motor-reflexes, and his experience of theatrical presentation as a 'montage of attractions', montage opened up new ways of modelling film form beyond the linearity of the dominant model. The complexity it suggested was to be embodied in such different examples as the spatial and temporal disjunctions of the massacre on the Odessa Steps in *Battleship Potemkin*, the lyrically fragmented closing of the bridge in *October*, the climactic animation of the cream-separator in *Old and New*.

Montage cinema then broke with traditional film form and involved spectators in new reflexive modes of reading cinema. But for all its multivalence and polyphony, montage in Eisenstein is always contained by larger-scale dramatic principles. It never reaches the degree of riotous profusion that creates the semiotic complexity of Vertov's* *Man with a Movie Camera*, for instance, perhaps the supreme example of the anti-realist drive of the Soviet montage aesthetic. For the disruptive and disintegrative powers of montage are contained in Eisenstein by a more classical impulse for organicism and coherence, which becomes more marked in Eisenstein's later work as montage cinema as a whole is overhauled by the return to Classicism, in the 1930s, in the form of Socialist Realism. By the time of Eisenstein's sound films this has become the case in two main ways. First, Eisenstein's concerns with montage at the level of film editing are displaced by an increasing interest in the internal organization

or montage of the image and of the shot, marking an increased concern with *mise-en-scène*. This is more than partly because the late historical dramas, *Alexander Nevsky* and *Ivan the Terrible*, now centre individual 'character' as never before in Eisenstein, thus emphasizing the centrality of the film actor, and the space and time in which he moves. Editing in these later works thus sacrifices its disruptive potential in the service of the coherence of the pro-filmic event, preferring to assume instead a heightened function of ensuring complex but classical continuity of dramatic space and time. It is in this period that Eisenstein can look back on *Battleship Potemkin* as a model of organic unity and symmetry. Second, the organicism of Eisenstein's late works is also determined by his acceptance of a classical aesthetic of coherence for the combination of sound and image. Sound, like montage, is used to enrich and reinforce, rather than to disrupt. The call for contrapuntal use of sound embodied in Eisenstein's, Pudovkin's*, and Alexandrov's 1928 manifesto instead gives way to the sumptuous synchronicity of the late films, particularly in their plangent and emotive use of scores by Prokofiev*. In his book *The Film Sense*, Eisenstein is even able to claim a note-to-image correspondence between the music-track and picture-track of a segment of *Alexander Nevsky*. It is perhaps the tension between these two modes – the disruptive montage aesthetic of the 1920s compared with the organic classicism of the later period – that focuses the importance of Eisenstein for ideas about the differing possibilities of film form, and of the ideological systems underpinning them.

Philip Drummond

Eisenstein, *Izbrannyiye Proizvededea v shesti tomakh*, ('Selected Works', 6 vols, 1964–71); *The Film Sense* (1942); *Film Form* (1949); *Notes of a Film Director* (1959); *Film Essays* (1968); See: Yon Barna, *Eisenstein* (1973); Marie Seton, *Eisenstein* (2nd edn, 1978); Jean Mitry, *Eisenstein* (1975); Leon Moussinac, *Sergei Eisenstein* (1970); Peter Wollen, *Signs and Meaning in the Cinema* (3rd edn, 1972). See also: Jay Leyda, *Kino: A History of the Russian and Soviet Film* (2nd edn, 1973); Sylvia Harvey, *May '68 and Film Culture* (1978).

135

EISLER, Hanns 1898–1962

Austro-German composer

Born the second son of the Austrian liberal philosopher Rudolf Eisler in Leipzig, Hanns moved with his family in 1901 to Vienna. Here, after grammar school (1908–15) and military service with a Hungarian regiment (1916–18), he took his formal musical training, first at the conservatory, then privately with Arnold Schoenberg*. After this important and influential apprenticeship with Schoenberg and subsequent success at avantgarde music festivals, Eisler moved to Berlin (1925) and renounced the ideals of his teacher, forcing an ideological break with him (1926).

From then on he assumed the role of politically committed composer, as did so many artists in the Weimar Republic, and it is for the conscious politicization of his art that he is perhaps best known. This was achieved to a large extent through his collaboration with the poet and playwright Bertolt Brecht*, who did much to boost his reputation; but even in this capacity as Brecht's composer he has been overshadowed by Kurt Weill*, who, through his music to a handful of stage works, has gained much recognition and popularity. Eisler's settings of Brecht far outnumber Weill's, however, and represent in their common sense of purpose an outstandingly prolific and productive artistic partnership. Eisler's influence on Brecht's early development towards Marxism, both in the realm of theory and in the practice of didactic theatre (the *Lehrstück*), is proving to have been considerable. His intention was to write music which he hoped would advance the cause of socialism, and it is this intention which determines and characterizes his many-sided output.

Eisler's early works (Opp. 1–11) betray many affinities to the idiom of the Second Viennese School (Schoenberg, Webern* and Berg*) – intensely chromatic musical material, the use of the twelve-note method and an aversion to unnecessary ornament; but already in these works elements appear which suggest opposition and criticism. These are most clearly heralded in the *Zeitungsausschnitte* (*Newspaper Cuttings*), Op. 11 (1922–6), which employ banal texts expressing aggression and caricature and a musical language embracing both freely-dissonant and tonal writing. Eisler's stylistic eclecticism, apparent in so much of his work, is a product of concerning himself not just with the purely aesthetic aspects of music but also with its uses and functions in society. His musical output, therefore, is not easily classifiable into stylistic periods, but rather into genres, each of which uses the musical means suitable for its particular function. Throughout the four stages of his career – Vienna (1923–5), Berlin (1925–33), exile in Europe and the USA (1933–49), German Democratic Republic (1950–62) – he devoted himself mainly to writing *angewandte* ('applied') music: over six hundred vocal works, including revolutionary songs, ballads, choruses and cantatas, and many stage works and film scores, which also provide the basis for much of his purely instrumental music.

His compositional practice was supported by a powerful intellect which found expression in his work as an essayist and theorist of strikingly original and precise formulation. His writings document a pioneering attempt to formulate a dialectical materialist theory of music, and along with his book *Composing for the Films* (1947), written in collaboration with Theodor Adorno*, he made a significant contribution to the sociology of music. His political persuasions brought him before the Committee of Unamerican Activities in 1948, and he was forced to leave the USA despite international protest. Because of its applied nature, some of his music, especially the *Kampfmusik* (music written directly for political agitation), has proved to be ephemeral, but there is much, partly because of political pressures, that has been unjustly suppressed or neglected.

Stephen Hinton

A complete edition of Eisler's work is being prepared by VEB Deutscher Verlag für Musik, Leipzig. A selection of Eisler's writing is available in English translation in *Hanns Eisler: A Rebel in Music*, ed. Manfred Grabs (1978). See also Eberhardt Klemm, *Hanns Eisler. Für Sie porträtiert* ('Hanns Eisler. Portrayed for you', 1973).

136
ELGAR, Sir Edward (William) 1857–1934

British composer

At a period when it was assumed that England was 'Das Land ohne Musik' and where only foreigners would compose or play, Elgar was born to an obscure piano tuner's wife a few miles from the cathedral city of Worcester. Recognition was slow in coming to this composer who was almost entirely self-taught. He learnt his craft partly by helping his father at the organ of St George's Roman Catholic Church, by playing violin in the Worcester Festival Choral Society's orchestra, by his careful copying and paraphrasing of the works of the great masters, by his visits to Germany where he listened to Wagner, and by his somewhat strange appointment as Band Instructor to the City of Worcester Pauper Lunatic Asylum. He did not receive the normal instruction of a young musician of the time and was always somewhat self-conscious and even bitter on this account. Nevertheless he not only built up a formidable technique worthy to place alongside the giants in Germany such as his contemporary Richard Strauss*, but, as has now become much clearer, he became a composer with a recognizable style of international standing.

Indeed Elgar changed from a provincial nobody to a world-famous genius round about the turn of the century when he completed his now famous *Variations on an Original Theme* (Op. 36). It is probable that when he wrote the word 'Enigma' on the first page of the score he was thinking of his attendance at St Joseph's, Malvern, on Quinquagesima Sunday, 1899, when he heard the words of St Paul, ending with 'aenigmate', in which we are like 'men looking at puzzling reflections in a mirror. The time will come when we shall see reality whole and face to face.' In this composition Elgar wrote character-sketches of his friends 'pictured within' – perhaps a mirror is implied here. The 'breakthrough' (for the second part of St Paul's lines) came sooner than was expected. The *Variations* were performed with resounding success in June 1899. The conductor was, of course, foreign, an Austrian, Hans Richter (1843–1916). Another man of German blood who helped to put Elgar on the international map was Julius Buths (1851–1920). This time the inadequacies of British choral societies of the time are seen to be painfully obvious. *The Dream of Gerontius* (Op. 38 and based upon a poem by Cardinal Newman) was too 'modern' for the Birmingham Festival performers in 1900 and it was due to Buths that a successful second performance was given in Düsseldorf the following year, which led Strauss later to refer to Elgar as the 'first English progressive musician'.

If Elgar's music was not violently revolutionary it was certainly new and frequently upsetting to many of the conventional members of Edwardian society. Now, however, well into his forties, the composer was accepted both artistically and socially. He continued to live in the world of the Three Choirs Festival (where his music is especially cherished) and from 1904 to 1911 he and his wife and one daughter occupied a house called Plas Gwyn on the outskirts of Hereford, but he was much in demand in London – about which he had written colourfully in *Cockaigne* (Op. 40). Works of this period include the two fine Symphonies (No. 1 in A flat, 1908; No. 2 in E flat, 1911) and the Violin Concerto (Op. 61) which, together with some passages in the two oratorios, *The Apostles* (Op. 49, 1903) and *The Kingdom* (Op. 51, 1906), contain his maturest and most characteristic music.

Elgar was knighted in 1904 and was also given a Festival to himself that year. Gradually his name became associated with the more extrovert side of the buoyant and confident British Empire. The trio tune of the first of a series of five *Pomp and Circumstance* military marches was put into the *Coronation Ode* (Op. 44) in 1902 and later became a song in its own right as *Land of Hope and Glory*.

Despite Elgar's clear love of outward pageantry, there was another dreamy and introspective side to his nature, never far from the surface, giving a tinge of whimsical melancholy even to his happy children's music. The tunes from the two suites, *The Wand of Youth* (Op. 1) date back to his earliest years, but were published in 1907 and 1908. *The Nursery Suite*, a similar work put together as late as 1931, was dedicated to H.R.H. Queen Elizabeth II and Princess Margaret when the sisters were children. The nervous melancholy broke through with the onset of the First World War. The world's values would never be the same and

Elgar knew it. He was wrong to think that future generations would not care for his music but he was right to suppose that post-war composers would write experimental heartless non-national works instead of music which might stir, exalt or ennoble. Works such as the *Introduction and Allegro* for strings (Op. 47, 1905) and *Falstaff* (Op. 68, 1913) have sad interludes in otherwise jaunty and optimistic settings, the one a nostalgic reminiscence of Welsh voices singing over the hills at Llangranog in Dyfed, the other of a young Falstaff, a 'Dream Interlude'. Whereas the former work ends with a flourish, the latter paves the way for the desperately unhappy ending to the Cello Concerto (Op. 85). Although performed before the death of his wife in 1920, it is full of foreboding; the composer wrote nothing more of significance and his style became less adventurous.

Elgar's impact has grown steadily. At one time it was thought that Debussy* was inevitably more important since he broke the conventions in harmonic progression and in form. Elgar was then being judged by the classical romantic standards which would apply to Brahms. Just as *The Dream of Gerontius* represented a break with the recitative and aria tradition of English choral music, so the Symphonies broke with traditional sonata form in many respects, especially with regard to the key scheme in the first. It is now recognized that his use of mosaic-like units in, say, *The Apostles*, is much nearer to the structuring of *La Mer* (1905) than was realized and his reacting against the rules of the textbooks was no less fierce than that of the Frenchman. His musical language was, however, steeped in the Germanic tradition. An English tradition? There was none. The only British composer immediately before him of stature was Arthur Sullivan – who studied, as he did, in Leipzig.

Professor Ian Parrott

Most of Elgar's works are published by Novello or by Boosey. See: P. M. Young, *Elgar O.M.* (1955); Diana M. McVeagh, *Edward Elgar: his Life and Music* (1955); Michael Kennedy, *Portrait of Elgar* (1968); Ian Parrott, *Elgar* (2nd edition 1977).

137
ELIADE, Mircea 1907–

Romanian historian of religions and novelist

Mircea Eliade was born and educated in Bucharest. After taking his MA in 1928 he was awarded a scholarship which enabled him to live in India for four years where he studied Sanskrit and Indian philosophy at the University of Calcutta before spending six months in the *ashram* of Rishikesh in the Himalayas. On his return to Romania he took his PhD with a dissertation on Yoga, and was appointed an assistant Professor in the Faculty of Letters at the University of Bucharest. In the pre-war years he published several books and articles on the history of religions and folklore as well as a number of novels and short stories and, in 1938, founded the review *Zalmoxis* dedicated to religious studies. In 1940 Eliade was made cultural attaché to the Romanian Legation in London, being transferred to Lisbon in 1941 where he remained for the duration of the war. The experience of the period surrounding the war years forms the background to his epic novel *Forêt Interdite* ('The Forbidden Forest', 1955). In that novel, which Eliade considers his best book, he explores the theme of man's quest for an escape from time and the terror of history which is central to his understanding of the nature of religious experience. After the war Eliade went to Paris as a visiting professor at the École des Hautes Études of the Sorbonne, and in the following years lectured at many European universities. To this period in France belong many of the books on which his wider reputation rests, most notably *The Myth of the Eternal Return* (*Le Mythe de l'Éternel Retour*, 1949, trans. 1954). In 1957 Eliade was appointed as a professor of the History of Religions at the University of Chicago in succession to Joachim Wach and in 1962 was made Sewell L. Avery Distinguished Service Professor. In addition to his books on the history of religion and the meaning of religious symbols Eliade has published several works of fiction and a selection from the journal which he kept between 1945 and 1969 (*Fragments d'un journal*, Paris 1973), part of which appeared in English in 1978 under the title *No Souvenirs*.

Eliade's work combines a remarkable grasp of empirical material with an apparent insight into the nature of religious experience which owes much to his years of study in India. At the centre of his approach is a conception of religious symbolism as a fundamental form of creative response to the pressures of human existence in the cosmos, and much of his wider cultural influence has derived from his ability to trace the covert forms in which archetypal myths have survived in the modern world. 'The religious symbol,' he writes, 'translates a human situation into cosmological terms and vice versa, more precisely, it reveals the continuity between the structures of human existence and cosmic structures. This means that man does not feel himself "isolated" in the cosmos, but that he "opens out" to a world which, thanks to the symbol, proves "familiar".' The cultural resonance of this theory must be understood in the context of a concern with the existential meaning of symbols which is characteristic of much twentieth-century thought and which links such otherwise disparate intellectual endeavours as the depth psychology of Freud* and the political science of Eric Voegelin*. As historian of religions the scholar is summoned neither to believe nor disbelieve the claim of a doctrine or the narrative of a myth. Rather he

must 'decipher in a "fact", conditioned as it is by the historical moment and the cultural style of the epoch, the existential situation that made it possible.' It is on this basis that Eliade makes his ambitious claim that the history of religions can play a central part in the creation of a new humanism that transcends the European-centred humanism of the past, for 'by attempting to understand the existential situations expressed by the documents he is studying, the historian of religions will inevitably attain to a deeper knowledge of man'.

Eliade has been criticized by some anthropologists, such as Edmund Leach*, on the grounds that his use of evidence is too uncritical to justify the speculative conclusions which he draws from it and that he uses the apparatus of scholarship to justify a personal mysticism. Others, such as the philosopher Paul Ricoeur, find this interpretative approach to religious experience and symbols a valuable extension to our understanding of man and his cognitive relationship to the surrounding universe. At the heart of such disputes is a division over the nature of the human sciences and the methods appropriate to their advancement, a division in which Eliade is aligned with those who draw on the insights of the phenomenology of Husserl* to justify their quest to identify essential structures of human existence beyond or behind the shifting surface of events. Since there is no sign of an end to this often bitter dispute Eliade's work will remain controversial in academic circles. What can scarcely be questioned is his success in introducing a vast reading public to a fascinating area of investigation, a success which results from a vivid literary style as well as from the intrinsic interest of the data.

David J. Levy

For a full bibliography of Mircea Eliade's writings up to 1968, see *Myths and Symbols, Studies in Honor of Mircea Eliade*, ed. Joseph M. Kitagawa and Charles H. Long (1969). Eliade's major books include: *Patterns in Comparative Religion* (*Traité d'histoire des religions*, 1949, trans. 1958); *Images et symboles* ('Images and Symbols', 1952); *Le Yoga. Immortalité et liberté* ('Yoga. Immortality and Freedom', 1954); *Mythes, Rêves et mystères* ('Myths, Dreams and Mysteries', 1957); *The Sacred and the Profane* (1959); *Aspects du mythe* ('Myth and Reality', 1963); *The Quest* (1969). See also: Guilford Dudley III, *Religion on Trial: Mircea Eliade and his Critics* (1977); John A. Saliba, *'Homo Religiosus' in Mircea Eliade: An Anthropological Evaluation* (1976).

138
ELIOT, Thomas Stearns 1888–1965

US/British poet, critic and playwright

T. S. Eliot was arguably the most important English

poet and critic of the twentieth century (he was baptized into the Church of England and took out British naturalization papers in 1927). His long poem *The Waste Land* (1922) helped to crystallize the sense of spiritual desolation, social chaos and failure of linguistic nerve that became widespread in the West, especially in the aftermath of the First World War, and thus to define some fundamental aspects of literary modernism's pervasive negativity and pessimism. Certain phrases from his essays – 'dissociation of sensibility' (to define the seventeenth-century break he alleged had occurred in 'the English mind'), 'objective correlative' (coined to help explain *Hamlet*'s failure) – quickly passed (to Eliot's embarrassment) into the common stock of critical phraseology. As editor of the *Criterion* (1922–39) he pushed his own poems (*The Waste Land* first appeared in the *Criterion*'s opening number), the European and American authors he admired, his discoveries in the next generation of English poets (notably Auden* and Spender*), and his own critical and political preferences, into the centre of English intellectual life. As a member (from 1925) of the publishing firm of Faber's he helped to build up what quickly became England's central corpus of published poets (Auden, Barker, MacNeice, Pound*, Read, Sassoon, Spender). It was to Eliot as editor and publisher, as much as to his work as poet and critic, that the definition of modernist poetry in English is owed: *The Faber Book of Modern Verse*, edited by Michael Roberts (1936), was only one among several of Eliot's central signposting activities.

In an unguarded moment in the Preface to *For Lancelot Andrewes: Essays on Style and Order* (1928) Eliot defined his 'point of view' as 'classicist in literature, royalist in politics, and anglo-catholic in religion'. An Englishing of a description of the policies of Charles Maurras's right-wing French monarchist movement, *Action Française*, the formula (which Eliot occasionally attempted to blur) was an apt summary of the position put by his poems and essays. It remained true for the rest of his life and work. A writer must have a living relation to the tradition, he argued, in 'Tradition and the Individual Talent' (in his first volume of essays, *The Sacred Wood*, 1920), and before long Eliot had settled on the early seventeenth century (roughly Shakespeare and the Metaphysicals) as the centre of an ideal tradition, a time when English literature was continuing Dante's Christianity with the intellectual sprightliness of an un-Victorian amalgamation of thought and feeling such as he admired in some modern European authors (notably Jules Laforgue). The sermons of Jacobean Bishop Lancelot Andrewes epitomized for Eliot the preferred prelapsarian blend of monarchism (they were preached to King James), Anglicanism (Andrewes was Bishop of Winchester), and classicism (his discourses, formidably learned, quote freely from the ancient tongues). Pre-Civil War, they helped

undergird Eliot's notion that the great English poetic tradition had been destroyed by the onset of parliamentary democracy, the abolition of the peerage and the episcopate, and by the killing of King Charles. So Eliot's work did not only keep expressing anti-democratic and anti-humanist, anti-Romantic and anti-Semitic sentiments, it continually sought to reconnect his readers to the contrasting Andrewes tradition that would be a salvation from the modern plight. It was an educational task that he sought to effect through two parallel activities: by quoting and remodelling bits of the admired literature in his poems (Andrewe's sermons, for instance, are extensively used in 'Gerontion', 'Journey of the Magi' and *Four Quartets*), and by making parallel references to and explanatory comments on those same authors and passages in his essays (he called them 'workshop' criticism), on Elizabethan and Jacobean poets and dramatists and on Dante. And, of course, in their admiring explanations about, e.g. seventeenth-century poetic borrowings, or mysterious poets, or gathering flowers in gardens, the essays managed in passing to keep assigning the highest value to T. S. Eliot the stealing poet, the would-be impersonal writer who recalls 'the hyacinth garden', and so on.

Eliot continually tries like this to have things several ways. He deplores the dissociation of poetic sensibility, the breaking of the tradition, and yet pronounces the likelihood 'that poets in our civilization as it exists at present, must be difficult. . . . The poet must become more and more comprehensive, more allusive, more indirect, in order to force, to dislocate if necessary, language into his meaning.' And in practice his best work is achieved early on, in the disjunctive, perturbed and pre-Christian 'Love Song of J. Alfred Prufrock' in *Prufrock and Other Observations* (1917) and *The Waste Land*, rather than in the smoother, liturgically sponsored approaches towards Christian assurance and reassurance that begin with *Ash Wednesday*. The early poems are never freed from the worryingly apocalyptic cities and urbanized moral despondencies they inhabit, particularly the London of sexually licentious sinners that Eliot has updated out of the pages of eighteenth-century satire, particularly Alexander Pope's (an exuberantly disgusting world the English Augustans themselves inherited from the Romans), and that Eliot only begins to tear himself free of in *Ash Wednesday*. They are preoccupied with a sense of the disjunction of the self. Prufrock is a split man, in the Romantic tradition of The Double, a good Dr Jekyll burdened by his Conradian 'Secret Sharer', a Doppelgänger self, an evil Mr Hyde. The 'Unreal city' passage of *The Waste Land*, which by dint of quotations from Dante amalgamates the City of London with Hell, even drags the reader into the narrator's Double relationship with the dead man Stetson. 'You' (in Baudelaire's words) 'hypocrite lecteur! – mon semblable – mon frère!'

The pervasive spiritual dryness and death, manifestations of the original sin T. E. Hulme instructed his contemporaries in, have resulted in the breaking of civilizations ('London Bridge is falling down'), the collapse of the poetry into the hard, dry imagistic bits ('These fragments. . .') that T. E. Hulme associated with Classicism, a reduction of the people to mere bits of once whole bodies and selves (this is a poetry of cut-off heads, of eyes, claws, 'butt-ends', hands, arms, fingers), a disuniting of experience into unconnectedly separate things (the typist 'lays out food in tins', her clothes are a jumble of 'Stockings, slippers, camisoles and stays'; her 'drying combinations' merely mock her fragmentedness; the narrator 'can connect/Nothing with nothing'). And yet this world of just those rootless sinners and wretched cosmopolitans that Eliot came so strongly to deplore in his social criticisms in *After Strange Gods* (1934) and after, the gang of flat characters thronging the earlier poems (fictions quite aware of their considerable debt to Dostoevsky, Dickens, James and Conrad*), people judged to be so morally and spiritually wanting and granted, like many of Ben Jonson's or Pope's or Dickens's Londoners, not much more than a name – Fresca, Mrs Cammel, Mr Silvero, Hakagawa, Mr Eugenides, Bill, Lou, Mary – manages to be far more agreeably enticing, lives with a far more exciting energy than the tired-out penitent who narrates *Ash Wednesday*, the dutiful proletarian mouthers of churchy or anti-churchy sentiments in *The Rock* (1934), or the clutches of dulled members of the bourgeoisie who inhabit all of Eliot's plays but *Murder in the Cathedral* (1935). The later Eliot – whether composing a grindingly slow drama like those that followed *The Family Reunion* (1939), or giving one of his loftily Parnassian lectures, or just reading his poems on gramophone records – seemed scarcely even to hanker for the fire and energies of his first essays and poems. He had settled early on for tired old age.

There are isolated successes after *The Waste Land*. *Murder in the Cathedral* proved that Eliot could make temptation a dramatically engaging business. Parts of *Four Quartets* are superb, particularly the stories of ghosts (intended as vehicles for the Holy Ghost) – the ghostly children in 'Burnt Norton', the ghostly ancestors in 'East Coker', the ghostly 'double' in 'Little Gidding'. As in the earlier poems, the 'impersonal' poet is best when he is reflecting quite personally on his own sinfulness or childnessness, on his ancestor Sir Thomas Elyot or his spiritual encouragements during the Second World War Blitz on London. But when he turns to word-spinning assurances on the Lancelot Andrewes plan he becomes unconvincing. Eliot's faith is best expressed – as in 'Journey of the Magi' – doubtingly.

In '*Ulysses*, Order, and Myth' (1923) Eliot praised Joyce* for joining in the effort of psychology, ethnology and Frazer's *The Golden Bough*, 'to make possible what was impossible even a few years ago. Instead of narrative method, we may now use the mythical method. It is, I seriously believe, a step toward making the modern world possible for art.' Eliot's early work successfully mythicized 'the modern world', particularly the modern London Eliot had adopted as his home. When he swapped *The Waste Land*'s opportunistic mixture of ethnology, *The Golden Bough*, mythical ideas out of Jessie Weston's *From Ritual to Romance*, bits of Buddhism and Christianity, fragments of this and that reading, for a fully-fledged attempt to bring an exclusive Christian myth alive, he not only (deliberately) stopped making the modern world possible for his art, he proved that his art didn't really make a convincingly possible home for his Christianity.

Valentine Cunningham

Works include: *Complete Poems and Plays* (1969); *The Waste Land: A Facsimile and Transcript*, ed. Valerie Eliot (1971). See: Hugh Kenner, *Invisible Poet* (rev. 1965); Northrop Frye, *T. S. Eliot* (rev. 1968); B. C. Southam, *A Student's Guide to the Selected Poems* (1968); *Selected Prose of T. S. Eliot*, ed. Frank Kermode (1975); Stephen Spender, *T. S. Eliot* (1975); Helen Gardner, *The Composition of Four Quartets* (1978).

139

ELLINGTON, Duke 1899–1974

US jazz composer

Edward Kennedy 'Duke' Ellington, as his nickname implies, brought distinction to jazz. Partly it was social distinction, taking the American Negro's music into Carnegie Hall, Westminster Abbey and the White House, but primarily it was musical distinction: the creation of a substantial body of work that challenged comparison with that of modern European composers without losing touch with its own indigenous origins.

Ellington was a pianist who composed for the jazz orchestra he led. Born in 1899, he had a five-piece band by 1923, which attained a distinctive character with the addition of growl-trumpeter 'Bubber' Miley in 1925. Accompanying floor-shows at the Cotton Club after 1927 developed this 'jungle music' image with *Black and Tan Fantasy* and *The Mooche*, balanced by more lyrical pieces such as *Creole Love Call* and *Mood Indigo*. He began recording in 1924, and when he visited Europe in 1933 it was to find himself famous. His music was already evolving: *Reminiscin' in Tempo* (1935) showed that Ellington had begun to listen to Ravel*, Debussy* and Delius*, with whom he had already been compared. But his compositions lost none of their excitement; by 1940 his superb orchestra had reached another peak with *Ko-Ko*, *Harlem Airshaft*, and many others.

The individuality of Ellington's music lay in his adaptation of the jazz idiom to impressionist moods, and in the originality of his scoring, but he depended heavily on a long line of inventive soloists (Miley, Joe Nanton, Johnny Hodges, Cootie Williams), some of whom stayed with him for decades. In 1939 he recruited the arranger Billy Strayhorn, and a remarkable collaboration ensued until the latter's death in 1967, so that the responsibility for any 'Ellington' piece was never entirely clear.

During the second half of his career his repertoire became more extended. His stature as a Negro composer was increased by the suites *Black, Brown and Beige* and *New World A-Comin'* (both 1943), but his post-war inter-continental travels produced *The Far East Suite* (1964) and *The Latin-American Suite* (1968). There were also the three Sacred Concerts (San Francisco 1965, New York 1968 and London 1973) that were repeated all over Europe. His orchestra never abandoned its jazz character, however, and maintained a gruelling schedule of commercial engagements till within a few months of Ellington's death in 1974.

The range and originality of Ellington's music brought him world-wide acclaim. Paradoxically, his recordings are permanent masterpieces, but their scores are neglected or lost, and in any case could not be played by another group. Despite the ambition of his concert pieces, he was most successful as a miniaturist; the suites have undeniable *longueurs*. As his great soloists aged or fell away, some of the excitement waned, but Ellington himself, disregarding post-Parker* experiments, maintained his tireless creativity and his orchestra's unique timbre. André Previn said that whereas most arranged jazz could be analysed, 'Duke merely lifts his finger, three horns make a sound, and I don't know what it is.' Or as Ellington himself said, more simply, 'The band you run has got to please the audience. The band I run has got to please me.'

Philip Larkin

The Works of Duke Ellington (French RCA) is a variorum edition of Ellington's recordings for Victor; *The Complete Duke Ellington* (French CBS) does the same for his work on other labels such as Columbia and Brunswick. Numerous selections have been issued. *Duke Ellington's Story on Records 1925–1945* by Luciano Massagli and others (5 vols, Milan 1966) is an exhaustive discography for the period indicated; J. G. Jepsen's *Jazz Records 1942–1965: Vol. 3 Co – El* (Denmark 1967) provides further guidance. See also: Stanley Dance, *The World of Duke Ellington* (1971); Duke Ellington, *Music is My Mistress* (1974); and Derek Jewell, *Duke: a Portrait of Duke Ellington* (1977).

140
ELLIS, Henry Havelock 1859–1939

British writer

Born in the year which saw the publication of *The Origin of Species*, Henry Havelock Ellis quickly broke out of conventional medicine to shock Victorian England with his encyclopedic seven-volume work *Studies in the Psychology of Sex*. One of the last representatives of the days when one man could attempt to embrace a universal view, he wrote more than fifty books covering such diverse subjects as medicine, eugenics, love, literature, criminal law and, above all, sex. His influence permeated many areas of social thinking and his works played a considerable part in changing attitudes towards homosexuality, the relations between the sexes and sexual patterns of behaviour.

Ellis's father was a sea captain and he received news of his son's birth on 2 February 1859 while anchored off Singapore from a month-old copy of *The Times*. Ellis's mother, Susannah Ellis, who came from East Anglian stock, sheltered a sensitive nature behind a tough façade but intellectually both parents were mediocre. It was to his grandparents, not his parents, that he owed his more remarkable characteristics. These quickly became evident in his teens. At the age of sixteen he set sail aboard his father's ship for Australia and there, in Sydney, took a job as a schoolteacher. One day, in the outback he suddenly decided that no small part of the trouble in the world was the result of the distortion of the sexual instinct. 'A resolve slowly grew up within me: one part of my life work should be to make clear the problems of sex.' One other decision was also taken in Australia: he would first become a doctor.

His long-drawn-out medical training in England was interrupted by the arrival of a small vivacious person destined to haunt his early love life and reveal his own true nature – Olive Schreiner. Now a handsome, shy, bearded young man, he found himself subject to fits of impotence and his sexual relationship with Olive Schreiner was unsatisfactory. Clearly suffering from acute anxiety neuroses all his life they found substitute relief in frequent stomach trouble. His passivity occasionally reached pathological proportions and his extravagant shyness prevented him from giving a single public lecture.

It is surprising that the power of his relationship with Olive Schreiner did not wreck his medical studies. Instead his interests seemed to widen and soon he was writing articles on anthropological and literary subjects, and suddenly launched into editing a number of Elizabethan dramatists under the title of The Mermaid series.

His first important book, *The New Spirit*, appeared in 1890 and set out to 'promote the increase of natural knowledge and to forward the application of scientific methods of investigation'. Fast on its heels came *The Criminal* (1890) which revealed that his theories of human nature were deeply rooted in the biological origins of human behaviour. It analysed the physiological characteristics of criminals from an anthropological point of view and assessed their intelligence, moral insensibility and emotional stability.

The year 1891 brought a dramatic change in his personal life – on 19 December he married Edith Lees, a short, dynamic person who quickly revealed Lesbian tendencies. Over the next few years she gave him as much pain as happiness. Ellis had by now collected a considerable amount of information about the sexual life of men and women friends, among them a number of homosexuals. Having taken an undistinguished degree in medicine, he concentrated his attention on sexual research and literary studies, producing first *Man and Woman* (1894). This led naturally into the first volume of his life's work, *Sexual Inversion* (1897). Until *Sexual Inversion* appeared, every printed case of homosexuality concerned criminals or madmen, the correctness of Victorian values insisting that anything so horrible must be abnormal if not criminal. Now Ellis revealed its presence in otherwise unblemished people. This first volume of the *Studies* was not only revolutionary to that extent: it brought a quite different attitude to bear on the whole problem. Distinguishing between inborn and acquired homosexuality, Ellis argued that society should 'refrain from crushing . . . beneath a burden of shame' those who were *born* homosexual.

The police quickly took action against *Sexual Inversion* on the grounds that it was obscene, and Ellis narrowly escaped penalties which could have been severe.

Six other volumes of the *Studies* followed over the next thirty years, from *The Evolution of Modesty* (1899) which dealt with the phenomenon of *Sexual Periodicity* and *Auto-Eroticism* (1899) to the *Analysis of the Sexual Impulse* (1903) and *Sex in Relation to Society* (1910). The importance of the earlier volumes (frequently revised and expanded) lay in their value as a comprehensive encyclopedia of physiological fact and sexual behaviour. In the tradition of natural history he had given an elaborate picture of one side of man's nature and had broken open a conspiracy of silence about sexual matters. In the sixth volume he expressed his own philosophy which said that only after the birth of a child had the state any right to interfere with sexual relations between consenting adults.

In the end his credo came to this: socially sanctioned trial marriages were to take place on a widening scale, monogamy was not necessarily to have religious sanctions, marriage was to admit *affaires* and divorce to be by mutual consent.

Such views shocked the embalmed correctness of Victorian society but it is some measure of Ellis's wisdom and influence that today they have become the received opinion of a large section of the population. His enlightened work on homosexuality undoubtedly laid the foundations for the 1967 Sexual Offences Act. However, he never, unlike Freud*, distilled a theoretical model from his work. None the less he stands as the leading English pioneer on the modernization of sex and the renovation of relations between the sexes, but women's liberation has now entered new conceptual fields and finds much of his work dubious.

Vincent Brome

Ellis's other books include: *The Nationalization of Health* (1892); *Affirmations* (1898); *A Study of British Genius* (1904); *The Task of Social Hygiene* (1912); *The Dance of Life* (1923); *From Rousseau to Proust* (1936); *My Life* (1940). See also: Houston Petersen, *Havelock Ellis, Philosopher of Love* (1928); Arthur Calder-Marshall, *Havelock Ellis* (1959); Vincent Brome, *Havelock Ellis, Philosopher of Sex* (1979).

141
EMPSON, Sir William 1906–

English critic and poet

Astonishingly perceptive if occasionally too perversely brilliant, *Seven Types of Ambiguity* (1930) – its author a graduate student of only twenty-four years old – was the first major critical product of that mode of close and unsentimental reading of English poetry first initiated in the young Cambridge English Faculty of the 1920s by I. A. Richards*. Educated as a mathematician, Empson, who was Richards's pupil, was typical of the young poets and critics, many of them scientists, grouped about the Cambridge student magazine *Experiment*, who brought a cool rationalism and the spirit of the laboratory to bear on the reading of poems that anti-scientific romantics and woolly belles-lettristes seemed to have made their own ('And if one is forced to take sides, as a matter of mere personal venom, I must confess I find the crudity and latent fallacy of a psychologist discussing verses that he does not enjoy less disagreeable than the blurred and tasteless refusal to make statements of an aesthete who conceives himself to be only interested in Taste'). *Seven Types* made a sensation and it made critical history. It proved that Richards's road was richly pursuable. Very quickly, especially in the USA under the banner of the New Criticism (the so-called Chicago School), the presence of verbal ambiguities in a literary text became a sure sign of literary quality, and discerning them a *sine qua non* of respectable critical activity. And since, broadly speaking (and adjusted to the demands of more recent structuralist and 'deconstructive' assumptions), these notions still hold good, Empson's role in the generating of modern Anglo-American literary criticism can be said to be as importantly influential as I. A. Richards's own.

Nothing after it could match the splash *Seven Types* made – though *The Structure of Complex Words* (1951) is perhaps just as critically instructive. Nevertheless Empson's recurrent wish innovatively to startle was steadily kept up in *Some Versions of Pastoral* (1935) and also in *Milton's God* (1961), largest of his many published denigrations of Christian literature for what he argues is Christianity's wicked and cruel sadomasochism. In this sturdy rationalism, as in so much else – in the desire to bond literary criticism and scientific method, in the considered slanginess and colloquiality of his prose and poetic styles (on the one hand) and (on the other) the laconically Augustan polish of his poetic forms in the coolly finished manner of Robert Graves*, in his poetry's Donne-like attempt (instructed by T. S. Eliot's* 'classicism') to combine expressions of feeling with a harder-edge ratiocination (drawing particularly on what often prove for 'literary' readers extremely recherché bits of scientific knowledge) – Empson was a child of the 1920s (and 1920s Cambridge in particular) that initiated him into early adulthood. And yet, hero of the 1930s 'Auden* Generation' of poets though the author of *Seven Types* became (he was even blurred in with them as a contributor to the *New Signatures* anthology, 1932), he refused to endorse their enthusiasm for proletarian literature on the Soviet model (hence *Some Versions of Pastoral*), or their relish for apocalyptic strains (see his poem 'Just a Smack at Auden'): he was not nor would he become (Julian Symons's phrase) a 'Pylons-Pitworks-Pansy poet'.

For a poet who wrote so little so early (his slim *Collected Poems*, 1955, consists mainly of his *Poems*, 1935, and *The Gathering Storm*, 1940) his verse too has been remarkably influential. His ear for colloquialisms, his achieved formal finish, his knack of hitting on the precise adjective: it was clearly Empson's verse which helped transmit those disparate merits of Hardy, Graves, and Auden to his great successor as their deft mixer, Philip Larkin*.

Valentine Cunningham

See: Roma Gill (ed.), *William Empson: The Man and his Work* (1974); Philip Gardner, *The God Approached: A Commentary on the Poems of William Empson* (1978).

142

EPSTEIN, Sir Jacob 1880–1959

US/British sculptor

In the eighteenth and nineteenth centuries sculpture took very much a second place to painting as the medium for fine art in Europe. A renaissance of sculpture was brought about single-handedly by the French artist, Auguste Rodin, during the period from his exhibition of *The Age of Bronze* in 1877 to his death in 1917. His first great successor was the Rumanian-born Constantin Brancusi* who from 1907 onwards rapidly modified the tradition of sculpture revived by Rodin (that of Michelangelo) and gave it a new and modern form. This was in turn immediately taken up by Epstein and carried to Britain where it found a fertile soil and led to the emergence in the 1930s of two world-class sculptors, Henry Moore* and Barbara Hepworth* and to the development of a school of sculpture in Britain which has flourished mightily in the postwar period. Epstein was the father of modern British sculpture and, more generally, one of the pioneers of modern sculpture in the whole Western world, both through the force of his style and to some extent through the intense controversy aroused by his work throughout his life which firmly established in the public mind the idea of the artist as sculptor.

Epstein was born in New York, USA, on 10 November 1880 of Polish-Jewish parentage. He attended the Art Students League *c.* 1896. In 1902 the proceeds of a commission to illustrate Hutchins Hapgood's *The Spirit of the Ghetto* enabled him to go to Paris. He studied at the École des Beaux Arts and Académie Julian, then settled in London in 1905 becoming a British citizen in 1907. In the same year he received his first major commission, to carve eighteen over-life-size figures for the sides of the British Medical Association building in the Strand. These figures were later virtually destroyed because, apparently, they became unsafe but the remnants can still be seen *in situ*. Photographs of them in their original state reveal that Epstein was still at this stage under the influence of Rodin but they already have a highly personal expressive power as well as being fully accomplished technically. Their theme is, broadly speaking, the cycle of life with particular stress on procreation, something which remained central to Epstein's art. This theme and the emphatic nudity through which it was expressed resulted in the first of the public rows over Epstein's art and accounts of this and later controversies can be found in Epstein's autobiography *Let there be Sculpture* (1940).

In one respect, however, the Strand statues (as they are known) marked a break with Rodin; they were carved by Epstein himself whereas all Rodin's marbles were carved by professionals from the master's maquettes, a not uncommon procedure at the time. Indeed, the fact that the Strand statues are carvings rather than bronzes is in itself significant. Rodin, like all nineteenth-century sculptors, was essentially a modeller in clay for eventual casting in bronze and attached no importance to carving as a creative process in its own right. The revolution in sculpture brought about by Brancusi and pursued by Epstein was in part the result of their adoption of carving and specifically *direct carving* as a means. Carving *directly*, the sculptor works on the block with his own hands and without a maquette so that the final form of the sculpture evolves through the process of its making. In fact Epstein did make maquettes for the Strand statues but their strength and vitality undoubtedly stem partly from having been carved by their inventor's own hand. In any case, also in 1907 Epstein made a smaller carving which appears to be fully direct, *Rom*, a head of a child based on Romilly John, son of Augustus John*, now in the National Museum of Wales, Cardiff. He followed this in 1910 with a large *Maternité*, a *A Sun God* and *Sunflower*. These works are increasingly simplified in form, particularly the *Sunflower* (private collection, London), and show the influence of archaic (Egyptian) and primitive (African) art which Epstein studied both in Paris and London and, in the case of African art, had also begun to collect. These influences were another vital ingredient in early modern sculpture.

In 1908 Epstein had been commissioned to produce a monument for the tomb of Oscar Wilde in Père Lachaise cemetery in Paris. He eventually carved it in London from a twenty-ton block of Hopton Wood stone in 1911–12 and took it to Paris for installation. The Wilde monument is a highly personal tribute to the poet, showing him in Epstein's own phrase as 'a winged demon angel' carved in high relief into the side of the massive block. This sculpture caused another major row, again because of its nudity, the cemetery authorities refusing to allow it to be unveiled until a cache-sexe was provided. However, the really crucial event of this visit to Paris was Epstein's meeting with Brancusi, then in the full flood of his first maturity. The impact of his work on Epstein was profound, Epstein receiving from a greater artist abundant confirmation of the rightness of the direction he was himself already taking in some of his work. On his return to England he shut himself away in a remote part of Sussex called Pett Level and, for three years, until 1916, produced a group of carvings which constitute his great contribution to the early history of modern sculpture. The most important among them are the three groups of mating doves (second group in the Tate Gallery, London), the two large marble Venuses standing on mating birds (Baltimore and Yale University), the pregnant female *Figure in Flenite* (Epstein's term for the stone called serpentine) in the Tate Gallery and the *Mother and Child* (Museum of Modern Art, New York). During these few years he also produced one major work of a different kind, *The Rock Drill*. This was the result of the influence of the Futurism of Marinetti* and of Epstein's brief association with the British cubo-futurist group, the Vorticists, led by Wyndham Lewis*. This sculpture consisted in its original state of a mechanistic plaster figure of a man mounted on a real mining drill and was undoubtedly one of the great works

of Futurist sculpture. It is also important as an early contribution to that other major technique of modern sculpture besides direct carving – construction (see Picasso*, Gabo*). Epstein soon dismantled it and preserved only the torso which, cast in bronze, is now in the Tate Gallery.

After the hiatus of the First World War Epstein continued to produce, at regular if longish intervals, great monumental carvings on primitive and religious themes and continued to arouse controversy. However, he also began to work increasingly in bronze in a relatively naturalistic style, concentrating particularly on portrait busts of the famous and fashionable.

Simon Wilson

See R. Buckle, *Jacob Epstein Sculptor* (1963).

143
ERNST, Max 1891–1976

German/French artist

Ernst, 'the compleat Surrealist', was both the most versatile of the Surrealist artists and the one whose work was most central to the movement as a whole. He had a foot in both the main artistic tendencies within the movement, the quasi-abstraction of, for example, Miró*, and the illusionism of, for example, Dali*. While the range of his technical inventiveness was exceptional, his most outstanding ability lay in the creation of images possessing an extraordinary psychological, magical and poetic power. Among his wide-ranging interests perhaps the most prominent were those in the theories of psychoanalysis, psychology and the occult.

Much more even than with most artists, Ernst's childhood experiences were crucial for his work: for example, his obsession with birds and forests. He was born into a bourgeois artistic family at Brühl near Cologne, an area where, as he said, 'many of the important crossroads of European culture meet'. After studying philosophy at Bonn University, he took up painting just before the First World War. After the war, 'Dadamax' was the principal figure in Cologne Dada. As well as wood-reliefs, he created collages, often including mechanical imagery in bizarre juxtapositions. From 1922 in Paris, he made paintings strongly influenced by De Chirico*, which constituted the main link between Dada and Surrealism: of these the masterpieces were *Oedipus Rex* (1922) and *Two Children Are Threatened by a Nightingale* (1924), both showing his interest in Freud*. Ernst was in the Far East when Breton's* *Surrealist Manifesto* (1924) was published; on his return, he experimented with a less perspectival, more textural and abstract idiom, reflecting Breton's call for 'psychic automatism' to reveal directly the workings of the unconscious. He invented *frottage* – rubbings, from surfaces like grainy wood, whose patterns provoked visions which he then worked up: a portfolio of drawings made this way were published as the *Histoire Naturelle* (1926). From this developed a series of paintings of *Forests*, recalling German artists like Altdorfer, usually with ambiguous (and alchemistic) sun/moons. Rubbings employing twine led to a series of monstrous *Hordes*, closely related to which is the sinisterly sexual *One Night of Love* (1927). Under Giacometti's* influence, he took up sculpture seriously in the 1930s, as well as producing his most emotionally disturbing book of collages, *Une Semaine de Bonté* (1934). Among his paintings of this time were ones of mysterious cities, remnants of archaic civilizations, in the foreground of which weird vegetation flourished. The technique of *decalcomania* – using Rorschach-like blots – led to paintings with even more fantastic vegetation, suggesting insect-filled jungles or the ocean bed, among the greatest of which was *Europe After the Rain* (1940–2). In 1941 he fled to America, there meeting Dorothea Tanning, whom he married in 1946. In 1953 he returned to Paris, becoming a French citizen in 1958. With certain exceptions, his works since the war were less powerful – certainly less revolutionary – than those produced during the rise and flowering of the Surrealist movement.

Ernst's influence on subsequent art has been subtle and far from direct. He was, for example, much less relevant for the immediate post-war development of Abstract Expressionism than were the quasi-abstract Surrealists, who provided a way forward in terms of a specifically pictorial language. Formal considerations, though important, were always secondary to him. Evident throughout his work is the mind of a philosopher-poet (he did in fact write poetry), a seeker of treasure in strange, forbidden lands. He was perhaps the most important inheritor in the first half of the twentieth century of the spirit of German Romantic art; and if this fact distinguished him, despite his centrality in the Surrealist movement, from its other leading figures, it also accounted in part for his unsurpassed success in one of Surrealism's principal aims – the pursuit of the 'marvellous'.

Gray Watson

Other books by Ernst include: *Les Malheurs des immortels*, with Paul Eluard (1922); *La Femme 100 têtes* (1929); and *Vus à travers un tempérament* (1953). Books about Ernst include: Patrick Waldberg, *Max Ernst* (1958); John Russell, *Max Ernst – Life and Work* (1967); Uwe Schneede, *The Essential Max Ernst* (1973). See also: William S. Rubin, *Dada and Surrealist Art* (1968); and Roger Cardinal and Robert Stuart Short, *Surrealism – Permanent Revolution* (1970).

144

EVANS-PRITCHARD, Sir Edward Evan 1902–73

British social anthropologist

One of the most widely influential social anthropologists of his day, Evans-Pritchard's career invites comparison with the scholar adventurers of the nineteenth century. The son of a high-church Anglican clergyman, he was educated at Westminster and Exeter College, Oxford, where the armchair anthropologist R. A. Marrett ('that genial boaster') was a fellow. At Oxford he developed a concern for history which took concrete form in his own historical writings and in his successful endeavour to create a climate of opinion favourable to the synthesis of history and social anthropology. But, not wanting to become 'just an intellectual', he undertook graduate studies at the London School of Economics (where, with Raymond Firth, he was the first of Malinowski's* students), as a preparation for fieldwork. His immediate supervisor, C. G. Seligman, had initiated systematic research among the peoples of southern Sudan, and it was this that launched Evans-Pritchard on his first ethnographic project – among the Azande of south-western Sudan, bordering on what is now Zaire. His fieldwork was intensive, and of long duration under difficult conditions. For it, he was awarded a PhD in 1927. Then, in 1930, at the request of the Sudan government, he began a series of trips among the Nuer, a pastoral people inhabiting the pastoral region of the central south. In the same period (1926–36) he carried out shorter researches among the Anuak of the Sudan–Ethiopian borderland, and the Luo of western Kenya. In 1935 he returned to Oxford, and was married in 1939; but when war broke out the same year he joined the British army and organized a force of Anuak irregulars to combat the Italians in western Ethiopia. After the Axis defeat in North Africa he served as a liaison officer between the British military adminstration and the Arab Bedouin. Following an arduous camel journey, he converted to Roman Catholicism: 'I could not have faced the dangers I had to face . . . had I not known that I had divine support,' he later explained. When the war was over he was appointed, after a brief spell at Cambridge, to the Chair of Social Anthropology at Oxford, in succession to A. R. Radcliffe-Brown* – a post he occupied until 1970.

Evans-Pritchard's fieldwork led to six major monographs, several collections of essays and texts, and numerous papers; his theoretical impact was revolutionary. In a very broad sense he was a functionalist, holding that human beliefs and social practices 'must be seen as a relation of parts to one another within a coherent system, each part making sense only in relation to other institutional systems, as part of a wider set of relations'. His first monograph, *Witchcraft, Oracles and Magic among the Azande* (1937), demonstrated the inner coherence and self-validating character of an 'exotic' belief system in its relation to the social system as a whole: this book has directly influenced studies of European witchcraft, and philosophical discussions on the social embeddedness of knowledge. His next major work, *The Nuer* (1940), concerned power and politics in a society without government; here he pointed out the interlinked and systemic character of ecology and economy, perceptions of space and time, political relations between local groups, and the factors which made for relative stability in the absence of formal institutions; this argument was continued in *Kinship and Marriage among the Nuer* (1951) where he proceeded to show how kinship, marriage practices, incest prohibitions, and the like, were all a part of the same system as well. *The Sanusi of Cyrenaica* (1949) advanced the analysis of the nature of power and politics by showing the role of an Islamic religious brotherhood in crystallizing the political consciousness of otherwise divided desert pastoralists in the face of foreign intrusion. This book demonstrated Evans-Pritchard's hostility to colonialism in its Italian form and what, at least by this time, was his ambivalent attitude to that of the English.

His last central work, *Nuer Religion* (1956), marks a change of mood. It is a detailed and carefully reasoned sociological account of religious belief, showing, as had been done with regard to politics in *The Nuer*, how belief, or at least its expression, is relative to circumstance and social milieu. But it is a good deal more besides since, in some way, it is his own public testament. The Nuer, though not monotheists by a narrow definition of a term, have a nomad's perception of deity. Evans-Pritchard was deeply involved in an attempt to understand the symbolism through which they expressed their sense of relationship to it; he felt that, when all sociological factors were considered, something else remained behind as an irreducible core. What he thought this to be can only be construed as an immanent consciousness of God; with regard to Christianity he said that 'nothing could have been revealed about anything if men had not already had an idea about that thing.' The conclusion to *Nuer Religion*, after all analysis was complete, is that here 'the theologian takes over from the anthropologist'.

Evans-Pritchard was not inclined to be explicitly theoretical, yet his influence in this area was profound; his works have accumulated praise through the re-analyses and new research which they have inspired. His own view, however, was that sweeping theoretical pronouncements are antithetical to the spirit of the subject and the complexity of its subject-matter. His own work received some of its inspiration from nineteenth-century figures such as the legal historian, Sir Henry Maine, the historian of Semitic religion Robertson Smith, and the classicist Fustel de Cou-

langes. Also evident is the influence of the French social theorist Durkheim* and the imaginative group of collaborators around him; in recognition of this, Evans-Pritchard inspired among his students a series of translations of French anthropological classics. He also devoted some effort to showing that the errors of the past, no matter how outrageous, are the key to the relative truth of the present, if only through their demolition. And in the end he came to reject the idea that social anthropology is, or even can be, a 'social science'; he saw it as a humanity akin to history, and his functionalism became that of the linguist who sees meaning as emergent from systemic interrelationships. He specifically rejected the scientism of his predecessor, Radcliffe-Brown, who retorted that 'scientific methodology is something you are not very strong on'.

Evans-Pritchard's work has found an echo within various branches of social anthropology, and in other areas of study such as social history and philosophy. Through his central position at Oxford University he inspired a generation of British social anthropologists, as well as many who came there from abroad. Like many travellers he was a reticent man, and taught more by example than by precept. Rejecting pleas to write anything substantial of an autobiographical nature, he said: 'I have led a pretty vigorous and variegated life and I do not wish to lie to myself or embarrass my children.'

Dr Michael Kenny

Other works include: *The Political System of the Anuak of the Anglo-Egyptian Sudan* (1940, repr. 1977); *Social Anthropology and Other Essays* (1962); *The Azande: History and Political Institutions* (1971); *Man and Woman among the Azande* (1974). See also: T. O. Beidelman (ed.), *Bibliography of the Writings of Sir Edward Evans-Pritchard* (1974).

145
EYSENCK, Hans Jurgen 1916–

British psychologist

Born in Berlin (father a comedian, mother a silent-movie star), Hans Eysenck wanted to be a physicist but on coming to England shortly after Hitler's* rise to power he found that it was only possible for him to study psychology at the University of London. He obtained his PhD in 1940 and was senior research psychologist at Mill Hill Hospital, London, from 1942 to 1946. He then became the director of the department of psychology at the Maudsley Hospital and in 1955 was appointed the first professor of psychology at the recently instituted Institute of Psychiatry in London. Apart from brief spells as a visiting professor at Berkeley and Philadelphia, Eysenck has spent all his academic life in Britain. He has been editor-in-chief of *Behaviour Research and Therapy* since it was first published in 1963.

A prolific writer (he has written some twenty books and over five hundred articles in international journals) and a controversial theorist and popularizer of psychology, Eysenck devoted his early work to clarifying the nature of the relationship between personality and learning (*The Scientific Study of Personality*, 1952). Drawing on the theories of Pavlov, McDougall and J. B. Watson*, he conceptualized this relationship in terms of excitatory and inhibitory states of the central nervous system. Using a specially designed personality inventory (*Manual of the Eysenck Personality Inventory*, 1964), he described two dimensions of personality – an extraversion–introversion continuum (in which there are echoes of Jung's* personality archetypes) and a neuroticism–normality continuum. Eysenck has since argued that these personality dimensions are largely determined by hereditary factors (*The Biological Basis of Personality*, 1968). Subjects with high extraversion scores are characterized by rapid development of central inhibition – stimulant drugs, for example, have little effect on them but they respond to small doses of depressants with marked changes of behaviour. Introverted subjects, in contrast, show quite the reverse behaviour (*Experiments with Drugs*, 1963). Eysenck regards neurotic reactions as conditioned emotional responses and argues that the two major personality patterns, neuroticism (N) and introversion, are closely related. Persons high on neuroticism, according to this theory, are characterized by strong, long-lasting emotions; these are typical reactions in painful or fear-producing situations. Such individuals are more likely to form long-lasting conditioned emotional responses (phobias, anxiety, obsessional symptoms) under these conditions; they are predisposed to become neurotic in ways that the low N scorer, with his inadequate emotional responses in similar situations, is not. Equally, introverts, who are believed to have a high level of cortical arousal, form conditional emotional responses more quickly and more strongly, and extinguish them less readily than do extraverts; this, according to Eysenck, makes them more likely to form those conditioned emotional responses which in his theory constitute the neurotic disorder.

While the so-called 'dysthymic' disorders (anxiety state, phobias, obsessive-compulsive disorder and reactive depression) are linked to introversion/high neuroticism, another group of disorders (hysteria, psychopathy, personality disorder and criminality) is linked by Eysenckian personality theory to extraversion/high neuroticism (*Crime and Personality*, 1964). For the dysthymic disorders, Eysenck believes that the optimum treatment involves the application of a wide range of behavioural techniques including desensitization, relaxation and modelling. These methods have in common the notion that since neurotic symptoms are conditioned maladaptive responses, treatment should consist of a process of unlearning and relearning, of a deconditioning of the inappropriate response and a reconditioning of an appropriate one. In the case of psychopathy and criminal behaviour, however, the behavioural task is not the extinction of superfluous and maladaptive emotions but the establishment of socially acceptable conditioned responses, which Eysenck argues can be achieved by such techniques as aversion therapy and token economy systems (*The Causes and Cures of Neurosis*, with S. Rachman, 1965).

In a series of popular paperbacks, Eysenck published his learning theory model of psychology and his insistence on the value of intelligence testing (*Uses and Abuses of Psychology*, 1953; *Sense and Nonsense in Psychology*, 1957; *Know your own I.Q.*, 1962; *Fact and Fiction in Psychology*, 1965). He has supported Arthur Jensen's view that intelligence is largely inherited and that racial differences in intelligence test results are mainly due to genetic factors (*Race, Intelligence and Education*, 1971).

Eysenck has also fiercely attacked psychoanalysis, arguing that its elaborate theoretical explanations of neuroses are redundant, that its therapeutic claims are suspect and that its results are no better than what is achieved through the process of spontaneous remission (*Handbook of Abnormal Psychology: an Experimental Approach*, 1960). This controversy has continued right up to the present day (*The Experimental Study of Freudian Theories*, with Glenn Wilson, 1973). Eysenck, however, clearly relishes public disputation and over the years has written widely on the application of his behavioural and genetic views to such topics as smoking, crime, politics, sexual deviation and the effects of the mass media.

Anthony W. Clare

Other works: *Dimensions of Personality* (1947); *The Structure of Human Personality* (1953); *The Psychology of Politics* (1954); *Behaviour Therapy and the Neuroses* (ed., 1960); *Smoking, Health and Personality* (1965); *Psychology is about People* (1972); *Encyclopaedia of Psychology* (3 vols, ed., 1973); *The Measurement of Intelligence* (1973); *Case Studies in Behaviour Therapy* (ed., 1976); *Sex and Personality* (with S. B. G. Eysenck, 1976); *Psychoticism as a Dimension of Personality* (1976); *You and Neurosis* (1977); *Sex, Violence and the Media* (with D. K. B. Nias, 1978).

146

FAULKNER, William 1897–1962

US novelist

William Faulkner was born in New Albany, Mississippi, and grew up in nearby Oxford. His first book – a collection of poems called *The Marble Faun* – was published in 1924. On moving to New Orleans in 1925 he met Sherwood Anderson*, and it was partly as the result of Anderson's influence that he turned to fiction. His first novel, *Soldier's Pay*, appeared in 1926, and was favourably reviewed, but brought little financial reward. After writing a satire, *Mosquitoes* (1927), Faulkner returned to Oxford, and began to shift his attention to his homeland. Its romantic past and present decadence were to provide the material for nearly all his major fiction. The initial result was *Sartoris* (1929), a novel in large measure based on the history of the Faulkner family. It was followed, in the same year, by *The Sound and the Fury*, whose technical inventiveness was greeted with some excitement in literary circles, but which failed to reach a wider public.

The years 1929–36 were enormously productive, and saw the publication of much of Faulkner's most important work – *As I Lay Dying* (1930), *Light in August* (1932), *Absalom, Absalom!* (1936) – together with the less remarkable *Pylon* (1935). It was *Sanctuary*, however, that in 1931 brought Faulkner popular success. A gruesome story of rape, murder and mob violence, it shocked, and aroused indignation. But sales were high, and with notoriety came the opportunity to write scripts for Hollywood. Faulkner was to work for Hollywood, if rather sporadically, for over twenty years, whilst continuing to live in Oxford. He wrote relatively less fiction during this time. *The Unvanquished* came out in 1938 and was followed by *The Wild Palms* (1939), *The Hamlet* (1940), *Go Down, Moses* (1942), *Intruder in the Dust* (1948) and *A Fable* (1954). *The Town* (1957) and *The Mansion* (1959) concluded the Snopes trilogy begun with *The Hamlet*. Faulkner's last novel was *The Reivers* (1962).

During the 1940s, Faulkner's reputation declined, and it was only with the award of the Nobel Prize for Literature in 1950 that interest in his work revived. His stock has remained high since. His importance as innovator has been generally recognized. His experiments with narrative chronology, and his use of 'stream of consciousness' and 'multiple perspective' techniques beg comparison with the work of contemporaries like Virginia Woolf* and James Joyce* – *Ulysses* was an important influence on Faulkner. But from *The Sound and the Fury* to *The Wild Palms* experimental devices serve singular ends, and Faulkner's complex, involuted prose style is likewise peculiar to him. Perhaps his most original achievement is his use of style and technique to unsettle habits of thought and perception. The vision offered by the best novels is often unfamiliar, primeval – a disturbing refutation of the cosily humanized world of civilized man.

Faulkner's significance is partly that of a successful regional novelist. He is conspicuous as the most prominent figure in the 'Southern renascence' during this century. Most of his novels are set in the fictional Southern county of Yoknapatawpha, and, from *Sartoris* onwards, Faulkner's chief concern was with the South. It was a South impotent and backward, defeated in war, but inheriting a set of impossibly romantic ideals. Faulkner's attitudes to it are complicated and ambivalent, those both of critic and apologist. He attacked its intolerance and bigotry, yet his work is often coloured with the very puritanism he satirized. He cherished its legends of heroic endeavour, but he was able soberly to disengage himself from them and to demonstrate their futility. *Absalom, Absalom!*, for instance – itself a myth – is also a careful analysis of the process by which myths are born and nourished. Faulkner censured the parochialism of the post-bellum South, whilst finding in it the basis for a critique of the urban and commercial culture dominant in America. Hostile to views on the racial question espoused by the conservative white South, his own attitudes to the Negro, and to Negro culture, were commonly less reformist than romantic – to the point, some have complained, of evasiveness.

In his Nobel Prize address, Faulkner spoke of 'the old universal truths – love and honor and pity and pride and compassion and sacrifice'. Commentators hopeful of finding consoling faiths in Faulkner's work have affirmed his allegiance to such truths. Others have suspected that it is only endurance that he can recommend with conviction. But the novels cannot be reduced to a simple ethic. Possibly more fundamental to Faulkner is a deep-seated and pessimistic distrust of human unruliness. For Faulkner, it is at best precariously subject to the limits of law and the constraints of civilization.

It was in France that Faulkner's novels first met with a reception that was appreciative and intelligent, and they exerted an acknowledged influence on developments in French fiction after 1930, from André Malraux* to Claude Simon. His impact on American writing came somewhat later, but has been felt in the work of writers as various as Norman Mailer*, Thomas Pynchon* and John Hawkes, as well as post-war Southern fiction (William Styron, Truman Capote*). No writer of importance, however, has followed him in blending modernist experiment with the evocation of a circumscribed but densely imagined provincial world, and a disabused and penetrating quality of insight.

Andrew Gibson

Other works: *A Green Bough* (1933) is a collection of poems; *These Thirteen* (1931), *Doctor Martino and Other Stories* (1934) and *Knight's Gambit* (1949) are collections of stories; *New Orleans Sketches* (1958) is a collection of short pieces first published in the New Orleans *Times-Picayune* in 1925; *Requiem for a Nun* (1951) is a play with narrative interludes. On Faulkner: J. Bassett (ed.), *William Faulkner, The Critical Heritage* (1975); J. L. Blotner, *Faulkner, A Biography* (1974); C. Brooks, *William Faulkner, The Yoknapatawpha Country* (1964) and *Towards Yoknapatawpha and Beyond* (1978); Michael Millgate, *The Achievement of William Faulkner* (1966); Olga Vickery, *The Novels of William Faulkner* (1959).

147
FELLINI, Federico 1920–

Italian film-maker, scriptwriter

The neo-realist style of film-making in Italy, in which society was accurately observed and morally judged, gave way in the 1950s to a more personal, intimate style. It was at this moment of transition that Fellini, after a career as journalist, gag-writer and film scriptwriter (notably for Rossellini* and Pietro Germi), began making his own films. Whether he looked outwards towards society, or inwards towards the psyche, he expressed what he saw with great intensity, imposing an inner world of feeling on the objective world, and progressively concentrating more and more on the landscape and history of his own psyche.

For the neo-realists, meaning came before the image. For Fellini the image came first, and his screen is always filled with spectacle. A recurring image in his films is the parade or procession, in which characters who are the vehicles of his memories and obsessions stream across the screen, often as in a dream. He gained total personal control over the development of his films, a relative freedom from non-artistic constraints which he learnt from Rossellini's example, but which he exploited not for the purpose of accurate chronicling, like Rossellini, but for self-expression, autobiography – some have said narcissism.

There is an early Fellini, in which stand out *I vitelloni* (1953), *La strada* (1954) and *The Nights of Cabiria* (*Le notti di Cabiria*, 1956): the first a wry and affectionate portrayal of young men watching their dreams crumble in a provincial seaside town, the other two portrayals of women (played by his wife Giulietta Masina) who are at once victims of squalor and exploitation, and at the same time, in their innocent and intuitive natures, bearers of some mysterious grace. Already one of Fellini's fundamental themes is central: that of the contrast between innocent spirituality and material corruption.

Two of Fellini's finest films make up a sort of middle period: *La dolce vita* (1959) and *8½* (1962). The first looks at the high life of Rome through the eyes of a journalist who never loses his slightly provincial perspective. The sensual indulgence and moral vacuity depicted, the sheer volume of vivid scenes, packed with fairly accessible symbolism, a rather cynical sentimentality, and those occasional illuminations of innocence and candour, made the film notorious and yet widely admired. *8½* examines a film director about to make a film, but who feels tainted and adrift. The forces and experiences that have gone to make his personality are given symbolic expression (owing much both to Freud* and to Jung*) as the camera surveys his psyche and his past. The final integration, the solution to the impasse, is found in an acceptance of all these forces, visually conveyed with a marvellous parade of characters through a film set. In this black and white film Fellini makes strikingly original use of a very wide range of tonal contrasts.

With *Juliet of the Spirits* (*Giulietta degli spiriti*, 1965), Fellini used colour, and used it in a characteristically vivid, expressionist way. Though his basic themes do not change, the later films are more fragmentary in construction, less narrative, and particularly in the case of *The Clowns* (*I clowns*, made for television, 1970), *Roma* (1971) and *Amarcord* (1974), essentially autobiographical. *Fellini Satyricon* (1969), Fellini's adaptation of Petronius' novel, attempts to view ancient Rome through myth and ritual, whereas *Roma* projects Fellini's personal experiences and curiosities concerning the city on to a further deformed version of the backcloth that had served for *La dolce vita*. The obsession with sex, with the repressive nature of a Catholic childhood, the yearning for a return to a chaste, maternal bosom, a joyful, fascinated disgust with the grotesque, and lyrical exaltations of purity and innocence – a veritable mythology of 'being' – are the themes that run through all Fellini's films. Even *Casanova* (1976), a subject he took on only to find that it disgusted him, became a treatise on the theme of the alienated lay, wrapped in the visual splendour of Fellini's indulgent spectacle.

Analysis of themes does not get to the power and vitality of Fellini's art. In Italy, Catholic critics have praised him as the artist who best expresses man's dissatisfaction with the things of this world. Left-wing critics bluntly call his individualist self-analysis petit-bourgeois, and quite justly dismiss his oratory. *Orchestra Rehearsal* (*Prova d'orchestra*, 1978) attempts political allegory, and in Italy has met with some ridicule. But post-war Italian culture, especially cinema, almost demands ideological commitment from the artist, and this is particularly unfair to Fellini, an artist who lives in a vivid imaginative world of subliminal images, allusions, metaphors, symbols – ambiguous, incoherent, and yet welded together into one of the most potent reflections of turbulent life that the cinema has produced.

Christopher Wagstaff

Other films include: *Lo sceicco bianco* (*The White Sheikh*, 1952); *Il bidone* (1955); *Le tentazioni del dottor Antonio* (*The Temptations of Doctor Antonio*, 1961 – an episode in *Boccaccio '70*). Books on Fellini: Pio Baldelli, *Cinema dell'ambiguità* (1971); Suzanne Budgen, *Fellini* (1966); Franco Pecori, *Fellini* (1974); Peter Bondanella (ed.), *Federico Fellini, Essays in Criticism* (1978).

148
FERMI, Enrico 1901–54

Italian/US physicist

Fermi largely taught himself mathematical physics, while still a schoolboy, by reading the various classical treatises on the subject which were recommended by a judicious friend of his family. He obtained his doctorate from Pisa at the age of twenty-one, and after a couple of years abroad, visiting some of the centres of European mathematical physics, he returned to Florence and then to Rome, to the first chair of theoretical physics in Italy. He remained there until 1938, during which time he built up a prestigious Italian school of theoretical and experimental subatomic physics. Fermi's wife was Jewish and in 1938 he left for the United States to escape from Italy's fascist racial laws. Fermi became one of the fathers of the US atomic bomb project, working first at Columbia, then at Chicago, then at Los Alamos. At Chicago he was responsible for the building of the first chain-reacting pile, and he returned to that university after the war where he attracted a galaxy of brilliant students.

Fermi is the only twentieth-century physicist who has been really outstanding both as a theoretician and as an experimentalist. Largely self-taught, his own advice to students was to cut their teachers' lectures and to spend their university years mastering the subjects on their own in the library. At twenty he introduced the use of Fermi co-ordinates into general relativity. At twenty-four, capitalizing on Wolfgang Pauli's discovery of the exclusion principle, he invented Fermi–Dirac statistics, which did for the electron and particles with half-integral spin what the recently invented Bose–Einstein* statistics were to do for the photon and particles of integral spin. But this way of describing the achievement only came later, following P. A. M. Dirac's contribution; at the time Fermi's statistics seemed more like a rival theory to Einstein's of the non-classical behaviour of gases at high densities and low temperatures. Fermi soon realized the application of his theory to the behaviour of electrons in atoms, in accordance with the new quantum theory, thereby creating the Thomas–Fermi atomic models. By the age of thirty he had mastered and contributed to the newly emerging quantum electrodynamics and, in a brilliant review article, he was perhaps the first to explain to the generality of physicists how it was that the new theory reproduced all the effects for which photons had previously been invoked, without itself requiring any localized particulate nature for its light quanta. Many teachers of today's undergraduate physics courses could benefit from the reading of this paper.

But Fermi's greatest theoretical achievement came a couple of years later, in 1933, when he created a theory of the emission of electrons and neutrinos by nuclei in atomic disintegrations, which showed a deep analogy to the theory of the emission of light quanta by excited atoms. Fermi's theory has stood the test of time with astonishingly little modification and also directly inspired Hideki Yukawa's theory of nuclear forces. These were really the last great fundamental theoretical breakthroughs in physics, until the development of gauge theories of all physical forces in the late 1960s and early 1970s. And even these theories really amount merely to carrying a little further the deep analogy between electromagnetic and other physical forces to which Fermi here first drew attention.

In experimental physics Fermi was the first to use neutron beams to induce artificial radioactivity and to appreciate theoretically and confirm experimentally the counter-common-sensical fact that slowly moving neutrons would be more effective here than faster, more energetic ones. (The explanation is that resonance will enhance the effects when the wavelength of the neutrons is long enough to be comparable with the size of the bombarded nuclei.) In pursuing the associated experimental programme, Fermi and his co-workers produced artificial nuclear disintegration (in uranium and thorium) for the first time, but neither they nor anyone else realized at the time that they had done so. When theoretical understanding did come, Fermi was among the first to appreciate the tremendous consequences, and to suggest the production and separation of the still-undiscovered element plutonium as an alternative to the use of U235-enriched uranium in a possible atomic bomb. He subsequently worked on both projects, but mainly on the latter, and this work, leaning very heavily on his own technique of slowing down neutrons, culminated in the construction of the first chain-reacting pile, at Chicago in December 1942. Fermi later actively participated in the test of the first atomic bomb and was a member of the committee advising on the use of the bomb. But he also showed an early interest in possible peace-time uses of nuclear fission and in particular in the possibility of breeder reactors. His research and teaching career after the war was cut short by his early death.

Jon Dorling

See the *Collected Papers* (1965); and Laura Fermi, *Atoms in the Family* (1954).

149

FIRBANK, (Arthur Annesley) Ronald 1886–1926

English novelist

Only recently has Ronald Firbank's writing moved beyond cult status and been generally acknowledged as far more than delightful nonsense. His audacity had much to do with inventing the modern novel and his influence has been very widespread, though typically oblique, and more practical than theoretical. Writers respect him far more than do academics. His approach was simple. He ignored naturalist tradition altogether and, in so far as he draws anything from tradition at all, went back to the social novels of Jane Austen.

But he is quintessentially modern: streamlined, kinetic, tactile, post-Freudian* in outlook. He wrote by inference rather than statement, using dialogue rather than narrative, in a highly wrought style that is both exotic and intimate. His close-knit, contrapuntal surface, however, is only the iridescent, comic manifestation of a complete, even tragic, universe to be descried below the waterline by the mind's eye. Cyril Connolly* wrote that Firbank's 'air of ephemerality is treacherous in the extreme' and it is indeed this deliberately submerged weight beneath the play of absurdities which makes Firbank a great writer in the way that, say, P. G. Wodehouse* is not.

In his own time Firbank was considered obscure, affected, unimportant. Nearly all his novels were published at his own expense and attracted few reviews. His impious sense of humour and surrealistic disregard for convention, both in word and in life; the vagueness of his education (brief periods at Uppingham and Trinity Hall, Cambridge, and tutors in France and Spain); the private income derived from his grandfather, a nouveau riche railway magnate, enabling him to meander with apparent purposelessness throughout Europe, North Africa and the Caribbean; his ill-health; his recourse to alcohol and marked distaste for solid food; his theatrical homosexuality; and the sheer slimness of his novels; all this has inclined the critical establishment to dismiss his work as the avocation of an effete playboy. In fact no writer ever pledged his resources more resolutely to his art than Firbank. The novels were assembled, mosaic form, from many notebooks, the results refined again and again. Important events – and there is an abundance of them because his imagination was prodigiously inventive, and the books are packed with outlandish incident and character – usually take place 'off stage', often coming to notice only in the course of one of his bizarre yet remarkably plausible conversations. This light and very elliptical technique, in which even an eccentricity of punctuation is made to express an entire frame of mind, in which nothing is random and everything is honed to the detail which expresses the essential, created an *oeuvre* of sustained mercuriality without parallel in English. Never before was the language of fiction so delicately, efficiently suggestive. Mayfair, Cuba, Hapsburg Vienna, Bath and Wells, the Orient and the Mediterranean interpenetrate in a world of dazzling wish-fulfilment myths which can only be described as 'Firbankian'. None of this could have been achieved without extreme concentration, great strength of character in the face of derision or neglect, a clear and observant intellect, and compassion, qualities that his acquaintances (he had no close friends) hardly ever suspected in him.

Firbank's key work began in April 1915 with the appearance of *Vainglory*. It established the basis of his syncopated method of design and had sold 179 copies by the end of the year. This was quickly followed by *Inclinations* (1916), *Caprice* (1917), *Valmouth* (1919), *The Princess Zoubaroff* (a play, 1920), *Santal* (1921), *The Flower Beneath the Foot* (1923), *Prancing Nigger* (1924), and his last completed book, *Concerning the Eccentricities of Cardinal Pirelli*, published posthumously in 1926. It was an extraordinary 'present' to English literature and not only created a form for the modern novel which leads to development (whereas Joyce's* legacy seems to be of a terminal kind) but also founded the modern comic style. Evelyn Waugh*, Ivy Compton-Burnett, Noël Coward*, Graham Greene*, Muriel Spark, Joe Orton*, William Burroughs*, Tom Wolfe*, Richard Brautigan, Hunter Thompson, and the black comedy school of contemporary America, as well as some 'absurd' writers of Europe (especially the young Samuel Beckett*), are only some of its offspring. Firbank's own description of his writing is accurate: 'aggressive, witty and unrelenting'. He died in Rome from a disease of the lungs.

Duncan Fallowell

See: *The Complete Ronald Firbank* (1961); *The New Rhythm & Other Pieces* (1962). About Firbank: Miriam Benkovitz, *A Bibliography of Ronald Firbank* (1963) and *Ronald Firbank: a Biography* (1969); Brigid Brophy, *Prancing Novelist* (1973); *Ronald Firbank: Memoirs and Critiques*, ed. Mervyn Horder (1977).

150

FITZGERALD, Francis Scott Key 1896–1940

US writer

Although his merit as a short-story writer had been shown in *Tales of the Jazz Age* (1922), it was not until the publication of *The Great Gatsby* (1925) that F. Scott Fitzgerald was revealed as a serious novelist. The titles of his earlier best-selling novels, *This Side of Paradise* (1920) and *The Beautiful and Damned* (1922), give some indication of their contents. Their theme is romantic disillusion, and their tone a strange mixture of sophistication and naïveté. With *The Great Gatsby*, however, the style tautened and the angle of vision changed. It became apparent that, warring with the romantic dream, there was a sharp critical intelligence.

Fitzgerald's fourth novel, *Tender is the Night* (1934), his most ambitious and in some ways his best, shows him even more firmly at grips with the problems of the Jazz Age, the inner tragedy of which he understood as well as anyone. By the time it appeared, however, America had moved into the 1930s, and the Depression. Violence and crudeness became the order of the day, and it is possible that Fitzgerald's bewildered attempts to comprehend *Tender is the Night*'s lack of success in this alien atmosphere hastened his early death. Fitzgerald had to be the toast of the town; he found it difficult to work at his art alone and ignored, like Melville in his later years. It is this flaw – if flaw it be – which makes him at once so pathetic and so sympathetic.

He was born in St Paul, Minnesota, the son of Edward and Mary McQuillan Fitzgerald, and was christened Francis Scott Key after the author of 'The Star Spangled Banner', to whom he was distantly related. After two years at the Newman School in New Jersey, he went to Princeton a year before the outbreak of the First World War. There he led a busy social life, becoming a member of the Triangle Club, writing an operetta in his freshman year, contributing to the student magazines, and collaborating with his fellow-student, Edmund Wilson*. In 1917 he joined the army, was commissioned, and became aide-de-camp to General J. A. Ryan at his staff headquarters in the South. The war ended before he was sent overseas, but into this period he managed to cram a great many social activities. He also wrote his first (unpublished) novel,

The Romantic Egoist, and became acquainted with Zelda Sayre, whom he married in 1920.

Beneath the bright surface of Fitzgerald's life, however, there was practical ability and a shrewd grasp of affairs. While working as an advertising copy-writer, from 1919 to 1920, he wrote his first short stories and revised *The Romantic Egoist*. With the publication of this revised version as *This Side of Paradise* he became an immediate success. He settled on Long Island, the scene of *The Great Gatsby*, and continued writing stories, mainly for the *Saturday Evening Post*. During the next four years he published *The Beautiful and Damned* and *Tales of the Jazz Age* and wrote an unsuccessful play, *The Vegetable*. He mixed with the rich, whose lives fascinated him, and tried to live up to their standard. In one year he is reputed to have spent $36,000 which, although no large sum compared with the extravagance of the bootleggers and gamblers, is high enough for a writer who has nothing but his wits to live on. His wits, in fact, were Fitzgerald's fortune. He had the ability both to charm his contemporaries and to sum them up in a single apposite phrase. He could not spell, but he wrote like an angel.

In 1924, he moved with his wife and small daughter to Paris and the Riviera. After a few years, his drinking and social activities became more desperate. The high-spirited charmer of Long Island and New York became a sordid brawler. The ugly scene in *Tender is the Night* when Dick Diver is arrested by the French police has the ring of truth. Out of this period, however, came his best work: *The Great Gatsby, All the Sad Young Men* (1926) and finally, after a long gap, *Tender is the Night*.

After the publication of *Taps at Reveille* (1935), Fitzgerald went to work in Hollywood, where he wrote the unfinished *The Last Tycoon*. For varying periods he managed to stop drinking, but he was an ill man, and although a hypochondriac by nature, had incipient tuberculosis and a heart ailment. Zelda had finally succumbed to the schizophrenia which had been latent but unsuspected when Fitzgerald married her, and, added to this worry, there was his constant fear that his talent was drying up. The last disastrous episode of his life, his visit as a film script writer to Dartmouth College, is recounted by Budd Schulberg in *The Disenchanted*. These last years are also touched on in Sheilah Graham's *Beloved Infidel*, and are documented in Fitzgerald's own words, with a memoir by Edmund Wilson, in *The Crack-Up* (1945). He died on 21 December 1940 in Hollywood.

Unlike Sinclair Lewis*, Fitzgerald never wrote directly of Minnesota in his novels, and only occasionally in his short stories. His life was in the East and it was his, in a sense, misfortune to be romantic about great wealth. His remark in *The Rich Boy*, 'Let me tell you about the very rich. They are different from you and me', is reported to have led Ernest Hemingway* to reply, 'Yes, they have more money.' But Fitzgerald's star-struck infatuation has validity, for all the cynical light that Hemingway's comment casts upon it. His preoccupation with the life and status which great wealth can bring is the American equivalent of the English novelist's preoccupation with rank and manners, and had a special appeal in an age when American society was in a stage of transition.

In his career as a novelist, Fitzgerald mirrored his kind and his period as clearly as Jane Austen mirrored hers, and in his defeat ('There are no second acts in American lives') he summed up a peculiarly American failure: the inability to stay the course. But Fitzgerald was more than a writer of documentaries. He had an extraordinary ear for conversation and for the nuance of social behaviour. It is not 'good characterization' in the old-fashioned sense, but something much more intimate, a power of conveying verisimilitude through – as he says of Dick Diver – 'a trick of the heart'. His phrases are very fine, and have a poetic as well as a descriptive quality. Delicate, sensitive, with his finger on the pulse of the life which flowed around him, Fitzgerald's sensibility was of the Jamesian type. What he lacked, however, was Henry James's range and, finally, the deadly seriousness of the dedicated artist which comes from putting art before life. Whatever disguise he wears, it is almost always himself that Fitzgerald writes about. And for this reason, if for no other, a shadow is cast over the work of a writer who had the potentiality of a great novelist. As in the case of Hemingway, it is only in his short stories that he was able to make form and subject fuse into a perfect whole, and it is perhaps significant that the novel which comes nearest to achieving this is his shortest, *The Great Gatsby*.

Geoffrey Moore

Recommended critical books are: Arthur Mizener, *The Far Side of Paradise* (1951); Alfred Kazin (ed.), *F. Scott Fitzgerald: The Man and His Work* (1951); James E. Miller, *The Fictional Technique of F. Scott Fitzgerald* (1957); A. Turnbull, *Scott Fitzgerald* (1962); and W. Goldhurst, *F. Scott Fitzgerald and his Contemporaries* (1963).

151
FOKINE, Michel Mikhaylovich 1880–1942

Russian dancer and choreographic innovator

Son of a St Petersburg businessman, Fokine entered the Imperial Ballet School in 1889 and made astonishing progress under P. Karsavin, P. A. Gerdt and N. Legat. He graduated in 1898, entered the Imperial Ballet and immediately took leading roles: a precedent in living memory.

Fokine's creative work begain in 1905 with *Acis et*

Galatée for the Annual Pupils' Display (one of them was Nijinsky) in which he told a Greek story in terms other than the classical style. Fokine next created the 'plastic poem' *Le Cygne* (1905) for Anna Pavlova, recently another student; but in 1907 he was permitted to choreograph *Le Pavilion d'Armide* in a new production at the Maryinsky, which succeeded after initial jealous interventions.

In 1909 Fokine created *Chopiniana* and *Cléopâtre* and succeeded Marius Petipa as Maître de Ballet of the Maryinsky. Serge Diaghilev* saw in Fokine the collaborator he needed, and invited him to Paris with the Imperial Ballet's first tour to Western Europe. From then on Fokine became Diaghilev's principal choreographer: both sought to revolutionize their art and did so through Fokine's ballets, thirteen of which confirmed his complete break from tradition. He collaborated with leading artists of the day, notably Léon Bakst and Alexandre Benois, and with the composers Stravinsky*, Ravel*, Richard Strauss*.

During the First World War Fokine worked again in Russia, and in 1918 he and his wife Vera began teaching and reproducing his ballets in Scandinavia. He then worked for the theatre in London and New York with Basil Dean and Max Reinhardt*; he lectured and also taught. From the late 1920s Fokine's desire to teach and to invest his pupils with his concepts came uppermost in his life, but he also supervised, most strictly, new productions of his famous ballets and created a very few new ones. He died in New York in 1942.

Michel Fokine released the classical Russian ballet from its self-imposed restrictions and clichés of nearly two hundred years (such as balletic mime) by allowing the Dance to give complete unity and meaning to every story through movement, music and design, but also through unexaggerated physical gesture. As well as being a superb dancer, his contribution to posterity is as the greatest dance reformer since Noverre, and as the most important choreographer of the twentieth century.

Alan Jefferson

Principal works for St Petersburg: *Les Sylphides* (1908); *Carnaval* (1910). For Diaghilev in Paris unless otherwise stated: *Polovtsian Dances* from 'Prince Igor' (1909); *Schéhérazade* (1910); *L'Oiseau de Feu* (1910); *Spectre de la Rose* (Monte Carlo 1911); *Petrouchka* (1911); *Thamar* (1912); *Daphnis et Chloë* (1912); *Coq d'Or* (1914); *Josephslegende* (1914). About Fokine: R. Buckle, ed., *Fokine* (1961); L. Sokolova, *Dancing for Diaghilev* (1960); C. Beaumont, *Michel Fokine and his Ballets* (1935); and *The Complete Book of Ballets* and *Supplement* (1937 and 1942).

152
FORD, Ford Madox 1873–1939

British writer

A central figure in the international movement that has come to be known as 'modernism', Ford Madox Ford was surrounded by cosmopolitan, scholarly and artistic influences from his earliest years. His father, Franz Xaver Hüffer, author of *The Troubadours: A History of Provençal Life and Literature* and music critic for *The Times*, had taken his doctorate at Göttingen before emigrating to England where he became a naturalized British subject, changing his name to Francis Hueffer. From his father Ford inherited his life-long love of France (he also wrote a book on Provence), his zest for encyclopedic detail and his ability for hard work – he wrote seventy-eight books in the course of his life.

When his father died at the age of forty-three, the fifteen-year-old Ford Herman Hueffer and his mother went to live with his grandfather, Ford Madox Brown, one of the most eminent of Victorian painters, mentor to the Pre-Raphaelite Brotherhood and genial host to all the celebrities of Victorian art and letters. In his studio the young Ford heard first-hand anecdotes of Carlyle, Ruskin, Browning, Gladstone, Tennyson – 'the bitter, enormous, greybeard assembly of the Victorian Great' as he later called them. The later, more rebellious generation included Swinburne, who was often drunk and placed in the bath to sober up, and Oscar Wilde whom Ford found 'heavy and dull'.

Under his grandfather's influence Ford developed an allegiance to art which never left him, a tendency to create instant mythology from brief encounters with the famous and a taste for anarchic politics which led to his later pacifism and attempts at self-sufficiency farming. Although he claimed to be inhibited by the profusion of talent surrounding him, he published his first book when he was seventeen, a children's story, *The Brown Owl*, which, he said, made more money than any other book he wrote.

Apprenticed as he was – but with little other formal education – Ford soon moved to the centre of Edwardian literary life where he collaborated closely with the novelist, Joseph Conrad*, and founded *The English Review*. Here he published the first short stories and poems of D. H. Lawrence* and maintained close contacts with writers as diverse as Ezra Pound*, H. G. Wells*, Arnold Bennett*, Wyndham Lewis* and John Galsworthy*. This period ended abruptly with the First World War in which Ford served as an infantry officer. After the war and some years farming in Sussex, Ford went to Paris where, in 1924, he started *The Transatlantic Review*, a journal as influential as his previous one. He championed a new generation of writers including Gertrude Stein*, Ernest Hemingway*, Jean Rhys and James Joyce*. During these years he also wrote his four-volume novel centred around his war experiences: *Some Do Not* (1924), *No More Parades* (1925), *A Man Could Stand Up* (1926) and *Last Post* (1928). The last years of his life were mainly spent in the United States where in addition to teaching he encouraged the work of Allen Tate, William Carlos Williams*, John Peale Bishop and Eudora Welty. He returned to France and died at Harfleur on the eve of the Second World War.

Ford has always been prized by a minority for *The Good Soldier* (1915) and for his four-volume sequence collected under the title *Parade's End* (1950), and to a lesser extent for his historical trilogy *The Fifth Queen* (1906). He has also been admired as a successful editor, essayist and writer of memoirs. What he has not received full credit for is his role in the development of modernism. Next to Ezra Pound, whose friend he was, he is a pivotal figure in the development of new techniques and awareness of form as well as in the certainty and authority with which he encouraged others to move into the future.

Part of the reason for his neglect is of his own making. Surrounded as he was by cosmopolitan influences, Ford created a hero for *Parade's End* who seems a burlesque of the English upper classes. Christopher Tietjens embodies all Ford's agonies and prejudices about his national and social identity. European by instinct, at war with his father's country, Ford's reaction was to present a Tory squire with an eccentric patriotic seriousness which makes his subject-matter as weird as his presentation is modern. Yet the opening chapter of *No More Parades* is perhaps the finest piece of writing to come out of that war.

Only in *The Good Soldier* (or *The Saddest Story* as Ford wanted to call it) do content and technique coalesce with a perfection that has been equalled by few other modern writers. To call it 'the best French novel in English' is unflattering praise. For all its precise engineering, it probes the irrationality of emotion with great power. If everything in Ford's memoirs is seen through rose-coloured spectacles and everyone is larger than life, the light in this novel is absolutely clear and the characters the opposite of heroic. Adopting the persona of a naive American narrator, Ford avoids the self-indulgence that appears elsewhere in his work. There is a scrupulous attention to detail that makes every sentence specific and evocative. In this novel the meticulous craft of the novelist is inseparable from the vision of the artist.

As the early years of twentieth-century literature are reassessed, Ford's importance becomes clearer. His omnivorous appetite for good writing in all its forms and his generous encouragement to writers, known and unknown, earn him the title of 'a man of letters'. He was influential at the centre of Edwardian London, Paris in the 1920s and America in the 1930s. As a novelist he is, at his best, the equal of Virginia Woolf* and Henry James, whose techniques of interior consciousness, relative point-of-view and simultaneity of action he developed. In particular, his use of Impressionism – small dabs of conversation and action – keeps the reader guessing until, as he wrote, 'in the last few lines you will draw towards you the master-string of that seeming confusion . . . and the whole design of the network will be apparent.'

In many ways eccentric and too muddled to construct a consistent persona ('if he were placed naked and alone in a room without furniture, I would come back in an hour and find total confusion', Ezra Pound said of him), Ford changed his German name after the First World War, refusing, characteristically, to do so while he was 'fighting his aunts and uncles'.

John Daniel

Ford's other books include: *Ford Madox Brown* (1896); *Joseph Conrad: A Personal Remembrance* (1924); *Collected Poems* (1936); *The March of Literature from Confucius' Day to Our Own* (1938). See also: *Letters*, ed. R. M. Ludwig (1965). The major biography is *The Saddest Story* by Arthur Mizener (1972). See also: John A. Meixner, *A Critical Study of Ford Madox Ford's Novels* (1962); Grover Smith, *Ford Madox Ford* (1972); Frank Macshane, *Life and Works of Ford Madox Ford* (1965); Sondra J. Stang, *Ford Madox Ford* (1977).

153
FORD, Henry 1863–1947

US industrialist

Possessed of a minor local reputation in Detroit as a racing driver and dabbler in motor manufacturing, Ford vaulted into national prominence in 1901 as a result of his exploits on the racing circuit. Soon relegating to second place his concern with racing and racing cars he had by 1903 founded the Ford Motor Company and had turned his attention to the production of vehicles for the commercial market. Early on he expressed his intention to produce a car 'so low in price that no man making a good salary will be unable to own one'. Introducing the famous Model 'T' on 1 October 1908, he sold a million cars within the next seven years and 15 million before the end of 1927. The extent to which he had realized, and even exceeded, his dreams was nowhere more eloquently, if poignantly, revealed than in the poverty-induced but motorized migrations of the Depression decade of the 1930s. Despite his displacement as the major automobile manufacturer in the United States the Ford brand name still today has a world-wide recognition rivalled at all closely only by that of Coca-Cola. He, above all, personifies the Automobile Age.

It was not only the car but the manner in which he produced it which invests Ford's career with such significance. His business success did not rest primarily upon design innovations, although the Model 'T' was innovatory in many respects. Indeed, he was in the 1920s and 1930s to lose his domination of the market in part because he was not sufficiently innovatory. His engineering creativity found a different kind of expression: in the mobilization of existing practices, techniques and knowledge to produce a concentrated attack upon the manufacturing process. To all intents and purposes the inventor of the continuous assembly line, a line increasingly automated and running ever faster, Ford made possible the high-volume, low-unit-cost production needed to create and satisfy a mass market. This concept involved also the recognition that in a consumer-oriented society production and marketing were equal partners. Just as he had rationalized the production process so Ford sought to rationalize marketing. He created highly sophisticated dealer networks, promoted massive advertising campaigns, and made well-timed price-cutting an essential element of his strategy. He encouraged public tours of his many factories, especially of the massive Highland Plant in Michigan which was opened in 1911. The public came in large numbers to marvel at the success with which this sorcerer's apprentice appeared to have harnessed the many forces unleashed by recent advances in technology.

Ford's almost heroic stature as one who served rather than exploited the consumer had first emerged during his court struggles over the Selden Patent. The Selden Patent allegedly covered vital elements in the manufacture of internal combustion engines and, if enforced, it appeared to threaten the free and rapid development of an important new area of technology. Many of Ford's rivals had succumbed to the claims of the controllers of the patent and had entered into licensing arrangements; Ford refused to do so and embarked upon a long battle in the courts which, after initial setbacks, he won in 1911. He was hailed as the defender of the small man, the entrepreneur and individualist against the evil machinations and ambitions of big business and monopoly. His marketing strategies reinforced that image and so, at least until the 1930s, did his labour practices. In 1914 he startled the business community, not just within the United States, but around the world, by introducing the five-dollar day in his plants. More than doubling the pay of his workers, and leaving his competitors far behind, Ford thereby squared the circle by completing the system, the chief advocate of which he was to become, of high wages, high productivity and low prices. That system promised an effective alternative to socialism by holding out the prospect of harmonizing the interests of manufacturer, employee and consumer, their mutual antagonism dissolved in the solvent of universal prosperity.

Most highly esteemed by the public and at the peak of his powers between 1914 and 1927, Ford's eminence remained significant through the Second World War and into the late 1940s. But his reputation had become somewhat tarnished as his public persona began to reflect the ambiguities and ambivalences of his more private personality. Sharp financial practices in the 1920s, his virulent opposition to labour unionization in the 1930s, his manifest anti-semitism, and his opposition to the Second World War, combined to lessen but not to destroy his public standing. An enigmatic character, Ford coupled ruthlessness in business with a gentle and loving marriage; anti-semitism with liberal employment practices with respect to black people; a commitment to high wages with hostility towards unions and their practices; a hostility to tradition ('History is more or less bunk') with the founding of a major museum of Americana. Yet, however complex the man, and however apparently inconsistent his behaviour, it is not difficult to isolate Ford's major contributions to the culture of the modern world.

Mass-production and consumer-oriented societies have been made possible by the wide application of the techniques he pioneered. Even today, however, despite the extension of those techniques to other industries, automobile manufacturing lies at the heart of many advanced economies. Social organization in both its physical and cultural aspects has, moreover, been powerfully shaped and coloured by wide ownership and operation of motor vehicles. For many years few doubted the liberating nature of those developments. Although their essential benevolence has recently been brought into question they still represent the aspirations of a major portion of the world's inhabitants. If any one man can be said to have played a vital role in generating those aspirations, and in holding out a realistic promise of their universal attainment, whether for good or ill, then that man was Henry Ford.

Dr Duncan MacLeod

See: Henry Ford and Samuel Crowther, *My Life and Work* (1922); Allan Nevins and Frank Ernest Hill, *Ford* (3 vols, 1948); William Greenleaf, *Monopoly on Wheels: Henry Ford and the Selden Automobile Patent* (1961); David L. Lewis, *The Public Image of Henry Ford. An American Folk Hero and his Company* (1976); Keith T. Sward, *The Legend of Henry Ford* (1948).

154
FORD, John 1895–1973

US film director

A succinct pointer to the significance of John Ford's career is that in 1973 he received the first Life Achievement Award given by the American Film Institute.

This suggests both the longevity of that career (director credit on over 130 films between 1917 and 1965) and its absolute, quintessential Americanness.

The most obvious sign of the latter is the vital link between Ford and the Western, *the* American genre, of which Ford's work virtually constitutes a history. From silent two-reelers, through *Stagecoach* (1939) and *My Darling Clementine* (1946), via the John Wayne cavalry trilogy of *Fort Apache* (1948), *She Wore a Yellow Ribbon* (1949) and *Rio Grande* (1950), to the melancholy, sometimes bitter, tones of *The Searchers* (1956) and *The Man Who Shot Liberty Valance* (1961), within the rockscapes and desert of Monument Valley Ford made nonsense of the false division between genre and 'art'. This achievement alone would guarantee Ford's pantheon status.

But the Westerns can be located within a wider ranging version of American history which encompasses the 'biography' of *Young Mr Lincoln* (1939), the Revolutionary War in *Drums along the Mohawk* (1939), the Okie dustbowl setting of *The Grapes of Wrath* (1940), or the Second World War naval drama of *They Were Expendable* (1945). History here is never simply people rather than events, but the exploration of dynamic oppositions around three basic points: the individual (often the loner, the outsider), the group (family, community, society) and all that lies outside (Indians, the wilderness). Also, Ford's history is rarely jingoistic celebration; more often it is, despite his own disclaimers, a poetic vision of defeat.

Ford's style evolves towards simplicity. This is significant. His critical reputation resulted from rather Europeanized films like *The Informer* (1935) and even *Stagecoach*, which now seem burdened by Dudley Nichols's literary, overly symbolic scripts and a portentous 'Expressionist' visual sense. It now seems extraordinary that, as a result, Ford was valued as an 'artist' who worked within, and transcended, the Hollywood 'system'. Critical recognition of that system's virtues, i.e. the virtues of mainstream, generically based American popular cinema, now enables Ford to be located, without disparagement, alongside other Hollywood 'professionals', such as Howard Hawks* and Raoul Walsh, whose filmographies tread similar paths. Ford's later work is characterized by a classical economy of expression, centring on performance, milieu and narrative. This economy finds its perfect counterpart in the acting styles of Henry Fonda, James Stewart and, above all, John Wayne. Wayne has come to signify what he does largely through his performances for Ford.

Two other factors should be noted. First, Ford's silent era work remains largely uncharted territory. He went to Hollywood in 1913, and worked for several years on shorts and serials with his brother Francis. Between 1917 and 1931 he was a contract director, first with Universal, then Fox, making comedies, melodramas, adventure films and Westerns. Before *The Iron Horse* (1924), the best known of his silent films, he had already directed over thirty-five features. Second, Ford was born into a large Irish émigré family. *The Informer*, *The Plough and the Stars* (1936), *The Quiet Man* (1952) and *The Rising of the Moon* (1957) all share an Irish setting, and Ford himself has been characterized as an Irish-Catholic conservative. Certainly a sense of Irishness vitally inflects the distinctive strain of humour which runs through his work.

Jean-Luc Godard* has written of the dilemma facing the critic who confronts the powerful emotional pull of Ford's work, but is distanced from its investment in a traditional, conservative American ideology. One hates John Wayne for McCarthyism, but loves him when he lifts up Natalie Wood at the end of *The Searchers*, says Godard. Paradoxically this is perhaps why progressive devlopments in film theory are often marked by returns to Ford's work at crucial points. Thus Peter Wollen's structuralist version of auteurism in *Signs and Meaning in the Cinema* (1969) takes Ford as one focal point. *Cahiers du Cinéma*'s 1970 rereading of *Young Mr Lincoln*, their attempt to expose the cracks and contradictions in its apparently seamless ideological stance, constitutes perhaps the single most important example yet of filmic textual analysis. One can virtually trace the history of film criticism through responses to Ford, the championing of different periods of his work by groups of critics at various times. Ford's *oeuvre* is so embedded in, almost synonymous with, the institution of classical American cinema, that any attempt to understand that institution cannot really avoid Ford. Orson Welles* made this point, when asked which American directors most appealed to him: '. . . the old masters. By which I mean John Ford, John Ford, and John Ford.'

Steve Jenkins

See: Peter Bogdanovich, *John Ford* (1970); Andrew Sinclair, *John Ford* (1979).

155
FORSTER, Edward Morgan 1879–1970

English novelist

E. M. Forster is one of those writers who have suffered to some extent from the reputation which admiring readers and friends have forced on them. The Cambridge and Bloomsbury circles in which he moved dearly wanted him to be an intellectual and his public, helped by his last incarnation as the revered honorary fellow of King's College, subscribed to this idea. Yet anyone who opens *Aspects of the Novel* (1927) in expectation of lucid insights based on broad and objective reading is likely to be disappointed. Much of the apparently 'intellectual' content of the novels is no more

than the diluted ethic of that Edwardian homosexual and philhellene milieu in which Forster himself matured.

Edward Morgan Forster was reared, like others of the Bloomsbury group, in a family with strong evangelical traditions and a connection with the Clapham Sect. The spectres of guilt, duty and a general atmosphere of sternness in conflict with levity are thus never wholly absent from his work. He was educated at Tonbridge School and at King's College, Cambridge, where the somewhat romanticized hellenism of Goldsworthy Lowes Dickinson offered a powerful appeal.

The experience of travel in Italy produced two good novels, *Where Angels Fear to Tread* (1905) and *A Room with a View* (1908), both of them expressing what was to become a favourite theme with him, the need for strong and fulfilling human relationships summed up in the slogan 'Only connect'. His attack on narrow-mindedness, intolerance and philistinism was carried still further in *Howard's End* (1910), generally accepted as his finest artistic achievement. Despite its heavily charged plot and diffuseness of interest, it is infinitely more successful than *The Longest Journey* (1908) with its powerfully evangelical overtones and unconvincing analyses of marital experience.

Most absorbing of all Forster's works, and by far the most ambitious, is *A Passage to India* (1924), based on his visits there in 1911 and 1921. The novel is both an extended comparison of English colonial attitudes with those of the Indians themselves, and an account of the complex relationship of Dr Aziz to Fielding and Mrs Moore. The search for mutual understanding colours the entire novel, which closes with gestures ultimately symbolic of failure. Forster's liberal humanist message is not, however, overstated, and his brilliant ear for cliché and for second-hand phraseology tinges the book with a welcome vein of comedy.

The fact that his interests and preoccupations may nowadays seem rather too obviously attached to a particular era, and the likelihood that his homosexuality may have slanted or even distorted his viewpoint, need not blind us to his real merits as a writer. The posthumous publication of *Maurice* (1971) and a clutch of ungathered stories, principally on homosexual themes, did little either to enhance or diminish a reputation based, like that of Jane Austen, on a mere handful of novels. Still more telling, perhaps, is the fact that his literary fame owed practically everything to works written during the first forty years of his life. He is not a profound thinker or an original critic, but as a writer who continually demolishes cant and humbug, asserts the validity of tenderness and sympathy, and shows a sincere devotion to his craft, he holds a secure place in the history of the modern novel.

Jonathan Keates

Other works: stories, *Collected Tales of E. M. Forster*

(1947); essays, *Abinger Harvest* (1936) and *Two Cheers for Democracy* (1951). See also: Lionel Trilling, *E. M. Forster: A Study* (rev. 1965); Wilfred Stone, *The Cave and the Mountain* (1966); P. N. Furbank, *E. M. Forster* (2 vols, 1979); Lionel Trilling, *E. M. Forster* (1967).

156
FOUCAULT, Michel 1926–

French social historian

Born in Poitiers, Foucault studied under Althusser* at the École Normale Supérieure, and held a number of academic posts before becoming a professor at the Collège de France. Since 1961, he has published major studies of the discourses and institutional practices which define madness and the asylum, illness and the teaching hospital, modern punishment and prisons, sexuality and the governmentality of sex. The most recent studies insist that discourses and institutional practices are always implicated in the exercise of power and, thus, Foucault's texts can be read as an attempt at a new kind of analysis of power. If power is about who does what to whom, Foucault provides the first analysis of power which puts the question of 'does what' in a privileged and primary place. Foucault's concept of what power does has changed radically in twenty years and these changes can be summarized by comparing and contrasting Foucault's earliest and most recent study.

Madness and Civilization (*Histoire de la folie*, 1961, trans. 1967) is a history of madness in the eighteenth century. This text conceptualizes power negatively as something which works by establishing lines of division and exclusion. Here power is defined as that which differentiates. The differentiation works in discourse or madness which the classical age defines as 'unreason' or the excluded negative of reason. The differentiation also works practically through the construction and operation of institutions like the eighteenth-century 'houses of confinement' which excluded madmen from society. This negative concept of power is turned upside down in Foucault's most recent work which promotes a new concept of power as that which enjoins an interminable seeing, saying and doing.

Discipline and Punish (*Surveiller et punir*, 1975, trans. 1977) is a history of the introduction of imprisonment as the standard punishment for criminals in the early nineteenth century. It is also more generally a history of 'the modern spirit of punishment' in schools, factories and hospitals as well as in prisons. This text conceptualizes power positively as a matter of strategy and technique. A strategy is a kind of programme materialized in a definite technology of power which is used against the delinquent, ill, ignorant or unproductive. Here power is defined as a set of techniques. First,

there are methods of acquiring and storing knowledge, the examinations and the dossiers necessary to a strategy of surveillance. Second, there are the methods of training whereby everybody inside and outside the army is condemned to endless rifle drills; these are the disciplinary techniques which Foucault finds everywhere in modern society.

If there are important differences between the early and late texts, all Foucault's studies problematize only a small area of governmentality. They ignore the early twentieth-century modernization which defined social and economic policy as distinct and definite spheres of state action in capitalist economies. Contemporary social policy gives people money subject to various conditions, while contemporary economic policy finds macro-economic points of intervention and continuously manipulates Keynesian* aggregates or monetary variables. These developments have displaced institutional confinement which is now a side-show. Foucault's unfinished work *History of Sexuality* (*La Volonté de savoir*, 1976, trans. 1978) does very generally characterize modern governmentality as a kind of 'biopouvoir' concerned with the welfare of population. But this conceptualization would have to be developed before it could deal with contemporary techniques of economic management or social security.

In the area that they do problematize, Foucault's existing studies are marred by a descriptive eclecticism. Foucauldian analysis has always been concerned with the relations established between and among heterogeneous elements in knowledge, in economic and social practices, and in personal existence. *The Archaeology of Knowledge* (*L'Archéologie du savoir*, 1969, trans. 1972) was a theoretical text which tried to systematize the analyses of the earlier substantive studies. It conceptualized the conditions of existence of discourse as so many regular relations between such heterogeneous elements. The subsequent study of modern punishment argues that strategies establish rational calculations amongst heterogeneous elements and it also supposes that disparate techniques hang together in terms of 'coherence of results'. The possibility of regularity and rational calculation, just like the existence of coherent results, is an article of faith.

Further difficulties are created by the schematism which is most apparent in *The Order of Things* (*Les Mots et les Choses*, 1966, trans. 1970), a history of the variation in the representational presuppositions in the human sciences. This study differentiates renaissance, classical and modern 'epistemes', or representational stages, in terms of the variable articulation of signifier and signified. The stages of discourse and institutional practice are differently accented and specified in the substantive studies of madness, clinical medicine and punishment. The unfinished history of sexuality promises an altogether more complex analysis of multiple strategies and polyvalent techniques. But, in one way or another, all the other studies endorse the notion of one early nineteenth-century transition to modernity after which not very much happened. This is a grossly uninformative basis for any analysis concerned with, for example, what is done in modern hospitals or prisons.

Either Foucault's studies are schematic and fail to conceptualize the differences in the way in which power is exercised, or they are eclectic and incorporate those differences in such a way as to undermine the credibility of the analysis. The studies must move between these two poles because of the way in which they are constructed.

Foucauldian analysis relies on corroborating examples extracted from a random collection of sources. This procedure can only be justified on the assumption that there are characteristic mechanisms of the age which are self-evident in all the signifying material on, for example, madness or punishment. In this case Foucauldian analysis is completely circular because its schematic conclusions are present at the beginning of the analysis in the form of quasi-methodological assumptions. Foucault's studies only illustrate and articulate their initial presuppositions with so many striking vignettes – the ship of fools, the torture of Damiens, the regicide and so forth. Because it is preoccupied with corroborating examples, Foucauldian analysis cannot pose or answer serious questions about the non-realization of strategies or the complex articulation of polyvalent techniques.

Karel Williams

Other works: *L'Ordre du discours* (1972); *Moi, Pierre Riviers* (*I, Pierre Riviere*, 1973, trans. 1975); *Language, Counter-Memory and Practice* (1977). See also: J. Donzelot, *La Police des familles* (1977); C. Gordon, 'Other Inquisitions', in *Ideology and Consciousness* (Autumn 1979); K. Williams, *Pauperism to Poverty* (1980).

157
FREUD, Sigmund 1856–1939

Austrian psychoanalyst

Sig(is)mund Freud was born at Freiberg in Moravia (now Pribor in Czechoslovakia), the first child of the third marriage of Jakob Freud, a Jewish wool merchant. In 1859, when Sigmund was aged three, the family moved to Vienna, where they lived in considerable poverty, relieved at times by gifts from the two sons of Jakob's first marriage, who had settled in Manchester and done well.

At school he had a brilliant career, was head of his class for six successive years, and left with a thorough knowledge of Latin, Greek, French, English, Italian and Spanish – in addition to German and Hebrew. According to one of his sisters, the whole life of the Freud family was subordinated to Sigmund's studiousness, which required that his five younger sisters keep quieter than it is natural for young girls to be. In Freud's view he was the 'indisputable favourite' of his mother, who in later life used to refer to him as 'mein goldener Sigi'.

In 1873 Freud entered the University of Vienna as a medical student, qualifying as a doctor in 1881, having in the intervening nine years spent periods as a research worker in the zoology and physiology departments of the university. In the latter he worked under Ernst Brücke, a leading member of Helmholtz's School of Medicine, a scientific movement dedicated to the elimination of all religious and vitalist concepts from the biological sciences. 'No other forces than the common physical and chemical ones are active within the organism' began a solemn oath to which Brücke had pledged himself as a young man. Brücke was undoubtedly one of the main intellectual influences on Freud, whose life-long ambition was to construct a scientific psychology which would explain all mental activity in terms of the attraction and repulsion of quantifiable forces, i.e. which accorded with the laws of physics and chemistry and was strictly determinist, all mental events being explicable as the effects of prior causes.

After qualifying in medicine in 1881, Freud continued his research work for a further fifteen months, publishing, among others, a paper which entitles him to be included among the discoverers of the neurone theory, a concept on which all modern neurology is based. However, in 1882, Brücke advised Freud to abandon his career as a research worker and to practise medicine, his reasons being Freud's bad financial position and the dearth of opportunities for academic advancement in the field of pure research. Freud accepted this advice, largely because he had just fallen in love and wished to marry and have children. So, in 1882, preparatory to entering private practice and marrying, Freud began three years as a resident in the Vienna General Hospital, spending five months in the psychiatric department. In 1885 the university gave him a travelling scholarship which enabled him to spend six months in Paris studying under Jean-Martin Charcot, the famous neurologist who had demonstrated that hysterical symptoms could be both induced and removed by hypnosis. Charcot was the second major intellectual influence on Freud, since from him he acquired his interest in hysteria and psychopathology. Then in 1886, his years of training over, Freud set up his plate as a specialist in nervous diseases and, a few months later, after a long engagement, he married Martha Bernays.

In view of the role played by sex in Freud's psychoanalytical writings, his own sex life and marriage have, understandably, been the object of considerable curiosity. According to Ernest Jones's* *Life*, Martha Bernays was not only the greatest but also the only love of his life, and no evidence has been discovered to support the suggestions that he may have had affairs with his sister-in-law Minna Bernays, who became a member of his household in 1896 and never married, or with Lou Andreas-Salomé, the friend of Nietzsche and Rilke*, who was his pupil from 1911 to 1913. There is however ample evidence that both these women understood and appreciated Freud's ideas better than his wife Martha did and that Freud's sexual drive faded earlier than it does in most men. It is one of the ironies of history that the man who made sex a discussable topic was personally reticent and whose theories supported sexual liberation was self-disciplined to a fault.

In the 1880s most of the patients referred to a specialist in nervous diseases were neurotics with no physical illness of any kind, and all the treatments available, apart from hypnosis, were useless – and hypnosis smacked of quackery and mumbo-jumbo. Freud was, therefore, displaying moral courage when in 1887 he adopted hypnotism as his treatment of choice and a return to scientific respectability when, some time between 1892 and 1896, he replaced hypnosis with 'free association', instructing the patient to say whatever came into his head in the hope that such undirected thought would lead to revival of the repressed traumatic event that had caused the illness. The theory behind this cathartic form of treatment was that neurotic symptoms are physical expressions of a repressed emotion and vanish if the original painful experience is recollected and the accompanying 'strangulated' emotion is belatedly expressed. Examples of this process were given in Freud's and Breuer's *Studies on Hysteria* (*Studien über Hysterie*, 1895), which also included an attempt to explain how a repressed emotion could be converted into a physical symptom. This book is usually regarded as the first psychoanalytical work, since it introduced the concepts of trauma, repression, the unconscious, conversion and abreaction.

Josef Breuer, Freud's collaborator in this book and, incidentally, his patron, took fright however at two of its implications: patients who benefited from the form of treatment described in it became passionately attached to their therapist, and the pathogenic, traumatic experience seemed often to be sexual. Freud none the less continued undeterred by these moral hazards, eventually formulating the concept of transference to explain the former, and his theory of infantile sexuality to explain the latter.

Breuer's withdrawal from the scene when confronted with transference and sexuality is one of the two reasons why psychoanalysis was the sole creation of one person, Freud, and not, as most advances in knowledge are, the collaborative achievement of a group. The other was the peculiar course of events that took place privately inside Freud's mind during the years 1894–1902. In Freud's own writings, and in psychoanalytical literature generally, this is referred to as his self-analysis, but Ellenberger styles it, more correctly, a creative mental illness. During it Freud suffered from heart symptoms, was obsessed by his own dreams, suffered from feelings of total isolation which were only alleviated by his correspondence and occasional meetings with Wilhelm Fliess, a Berlin nose and throat specialist (on whom all authorities agree he had a transference), mourned the death of his father who died in 1896, and wrote his magnum opus, *The Interpretation of Dreams* (*Die Traumdeutung*, 1900). At the end of it he emerged certain that he had discovered three great truths: that dreams are disguised fulfilments of unconscious and (mostly) infantile wishes; that all human beings have an Oedipus Complex, wishing to possess the parent of the opposite sex and to kill the parent of the same sex; and that children have sexual feelings. He was also convinced that he was despised, rejected and misunderstood.

This private source of so many psychoanalytical ideas has, understandably, proved an embarrassment to psychoanalysts, especially as the full extent of the subjective origins of psychoanalysis only became apparent in the 1950s, when a selection of Freud's letters to Fliess was published. Jones, who had access to all the letters, many of which remain unpublished, describes Freud's relationship with Fliess as 'the only really extraordinary experience in Freud's life', as a 'passionate friendship for someone intellectually his inferior' from which Freud extricated himself by 'following a path hitherto untrodden by any human being, by the heroic task of exploring his own unconscious mind'; but for others it has initiated a process of sifting the grains of truth from the chaff of personal contingencies. It would seem, for instance, that although Freud was right about the Oedipus Complex and infantile sexuality, he was misled by his father's recent death and by his all too perfect relationship with his mother, who survived until he was seventy-four, into attaching too much importance to fathers and too little to maternal deprivation. It would seem too that the widely accepted story that Freud encountered opposition and neglect is a myth born of his conviction of being despised and rejected. In fact Freud never had any difficulty in placing his papers in learned journals; the *The Interpretation of Dreams*, which according to the myth passed unnoticed, was politely and often appreciatively reviewed in all the appropriate places.

From 1900 to 1920 Freud devoted his life to expounding, amplifying and propagating the insights and illuminations he had acquired during the 1890s. During these two decades he wrote some eighty papers and nine books of which the most important are perhaps: (1) *The Psychopathology of Everyday Life* (*Zur Psychopathologie des Alltagslebens*, 1904), in which slips of the tongue and other faulty actions were shown to be unconsciously determined; (2) *Three Essays on the Theory of Sexuality* (*Drei Abhandlungen zur Sexualtheorie*, 1905), in which he discussed (a) the sexual perversions and their inverse relation to neuroses, (b) infantile sexuality, arguing that infants have erotic sensations from the beginning of life and that their sexual instinct goes through a series of developmental stages (oral, anal and phallic) during childhood, and (c) the psychosexual effects of puberty; (3) *Totem and Taboo* (*Totem und Tabu*, 1913), a speculative anthropological work, in which he interpreted the universal taboo on incest as a reaction to the Oedipus Complex, and the Oedipus Complex itself as the result of a primal crime – he assumed, following Darwin and Robertson Smith, that primitive man lived in hordes dominated by one powerful male who refused the other younger males access to the females, and went on to propose that the younger males periodically banded together, slew and devoured the father, and instituted totemic feasts to commemorate this primal crime. Freud himself referred to this speculation as a Just So Story and it can be regarded as an instance of his overestimation of the father; it is just as plausible to assume that the earliest human groups consisted of women and their children with loosely attached, visiting males and were matriarchal not patriarchal; (4) *Introductory Lectures on Psychoanalysis* (*Folge der Vorlesungen zur Einführung in die Psychoanalyse*, 1915–17; trans. 1952), in which he expounded psychoanalytical theory in ordinary language for a lay audience. It contains his clearest account of sexual symbolism and the view of psychoanalysis given in it is the one which has passed into popular consciousness.

During these two decades Freud also established the Psychoanalytical Movement. He founded the Vienna Psychoanalytical Society in 1902, the International Psychoanalytical Association in 1910, and the International Psychoanalytical Press in 1919. He also devoted considerable energy to acquiring disciples who would propagate his ideas outside Vienna and to protecting the purity of his theory from those whose thinking led them into heresy, notably Adler* and Jung*, both of whom seceded to form schools of their own. It is no secret that clashes of personality and temperament entered into their dissensions or that Freud had a tendency to quarrel with the very person whom he was grooming to become his heir.

In the early 1920s, however, Freud's thinking took a surprising turn. He proposed two ideas, one of which can be traced back to his earliest writings, the other of which was original and almost certainly misguided. The first was that the mind can be conceptualized as a tripartite psychic apparatus, the three parts being the *id* (or it) which contains unorganized, unconscious instinctual impulses, the *ego* which is 'that part of the id which has been modified by the direct influence of the external world . . . [and] represents what may be

called reason and common sense', and the *super-ego*, which is part of the ego from which self-criticism, self-recrimination and self-hatred arise; and that, further, the ego uses defence mechanisms to master id-impulses unacceptable to the super-ego and develops anxiety as a danger signal whenever it is threatened by one. To some analysts, notably Wilhelm Reich*, this idea seemed a retreat and a betrayal of all Freud had previously stood for, since he seemed to have changed sides: instead of seeking to liberate the instinctual wishes striving for expression, he seemed to be siding with the ego in its attempts to control unruly impulses. This view of psychoanalysis, the seminal statements of which are Freud's *The Ego and the Id* (*Das Ich und das Es*, 1923), his *Inhibitions, Symptoms and Anxiety* (*Hemmung, Symptom und Angst*, 1926) and his daughter Anna Freud's *The Ego and the Mechanisms of Defence* (1937), has, however, become the orthodox version among psychoanalysts themselves (except perhaps in Britain where the object-theories of Winnicott*, Fairbairn and Melanie Klein* are equally influential) and it is tempting to correlate this with the fact that psychoanalysis has ceased to be a subversive movement and become a respectable profession.

The second idea, proposed by Freud in *Beyond the Pleasure Principle* (*Jenseits des Lustprinzips*, 1920), was that human beings possess a death instinct, a built-in self-destructive wish to die, to revert to the inanimate state. As Jones pointed out, the idea is based on a confusion between *telos* and *finis*; the fact that we all do die does not imply that we wish to die or live in order to die; intention cannot always be deduced from consequence. This idea of a death instinct, unlike those of defence mechanism and signal anxiety, has, however, not been absorbed into the mainstream of analytical thought: even those who have used it, such as Melanie Klein, did so in a sense remote from Freud's original theory.

In view of its peculiar irrationality it is tempting to relate Freud's postulation of a death instinct to the disillusioning effect of the First World War, though that was evidence for a destructive, not a self-destructive, instinct, and to intimations of his own mortality. Freud was sixty-four in 1920, all his life he had prophesied his own early demise, and in 1923 he developed cancer of the upper jaw, for which he had numerous operations, as a result of which he was in pain and had to wear a prosthesis impeding speech for the last sixteen years of his life. He continued none the less to see patients and to write until shortly before his death in London on 23 September 1939, his last book, *An Outline of Psycho-Analysis* (1938), being a definitive summing-up of his life's work.

'An important Jew who died in exile. . . . To us he is no more a person/Now but a climate of opinion' wrote W. H. Auden* in 'In Memory of Sigmund Freud' shortly after his death, and many of Freud's ideas –

the unconscious, libido, repression, the Oedipus Complex, even the word Freudian itself – have passed into general currency to mean more or less what he himself meant by them. His influence can be discerned in the greater respect shown by modern parents for the feelings and rights of their children, in the reluctance of parents and teachers to strike patronizing superior attitudes, and in the widespread realization that concern and understanding are more appropriate responses to anti-social behaviour than is moral indignation; a distrust of self-righteousness and an awareness that private suffering may lie at the back of public misdemeanour constitute his major legacy. But in the forty years that have passed since his death it has become apparent that his work was not quite so original as he himself seems to have believed, the ideas he dismissed as heretical were not so foolish or pernicious as he himself thought, and he himself has emerged as a person stranger and less explicable by his own theories than he himself realized.

Dr Charles Rycroft

All Freud's psychoanalytical writings are translated in the *Standard Edition of the Complete Psychological Works of Sigmund Freud* (1953–66), ed. James Strachey. The 'official' biography is Ernest Jones, *Sigmund Freud: Life and Work* (3 vols, 1954, 1955, 1957). See also: Vincent Brome, *Freud and his Early Circle* (1967); Henri F. Ellenberger, *The Discovery of the Unconscious* (1970); Richard Wollheim, *Freud* (1971); Max Schur, *Freud: Living and Dying* (1972); David Stafford-Clark, *What Freud Really Said* (1975); Paul Roazen, *Freud and his Followers* (1976); Ronald W. Clark, *Freud: The Man and the Cause* (1980).

158
FRIEDAN, Betty 1921–

US feminist

Born in Peoria, Illinois, population 100,000, the symbol of the conservative heartland of America, Betty Friedan more than any other struck the spark that started the contemporary women's revolution in the United States. Daughter of a housewife and jeweller, Mirian Horowitz Goldstein and Harry Goldstein, she remembers most from her youth the influence of her mother's thwarted professional ambition and her own refuge in books to compensate for exclusion for being a Jew. It was a grand personal victory when she went back to Peoria in 1978 to lead a torchlight parade of feminists supporting the Equal Rights Amendment, more important probably than the countless audiences of thousands she had by then rallied to countless feminist causes in America and throughout the world.

Friedan's first contribution to the renewal of American feminism was her book *The Feminine Mystique* (1963). At the time of its publication, feminism had been dormant in America for forty years. Yet the book stirred highly charged responses from thousands of women, numbers of women reporting from its first year of publication to this day that it changed their lives. In the book, Friedan identified 'the problem that has no name' among women as that of writing 'occupation: housewife' on the census form. The 'feminine mystique' is that there is but one way to be authentically a woman in the American controlling mythology and that is to be a housewife-mother. Everything that does not conform to this mystique of submission, domesticity and relationship is perceived in myriad subtle ways as deviant in women. Friedan documents this conclusion with abundant evidence from popular literature, psychology, the history of feminism, social science and educational theory. All conspire to keep women subordinate and in the home, she indicates. Her solution to the mystique is self-supporting work for women outside the home.

Friedan had been a working freelance journalist before the publication of *The Feminine Mystique*, but her own personal dominant identity had been as a housewife. She had been married to Carl Friedan whom she divorced in 1969. They had three children, Daniel, Jonathan and Emily. Educated at Smith College, she studied further at the University of California, Berkeley, and at the University of Iowa, but she gave up a professional direction in psychology for marriage and family.

Following the impact of *The Feminine Mystique*, Betty Friedan took a leading role in organizing the first new American feminist group, the National Organization for Women (NOW), and was its first president from 1966. That organization has continued to be the most highly visible and widely respected of the feminist groups in America. Through NOW and other organizations such as the National Women's Political Caucus which she also helped found, Friedan has advocated and worked for an enormous range of issues on behalf of women, issues such as sex-desegregation of wanted advertising in newspapers, sex-desegregation of institutions, the right of women to abortion, fairness for women in divorce, entry of women to educational institutions and professions, equal pay for women, the Equal Rights Amendment. She has constantly been in the vanguard of all phases of women's movement activity in America, and she has grown more radical along with the movement in the 1970s. In 1975, she organized a counter-demonstration at the Mexico City United Nations meeting for International Women's Year, insisting that the United Nations meeting was a co-optation of women rather than one genuinely attending to women's issues.

In 1976, she published a second book, writings collected from a decade of women's movement involvement, *It Changed My Life*. On her fiftieth birthday, she was quoted as saying, 'I celebrate putting it all together, finally, this half century that is me . . . the net I've cast for "herstory" . . . it is a lot of fun making a revolution.'

Gayle Graham Yates

159
FRIEDMAN, Milton 1912–

US economist

Milton Friedman is undoubtedly the most influential economist in the Western world since Keynes*. His influence is partly a reflection of, and partly a cause of, the shift in the priorities of economic policy pursued by the governments of the advanced industrialized countries, and in the methods of such policies.

Keynesian economics – both the theory and the policies derived from it – was born in the Great Depression of the 1930s, and was a major factor in the remarkable levels of employment, output and economic growth which the Western world enjoyed for very nearly three decades after the war. But throughout this period and throughout the world, the general level of prices has been rising too, admittedly at varying rates in different countries, without a break. By the early 1970s the rate of inflation had accelerated to an uncomfortable speed, and many Western politicians, whether in or out of office, sensed that electorates were as worried, even frightened, by rapid inflation as their parents were by widespread unemployment.

Keynesian economics had emphasized that economies dominated by private enterprise had no natural stabilizing forces. Stability at any level of output and employment, let alone at maximum output and full employment, could be achieved only by fiscal policy, i.e. changes in taxation and government spending. This so-called 'fine-tuning of the economy' was alone unlikely to produce price stability as well as high employment. Indeed many economists and politicians feared that these were incompatible. A choice – or to use the jargon a 'trade-off' – existed between high employment and rapid, perhaps accelerating, inflation, and governments must and could make that choice.

Some governments and many economists held that we could enjoy the best of both worlds by arguing that prices rose because prices were raised. Prices were raised because costs rose – but costs were mainly wages, which rose because the cost of living, i.e. consumer prices, rose. The wages–prices–wages spiral could be halted. If unemployment was unacceptable, governments must intervene directly in the wage-setting and price-setting processes.

Governments of both left and right experimented with prices and incomes policies of differing forms, complexity, duration and success. Such policies were found irksome by and were unwelcome to both managers and unionists, the major beneficiaries of high employment who are arguably least harmed by (moderate) inflation.

Thus a divide in political economy opened up between the expansionists who were necessarily interventionists, and the non-interventionists who wanted to minimize the economic role of governments. The intellectual power-house of such *laissez-faire* theorizing has long been the Chicago School of economists. The core of this School's theories of inflation, which centre on both the analytical and statistical work of Friedman, is quite simply that inflation is always and everywhere a monetary phenomenon. To Keynesians (although not Keynes himself) who argued that 'money does not matter', Friedman retorted that 'money matters most' or even (and certainly his disciples argued) that 'only money matters'.

The origins of this view lie in the distant past of economic theorizing, certainly in the eighteenth-century writings of the Scottish philosopher David Hume. He argued that the general price level is simply the rate of exchange of a flow of goods and services against a stock of currency. If any commodity becomes more abundant, it becomes cheaper relatively to all other things. Hence if the stock of money increases, the value of each unit of money in terms of goods and services – its purchasing power – will fall, i.e. the general price level will rise. This view was translated by Irving Fisher (a nineteenth-century American economist) into an instantly memorable formula – M.V = P.T – called the Fisher 'quantity theory of exchange'. It is by definition true that the total value of expenditure (the amount of money, M, times the number of occasions an average unit of currency changes hands, or its velocity of circulation, V) is identically equal to the total value of purchases (the number of transactions, T, times the average price level, P). It was argued that the number of transactions was constant over short periods, and the velocity of circulation is determined by such institutions as payment periods and banking habits. Hence any change in the price level must be caused – or at least accompanied by – a proportionate change in the stock of money. In his massive *A Monetary History of the United States 1867–1960* (with Anna J. Schwartz, 1963) Friedman sought to establish statistically that all the major economic fluctuations in the US over this period were not inherent in the workings of advanced capitalism, but were due to monetary mismanagement.

His conclusion was not, as might be expected, that governments should intervene by discretionary monetary policy more wisely: he doubted that anyone knows enough, soon enough, in order to 'fine-tune' the economy successfully by monetary policy (which is too potent), let alone by fiscal policy (which, apart from its monetary side-effects, is impotent). He further claimed to have established that even monetary changes work only with a long (over two years) and variable time-lag. Money supply changes are therefore positively dangerous in the short run, and a further source of instability. For discretionary policy, he wanted to substitute a 'money-supply rule' whereby the monetary authorities, i.e. the national central bank, would expand the stock of money at the same rate as the growth of productive capacity. The average price level would thus *become* stable, since any general rise or fall in prices would set up contractionary or expansionary forces to return to stability.

As with all schools of thought, there are fanatical believers, worldly-wise practitioners, and sceptical, even cynical, opponents. Friedman has undoubtedly succeeded in restoring monetary management to the centre of economic policy in many Western countries. In particular, his theories appeal strongly to Conservative politicians in the UK, and to right-wing parties elsewhere. This may be partly due to their political overtones and implications, e.g. a major factor in the growth of the money supply is the level of government borrowing. This can most usefully be limited by reducing government spending. Equally, the policy makes direct intervention in prices and incomes unnecessary.

Crude 'monetarism' which argues that 'control of the money supply alone is necessary and sufficient' has not yet been tested in an advanced industrialized economy with large areas of monopoly power in both product and labour markets, enjoying a high level of employment.

Friedman is a prolific author in the fields of economic and political theory, and in popular economic debate, and is a formidable public speaker. He has spent almost all his working life as a professor at Chicago from 1948 to 1976, and as a member of the research staff of the National Bureau of Economic Research since 1948. During the war, he worked in the Tax Research Division of the US Treasury, and the Division of War Research at Columbia University. In 1976 he was awarded the Nobel Prize for Economics.

Roger Opie

Other works include: *Essays in Positive Economics* (1953); *A Theory of the Consumption Function* (1957); *Capitalism and Freedom* (1962); *Price Theory* (1962); *Inflation, Causes and Consequences* (1963); *A Programme for Monetary Stability* (1969); *The Optimum Quantity of Money and Other Essays* (1969); *A Theoretical Framework for Monetary Analysis* (1971); *There's No Such Thing as a Free Lunch* (1975).

160

FRISCH, Max 1911–

Swiss novelist and playwright

The son of an architect, Frisch, having spent a few years as a journalist, finally also qualified as an architect. The municipal baths in Zürich, his native city, are a permanent reminder of his competence in this field, which he only left after having become prominent as a writer.

The publication of some of his early stories and a novel led to an invitation from the 'dramaturg' (literary manager) of the Zürich Schauspielhaus, Kurt Hirschfeld, to try his hand at drama. Frisch's first plays were expressionistic, lyrical attempts to come to terms with the Second World War: *Nun singen sie wieder* ('They are singing again', 1945); *The Great Wall of China* (*Die chinesische Mauer*, 1946); *Als der Krieg zu Ende war* ('When the war was over', 1949). Frisch's preoccupation with the peculiarly Swiss problem of a claustrophobic existence in an excessively well-ordered bourgeois country found expression in his first major play *Count Oederland* (*Graf Oederland*, 1951, third, revised version, 1961) which shows a highly respected official, a public prosecutor, suddenly breaking out of his confined existence to become the leader of a terrorist revolution.

Another of Frisch's principal themes, the problem of human identity, is dealt with in the novel, *I'm not Stiller* (*Stiller*, 1954, trans. 1958) and in the remarkable play *Don Juan or the Love of Geometry* (*Don Juan oder Die Liebe zur Geometrie*, 1953). Far from being the archetypal seducer this Don Juan merely wants to be left alone to devote himself to geometry; but having, for that reason and because he is too honest to promise eternal love, refused to go through with his marriage to Donna Anna, he acquires the reputation of a wicked libertine and is accordingly pursued by randy women. To escape this image, which destroys his opportunity to be left to himself, he stages his famous descent into hell so that he can disappear and start a new life with another identity: but this, in turn, enables the most cunning and persistent of the women who are after him to blackmail him into marriage. So, while alive, he remains trapped by women; and dead, cannot escape the legend he has himself created.

Stiller, the hero of the novel of that title, is a modern man who vainly tries to escape from his former self. In another important novel, *Homo Faber* (1957), Frisch attempted a modern version of the Oedipus story: his hero falls in love with his own daughter.

The play *Biedermann und die Brandstifter* (1958, in the US *The Firebugs*, in Britain *The Fireraisers*) dramatizes the guilt complex of capitalist, bourgeois society, whose bad conscience about the social injustice it causes prevents it from taking effective steps against totalitarian revolution which will destroy all freedom: Biedermann, the archetypal bourgeois, a manufacturer of hair tonic who has cheated an inventor and driven him to suicide, is afflicted with such a bad conscience that he takes some tramps into his home and is too cowardly and embarrassed to stop them from stacking his attic with drums of petrol. And, when they finally compel him to do so, he himself puts the match to the inflammable material which will burn down his house. The play has been seen as an allegory of the capture of Germany by Hitler*, and of President Benes's inaction in face of the take-over of Czechoslovakia by the Communists in 1948. *The Firebugs* became Frisch's most successful play outside the German-speaking world.

Frisch returned to the subject of guilt for the horrors of our time, combined with the problem of human identity, in the play *Andorra* (1961). Andorra, the smallest of mountainous countries, here obviously represents that other small and complacent mountainous country, Switzerland. Would the Swiss, who feel themselves morally superior to the Germans because they had no part in the genocide of the Jews, have acted differently from them had they been taken over by Hitler? The hero of the play, Andri, is a boy whose father conceals his illegitimate birth by pretending that he is a Jewish child whom he has taken home with him after a visit to a country ruled by anti-Semites, to save him from persecution. So Andri grows up believing himself to be a Jew and being treated as such by all the neighbours. When the anti-semitic great power invades Andorra, Andri's father confesses that he is his own child and not a Jew. But now it is too late: Andri has become a Jew, he feels himself a Jew, for we are what others think we are. And so he is killed by the invaders, with none of the Andorrans having the courage to protest.

Frisch's third major novel, *A Wilderness of Mirrors* (*Mein Name sei Gantenbein*, 1964), and his play *Biography, a Game* (1967) return to the problem of human identity, the question whether man can choose his own fate; and his inability to know the truth about himself. Gantenbein, the hero of the novel, pretends that he has gone blind in order to gain certainty, by seeing it with his own eyes, that his wife is deceiving him. Kuermann, the hero of *Biography* is given the chance of playing a game which would allow him to restart his life from any point in the past at which he feels that it might have gone wrong, only to find that he, being the man he is, simply cannot escape his ultimate fate. The play *Triptychon* (*Triptych*, 1978) is an attempt to explore, and come to grips with, the idea of death.

Frisch has also published two volumes of his diaries which show most graphically how the ideas for his major works originated in personal experiences and observations. His novel *Montauk* (1976) is also a daringly frank excursion into near-autobiography: it describes a brief affair between an ageing Swiss author and the young woman assigned by his publishers to look after him during a visit to New York.

Frisch's works are characterized by penetrating intelligence, great originality in the handling of complex ideas and a deep concern with the major problems of our age.

Martin Esslin

Frisch's plays are available in translation in *Three Plays* (1962, containing *The Fireraisers, Count Oederland* and *Andorra*) and *Four Plays* (1969, containing *The Great Wall of China, Don Juan, Phillip Hotz* and *Biography*). See also Michael Butler, *The Novels of Max Frisch* (1976); the best general account of Frisch in German is contained in Hans Baenziger, *Frisch and Duerrenmatt* (1960, revised 1971).

161
FROMM, Erich 1900–80

German/US social psychologist and psychoanalyst

Erich Fromm was born in Frankfurt. He studied psychology and sociology at the Universities of Frankfurt, Munich and Heidelberg. After obtaining his PhD at Heidelberg in 1922 he went on to train as a psychoanalyst at the Berlin Institute of Psychoanalysis. In 1933 he left Germany for the USA where he was at first attached to the Chicago Psychoanalytic Institute, and later moved to New York City. In 1942, dissatisfied with what he felt to be the 'bureaucratic and often fanatical spirit' which he said took over the leadership of the psychoanalytic movement in the USA, Fromm, together with Clara Thompson and Harry Stack Sullivan, founded the William Alanson White Institute of Psychiatry.

Throughout his long professional career, Fromm was an indefatigable writer. His early sociological training continued to influence his work, and he became wellknown as one of the few thinkers who have attempted to link the ideas of Sigmund Freud* with those of Karl Marx. In 1941, the publication of his *Escape from Freedom* (known in Britain as *The Fear of Freedom*) made Fromm's name known to a wide English-speaking public.

Though acknowledging Freud's genius, and remaining within the orbit of psychoanalysis, Fromm's emphasis was upon the social factors which made possible or marred human fulfilment rather than upon man's relation with his instincts. Fromm rejected both capitalism and communism, believing that both made men into robots. A society based upon the acquisition of wealth could never satisfy man's needs; but neither could a society based upon exploitation and control, as he thought was the case with the various forms of totalitarianism. Fromm believed that Marx's original insights as a radical humanist were completely distorted by modern communism into a 'vulgar forgery'.

Indeed, perhaps surprisingly, Fromm found 'a remarkable kinship in the ideas of the Buddha, Eckhart, Marx and Schweitzer'.

Fromm's vision of society was one 'in which man relates to man lovingly, in which he is rooted in bonds of brotherliness and solidarity, rather than in the ties of blood and soil; a society which gives him the possibility of transcending nature by creating rather than by destroying, in which everyone gains a sense of self by experiencing himself as the subject of his powers rather than by conformity, in which a system of orientation and devotion exists without man's needing to distort reality and to worship idols.'

Fromm had a far wider and deeper knowledge of history, sociology and religion than did most of his psychoanalyst colleagues. He also took a critical interest in the writings of Konrad Lorenz* and the other ethologists. *The Anatomy of Human Destructiveness* (1973) is a lengthy and valuable examination of the various personal and social factors which lead to men becoming sadistic and destructive, and includes character studies of Hitler*, Himmler, and Stalin*. *The Forgotten Language* (1952) is an exploration of symbolism in dreams, fairy tales, and myths in which Fromm criticized the dream theories of both Freud and Jung* as being one-sided, and in which he put forward the view that symbolic language is 'the one universal language the human race has ever developed'.

Fromm's importance is twofold. First, he was one of the earliest psychoanalysts to show that psychoanalytic ideas could fruitfully be applied to the study of society as well as to the study of the individual within his family setting. Second, he amply demonstrated in his work that it was possible to be deeply indebted to Freud and to Marx without being a convert or disciple of either. Fromm, throughout his long life, was invariably an advocate of humanity, compassion and love. He never lost his faith that a society could be created in which men could find fulfilment of their human needs; 'a society centred round persons rather than round things'.

Anthony Storr

Other works include: *Man for Himself* (1948); *Psychoanalysis and Religion* (1951); *The Sane Society* (1956); *The Crisis of Psychoanalysis* (1971); *To Have or To Be* (1978).

162
FROST, Robert 1874–1963

US poet

Robert Frost was born in San Francisco. At the age of ten, however, he was taken to New England, the home of his forebears. There, but for three years in Britain (1912–15), he remained all his life, mostly in New Hampshire and Vermont. In 1892 he entered Dartmouth College, but left before graduating to work at various jobs. In 1895 he married, and in 1897 entered Harvard where, for two years, he studied the classics.

Never one for much formal education, Frost left Harvard as he had done Dartmouth, and began on a career of farming, supplemented by teaching. He had a book of poems, *Twilight*, privately printed in 1894 and some more of his poems were published in magazines. Despairing of a favourable reception in America, however, he took his wife and family to England. There, the 'Georgian' poets were his friends, and it is possible that he influenced them, particularly Edward Thomas, as much as they influenced him. His first two books, *A Boy's Will* (1913) and *North of Boston* (1914), were published in England and reprinted in America through the representations of Ezra Pound* to Harriet Monroe, the editor of *Poetry*. Frost returned to America to find his reputation made. From 1916 to 1938 he was 'poet in residence' at Amherst College and, as an honoured public figure as well as an outstanding poet, lectured widely. He died on 29 January 1963.

The best of Frost's work may be found in *North of Boston, Mountain Internal* (1916), and *New Hampshire* (1923). Here are the great dramatic poems 'Home Burial', 'The Death of the Hired Man' and 'The Axe-Helve', as well as brilliantly observed and realized lyrics like 'Mending Wall' and 'Birches', which, as with all Frost's best poems, are profoundly philosophical for all their homely diction. The later books, from *West-Running Brook* (1928) to *Steeple Bush* (1947), reflect what is also found in the blank-verse plays, *A Masque of Reason* (1945) and *A Masque of Merch* (1947): namely, a more abstract interest and a more public manner.

Some critics have felt that Frost professionalized his earthy charm and homely philosophy. Louise Bogan said that he 'began early by imperceptible degrees to slip over from bitter portrayal of rural facts into a romantic nostalgia for a vanished way of life. . . . Frost's final role – that of the inspired purveyor of timeless and granitic wisdom – has proved acceptable to all concerned, including the poet himself.' That there is an element of the conscious cracker-barrel philosopher in his work is undeniable, and that he knew very well what he was about is suggested by the following lines from 'New Hampshire':

I choose to be a plain New Hampshire farmer
With an income in cash of say a thousand
(From say a publisher in New York City).
It's restful to arrive at a decision,
And restful just to think about New Hampshire.
At present I am living in Vermont.

Of his own work he said, 'To me, the thing that art does for life is to clean it, to strip it to form' and, in the Preface to his *Collected Poems* (1930), 'like a piece of ice on a hot stove, a poem must ride on its own melting. A poem may be worked over once it is in being but may not be worried into being.'

In critical retrospect Frost's poetry is undeniably deeper and tougher than it seems. The simple language, the conversational manner, and the near-whimsy of some of the observations tend to obscure the fact that he was no pantheistic romantic. Death and despair loom large. As Randall Jarrell put it in *Poetry and the Age*, 'The limits which existence approaches and falls back from have seldom been stated with such bare composure.' The wry humour which endeared him to a wide audience masks a pessimism which is akin to E. A. Robinson's. Like so many other New Englanders, he saw the skull beneath the skin, and his mind turned easily to metaphysics and symbolism. In this respect he was of the company of Emerson, Thoreau and Emily Dickinson, a true Yankee, gnarled, aphoristic and – for all the seeming directness of his manner – essentially oblique in his comments. Local in reference, he is universal in implication. It may well be, as F. O. Mathiessen said in his Introduction to *The Oxford Book of American Verse*, that 'When the history of American poetry in our time comes to be written its central figures will probably be Frost and Eliot*.'

Professor Geoffrey Moore

Recommended critical books are: Lawrance R. Thompson, *Fire and Ice: The Art and Thought of Robert Frost* (1942); Robert A. Greenberg and James G. Hepburn (eds), *Robert Frost: An Introduction* (1961); James M. Cox (ed.), *Robert Frost: A Collection of Critical Essays* (1962); John R. Doyle, Jr, *The Poetry of Robert Frost: An Analysis* (1962); Elizabeth Isaacs, *An Introduction to Robert Frost* (1962); Reuben Brower, *The Poetry of Robert Frost: Constellation of Intention* (1963); Radcliffe Squires, *The Major Themes of Robert Frost* (1963); John F. Lynen, *The Pastoral Art of Robert Frost* (1964); Lawrance R. Thompson, *Robert Frost* (1964); Philip L. Gerber, *Robert Frost* (1966); and Richard Thornton (ed.), *The Recognition of Robert Frost* (1970).

163
FRY, Roger Elliott 1866–1934

British art critic and artist

On leaving Cambridge Roger Fry rejected the scientific career for which he seemed well suited, and resolved to devote himself to painting. As an artist he seldom achieved the recognition he sought, but his studies of Italian Renaissance art earned him respect; he helped to re-establish the *Burlington Magazine*, was offered the Directorship of the National Gallery, and accepted the post of Curator of Paintings at the Metropolitan Mu-

seum in New York. At this point he was captivated by the work of contemporary French artists, in particular Cézanne. In 1910 he left the Metropolitan Museum and met Clive and Vanessa Bell, with whose assistance he organized a provocative exhibition at the Grafton Gallery in London, entitled 'Manet and the Post-Impressionists'.

This exhibition aroused an unprecedented furore among both critics and fellow-artists. The 'primitive' forms and colours of Gauguin, Cézanne and Van Gogh, who were all strongly represented, evoked animosity against their promoter and apologist. Critical reaction to his second 'Post-Impressionist' exhibition of 1912, which included English and Russian contributors and a notable Cubist element, was scarcely less hostile. Yet Fry's enthusiasm and sincerity, combined with a reputation for connoisseurship established in less controversial fields of art history, gradually induced his audiences to consider afresh the limits and purposes of visual art.

In July 1913 Fry initiated the Omega Workshops at 33 Fitzroy Square in London. Here Duncan Grant, Vanessa Bell, Fry and others produced boldly figured and vividly coloured fabrics, furniture and pottery, drawing inspiration from *Les Fauves* and from Cubism. Each piece carried the Omega motif, while its designer remained anonymous. The Workshops operated through the war years, widely publicized but seldom profitable; they were disbanded in 1919. Fry developed a broad range of interests, from children's painting to lithography and handwriting, but continued to work passionately in the cause of the art he admired, through exhibitions, lectures and publications. He maintained his own endeavour as a painter, thereby sharpening his critical and theoretical writings. 'An Essay in Aesthetics' (1909) is a lucid characterization of art as 'the expression of the imaginative life' and thus as the occupant of a realm apart from reality, which it has no duty to mirror. He remained closely involved in the lives and activities of the Bloomsbury Group; Virginia Woolf*, to whom he had been a close friend in his last years, became his biographer.

Patrick Conner

Fry's *Vision and Design* (1920) includes his 'Essay in Aesthetics' together with subsequent retractions from the position there adopted. Other important essays are to be found in *Transformations* (1926) and the wide-ranging *Last Lectures*, ed. K. Clark (1939). Among his monographs, *Cézanne: a Study of his Development* (1927) is outstanding. Virginia Woolf's *Roger Fry* (1940) illuminates the effects of his Quaker upbringing; *The Letters of Roger Fry* are thoroughly edited by Denys Sutton (2 vols, 1972). See also *Vision and Design: the Life, Work and Influence of Roger Fry 1866–1934*, an Arts Council exhibition catalogue

(Nottingham University 1966); Frances Spalding, *Roger Fry: Life and Art* (1980).

164
FULLER, Richard Buckminster 1895–

US architect, engineer, philosopher and inventor

Buckminster Fuller, a great-nephew of Margaret Fuller, was born into a Nonconformist family in Milton, Massachusetts. Popularly known for his geodesic domes, these and other inventions are only a particular manifestation of his philosophy and approach to design. It is arguably the radical nature of the thinking process leading to his inventions and his global approach to design problems which will prove to be of the greatest value to mankind.

His rejection of conventional thinking started early and led to his being expelled from Harvard in 1914. After a brief but important experience in the US navy he worked for a while on a building system invented by his father-in-law. The death of his first child in 1922 and the loss of financial control of the building company in 1926 led him to rethink fundamentally the direction of his activities and he resolved to treat his whole life as an experiment. As at other points of crisis he turned outwards from personal problems to face global issues. A critical year was 1927 in which he privately published *4D*, attacking the stagnation of the building industry, pleading for a global approach to energy and resource problems and proposing light-weight mass-produced housing (the 'Dymaxion house') for delivery by air. There followed further Dymaxion housing proposals (1929), the building of a prototype Dymaxion car (1933), a mass-produced Dymaxion bathroom unit (1937) and a soft-tool version of the Dymaxion house (1945). Following his geodesic patent (applied for in 1951) and the successful and widely reported building of the Ford Motor Company dome in 1953, there was a world-wide epidemic of dome constructions culminating in the US pavilion for Montreal's Expo 67.

He maintained a chronofile (*Explorations*, ed. M. McLuhan*, 1967) documenting his life's experiment and this preoccupation with his own experience is central to Fuller's thinking (see also *No More Second Hand God*, 1962). In a letter to John McHale in 1955 he described the significance of his childhood experiences of boat-building and fishing technology and his interest in logistics in the navy. These experiences can be seen reflected in his utilization of tension structures (tensegrity patent applied for in 1959), his geodesic structures and his interest in problems of the world availability of resources.

His concern about world energy and resource problems first reached a wider audience with the publication of *Nine Chains to the Moon* (1938). He regarded making the world work as a design problem rather than a political responsibility and in an attempt to involve design students Fuller founded in 1961 the World Design Science Decade 1965–75. There followed a series of publications including an *Inventory of World Resources, Human Trends and Needs* (1963), a *Comprehensive Design Strategy* (1967) and the *Ecological Context* (1967). What Fuller refers to as 'comprehensive anticipatory design science' was to be employed to reform the environment rather than man and this was to be accomplished by employing the principle of 'synergy' to achieve more with less resources. World resources and patterns were to be modelled using a 'World Game' based on the game theory of Von Neumann*. Having observed that 'spaceship Earth' had come without an instruction book, Fuller provided the *Operating Manual for Spaceship Earth* (1969).

Although he has come to enjoy world-wide recognition and honours including the Charles Eliot Norton Professorship of Poetry at Harvard (1962) and the Royal Institute of British Architects' Gold Medal (1968), Fuller's philosophical and political views are still generally misunderstood and frequently misrepresented. Some of his published works are unedited transcripts of talks often lasting four hours and delivered without notes. Other publications are carefully written employing a private code of precise meaning which is more easily understood when printed as verse (see *Untitled Epic Poem on the History of Industrialization*, 1962; *Intuition*, 1970). Recurrent themes and preoccupations of Fuller are set out as forty strategic questions and fourteen dominant concepts in *Comprehensive Thinking, World Design Science Decade, document 3* (1965; more accessibly *Utopia or Oblivion*, 1969). Whilst his inventions are well documented by others (Robert W. Marks, *The Dymaxion World of Buckminster Fuller*, 1960; John McHale, *R. Buckminster Fuller*, 1962) his philosophical ideas have not yet received the quality of critical comment and elucidation that they deserve.

John Frazer

Other works include: *Education Automation* (1962); *Ideas and Integrities* (1963); and *Synergetics* (1975). See also *The Buckminster Fuller Reader*, ed. James Mellor (1970).

165
FULLER, Roy Broadbent 1912–

English poet

Roy Fuller was born in Oldham, left school at sixteen to train as a solicitor, and earned his living for many years as solicitor to the Woolwich Equitable Building Society. His background was thus markedly different from the public-school-and-Oxford environment that shaped the most prominent poets of the 1930s. Yet Fuller's first collection *Poems* (1939), showed how enthusiastically he adopted the didactic style and morally righteous attitude practised by Auden*, of whom he wrote in *Professors and Gods* (1973): 'From Auden, as from a schoolboy hero, one took a tone of voice, catch phrases, beliefs – the very cut of one's poetic personality.'

During the Second World War, Fuller served in the Fleet Air Arm of the Royal Navy and the experience of collective responsibility made him suspicious of the customary poetic posture of infallibility. In the title poem of *The Middle of a War* (1942) he sounded the self-critical note that was to become so characteristic of his later poetry:

My photograph already looks historic.
The promising youthful face, the matelot's collar,
Say 'This one is remembered for a lyric,
His place and period – nothing could be duller.'

Fuller has never actually been a dull poet but he has displayed extreme caution, favouring the traditional forms of poetry and relying on detailed observations rather than vague speculation. In his post-war collection *Epitaphs and Occasions* (1949) Fuller added irony and satire to his repertoire but his most persistent concern was with the kind of personal honesty he expressed in his poem 'To My Son' (the poet John Fuller who was born in 1937) where he delicately rejected authoritarian assumptions.

Chronologically Fuller was a late arrival in the 1930s; stylistically he was the quiet outsider in the 1940s when British poetry succumbed, under the influence of Dylan Thomas*, to a neo-Romantic revival. It was in the 1950s, when the Movement poets had re-established decorum in poetry, that Fuller came into his own again as a substantial poet with a sardonic outlook. *Brutus's Orchard* (1957) was a self-portrait in some depth and Fuller took a grim delight in minimizing his own achievements. He confronted the flattering image of himself in the double-sonnet 'Sitting for a Portrait' with the mocking couplet:

So this is what I am. Or rather what
I hoped I was – and wished that I was not.

'At a Warwickshire Mansion', a fine poem on the transitory nature of art, concluded with the defeat of artistic aspiration by social reality. Throughout the book there was an air of defeatism that was nevertheless articulated with triumphant craftsmanship. Poetry, Fuller sadly implied, was a pleasant but peripheral phenomenon most people could do without.

Fuller has never been a demonstrative figure in modern English poetry, preferring to play a secondary and self-conscious role as the talented part-timer. Later collections like *Buff* (1965) and *From the Joke Shop* (1975) reinforced his pessimistic vision of a world where the artist is apparently irrelevant. In the second of these collections Fuller broods on his retirement, contemplates his inadequacies, scrutinizes the ageing process, is saddened by the death of his master Auden, and makes a virtue of necessity with conversational asides like 'it's booze/And cigarettes make bearable our lives' ('Reading at Night about Marcus Aurelius'). For a man seemingly obsessed by his own failures he has been a remarkably successful and prolific writer, producing not only poems but novels including *Fantasy and Fugue* (1954) and *The Ruined Boys* (1959), and, as Oxford Professor of Poetry, the shrewd criticism of *Owls and Artificers* (1971).

Alan Bold

Roy Fuller's selection of his first six volumes comprises his *Collected Poems 1936–1961* (1962).

G

GABO, Naum 1890–1977

Russian/US artist, sculptor

Born Naum Neemia Pevzner in Bryansk, Russia, Gabo became a central figure of international Constructivism in the 1920s contributing significantly to the development of creative thought and work in Russia, Germany, England and the United States of America. Gabo's early training was scientific. He enrolled at the University of Munich in 1910 as a medical student and subsequently studied natural sciences and engineering in Munich. During 1911–12 Gabo also attended Wölfflin's lectures in the history of art and became increasingly interested in creative work. His first constructions, figurative works with a Cubist flavour to them, followed in 1915. Subsequently his art, progressing as a process of meticulous investigation, led to constructions that displayed all the precision of an engineer in the distribution of modern materials (metals, glass, plastics), yet the function of the structures devised by Gabo was aesthetic and not mechanical usefulness, reflecting, embodying and exemplifying instead the concepts of space and perception outlined in Gabo's essays and in his book *Of Divers Arts* (1962) in particular.

Creative work, for Gabo, was not a stylistic consideration, rather it was the exploration of modern materials, of spatial concepts and relationships, and ultimately an investigation of the nature of creativity. In many ways these attitudes brought Gabo into line with Russian Constructivists of the early post-Revolutionary years. When, in 1920, Gabo together with his brother Anton (Antoine) Pevsner, exhibited constructions on the Moscow Tverskoy Boulevard and published their *Realistic Manifesto*, their closeness to Tatlin*, the Stenberg brothers and other sculptors was apparent yet limited. Gabo did not share other constructivists' belief in the necessary subjugation of individual creativity to political ends (the position expounded by Rodchenko), nor indeed the evolution of construction from purely material and no longer aesthetic criteria. Gabo believed in intuitive investigation that led to the manipulation of modern materials according to predetermined aims. He studied form in terms of structure and studied the structure of perception itself. As a result certain themes have recurred in his constructions, which more than once he compared to flowers, trees and to other organic structures. For example, his works often evolve outwards from a central axis or core that is mathematically precise and determined by the intersection of flat or curving planes. Materials provide a means of articulating empty space although every allowance is made for their inherent qualities. In so far as constructions emerge from a central core, their outer edge may be established at differing points so that relationships rather than ultimate positions or masses are what is defined. Similarly their engineering precision reveals Gabo as a supreme craftsman, yet a sign of this is the degree to which his constructions escape the confines of personal style and may be reproduced, some of them on different scales or in different materials, without damage to the spatial concept embodied in the original.

In 1922 Gabo left Russia for Berlin where a number of his works were exhibited at the First All-Russian Exhibition at the Van Diemen Gallery. He continued to live in Berlin until 1932 when he moved to Paris. His constructions included stage works, notably for *La Chatte* which Gabo designed with Pevsner for Diaghilev's* Ballets Russes in 1926–7, and architectural projects both for monumental sculptures to stand in an architectural context (leading ultimately to the Bijenkorf monument erected in Rotterdam in 1957), but also for buildings themselves in Gabo's designs for the Palace of the Soviets competition of 1931.

Gabo was a member of the Abstraction-Création group from 1932 to 1935 and after settling in England in 1935 he collaborated with Ben Nicholson* and Leslie Martin on the book *Circle* (1937). He moved to New York in 1946 and two years later exhibited with Pevsner at the Museum of Modern Art there. He became a Professor at Harvard University Graduate School of Architecture in 1953 and an increasingly renowned figure internationally.

In Gabo's work self-expression gave way to investigation of the nature of space and the manipulation of materials. Empty space is, in fact, the precise material of his constructions and his distribution of plastics, glass and metals a system of articulating and elucidating that space. There is, inherent in Gabo's achievement, an example of scientific and creative thought simultaneously at work: engineering and mathematics were not alien to Gabo's work. There is a vision, too, of a further unity, between the constructions of man and the structures of nature.

Dr John Milner

See: Herbert Read and Leslie Martin, *Gabo* (1957); Teresa Newman, *Naum Gabo – The Constructive Process* (1976).

167
GALBRAITH, John Kenneth 1908–

US economist

J. K. Galbraith is an economist for the man-in-the-street. He has been a Professor of Economics at Harvard since 1949, has contributed to professional journals, and published his first book – *The Theory of Price Control* – in 1952. But in the main he has written, and prolifically, to and for the layman. His wit and irony and his capacity to coin a telling phrase have made him probably the most-quoted economist after Marx and Keynes*. 'The Affluent Society', 'private affluence and public squalor', 'countervailing power', the 'new industrial state and its technostructure' are the common currency of informed day-to-day debate.

He was born in Ontario, Canada, in 1908. After graduating in agriculture from Toronto University, he took a PhD in California and became a research fellow at Cambridge (England). His professional life was spent as Paul M. Warburg Professor of Economics of Harvard until he retired in 1975. He has as well spent many years in public service – work which has both shaped and reflected his approach to economics. From 1941 to 1943 he was in charge of wartime price control at the US Office of Price Administration, an experience which has crucially affected his attitudes to, and explanation of, the causes and nature of and the cures for inflation in an advanced and highly concentrated economy. In particular it gave him insights into the process by which large corporations set their goals and consequently their prices.

He became for the next five years an editor of *Fortune* magazine, work which both extended his acquaintance with industry into peacetime and which importantly influenced his writing style. He was Director of the Office of Economic Security Policy in the State Department at the end of the war.

Politically a Democrat like so many American academic economists, he was an influential adviser to the Democratic Party over the years, and a key member of the Kennedy* presidential campaign. When Kennedy became President, however, Galbraith was thought to be too controversial a figure to remain in Washington as a senior government adviser and was instead sent in 1961 as US Ambassador to India. Directly responsible for the largest American overseas

effort in economic development, he wrote a colourful *Ambassador's Journal* (1969) and started to analyse the problems of developing countries as sharply and wittily as he had those of the advanced economies.

Galbraith has made his impact by addressing himself to the layman and by engaging in public and political controversy. In this arena, his weapons have been a caustic wit, a devastating sense of irony, and a literary style that seems to produce a telling phrase on every page. He is a leading exponent of an institutionalist approach to political economy rather than the mathematical approach to economics. He has written, remarkably in a subject so widely regarded as 'dismal', a number of world-wide best sellers, not least *The Great Crash: 1929* (1955) which was a hilarious, biting history and analysis of the Wall Street boom and financial crisis that ushered in the Great Depression.

The main line of his thinking can be traced from his *Theory of Price Control*, based on his reflections on his wartime experience, to *American Capitalism: the Concept of Countervailing Power* (1952) to *The Affluent Society* (1958) to *The New Industrial State* (1967). The central theme is methods by which and the extent to which the typically large industrial, commercial and financial enterprise has freed itself from all outside control. Shareholders and non-executive directors were long ago made unimportant by the widening spread of share-ownership, and the concentration of power in the hands of technically trained professional managers. The increasing concentration of power within corporations was matched by a similar concentration of power by those corporations over the markets and hence over the whole economy.

All was not gloom and despondency. Galbraith demonstrated that these monopolistic enterprises, whose conduct departed so widely from the textbook norms of competition, were the most advanced and most rapidly advancing sectors of capitalism, whereas the textbook 'competitors' – industries composed of large numbers of small firms – were typically technically backward, earning low profits and paying low incomes. In any case, large corporations tended to generate 'countervailing power' amongst their suppliers or their customers. Big buyers led to big sellers, and vice versa.

This theme is developed to analyse the omnipotence of the managerial and technical elite in advanced enterprises. It matters not who owns the enterprises – 'the technostructure of the new industrial state' sets the goals, takes the decisions, distributes the rewards, according to its own judgments of its own best (long-term) interests. Its power inevitably and naturally spreads from the enterprise to the markets in which it buys and sells. Market forces, far from being autonomous, independent, anonymous and finally decisive, turn out to be other managers pursuing their own (even if competing) interests.

The technostructure's success, and hence its ethos,

has spread to provide the yardsticks for judging economic performance. 'Private affluence amid public squalor' is as much the mark of successful advanced capitalism as 'poverty in the midst of plenty' was the mark of the failed capitalism of the Great Depression. Galbraith's scathing analysis of the supremacy of 'market values' has become an important ingredient in the thinking of environmentalists, and the anti-growth schools, by undermining the very criteria of economic advance, viz. the level and growth and content of 'national product'.

Galbraith, as a Keynesian, has no doubts that capitalist economies can be stabilized at high, even full, employment: the rate of growth of output has been and can continue to be spectacular. He questions not how much they can produce, but the *content* of that output – and he doubts that prices will ever stop rising, unless sellers are stopped from raising them.

Roger Opie

Other works include: *Journey to Poland and Yugoslavia* (1959); *The Liberal Hour* (1960); *A Contemporary Guide to Economics, Peace and Laughter* (1971); *Economics and the Public Purpose* (1974); *Money* (1975); and *The Age of Uncertainty* (1976), the book of the television series.

168
GALSWORTHY, John 1867–1933

English writer

Galsworthy had every conceivable reason to feel pleased with himself. Son of a resourceful Devonshire lawyer, he was sent to Harrow and New College, Oxford, with the intention that he should follow his father's profession. In the classic tradition of the dilettante lawyer with literary aims he actually did begin to dabble in the business, but a meeting with Conrad*, following a visit to Africa, was influential in determining both men to pursue a writing career. In 1905 Galsworthy married his cousin's ex-wife Ada Cooper, and the first-hand experience of the pressures of marriage and the intricacies of divorce (at that time social as well as legal) had an undeniable effect on certain features of the plot of the *Forsyte Saga*.

The Forsyte novels, for which he is best known, began in 1906 with *The Man of Property*. In the figures of Soames and the members of his cohesive family, Galsworthy undertook a detailed analysis of Edwardian bourgeois life, meaning to expose the power of money and the various forces of social hypocrisy. His readers appear to have taken him seriously enough, and he was placed on a par with Shaw* and Wells* as a modern novelist dealing with significant questions of the day.

Galsworthy's was not the first English *roman fleuve*.

Trollope and others had trodden the path he was to follow, but Émile Zola's *Rougon-Macquart* cycle seems to have been equally influential. The realism cultivated from his reading of French literature was softened, in Galsworthy's novels, by an admirable compassion for his principal characters. The success of the first three Forsyte books emboldened him to begin a second trilogy, *A Modern Comedy*, which took the family into the 1920s. A further three novels concluded the cycle in 1931–3.

Since the Second World War Galsworthy's literary reputation has slumped disastrously, despite the incredible hold exerted on television audiences on both sides of the Atlantic during the late 1960s by the serialized novels. Revivals of his plays, Ibsenesque explorations of such topics as strike action and anti-Semitism, have proved fairly effective, but it is doubtful if his status as a major Edwardian novelist will ever be recovered. His own slightly too reticent and easy-going personality may have something to do with his consistent failure to convey sufficient intensity or involvement with his subject. As a stylist he rarely achieves distinction, and is frequently guilty of bathos and cliché. His chosen situations and themes have a certain faded interest, but he is unlikely to charm any save students of Edwardian manners and seekers after period. The winning of a Nobel Prize is, of course, no guarantee of any writer's enduring worth.

Jonathan Keates

See: Catherine Dupré, *John Galsworthy* (1976); Rudolf Sauter, *Galsworthy the Man* (1967); Margaret Morris, *My Galsworthy Story* (1967).

169
GANDHI, Mahatma (Mohandas Karamchand) 1869–1948

Indian politician

A politician, saint, social and economic reformer, an originator of *satyagraha* (holding on to truth), a non-violent form of popular agitation and struggle, and an early advocate of 'Small is beautiful', Mohandas (son of) Karamchand Gandhi left a lasting impression on the political culture of the Indian sub-continent, and accelerated the pace of socio-religious reform among the Hindus of the sub-continent. He dominated Indian politics for nearly three decades, from 1919 to 1948; and yet he described himself as 'a man of religion in the garb of a politician'. While his opponents knew him to be a clever tactician and shrewd negotiator, the masses revered him as a spiritual figure, a Mahatma: Great Soul.

He was born in 1869 of a middle-class *bania* (trading caste) family in Porbandar, a small port in the western state of Gujarat. A shy and diffident boy, he had an arranged marriage at thirteen to Kasturba, a girl of the same age. At eighteen he went to London to study law, and was called to the bar two years later. His strict vegetarianism brought him into contact with such leading British vegetarians of the time as the playwright George Bernard Shaw* and theosophist Annie Besant. They introduced him not only to the works of John Ruskin, Leo Tolstoy, and David Thoreau, but also the *Bhagavad Gita*, an important Hindu scripture. These early influences were at the root of what was later to emerge as Gandhism – a set of socio-economic theories which, if practised to the full, would re-create the world of the past, inhabited largely by self-sufficient village communities.

After an unsuccessful attempt to practise law in India, he went to South Africa in 1893 as a clerk with an Indian firm in Durban. Here he fought for the rights of the Indian settlers, established the weekly *Indian Opinion* (1903), and put into practice some of the concepts advocated by Tolstoy and Ruskin by founding a co-operative farm at Phoenix near Durban (1904). He synthesized the Hindu tactic of *dharna* (squatting in front of a house/office to draw attention) with the ideas contained in Thoreau's essay 'Civil Disobedience', and forged the tool of *satyagraha*, which combined passive resistance against and non-co-operation with the authorities. He initiated the *satyagraha* movement against the racist laws of South Africa in 1907 and struggled on, sporadically, until the government agreed to compromise, six years later.

On his return to India in 1915 he helped the British in their war effort. He settled down at an *ashram* (retreat) near Ahmedabad, and did not play a leading role in nationalist politics until after the Amritsar massacre in April 1919. Then, as a leader of the Indian National Congress, he gave a call for non-co-operation with the British government. This meant boycotting all the official institutions and refusing to pay taxes. Tens of thousands of people followed his lead, and were imprisoned. The consequences of this movement went beyond politics. The collective courting of jail by a group of people, often with a petty-bourgeois urban background, banished the fear among the populace of being imprisoned for a just cause. The participation of many women in the movement, actively encouraged by Gandhi, gave an impetus to women's emancipation in general. These actions inspired novelists and poets to inject social and political themes into their works – an unprecedented phenomenon.

In the mid-1920s, Gandhi turned his attention to the practice of untouchability among Hindus. He tried to break taboos against the Untouchables, the Outcastes, by having them serve food to the caste Hindus, and by encouraging the latter to sweep streets, a job traditionally performed by the Outcastes. He gave a lead by doing the menial tasks, associated with the Untouch-ables, at the *ashram* near Wardha, in Maharashtra, that he established in the early 1930s. Here he founded the English weekly *Harijan* ('Children of God'), a name he coined for the Untouchables. In addition he undertook a series of 'fasts unto death' either to pressurize the orthodox Hindu leaders into softening their attitudes towards the Outcastes, or merely to 'persuade' his political opponents. This practice continues. Vinobha Bhave, one of his disciples, undertook a 'fast unto death' in 1979 to force the Indian government to outlaw cow slaughter throughout the country, an irrational demand.

Although a pacifist, Gandhi did not remain neutral when wars broke out. During the Second World War he opposed Hitler* and Nazism. But he insisted that if the Allies were really fighting for democracy and freedom then Britain should grant independence to India immediately so that an independent India could then join the war against Nazism. When this demand was turned down he launched the 'Quit India' movement against the British in August 1942.

By the end of the next five years the British had departed, leaving behind a sub-continent partitioned into the independent states of India and Pakistan. The inter-religious rioting that took place before and after the partition in August 1947 heightened the historic animosity between Hindus and Muslims. It was in this atmosphere of feverish communal tension that Gandhi, an advocate of Hindu–Muslim amity, was shot dead by a Hindu fanatic, Nathuram Godse, in Delhi on 30 January 1948.

A prolific writer, Gandhi expressed himself simply and directly in both Gujarati and English. He used the three weeklies that he edited (*Indian Opinion*, *Young India*, and *Harijan*) as vehicles to guide his followers and expound the various theories and causes that he came to propagate. These ranged from nature cure to *brahmacharya* (celibacy) to home rule to *ahimsa* (nonviolence) to opposition to industrialization and urbanization and the corporate state, and his yearning for a world peopled by communities living in self-sufficient villages.

Dilip Hiro

See: Gandhi, *The Story of My Experiments with Truth* (2 vols, London 1929); *The Collected Works of Mahatma Gandhi*, 40 vols until May 1929 (Delhi 1958–), with 40 more vols to come. About Gandhi: C. F. Andrews (ed.), *Mahatma Gandhi: His Own Story* (1930); L. Fischer, *The Life of Mahatma Gandhi* (1950); J. Eaton, *Gandhi, Fighter without a Sword* (1950); D. G. Tendulkar, *Mohandas Karamchand Gandhi* (8 vols, revised edition, Delhi 1963); J. V. Bondurant, *Conquest of Violence: The Gandhian Philosophy* (1965); E. H. Erikson, *Gandhi's Truth: On the Origins of Militant Non-violence* (1969); H. Alexander, *Gandhi Through Western Eyes* (1969); G. Woodcock, *Gandhi* (1972).

170
GARCÍA MÁRQUEZ, Gabriel 1928–

Colombian novelist

Probably the best known Spanish American contemporary novelist. His early short stories, written partly under the influence of Faulkner*, are abstract and rather artificial. However, in *Leaf Storm and Other Stories* (*La hojarasca*, 1955, trans. 1972), he created the township of Macondo, around which much of his later work gravitates. In this first novel and in *No-one Writes to the Colonel* (*El coronel no tiene quien le escriba*, 1958, trans. 1971) and *In Evil Hour* (*La mala hora*, 1962, trans. 1980), which constitute the first phase of his production, the emphasis is on moral corruption, social decay and political oppression, relieved by individual acts of resistance to the depressing conditions in which the characters live. However, these works mark a break with the preceding pattern of social protest in the Spanish American novel, not only because they reach out to a more universal plane of meaning (*Leaf Storm*, for instance, is modelled on Sophocles' tragedy *Antigone*), but also because of their often ambiguous presentation of reality, their unusual symbolism and their occasional inclusion of elements of fantasy and humour.

Big Mama's Funeral (*Los funerales de la Mamá Grande*, 1962) in *No-one Writes to the Colonel* constitutes another giant stride forward in the Spanish American novel which until the emergence of García Márquez had, with few exceptions, tended to reject humour as incompatible with the high civic responsibilities of writers who saw their first duty as that of stirring the conscience of their readers. The theme of the novel is a traditional one: the immense power and influence of the landed oligarchy in Latin America. But instead of mounting the usual frontal attack on the rural landowners for their exploitation of the peasantry and their manipulation of the local authorities, García Márquez ridicules them, adapting for the purpose techniques of grotesque exaggeration and comic enumeration which he had learned from Rabelais. The result is a carnivalesque satire, written without bitterness or aggressiveness, but which never allows the reader to forget the author's basic aim.

The difference between *Big Mama's Funeral* and *One Hundred Years of Solitude* (*Cien años de soledad*, 1970, trans. 1976), García Márquez's acknowledged masterpiece, lies in the fact that the former is based essentially on a hilarious deformation of observed social conditions, while the latter moves much further away from reported reality towards created reality and unbridled fantasy. No general consensus about the meaning of the work, which chronicles the fortunes of several generations of the Buendía family, the founders of Macondo, has emerged. One feature of the novel is its tendency to blur the distinction between the real and the imaginary and to undermine the confidence with which we differentiate between them. In this sense a theme of the novel is fiction itself. *One Hundred Years of Solitude* is also a metaphor of the human condition. The iron determinism which governs the lives of the characters, the solitude, the violence, the curse under which the Buendías labour, all illustrate García Márquez's underlying tragic vision. At another level Macondo is presented as a metaphor of Latin America's historical development, at first idyllic and primitive; then with a rudimentary social organization imposed from without (as in the colonial period); next, succumbing to the civil strife of nineteenth-century Latin America, finally falling victim to the economic imperialism characteristic of our day. The circularity of time in Macondo implies an attempt to escape from history seen as dynamic linear progress. The biblical parallels, especially with Genesis and Exodus, indicate a Fall, but no Redemption. Yet this is a very funny book. Its serious themes are enveloped in an atmosphere of fantasy, of magical and miraculous events and playful, often erotic, humour. The method produces a blend of tones which is completely original and unique in Spanish American fiction, where it is sometimes known as 'magical realism'.

After *Innocent Eréndira and Other Stories* (*La increíble y triste historia de la cándida Eríndera y de su abuela desalmada*, 1972, trans. 1978), an ironic parody of the conventional fairy-tale love story, García Márquez published *The Autumn of the Patriarch* (*El otoño del Patriarca*, 1975, trans. 1975), in which he caricatures the archetypal Latin American military dictator, mythicized, almost deified, yet at the same time comic and even pathetic.

All García Márquez's work reflects the struggle within the author of a deep attachment to life expressed via the humour and (more ambiguously) the love element in his novels, and an equally profound rejection of life whose expression is the solitude of his characters and the determinism to which they are subjected.

D. L. Shaw

See: Luis Harss, *Into the Main-Stream* (1967); D. P. Gallagher, *Modern Latin American Literature* (1973); G. Brotherston, *The Emergence of the Latin American Novel* (1977). In Spanish: M. Vargas Llosa, *Gabriel García Márquez: historia de un deicidio* (1971).

171

GELLNER, Ernest 1925–

British philosopher, sociologist and anthropologist

Born in Paris, Ernest Gellner was educated in Prague and in England. From Balliol College, Oxford, he took his PhD in Social Anthropology at London University, becoming first a lecturer at the London School of Economics in 1949, then Professor in 1962, first in Sociology and then in Philosophy. He is among the most original and the most knowledgeable of modern philosophers and social theorists, offering fundamental critiques of epistemological presuppositions. His writing is analytical, witty and polemical – virtues not always welcomed.

His first book, *Words and Things* (1959), made him appear as an *enfant terrible* for he not merely said that the great Oxford school of linguistic philosophy (*vide* Austin*) was boring, but that it was pointless; and what little point it had could be seen best, sociologically or anthropologically, as fulfilling a culturally conservative, ideological role rather than as critical analysis. 'Linguistic philosophy,' he said, 'tries to make us take the world for granted and to think only about the oddity of philosophy emerging in it, rather than to think philosophically about it.' He accused British philosophers of disguising preconceptions as procedural rules and said that they offered 'the argument from impotence', that is 'the idea that philosophy must only be concerned with the *how* and not the *what*'. 'Philosophy is,' he agreed, 'partly a matter of making explicit our concepts', but it must also be concerned with evaluating them. And while philosophy must examine the logical structure of generalizations, it must also seek to add to the stock of true generalizations.

Gellner, though highly critical of some aspects of Karl Popper's* teaching, shares his concern with the discovery of knowledge, not simply the critique of knowledge, or worse, to Gellner, the critique of mere words. As his *Saints of the Atlas* (1969), a study of politics and tradition among the Berbers, shows, he is not merely interested in other cultures, but obviously believes that the social philosopher carries no conviction who has not undertaken laborious fieldwork himself, particularly in a culture with very different concepts. But typically Gellner has argued against what he calls 'contextual charity' as the dominant tradition of social anthropology: we must emphasize with different concepts to understand how a system works, but having understood we can still say that some of the beliefs are untrue or absurd.

In *Thought and Change* (1964) he made a contribution to the sociology of development, a kind of reformulated evolutionary theory of steps or stages, claiming that, for good or ill, there are only two conditions for valid social order in the modern world: that a society can successfully maintain industrial affluence, and that rulers are co-cultural with the rest of society (i.e. not alien). It should be noted how minimal these conditions are. While critical of ideological presuppositions in allegedly neutral modern philosophy and while in favour of judgment and evaluation, Gellner has never advanced any clear political philosophy himself except, which may be as far as he thinks anyone can go, a

clear concern for Popper's principle of openness and for the holding of theories hypothetically – say simply liberty. Yet he is sceptical of claims that liberty presupposes a free market, appearing pragmatically to accept mixed economies.

Three volumes of essays have appeared, *Cause and Meaning in the Social Sciences* (1973) (which included an almost classic attack on relativism), *Contemporary Thought in Politics* (1974) (much concerned with the relationship between democracy and industrialization), and then his various reflections on the connections between philosophy and life, *The Devil in Modern Philosophy* (1974). In the same year his most ambitious book to date appeared, *Legitimation of Belief*. In it he discusses the strange paradox of the steady advance in objective knowledge since the time of Descartes but the decline in people's comprehension of the world. He thinks that the rejection of theological or scientific monism for pluralism has gone too far, or rather that in accepting the virtues of political pluralism we have underestimated both the internal incoherence and the external consequences of philosophical pluralism. Most of the book is concerned with three 'hanging judges': (i) *empiricism*, which claims that knowledge is only valid in terms of experience or sensations; (ii) *materialism*, which claims that knowledge is only valid if it can specify some publicly replicable structure, like a machine; or (iii) *logical form*, which he sees as the foible of modern philosophers that knowledge must conform to logical forms of rules that they have certified as valid. *Our* sensations are authentic, but there is an *external* world. The book faces this basic dilemma.

At the end of *Legitimation of Belief* he wishes to offer us, in 'our shipwreck', no more than 'a raft of four planks': the empiricists' insistence that 'faiths must not fill out the world' but must be judged by evidence not under their own control; the relativistic acceptance of 'ironic cultural nationalism' in styles of life, but not of real knowledge of real convictions (i.e. such as convictions about how we should behave towards other lifestyles); the mechanistic insistence that we must believe in impersonal, structural explanations; and 'truncated evolutionism', not Darwin and the survival of the fittest but a humane commitment to the specific development of industrial civilization, whose consequences are irreversible but whose forms can vary.

Professor Bernard Crick

See Bryan Magee (ed.), *Men of Ideas: Some Creators of Contemporary Philosophy* (1978).

172
GENET, Jean 1910–

French poet, novelist, dramatist

Genet's father was unknown, his mother a prostitute

who abandoned him to be brought up by the state. When his foster parents caught him stealing and called him a thief, he decided to turn this insult into a virtue and to make a career as a thief. Much of his childhood was spent in reform schools, where his first homosexual encounters took place. He escaped and joined the French Foreign Legion, only to desert again soon afterwards. Living off theft and prostitution, he wandered from one part of Europe to another, often in prison or on the run from the police.

His first novels were written in prison: *Our Lady of the Flowers* (*Notre-Dame des Fleurs*) at Fresnes in 1942 and *Miracle of the Rose* (*Miracle de la Rose*) at the Santé prison in 1943. These are novels of homosexual eroticism written in sumptuously poetic prose. They are theatrical novels in the sense that they portray people constantly preoccupied with appearances, both their own and others'. Even more, they suggest an almost mystical belief in the sudden transformation of outward appearances in such a way as to reveal another reality visible only to the eye of the believer. *Miracle of the Rose* contains a celebrated account of a scene in the courtyard of Fontevrault prison in which a notorious bandit steps out from the condemned cell and suddenly his chains are transformed into a garland of roses.

In 1947 Genet's reputation was established with the publication of two more novels and the performance of *The Maids* (*Les Bonnes*) produced by Jouvet in a double bill with a play by Giraudoux. His last novel *The Thief's Journal* (*Journal d'un Voleur*) appeared in 1949, which was also the year when he produced his own play *Deathwatch* (*Haute surveillance*). Since then, Genet has written three major plays: *The Balcony* (*Le Balcon*, 1956); *The Blacks* (*Les Nègres*, 1958); and *The Screens* (*Les Paravents*, 1961), and nothing more.

In the 1960s and 1970s he has championed the causes of various urban terrorist groups including the Black Panthers, the Fedayeen and the Baader-Meinhof gang. He has described himself as 'a black whose skin happens to be pink and white' and his early identification with the criminal classes has shifted to an identification with the oppressed, the dispossessed and the coloured.

Genet's life presents an extraordinarily consistent attempt to turn bourgeois morality on its head. He is at least partly the creation of Sartre* who, when asked to write a short introduction to Genet's work, produced a six-hundred page essay explaining the phenomenon that was Jean Genet in Existentialist terms. This appeared as volume I of Genet's complete works. For Sartre, Genet had aspired to a kind of saintliness by his single-minded devotion to evil and his systematic reversal of received moral codes.

Genet's writing style is different from that of Sartre, being poetic rather than discursive, baroque rather than austere. Although he has written about social outcasts, it is difficult to extract a socialist message

from his works. In fact he has expressed admiration for an SS torturer and regret at the closure of the Cayenne convict settlement. But his work has always been seen as subversive by the Establishment. His first novels were not available to open sale; performances of his plays all provoked some degree of protest and the production of *The Screens* at the Odéon in 1966 led to demonstrations and street battles.

By his own definition, his method is to draw the reader or the spectator into imaginative sympathy with a character or attitude which turns out to be diametrically opposed to his normal assumptions or standards. But neither in fiction nor on the stage does Genet match the crude extremes of, say, Burroughs* or Arrabal*. His work has a greater range and depth, commenting on social, political and spiritual aspects of life. His plays embody a very brilliant interplay of different levels of illusion which suggest both the interdependence and the potential treachery of all social roles, stressing the links between the power and theatricality. They also point to the inadequacy of common notions of reality. In many ways they approach the ideals of Artaud*, being characterized by an absence of traditional psychology, ritualized movements and actions, interchanges of identity and a carefully worked contrast between the sumptuousness of poetic dialogue and the sordidity of dramatic situation. They also demand an exploitation of the whole theatre space and aim for a Powerful, disturbing effect on the audience. Genet has expressed contempt for most Western theatre because it offers entertainment instead of communion. He has expressed admiration for the Roman Catholic Mass and for children's games.

His plays have provided opportunities for directors like Roger Blin and Peter Brook* to put the theories of Artaud to the test and have resulted in some very brilliant productions. But he is an uncomfortable figure: the Left has never quite forgiven him for writing a panegyric of Nazi killers; the Right will never forgive him for casting dirt on the French army in Algeria. He remains an unclassifiable figure, but a challenging one.

David Bradby

Oeuvres Complètes (from 1951). Many of his works have appeared in English translation published by Faber. See also: Richard Coe, *The Vision of Jean Genet* (1968); Philip Thody, *Jean Genet, a Critical Appraisal* (1968).

173
GERSHWIN, George 1898–1937

US composer

George Gershwin was an American composer no less remarkable for historical significance than for intrinsic ability. Born in 1898 of Jewish parentage, in the heart of New York, he was a natural who flourished in what might have seemed a musical desert. Nurtured off Broadway, he first made a living by plugging other people's songs at the piano, in music emporia; and found himself creating his own numbers almost fortuitously. It never occurred to him that distinctions might be drawn between making songs and selling them; and intuitively he was right in believing that, although commercial art operates in order to make money, it will do so best if the dreams it proffers bear some relation to people's emotional needs. The musical comedy numbers of Gershwin, especially those for which his brother Ira wrote such witty lyrics, accept the clichés of Tin Pan Alley while imbuing them with an irony – a recognition of 'other modes of experience that may be possible' – that makes them at once comic and deeply moving. 'The man I love' (1924) can stake a claim to being the most affecting pop song of the jazz era because, starting from the adolescent moon-June cliché, it admits that the dream, though true to the cravings of the human heart, isn't likely to be true in fact. What happens in the music makes the girl grow up; and we grow with her. The music tells us that, though she won't find her Prince Charming, she'll almost certainly find a guy she mistakes for one; and that the mistake matters less than the fallible aspiration.

The memorability of Gershwin's tunes has ensured that no show-biz composer has created so many tunes so widely known to so many people; at the same time the subtlety of the composer's melodic and rhythmic structures and the often quite complex ambiguities of his harmony and tonality have ensured that the tunes are 'news that *stays* news'. There's enough art in Gershwin's commercial numbers to explain why it was possible for his career to climax (in 1935) with a large-scale work, *Porgy and Bess*, which starts from the conventions of the Broadway musical, yet becomes a fully-fledged and genuinely grand opera. Part of Gershwin's talent was to have recognized in Dubose Heyward's novel his own essential theme: for the book is a parable about alienation, oppression, and the inviolability of a radical innocence of spirit, even in a corrupt world. Gershwin was not, like Porgy, a Negro, nor, in the material benefits of life, was he in any way deprived. He was, however, a poor boy who made good: an American Jew who knew about spiritual isolation and had opportunities enough to learn about corruption. He was not, like Porgy, a physical cripple; he was, however, an emotional cripple, victimized by the nervous maladjustments typical of his generation, and by the usual escapes from them. So, in his opera, he sang with honest strength of the malaise inherent in the twentieth-century pop song itself: telling of the impact of the world of commerce on those who once led, would like to have led, the 'good life', based on an intimate communion between man and nature. Significantly the veracity of the pentatonic roulades and painful false relations of the Negro blues is endemic in Gershwin's melody and harmony; and comes to terms both with the commercial clichés of Tin Pan Alley (as represented by the beguiling numbers of the light-skinned villain, Sportin' Life), and also with the operatic conventions of 'Western' art, which seek a synonym for Order and Civilization.

The pervasiveness of the black blues within Gershwin's white music bears on the fact that he has been so important a figure in the evolution of jazz as an urban folk art; *Porgy and Bess* has itself spawned jazz improvised composition of extraordinary intensity, from the versions of Ella Fitzgerald and Louis Armstrong* to those of Miles Davis*, Cleo Laine and Ray Charles, and Oscar Petersen. Yet Gershwin did not regard the 'folk' aspects of his work as alien to his aspiration towards 'art'; and it's a fact that his early success (initiated by Paul Whiteman) as a composer of 'concert' music abetted his later triumphs in the pop field. Academic musicians are still apt to say that, whereas the tunes in *Rhapsody in Blue* (1924) and the *Concerto in F* (1925) are marvellous, they're not improved by the synthetic symphonic treatment. There must be something wrong with this argument, for after more than fifty years these 'synthetic' pieces continue to be frequently performed whereas literally hundreds of (often critically lauded) piano concertos composed during the period have gone the way of all flesh. Gershwin himself, who wrote the concerto in 1925, while working on the musical *Tiptoes* (1925), didn't think it odd that the first movement, which 'represents the young, enthusiastic spirit of American life', should be both in Charleston rhythm and in sonata form. The structure of the concerto proves as durably 'organic' as that of *Porgy and Bess*; and there are affinities between the two experiences, in that the finale of the concerto recaptures the gaiety of a (Porgy-like) child, while the blue sevenths of the haunting slow movement are nostalgic for a lost Eden. One of the names Americans of the 1920s and 1930s gave to that Eden is 'Paris': as is evident in the nocturnally bluesy section of Gershwin's most mature concert work, *An American in Paris* (1928), which earned the 'artistic' accolade of performance at the International Festival of Contemporary Music!

Intrinsically Gershwin matters because he was a genius, and there aren't many of them in any society. Historically he matters because he was the first, and remains the most potent, composer to fuse the vital *instinct* of black jazz as an urban folk art with the more will-dominated *creativity* of Western art music and with the *production* of an industrial technocracy. Such an achievement is basic to our future, if we're to have one. The pity is that Gershwin died before he'd attained forty.

Wilfrid Mellers

Gershwin wrote the scores for many musicals, including: *Lady be Good* (1924); *Oh Kay!* (1926); *Strike up the band* (1927); *Funny Face* (1927); *Girl Crazy* (1930); and *Of thee I Sing* (1931). Other works include: *Second Rhapsody for Orchestra and Piano* (1932); *Cuban Overture* (1932). See also: Wilfrid Mellers, *Music in a New Found Land* (1964); Charles Schwartz, *The Life and Music of Gershwin* (1973).

174
GIACOMETTI, Alberto 1901–66

Swiss sculptor and painter

Alberto Giacometti was born in Borgonovo and spent his childhood in Stampa, both near the Italian border. His father, Giovanni, was a painter, and it was from him that he first learnt the art of drawing. In 1919 he enrolled at the École des Beaux Arts in Geneva, but left after three days to attend the École des Arts et Métiers instead. In 1922, having travelled for two years through most of Italy with his father, he arrived in Paris, where he attended the classes of the sculptor Antoine Bourdelle at the Académie de la Grand-Chaumière, and where he settled for the rest of his life. For a period, between 1929 and 1935, he joined the Surrealists, but he was never a man to be easily identified with a particular school or group – a characteristic that in time became transformed into a legend of personal integrity. Separating from the Surrealists he concentrated for five years on the study of nature. In 1937 he abandoned painting in favour of drawing and sculpture – only to resume it again after the war, most of which he had spent back in Geneva working from memory on sculptures which grew smaller and smaller until they were barely an inch high. But he continued to sculpt, and the figures he now produced – increasingly tall, but uncompromisingly thin, and extraordinary in their eerily erect dignity – are the ones that have come to stand for his name. From 1949 he also began the series of sculpted groups, conceived first as separate figures, but later joined on a solid base. His international recognition was established in the 1960s, when he won the Carnegie Foundation Award (1961), the Grand Prix at the Venice Biennale (1962) and the Guggenheim International Award (1964). He died at Chur, in Switzerland, of a heart disease.

The upright oblong format is present in most of Giacometti's work, both painting and sculpture. Depending on the height of the piece in question, and the distance from the viewer, the emphatic verticality could suggest either intricate intimacy, as in the stick-like figurines, or monumental sparseness, as in the later public commissions (for example, *Standing Women* in the Chase Manhattan Plaza in New York, 1960–5). The artist's choice of elongation, partly derived from Etrus-

can tomb statuettes, was less the application of a specific theory, more the result of a painstaking search for truth. Giacometti's work evolves around several ambiguously related ideas: the Surrealist notion of objective chance, projection of desire, silent disruption of the continuities of space and time. In addition he perhaps inherited, from the Cubists, the idea of the confrontation of opposites, and the concept of the transparency of sculpture. But his relations to formal theories are curiously mirrored by his own stylistic idiosyncrasy: the idea of distance as part of the object, and the onlooker's active role in the composition of the piece.

Thematically his work consists of still lives, landscapes, portraits, animals, nudes, arms, legs, heads, and abstract objects. But beyond question his central pursuit is the representation of the *presence* (not the simple likeness) of a human being; and it is this quest that leads him to explore a new ground, between the fixity of conventional figurative sculpture, and the fluidity of abstraction. And indeed Giacometti's career began with a fascination for two opposing traditions: the strictly mimetic and the magically evocative. He was not alone in his generation in this respect, but he is perhaps the only artist who successfully refused to accept a solution to the dichotomy based on a preference for either of its poles. The peculiarly tortured aspect of much of his best work is perhaps a result of this. 'Art and science', he said, 'mean trying to understand. Failure or success play a secondary role.' Like all great artists he sought to grasp reality, but sought to grasp it in the hardest place – the face; as he wrote in a poem, *Le Rideau brun* ('Brown Curtain', 1922), 'the more one looks at it, the more it closes itself off and escapes by the steps of unknown stairways'. Typically he loved the elusive *Madonna with Angels* of Cimabue, because it came 'closest to truth'.

Early works, represented by *Torso* (1925), *The Spoon Woman* (1926) and *The Couple* (1926), were abstract 'objects' with no indication of what was to come. His first concerted attempt to free himself from that manner was the deployment of the cage to envelop an object or figure in a frame that sets it off from the real world, as in *Man* (1929) or *Suspended Ball* (1930–1). The ball, suspended by a wire in an actual cage, adds the rhythm of movement to the rhythm of forms if set in motion, thus confronting measurable time with moving form. This strategy was developed through a series of pieces (*Caught Hand*, 1932, *The Palace at 4 a.m.*, 1932–3, *The Nose*, 1947) which explore the possible effects of separation and recombination. *Caught Hand* also introduced the theme of torture, as a symbol of existence, which led to *Point to the Eye* (1932) and *Woman with the Throat Cut* (1932). At the same time Giacometti was experimenting with other forms of movement. In *Man, Woman and Child* (1931), *Circuit for a Square* (1931) and *No More Play* (1932–3) he introduced tracks on boards with small horizontal or vertical figures, inviting the viewer to alter the composition by moving the form. *Circuit*, in which a ball cannot reach the hole which lies next to its path, can be seen as a metaphor for paradise lost (Hohl). But perhaps the most obviously Surrealist sculpture is the *Disagreeable Object* (1931), a smooth worm-like form spiked at one end.

Giacometti's separation from the Surrealists cost him friends and art dealers, but it was necessary if he was to pursue the theme that engaged him for the rest of his life: the perception of an Other through the distance which is part of that Other. If the terminology echoes Sartre*, that is no accident, for it was Sartre who became his champion and in two important essays – 'The Search for the Absolute' (1948) and 'The Paintings of Giacometti' (1951) – provided a key to the artist's 'difficulty'. Above all, in his mature work, Giacometti confronts the inaccessibility and solitude of his subjects as a psychological phenomenon; or, as Sartre observed, 'Distance, to his eyes, far from being an accident, is part of the innermost nature of the object.' This summarizes the meaning of the great sculptures – *City Square* (1948), *Three Men Walking* (1949), *The Forest* ('Composition with Seven Figures and a Head', 1950), *Figure from Venice I–IX* (1956) and *Tall Figures* (1960). Here the distance is no longer achieved by artifice, as in the 'cage' period, but emanates from the pieces themselves. Because it is a psychological emanation, it is untraversable. It is a distance which only the spoken word can cross, as Giacometti himself put it on one occasion, or on another a gleaming floor that cannot be trodden. His faces are characteristically pointed dead ahead, without the least trace of visible humour. The severity of the long curving jawbones, which continue to encompass generally reduced crania in a single line, is to a degree contrasted by the deliberately unpolished surfaces, which allow for a subtle movement of light if the viewer himself moves but fractionally, and which perhaps account for an unexpected tenderness.

Sartre also drew attention to Giacometti's dual existence as a painter as well as sculptor, showing that when he sculpts he confers on his statues an imaginary and fixed distance, whereas when he paints he uses the space between a figure and the frame as a true void. Giacometti himself referred to the fluidity between the two media when, apropos the *Nine Figures* (1950), he said: 'I had very much wanted to paint them last Spring' – but modelled them instead.

Dr Slavka Sverakova

See: R. J. Moulin, *Giacometti Sculptures* (1962, trans. 1964); Jean Genet, *Alberto Giacometti* (Zürich 1962); P. Selz, *Alberto Giacometti* (1965); M. Leiris, *Alberto Giacometti* (trans. 1971); J. Lord, *Alberto Giacometti: Drawings* (1971); R. Hohl, *Alberto Giacometti* (1972).

175
GIDE, André-Paul-Guillaume 1869–1951

French writer, intellectual, moralist

Born into a Protestant upper middle-class family and dominated by a puritanical mother, Gide, always a highly strung youth, sought consolation in the pleasures of botany, music and imaginative literature. From an early age he saw himself as the product and victim of contradictory and conflicting tensions – religious, social and moral. The strictness of his religious upbringing stands in contrast to the Dionysiac fervour of his sexual emancipation in North Africa in the mid-1890s. He was then, after a brief flirtation with Catholicism in 1905 and a further religious crisis in 1915, to develop a form of liberal humanism, which itself underwent a brief Communist phase. His social and moral ideas were generally more consistent – from the modish non-conformism of his Symbolist youth, he pursued his Romantic revolt against the bourgeoisie while refusing to underwrite the Dadaists and early Surrealists. Championing homosexuality in the 1920s, he became a fellow traveller in the early 1930s, only to reassert his independence and individualism in *Return from USSR* (*Retour de l'URSS*, 1936, trans. 1937). Never the darling of the French literary establishment, he remained on the fringe until his death in 1951, four years after being awarded the Nobel Prize for Literature.

Gide's commitment to his art was absolute. His range was considerable, beginning with his rather self-conscious exploration of Symbolist themes in his early works and the lyrical fervour of *Fruits of the Earth* (*Les Nourritures terrestres*, 1897, trans. 1949) and moving to the more tightly controlled classicism of his *récits* and the burlesque humour and irony of his *soties*. He experimented with every genre – poetry, plays, prose poems, moral treaties, literary criticism, social and political journalism and, above all, novels. In addition, the long correspondences with many leading literary figures add a further dimension to his self-portrait. All of this is seen in fragmentary form in his diaries, and reconstructed in his autobiographical works.

Gide's reputation rests mainly with his three *récits*, *The Immoralist* (*L'Immoraliste*, 1902, trans. 1930), *Strait is the Gate* (*La Porte étroite* 1909, trans. 1924) and *La Symphonie pastorale* (1919, trans. 1931), recognized by many as models of the genre. These spare, unilateral monodies are all ironical works which dramatize extreme attitudes in a critical fashion. 'L'oeuvre d'art, c'est une idée qu'on exagère' ('the work of art involves the exaggeration of a single idea'). Each of the heroes, Michel, Alissa, the pastor, is deliberately presented as a logical extreme. In the light of their hubris, or lyrical excess, Gide hopes to convey psychological depth and illustrate significant moral dilemmas. All these works employ the first-person narrative mode and are an idiosyncratic amalgam of melodrama, understatement, discreet irony and, in addition, the patterning and rhythm of classical tragedy.

But it is in his polyphonic mode that Gide is perhaps least appreciated – by Anglo-Saxon readers, at least, who sometimes dub his novels as cerebral, desiccated and stylized in the extreme. Indeed, Gide read long and hard in other literatures in his search for a new novel form. His wide experience of the nineteenth-century French novel – Stendhal, Balzac, Flaubert, Barrès, Zola – was complemented by his study of Tolstoy and Dostoievski, the nineteenth-century English novel from the Brontës to Stevenson and Conrad*, but more significantly perhaps by his new look at the eighteenth-century picaresque tradition. Gide, in association with his protégé, Jacques Rivière, at the *Nouvelle revue française* (founded in 1908), was a leader in the movement to revitalize the novel form. In *The Vatican Cellars* (*Les Caves du Vatican*, 1914, trans. 1925) he crossed the picaresque adventure novel and the detective novel with Molièresque farce and produced in the process a deconstruction of the Balzacian realist novel – decentralized in form. His only full-scale novel, *The Counterfeiters* (*Les Faux-monnayeurs*, 1926, trans. 1927), is even more open-ended, the amalgam of many different novel-types and the focal point of many dramas. He shows his preference for Dostoievski over Tolstoy in what close analysis reveals to be a strange conglomerate, but which in fact, due to its technical brilliance, possesses an ease of manner and a sense of natural growth. Praised somewhat stintingly by most critics (see E. M. Forster*, *Aspects of the Novel*), this novel is a major achievement of twentieth-century fiction.

Admired by the Symbolists in the 1890s, wooed by the Catholic Claudel and the materialist Gourmont before 1914, and briefly idolized by the Dadaists, Gide became in the 1920s the public champion of homosexuality and the apostle of youth, who 'discovered' the iconoclastic *Les Caves du Vatican* and the neo-Nietzschean song of songs, *Les Nourritures terrestres*.

Following his interest in social problems, he associated himself in the early 1930s with the Communist Party. However, the intellectual honesty and the anti-Stalinism* of his *Retour de l'URSS* had reverberations in French intellectual life up to 1939. Always on the fringe of any establishment, appalled by the demands of 'le grand nombre' ('the many'), his heart went out to 'le petit nombre' ('the few'), the young and the oppressed.

His contribution to intellectual life was fully acknowledged by the generation of Malraux*, Sartre* and Camus*. His reappraisal of the novel complements the work of Proust*, Joyce* and Dos Passos* and conditioned the theories of the French new novelists, Sarraute*, Robbe-Grillet* and Claude Simon. Steeped in European culture, seeing life as a long voyage through books, men and countries, Gide is heir to a long humanist tradition – a latter-day Montaigne, by Nietzsche out of Racine.

Christopher Bettinson

Other works include: *Journal, 1899–1939* (1939), *Journal, 1939–49* (1954, both vols trans. 1953); *Souvenirs* (1954, containing the autobiography *Si le grain ne meurt*, 1926, and *Voyage au Congo*, 1927); *Thésée* (1946, 'Theseus' in *Two Legends: Oedipus and Theseus*, trans. 1950). See: K. Mann, *André Gide and the Crisis of Modern Thought* (1948); J. O'Brien, *Portrait of André Gide* (1953); G. Brée, *Gide* (1963); G. W. Ireland, *André Gide – a Study of his Creative Writings* (1970); Christopher Bettinson, *Gide: a Study* (1977).

176
GINSBERG, Allen 1926–

US poet

Born (Newark, NJ) in Fire-Tiger year 3 june, son of Naomi & the poet Louis Ginsberg, he grew up near William Carlos Williams* in Paterson NJ (where at 7, Grammar School, 'Miss Morgan gave me my start in literature'). Said to have travelled 'more than any other writer in the history of America' the vision he gave two decades (50s & 60s) of an alternative society came even more from journeys inward. His public presence erupted twice – either side a 4-year visit to the Far East: first as leader of the Beat Scene from '55 (*HOWL!*) to 1961, and then as the creator of Flower Power from 1965 (spring: his mayday coronation by 100,000 students in Prague; autumn: the Berkeley Flower Power speech) through its peak in '67 (january: the San Francisco First Gathering of the Tribes for a Human Be-in; easter-day: the First Greater New York Be-in; summer: London Dialectics of Liberation; october: the Circumambulation of the Defense Department). Often assessed on this double euphoria, his real contribution to poetry and the transformation of culture lies in the years before each.

Up at Columbia University ('44–'48) the 8 years ending '53 began with a mutual creation of the beat generation quartet: Ginsberg, Burroughs*, Kerouac*, & (from jan '50) Corso, plus Herbert Huncke (a beat in the 1965 layabout sense who introduced the word to them). They ended with all 5 reassembled & included AG's stay in the Columbia Psychiatric Institute (he pleaded insanity after Huncke got nicked for profitable kleptomania) where, with Bhagavad-gita confiscated, he met Carl Solomon (mad holy hero of *HOWL!* – his uncle owned Ace Books, hence Burroughs got *Junkies* published '53); a trip to Dakar (poem-cycle *Doldrums*); & a year at home (the *Empty Mirror* poems). These were the years crucial to AG's development first as a poet & then, through that, as a contemplative. As poet they were years of influence by Whitman & W. C. Williams, of 'encounter' with Blake's voice in summer '48 reading Ah Sunflower, of work on the real inner-language meaning of myth, of mind extensions on pot & of forging a new poetics in extended rhythm – breath-pattern from the language of jazz, hebrew cantillation & a 40-page sentence from Neal Cassady. As contemplative, the flicker between catching his mind 'moving naked in time' into a no re-Vision text, & the satori of catching mind, follows the inner map (eastern & christian) where the first lap of the journey is precisely from nature into mind. 'The beat generation is a holy generation': AG found out only later how wide & deep Kerouac's reading in buddhism had been though no one remembers when he coined that label first printed '52 by John Clellon Holmes (in his novel Go & in The NY Times same year nov 16: 'JK said years ago "This is really a beat generation" '). Via Florida, Yucatan & AG took a year to reach the West coast with W. C. Williams' introduction to Rexroth.

The next 8 years ('54 till his visit '61 to the Far East) began in SF with Neal Cassady ('Dean Moriarty' of On the Road), Peter & Julius Orlovsky (met xmas '54) & Kerouac (arrived same winter). To their Dionysus, the San Francisco Renaissance were Apollo in touch with Charles Olson* & the Black Mountaineers. They included Ferlinghetti (City Lights bookshop); Rexroth who introduced the Six Gallery reading of HOWL! & Lamantia, Whalen, McClure & Synder who read before him that evening. Some of these broke with him after HOWL! was published, tried & acquitted, but with Gary Snyder (& Kerouac) AG's poetic intuition of mind's nothing-centre sharpened into zen: the second leap from mind to the Void it reflects. He read deep in the sutras, made 'pious investigation' of pot, researched its literature & took off for the land of the Bo tree – but not before invitations from Stanford Research ('59) to try LSD & ('60) from sir Humphrey Osmund (who had taken peyote with Chief Frank Takes Gun & given it to Aldous Huxley*) to try psilocybin mushroom, & not before turning Robert Lowell*, Gillespie & Monk on to LSD & what they returned to in '65 was the LSD revolution, a Guggenheim Poetry Fellowship grant that gave them 5 months to travel America before the first joint reading (march '66) of the two Ginsberg's & being asked advice by senators in Narcotic Legislation. That same year AG became a charitable tax-exempt foundation (The Committee on Poetry. Orlovsky president, himself treasurer), made Charles Rothschild his agent, & emerged a generous patron to artists & benefactor through readings to the Tibetans in exile like Trungpa Rinpoche the abbot-poet in America & the tulku Sogyal Rinpoche in the congenial line of the ecumenical rimed ('no biundary') school.

AG has had an often seminal role in most (at least pre-punk) areas where culture actually feels the transformation: human rights, protest, psychedelics, gay lib, music, yoga, earth-friends & the wider ecumenism between major religions. When the vehicle he assembled for his vision – from american indians, veda, zen, from tantra, torah, tibet & tao – falls apart, something from that vision, transplanted, re-embodied, will still be growing into what we are making.

Sylvester Houédard

Other works include: *HOWL! & Other Poems* (1956); *Kaddish & Other Poems* (1958–60) (1961); *Empty Mirror: early poems* (1961); *Reality Sandwiches 1953–1960* (1963); *The Yage Letters* (1963); *The Change: Kyoto-Tokyo Express july 18* (1963); *Planet News 1961–1967* (1968); *Airplane Drea,s* (1968); *Ankor Wat* (1968); *Indian Journals* (1970). See: Jane Kramer, *Paterfamilias. Allen Ginsberg in America* (1970).

177
GODARD, Jean-Luc 1930–

French film and video maker

Born in Paris, son of a doctor, Jean-Luc Godard was educated in Switzerland and at the Sorbonne. While still a student he developed his passion for the cinema, frequenting the Left Bank ciné-clubs, writing reviews and articles (many for the short-lived *Gazette du cinéma* which he co-founded with Eric Rohmer and Jacques Rivette) and making occasional tiny appearances in the amateur films shot by his friends. Back in Switzerland in the early 1950s he made his first two shorts, *Opération béton* (1954), a twenty-minute documentary about the building of the Grande-Dixence dam, on which he worked for a while as a labourer, and *Une Femme coquette*, shot in Geneva in 1955 from a Maupassant short story: a woman decides to deceive her husband with the first man she meets in the park.

On his return to Paris, Godard's career took on a new importance as he established himself as a major film critic with articles and reviews in the magazines *Cahiers du cinéma* and *Arts* and made three further short films in which the characteristic preoccupations of his subsequent features are already apparent: *Tous les Garçons s'appellent Patrick*, *Charlotte et son Jules* and *Une Histoire d'eau* (all 1957–8). This intense activity was part of the necessary preparation for Godard's participation in the eruption of young French talent and originality, journalistically named the New Wave, which startled the film world at the Cannes Film Festival in 1959.

During the period 1960–7 Godard worked within the French commercial film industry and in a context of enormous international publicity to make fifteen full-length feature films of his own and to contribute episodes to seven collective works. In this series of works, ranging from the affectionate gangster film parody *À Bout de souffle* (1960) to the virulent *Weekend* (1967), all the problems of language and communication (both verbal and filmic) are probed in an increasingly jagged and aggressive elliptical style. Throughout this masterly sequence of films Godard explores simultaneously his own relationship to his chosen medium of expression, the social and emotional interconnnections of his characters among themselves and also the fundamental alienation of the individual within modern urban society. In the early films *Vivre sa vie* (1962), *Le Mépris* (1963), *Une Femme mariée* (1964) and the exuberant *Pierrot le fou* (1965) – where there is always the possibility, however tenuous, of some resolution through love – the visual style is lively and full of little surprises and incidental delights. But when, in the later films, an analogous investigation is made into the possibilities offered by political commitment, the mood darkens, whether the ostensible subject is the predicament of the French Left (*Made in USA*, 1966), Mao's* teachings (*La Chinoise*, 1967), or Black Power (*One Plus One*, 1968). Even in his most resolutely political films of this pre-1968 period Godard retains, however, more than a trace of romantic idealism, and political issues are still formulated in simplistic terms (as in his celebrated definition of political film-making as 'Walt Disney* with blood'). The tone of these films remains unmistakably personal, but the despair imposes itself ever more strongly from the joyful vivacity of *Une Femme est une femme* (1962) to the bleak hopelessness of *Masculin féminin* (1966).

Since 1968 almost all of Godard's work has been outside the confines and constraints of the commercial film and television industries. The resulting frustrations – a succession of unfinished works planned or begun in the USA, Canada, Cuba and the Middle East – contrast strongly with his earlier effortless ability to find outlets for his work. The sincerity of Godard's commitment to alternative structures of production cannot be questioned, but his increasing distance from any kind of audience is equally apparent.

The events of May 1968 in Paris brought a new political focus and commitment to his work and, for the next four years, he made a series of films which are radical in both form and content. Paradoxically he financed most of these by using his personal renown as a key figure in the European art cinema, while simultaneously playing down his own role as a film author and eventually submerging his identity in the anonymity of the 'Dziga Vertov* Collective'. During this period he had the unique distinction of making films financed and subsequently rejected by four successive national television institutions: *Le gai savoir* (France, 1968), *British Sounds* (Britain, 1968), *Lotte in Italia* (Italy, 1969), *Vladimir und Rosa* (West Germany, 1970). The most notable films completed and given some kind of showing at this time – though hardly at all in France – are the Czech-made *Pravda* (1969) and *Vent d'est* (1969), co-scripted with a key figure of May 1968, Daniel Cohn-Bendit.

In 1972 Godard and his prime collaborator in the Dziga Vertov Collective, Jean-Pierre Gorin, made a brief return to the commercial cinema with *Tout va bien* (1972), in which the contradictions of Godard's stance are very apparent. Subsequently Godard has worked largely in video, in collaboration with Anne-Marie Miéville. Two major films emerged from the litt-le-seen video material produced at Grenoble (1973–7) – *Numéro deux* and *Ici et ailleurs* (both 1975) – but Godard's subsequent work at Rol in Switzerland has been largely in video and has effectively cut him off from any influence on current developments in world cinema until the film *Sauve qui peut (la vie)* in 1980.

While Godard's later experiments are invisible because they remain largely unseen, his earlier innovations are almost equally concealed by the extent of his impact on world film-making which has made them appear familiar and almost conventional. In retrospect it is difficult to dispute the view that, of all the new film-makers to emerge in the late 1950s and early 1960s, Jean-Luc Godard was the most influential. Some of his contemporaries, such as Alain Resnais*, were equally radical, but whereas a film like *L'Année dernière à Marienbad* (1961) still looks like an avant-garde film, the lessons of Godard's work in the early 1960s have been absorbed into the mainstream of contemporary cinema. Though a film as revolutionary in its time as *À Bout de souffle* can now, some twenty years later, seem to resemble a routine made-for-television gangster film in its cutting techniques and throwaway style, many of Godard's works from that incredibly productive period – among them *Une Femme est une femme*, *Pierrot le fou* and *Weekend* – still retain their power to surprise and delight us.

Dr Roy Armes

Other films are: *Le petit soldat* (1960); *Les Carabiniers* (1963); *Bande à part* (1964); *Alphaville* (1965); *Deux ou trois choses que je sais d'elle* (1966); *Jusqu'à la victoire* (unfinished, 1970); *Lettre à Jane* (1972). Video series include: *Six fois deux*; *Sur et sous la communication*; *France, tour, détour, deux enfants* (all 1975–7). See: Richard Roud, *Jean-Luc Godard* (1967); Ian Cameron (ed.), *The Films of Jean-Luc Godard*; Tom Milne (ed.), *Godard on Godard* (1972); Royal S. Brown (ed.), *Focus on Godard* (1972); James Roy MacBean, *Film and Revolution* (1975).

178
GODEL, Kurt 1906–78

US mathematician

Godel was born in Brno, Czechoslovakia and educated

at the University of Vienna, where he took his PhD in 1930. He settled in the United States in 1940, and was naturalized in 1948. From 1953 to the end of his life he held a chair at the Institute for Advanced Study, Princeton.

It was in 1931 that his paper 'Über formal unentscheidbare Sätze' ('On Formal Theoretical Advances') was published. It hit the mathematical world like a thunderbolt. Von Neumann* stopped a lecture series in its tracks and began to lecture on the work of Godel. David Hilbert was reported as being 'very angry' that the young Godel had upset the applecart of his famous 'Hilbert Programme', which envisaged the eventual formalizatiion into one categorical system of the entire body of mathematics. What Godel had proved was that no complete, final, categorical formalization of mathematics was possible in principle. It could be shown that mathematics was capable of transcending any state of mathematics given beforehand. There was no 'final state of mathematical knowledge' any more than there was a 'final prime number', a fact, incidentally, proved by Euclid more than two thousand years before. It was Euclid who first introduced the idea of systematic rigour into mathematics; working from a few basic axioms and definitions, the whole body of geometry known to the Greeks could be built up. But in the nineteenth century rigour problems in mathematics reappeared. First it was shown that Euclid's Twelfth Axióm was not a necessary truth. It could be negated, giving new kinds of so-called 'Non-Euclidean' geometry. Then Cantor proved the remarkable result that it was impossible in principle ever to put the infinite, non-terminating decimals into a final, categorical order. For suppose it could be done, we would have a sequence listed systematically, something like this:

$$.a_1a_2a_3a_4a_5a_6a_7 \ldots$$
$$.b_1b_2b_3b_4b_5b_6b_7 \ldots$$
$$.c_1c_2c_3c_4c_5c_6c_7 \ldots$$
$$.d_1d_2d_3d_4d_5d_6d_7 \ldots$$

[We concentrate on decimals between 0 and 1. Each letter stands for a single digit.]

Now form the infinite, non-terminating decimal

$$.\bar{a}_1\bar{b}_2\bar{c}_3\bar{d}_4\bar{e}_5 \ldots$$

The bar over the top is used to indicate that each digit has been changed (by adding 1, except in the case of 9, which is replaced by 0). It is not difficult to see that this new decimal differs from every decimal in the previous list. It differs from $.a_1a_2a_3a_4a_5 \ldots$ in the *first* decimal place, it differs from $.b_1b_2b_3b_4b_5b_6 \ldots$ in the *second* place, and so on.

Godel showed, by a much more complicated argument involving the numbering of mathematical symbols, that if mathematics was all deducible from a given set of axioms, its provable formulae would be capable of being put into a single categorical list; like the alleged list of infinite decimals. But then it could be shown that the list was not complete. There were other formulae, evidently true, which, it could be shown, did not appear anywhere on the list. So mathematics was an intrinsically incompletable enterprise: the assumption of its completability led to a contradiction.

Godel's result has still not been assimilated into a fully satisfactory view of mathematical proof. There are still many parts of mathematics in which serious doubts arise about the rigour of the arguments, and the process of axiomatization reduces these doubts to doubts about the consistency of sets of axioms. But how can one ever be sure that a set of axioms is consistent, if there is no final mathematical axiom system to serve as touchstone? This is the difficulty which Godel's theorem underlined.

In 1940 Godel produced a monograph, *The Consistency of the Continuum Hypothesis*, which showed that the body of mathematics is at least as relatively consistent as the continuum (the system of infinite decimals): if the former is inconsistent, so is the latter, and vice versa.

Christopher Ormell

See also: *Rotating Universe in General Relativity Theory* (1950). For a lucid account of Godel's work, see Ian Stewart, *Concepts of Modern Mathematics* (1975).

179
GOLDING, William Gerald 1911–

English novelist

William Golding's reputation has grown considerably since the early 1960s. The symbolist and notion-monger who did not always escape derision has become the admired subject of critical dissertations and extensive reappraisals, and several much younger writers, notably Alan Garner, have testified to their admiration of his work. Of all contemporary English novelists he is perhaps the most substantially rooted in the preoccupations of his own century. Existentialism, for example, finds more than a mere echo in such books as *Free Fall* (1959) and *Pincher Martin* (1956), while a neo-Wellsian* view of human development is reflected in *The Inheritors* (1955), and *Lord of the Flies* (1954) is easily accepted by many as a grim backward glance at totalitarianism.

It is this last novel which has earned Golding his broadest popularity. Originally a reinterpretation of R. M. Ballantyne's Victorian adventure story *The Coral*

Island, it concerns the creation of a sinisterly adult hierarchy among a group of schoolboys cast away on an uninhabited island. Golding's personal experience of children, and his consequent refusal to sentimentalize them, derived from his years as a schoolmaster at Bishop Wordsworth's school, Salisbury, where, aged forty-three, he began writing novels after beginnings as a dramatist and poet.

His early life, poised between his family's rationalism and his own concern with religious influences, was surely instrumental in shaping his predominant interest, as a writer, in man's discovery of his own nature. Especially potent are the ideas of grace, sin and guilt which recur from novel to novel, most successfully in the metaphysical culture fashioned by the protagonists of *Lord of the Flies*, a civilization whose bonds finally crack with the murder of the wise and myopic Piggy.

Objections to Golding nearly always culminate in complaints at the arch way in which he manipulates symbol. Notable in this respect was the response to *The Spire*, a book based on the completion of the spire of Salisbury Cathedral and generally darker and denser in texture than any he had written before. Yet such cavilling becomes insignificant beside considerations of his technical boldness, and his comprehensive views of an errant and bewildered humanity. Among the shriller and infinitely more parochial voices of the modern English novel, Golding's quietly authoritative tone commands immediate and enduring respect.

Jonathan Keates

Other works include: *Poems* (1934); *The Pyramid* (1967); *Darkness Visible* (1979).

180
GOODMAN, Paul 1911–72

US writer

Paul Goodman's ideas represent an original and challenging contribution to literature, politics and psychology. They raise many questions about the function of art, the nature of instincts and the interaction of culture and personality.

In 1931, after graduating from City College, New York, Goodman committed himself to a libertarian career. He improvised continually both in politics and in writing, and by the 1940s was unique in his number of interests: Reichian* sexual liberation, psychodrama, major contributions to the periodical *Politics*, and fiction. Refused tenure by Black Mountain College because of his committed bi-sexuality, Goodman did teach at the Spanish Anarchists Hall, New York, with Robert Duncan, James Baldwin* and the Becks.

Ill-health helped Goodman avoid the draft but in any case: 'I was having a disagreement with the selec-

tive service and was set to go to jail, though this was entirely against both my prudent principles and my wishes. My philosophical and political position was dodging.'

After *Gestalt Therapy* (1951) Goodman created the Gestalt School of psychoanalysis together with Fritz Perls. Its basis was the Gestalt, 'the whole', an idea of 'the irreducible unity of the socio-cultural animal and physical field in every concrete experience'. But in the 1950s his only outlets were minority periodicals and his sexually honest autobiographical journal *Five Years* (1966).

With *Growing Up Absurd* (1966), on youth culture, Goodman was suddenly popular. He became a mentor and spokesman for the 1960s counter-culture, teaching at San Francisco's 'Experimental College' and publicly supporting draft resisters.

Goodman's popularity as educationalist and activist has obscured his contribution to literature and anarchism. He writes in the classic American tradition of his admired Thoreau in challenging writers to recognize their responsibilities as citizens. The key texts are *May Pamphlet* (1946), the modern equivalent of Thoreau's *On Civil Disobedience*; *Kafka's Prayer* (1947), the first American psychobiography to mix ego-psychology with literature; and the epic novel of communitarian culture, *The Empire City* (1959).

Goodman's aim was to describe and theoretically underpin a libertarian life-style. Although an American romantic, he rejected *laissez-faire* ethics defining happiness as 'freely explored natural instincts in a community of mutual aid' opposed to 'official' happiness which is merely social engineering with financial inducement. Similarly in literature, by using intrusive narrators, surrealist dialogues and random plots Goodman tried to set up a dialogue with his reader. He left the more precise emotions to his lyrics and the most intense poems are those on the death of his son in *Collected Poems* (1972).

Gestalt Therapy is in direct line to the encounter groups of the early 1970s; Goodman's plan for negative government anticipates Ivan Illich*, and the free school movement depends on Goodman's pioneering work and his friendship with A. S. Neill. But Paul Goodman's greatest importance lies in constructing a coherent anarchist ideology.

Maggie Humm

Goodman's other books include: *Communitas* (1947), the influential town-planning critique; *Three Plays* (1965); and the social essays *Utopian Essays* (1962), *People or Personnel* (1965), *Like a Conquered Province* (1967), and *New Reformation* (1970); *Nature Heals, the Psychological Essays; Creator Spirit Come: The Literary Essays; Drawing The Line, The Political Essays*, all ed. T. Stoehr (1977). See also: T. Roszak, *The Making of a Counter-Culture* (1969); B. Vincent, *Paul Goodman et la reconquête du présent* (1976); David deLeon, *The American as Anarchist* (1979).

181

GORKY, Maxim (Aleksey Maximovich Peshkov)
1868–1936

Russian writer

Born in Nizhny Novgorod, since renamed Gorky, on the Volga, his father died when he was four and he was brought up in his mother's family. His grandfather was the owner of a small dye works, a tight-fisted, domineering man who subjected the young Gorky to frequent beatings. His grandmother was a kindly, protective influence, from whom the boy first learned a fondness for folk tales and acquired his first taste for literature. The greed and feuding which marked the relations between the grandfather and his sons, the 'uncles' of Gorky's brilliant autobiographical picture of his early life, *My Childhood* (*Detstvo*, 1913), were symptoms of the financial crisis about to overtake the family and turn them into paupers. Gifted though he was with a phenomenal memory, Gorky had barely any formal schooling and when, at about eleven years of age, he was 'sent out to work' – see *My Apprenticeship* (*V lyudyakh*, 1916) – he had no accomplishments save a largely self-taught ability as a reader and a memory crammed full of his grandmother's stories. His young life then became an untidy saga of apprenticeships, lengthy trips on the Volga and journeyings over southern Russia and the Ukraine – the years and experiences which he later bitterly entitled *My Universities* (*Moi universiteti*, 1922) and formed the final part of his famous autobiographical trilogy. In the 1890s, when his wanderings were over and he took his first steps as a writer, he chose to remember his father's name, Maxim, and to proclaim the bitterness of his early years by adopting the pseudonym Gorky ('bitter'), so that his fame as a writer has become international and assured under the harsh soubriquet of 'Maxim the Bitter'.

His first story 'Makar Chudra', was published in Tbilisi in 1892. It combined realistic setting and portraiture with a romantic internal narrative and set the tone for many other similar types of tale Gorky published during the decade. The realism, though often poetic in its evocation of the natural scene, derived from his experiences during his years of footloose wandering, but the romanticism sprang both from his respect for such eccentric, freedom-loving figures as gypsies or vagabonds and his conviction that mankind needed a romantic ideal in order to escape from the squalor and indignity of capitalist society. In verses, allegories and short stories Gorky celebrated mankind's aim to be free from acquisitiveness and poverty, but his was a vision of freedom with Nietzschean overtones.

It also proclaimed a Promethean heroism, exemplified in Danko who sacrifices his heart in order to lead his people to freedom, or, like the hero of 'Chelkash' (1895), it proclaimed a repudiation of bourgeois standards in the name of freedom. If Gorky's picture of the 'barefoot' migrant workers (the *bosyaki*, as they were known) was often depressing, it also depicted in manifold ways a society undergoing the initial strain of moving from an agricultural to an industrial, urban economy.

Through the portrayal of many victims of social and economic change, of which the most remarkable instances in his stories of the 1890s were 'Konovalov', 'Former People' ('Byvshiye lyudi') and 'The Orlov Couple' ('Suprugi Orlovy'), Gorky extended his search for a positive hero from among the *bosyaki* to the dissident bourgeoisie in the hero of his first novel *Foma Gordeyev* (1899) and the talkative bourgeois intellectuals of his first play *Smug Citizens* (*Meschane*, 1902). This last work contained, for the first time in Gorky's work, the figure of a young proletarian hero whose defiance appeared to be based on the revolutionary political consciousness of his class. Though his second and most famous play *The Lower Depths* (*Na dne*, 1903) explored the disillusionment and degradation of human beings at the bottom of society who are misled by a Christ-like figure's message of comfort, his most famous novel *Mother* (*Mat'*, 1906) emphasized by contrast the revolutionary potential of the working class through achieving political consciousness and leadership. The crude didacticism of the work, modified though it was in later editions, alienated the intelligentsia of the period and brought a decline in Gorky's popularity. Between 1906 and the First World War he lived outside Russia, mostly on Capri, devoting himself to chronicle-type studies of Russian provincial life (*The Life of Matvey Kozhemyakin*, 1911–12) and his autobiography, but also writing a minor masterpiece, *A Confession* (*Ispoved'*, 1908), an interesting short novel on the theme of 'God-building'.

During the October Revolution and the Civil War, though a supporter of the Bolsheviks, Gorky did much to help fellow-writers regardless of their political affiliations. His quarrel with Lenin* over the question of the technical intelligentsia and poor health combined to send him into a second exile on Capri and it was there that he remained for a dozen or so years, despite his triumphant official return to Soviet Russia in 1928. The final years of his life as a writer were noteworthy for probably his best novel *The Artamonov Affair* (*Delo Artamonovykh*, 1925), two outstanding plays *Egor Bulychov and Others* (1932) and *Dostigaev and Others* (1933), and his most conspicuous failure, the unfinished chronicle novel, *The Life of Klim Samgin*. He died in mysterious circumstances in 1936.

In the Soviet Union and throughout the Communist world Gorky has become known as the father of Socialist Realism. As the first Russian writer to depict the struggle of the factory proletariat, especially in his novel *Mother* and his play *Enemies* (*Vragi*, 1906), he deserves this title, but neither by origin nor by experience was he strictly speaking a member of the industrial proletariat. His strengths as a writer derived from the freshness and brilliance of his visual powers, the fecundity of his characterization and the compassion that he brought to his portrayals of humanity in the lower depths of society. Long-windedness, formlessness and a lack of intellectual interest were his principal weaknesses. The Volga and its major cities provided the setting for his greatest work, and commitment to that world rather than to a specific political attitude was the mainstay of his achievement. The merchants and the rich mercantile life of the Volga, the intellectuals, mostly of bourgeois origin, who protested vainly at the mercantilism of the period – these types figured almost as prominently in Gorky's work as did the 'former people' and other victims of capitalism.

Gorky's is by and large a world divided between the grasping, Old Testament ethos of his grandfather and the compassionate New Testament idealism of his grandmother. The vision of a world transformed owes much in his work to the imagery of folk-tale and legend which he first received from his grandmother. In this, as in so many other ways, the durability of his reputation has come to rest upon the autobiographical element in his writing, just as the image of the man himself, Maxim Gorky, has transcended the literary images with which he is associated. His advocacy of the transforming power of work, so appropriate to a Soviet Union in the throes of the First Five-Year Plan, turned him towards the end of his life into a Soviet establishment figure, but this statuesque, official version of his reputation has yielded to a more lasting version based on the roguish nonconformism and bitter vitality of his power as a writer.

Professor Richard Freeborn

Other works: *Three of Them* (London 1905); *Twenty-six Men and a Girl and Other Stories* (London 1928); *Reminiscences of Tolstoy, Chekhov and Andreyev* (London 1934); and *Untimely Thoughts: Essays on Revolution, Culture and the Bolsheviko* (London 1970). About Gorky: an early biography is among the best, A. Kaun, *Maxim Gorky and his Russia* (London 1932). General introductions are offered by F. M. Borras, *Maxim Gorky the Writer: An Interpretation* (1967); R. Hare, *Maxim Gorky: Romantic Realist and Conservative Revolutionary* (1962); and D. Levin, *Stormy Petrel* (1967). Some detailed analysis of his work is offered in I. Weil, *Gorky: His Literary Development and Influence on Soviet Intellectual Life* (1966). Bertram D. Wolf provides a good account of Gorky's relationship with Lenin in *The Bridge and the Abyss* (1967). A more recent digest of Gorky's life and work is G. Habermann, *Maksim Gorki* (1971).

182

GRAMSCI, Antonio 1891–1937

Italian Marxist

Born to a modest Sardinian family, Gramsci won a scholarship that enabled him to go to Turin, the red centre of Italy, to study philology. There he joined the Socialist Party (PSI) and was soon contributing extensively to several of the party's publications. In 1919 he founded, with Palmiro Togliatti, the *Ordine Nuovo*, a socialist weekly that rapidly became the organ of the movement to establish workers' councils in the factories, and which was a leading force during the strikes of 1920. In 1921, disillusioned with the PSI's failure to provide its full support for the Turin movement, Gramsci participated in the creation of the Italian Communist Party (PCI) at Livorno. From 1922 to 1924 he worked at the Secretariat of the Comintern, first in Moscow and then in Vienna. Back in Italy he became leader of the PCI, until in 1926 he was arrested by the fascist government and sentenced to twenty years' imprisonment – despite the immunity he should have gained by being a Member of Parliament. The rest of his life was spent in jail. There, struggling against illness, he recorded his reflections in twenty-nine notebooks which have become a landmark in Marxist thinking.

Like the majority of intellectuals of his generation Gramsci began under the influence of the idealist philosopher Benedetto Croce*: it was the impact of the Russian Revolution that turned him towards Marxism, and in particular Lenin's* interpretation of Marx. Whereas the Second International had presented the socialist revolution as the mechanical and unavoidable consequence of the development of the economic contradictions inherent in capitalism, Lenin had rejected this economistic conception in favour of a political practice that saw politics as the conscious intervention in history of organized social groups. In his own work Gramsci concerned himself with the need to develop, at the level of theory, the implications of Leninism, so as to provide the bases for a re-elaboration of historical materialism in terms of 'a science of history and politics'. This led him to evolve a new strategy for socialist revolution, on which his importance rests.

The cornerstone of Gramsci's thought is his theory of hegemony. Hegemony, which he defined as 'political, intellectual and moral leadership', consists in the capacity of a dominant class to articulate its interests and the interests of other social groups, and to become in that way the leading force of a 'collective will'. The latter is forged through ideological struggle because it is cemented by a common view of the world that Gramsci calls an 'organic ideology'. Hence the strategical importance Gramsci attached to intellectuals: in the process of establishing the hegemony of a class they are the ones who elaborate those organic ideologies which are conceived as the articulation, around an organizing principle provided by the hegemonic class, of a series of ideological elements expressive of allied groups and of the national tradition and culture.

The nature of ideology, therefore, in Gramsci's hands, already differs radically from the traditional interpretation of Marx, which sees ideology as 'false consciousness'. For Gramsci ideology is 'the terrain where men become conscious of themselves and of their tasks', the terrain where they are constituted as 'subjects'. In fact the notion of hegemony implies a much wider conception of politics, which is no longer understood as being exclusively an activity of domination exercised at the level of the state (political society). Rather, Gramscian politics includes a positive aspect of moral and intellectual direction, and so acquires a character of universality, the power of creation of values. His equation, philosophy = ideology = politics, does not mean the reduction of philosophy to a mere political ideology, but the attribution to politics of a philosophical aspect of the definition of the general interest of a society. It is also this enlarged conception of politics that provides the meaning of the controversial notion of the 'integral state' that Gramsci defines as including both civil and political society, hegemony and coercion.

The socialist revolution, therefore, should not simply be pursued through a frontal attack on the state ('war of movement'): rather that final stage must be prepared by a long and difficult period of 'war of position', during which the working class should be able, through political and ideological struggle, to disarticulate the system of alliances of the bourgeoisie, and to create a new national-popular collective will in which it will be the hegemonic force.

This strategy of 'war of position' is often presented as the one expressing, or adapted to, the specific conditions of advanced capitalist societies; and it is for this reason that Gramsci is called 'the theorist of the revolution in the West'. But its field of application is certainly wider and what Gramsci provides through the concept of hegemony is in fact the key to the conception of a democratic socialism. The idea of a democratic socialism based on a wide popular consensus around the working class has had an important influence on the strategy of the PCI, and from that point of view Gramsci can be considered as the theoretical forerunner of 'Eurocommunism'. This is, indeed, one of the reasons for the increasing interest in his writings. From being virtually unknown outside Italy he has become, since the late 1960s, one of the most important Marxist thinkers of the century. However, all the potentialities present in his elaboration of the concept of hegemony are far from having been fully exploited. This is particularly true with regard to his intuition that social antagonisms do not simply take place between classes as economic agents, but between complex popular forces constituted through a plurality of antagonisms emerging at the political and ideological levels, and that political struggle cannot easily be reduced to 'class-struggle'. Such a position is unacceptable to the orthodox Marxists, the 'hard-liners' who accuse Gramsci's strategy of representing a compromise that merely procrastinates the revolution indefinitely. But more and more Marxists are beginning to realize the shortcomings of the orthodox position and the need to overcome them. In the elaboration of a Marxism free from reductionism and economism – that would invalidate the liberal claim that those shortcomings are inherent in the Marxist conception and cannot be overcome – Gramsci's place will indeed be of prime importance.

Chantal Mouffe

See: *Quaderni del Carcere*, ed. Valentino Gerratana (1975), the best edition of the Notebooks. In English: *Selection from Prison Notebooks*, ed. Hoare and Nowell Smith (1971); *Selection from the Political Writings, 1910–1920 and 1921–1926* (2 vols, 1978 and 1979). About Gramsci: A. Davidson, *Antonio Gramsci: Towards an Intellectual Biography* (1977); J. M. Cammett, *Antonio Gramsci and the Origins of Italian Communism* (1967); C. Buci-Glucksmann, *Gramsci and the State* (1979); C. Boggs, *Gramsci's Marxism* (1976); James Joll, *Gramsci* (1977); *Gramsci and Marxist Theory*, ed. C. Mouffe (1979); Anne Showstack Sassoon, *Gramsci's Politics* (1980).

183

GRASS, Günter 1927–

German writer

Grass advanced from the small, but influential, German literary scene around the Group '47 to international recognition with Ralph Manheim's translation into English in 1961 of The Tin Drum (*Die Blechtrommel*, 1959), receiving both extravagant praise and expressions of disgust. Most amazing about this success was that most reviewers were able to unite on very little about his novel other than that it was dazzling though not yet quite understandable. Serious critics were still not sure that obscenity, vulgarity and, simply, childishness had a place in serious literature. However, there was no denying that the publication of his first novel was both a literary and a historical event, for Grass was of the generation of the Hitler Youth. In 1945 he was a teenage prisoner of war, later a black marketeer, a stone-cutter chiselling tombstones and a jazz timpanist on snare and washboard. At the end of the otherwise quiet 1950s, his voice seemed loud and disturbingly alone in Germany, making 'wicked' insinuations about the character and continuity of his native country's recent history.

That Grass was born on 16 October 1927 in Danzig (now Gdansk, Poland) is more than biographical incident; often mischievous autobiography is a central element. When he wrote about that era and area he fulfilled the highest critical expectations, that is to say, when his novels moved to post-war West Germany his genius ebbed. An admirer of James Joyce* and Marcel Proust*, he likewise rose above sentimentality in feeling exiled from place and time. His characters in the 'Danzig trilogy', *The Tin Drum, Cat and Mouse* (*Katz und Maus*, 1961, trans. 1963) and *Dog Years* (*Hundejahre*, 1963, trans. 1965), were the little people, the lower middle class who filled the ranks of Hitler's* following. Capably reproducing their dialects, Grass made his picaroons mouth the 'Great Ideas' of that time with ignoble unpretentiousness.

Grass's father was a grocer in the lower-class Danzig suburb of Langfuhr; his mother, a Kaschubian, an exotic tribe that filters into his writings and recipes. Grass never finished school, a fact, he remembers, 'that kept me from getting a job as a night-time radio programme director and from putting my writings on a shelf somewhere, to gather dust'. After serving in the armoured infantry, he worked as a farm labourer and in a potash mine. He studied painting and sculpture at the Art Academies in Düsseldorf and Berlin, had some minor glory at exhibitions and he still designs the dust jackets for his books. He met his wife, a ballet dancer, while hitch-hiking through Switzerland. They moved to Paris in 1956 where he finished writing *The Tin Drum*.

Grass returned to Berlin, where he still lives with his wife and four children. He has had to fend off innumerable attempts by right-wing groups to have his books banned for their earthiness and grotesque caricatures of Germans. The Bremen Senate refused him the city's literature prize (already awarded to him by the Art Committee) because they felt his book was a disgrace – specifically, they took offence at the blunt descriptions of sex. In 1960 he received the Berlin Critics' Prize. For a while he worked as consultant and speech writer for Willy Brandt's mayoral campaign. Later, he would drive up and down Germany in a Volkswagen bus making speeches for the Social Democrats. A French panel in 1962 selected *The Tin Drum* as the best foreign language book of the year. In 1965 he was awarded the Federal Republic's most prestigious literary accolade, the Georg Büchner Prize. A plaster bust of him can be found in the Regensburg Memorial Temple, Valhalla. He has been elected to the German Academy of Arts and the American Academy of Arts

and Sciences. In short, he is an established gadfly; his books are banned in the German Democratic Republic; his favoured audience, the young non-orthodox left, see him as a middle-age reformer; the German masses who perhaps know something about him wish he had been a prophet in some other country.

The hero of Grass's picaresque first novel begins by saying: 'Granted: I am an inmate of a mental hospital.' He relates the story of his decision to stop growing at the age of three. He remains a three-foot dwarf until 1945, when he grows another eleven inches but is then cursed with a hunch-back. Often, Oscar Matzerath thinks he is Jesus of Nazareth (the two names rhyme in German). He is a little tyrant, always able to have his way because he has the rare talent of being able to shatter glass with a stupendously shrill voice. Oscar always has his tin drum at his side with which he can conjure up spirits and even throw political rallies into confusion by drumming a different beat. At one level, this is Oscar the resistance fighter and, at another level, it is an allusion to the epithet given to Hitler, the drummer (in the German sense of rabble-rouser). During the war, Oscar is able to combine his two extraordinary talents and joins a troupe of midgets, part of a propaganda company entertaining the troops at the front. His size evokes pity. After the war, neither the Soviets nor the Americans even think of holding little Oscar responsible for anything that has happened.

Grass has a peasant's instinct for the tangible, earthy image and craftsman's sense of conservative style. Oscar and Danzig are both a microcosm and a macrocosm of Germany and Central Europe. The novel is packed with historical allusions, e.g. Germans refusing to grow up to the responsibilities of democracy in the Weimar Republic or not bearing their guilt after the Holocaust. With seeming ease Grass parodies German propaganda, philosophy and literature, exposing the penchant for inscrutable abstractions. Oscar hangs his drum around a statue of Jesus, begging Him for a little miracle in these hard times under Hitler. But Jesus remains still. The implication is that the churches never played a significant tattoo of protest when they were called upon to do so.

In *Local Anaesthetic* (*Örtlich betaeubt*, 1969, trans. 1970) a teacher in a dentist's chair tries to decide what to do about one of his brightest pupils. The young man is plotting a public immolation of his pet dachshund to protest against the use of napalm in Vietnam. 'But why a dog?' his teacher asks. 'Because Berliners love dogs more than anything else.'

In *The Flounder* (*Der Butt*, trans. 1978) the reader is carried through Baltic culinary and sexual history, exploring the themes of male/female domination, as a mythical omniscient fish is placed on trial before a feminist tribunal.

Grass is aware of his image as a 'committed writer' and as the 'conscience of the nation', descriptions which he reformulates as a 'literary court jester' – a creature whose powers must serve such many-sided interests (political, aesthetic, personal) that the contradictions in those roles will deflect and limit effectiveness. If he is sceptical about the political force of one individual's attraction, he is hopeful about the influence of art and artists as such: 'Something we must get through our heads is this: a poem knows no compromise, but men live by compromise. The individual who can stand up under this contradiction and act is a fool and will change the world.'

Frank Steele

Other novels: *From the Diary of a Snail* (*Aus dem Tagebuch einer Schnecke*, 1972, trans. 1973); *Das Treffen in Telgte* (1979); *Kopfgeburten – oder die Deutschen Sterben aus* (1980). Plays include *The Wicked Cooks* (*Die bösen Köche*, 1957, trans. 1967) and *The Plebeians Rehearse the Uprising* (*Die Plebejer proben den Aufstand*, 1965, trans. 1966). *Selected Poems* (trans. 1966); *New Poems* (trans. 1968). See also: W. Gordon Cunliffe, *Günter Grass* (1969); John Reddick, *The Danzig Trilogy of Günter Grass* (1974); Kurt Lothar Tank, *Günter Grass* (trans. 1969).

184
GRAVES, Robert Ranke 1895–

English writer

Robert Graves was born on 24 July 1895 in London where his father, the Irish poet Alfred Perceval Graves (author of the popular song 'Father O'Flynn'), was a schools inspector. He won a scholarship to Charterhouse and from there planned to go up to Oxford. However, when England declared war on Germany Graves enlisted with the Royal Welch Fusiliers. His experience of the trenches led to the realistic war poems in *Over the Brazier* (1916), though he later repudiated these poems. On 24 July 1916 he was reported dead of wounds received at the Somme and was thus able to read his own obituary in *The Times*. His apparent resurrection was described in his poem 'The Survivor' from *Poems and Satires* (1951).

In January 1918 the shell-shocked poet married Nancy Nicholson, an eighteen-year-old feminist who refused to use her married name. Graves had too many medical and marital difficulties to take his BA at St John's College, Oxford, but was permitted to submit a newly published critical work *Poetic Unreason and Other Studies* (1925) as a B.Litt. thesis and graduated in 1925. The following years Graves and Nancy – with their four children and the American poet Laura Riding – sailed for Cairo where Graves was Professor of English for a year. After they returned to England Graves left Nancy with the children and went with Laura Riding

to Deya, Majorca. His break with England was immortalized in the title of his classic autobiography *Goodbye to All That* (1929, revised 1957).

Like Nancy, Laura Riding was a militant feminist and had a decisive influence on Graves who began to assert the feminine principle as the supremely creative impulse. Two years after the successful publication of his historical novels on Imperial Rome – *I, Claudius* and *Claudius the God* (1934) – Graves left Majorca on the outbreak of the Spanish Civil War and spent the Second World War in England as three of his children had joined the armed forces. When the war ended he returned to Majorca; he had parted from Laura Riding but her influence permeated his major mythographical work *The White Goddess* (1948, amended and enlarged 1952).

Graves had decided that the survival of poetry depended on the celebration of women as earthly representatives of the eternal Muse – the White Moon Goddess. To defend the tradition of love-poetry against the prevailing anti-romantic tendency of modernism, he erected an elaborate and controversial theoretical edifice in its honour. The White Moon Goddess symbolized the three stages of womanhood (mother, mate and mourner): poetry was to be achieved by religious invocation of the Goddess through a woman possessed by her, and indifference to the Goddess meant creative death. His key poem on the Goddess theme was 'To Juan at the Winter Solstice' from *Poems 1938–1945* (1946); the Juan of the title was a child of Graves's second marriage to Beryl Pritchard with whom he had resettled in Majorca.

Graves's output has been prodigious; he has written more than a hundred books of fiction, mythography, criticism, translation and poetry. His tenacious belief in the necessity of love-poetry and his aristocratic bearing have made him perhaps the most romantic figure in modern English poetry. Yet his romanticism is expressed with a fastidious regard for language and a classical severity of style. He has received many honours – he succeeded Auden* as Professor of Poetry at Oxford in 1961 and was awarded the Queen's Gold Medal for Poetry in 1968 – but has remained an aloof and somewhat anachronistic man of letters.

Alan Bold

Graves's *Collected Poems* was first published in London in 1938 and has been rigorously revised and updated at regular intervals ever since; his literary criticism includes *The Common Asphodel* (1949) and *The Crowning Privilege* (1955). See: Douglas Day, *Swifter than Reason* (1963); Michael Kirkham, *The Poetry of Robert Graves* (1969).

185

GREEN, Henry 1905–73

English novelist

'Henry Green' was the pen-name of Henry Vincent Yorke, a businessman who in later life inherited the managing directorship of his father's engineering form. Green began his first novel while at Eton, and he was still a student at Oxford when it was published. Despite some occasional gaucheness, *Blindness* (1926) is a remarkable imaginative achievement. It tells how a young man, John Haye, comes to terms with the loss of his sight after a senseless accident. It does so with a total lack of sentimentality. Such is Green's assurance that he seems unaware that there are pitfalls to be avoided. Right from the start, he displays the detachment that is a notable feature of his writing. He is the least intrusive of authors. *Blindness* is John Haye's book, the book of a man who learns to see with words.

Green's second novel, *Living* (1929), is his most original. He wrote it after working for a few months on the shop floor in the family business, where he made the acquaintance of working men. As he recounts in his autobiography, *Pack My Bag* (1940), he was delighted and stimulated by what the men had to say, and particularly by the way they said it: their speech, to his ever-alert ears, was as inventive as it was unselfconscious. *Living* is one of the few works of fiction in English to deal with people *working*. It celebrates the resilience of factory workers, fated to live in mean houses and to toil for long hours for meagre wages, without a hint of didacticism. *Living* is a true novel, not an exercise in moral outrage.

In *Party Going* (1939) Green is among his own kind – socially, that is. The idle rich are looked at in this comedy of manners with the same eye that examined the industrious poor in its predecessor. No judgments are made, however, on the bright young things who are forced to stay in a hotel near Victoria Station because of the fog that has delayed their departure to France. There is a suggestion of menace, of gathering darkness, behind the flippancy and casual cruelty of the entrenched week-enders – it is present in the novel's opening sequence, in which a pigeon falls dead in front of the eccentric Miss Fellowes, who takes the carcass to the ladies' lavatory, where she washes it clean.

During the Second World War, Green worked in London in the Fire Service. Once again, he found himself among 'ordinary' people. Convinced that his own death was imminent, he wrote his three best books in quick succession: *Caught* (1943), *Loving* (1945), and *Back* (1946). *Caught* contains memorable descriptions of the Blitz, but more memorable still is the sense of dislocation, of madness all about and all around, that comes with war: this sense pervades the narrative. *Loving* is the happiest, and most lyrical, of Green's

extraordinary books – it is set in a country house in Ireland, where the somewhat seedy butler, Charley Raunce, is surrounded by women. Love comes to this disreputable character, as it often does in Green's work to other not especially deserving people: it touches him with grace for a while. The last scene of *Back*, the hero of which is also called Charley, is the most sensuously beautiful passage in his entire *oeuvre*: without indulging in specific sexual details, Green conveys that feeling that lovers have of time having stopped, of tenderness triumphing over mere communication.

Three more novels followed: *Concluding* (1948), *Nothing* (1950), and *Doting* (1952). *Concluding* is about a scientist, Mr Rock, through whose eyes Green shows the reader a world both lovely and sinister; the last two books, written mainly in dialogue, contain typically funny and deliciously irrelevant Green asides, but are thin on detail – his people now are shadows. But perhaps that is the point.

Green's distinction and originality can best be demonstrated by some words of his own. In *Pack My Bag*, he describes the function of prose: 'It should slowly appeal to feelings unexpressed, it should in the end draw tears out of the stone, and feelings are not bounded by the associations common to place names or to persons with whom the reader is unexpectedly familiar.' He is a master of unexpressed feelings, of bright language used as camouflage. He allows his people to be wholly themselves. He looks on the kindly and the mean alike with the same disinterest.

Paul Bailey

See: John Russell, *Henry Green: Nine Novels and an Unpacked Bag* (1960).

186

GREENE, Graham 1904–

British novelist

After an education at Berkhamstead School (where his father was the headmaster) and Balliol College, Oxford, where he read History, Graham Greene was for a time a sub-editor on *The Times* and film critic for the *Spectator*. During the Second World War he was involved in intelligence work in West Africa; in the autobiography of his early years, *A Sort of Life* (1971), Greene comments on the affinities between the spy's trade and the writer's. An insight into this author's temperament can be found in the same book where he describes how he played Russian roulette as an antidote to boredom. He continues, 'It was the fear of boredom which took me to Tabasco during the religious persecution, to a *léproserie* in the Congo, to the Kikuyu reserve during the Mau-Mau insurrection, to the emergency in Malaya and to the French war in

Vietnam.' Greene is unusual among English novelists, often rightly accused of parochialism, in the range of his settings and his political sense, the two drawing together in the list above. A feeling of despair, allied to boredom, descends frequently on his protagonists and is only modified – sometimes aggravated – by the Catholicism of many of them. Greene himself was received into the Catholic church in his twenties and the church and its rituals are in the background of much of his work. Often the religious consciousness serves only to heighten the certainty of damnation. The landscape – 'Greeneland' – of his books can be hellish: one of the characters in the lurid *Brighton Rock* (1938) misquotes slightly from Marlowe's *Dr Faustus*, 'Why, this is Hell, nor are we out of it.' It is a claim that Greene seems determined, sometimes wilfully, to substantiate. Those squalid locales, Haiti for instance in *The Comedians* (1966) or the American states in *The Power and the Glory* (1940) and *The Honorary Consul* (1973), are matched by the frayed despotisms that rule over them. The two latter novels, their publications separated by more than thirty years, both feature priests who have lapsed from the church, one into a literal fatherhood, the other into revolutionary action, but their erratic courses as they try to escape the demands of their creeds are sympathetically presented as preferable to the arid piety enjoined by a rich and reactionary church. Greene's 'damned' heroes are closer to salvation, essentially because of their doubt, self-abasement and unorthodoxy, than the bishops who dine with the generals.

Greene has provided the category 'entertainments' for some of his books. The pleasantly anecdotal *Travels with my Aunt* (1969), the mocking spy story *Our Man in Havana* (1958), the short stories in the collection *May We Borrow Your Husband?* (1967) illustrate a sardonic and urbane quality and a lightness which are not so evident in the earlier thriller-type novels like *Stamboul Train* (1932). Throughout his writing life Graham Greene's interest has centred 'on the dangerous edge of things', a phrase from lines by Browning that Greene would choose as 'an epigraph for all the novels I have written'. From this comes his concern with spies, murderers, men fallen from grace. For all its topicality – and occasional prescience, as in *The Quiet American* (1955) – Greene's oeuvre is consistent in its interests and anxieties. In recent years his popular reputation has grown to a degree unusual for a serious novelist and critical esteem has been largely maintained, although he has sometimes seemed to be re-working the same ground with a conscious self-parody. It is perhaps significant that his most recently published novel, *The Human Factor* (1978), is set in the town of his childhood and deals with the ambiguities of loyalty, a favourite subject.

Philip Goden

Graham Greene's other novels include: *The Heart of the Matter* (1948); *The Third Man* (1950); *A Burnt-out Case* (1961).

187
GREER, Germaine 1939–

Australian writer, journalist and feminist

The eldest of three children of a conservative, middle-class Melbourne family, Germaine Greer had an intensely unhappy childhood marked by her mother's persistent violence towards her and her father's frequent absence. After attending the Star of the Sea Convent, Melbourne, she went to the University of Melbourne, graduating in 1959 in English and French. A year later she started graduate work at the University of Sydney, obtained an MA in English and continued work in that department as a senior tutor. In 1964 a Commonwealth Scholarship to Newnham College, Cambridge, offered the opportunity to leave Australia. A successful PhD thesis on Shakespeare's Early Comedies led to her appointment as a lecturer in English at the University of Warwick, specializing in Elizabethan and Jacobean Drama – a position she held intermittently between 1967 and 1973.

During the late 1960s Greer became actively involved with the London 'underground' scene, writing for papers like *It* and *Oz* and co-founding *Suck*, a radical pornographic paper published from Amsterdam, as well as contributing to more conservative weeklies like the *Spectator* and the *Listener*. The combination of her dazzling appearance, erudition and fondness for sharp repartee made her an obvious choice for mass media, as a TV personality, broadcaster and popular journalist.

Greer's relatively late entry into the feminist arena in 1970 arose from a suggestion by her agent that she write a book on the failure of women's emancipation. Although Greer was associated with radical activity, *The Female Eunuch* (1970) is not in the political tradition of English feminism or in keeping with its emphases on collective action and non-hierarchical structures. More aligned with American feminism, *The Female Eunuch*'s highly autobiographical, anarchic nature, wit, pace and apparent controversiality made it attractive and accessible to both women and men – sold by the million and translated into twelve languages.

Greer's central thesis is that society symbolically castrates women, perpetuating their status as consummately inferior beings and thus maintains a state of oppression which enslaves men as well as women. An exercise in individual 'consciousness-raising', Greer follows the dictum of the personal as political, with liberty and communism being possible through individual intervention, without revolutionary strategy.

The book divides into sections, 'Body' and 'Soul' examining how the stereotype of the 'Eternal Feminine Woman' has been created. Greer argues that the negation of the female libido – sexual and life-giving energy – is the product of conditioning. Women are conditioned by the basic assumptions male-orientated society makes about the female body, mind and sexuality and the way these are reinforced – by rearing and status in the nuclear family, education, the undervaluation of women's work and the pressures of capitalist consumer society. On 'Love', Greer considers that love is essentially narcissistic (self-esteeming), and that the castration of women has been carried out in terms of a masculine–feminine polarity, in which women have been systematically deprived of their narcissism and men have usurped their power and energy, thus reducing all heterosexual contact to a sadomasochistic pattern. What passes for love in our society are perverted forms of mutual dependence, reinforced by 'Altruism', 'Egotism' and 'Obsession' and upheld by 'Romance', 'The Middle Class Myth of Love and Marriage' and the 'Family', each distortion or fantasy being treated separately. Using examples from history, literature and popular culture, Greer traces how society arrived at these present forms of sanctified oppression. Criticizing the nuclear family and the institution of marriage, Greer views the isolated mother–child relationship as the model for exploitative, possessive adult relationships, suggesting alternatively a structure similar to the pre-industrial extended family. Examining male–female antagonism in the section on 'Hate', Greer regards their polarized positions as creating circular systems of oppression. She argues that female conformity to stereotyping is the prime motivator for female self-loathing as well as for men's hatred towards them. Equally men's violence both physical and psychological to women is counteracted by women's psychological oppression of men, to which Greer sees parallels in some aspects of the Women's Liberation Movement.

Greer's anarchic position on feminism and cultivated media persona have made her both identified with and alienated from the Women's Liberation Movement. Her other major published work is *The Obstacle Race* (1979) – the fortunes of women painters and their work – a historical and sociological survey of women painters from the Middle Ages to the twentieth century. Germaine Greer works as a journalist, broadcaster and university lecturer, dividing her time between Tuscany, London and the USA.

Monica Petzal

188

GRIFFITH, David Wark 1875–1948

US film director

When D. W. Griffith joined the Biograph film company in 1908 the narrative fiction film was essentially 'theatrical' in two ways. First, the plots of most films were lifted from stage melodramas. Second, in terms of form, the action was filmed with a single static camera, placed in a centre orchestra position, with each shot corresponding to a complete scene. It is generally accepted that between 1908 and 1913, in the (approximately) 450 one- and two-reel shorts he directed for Biograph, Griffith defined the elements which have, ever since, constituted the 'syntax' of narrative cinema, and which broke the formal theatrical tie. The Griffith films of this period contain close-ups, longshots, fade-outs, iris shots, soft-focus, back lighting, moving camera, and, perhaps most important, rapid cutting and parallel montage. Whilst he was definitely not the first to use many of these devices (despite his claims to the contrary) he was certainly the single figure most responsible for developing their usage in terms of dramatic and psychological effect. However, it is also significant, as regards Griffith's later career, that the plots and characters of these films remained almost entirely rooted in the conventions of the nineteenth-century stage melodrama.

Griffith wanted to make longer, more spectacular pictures to rival contemporary Italian productions and, after overspending problems on the four-reel biblical epic *Judith of Bethulia* (1913), he left Biograph. Under conditions of greater independence he made *The Birth of a Nation* (1915) and *Intolerance* (1916), the two films which, in conventional cinema history, massively overshadow in importance any other works in his filmography. The former, a Civil War drama, is, in its blending of the personal and the epic, the summation thus far of Griffith's art of narrative construction, and effectively established him as the cinema's first 'director as artist'. It is also a profoundly reactionary work, a racist celebration of the Ku Klux Klan, and a vision of the Old South as a model society (Griffith was born and raised in Kentucky, the son of a Confederate officer). *Intolerance* interweaves four narratives (stories set in the present, Judaea at the time of Christ, sixteenth-century France, and Ancient Babylon) in 'A Drama of Comparisons', supposedly illustrating the 'theme' of intolerance through the ages. Parallel montage is here developed to link events occurring within disparate narratives. The massive spectacle of the Babylonian sets is still impressive, as are the fine female performances, but the central idea justifies Eisenstein's* claim that Griffith's 'tender-hearted film morals go no higher than a level of Christian accusation of human injustice'.

Despite its later enormous critical reputation and

significance, *Intolerance* was a financial disaster. Griffith's subsequent work, up to the mid-1920s, can be characterized as melodrama and romance on a smaller and simpler scale. Relationships may be set against a larger historical background – the First World War in *Hearts of the World* (1918), the French Revolution in *Orphans of the Storm* (1921), the War of Independence in *America* (1924) – but there is no sense of the latter interest swamping the former. Events and numbers of characters are pared down in rural dramas like *True Heart Susie* (1919) and *Way Down East* (1920), and in *Broken Blossoms* (1919), set in a foggy, atmospheric re-creation of London. The results, despite occasional lapses into bathos and unsubtle humour, seem more impressive now than the 'monumental' qualities of the epics.

Several of the above titles were produced by United Artists, founded in 1919 by Mary Pickford, Douglas Fairbanks, Chaplin* and Griffith, with a view to producing and distributing 'quality' product, but Griffith's career from approximately 1925 onwards is basically a tale of alienation from the Hollywood system and its values. He directed eight movies between 1925 and 1931, but reassessment has so far rescued from critical oblivion only *Sally of the Sawdust* (1925, with W. C. Fields), and his two sound films, *Abraham Lincoln* (1930) and *The Struggle* (1931). The latter title is a particularly powerful study of a descent into alcoholism. Otherwise Griffith's essentially Victorian sensibility seems hopelessly at odds with the kind of Jazz Age material he was forced to deal with, particularly at Paramount.

However, rather ironically, current critical interest centres precisely on aspects of this 'Victorianism'. His cultivation of the 'childwoman' image, with actresses such as Lillian Gish, has obvious historical importance *vis-à-vis* Hollywood's investment in, and cultivation of, female stereotypes. And, most important, Griffith's work can be seen as the vital link between the nineteenth-century roots of melodrama and the absorption and development of that mode throughout the whole history of the American cinema.

Steve Jenkins

See: Paul O'Dell, *Griffith and the Rise of Hollywood* (1970); Robert M. Henderson, *D. W. Griffith – his Life and Work* (1972).

189

GRIS, Juan 1887–1927

Spanish painter

José Victoriano González, known to painting as Juan Gris, was born in Madrid in 1887. Together with Picasso* and Braque*, Gris was one of the principal figures of the movement known as Cubism, which, although it can now be seen as a logical development from late nineteenth-century painting, was still perhaps the most revolutionary epoch in Western art since the Renaissance.

Six years younger than Picasso and Braque, Gris arrived in Paris in 1906 to live in the same Montmartre building as his compatriot. Here, while earning his living as a graphic artist and draughtsman, Gris made the acquaintance of many young artists, among them Daniel-Henry Kahnweiler, who was to be both his patron and at a later date his exemplary biographer. Familiar with Picasso's and Braque's early essays in Cubist techniques, Gris first revealed his own works in this form in 1911. Rather than imitating the style of his friends, however, Gris had evolved his own Cubist technique through a study of Cézanne and perhaps also his early training in the sciences. The essential nature of his sober and analytical approach to painting is clearly revealed in several important early works, notably *Portrait of Picasso*, *The Artist's Mother*, and several still-lives.

Gris's art developed rapidly over the following years, solving the problems presented by his artistic imagination in economical and ingenious ways. Imaginative use of light and *chiaroscuro*, a willingness to employ effective colour contrasts, the gradual emergence of a vital linear framework as an essential component of his canvases, the introduction of collage – all these are to be found in the work of Gris by 1915. His essentially austere and original mind led to his being recognized as a highly independent artist, but one who at the same time, as his colleagues remarked, understood the rational artistic basis of Cubism perhaps more profoundly than any other.

Although he experimented with subjects more familiar in French painting of the Impressionist period, such as *Still Life Before an Open Window: Place Ravignan* (1915), in general Gris was content to work within the confines of the still-life tradition, exploring the problems and possibilities of the representation of everyday objects and their relationships one to another with dedication and inventiveness.

The end of the First World War at last saw the beginnings of serious critical appreciation of the Cubists and their work, but Gris was now starting to sense, and be alarmed by, the directions in which painting was moving as a result of their innovations. Picasso's protean and innovatory talent had always been far removed from his own single-minded and narrower vision, and he now too felt distanced from Braque both artistically and personally. Gris's last years revealed his art at its most mature, with an increasing preoccupation with that most Spanish of themes, the fundamental natures of illusion and reality and their representation. He contracted pleurisy in 1920, and his last years were darkened by ill-health, aggravated by exhausting work as a designer for the Russian impresario Diaghilev*.

The work of Juan Gris, although limited in subject-matter in comparison with his great contemporaries, is of vital importance in the history of twentieth-century art. In both his work and his lucid verbal exposition of the nature of Cubism, it becomes clear that what for some might have seemed an assumed and temporary style of painting was in reality a serious attempt to 'represent the world' in the spirit of the time, and thus in a new and fresh way. 'Cubism is not a manner but an aesthetic, and even a state of mind; it is therefore inevitably connected with every manifestation of contemporary thought.' Juan Gris's friend and biographer, Kahnweiler, assessed his achievement thus: 'With Gris, as with Raphael, I feel a truly classical aspiration: the creation of a static art, painting which is measured, restrained, calm and pure, which resumes and yet renews the work of earlier times.'

R. P. Calcraft

See: R. Rosenblum, *Cubism and Twentieth Century Art* (1959); *Juan Gris: His Life and Work* (trans. 1969); D. Cooper, *The Cubist Epoch* (3rd edn, 1970).

190
GROPIUS, Walter 1883–1969

German architect

Alongside Frank Lloyd Wright*, Le Corbusier* and Mies van der Rohe*, Walter Gropius is one of the great 'Modern' architects. He helped to evolve an architectural style for the twentieth century which, rejecting nineteenth-century historicism, derived its inspiration from the contemporary world of mechanization and mass-production. This pursuit of a new aesthetic idiom, combined with a burning interest in a new form of visual education which sees the arts as a totality headed by architecture, characterizes Gropius's contribution to the twentieth-century environment. In particular he is remembered as the prime mover of the Bauhaus.

Born in Germany in 1883, Gropius's early architectural theories reflect the ethical and aesthetic goals of William Morris and the English Arts and Crafts Movement – ideas which were transported to Germany by Herman Muthesius and expressed in his book *The English House* published in Germany in 1906. After studying architecture at the universities of Berlin and Munich, Gropius worked as Chief Assistant to Professor Peter Behrens in his Berlin architectural practice from 1908 to 1910. These years coincided with the early existence of the Deutscher Werkbund – an institution set up to encourage links between art and industry and to replace nineteenth-century ideas about standardization

and anonymity. Behrens's work for the A.E.G. company reflected totally these new concerns and undoubtedly influenced Gropius in his search for a new architectural language. The traditional brick walls and pitched roofs of his designs for housing for farm workers of 1906 are soon replaced, in his famous Fagus Shoe-Last Factory of 1911 (built in collaboration with Adolf Meyer), by a flat roof, and a steel-frame structure supporting large panes of glass. This was the first true use of a curtain wall; through the use of the frame construction, the wall became simply a screen stretched between the upright columns. The visual effect is one of transparency and weightlessness bestowing a new significance to the built structure. The Werkbund Exhibition Model Factory, built in Cologne in 1914, displays the same concerns and contributes the first rounded glass wall surrounding a circular staircase to the growing architectural syntax of the International Modern Movement.

On his return from the Western Front in the First World War, and following a brief involvement with a German Expressionist group in Berlin in 1918–19, Gropius was summoned, at the urging of Van der Velde*, to Weimar to become director of a new art school called the 'Staatliches Bauhaus Weimar' which was formed from two existing institutions – the School of Applied Art and the Academy of Art. It was during this period, until his resignation from the Bauhaus and his resumption of private practice in Berlin in 1928, that Gropius consolidated his theories of architecture and of art education and designed one of his most important buildings – the Bauhaus at Dessau.

In 1919 Gropius wrote a Manifesto for the Bauhaus which was accompanied by a woodcut by the German painter Lionel Feininger – one of the several expressionist artists (who also numbered Paul Klee* and Wassily Kandinsky*) to be employed by Gropius at the Weimar Bauhaus. In this piece of polemical writing he set out his ideas about architecture being the queen of the arts and about the necessity of all designs for mass production being based in the crafts. These ideas dictated the structure of art education at the Bauhaus. This consisted of a foundation course which encouraged experimentation in basic form, colour and composition, followed by time spent in a materials workshop – wood, metal, etc. – in which results learnt from the earlier course could be applied to the design of three-dimensional objects which were seen as prototypes for mass production. Well-known names among the staff and students at the Bauhaus included Moholy-Nagy, Mies van der Rohe, Josef Albers* and Marcel Breuer.

Gropius never succeeded in establishing an architectural school at the Bauhaus during his reign – this was left to his successor Hannes Meyer. The Bauhaus building which was constructed in Dessau in 1925 is the high point of Gropius's early architectural career.

Built on a reinforced concrete frame, it is a simple, flat-roofed building housing both work and residential facilities for the students and is characterized internally by an extreme flexibility. Other designs by Gropius during the Bauhaus period include the Sommerfeld Residence of 1921, the Chicago Tribune Building of 1922, the Municipal Theatre of 1922, the Törten development of 1926–8, the prefabricated house for the Werkbund Housing Exhibition of 1927, the Total Theatre of 1927 and the Megastructure of 1928. All contribute unique features to early twentieth-century architecture. In 1930 Gropius designed a car called the Adler Cabriolet.

During the years leading up to the Second World War and the expansion of Nazism in Germany Gropius came first to England, working in partnership with Maxwell Fry (1934–7), and then, in 1937, went to the USA to become Professor of Architecture at Harvard University. This marks the beginning of the final stage of his career during which time he worked for a while with Marcel Breuer and with the 'Architects' Collaborative' which he formed in Massachusetts in 1945 and which was responsible for the Harvard Graduate Centre. He continued to design right through the period, concentrating on private residences and academic centres. Some of his larger projects include the Pan Am Building in New York (1958–63), the US Embassy in Athens and the Gropiusstadt in Germany (1959–71). The aesthetic idiom for all these buildings is either a reworking of his early forms or an extension of them into high-rise structures which combine all the technical and aesthetic discoveries of the 1920s. Above all Gropius's work is characterized by a strong consistency which has had an enormous influence upon the twentieth-century architectural environment.

Penny Sparke

Works by Gropius include: *The New Architecture and the Bauhaus* (trans. 1936) and *Scope of Total Architecture* (trans. 1956). See also: Sigfried Giedion, *Walter Gropius, Work and Teamwork* (1954); James Marston Fitch, *Walter Gropius* (1960); and Hans M. Wingler, *Bauhaus – Weimar – Dessau – Berlin* (1969).

191
GROTOWSKI, Jerzy 1933–

Polish theatre director

The post-war period has seen a rapid growth in the reputation of Polish theatre, several of its writers and directors achieving international status. None has been more influential than Jerzy Grotowski, 'the father of experimental theatre'. Born in Rzeszós, he was educated at the Higher State Theatre School, graduating in acting and directing. He went on to spend a year at the State Institute of Theatre Art in Moscow. In 1957 he became a director at the Stary Theatre in Cracow, his first production being of Ionesco's* *The Chairs*, and in 1959 joined the Theatre of 13 Rows, in Opole. This later changed its name to the Institute for Research on Actor's Method-Theatre-Laboratory, and moved to Wroclaw in 1965. It is with this company that Grotowski has created the majority of his most important work. In 1966 he collaborated with the Royal Shakespeare Company in London, and has also made several working-visits to France and the United States. Since 1966 he has run Pan-Scandinavian acting courses, first in Holstebro, and subsequently in Stockholm. Grotowski has received many awards, both at home and abroad, and in 1967 won the Golden Prize at the International Festival of Theatres in Belgrade.

As the name 'Theatre-Laboratory' suggests, Grotowski is interested in theatre not simply as a performance art-cum-entertainment, but as a subject for detailed quasi-scientific research, with the aim of reaching a deeper understanding of the theatrical experience. He has inspired a number of similar ventures in Western Europe, notably Peter Brook's* International Centre of Theatre Research. Grotowski himself is best known in the West for the book *Towards a Poor Theatre* (1968), a collection of essays and interviews detailing the aims and achievements of the Theatre-Laboratory. He argues for the development of a 'poor' theatre as a response to 'Rich Theatre' ('rich in flaws'), which relies on 'artistic kleptomania, drawing from other disciplines, constructing hybrid-spectacles, conglomerates without backbone or integrity'. He sees deliberate poverty as a means towards infinite variety and the transformation of the traditional dichotomy of the performer–audience relationship into a dialectic. In *Kordian* (1962), for example, spectators sat on beds and chairs within the set of a mental hospital, and were treated as patients. Grotowski eschews all theoretical determiinism, seeking instead the correct spectator–actor relationship for any given performance.

While Grotowski often uses the work of major authors as the basis for his productions, he does not hesitate to alter radically the text and externals of a play (i.e. transferring the action of Wyspianski's nationalistic *The Acropolis* from the Royal Castle in Cracow to a Nazi concentration camp). Accepting that a text 'becomes theatre only through the actor's use of it', Grotowski replaces 'literature' (the written word) with 'performance' (the actor's body). This demands a high level of commitment from the actor, who must be brought to a point where performing is no longer voluntary, but inevitable, 'a state in which one does not "want to do that" but rather "resigns from not doing it"'. (Grotowski's debt to Stanislavsky* is obvious, and acknowledged by him.) Rejecting pre-performance artifice such as make-up, Grotowski's actors develop muscular control to the extent that their faces become endlessly changeable masks. When sufficient physical and psychological control has been attained, the actor is capable of a 'rebirth'. This, according to Grotowski, is the experience he shares with his audience and fellow-actors.

During the 1970s Grotowski claimed to have left theatre behind. Too little is known in the West about recent works such as *Undertaking Mountain* (1977) and *Undertaking Earth* (1977) for them to be adequately assessed, but clearly, in their almost total rejection of theatrical conventions (including audiences), these projects are a continuation of Grotowski's earlier concern for the realization of life itself as a creative activity.

While Grotowski is the main inspiration for the work of the Theatre-Laboratory, he acknowledges a debt to his many colleagues, particularly the architect Jerzy Curawski and the actor Ryszard Cieslak. Amongst the Theatre-Laboratory's major productions have been *Cain* (1960), *Faustus* (1963), *Hamlet* (1964), *The Constant Prince* (1965), and *Apocalypsis cum figuris* (1968–73).

Paul Nicholls

192
GUEVARA, Che (Ernesto Guevara de la Serna)
1928–67

Argentine revolutionary

Che Guevara has become the archetype of a modern revolutionary hero. His image adorns T-shirts and posters; his death provoked two films shown simultaneously around the world. Yet his political philosophy is as little known as his face and beret are familiar.

Guevara was an Argentine, born to a middle-class radical family. He completed a medical course at Buenos Aires University, interspersing his studies with travels around the continent. His very severe asthma put few constraints on his mobility; he travelled under all conditions, taking a series of jobs from mine guard to bookseller.

Growing up in an Argentina dominated by Peronism, there was no political channel for his obvious discontent. He was uneasy with Peron's demagoguery and there was in Argentina no mass socialist alternative. Perhaps his stay in Guatemala was a more definitive experience. Having seen Bolivia in the wake of its 1952 Revolution, Guevara was in Guatemala when the radical democratic regime of Jacobo Arbenz was overthrown by force of arms – arms supplied directly by John Foster Dulles's US State Department. That experience reinforced Guevara's conviction that, faced with a well-armed adversary supported by imperialism, revolutionaries must be prepared for armed struggle.

From Guatemala he went to Mexico, where his wife Hilda Gadea introduced him to the Cuban exiles of the 26 July Movement. He was among the eighty-two people who landed on Cuban soil from the *Granma* in December 1956. Ambushed by Batista's army, only twenty survived; Guevara was among them, and joined the guerilla army in the Sierra Maestra.

The experience of that struggle is documented in Che's *Reminiscences* and his *Guerrilla Warfare*. According to Fidel Castro* Che was a courageous fighter, distinguished by his 'resolute contempt for danger', and it was he who led the victorious 26 July Movement into Havana on 2 January 1959.

As a theorist of revolutionary guerilla warfare, Che has few equals. *Guerrilla Warfare* is a response to – and a reaction against – a theory of socialist change which emphasized the need to pass through a series of prior stages of development before reaching the socialist revolution. This theory, sustained by the Communist parties since the late 1930s, had few attractions for Che – especially after the Guatemalan experience. Like so many Latin American revolutionaries, Che had emerged from a period dominated by a populism whose ambiguities and compromises offered no solution to Latin America's central problem – its subordination to the interests of imperialism. In his view, their vague commitment to 'creating the conditions for change' only postponed the inevitable struggle indefinitely.

In Che's view, where the conditions for revolution did not exist, it was the vanguard (an *advance* guard in his terms) which would by its actions create the conditions; the guerilla group, or *foco*, was to provide a catalyst for revolution. It is in this sense that Che is a theorist of revolutionary war, and not merely a tactician.

This aspect of Che's life and work is well known in the West – particularly through the work of Regis Debray. Yet in the controversies that developed in post-Revolutionary Cuba, Guevara evolved and argued for an alternative strategy whose implications were more far-reaching and contentious than his theses on guerilla war. For in the economic debates, on the question of the relationship with Russia, and the nature and implications of Third World solidarity Che's position (for all its idealism) did challenge the received ideas about socialist construction and the excessively mechanical perceptions of the model of economic development.

In late 1959, Che was appointed Director of the Cuban National Bank; eighteen months later, as Minister of Industry, he was to play a key role in the major debates on economic policy and its political consequences.

In the immediate aftermath of the Revolutionary victory, Cuba's response to economic problems had been essentially pragmatic; the largely American-owned sugar estates were nationalized, the essential services taken into state ownership, wage levels raised and unemployment eliminated. While this took up the slack in the economy, it did nothing to attack the fundamental *structural* problems that beset Cuba; and it became clear, especially after the imposition by the United States of an economic blockade from late 1960 onwards, that the expansion of the economy was no substitute for a development policy. The search for a planning policy moved the Cuban government closer to the Russian model of economic growth and its Cuban advocates – the Cuban Communist Party.

By 1963, however, the Cuban government's disillusionment with Russia over the Missile Crisis, coupled with a growing dependency on Russia, provoked a new debate over development strategies. In the course of that discussion, Guevara emerged as the spokesman for an alternative strategy linking the economic and the political levels.

In brief, the Cuban Communists had argued that the central planning should operate on the principle that each individual enterprise or branch of the economy should raise its level of productivity and maintain its profitability. To achieve that, it would be necessary to introduce work quotas and combine them with material incentives to encourage productivity. At the same time, this would involve a reintroduction of some market mechanisms (particularly in commerce) and a growing differentiation within the workforce.

Against this, Che argued a model that was closer to the Chinese than the Russian experience. Market relations, he believed, should be eliminated. The economy should be treated as a single unit within which resources were distributed according to need, and the society as a whole should take collective responsibility for accumulation and economic development.

The political implications were profound, and related closely to Che's rejection of the concept of a revolution by stages. As he had insisted in his famous essay 'Man and Socialism in Cuba', the socialist transformation of Cuban society should occur simultaneously with its economic development. As an instrument of this policy moral incentives (social solidarity, revolutionary commitment, 'moral' rewards) should replace material recognition, as money was progressively eliminated.

If the Communist plan involved a *de facto* integration into the Eastern European bloc, Che's strategy required the creation of a Latin American – indeed a Third World – structure of mutual support and exchange. Hence the call for 'one, two, three many Vietnams', a policy expressed in the period between 1963 and 1968 in the concept of Latin American Solidarity (OLAS) and the firm commitment to the export of the Cuban revolution which flowed into support for those pursuing the guerilla struggle throughout Latin America. In this Che, as the theorist of the Cuban revolutionary *method*, became a key figure.

The debate over moral and material incentives reflected two concepts of revolutionary change – in Che's case, a still not fully evolved theory of permanent revolution which was both a political position ('Man and socialism') and a response to scarcity, through its socialization. By contrast, the acceptance of differentials involved an implicit concept of revolution by stages to which Che's theory and practice had been consistently opposed.

It was perhaps inevitable that Che should follow the logic of his own position and return to the armed struggle, first in the Congo and later in Bolivia, which, he had argued, was ripe for revolutionary change. Tragically, Bolivia (and Che's *Bolivian Diary*) demonstrated the limitations of Che's politics, his tendency to overstate the catalytic role of the vanguard and to underestimate the importance of a mass vanguard organization which was itself the product of struggle. Typically, too, his concept of the guerilla *foco* rested on peasant support, and said little of the role of the working class. In Bolivia the limited support of the peasantry and the failure to establish a clear link with the workers, and in particular the militant and highly organized miners, led to the isolation of the guerillas. In what became an exclusively military confrontation between the guerillas and a Bolivian army trained in counter-insurgency by the United States, the outcome could not be long in doubt. In October 1968, Che was trapped and captured; rather than attempt to hold a prisoner who would rapidly become a symbol of the continuing struggle against imperialism, his captors killed him on the spot.

Che's death closed finally that alternative course for revolutionary construction. His epitaph, sadly, was the Venezuelan guerilla leader Douglas Bravo's criticism (in 1970) of the Cuban regime. Cuba, he said, had abandoned the guerilla struggle. It was undoubtedly true. For it had become clear by then that the guerilla strategy had failed. And perhaps Che, while he had raised key questions about the transformation of the consciousness of the masses through struggle, and himself led an exemplary life, had forgotten Lenin's* dictum that the emancipation of the working class must be the act of the workers themselves.

Mike Gonzalez

See: Che Guevara, *Reminiscences of the Cuban Revolutionary War* (trans. 1968); *Guerrilla Warfare* (trans. 1967); *Bolivian Diary* (trans. 1969); *Venceremos*, ed. John Gerassi (1968). See also: R. Debray, *Revolution in the Revolution* (1968); M. Lowy, 'The Marxism of Che Guevara', in *Monthly Review* (1973).

193
GUILLÉN, Jorge 1893–

Spanish poet

Jorge Guillén was born in Valladolid. From 1917 to

1923 he was 'lecteur d'espagnol' at the Sorbonne in Paris, and from 1929 to 1931 he was lecturer in Spanish at Oxford. He left Spain for America in 1938 and was Professor of Spanish at Wellesley College, Massachusetts, from 1940 to 1958. In 1957–8 he was the Charles Eliot Norton Professor of Poetry at Harvard. In recent years Guillén has lived more or less permanently in Málaga, Spain. Jorge Guillén was awarded the Premio Miguel de Cervantes in 1976, Spain's first public recognition of one of her greatest poets.

Guillén belonged, with Lorca*, to a group of poets called the Generation of 1927, but he points out that they were united more by a spirit of poetic creativity than by the regulations of a school. The group were inspired not only by Spanish predecessors but also by contemporary English and American writers. Most of the group left Spain during or after the Civil War, but continued to write in exile.

Guillén's personal criteria for poetry are well documented. He opted for 'not quite pure' poetry, poetry and 'other human things' as distinct from the topical but impracticable tenet of Valéry* – *poésie pure*. Moreover, he believed that the poet should create with words as conscientiously as the painter with colours and the sculptor with stone.

Guillén was particularly fascinated by the concept of a unified work, implicit in Baudelaire's *Les Fleurs du Mal* and Walt Whitman's *Leaves of Grass*. His first volume of poems, published in Spain in 1928, heralds the beginning of fifty years of constant creativity, culminating in the complete *oeuvre* which was his goal. *Aire nuestro* ('Our Air', 1968) is the overall title of Guillén's poetic work and includes five volumes, *Cántico* (1950), *Clamor* (I, 1957; II, 1960; III, 1963); *Homenaje* (1967), *Y otros poemas* (1973), and *Final* (1981).

Cántico means a hymn of praise, of joy, and the object to which Guillén directs his sense of joy, and which is also its impulse, is Creation. Essentially Creation is good. The evil side of man's nature is acknowledged but kept within limits; it provides the chorus in the background over which the joyous voice rises. The world offers visible shapes for man's perception, light by which to see, and air by which to breathe and live. Moreover, *Cántico*'s subtitle is *Fe de Vida*, signifying not only the poet's 'faith in life', which is Guillén's starting point, but also the poems of the whole volume, which is a monument to the value of affirmation.

Clamor's subtitle is *Tiempo de historia*. The minor voices of *Cántico*, chaos, evil and death, come forward. Guillén shows us man's world and, in addition, how to come to terms with it, in full knowledge of the difficulties involved. There is no exhortation to mystic flight or diabolic negation, but rather simply to be *human*. And in this we find our salvation, for *Clamor* is dedicated 'To my children, to possible hope'.

Homenaje is a homage by Guillén, and by extension the reader, to the great creative achievement of man.

The poems include homages, glosses, or variations upon the Bible, Greek and Latin classics, and creative writers and philosophers of the civilized world. This volume is dedicated 'To all the muses', and together title and dedication indicate both a general sense of inspiration and also a sense of the conscious involvement of man with man.

Y otros poemas ('And Other Poems') is dedicated 'In my memory, to my father, fire of which I am a spark', suggesting the debt of life that each of us owes to previous generations. The protagonist throughout Guillén's poetry is every reader. Indeed, *Aire nuestro* is dedicated initially 'To whomever may read', the general nature of which has become, in the final dedication, the more specific 'To my friend forever, the future friend'.

Guillén's poetry is characterized by clarity of structure and concision of vocabulary. Each poem is a carefully constructed form in which metre, assonance, rhyme and symbol exactly parallel both the apparent and the essential nature of object or emotion described. Guillén's poetry is undoubtedly difficult because of its unique precision of language, yet its universality is immediately apparent. *Aire nuestro* in fact celebrates the whole of man's life: the effort to be (*Cántico*), to live courageously (*Clamor*), to create (*Homenaje*), and to reflect (*Y otros poemas*). Archibald Macleish's well-known comment on *Cántico* may stand with equal justification as a fitting tribute to the whole of *Aire nuestro*: 'Posterity, if it comes upon the great resounding Yes of *Cántico* among the tumbled fragments of our time, will not believe that No was all we had to answer to the world.'

Elizabeth Matthews

Other works: *El argumento de la obra* ('The Argument of the Work', 1961); *Language and Poetry* (revised versions of the Charles Eliot Norton Lectures); *Federico en persona* ('Federico García Lorca in Person', 1959). See: R. Gibbons and A. L. Geist, *Guillén on Guillén* (1979); I. Ivask and J. Marichal (eds), *Luminous Reality: The Poetry of Jorge Guillén* (1969).

194
GUNN, Thomson William 1929–

English poet

Thom Gunn was born on 29 August 1929 in Gravesend, the son of a successful journalist. In 1937 the family settled in Hampstead where Gunn attended University College School; when he was fourteen his mother died. Before going to Trinity College, Cambridge, Gunn did his National Service in the army which he found, apart from enjoying the discipline of basic training, 'the most boring two years in my life'. For six months after that he worked in Paris, attempting to write a Proustian* novel. When he abandoned that project he returned to poetry, his first love. Gunn published his first collection *Fighting Terms* (1954, revised 1962) while still a Cambridge undergraduate. The title was significant, for while Gunn relied heavily on the traditional iambic pentameter there was a combative quality about the subject matter. The first poem in the book, 'The Wound', was ostensibly spoken by a wounded soldier.

After spending some time in Rome on a studentship, Gunn obtained a fellowship at Stanford University where he worked under the poet and critic Yvor Winters who influenced him to consider consciously the importance of the existential will. Gunn's earliest poetic influences had been Shakespeare and Donne; in America he discovered the poetry of Wallace Stevens*, William Carlos Williams* and Hart Crane*. All these factors combined to make *The Sense of Movement* (1957) one of the most important collections to appear in the 1950s. The most famous poem in the book, 'On the Move', is set in the San Francisco peninsula and describes the urge towards identity of a motorcycle gang. At the time Gunn was unfairly castigated for identifying too easily with the toughs of the poem; in fact the formally patterned verse is directed towards the existential conclusion that excessive energy is only what Gunn calls 'a part solution, after all'. Apart from the thematic obsessions of the book – much of which displayed a pronounced leather-fetishism – Gunn showed he was a poet equally at home with the accentual verse of 'On the Move' or the syllabic lines of 'Vox Humana'.

In 1958 Gunn accepted a teaching post at the University of California, Berkeley, and in 1960 settled in San Francisco where he has lived ever since. *My Sad Captains* (1961) contained further experiments with syllabic verse and also showed, in poems like 'In Santa Maria Del Popolo', a disavowal of the aggressive attitudes adopted in his earlier poems. Gunn was no longer so anxious to flex his metaphorical muscles and yet the book was seen, by English critics, not so much as a progression but a denial of his roots in the English poetic tradition. Gunn briefly returned to London in 1964 to work with his brother, the photographer Ander Gunn, on *Positives* (1966), a book combining verbal and visual elements. Back in San Francisco he published *Touch* (1966) containing 'Misanthropos', his most ambitious poem to date. This long narrative depicts the return to consciousness of a survivor who assumes he is alone in a hostile world.

Gunn's experience of the 1960s, as a citizen of San Francisco when it was widely publicized as the centre of the psychedelic universe, was presented in *Moly* (1971). Collectively the poems evoke a chemically-induced spirituality: Homer's magic herb 'the moly', which saved Odysseus's men from Circe, is clearly identified with the hallucinogenic drug LSD. However

there is no lack of formal control in *Moly* and the key-poem 'Sunlight' shows Gunn at the height of his poetic powers:

> Enable us, altering like you, to enter
> Your passionless love, impartial but intense,
> And kindle in acceptance round your centre,
> Petals of light lost in your innocence.

That sums up Gunn's search for a vision of innocence uncontaminated by rigid intellectual categories, a search he continued in his collection *Jack Straw's Castle* (1974).

Alan Bold

Gunn's poetry is examined in Alan Bold's *Thom Gunn & Ted Hughes* (1976).

195
GURDJIEFF, George Ivanovich 1877–1949

Russian mystic and teacher of the occult

Gurdjieff was born in Alexandropol (now Leninakan) of Greek and Armenian parents. Soon after his birth the family moved to Kars, where his father worked as a carpenter. The father's most important function was that of local 'bard'; he recounted endless stories and recited long epics, including the epic of *Gilgamesh*, which had a profound influence on the young Gurdjieff and contributed greatly to his determination to look for some source of esoteric knowledge, which was to be the mainspring of his activity for much of his life. After a period in the municipal school at Kars, Gurdjieff gained most of his education from tutors selected for him by the Dean of the Cathedral. The result was a broadly based scientific and medical education, which the Dean considered to be a necessary complement to studies leading to the priesthood, the calling for which Gurdjieff was intended by his family. Gurdjieff himself had other ideas, however, and from an early age travelled extensively in his quest for hidden knowledge. It is by no means easy to establish the facts concerning Gurdjieff's travels during the first half of his life, despite the many autobiographical intimations scattered throughout his books, particularly in *Meetings with Remarkable Men* (trans. 1963). Some expeditions were undertaken in company with a group of people who called themselves 'Seekers of Truth'; among them were journeys across the Amu Darya (formerly the Oxus) to Samarkand, Bokhara and Tashkent, and to India and Tibet. There is evidence that Gurdjieff remained alone in Tibet for some time during the years 1900–2 and that he visited lamaseries which would not normally have been open to visitors from the west; it is equally certain that at different times he spent long periods in Sufi monasteries in Central Asia where he acquired much of the knowledge which was to form the basis of his later teaching method, and was able to study the ritual dances and rhythmic movements which constituted an important component of this method.

From 1905 onwards Gurdjieff undertook no further expeditions of the same kind. He spent the years from 1905 until 1907 in the Caucasus where he was known variously as a professional hypnotist, a 'healer' and a teacher of the occult. Towards the end of this period he established in Tashkent a 'circle' of people, an organization which was in some respects the prototype of that which he was to set up in Western Europe.

The record of his life becomes more certain from his arrival in Moscow in 1912. He acquired an estate near Moscow and began to make preparations for establishing an 'Institute for the Harmonious Development of Man'; he also met and married Countess Ostrowska, a lady-in-waiting to the Tsarina, who remained with him until her death in 1927. The outbreak of war in 1914 increased the difficulty of organizing such an institute as Gurdjieff had in mind, but he continued to work with groups of people and in 1915 Ouspensky* came into contact with him and became one of his principal helpers. An account of their meeting and of the ideas which Gurdjieff expounded in the course of the next year or so is to be found in Ouspensky's *In Search of the Miraculous* (1949). The revolution of 1917 caused Gurdjieff to leave Moscow and, after a period spent in the Caucasus, he made his way to Constantinople, where he was rejoined by a number of his pupils, including Ouspensky. A branch of the 'Institute for the Harmonious Development of Man' was opened, with a programme which included, in addition to lectures by Gurdjieff, instruction in the dances and movements, to which a number of the pupils had already been introduced. The music which accompanied the movements was remembered or composed by Gurdjieff himself and was considered by him to play an important role in his teaching. The Institute continued to function in Constantinople until 1921, when Gurdjieff moved with some of his followers to Berlin. The uncertainty of conditions in Germany led him to look to England as a possible permanent home for the Institute, particularly as Ouspensky was already settled there. Official permission to set up the organization in London was not, however, forthcoming and Gurdjieff finally decided upon France as the home for his institute. A large house with extensive grounds, Le Prieuré, at Fontainebleau was acquired and from 1922 until 1936 this remained Gurdjieff's headquarters.

A considerable number of people, some of them well-known, went to Fontainebleau for long or short periods to benefit from Gurdjieff's teaching and the regime of the Institute. This consisted of many hours of intense physic labour, long periods of practice of the exercises and movements, interspersed with occasional lectures from Gurdjieff, and the living of daily life in somewhat Spartan conditions under the watchful eye of a teacher who missed no detail of individual motive and behaviour.

In 1924 Gurdjieff took a band of his pupils to America where demonstrations of ritual dances and movements were given in New York and other cities. As a result much interest in his ideas was aroused and groups were formed for the purpose of working on the lines which he put forward. Soon after his return to France he was involved in a serious motor accident. This event caused the suspension of active work at the Institute. Upon his recovery Gurdjieff decided that the knowledge that he possessed should be given out in written form and he embarked on the task of committing to paper a long series of texts which should serve as study material for those who wished to follow his ideas. These were circulated privately among groups of people who were studying his method, first at Fontainebleau and later in Paris before and after the Second World War, and also in America and elsewhere. Gurdjieff himself continued to teach, particularly from 1934 onwards, and after the war returned also to the teaching of the movements, introducing new versions of many of the exercises. Gurdjieff died in Paris in 1949 and was buried at Fontainebleau.

The writings of Gurdjieff were not published during his lifetime but since his death they have appeared in several languages: the English titles are *All and Everything* (1950), *Meetings with Remarkable Men* (1963) and *Life is Real Only Then, When 'I Am'* (1975). Of the vast range of ideas presented in these books and used by Gurdjieff in his teaching many are treated in Ouspensky's writings and in other books listed in the bibliography below but there is a sharp contrast between Gurdjieff's own writing and these accounts; they appear over-systematized and intellectualized when compared with, for example, *All and Everything*, which is difficult to read, being full of unusual constructions and neologisms, but makes a great impact on the reader. Among the ideas which Gurdjieff most frequently stressed for his pupils were the distinction between knowledge and being and the need to try to achieve a balance between them; the role of essence and personality and the conditioned nature of the latter; the tendency for emotion to interfere constantly with the working of the other components of the human psychological make-up and the need for continual awareness and observation of the working of the machine which runs the daily life of the ordinary human being.

Dennis Fry

See also: *Views from the Real World: Early Talks in Moscow, Essentuki, Tiflis, Berlin, London, Paris, New York and Chicago, as recollected by his Pupils* (New York 1973; London 1976). About Gurdjieff: K. Walker, *A Study of Gurdjieff's Teaching* (1957); C. S. Nott, *Teachings of Gurdjieff* (1961); R. Lefort, *Teachers of Gurdjieff* (1966); J. G. Bennett, *Gurdjieff: Making a New World* (1973).

H

196
HAMILTON, Richard 1922–

English artist

During the early 1950s, Richard Hamilton, along with a number of contemporaries (among them the architectural historian Reyner Banham, the architects Alison and Peter Smithson, the artists John McCale and Eduardo Paolozzi, and the critic Lawrence Alloway), was a member of an off-shoot of the ICA (Institute of Contemporary Art) called the Independent Group which was single-handedly responsible for the change-over in British Art from Establishment to Pop.

This radical break came about through a growing dissatisfaction with current British art values and a desire to move into new areas of popular culture – sci-fi, mass-market films, pulp novels, advertisements – and technology. Hamilton was ideally prepared for this discussion. His early experiences in the advertising department of an electrical engineering firm in 1936 and as a jig and tool draughtsman from 1941 to 1945, combined with studying art, first at evening class and later at the Royal Academy Schools (from which he was expelled) and at the Slade School of Fine Art, put him at an arm's length from the fine art establishment and encouraged him to look at things from a different perspective. In 1952–3 he taught design at the Central School of Arts and Crafts, and from 1953 to 1966 at the University of Newcastle-upon-Tyne. His artistic interests, up to the 1950s, lay in a large variety of areas – always in search for a technical format for artistic creativity. Theories of organic growth and later of mechanical motion inspired him to evolve diagrammatic equivalents and he became interested in Marcel Duchamp's* dynamic version of Cubism. In 1956 all this changed and Hamilton produced a collage of magazine cut-outs as a programme cover and poster for the I.G. exhibition at the Whitechapel – 'This is Tomorrow' – which he called *Just What is it that makes Today's Home so Different, so Appealing?*

This anthology of mass-media imagery and presentation techniques determined Hamilton's production for the next decade. He became more and more interested in the ad-man's techniques of persuasion and the iconographic content of popular imagery and this emerged in works like *Hommage à Chrysler Corp* (a study of car advertising) of 1957, *Here is a Lush Situation* of 1957, and *She* of 1958–61.

Recurrent icons – the sex symbol, the film goddess, the fashion model, the pop star, the famous politician and consumer goods – recur through Hamilton's work of the 1960s and he becomes increasingly involved in mass-media communication techniques as well as in its images. Studies of close-up photography provide a starting point for *Whitley Bay* of 1965 and *Trafalgar Square* of 1965–7 and, in his studies of the Guggenheim Museum (1965–7), it is the communicative power of the image that inspires the work. Also in 1965–6 Hamilton made a reconstruction of Marcel Duchamp's *Large Glass* showing his continued debt to that genius. It is, however, in the 1950s that Hamilton's work is at its most provocative and it inspired two further generations of painters to develop his ideas.

Penny Sparke

Writings by Hamilton include: '*Hommage à Chrysler Corp*' in *Architectural Design*, March 1958: 'Persuading Image' in *Design*, February 1960; 'Urbane Image' in *Living Arts*, 2, 1963. See also: Lawrence Alloway, 'The Development of British Pop', in L. Lippard (ed.), *Pop Art* (1966); C. Finch, *Pop Art – Object and Image* (1968); J. Russell and S. Gablik, *Pop Art Redefined* (1969); and *Richard Hamilton*, Catalogue to the Tate Gallery Exhibition (1970).

197
HANDKE, Peter 1942–

Austrian novelist and dramatist

Handke's first work appeared in little magazines while he was studying law at the University of Graz (1961–5), and before the end of the 1960s he had won a reputation as an *enfant terrible* for his provocative writings and public persona. But the integrity of his work and its underlying seriousness of purpose soon gained respect to the extent of his winning the German Academy's 1973 Georg Büchner prize and of being, in John Updike's* words, 'widely regarded as the best young writer, and by many as the best writer altogether, in his language'.

Handke has essayed most forms of writing, but it was as an anti-theatrical playwright that he made his first impact. In *Offending the Audience* (*Publikums-beschimpfung*, 1966, trans. 1969) four 'speakers' coolly inform the audience that what they are watching is not a play but simply a stage with four people on it; they then alternately insult the audience and compliment them on their 'performance', a strategy that provoked extreme reactions wherever it was played. Further plot-less, character-less, one-act pieces followed until *Kaspar* (1968, trans. 1969), *The Ride across Lake Constance* (*Der Ritt über den Bodensee*, 1971, trans. 1973) and *They are Dying Out* (*Die Unvernünftigen sterben aus*, 1974, trans. 1975), all full-length, gave the lie to suspicions of char-latanism and established Handke's consistent concern with the problem of truly individual expression in a world already over-stocked with ready-mades. In the best of these plays, *Kaspar*, an innocent *tabula rasa* based on the historical Kaspar Hauser, who was kept from contact with the world until almost an adult, is indoc-trinated with conformist language and behaviour be-fore lapsing into incoherence as he struggles for self-expression. The play demonstrates a corollary of Wittgenstein's* views of language: that, as language is necessary for the expression of thought, he who controls language also controls thought.

Wittgenstein also seems to have influenced Handke's novels – stylistically at least – in their tendency to approach a phenomenon over and over again from different angles in search of its absolute reality (a preoccupation, along with a rejection of conventional character and plot, which Handke shares with Robbe-Grillet* and other *nouveaux romanciers*). As with the plays, initial critical reaction was hostile, but Handke's deadpan, ultra-objective accounts of characters in ex-treme states of mind moving through 'normal' yet alien landscapes have won increasing acclaim – and sales – especially in Germany and the USA. In *The Goalie's Anxiety at the Penalty Kick* (*Die Angst des Tormanns beim Elfmeter*, 1970, trans. 1977) a murderer is on the run from a pointless, spur-of-the-moment killing. *Short Let-ter, Long Farewell* (*Der kurze Brief zum langen Abschied*, 1972, trans. 1977) is the first-person account of a young Austrian writer's journey across the USA in search of his estranged wife, a journey which allows Handke to pay incidental homage to a number of his literary heroes, among them Faulkner*, Chandler* and Patri-cia Highsmith. *A Moment of True Feeling* (*Die Stunde der wahren Empfindungen*, 1975, trans. 1977) concerns anoth-er murderer, a press attaché at the Austrian Embassy in Paris, but despite nods in the direction of Kafka* the careful depiction of tedium becomes itself danger-ously tedious. In *The Left-Handed Woman* (*Die linkshänd-ige Frau*, 1976, trans. 1980), based on an original screenplay which Handke himself had filmed, an ap-parently happily married young mother, having sud-denly asked her husband to leave her, has to cope both with her new-found independence and with a sense of disorientation, which is described in a style exactly matching the dispassionate eye of a camera.

In the middle of this sequence, spurred by his mother's suicide, Handke wrote an unsentimental yet affecting memoir of her life – not unlike that of his fictional characters. *A Sorrow Beyond Dreams* (*Wunschloses Unglück*, 1972, trans. 1976) shows his technique at its best.

Handke has also published poetry, essays, stories, radio drama, a television play and a long journal of the eighteen months of his domicile in Paris, *Fantasies and Prejudices* (*Das Gewicht der Welt*, 1978, trans. 1979). Whatever the medium, however, Handke's concern is to demonstrate that experience is a succession of ready-made, pre-ordained components, whose deadening effect must be painstakingly countered. Hence the per-sistent dialectic in his work between conventional and unconventional forms. Though his work can be diffi-cult, in the breadth and variety of his experimentation and the uniqueness of his best prose and drama, Handke is one of the most exciting and original of the post-war generation of European writers.

Nicholas Hern

See: N. Hern, *Peter Handke* (1971).

198
HAŠEK, Jaroslav 1883–1923

Czech writer

Jaroslav Hašek was born in Prague, both his parents coming from southern Bohemia. Josef, his father, worked as a mathematics teacher and later as a bank clerk. His mother, Kateřina, was the daughter of a water-bailiff. In 1896 Josef died, the family was left without means of support, and Jaroslav was obliged to leave grammar school and work in chemists' shops until 1899, when he enrolled at the Commercial Acad-emy, possibly because that institution was not simply a place for business training. On its staff were several established writers, who might have expected to influ-ence Hašek's career as a writer. However, when in the following year he began contributing satirical pieces to newspapers, he adopted the style of the business letter. Much later he would give as an example of his early style the sentence: 'With your esteemed letter to hand I beg to inform you that your esteemed sack of coffee reached us in good order.' At the same time he made several journeys with his brother Bohuslav to Moravia, Slovakia and the border areas of Hungary and Poland, where his ability to observe and listen to folk anecdotes led him to a new stylistic source – the ordinary. Many of the stories in the sixteen volumes of short stories published before the First World War are based on ordinary situations and told in ordinary language. This enabled him simultaneously to satirize peasant gullibility and attack the trickster who exploited peasant misery. A third influence, on Hašek's character as well as his writing, was life in Prague, where he took part in both organized and unorganized demonstrations against the German ruling class and the bureaucracy of the Austro-Hungarian empire. A file kept by the police on Hašek reveals that he was drunk and disorderly with unpalatable monotony.

In 1910 he met and married Jarmila Meyerova, while working on the anarchist paper *Progressive Youth* (*Nová Omladina*). To pacify his father-in-law he abandoned the anarchist movement to become editor of *Animal World* (*Svět Zvířat*). As another precondition to the marriage he also temporarily abandoned alcohol. The only other occasion in his life when he managed to break the habit was in 1919. Drafted into the Austro-Hungarian Army at the beginning of the war he was soon captured by the Russians. As a prisoner in Russia he joined the Czech liberation army, but when he returned to Prague at the end of the war and the beginning of the new Republic of Czechoslovakia he did so as a Bolshevik committed to socialist revolution. A coup in Kladno had been masterminded in Moscow, but four days before Hašek's arrival there the revolutionary leaders were arrested. Hašek's response was to drink. Had the revolution succeeded he would probably have become an early dissident, for the only consistency in his politics was a temperamental dislike of authority. In the imperial parliamentary elections of 1911 he had presented himself as a candidate for the 'Party of Moderate Progress within the Bounds of Law', calling for the rehabilitation of animals by making an end to the convention of giving their names to human beings. His manifesto contained statements like 'We still need fifteen votes – Everyone who votes for us will receive a pocket aquarium.'

In 1911 Hašek also embarked on the project for which he is best known, *The Good Soldier Schweik*. This appeared in three versions: 'The Good Soldier Schweik and Other Stories' (1912), 'The Good Soldier Schweik in Captivity' (1915), and *The Adventures of the Good Soldier Schweik* (*Osudy dobrého vojáka Švejka za světové války*, 1921–3, trans. 1930). Four out of an intended six volumes of the last, the fullest, version were completed when he died. In its various forms this work made him popular with working people, and later with readers from all walks of life, to the extent that the Czech language adopted the noun 'švejkovina' to describe humorous behaviour directed against the authorities. Schweik himself is a character living in eternal conflict with his superiors and represents the resistance of the Czech people against bureaucracy. He also represents a common-sense attitude towards war: 'For Christ's sake don't shoot!' he exclaims at the enemy across a battlefield. 'There are people over here!' Comparable to Sancho Panza, he is a burlesque caricature of the man who pretends to be stupid in order to expose the conceit, mindlessness and arrogance of those in power. The novel itself is composed of short, anecdotal stories held together by a handful of central characters – Schweik, Lieutenant Luáš, Major Wenzel, cadet Jan Biegler, Lieutenant Dub and Mrs Müller. Its humour is based on two seemingly incongruous elements: an uninhibited, adolescent surrender to the emotion of the moment, and a gargantuan vitality undermined by a deep sense of despair.

The Good Soldier Schweik belongs to an *engagé* type of literature inherited from the nineteenth century, although, in its monumental haphazardness, some critics have seen a prefiguration of the 'accidental forms' of more self-consciously modernist twentieth-century writing. Hašek himself seems to have been completely indifferent to 'high art' and scholarship. In some 1,200 contributions to newspapers and journals he invented most of the events which he supposedly witnessed and reported, seldom relating anything to a particular townscape or countryside. His interest focused on people and animals. To posterity he left an unfinished demotic masterpiece, and an unexplained life. To some he appears as a bohemian without depth, to others as a reckless architect of his own unhappiness. Ironically, when he died people did not believe it, thinking it was just another of his hoaxes. His funeral was organized by a nationalist organization who had regarded Hašek as a traitor. The only happy period of his life was the time spent in Russia, when he fought not against but for a cause. Although he could not lead a revolution, it was only when he thought of taking part in one that he found the necessary self-discipline to mirror a norm of behaviour.

Dr Slavka Sverakova

See: M. Brod, *Prager Sternenhimmel* (1966); C. Parrot, *The Bad Bohemian* (1978).

199
HAWKS, Howard Winchester 1896–

US film director

Of all the directors brought into the limelight by French cinema critics in the 1950s, Howard Hawks is the one whose work most deserved acclaim and most repays close scrutiny. Ironically, for a director of popular and often profitable films, his oeuvre has the kind of thematic coherence that is more usually associated with literature of classical music, with a similar self-inspiring sense of irony, and a comparable formal purity.

Howard Winchester Hawks began his career in the props department of Mary Pickford's film company, after serving as an airman in the First World War.

Rising through the editing department, he became a script-writer in his mid-twenties and directed his first feature (*The Road to Glory*) in 1926. A series of uneven silent features followed, though with *A Girl in Every Port* (1928) he brought to life one of the cinema's greatest actresses, Louise Brooks (who was subsequently cast in Pabst's screen classic, *Pandora's Box*). Despite studio misgivings, he directed his first sound film in 1930, and two years later shot to prominence with *Scarface* (1932), a *succès de scandale*, and the definitive example of the gangster cycle which it spawned. This was also the first of Hawks's many successful collaborations with hardbitten ex-journalist and screenwriter Ben Hecht – *Scarface* was reputedly written in ten days.

Hawks's career in the 1930s is characteristically varied, but in every case betrayed an eye for talent that had little to do with the studio system: William Faulkner's* first screen script (*Today We Live*, 1933) was for Hawks. And the decade culminated in three extraordinary collaborations with the mercurial Cary Grant: *Bringing Up Baby* (1938), *His Girl Friday* (1940), *Even Angels Have Wings* (1939). What is so hard to conceive, and remains a distinguishing feature of his career, is the diversity of the projects – in this case a screwball comedy, a headlong farce, and a semi-tragedy. This last (*Even Angels*) reveals Hawks's central strength, an optimism (improbable in this tale of loneliness and courage among airmen) born of looking into the dark heart of things, and an irony (intimated by the title) which is anything but glib.

Strangely enough, the comparison that springs constantly to mind is that of Shakespeare's mature comedies, for Hawks's heroines have a comparable seriousness beneath their life-enhancing resilience, and his heroes the same complex instinct towards self-knowledge and integrity. Thus *To Have and Have Not* (1945), spawned by the war propaganda effort and adapted (by Faulkner, admittedly) from one of Hemingway's* most garrulous and least engaging novels, is an almost tragically intense moral text: Bogart (an apolitical and apparently cynical gun-runner) grimly maintains the fine line between 'right' and 'wrong' despite the immense conflicting demands of private loyalty, nationality and survival. In *The Big Sleep* (1946) which, because of its dark stylistic skill and Bacall's performance, is probably Hawks's best-known film, the Bogart character faces a choice so internal that it is virtually metaphysical – whether to acknowledge *to himself* that the woman he loves is herself part of the night-living corruption against which he is struggling.

Doubt and self-doubt; respect and self-respect; Hawks's emphasis is committedly humanist, ambivalent and incapable – despite the apparent stylistic ease – of simplification. What matters is choice, because right choices make for integrity and self-respect; and integrity in turn permits right choices. Only the will-power of the individual, a constant struggle, permits the inner freedom that is essential to making real choices. What distinguishes will-power from an overweaning will *to* power (and what is so lacking in Hawks's close colleague and polar opposite Ford*) is a caustic wit. Humour in Hawks goes with humanity and, surprisingly (in view of the way he has been attacked for chauvinism), with *women*. From the aggressive Katharine Hepburn in the 1930s, to the laconic Bacall in the 1940s, to the ironical Angie Dickinson in *Rio Bravo* (1959), Hawks's women (or, more abstractly, their freewheeling sexuality) put at risk the most rigid social and sexual roles. Cary Grant in *I Was a Male War Bride* (1949) is forced by an obstructive bureaucracy into adopting a female persona to win his wife; and in *Red River* (1948), one of the great traditional Westerns, it is the irruption of a woman (Joanne Dru) which saves the film from Oepidal tragedy as John Wayne and Montgomery Clift prepare to fight to the death.

Though the eleven-year period 1938–49 was perhaps the fertile peak of his career, Hawks's work in the 1950s bristles with inspired moments and ideas, like his first venture into science-fiction in 1951, *The Thing* (on which he is credited as producer only, but seeing is believing). And in 1959, with *Rio Bravo*, Hawks (aged sixty-three) married comic and tragic themes wholesale for the first time. A Western? a comedy? a drama of inner growth? *Rio Bravo* is all these things, a film which humanized the rigid self-assurance of John Wayne as thoroughly as the earlier *Red River* had implicitly criticized it.

Hawks 'discovered' (among others) Louise Brooks, Carole Lombard, Lauren Bacall, and Montgomery Clift. It is surely no coincidence that the three actresses were so much more than the pretty comediennes Hollywood at the time required, nor that Clift was one of the most spiritual and tragically self-aware actors the cinema has seen. Hawks was a great director of actors; a master of genres; a man sensitive to good scripts and to the ideas of others. But above all, in an art where so much tends to artifice, the cinema of Howard Hawks is unique for never faking: there is never an unnecessary close-up to signal emotion; never an arbitrary cut to hasten the action; never, even in his failed films, a sense of portentous self-indulgence. It is an extraordinary record in an art form which is also an industry.

Chris Auty

See: Robin Wood, *Howard Hawks* (1960); David Thomson, in *A Biographical Dictionary of the Cinema* (1975).

200

HAYEK, Friedrich-August von 1899–

Austrian economist

Hayek's thought lies in the long tradition of Central European liberalism. He himself was trained in the prestigious Austrian School which under L. von Mises had strongly opposed Marxian analysis in the nineteenth and early twentieth century. His views returned to political prominence after he was awarded a Nobel Prize for Economics in 1974, but more significantly with the growth of monetarism in economic theorizing and the revival of 'free market policies'. In particular the British Conservative Party, while it was in opposition from 1974 to 1979, embraced much of his philosophical stance and adapted their programme in office accordingly. As a persistent critic of Keynesian* theories and, even more, of policies, he has lived to see a world-wide abandonment of avowedly Keynesian 'demand-management'.

Hayek was born in Vienna in 1899. On graduating from the University in 1921, he entered the Civil Service until he returned to academic life in 1926 as Director of the Austrian Institute for Economic Research. He accepted the Tooke Chair of Economic Science at London University in 1931, became a naturalized Briton in 1938, but moved to the United States in 1950. There he took up a chair in social and moral science at the University of Chicago, a highly congenial intellectual home for his developing political philosophies. In 1960 he returned to Europe to take up his last chair at the University of Freiburg until he retired in 1970.

Hayek's first published works were fiercely theoretical, even esoteric. He was very much an economists' economist. It was partly his experience of the shattering inflations of the early 1920s that led him into the field of monetary economics and the problems of economic instability. Hence, he concentrated on these issues in *Prices and Production* (1931), *Monetary Theory and the Trade Cycle* (1926 and 1933), and *Monetary Nationalism and International Instability* (1937). His major contribution came, however, from his two works *Profits, Interest and Investment* (1939) and, more importantly, *The Pure Theory of Capital* (1941), drawing on his 'Austrian School' background and long traditions in this field, and working in the highly anti-Keynesian atmosphere of the London School of Economics of the 1930s. The essence of this stage of Hayek's work lies in his analysis of the disproportions that arise in a decentralized economic system between resources devoted to the production of capital goods – plant, machinery, equipment – and the volume of demand for consumer goods to be produced by these capital goods.

Although his work was highly intricate and immensely thorough, it can be held to have had little or no influence on policy, swept aside as it was by the tidal wave of Keynesian ideas and analysis, although it has resurfaced in the post-war flowering of esoteric capital theory.

Hayek's influence does, however, start in this period, not on policy at all but on ideas. His first major political statement, *The Road to Serfdom*, was published in 1944, and Keynes wrote of his 'broad sympathy with its sentiments'. Both authors were, after all, old-fashioned Liberals in politics. Hayek saw the seductive path – from the welfare state to collective attempts to increase and redistribute income, wealth and welfare, and to state-centred full-employment policies – as leading inevitably to the destruction of personal freedom in the serfdom of socialism.

His later published works (and indeed the study-area of his Chicago Chair) show the direction and concerns of his thoughts. *The Political Ideal of the Rule of Law* (1955) led to *The Constitution of Liberty* (1960) and three volumes on *Law, Legislation and Liberty* (1973, 1976, 1979). The essence of this message is the view that individual freedom is inseparable from economic freedom, and that socialism is the surest way to lose both. But the road to socialism is a seductive and slippery slope. The only preserver of freedom, therefore, is not a set of economic policies, for there are only two legitimate forms of government power – 'to provide a framework for the market, and to provide services that the market cannot provide'. The free market – for goods, capital and labour – is the final guarantee of freedom because it guarantees the free expression of choice of individuals and not collective choice. He would even introduce free choice in the supply of currency – an area in which a state monopoly of control could be regarded as the hallmark of an independent nation state.

The reluctance of politicians to implement his ideas he understands. He is concerned with ideas, not with policies. 'My aim is to make politically possible what is politically impossible.' A test bed for these ideas could well be the performance of the British economy and hence of British society in the 1980s.

Roger Opie

201

HEIDEGGER, Martin 1889–1976

German philosopher

Though condemned as a purveyor of literal nonsense by men as eminent as Rudolf Carnap* and Karl Popper*, Heidegger's influence has been pronounced in fields ranging from theology (Bultmann*) to psychotherapy (Binswanger). Furthermore, a much used and sometimes abused 'existentialist' vocabulary of 'authenticity', 'anguish' and man's 'being unto death', though popularized by the work of Sartre*, derives from Heidegger's early but most influential book *Being and Time* (*Sein und Zeit*, 1927, trans. 1962). The heyday of existentialism passed with the 1950s but the direct influence of Heidegger has continued to grow.

The radical intellectual impact of Heidegger's work stands in marked contrast to the external quiet of a life passed in study and teaching in southern Germany. The philosopher was born into a Catholic family at Messkirch in the Black Forest. He attended school at Constance and at Freiburg and, from 1909 to 1916, studied theology and philosophy at Freiburg University. The presentation of his dissertation on Duns Scotus qualified him to teach and in 1922 he became an associate professor at Marburg. *Being and Time* appeared in 1927 with a dedication to Edmund Husserl*, whom Heidegger succeeded as Professor of Philosophy at the Albert-Ludwig University in Freiburg the following year. In 1933, following Hitler's* appointment as Chancellor, Heidegger became Rector of the University. Though he resigned the rectorship in February 1934, the period of tenure was marked by a number of statements in which the characteristic vocabulary of *Being and Time* was blended all too easily with the 'blood and soil' jargon of Nazi ideology. Disillusion with the regime came swiftly but following Germany's defeat the Allied authorities forbade Heidegger to teach until 1951. Neither the war nor the teaching ban interrupted Heidegger's single-minded philosophical quest, to explore the meaning of that most problematic and ubiquitous term, Being. Throughout the post-war years, which he spent living in the Black Forest, Heidegger published a series of works, mostly in the form of brief essays. Their subjects were various (the Pre-Socratics, the nature of the work of art, poetry and the significance of technology) but the dominant theme remained the same, a concern with the meaning of Being and with language as a speaking of the truth of Being.

Though Husserl was the major philosophical influence on the young Heidegger, his interest in ontology contrasted from the beginning with the older man's concern with the analysis of consciousness. In *Being and Time* he uses the phenomenological approach to shed new light on central ontological issues, first raised by the earliest Greek thinkers but, according to Heidegger, lost from sight in the over-formalized terminology of later metaphysics. Thinking about Being must consist in concrete phenomenological analysis of *How* beings are and not *what* or *why*, and in *Being and Time* he analyses man's particular mode of being in the world, *Dasein* (literally 'being-there'), as an approach to the understanding of Being itself.

Dasein is that being for whom its being is a problem. Uniquely *Dasein* is aware that sometime he will die and cease to be. He is a temporally bound being and the horizon of being in time is death. Heidegger conceptualizes the relationship between *Dasein* and other beings not as one of knowing subject and known object but as a multifarious involvement summed up in the notion of 'care'. *Dasein* cares about his existence. He is also beset by 'anxiety' (*Angst*). Anxiety must not be confused with fear, for fear is fear of some particular object while anxiety arises from being in the world as such and, in particular, the consciousness of mortality. In anxiety, '*Dasein* finds itself face to face with the nothing of the possible impossibility of its own existence.' The essence of man is to exist in a particular way that uniquely exposes him to awareness of the truth of Being and the horizon of death. But man can shield himself from such awareness. Language which might articulate the truth can become a veil that hides it. When this happens *Dasein* is living inauthentically, cut off from the true problems and mysteries of his existence.

Such themes were readily integrated in the literature of an insecure age, but the analysis of *Dasein* did not satisfy its author. In his later works Heidegger turns to a less human-centred approach to ontological issues. To Sartre's statement: 'We are precisely in a situation where there are only human beings', Heidegger replies: 'We are precisely in a situation where principally there is Being', and the path to the understanding of Being is one that seems to bypass the concerns of humanism. Man, at most, is the 'shepherd of Being', who articulates its truth through language, but only in so far as language remains in contact with engendering experience. It is Heidegger's relentless concern with avoiding the abstractions of traditional philosophy that accounts for much of the difficulty of the later arcane texts. He seems to many, admirers and critics alike, to be entering an area that falls outside the limits of what can be thought or said. Yet in the very effort to transgress these limits Heidegger has revitalized central questions of philosophy and the human sciences, and this is likely to remain his most significant contribution to modern culture.

David J. Levy

There is a useful bibliography of Heidegger's vast output in Walter Biemel, *Martin Heidegger: an Illustrated Study* (1977), while *Martin Heidegger: Basic Writings* (1977) makes available several of his key essays. See also: George Steiner, *Heidegger* (1978); and Michael Gelven, *A Commentary on Heidegger's 'Being and Time'* (1970).

202
HEISENBERG, Werner 1901–76

German physicist

The founder of Quantum mechanics and the inventor of the uncertainty principle, Werner Heisenberg was born in Würzburg and brought up in Munich, where he entered the University in 1920 to study physics under Arnold Sommerfeld. After a brief stay at Göttingen University he took his doctorate in 1923 with a dissertation on turbulence in fluid streams. In 1924 he returned to Göttingen as assistant to Max Born. Later that year he moved to Copenhagen to pursue research under Niels Bohr* and remained there until 1927.

After 1913 the Quantum Theory made considerable progress, but by 1924 it was running out of steam, largely owing to its lack of a coherent and systematic mathematical foundation: it consisted largely of a set of piecemeal modifications to classical physics that took account of the quantum of action. What was needed was a new mechanics, a Quantum mechanics that would be valid for the microphysical, as well as for the macrophysical, realm. In the summer of 1925 Heisenberg discovered the foundations of just such a mechanics. His theory was rapidly developed by Max Born, Pascual Jordan, and P. A. M. Dirac to form matrix mechanics, the basis of which is a non-commutative algebra in which observable physical quantities are represented by matrices, i.e. sets of numbers arranged in rows and columns. In 1926 Erwin Schrödinger* invented wave mechanics which, though very different from matrix mechanics, led to the same results.

In the spring of 1927, while a lecturer at Bohr's institute, Heisenberg followed up his great work with his discovery of the uncertainty relations, $\Delta q \, \Delta p = h/2\pi$ and $\Delta E \, \Delta t \sim h$, which are of central importance in Quantum mechanics. Heisenberg took these relations as an expression of a fundamental limitation on the accuracy with which position and momentum (q and p) and energy and time (E and t) can be simultaneously measured: simultaneous measurement of these quantities must always involve an inaccuracy at least as great as the value of the quantum of action h. This is Heisenberg's *uncertainty principle*.

The exact physical significance of the uncertainty relations is still a controversial question. Most physicists, though by no means all, believe that the uncertainty principle provides the correct interpretation of the uncertainty relations. The basis of the uncertainty principle, however, is itself a disputed question. Heisenberg believed that the uncertainty is due to the unavoidable disturbance of the object by the process of measurement. All observation involves an interaction between the object and the instrument of observation. For macrophysical objects this interaction is usually negligible, but for microphysical objects it generally involves a considerable disturbance.

In a penetrating analysis Bohr showed that the uncertainty is due not simply to the unavoidable measurement disturbance, as Heisenberg had thought, but to the fact that the amount of the disturbance cannot be accurately ascertained. Although Heisenberg accepted Bohr's analysis, there are certain differences in their views. Heisenberg sees Quantum mechanics as being concerned not with nature as it is but with nature as exposed to our methods of questioning. He stresses the fact that observation of the microphysical world is possible only at the expense of interfering with it. For Bohr, however, the disturbance involved in observation is of secondary importance. The central point for Bohr is logical rather than epistemological: the concepts of exact position and exact momentum, he thinks, are, though equally indispensable for quantum mechanics, strictly speaking incompatible in that they presuppose mutually exclusive conditions for their meaningful applicability – they are in that sense complementary.

The consequence of the uncertainty principle is clear, viz. the statistical character of Quantum mechanics: we cannot predict the behaviour of microphysical objects, since we cannot obtain sufficiently accurate information about their exact simultaneous position and momentum. The philosophical significance of the uncertainty principle is, however, far from clear. Some are inclined to the view that the principle restricts only the simultaneous observability of exact position and exact momentum; microphysical objects, for all we know, may *have* an exact simultaneous position and momentum and a causally determined behaviour. Others, including Heisenberg, who are influenced by the philosophy of positivism, hold that since exact position and exact momentum cannot be simultaneously measured, microphysical objects cannot be said to have an exact simultaneous position and momentum, for the positivistic reason that what cannot be observed cannot meaningfully be said to exist. Whether the behaviour of microphysical objects is causally determined is, on this view, a meaningless question. Bohr too held that an object (even a macrophysical object) cannot meaningfully be said to have a definite simultaneous position and momentum, not for the epistemological reason that no such property is observable, but for the logical reason that the concept of such a property is basically incoherent.

Heisenberg was awarded the Nobel Prize for Physics in 1932 for his contribution to the development of Quantum mechanics. He continued to make important contributions to physics, particularly in the fields of ferro-magnetism, nuclear theory and elementary particle theory. In the 1950s he strove to develop a unified field theory based upon an equation reflecting a set of basic mathematical symmetries that would account for all the dynamic properties of matter.

He was Professor of Theoretical Physics at the University of Leipzig from 1927 to 1941. Although privately unsympathetic to the Nazi regime he remained in Germany throughout the Second World War, seeing it as his duty to work for the preservation of German physics and its future reconstruction. From 1941 to 1945 he was Director of the Kaiser Wilhelm Institute for Physics at Berlin, where he worked with Otto Hahn on the development of a nuclear reactor. After the war he became Director of the Max Planck Institute for Physics, first at Göttingen and later at Munich. After the war he played a prominent part in the promotion of scientific research in Germany. He married Elisabeth Schumacher in 1937; they had three sons and four daughters.

Heisenberg has an important part in twentieth-centry thought: the notion of uncertainty or indeterminacy which he introduced is, like Einstein's* concept of relativity, one of the major ideas of the century; it has changed not only physics but our entire world picture.

D. R. Murdoch

Heisenberg's great papers on Quantum mechanics and the uncertainty relations are: 'On the quantum-theoretical re-interpretation of kinematic and mechanical relations' ('Über quantentheoretischen Umdeutung kinematischer und mechanischer Beziehungen'), Zeitschrift für Physik, 33, 1925, and 'On the visualizable content of quantum-theoretical kinematics and mechanics' ('Über den anschaulichen Inhalt der quantentheoretischen Kinematik und Mechanik', Zeitschrift für Physik, 43, 1927. See also: The Physical Principles of the Quantum Theory (1930), and the collections of his essays, Philosophic Problems of Nuclear Science (1952); Physics and Philosophy (1959), and the semi-autobiographical Physics and Beyond (1971); Patrick A. Heelan, Quantum Mechanics and Objectivity (1965); Max Jammer, The Conceptual Development of Quantum Mechanics (1966).

203
HEMINGWAY, Ernest 1899–1961

US writer

Perhaps the best known of all the serious American novelists, Ernest Hemingway has suffered to some extent from his very popularity. In Europe his terse vitality of style, and tough, seemingly limited, subject-matter have tended to arouse either uncritical admiration or uncomprehending antagonism. Americans, however, steeped as they are in the allegorical-symbolistic undertones of their literary heritage, have been in a better position to appreciate the subtler points of Hemingway's achievement. This appreciation was summed up in 1952 with the appearance of two first-class critical works: Philip Young's Ernest Hemingway (1952) and Carlos Baker's Hemingway: The Writer as Artist (1952). The merit of these studies is that they effectively 'place' Hemingway for the uninitiated reader in terms of his literary inheritance and artistic method. A further book, Charles A. Fenton's The Apprenticeship of Ernest Hemingway (1954), provided de-

tailed information about Hemingway's early days, and suggested a number of causes for his disillusioned and fatalistic attitude towards life.

Hemingway, Fenton suggests, was sickened by the hypocrisy of his birthplace, Oak Park, Illinois, whose Christian charity stopped where its churches, tree-lined avenues and white-framed houses gave way to the slummy taverns and crime-ridden streets of Cicero. Appearances to the contrary, he was as sensitive as he was idealistic, and quite unprepared for his early introduction into the world of brutality and violence. Later, Hemingway the young artist became obsessed by the stark American contrast between the world of innocence and the world of corruption. Unfortunately, he seems to have remained more or less at this stage most of his life. In the uncompromising severity of his clear and simplified view of human existence he seems typical of the American Puritan from Cotton Mather to John Foster Dulles.

Hemingway's 'initiation' is symbolized in In Our Time (1925). The story of Nick and the squaw is typical. Up in the woods of Michigan with his doctor father (as Hemingway often was in his boyhood) he is called upon to assist at a caesarean operation performed with a jack-knife. This would have been initiation enough, but the dénouement of the story is the discovery that the squaw's husband, unable to bear his wife's pain any longer, has quietly cut his throat in the bunk above. Hemingway's education was continued in Kansas City, where he went to be a reporter, following accident ambulances; it was completed at the age of eighteen, when, at Fossalta in Italy, in the Ambulance Service during the First World War, he 'received 227 separate wounds from a mortar shell and was hit simultaneously in the leg by a machine gun round' (Fenton).

Invalided back to the United States in 1919, Hemingway worked in Chicago, and in Toronto for the Star. In 1922 he was back in Europe, again as a foreign correspondent. Much of the time he spent in Paris, but he also reported the Graeco-Turkish war and the Lausanne Conference. During this period he had been publishing youthfully cynical and blasphemous poems, a typical example of which is:

> I know monks masturbate at night
> That pet cats screw
> That some girls bite
> And yet
> What can I do
> To set things right?

(He was delighted, he records in Green Hills of Africa, 1935, to meet an Austrian who knew him as a Dichter because he had read some of Hemingway's poems in Der Querschnitt.) In Our Time, which, in a series of sharp vignettes of Middle Western life interpolated with war experiences, charts Hemingway's disillusionment, helps to explain what threw him back on the philosophy of 'Good is what you feel good after, bad is what you feel bad after.' The first major success was *The Sun Also Rises* (1926), backed three years later by *A Farewell to Arms* (1929). The novels after that were *To Have and Have Not* (1937), *For Whom the Bell Tolls* (1940), *Across the River and Into the Trees* (1950) and *The Old Man and the Sea* (1952), together with the non-fiction books, *Death in the Afternoon* (1932) and *Green Hills of Africa*. It could be claimed, however, that Hemingway's artistry is seen at its best in his short stories, from 'The Three Day Blow' and 'In Another Country' to 'The Short Happy Life of Francis Macomber'. By the time of his death in 1961, no new work had appeared since *The Old Man and the Sea*, but *A Moveable Feast* (1964) and *Islands in the Stream* (1970) were published posthumously.

Hemingway was a literary artist of high calibre. The surface realism of his work is so convincing and interesting for its own sake that it has obscured the fact that, like many other American novelists – Cooper, Hawthorne, Melville and James, for example – he used the novel form in order to pose philosophic questions about life. This is perhaps why his characters sometimes seem so 'flat'. Jake and Brett, Lieutenant Henry and Catherine, Jordan and Maria do not really 'come to life'. Whether or not this makes Hemingway a flawed novelist is a question for debate. His work brings into focus the distinction which exists between the novel in America and the novel in the rest of the world. The emphases and preoccupations of the novelist in America are different, and they are different because the nation from which they spring, with its idealistic Founding Fathers and violent modern conditions, is unique in the annals of the Western world.

Geoffrey G. H. Moore

See: J. K. M. McCaffery (ed.), *Ernest Hemingway: The Man and His Work* (1950); S. Donaldson, *By Force of Will* (1977); R. B. Harmon, *Understanding Ernest Hemingway* (1977); M. J. Bruccoli, *Scott and Ernest* (1978); A. Burgess, *Ernest Hemingway and his World* (1978).

204
HENZE, Hans Werner 1926–

German composer

The period immediately after the Second World War was one of great change in German music, for suddenly scores became available which had been suppressed by the Nazis and the music of Schoenberg*, Stravinsky* and others could at last have an influence on German composers. Henze was one of the first to take advantage

of the new freedom. Following the example of Wolfgang Fortner, with whom he studied in the late 1940s, he made efforts to combine Schoenberg's serialism with Stravinsky's neo-classicism in such works as his first symphony and first violin concerto (both 1947). Equally important to his subsequent development, however, was the close association with the theatre which he began in 1948 by taking an appointment at the Deutsche Theater, Konstanz: within the next five years he had completed four ballets and four operas, the latter including a version of the Manon Lescaut story as *Boulevard Solitude* (1951).

During the same period Henze was briefly attracted by the rigorous serial methods being developed by Boulez* and Stockhausen*. In his second quartet (1952) he came close to their concerns, but the next year he took the decision to free himself and settle in Italy, where he has since remained. He broadened his style to embrace a rich flood of lyrical melody and colour, expressed most abundantly in his opera *König Hirsch* (1953–5), which was later revised as *Il re cervo* (1962). During the next few years he continued to produce music of nostalgic Mediterranean warmth – the Hölderlin cycle *Kammermusik* for tenor, guitar and eight instruments (1958) is typical – but he could range also as far as the militarist world of his Kleist opera *Der Prinz von Homburg* (1958) or the romantic waterscapes of his full-length ballet *Undine* (1956–7), which was choreographed by Frederick Ashton.

The early 1960s saw the culmination of Henze's 'southern' manner, with its roots in early nineteenth-century Italian opera as much as in the German tradition. Apart from his fifth symphony (1962) he wrote little abstract music at this time but instead concentrated on operas and cantatas, the latter including ecstatically lyrical settings of Rimbaud in *Being Beauteous* for soprano, harp and four cellos (1963), Tasso in *Ariosi* for soprano, violin and piano duet (also 1963) and Virgil in *Musen Siziliens* for chorus, two pianos, wind and percussion (1966). The operas of this period include the satirical comedy *Der junge Lord* (1964) and two works to librettos by W. H. Auden* and Chester Kallman: *Elegy for Young Lovers* (1959–61), a tragedy of art and love in an alpine setting, and *The Bassarids* (1965–6), a reworking of *The Bacchae* as a continuous two-hour operatic symphony.

After completing *The Bassarids* Henze became dissatisfied with his role as a purveyor of new operas for essentially bourgeois audiences in Germany: the conflicts in his mind at this time are recorded in his second piano concerto (1967). In 1968, following in the wake of world-wide student unrest, he declared himself on the side of revolutionary socialism and began, with the oratorio *Das Floss der Medusa* (1968), a series of works attacking bourgeois convention and eulogizing sons of the oppressed. He found a sympathetic environment in Cuba, where in 1969 he composed his sixth symphony, heavily indebted to the rhythms and sounds of Cuban music, and where he found the materials for his *El cimarrón* (1970), the story of a runaway slave in songs for baritone and three players.

When he returned to the opera house, with *We Come to the River* (1974–6), it was with several such smaller-scale works behind him, and the new piece, to a text by Edward Bond*, has more in common with these works of commitment than with Henze's earlier operas. However, he had departed somewhat from the intransigent political stance taken in every work of 1968–70: there had been, among other things, two big symphonic poems, *Heliogabalus imperator* (1971–2) and *Tristan* (1974), both of which show his fertile orchestral invention and his unrivalled ability to draw from a wide range of musical sources.

Since completing *We Come to the River* Henze has made a return to chamber music, which he had neglected since the early 1950s: a set of three quartets, nos 3–5, was finished in 1976. However, the ballet *Orpheus* (1979), again created in collaboration with Bond, proved that he was not long to be detained from the theatre.

Paul Griffiths

Other works: *Apollo et Hyacinthus* for contralto, harpsichord and eight instruments (1949); *Nachtstücke und Arien* for soprano and orchestra (1957); *Novae de infinito laudes* for soloists, chorus and orchestra (1962); Double Concerto for oboe, harp and strings (1966); Double Bass Concerto (1966); *Der langwierige Weg in die Wohnung der Natascha Ungeheuer*, music theatre (1971); Violin Concerto no. 2 (1971); *La Cubana*, music theatre (1973); *Voices* for mezzo-soprano, tenor and chamber orchestra (1973). Writings: *Essays* (Mainz 1964). About Henze: Klaus Geitel, *Hans Werner Henze* (Berlin 1968).

205

HEPWORTH, Jocelyn Barbara 1903–75

British sculptor

Barbara Hepworth was one of a small group of artists – the most important of whom were herself, the painter Ben Nicholson* and the sculptor Henry Moore* – whose combined achievements during the 1930s were largely responsible for giving British art a central place in the modern movement, despite public indifference amounting at times to hostility. After the Second World War she went on to become an abstract sculptor of international reputation.

She was born at Wakefield, the eldest child of H. R. Hepworth, a civil engineer and later County Surveyor to the West Riding of Yorkshire, whom she would sometimes accompany on his motor tours through the Pennine landscape – journeys which she later recalled made a deep impression upon her. Responsiveness to natural form remained a rich source for the making of her sculpture and can be sensed most powerfully in those works which she carved in wood or stone. At the age of sixteen she won a scholarship from Wakefield Girls' High School to Leeds School of Art, where Henry Moore was a fellow student. In 1921 both artists transferred to the Royal College in London. In 1924 she travelled to Italy on a West Riding Scholarship, where she met the sculptor John Skeaping, a scholar at the British School in Rome. The couple were married in Florence in May 1925. They returned to London in 1926 and exhibited together at the Beaux-Arts Gallery in 1928 – her first important exhibition.

Throughout this period, Hepworth, like Moore, developed a strong preoccupation with 'direct' carving, a practice which had been revived in the decade or so before the First World War by Brancusi*, Epstein*, Gaudier-Brzeska and others. The doctrine of 'truth to materials' – of respecting the intrinsic properties of different types of stone or wood – was central to the work of Hepworth and Moore up until the 1950s, when both artists began to cast extensively in bronze – though Hepworth always insisted that she was primarily a carver. Her earliest surviving carvings, which date from the late 1920s, are on the whole stylized treatments of the human figure which also reflect an interest in primitive art. During the early part of the 1930s her work became freer and more abstract, though still based loosely on the human anatomy. The white alabaster *Pierced Form* of 1931 (destroyed during the war) was the first sculpture to explore the relationship of solid to void and of exterior to interior by incorporating in it a hole. From this sensuous, organic phase, which has close affinities with Moore's work of the same period, Hepworth progressed in about 1934 to a completely abstract sculpture of elementary geometric – or as she described them 'constructive' – forms.

Hepworth's meeting with Ben Nicholson in 1931 (they married two years later, after divorce from Skeaping) marked the beginning of one of the most mutually beneficial relationships in the history of British art. Together they visited Paris, where they made pilgrimages to the studios of Picasso*, Braque*, Brancusi*, Mondrian* and Arp*. The purity of Brancusi's sculpture, with its reliance on simple archetypal shapes, profoundly affected Hepworth. In 1933 she and Nicholson joined *abstraction-création*, an association of artists of all nationalities dedicated to the promotion of non-objective art through exhibitions and an annual review (1932–6). Such contact with the Parisian avant-garde was one of the main reasons for that renewal of communal artistic activity in England which began in 1933 with the formation of the group Unit One and continued through various publications and organizations, some more politically committed than others, until the outbreak of war. Further impetus was provided by the presence in London from about 1935 of certain refugee artists and architects from the continent, amongst whom were Gropius*, Moholy-Nagy, Gabo* and later Mondrian. The progressive ideals of these artists are embodied in the publication *Circle* (1937), subtitled 'International Survey of Constructive Art', in which abstract art takes its place in a broad aesthetic and social programme embracing technology and architecture – in short, the 'constructed' environment. *Circle* was edited by Nicholson, Gabo and the architect Leslie Martin; Hepworth was closely involved in its preparation and contributed photographs of her work and a statement of her beliefs.

Shortly before the outbreak of war, Hepworth, Nicholson and their triplets (born in 1934) moved to St Ives in Cornwall, where they were soon followed by Gabo and his wife. Owing to a variety of reasons, including the scarcity of material for sculpture, Hepworth's output during the first half of the war was limited to making geometrical abstract drawings in pencil and gouache in which she worked out ideas for a sculpture using both colour and strings – ideas which were later realized in a series of hollowed-out wooden ovoids of extraordinary clarity and perfection of shape. Some of these – for example, *The Wave* (1944) – are equivalents for natural rhythms, a reaction to the new environment of caves, wide curving bays and the sea. The megalithic landscape between St Ives, Penzance and Land's End became the inspiration for a number of major sculptures executed over the next thirty years, culminating in the two monumental bronze groups *Family of Man* (1972) and *Conversation with Magic Stones* (1973). The relationship of figure to landscape was an important theme in her post-war work.

However abstract, Hepworth's sculptures nearly always suggest a human presence or a relationship of one person to another. Her interest in the human figure can be seen in the beautiful series of Operating Theatre drawings which she made in 1948–9. In 1949 she also moved into the studio at St Ives where she worked permanently from 1951, after the dissolution of her marriage to Nicholson, until her death in a fire in 1975.

Richard Calvocoressi

See: *Barbara Hepworth, Carvings and Drawings*, ed. Herbert Read (1952); *Barbara Hepworth: Drawings from a Sculptor's Landscape*, ed. Alan Bowness (1966); *A Pictorial Autobiography* (1970); *The Complete Sculpture of Barbara Hepworth 1960–69*, ed. Bowness (1971). See also: J. P. Hodin, *Barbara Hepworth* (1961); *Barbara Hepworth* (Tate Gallery catalogue, 1968); *Barbara Hepworth: Late Works* (Edinburgh International Festival, 1976).

206
HESSE, Hermann 1877–1962

German novelist and poet

Born in the Black Forest into a family with a tradition of missionaries and scholars in India, Hesse lived sporadically in his youth in Basel, where he also worked in a bookshop for three years. He made a trip to India in 1911 and took up permanent domicile in Switzerland a year later. During and after the Great War he underwent psychoanalytic treatment for nervous collapse by Jung* and his pupil, J. B. Lang. In 1919 Hesse moved to Montagnola in the Ticino, which was to be his home until his death. He married three times but shunned the business of the literary world, its groups and movements, preferring – like his heroes – an existence of voluntary withdrawal, embarking on journeys into his self, discovering hidden layers of the personality through dreams and engrossed contemplation.

Hesse's thought was influenced by men like Kierkegaard and Jakob Burckhardt, and especially Nietzsche. The latter, together with other 'visionaries' like Blake and Dostoievski, are seen as key 'loners' in modern culture by Colin Wilson in *The Outsider* (1956) where a chapter, 'The Romantic Outsider', is devoted to Hesse. His relations with fellow-writers were cordial and often of close affinity (e.g. with T. S. Eliot* and Thomas Mann*) and his already high reputation – he received the Nobel Prize for Literature in 1946 – was given a fresh and unexpected boost when his work became posthumously the gospel of the West Coast 'hippie' cult, Timothy Leary* to the fore, in the late 1960s. Hesse's ascetic, withdrawn lifestyle reinforced the myth, and this notoriety fed renewed interest in his writings in Europe.

Hesse's search for individual ways of achieving a harmonious personality appealed to a young generation rebelling against the consumerist conformist values of their elders. The attainment of a higher state of being does not occur overnight; it is a long, painful, though evolutionary process of shedding preconceptions and outer 'skins' and proceeding through organic stages to ultimate harmony. Hesse's own life and writings were a blue-print for this journey into the interior or 'inner way', starting with his early phase of Romantic restlessness where his vague yearnings, sensitive reactions and aesthetic ambitions were projected on to his heroes. In *Peter Camenzind* (1904, trans. 1961) the wandering outsider figure, the footloose vagabond in flight from society, appears. Already evident, too, is a recalcitrant dissatisfaction with and isolation from the establishment and its cultural values, particularly – from bitter personal experience – its stultifying educational system; Hesse ran away from school in Maulbronn, an event still powerful enough to inspire *Under the Wheel* (*Unterm Rad*, 1906, trans. 1958).

This hallmark of the young Hesse, the desire for experience untrammelled by the inhibitions of institutionalized society, elicited a liberation of thought and behaviour in personal responses, love and sexual matters. On the face of it this may appear as a licence for 'permissiveness', but it actually expressed Hesse's urgent need to break out of the constrictions of accepted morality to open the way for the development of a healthier, balanced personality. The rejection of worn-out morals coincided during the First World War with the infiltration into Hesse's life and work of the psychoanalytic techniques of Freud*, Stekel and others. From Nietzsche came the idea of the lost God and empty worldly values, from his trip to India (prompted by 'sheer inner distress') the burgeoning study of Indian and Chinese thought, and from his own life the nervous illness of his first wife and the breakdown of their marriage that had serious repercussions on Hesse's mental state. The protracted treatment he received from his friend Dr Lang contributed to the transmutation of psychoanalysis into literature in *Demian* (1919, trans. 1923), a novel documenting the stages in the emergence of a reborn personality. Emil Sinclair, the hero, is guided by his mentor Demian along the way to discover his own self in a contemplative search that entails – as in most of Hesse's novels – the investigation of the individual psyche and the neglect of action and external reality.

Despite his absorption with the individual and inner problems Hesse was by no means abstracted or publicly reticent during the Great War. Vigorously pacifist, he kept up a stream of political essays, open letters, and hortatory calls to the warring nations, and worked especially hard on behalf of prisoners-of-war. His ideas had a notable influence on Eliot's assessment of Western culture in *The Waste Land*, and the warnings of cultural doom Hesse voiced are transformed in his most famous work, *Steppenwolf* (*Der Steppenwolf*, 1927, trans. 1929), into the desolation of the lone hero, Harry Haller, whose discontent with a stifling and neurotic bourgeois society leads him to shun it. But Haller's real agony is internal, in his struggle to balance his 'wolfish' and 'human' psyches, his instincts and ideals. The depiction of his anguish that leads him through despair to a release in a symbolic death reflects imaginatively the stages of a therapeutic psychoanalytic cure. Hesse stressed that the story certainly recounted 'sufferings and distress, but was by no means the story of a despairing man, but one full of hope'. The rebirth of Haller's identity is brought about in the incidents of the climactic Magic Theatre, the door to which is opened by the use of drugs and in which metaphors from the armoury of psychoanalysis – mirrors and images, violence and murder, sexual bipolarity, music and art – are played out until Haller emerges from his mental and emotional chaos to a new potential for balance and serenity.

Serenity ('Heiterkeit') becomes the key word in the mature Hesse. Around 1930 a fresh dimension in his thought came with his renewed interest in the inward-turning, contemplative spirit of the East which gave a new and precise focus to what had always preoccupied him, namely personal religious experience. Stirrings of this Eastern attitude are evident in *Siddhartha* (1922, trans. 1951), a novel highly regarded by Henry Miller*, and *The Journey to the East* (*Die Morgenlandfahrt*, 1932, trans. 1956), which showed how Hesse had moved beyond conflict with society into a sort of secular mysticism. Hesse's engagement with Eastern thought culminated after eleven years of gestation in his last major work, *The Glass Bead Game* (*Das Glasperlenspiel*, 1943, trans. 1970), which recounts the life of the *magister ludi*, Josef Knecht, in the pedagogic province of Castalia. Here a secularized religious order seeks through teaching and example to instil in its young charges the 'search for wholeness' that, if successful, leads to an 'awakening' ('Erwachen'), a true understanding and a tranquillity transcending the arbitrary values of the world that only clog the personality. The path that leads both upwards and inwards to this fulfilment is in three stages, reflecting again the themes that dominate Hesse's whole output: the innocence of the child (*Peter Camenzind*) is followed by the guilt and despair of the man (*Steppenwolf*), leading in turn either to downfall or to life itself, the latter exquisite state achieved through abnegation and self-denial, overcoming yet accepting the world. The disintegration of the self into innumerable personae, already adumbrated in *Steppenwolf*, is a prerequisite for this progression that contains many echoes of *Bhagavad Gita*, the *Upanishads* and the practice of Yoga.

In addition to search the motifs of 'play' and 'service' are other essential elements in this process; although the pedagogic province is the home of the spirit ('Geist') and the desired awakening occurs through meditation at moments of intense feeling and insight, Hesse nevertheless seems to recognize that this state of felicity can also end in impotence, rigidity and lifelessness. The model of perfect attainment postulated in Castalia is therefore one where a symbolic unity of the *vita contemplativa* and the *vita activa* is achieved by Josef Knecht, the supremely serene sage and teacher of the young, who drowns after following his star pupil into a glacial mountain lake.

Like Goethe's *Faust*, Hesse's hero too finds ultimate fulfilment, even salvation, in service to humanity. In articulating the total dedication to the search for awakening, in harmony with one's fellow-men and eschewing strife, Hesse opened up a path that could lead to wisdom, serenity and happiness for many troubled individuals.

Professor A. V. Subiotto

Other works include: *Knulp* (1915, trans. 1971); *Klingsor's Last Summer* (*Klingsors letzter Sommer*, 1920, trans. 1970); *Narziss and Goldmund* (*Narziss und Goldmund*, 1930, trans. 1959); *If the War goes on. . .* (*Krieg und Frieden*, 1946, trans. 1970). See also: Hugo Ball, *Hermann Hesse: Sein Leben und Werk* (1947); Theodore J. Ziolkowski, *The Novels of Hermann Hesse* (1965); Mark Boulby, *Hermann Hesse: His Mind and Art* (1967); Walter Sorell, *Hermann Hesse. The Man who Sought and Found Himself* (1974); Ralph Freedman, *Hermann Hesse: Pilgrim of Crisis. A Biography* (1979).

207

HEYDERDAHL, Thor 1914–

Norwegian anthropologist

Thor Heyerdahl has revolutionized our appreciation of human mobility in the ancient world. Up to his time prehistorians had tacitly equated contact with land routes, that were necessarily interrupted at the sea's edge. Heyerdahl, by practical demonstration, showed that the high seas were pathways quite as much as, or even more than, they were barriers. Furthermore, he proved several types of primitive craft to be fully capable of traversing long sea roads at extremely early dates.

Heyerdahl was born in Narvik in Norway. He studied zoology and geology at the University of Oslo, spending his vacations fishing, mountaineering and dog sledging and writing articles about his adventures for Norwegian newspapers. After graduation, he and his wife spent a year on Fata Hiva in the Marquesas doing zoological research and compiling the first Norwegian-Marquesan dictionary. Heyerdahl became fascinated by the island's rock carvings, stone figures and legends, which suggested to him that the Polynesians had originated in South America. Thereafter, abandoning zoology for ethnology, he conducted library research in the University of Oslo that led him to the belief that not only South American Indians but also Indians from the Pacific North-west had reached Polynesia. Then in 1939 he excavated rock carvings in British Columbia and studied legends and megalithic structures in Peru. Traditions of a fifth-century AD pre-Inca king, Virakocha, originally known as Kon-Tiki, who was said to have sailed into the sunset, were equated by Heyerdahl with the Polynesian *tiki*. The war interrupted his speculations. He joined the Norwegian Air Force in Canada and later became an officer in a special parachute unit operating in Arctic Norway.

Peace found him in New York unsuccessfully attempting to have published a manuscript on Polynesia and America. This rebuff convinced him that only by actually making an ocean crossing in a reconstructed *balsa* could he demonstrate the practicability of his theory. So was constructed the famous balsa-wood raft *Kon-Tiki*, in which Heyerdahl and his five companions, Haugland, Hesselberg, Raaby, Waltzinger and Danielson, sailed 4,300 miles from Ecuador in 101 days, to be finally wrecked on the reef of Roroia in the Polynesian Tuamotus. Not until later did he elucidate the dagger-board steering principles of Inca sailing rafts (identical with Brazilian *jangardas* and Taiwanese fishing rafts), which would have enabled them to avoid the accident. Nevertheless, the voyage vindicated beyond all doubt the trans-Pacific capability of Peruvian *balsas*.

It is unnecessary to enlarge on the success of the *Kon-Tiki* (1950) book and film or the *Kon-Tiki* Museum in Oslo. The once rejected manuscript was published in enlarged form as *American Indians in the Pacific: the Theory behind the Kon-Tiki Expedition* (1952).

In 1953 Heyerdahl led an archaeological expedition to the Galapagos Islands and, in 1955–6, the important Norwegian expedition to Easter Island, where a wealth of archaeological and ethnographic data was gathered. A popular work *Aku-Aku* (1958) dealt with but did little to illuminate the work of this expedition. The subsequent official *Reports of the Norwegian Archaeological Expedition to Easter Island and the East Pacific*, Heyerdahl and Ferdon (eds), published in 1961 and 1966, failed to bear out Heyerdahl's American thesis. Easter Island culture, including the great statues, was found to be Polynesian in inspiration. By this time systematic archaeological and linguistic studies had demonstrated the ultimately Asiatic heritage of Polynesian man, while allowing for secondary Amerindian contacts, either by Peruvian *balsa* or Polynesian double canoe.

But Heyerdahl's main point, the feasibility of transoceanic voyaging in early craft, had been well and truly demonstrated. To drive it home he next turned his attention to the Atlantic. His *Ra I* and *II* were reedbundle boats of Egyptian type, constructed with the aid of reed-bundle boat builders from Lake Chad and Lake Titicaca. *Ra I* sank short of its goal but *Ra II* successfully crossed the Atlantic from Safi to Barbados (*The Ra Expeditions*, 1971). Then in 1978 the indefatigable Norwegian set out with eleven companions over the Indian Ocean in *Tigris*, a similar reed-bundle boat to *Ra*. Sailing from Shatt Al Arab in Iraq, they called at Bahrain, Muscat and Karachi, before crossing the Gulf of Aden to Djibouti – a passage of 144 days in all.

While some of Heyerdahl's particular contact theories may have only limited significance, his achievement in broadening the horizons of prehistory cannot be overestimated. Often at the risk of his life he has added an entirely new maritime dimension to our vision of the ancient world.

David H. Lewis

208

HINDEMITH, Paul 1895–1963

German composer

Paul Hindemith was born in Hanau-am-Main, the son of a master painter. In 1909 he enrolled at the Hoch Conservatory in Frankfurt, studying the violin under Adolf Rebner and later, from 1913, composition under Arnold Mendelssohn and Bernhard Sekles. In 1915 he was appointed leader of the orchestra of the Frankfurt Opera, a post he occupied until 1923. He came to prominence in the world of music in 1921, first of all in association with the premiere in Stuttgart of his two one-act operas *Mörder, Hoffnung der Frauen* (text by Oskar Kokoschka*) and *Das Nusch-Nuschi* (text by Franz Blei), which created a furore, and then through the performance of his String Quartet Op. 16 at the Donaueschingen Festival of contemporary chamber music. The Donaueschingen Festivals played a very important part in Hindemith's development over the following years. From 1923 onwards he was on the programme committee and his initiatives in that role, which he also exercised at the Baden Baden festivals from 1927 to 1929, had a decisive influence on the rising generation of young composers. In addition to his astonishing activity as composer and musical administrator, he was also busy in the concert hall as a viola player, both as soloist and as a member of the Amar Quartet, which vigorously promoted the cause of new chamber music in the 1920s. During the early part of that decade nearly all Hindemith's compositions were in the field of chamber music and song, but as his reputation became established he turned to the larger forms, to opera and to full-scale orchestral works. In 1926, in collaboration with the writer Ferdinand Lion, he wrote the opera *Cardillac* (after a novella by E. T. A. Hoffmann, *Das Fräulein von Scuderi*). Three years later the world premiere of the opera *Neues vom Tage* took place in Berlin. But Hindemith continued to attach equal importance to the whole range of music; he was especially concerned to win the interest of the lay public for new music, to which end he composed film music and occasional pieces for which he coined the generic name *Gebrauchsmusik* ('music for use'), and he worked with Bertolt Brecht* on *Das Lehrstück* (1929) and *Lindberghflug* (a radio play in which Kurt Weill* also had a hand). Hindemith's status in the musical life of the 1920s was acknowledged by his appointment as teacher of composition at the Musikhochschule in Berlin in 1927.

By 1930 he was at the pinnacle of his career, and in 1931 he composed the oratorio *Das Unaufhörliche*, in close collaboration with the poet Gottfried Benn. The year 1933 signified the great divide in his life and work, as it did for so many other German artists. His music was consigned by the Nazis to the category of 'degenerate art'. His position became steadily more difficult, though there were periods when it seemed to stabilize and he was allowed to travel abroad; visits to Turkey, at the behest of the Turkish government, resulted in his 'Proposals for the Reorganization of Music Life in Turkey'. Relations with the National Socialist authorities came to a head over his opera *Mathis der Maler* and the symphony of the same title, which Furtwängler performed in spite of the Nazi ban on Hindemith's work. Eventually, in 1937, emigration was the only course open to Hindemith and he left Germany, initially for Switzerland, and after travelling extensively he settled in the USA in April 1940. He was on the faculty of Yale University until 1953, teaching composition and organizing countless performances of 'early music' with the university's Collegium Musicum.

After the end of the war, he made his first return visit to Europe in 1947. He placed his world-wide fame at the service of the restitution of German culture. In 1951 he accepted the chair of music at the University of Zürich, and two years later settled in Blonay-sur-Vevey on Lake Geneva. From here he made numerous forays as a conductor, giving concerts in many countries. His creative tempo slowed markedly. The world premiere of his opera about Johannes Kepler, *Die Harmonie der Welt*, took place in Munich in 1957. In 1961 his last opera appeared, *The Long Christmas Dinner*, on the play by Thornton Wilder. His final work was the Mass for *a cappella* choir of 1963. He died in Frankfurt am Main.

Hindemith was a composer of extraordinary versatility. His oeuvre embraces almost all the traditional genres, ranging from opera and oratorio, through symphonic and other orchestral works, chamber music and song to sonatas for one and two instruments. In the 1920s his music was a by-word for the anti-romantic and the disrespectful. While some felt it to be destructive and others to be a symbol of potent genius, all who heard it were struck by the reckless vitality with which Hindemith broke away from the romantic aura surrounding 'art' and employed music to express the feelings of the new age. Works representing this innovatory attitude are the *Kammermusik Nr. 1* Op. 24, No. 1, which uses what was then a well-known fox-trot in the 'Finale 1921', and the *Suite 1922* Op. 26 for piano. The popular dance music of the time – Shimmy, Boston and Ragtime – and the influence of jazz give the *Suite* a character that is familiar and everyday and, at the same time, satirical. The work's strident aggression goes hand in hand with the young Hindemith's characteristic tendency to attack the bourgeois concept of music. His brash and tempestuous nature had another side to it, however; in the Nocturne of the *Suite 1922*, in the slow movement of the *Kammermusik Nr. 1*, in the important song-cycle *Die junge Magd*, Op. 23, No. 2 for female voice, 2 violas and 2 cellos (1922), there is a sensibility which suggests that the combativeness is less an expression of self-assurance than a kind of defensive measure against dangers and pressures that Hindemith may well have inwardly realized lay before him. Thus it is no accident that he soon found it necessary to channel the vehemence of his melodic kinetic impulses into more controlled structural uses. The change can be seen taking place in his String Quartet No. 3, Op. 22. The fugato structure of the first movement and the part-writing of the last reveal a conscious determination to restrain the melodic vigour within the bounds of polyphonic order. With the Rilke* song-cycle *Das Marienleben* (1923), the new stylistic concept is realized on a higher level of accomplishment. The music does not serve to convey an atmosphere: it is 'pure composition', although it is still too much of an experiment for it to be called an exemplar built on classical models.

Hindemith had now established the essentials of his future concept of style. He was now led to pay ever greater attention to the baroque era, where he found an affinity to his own wishes and ambitions. The link with the past did not consist solely in his interest in polyphony and the evolving continuity of musical form: the crucial factor was the concertante principle. This is manifested in a whole series of compositions, above all in the group of concertos which make up his Op. 36 *Kammermusik* set (1924–7), in the Concerto for Orchestra Op. 38 (1925), in the pieces entitled *Konzertmusik* of *c.* 1930, and in his opera *Cardillac* (1926), whose points of reference lie with Handel, Mozart and Verdi. According to Hindemith's first biographer, Heinrich Strobel, the significance of *Cardillac* lies in 'the way the numbers develop as purely musical constructs out of the highly characterized themes, while maintaining the closest possible relevance to the scene'.

In 1936–7 he sought to provide a theoretical basis for the view of music that he had hitherto demonstrated by example, and wrote *Die Unterweisung im Tonsatz* (*The Craft of Musical Composition*, 3 vols, 1937–8 and 1970, vols 1 and 2 trans. 1941, rev. 1945). According to this the nucleus of his stylistic concept is 'melodic tonality', the conception of musical forms governed by linear dictates, wherein the melodic lines are so laid out that they lead to chord-group hierarchies, which can be understood as a kind of 'expanded tonality'. In leading the tonal system back to the 'natural order' of the notes, Hindemith's theory is in effect counter to Schoenberg's* twelve-note thinking. Hindemith never adopted serial techniques; on the contrary, he was, particularly later, to express vehement opposition to serialism on the model of Schoenberg and Webern.*

Hindemith's concept of style, which admittedly experienced numerous changes in musical practice, is also above all a consequence of a claim for artistic ethics which he formulated most emphatically in the operas *Mathis der Maler* (1934–5) and *Die Harmonie der Welt* (1957, but first conceived in the late 1930s), which refer to contemporary world problems and to the artist's role in real political conflicts. There is no mistaking the connection Hindemith made between his stylistic ideal and the restitution of the 'old' concept of music, in which there is a place for all the manifestations of music, art music just as much as music for use. This is the light in which the chamber music of the 1930s through to the 1950s – a series of compositions for all the traditional instruments – should be seen. Indeed, the search for and rehabilitation of the 'old' concept of music links up with the example Hindemith set in writing for children and amateurs (*Wir bauen eine Stadt, Plöner Musiktag, Gebrauchsmusik*). For Hindemith, being a musician meant the lifting of the barriers between art music and amateur music, and between creation and interpretation.

Dr Dieter Rexroth
(translation by Mary Whittall)

See: Ian Kemp, *Hindemith* (1970), and Geoffrey Skelton, *Paul Hindemith, the Man Behind the Music* (1975)

209

HITCHCOCK, Sir Alfred Joseph 1899–1980

British/US film director

Hitchcock's career in cinema is in many ways unique: no other British director established himself so securely in Hollywood, and few others of any nationality have earned a descriptive tag ('The Master of Suspense') or become such a familiar public figure. Born in London, he began working in the customary minor capacities in the early 1920s, designing title cards, serving as assistant director and art director, all the while acquiring a fascination with the mechanics of cinematic illusion. By 1925 he was a full-time director: his material was mostly drawn from popular stage plays, yet he quickly and effectively mastered the grammar of silent cinema. *The Manxman* (1928) remains a stunning example of story-telling through the manipulation of visual symbols. And in *The Lodger* (1926), with stage matinée idol Ivor Novello as a suspected Jack the Ripper, he showed his early interest in crime and the harassment of the innocent.

In *Blackmail* (1929) Hitchcock pounced on sound as another tool to convey mood and propel the plot imaginatively. Then in 1934, with *The Man Who Knew Too Much*, he began a run of six solid thrillers for Gaumont-British, which have retained all their pungency. *The Thirty-Nine Steps* (1935) has many key Hitchcock ingredients – an innocent hero pursued by both police and enemy spies all over Britain, handcuffed for some of the way to a resentful heroine (Hitchcock has always treated male/female relationships somewhat icily). And

Sabotage (1936), derived from Conrad's* novel *The Secret Agent*, is quite the equal of its Hollywood successors in its power to generate audience jitters and deep unease.

Rebecca (1940) was his first American film, and Hitchcock luxuriated in the superior technical facilities Hollywood could offer. Yet there were losses as well as gains – none of his American films had that quirky response to everyday life found in his earlier work. Hitchcock took some time getting acclimatized. *Shadow of a Doubt* in 1943 found him beginning to explore small-town manners, but elsewhere he marked time with propaganda-slanted entertainments like *Lifeboat* (1943) or the bizarre melodrama of *Spellbound* (1945).

Then in 1951 came *Strangers on a Train*, in which an unhappily married tennis champion becomes ensnared in a psychotic's murderous trap: Hitchcock's use of Washington society and character psychology was ingenious and unerring. His best films were now probing deeper into fears and motivations: *I Confess* (1952) was a bleak study in tormented conscience, while *Rear Window* (1954) and *Vertigo* (1958) provided a sexual dimension to the problems faced by James Stewart's two heroes – a voyeur who discovers a murder through a neighbour's window, an ex-detective hounded by his love for a neurotic girl he failed to save from death. Even *North by North West* (1959) contained worried reflections of depersonalized modern life beneath its surface escapades.

In *Psycho* (1960) Hitchcock's love of teasing his audience reached a spectacular consummation. This deeply deceptive story of Norman Bates (played by Anthony Perkins), his motel, and his beloved mother was told with fiendish skill. The vicious murder of a woman taking a shower, immaculately pared through precision editing, has spawned countless imitations. In *The Birds* (1963) Hitchcock had a field day manipulating the mysterious attacks of massed birds, though the film's technical daring interfered with its emotional resonance. Since then his output received mixed responses: what some interpreted as laxity and slipping standards others kindly regarded as the relaxed approach suitable to old age. *Marnie* (1964), *Torn Curtain* (1966) and *Frenzy* (1972) certainly have superior sequences, yet their narrative momentum is erratic. But Hitchcock's reputation still remains unassailable: no one has ever used the elements of cinematic storytelling so artfully or so disturbingly.

Geoff Brown

210
HITLER, Adolf 1899–1945

Austro-German politician

Adolf Hitler was born in Braunau on the Inn as a national of the Austro-Hungarian Empire. He died, as Reich Chancellor of Germany, on 30 April 1945, in a bunker beneath the rubble of Berlin. He had been Germany's leader since 1933. Originally he had wanted to become an artist but two rejections from the Vienna Academy of Fine Arts changed his mind. In 1913 he left Austria for Munich where the following year he volunteered for a German regiment and went into the First World War. He was twice decorated for bravery and, in 1918, was wounded in a British gas attack. Whilst in hospital he learned that the Kaiser's Germany had been defeated and that Socialists now ruled the land. Hitler, who had gone into the war a dreamer and a drifter, emerged from it as a highly politicized demagogue.

After recovering, Hitler was employed as a political instructor by his old regiment and it was in this post that he first came across the small Fascist party which he joined and then led. His success was the result of his skill in politics for he combined a polished demagogic style with an easy political logic, one which made a new and complex world situation seem the simple result of a Jewish–Marxist conspiracy. Indeed, it was from this concept that the subsequent history of the Third Reich was to flow even though the road to power was not easy.

In the Fascist manner Hitler first tried to ape the March on Rome tactic of his forerunner and idol Mussolini*. But Hitler's attempt to putsch ended in a nine-month gaol sentence and the need to rethink strategy. Since Weimar Germany was a democracy, the Nazi leader reasoned, power had to be won by methods which were appropriate to it: the party would have to become a mass movement and democratic privileges might be exploited to the point of illegality. In addition, Nazis would have to peddle a coherent ideology and Hitler himself set about trying to provide the latter. In fact his intellectual contribution was minimal for *Mein Kampf* (1924) was no more than a rambling account of his own version of the Social Darwinism and Anti-Semitism of others badly glued to an attempt at making his own life appear a suitable symbol for a future Germany. His spoken ideas were generally banal although they could, on occasions, seem remarkably apposite.

Hitler came to realize that in an era of mass communication the communicator-politician supported by dedicated followers could flourish and so, within ten years, he became Germany's dictator. He was helped by the Nazis' open use of political terrorism (which none the less never won for him the majority of Germans) and the world economic crisis of 1929. Once in power, he dismantled the achievements of the Weimar: he banned all parties except his own, he transformed the economy and he institutionalized the violent intimidation of all opposition. Indeed, the spiritual site of the Third Reich was not located, as popular myth would have it, in Wagnerian idylls or licentious excess but in the concentration camp and the Gestapo cell.

A special part in all this was played by Hitler's persecution of the Jews. It enabled him not only to prove his ruthlessness but also to fabricate a kind of national identity. So-called Aryan Germans (and Europeans in general) were invited to define themselves as those who did not have to wear yellow stars, resettle themselves in ghettos and vanish suddenly to the east and its gas chambers.

To suggest that the reality of the Third Reich was very different from the image its leadership tried to create is, however, to fail to explain adequately why the Nazis' own image proved so strong. For Hitler appeared to have abolished class conflict, to have enabled the Germans to go back to work, to have provided law and order at home and stood up for Germany in international affairs. Equally, the Nazis' desolation of German cultural life, not least by their elimination of the Jews, seems less significant than their support of obvious bourgeois art and traditional values of propriety and rural harmony. One answer is simply that Hitler and his henchmen possessed such understanding of the nature of mass communication and such mastery of its techniques that any myth they chose to create was bound to be effective. The very notion that National Socialism was a German phenomenon rather than a straightforward variety of European Fascism is a case in point. Nazi attitudes were, more often than not, Fascist ones, originating from a response to the overthrow of the old world by the Great War and its aftermath by those who contrasted the glory of comradeship under arms and patriotic death to the chaos of Marxist revolution.

Hitler's individual impact was very different from what it seemed and has been made to seem. He was but a figurehead in most areas of politics, convinced that the correct appearance would always be taken as the correct action and that its consequences would be attributed to something for which he could not be held responsible. Hitler's most important offering, then, was that he realized that in the new politics of Nazism, propaganda or the interpretation of reality was interchangeable with leadership, or the shaping of reality. That the results would one day catch up with him was exemplified by his death. For to commit suicide by shooting himself in the mouth was to destroy himself through the same organ that had brought him his fame, the source of his demagogic appeal. Hitler verbalized the intentions of the Nazis and they intended him to be their leader and run their affairs. This is the cause of the exaggeration of his personal role.

The Thousand Year Reich, that figment of Nazi imagination, lasted a little over twelve years. National Socialism did not create a new Germany for it brought only the destruction of an existing alternative one, based on Fascist ideals of violence, anti-Marxism and

racial exclusiveness. Indeed, the destructive power of Nazi policies, which was a result of the dynamism inherent in the movement, led directly to war and defeat. Each Nazi campaign was designed to engender another campaign, another struggle, another test. There was only one exception, of course: the final solution of the so-called Jewish problem, perhaps the most consistent Nazi aim and one to which all real strategic goals were subordinated.

Hitler was remarkable as a violent demagogue, the leader of a political movement which imposed on human lives an unrealizable set of policies. He could no more be appeased than Germany become a nation of blond blue-eyed giants. Claiming to uphold German nationhood, he in fact destroyed it; pretending to be close to the German people, he in fact prescribed their destruction since their defeat by the Allies would render them valueless. Hitler and his state are not a monument to the values he maintained he was promoting but rather to a more abstract and frightening truth: political manipulation by a violent movement with a violent leadership outpaced mankind's comprehension of the extent to which political reality was being fabricated.

Dr Anthony Glees

See: H. R. Trevor-Roper (ed.), *Hitler's Table Talk* (1953); Ernst Nolte, *The Three Faces of Fascism* (1965); George Mosse, *The Crisis of German Ideology* (1966); Alan Bullock, *Hitler* (1971).

211
HOCHHUTH, Rolf 1931–

German playwright

Hochhuth, who left school at the age of sixteen, is largely self-educated; a voracious reader, he decided to become a bookseller to have easy access to reading matter. He had been fourteen years old when American troops occupied the little town of Eschwege in Northern Hesse (very close to today's border between East and West Germany) where he grew up; he became deeply preoccupied with the origins of the war and the problem of war guilt. So he delved into the study of contemporary history which finally led him to write the play which not only brought him into world prominence but also created one of the most intense and stormy controversies ever caused by a piece of theatre, a debate which shook the Roman Catholic Church to its foundations.

This play, *Der Stellvertreter* (*The Representative* in Britain, *The Deputy* in the US), first performed by Piscator in Berlin in 1963, raises the question why Pope Pius XII remained silent about Hitler's* genocide of the

Jews, although he knew about it. A word from him condemning the holocaust would have stopped Hitler. And if it had failed to do that and Hitler had turned against the Church, should not Christ's representative on earth have been ready to be crucified, as Christ was? Hochhuth embodied these questions in a vast tragedy, written in the traditional style of classical German drama as developed by the great eighteenth-century romantic playwright Schiller. While the Pope is in the centre of this tragedy, his attitude is contrasted with that of a Catholic priest who goes to his death in Auschwitz, and an SS officer who joins the resistance against Hitler when he realizes what is being done.

Der Stellvertreter was produced throughout the world and everywhere led to violent demonstrations and bitter controversy. It was the first major world-wide success by a German playwright of the post-war generation and established a powerful new trend towards 'documentary drama'. Hochhuth's second play, *Soldiers* (*Soldaten*, Berlin 1967), created an uproar of similar proportions. This time the tragic figure at the centre was Winston Churchill, whom Hochhuth reveres as the champion of freedom in the fight against Hitler but regards as enmeshed in a tragic conflict between ends and means. To win the struggle against supreme evil, Churchill, as Hochhuth sees it, had to use evil means: mass 'terror' bombing of innocent civilians and even political murder. Hochhuth's play suggests that Churchill ordered the murder of the Polish leader, General Sikorsky, in an air accident at Gibraltar, because Sikorsky's uncompromising stand against Soviet demands endangered the alliance with Stalin*. The latter, highly contentious, accusation resulted in a libel action brought by the surviving pilot of the crashed aircraft which involved the author and the producers of the play in London in a costly financial settlement.

Hochhuth's later plays, always based on a mass of voluminously documented material, are: *Guerillas* (1970), a highly fanciful documentary on the theft of a US atomic submarine in order to blackmail the American government into a more liberal policy; *Die Hebamme* (*The Midwife*, 1971), which shows the sufferings of the homeless in prosperous post-war Germany; *Lysistrata und die NATO* (1975), in which the women of a Greek island repeat the sex strike of their ancestresses depicted in Aristophanes' comedy but go one better by not only refusing to sleep with their husbands but actually sleeping with the NATO officers instead; *Tod eines Jaegers* (*Death of a Hunter*, 1977), a long monologue depicting the last hours of Ernest Hemingway* before his suicide.

Hochhuth, who now lives in Vienna, is one of the few German writers who does not disdain to descend into the political arena and to use his prestige to exercise a real political influence on events and to open the debate on topics of major importance. His courage and integrity are beyond doubt.

Martin Esslin

There is a useful study of Hochhuth in German by Siegfried Melchinger (1967). The story of his first great success is documented in *The Storm over the Deputy*, ed. Eric Bentley (New York 1964).

212

HO CHI MINH 1890–1969

Vietnamese political leader

Ho Chi Minh, the name which the great Vietnamese patriot assumed for political reasons and by which he has come to be universally known, was born in Nghe An Province, Vietnam. While he was at Quoc Hoc College in Hue he engaged in underground work with one of the nationalist movements. Knowing French civilization only in its colonial form of misery for his fellow countrymen, Ho Chi Minh wished to find out what was actually meant by such terms as *liberté, egalité* and *fraternité*. He wanted to study the new revolutionary theories and experiences of the time.

He shipped aboard a French liner as kitchen help, and, as cook and gardener in Le Havre, photographer's assistant in Paris, waiter and stoker in London, hired labourer in Brooklyn, he visited many countries and learned that 'our friends are the working class, the labouring people in all countries: our enemy is imperialism wherever it may be'.

The October Revolution had a profound influence on him and he found Lenin's* *Theses on the National and Colonial Question* inspiring. 'Here's what we need. Here's our road to liberation.' In 1919 he sent to the Peace Conference at Versailles his famous eight-point petition demanding recognition of the Vietnamese people's right to freedom, democracy and self-determination which burst like a bomb-shell on French public opinion. He participated in the founding of the French Communist Party in 1921 and was elected to the Presidium of its First National Congress. He pointed out the close relationship between colonial revolution and proletarian revolution in the 'mother country' and explained that the colonial revolution was an inseparable part of the world revolution.

In 1924 he went to China where he founded the Vietnam Revolutionary Youth Association to train young people to go into the factories and mines and among the peasants of Vietnam to spread revolutionary ideas. His book, *The Revolutionary Road*, applied Marxism-Leninism to the concrete conditions of Vietnam in a creative way. In February 1930, on Kowloon Island, Hong Kong, he convened the founding congress of the Communist Party of Vietnam. The Outline

Strategy which he drafted called for 'a new type bourgeois democratic revolution which would advance to a socialist revolution without passing through the stage of capitalist development, its task to overthrow French imperialism and the feudal landlord class, win complete independence for Vietnam, give land to the peasants and set up a worker-peasant-soldier government'.

In 1940 the Japanese invaded Vietnam and the French handed over the country. Ho Chi Minh summoned the people to rise in a general insurrection against both the Japanese and French collaborators. In the liberated area the Vietnam National Committee for Liberation was set up with Ho Chi Minh as President and this was the Provisional Government of the Democratic Republic of Vietnam which was declared independent on 2 September 1945 in Hanoi.

Ho Chi Minh's position was confirmed in the general elections held the following year. But there were American troops in the north helping Chiang Kai-shek and British troops were helping the French stage an imperialist come-back. In his directive of December 1946, *Resistance of the Entire People*, Ho Chi Minh laid down the ground rules of protracted, all-sided, self-reliant people's war. He called on the people to 'wipe out the French colonialists and defeat the US interventionists who had begun to help them'. On 7 May 1954, was fought and won at Dien Bien Phu one of the decisive battles of history which ended French colonialism in south-east Asia.

When the US, in defiance of the Geneva Agreement, moved in with ever more massive military force and began turning the southern half of Vietnam into a new-type colony, Ho Chi Minh called on the Vietnamese people to take up two great tasks simultaneously: to build up the north and take it to socialism; to achieve reunification of the country and complete the people's national democratic revolution. In March 1964, a special political conference was convened by Ho Chi Minh to greet the victories being won by the South Vietnam National Front for Liberation formed in 1960.

Ho Chi Minh died on 3 September 1969, nearly six years before the final liberation victory he had done so much to prepare for. In one of his poems he wrote:

Our mountains will always be, our rivers will always
  be, our people will always be,
The American invaders defeated, we will rebuild our
  land ten times more beautiful.

William Ash

See: *Prison Diary, Poems* (Hanoi 1965); *Selected Writings: 1920–1969* (Hanoi 1977); also: Committee for the Study of the History of the Vietnam Workers Party, *Our President Ho Chi Minh* (1976).

213

HOCKNEY, David 1937–

British painter

From *enfant terrible* to golden boy of the colour supplements and now one of England's most established artists, Hockney's career has been a brilliant success story. Arriving in London in 1959 from his native Bradford, he already achieved public notice while a student at the Royal College. Like many of his generation, he reacted against the dominance of abstraction; critics were misled, however, in taking the inclusion of certain motifs, for example tea-packets, in his work as justification for labelling him a Pop Artist. His concerns have, rather, always been personal and autobiographical – in a sense, very traditional. At first, he felt very strongly the need to reconcile this with the main tenets of modernist painting, especially flatness. Much of his work explored, with great wit, the contradictions between the two-dimensional surface and three-dimensional illusion: this underlay his playing with several 'styles', for example the Egyptian – as in *The First Marriage* (1962). Such explorations helped him to develop, with remarkable consistency, towards a type of realism with which he felt instinctively in tune – the smooth, somewhat photographic style for which he is most famous. The year 1964 represented a watershed: in that year he began to use acrylic paint and he discovered California. The geometry of Californian architecture provided his paintings with a strong, slightly graphic, construction which did not conflict with a naturalistic reading. He frequently painted swimming pools, partly because the depiction of water, like glass and other transparent substances, posed a fascinating challenge, and partly because they were a convenient setting for his principal interest, the male human figure.

Perhaps Hockney's greatest contribution to cultural change has been his frank avowal of homosexuality, in that it is hard to think of any reputation, in England at least, which has done much more to liberalize public opinion on this matter. His influence in the specific sphere of art, by contrast, has been essentially conservative or, better, conciliatory. Not much in sympathy with the aims of avant-gardism, he is above all a superbly talented practitioner of recognized skills. A lover of opera, he has designed a number of sets, including for *The Magic Flute* at Glyndebourne. His graphic works, including several small books, are of a very high quality. Particularly evident is his talent as a draughtsman: he has produced many drawings, some in coloured crayon, which capture the atmosphere of certain situations and the characters of several close friends (as well as his parents) with extraordinary accuracy and feeling. A painting with a similar quality is *Mr and Mrs Clark and Percy* (1970 –1). In some ways, it is a quality shared with good short-story-telling; nor would the literary analogy be offensive to Hockney. Much admired abroad, there is nevertheless something about his art which is very English and in particular Yorkshire. From that county no doubt derives his plentiful common sense, enabling him to be straightforward about what matters to him and cynical about what he believes to be pretentious in many of the modern art world's attitudes.

Gray Watson

The only major book about Hockney is written by Hockney himself: *David Hockney* (1976). Books of his drawings include: *72 Drawings* (1971); *Travels with Pen, Pencil and Ink* (1978). See also the catalogues to his exhibitions at the Whitechapel Gallery, London (1970), and the Musée des Arts Décoratifs, Paris (1974). Hockney is the subject of the film *A Bigger Splash* (dir. Jack Hazan, 1974).

214
HOLST, Gustav 1874–1934

English composer and teacher

Gustav Holst was born in Cheltenham and christened Gustavus Theodore von Holst after his Latvian-born grandfather Gustavus (who taught the harp and composed pieces for it) and his great-uncle Theodore (a painter). The 'von' was an embarrassment during the First World War, and he dropped it.

Like Vaughan Williams*, Holst developed with difficulty a style of composing which could enable him to express his individual vision. After some academic training, and lessons in composition with Stanford, he freed himself from the German musical language then predominant in England, seeking a personal idiom in other sources, in aspects of the English musical heritage – the characteristics of folk-song and early rhythmic polyphony. The richness and scope of his creative work reflected the wide range of his interests, which extended to Sanskrit, philosophies and poetry of the East, and astrology. A bold experimenter in musical styles (including polytonality) he cultivated towards the end of his life an austere, concentrated idiom such as is found in *Egdon Heath* (1927), a symphonic poem inspired by Thomas Hardy's description of a Dorset landscape. But his best-known orchestral work is *The Planets* (1914–17), a large-scale, richly orchestrated suite in seven movements. In this, Holst imaginatively portrays in musical terms the character and astrological significance of the different planets, from Mars, the bringer of war, to Neptune, the mystic. It is on this work that Holst's reputation as a composer largely rests. Equally characteristic, however, are certain more classically conceived works such as the *St Paul's Suite* for strings

(1913) and the Double Concerto for two violins and orchestra (1929), besides the overtly oriental impressions of *Beni Mora* (1910) and the *Japanese Suite* (1915).

In Holst's vocal music, his explorations were equally far-reaching. The choral *Rig Veda Hymns* (1908–12) must have sounded quite un-English in 1912. Modes akin to Indian ragas were used, irregular rhythms, and a triadic harmony quite unconventional in its progressions. The large-scale choral-and-orchestral *Hymn of Jesus* (1917) takes its text largely from the apocryphal Acts of St John, and the inspiration derives from plainsong (akin to folk-song in its modality), *ostinato* procedures, and stark medieval textures: in all, a work of the profoundest originality. Other choral compositions explore chromaticism in a highly original way; but Holst's style achieves one of the finest and most balanced expressions in the *Ode to Death* (1919), to words by Walt Whitman.

In opera, Holst brought a freshness of outlook which led to some fine music; but there was not always a strong enough dramatic sense to hold the stage. The early *Savitri* (1908), quite unlike any other English operatic work, is based on an episode from Hindu scriptures, translated by the composer. In contrast to its austere beauty and economy, there are the comic operas *The Perfect Fool* (1918–22) and *At the Boar's Head* (1924). Most satisfying in this field is undoubtedly *The Wandering Scholar* (1929–30), based on a Chaucerian episode from Helen Waddell – a late work, truly operatic in its complete unity of dramatic text and music.

Besides his importance as a composer in his own right, Holst was a pioneer, opening up new paths in English music which were further explored by other composers. His influence on Vaughan Williams, Rubbra, and Britten*, for example, was immense. Holst was a many-sided musician – composer, teacher, organizer, pianist and trombonist – somebody who *lived* music to the fullest degree, and who had the gift of communicating his experience and enthusiasms to others. His work as a teacher was of great importance, particularly in his London posts as music master of St Paul's Girls' School, Hammersmith, and as musical director at Morley College 'for working men and women'.

David Cox

See: Imogen Holst, *Gustav Holst: a Biography* (1938) and *The Music of Gustav Holst* (1951).

215
HOOK, Sidney 1902–

US philosopher, publicist

Born in New York City, educated in local schools, at City College and at Columbia University, Hook spent almost his entire teaching life, save for several spells as Visiting Professor, at New York University. Since his retirement he has been attached to the Hoover Institution for the Study of War, Revolution and Peace.

He was a devoted pupil of John Dewey*, going on to join Dewey in most of his public campaigns and commitments. One product of Hook's early Trotskyist* associations was a study, in its time outstanding, *Towards an Understanding of Karl Marx* (1933). However, although Hook still claims to be some sort of democratic socialist, this early Marxist phase was soon left behind. But two later books have dealt with *The Ambiguous Legacy: Marx and the Marxists* (1955) and *The Hero in History* (1943). The latter treats a question crucial to the Marxist or any other similar theory of historical development. Hook argues, using the elegantly chosen example of Lenin's* role in the October Coup against the democratic successors of the last Tsar, that the role of a particular world-historical individual must be too great to be contained within the compass of any such theory.

Hook has also done traditional work in some mainstream philosophical areas. He produced, for instance, a volume of essays on *The Quest for Being* (1961), and studies of *Education for Modern Man* (1963) and of *The Metaphysics of Pragmatism* (1927). In addition he edited a commemorative volume, *John Dewey, Philosopher of Science and Freedom* (1950). Yet there is no doubt that his main work has been the intellectual defence of freedom against every sort of tyranny, whether traditional or totalitarian; and against what he likes to call 'ritualistic liberals', and other witting or unwitting sellers of the pass. In this cause Hook has served on many committees, including the American Committee for Cultural Freedom, the Congress for Cultural Freedom, and the International Conference for the Rights of Man; and published an endless flow of articles and books, among them *Heresy – yes, Conspiracy – no* (1953), *Political Power and Personal Freedom* (1959), *Paradoxes of Freedom* (1962), and *Academic Freedom and Academic Anarchy* (1970). His battle colours are run up in his entry for *Who's Who in America*: 'It is better to be a live jackal than a dead lion – for jackals, not men. Men who have the moral courage to fight intelligently for freedom have the best prospects of avoiding the fates both of live jackals and of dead lions. Survival is not the be-all and end-all of a life worthy of man. Sometimes the worst thing we can know about a man is that he has survived. Those who say that life is worth living at any cost have already written for themselves an epitaph of infamy, for there is no cause and no person they will not betray to stay alive.'

Professor Antony Flew

Sidney Hook and the Contemporary World (1966), ed. P. Kurtz.

216
HORKHEIMER, Max 1895–1973

German social theorist

Initiator of the theoretical current loosely labelled the 'Frankfurt School', and a crucial figure of what is known, even more loosely, as 'Western Marxism', Max Horkheimer was born into an entrepreneurial Jewish family of Stuttgart. Breaking with tradition (partly as a result of service in the disintegrating Imperial Army), he pursued an academic career, his formative influences being: the multi-talented neo-Kantian, Hans Cornelius; the founder of phenomenology, Edmund Husserl*, and Martin Heidegger*, whose 'Existence Philosophy' seemed to express the anguish of a generation. None of this was regarded as incompatible with an overriding commitment to Marxism (epitomized for Horkheimer by Rosa Luxemburg*: had not Marx himself argued that the proletariat would abolish philosophy precisely by 'actualizing' it?)

Having been instrumental in establishing Germany's first Institute for Social Research in Frankfurt in 1923, Horkheimer became its Director in 1930, simultaneously assuming Germany's first chair in Social Philosophy, and editing, from 1932, the *Zeitschrift für Sozialforschung* ('Journal of Social Research'). In his own contributions to the journal, Horkheimer formulated the programme of a 'critical theory of society': to identify, at all levels, the contradictions of capitalist society, and, via a 'dialogue' with the workers' movement, to intervene as a practical force in the struggle for classless society. But even as this conceptualization of the theory–praxis nexus was being distilled, the rise to power of the Nazis (which forced the Institute to migrate to New York), together with the Stalinization* of the USSR and the culture shock of New Deal America, served to transform 'critical theory of society' into an increasingly abstract account of a universal conflict between 'Reason' and 'Manipulation'. This was particularly evident in the last few issues of the journal, which, with the fall of Paris, came out in English as *Studies in Philosophy and Social Science*.

In 1941, the journal was discontinued altogether, and Horkheimer's break with his original programme was symbolized by his departure for California. Together with his close friend, Theodor W. Adorno*, he now worked on what he considered a far more radical project, the *Dialectic of Enlightenment*. The current barbarization of Europe, together with the 'culture industry' of the USA, was no longer seen simply as an expression of the irrationality of capitalism, but in terms (greatly indebted to Husserl's *Crisis of European Science*) of a concept of 'Reason' dating from the Enlightenment: the latter, prefigured in Greek philosophy, had dispelled the 'dark forces' of myth and religion in favour of an instrumental rationality that viewed nature solely as an object for domination. Blind to its own genesis and consequences, the Enlightenment was itself a mythology, and one so deeply rooted and concealed that not even Marx had been able to break its spell.

Partly for financial reasons, partly out of personal commitment, Horkheimer had also taken up contact with the American Jewish Committee, whose Department of Scientific Research he headed, editing the *Studies in Prejudice* (1949–50). But in 1949 he was persuaded to return to Frankfurt as Professor of Philosophy and Sociology and as Director of the Institute for Social Research, newly established in its native town. Horkheimer retired his chair in 1959, leaving the Directorship of the Institute to Adorno, but he continued to play a role in the affairs of the University until his death in 1973. By then, the student anti-authoritarian movement, which had avidly seized on his essays of the 1930s outlining the revolutionary theory–praxis nexus, had served to transform Horkheimer into a liberal and a staunch defender of the Establishment (including the Pope, the Pentagon and the Shah of Iran). Whereas his former Institute colleague, Herbert Marcuse*, not only sanctioned but actively contributed to the Marx renaissance of the last decade, the utilization of 'critical theory of society' in this regard was a matter of deep regret to Horkheimer, who died a lonely and bewildered old man.

Phil Slater

Horkheimer's seminal essays of the 1930s are collected in *Critical Theory* (1972). The highly readable *Eclipse of Reason* (1947) can be recommended as an introduction to the more demanding collaborative work with Adorno, *Dialectic of Enlightenment* (1947, trans. 1972). See also *Verwaltete Welt* ('Administered World', 1970). About Horkheimer and his circle: Martin Jay, *The Dialectical Imagination* (1973); and Phil Slater, *Origin and Significance of the Frankfurt School* (1977).

217
HUGHES, Ted (Edward James) 1930–

English poet

Hughes was born in Mytholmroyd, in the Calder Valley, on the Yorkshire side of the Pennines. Although he left his birthplace at the age of seven, it was a vital formative influence: growing up with a harsh, vigorous, non-standard form of spoken English, and close to some of the wildest country in England, shaped his poetic voice and his vision. He was educated at Mexborough Grammar School in South Yorkshire and Pembroke College, Cambridge, where he changed from English to Anthropology. The rejection of academic study of literature in favour of a discipline that took him beyond his own civilization was a significant choice. An abiding early influence was *The White Goddess* by Robert Graves*.

In 1956 he married the American poet Sylvia Plath*. In 1961 they settled in Devon with their two children. In this period his first two volumes, *The Hawk in the Rain* (1957) and *Lupercal* (1960), were published. He was immediately recognized as a powerful new voice. Some reacted as if English poetry had been invaded by a barbaric, primitive force. His language, though highly literate, was harsh, physical, aggressive and energetically mimetic. It related to tradition via Dylan Thomas* and Gerard Manley Hopkins, by-passing the dominant urbane and ironic mode of modern English poetry. His subject, of which this style was the natural expression, was, and is, the continuity, broken in consciousness and culture but affirming itself in the biological and unconscious self, between humanity and the natural world beyond. This entailed a particular stress upon and empathy with predatory violence – in such poems as 'The Jaguar', 'Pike' and above all 'Hawk Roosting'. At the same time, for example in 'The Thought-Fox', 'Pike' and 'The Bull Moses', he showed great delicacy and subtlety, and there is a deeply meditative quality in much of his best work. 'Violence' is a word that has always bedevilled Hughes criticism. He has said that his work is about not violence but vitality, and that what his critics call violence is an integral quality of great poetry, to be found in Shakespeare, Homer, Aeschylus and the Bible.

In 1962 Hughes and his wife separated and in 1963 Sylvia Plath committed suicide. For some time he wrote no poetry and his next major volume, *Wodwo*, did not appear until 1967. This contains some of his best nature poems, such as 'Skylarks' and 'Thistles', and also some more overtly ambitious metaphysical poems, of which the best are perhaps 'Stations', 'The Green Wolf' and 'Wodwo' itself. 'Full Moon and Little Frieda' is one of his most tender poems. The book also contains five stories and a play. Many of the poems express a darker, less celebratory view of nature, and a profound preoccupation with death.

With *Crow* (1970) he began a new phase of connected, mythical work. It is his harshest book, a sequence of poems, many of them narrative in form, linked by Crow, a protean figure influenced by American Indian Trickster mythology, and the antagonist of the Christian God. *Crow* severely divided Hughes's critics. His admirers see it as a bold attempt at unillusioned poetry, with a new energy and simplicity of language; his detractors find it crude and nihilistic. Unfortunately it has remained incomplete and Hughes has confused matters by speaking of its 'super-simple, super-ugly' style, which does scant justice to its subtlety and variety.

In 1970 he married Carole Orchard and in 1971

collaborated with Peter Brook* on *Orghast*, a drama written in a language invented by Hughes. Two major 'mythical' works have followed *Crow*. *Gaudete* (1977) is a narrative poem about Dionysiac disruption in a beautifully and powerfully evoked English countryside. It is flawed by a tendency to caricature and a crude use of the occult. More successful is *Cave Birds* (1978), a more connected sequence than *Crow*, with drawings by the American artist Leonard Baskin. A drama of psychic rebirth, it demonstrates a renewed richness and complexity of language, and a more hopeful view of the human condition. The Mother Goddess celebrated by Graves is a prominent figure in both these works.

Hughes's work in the 1970s, which also includes *Season Songs* (1975) and *Moon-Bells* (1978) – both 'for children' but not exclusively so – *Remains of Elmet* (1979, a sequence about the Calder Valley) and *Moortown* (1979, including a powerfully direct autobiographical sequence about farming), has been prolific, varied, and marked by a more overt tenderness and humanity. His mastery of a range of voices, from the mythic-archetypal to the practically realistic, is that of a major poet at the height of his powers.

Dr Neil Roberts

Selected Poems 1957–1967 (1972) contains most of the best poems in the first three volumes. Other works for children: *Meet My Folks!* (1961); *How the Whale Became* (1963); *The Earth-Owl and Other Moon-People* (1963); *Nessie the Mannerless Monster* (1964); *Poetry in the Making* (1968); *The Iron Man* (1968); *Moon-Whales* (1976). Fiction: 'The Head', in *Bananas* 11 (1978). See also: Keith Sagar, *The Art of Ted Hughes* (1975, revised 1978); and A. C. H. Smith, *Orghast at Persepolis* (1972).

218
HUIZINGA, Johan 1872–1945

Dutch historian

The son of a professor of medicine at the University of Groningen, Johan Huizinga studied at that university and (briefly and none too successfully) at Leipzig. When he took his doctor's degree in 1897 it was as a specialist in Indo-Aryan philology. Although he took a post as a history teacher in a Haarlem school, for several more years his research interests remained in the oriental field. Huizinga then decided to turn to history, undertaking a study of early town history under the guidance of Professor P. J. Blok, which began to appear in 1905 under the title *The Origins of Haarlem*. In that same year Blok secured his appointment to the chair of history at Groningen; in 1915 he moved to the chair of general history at Leiden, where he remained until the university was closed by the Germans in 1942.

Huizinga was briefly imprisoned in a concentration camp, then released to live under surveillance in a small village near Arnhem, where he died shortly before the liberation of Holland.

The indirect route by which Huizinga became a professional historian explains much of the special character of his work. His wide range of cultural and linguistic knowledge, combined with his experience of teaching school children over an extensive syllabus, gave his writing unusual breadth, even when he was dealing with relatively narrow topics. Never a master of the precise archival skills perhaps overvalued by many of his contemporaries, he compensated for these by his analytical powers (partly derived from philology), by his intellectual enterprise and independence, and by his discriminating appreciation of the arts. His most famous book, *The Waning of the Middle Ages* (1919, trans. 1924), had its genesis in his admiration for the art of the Van Eyck brothers. Exhibitions of their work, and that of other fifteenth-century masters, had made a considerable stir in the early years of the century, when Huizinga conceived the idea of writing of the later Middle Ages as 'an epoch of fading and decay'. The book's real strength, however, lies not in its 'thesis', but in its texture and its detail. Primarily a study of the highly wrought and artificial culture of the Burgundian and French courts, it is yet full of insights into the mentality of the fourteenth and fifteenth centuries in a much wider context. As the invocation of a moment in time it remains one of the masterworks of twentieth-century cultural history, showing Huizinga's rare ability to re-create the past intuitively, while controlling that intuition by intelligence and discrimination. The same qualities are apparent in the long essay *Dutch Civilization in the Seventeenth Century* (1941, trans. 1968), perhaps the most perfectly balanced of all his writings. Even here Huizinga's critics, while always respectful of his achievement, have pointed to a missing dimension in his work. Never truly interested in politics or political history (a distaste perhaps inherited from his Mennonite ancestors), his perception was less acute when explanations of change were needed, even in the cultural field. Valid enough in its own terms, such criticism may rather miss the point; Huizinga's very personal approach, while it may have limited his work, was also the source of its distinctive qualities.

Among Huizinga's other important works are his biography of *Erasmus* (1924, trans. 1924), a short, unpretentious book which remains one of the most sensitive portraits of the great Burgundian humanist, and the enigmatic late work *Homo Ludens* (1938, trans. 1949). The latter must be reckoned a stimulating failure; the idea of isolating and analysing the play element in culture was a brilliant one, but the execution too eclectic and haphazard. Above all Huizinga failed to benefit from the advances (admittedly then very recent) in such subjects as psychology and zoology, not to mention games theory itself. Despite such weaknesses, *Homo Ludens* remains a tribute to its author's intellectual adventurousness, a book whose challenge has too rarely been taken up since. Indeed, Huizinga founded no school of historians, and some of his pupils were among his sternest critics. Like Burckhardt (who greatly influenced him) his effect was of a much more general kind; cultural history as a discipline will always recognize him as one of its greatest pioneers.

Robin Briggs

Huizinga's complete works were published in Dutch as *Verzamelde Werken* (7 vols, Haarlem 1948–53). Other books in English translation include: *In the Shadow of Tomorrow* (1936); and the volumes of essays *Men and Ideas* (1960).

219
HUSSERL, Edmund 1859–1938

German philosopher

The philosopher known as the 'father of phenomenology' began his career as a mathematician. Husserl was born at Prossnitz (Prostějov) in Moravia and studied physics, mathematics, astronomy and philosophy at the Universities of Leipzig, Berlin and Vienna, receiving his doctorate in Vienna in 1882 for a dissertation on the calculus of variations. This was followed by a period in Berlin as assistant to the mathematician Karl Weierstrass. Then, in 1883, Husserl went back to Vienna to study with the philosopher and psychologist Franz Brentano who was to be one of the formative influences on the development of his thought. Later he went to Halle to study with one of Brentano's pupils, Carl Stumpf, and in 1887 became a lecturer at Halle University. His new interests were reflected in his first book, *Philosophie der Arithmetik* (1891), an attempt to clarify the presuppositions of mathematics by establishing their basis in the structure of the human mind. His analysis was dissected in a famous essay by Gottlob Frege who pointed out that Husserl had confused logical and psychological considerations. Subsequently, Husserl revised his approach, and in his *Logical Investigations* (*Logische Untersuchungen*, 1900–1, trans. 1970) undertook the critique of psychologism indicated by Frege, while continuing to seek to establish the conditions of knowledge by examining the nature of the fundamental relationship between consciousness and the world. He went on to develop the philosophy known as phenomenology, that is, a philosophy of consciousness which was critical of both empiricism and rationalism and which accorded priority to description and intuition over reflection. It was important that phenomenology be purified of psychological factors; accordingly, in his *Ideas: General Intro-*

duction to Pure Phenomenology (*Ideen zu einer reinen Phänomenologie und phänomenologischen Philosophie*, 1913, trans. 1931), where we find the elucidation of the major phenomenological concepts, Husserl developed the method known as the reduction (*epoche*), by which all empirical and metaphysical presuppositions are suspended in order to bring to light the essential structures of the meaning-bestowing consciousness. *Ideen* presents a theory of phenomenology as a universal science of meanings, no longer just a method, but a transcendental, idealist philosophy. It was written during Husserl's period as Professor of Philosophy at Göttingen (1901–16) when, for the first time, he began to attract students from all over Germany, and from other countries as well, and the phenomenological 'school' came into existence. From 1916 to 1928, Husserl held a chair at Freiburg, to which he was succeeded by his pupil Heidegger*, whom he saw as his philosophical heir, though it was not long before differences between them became apparent. The outbreak of the First World War had a considerable impact on Husserl's thought. He felt that the old European culture and values were disintegrating, and in his lectures emphasized the role of phenomenology in the renewal of Europe. After his retirement he continued to write and give public lectures on this theme. His last work, *The Crisis of European Sciences and Transcendental Phenomenology* (*Die Krisis der europäischen Wissenschaften und die transzendentale Phänomenologie*, 1936, trans. 1970), analysed the 'crisis of European Man' and reiterated his ideal of a scientific philosophy. His extensive unpublished manuscripts, now in the Husserl Archives at Louvain, were smuggled out of Germany during the Nazi regime, for posthumous editing and publication.

Husserl thought of phenomenology as a transcendental philosophy, but it has also been described as a radical empiricism. Depending on the emphasis of the interpreter, it can be seen as a realist or as an idealist philosophy, as a method, or as a system, and no doubt this ambiguity accounts for the diversity of the philosophical work inspired by Husserl. Although the intelligibility of his fundamental concepts has been radically challenged, Husserl's thought has none the less been enormously influential. Phenomenology is now one of the main currents of contemporary European philosophy; it includes French and German existentialism among its heirs. It has also had a significant influence on other disciplines, notably psychology, psychopathology, sociology, history and religious studies.

Margaret Whitford

For Husserl's complete works, see *Husserliana* (The Hague, 1950–). See also: *Formal and Transcendental Logic* (*Formale und transzendentale Logik*, 1929, trans. 1969); *Cartesian Meditations* (*Cartesianische Meditationen*, Paris 1931, trans. 1960); *Experience and Judgment* (*Erfahrung und Urteil*, 1939, trans. 1973). About

Husserl: Herbert Spiegelberg, *The Phenomenological Movement* (2 vols, 1960); Quentin Lauer, *Phenomenology: Its Genesis and Prospect* (1965); Marvin Farber, *The Aims of Phenomenology. The Motives, Methods and Impact of Husserl's Thought* (1966); Paul Ricoeur, *Husserl: An Analysis of his Philosophy* (1967); Edo Pivčević, *Husserl and Phenomenology* (1970); and Maurice Natanson, *Edmund Husserl: Philosopher of Infinite Tasks* (1973).

220

HUXLEY, Aldous Leonard 1894–1963

British novelist

Grandson on his father's side of T. H. Huxley, eminent Victorian champion of the new biology; on his mother's side the great-grandson of Dr Thomas Arnold of Rugby, the great-nephew of Matthew Arnold, the newphew of Mrs Humphrey Ward, novelist and reformer; the third son of Leonard Huxley, editor of *Cornhill Magazine*, and Julia Arnold Huxley, founder of Prior's Field, a school for girls; youngest brother of Julian Huxley, the biologist – few writers indeed can lay claim to a legacy of such learning and distinction as that into which Aldous Huxley was born.

His childhood was spent at Laleham, near Godalming in Surrey. While at Eton he contracted a serious eye ailment (*keratitus punctata*) that rendered him nearly blind and ended his plans to pursue a career in biology. His older brother Trevenan took his own life in August 1914, an event which affected Aldous deeply. His first publications were poems (collected in *The Burning Wheel*, 1916) written while he was an undergraduate at Balliol College, Oxford. In the next few years he worked intermittently as a schoolmaster at Eton, was a frequent guest of Lady Ottoline Morrell at Garsington, and became an editor on the *Athenaeum* under John Middleton Murry*.

During the 1920s Huxley's keenly witty and urbane novels earned him a vast and ardent following, and like his American counterpart, F. Scott Fitzgerald*, he became identified with the era whose hysterical nihilism roused in him both fascination and revulsion. The earliest novels, *Crome Yellow* (1921) and *Antic Hay* (1923), were country-house farces in the Peacockian manner brought up to date. These works involve a cast of grotesques, constituted largely of predators and their all too eager victims, who assemble to pursue their respective lusts: for power, learning, sexual conquests, diversions of all kinds. Whether or not the pursuits are successful, there is a general air of futility about it all, and an underlying loneliness that belies the festive occasion. 'Parallel straight lines,' muses a character in *Crome Yellow*, 'meet only at infinity. . . . Did one ever establish contact with anyone? We are all parallel

straight lines.' The remark typifies the satirical vantage point of these works, which proved influential upon younger novelists such as Evelyn Waugh*, Henry Green* and Anthony Powell*.

Huxley's view of the contemporary world darkened considerably near the end of the decade. *Point Counter Point* (1928) is a devastating portrait of the utter baseness and hollowness of modern life. Technically it marked an important advance in his fiction. Where the 'parallel lines' of the earlier novels were embodied in characters whose ideas, and attempts at communication, failed to connect, here the same image governed the very structure of the novel, through a sustained contrapuntal arrangement of several plots, intercalated with entries in the journal of the novelist-surrogate, Philip Quarles. One of these entries, manifestly an apologia for Huxley's works to date, is worth noting: 'Novel of ideas. The character of each personage must be implied, as far as possible, in the ideas of which he is the mouthpiece. . . . The chief defect of the novel of ideas is that you must write about people who have ideas to express – which excludes all but about .01 per cent. of the human race. Hence the real, the congenital novelists don't write such books. But then, I never pretended to be a congenital novelist.' Of all the novel's characters produced according to this recipe, the most important – if also the least convincing – is Mark Rampion, who was modelled after Huxley's close friend D. H. Lawrence*. The novel was written during a period in which Huxley was much influenced by Lawrence's vitalist-cum-primitivist creed, and Rampion was intended to be the lone 'life-worshipper' in a gallery of death-obsessed hedonists, charlatans, and fanatics.

Brave New World (1932), despite its veneer of comic-satiric fun and its verbal play ('Ford's in his flivver, all's well with the world'), marked the culmination of Huxley's 'dark' period. Thrown off perhaps by the book's deceptively light anti-utopian beginning, some have professed bafflement at its abruptly tragic ending. In fact the suicidal, guilt-ridden despair of John 'the Savage' is an index of the author's own state of mind at a time when, after the death of Lawrence, he cast about for something to believe in and came up empty-handed.

The 1930s amounted to the crossroads of Huxley's career. He had already begun to turn away from 'pure' satire and from the kind of novel in which ideas were juxtaposed for their own sake, towards the more explicitly didactic novel, the moral apologue, which would become the dominant mode of all his subsequent fiction. In the later, more affirmative novels such as *After Many a Summer Dies the Swan* (1939), *Time Must Have a Stop* (1944), and especially *Island* (1962), the play of diverse ideas gave way to the exposition of Huxley's own ameliorative creed – a kind of rationalist mysticism – as the answer to the world's ills. Few of these works (all written after his emigration to Southern California in 1937) satisfy as novels, and Huxley's reputation underwent a precipitous decline from which it is only now starting to recover.

Evidence of this recovery in esteem is the current revaluation of *Eyeless in Gaza* (1936). Once considered the prime exhibit of Huxley's decline as a serious writer – the common view of those readers who felt betrayed by his apparently abrupt forsaking of the 1920s ethos which, in their eyes, he had epitomized in all its contradictions – the work can now be recognized for what it is: his best and most ambitious novel. The book recounts the conversion experience of Anthony Beavis, a world-weary, psychologically spent aesthete who, after several encounters with violent death during a trip to revolutionary Mexico (loosely based on Huxley's own journey, described in *Beyond the Mexique Bay*, 1934), discovers in himself the will to live, and the concomitant need to love and to serve his fellow men. No description of its theme, however, can do justice to the brilliance of the work's structural design, or to the emotional authenticity (unusual in Huxley) that anchors the astonishing array of ideas and experiences upon which Beavis broods as he makes his agonizing pilgrimage toward spiritual rebirth. Though he was never again to attain its heights, it is clear that this was the novel Huxley had to write if he was to survive the nihilistic despair to which his earlier works, especially *Point Counter Point* and *Brave New World*, had brought him.

Throughout a long and distinguished career Huxley also produced numerous volumes of short fiction, essays, poetry, travel books, plays, and a fine biography, *Grey Eminence* (1941). These works bear ample testimony to his vast erudition and his unceasing curiosity about science, art, politics, economics, religion, and many other subjects. All are of interest. But it is for his novels that Huxley will be best remembered, and of these *Eyeless in Gaza* is his one major achievement.

Ronald G. Walker

Other works by Huxley include: *Those Barren Leaves* (1925) and *Ape and Essence* (1949), both novels; *Collected Short Stories* (1957); *Leda* (1920), *Limbo* (1920), and *The Cicadas* (1931), collections of poems; *The Genius and the Goddess* (1955) and *The Giaconda Smile* (1948), both plays; *On the Margin: Notes and Essays* (1923), *Do What You Will* (1929), *Music at Night* (1931), *The Olive Tree* (1936), *Ends and Means* (1937), *The Art of Seeing* (1942), *The Perennial Philosophy* (1945), *Brave New World Revisited* (1958), and *Collected Essays* (1959), essays and journalism; *Letters*, ed. Grover Smith (London 1969). About Huxley: Sybille Bedford, *Aldous Huxley: A Biography* (1973); Jerome Meckier, *Aldous Huxley: Satire and Structure* (1969); George Woodcock, *Dawn and the Darkest Hour: A Study of Aldous Huxley* (1972). See also: Ronald G. Walker, *Infernal Paradise: Mexico and the Modern English Novel* (1978).

I

221

ILLICH, Ivan 1926–

Austrian social critic

Best known for a complex of ideas brought together under the banner 'deschooling society', Ivan Illich was born in Vienna. He studied theology and philosophy at the Gregorian University of Rome, and, for his PhD, history at the University of Salzburg. In 1951 he became assistant pastor in an Irish-Puerto Rican parish in New York City, and from 1956 he was vice-rector of the Catholic University of Puerto Rica, where he organized an intensive training centre for American priests in Latin American culture. When in 1960 this work was brought to an abrupt halt after he spoke out against the church's attitude towards birth control, Illich went to Mexico to set up the Intercultural Centre for Documentation (CIDOC), a storehouse for all kinds of information about Latin America. From 1962 to 1976 Illich directed its research seminars, and from 1968 'deschooling' was the main discussional theme. His book *Deschooling Society* (1971) brought his ideas to the general public, and became one of the basic texts of the alternative schooling movement of the early 1970s.

Originally Illich argued that if schools could not provide the education needed in Latin American countries (mainly because there were not enough to go round), a system should be evolved by which learners could be made more responsible for their own learning–teaching arrangements. This produced the notion of a learning network, in which learners and teachers are matched.

In *Deschooling Society* Illich expanded on these ideas and applied them to America and England. While others (viz. Charles Silberman in *Crisis in Education*, 1970) responded to what many believed to be the imminent breakdown of education in the West by putting forward policies designed to shore up a crumbling system, Illich sought to demolish what he maintained could not work: giving more of the same was not enough. Instead he defined a good educational system as having and fulfilling three purposes: it should provide learners with access to available resources at any time in their lives; it should assist people who want to share their knowledge to find those who want to learn it from them; and it should 'furnish all who want to

present an issue to the public with the opportunity to make their challenge known'. Such a free-for-all, in which it was stipulated there would be no obligatory curriculae or discrimination based on the possession of certificates and diplomas, would, Illich acknowledged, require new kinds of constitutional guarantees. But these, combined with the proper use of modern technology and the abolition of the huge professional apparatus of educators and buildings (supported by regressive taxation) would make for 'free speech, free assembly, and a free press truly universal and, therefore, fully educational'.

Obviously such a strategy provoked many criticisms (e.g. Herbert Gintis in *Harvard Educational Review*, February 1972), but despite these, Illich, with his obsession for rearranging social priorities and hence remoulding society itself, was naturally led to apply it in other areas. Thus transport, technology and medicine were brought within his ken. Modern medicine, he argued (in *Limits to Medicine*, 1976), with its high degree of institutionalization, sickens as much as it cures. The development of a few, sophisticated means of rapid transport results in more people not being able to move at all: 'Motorways expand, driving wedges between neighbours and removing fields beyond the distance a farmer can walk' (*Energy and Equity*, 1974). And technology 'has translated human survival from the performance of organisms into the results of technical manipulation' (*ibid.*).

All Illich's arguments point in the same direction: a need for de-institutionalization and disestablishment. Often dismissed as either an anarchist-*manqué* prone to overstatement, or a 'charismatic hero in a disenchanted world' (Margaret Fay in *Higher Education Review*, Summer 1974), his work remains important for having helped focus public attention on the discrepancies between what certain institutions set out to do (educate, heal, provide welfare) and what they in fact achieve. His concentration on their destructive by-products, however, has not generally proved a warrant for the new social forms he seeks.

Peter Lund

Illich's other books include: *The Church, Change and Development* (1970); *Celebration of Awareness* (1971); *Tools for Conviviality* (1973); *After Deschooling, What?* (1974); *Imprisoned in the Global Classroom* (1976).

222

IONESCO, Eugène 1912–

Romanian/French dramatist

The child of separated parents, a Romanian father and a French mother, Ionesco lived in France until 1925 with his mother but then had to return to Romania because his father had won legal custody of the children. He studied French at the University of Bucharest, where he experienced horror and growing isolation amidst the rise of fascism, both emotions that were to colour his later work. In 1938 he went to Paris on a research scholarship, returned to Romania on the outbreak of war, but in 1942 was back in Paris, where he has lived ever since.

In 1948, he started to learn English. In his language phrase book he discovered a strange world in which disembodied voices, with names like Mr Smith or Mrs Smith, would tell each other extraordinary facts such as that the ceiling is up but the floor is down. He adopted this style for his first play *The Bald Prima Donna* (*La Cantatrice Chauve*, 1950), believing that he had written 'the tragedy of language'. He was amazed when audiences laughed and followed this play with several more which exploit the same tendency of language to become reified, to turn into an unmalleable object obstructing communication. The characters in these plays are deprived of all humanity; through them, human behaviour is depicted solely by means of its external manifestations, so that it resembles the inexplicable antics of mechanical puppets.

Towards the end of the 1950s, Ionesco introduced into his plays a character named Bérenger, with whom it is easier for an audience to identify. Naive, imaginative, alternately ecstatic or depressed for reasons he cannot identify, Bérenger is a frankly autobiographical figure. But Ionesco's plays continued to be situated in unreal, dream-like circumstances, even when they come closest to making political comments, as in *Rhinoceros* (1960). When accused by Kenneth Tynan of formalism, Ionesco engaged in a long polemic supporting his conception of theatre, claiming that however good its intentions, political plays were always dangerous, that 'committed theatre leads straight to the concentration camp' and that the only way a dramatist can change the world is by 'renewing language, which is to renew our conception and vision of the world'. Supporters of Brecht* and committed theatre claimed that Ionesco destroyed language rather than renewed it, but Ionesco insisted that he wanted to create an 'abstract theatre', to 'present events that were disincarnate', to invent actions that bore no relation to reality but existed as autonomous creations. His plays in the 1960s made increasing use of dream material.

The dominant theme in his work is the anguish of separation and the lack of apparent meaning to human existence. This is set against rare moments, especially in childhood memories, when 'a perfect marriage of earth and heaven takes place'. He believes that there is a direct link between literature and neurosis and that the main achievement of the avant-garde theatre of the 1950s was to concretize and embody a sense of anguish instead of writing *about* it as the Romantics had done.

In 1966 when *Hunger and Thirst* (*La Soif et la Faim*) was produced at the Comédie Française, the avant-garde theatre acquired a symbolic respectability and this was followed, in 1970, by Ionesco's election to the Académie Française. His early plays have become world-famous and were probably more influential even than those of Beckett* in shaping a general understanding of what is meant by the Theatre of the Absurd. But they rely to a considerable extent on the shock of the unexpected for their impact and in his latter work Ionesco has found it difficult to equal his early successes. His plays have lost their anarchic freedom and have taken on a more literary form, often becoming excessively verbose. The outstanding quality of his drama is its exploitation of striking dramatic images, like the expanding corpse of *Amédée* (*Amédée, ou comment s'en débarrasser*, 1954) or the transformation of people into rhinoceroses in *Rhinoceros*. In the light of this strong visual imagination, it is perhaps surprising that he has made only one film, *Slime* (*La Vase*, 1971); he has also written one novel, *The Hermit* (*Le Solitaire*, 1973).

David Bradby

Théâtre (from 1954); *Notes et Contre-notes* (1962); *Journal en Miettes* (1967); *Présent passé, passé présent* (1968). See also: Claude Bonnefoy, *Entretiens avec Ionesco* (1966); Richard Coe, *Ionesco* (1961).

223

IQBAL, Sir Muhammad 1873–1938

Pakistani/Indian poet and philosopher

A leading Indian Muslim thinker and poet, Muhammad Iqbal formulated the political theory which led to the founding of Pakistan in 1947. He was born in Sialkot, a town in northern Punjab, and educated at Government College, Lahore. In 1905 he went to Cambridge, and then to the University of Munich, to study philosophy and law. After qualifying as a barrister in London he returned to Lahore, in 1908, where he taught at Government College, and practised law. A poet of outstanding quality and power, he published eleven volumes of poetry in Urdu and Persian. His early work, in Urdu, was in the traditional style of romantic lyricism. This changed as his sojourn in the

West, and study of philosophy, strengthened his belief in Islam, the religion his ancestors, Kashmiri Hindus, had adopted. He then used poetry as a vehicle to convey his socio-religious philosophy.

Believing that the Islamic doctrine was flexible enough to adapt to the modern age, he reinterpreted the message of the Koran in his poetry. His study of western civilization led him to reject its materialism but accept its values of freedom and individualism. Out of this arose his philosophy which, while stressing the superiority of Islamic spiritualism, urged the faithful to seek freedom and full development of self. *Asrar-e-Khudi* ('Secrets of the Self'), his long narrative poem in Persian, published in 1915, established him as a poet-philosopher; and *Peyam-e-Mashriq* ('Message of the East'), his collection of poems published a year after he was knighted in 1922, is regarded as a rejoinder to Goethe's *West-Östlicher Diwan* ('The West-Eastern Divan'), which first appeared in 1819.

He tempered his support for the ideas of individualism and freedom by stressing that a proper development of self was best achieved by an individual placing himself at the service of his community. Since he came to regard the Muslims of the Indian sub-continent as a distinct community, inspired by the traditions of Islam, he aired the idea of a separate homeland for them, in 1930, in his capacity as the president of the Muslim League. This concept was transformed into a fully-fledged demand by the Muslim League in 1940, and realized seven years later in the form of an independent Pakistan.

His mature social philosophy and fertile poetic imagination found their best expression in his fantasy-poem *Jawed Nama* ('The Song of Eternity', 1932): a journey during which he engaged in political, social and religious discourse with the inhabitants of the various spheres lying interspersed between the earth and the heaven.

Though his poetry was translated into the languages of the Indian sub-continent and the Islamic world during his lifetime, and widely read by both Muslims and non-Muslims, the first translation of his poems in English did not appear until two years after his death in 1938.

Dilip Hiro

Poetry: in Persian: *Asrar-e-Khudi* ('Secrets of the Self', 1915, trans. 1940); *Rumuz-e-Bikhudi* ('Mysteries of Selflessness', 1918, trans. 1953); *Zabur-e-Ajam* ('Persian Psalms', 1927, trans. 1948); *Jawed Nama* ('The Song of Eternity', 1932, trans. 1966); in Urdu: *Bang-e-Dara* ('Call of the Bell', 1924); *Bal-e-Jibril* ('Blow of Gabriel', 1935); *Zarb-e-Kalim* ('Blow of Moses', 1937). Essays: *Reconstruction of Islamic Thought in Islam* (1934). About Iqbal: S. A. Vahid, *Iqbal: His Art and Thought* (1959); A. M. Schimmel, *Gabriel's*

Wing (1963); K. G. Saiyidain, *Iqbal's Educational Philosophy* (1965).

224

ISHERWOOD, Christopher William Bradshaw
1904–

English writer

Christopher Isherwood was born at Wyberslegh Hall, Cheshire. He was educated at St Edmund's Preparatory School, where he met his friend and future collaborator, W. H. Auden*, and at Repton, where he formed a lifelong friendship with the writer Edward Upward. His schooldays, although academically and socially successful, were overshadowed by the First World War and the death of his father (a professional soldier) in action in 1915. In 1923, Isherwood went up to Corpus Christi College, Cambridge, with a scholarship in history. He did little or no academic work as an undergraduate, putting his energies partly into writing and partly into the creation of 'Mortmere', the mythical surrealist world invented and sustained by himself and Upward. He left Cambridge without a degree (deliberately writing nonsense in the examinations) and supported himself mainly by short-term jobs while he concentrated on writing. In 1928, he left for Berlin, where he stayed for five fruitful years – apart from the publication of *The Memorial* in 1932, the events and experiences of the period formed the basis of his most successful writings of the 1930s. When the Nazis seized power in 1933, Isherwood left Germany and until 1939 lived peripatetically, mostly in Europe. Fame and success came with the publication of *Mr Norris Changes Trains* (1935). It was followed by the stories, including 'Sally Bowles' (1937) which were incorporated into *Goodbye to Berlin* (1939), on which the plays *I am a Camera* (1951) and *Cabaret* (1966, filmed in 1971) were later based. The 1930s also saw the major collaborations between Auden and Isherwood: the plays *The Dog beneath the Skin* (1935), *The Ascent of F6* (1936) and *On the Frontier* (1938), and the travel book *Journey to a War* (1939), about the Sino-Japanese war, Isherwood being responsible for the prose diary part of the book.

In 1939, Isherwood went with Auden to the United States, where he soon settled in Los Angeles, which has become his permanent home. He effectively repudiated his leftist Popular Front stance, becoming a pacifist and a convert to Vedānta, an allegiance he has maintained ever since. He has also, of recent years, become an outspoken champion of the rights of homosexuals. Both stances have considerably influenced his later writings.

Isherwood began his novelistic career as a 'modernist' writer. His first novels, *All the Conspirators* (1925) and *The Memorial*, show the influence of Joyce* and Woolf*, especially the latter. Planned by Isherwood as 'a drawing-room epic about the effects of the War on my generation', *The Memorial* shows a group of neurotic characters damaged not so much by the war as by the myths generated about and by it.

With *Mr Norris Changes Trains*, however, Isherwood abandoned the multiple subjectivities of the 'modernist' novel for a 'realist' approach. Here, an excitingly seedy and dangerous world is viewed through the naively candid eyes of 'William Bradshaw', the first of Isherwood's semi-autobiographical 'I'-narrators. He is replaced in *Goodbye to Berlin* by 'Christopher Isherwood' (or 'Herr Issyvoo'), who was to figure in many later writings. Apparently a simple and objective 'camera', he is really an ironically conceived persona whose naivety is the object as well as the lens of the irony that shapes the book. *Goodbye to Berlin* and *Mr Norris* are often considered as a brilliant portrait gallery – notably the pictures of 'Mr Norris', 'Sally Bowles', the slum family 'Nowaks' – but the book derives its force at least as much from the ironic interplay between the narrator's naive vision and the author's greater understanding of what it is he sees.

'Christopher Isherwood' appears also in the autobiographical novels *Prater Violet* (1944) and *Down There on a Visit* (1962), but he has disappeared from Isherwood's more recent writings. In what many think his best novel, *A Single Man* (1964), Isherwood adopts an 'objective', present-tense third-person narration. Its hero, George, an ageing homosexual Englishman in California, is treated not as a unified identity whose point of view focuses the novel, but as a collection of different personalities or impulses whose true being is impersonal. (The influence of Vedānta can be clearly discerned here.) Isherwood has been able in this book to combine a coldly objective stance with a powerful fantasy element (George's day-dreams are quite as grotesque as 'Mortmere').

Isherwood has also written several autobiographies. The first, *Lions and Shadows* (1938), covering the years of his late adolescence, is a brilliant portrait gallery in which Auden, Upward, Stephen Spender* and Isherwood himself appear as vivid caricatures, the younger Isherwood being treated with mocking irony by a mature narrator. This ironic distancing of his younger self is carried to a logical extreme in *Kathleen and Frank* (1971), a memoir of Isherwood's parents, and *Christopher and his Kind* (1977), in both of which Isherwood's younger self is called 'Christopher' (not 'I') and is treated as if he were quite separate from the author. In both books, Isherwood has rewritten the story of his youth, replacing the mild leftish liberalism of *Lions and Shadows* with an insistence that the significant element of his life is his homosexuality.

Isherwood is primarily an autobiographical writer. Many of his novels are narrated as memoirs, and his characters are frequently versions, often exaggerated or distorted, of real-life originals. In the 1930s, he was regarded as a realist who told the truth objectively; it can be seen now that he is rather a mythologizer of his own past. His works can be seen as a succession of reshapings of his own life, dramatized through characters (including himself) who embody aspects of the meanings which, at different times, he has seen in it. His personal revolt against patriotic pieties which informed both the parodied Englishness of 'Mortmere' and the modernism of the early novels changed to a broadly political stance in the 1930s, which in turn has given place to a drama of homosexual revolt and Hindu philosophy. Isherwood's writings are often used as source-material for literary history, especially of the 1930s, but although each of the versions of his past contains some truth, it would be naive to take any of them as literally true. Isherwood's success lies not in his fidelity to reality, but in the vigour, liveliness and interest of the characters and *personae* he has created.

Janet Montefiore

Other works: novels: *The World in the Evening* (1954); *A Meeting by the River* (1967); travel: *The Condor and the Cows* (1949). *Exhumations* (1966) includes much early work. See: Alan Wilde, *Christopher Isherwood* (1971); Brian Finney, *Christopher Isherwood, A Critical Biography* (1979).

225
IVES, Charles Edward 1874–1954

US composer

The son of an ex-civil war bandmaster, Ives came from a New England Puritan background and spent his early years in Danbury, Connecticut. His relationship with his father George Ives was both an emotionally and intellectually satisfying one, for Ives senior not only gave his son instruction in practical and academic musicianship but also encouraged an interest in more experimental ways of employing the tools of sound, texture and timbre, in order to construct a new kind of music. Taking harmony and counterpoint of the German romantic tradition as a departure point Charles Ives composed with the materials that he had grown up with, namely the sounds of the marching band, barn dance, revivalist hymn and 'nigger minstrelsy', liberally sprinkling his scores with quotations from these home-grown sources. His arrival at Yale University in 1894 proved a great cultural shock, for his tutor was to be the Leipzig trained Horatio Parker, one of the nation's most respected composers and pedagogues. Parker appears to have contributed little to his pupil's musicality other than consolidate what Ives had already thought to be the case, that the whole of American musical society was dominated by a German academicalism which had little to offer to the making of a specifically indigenous musical style. However, his time at Yale was not wasted for he found part-time employment as a church organist and choirmaster, stood in as a bar pianist at beer-halls and frequented the local theatres; thus he could add choral music, early ragtime and popular song and dance to his musical experiences. At the turn of the century a career as a professional musician was considered precarious and in Ives's milieu unrespectable. Accordingly, on his departure from Yale he entered the insurance business as a broker and within a short space of time had teamed up with a partner to form one of the most successful independent agencies in New York which was eventually to become the Mutual Life Insurance Company. A succession of heart-attacks caused him to retire early from business practically a millionaire.

Ives was influenced, as his father had been, by the pragmatic philosophy of the Transcendentalists and was well acquainted with the prose and poetry of America's major authors. Though not politically active, he was a strong believer in American democratic principles and besides drawing up draft amendments to the Constitution, held protracted correspondence with prominent senators and two presidents as well as writing political pamphlets for distribution to those who expressed any interest. Such was Ives's passionate ardour for all that occurred around him, coupled with an intellectual conditioning steeped in the Puritan aesthetic, that they not only provided the stimulus for spiritual and emotional conflict in Ives's personal life but also the unique creativity which was an attempt to resolve this dilemma.

Charles Ives's musical output spans the years 1888 to 1927 although after 1921 he virtually ceased composing. The 141 songs not only cover the whole of his creative life but also demonstrate every facet of his compositional style. His choice of texts is eclectic for it not only covers the English and American Romantic poets but also French and German verse of the same period as previously set by Schubert, Schumann, Brahms and others; neither was he averse to setting the contemporary poetry of Brooke*, Kipling*, Vachel Lindsay and even epithets from newspaper columns. The Psalm settings for chorus of 1894–1901 reflect his early preoccupation with experimental rhythmic and harmonic textures reaching a peak of complexity in the *Harvest Home Chorales*. Such innovations were continued in the chamber pieces *Central Park in the Dark* and *The Unanswered Question* (both 1906) where independent rhythmic textures in different sections of the orchestra are heard simultaneously. To a much greater extent this also occurs in the later pieces for full orchestra collectively entitled *New England Holidays* (1904–13), in the two orchestral sets (1903–15) and especially in the massive Fourth Symphony (1909–16) which invariably requires two conductors for successful performance. Besides producing four violin sonatas, two string quartets and many smaller experimental works for chamber groups and theatre band the composer has endeavoured to express the aesthetic of the Transcendentalist writers in the second piano sonata entitled *Concord 1840–1860*; its four movements are called Emerson, Hawthorne, The Alcotts, and Thoreau.

During his composing life Charles Ives worked in complete isolation from contemporary European developments and as a result had to wait thirty years for national recognition. However, since his death both his innovative techniques and his individual aesthetic stance have exerted a major influence on experimental composers of the post-war period in America and Europe.

Michael Alexander

Principal writings: *Essays before a Sonata, The Majority, and Other Writings by C.I.*, ed. H. Boatwright (1970); *Charles E. Ives Memos*, ed. J. Kirkpatrick (1971). See also: F. R. Rossiter, *Charles Ives and His America* (1976); H. and S. Cowell, *Charles Ives and His Music* (reprint 1974); R. S. Perry, *Charles Ives and The American Mind* (1974); D. Wooldridge, *From the Steeples and the Mountains* (1975); *An Ives Celebration*, ed. H. Wiley Hitchcock and V. Perlis (1977); H. Wiley Hitchcock, *Ives* (1977); *Charles Ives Remembered*, ed. V. Perlis (1976).

J

226
JAKOBSON, Roman Osipovich 1896–

Russian/US linguist

Roman Jakobson took his first degree, in Oriental languages, at Moscow University, where he founded the Moscow Linguistic Circle in 1916. Jakobson was heavily influenced by avant-garde movements in the arts, and in particular by the Russian Futurist poet Velemir Khlebnikov. From 1920 he studied and taught in Prague, and in 1933 moved to Brno; he and his close associate N. S. Trubetzkoy, another Russian émigré, became two of the leading figures in the Linguistic Circle of Prague, which was perhaps the chief single centre of linguistic thought during the dozen years before it was dispersed by the Nazi occupation of Czechoslovakia. Jakobson spent the period 1939–41 in Scandinavia, where he wrote one of the key items of his large oeuvre: *Child Language, Aphasia, and Phonological Universals* (*Kindersprache, Aphasie und allgemeine Lautgesetze*, 1941). When in 1942 the École Libre des Hautes Études was founded in New York by refugee scholars from Europe, Jakobson was invited to a chair in linguistics; here he formed a close intellectual relationship with Claude Lévi-Strauss*. In 1949 Jakobson moved to Harvard, and from 1957 was affiliated also with the neighbouring Massachusetts Institute of Technology.

Jakobson's intellectual interests are extremely diverse, extending from phonological and grammatical analysis of a wide range of languages, through the mathematics and physics of speech, to structuralist poetics and studies of Slavonic folklore. However, a single red thread runs through his work: the notion that abstract structural invariants underlie the superficial diversity of cultural products (such as languages or poetic genres). The notion of simple abstract patterns below the surface of complex concrete realities was common ground for members of the 'structuralist' movement; the idea that these patterns were invariant, while anticipated in particular fields (e.g. by Vladimir Propp's analysis of Russian folk-tales), as a general guiding principle was Jakobson's special contribution to the structuralist tradition.

Jakobson's *Child Language*, for instance, argues for structural invariants among the sound-systems of different languages, an area that had often been seen as a paradigm case of cultural diversity. According to Jakobson, the multifarious phonetic distinctions found in the world's languages can be reduced to a small set of binary oppositions arranged in a fixed hierarchy; children invariably acquire the distinctions in the order implied by the hierarchy, and the phonological systems of adult languages differ only in the extent to which this progressive differentiation is allowed to proceed along various branches of the hierarchy. Individuals who lose the power of speech invariably mirror the progress of the child, in reverse.

Jakobson represents the chief personal link in America between the American and European traditions of linguistics. His most lasting achievement may have been to render certain rationalist attitudes to language and culture 'thinkable' for Americans, and thus to stimulate younger men within his ambit (most notably Noam Chomsky*) to embark on programmes of research which they could scarcely have conceived apart from his influence. The unlimited diversity of cultural products had been axiomatic within the American scholarly tradition founded by Boas*; and indeed, to behaviourists for whom the term 'mind' was taboo, there seemed to be no locus in which hypothetical invariants might reside. Jakobson suddenly made it respectable to suppose that men might be born with minds having fixed properties, which would be reflected in their culture. But although this branch of scholarship was inspired by Jakobson, its concrete results have been worked out by others. Jakobson has repeatedly been criticized for basing his theories about linguistic universals on very meagre evidence, and to a large extent his theories have been abandoned even by the scholars who can be seen as his followers.

Geoffrey Sampson

Most of Jakobson's publications are assembled in *Roman Jakobson, Selected Writings* (The Hague 1962–), a series expected eventually to run to seven volumes. See: *Roman Jakobson: a Bibliography of his Writings* (The Hague 1971); Elmar Holenstein, *Roman Jakobson's Approach to Language: Phenomenological Structuralism* (1976).

227

JANÁČEK, Leoš (Eugen) 1854–1928

Czech composer

The son of a Moravian schoolmaster and organist, he was a boy chorister at the Abbey of St Augustine in Brno (1865–9), which was then directed by Pavel Křížkovsky, a noted composer of church music. Janáček continued his education at the Brno Teachers' Training College (1872–4) and at the Prague Organ School (1874–5). He also went for brief periods of study to the conservatories of Leipzig (1879) and Vienna (1880), but found the German approach unsympathetic.

By this time Janáček had already begun to make a local reputation in Brno as a composer of choral music in the Křížkovsky tradition. In the 1880s he began to widen his scope, and in 1887 he produced his first opera, *Šárka*, though this was not staged until 1925. In it he treated a mythical theme in a manner close to that of Dvořák, whose influence is also clear in the set of *Lachian Dances* for orchestra (1889–90). However, his second opera, *The Beginning of a Romance* (1891), makes a more direct use of the Moravian folk music which he had been collecting since 1885, abandoning the Dvořákian effort to civilize such material within a symphonic style.

Janáček progressively refined his method of using folk elements in the cantata *Amarus* (1897) and in his third opera, *Jenůfa* (1894–1903), a passionate tale of love and jealousy set in a Moravian village. This was several times revised before its Prague première, in 1916, which belatedly brought its composer national and soon international recognition. In a sense this event marked the beginning of his career, at the age of sixty-one. Another opera, *Fate* (1903–4), had been completed soon after *Jenůfa*, but this was not performed until 1934, and the great majority of Janáček's finest works came in the twelve years after the Prague performance of *Jenůfa*.

Among those works are the orchestral rhapsody *Taras Bulba* (1915–18), based on episodes of love and death from Gogol's treatment of the Cossack hero, and the *Sinfonietta*, boldly scored for an orchestra including twelve trumpets (1926). There was also the powerful *Glagolitic Mass* for soloists, choir, organ and large orchestra (1926) as well as a variety of chamber pieces, including two string quartets, both of a private, autobiographical character: the first (1923–4) is subtitled 'Kreutzer Sonata' in reference to Tolstoy, the second 'Intimate Letters' (1928). In other works of this period Janáček disregarded conventions of form and genre, especially in the *Diary of a Young Man who Disappeared* for tenor, contralto, female voices and piano (1917–19), in the set of *Nursery Rhymes* for voices and instruments (1925–7), and in two miniature piano concertos:

the Concertino for piano and six instruments (1925) and the Capriccio for left-hand piano and eight wind (1926). But then all of these late compositions are highly individual, sometimes even quirky, being based on short, irregular phrases of modal character and strong personality.

Janáček used the same features of style in the five operas he wrote after 1916, and these show also the full fruits of his research into Moravian folk music. That research, coupled with the work he had done in noting down the pitch inflections and the rhythms of speech in Moravia, had provided him with the material upon which he could build an operatic style suited to his own language, as Mussorgsky had done. It was no longer necessary for him to justify his procedures by using a local setting, as he had in *Jenůfa*: the Moravian elements had been thoroughly absorbed into a vigorous personal style. His five late operas are widely varied in dramatic tone and location, but they all show his ability to follow the words (usually his own) naturally yet with high intensity in a manner that benefits from folk models but by no means sounds picturesquely ethnic.

These operas also demonstrate Janáček's unerring skill in depicting his characters and their emotions by means of swift, imaginative strokes, and in achieving potent dramatic effects through his very original use of the orchestra, involving, as in his contemporary orchestral and chamber works, stark sonorities and the rapid development of pungent motifs. Again like other compositions of the same period, they display his relish of the bizarre and unusual. *The Excursions of Mr Brouček* (1908–17), Janáček's only comedy, is a fantasy which finds a commonplace man transported to the moon in the first act and to the fifteenth century, the time of the Hussite wars, in the second. *The Cunning Little Vixen* (1921–3), which benefited from the composer's keen ear for animal sounds, is a quite unpatronizing story of woodland creatures. *The Makropoulos Case* (1923–5) reveals the empty fate of a woman who has magically prolonged her existence for three hundred years, and *From the House of the Dead* (1927–8), which was left unfinished, is an austere setting of incidents from Dostoevsky's prison-camp novel. Yet despite all these examples of a taste for the extraordinary, Janáček was stimulated above all, as *Katya Kabanova* (1919–21) eloquently proves, by the inner lives of real human beings and by the tragedy of their destinies, and it was in this version of Ostrovsky's play *The Storm* that he produced his greatest achievement.

Paul Griffiths

About Janáček: Jaroslav Vogel, *Leoš Janáček: his Life and Works* (1962); Hans Hollander, *Leoš Janáček: his Life and Work* (1963); Erik Chisholm, *The Operas of Leoš Janáček* (1971); Michael Ewans, *Janáček's Tragic Operas* (1977).

228

JASPERS, Karl Theodor 1883–1969

German existentialist philosopher

Jaspers studied law at Heidelberg and Munich before devoting himself to the study of medicine at Berlin, Göttingen and Heidelberg. In 1909, the year in which he was registered as a doctor, he joined the psychiatric clinic of Heidelberg University as a research assistant to the neuropathologist Franz Nissl. Pursuing his own methods of inquiry he wrote *General Psychopathology* (*Allgemeine Psychopathologie*, 1913, trans. 1965), an important and distinguished attempt to provide psychopathology with a systematic symptomatology. However, with his appointment as Assistant Professor of Psychology at the same university in 1916 his interests again shifted, and in 1922 he took the chair of Philosophy. For political reasons (his wife was Jewish) he was dismissed by the National Socialists in 1937, after several years of persecution. Reinstated in 1945, he transferred, from 1948 until his retirement in 1961, to the University of Basel. He died in Switzerland, having renounced his German citizenship.

While it would be possible to review Jaspers's philosophy under the headings of psychology, epistemology, theology and philosophical logic, it is evident from the ontological draught characteristic of his thinking in each of these areas that his fundamental and unifying theme is the question of Being, realistically conceived.

Jaspers's approach to Being is 'existentialist', in the sense that it repudiates any ontology which is not an elucidation of the 'sense of being' that is potential in the ties of a concrete human existence with the world. In this sense, Jaspers's method is descriptive, although not strictly phenomenological, if this epithet implies the use of the theoretical and methodological baggage derived from Husserl*, as by Heidegger*, Sartre* or Merleau-Ponty*. Nor does Jaspers follow other existentialists in affirming that Being 'speaks' to us only at the level of intentional consciousness.

Jaspers distinguishes between Being as such and being-an-object. The latter category includes the objects of perception and scientific investigation, whereas the former, which is not a sum of empirical beings, is inaccessible to science and constitutes the domain of philosophy. But since only empirical beings are determinable by objective thought, it follows for Jaspers that the primary question is not '*What* is being?' – which in asking after determinateness relegates Being to an empirical being – but '*How* can we and how must we think of Being if we want to speak to Being?' This emphasis on techniques of invocation, rather than of definition, makes philosophy an activity whose purpose is to render Being transparent, a process in which reason serves as a midwife who effaces herself, as it were, at the moment of birth. Being intimates itself as

an Encompassing, within which Jaspers discerns seven modes which, he claims, are systematically connected. This is not indicative of a real multiplicity within Being, but expresses the finite nature of our various approaches to it. The characteristic feature of any mode of the Encompassing is the fusion of object-being and subject-being. For example, through reflection on himself the thinking subject understands himself to be encompassed within an impersonal principle which participates in his act of knowing but which cannot be appropriated by the act, since for a subject to objectify itself for itself would be for it to cease to be a subject. From this point of view of unity between the self and the non-self, the duality between the two that is characteristic of the relation of empirical knowledge appears as a deficient mode of being. The problems of communication thereby posed lead Jaspers to the view that any philosophy must embrace a philosophy of philosophizing, which in his case appeals to the reader to participate in a communion through which the meaning of Being is sensed 'between the lines' of the objective discourse with which no philosophy can ultimately dispense.

Jaspers terms *Existenz* the dimension of human life (and mode of Being) which in striving to know Being aspires to authentic selfhood, and so ceases to be preoccupied with psycho-physical existence (*Dasein*) in the world of things. That *Existenz* dwells within Being is again attested to by its capacity to transcend and encompass the schisms which characterize ordinary psychological life: man is a temporal being who hankers after eternity; yet in becoming aware of itself as a consciousness in time, *Existenz* enters into a mode of Being which is neither temporal nor timeless. 'Historical consciousness' is the locus where the experiences of time and eternity take place together.

Similarly, communication between selves is an 'existential' event only where it has the effect of promoting loneliness to a luminous solitude: the persons remain as distant from each other as Being, in uniting them, remains transcendent to them.

The goal of both philosophy and of life is the 'illumination' of *Existenz*'s authentic orientation towards Being. In this, man is helped by Pascal's ciphers ('the footsteps of God'), which announce the presence but not the nature of Being, as well as by the 'ultimate situations' to which Jaspers attributes ontological import. But the first condition of authenticity rests with human choice.

Despite lapses into sentimentality, repetitiousness and obscurity, Jaspers's thought is on the whole systematic. It is also often original (being preceded in its general orientation only by Kierkegaard) and contains many refreshing recastings of old philosophical themes. But it remains a dead formalism to the attitude which does not respond spiritually to something like 'intimations of eternity', or intellectually to the claim that

Being is the Protean ground of the mysterious analogous relations obtaining between the different meanings of the word 'is' in the various forms of predication.

Dr Roger McLure

Jaspers's many works include: *Philosophie* (3 vols,
1932); *Reason and Existence* (*Vernunft und Existenz*, 1935,
trans. 1955); *Nietzsche* (1936, trans. 1965); *Descartes
und die Philosophie* (1937); *Philosophy of Existence*
(*Existenz philosophie*, 1938, trans. 1971); *The Origin and
Goal of History* (*Vom Ursprung und Ziel der Geschichte*,
1949, trans. 1953); *The Way to Wisdom* (*Einführung in
die Philosophie*, 1950, trans. 1951); *The Great Philosopher*
(*Die grossen Philosophen*, 1957, trans. 1962). See: J. H.
Blackham, *Six Existentialist Thinkers* (1956); P. A.
Schlipp (ed.), *The Philosophy of Karl Jaspers* (1957); S.
Samway, *Reason Revisited* (1971).

229

JOHN XXIII 1881–1963

Pope

Widely regarded on his election as merely a transitional
pope, John XXIII probably did more in a shorter time
than any of his predecessors to bring about a radical
change in the policies and the image of the papacy.
More and more power within the Roman Catholic
Church had come to be concentrated in the hands of
the pope and his immediate circle of advisers and officials; John XXIII's pontificate decisively reversed
this trend and made not just bishops but also ordinary
priests and laypeople aware of their shared responsibilities for the Church's doctrine and practice. Uniformity gave way to diversity in unity. In the process
John XXIII brought about a dramatic improvement
in the prospects for Christian unity by helping the
Roman Catholic Church to become much more the
kind of Church with which other Churches might be
able eventually to contemplate union.

In all this what was most important was not what
to the outsider might seem the most striking changes
brought about as a result of his pontificate – for example, the virtual abandonment of Latin as the
language of worship in favour of modern vernaculars.
Such changes could have been brought about by papal
decree, and in fact Pius XII had already introduced
some fairly far-reaching changes in this way. What
John XXIII did was to put an end to the practice of
the papacy acting in splendid isolation on behalf of the
Church as a whole. Instead he called together the
bishops of the entire Church to work out what needed
to be done in a world where the Church was in danger
of becoming regarded more and more as an irrelevant
archaism, a piece of living history, and where its message, the gospel, was in danger of going unheeded and
unheard.

This summoning of a general council came as a
surprise to most people both inside and outside the
Church. In the wake of the definition of papal primacy
and infallibility by the First Vatican Council in 1870,
it was commonly assumed that a general council was
something that could now be dispensed with. John
XXIII's achievement was to bring the bishops in –
and with them the local churches they presided over
– to balance what in both theory and practice had
become a lop-sided Church.

Nor was John XXIII's impact confined simply to
the Church. The whole world responded to this ap-
proachable, human, and lovable old man in the see of
Peter. He was to an eminent degree what the Italians
call *simpatico*. He took seriously his duties as Bishop of
Rome, as was shown the first Christmas of his pontificate when he visited children in hospital and the
inmates of the Regina Coeli prison. He was moreover
a man of reconciliation. He set up the Secretariat for
Promoting Christian Unity to develop relations between Rome and the other Christian Churches. Nor
was reconciliation confined to fellow-Christians divided from Rome by the great schism between east and
west or by the Reformation, or even to fellow-believers
(as with the removal from the liturgy of expressions
offensive to Jews and Moslems). A dramatic change
from the cold-war stance of the previous pontificate
was indicated when in March 1963 he met Alexis Ad-
zhubei, editor of *Izvestia* and son-in-law of the Soviet
Prime Minister, Nikita S. Khrushchev. And this shift
in Catholic attitudes towards Communists was reflected in his encyclicals *Mater et Magistra* (1961) and *Pacem
in Terris* (1963) with their cautious approval of Catholic
co-operation with those previously held to be beyond
the pale.

For this pastoral ministry of reconciliation and *ag-
giornamento* – his term for the task of bringing the
Church up to date – John XXIII's background and
previous career provided an admirable preparation.
Born Angelo Roncalli at Sotto il Monte, near Bergamo,
where his father was a peasant share-cropper, he enjoyed the background of a secure and stable Catholicism which was far from showing the neurotic
defensiveness all too common elsewhere in the face of
modern developments. His early years as a priest were
spent as secretary to Bishop Giacomo Radini-Tedeschi
of Bergamo, one of the pioneers of the social Catholicism which, despite the obstacles of Vatican insistence
on Catholic non-participation in Italian public life following the loss of the Pope's temporal power and despite subsequently a measure of official disapproval
and interference in the wake of the modernist crisis,
was to lay the foundations of the Christian Democratic
movement. In 1925 Monsignor Roncalli began his career as a papal diplomat as apostolic visitor (from 1931

apostolic delegate) to Bulgaria; in 1934 he was appointed apostolic delegate to both Turkey and Greece; and in 1944 he became nuncio to newly liberated France. In all these posts Roncalli gained the confidence and affection of those he came into contact with, and in the first two he developed an understanding and love of the eastern Orthodox Churches. Throughout his displayed a remarkable gift for diplomacy: in France, for example, he was faced with the demand for the sacking of thirty-three bishops accused of having shown too much favour to the Vichy regime, but in the event only three bishops had to resign. In 1953 he was made a cardinal and appointed patriarch of Venice, his first purely pastoral post since his service as a chaplain (originally as a medical orderly) in the First World War.

When elected Pope in 1958 he was within a month of his seventy-seventh birthday. His decision to hold a general council, announced the following January, was put into effect within a remarkably short space of time, and the Second Vatican Council met in St Peter's on 11 October 1962. From the start the 2,300 or so bishops from all over the world refused simply to act as rubber stamps for decisions taken by the Roman Curia, the Pope's civil service, which many of them thought had become too arrogant and too powerful. Already this first session foreshadowed what was to emerge: freedom within the Church and toleration of a diversity of viewpoints, a less authoritarian and more open Catholicism, a willingness to learn from the modern world instead of condemning it out of hand and claiming to be able to prescribe all the answers to mankind's problems in advance.

But John XXIII was not to see the conclusion of what he had set in motion. His successor, Paul VI (Giovanni Battista Montini), Pope from 1963 to 1978, saw the council to its conclusion and in general carried through the revolution brought about by John XXIII – though he was liable to clamp down on what he judged dangerous tendencies, as with his ban on the discussion by the council of the possibility of married priests and his withdrawal from the council's competence of the question of birth control. This latter issue was to blow up in his face when in 1968 he reaffirmed Pius XI's condemnation of artificial birth control as wrong in itself, a condemnation which the majority of Catholics found themselves unable to accept – and said so. The resulting dispute can be seen as having consolidated the work of the Second Vatican Council by forcing the Church to live with unresolved tensions and differences in its midst.

The Catholicism of the 1970s may not be quite what John XXIII envisaged when he threw open the Vatican's windows. His motto was 'obedience and peace', and he could best be described as an unfrightened conservative. In other words, he trusted God and his fellow-men rather than his own preconceived ideas,

and was willing to embark on radical change if this could be shown to be what was demanded by the gospel.

Robert Nowell

See: John XXIII, *Journal of a Soul* (*Il giornale dell'anima e altri scritti di pietà*, 1964, trans. 1964); Zsolt Aradi, with Michael Derrick and Douglas Woodruff, *John XXIII, Pope of the Council* (1961); Leone Algisi, *John XXIII* (*Giovanni XXIII*, 1959, trans. 1963); Ernesto Balducci, *John, 'the transitional Pope'* (*Papa Giovanni*, 1964, trans. 1965); E. E. Y. Hales, *Pope John and his Revolution* (1966); Meriol Trevor, *Pope John* (1967); Paul Johnson, *Pope John XXIII* (1975). See also: 'Xavier Rynne', *Letters from Vatican City* (1963), *The Second Session* (1964), *The Third Session* (1965), *The Fourth Session* (1966).

230
JOHN, Augustus Edwin 1878–1961

Welsh artist

Augustus John was the third child of a Pembrokeshire solicitor, while his mother (who died when he was six) came from an almost endless line of Sussex plumbers called Smith. This name John improved to 'Petulengro' which, meaning blacksmith, might be taken as its Romany equivalent. Here was the origin of that mysterious gypsy flavour which was to spice John's flamboyant reputation. He had invented it to distinguish himself from a disconcertingly respectable paterfamilias who had warned his children never to speak to gypsies in case they were kidnapped – a destiny Augustus longed for. 'We are the sort of people,' he later confided to another Welsh artist, Nina Hamnet,, 'our fathers warned us against.'

John was sent to local schools in Tenby and aired and exercised by a governess optimistically described as 'Swiss'. The break came in 1894 when, aged sixteen, he went to the Slade School of Fine Art in London – to be followed the next year by his elder sister Gwen (who herself became a fine artist). His start there was conventional, but in the summer of 1897 a serious accident accelerated his career. While bathing off the coast of Tenby, he dived off a cliff, smashed his head on a rock and emerged from the waves, so legend insists, a genius.

Whatever the cause, he now became a dramatically changed figure; a wild, bearded, anarchical creature and 'a great man of action', as Wyndham Lewis* described him, 'into whose hands the fairies had placed a paintbrush instead of a sword'. He lived and worked with feverish impatience, outpacing his uncertainties and producing drawings that were, in the opinion of John Singer Sargent, beyond anything that had been seen since the Italian Renaissance. It was the beginning of what Virginia Woolf* called 'the age of Augustus John'.

Early in 1900 he married Ida Nettleship and his life developed into an agitated tale of two cities, London and Paris, and two 'wives', Ida and Dorelia McNeill who after Ida's death in 1907 took her place as his common-law wife and *femme inspiratrice*.

Up to this time John had been a Slade School prodigy whose reputation rested chiefly on his virtuosity as a draughtsman, whose work was regularly on show at the New English Art Club and whose influence on students was extended by his occupation first as instructor at the School of Art in Liverpool (1900–2) and then as co-principal with William Orpen of the Chelsea Art School (1903–7). But increasingly he was working in oils and tempera. From his early exemplars, Hals and Rembrandt, whose work he had studied in London, he turned to Puvis de Chavannes, Gauguin and Picasso* whose paintings he had seen in Paris. Then in 1910, following a tour through a number of Italian galleries, he became convinced of the modernity of the Italian Primitives. After nine months abroad, he showed his work at an exhibition, 'Provençal Studies and Other Works', that opened in London at the same time as Roger Fry's* 'Manet and the Post-Impressionists' and attracted almost as much hostility.

Fry and John, who had reacted similarly to the Italian painters, went on to distil from their experience a different lesson, John's concept of 'meaningless' beauty being incompatible with what became known as Fry's gospel of 'significant form'. For the next four years, sometimes in company with J. D. Innes and Derwent Lees, on the west coast of Ireland, in north Wales and through Provence, John painted a series of landscapes and figures in landscape that tell no story but reflect life as in a ballet. 'The technique appears to be, at its simplest, to make a pencil drawing on a small board covered with colourless transparent priming, then the outlines are washed in with a generous brush loaded with pure and brilliant oil colour,' wrote David Piper; 'the lines . . . are those of any John drawing, subtly lapping and rounding the volume they conjure up, but they are obliterated by the oils, and the result for effect relies in the inscape of colour, on contrasting colour, and the broad simplified pattern.'

This style of painting, which contributed to a small Symbolist Movement in British painting, was terminated by the war which turned John, as part of his agreement to work for the Canadian War Memorials Fund, into a Canadian Major with an alarming likeness to George V. But it was not a good war for John. He emerged as an erratic painter of celebrities. His best portraits were of exotic women (Lady Ottoline Morrell, Marchesa Casati, Guilhermina Suggia) who tended to amuse as well as excite him; or of writers and artists he admired (Thomas Hardy, Arthur Symons, Joseph Hone, William Nicholson, Matthew Smith); or of his own proliferating family.

As King of Bohemia he held court in Chelsea, at the Café Royal and in the Dorset and Hampshire countryside where Dorelia made homes for him. But the rebel became an RA, the anarchist an OM and the British public promoted him to a Grand Old Man.

His death on 31 October 1961 marked the end of an era, but the era had vanished first. Like a Canute, John had held up his hand to halt the tide of prowling industrialism; and such was his influence on style and fashion that, for a time, he appeared to succeed. The waves held back; there was a frenzied pause: then the sea of modern life flooded past him. But in the interval, in his finest paintings and drawings, he had captured that interval forever.

Michael Holroyd

John's autobiography was published in two volumes, *Chiaroscuro* (1952) and *Finishing Touches*, ed. Daniel George (1964). The definitive edition came out (with an Introduction by Michael Holroyd) in 1975 under the title *The Autobiography of Augustus John*. About John: Sir John Rothenstein has produced a number of books about John, in particular No. 2 in the British Artists Series (1944) and No. 79 of *The Masters* (1967); Lord David Cecil (ed.), *Fifty-Two Drawings* (1957); the authorized biography was written by Michael Holroyd (1974–5) who also collaborated with Malcolm Easton in *The Art of Augustus John* (1974); in 1975 Malcolm Easton and Romilly John produced *Augustus John* for the National Portrait Gallery; the latest art book on John is by Richard Shone (1979).

231

JOHNS, Jasper 1930–

US painter

Born in Augusta, Georgia, Johns studied at the University of Southern Carolina. In 1949 he served in the US Army in Japan, then moved to New York where from 1952 to 1958 he worked in a bookstore and, with Robert Rauschenberg*, as a window display artist for Tiffany's. Painting with little outside influence Johns chose flags, targets, alphabets and numerals – 'things the mind already knows,' he explained. Johns was making painting serve philosophy, yet in no sense illustrate ideas or arguments. Nor was the sensuous side of painting neglected. The subtlety of inflection of encaustic – painting into wax – was a constant reminder of the distance between signifier and signified, language and reality. Work for the 1958 one-man show at Castelli was made in three years; in 1954 Johns had destroyed all but a few of his pieces. Their preoccupations were to remain with him throughout his career: the play between different ways of looking; the defences of art-objects not only against visual ransacking but also against their innate expressivity; the paradoxical dialectic between recognizable, *a priori* structures, icons which become increasingly strange as the mind fails to encompass them, and the brute *Dinglichkeit* of illusions, or rather of objects as springboards for illusions. In an early interview Johns said: 'I am concerned with a thing's not being what it was, with its becoming other than what it is, with any moment in which one identifies a thing precisely and with the slipping away of that moment, with at any moment seeing or saying and letting it go at that.'

The first crisis in Johns's career occurred when his stock of 'flat' images was exhausted. But in 1959 he was introduced to Marcel Duchamp* and from 1961 onwards began reading Wittgenstein*. Both affected his work in the 1960s, typified by a broad painterly style, suspended objects and names of subjects and colours stencilled on to the canvas. A consuming interest in process and change overtook not only the new paintings but also the procedure of the career itself, with motifs pursued, rehearsed and ransacked in an act of ceaseless redefinition. After denying the rampant individualism of Abstract Expressionism – 'I worked in such a way that I could say it's not me,' Johns remarked – then moving through an intensification of that irony and *maniera* inherent in American 1960s art, he arrived at that complex obsession with exhaustion which prepared the ground for the mathematical systems of 'epistemic' post-minimalism. Like the lives of Duchamp or Joyce*, whose artistic decisions resemble a cultural equivalent of military strategies, Johns seemed to have cleared an area in which he could enrich his chosen form. The cross-hatched motif of *The Barber's Tree*, *The Dutch Wives* and *Weeping Women* was remembered from a brief but vivid experience. 'I was riding in a car . . . when a car came in the opposite direction . . . covered in these marks. . . . I only saw it for a moment . . . but I immediately thought that I would use it for my next painting.' All of Johns's major themes are present in the finished pictures – a Puritan mistrust of the mendacity of visual forms and a counterbalancing, defensive desire to employ them, a concern with beginnings and endings of events and the arbitrary but blinding effect of a shifted point of view. Like the mature style of Henry James or Milton, Johns's manner, which IS the painting, is both an approach and a tool for understanding that approach. Johns is not recording the existence of anything but locating his subject, sensing its presence, then registering it by providing a visual parallel to the act of permitting it to impinge on his consciousness. In his monograph on Johns, Michael Crichton seriously suggests a biological reason for his lateral thinking. Perhaps they amount to the same thing, an originality so powerful that the very foundations of the art they are using are exposed, questioned and miraculously rearranged. Jasper Johns himself has said: 'I don't know anything about art.' And on another occasion, 'I'm just trying to find a way to make pictures.'

Stuart Morgan

See Leo Steinberg, *Jasper Johns* (1963); Max Kozloff, *Jasper Johns* (1969); Richard Field, *Jasper Johns: Prints 1960–1970* (1970) and *Jasper Johns: Prints 1970–1977* (1978); Michael Crichton, *Jasper Johns* (New York, Whitney Museum/New York Graphic Society, 1978).

232
JONES, Alfred Ernest 1879–1958

British psychoanalyst

One of the founder members of the psychoanalytical movement, Ernest Jones lived through its long history to become President of the International Psychoanalytical Association and biographer of Sigmund Freud*. For fifty years he was – in effect – the man behind Freud, working in the early years as a member of the Vienna circle, then as committee catalyst and finally as the powerful administrative manipulator whose influence appeared at all points and moulded many aspects of psychoanalytical history.

Born of humble parents at Rhosfelyn in Wales, he made the interesting statement about his early years: 'The practice of coitus was familiar to me at the ages of six and seven, after which I suspended it and did not resume it till I was 24.' A certain irony underlies a childhood which so vividly evoked one of the revolutionary principles – infantile sexuality – which was to distinguish the doctrines of the man destined to become his – the word Master has too mystical a ring. Educated at Swansea Grammar School and University College, Cardiff, his early medical career was very successful but key appointments which should have been his on merit were given to rivals for reasons of medical politics. His meeting with Sigmund Freud in April 1908 at the Congress for Freudian Psychology was historic. From then onwards a new direction appeared in his life but there were many doubts and deviations before he was finally committed to psychoanalysis.

Unable to attend the International Congress in 1910, he was present at the 1911 Congress and from then on took a more active and influential part in the development of the movement. Collaborating with Brill in America, they founded the New York Psychoanalytical Society and the American Psychoanalytical Association in 1911. When Jung*, Adler* and Stekel broke away from the early circle it was Jones who mooted the idea of a committee which would form an Old Guard around Freud committed to the major concepts of psychoanalysis: sexual libido, infantile sexuality, repression and the unconscious. A maladroit administrator, Freud needed someone who could fulfil the role of chief executive, and Jones's first-hand knowledge of the Movement, his status as a pioneer member and his negotiating skills made him the best candidate.

He published a number of papers between the years 1911 and 1920, the most important among them his *Collected Papers on Psychoanalysis* (1912). Delivered before the British Psychological Society (29 January 1916), one of his most original contributions was a paper 'The Theory of Symbolism'. Symbolism in psychoanalytic terms, he wrote, was an attempt to overcome the inhibition of 'feeling-ideas' and always constituted a regression to a simpler mode of 'apprehension'. When the regression was relatively superficial, involving at most the pre-conscious, the result became metaphorical. Pressed deeper to the level of the unconscious 'the result was symbolism in the strict sense'.

Following the death of his first wife, his marriage to Katharina Johl in October 1919 was very successful and – he claimed – brought him luck because psychoanalysis struck firm and healthy roots in Britain when he founded the British Psychoanalytical Society in that year.

Ernest Jones was active in advancing the status as well as the development of psychoanalysis. A special committee, set up between 1926 and 1929 by the British Medical Association to consider psychoanalysis, produced a favourable report, largely because of his firmness and tact. Perhaps the most spectacular diplomatic feat in his life occurred in 1938 when he faced the Nazis in Vienna to bring Freud safely back to London.

A complete list of Jones's contributions to psychoanalytic journals would fill many pages but his best work is represented in four books, *Papers in Psychoanalysis* (1921), *Essays in Applied Psychoanalysis* (1923), *On the Nightmare* (1931) and *Hamlet and Oedipus* (1949). In Chapter 2 of the last of these he states that the central mystery of Shakespeare's play is Hamlet's hesitancy in seeking revenge for his father's murder. In this closely reasoned and scholarly book he examines a wealth of previous explanations and discusses them with polemical adroitness. His own interpretation follows the classic pattern. Hamlet had bitterly resented sharing his mother with his father, but repressed the wish to have him put 'out of the way'. His father's murder reactivated his own wish and produced the double guilt of patricide and incest, a combination so intolerable that he faltered in his resolve to take revenge.

In later years Jones became involved in the Melanie Klein* split with Freud, his sympathies with her theories causing some friction. Among other reformulations, she reinterpreted the processes of introjection and projection in infancy which led, according to Jones,

to deeper insights into the origins of the super-ego. Some of his clinical work anticipated parts of her theory of the need to assimilate the depressive position.

As President of the International Psychoanalytical Association between 1920 and 1924 and again from 1932 to 1944, he presided over the biennial Congresses and conducted a large correspondence. At this stage some people found his personality abrasive, but they were a minority. It became customary for him to read the first paper at each International Congress and he did this for the last time in Paris in 1957, a year before his death.

Vincent Brome

See also Jones's *Sigmund Freud, Life and Work* (3 vols, 1953–7).

233
JONES, Everett LeRoi/Imamu Amiri Baraka 1934–

US author and Afro-American activist

Few black American literary contemporaries have been so prolific, or so willing to attempt new varieties of form, as LeRoi Jones/Amiri Baraka, an established presence as poet, dramatist, Jazz historian, essayist, short-story writer, novelist, editor and anthologist. Since the 1960s, and the transforming impact of Civil Rights and the widespread black power revolts against America's inherited racial order for which Malcolm X* and other radicals were spokesmen, he has also given his energies increasingly to urban politics, visible and often controversial activity which took him out of his early Beat and Lower East Side New York years into militant black nationalism, and latterly Third World Marxism and Maoism*. Raised in moderate affluence in Newark, New Jersey, he attended a token integrated High School, before winning scholarships to Rutgers (1951), then Howard University (1952), from which he took his BA in 1954 and which he later castigated as a 'sick' institution for turning out black bourgeois students. He did graduate work at the New School for Social Research and Columbia; served as a gunner and weatherman in the US Air Force (1954–7); edited, with Hettie Cohen, whom he married in 1958, the important avant-garde poetry magazine *Yugen* (1958–62); began Totem Press Books as his own poetry was beginning to appear in a host of small publications; visited Cuba (1960) and took up teaching appointments at Columbia University, then the University of Buffalo and The New School. In 1965, he left Newark and his family for Harlem, where he became Director and resident playwright of the Black Arts Repertory Theater (Federally financed) from which, after bitter argument and recriminations, he returned to Newark and started 'Spirit House' to bring together black arts and the community. There he re-married, in 1966, Sylvia Robinson/Ameena Baraka; received in 1967 a two to two-and-a-half-year sentence for alleged participation in a city riot (of which he was later acquitted); and again, in 1967 in Newark, was a shaping force in organizing the National Black Power Conference. He became deeply involved in Jihad publications – broadsheets, agitprop, essays and poems, work by black authors for a black readership. In 1969, he inspired the Pan-African Congress in Atlanta (and edited its transcripts); supported the campaign of Kenneth Gibson as Newark's first black mayor (support he later regretted); took a leading part in the Black American Congress in Gary, Indiana, in 1972; and from the mid-1970s moved towards Maoism, repudiating the nationalism of his earlier allegiances and figures like Ron Karenga. Throughout, he has maintained his considerable literary output, a vital, undeniable strength in the emergence of post-war black American writing and thought.

Of Jones's main collections of poetry to date, *Preface to a Twenty Volume Suicide Note* (1961) reveals him at his most domestic – intimate in exploring the meanings of his recent marriage and impending fatherhood, nostalgic for the lost radio and screen figures of his youth, excited by new Greenwich Village friendships. 'Blackness', at this stage, meant a condition largely at the periphery of things. As he writes in the concluding lines of 'Notes For A Speech', 'You are/as any sad man here/American.' The poems in *The Dead Lecturer* (1964) speak from a more resolved set of black racial perspectives, still often lyric with their inspiration in Blues and Jazz, but bolder, and nowhere more so than in BLACK DADA NIHILISMUS, verse pitched in a powerful, exorcizing voice, which also confirmed Jones's repudiation of his East Side Bohemian phase. With *Black Magic, Poetry 1961–1967* (1969), which gathered three previous volumes into one, *Sabotage, Target Study*, and *Black Art*, Jones's manner became that of a poet in yet fuller possession of his powers, seeking in black history the very ground condition of his art. He writes, for instance, in 'Race', a poem from *Black Art*:

Our strength is in the drums,
The sinuous horns, blow forever beautiful princes,
   touch
The spellflash of everything. . . .

The recovery of black confidence, from Jazz, from Africa, from everyday black American life, marks an essential theme in Jones's later poetry, especially in *In Our Terribleness* (1970), a major transitional collection of his prose and verse, and *Hard Facts* (1975), a sequence of Marxist compositions.

Jones's drama has earned him contradictory rewards, genuine acclaim as an innovator and stylist, yet frequent abuse, especially from offended white audiences. In *Dutchman* (1964), probably his best known play, he wrote a small masterpiece, a journey allegory set on the New York subway about black manhood, racial and sexual defeat. Its companion piece, *The Slave* (1964), offers a vision of confused rebellion, white America under conditions of uncertain siege. In plays like *The Baptism* (1967) and *The Toilet* (1967), deliberate 'unsavoury' writing, Jones's preoccupations are religious, and with group violence towards homosexual feeling. The subsequent work, Jihad publications like *Arm Yourself or Harm Yourself* (1967) and *Slave Ship* (1967), or *Experimental Death Unit* (1965), *A Black Mass* (1966), or *The Great Goodness of Life* (1967), or *Jello* (1970), and the plays published in *The Motion of History* (1978), depict the need for genuine community purpose, shared black political direction in America. Whether performed before white or Harlem and Newark black audiences, Jones's plays rarely fail to disconcert, seeking to arouse awareness in idioms which use the theatre as a focus for serious racial change.

Those same idioms prevail in Jones's experimental fiction, *The System of Dante's Hell* (1965) and *Tales* (1967), both intricate prose narratives, which catch a gallery of individual black stances and moods. *Dante's Hell* adapts the *Divine Comedy*'s 'Hell' to contemporary America, fallen contemporary sinners incarcerated in the modern ghetto Western city. *Tales*, arguably a novel as much as a short-story collection, evokes a haunted world of young male/black life discovering its meaning and debates the relationship of literary aesthetics with actual living. Jones's other prose, his landmark *Blues People: Negro Music in White America* (1963) and *Black Music* (1967), both of which rank with the best existing analyses of Blues and Jazz (a full-length study of John Coltrane is promised), and his essay collections, *Home: Social Essays* (1966) and *Raise Race Rays Raze: Essays since 1965* (1971), when taken with the occasional pieces, his reviews and pamphlets, his Introductions and frequent journal correspondence, confirm another essential dimension of his talent. Essays as fine as 'Cuba Libre' (1960), written in the immediate wake of Castro's* revolution, or 'The Myth Of A "Negro Literature" ' (1962), a plea for an ungenteel and live black literary tradition, or the astonishing verve of his Jazz pieces, continue to deserve wide recognition.

Jones/Baraka, as his composite name suggests, has been an evolving thinker and activist, of late unwilling to let his art part company with his essential political and black-community commitments. His frequent skirmishes with the law, and his roles in different black movements, right through to his present Marxism, argue a fierce individual seriousness about black needs. Yet for all that Jones's politics have taken different forms, like his literary work, what remains unaltered is the legitimacy of his talent, his formidable articulate energy.

A. Robert Lee

See: Theodore Hudson, *From LeRoi Jones to Amiri Baraka: The Literary Works* (1973); Kimberley Benson, *Baraka: The Renegade and the Mask* (1976); Werner Sollors, *Amiri Baraka/LeRoi Jones: The Quest for a 'Populist Modernism'* (1978); Letitia Dace, *LeRoi Jones (Imamu Amiri Baraka): A Checklist of Works by and About Him* (1971); C. W. E. Bigsby (ed.), *The Black American Writer* (1969); Addison Gayle (ed.), *The Black Aesthetic* (1972), *Black Expression* (1969) and *The Way of the New World: the Black Novel in America* (1976); and Eric Mottram, 'Toward the Alternative: the Prose of LeRoi Jones' in A. Robert Lee (ed.), *Black Fiction: New Studies in the Afro-American Novel since 1945* (1980).

234
JOYCE, James Augustine 1882–1941

Irish writer

James Joyce was the greatest master of the heroic age of Modernist literature. He was the near-contemporary of Picasso*, Schoenberg* and Webern*, and his career coincided with the heroic ages of Modernist painting and music. Joyce, however, was no self-proclaiming modernist; he signed no manifestos and joined no groups (though he did have a small circle of admirers in Paris); if anything, he thought of himself as the reincarnation of Henrik Ibsen and of the tragic artist-heroes of Ibsen's plays, preferring solitude, 'silence, exile and cunning'.

Joyce was born at Rathgar, Dublin, on 2 February 1882, into a fairly prosperous Catholic middle-class family. As he recounts in his fictional autobiography, *A Portrait of the Artist as a Young Man* (1916), he was sent at the age of six to Clongowes Wood College, a boarding school run by the Jesuits for the Catholic elite. He stayed at this school for only three years, since his father's fortunes declined. Thereafter he was educated briefly at a Christian Brothers School (which he did not mention anywhere) and later was admitted without fees to an excellent day school, Belvedere College, which was also run by the Jesuits. His sexual precocity, terror at a sermon on hell, repentance, thoughts about becoming a priest and eventual loss of faith are recounted dramatically in *A Portrait*, as are some of his intellectual adventures at University College, Dublin. He studied modern languages, but did not do well academically, despite his great linguistic talents and his extraordinary memory. He was too busy educating himself in literature of all ages and in beginning his career as a writer. In 1899 just after his eighteenth birthday he had an article, 'Ibsen's New Drama', published in the London *Fortnightly Review*: when this was shown to the aged playwright he praised it for its understanding of his last play *When We Dead Awaken*. When he graduated BA in 1902 he decided to go off to

Paris to study medicine, but soon gave up that idea. He was recalled to Dublin in 1903 because his mother was dying (as commemorated vividly in *Ulysses*, 1922) and hung around Dublin for a year doing various odd jobs, including teaching. In 1904 he met a girl called Nora Barnacle, and on 16 June fell in love with her on an excursion to the Head of Howth: this is the date commemorated as 'Bloomsday' in *Ulysses*, and indeed his relationship with Nora is one of the main themes of that novel. He persuaded her to go abroad with him, but refused as a matter of principle to go through any ceremony of marriage until 1931.

From 1904 to 1915 Joyce with his family spent most of his time in Trieste, working in the Berlitz school of languages. He became friendly with a Jewish businessman called Ettore Schmitz, who, thanks to Joyce's encouragement, wrote distinguished novels under the name of Italo Svevo*. In those years he wrote the stories of *Dubliners* (published after much difficulty in 1914) and began *A Portrait of the Artist as a Young Man*. This also ran into publishing difficulties (censorship by the printers) and was not published until 1916, by which time Joyce had begun *Ulysses*. In 1920 the Joyces went to Paris, where they remained until 1940. *Ulysses* was serialized in the *Little Review* from 1918, published in Paris in 1922 and promptly banned in Britain and the USA. Joyce was now world-famous but a figure of scandal in the literary world: unlike his countrymen W. B. Yeats* and Shaw* he did not receive the Nobel Prize. In 1923 he began *Finnegans Wake* and laboured at it until he corrected the last proof in 1938: it was published early in 1939 and fell flat. Joyce, who had worked on through severe eye troubles and anxiety about his daughter's failing mental health, was bitterly disappointed. When the Nazis invaded France Joyce moved to Zürich again, where he died on 13 January 1941.

His biography could be extended indefinitely without irrelevance, because almost everything in the life appears in the works, if only as a humorous detail. The young Joyce becomes Stephen Dedalus of *A Portrait* and *Ulysses*, but Leopold Bloom is closely based on the middle-aged Joyce; the analogues in *Finnegans Wake* are Shem, the dissolute Bohemian writer, and H. C. Earwicker, husband and father. Joyce, unlike Shakespeare, was not a great inventor of other lives and scenes: he used his own life and the social milieu of Dublin, through which he took an imaginary walk every day of his exiled life. He was first and foremost a realist or naturalist (these terms cannot be made precise) and his early work is an extension of the fiction and drama of the great nineteenth-century masters Flaubert, Ibsen and Chekhov. The *Dubliners* are highly successful exercises in this mode: every linguistic and visual detail is sharp and meaningful. The reader, however, should be warned that every story contains a trap for the unwary. Critics have discovered that the old priest in the first story has syphilis, that Frank in 'Eveline' is a deceiver, that every single ecclesiastical fact in the wonderful, funny 'Grace' is wrong, and there will be more discoveries like those to come. Realism is predominant in *A Portrait*, an unequalled description of a Catholic education and of an era of Dublin's history; and realism reaches its heights in the first half of *Ulysses*, and is thereafter abandoned.

What takes its place is *parody* (under which may be included pastiche), of which Joyce is the greatest master in English literature. Parody underlies his brilliant modulation of style to correspond with the subject. *A Portrait* begins with baby-talk, shifts to the objective reportage of a small boy, shows the awakening of the adolescent imagination in Romantic flashes: the clerical passages draw on Newman, the aesthetic ones on Pater; the discussion on art and politics at the university are in a sparse Ibsenic dialogue; while the last passage, though disguised as a diary, is in fact written in the stream-of-consciousness technique Joyce had begun to devise for *Ulysses*. The development of style is thus parallel to the development of the artist's character. In *Ulysses* parody is largely absent from the first half, which presents the interior monologue of Stephen and of Bloom, combined with highly vivid imagery. These early chapters were apparently written slowly and revised with great care. But beginning with the 'Cyclops' chapter (set in Barney Kiernan's pub) Joyce began to write at a much greater speed and fell back into his favourite mode. The funniest parodies, mostly of bad journalism, are in 'Cyclops'; the most pedantic are in the 'Oxen of the Sun', where he imitates every major shift of English prose style from Mandeville and Malory to Carlyle. The ultimate in parody is the 'Ithaca' (penultimate) chapter, where he takes off every kind of non-literary, flat, denotative prose, from scientific textbooks to house-agent's reports; this chapter, in which every conceivable fact about Bloom is set down, is also a joke at the expense of nineteenth-century naturalism. Joyce called it the ugly duckling of the book, and his favourite chapter: it certainly possesses a strange spectral imaginative fluorescence. *Finnegans Wake* is *all* parody, though because of the strange Jabberwocky language it is not always easy to see what is being parodied. But every sentence of the book is based on some earlier literary or popular work: after a while one can begin to hear the voices of Swift or Dickens or the broadside ballad-singers or Wagner or Wyndham Lewis* or Yeats, emerging from the constant babble of puns. To read *Finnegans Wake* is a labour of great difficulty, from which every intelligent reader has a perfect right to be excused; but it can turn for some into a great delight, once the problem of identifying parodied styles and underlying myths can be tackled.

Joyce is the great mythological writer of his period, only equalled in this respect by Thomas Mann*. A myth, defined rather loosely, is a story about god or

the gods or ancient non-historical heroes, and one which is still felt to be of value. In *A Portrait* Joyce used the myth of Daedalus, the architect of the Cretan labyrinth, who escaped by inventing human flight: his son Icarus perished in his first flight. Joyce uses this story to represent the situation of the modern artist, who must escape from the labyrinth of family, nationalist politics and religion. From the point of view of the normal everyday world the artist falls like Lucifer (another mythological constant in Joyce); but from the point of view of the artist this is a fall *upwards*, from darkness into light. Of course, the young artist may not succeed like Daedalus, the 'old artificer', but fail and die young like Icarus; the possibility of failure and death is very strongly presented in *Ulysses*. For his greatest novel Joyce wanted a myth to buttress his portrait of the mature, married, 'all-round' man and found in the Homeric figure of Odysseus, who appears no longer as warrior at Troy but as adventurer, husband and lover, ingenious, occasionally rash, and with a hundred other qualities recognizable in contemporary man. Every chapter of *Ulysses* is based on a Homeric episode, and all kinds of correspondence between ancient and modern are worked out with the greatest felicity. The virtuosity should not conceal the main point, which is that the world and human nature do not change: the great myths of Zeus, Odysseus, Aeneas, Hamlet, Siegfried, Tristan and Isolde are always relevant to the human condition. There is no controversy among critics about the use of Homer in *Ulysses* but it is still not generally accepted that Joyce used the Christian and Jewish Biblical myths in the same way: a non-believer in religion, he gave a radical reinterpretation of the Biblical stories to show their relevance to the life and work of the modern artist. Every chapter of *Ulysses* refers, when Stephen is present, to some episode of the New Testament and to the liturgy, and when Bloom is present, to the Jewish Bible from Genesis to the later prophets. This most powerful and resonant part of Joyce's mythological writing has not been generally recognized, because such a ruthless reinterpretation is offensive to some believers and largely unintelligible to non-believers. The myths employed in *Finnegans Wake*, sometimes with even greater poetic intensity, are too numerous to list; but the myths of Genesis are perhaps predominant, followed by the Wagnerian myths of the *Ring* and *Tristan*.

The importance of Wagner to Joyce can hardly be overstated. The young Dedalus at the end of the *Portrait* is the young Siegfried, 'forging the uncreated conscience of my race'; the reforged sword, Nothung, a symbol of the artist's need to destroy and re-create, turns up after several hundred pages of *Ulysses*. Wagner was the greatest mythologist of the nineteenth century, using the ancient Germanic stories to illuminate the present and indeed the future of mankind. Wagner was also vastly more sophisticated than the French or Italian operatists of his century in the symphonic construction of his 'musical dramas'; he aimed at producing a continuous musical texture, embodying basic themes or leitmotivs. *Ulysses* and *Finnegans Wake* are based on this principle: they contain a number of thematic statements which keep reappearing in different contexts and subject to different transformations. In *Finnegans Wake* the transformations are more difficult to follow, because of the licence of punning language, but many of the themes will easily be detected. A knowledge of Wagner, and indeed of all opera, is a great help to an understanding of the work, since Joyce finally showed greater devotion to music than to literature.

Joyce was himself not a great inventor of myths and must therefore take a lower place in the hierarchy of imagination than Kafka*. He will perhaps one day cease to be admired for his technical skills and inventions. But he will perhaps always continue to be read, as may his disciple Samuel Beckett*, for his humour and his simple humanity.

Professor Matthew Hodgart

Other works include: *Exiles* (play, 1918); *Collected Poems* (1936); *Letters*, ed. Stuart Gilbert and Richard Ellman (3 vols, 1957–66). See: Harry T. Levin, *James Joyce, a Critical Introduction* (1941; 2nd edn, 1960); Richard Ellman, *James Joyce* (1959) and *Yeats and Joyce* (1967); Frank Budgen, *James Joyce and the Making of 'Ulysses'* (2nd edn, 1960); Anthony Burgess, *Here Comes Everybody: an Introduction to James Joyce for the Ordinary Reader* (1965); William Y. Tindall, *A Reader's Guide to 'Finnegans Wake'* (1969); Robert H. Derning, *James Joyce: The Critical Heritage* (2 vols, 1970); Charles Peake, *James Joyce: The Citizen and the Artist* (1977); M. J. C. Hodgart, *James Joyce: A Student's Guide* (1978).

235
JUNG, Carl Gustav 1875–1961

Swiss psychiatrist

C. G. Jung was an original thinker who made notable contributions to the understanding of the human mind. Jung was born in Kesswil, Switzerland, on 26 July 1875. His father was a pastor in the Swiss Reformed Church. He remained an only child for the first nine years of his life, and, since he was far ahead of his contemporaries at the village school to which he was first sent, remained somewhat isolated emotionally during most of his childhood. At the age of eleven, he went to school in Basel, and later became a medical student at the University there. He had almost decided to specialize in surgery when he came across a textbook of psychiatry written by Krafft-Ebing. Reading this

book made Jung decide that he must specialize in psychiatry which, at that time, was a poorly regarded branch of medicine. In 1900, he obtained a post in the Burghölzli mental hospital in Zürich. In 1905 he was appointed lecturer in psychiatry at the University of Zürich. In 1907 Jung first encountered Freud*, with whom he actively collaborated for the next six years. In 1909 Jung gave up his hospital appointment in favour of his growing private practice; and, in the same year, travelled with Freud to the United States to lecture at Clark University, Massachusetts. Increasing divergence between the two men led to Jung's withdrawal from the psychoanalytic movement; and, in April 1914, Jung resigned his position as President of the International Psychoanalytical Association. He also gave up his academic post at the University of Zürich, feeling that he could not continue to teach until he had more clearly formulated his own, individual point of view. Henceforth he devoted himself to his practice and to research. Jung's psychology became known as 'Analytical Psychology' in contrast to Freud's 'Psychoanalysis'. As the eighteen volumes of his *Collected Works* attest, Jung was an indefatigable writer. The rest of his long life was outwardly uneventful. From time to time, after he became world-famous, his routine was interrupted by travels to India, Africa, the United States and other parts of the world; but, for the most part, he continued to live and work at his home in Küsnacht, by the lakeside of Zürich. Jung died at the age of eighty-five on 6 June 1961.

When Jung started work in the Burghölzli hospital, associationist theories of mental functioning held the field. Jung transformed the tool of word-association tests from a means of investigating contrast, contiguity and so on into a way of uncovering personal problems and emotional preoccupations. In using the tests in this way, Jung provided experimental support for Freud's concept of repression; for his subjects were often unaware that their hesitations in response to stimulus words revealed their inner life. It was this work which led to Jung's introduction of the word 'complex' into psychiatry. It also led to correspondence with Freud, whose first surviving letter to Jung acknowledges the latter's paper 'Psychoanalysis and Association Experiments'.

In 1906, Jung published *The Psychology of Dementia Praecox* which was the first notable attempt to apply psychoanalytic interpretation to the phenomena of insanity. He sent the book to Freud, who promptly invited Jung to visit him in Vienna. It was Jung's research into schizophrenia which led to his conception of a 'collective unconscious'; that is, a deeper layer of mind, common to all men, which lay beneath the merely personal. Jung was widely read in history, and also in comparative religion. His efforts to understand the bizarre delusions and hallucinations of the insane led him to compare them with the myths and religious beliefs of primitive people. He found many parallels. In Jung's view, this myth-making substratum of mind could not be explained in terms of the personal vicissitudes of childhood, as were the neuroses described by Freud. The child was not born into the world with a mind like a blank sheet of paper upon which anything could be inscribed. The child was already predisposed to feel and think along the same lines as had his ancestors since the beginning of time. The unconscious was not just a part of the mind to which unpleasant experience was banished: it was the very foundation of our being and the source not only of mental disturbance but also of our deepest hopes and aspirations.

At least part of the divergence between Jung and Freud was the result of their different clinical experience. Freud did not work in a mental hospital, and had little experience of insanity; whereas Jung continued to be interested in schizophrenia throughout his life. Jung concluded that the delusional systems of schizophrenia served a positive function. First, delusional systems were explanatory devices which served to make sense out of the sufferer's experience and to preserve his self-esteem. An obvious example is the familiar type of paranoid system, which explains the individual's plight as the consequence of the machinations of others, thus relieving the sufferer from responsibility whilst attributing to him an undeserved importance. Second, delusional systems often contained material which resembled myth, and to which parallels could be found in various forms of religious belief, even though the patient might never have encountered any such parallel. Jung concluded that the collective, myth-creating level of mind, in both normal persons and in the insane, had the function of making sense out of the individual's experience and giving meaning to his existence. In later life, Jung concluded that the real cause of much mental suffering was the fact that the individual had become alienated from this level of mind, with the result that he lost any sense of significance in his life. In this way, Jung anticipated the point of view of the existentialist analysts. In a letter to Freud in 1910, discussing the possibility of joining a new ethical society, Jung wrote: 'What sort of a new myth does it hand out for us to live by? Only the wise are ethical from sheer intellectual presumption, the rest of us need the eternal truth of myth. . . . 2000 years of Christianity can only be replaced by something equivalent.'

In 1912, just before his break with Freud, Jung published *The Psychology of the Unconscious*, later to become known as *Symbols of Transformation*. This was the first major work in which his own distinctive point of view was made manifest. During the next few years, Jung went through a period of profound upheaval which is vividly described in his autobiography. He described himself as being 'menaced by a psychosis'. This 'midlife crisis', as it would now be called, proved to be very important for his subsequent development. The self-analysis which he was forced to pursue during the years of the First World War shaped the whole course of his subsequent psychological theorizing, and also influenced his technique of psychotherapy. He wrote: 'The years when I was pursuing my inner images were the most important in my life. In them, everything essential was decided.' He managed to retain his hold on reality, partly because he was supported by his wife and family, and partly because he learned to objectify his own fantasies by painting them and writing about them. In later life, he encouraged his patients to use the same techniques in coming to terms with their own psychopathological material. Emerging from this period of mental turmoil, Jung started to reflect upon how it was that such men as Freud, Adler* and himself could study the same psychological material and yet come to such different conclusions about it. These reflections led to the theme of his next major work, *Psychological Types* (1921), in which his concepts of Extraversion and Introversion were delineated. Jung saw that men approached the study of the mind, and life in general, from different basic attitudes. The extravert was primarily interested in the world of external objects; the introvert in what went on within his own mind. Both attitudes were necessary for a full comprehension of reality; but men were usually one-sided, and tended to one or other extreme. From his concept of types sprang Jung's idea that neurosis arose from a one-sided development of the individual, and his valuable conception that the unconscious compensated for the one-sided development of consciousness. Neurotic symptoms were not always residues of childhood experience, as Freud supposed, but were often attempts on the part of the mind to correct its own lack of equilibrium, and therefore pointers to a new and more satisfactory synthesis. This point of view is in accord with modern ideas on cybernetics, and with the recognition by physiologists that the body is a self-regulating entity. It follows from this conception that there must be an ideal state of synthesis or integration towards which the human being is striving, even though it may never, in practice, be attained. In Jung's view, this search for integration or wholeness was characteristic of the second half of life; and it is in dealing with the problems of older people that Jung's psychological ideas have proved most effective. Many of Jung's patients were successful people who did not fall into the conventional categories of neurosis, but who complained that life no longer held any meaning for them. Jung treated such people by encouraging them to pursue the products of unconscious fantasy, whether these manifested themselves in dreams or day-dreams. He encouraged them to enter into a state of reverie in which consciousness was not lost, but in which judgment was suspended. His patients were urged to write or paint the fantasies which came to them whilst in this condition; a technique which became known as 'active imagination'. In this way a process of psychological development was initiated which Jung named the process of individuation. This might be described as a kind of Pilgrim's Progress without a creed; aiming not at heaven, but at integration and wholeness, a condition which his patients expressed in paintings resembling the patterns known as Mandalas, which are used in the East for meditation. Although individuals might differ very widely from one another, the paths they pursued in their exploration of the unconscious shared some landmarks in common. In the course of analysis, patients would encounter various typical, 'primordial images' which Jung named 'archetypes'. These images are the same kind of figures which are familiar in myth and fairy story: heroes, heroines, demons, witches, gods and goddesses. A characteristic encounter is with the Shadow; that is, with a personification of the least acceptable parts of human nature, often symbolized by a sinister, dark 'other' who is felt to be terrifying or alien. The primordial image of the opposite sex is named Animus in women, Anima in men. A typical anima figure is Rider Haggard's 'She'. 'She' is not only spectacularly beautiful, but also an immortal priestess with access to arcane wisdom. She is clearly not an actual woman, but an image of Woman, a distilled essence of all that is most fascinating and seductive about women for men. Jung maintained that, in order to attain integration, the individual must recognize and differentiate himself from the immensely powerful influence of such archetypal images which, all too often, are projected upon actual people in the external world.

The greater part of Jung's later work is concerned with the process of individuation. Having formulated the idea, Jung set about looking for parallels from the past. Jung believed that man's essential nature did not alter much in the course of centuries, and that there must therefore be evidence that the men of old were looking for the same integration as were his patients in the present. He found his main parallel in alchemy.

Alchemy is interesting psychologically just because there is nothing in its scientifically. The alchemists were looking for something (the philosopher's stone) which had no real existence, but which, for them, was of extreme importance. The symbolism in which the alchemists expressed their search was found by Jung to be remarkably similar to that produced by his patients, and he chronicles much of his research in this field in *Psychology and Alchemy* (1953).

In his later years, Jung became interested in the problem of time. He came to the conclusion that events were linked, not only in a causal sequence, but also by their simultaneous occurrence. Throughout his life, Jung was interested in what he called 'meaningful coincidences'; and he finally came to believe that there was an acausal principle of equal importance with causality which he named 'synchronicity'. This aspect of his work has not been generally accepted.

In spite of the fact that Jung became something of a cult figure amongst the young of the Western world during the 1960s and 1970s, his work has never been very widely appreciated. Moreover, some of his contributions have been taken over by others without acknowledgment, or perhaps without realization of their origin. This is especially true of the so-called Neo-Freudians. For many years Jung was reluctant to allow his teaching to become formalized within an institutional framework; but centres at which analysts are trained in his methods exist in Zürich, London, various cities in the USA, and some other European countries. His impact upon psychiatry has been small; but his influence upon the practice of psychotherapy has been greater, particularly as regards a more flexible approach than that of orthodox Freudian analysts, together with the use of painting, modelling, and writing as adjuvants to talk. Jung's emphasis upon the spiritual, as opposed to the physical, is a valuable counterbalance to Freud's insistence upon the body. Distinguished people from spheres other than psychiatry and psychotherapy have paid tribute to Jung's influence. Among them are the writers Hermann Hesse* and J. B. Priestley; the historian Arnold Toynbee*; the physicist W. Pauli; the art historian Sir Herbert Read. Jung is certain of a place in history; but the ultimate significance and impact of his ideas are as yet undetermined.

Anthony Storr

Jung's works are translated in the *Collected Works* (18 vols, 1953–71). See also: *Memories, Dreams, Reflections* (1963); C. G. Jung, Marie-Louise von Franz, J. L. Henderson, Jolande Jacobi and Aniela Jaffe, *Man and his Symbols* (1964); and William McGuire, ed., *The Freud/Jung Letters* (1974). About Jung: Frieda Fordham, *An Introduction to Jung's Psychology* (1953); Raymond M. Hostie, *Religion and the Psychology of Jung* (1957); Anthony Storr, *Jung* (1973); Antonio Moreno, *Jung, Gods and Modern Man* (1974); Marie-Louise von Franz, *C. G. Jung; His Myth in Our Time*; Volodymyr Walter Odajnyk, *Jung and Politics* (1976); Vincent Brome, *Jung: Man and Myth* (1978).

K

236

KAFKA, Franz 1883–1924

Austrian novelist

The timid, reticent son of a robust self-made business-man, Kafka was born in Prague, and educated at the German Gymnasium and then the German University, where he read law. After receiving his doctorate he worked from 1908 until 1922 for the 'Workers' Accident Insurance Institute', where his duties were to write reports concerning the dangers of various trades and recommending methods of accident-prevention. Until 1915 Kafka lived with his parents, helping in their shop during his spare time, a fact which, combined with the exigencies of his profession, left him with little time for writing. He was thus compelled, to the eventual detriment of his health, to do his writing at night, and in 1909 and 1910 published a number of short prose pieces in literary journals. Through his close, lifelong friend the writer Max Brod, Kafka, in August 1912, met Felice Bauer, a young woman from Berlin, with whom, for the next five years, he pursued a troubled relationship involving him in profound vacillation. Twice engaged to Felice, Kafka found himself torn between reluctance to bear life alone and the fear that marriage would involve a threat to the solitude which he saw as a necessary precondition of his art. In the event, Kafka never married, although a number of women in addition to Felice played an important part in his emotional life, including Dora Dymant with whom, towards the end of his life, he lived for a short time in Berlin. But the quickened development of tuberculosis, which had been diagnosed in 1917, caused him to return to Prague and thence to a sanatorium in Vienna, where he died in 1924, leaving instructions to Max Brod that his unpublished writings should be burned. Brod disobeyed, thus rescuing from oblivion the three unfinished novels, *America* (*Amerika*, largely written 1911–14, trans. 1949), *The Trial* (*Der Prozess*, 1914–15, trans. 1937), and *The Castle* (*Das Schloss*, 1922, trans. 1930, rev. 1969).

During his lifetime, Kafka published only a proportion of his shorter fiction in various collections. Late in 1912, he wrote the two stories which are generally regarded as his first mature achievement, *The Judgment* (*Das Urteil*, trans. 1928) and *The Metamorphis* (*Die Verwandlung*, trans. 1961). Each is the history of its hero's regression from the confident certainties of 'normal' life to a state of overwhelming psychic bewilderment and finally death: in the first story the protagonist unquestioningly accepts the death sentence passed upon him for his dishonesties and inadequacies by a spectacularly rejuvenated father; in the second, the hero is transformed overnight into an enormous beetle while retaining a lucid human consciousness as ironic accompaniment to his physical degradation. In both cases – and this is a recurrent feature of much of Kafka's work – the punishment unconsciously incurred by the protagonist seems monstrously disproportionate to any ascertainable crime. Yet the works transcend the status of mere paranoid fantasies by virtue of two factors: the meticulous lucidity of the writing and the gain in metaphoric range occasioned by the disconnection of effect from cause. The described effect thus acquires the status of free-standing or unascribed metaphor, so that the area of suggestivity which radiates from the central situation is vastly enlarged.

In the relatively immature novel, *America*, Karl Rossmann's emigration to the USA is in itself a punishment, inflicted by his parents: so that in the bizarre adventures which ensue (in which the hero is on a number of occasions actually or implicitly brought to trial) the causes of events, no matter how grotesquely refracted, are at least dimly perceptible. But in Kafka's most famous work, *The Trial*, the protagonist, Josef K, is suddenly arrested for no apparent reason, and finds himself plunged into a world in which absurd appearances correspond to no ascertainable reality, where explanations make a mockery of logic and where the individual is subject to a power whose mechanisms are obscure and whose ultimate nature remains wholly inscrutable. Josef K, a victim of the ineluctable force known simply as The Law, is both constrained and attracted by it. Armed only with the hopelessly inadequate powers of human perception and language, he seeks unsuccessfully to establish the nature of his guilt and, though still questioning, submits passively to a grotesque execution.

In *The Castle*, the hero, here called simply K., has in common with his namesake in *The Trial* the fact that he undergoes, *vis-à-vis* an oppressive authority, a progression from defiant arrogance to a relative humility. At the beginning of the work K. has arrived at a nameless village in order to take up a post as land-surveyor. More hindered than helped by the intricate network of bureaucracy which is the castle's representative presence in the village, K. finds that in effect no conscious exercise of will or intention can in any way advance his aims. His position in the village, he is told, is paradoxical: he has been appointed land-surveyor, but none is needed. Officials whom K. tries to contact for clarification of his position prove elusive, even fugitive; the two assistants assigned to him seem to K. childish to the point of imbecility; and, humiliated by being given a menial position as school caretaker, K. is, in effect, left to fumble his own way through the maze of irrationality that constitutes the life of the village. Thus the world into which he enters unremittingly challenges his expectations, his will, his entire sense of himself. Any achievement, he is told in a crucial interview with the official Bürgel, would be inadvertent: having accidentally slipped through the castle's protective net, he would find himself able to command all he wished. But this information – which is in any case couched in a plethora of cautious subjunctives (for Bürgel is in effect describing theoretically the position in which K. actually finds himself at this point) – comes ironically at a moment where K. is too drugged and fatigued to make use of it: unable, that is, to enforce a will which he has by this time effectively abandoned. Shortly after this, the novel breaks off, unfinished: but a note communicated by Max Brod roughly summarizes Kafka's intended ending – at the moment of K.'s death a message arrives from the castle with the ironic information that K. has no official right to live in the village, but will 'in view of certain peripheral circumstances' be permitted to do so. The nature of these 'peripheral circumstances' is, of course, not clarified: but it is a reasonable negative inference that the circumstances are peripheral to anything which K.'s assertive ego, or his ego-related perceptions, may be capable of establishing.

The hallmark of *The Castle* then, as of Kafka's work as a whole, is ambiguity. The castle itself is no more an image of Divine Grace than it is of ultimate Evil: it is a symbol whose range of implication encompasses both these possible extremes. More importantly, the central feature of the novel is less the castle itself *qua* symbol than the castle *as apprehended by K.* But to what extent is K. possessed of a consciousness adequate to the task imposed upon it? Is consciousness itself, refracted and distorted by the pressures of immediate vicissitudes and the clamorous demands of self-interest, an adequate instrument for the apprehension of the world in which we find ourselves? Conversely, does the castle itself, in concrete actuality, exist at all? – or is it no more than the focal point of a web of errors, half-truths and conflicting assertions?

Kafka's work raises far more questions than it ever answers. ('To ask questions is the main thing,' Josef K is told by his advocate.) Not surprisingly, then, Kafka has been more widely and more variously interpreted than almost any other modern author. His fascination has remained undiminished by any changes in literary fashion: and it is perhaps a wholly appropriate irony that Kafka's work should have proved, in its very elusiveness, more relevant to the bewilderments of twentieth-century man than that of many writers who speak with louder voices and more confident tones.

Corbet Stewart

See: *Gesammelte Schriften*, ed. Max Brod and Heinz Politzer (1945–7). Translations of the novels are by Willa and Edwin Muir. See also: *The Complete Stories*, ed. Nahum N. Glatzner (1971); *Letters to Felice*, ed. Erich Heller and Jürgen Born, trans. James Stein and Elizabeth Duckworth (1974). About Kafka: H. Politzer, *Franz Kafka. Parable and Paradox* (1966); A. Thorlby, *Kafka: A Study* (1972); R. Gray, *Franz Kafka* (1973); R. Sheppard, *On Kafka's Castle* (1973); E. Heller, *Kafka* (1974); F. Kuna, *Kafka: Literature as Corrective Punishment* (1974).

237

KANDINSKY, Wassily (Vasilii Vasilievich) 1866–1944

Russian painter

Kandinsky was amongst the pioneers of Abstraction in twentieth-century Western European art. The evolution of his work comprised a step-by-step investigation of the expressive powers at the disposal of the painter. The changes of form and technique that characterize his development reveal his sensitivity to the innovations and achievements of contemporaries, yet the driving force of his evolution remained an ultimately spiritual search, for which painting provided Kandinsky with a means of expression that he was able to manipulate with brilliance and originality. He became committed to painting relatively late after studying law and economics at the University of Moscow. In 1895 a painting by Monet of *Haystacks*, which Kandinsky saw in Moscow, impressed him with the force of a revelation. In addition recent travels into northern Russia had brought Kandinsky into close contact with a vigorous folk-art tradition. As for many Russian painters active in the 1890s, the simultaneous impact of a vital indigenous Russian tradition and a new awareness of the brilliant colour and virtuoso handling of French Impressionist and Post-Impressionist painting led to vigorous painting that reflected Russian themes in a welter of rich colour. Kandinsky's early studies reflect this, echoing too the decorative swirls of the *Jugendstil* which was evident both in Moscow, particularly in the works of the architect Shekhtel, but also in Munich where Kandinsky entered the studio of the painter Anton Ažbé in 1897. Russians excited by vigorously handled strong colour had preceded him: Igor Grabar, Alexei von Jawlensky (Yavlensky) and Marianne von Werefkin (Verefkina) comprised a group there. Kandinsky remained until 1899 producing brilliantly coloured evocations of garden scenes and Russian folk stories that were often fantastic. Kandinsky, however, brought to these works a sense of an allegory of conflicting forces, at first distinctly medieval but subsequently a timeless battle between colossal opposing elements. This theme recurred throughout Kandinsky's life. Kandinsky also painted directly from observation. Whilst in Munich he was prolific in both kinds of painting. His observed works flourished in particular in his period at Murnau with the painter Gabriele Münter. Colour became increasingly assertive and painterly conventions were steadily broached to expressive ends. His expressive colour was comparable in its saturation and its dynamic application to that of the French Fauve painters. Like them, Kandinsky exhibited at the 1905 Salon d'Automne in Paris. Whilst he appears never to have abandoned depiction entirely, Kandinsky investigated with increasing daring and success the extent to which colour and line could be made to sustain an expressive and an emotive role: the purpose was to embody spiritual experience and make it communicable through painting.

His first major text upon painting concerns precisely this (*Über das Geistige in Der Kunst*, 1912; trans. *Concerning the Spiritual in Art*, 1914). He was necessarily acutely aware of his material means in order to employ them to provide a spiritual, expressive and emotional resonance. This attitude made Kandinsky a central figure of the Expressionist movement in Germany. His articulate theories led him to group ventures in publishing as well as exhibiting: with Klee*, Marc, Macke and others he was a vital force of the *Blaue Reiter* (from 1911) and its almanac (1912). He also became a theorist in the field of art education and believed that the psychological and spiritual power of the painter's means could be studied systematically and communally. His awareness of the Theosophical Society is perhaps reflected in this. The First World War caused Kandinsky's return to Russia. The Bolshevik Revolution of 1917 raised Kandinsky to a position of power concerning the establishment of new kinds of museum and new art education in Russia. His conviction that artists were the discerners, and even the moulders, of the forms appropriate to their age, poised upon the verge of widespread application in Russia before Kandinsky abandoned his post at the Institute of Artistic Culture in Moscow, was the psychological bent of his ideas and painting as opposed by Constructivists (see Tatlin*), and, in 1921, he accepted the invitation of Walter Gropius* to put his principles into practice at the Bauhaus in Weimar. Kandinsky's second major theoretical book *From Point and Line to Plane* (*Punkt und Linie zu Flache*, 1926; trans. 1947) reflects his teaching

there. His investigation of the painter's means was meticulous and thorough: it led him to publish his theories and to devise teaching systems. Yet its aims, its goal at the time of his death in Paris in 1944, remained a spiritual evolution through the clarity of his means: he still sought the forms appropriate to the unfolding future, convinced of a spiritual ascent for humanity within which the painter, the creative man, played a vital and progressive role.

Dr John Milner

See: Wassily Kandinsky and Franz Marc, *The Blaue Reiter Almanach* (1974); Will Grohmann, *Wassily Kandinsky – Life and Work* (1959)

238
KAWABATA YASUNARI 1899–1972

Japanese writer

Kawabata Yasunari was born near Osaka in 1899. He was orphaned in infancy, and soon lost his grandparents and only sister as well. He finished primary and middle school near Osaka, and went on to the elite First Higher School in Tokyo, and to Tokyo Imperial University, from which he graduated in 1924. His earliest publications were in student magazines. The story that brought him fame, 'The Izu Dancer' (*Izu no Odoriko*), was published in 1926.

The years after his graduation from the university are known as his 'Izu period', the best of his early writings being about the Izu Peninsula, south of Tokyo. The Izu period was followed by an Asakusa period, when his chief interest was the Asakusa district of Tokyo, the liveliest of the plebeian entertainment centres. Just before the outbreak of the Second World War came his 'snow-country period', when he was fascinated with the snowy regions on the western slope of the main Japanese island.

He wrote little during the war. After the war he was for some years president of the Japanese P.E.N. The post-war years might be called his Kamakura period. He lived in and wrote about Kamakura, an old political and cultural centre south of Tokyo. In 1968 he became the first and thus far the only Japanese Nobel laureate in literature. He died on 16 April 1972. The usual view is that he killed himself, although some hold that his death was accidental.

In his early years he was much under the influence of avant-garde European literature. The influence on some of his writings is overt. The best of it, however, such as 'The Izu Dancer', is delicately lyrical, putting him firmly in the Japanese tradition, in which lyric verse and the lyrical mode in prose have been dominant. The looseness of form, the abrupt transitions, and the frequent difficulty in establishing the relation between successive statements may be ascribed to a surrealist influence. They may as well be ascribed, however, to Japanese antecedents, most particularly the linked verse (*renga*) of the Middle Ages.

Snow Country (*Yukiguni*, trans. 1956), written sporadically over several years, with revisions, from 1935, and completed in 1947, is widely held to be his best novel, and certainly it illustrates as well as any his themes and methods. It is essentially about loneliness and the impossibility of love. A Tokyo dilettante has a desultory love affair with a 'snow country' geisha, and presently he stops visiting her, and that is that. The inconclusive ending is characteristic of Kawabata, and so is the looseness of form. It is often difficult to know whether or not one of his works is in fact finished, and the list of his unfinished works is impressive. A sketch or tableau would form the nucleus of a story, which might or might not be expanded into a novel. If it did become a novel, the movement from episode to episode was most commonly by a process of flexible but controlled association, as with a *renga* sequence.

Kawabata's great achievement was a fusion of the traditional and the modern so complete that it is difficult to assign elements to either source. The looseness of form suggests the modern rebellion against the well-plotted novel, but it also suggests *renga* and the discursive lyrical essay, a form held in high esteem by the Japanese for almost a millennium. So too it is with the themes, loneliness and lovelessness, and cold, wasted beauty set off by shocking ugliness – they are modern and ancient as well. Kawabata's characterization tends to be so delicate that the characters, almost wraith-like, are constantly on the point of fading back into the natural background, which sometimes seems the principal concern, the real reason for the story.

Edward Seidensticker

Kawabata's complete works, in fifteen volumes, were published in Tokyo (1969–74); a new edition, in thirty-five volumes, is planned from 1980. A partial translation of 'The Izu Dancer' appeared in *Atlantic Monthly* (January 1955). Other English translations: *Thousand Cranes (Sembazuru,* 1959); *House of the Sleeping Beauties (Nemureru Bijo,* 1969); *The Sound of the Mountain (Yama no Oto,* 1970*); The Master of Go (Meijin,* 1972); *The Lake (Mizuumi,* 1974); *Beauty and Sadness (Utsukushisa to Kanashimi to,* 1975). *Koto* ('The Old Capital') has been translated into several European languages, but not English. See also: Edward Seidensticker, 'Kawabata Yasunari' in *This Country* (1979).

239

KEATON, 'Buster' (Joseph Francis) 1895–1966

US film-maker

Buster Keaton's great tragedy was to be making films at the same time as Charlie Chaplin*, whose shadow obscured Keaton's genius during their own time and in the following decades. Only recently with the rise of the importance of the Director has Keaton taken his rightful place as one of the major 'auteurs' of the twentieth century, far superior to his comic rivals such as Mack Sennett, Harold Lloyd, and even Chaplin in his visual eye and other directing skills.

Keaton, like so many other early American show-business greats, was almost literally 'born in a trunk', performing for the first time with his vaudevillian parents at the age of three, and his only real education was that earned in the school of hard falls of his parents' acrobatic act which moved from medicine shows to burlesque to vaudeville. When his father's drinking made the act too dangerous, Keaton joined Roscoe 'Fatty' Arbuckle's company, making fifteen films with the notorious film comedian between 1917 and 1919. When Arbuckle's career collapsed, Keaton starred in almost two dozen shorts for Joseph Schenck, many co-directed with Eddie Cline. They included some of Keaton's best work, such as 'Cops', 'The Haunted House', 'The Electric House', and others. Keaton gradually assumed total control of his film unit and eventually began to make feature films beginning with *The Three Ages* in 1923. MGM distributed his first seven features with Keaton in full control as producer, co-director, and star, the best of many superb comedies probably being *Sherlock Jr.* and *The Navigator.* In 1926 he joined United Artists where he made his masterpiece *The General.* His last silent film was *Spite Marriage* for MGM. The sound revolution is generally credited with destroying his career, though personal problems culminating in a year in a psychiatric clinic in 1937 undoubtedly contributed. His talkies were mostly commercial failures and he clung for the rest of his life to the fringes of the film industry making brief appearances in anything from Billy Wilder's *Sunset Boulevard* and Chaplin's *Limelight* to Stanley Kramer's *It's A Mad, Mad, Mad, Mad World* and other real circuses. Ironically, at the end of his life his talent and his comic persona were again being more fully recognized by his appearance in *A Funny Thing Happened on the Way to the Forum* and a short film expressly written for him by Samuel Beckett*.

While many silent comedy stars were justly famous for their physical grace and athletic ability, Keaton always took special pride in his acrobatic skills and grace. Keaton not only almost never used a double or stunt man, he often did other characters' stunts, even literally 'breaking his neck' in the process. From driving a speeding motorcycle while seated on the handlebars to diving into a net from a suspension bridge 75 feet high, Keaton always astonished his audience; but his best stunts were also integral to his character and plot, perhaps the most astonishing and beautiful being the one in *The General* where the forlorn Johnnie Grey, in despair over his lost love, rides off emotionlessly oblivious on the driving bar of his engine.

While his shorts are as acrobatic and cinematically inventive as the best work of their time, Keaton's real genius can be seen most clearly in the ten feature films that he either directed or co-directed. Unlike many of his comic rivals, Keaton strove for logical progression in his narrative rather than a series of seemingly improvised anecdotes connected by the presence of the comedian. The structure of *The General* illustrates this perfectly. Keaton is able to use the whole panorama of the Civil War for his hero's efforts to win the woman he loves. The two train chases (one going North, the other returning South) provide the visual and narrative centre for the film. Everything that happens in the first chase recurs with subtle twists in the second, making the second chase not only new but at the same time organically related to the earlier part of the film. In *Seven Chances* Keaton is pursued by two different kinds of crowds: the first a gaggle of prospective fortune-hunting brides, the second 1,500 studio-made rocks that he accidentally dislodges. The two separate chases are united when the avalanche dissipates the racing women, and then, after Keaton successfully eludes rocks ranging in size from bowling balls to giants eight feet in diameter, a last-minute little stone drops him in his tracks just as he will be caught by the late-arriving heroine at the end of the film. Keaton's instinctive love of form worked all this out at the last minute, since the avalanche was a last-minute addition to the film. A certain passion for order and balance thus always prevails in Keaton.

Order and balance also contribute to the lack of sentimentalism in Keaton's persona and stories. The Keaton persona, often outnumbered by villains and fate, always prevails through sheer movement and stubbornness. Even women are never sentimentalized as marital love objects. The heroine of *The General* is stuffed into a burlap bag and tossed into a freight car, among other indignities, and finds herself totally out of place in the engine cab trying to use a broom or throwing away firewood because it has a knot-hole in it. When she proudly hands Keaton a small woodchip for the fire, in reasonable anger he reaches out to strangle her and changes the gesture to a quick kiss – one of Keaton's most effective demonstrations of his humanity without excessive sentiment. His large, expressive eyes said far more than the most frenetic twistings of facial muscles of other stars of the silent era, for Keaton knew how important eyes were in film. And while those eyes expressed the pain and bewilderment

of his condition, his body whirred constantly to avoid disaster, and to set things right.

Professor Charles Gregory

Other works: *My Wonderful World of Slapstick* (1962); see: R. Blesh, *Keaton* (1966); D. Moews, *Keaton: The Silent Features Close-Up* (1977); Donald McCaffrey, *Four Great Comedians* (1968); David Robinson, *Keaton* (1969); J.-P. Lebel, *Buster Keaton* (1967); E. Rubenstein, *The General* (1973); A. Sarris, *Interviews With Film Directors* (1967); K. Brownlow, *The Parade's Gone By* (1968).

240
KENNEDY, John Fitzgerald 1917–63

US president

John F. Kennedy was born on 29 May 1917 in Boston, New England, and he was assassinated on 22 November 1963 in Dallas, Texas, as the 35th President of the United States. His killing created an indelible political trauma not simply because it was never satisfactorily explained but also because it put a new perspective on what he had achieved in his brief career. It seemed that a young idealist had been sacrificed to the atavistic violence of old America, a progressive slain to appease anti-Communist, anti-Black illiberal adventurers. Kennedy himself denied high-mindedness: 'Never fight on principle,' he declared, 'fight the other candidate.' Yet, as he once confided to his wife Jacqueline, he was 'an idealist without illusions' and so it is possible that even if his murder made his presidency seem more idealistic than it was, he was none the less one of the great political reformers of modern politics.

He was the second son of a very rich Irish American whom Franklin Roosevelt had made Ambassador to Britain before the Second World War. The family had strong roots in the Democratic Party and politics were a family profession. At first it had been intended that the eldest son Joe Jnr should go for high office but his death in the war caused his mantle to pass to the more thoughtful and introspective JFK.

Kennedy attended an exclusive school, followed by study at Harvard, Princeton, Stanford and the London School of Economics. It was an education intended to enhance his chances of social leadership which were, in any case, very good ones on account of his father's wealth. In the Second World War JFK volunteered for active service despite an earlier back injury. Here he showed considerable bravery when his boat was cut in half by a Japanese destroyer. He swam to safety through burning seas pulling a severely injured shipmate with him.

His health was badly undermined by this experience and he remained a sick man. He suffered from a major internal complaint and was often in pain. This, added to a number of tragic deaths within the Kennedy family, gave him a detached view of his own existence, an advantage for any politician.

JFK's political success was both dramatic and rapid. He became the youngest Congressman in the House, and, in 1952, he was elected to the US Senate as a Senator for Massachusetts. Only four years later he came close to gaining the Democratic Vice-Presidential nomination and four years after that he was elected President. He defeated the then Vice-President, Richard M. Nixon, by no more than 120,000 votes (out of an electorate of 49 million) after a campaign which the Kennedy staff had planned brilliantly, laying special emphasis on good media relations.

Two factors had caused many Americans to be wary of the JFK image. The first was his Roman Catholic faith: during the campaign Kennedy was repeatedly asked to pledge that, were he elected, he would not take orders from the Pope, or allow Catholic views of morality to influence legislative measures. Secondly, Kennedy was young. At the age of forty-three he would be the youngest President of the United States and a stark contrast to the sitting tenant, Eisenhower, who was the oldest. Yet JFK managed, thanks to a combination of wit, eloquence and intelligence, to capitalize on his youth, to indicate, in the words of his striking inaugural address, that 'the torch has been passed to a new generation'.

Kennedy and his supporters claimed they would offer America a 'new frontier'. New perspectives would be given to domestic politics (although at this stage a fair deal for Blacks was not emphasized) and also to American ambitions throughout the world where a greater readiness to face up to the Soviet challenge was promised. 'Softness' towards the Russians had allowed them to infiltrate a number of hitherto neutral areas including, of course, outer space where the USSR's satellites had altered the strategic balance between the two powers.

Superficially, then, what Kennedy promised appear to have little to do with liberal or radical thinking. Rather, he promised to do more effectively what others had tried to do before. But this was not what came to pass, for both at home and abroad the young President was forced to respond to challenges more hazardous than had been anticipated, challenges that ultimately helped change America and the world. The first came from the USSR. There can be no doubt that Khrushchev, the Soviet leader, hoped to exploit the President's inexperience in order to strengthen the Russians' position in all areas. After an early skirmish over Berlin, Khrushchev tried to install nuclear missiles on Cuba in 1962. Kennedy, however, refused to accept such a move and, in the autumn of that year, he demonstrated an absolute willingness to take the world to war in order to maintain the status quo. This show of force

perhaps ironically impressed the Russians so that peace was kept intact and the prospect for later agreement became much better.

The second challenge was a domestic one. It came from Black Americans who were now demanding with some force the same civil rights enjoyed by Whites. Kennedy had initially been unconcerned by the grave injustices done to the Blacks. But the courage they demonstrated in seeking equality in all spheres of public life and the exceptional leadership provided by Martin Luther King* encouraged Kennedy to face up to his responsibilities. He used the full authority and power of his office to establish Black rights in education, housing and in politics generally. Blacks had to risk their lives to gain his support but once gained they could count on it. It was not insignificant that Dr King was destroyed in the same way as his white colleague.

Kennedy had by November 1963 changed a number of things, but his 'new frontier' appeared less new and less inspiring than many had hoped. There was growing concern at American interference in the politics of South-East Asia which appeared sinister. He seemed to act only when forced to by others and to avoid fighting for principles, however noble. But that day in Dallas showed this judgment was too simplistic to account for the impact he was to have. America now seemed to be on the side of the young and of change; the fathers had yielded to their sons. Although he had been rich and successful he had none the less established that the underprivileged and unemployed had social rights too. Kennedy the man may have been the product of old America. But Kennedy the President stood for something new. When, in front of millions, he was killed, it had seemed as if the most reactionary forces in politics would be his heirs. In fact, however, this was not so. What he had managed to do, and what had happened to him for doing it, showed how much he had actually accomplished. To be an idealist without illusions was not only a fitting aim for a President, it now appeared the only honourable response to the dangerous world of the 1960s.

Dr Anthony Glees

By J. F. Kennedy: *Why England Slept* (1961); *Profiles in Courage* (1965). See also: T. H. White, *The Making of the President* (1960); A. M. Schlesinger, Jnr, *A Thousand Days* (1965); T. C. Sorensen, *Kennedy* (1965); Pierre Salinger, *With Kennedy* (1966).

241
KEROUAC, Jack 1922–69

US writer

Jack Kerouac was born in the industrial town of Lowell, Massachusetts. Educated in Catholic schools, he reached Horace Mann school and Columbia University, New York, largely through his football prowess. Apart from brief spells in the Merchant Marine and army, he lived by his writing. The early years are dramatized in *The Town and the City* (1950), *Doctor Sax* (1959), *Maggie Cassidy* (1959) and *Visions of Gerard* (1963). Subsequent life in New York, at sea, in Mexico, Tangier, France, London and San Francisco is the material of *On the Road* (1957), *The Subterraneans* (1958), *The Dharma Bums* (1958), *Tristessa* (1960), *Big Sur* (1962), *Desolation Angels* (1965), *Sartori in Paris* (1966) and *Vanity of Duluoz: An Adventurous Education 1935–1946* (1968). Most of this work comprises what Kerouac came to call *The Duluoz Legend*, a huge Proustian* compendium of reminiscences and transformations of memory. Concurrent with these fictions, Kerouac published a number of supplementary works including *Lonesome Traveller* (1960, travel sketches), *Book of Dreams* (1961, a record of his imaginative resources), the poetry in *Mexico City Blues* (1959), *Rimbaud* (1960), *Pull My Daisy* (1961) and *Scattered Poems* (1972), and a number of uncollected pieces on jazz and the writing process. A number of recordings testify to his gifts as a reader and singer of his own works. Within this large lifetime's creativity stands his masterpiece, *Visions of Cody* (written in 1951–2, published in 1973; a very shortened version appeared in 1960).

Vanity of Duluoz (written in 1967) draws on his life as school and college football star and wartime serviceman, and on early intuitions and realizations of a literary career. It records his first published novel, *The Town and the City* (written 1946–9) which creates the Martin family out of his own family and that of friends (see his note in Ann Charter's *A Bibliography of Works by Jack Kerouac*, 1975), a work in the traditions of Sherwood Anderson* and Thomas Wolfe*, fictions of small-town experience and regional location, and the youthful hero's necessary departure for the city where ambition may be realized. *Doctor Sax* records in brilliantly inventive style the complex fantasy life of himself and his boyhood friends in Lowell, a first intimation of the interplay of fiction and day-to-day life for his creative imagination, before the severe realization that writing is a discipline. *Vanity of Duluoz* records his abrupt experience that professional sport is part of a corrupt system which includes military coercion. The autobiographical hero's discharge from the military service in 1943, after acting mad by the standards of the officers, is a main instance of Kerouac's responses to the stupidities of the Establishment. The 'lost dream of being a real American man' through the open road tradition – 'an adventurous education, an educational adventurousness' – is the core of *On the Road* (written in 1951), whose plot generates, through Sal Paradise's writer and intellectual's relationship with the proletarian and petty-criminal life of Dean Moriarty, ways of release from bourgeois consciousness. Their automo-

bile mobility in search of freedom of action and speech is written in a free-wheeling associative style, later theorized in 'Essentials of Spontaneous Prose' (*Black Mountain Review*, no. 7, 1957; reprinted in *A Casebook on the Beat*, edited by Thomas Parkinson, 1961). This essay delineates the origins of Kerouac's methods in the breath-lengths of speech and jazz, and the notational ideas in the poetry of William Carlos Williams*, as well as certain states of consciousness which release the writer from censor of inherited forms.

The 'Beat Generation' of writers (essentially Kerouac, Allen Ginsberg*, Gregory Corso and William Burroughs*) were part of a resistance to the years of civil repression under the Eisenhower–Kennedy*–Johnson–Nixon regimes, what Kerouac described as 'a potboiler of broken convictions, messes of rioting and fighting in the streets, hoodlumism, cynical administration of cities and states, suits and neckties the only feasible subject, grandeur all gone into the mosaic mesh of Television'. But for Kerouac, resistance had to be gained against his bourgeois-Catholic upbringing. From Burroughs he learned of Spengler's* history of western decadence and barbarism (the rejuvenating *fellahin* are as constant in Kerouac as in another of his masters, Gary Snyder). He recognized Céline's* bitter criticism of America and the West, the aristocratic integrity of Renoir's* *La Grande Illusion*, Tolstoy's peasant rejuvenators, the vision of the *poète maudit* in Rimbaud and Cocteau*, Gide's* *acte gratuite* as 'abandonment of reason and return to impulse', and much more, as he inherited the responsibilities of the artist in the European great tradition. The *élan vital* principle fuses with Emerson's 'self-reliance' to become 'a holy idea [of] "self-ultimacy" '. His friend Neal Cassady, the Moriarty of *On the Road*, exemplifies a liberated anti-bourgeois life, which Kerouac rejoined by working with him as a railroad brakeman for a time. But he needed to research his Breton origins as well (*Sartori in Paris*) to 'redeem this runaway slave of football fields'.

To summarize his experience he conceived an American *Forsyte Saga* – the Duluoz saga – as 'a lifetime of writing about what I've seen with my own eyes, told in my own words . . . as a contemporary history record for future times to see what really happened and what people really thought'. But his perspective is the Buddhist void as given in *The Scripture of The Golden Eternity* (1960); the boyhood Catholicism (*Visions of Gerard*) and the mobile search for IT in *On the Road* are modified by the vision of an oriental stillness within motion, of the artist's creativity taking place in a meaningless universe. The search for IT – the force which sustains exuberant spontaneity and charisma – is challenged from an alternate tradition which has had a profound effect on American culture at least since the nineteenth-century Transcendentalists (Kerouac gained much of his Buddhist insight from Gary Snyder, the poet and orientalist who features as Japhy Ryder in *The Dharma Bums*).

Kerouac died the year after publishing *Vanity of Duluoz*: an abdominal haemorrhage had been aggravated by a general condition from his alcoholic life. This last book contains a lament for human life over 'a million years on this planet'. Our lives are 'sacrifices leading to purity in the after-existence in Heaven as souls divested of that rapish, rotten, carnal body'. The 'beat' natural joy in 'digging everything', whatever the doomed melancholy of artists, is lived out in *karma*, the inescapable contingencies of existence and 'the mental garbage of "existentialism" and "hipsterism" and "bourgeois decadence" '. 'Wars as social catastrophes arise from the cruel nature of bestial creation, and not from "society".' Writing is born from damnation. Kerouac had come a long way from his earlier confidence, but within his 'serious exuberance' (his phrase for jazz) and the loving records of boyhood and adolescence, there had always existed the threat of death and disease in *Tristessa* and *Visions of Gerard*, and passing love and friendship in *Maggie Cassidy* and *Desolation Angels*. Neither sexual nor religious experience gave him much happiness beyond initial satisfactions. The stylistic invention of earlier work declined into a sober flatness concomitant with his later vision. But *Visions of Cody* remains, a fine and large collection of his best achievement, written – as Allen Ginsberg says in his prefatory essay, 'the Great Rememberer' – out of 'tender brooding compassion for bygone scene & Personal Individuality oddity'd therein ... a giant mantra of Appreciation & Adoration of an American Man, one striving heroic soul'. In Kerouac's words: 'I struggle in the dark with the enormity of my soul, trying desperately to be a great rememberer redeeming life from darkness ... this record is my joy.' The marvellous prose emerges from a rich experience of life, of the twentieth-century masters, of drug-transformed consciousness, and of transcribed tapes of energetic speech. Ginsberg accurately places it in the mainstream of American arts between 1940 and 1960, which include Abstract Expressionism, 'projective verse' and Frank O'Hara's 'personism', but also within that 'Disillusionment with all the heroic Imagery of U.S.' arising out of Kerouac's 'experience on the street with Nationalist Imagery of previous generations, & his familiarity, sympathy & Disillusionment with the American myth'. By 1952 the 'beat writers' were 'lonely at wit's end with the world & America – the "Beat" generation was about that time formulated, the Viet Nam War was just about to begin its U.S. phase, the exhaustion of the planet by American Greed & Lust'. Kerouac's last writing, an essay called 'After Me, the Deluge' (*Washington Post*; reprinted in *Sixpack*, nos 3/4, 1973) parades a regret for responsibility for the 'Beat' antecedence of 'hippies' and 'yippies', and a rejection of the 'shiny hypocrisy' of both the radicals and the Es-tablishment, both the North Vietnam leaders and the American military-industrial complex: 'I think I'll drop out. Great American tradition – Dan'l Boone, U.S. Grant, Mark Twain – I think I'll go to sleep and suddenly in my deepest inadequacy nightmares wake up haunted and see everyone in the world as unconsolable orphans. . . .'

Eric Mottram

Other works include: *Pic* (novel, 1971). See: John Clellon Holmes, *The Beat Boys* (*Go*, 1952) and *Nothing More to Declare* (1968); 'Jack Kerouac at Northport' (interview) in *Athanor*, nos 1–111 (1971–2); Bruce Cook, *The Beat Generation* (1972); Ann Charters, *Kerouac: A Biography* (1974); John Tytell, *Naked Angels: The Lives and Literature of the Beat Generation* (1976); Barry Gifford and Lawrence Lee, *Jack's Book: An Oral Biography of Jack Kerouac* (1979).

242
KESEY, Ken 1935–

US novelist

Kesey spent his youth in Oregon timber country, became a wrestling champion at the University of Oregon, and at Stanford University, California, attended writing classes under Malcolm Cowley and Wallace Stegner. Working in a mental hospital he became sympathetically involved with the patients, organizing parties, loaning them his car for a night out, and, when an attendant refused to stop bullying a catatonic patient, threw him through a shower-room door. Kesey was discharged with the label: 'Not interested in patient welfare.' During the 1960s he wrote two novels, became a cult figure in the hippie sub-culture of drug and high-decibel communities in the San Francisco Bay Area, and set up a pot-smoking, LSD-partying community in Palo Alto. Arrested in 1965, he managed to vanish via a faked suicide, but was hounded from the country, re-arrested, and imprisoned in 1966. His pop status increased, then waned severely, since when he makes fairly well-publicized reappearances.

Through Cowley, *One Flew Over the Cuckoo's Nest* was published in 1962, and became a best-seller over the decade. With the royalties, and money from the Broadway version (and later a film), Kesey has lived well. In the 1960s he bought a bus, painted it in fashionable psychedelic designs, employed Neal Cassady (the manic driver in Kerouac's* *On the Road* of the previous decade), and drove across the country, apparently abandoning fiction. But his first novel deals with the techniques of possible survival and escape from an oppressively enforced society which reduces varied life to the routines required by authority – in this case, the boss, Big Nurse, and her lunatic asylum staff. The narrator, Chief Bromden, escapes to tell the tale of how the red-headed Irish protestor McMurphy succeeds in wrecking the establishment before he is forcibly lobotomized by the Combine. At least he has enabled the patients to enjoy themselves, however briefly. Kesey's second novel, *Sometimes a Great Notion* (1964), had little of the success of the first, but it, too, concerns a violent break for individual freedom against majority coercion. Using the large-scale manner of Thomas C. Wolfe*, it tells of the two Stamper brothers' lurch towards independent manhood by acting against a strike in the timber industry. They float their logs downstream, a social confrontation with the community which ends in a sort of victorious and deathly defeat. The huge book is propelled by a compulsive necessity and massive *macho* energy, but it remains a bulky high adventure story of masculinity in a traditional family, pastoral setting.

Meanwhile, Kesey shot 60,000 feet of film and set up his pleasure dome at La Honda, south of San Francisco, calling himself the Navigator and giving light and music shows infused with LSD. He organized the 'Acid Test', a psychedelic discoteque, in the 1964–5 years when acid became popular on the West Coast – spiked punch was served, it is said, to unsuspecting 'squares' who 'freaked out'. He also used his camera and tape-recorder continually, with drug aids: 'To discover something new, you have to put yourself in a position when an accident can happen to you.' Once acid became trite, he moved on. In prison – or rather, in the San Mateo sheriff's honour camp, in the redwood forests – he painted, wrote his notebooks, and planned a book on justice. His earlier aim, to form an exemplary mobile family group called the Merry Pranksters, appeared in the documentary fiction *The Electric Kool-Aid Acid Test* by Tom Wolfe in 1968. Travelling across America in a bus called 'Further', he enacts one more version of 'the open road' obsession, attempting to incorporate the current transformations of both Timothy Leary* and the Hell's Angels – without their concurrence. As Tom Wolfe wrote in the *New York Times Book Review* in 1968, Kesey's bus was totally American – a family car, an '18-foot gleaming dreamboat' in which to achieve 'all the freedom, the free time, the gadgets, the TV, the movies, tapes, sound systems' denoting the good life, and the effort at ecstasy against the inherent boredom of the conformist society of labour and sobriety.

In 1973, *Kesey's Garage Sale* offered a retrospective presentation of his ideas and beliefs in a broadly ecological context – one section was *The Last Supplement to the Whole Earth Catalog*. Another section concerned the myth of how he wrote his first novel. A section of letters is followed by an interview with Paul Krassner (editor of the *Realist*, an abrasive satirical journal of the period). The book's form combines print and picture

information, characteristic of methods put forward by McLuhan* and others in the 1960s.

When Kesey's visit to New York was reported in 1979, he turned out to be a married man with four children and living on a dairy farm near his Oregon boyhood home, finding Wolfe's book and his early reputation 'a nuisance', but looking forward to riding at the head of the local Rhododendron Festival parade as Grand Marshal, on a white Harley Davidson motorcycle.

Eric Mottram

243
KEYNES, John Maynard 1883–1946

British economist

A. C. Pigou, one of Keynes's tutors at Cambridge, once said of him that 'he was, beyond doubt or challenge, the most interesting, the most influential and most important economist of his time' (Pigou, *John Maynard Keynes*, 1949). Indeed the revolution in economic theory, the break with the 'classical' tradition, that he brought about is thought to be the only theory change in the social sciences that comes close to Kuhn's* theory of scientific revolutions. Possibly more important however, and certainly more important to him, was his influence on post-war governmental economic policy throughout the whole of the Western world. In fact the post-war boom, the most sustained period of rapid expansion in history, is often referred to as the 'Keynesian Era'.

It is impossible to tell to what extent this was due to Keynes. His theory certainly dominated economic thought and government policy for the thirty years from 1945 to 1975. It was his 'Demand Management' which had substituted small and short wobbles in economic activity for the classic cycles. This led many to believe that Keynes's dream of regulated capitalism had come true and at last continuous growth could be assured. Ironically, it was this total victory of the 'Keynesian Revolution' which contributed a great deal to its downfall. Keynesianism dominated the policy of both Labour and Conservative governments in Britain for the thirty-year period. It was government commitment to full employment and Trade Unionists' 'proven' conviction that it was here to stay that has finally brought the era to an end.

John Maynard Keynes was born in Cambridge to John Neville and Florence Ada Keynes. He was educated at Eton and won a scholarship in mathematics and classics to King's College, Cambridge, where he graduated as 12th Wrangler in mathematics. After his degree he studied economics under Alfred Marshall for the Civil Service entrance examination. The young Keynes was profoundly influenced by Marshall, especially by his conviction that in order to explain booms and slumps monetary economics should be separated from the rest of economics. He decided to specialize, at Marshall's prompting, in money and banking.

Marshall was sufficiently impressed by Keynes's ability that he expressed hopes that Keynes might become a professional economist. However in 1906 Keynes entered the Civil Service and requested to be posted to the then small and intimate India Office. There he became especially interested in Indian currency and finance, which formed the basis of his first book in economics – *Indian Currency and Finance* (1913). In 1908 Marshall offered him a lectureship in economics at Cambridge which he accepted. In 1912 Keynes became editor of the *Economic Journal* through which he was able to exercise great influence over younger generations of economists.

Soon after the outbreak of war Keynes was invited to join the Treasury and by 1917 he was head of the External Finance Department. In early 1919 he was sent to Paris as principal representative of the Treasury at the Peace Conference. However, he found himself in fundamental disagreement with the terms in the Treaty dealing with reparations. In June he resigned, returned to England and wrote *The Economic Consequences of the Peace* (1919). This book, which brought him immediate and international recognition, made him unacceptable to British official circles for nearly two decades.

During his undergraduate days Keynes became a member of a small intimate group, including Leonard Woolf and Lytton Strachey*, called 'The Apostles', which later formed the Bloomsbury Group. Although closely connected with the Webbs*, Shaw* and other socialists, he remained almost wholly ignorant of Marx. Indeed he proclaimed that, as an 'immoralist', 'The class war will find me on the side of the educated bourgeoisie.' However, he was a profound and effective critic of unregulated capitalism, writing in 1924, 'Capitalism in itself is in many ways objectionable' (*The End of Laissez-Faire*, 1926). He recognized that capitalism possessed enormous expansive powers and it was his wish to save capitalism from itself.

It was through the Bloomsbury Group that he met many of the great artists of his time. His love of art and his anxiety that it should reach an audience as wide as possible, as well as his life-long friendship with the painter Duncan Grant, led him to be instrumental in the creation of the Arts Council.

In 1925 he married Lydia Lopokova, a famous dancer with the Imperial Ballet of St Petersburg and later in Diaghilev's* company. 'Oh, what a marriage of beauty and brains, fair Lopokova and John Maynard Keynes,' it was said at the time. However, Keynes soon lamented to Lytton Strachey, himself brilliant but hideous, that beauty and intelligence were rarely combined, and that it was only in Duncan Grant that he found such a satisfying combination.

The corner-stone of what Keynes described as 'Classical Theory' was Say's Law (formulated by the French economist Jean-Baptiste Say, 1767–1832), which states that supply creates its own demand. In other words, all income is spent. Money withheld from expenditure on consumer goods is saved but not hoarded. No rational householder would hold idle balances which yield no income. Instead he would use the accumulated balance directly, or lend it to others to use in order to purchase capital goods, i.e. to invest. The flow of savings and the flow of investment which are the supply of and the demand for 'loanable funds' are brought into balance, as in any other market, by changes in price, in this case in interest rates.

In 1935 Keynes wrote to George Bernard Shaw, 'I believe myself to be writing a book on economic theory which will largely revolutionize – not, I suppose at once, but in the course of the next ten years, the way the world thinks about economic problems.' Keynes's first task in his *General Theory of Employment, Interest and Money* (1936) was to show that in certain circumstances hoarding of money would take place; he argued that money was not only a medium of exchange but also a store of value available for the 'speculative' purpose of buying assets at some future unknown date.

Because of the reciprocal relationship between interest rates and the capital value of paper assets, Keynes argued that at low rates of interest (when it was generally thought that they would rise) people would prefer to hold money balances rather than risk a capital loss since in any event they were not forfeiting much interest-income. In other words, surplus speculative balances will be willingly held, in what Keynes christened the 'Liquidity Trap', without driving down the interest rate to a market-clearing level. Furthermore this same trap could very likely render monetary policy aimed at raising expenditure, output and employment ineffective. Thus it could be said that Keynes's *General Theory of Employment, Interest and Money* put forward a general theory of unemployment based on a new theory of the working of interest rates derived from a different view of money. It was a theory of *unemployment* to the extent that it could explain the level of employment, which was a function of an ever-changing cycle of total spending.

It was Keynes's abhorrence of the effects of unregulated capitalism and the human waste of unemployment which spurred him towards finding a method by which state intervention could leave intact the great expansive powers he recognized in capitalism, while at the same time forestalling its anarchic effects.

Once he had analysed money and freed saving and investment from their neo-classical identity, it was essential to discover their determinants. Savings, Keynes argued, were simply the residue of income after consumption. But as income rose consumption would not rise as much. Thus savings would rise in absolute terms and also as a proportion of income. Investment on the other hand was to some degree determined by interest rates as the neo-classicists had argued, but more important by far was the entrepreneurs' anticipated future return from that investment. Such expectations are volatile and self-reinforcing.

At the time the *General Theory* was published, the cause of the depression was held to be too high wages, which prevented any fall in prices, and too high interest rates which prevented any rise in investment. His analysis had shown why interest rates would fall no further and also that such a fall was not effective in raising investment. He also demonstrated that a fall in money wages would reduce consumer demand even further, which would make entrepreneurs even less willing to invest.

However, it was only by using Richard F. Kahn's recent invention of 'the multiplier' that Keynes was able to demonstrate the logic of what many people, including Lloyd George in the UK and Roosevelt in the USA, had argued intuitively, viz. that the state itself should carry out investment. The multiplier is the ripple-effect that any increase in investment will have on the level of total economic activity. A proportion of the income generated first by the purchase of extra capital goods will in turn be spent on consumer goods, and that income too will be spent in part, thus generating more income than the initial outlay. Therefore the state could, even by simply employing people to dig holes and fill them up again, generate more income in the economy than the initial expenditure and by so doing induce businessmen to invest. By this method, Keynes argued, it would be possible to raise the economy to stable full employment. Conversely, if expansion were too vigorous, fiscal policy could damp down demand by cutting government expenditure and, through higher taxes, private expenditure as well. This practice of government intervention has in recent years come to be known as 'Demand Management'. Thus in opposition to Say's Law, Keynes postulated that demand will create its own supply.

Keynes, through his *General Theory*, had provided a theoretical justification for the sort of state intervention in the economy that many people had arrived at through common sense. However, it was the practical experience of the economic effects of rearmament expenditure and even more those of total war which persuaded post-war governments as well as academic theorists to embrace the Keynesian analysis as well as the politics.

In 1940 Keynes was invited by the Chancellor of the Exchequer to become once again an adviser to the Treasury. He was chiefly responsible for a new concept of policy instituted in the Budget of 1941, aiming to prevent inflation by raising taxation enough to equate civilian expenditure to the goods and services available. In 1943 Keynes began to turn his attention to the problems of peace and in 1944 as leader of the British delegation at the International Conference at Bretton Woods, was the main architect of the International Monetary Fund and the International Bank for Reconstruction and Development. In May 1944 the coalition government published a White Paper on *Employment Policy*. Although Keynes contributed little in person to this document, its publication, together with a peerage awarded him in 1942, showed that his ideas had become acceptable to the British Establishment.

Keynes first suffered from heart trouble in 1937. Between the autumn of 1944 and early 1946 he was chief negotiator of the 'Lend-Lease' aid programme from the USA. But when he finally returned in April 1946 he was near collapse and died a few days later on Easter Sunday, 12 April 1946, at his home in Sussex.

Keynes, through his *General Theory*, essentially achieved his aim in that liberal Western capitalism was given a new lease of life. Evidently it was not all his doing in that Western capitalism was due for a period of expansion after fifteen years of slump and a world war. However, his policy prescriptions certainly helped to spawn the strongest and longest expansion of the Western economies in history. Through rising living standards and full employment social tensions were eased, such that a peaceful intellectual revolution was substituted for a bloody one.

Since the late 1960s, however, it has become evident that he was not the final saviour of capitalism.

His triumphant professional life was not enough to engage his talents to the full. As well as his prolific writings in theoretical and applied economics he wrote innumerable articles and published some in *Essays in Persuasion* (1931) and *Essays in Biography* (1933). He speculated actively in commodities, currencies and the Stock Exchange. He was a brilliantly successful bursar of his college, chairman of an insurance company and later a director of the Bank of England. He was a life-long bibliophile, a lover of the ballet, chairman of the National Gallery, and founder of the Arts Theatre in Cambridge. He was a supreme example of the Universal Man.

Roger Opie

Other writings include: *A Treatise on Probability* (1921); *A Revision of the Treaty* (1922); *A Tract on Monetary Reform* (1923); *A Short View of Russia* (1925); *A Treatise on Money* (1930); *How to Pay for the War* (1940). *The Collected Writings of John Maynard Keynes* are being issued by the Royal Economic Society in 24 volumes (from 1971 onwards). See also: (Sir) R. F. Harrod, *The Life of John Maynard Keynes* (1951); Michael Stewart, *Keynes and After* (1974); *Essays on John Maynard Keynes*, ed. Milo Keynes (1975); *The End of the Keynesian Era*, ed. R. Skidelsky (1977); and E. S. and H. G. Johnson, *The Shadow of Keynes* (1979).

244

KING, Martin Luther, Jnr 1929–1968

US racial leader

Born in 1929, Martin Luther King, Jnr, was only twenty-six years old when the Montgomery Bus Boycott thrust him into the midst of America's civil rights struggle. A little over a year later he achieved fame – the cover of *Time* magazine, the Spingarn Medal for his contributions to race relations, and a flurry of honorary degrees. In 1964 he became the youngest winner in the history of the Nobel Peace Prize.

Success at an early age could not have been completely unexpected. King had graduated from Morehouse College at nineteen, finished divinity school at the head of his class at twenty-two, and completed his PhD degree at Boston University at twenty-six. When black residents of Montgomery, Alabama, began their spontaneous boycott of segregated buses, however, King was nothing more than the young, rather shy pastor of the largest black Baptist church in the city. He was not an activist seeking an occasion; the occasion sought him. Before taking a public stand, King had to convince himself, and for this reason it would be easier for him to convince others. King was schooled in theology and philosophy, but he had prepared himself to be a minister. He had no programme and no commitment to a theory of change. Beginning with a strong Christian faith in the power of love and a black American tradition of non-violent protest against white oppression, Martin Luther King also came to appreciate the example and teachings of Mahatma Gandhi*. Before the Montgomery Boycott was successfully concluded, King had articulated a philosophy of non-violent direct action whose spirit, he said, came from Jesus and whose technique came from Gandhi. King, however, was never an organizer, planner, or administrator. In January 1957 he and some sixty other black leaders, mostly preachers, met in Atlanta to form the Southern Christian Leadership Conference (SCLC) in an attempt to co-ordinate the many civil rights efforts and ambitions spawned by the success in Montgomery. The SCLC would be Martin Luther King's official organization throughout the remainder of his thirteen-year career, but it never controlled or directed the Civil Rights Movement. King became *the* civil rights leader and a man of immense national and international prestige, but his influence and contribution were predominantly spiritual.

Almost all the civil rights campaigns of the late 1950s and 1960s began as local campaigns, led by established local leaders and manned by local blacks, especially students. Rarely could these campaigns win success, however, unless they achieved national awareness. Here was the critical role of Martin Luther King. Only he had the prestige and influence to elevate a local crisis to the attention of the news media and the federal government. Only he could attract sufficient white support to provide the stamp of 'legitimacy'. His devotion to non-violence, his emphasis upon love, and his openness to compromise made him appear responsible and moderate and, therefore, respectable. But King's role as a symbolic and spiritual leader meant that he often had little power to control the movement he represented. The inability of the SCLC to define a coherent programme of action in the late 1950s, for example, led to impatience among many black students and thus to the birth of the sit-in movement in 1960. King endorsed the sit-ins and for a time brought the Student Non-violent Coordinating Committee (SNCC) under the loose umbrella of the SCLC. In this way, he maintained his important position, but as one observer commented, 'It was not leadership but agility that put him there.' The popularity of the student sit-in movement among local black communities put great pressure on King. Expectations had been raised, and blacks looked expectantly to Martin Luther King. His instincts, agility and prestige served him well, but on occasion, as with the demonstrations in Albany, Georgia, in 1961–2, they failed. In Albany, a lack of planning and background information had caused King to step into a virtually impossible situation. His prestige slipped, particularly among more aggressive civil rights groups such as SNCC and the Congress of Racial Equality (CORE).

If King and the SCLC had a tactical civil rights plan, it was to maintain tension on the South's caste-like system of segregation and discrimination. Unless pressure was applied, there was no impetus to change. By 1963 King needed a productive crisis. Dissent was growing among black activists, and civil rights legislation was making little progress in Washington. Consequently, King turned his attention to a massive demonstration assault on Birmingham, Alabama, perhaps the most segregated city in the South. For two months marches confronted the forces of white resistance. Violence flared and eventually over 2,400 civil rights demonstrators, including King, were jailed. The two sides finally reached a compromise in Birmingham, but not before the full weight of John F. Kennedy's* presidency was thrown into the fray. In addition, the crisis renewed Kennedy's support for a comprehensive new civil rights law and also raised recognition of Martin Luther King's leadership to new heights. In an eloquent and widely publicized 'Letter from Birmingham Jail', King had defended his direct action tactics and articulated his goals in a fashion that contrasted dramatically with the harsh and primitive measures of his segregationist opponents. In the sensitive months following Kennedy's assassination in November 1963, Martin Luther King's prestige reached its peak – the passage of the Civil Rights Act of 1964 and the awarding of the Nobel Peace Prize.

Still, however, there was tension within the ranks of the civil rights movement. On the one hand, many SNCC and CORE workers continued their criticism of King's willingness to compromise short of his declared objectives, and they turned more and more away from co-operation with whites in favour of various brands of 'black power'. On the other hand, King was being pressured to give attention to the ghettos of the North where violence and the black nationalism of Malcolm X* were on the rise. Furthermore, he was also beginning to feel the pull of a growing anti-Vietnam war movement. In effect, many blacks had come to feel that the accomplishments associated with King's leadership had not sifted down to the black masses. King responded to these pressures by taking his non-violent programme to Chicago in an effort to force improvement in inner-city housing and employment practices. He attained little success and his prestige suffered. Advocates of protest violence and black power gained voice and urban rioting increased. Meanwhile, in April 1967, King had reluctantly taken a public stance against the war in Vietnam – a position he had maintained privately for many months. The decision to go public further diminished his leadership role in the increasingly fragmented civil rights movement. Conservative black workers in the National Association for the Advancement of Colored People (NAACP) and National Urban League criticized King sharply, and he lost his once considerable leverage with the Lyndon Johnson administration.

By 1967 Martin Luther King's approach to bringing meaningful social change in the United States showed the strains of his twelve-year struggle. In *Where Do We Go from Here?*, published in that year, King had embraced a modified version of black power. But while he was no longer the shy, rather naive young black minister who had been drawn into the Montgomery Bus Boycott, he still relied heavily upon Christian oratory and clung hopefully to his belief in Ghandian non-violent techniques. King began to put together plans for what he hoped would be a massive 'Poor People's March' on Washington in the summer of 1968. Many advisers warned him of the probability of violence in such a march, but King rejected their advice and pushed ahead in what seemed an almost desperate effort to re-establish the viability of non-violent demonstrations. While planning was going on, however, a plea came from striking Memphis, Tennessee, garbage workers. They wanted King's support. Here was an opportunity to re-establish his own sagging prestige and, therefore, to enhance the chances for success of his Poor People's March. It was in Memphis on 4 April 1968 that Martin Luther Jnr fell victim to an assassin's bullet. In addition to a floundering and fragmented civil rights movement, King left his wife, Coretta Scott King, and four children. His personal prestige was still huge, but his special capacity as an

effective spiritual leader had deteriorated significantly from its peak in 1964.

Professor Lester C. Lamon

King's other works include: *Stride Toward Freedom* (1958); *The Measure of a Man* (1958); *Strength to Love* (1963); *Why We Can't Wait* (1964); *The Trumpet of Conscience* (1968). See also: David L. Lewis, *King: A Critical Biography* (second edition, 1978); and C. Eric Lincoln (ed.), *Martin Luther King, Jr.: A Profile* (1970).

245
KIPLING, Joseph Rudyard 1865–1936

British writer

Rudyard Kipling was born in Bombay, the son of Alice and Lockwood Kipling (who later became curator of the Indian Museum and director of the Art Institute at Lahore). After an idyllically happy early childhood, he was sent back at the age of six to England with his sister, and spent six bitterly wretched years at a foster-home in Southsea he later referred to as 'The House of Desolation'. In 1877 he was sent to the recently founded United Services College at Westward Ho!, Devon, on which the stories of *Stalky and Co.* (1899) were later based. At sixteen Kipling left school and rejoined his family in India to work as a journalist. The next seven years, at Lahore and Allahabad, stimulated some of his finest early work and remained a continuing inspiration for much of his writing life. Beginning with the witty light verse of *Departmental Ditties* (1886), he wrote many of his classic short stories. The first collection of these to be published in England – *Plain Tales from the Hills* (1888) – was immediately acclaimed, and in 1889 Kipling left India to pursue a literary career in London. His success was quickly assured, but he soon learnt to dislike the metropolitan *literati*. Throughout his life he was to maintain the attitude of a plain experienced man of action, despite an unquestioned dedication to his art. His friendships included Stanley Baldwin, Lord Milner and Max Aitken (later Lord Beaverbrook), but few fellow writers.

The years between 1890 and 1902 were the zenith of Kipling's popularity. During this time he published three superb collections of mainly 'Indian' short stories: *Life's Handicap* (1891); *Many Inventions* (1893); and *The Day's Work* (1897), which included his finest fable 'The Bridge Builders'. These were followed by *Kim* (1901), his only full-length romance, the story of a boy who moves within the 'daylight' world of the British in India, and the dark, rich, friendly world of the native Indians, equally at home with the 'Great Game' of spying for the British and with the mysticism of the Buddhist lama whose disciple he becomes. The same period also witnessed Kipling's children's classics: *The*

Jungle Book (1894); *The Second Jungle Book* (1895); and the brilliant fables of *Just-so Stories* (1902); while in verse were published *Barrack Room Ballads* (1892 and 1896), 'vernacular' poems inspired by his knowledge of military life in India and by the London music-halls, and of their kind unsurpassed in the English language. In addition, Kipling established himself as a public spokesman on behalf of a Tory populism characterized by the ideals of patriotism, the glory of the Empire, and the value of hard work and dedication to one's duty in all classes. Of particular note in this context are the hymn 'Recessional' (1897, published in *The Times* for Victoria's Diamond Jubilee), warning Britons against pagan pride in their inevitably transient empire, and the song 'Absent-Minded Beggar', which raised £250,000 for the wives and dependants of soldiers fighting in the Boer War.

By 1897 Kipling was settled in Sussex where, apart from occasional spells of foreign travel, he remained for the rest of his life. This followed an unhappy five years in Vermont after his marriage, in 1892, to the American Caroline Balestier. During the Edwardian period Kipling became if anything even more firmly identified with the English ruling class, although he steadfastly refused official status, declining both the Laureateship and the Order of Merit. His fiction of this 'middle period' deals less with alien cultures and more with the mundane world of solid, hard-working non-intellectuals, with the problems of administration, and with the marvels of technology. 'Below the Mill Dam' (from *Traffics and Discoveries*, 1904) and 'The Mother Hive' (from *Actions and Reactions*, 1909) are his most skilful political fables, while other stories, such as 'They' and 'Mrs Bathurst' (from *Traffics and Discoveries*), 'The House Surgeon' (*Actions and Reactions*) and the coldly terrifying 'Mary Postgate' (*A Diversity of Creatures*, 1917), brilliantly combine surface commitment to modern actuality with profound explorations into the recesses of the psyche.

During the First World War Kipling threw himself passionately into German-hating propaganda (his war verses have a rage and shrillness unparalleled elsewhere), but he was also deeply disillusioned by the sordid waste of life (his son John was killed at Loos in 1915) and embittered both by the conduct of the war and its aftermath. In the sense that his later fiction is concerned more with suffering, and less with the action of his earlier work, the spiritual damage was permanent. The war is often the background and partial cause of the suffering (as with 'The Janeites' and 'The Gardener', in *Debits and Credits*, 1926); but at least as often this is treated simply as an inevitable part of the human condition (as with 'The Wish House', in *Debits and Credits*, or 'Dayspring Mishandled' in *Limits and Renewals*, 1932). At the same time Kipling's interest in historical settings, of the kind that he had used in the children's books *Puck of Pook's Hill* (1906) and *Rewards and Fairies* (1910), was rekindled in stories like 'The Eye of Allah' and 'The Church that was at Antioch'.

Many of Kipling's late stories are masterpieces of technical narrative complexity, and serve to remind one of their author's versatility, energy and mastery of form – qualities in fact that are apparent in nearly everything he wrote. What is less consistent in Kipling's work, however, is the *persona* behind it. The more one reads of him, the more elusive his character becomes. His stories frequently employ a narrating 'I' (just as most of his poems are best read as dramatic monologues) – yet this 'I' has a whole range of personalities and its only regular qualities are that it is invariably possessed of an 'insider's knowledge' about whatever world it narrates, and that it is (usually) compassionate. The kind of difficulties Kipling offers his interpreters are exemplified in 'Mary Postgate', a story in which a middle-aged governess, in revenge for the wartime death of her pupil, watches the death agony of a German pilot, refusing to help him and taking an unmistakably sexual pleasure in the experience. This can be seen as the vilest kind of war propaganda or as a masterly piece of compassionate psychological realism.

Not surprisingly, in the light of this, responses to Kipling have been extreme, and, despite the technical brilliance of his writing, his importance has been cultural rather than literary, at least in the English-speaking community. (Elsewhere, among major writers, both Brecht*, who translated *Barrack Room Ballads* into German, and Jorge Luis Borges* have acknowledged his influence.) To the conservative middle classes whom he often celebrated (while implicitly criticizing their narrow outlook), he embodied the pieties of patriotism and tradition; while to liberals and the progressive left he stood for everything they hated: reactionary politics, jingoism, brutality and cultural philistinism. One reason for this simplistic caricature of a complex man is the intertwining of 'Kiplingesque' values with the (assumed) ideology of the English public schools. The intellectual left, particularly of the 1930s, were much affected by public school experience, values and mythology, a parodic and partially distanced version of which the poets made their own, and consequently, to the extent that these values continued to affect them, their outlook was inversely shaped by Kipling. The jibe of Orwell* that Auden* was 'a sort of gutless Kipling' (in *The Road to Wigan Pier*) is typical: the comparison is an insult, and yet not only is Kipling a landmark, but the word 'gutless' reproduces the values which are ostensibly rejected.

Janet Montefiore

Other works include: *The Light that Failed* (novel, 1890); *The Naulakha* (novel, 1892, with his wife); *Captains Courageous* (novel, 1897); *Something of Myself* (autobiography, 1937); *The Verse of Rudyard Kipling* (collected verse, 1940). See: Charles Carrington, *Kipling: his Life and Art* (1955); J. M. S. Tompkins, *The Art of Rudyard Kipling* (1959); *Kipling's Mind and Art*, ed. A. Rutherford (1964, including essays by Orwell, Edmund Wilson and Lionel Trilling); Angus Wilson, *The Strange Ride of Rudyard Kipling* (1977).

246
KIRCHNER, Ernst Ludwig 1880–1938

German painter

The son of a chemistry reacher in Aschaffenberg in the Rhineland, but of Prussian descent, Kirchner spent four years (1901–5) qualifying as an architect at the Dresden Institute of Technology before cutting loose as a painter. In 1905, with his fellow students Erich Heckel and Karl Schmidt-Rottluff, and the more superficial Max Pechstein, Kirchner founded *Die Brücke* – 'The Bridge' – a group which remained active, publishing manifestos and graphics, until 1913. Aiming at a Nietzschean 'revaluation of all values', this band of youthful bohemians lived, worked, and (together with their women friends) sometimes slept in common, anticipating the drop-out 'families' of our own time. At first their paintings were almost indistinguishable from one another, a heightened Impressionism reminiscent of Van Gogh, and close to the early work of Emil Nolde* – who, ten years older, briefly joined the group as an admired mentor. But by 1906 Kirchner had seen Fauvist works by Matisse*, with their potentially ferocious intensity and immediacy of colour; Gauguin, and the art of the South Seas, had contributed a primitivistic element; and Munch* helped point him towards a psychological art. The resulting synthesis has a peculiar sour, sophisticated brilliance. In *Self-portrait in a Striped Dressing-gown* (1907) the young artist seems to declare his dissipation, his narcotic and exhilarated despair, while in the background the child-model in her underwear carries overtones of sexual depravity. This sexual emphasis is continued in his graphics of brothels and (influenced by the Japanese) sexual postures, as well as in the many paintings of the friends, frolicking naked together on the island of Fehrmarn.

In 1907 Kirchner had painted his first large street scene, still reminiscent of Munch, but when he moved to Berlin in 1911 the street, and specifically the streetwalkers, triggered a series of masterpieces that establish him as perhaps the greatest of all twentieth-century painters of The City. The war and conscription cut short his brief flowering. *Soldiers under a Shower* (1914) shows Kirchner responding to the humiliations of Prussian discipline, the naked spindly figures herded beneath a vast boiler, barked at by a uniformed officer – an image unmistakably prophetic of the gas-chambers. In 1915, still under training, he suffered a complete mental and physical breakdown; he was sent off to the mountains, but never fully recovered. His alpine landscapes have been admired, but are relatively heavy-handed, while most of the other later work – including a disastrous flirtation with Picasso* – is unworthy. Kirchner also repainted many early masterpieces, with unfortunate results. Like so many of the great figures of Expressionism, he became famous only when his creative years were past. He suffered from the Nazi defamation of his all-too-obviously 'degenerate' art, and in 1938 in Davos, after holing several of his own pictures, he shot himself.

Kirchner once said his whole work was 'the life-story of a paranoid', and it is the expression of this complex, acid, spiteful temperament, in a racy, nervy calligraphy, that gives his art its special edge. In *Potsdamer Platz* (1914), the prostitutes stand almost life-size on their island, while tiny bowler-hatted men lurk at the periphery; in *Red Cocotte* (1914), the exotic plumed tart crosses the street, silhouetted against the menacing, anonymous, predatory males.

Perhaps Kirchner is strongest of all in his graphics, with their 'hieroglyphic' language so well described by 'L. de Marsalle', the fictitious French art critic invented by Kirchner to praise his own work. 'The images are not in themselves representations of definite objects; their significance lies in their placing, their size, their juxtaposition with others on the page. They are *hieroglyphs*, in the sense of reducing natural forms to simplified flat shapes.' The tense threatening angularity of Kirchner's urban spaces was very influential, as we can see in a film like *Caligari*, and it still rings true. When Munch first saw *Die Brücke* graphics, he commented: 'May God protect us, we are approaching difficult times.' Kirchner, that 'difficult man', transcended his personal predicament to speak for many who would suffer in our contemporary 'Jungles of the Cities'.

Timothy Hyman

See: Will Grohmann, *E. L. Kirchner* (1961); Annemarie Dube-Heynig, *E. L. Kirchner, Graphik* (1961); *Painters of the Brücke* (Arts Council of Great Britain, 1964); Enrico Crispoli, *Ernst Kirchner* (no. 137 in the Fabbri series 'I Maestri di Colori', 1966); *Kirchner* (Marlborough Gallery Catalogue, 1969).

247
KLEE, Paul 1879–1940

Swiss-German artist

Born near Berne in Switzerland, Paul Klee hesitated for a long time as to whether to be an artist, a poet or a musician; he finally left home to study at an art school in Munich. He soon felt the urge to shed the strict training of the hand which classical art studies entail, and entered upon a lifelong practice of experimentation, trying out dozens of fresh techniques and styles, some inspired by the artless drawings of children or the insane, others by the work of such artists as Van Gogh and Ensor. The scratchy, fantastical manner of his early drawings reflects a talent straining away from all orthodoxy. 'I want to be as though new-born' reads an entry in his diary.

In 1901 Klee had visited Italy and busied himself with relatively out-of-the-way attractions such as Byzantine mosaics, the Pompeii frescoes and a marvellous aquarium in Naples, whence sprang an enduring fascination with the dim forms of marine life. His travels were always occasions to gather primary impressions which he then allowed to germinate in their own time, eventually to surface as artistic forms. After a period back in Berne, Klee married in 1906 and returned to Munich, where he became a member of the Blauer Reiter circle with Kandinsky* and Franz Marc. Already a virtuoso draughtsman and water-colourist, Klee now came to contemplate the suggestive potential of graduated tones of colour, revealed most dramatically upon his discovery of Cézanne in 1910. He was beginning to grasp that the art of painting might be based on fidelity to the palette itself rather than to any pre-existing subject-matter.

A visit to another great colourist, Robert Delaunay, in Paris was followed in 1914 by a journey to North Africa. Lasting less than a fortnight, this journey was to be the climax of Klee's quest for the full understanding of his artistic orientation. The town of Tunis manifested itself as the perfect model for a vision of painting in which architectonic shapes could be synthesized with orchestrated zones of luminous colour. The harmonic vibrancy of the place created an impression which was to radiate throughout Klee's subsequent work. The mosaic patterns made up by the cubes and cupolas of the Arab buildings, the textures of parched earth and hot walls, the lush oases, the moon rising over the desert sands – these elements of an exotic reality nourished a language of shapes and colours which was to become Klee's native idiom. 'It is all sinking so deeply and calmly into me,' he recorded in his diary. 'Colour has taken possession of me. That is the significance of this happy hour: colour and I are one. I am a painter.'

By 1920 Klee was an artist of repute and was engaged by Walter Gropius* to teach at the Bauhaus in Weimar, along with the painters Lyonel Feininger, Oskar Schlemmer and Kandinsky, the latter already an intimate friend and co-explorer in the realms of pure colour and form. Klee's work with students encouraged him to systematize his intuitions concerning the construction of forms and the relationships of line, tone value and colour. The *Pedagogical Sketchbook* (*Pädagogisches Skizzenbuch*, 1925, trans. 1953) is a résumé of his teaching on graphic procedures and deals with the dynamics of the dot, the line, the spiral, the square and so forth. Pedagogic practice merely confirmed Klee's ingrained habit of self-scrutiny, of making conscious that which was primarily instinctive. In this Klee came close to the Surrealists, with whom he exhibited in Paris in 1925: but against their unbridled 'psychic automatism' he favoured a mode of 'psychic improvisation' whereby the spontaneous gestures of pen or brush are studied, interpreted, even supervised by a purposive, lucid intelligence.

In the 1930s, Klee came up against antagonisms at the Bauhaus and in Germany at large, and in 1933 decided to move back for good to Switzerland. The Nazis in due course suppressed all his works in public galleries after derisively showing Klee in their 1937 exhibition of 'degenerate art'. Re-settling in Berne, the artist fell victim to a malignant skin condition but continued to produce at a phenomenal rate: during 1939 he completed 2,000 works. He died in 1940 in a clinic near Locarno.

Klee left behind an extraordinary *oeuvre* of some 9,000 works, primarily water-colours, drawings and oil paintings, in a great range of styles. Most of his pictures are on a diminutive scale, neat miniatures in which daring experimentation is almost hermetically sealed. Each image is the tiny encapsulation of a happy solution to a particular aesthetic question.

Klee's approach was markedly different from that of his Expressionist contemporaries. He was drawn to a type of abstraction in which identifiable shapes from the real world – his favourite motifs are birds and fishes, trees, parks and cities, human figures and far-away landscapes – are rendered in spidery lines that suggest a kind of kabbalistic picture-writing. It is an idiom of intellectual signs rather than of emotions, and is indeed based on Klee's understanding of the conceptual rather than expressionistic mode of child art. Some works are self-conscious displays of verbal signs: *Villa R* (1919) and *Vocal Fabric of the Singer Rosa Silber* (1922) present letters from the alphabet as visual configurations in their own right. At one time Klee did a series of 'inscription pictures' in which poetic texts are rendered in capitals upon ribbons of colour to create a lilting synthesis of word and image. *Leaf from the Town Records* (1928) depicts a manuscript whose 'text' consists of interlinked runic figures suggesting turrets, flags, domes and city walls; the title of the work underlines the draughtsman's claim to equate the pictorial with the written sign. In due course Klee adumbrated a set of simple figures – squares, triangles, dots, squiggles, arrows – which were the letters of his personal alphabet.

Another analogy which asserts itself in the context of Klee's semi-abstract paintings is that with the set of notes which are arranged and rearranged in a musical composition. *Highway and Byways* (1929) presents a wide road stretching to the horizon across a plain built up to either side in rich ochre, pale green and purple strips, some thick, some thin. Inspired by a visit to Egypt, this landscape is in transition from being the transposition of a real spatial experience to being a prodigiously organized exercise in the polyphonic combination of colour tones and geometric shapes across the picture surface.

Klee's conception of Nature springs from the notion that the artist is himself a fragment of the totality of things: 'The artist is a man, himself nature and a part of nature, within nature's space.' His task is therefore not to reproduce idly what he sees, but to attune himself to natural processes and translate these formative energies into the idiom of aesthetic signs. The artist should not linger over surface perceptions: after all, 'the visible is only an isolated case'. His picture must be the record of a meditation upon deeper, invisible truths; he fashions not a mirror of natural creation but its emblem. 'He transcends reality, dissolves it, in order to reveal what lies behind and inside it.'

The canvas *Blossoming* (1934) consists of a framework of irregular multi-coloured squares, their tonal values meticulously graded so that the eye is first drawn to the brilliance at the centre, then out to the surrounding areas of progressive darkness. The movement of the viewer's eye, from brightness to darkness, from centre to circumference, corresponds to the dimly sensed motion of natural growth. The picture is a geometrical allegory of blossoming rather than a direct representation of any flower. Similarly *Untamed Waters* (1934) shows us not literal turbulence but an ideogram in which lines of flow are stylized into intertwined ribbons of blue, turquoise, rust and pink: the literality of water in motion is transcended in an image of thrusting currents held in suspense, convulsive lines soothed by calm water-colour hues.

Klee's art often seems to drift away from all immediacy. Thus the wistful portrait of the *Man in Yellow* (1921), with its caricatural reduction of facial features to a few slickly curled lines and the breathless way Klee floats this yellow figure on to the green depths of the background, evokes a presence which is remote, unreal. *The Tightrope Walker* (1923) is a vaguely comic portrayal of a spotlighted manikin with bird-like face easing his way silently along a thin rope with a balancing pole; fussy paraphernalia – rope-ladder, safety-net and the like – dangle irrelevantly beneath. The black lines representing these are inscribed over an unearthly pink ground, a typical combination for Klee, who loved to draw in spiky transparent configurations over an initial wash of glowing water-colour. The effect of this little image is to evoke a feeling of diminished gravitational pull: the tightrope walker is like Klee himself, delicately stepping from the world of substance on to the higher plane of art. This sure-footedness, this discretion, this cool remoteness seem characteristic:

they place Klee in the lineage of a Mozart rather than of a Beethoven, and can make some of his pictures come across as things to be peeped at, quaintly seductive windows on to a fantasy world, rather than the solemn repositories of the semi-mystical teachings of the theoretical writings.

Klee was active in so many different styles and his example has been so subtly pervasive that it is impossible to pin down the exact range of his artistic influence: there are touches of Klee in the work of artists as disparate as Bissier, Wols, Dubuffet*, De Staël and Hundertwasser, to name but a few. And perhaps because Klee never relinquished the child-like manner, his images have also been among the most popular in twentieth-century art, doing much to accustom a reluctant public to the formidable modernist proposition which the artist once formulated, simply yet boldly, in the aphorism: 'Art does not reproduce the visible – it makes visible.'

Roger Cardinal

Writings by Klee: *Tagebücher* (*Diaries*, 1957); *Notebooks*, vol. I *The Thinking Eye* (*Das bildnerische Denken*, trans. 1961) and vol. II *The Nature of Nature* (*Unendliche Naturgeschichte*, trans. 1973); *On Modern Art* (*Über die moderne Kunst*, trans. 1948). On Klee: C. Giedion-Welcker, *Paul Klee* (1952); W. Haftmann, *The Mind and Work of Paul Klee* (*Paul Klee: Wege bildnerischen Denkens*, trans. 1954); W. Grohmann, *Paul Klee* (1954); G. di San Lazzaro, *Klee* (1957); J. S. Pierce, *Paul Klee and Primitive Art* (1975).

248

KLEIN, Melanie 1882–1960

Austrian psychoanalyst

Melanie Klein was born in Vienna in 1882, the youngest of four children in a Jewish family. Her father, originally trained as a doctor, later became more successful as a dentist which considerably improved the material well-being of his family. She described her childhood as being happy, but always felt closer to her mother than her father, who remained a rather distant figure. However, she was much affected by the early deaths of two of her siblings and the impact of this loss remained with her throughout her life. She had planned to study medicine but this was prevented by her engagement at nineteen and subsequent marriage at twenty-one to a businessman whose work involved travel. She always regretted this lost opportunity, but studied Humanities instead. Her marriage proved to be an unhappy one, partly because she missed the intellectual stimulation of Vienna. She had three children, two boys and a girl.

In 1910, whilst living in Budapest, she discovered

Freud's* work. Her interest and excitement in this led to her personal analysis with Sándor Ferenczi, who encouraged her in her desire to analyse children. Her increasing commitment to psychoanalytic work eventually contributed to her separation from her husband in 1919, and divorce in 1922. She moved to Berlin and was much influenced by Karl Abraham, whom she persuaded to give her further analysis. Although this was interrupted after only nine months by his sudden death, this period with him deepened her analytical thought and modified the direction of her work. There followed a difficult period for Klein in Berlin, largely produced by her conflicting ideas with Anna Freud, whose analytical work with children was considered to be more orthodox. She came to England in 1926, where she worked as a psychoanalyst for the rest of her life. She died in London in 1960.

Klein's contribution to the psychoanalysis of adults and children was to underline the importance of object relationships as determinants of personality. Her work emphasized the important role of phantasy in the first two years of life, as well as the importance of early two-person relationships. A baby's love and hate are directed initially towards the mother, who represents the child's whole world. The lack of cohesion of the early ego leads to a splitting of impulses into good and bad. During the first three to four months of life the dominant features of psychological activity are feelings of omnipotence and persecution, and the mental mechanism of splitting the mother image into good and bad. This is called the *paranoid schizoid position*. As the ego becomes more integrated this mechanism of splitting decreases, so that the good and bad aspects of the mother and of her internal image can be synthesized. The child fears that his aggressive wishes and impulses towards the mother he also loves may be directly damaging to her, since a wish and an act are the same thing to him at this stage of development. This leads to feelings of guilt, concern and sadness, or the *depressive position*. This is slowly worked through as the child's knowledge of the world increases, but these depressive and persecutory anxieties may return when internal or external pressures become intense. The essential difference from Freudian theory, where satisfaction of instincts is of fundamental importance, is this focus on early object-seeking and relating. Klein's practical contributions are the play technique evolved in the analysis of children, and the way early object relationships are relived in transference during the psychoanalysis of adults.

Klein's work has always been surrounded by controversy and criticisms, largely that she attributed too much complexity to a child's early mental activity which is not in keeping with the facts about an infant's abilities in the early years. However, there have recently been suggestions from research that the infant's perception is more advanced than had previously been suspected.

Dr David Sturgeon

Melanie Klein's works include: *The Psycho-Analysis of Children* (1932); *Contributions to Psycho-Analysis 1921–1945* (1948); 'On the Theory of Anxiety and Guilt', *Int. J. Psycho-Anal.*, vol. 29; *Envy and Gratitude* (1957); *Narrative of a Child Psycho-Analysis* (1961). See also: Hanna Segal, *Klein* (1979).

249
KLEIN, Yves 1928–62

French artist

In 1946, lying on the beach at Nice, Klein made a 'realistico-imaginary' voyage and signed his name on the other side of the sky. From that experience dated his ambition to express the infinite in art. The pure cloudless sky was for him not only the symbol of 'existential space' but also of the 'immaterial' and of 'absolute freedom'.

Klein's vision was optimistic and Utopian, believing as he did in a future technological Garden of Eden. But to achieve this it was first necessary to transform the sensibility of mankind and this was the central purpose of his art. Such a transformation did not entail, as it has for most avant-gardistes, a total break with the past. On the contrary, all existing traditions contained truths which could be used. His own creative development was facilitated by the practice of judo: 'Judo has helped me to understand that pictorial space is above all the product of spiritual exercises.' Nevertheless, as 'an Occidental, a right-thinking Christian', he did not believe that the answer lay in the wholesale espousal of Eastern systems. The principal answer which he proposed was: pure colour. From 1956 he produced his monochrome paintings. Finding that differently coloured monochromes hung together were seen comparatively and hence polychromatically, he limited himself principally to one colour – a deep ultramarine which he later (1960) patented as International Klein Blue (IKB). Despite their resonance, however, his blue paintings were not in themselves finished artworks but 'only the title-deeds' proving him to be an artist. His real art, the transformation of sensibility, consisted also of his many activities. His *anthropométries*, for example: in 1960 he directed three nude models as they imprinted IKB paint on to canvases before an audience while twenty musicians played his one-note *Symphonie Monotone*. In the same year, Klein threw himself off a first-floor parapet, injuring himself in so doing, to create *A Man in Space*; this action was recorded in his *Newspaper of a Single Day, Sunday* (27 November 1960). Fascinated by air, he was also fascinated by fire, creating in 1961 a gas-fuelled *Fire Fountain* and *Fire Wall*, as well as numerous *Fire Paintings*. His involvement with the elements was alchemistic. Not surprisingly, therefore, he executed a number of works in gold, the 'monogolds'. But the metal must be abandoned for its 'immaterial' equivalent, as demonstrated in Klein's sale, for gold, of *Immaterial Pictorial Sensitivity Zones* (1959–62); while he threw away or destroyed half the gold, the 'buyer', was obliged to destroy the receipt if his proprietorship was to be validated. In 1962 Klein began work on a project intended to contain IKB-coloured plaster-casts of his friends against gold backgrounds with, in the centre, a gold plaster-cast of himself against an IKB background: its completion was prevented by his early death.

The posthumous reputation of 'Yves, le Monochrome' has been complicated, and greatly enhanced, by the rise of Conceptual Art and Performance Art, both of which he prefigured to a remarkable degree. Perhaps no artist of his generation had a clearer understanding than he of the direction in which art needed to develop if it were to fulfil its properly investigative and didactic function.

Gray Watson

See: Pierre Restany, *Yves Klein, le Monochrome* (Paris 1974); also the catalogues to his exhibitions at the Jewish Museum, New York (1967), and the Tate Gallery, London (1974).

250
KODÁLY, Zoltán 1882–1967

Hungarian composer, ethnomusicologist and music educationist

As the son of a station master he was taken in his youth to different parts of Hungary and so gained a knowledge of the diversity of the country's folk music; he also inherited his parents' enthusiasm for classical music. He studied under Hans Koessler at the Royal Academy of Music in Budapest (1900–4), where he was a contemporary of Bartók*, and where in 1907 he took a teaching post. With Bartók he began collecting folk-songs in 1906, and in Hungarian folk-music he found the basis for a distinctively nationalist style. His early works, which include a Sonata for cello and piano (1909–10), a Sonata for cello alone (1915) and the first of two string quartets (1908–9), show his adoption of folk elements into a rhapsodic and primarily melodic style.

Unlike Bartók, Kodály showed little interest in the advanced musical trends of his time, preferring to retain a close connection with Hungarian folk-music. That connection is strong and clear in the four major

works he wrote during the inter-war period, all of which won immediate and lasting success: the *Psalmus hungaricus* for tenor, chorus and orchestra (1923), the opera *Háry János* (1925–7), source of a popular orchestral suite, the *Dances of Maroesszék* for piano (1927) or orchestra (1930), and the *Dances from Galanta* for orchestra (1933). The picturesque colourfulness of these scores is also a feature of the 'Peacock' Variations (1938–9) and the Concerto for Orchestra (1939).

Kodály remained in Hungary during the Second World War and afterwards, when he became a national figure in the new socialist state. He was now able to put forward ideas for reforming music education by emphasizing the practice of singing at sight, and he produced an enormous quantity of choral music for children and amateurs; the Symphony of 1961 is one of his few 'professional' works from this period.

Paul Griffiths

Other works: *Summer Evening* for orchestra (1906, revised 1929–30); Sixteen Songs for voice and piano (1907–9); Ten Pieces for piano (1907–9); Duet for violin and cello (1914); *Belated Melodies* for voice and piano (1912–16); String Quartet no. 2 (1916–18); Serenade for two violins and viola (1919–20); Five Songs for voice and piano (1916–23); *Budavári Te Deum* for soloists, chorus and orchestra (1936). Writings: *A magyar népzene* (1937, third edition 1951, trans. Ronald Tempest and Cynthia Jolly, *Hungarian Folk Music*, 1960). About Kodály: László Eösze, *Zoltán Kodály, his Life and Work* (trans. 1962); Percy M. Young, *Zoltán Kodály, a Hungarian Musician* (1964).

251
KOESTLER, Arthur 1905–

Hungarian/British writer

Arthur Koestler was born in Budapest at a time when the Austro-Hungarian Empire still straddled much of central and south-eastern Europe. He witnessed its demise as a young man and, like many intellectuals in the inter-war years, believed he was about to experience the collapse of Western civilization itself. As a young man Koestler studied at the University of Vienna but left in 1925, before completing his degree, to live in Palestine. After working on a kibbutz Koestler began to work as a journalist, later returning to Europe to continue his career. He became foreign editor and assistant editor-in-chief of Berlin's *BZ am Mittag*.

The inter-war years were intensely political in the sense that politics dominated the discourse of Western intellectuals to a hitherto unparalleled extent. With the failure of conventional political movements to solve the acute economic problems of the day intellectuals began increasingly to move to the polar extremes, the fascists and the communists. Koestler chose to join the latter, becoming a member of the German Communist Party (KPD) at the end of 1931. In his fervent attachment to and subsequent disenchantment with communism Koestler represents, in many respects, the values, aspirations and eventual disillusionment of the young men of the 'pink decade'. Koestler's personal experiences, set out briefly in a collection edited by Richard Crossman, *The God That Failed* (1942), and chronicled in detail in the autobiographical *The Invisible Writing* (1954), provide a detailed account of Koestler's progress; his, in many respects, is the story of a generation of intellectuals, hence its abiding interest.

Koestler describes his work for the KPD in rather limp terms. In the early days it was clearly the social and intellectual life of the party cell, the sense of comradeship, which caught his imagination. Yet even early on he was distrustful of the party's reluctance to encourage open discussion among individuals. Unquestioning obedience to the party line was necessary for, as he was told, the front line was no place for discussion and, wherever he might be, a communist was always in the front line! More serious doubts began to trouble Koestler after 1934, when at the 7th Congress of the Comintern, the Soviet Union reversed its policy towards Western social democratic parties with the formation of the Popular Front. Moreover he found his own trips to the Soviet Union disillusioning. Eventually the KPD was crushed by the Nazis, whilst Koestler was in the Soviet Union. He took up residence in Paris. His disenchantment was further nourished when, during the Moscow purges and show trials which began about this time, many of his own acquaintances were charged with offences of which he knew them to be innocent. At the outbreak of the Civil War Koestler went to Spain as a correspondent for Hungary's *Pester Lloyd* and the *News Chronicle*, though unofficially he was a communist propagandist. He was imprisoned by the falangists and spent three months in a death cell before being released. He subsequently wrote *Spanish Testament* (1937) based on his experiences. By this time, though, he found it impossible to support the communist policy of hostility to its former anarchist and Trotskyist* allies. In 1938 he left the communist party. During the Second World War Koestler fought with the French Foreign Legion and with the British Army. He subsequently became a British citizen.

Koestler's disillusion with Soviet communism inspired three influential novels, the *Gladiators* (1939), *Darkness at Noon* (1940) and *Arrival and Departure* (1943). In each Koestler sought to expose what he took to be irreconcilable incompatibilities in the very nature of revolution. In the *Gladiators* he portrays the events of the slave uprising led by Spartacus between 73 and 71 BC in such a way that Spartacus becomes not simply a historical figure but a prototype proletarian revolutionary leader. Though the rebellion succeeds, attempts to establish an egalitarian state fail and all the old trappings of oppression return. Eventually Spartacus crucifies as traitors twenty of his revolutionary comrades, and we know that defeat is inevitable. The moral is clear: revolutions are doomed to fail because the leader must have absolute power to channel undifferentiated rebellion into revolution, but absolute power isolates and eventually corrupts the leader, and thus the revolution.

Darkness at Noon is also an account of a failed revolution, or more correctly of the consequences of such failure, in the Soviet Union of Joseph Stalin*. It concerns the arrest, imprisonment, and subsequent trial for treason of a member of the old revolutionary vanguard. Rubashov accepts his basic guilt, for he no longer believes in the infallibility of the party and the party persecutes the seeds of evil not only in a man's deeds but in his thoughts, admitting no private sphere to the individual, not even in his skull. Yet it is precisely in terms of individual values that Rubashov rejects the validity of the revolution. The objectives of the revolution had been to abolish needless suffering, yet to achieve this in the long term seemed to involve an enormous increase of suffering in the short term. In practice, Rubashov concludes, the short term becomes infinitely extendable. The party, created as a means to achieve the objective of the revolution, becomes instead an apparatus for maintaining strict obedience to itself, becomes in short the end and not the means; thus the revolution carries within it the seeds of its own destruction. For Rubashov the significance of the failure resides in the fact that by emphasizing party infallibility the revolution diminishes the individual. Yet no mathematical formula could balance public 'necessity' and individual values. Rubashov's final acceptance of the role cast for him in the show trial by the party in no way diminishes his conviction that ends and means have become disastrously and inevitably confused.

The third novel, *Arrival and Departure*, is an attempt to analyse the revolutionary 'type'. Koestler seems to want us to believe that the impulse to revolt is seated in some psychotic trauma quite unconnected with any social or political structure. The revolutionary 'hero' of the novel, Peter, is slowly allowed to realize, through psychoanalysis, that he has no true commitment whatever to the cause of revolution. Thus to put it shortly, Koestler is telling us that the archetypal revolutionary figure is psychotic. Demonstrably impossible to substantiate, what such an hypothesis would tell us if correct is something of a mystery; it would not, after all, alter the course of history one iota. Indeed, though self-knowledge might have made Peter himself a sadder and a wiser man, it does not prevent him from doing exactly what he had originally intended in the novel.

So in all three novels, Koestler explains why he thinks revolutions will always fail. He does not, according to George Orwell*, differentiate between revolutionary movements nor between levels of failure; does not realize, says Orwell, that all failures are not the same failure. Koestler spoke of the novels as recording 'a bewildered pilgrim's progress from the illusions of the pink decade'; as such, they were widely read after 1945 and very influential. Koestler had looked to communism to provide a comprehensive plan to improve the lot of mankind but rejected its monolithic and coercive character. Yet as his essays *The Yogi and the Commissar* (1942–4) and his essays on Mahatma Gandhi* clearly show, he did not come to believe that societies could only be improved by individual effort 'from within' of all the citizens; he did not, that is to say, reject the commissar for the yogi. What he did was to retreat from politics altogether, seeking elsewhere a plan for the betterment of mankind. In fact, Koestler turned to science.

Koestler's scientific writing, whilst it has always aroused great interest, has not been as influential as were his political works. He has written on many varied topics especially on the 'life sciences'. His approach to the nature of scientific discovery is to argue the existence of some systematic, natural design which is working towards mankind's ultimate benefit. Man does not understand this design, though if he could come to do so, it would be greatly to his advantage. Yet the application of mechanistic orthodoxies is not the way; scientific discovery has a uniquely human quality and discoveries are made as if in a fit of absence of mind – hence his description of the early astronomers as *Sleepwalkers* (1959). For Koestler, as he shows in *The Ghost in the Machine* (1967), the slavishly orthodox reductionist scientists, of whom he takes the behaviourists to be the exemplars, are simply the scientific equivalent of his 'commissars' (see *The Alphbach Symposium*, 1968). In line with his belief in some systematic natural design, Koestler abhors theories of randomness and contingency, such as underpin Darwin's evolutionary theories. In his *The Case of the Midwife Toad* (1971) he takes up a solidly pro-Lamarckian stance on evolution.

Koestler's belief in the existence of a natural, sequential order in nature has dominated his scientific writing, just as a faith in a systematic, ordered society opposed to 'randomness' dominated his political thought when he was a young man. He rejected communism because it forgets individual values; he has continued to battle against what he sees, rightly or wrongly, to be the same tendency among the scientific 'establishment'. There is a scheme of things, says Koestler, and its true centre is the individual human being.

Dr S. J. Ingle

Other works include: Autobiography: *Scum on the Earth* (1941); *Arrow in the Blue* (1952); Novels: *Thieves in the Night* (1946); *The Age of Longing* (1970); Essays and scientific works: *The Lotus and the Robot* (1966);

The Roots of Coincidence (1972); *The Heel of Achilles* (1974); *Janus: A Summing Up* (1978). See: J. A. Atkins, *Arthur Koestler* (1956); Jenni Calder, *Chronicles of Conscience* (1968).

252

KOKOSCHKA, Oscar 1886–1980

Austro-German artist

Throughout his life Kokoschka's art was dominated by a nervous tension of line which commenced during his days as a student at the Vienna School of Arts and Crafts at the time when *Jugendstil* was strongly in evidence there. The medieval and Gothic influences inherent in the movement produced ornamental art of a lively quality together with utopian ideas of a new society based on work through a guild system. Kokoschka belonged for a while to Josef Hofmann's Wiener Werkstätte. After 1906, upon seeing the work of Van Gogh, Kokoschka's painting and drawing became more emotional and expressive. The publication of Wilhelm Worringer's book *Abstraction and Empathy* in 1908 deepened this tendency towards reverence for life and the feeling for imagination as a prophetic faculty. Although choosing to be figurative in style and not inclining towards abstraction, Kokoschka was none the less opposed to the objectivity of naturalism and sought a form that conveyed a subjectivity stronger and more aggressive than that of Symbolism.

In common with the other German Expressionists such as the Brücke group and also the Norwegian Edvard Munch*, with whom he exhibited at Herwarth Walden's Der Sturm gallery in Berlin, Kokoschka's work conveyed a deep pessimism. Despite this there was also displayed a love of flux, of excess, spontaneity and visionary qualities of the imagination. At times dealing with the relationship of eroticism to sadism, Kokoschka's woodcuts and drawings show violent distortions of form. Themes of conflict of the sexes, vulnerability of the artist, woman as *femme fatale* and even murderess, and the loneliness of religious man in a world without religion were dwelt upon from a highly personal viewpoint where is expressed sympathy with suffering humanity.

The oil painting *The Tempest* of 1914 is a freely painted work depicting a sleeping woman lying against a stiffly wide awake man. The couple float wreathed by swirling shapes in a vast blue space and the combination of violent movement with racked stillness and empty space sets up intense physical and psychological tension.

After the First World War, Berlin was in a desperate state of fear and hunger. Expressionist work held sway for a few years but by the early 1920s a new formalism was gaining ground. Kokoschka spent long periods travelling through Europe, Russia, North Africa and the Near East before settling in England between 1935 and 1953. He drew and painted many sensitive portraits and landscapes, the latter usually from very high viewpoints giving a panoramic effect and suggesting that the works are in part at least from imagination. Frequently the scenes include mountains or a broad river. During the later 1950s and early 1960s Kokoschka taught at the Salzburg School of Seeing. As a man of great compassion he seems to have inspired affection in numbers of people who knew him well, yet essentially, and his work conveys this feeling, he was a man who remained with an unassuaged sense of loneliness.

Pat Turner

Writings by Kokoschka include contributions to Walden's magazine *Der Sturm*, three plays, including *Mörder Hoffnung der Frauen* ('Murder, Hope of Women', 1907) and an autobiography, *My Life* (trans. 1974). See: J. Russell, *Oskar Kokoschka: Watercolours, Drawings, Writings* (1963). See also: H. M. Wingler, *Oskar Kokoschka* (1958); J. P. Hodin, *Kokoschka* (1966).

253
KOLAKOWSKI, Leszek 1927–

Polish social philosopher

By far the most interesting and powerful philosopher to have emerged anywhere under Leninist* rule, Kolakowski has also written literary criticism, plays and fables, and is married to a psychiatrist. Kolakowski began his university studies in 1945 under Kotarbinski and other survivors of the old Warsaw school. As a Communist Party member he played a leading part in the events leading up to the 1956 Polish thaw – 'the Spring in October'. In 1966 he was expelled from the party, and in 1968 dismissed from his chair at the University of Warsaw. He has since been elected to a Fellowship at All Souls' College, Oxford, and has served as a Visiting Professor in the Universities of Montreal, Yale and California.

His essays on *Marxism and Beyond* (trans. 1968) introduce into the tradition of historical materialism a more than existentialist emphasis upon the ineluctable responsibility of every individual: history and its movements are made by, indeed are, the several actions of flesh-and-blood particular people who always could have done, or not done, other than they did, or did not do. Kolakowski has since come first to accept and now to insist that socialism – in the traditional Clause IV sense of state or public ownership and direction of all the means of production, distribution and exchange – is in practice incompatible with the elementary freedoms of a liberal society. His main work has been a comprehensive and definitive review of the *Main Currents of Marxism* (trans. 1978), in three large volumes: *The Founders*; *The Golden Age*; and *The Breakdown*. It is altogether characteristic of Kolakowski that the first chapter of the first, on 'The Origins of Dialectic', puts Marx as a German philosopher into an illuminating and unfamiliar perspective of Christian and pre-Christian philosophical theology.

Professor Antony Flew

254
KOONING, William de 1904–

US artist

Willem de Kooning was born in Rotterdam, studied at the Academy there, and in 1926 emigrated to the United States as a stowaway. He took a studio in New York where he became friends with Arshile Gorky, and in 1935 worked on the federal WPA (Works Progress Administration) project. He was a leader of what subsequently became known as 'Abstract Expressionism', and it was his vigorously physical approach to painting, the seemingly endless search for the right 'fit', each stage of the process a challenge to ever bolder revisions, that provided the model for Harold Rosenberg's existentialist interpretation 'Action Painting'. De Kooning's influence was at its height in the 1950s (his first one-man show was not until 1948) but his art has developed uninterrupted from the 1930s to the present.

The early paintings – tense abstractions drawing on Mondrian* and Miró*, and solitary figures disintegrating into melancholy but luminous backgrounds – have a hard and repressed quality. Opaque planes alternate with transparent apertures across the surface, and focal points (such as the eyes, the exposed shoulder-joints, the vase in the beautiful portrait, *The Glazier* of 1940) control the eye's travel. Only the sinewy contour, an incisive line that seeks out its own shapes – shapes that become distinctively de Kooning's own and reappear through all his phases – disturbs the stillness. Gradually the paintings gain in fluency, as the implied formal metamorphoses of the image, the restless ambiguity of its space, become fused with physical momentum – the thrusts and drips of the brush, the energized glare of heightened colour – of the painting process. A series of paintings of women became increasingly urgent or 'pressured', the line thrusting and looping, the colour rising to pinks, reds, yellows, blues, until the figure dissolved in a swirl of disembodied limbs (e.g. *Pink Angels* of 1945). There followed a magnificent group of black paintings with white linear motifs (deriving from the alphabet or landscape details) carrying a continuous rhythm of light and texture across the entire surface (see *Light in August*, 1946, or *Dark Pond*, 1948, for example). It was at this time that Pollock* and de Kooning were at their closest, both using dripped black enamel paint across allover undifferentiated fields. But de Kooning's shapes came to re-establish their identity, to separate from the pattern in sharp juxtaposition (they were frequently derived from collaged drawings, a practice that was to remain constant), with white and flesh tints now predominating over black (e.g. *Attic* of 1949) culminating in *Excavation* of 1950, where flashes of eyes, teeth, lips intersperse the seething crush of form.

De Kooning's grimacing goddess/pin-up, *Woman I* of 1950–2, his best known work, surprised many of his followers who took abstraction to be an irreversible step. Both hilarious and hysterical, the painting marked an extreme of painterly ferocity, the brush gouging, tearing, slapping the surface. The *Women* series evolved into gritty 'urban' abstract paintings (e.g. *Easter Monday* of 1956), with the same high velocity and impacted scaffolding, giving way to much simplified landscape images (e.g. *Suburb in Havana*, 1958) of boldly gestured verticals, diagonals and horizontals. Hereafter his paintings became calmer and more pastoral (he moved to the countryside outside New York in 1963), reaching new extremes of loose watery handling and soft exultantly erotic colouring (e.g. *Clam Diggers*, 1964, or *Untitled II*, 1976). Figures shimmer and dissolve into landscape, and landscape merges into gestural rhythm, so that the figurative/abstract polarity has little meaning. Counteracting the elusive immateriality of these images perhaps, de Kooning has more recently been preoccupied with aggressively massed clay sculpture.

If the earlier work synthesized cubist linear discipline and surrealist freedom, this late work can be seen to incorporate the sensuality of Rubens or Boucher, the rich physicality of Courbet, and yet it remains as toughly measured, and free of the rhetoric of Expressionism, as ever. It's arguable that it's the unlikely compass of de Kooning's art, combined with its pressing vitality, each phase a complete renewal, that puts it on a par with Picasso* and Matisse*. And like them, his importance is not as an innovator but as an artist who embodied, to a spectacular degree, an irrepressible inventiveness.

James Faure Walker

See: Harold Rosenberg, 'The Tradition of the New' in *Horizon* 1959 and *William de Kooning* (1974); also *William de Kooning*, exhibition catalogue of the Museum of Modern Art (NY, 1968).

255
KRAUS, Karl 1874–1936

Austrian satirist, journalist and poet

Karl Kraus was born in the small Bohemian town of Jičín to wealthy German Jewish parents. When he was three the family moved to Vienna where Kraus was to spend the rest of his sixty-two years. After a brief period of study at the University and an unsuccessful attempt to make a career as an actor, Kraus turned to journalism. In his early years he wrote on a wide range of topics for an equally wide range of journals in Austria and Germany including Vienna's famous liberal paper, the *Neue Freie Presse*, which, with its editor Moritz Benedikt, was to be a major target of his later campaigns against the corruption of language in a decaying civilization. In 1899 Kraus founded his own periodical, *Die Fackel* ('The Torch'), which he was to edit for the rest of his life. Not only did practically all Kraus's work first appear in its pages but, from 1910 onwards, he wrote every word of the journal himself. *Die Fackel* was the prime medium of Kraus's influence on the cultural life of Vienna during his lifetime and Schoenberg* and Wittgenstein* were among its many admirers. Culturally committed to a tradition of enlightened conservatism which seemed destined to perish in the ideological maelstrom of the new century, Kraus became sympathetic to the Austrian Social Democratic Party after the débâcle of the First World War. Later, though, he transferred his always provisional support to the authoritarian regime of Engelbert Dollfuss as the only possible barrier to the takeover of Austria by Nazi Germany. Hitler's* accession to power in 1933 and the murder of Dollfuss the following year deepened Kraus's pessimism about the prospects for the survival of civilization. Devoted with an almost religious zeal to the preservation of the purity of language from political and journalistic distortion, he recognized the apparent impotence of his struggle. As he wrote in his final poem, written after Hitler's accession to power:

One speaks only in one's sleep.
And dreams of a sun which used to laugh.
It passes away:
Afterwards it was all the same.
The Word fell asleep, as that world awoke.

Kraus died of heart disease on 12 July 1936 and less than two years later Hitler entered Vienna.

Kraus's main influence, which was to be renewed in the post-war years, has been as a satirist and cultural critic. He once described his goal as 'to pin down the Age between quotation marks'. Indeed, during the First World War, Kraus only escaped imprisonment because of the impossibility of prosecuting successfully a critic of the war whose major weapon was the quotation of the words of its supporters. In his unwieldy masterpiece, the almost unactable play *The Last Days of Mankind* (*Die letzten Tage der Menschheit*, 1922, trans. 1975), the characters are the real historical figures and the words drawn largely from their speeches and writings as reported in the press. J. P. Stern has described the play as 'the most massive indictment of modern war to be found in European literature'. In Kraus's last important work, *The Third Walpurgis Night* (*Die Dritte Walpurgisnacht*), written in the months following Hitler's appointment as Chancellor but not published until 1952, a similar technique of literary collage is employed in an effort to render the fact of evil in the inadequate yet irreplaceable medium of language. Kraus juxtaposes the complex yet lucid style of his own prose with the terrible simplifications of both supporters and opponents of the Nazis. The corruption of language, Kraus held, is both the mark and the medium of the degradation of man and society to a state of savagery, and the bitterness of his attacks on so many of his contemporaries among writers and journalists reflects their alleged responsibility for the terrible course of events.

In his work and person Kraus seems to symbolize the resistance of an admirable Central European culture from which we derive so much of our own cultural identity. The Vienna of Karl Kraus was the city of Freud*, Wittgenstein, Schoenberg. That it was also the city of Adolf Hitler strikingly underlines the vulnerability of the foundations on which civilization rests.

David J. Levy

Karl Kraus's works have been published in twelve volumes in German (1952–64). In English see Frank Field, *The Last Days of Mankind, Karl Kraus and his Vienna* (1967); Erich Heller, *The Disinherited Mind* (1957).

256
KUHN, Thomas Samuel 1922–

US historian and philosopher of science

Born in Cincinnati, USA, Thomas Kuhn set his sights, originally, on a career as scientist, and after taking his degree at Harvard he worked for a time in the Radio Research Laboratory. But life in a large laboratory fell far short of his youthful idea of a research career. He was hampered on the one side by intellectual constraints, on the other side by social pressures. Professional science was more frustrating, less interesting than he had imagined. He escaped, becoming a junior fellow of Harvard in 1948, and a member of the Faculty of the History of Science in 1951. By 1961 he was a Professor in the History of Science at Berkeley, and in 1964 he moved to a similar chair at Princeton.

The fruit of his years of research and reflection on the role of science in the development of human cognition was his book *The Structure of Scientific Revolutions* published in 1962. It was an intellectual *tour de force*; a new voice; a new viewpoint on science at once unique,

wide-ranging and devastatingly near the truth. Although it is a book 'about' science, rather than 'of' science, it has probably done as much to colour our awareness of the meaning of science as any single scientific event in the post-war period.

Until Kuhn produced his essay, it was customary for philosophers and historians to treat the development of science with a certain amount of idealization. Science, it was agreed, represented a systematic attempt to marshal rational thought and purposive experiment to the task of understanding the physical and the biological. It was natural, therefore, to think of science as itself being a systematically rational enterprise. But Kuhn showed that, when examined in detail, step-by-step, science was a far less rational exercise than had previously been supposed. Science and scientific communities, he argued, are as much structured to resist breakthroughs as they are to compel them. Any scientific theory functions as a 'paradigm': a point of view (and a method of analysis based on that point of view) which is thought to be worth following. But why is it thought to be worth following? On what grounds does the credibility of a particular paradigm ultimately rest? The official, pre-Kuhnian view was that credibility rested on the balancing of empirical evidence and the fielding of logical argument. But Kuhn showed that, to a surprising extent, the leading paradigms which have been followed in science have not been, initially, very satisfactorily grounded *either* in evidence *or* in deductive argument. They have been, rather, imaginative leaps: hunches, which have given people the feeling 'that something like this must be true'. In a word, scientists have adopted paradigms for reasons which they have been unable fully to render into the public discourse.

Similarly, relationships between scientific schools of thought seem to have been frequently less than satisfactory. Kuhn introduces the idea of the 'incommensurability' of old and new scientific points of view: there is no common ground, he argues, between paradigms. If paradigms were fully rational, there would be such common ground; but as they are not, there is none. And education does not escape Kuhn's witheringly accurate glance. Typically the insights and methods of a particular paradigm are transmitted in the classroom by the primitive pedagogy of 'Do it this way and follow me!'

Nor is the life of science quite what previous theorists thought it was. Kuhn distinguishes 'normal' science from 'revolutionary' science. Normal science, Kuhn suggests, operates in an hierarchical way, defensively, with some complacency. It consists, not in any earth-shattering intellectual adventure, but in the patient application of existing paradigms to new cases, and to new variations of old cases. Most normal science is successful. Most science is normal science.

Kuhn's book, then, has altered the vocabulary, the

perspectives, the frontiers, of our whole conception of science, of science's contribution to knowledge, of science's place in society. Kuhn perceived what previous theorists had overlooked; but it is, in the end, his unique blend of theoretical generalization and historically accurate particularity which creates the total impact. And Kuhn's theory can be applied, with minimum modification, to almost any field.

Kuhn's philosophy of science has the unfortunate characteristic that the more successful it is, the more it creates the pre-conditions for its own reversal. Once it has been widely perceived that science has operated irrationally in the past, the chances that it will continue to do this inevitably diminish. Scientific education is only one area where scientists have tried to remedy the unsatisfactoriness revealed by Kuhn. Some scientific empires (e.g. Barrow's) have been given up without revolution. This does occasionally happen, as it does in the political arena (India, French Africa). And there is mathematics. Kuhn overlooks the Peircean interpretation of mathematics as 'the science of hypothesis', the science whose role is, in effect, to be unimpressed by paradigms.

It is a measure of the importance of Kuhn's thought that it has shaken scientists' belief in their own rationality. Science will never be quite the same again; scientists will be more self-critical; more on their guard against the irrational bewitchments of a paradigm. This is less than satisfying for Kuhn, but healthier for science.

Christopher Ormell

Kuhn's other works include: *The Copernican Revolution: Planetary Astronomy in the Development of Western Thought* (1957); *Sources for the History of Quantum Physics* (1967).

L

257

LACAN, Jacques 1901–

French psychiatrist and psychoanalyst

Lacan published his doctoral thesis on 'Paranoiac psychosis and its relationships with personality' in 1932. He made his entry into the psychoanalytic movement in 1936 with his paper on 'The mirror stage as formative of the function of the I', in which he shows the mediating role of the image of the body in the constitution of the subject. In the 1950s Lacan adopts a public position on analytic theory and practice. His teaching, an activity pursued over many years, up to and including the present time, has taken the form of fortnightly public seminars (still mostly unpublished), conducted on the margins of institutionalized psychiatry. The essential seminar texts, often elliptical and difficult because they expose the work of language, are brought together in *Écrits* (1966, trans. 1977).

Lacan's thinking integrates linguistics (Saussure*, Jakobson*), anthropology (Mauss*, Lévi-Strauss*), symbolic logic (Peirce), set theory and topology (the formal system to which he gives priority in psychoanalysis), and is a contribution to structuralism in the human sciences ('The unconscious is structured as a language'). It aims to return to the seminal experience of Freud* which, it maintains, cannot be overtaken in so far as it opens up the field of the unconscious. This return to Freud seemed necessary because of theoretical and practical distortions such as the active promotion of normative ideals, the idea that the purpose of analysis is to make people happy and well adjusted, the application of techniques for reinforcing the ego, the suggestion that one should try to identify with the 'good object', etc. Lacan strongly protests against the bastardization of Freudian concepts, for example 'transference', wrongly identified with the feelings of the patient, or 'resistance', confused with defensive attitudes. On the other hand, he re-elaborates the fundamental concepts of analysis. A reflection on the status of language, on desire and its interpretation, on the unconscious as the place of the Other, plays a vital part in the orientation of analytic practice, while his interpretation of psychosis as the foreclosure of the Name-of-the-Father is essential to the subsequent development of his conception of the subject. Via a rigorous positioning of the three orders of the 'real', the 'imaginary' and the 'symbolic', he confronts the human sciences with the need to re-examine the philosophical problem of Being and Truth. The work of Lacan also involves a very important dimension of critical reflection on Western culture and its ideology.

Lacan was, in 1953, one of the founders of the Société Française de Psychanalyse at the time when the Société Psychanalytique de Paris was in the grips of a power struggle over the question of the teaching of psychoanalysis. It was once again the crucial question of teaching and the transmission of psychoanalysis which led, in 1963, to the establishment of the École Freudienne de Paris, an association which has aimed to do away with hierarchy in the training of analysts, and laid the emphasis on the search for knowledge (but which Lacan moved in 1980 to dissolve). Lacan has been excommunicated by the International Psychoanalytic Association, but his ideas have their following in many countries.

The work of Lacan is profoundly original and subversive and has left its stamp on the whole theoretical edifice of psychoanalysis. Bearing as it does on literature, philosophy and ideology, it has had a considerable effect on current thinking.

Dr Bernard Lombart and Dr Michel Elias
(Translated by Annwyl Williams)

Other works include: *The Four Fundamental Concepts of Psycho-analysis* (*Les quatre concepts fondamentaux de la psychanalyse*, *Le Séminaire*, Book XI, 1973, trans. 1977); *Le Séminaire*, Book I, *Les Écrits techniques de Freud* ('The technical writings of Freud', 1975); *Le Séminaire*, Book II, *Le Moi dans la théorie de Freud et dans la technique de la psychanalyse* ('The ego in Freudian theory and in the technique of psychoanalysis', 1978).

258

LAING, Ronald David 1927–

British psychiatrist

Born in Glasgow in a three-room tenement, R. D. Laing attended school in that city before going on to read medicine in his local university. He graduated as a doctor in 1951 and spent the next two years in the British Army before returning to Glasgow for three years' further training as a psychiatrist. In 1957 he moved to London and joined the Tavistock Clinic and was director of the Langham Clinic from 1962 to 1965. From 1961 to 1967 he was involved in research into psychiatric disturbance in families with the Tavistock Institute of Human Relations as a Fellow of the Foundations Fund for Research in Psychiatry. In 1964, Laing founded the Philadelphia Association, a registered charity concerned with establishing a network of households where people in extreme mental distress might spend some time without having to undergo orthodox forms of psychiatric treatment. He is currently in private practice as a psychoanalyst.

Ronald Laing burst into prominence with the publication of his first book, *The Divided Self* (1960). In the preface to the first edition, he acknowledge his debt to the phenomenologists Jaspers* and Binswanger and to the existentialists Kierkegaard, Heidegger* and Sartre*. The book set out to demystify madness, break down the divide between the sane and the insane and provide an understanding of so-called 'mad' communication and behaviour. In particular Laing explored the role of the schizophrenic patient as 'outsider', estranged from self and society, and portrayed him as the inventor of a false self with which to cope and keep at bay the outside world and the inner despair. Such a model of madness envisaged schizophrenia as the final state of personal disintegration involving a total 'splitting' between the negated inner 'real' and the external 'false' self.

Laing subsequently wrote *Sanity, Madness and the Family* (1964), with Aaron Esterson, and *The Self and Others* (1961), in which he examined patterns of communications within the families of schizophrenic patients and focused particularly on the potential role of Gregory Bateson's notion of the 'double-blind'. However, it was the publication of *The Politics of Experience/ The Bird of Paradise* (1967) which marked a radical departure in Laing's thinking and elevated him into the role of a guru of the 1960s. In that book, Laing turned from the exploration of individual pathology to social sickness and the human condition in general. A conspiratorial model took shape in which the psychotic patient became both a scapegoat, driven into madness by a mechanistic and dehumanizing world, and a voyager, engaged in a semi-mystical journey of self-exploration, transcendence and growth. The book uncannily reflected ideas and passions prevalent in society at the time and contributed to the bracketing of the psychotic patient with the criminal, the racial outcast and the political dissident in a coalition of oppressed bearers of an authentic statement concerning the human condition. It also became a crucial text in the growing 'anti-psychiatry' movement by virtue of its portrayal of psychiatrists as agents of social control, psychiatric institutions as centres of degradation, and psychiatric

treatment as a process of invalidation and the reestablishment of a state of 'pseudo-sanity'.

Shortly afterwards, Laing went to Ceylon and India to meditate and familiarize himself with Buddhist and Hindu philosophy. His influence within psychiatry has been less extensive than it has outside – the widespread notion of the 'schizophrenogenic' mother driving her offspring mad, epitomized in the film *Family Life* (1971), owed much to Laing and his views on the value of hallucinatory experience were marshalled to support moves to legalize cannabis.

In recent years, Laing has become interested in the experiences of pre-natal life and birth itself and their impact on subsequent development of the person. He has made a film which is highly critical of current obstetrical techniques and practices and his latest book, *The Facts of Life* (1976), explores the notion that in adult life we are haunted by and re-enact our conception, foetal life and birth, the loss of the placenta and cord.

The overall impact of Laing's writings on psychiatry seems likely to be judged in terms of the emphasis he placed on the *experience* of madness at a time when psychiatry was more preoccupied with its *form*. It is his first book which remains a seminal work for its uniquely rich and imaginative exploration of the content of psychopathology.

Anthony W. Clare

Other works: *Reason and Violence* (with David Cooper, 1964); *Interpersonal Perception* (with H. Phillipson and A. R. Lee, 1966); *Knots* (1970); *The Politics of the Family* (1971). See also: Edward Z. Friedenberg, *Laing* (1973); Andrew Collier, *R. D. Laing: The Philosophy and Politics of Psychotherapy* (1977).

259
LAKATOS, Imre 1922–74

Hungarian philosopher

Born in Hungary to the family 'Lipschitz', he changed his name, first to 'Molnar' (with the arrival of the Nazis) and second to 'Lakatos' (with the departure of the Nazis). The second change, it is recounted, was brought about shortly after the war with the discovery of some old shirts bearing the monogram 'I.L.'. He was, by this time, a communist, and by 1947 he had risen to a high position in the Ministry of Education in Budapest. His revisionist views, however, led to his imprisonment for three years from 1950. In 1956 he fled to the West, and after taking a PhD at Cambridge, he joined the staff of the London School of Economics, eventually becoming a professor. He rose to prominence as a philosopher quite quickly, mainly as a result of his vivid series of articles 'Proofs and Refutations'

(1963–4). This was then followed by an equally striking piece of work, his long paper 'Criticism and Methodology of Scientific Research Programmes' (1966). After his death in 1974 two posthumous collections of papers were brought out: *Methodology of Scientific Research Programmes* (1977) and *Methodology of Science and Epistemology* (1977).

The main drift in the philosophy of mathematics before Lakatos was towards increased abstraction, ever greater formalization. Lakatos set the engines in reverse. Instead of looking at the formal genealogy of mathematical *answering*, he turned a spotlight of attention on to the informal genealogy of mathematical *questioning*. We can learn most, he suggested, not by looking at any individual mathematical question, but by looking at the gradual development of a 'line' of mathematical questioning. And when we do this we see that the fruitful development of such a line of questioning depends much more on intuition, heuristic and creativity than had previously been supposed. Seen in retrospect a branch of mathematics appears Olympian, elegant, timeless. But this carefully fostered impression stems from the polished expositions which mathematicians typically produce *after* they have finished the real work. When he is convinced that his results are valid, the mathematician prepares to announce them in the classical voice.

Lakatos did not simply argue his case in abstract terms: he brought the debate to life by embodying the argument in vivid dialogue, re-creating the gradual gestation of some early concepts of combinatorial topology. In this way he is able to show us, at first hand as it were, the yawning gulf between the ascertaining and the expounding of mathematical truth. And this gulf is not simply one of academic interest. By allowing ourselves to be impressed by the finished exposition, we arrive at a systematically misleading concept of mathematics: and because mathematics has so often been a source of pivotal examples in philosophy, logic, education, we are misled in other areas as well.

In general, Lakatos argued, mathematics is much more like the other sciences than had hitherto been supposed. And after 'Proofs and Refutations' he turned his attention increasingly to defend a generally Popperian* view of science against the assaults of Kuhn*, Stephen Toulmin, and others. Relativistic and sociological arguments seemed to imply that established science was no less arbitrary and irrational than discarded science. Was 'scientific rationality', perhaps, an illusion? In the struggle for dominance between rival schools of scientific thought, the claim to 'rationality' could be portrayed as just another rhetorical weapon, wielded equally by both sides.

Lakatos argued that it is the *series* of questions scientists ask (the 'research programme' they adopt) which ought to be our main concern. As scientists try to understand a particular puzzling phenomenon, they develop theories and perform experiments, which they interpret in certain ways; and these have the effect of gradually changing their view of the phenomenon in question. As the view changes, the questions which seem most relevant change too. And it is in this *problem shift*, Lakatos maintains, that we may discern the characteristics of progressive science. Any theory is inevitably in a dynamic relationship with the facts to which it relates. As new facts come to light the exponents of the theory are driven to redefine the questions which it prompts. After a period of time it can be seen that the live questions which are being asked are either relatively *more* interesting questions being asked with confidence, or *less* plausible questions being asked with resignation. This is the difference between – to use Lakatos's terms – a 'progressive' problem shift and a 'degenerating' one. It was rational to discard the theory of 'Caloric' after its problem shift had degenerated beyond recall.

Lakatos's intellectual vitality made him more than a mere academic theoretician: his mercurial mind made him a phenomenon as well. This has laid him open to charges of unsound reasoning; of selecting the evidence; of projecting a past which never did exist. He was not, therefore, always the best advocate of his own ideas. But by his demonstration that it is rational to believe in the rationality of science, he contributed a steadying insight to a perplexing age.

Christopher Ormell

See *Essays in Memory of Imre Lakatos* (1976), and *Mathematics, Science and Epistemology* (1976), reviewed by Nicholas Jardine in *Philosophy*, January 1978.

260

LANG, Fritz 1890–1976

German/US film director

Lang, the most important film director to make a successful transition from the German silent cinema of the 1920s to Hollywood in the 1930s, was born into a bourgeois Catholic family in Vienna in 1890. His early studies in architecture, encouraged by his father, a municipal architect, conflicted with his own interests in the visual arts, particularly the work of Klimt and Schiele, and in 1911–12 he left home to globe-trot before settling in Paris in 1913. Here he scraped a living as a commercial artist and became interested in the new art of the cinema. With the outbreak of the Great War, Lang escaped home to Vienna, where he joined up, was promoted to officer, and was wounded and decorated on more than one occasion. In military hospital he began to write film scenarios – three of them known to have been brought to the screen by Joe May during 1917 – and as an actor came to the attention of Erich Pommer's company Decla, which Lang joined in Berlin in 1919. Here he read and wrote scripts and also did some editing and bit-part acting before moving promptly into direction with *Half-Caste* (1919). In this first year with Decla Lang also directed *The Master of Love*, *Hara-Kiri*, *The Wandering Image* and the two-part adventure melodrama *The Spiders*, his first surviving work of the period. In 1920, rapidly emerging as a major young director, Lang married the writer Thea von Harbou, with whom he was to write the majority of his German films, and who also turned several of their scripts into successful novels. Following *Four Around a Woman* (1920, now lost) Lang directed eight films before fleeing Hitler's* Germany in 1933. Two of these deal with historical fantasy and legend. *Destiny* (1921) tells its stories of lovers separated by the Angel of Death through a triptych of flashbacks – to the Arabian Nights, to Renaissance Venice, and to Imperial China – while an epic German version of *The Niebelungen* is retold in Lang's two-part film, *Siegfried* and *Kriemhild's Revenge* (1924). Two of Lang's silent films of the 1920s deal on the other hand with futuristic fantasy in the science fiction genre. The spectacular and costly *Metropolis* (1926) recounts the story of a workers' revolt in a visionary city of the future, while *Woman On the Moon* (1928) presents a comic-strip account of a rocket trip to prospect for lunar gold. The other four films of the period draw from the contemporary world of criminality and post-war *angst*. The two parts of *Dr Mabuse* – *Dr Mabuse the Gambler: A Picture of the Times* and *Inferno: Men of the Times* (1922) – enact the exploits of an unscrupulous master criminal with skills in hypnotism and disguise. His talents are later transferred to his psychiatrist in *The Last Will of Dr Mabuse* (1932–3). Lang's other two chief criminals of the period are the master spy in *The Spy* (1928), and the pathetic child-murderer hunted down by both police and criminals in Lang's first sound-film, *M* (1931).

The Last Will of Dr Mabuse, drawing links between criminality, dictatorship and mind-control, was immediately banned by Goebbels, but Lang was none the less offered charge of the Nazi film industry on the basis of Hitler's admiration for *Metropolis*. Fleeing overnight to Paris, Lang was once more hired by fellow émigré Pommer, now with Fox, to make his only French film, *Liliom* (1933), a tragi-comic fantasy of fairground life starring Charles Boyer. Espoused to National Socialism, however, Thea von Harbou remained in Germany, and divorced Lang. After *Liliom* Lang joined the central European exodus to the United States, where he joined MGM. Here, on the basis of sophisticated work in the popular genres, he was rapidly to become established as one of the leading Hollywood directors and as one of the key *auteurs* discovered by emerging generations of film critics in the 1950s and 1960s in America and Europe.

The bulk of Lang's twenty-two Hollywood films are crime thrillers. These commence with the anti-lynching drama of his first American film, *Fury* (1936), and his drama of the consequences of wrongful conviction, *You Only Live Once* (1937), and then re-emerge in the middle and later 1940s with his celebrated murder dramas in the *film noir* style, full of narrative and visual panache and complexity and frequently reworking some of his German themes such as the 'guilty innocent' and the *femme fatale*: *The Woman in the Window* (1944), *Scarlet Street* (1945), *Secret Beyond the Door* (1948), *House by the River* (1949), *The Blue Gardenia* (1952), *The Big Heat* (1953), *Human Desire* (1954), *While the City Sleeps* (1955) and *Beyond a Reasonable Doubt* (1956).

In the 1940s Lang also directed a group of films dealing with the experience of war – *Man Hunt* (1941), from Geoffrey Household's novel *Rogue Male*, *Hangmen Also Die* (1943), co-written with Brecht*, a version of Greene's* novel *Ministry of Fear* (1941), *Cloak and Dagger* (1946), and *An American Guerilla in the Philippines* (1950). He made only three westerns – *The Return of Frank James* (1940), *Western Union* (1941) and *Rancho Notorious* (1952). His more off-beat work in Hollywood included the anti-realist musical romance with music by Weill*, *You and Me* (1938), his version of Odets's* fishing melodrama, *Clash by Night* (1951), and *Moonfleet* (1955), a smuggling yarn set in Britain, his first film in cinemascope and one of his rare films in colour. Lang's career as a director ended, as it had begun, in Germany, and consisted of a return to some of his early German themes. *The Indian Tomb* (1958) remade the two films written by Lang for Joe May in the early 1920s – *The Tiger of Bengal* and *The Indian Tomb* itself. His last film, *The Thousand Eyes of Dr Mabuse* (1960), similarly, extends the 1920s Mabuse theme to the contemporary world of industrial intrigue. In 1963, signalling his importance for film-makers of the new European cinema, the patriarchal Lang appears as himself in Godard's* film industry love-tragedy, *Contempt*.

Philip Drummond

See: Siegfried Kracauer, *From Caligari to Hitler* (1947); Peter Bogdanovich, *Fritz Lang in America* (1967); Paul M. Jensen, *The Cinema of Fritz Lang* (1969); Lotte H. Eisner, *Fritz Lang* (1976); Steve Jenkins ed., *Fritz Lang* (forthcoming).

261

LARKIN, Philip 1922–

English poet

Poet and novelist, born in Coventry, educated at St John's College, Oxford (Robert Graves's* old college) – in a generation *mirabilis* that included also John Wain and Kingsley Amis* – who has deliberately embraced an ordinary, provincial life (working as a university librarian in Belfast, then in Hull) and cultivated a principled provincialism of outlook and practice in his writing. His two novels, *Jill* (1946, rev. 1964, written in 1943–4 when he was only twenty-one) and *A Girl in Winter* (1947), both rightly rejected by their author as juvenilia, are of little interest now except as early indicators of Larkin's sense of the provincial self (*Jill* is about a northern working-class boy up at Oxford) and of the stimulus the bleaker, wintrier aspects of English life grant him. The poems of *The North Ship* (1945), a juvenile *mélange* now almost as toughly denigrated by their author as his novels, indicate rather more clearly Larkin's maturer direction. For among the soothing echoes of the earlier W. B. Yeats* and odd hints of a young poet too overpowered by Dylan Thomas* there appear clearly the formal polishings of Robert Graves and the adjectival precisions that come from having attended carefully to W. H. Auden*:

Who can confront
The instantaneous grief of being alone?
Or watch the sad increase
Across the mind of this prolific plant,
Dumb idleness?

Larkin's emerging personal voice, however, only achieved its complete definition much later, with *The Less Deceived* (October 1955) and *The Whitsun Weddings* (1964). Larkin lacks, of course, the prolific output frequently associated with major poets, and there is a marked levelling-out in his *High Windows* volume (1974), but *The Less Deceived* and *The Whitsun Weddings* poems have already achieved for him a central, even *the* central position, among English poets of the middle twentieth century.

Larkin's mature style is consciously in an English tradition. His poetry was considerably inspirited by his discovery (he dates it 1946) of Thomas Hardy's poetry, his realization of the possibilities of the best Georgian poets, particularly (though no doubt Georgianism was also filtered through Graves and Empson*) Edward Thomas. Larkin has rejected influences from overseas. He points to the failure of authors who 'change countries' ('Look at Auden'). He believes the styles and fashions imported and popularized by Pound* and Eliot* to be regrettable intrusions into the English tradition. Modernism of all kinds – in painting and music as well as in literature – he rejects (see his volume of jazz reviews, *All What Jazz*, 1970, whose Introduction is his major anti-modernist tract). He blames the academic industry of literary study for supporting much pretentious literary and critical nonsense (see, e.g., 'Posterity' in *High Windows*).

Larkin has been accused of standing for the impoverished achievement, the cowardly practice of a retreat-

ing islanded minimalism. His *Oxford Book of Twentieth-Century English Verse* (1973), with its carefully garnered harvest of the provincial and minor, its large welcome to the likes of Hardy, Betjeman*, and Walter de la Mare, was seized on to illustrate the meagreness of his stand. Admittedly, Larkin's modernist targets are the very largest ones ('whether . . . Parker*, Pound or Picasso*: it helps us neither to enjoy nor endure'). Granted, too, that the pervasive negativism so frequently noticed by his readers (his fondness, for example, for words beginning with *un-*, *in-* and *dis-*) settled in *High Windows* into a sometimes dismaying drizzle of envious (?) hostility towards the young and freer ('They fuck you up, your mum and dad'; 'Sexual intercourse began/In nineteen sixty-three/(Which was rather late for me)'). But the gains for his poetry purchased by Larkin's dedicated hostility to the modernistic macrocosm are impressively positive. He has become the laureate of the common bloke, the unheroic man in bicycle clips (see 'Church Going' in *The Less Deceived*), the quiet narrator of life in back-street digs on Saturday afternoons as seen from the railway train ('An Odeon went past, a cooling tower,/And someone running up to bowl': lines from 'The Whitsun Weddings' sometimes hailed as the essence of the so-called 'Movement' of the 1950s), the voice of the ordinary chap who would rather stay at home, listen to his Sidney Bechet records and ponder death (see 'Vers de Société' in *High Windows*). 'I love the commonplace,' he has said, 'I lead a very commonplace life. Everyday things are lovely to me.' This means accepting ordinariness – the truth of 'a real girl in a real place' that he celebrates in 'Lines Upon A Young Lady's Photograph Album' (*The Less Deceived*). It entails paying attention to the vernacular of 'Mr Bleaney' and his landlady (*The Whitsun Weddings*), to people who like bottled sauce, do the football-pools, go to Frinton in the summer and have sisters in Stoke. It's an impressive refusing not to face our common mortality (see, e.g., 'Dockery and Son' in *The Whitsun Weddings*). And its success depends on a lovingly close regard (and Larkin has written some very fine love-poems) for the intransigent stuff of the day-to-day – a quotidian reality that Larkin's language constantly animates as it unflaggingly presents us with toughly bitten-off metonymic gobbets of it for our continual delight and illumination.

Valentine Cunningham

See: *Phoenix: A Poetry Magazine*, Nos 11/12, Autumn and Winter 1973/4: Philip Larkin issue; David Timms, *Philip Larkin* (1974); Blake Morrison, *The Movement* (1980).

262

LASKI, Harold 1893–1950

English political theorist and publicist

Laski was born into a wealthy, orthodox Jewish family in the Manchester cotton industry, and showed early courage in marrying at the age of eighteen a gentile eight years older than himself. Their families disowned them. He began studying Eugenics at Oxford but then changed to History. Rejected for military service in 1914, he got a job at McGill University in Montreal, going to Harvard in 1916 where he remained until public and faculty opinion turned against him violently for public statements he made in support of the Boston police strike of 1920. Such controversies became the mark of the man.

While at Harvard his first book was published, *Studies in the History of Sovereignty* (1919); and thereafter he wrote a book nearly every year, as well as a stream of academic and popular articles. His first books, all conceived at Harvard, are commonly acknowledged to be his best and most scholarly, all turning on a criticism of the traditional theory of sovereignty. Laski, while stopping short of syndicalism or of Guild Socialism (like his contemporary G. D. H. Cole), held that all power is essentially plural. He saw 'the state' as a body co-ordinating corporations, such as churches once were and trades unions and political parties are now. On returning to England he taught at the London School of Economics, perhaps the most famous figure of its great, inter-war generation. His fame and facility as a lecturer and teacher soon outstripped his reputation as a writer.

As a writer, he was rhetorical and repetitive; and as a thinker, eclectic rather than original. He took his views on liberty from Mill, the idea of the general will from Rousseau and T. H. Green, the idea of corporatism from Figgis, and theories of class dominance from Marx. The amalgam was more convincing polemically than philosophically. His *Grammar of Politics* (1925) was, in many subsequent editions, his most widely read book. In it 'liberty' began as 'the absence of those conditions in the modern state that prevent me from becoming myself at my best' but ended as 'the existence of those conditions without which I cannot become myself at my best', a quite unexplained switch from a negative to a positive theory. His political activities were many, bringing him into public dispute with Sir William Beveridge, Director of the LSE, but earning him the affection, almost the idolization, of many students. His influence on the immediately pre- and post-war generation of Indian, Chinese and African nationalist students in London in incalculable. He was chairman of the Labour Party in 1945, and his view of the importance of the office was famously attacked by Sir Winston Churchill and as famously rejected by

Clement Attlee. He lost an unwise libel action, in which he claimed that newspapers had said that he advocated violent revolution rather than that he had warned it was unlikely that the British ruling classes would allow themselves to be expropriated by parliamentary means. Never in good health, he wore himself out campaigning in the 1950 General Election: a scholar in political harness, a once famous and now neglected figure.

Professor Bernard Crick

Other works by Laski include: *Political Thought in England: Locke to Bentham* (1920); *The Rise of European Liberalism* (1936); *Liberty in the Modern State*, Pelican edn (1937); and *Faith, Reason and Civilization* (1944). See also: Kingsley Martin, *Harold Laski: a Biographical Memoir* (1953); Herbert Deane, *Political Ideas of Harold J. Laski* (1955).

263

LAWRENCE, David Herbert 1885–1930

English novelist, poet and playwright

The reputation of D. H. Lawrence has suffered many vicissitudes but he is now placed among the greatest English writers. Condemned as a reactionary in the Marxizing 1930s, he became a major influence on English writing during the regionalist revival of the 1950s, largely on the strength of his third novel, *Sons and Lovers* (1913). This therapeutic venture into psychological realism, admired now for its exploration of adolescent sexuality, vivid dramatization of family conflicts (influenced by Freud*), the scrupulous authenticity of its local colour (the mining country of Nottinghamshire and Derbyshire where Lawrence grew up), and the new intensity it imparted to the genre of the *Bildungsroman*, earned Lawrence abuse as well as praise from his contemporaries, whose repeated accusations of 'formlessness' derived, as Lawrence well knew, from class resentment and sexual prudery. Much rewritten and in many places painfully confessional, *Sons and Lovers* is the record of a personal struggle between the son and the (bourgeois) mother and (working-class) father in a style which Lawrence himself criticized almost immediately as 'hard and violent' and 'full of sensation and presentation', no doubt referring in this way to the moral over-determination of certain episodes. The novel represented, however, a major artistic and personal breakthrough for its author, being much less self-consciously literary than his two earlier novels, *The White Peacock* (1911), a technically insecure work, the main interest of which lies in the way it prefigures the key motifs of his last novel, *Lady Chatterley's Lover*, and *The Trespasser* (1912), a Wagnerian mythological romance with a Dostoevskian finale, the product of an intense artistic sensibility working with second-hand materials.

Only when Lawrence had exorcized the 'cultured' mother and come to terms with his psychological problem, which he was able to do in *Sons and Lovers* with the help of Frieda, wife of his German tutor at Nottingham University College, with whom he eloped in 1912, could he mature as man and artist. A prolific poet, influenced by Whitman and praised by Pound* for his 'modernity' of image and movement, Lawrence, whose poems were very personal right up to the posthumous *Ship of Death* (1933) recorded his sense of liberation in the significantly entitled collection *Look! We have come through!* (1917), his third volume of verse. This maturation coincided with the First World War and a growing sense of disintegration and disorientation in European civilization. In 1913 he began writing *The Sisters*, a work of epic proportions charting the evolution of a family generation by generation from a mythic Genesis to an Apocalypse corresponding more or less with the war. In the first part of this work, *The Rainbow* (published in 1915 and suppressed at once as immoral on sexual and political grounds), Lawrence builds up a massive cyclical interpretation of history in which the organic rhythms of the life of a farming family within a rooted community are shown responding and reacting to the pressures of industrialization, with a consequent intensification, atomization, and individuation of consciousness as well as growing ideological conflicts. The emergence of a recognizably 'modern' (i.e. sharply individuated and explicit) expression of sexual desire and sexual anxiety, the search for a sexual identity, embodied above all in the novel's ultimate protagonist and heroine, Ursula, are accompanied by experimentation in the presentation of character which Lawrence, in a famous letter of 1914, compared to the techniques of the Italian Futurist poets and painters. F. R. Leavis's* high praise of the novel helped to establish it as a classic in direct relation to the English 'great tradition'; but it has more in common with Emily Brontë than with George Eliot and should in any case be read in relation to its 'sequel' (the continuation of the projected *Sisters* novel) *Women in Love* (1921), in which the intricately woven 'rainbow' of history and myth is unwoven, painfully and obsessively, and discontinuous, fragmentary, imagistic 'illuminations' take the place of God's covenantal bow in the clouds as the correlatives of modern consciousness, if and when this elusive entity can be discovered. The moralized landscapes of Lawrence's earlier work have receded (there are apocalyptic visions instead), together with *The Rainbow*'s apparatus of Victorian interpretation explicitly derived from Ruskin and others, though the quest for the sources of life, especially in the characters of Ursula (recognizably continuous with the Ursula of *The Rainbow*) and Birkin (a new, deliberately intermittent and 'unfinished' character) persists.

Through Birkin's anguished and self-contradictory scrutinizing of himself and others, and his complex theory of the two rivers, of 'life' and of 'dissolution', a 'polarization' of male and female principles is advanced as the antidote to the neurosis of the modern world.

As Keith Sagar has remarked, marriage might seem to have been the end of the quest, and many critics have taken this to be the case: but the novel itself makes this reading impossible, as do those which follow. Virtually an exile, Lawrence gave his wanderings literary form in a sequence of works (novels, short stores, travel writing, poetry) which constitute a loose synthesis of genres: journalistic commentary and travelogue go arm-in-arm with political philosophy and poetic descriptive writing, while through the whole runs a bitterly satirical note, often (as in *Women in Love*) implicating living persons. Italy engendered *Aaron's Rod* (1922), Australia *Kangaroo* (1923), and Mexico *The Plumed Serpent* (1926). Seldom have geographical exploration and literary improvisation gone so closely together. In the course of this 'third' phase of his career Lawrence returned to painting, the rudiments of which he had mastered as a boy and which he often wrote about, brilliantly if idiosyncratically. He regarded his own paintings as improvisations; influenced by Cézanne, whom Lawrence greatly admired and tried to 'rescue' from English art historians in his *Introduction to these Paintings*, they celebrate, in bold colours and forms, what Lawrence liked to call the 'phallic', which might be understood as a veneration for sexual desire and sexual tenderness liberated from dictatorial will.

Lawrence's last novel, *Lady Chatterley's Lover*, unpublishable in England during Lawrence's lifetime, is wholly shaped by the 'phallic' faith of the now impotent and ill Lawrence (the rejected title of his late story 'The Man who Died', which was originally 'The Escaped Cock', makes explicit the connection between resurrection and the phallus). All three versions of the text are characterized by an intense eroticism (though Lawrence himself characteristically eschewed this word). In the later rewritings, however, the political and naturalistic elements of the earlier are restructured as myth and symbol in close touch with folklore and fairy-tale. W. B. Yeats* spoke of the use of dialect by the aristocratic lady and her gamekeeper lover (a device related to the use of the infamous 'four letter words') as 'a forlorn poetry uniting their solitudes, something ancient, humble, and terrible'. The national scandal of the prosecution of Penguin Books in 1960 for finally publishing the uncensored text in England was a major cultural event. *Lady Chatterley*'s victory signalled a new 'permissiveness' in life and letters and for a time Lawrence became a cult hero of sexual liberation. This misrepresents him to the extent that the context of Lawrence's phallic religion is an apocalyptic radical Puritanism (Bunyan and Blake are among his forebears), and the apocalyptic eroticism of

Lady Chatterley's Lover, which defied literary and moral convention, is consistent with Lawrence's essentially religious veneration for the act of love as the core of what, for want of a better word, he called 'Life'.

Lawrence's output was as large as it was diverse. His short stories alone would have commanded a reputation. In recent years increased attention to his writings on art and his paintings, his plays (very effectively staged), his poetry, his very distinguished literary criticism, as well as the philosophizing he self-deprecatingly called 'pollyanalytics', has gone hand-in-hand with a new awareness of the dominant place he occupies in what is now called Modernism. The immensely rich and complex *Women in Love*, for example, now looks no less impressive and central in its way than Joyce's* *Ulysses*.

G. M. Hyde

Lawrence's other works include: Novels: *The Lost Girl* (1920); *St Mawr* (1925); and *The Virgin and the Gypsy* (1930). Short stories: *The Prussian Officer and Other Stories* (1914); *England, My England and Other Stories* (1922); *The Ladybird* (1923); *The Woman Who Rode Away and Other Stories* (1928). *The Collected Poems* (2 vols) were published in 1964. His *Letters* (ed. Aldous Huxley, 1932, and again in 2 vols by Harry T. Moore, 1962) are indispensable. Critical studies include: F. R. Leavis, *D. H. Lawrence: Novelist* (1955); Graham Hough, *The Dark Sun* (1956); Julian Moynahan, *The Deed of Life* (1963); H. M. Daleski, *The Forked Flame* (1965); George H. Ford, *Double Measure* (1965); Keith Sagar, *The Art of D. H. Lawrence* (1966); Colin Clarke, *River of Dissolution* (1969); Frank Kermode, *Lawrence* (1973). The standard biography is Harry T. Moore, *The Priest of Love* (1975), although the earlier three-volume *D. H. Lawrence: A Composite Biography* (1957–9) remains important.

264
LAWRENCE, Thomas Edward 1888–1935

Anglo-Irish author and adventurer

Best known as 'Lawrence of Arabia', what first drew T. E. Lawrence to the East was an interest in the past world of romance and archaeology. As the illegitimate son of an impoverished Anglo-Irish Baronet, the present world was unattractive. He studied at Oxford High School and at Jesus College, Oxford, where he read History. His interests were turned towards the Middle East by the Curator of the Ashmolean Museum, and, partly through a thesis on *Crusader Castles* (1936), for which he gathered material in 1909 while walking through Syria, he took a first-class degree. He then worked for several years on an archaeological site at Carchemish, finding time in January 1914 to spy for Britain in Sinai. During the First World War his knowledge of the Arab world led to his employment by British Intelligence in Cairo. He hoped that the Arabs would find freedom from Turkish rule within the British Empire, and when in 1916 the Arab Revolt began, Lawrence was soon established as official liaison officer attached to Prince Faisal.

As he won Faisal's confidence and respect Lawrence began to take an active part in guiding and directing Arab policy. He encouraged guerilla activities against the Hejaz railway, and the capture of Akaba, a port on the Red Sea, in July 1917 was a major success. In January 1918 he helped an Arab group to defeat some Turks at Tafileh; and in October he organized the civil Arab administration which took effective control of Damascus after the Turks had fled.

The Allies had made many conflicting promises, and Lawrence's attempt at the Paris Peace Conference to see that only those most favourable to the Arabs should be honoured ended in failure. Feeling that his role had been fraudulent, he began writing his powerful but often self-accusing *Seven Pillars of Wisdom* (1935), while in London he was glamorized as 'Lawrence of Arabia' in a series of popular lectures.

Diplomatic success as Churchill's adviser at the Colonial Office came too late to avert mental breakdown. By 1922 there were secure Arab governments in Transjordan and Iraq; but Lawrence, brooding upon his 'guilt', his illegitimacy, and upon a homosexual assault suffered during the war at Deraa, sought refuge as John Hume Ross in the Royal Air Force. His mental state improved, but deteriorated sharply when, in 1923, his identity was revealed by the Press and he was discharged from the service. As T. E. Shaw he joined the Tank Corps, where, to expiate his guilt, and to indulge in masochism, he arranged for a fellow recruit to birch him. After threats of suicide he was allowed to rejoin the RAF in 1925. He regained his mental balance and for ten years led a useful life, helping to develop fast launches, initiating service reforms, writing an account of life as a recruit in *The Mint* (1955), and translating the *Odyssey* (1932).

He died after a road accident in May 1935.

Richard Perceval Graves

The Letters of T. E. Lawrence, ed. David Garnett (1938); *The Home Letters of T. E. Lawrence and his Brothers*, ed. M. R. Lawrence (1954); *T. E. Lawrence by his Friends*, ed. A. W. Lawrence (1937); John E. Mack, *A Prince of our Disorder* (1976); Richard Perceval Graves, *Lawrence of Arabia and his World* (1976). Richard Aldington's *Lawrence of Arabia: A Biographical Enquiry* (1955) is the best known of several accounts that are hostile to their subject.

265

LAXNESS, Halldór 1902–

Icelandic writer

Nobel Prize Winner of 1955, Halldór Gudjónsson, although born in Reykjavik, grew up on the farm of Laxnes, a few miles to the north-east of the capital, and it was from this place that he later took his professional name. In the rural surroundings he imbibed the rich Icelandic traditions of song, folk-tale and saga, displaying from an early age an almost fanatical bent for writing. One of the most varied novelists of modern times, Laxness's achievement is as complex as it is ambiguous: determined to engage in issues broader than those provided by his Icelandic birth, he has none the less retained a loyalty to the culture of his country. Where a lesser writer would have fallen between two stools, Laxness has triumphed on both: in his writings local and international concerns serve to illustrate, not to inhibit, each other.

When his father died in 1919, Laxness broke off his schooling at Reykjavik High School and travelled abroad for the first time. Long periods in Europe exposed him to the gloomy post-war conditions there, and a sense of crisis, both general and personal, induced him to enter a Benedictine Monastery in the Grand Duchy of Luxembourg, in 1922. His intentions of taking holy orders, however, were never realized, as his religious inclinations were replaced by a thoroughgoing secularism. His literary breakthrough, *Vefarinn mikli frá Kasmír* ('The Great Weaver from Kashmir', 1927), forcing a complete breach with Icelandic literary tradition, involved the reader in provocative and paradoxical discussions of religion, society, woman, marriage and sexuality. This was followed by a period (1927–9) in the United States, which produced a book of essays (*Althýdubókin*, 'The Book of the People', 1929) characterized by an undogmatic socialism, marking a decisive readjustment in Laxness's interests towards social problems. His American experience also made him intensely aware of his own nationality, and of a fundamental solidarity with one of the smallest nations of the world. From then on he devoted himself as an author to his own people. Three novels, published in the 1930s, were a splendid fulfilment of this programme: *Salka Valka* (1931–2, trans. 1936), dealing with the life of a fishing village and the fate of a poor fishergirl in a time of social change; *Independent People* (*Sjálfstaett fólk*, 1934–5, trans. 1946), a monumental picture of a small farmer and his heroic battle for independence; and the tetralogy *World Light* (*Heimsljós*, 1937–40, trans. 1969), the story of a parish pauper and folk-poet. Each of these works attracted considerable controversy as they offered a critique of Icelandic society from a deliberately socialist viewpoint. The satire, however, is leavened by a strong sense of humour, the realism heightened into an imaginative and symbolic vision. Critics were probably influenced by two journeys Laxness made to the Soviet Union, and accounts of his travels he published at the time. In any case they were largely appeased by the trilogy *Íslandsklukkan* ('Iceland's Bell', 1943–6), a historical fresco of Icelandic life in and around the year 1700, a work that, coinciding with Iceland's secession from Denmark in 1944, firmly established its author as the national voice.

Even so, his patriotism remained critical, and *The Atom Station* (*Atómstödin*, 1948, trans. 1961) evoked all the former antagonism. Overtly a fierce attack on the politicians for allowing American military installations to be built in Iceland, it provided a brilliant study of the collapse of customary standards in the face of international politics and strategy. With *The Happy Warriors* (*Gerpla*, trans. 1958), Laxness once again turned to history, on this occasion to the remote past of the sagas, amalgamating the saga of the Norwegian King Ólafr Haraldsson (d. 1030) with a somewhat peculiar specimen of the Family sagas. In an archaizing language of his own stamp Laxness satirized caustically the Old Norse heroic ideal, while paying tribute to the art that embodied it.

In a book of memoirs, *Skáldatími* ('A Writer's Schooling', 1963) Laxness looked back on his early travels and dissociated himself emphatically from his communist ideals, claiming that Marx had only served to 'cripple the language of my youth'. His later fiction reflected his changed attitudes, in their style as well as their ideology. *The Fish Can Sing* (*Brekkukotsannáll*, 1957, trans. 1966), *Paradise Reclaimed* (*Paradísarheimt*, 1960, trans. 1962), *Christianity at Glacier* (*Kristnihald undir Jökli*, 1968, trans. 1972), *Innansveitarkronika* ('A Parish Chronicle', 1970) and *Gudsgjafathula* ('A Tale of God's Gifts', 1972) are told in a calm and detached 'chronicle' manner in which social criticism is no longer based on a formal concept of class struggle, but on a generalized distaste for the negative aspects of contemporary life. In particular the people of his youth are remembered for their calmness, generosity and moral integrity. There is an element of nostalgia in this, but it signals an unpretentious and undogmatic humanism.

Peter Hallberg

Laxness has described his childhood and youth in other books of memoirs *Í túninu heima* ('On the Grounds at Home', 1975) and *Úngur eg var* ('Young I was', 1976). His many other works include plays, poems, short stories and essays, and he has edited several Icelandic sagas. For a bibliography, see Haraldur Sigurdsson, in *Árbók Landsbókasafns*, 1971 (Year-book of the National Library, Reykjavik). See also: Peter Hallberg, *Halldór Laxness* (New York 1971).

266
LEACH, Edmund Ronald 1910–

British anthropologist

Sir Edmund Leach was born in 1910 and educated at Marlborough and at Cambridge, where he read Engineering. He worked briefly in China, then returned to England to study anthropology under Malinowski* at the London School of Economics. A short field-study in Kurdistan in 1938 resulted in a slight monograph which, however, foreshadowed his concern with the constancy of change and flux. In 1939 he travelled to Burma to study the Kachin. Caught up in the war, he served with Kachin irregulars until 1945. His field notes were lost, but combining his field experiences with the study of secondary sources he wrote a doctoral thesis, later published in revised form as *Political Systems of Highland Burma* (1954), by common consent his masterpiece. A later field-study in Sri Lanka provided the basis for a second major study, *Pul Eliya* (1961). At some stage in the 1950s Leach came under the influence of Lévi-Strauss's* work (which incidentally provided a new model of Kachin social organization). He was one of the first and perhaps the most important critics and interpreters of the new structuralist movement, contributing important analyses in his own right.

Leach always enjoyed challenge and controversy, and tried, perhaps not altogether successfully, to shock the British bourgeoisie in his pro-youth, pro-machine and anti-God Reith lectures, *A Runaway World?* (1968). A serious atheist, he was for some time president of the Humanist Association. His polemical and critical posture within the discipline was a source of constant stimulation and controversy, and can in part be recaptured through a reading of his collection of essays, *Rethinking Anthropology* (1961).

Leach held teaching positions at the LSE (1947–53) and Cambridge (1953–78), where he became Provost of King's College and was responsible for the admission of women and the abolition of High Table. In 1972 he was created Professor by personal title and elected to the British Academy, and in 1975 he was knighted.

Leach's two major monographs, on the Kachin and on the Sinhalese village he calls 'Pul Eliya', were presented as challenges to the sociological mood of British social anthropology represented by Radcliffe-Brown* and his followers. Leach felt that they took too positivistic and static a view of the shifting and unsystematic flow of social relations, and too mechanistic a view of ritual and ideology. Social order was rooted in the ecological realities, which endured and imposed themselves upon the actors; and in the ideological or ritual language in which the actors struggled to make sense of whatever actual arrangements they were constrained to form with one another. The actors, constrained by material factors but not by ritual or ideology, com-

petitively pursued their basic interests, these being variously and never closely defined. The language of ritual permitted them to explain themselves to themselves.

Developing these ideas partly as a series of polemics against the Radcliffe-Brown school of thought, Leach was not always consistent or even entirely coherent as a theorist; but he was usually suggestive, original and stimulating. The analysis of the interplay of lions and foxes, *gumlao* and *gumsa*, anarchy and state, among the Kachin has proved to have repercussions for our understanding of a whole series of political societies. A related essay on the political implications of Kachin marriage provided a vital rider to Lévi-Strauss's alliance theory and a model for numerous analyses by others.

In his later work Leach has been dominantly concerned with explaining, criticizing and adapting Lévi-Strauss's theories of classification and of myth. Despite Lévi-Strauss's own methodological reservations, Leach produced several analyses of biblical episodes which have been influential. Never an easy follower, Leach and Lévi-Strauss were often critical of each other; but despite various disclaimers, Leach is today not inappropriately generally labelled a structuralist.

This protean, energetic and idealistic man increasingly came to dominate British social anthropology in the 1970s, becoming both intellectually and institutionally recognized as the leader of the profession. His outstanding students include such important senior figures as Fredrik Barth, Nur Yalman and S. J. Tambiah, as well as several of the ablest younger anthropologists.

Professor Adam Kuper

See also: *Genesis as Myth* (1970); his characteristically impatient *Lévi-Strauss* (1970); and *Culture and Communication* (1976) which provides an introduction to structuralist analysis in social anthropology. A discussion of his career and contribution is to be found in Adam Kuper, *Anthropologists and Anthropology* (1975).

267
LEARY, Timothy 1920–

US cult figure

Born in Springfield, Massachusetts, Leary rejected the parental insistence of being trained at West Point military academy, studied psychology in the University of California at Berkeley, served in an army hospital in the Second World War, became assistant professor of psychology at the San Francisco School of Medicine, and finally lectured in psychology at Harvard University. While working in the Center for Research in Personality, Harvard sacked him in 1963; the faculty discovered he had become the leader of a group of researchers and volunteers working with psilocybin, a chemical derived from a mushroom sacred for many centuries to certain Amerindians. Leary had taken the mushroom at the behest of a University of New Mexico scientist at Cuernavaca in 1960, and the experience changed his attitudes towards consciousness and religion. Then he began to concentrate research on the uses of lysergic acid (LSD), and other drugs, towards forms of expanded consciousness, psychedelic experience, and religious illumination. During the 1960s Leary became one of the most powerful influences on American youth, particularly those of the campuses deeply engaged in critical action against the official imperial and domestic wars into which they had grown up. Leary's psychedelic messianism became part of American cultic life, contributing strongly to the breaking up of fixed inherited patterns of life. In the mid-1960s, the LSD 'trip' was featured in every newspaper and magazine. In 1963, *Esquire* ran an article on the work of Leary and Richard Alpert at Harvard, quoting the former's beliefs that drugs provided the consumer with 'transcendence of space-time, of subject-object relations, and the ego or identity'; they are 'mental vitamins, or mental health foods'. The first issue of the *Psychedelic Review*, organ of the International Foundation for Internal Freedom, appeared the same year, and Leary's Center was investigated by the Food and Drug Administration. *Playboy* magazine published a panel discussion on the issues, whose members included William Burroughs*, Leslie Fiedler, Alan Watts and Harry J. Anslinger, for thirty-three years commissioner of the Bureau of Narcotics. By 1966, two thousand people could pack a New York theatre for Leary's 'Psychedelic Celebration No. 1', presented by the League for Spiritual Discovery, at the same time as Leary's centre at Millbank, New York, had been raided and the subsequent charges dismissed. In his 'Death of the Mind Service', Leary preached 'the biochemistry', of the body bringing about 'a state of grace', and followed this up with 'The Reincarnation of Jesus Christ' and an 'LSD Mass', a performance in which he proclaimed, 'I am here to lead the broken-hearted', and so on, in Christ-like style. This same year he told a Senate subcommittee on juvenile delinquency that the use of LSD had run out of control, that a third of the nation's college students were experimenting with it. His slogan 'Turn On. Tune In. Drop Out.' (in an article syndicated by a widely distributed underground press organization) appeared everywhere – he intended good advice: 'Do not routinely and blindly expose yourself to stupor-producing, symbol-addicting environments.'

In 1968, the state declared him 'a menace to the community'. A year later he said a kind of farewell at the Village Gate Theatre in New York, backed by Allen Ginsberg* and Paul Krassner, among others. In 1970 Leary was sentenced to ten years' imprisonment (Lawrence Ferlinghetti's City Lights press published

his 'Memorandum' for bail), but escaped through the Weatherman Underground, and issued a statement from hiding calling on Americans to resist the Third World War waged by the government against its own people (he had been arrested an estimated fourteen times on drug charges). In 1971 his *Jail Notes* appeared with a preface by Ginsberg excoriating both the narcotics laws and Harvard University.

Leary next turned up in Beirut in 1970, hoping to contact Al Fatah, and then emerged in Algiers in 1971, hoping to ally with Eldridge Cleaver* there – but the Black Panther leader arrested him as a dangerous influence on the black revolt – 'we cannot afford to jeopardize our work toward revolution in Babylon', and in any case Leary's mind 'has been blown by acid'. In 1973, after a spell in Switzerland and Afghanistan, Leary was back in jail in Los Angeles.

His cult status is best described by Ginsberg: 'a hero of American consciousness. He began as a sophisticated academician, he encountered discoveries in his field which confounded him and his own technology, he pursued his studies where attention commanded, he arrived beyond the boundaries of public knowledge.' This is indeed the basis of his messianic politics, extended in jail to the necessity for 'world-wide ecological religious warfare'. *High Priest* (1968) speaks of the need to break fixed, trained motivation, attitude and preconception by transformation in personal consciousness. The book is a record of 'a psychedelic scholar-politician', a contribution to 'the psychedelic revolution . . . a religious renaissance of the young', and he includes important meetings with Charles Olson* and Arthur Koestler*, Ginsberg and Burroughs*, and other highly influential figures. The change came for him in 1961 when, under acid, he had to confront the stereotypical pointlessness of his family's life, and then, under an overdose, to realize the void in his own life and his own responsibility for change. He concluded later that 'psychedelic research is experimental philosophy, empirical metaphysics, visionary science. . . . The discovery of LSD is as important to philosophy and psychology and religion as the discovery of the microscope was to biology.' In 1962, after a trip in a Vedānta *ashram* in Boston, he began 'the slow invisible process of becoming a guru, a holy man'. The Harvard project became 'an ontological conspiracy' – 'the course of social conflict is usually neurological. The cure is biochemical.' Such is his basis for 'the religious, scientific quest', 'the great plan', through which we are to find courage to recognize new forms of energy (*The Politics of Ecstasy*, 1969). The notorious 'generation gap' is in fact 'an evolutionary lurch . . . a species mutation'. The LSD lesson is that you have to re-enact the evolutionary drama, 'go through the *whole* sequence yourself'. Leary admitted to over three hundred acid trips in order to 'suspend' social conditioning (but, he adds, Herman Kahn had taken acid, so that there is no guarantee of any radical identity change for the better. . .). Leary's faith lay with the young: 'No one over the age of fifty should be allowed to vote' and 'voting should be by the extended family. . . . We must return – advance to – the tribal unit of society.' The prelude to a better society is 'the retracing of genetic memories back down through the myriad, multi-webbed fabric of RNA-DNA memories'. Freedom from symbol systems addiction comes through 'cellular wisdom'. Leary's advice to the youthful reformer is 'become your own priest . . . your own doctor . . . your own researcher on consciousness', and to 'love God and every living creature as thyself'. In addition, he claimed, in the famous *Playboy* interview (reprinted in *The Politics of Ecstasy*), that 'LSD is the most powerful aphrodisiac ever discovered by man' – a highly disputable assertion, apparently. He totally denied that LSD led to any harmful effects on the body-mind system – again a disputed claim. Reviewing both these books in the *New York Times Book Review* in 1969, Rollo May, the American psychotherapist, observed that it was not surprising that hallucinogenic drugs should appeal to a younger generation 'beset with malaise and apathy'; and 'when the prospect of discovering God is combined with the joy of escape that drugs promise, you have a power whose attraction is great indeed.' May concludes that while drugs do 'clear away debris, the false faiths, the conventional hypocrisy', you still have to 'move on to something more complete'. Leary himself seems never to have discovered that condition beyond the *ashram*.

Eric Mottram

See: Leary, with R. Metzner and R. Alpert, *The Psychedelic Experience* (1964); Leary, G. M. Weil, R. Metzner (eds), *The Psychedelic Reader* (1965); Leary, *Psychedelic Prayers* (1966).

268
LEAVIS, Frank Raymond 1895–1979

English critic

Cambridge-born literary critic, whose lectures, seminars and tutorials in the Cambridge English School, combined with a stream of books and articles, especially articles in the periodical *Scrutiny* which he and his wife Q. D. Leavis conducted (1932–53), not only put Cambridge English studies on the map (after William Empson* left for the Orient and I. A. Richards* for Harvard, Leavis *was*, in most people's eyes, Cambridge English), but also dominantly influenced the assumptions and aims of teachers, especially school-teachers of English literature, in the middle years of the century. Personally extremely kind, Leavis was none the less always tough and frequently venomous

in the conduct of his critical discourse. Like Matthew Arnold he had a sharp sense of the power and pervasiveness of the enemy. The opposition was entrenched in the narrow-minded mediocrity of some senior members of the Cambridge English Faculty (who went on black-balling his wife and only slowly and grudgingly let him into a permanent university post), in the civilized glibnesses of Oxford literary criticism represented most annoyingly by the aristocratic gentilities of Lord David Cecil, in the entire London literary world as represented in and about Bloomsbury and the organs of British cultural exchange (the *Times Literary Supplement*, the BBC, the *New Statesman*, serious Sunday newspapers), and in the steady march of a technological culture. The old sore tone, the ancient grudges did tend to rankle on, long after many of Leavis's more personal struggles had been won – when practically no academic pulpit was closed to him (he became Reader in Cambridge, was 1967 Clark Lecturer at Cambridge, became a Professor at York, was frequently invited to Oxford), when the periodicals he derided would have snapped up even his most unconsidered trifles, when youthful audiences were only bemused by still sharp sneers at Professor E. M. W. Tillyard or Kingsley Martin, once editor of the *New Statesman*. But then, Leavis and his wife *had* early suffered real academic ostracism; the piano-seller's son had had a long struggle to get his voice heard over the suaver, though intellectually feebler, tones of the privileged members of the converging intellectual and social establishments; the 'persecution mania' of which he was often accused was rooted in *real* persecution when in the mid-1920s he was pursued by the Cambridge police, the Public Prosecutor, and (Leavis thought) the Home Secretary himself, for challenging the then ban on Joyce's* *Ulysses* by discussing it in his lectures. And, of course, what Leavis called 'technologico-Benthamite' industrial civilization showed no signs of abating. All the more reason then for the unrelenting verbal sharpness of eighteenth-century satire (some of Leavis's best essays were on Swift and Pope) and the steady moral determination of Dr Johnson (one of Leavis's most kept-up heroes). 'I believe,' Leavis quotes Henry James as saying (it's an epigraph to one of Leavis's collections of *Scrutiny* essays, *The Common Pursuit*, 1952), 'only in absolutely independent, individual and lonely virtue, and in the serenely unsociable (or if need be at a pinch sulky and sullen) practice of the same; the observation of a lifetime having convinced me that no fruit ripens but under that temporarily graceless vigour.' Leavis came to feel increasingly close, in fact, to William Blake (see *Nor Shall My Sword: Discourses on Pluralism, Compassion and Social Hope*, 1972).

The promptings and sources of Leavis's earliest critical work are not particularly original ones. The strength, though, of his early signposting essays in *New Bearings in English Poetry: A Study of the Contemporary*

Situation (1932) and *Revaluation* (1936) lies in the vigour with which he adapts and promotes T. S. Eliot's* classical position on poetry. And, very shortly, Leavis was to be found pursuing literary quality where Eliot (and Practical Criticism) had been reluctant to venture – in the realm of the novel. It is a major part of Leavis's distinction as a critic that he added, so to speak, Henry James to Arnold and T. S. Eliot, and was arguing for the central moral and social importance of great fiction while much of literary criticism was still stuck fast in increasingly routine and often decreasingly important 'Practical Critical' exegeses of poems. *The Great Tradition: George Eliot, Henry James, Joseph Conrad* (1948) was followed by *D. H. Lawrence: Novelist* (1955: this represented a severe departure from Eliot's views), by *Dickens the Novelist* (with Q. D. Leavis, 1970: a departure, in fact, from the Leavises' earlier, shared reluctance over Dickens's greatness), and by *Thought, Words and Creativity: Art and Thought in Lawrence* (1976).

The novel, and some novelists in particular – there was a steadily mounting concentration on the earlier works of D. H. Lawrence* – were represented as performing literature's chief function: conveying a sense of enriching 'life', of moral seriousness, of personal maturity; in short of virtue, weighed with a modern puritanism's determination. Just as many writers, lost leaders, fell from grace (Eliot and Auden* to name no others), so many novelists were considered too nasty and/or trifling ever to have made the grade. Lofty critical standards were justified as necessary, however, because the moral education of readers, and so the only hope of resisting the swamping onrush of technology, were at stake. To be sure, from his pamphlet *Mass Civilisation and Minority Culture* (1930) onwards, Leavis could sometimes sound altogether too Luddite for his ideas to seem even remotely practicable. His pleas for the mythic 'organic community' of the English village (hence the attractions of the sentimental villager in D. H. Lawrence, and the cult of T. F. Powys in the younger Leavis's circle) are in the end impossibly and wistfully unreal. What is more, his case for the élitist role of culture in society, as well as his developing stance on the unique centrality of English studies in the University (see *Education and the University: A Sketch for an 'English School'*, 1943), can seem as wilfully (even megalomaniacally) narrow as some of his literary preferences. Nevertheless, Leavis's passionate concern for the culture of England, especially as reflected in works of literature the educated common reader could be expected readily to respond to ('And I am English, and my Englishness is my very vision': a favoured quotation from Lawrence), his stern insistence on the intelligent play of the critical mind, his high-minded defence of the centrality in education of the humanities, particularly English literature (it earned him obloquy as well as fame when he rebutted C. P. Snow's glib assertion in the 1959 Rede Lecture at Cambridge that

there were 'Two Cultures', a scientific as well as a humane), all this made Leavis one of the twentieth-century's most powerful as well as one of its most attractive educators. As a force for the conservation of the best of the English past he takes his place in a long tradition of a very English kind of radicalism. Despite his having early on rejected Marx and what Leavis called 'Marxizing', his teaching nevertheless runs deep – especially as refracted by the Cambridge-educated Marxist Raymond Williams – into English (literary) Marxism. And it now seems not at all absurd to add him to the distinguished list of corrosive, prophetic, crankily conservative English radicals: Bunyan, whom he loved; Swift, the twists and turns of whose prose he dissected so tellingly; Cobbett, and Blake; D. H. Lawrence himself.

Valentine Cunningham

Other works: *'Anna Karenina' and Other Essays* (1967); *English Literature in Our Time and the University: Clark Lectures 1967* (1969); *Lectures in America*, with Q. D. Leavis (1969); *Letters in Criticism*, ed. John Tasker (1974); *The Living Principle: 'English' as a Discipline of Thought* (1975). See also: *The Importance of Scrutiny*, ed. Eric Bentley (1948); *A Selection from Scrutiny*, compiled by F. R. Leavis, 2 vols (Cambridge 1968). See: Francis Mulhern, *The Moment of 'Scrutiny'* (1979).

269
LE CORBUSIER (Charles-Édouard Jeaneret)
1887–1965

Swiss-French architect and painter

Of all the great architects of the Modern Movement, Charles-Édouard Jeaneret (Le Corbusier) had, perhaps, the most unlikely origins. He was born in La Chaux-de-Fonds, which as he liked to point out is over 1,000 metres above sea level, the centre of the Swiss Jura watch-making industry. His mother was a musician and his father, a stalwart of the town industry, had Jeaneret apprenticed at the age of thirteen as a watchmaker and engraver. However, he detached the retina of his left eye by drawing at night and his resulting bad eyesight (enshrined in his uniform of heavy glasses) prevented him pursuing this vocation: at the age of seventeen he gave it up to study building (in the local technical school) and to undertake some minor architectural commissions.

Early in this century he set out on a series of apparently aimless but serendipitous tours: to Budapest, Vienna and Berlin, and later to Greece and Turkey, where the architecture profoundly impressed him. In Vienna and Berlin, his *wanderlust* paid off when he found work with the Vienna Werkstätte and in Peter

Behrens's office, where Ludwig Mies van der Rohe* and Walter Gropius* were his contemporaries.

In between these two trips he worked in Paris with that great pioneer in concrete, the engineer-contractor and family friend Auguste Perret, and then in northern France designing houses, sluice-gates and other waterway architecture for the local Waterways Board. Jeaneret was always rather proud of his lack of conventional architectural training, and, in later years, was one of the only three 'unqualified' architects licensed to practise in France.

In 1919 he moved to Paris, where he lived the rest of his life, and set up a small office with his cousin, Pierre Jeaneret, who had undergone a more conventional architectural training. Perret introduced him to Fernand Léger* and Amedée Ozenfant and the transformation from Jeaneret to Le Corbusier had begun. The name 'Le Corbusier' Jeaneret chose under the direction of Ozenfant to distinguish clearly his new architectural self from the old. It refers to an annual task undertaken in the Middle Ages by the Jeaneret family of cleaning the crows' nests out of the local church steeple, probably their only previous architectural connection. With its adoption came a rigorously maintained lifestyle (painting and 'visual researches' before lunch, then a role change to the be-suited, be-spectacled after-lunch architect), and a complete change in his persona, for before this time he had never painted, and his architecture had generally been of little interest with the exception of the Dom-Ino concrete housing system (1914), where six columns, arranged as on a domino tile, support flat concrete slabs, thus allowing a special freedom of spatial division.

On Le Corbusier the painter and visual artist (as he now was), Léger's work left a profound mark. Le Corbusier painted, and later sculpted and designed murals and tapestries, within the 'Purist' style of 'Post-Cubism', broadening his approach and using brighter, plainer colours and strong, almost crude forms, sometimes with a particularly symbolic intention (e.g. his frequent use of the open hand). His painting is not particularly significant except in regard to his architecture. Indeed, it is almost as though his paintings, failing to live in two dimensions, take on life and vitality in the three-dimensional world of the built form, where the concrete realization of the crude forms and bright colours could flourish as massive monuments.

Le Corbusier's work as an architect may be divided into three categories: his building; his town-planning projects; and his theorizing. One of the earliest and clearest theoretical statements he made of his intentions was in a manifesto he composed with his partner-cousin (who is usually, and quite inexplicably, neglected) in 1926, and called *Almanach de l'Architecture Moderne* (translated as *Almanac of Modern Architecture*). In this, they call for five 'principles' in the new architecture: free supports, that is to say a column structure which

lifts the building off the ground ('pilotis'); roof gardens, i.e. using the new flat roof as a resource and a viewing platform; a free plan (as in the Dom-Ino house, where the walls may move freely within the space without being confined by the structure); horizontal windows, which 'express' the non-structural character of the external walls; and the free design of the façades of the building. (These five principles became Le Corbusier's operations manual and, together with his early experience of concrete and industrial buildings, essentially account for his architecture.) The five principles, and Le Corbusier's other theoretical works of the 1920s – he also wrote several other manifesto-type statements, especially in the magazine *L'Esprit nouveau*, and many justifications of his ideas and buildings – constituted a revolutionary architectural statement, a realization in architecture of a new aesthetic of particular honesty and utility which had its origin in the fragmented picture plane of the 'Cubists', and the novel consequent interpretation of the concept of transparency and thus spatial definition. Its effect was profound: it was almost as though Le Corbusier had single-handedly invented the Modern Movement – particularly that part of it we now call the Heroic Period of the International Style, and his importance and influence were enormous. Indeed it was through his work that the foundation of the Congrès Internationaux d'Architectes Modernes (CIAM), the formative architectural association of the century, came about, in which internationalist group of architects Le Corbusier was the energetic and highly esteemed flag-bearer.

He also wrote several books, the earlier statements of architectural theory being very polemical, as in *Towards a New Architecture* (*Vers une architecture*, 1923, trans. 1946), which espouses the 'Machine Aesthetic', and *When the Cathedrals were White* (*Quand les cathédrales étaient blanches*, 1937, trans. 1947). In later years, his theorizing became somewhat more ascetic and less polemical, culminating in the publication of *The Modulor* (*Le Modulor*, 1949, trans. 1954), an account of his proportional system. This book had a wide influence among architects in the 1950s, but was founded on a most peculiar view of mathematics and absolute size standards. Nevertheless its Fibionacci series of related lengths did provide variety in the somewhat sterile environment of the post-war pre-fab.

His building work can be assembled in four groups: the first consists of individual villas which he built for rich clients and in which he could explore some of the spatial freedom demanded in the *Almanach*, using free-standing walls, double volume spaces, and experimenting with roof gardens, an exploration that gave play to his machine aesthetic and which generated his famous aphorism 'A House is a Machine for living in'. (His meaning of Machine was more Platonic than ours, and his comment is mainly about aesthetics.) Of these, the villas Vaucresson (about which he said, 'Until the house at Vaucresson, he [i.e. Le Corbusier] had no creative ambitions of any kind'), La Roche, Stein and Savoye (now a French national monument), all built in the 1920s, are the most interesting. For these houses he also designed his famous furniture, much of it still in production.

The second group, social housing, actively involved Le Corbusier for most of his life span. Here he tried to express his vision of the contemporary city and lifestyle of what the historian Reyner Banham calls the 'First Machine Age'. Essentially he developed the large housing block, containing the street in the sky and the vertical street. These blocks were developed from about 1930, starting with the Pavillon Suisse in Paris and including his Salvation Army building, finding their most exact form in the 'Unité d'Habitation' built in Marseilles and duplicated elsewhere. These schemes almost all had strong town-planning overtones.

The third group includes the projects in what may be thought of as urban compositions (as opposed to town-planing). Le Corbusier had a megalomaniac streak, which not only led to a massive self-righteousness, but let him enjoy designing the largest of urban buildings. The first of these, in the 1920s, was the project for the League of Nations which, he tells us, was the competition jury's preferred scheme but was disqualified because it was not drawn in indian ink. He followed this with the (unbuilt) Palace of Soviets which included an auditorium for 14,000, which he claimed rather simplistically 'was acoustically faultless (tested by lightwaves)'. Other schemes include a sports stadium project, the Ministry of Education in Rio de Janeiro, and the initial planning of the United Nations building in New York: but the most celebrated is the new provincial capital Chandigarh in the Punjab, where Le Corbusier designed and built the whole administrative and juridical complex around a vast pool of water.

The final aspect of his building is a number of extremely individualistic one-off jobs. The most impressive of these (and they are superb) are the pilgrimage church at Ronchamp in the Vosges mountains, noted for its scrolled roof and windows puncturing the massive walls; the Dominican Training Monastery at La Tourette with its randomly articulated façade; and the Philips Pavilion built for the Brussels World Fair, the home of one of the world's first 'total art' shows. (These last two were largely designed by Iannis Xenakis, now better known as a composer for his stochastic music.)

One cannot conclude an account of Le Corbusier without discussing his town-planning projects. It was largely he who put forward and developed the ideas adopted by CIAM for the contemporary city. His was the driving force behind the vision of the vast separated blocks in the Elysian Fields that was the modernist's dream. These ideas he developed through various projects, for 'La Ville Contemporaine' – the initial design

as an isolated new town for three million people – to proposed applications involving large-scale rebuilding of several distinguished towns, including Paris (the Plan Voisin), Stockholm and Barcelona. None of these schemes was built, much to his chagrin, for they aroused great public anger; but they had an enormous influence on architects and planners and their effects can be seen in the vandalized tower blocks situated in seas of asphalt that are all too familiar nowadays. However, it is hardly fair to Le Corbusier to judge his ideas on these realizations, for they are not only unpleasant and extraordinarily bad buildings, they are also appallingly executed travesties of his ideas. Whether such ideas, attacked by some as megalomaniac and totalitarian, could ever work we are unlikely now to find out.

Le Corbusier built himself a pair of small 'primitive huts' on the Mediterranean coast where he went for privacy and contemplation. It was while there, swimming, in 1965 that he had a heart attack and drowned. He was married but had no children.

Dr Ranulph Glanville and Professor Sam Stevens

See: C. Jencks, *Le Corbusier and the Tragic View of Architecture* (1973); C. Blake, *Le Corbusier* (1964).

270
LÉGER, Fernand 1881–1955

French painter

More than any other major twentieth-century painter Fernand Léger reacted with delight and enthusiasm to the new optimism expressed in the machine aesthetic. But he also had first-hand experience of the harsh realities of the trenches during the First World War and it was this that turned him away from the dry Cubist manner of the pre-war years and led him to evolve a more deliberately simple method that he knew might be readily understood by simple people. He no longer thought of an art for an elite. His art would not be of the studio but of the street and would be quite acceptable to the man and woman in that street. In the trenches he had met ordinary people under extraordinary conditions and he was quite convinced of their worth.

Fascinated by the ever-changing urban scene, his belief that the new dynamism of the new century was to be found in the city led him to renew his interest in architectural space and he well understood the complexities of modern building, as part of his early training had been in an architect's office. His sense of decoration led to an art of contrast with the freely flowing forms of smoke and clouds used to accentuate the stark rigid metallic character of the frames used in the new construction.

The contemporary world around him was his starting point, though a careful study of the late works of Cézanne gave him a sound framework into which he could introduce the almost robot-like figures that were to become his trademark. They first appear in the important *Card Players* of 1917 (Kröller-Müller, Otterlo) reminiscent in subject matter of Cézanne but treated here with steel-like precision reflecting both the character of soldiers at war and the machinery with which they fight that war. Man and machine act as one and Léger merges them into a total unity epitomizing the essence of the new optimism.

Throughout his long life Léger's theme rarely strayed from the basic premise that man ought to be at one with the world that he has made and that he must learn to live in the present and not in the past. Like the Futurists, for whom he had much sympathy, he was a man of his time, though unlike the Futurists he approached everyday life with his feet firmly on the ground. The large painting *The Constructors*, painted in 1950 (Musée Nationale Fernand Léger, Biot), typifies this attitude of mind. The men who are building this electricity pylon are dwarfed by the vast metal structure but it is they who are responsible for it. Standing in infinite space clouds drift through the structure as it rises still higher into the sky. Not only are they dwarfed by the pylon but also by the forces of nature that surround them. But they are confident in their work and confident in the new technology that makes it possible. They take their obvious strength for granted. They are the heroes of the new century and Léger is their spokesman.

John Furse

See D. Cooper, *Fernand Léger* (Geneva 1949); *Léger and Purist Paris*, Exhibition Catalogue with texts by J. Golding and C. Green, Tate Gallery, London 1972.

271
LENIN (Vladimir Ilyich Ulyanov) 1870–1924

Russian revolutionary, statesman, publicist and theoretician

Lenin was born in 1870 at Simbirsk in the heart of Russia. He came from an educated and enlightened family: his father was a schoolteacher and so too was his mother for a while. Lenin was the second son in a family of six children and received the usual middle-class schooling of his time. Lenin's elder brother, Alexander, was a romantic revolutionary; he was executed for plotting to murder the then Tsar. Lenin was seventeen then and the execution left a deep impression on him. Lenin's elder sister too was active in the revolutionary movement. Soon after his brother's death Lenin enrolled as a law student in the provincial university of Kazan. His university career, however, did not last for long; he was sent down and confined to his mother's estate for playing a leading role in a demonstration against the government regulations to which students were subject. Lenin did eventually qualify as a lawyer but only to practise for a year or so. Throughout his life he remained a professional revolutionary.

Lenin embarked on his eventful political career by joining in the revolutionary groups which had started to develop all over Russia. After a couple of years of political activities in provincial towns he moved to St Petersburg (today's Leningrad), then the capital of Russia – also the main industrial city and naturally the hub of anti-government political activities. It was there that Lenin in 1894 published his first major political work: *Who the Friends of the People Are and How They Fight the Social Democrats (Chto Takoye 'Drusya Naroda', kak oni voyuynt protiv Sotsial-Demokratov?*, trans. 1946). The tract is a blistering attack on the Narodniks (populists in Russian) and has all the features which characterize Lenin's voluminous writings: written by way of a political intervention with a view to drawing specific conclusions to guide political activity. Lenin's style is to combine didactic arguments with withering polemics.

Lenin was not allowed to remain free to participate in political activities for long. After a year of imprisonment he was exiled to Siberia for three years; it was there that he married a fellow revolutionary, Krupskaya. Lenin used his period of imprisonment and exile to write his monumental *Development of Capitalism in Russia (Razvitiye Kapitalizma v Rossi*, 1899, trans. 1956). Though the work is scholarly in content as well as in style, it is, none the less, political. It is, like most other pre-1900 writings of Lenin, directed against the Narodniks.

To start with Narodism covered a heterogeneous group opposed to the autocratic political and economic order in Russia. But by the 1890s the label came to be applied exclusively to non-Marxists who saw in the village commune the foundation of the future Russian society. They regarded capitalism – large-scale manufacturing industry and modern farms – as an alien import grafted on to the Russian society.

What Lenin argued against the Narodniks was that capitalism was not only firmly implanted but also rapidly growing both in the Russian cities and the countryside. The village commune which was to serve as the foundation of the Narodniks' future Russia, Lenin demonstrated, was no longer a community of equal individuals. On the contrary it was stratified; a small minority of richer peasants (*kulaks*) prospered while the rest were becoming progressively poorer and forced to work for wages. From this Lenin drew the political conclusion that Russia, contrary to the Narodnik thesis, would not follow a path of economic and social changes radically different from the one already traversed by Western European countries. The implication was that in Russia, as in the rest of Europe, the leading political force was the working class and the appropriate form of political organization a Social Democratic Party, similar to those which had already developed in Western Europe.

From 1900 onwards one may divide Lenin's life and activities into three phases: (1) the period up to 1907, (2) the period of exile from 1907 to 1917, and finally (3) the period of revolution and the establishment of the Soviet Union from 1917 till his death.

The Social Democratic party was founded when Lenin was still in Siberia and it grew very rapidly in size and influence soon after its formation. During the period 1900–7 the question of differences between Marxism and Narodism was no longer important. The two main issues which occupied Lenin during this period were, first, the nature of the impending revolution and second, the aim and the organization of the Social Democratic Party.

Lenin was convinced of the imminence of revolution and so too were other Russian revolutionaries. There was a nation-wide uprising again the Tsarist autocracy and feudal lords in 1905 – an event which Lenin later termed the full dress rehearsal of the 1917 revolution. In his *Two Tactics of Social Democracy* (*Dve taktiki Sotsial-Demokraty v demokrat icheskoy revolyutsi*, 1905, trans. 1935) Lenin argued that the impending revolution would be bourgeois rather than socialist in character. For, according to him, the working class and the Social Democratic party because of conditions specific to Russia could not carry through the revolution to victory on its own and thus realize a socialist economy. That, Lenin went on to argue, did not mean that Social Democrats could not play a leading role in the impending revolution; on the contrary it was necessary for them to do so in order to make sure that all vestiges of autocracy and feudalism were wiped out. Thus for Lenin, though it may seem paradoxical, the impending bourgeois revolution was to be led by the socialist party rather than by bourgeois parties.

Within five years of its establishment the Social Democratic Party split into two factions, the *Bolsheviks* (majority, in Russian) and the *Mensheviks* (minority) – the labels which later came to designate two separate socialist parties. Lenin became the leader of the former and it was the Bolsheviks who led the October Revolution of 1917. The immediate cause of the split was the difference of opinion on the nature of the party, its internal organization and the condition of its membership. Lenin argued for the establishment of a tightly knit party led from the centre, and which restricted its membership to only those who actively participated in its activities. The Mensheviks, in contrast, wanted the Russian party to develop like other European Social Democratic parties – a mass political party covering a wide political spectrum which was willing to admit a variety of individuals ranging from active participants

to sympathizers. Lenin managed to win over the majority by a very slim margin. His conception of the party has become a legacy of the communist movement and it came in for criticism from diverse quarters, including Trotsky* and Rosa Luxemburg*.

The 1905 revolution shook the existing political and economic order but did not overthrow it. It led to the persecution of leading revolutionaries; Lenin like other Russian revolutionaries was driven abroad. He left Russia in 1907 to return to it in 1917 and spent most of his exile in Switzerland.

The Tsarist government, shaken by the 1905 uprising, tried to introduce a modicum of reforms: the commune was abolished and there was a half-hearted attempt on the part of the government to grant more power to the feeble assembly of elected representatives. The outbreak of the First World War soon put a stop to the process of economic and political reforms, and it was that which was decisive in shaping the course of events up to the October Revolution.

The outbreak of the war confronted the European socialist movement with the awkward problem of what attitude to adopt towards the war. Earlier the second International, as the socialist movement was then named, had decided that in the event of a war it would stand aside leaving the ruling classes of belligerent countries to fight it out. This was not, however, what the majority of socialists did when the war was declared. In Germany the majority of Social Democratic members of parliaments voted funds for the war. The war split the socialist movement and put an end to the second International.

Lenin argued that socialists should stand aside and refuse to take any part in the conduct of the war. For, as he explained, the war was an imperialist war – by that he meant that it was not the national boundaries of the leading European combatants but the division of Africa and Asia into colonies which was the main issue in the war. Therefore the war was not worthy of support by socialists for patriotic reasons. Lenin's theses on imperialism, publicized in his pamphlet *Imperialism* (*Imperializm*, 1917, trans. 1933), had a dual political significance. Apart from indicating to socialists the right attitude towards the war, they were based on the postulate that imperialism was a particular stage of capitalism. He analysed imperialism as a product of the internal dynamics of capitalism and went on to argue that imperialism had turned the whole world into a unified and interdependent system. From this Lenin drew the political conclusion that revolutions could no longer be regarded as just national affairs; and that socialist revolutions in advanced capitalist countries, bourgeois revolutions in semi-capitalist countries like Russia and the struggles of national liberation in colonized regions were all interlinked. This was an important innovation; because till then the prevalent conception was that socialist revolution would first take place in advanced capitalist countries like Germany and then later in other countries depending on the development of capitalism in those countries.

The war, which was opposed by all sections of Russian Social Democracy, sapped the Russian state of all its power. In February 1917 – when Lenin was still in Switzerland – an almost bloodless revolution ended the Tsardom. The political power then passed into the hands of not one but two governments: one formal in the shape of the provisional government (dominated by conservative and liberal parties); the other was informal and was founded on the Soviets – a revolutionary council of workers' representatives. Of them the St Petersburg Soviet was the most important; such assemblies had been established before during the 1905 revolution.

Lenin arrived in Russia in April of 1917 and he argued for the transfer of all power to the Soviets and thus ending the situation of dual power which existed then. At that time it was not the Bolsheviks but the Mensheviks and the Social Revolutionaries (heirs of the Narodniks) who dominated the Soviets. With the two governments the political situation was balanced on a knife-edge. It was the attempt by a General Kornilov to capture political power which finally shifted the balance in favour of the Soviets, because it was they who frustrated the attempted *coup d'état*. By the beginning of October 1917 the leadership of the Soviets had passed into the hands of the Bolsheviks. It was then that Lenin called for an immediate seizure of power. Lenin's call was initially opposed by the majority of Bolshevik leaders, but, as in so many other situations in 1917, he managed to have his way. Thus within a year Russia went through two revolutions: one bourgeois democratic (the February Revolution) and the other socialist (the October Revolution).

After the October Revolution Lenin became an undisputed leader of Russian socialism and also of a substantial section of the European socialist movement. The centre of revolution shifted from Germany to Russia; Lenin went on to establish the Third International (the international organization of communist parties) to replace the already fissured and demoralized Second International.

The new Soviet state had to fight a civil as well as an external war against Germany. It survived both of them but at a very heavy cost. The war lasted for two years and it was the period of what was then termed War Communism – meaning a strict regimentation of citizens and the direct administrative control of industrial production and of distribution. The war and the War Communism led to a near collapse of the Russian economy. In order to avert that Lenin boldly suggested rolling back the frontiers of the communist economy. This he did by proposing what has come to be known as the New Economic Policy. Lenin did not live long

enough to see the construction of the first socialist economy in the world. He died after being bedridden for a year and a half.

The significance of Lenin and the Russian revolution are intertwined; both of them have left a decisive imprint on the politics of the twentieth century. The Leninist political legacy which still captures the imagination of revolutionaries all over the world consists of three main elements: his conception of the revolutionary party, his refinement of the art of political calculation, and his conception of the state.

It could almost be said that Lenin spent all his political life determining what is possible and calculating what is needed to realize the chosen possibility. It was Lenin who made revolutions objects of calculation; it was in this respect that he added an entirely new dimension to Marxist politics.

Lenin's ideas on the state are elaborated in his famous *The State and Revolution* (*Gosudarstvo i revolyutsiya*, trans. 1919) which he wrote in the midst of revolution in 1917. In it he treated democracy and dictatorship as complements rather than as mutually exclusive alternatives. He argued that parliamentary democracy of capitalist countries was, none the less, a dictatorship of the capitalist class. Further, that the aim of a socialist revolution was to replace the dictatorship of the capitalist class with the dictatorship of the proletariat – a phrase which acquired an ominous meaning during the mass purges of the Stalin* era.

Athar Hussain

See: *Collected Works* in 45 volumes (English translation, Moscow 1960–70); the 3-volume *Selected Works* (Moscow 1967). See also: Adam B. Ulam, *Lenin and the Bolsheviks* (1965); Robert Conquest, *Lenin* (1972); Neil Harding, *Lenin's Political Thought* (1977); Christopher Hill, *Lenin and the Russian Revolution* (1978).

272
LÉVI-STRAUSS, Claude 1908–

French social anthropologist

A central exponent of Structuralism, Claude Lévi-Strauss was born in Brussels. His secondary education was acquired in Paris at the Lycée Janson de Sailly. In 1931 he graduated in Law and in Philosophy. After two years as a philosophy teacher in small country towns he left France for Brazil, where he lectured at the University of São Paulo (1934–9). During his stay he became interested in social anthropology and started travelling in the Matto Grosso and the Amazon. He returned to France in 1939, but left again after the settling of arms in 1940, this time for the USA. In New York Lévi-Strauss lectured at the New School for Social

Research, then, with other exiled French intellectuals, founded the École Libre des Hautes Études de New York. After a brief return to Paris at the end of the war he became Cultural Counsellor at the French Embassy in Washington (1945–8). Back in Paris he was appointed Associate Curator of the Musée de l'Homme (1949), Director of Studies at the École Pratique des Hautes Études (1950–74), and, from 1959, Professor of Social Anthropology at the Collège de France. A member of the Académie Française since 1973, Professor Lévi-Strauss is the recipient of many awards, and a member of British, American, Dutch and Norwegian Academies.

Lévi-Strauss's remarkable autobiographical travel account, *Tristes Tropiques* (1955, trans. as *A World on the Wane*, 1961, and as *Tristes Tropiques*, 1973), is littered with references to overcrowding and congestion of every sort. Time and again he exposes 'those outbreaks of stupidity, hatred and credulousness which social groups secrete like pus when they begin to be short of space'. The cardinal virtues Lévi-Strauss appreciates are discretion and good manners. Only Buddhism is allowed to qualify as an acceptable moral and intellectual system, although Amerindian myths share his own concern for privacy: they regard the world as overcrowded as soon as a man has got a brother or a woman a sister. For 'as the myths explain, a brother can be a hardship . . . his social function being usually limited to that of potential seducer of their sibling spouse.' This establishes Lévi-Strauss's claimed affinity with Rousseau, who wrote: 'The ancient times of Barbarity were the Golden Age, not because men were united, but because they were separated.'

Although Lévi-Strauss does not propose a global system of interpretation of the world, there is a remarkable consistency in his approach to widely different domains of human culture. His epistemological framework can be briefly described. Recent interpretations of the fate of the human race hesitate between two explanatory schemes: either the human environment, natural and cultural, is shown as a near perfect clockwork wherein any part of the system is strictly constrained by the others and every event occurs necessarily; or constraints are shown to be few and human cultures have repeatedly to face choices between various alternatives. Sociobiology and the other varieties of cultural materialism belong to the first scheme, while Lévi-Strauss's system belongs to the second. However to him the great diversity of human culture is not arbitrary; it exhibits combinations which result from the interplay of two types of constraints: the constraints which lie in the outer world and the constraints of the inner world, what Lévi-Strauss calls 'l'esprit humain', the human mind. The human mind is not a metaphysical entity, it is a material object: man's nervous system. Cultures result from the interplay between the outer world and the possibilities of

man's nervous equipment. This is why Lévi-Strauss regards structural anthropology as a variety of psychology: anthropology is necessarily 'cognitive' anthropology.

Although Lévi-Strauss has sometimes claimed to be a Marxist, his conception of history is essentially anti-historicist. To him there are no laws to history: history is a probabilistic process which he compares to roulette; favourable sets of throws will allow some cultures to engage in cumulative sequences, while unfavourable throws will mean for others stagnation or cultural regression. But as history is unpredictable it is therefore capital to keep a record of it, as accurately as circumstances allow. History provides the only experiments the anthropologist has at his disposal. This is one of the differences between the 'Sciences de l'Homme' and the other natural sciences. Another difference is that the natural sciences restrict their level of apprehension to that of *explanation*, while a Science of Man cannot do so without tackling also the level of *understanding*, otherwise it would be meaningless. But very seldom does the anthropologist know whether he is dealing with *explanation* or with *understanding*. Therefore the Sciences of Man cannot state propositions which are falsifiable like propositions in physics. Lévi-Strauss distinguishes however the Sciences of Man from the social sciences (law, economics, political science, social psychology, etc.), which are 'in cahoots' with their object.

A hypothesis which pervades most of Lévi-Strauss's work is that of exchange, or rather of gift and counter-gift as it was defined by Marcel Mauss*. Mankind is constituted of a collection of groups socially defined in kinship on the basis of natural reproduction. To a large extent the social tissue results from these groups refraining from using for their own sake their own women, their own words and their own commodities.

The Elementary Structures of Kinship ('*Les Structures élémentaires de la parenté*, 1949, trans. 1969) rests on 'the structuralist hypothesis . . . that in every society, even where marriage seems to result only from individual decisions dictated by economic or emotional considerations foreign to kinship, definite *types* of cycles tend to get constituted' (D. Sperber, *Le Structuralisme en anthropologie*, 1973). Elementary structures appear in societies where men refrain from marrying their own women (incest prohibition) for the benefit of other men who belong to other groups but are nevertheless traceable kinsmen of a particular kind, e.g. the bridal pair is of cross-cousins, children of siblings of different gender. Lévi-Strauss introduced as a conceptual tool the opposition between '*restricted*' and '*generalized exchange*'. In restricted exchange, two exogamous groups exchange women, the men of A marry women of B, while men of B marry women of A. In generalized exchange, men of A marry women of B, while men of B marry women of C, etc. Another contribution of *The Elementary Structures* and later texts is the emphasis on the *atom of kinship*. Kinship can only be analysed if the unit considered is not the nuclear family (parents and children) but an atom where the wife-giving group is taken into account. The representatives of the wife-giving group might be one mother's brother, but also any other suitable representatives (e.g. the mother's mother's brother in a society where men marry their mother's mother's brother's daughter's daughter).

The Elementary Structures is a vast survey of the societies where prescriptive marriage with definite kin is in force. Many critics have discovered inaccuracies in the ethnography whereon Lévi-Strauss's argument rests; others have insisted that formalization in such matters leads to a neglect of essential sociological features of the marriage systems described, for instance, alternative choices or infringements on the rules. Whatever the case, *Les Structures élémentaires* became a reference book of Anglo-Saxon anthropology long before it was translated into English, a rare achievement.

The exchange scheme is visible in other spheres of social life: some gift-cultures of the Pacific have established a kind of exogamous economy: I give all I have produced and I only consume what I have been given. In many ways verbal taboo is also giving my 'words' for others to use. Lévi-Strauss shows the exchange scheme as having a high operational value, castes appear for instance as reversed totemic groups: castes keep their women for themselves but exchange goods and services, while totemic groups exchange women but consume their own products (*La Pensée sauvage*, 1962; trans. as *The Savage Mind*, 1966).

Lévi-Strauss's near fascination for the formal properties of his object of enquiry has often upset his critics. Indeed once he has established the possible combinations, the 'group of transformations', of a particular social phenomenon, not only is he not much concerned in determining why this possibility has been chosen preferably to others (this is related to his probabilistic view of history), but he is not prepared to privilege empirical actuality over mere logical possibility. His reply to critics in a slightly different context on this latter point is disarming: 'what does this matter? For if the final aim of anthropology is to contribute to a better knowledge of objectified thought and its mechanisms, it is in the last resort immaterial whether in this book the thought processes of the South American Indians take shape through the medium of my thought, or whether mine take place through the medium of theirs' (*Le Cru et le cuit*, 1964; trans. as *The Raw and the Cooked*, 1969).

If in his enquiry of kinship Lévi-Strauss was preceded by anthropologists like L. H. Morgan or W. H. R. Rivers*, this is not the case for mythology; only the Russian formalist Vladimir Propp can be regarded as a forerunner of the French anthropologist's approach. The four volumes of *Mythologiques* (1964–72; *Introduction to a Science of Mythology*, 1969–79) constitute the illus-

trative programme, on Amerindian myths, of Lévi-Strauss's method of analysis. Myths are not to be deciphered, there is no latent message lurking behind their manifest meaning. Rather, the meaning of a myth resides in the fact that there are other myths. The myths of a particular culture constitute a mythological system and it is possible to discover the rules that account for the transformation of one myth into another. Similarly there are rules which account for the differences between two versions of the *same* myth in different cultures. The existence of such rules explains why for Lévi-Strauss there is no authentic version of a myth: the set of all possible versions constitute a group of transformations. Any version is as good as any other as long as it is felt by the native listener that 'it tells properly the same story': 'Therefore, not only Sophocles, but Freud* himself, should be included among the recorded versions of the Oedipus myth on a par with earlier or seemingly more "authentic" versions' (*Anthropologie structurale*, 1958; *Structural Anthropology*, 1963). The function of a myth is neither to be a charter – Lévi-Strauss regards this idea as a platitude – nor to *explain* the origin of things. It is true that myths often mention when such and such an animal or plant appeared for the first time, but this is not the function of the myth. Plants and animals are actors in myths, not the things to be explained. The function of myths – if there is any such thing – is to account for categories. The world seems to be torn apart by the contradiction between irreducible opposites like near and remote, right and left, up and down, nature and culture, etc. Myths are a reflection on the conceptual puzzles and attempts at mediation. Mediation might succeed, for instance by showing that it is possible to bridge the opposition by 'stuffing' the conceptual gap with intermediaries, or it might fail, 'either that the mediator joins one of the two poles and gets completely disjuncted from the other (and then not always from the same one), or that it gets disjuncted from both'. Although Lévi-Strauss's venture in *Mythologiques* is undoubtedly impressive critics have been very embarrassed at appraising it. His reading is obviously consistent, but as his own method entails, it is but one among many. Moreover, the limitations of the method show conspicuously when it is used by anthropologists less gifted than Lévi-Strauss himself.

It is tempting to locate Lévi-Strauss in a straight line of descent from Durkheim* via Mauss, but as he stressed himself repeatedly, he owes much more to Anglo-Saxon social anthropology than he does to the French school of sociology. In particular, Durkheim's 'attempt to use sociology for metaphysical purposes' is not congenial to him. Time and again Lévi-Strauss praised Rivers's, Radcliffe-Brown's* or Robert Lowie's contributions to anthropology. But most of all he has underlined his personal debt towards Boas*. This particular assertion of filiation does not seem to have been taken seriously by most reviewers, probably because of the discrepancy between Lévi-Strauss's theoretical achievements and Boas's conspicuous unpretentiousness in theoretical matters. But as Lévi-Strauss noted, it is Boas's excessive demands towards theory which prevented him from contributing decisively to it. The development of anthropology during the fifty years which separate Boas's and Lévi-Strauss's works might explain their different attitudes to theory.

But Lévi-Strauss's most decisive contributions seem to have resulted from outer influences, especially those of structural phonology (Jakobson*) and cybernetics (Wiener*) with which he became familiar through personal contact during his New York days. Later writings reveal his constant concern of keeping in touch with the latest developments in the natural sciences, particularly with neurophysiology.

Lévi-Strauss's influence on contemporary anthropology is so considerable that it is difficult to evaluate it properly. Among the anthropologists who have best understood Lévi-Strauss's lesson and have applied it to other objects in their own way are in Britain Edmund Leach* and Rodney Needham, in France Pierre Bourdieu and Dan Sperber, and in the United States Marshall Sahlins.

In the early 1960s in France, Lévi-Strauss's works became very fashionable. *The Savage Mind* in particular was read by a large public of laymen. A trend called Structuralism flourished then before it receded dramatically after the May 1968 'events' which resulted in a renewed interest in Marxist studies. Not all the stars of Structuralism were noticeably influenced by Lévi-Strauss. Jacques Lacan*, the psychoanalyst, borrowed the concept of 'symbolic function', and constituted his own topology of 'The Real', 'The Imaginary' and 'The Symbolic'. Roland Barthes* found some inspiration in Lévi-Strauss's approach to myth, especially visible in his *Système de la mode* (1967) and *S/Z* (1970). Foucault's* 'épistème', the spirit of the time in natural and human sciences, functions much like a Lévi-Straussian 'group of transformations'. Jacques Derrida* discovered in Lévi-Strauss's reading of Rousseau matter for his reflection on the role of writing in the constitution of modern metaphysics (*De la Grammatologie*, 1967).

Lévi-Strauss's original work is often seen as the disincarnated report of a coroner. But such interpretations miss altogether what is probably one of the distinctive qualities of his work: the very ethical premises whereon his whole approach rests. His sympathy for Buddhism is everywhere endemic, and his use of the conceptual opposition of nature and culture can only be understood in the light of his play 'L'Apothéose d'Auguste' (chapter 37 of *Tristes Tropiques*). The true meaning of his work appears clearly in his reply to the question, what should be deposited in a coffer for the benefit of archaeologists in the year 3000?: 'I will put in your

time-vault documents relative to the last "primitive" societies, on the verge of disappearance; specimens of vegetable and animal species soon to be destroyed by man; samples of air and water not yet polluted by industrial wastes; notices and illustrations of sites soon to be ravaged by civil or military installations' (*Anthropologie structurale 2*, 1973; trans. as *Structural Anthropology 2*, 1976).

Dr Paul Jorion

Other works by Lévi-Strauss include: *Race et histoire* (1952); *Le Totémisme aujourd'hui* (1962; *Totemism*, 1969); *Du Miel aux cendres* (1966; *From Honey to Ashes*, 1973); *L'Origine des manières de table* (1968; *The Origin of Table Manners*, 1978); *L'Homme nu* (1971; *The Naked Man*, 1980); *La Voie des masques* (1975). See also: Edmund Leach, *Lévi-Strauss* (1970); Catherine Clément, *Lévi-Strauss* (1970); E. Nelson Hayes and Tanya Hayes, *Claude Lévi-Strauss: The Anthropologist as Hero* (1970); Raymond Bellour and Catherine Clément, *Claude Lévi-Strauss* (1979).

273
LEWIS, Clive Staples 1898–1963

British writer

Ulster-born poet, novelist, scholar, critic, popular theologian, and don (first at Oxford, then at Cambridge). His poems, brittle, brightly argumentative, unmovedly cerebral, count for little (though Philip Larkin* put one breezily reactionary example, 'On A Vulgar Error', into his *Oxford Book of Twentieth-Century Verse*). Lewis's forte was expository prose: no English literary historian of the twentieth century can better his energetically clarifying (if occasionally wrong-headed) *English Literature in the Sixteenth Century* (in the *Oxford History of English Literature* series, 1954), his masterly unfolding of the medieval and renaissance *Allegory of Love* (1936), or his *A Preface to Paradise Lost* (1942). Lewis liked nothing better than explaining complexities of literary and linguistic history, or of theology, to less informed audiences. He was a superb and popular lecturer, preacher, and radio broadcaster (many of his books began as talks and lectures). Public modes of persuasion – vigorous, often blunt, sometimes hectoring ('knock-down and drag-out', his friend John Wain called them) – were what he favoured. In the more personal tutorial situation he had some notable failures (John Betjeman* was one: Lewis couldn't abide aesthetes). He is reported to have challenged one pupil to a sword-fight (Lewis won, with his broadsword). Until he married late in life he found the robust male company of groups like the Oxford Christians who called themselves The Inklings (chief among them, besides Lewis and his brother, were J. R. R. Tolkien* and

Charles Williams) most to his liking. Belief in vigorously expressed common-sense, a strong whiff of misogyny, beer and *Beowulf*, long rural tramps, pub-haunting and pipe-smoking: The Inklings recipe – it was the very atmosphere of Lewis's career as popular broadcasting theologian – was Muscular Christianity on the nineteenth-century Oxford and Cambridge, Charles Kingsley model. Lewis's most famous works of Christian apologetic – *The Problem of Pain* (1940), *The Screwtape Letters* (1942), *Mere Christianity* (1952) – are not subtle, even though he came to literary studies out of his philosophical work for Oxford Classical 'Greats'. They now seem strongly marked by their original wartime context in which simple reassurances were widely craved. In practice, Lewis failed to 'prove' very much: largely, perhaps, because *analogy* (Lewis was excellent at culling sharp illustrations, frequently from the zones of food and drink) masqueraded too frequently as *proof*. Of his two most persuasive theological arguments – one (it assisted his own conversion, as he explained in his autobiography *Surprised By Joy*, 1955), that the many ancient Dying God myths must have a real, historical archetype (i.e. Christ); the other (he put it in the sermon entitled 'Transposition'), that 'higher' systems sometimes have to use 'lower' systems for their expression – only the latter (Lewis suggested it as a possibly general way of tracing the supernatural in the natural) has worn well (modern anthropologists believe that myths never have 'originals'). More fruitful for Lewis's whole output was the interest in allegorical fictions. His first effort at a modern Christian allegory, *The Pilgrim's Regress: An Allegorical Apology for Christianity, Reason and Romanticism* (1933) was ponderously didactic, as unlike Bunyan's lively original as could be. The Christianized science fiction trilogy that began with *Out of the Silent Plant* (1939), and the seven tales in the Narnia series evinced a bettering of the technique. Lewis was also rather good at taking a fictional devil's part, as *The Screwtape Letters* proves. In general, though, his fiction was as aggressively anti-modern in kind and attitude as his theology, politics and literary tastes. And he gladly made the escapist passage into being a writer for the childish mind that seems particularly attractive to teachers whose business is Old and Middle English (Tolkien is another case of it). But there is no denying the wide appeal of his Narnia books nor their author's prolific diversity and his always attractively supple prose.

Valentine Cunningham

Other works include: *The Great Divorce* (1945); *The Abolition of Man* (1946); *The Four Loves* (1960); *Studies in Words* (1960; 2nd edn 1967); *Poems*, ed. Walter Hooper (1964); *Letters of C. S. Lewis*, ed. W. H. Lewis (1966); *The Weight of Glory, and Other Addresses* (1949); *They Asked for a Paper: Papers and Addresses* (1962);

Christian Reflections, ed. Walter Hooper (1967). See also: Humphrey Carpenter, *The Inklings* (1978).

274

LEWIS, (Henry) Sinclair 1885–1951

US novelist

Sinclair Lewis was born in Sauk Center, Minnesota, and educated at Oberlin College, Ohio, and Yale. After graduation, he worked as a journalist, and in various publishing houses. His first novel, *Our Mr Wrenn*, appeared in 1914. Lewis's early work (1914–19) bridged the gap between the two kinds of novel then prevalent in America: the sentimental gentility of Booth Tarkington and the 'Hoosier' school, and the stark naturalism exemplified in the novels of Theodore Dreiser* (who had a lasting influence on Lewis's writing). But the early fiction was greeted with little acclaim. Unimaginative in its allegiance to traditional American values and ideals, it gave little indication of the talent which was to make Lewis famous.

Recognition came with the publication, in 1920, of *Main Street*, which mockingly anatomized the provincialism of the small town in the American Middle West. The central themes of the novel – the philistinism and complacency, cant and hypocrisy of a vulgar and meretricious society – were those which were to preoccupy Lewis throughout the next decade. The novel enjoyed a *succès de scandale*, and secured for Lewis a reputation as iconoclast, and as America's foremost satirist. He was quickly classed with Hemingway*, Fitzgerald*, Sherwood Anderson* and Mencken (the latter a formative influence on Lewis) as one of the leaders of a generation of American writers in revolt. In *Babbitt* (1922), Lewis turned his attention to the urban middle class. He captured the idioms and rendered the lifestyle of the American bourgeois with a derisive exactitude which has since caused Babbitt's name to be enshrined in the dictionaries as a synonym for smug conformity. In *Arrowsmith* (1925), the satire was respectably offset by a new strain of idealism. But *Elmer Gantry* (1927), Lewis's scathing portrayal of the corruption of religious life in America, provoked outrage still more extreme than that generated by *Main Street*.

With fame came prosperity, the life of a celebrity in Washington, New York and Europe, and, in 1930, the Nobel Prize in Literature, which marked the climax of Lewis's career. Ten novels followed over the next two decades. The concern with a variety of social and political issues remained – prison conditions, organized philanthropy, the Negro question, the labour unions, communism and fascism. But the tone of the satirist yielded increasingly to that of the pamphleteer. The later novels failed to meet with the success of the major work, and critics have commonly agreed that they are inferior productions.

During the 1920s, Lewis was thought by many to be the leading American novelist. His impact was immense. To a massive reading public, at home and abroad, he seemed to offer a precise diagnosis of the cultural and moral ills of America – the malaise inseparable from the new materialism of the post-war years. His reputation has since waned, and his subsequent influence has been slight. His importance is now often judged to be chiefly historical. Accurate and pungent at its best, his satire is not distinguished by its subtlety. Its triumphs are easily come by. In so far as his work has a redeeming complexity, it is the result of a latent orthodoxy which was present in Lewis from the outset, and conflicts with the iconoclastic and ostensibly enlightened attitudes of the major novels. It draws him into sympathy with the very objects of his satire, and allows him to perceive the frustration and despair that lie beneath the jejune enthusiasms and vacuous pieties he otherwise mocks so vigorously.

Andrew Gibson

Other works include: *The Trail of the Hawk* (1915); *The Job* (1917); *Free Air* (1919); *Mantrap* (1926); *The Man Who Knew Coolidge* (1928); *Dodsworth* (1929); *Ann Vickers* (1933); *Work of Art* (1934); *It Can't Happen Here* (1935); *The Prodigal Parents* (1938); *Bethel Merriday* (1940); *Gideon Planish* (1943); *Cass Timberlane* (1946); *Kingsblood Royal* (1947); *The God-Seeker* (1949); *World so Wide* (1951). On Lewis: D. J. Dooley, *The Art of Sinclair Lewis* (1967); M. Light, *The Quixotic Vision of Sinclair Lewis* (1975); M. Schorer, *Sinclair Lewis, An American Life* (1971); M. Schorer (ed.), *Sinclair Lewis, A Collection of Critical Essays* (1962).

275
LEWIS, (Percy) Wyndham 1882–1957

British painter, novelist, critic

Of mixed British and American parentage, Wyndham Lewis was born on a yacht off Nova Scotia, and was educated at Rugby, the Slade School of Art, and privately as an art student in various European cities, including Paris and Munich. Originally primarily a painter, Lewis began writing in order to do justice to what he felt he must keep out of his painting to prevent it from being too 'literary'.

Lewis early developed an absurdist view of life, with the body seen as a primitive and 'wild' machine, to which an essentially alien mind was attached. This condition can be seen as either comic or tragic. The early writings on the theme were revised and collected in *The Wild Body* (1927). The stories concern peasant life in Brittany, and rigorously exclude sentiment. Ear-

ly pictures, executed in a style derived from Cubism, and as satires on Fauvism, depict primitives, but in a way that prevents sentimental identification with their mindless self-absorption; one can be a spectator or a participant, but not both. This theme is also the subject of Lewis's first novel, *Tarr* (1918). The unillusioned artist Tarr is unable to organize his life, and is no less absurd than the deluded German romantics Bertha and Kreisler, who live the myth of Bohemia.

Tarr satirizes romantic social conventions, but Lewis recognized that without shared values and myths life is mechanical and worthless. He felt that technology gave people control over their lives as never before, and that the artist should bring this revolution to public consciousness. Lewis criticized Cubist pictures for restricted subject-matter which detracted from major formal innovations, whereas Futurist pictures lacked formal rigour and evinced too uncritical an adulation of the machine. Breaking away from Roger Fry's* Omega Workshops in 1913, Lewis founded the Vorticist movement and edited its magazine *Blast* (2 issues, 1914 and 1915).

Lewis's Vorticist pictures are geometric abstractions from mechanical and architectural forms, conveying both the violence and excitement of the modern city. They are anti-formalist (in opposition to Fry) and exploit discords in colour and unpleasant paint texture (e.g. *Workshop* and *The Crowd*, both in the Tate Gallery). Vorticism was destroyed by the war, in which Lewis served on the Western Front and as an artist. The hatred of war and violence he acquired can be seen in his war pictures, which adapt the harsh and angular vocabulary of Vorticism for more realistic ends.

Lewis's revolutionary enthusiasm survived the war briefly, and it took some years to adapt his artistic means to his new sense of the world. The main achievements of the transition period (1919–25) are pencil portraits and figure studies that show his skill as one of the century's finest draughtsmen.

It seemed to Lewis in the 1920s that, instead of controlling their lives, people were passive and fatalistic, despite living in a largely man-made world. In a series of books he analysed this failure of will in the fields of philosophy, politics, popular culture and literature (*The Art of Being Ruled*, 1926; *Time and Western Man*, 1927; *Paleface*, 1929; *Doom of Youth*, 1932). *The Childermass* (1928), a fantasy of life after death, is a fictional presentation of the same theme, as is *The Apes of God* (1930) – a satirical and pessimistic masterpiece of the same order as Pope's *Dunciad*.

Lewis's reputation was permanently damaged during the 1930s. Fearful of another war, he wrote anti-war books showing sympathy to Fascist regimes and policies. But the coldness or 'brutality' of Lewis's style has been too readily equated with an authoritarian temperament; *The Revenge for Love* (1937), a novel, is humane and moving: one of the profoundest 'political' novels since Conrad*.

Lewis now tried to re-establish his reputation as a painter, with an exhibition (1937) of oils produced, despite serious illness, since 1933. The pictures express the same tragic sense of life evident in *The Revenge*, and show the influence of De Chirico* and the Surrealists. Together with the essays on art in *Wyndham Lewis the Artist* (1939), they influenced the generation of British painters then emerging. The oil portraits of 1937–9, notably of T. S. Eliot*, Ezra Pound* and of the artist's wife, are among the greatest of this century.

Lewis spent the war in the USA and in Canada, unwilling to watch Europe destroy itself again. Fantastic water-colours concerned with violence and creativity are the main result of this unhappy period, which forms the background of a fine tragic novel, *Self Condemned* (1954). Despite going blind in 1951 Lewis continued to write criticism and fiction, and some critics have seen this late work as his best. *The Human Age: Part II* (1955), ostensibly a continuation of the unfinished *Childermass*, explores the tragic consequences of Lewis's absurdist view of life in a time of mass-violence and genocide. Lewis had always seen himself as a 'detached' intellectual, though not an unconcerned one; without rejecting that role he now measured its human consequences. He died in 1957 before writing the final volume of *The Human Age*.

Lewis's work is difficult to evaluate, partly because of its immense scope. He is of major importance independently in each of the following areas: painting; art criticism and theory; literary criticism; fiction. Some critics have considered him of importance as a poet. His influence has been hidden but enormous, felt by figures as diverse as El Lissitsky and Graham Sutherland*, Marshall McLuhan* and George Orwell*, Samuel Beckett* and Anthony Powell*, David Storey and Saul Bellow*. His best work shows an incomparably energetic accuracy in the use of the medium, in presenting its subject and in embodying a unique and forceful personality.

Paul Edwards

Other works: Fiction: *Snooty Baronet* (1932); *The Vulgar Streak* (1941); *Rotting Hill* (1951); *The Red Priest* (1956); *Unlucky for Pringle* (ed. Fox and Chapman, 1973); *Collected Poems and Plays* (ed. Munton, 1979). *Blasting and Bombardiering* (1937) and *Rude Assignment* (1950) are autobiographical. Literary criticism: *The Lion and the Fox* (1927); *Men without Art* (1934); *The Writer and the Absolute* (1952); *Enemy Salvoes* (ed. Fox, 1975). Art criticism: *The Demon of Progress in the Arts* (1954); *Wyndham Lewis on Art* (ed. Fox and Michel, 1969). *Wyndham Lewis: Paintings and Drawings* (1971) by Walter Michel is the most comprehensive work on Lewis's paintings. Critical studies include: Hugh Kenner, *Wyndham Lewis* (1954); William H.

Pritchard, *Wyndham Lewis* (1968); Robert T. Chapman, *Wyndham Lewis: Fictions and Satires* (1973) and Geoffrey Meyers, *The Enemy: A Biography of Wyndham Lewis* (1980). *A Bibliography of the Writings of Wyndham Lewis* by B. Morrow and B. Lafourcade was published in 1978.

276

LICHTENSTEIN, Roy 1923–

US painter

Fascinated by American popular mythology and by the language of mass visual communication, Lichtenstein was central to the American Pop Art movement of the 1960s. His pre-war paintings had frequently depicted a certain side of his native New York: jazz musicians, Coney Island, etc. In 1949–50 his favoured subjects had been cowboys, Indians and all aspects of the Western myth. But it was only in 1961 that his painting style, hitherto mostly loose and expressionistic, changed into the impersonal, hard-edged look for which he is famous and which was the perfect tool for his ironic semantic analysis.

His first properly called Pop paintings were of Walt Disney* characters but he soon switched for his material to comic books like *Armed Forces at War* and *Teen Romance*, whose subject-matter was more emotionally charged. With deliberate humour, he exploited the powerful narrative impact of such images. At first sight, his paintings appear merely as massively enlarged reproductions; only then does the difference appear between his purpose and that of the 'originals'. Rather than story-telling, his aim is the creation of a unified work of art, in an almost Classical sense. From his student days at Ohio State University, he learned the central importance for art of 'organized perception'. *What* one happens to be looking at is far less important than 'building a unified pattern of seeing'. His work testifies that this is possible even from the most unpromising material and in so doing opens up hitherto unsuspected perspectives on that material, in terms of both technical and wider social factors. Particularly successful is his painting *Whaam!* (1963), whose overt subject is aerial combat but whose real subject is the exploration of one sign-system by means of another. Like many of Lichtenstein's pictures, this features an explosion, the attraction of which lies in the contrast between the amorphousness of the phenomenon and the concreteness of its conventionalized representation. He has even made solid sculptures of explosions. Almost Lichtenstein's trademark is the Benday dot, the commercial printing technique for simulating halftones, to whose artificiality attention is drawn by its being transferred, in his paintings, to a vastly larger scale than that for which it was intended. Benday dots appear not only in paintings with comic-derived imagery but also in a vast amount of Lichtenstein's other work, such as his series of ruined monumental architecture, for example *Temple II* (1964), his pastiches of modern masters, for example *Woman with Flowered Hat* (1963) after Picasso*, and his 1966–70 pastiches of Art Deco and 1930s mural painting, for example *Little Aviation* (1968). Again, he has also made sculptures with Benday dots.

In one sense, Lichtenstein's interests are abstract and formal. He certainly does not intend any social message as such. However, as he himself points out, the cool 'lack of sensibility' in his work relates directly to that 'kind of brutality' and 'aggressiveness' which he believes characterizes the 'world outside largely formed by industrialism or by advertising'.

Gray Watson

See: Tate Gallery Catalogue, London (1968); Diane Waldman, *Roy Lichtenstein: Drawings and Prints* (1969); Diane Waldman, *Roy Lichtenstein* (1971); John Coplans (ed.), *Roy Lichtenstein* (1972).

277
LONDON, Jack (John Griffith) 1876–1916

US novelist

The illegitimate son of an astrologer, Jack London was born in San Francisco and brought up by his mother and step-father, keeping the latter's name. Throughout his adult life he worked hard, like Hemingway* after him, to create a myth of himself and the short episodes experienced as an adolescent: working as an oyster pirate and on the Fishery Patrol, joining Coxey's Army in its march of protest on Washington against unemployment, going to the Arctic on a sealer, or to the Klondike rush for gold. These experiences became exaggerated into the major episodes in his life, and out of them emerged an ambitious writer of short stories and novels who worked in short bursts and spent the rest of the time with his friends and hangers-on, accumulating debts which had to be paid for by hackwork. The myth he clung to and disseminated was that of the self-made man, rising from drudgery and criminality to a hard-living outdoor man, traveller and intellectual, absorbing all the latest theories and combining radical socialism with evolutionism and determinism.

The fusion of the ideas of Herbert Spencer, Marx and Nietzsche with the stylistic influences of Kipling* and Robert Louis Stevenson produced vivid adventure stories riddled with philosophizing, wildly inconsistent and yet hauntingly revealing of the dilemmas and nightmares of the time. Captain Wolf Larsen in *Sea Wolf* (1904) is a Nietzschean super-man, immensely strong, resourceful, intelligent and articulate, who propounds a belief in the supremacy of power as the only meaning in the Universe, and yet is defeated by a brain tumour and a bourgeois greenhorn whom he kidnaps. Similarly, in the semi-autobiographical *Martin Eden* (1909), the seaman hero becomes a successful author only to reject the possibility of marriage into the middle classes and instead, in disgust and despair, he commits suicide. Such self-defeat suggests that evolution, conceived as a competition to find the fittest, is a metaphor inadequate to our life as a species, and that the elitism it entails is empty because it is nihilistic; there is no obvious purpose in power except the exercise of it.

London's best writing works by undercutting itself and hence suggesting further depths. His renowned animal stories, *The Call of the Wild* (1903), in which a pet dog becomes a sledge-dog and thence the leader of a wild pack, and *White Fang* (1906), in which a wild dog enters into a close, but ambiguous relationship with a man, explore his ambivalent attitude towards predatory and aggressive drives. This takes the form both of an admiration for them and a fear of the ruthless and unstable consequences. Closer to contemporary problems, his documentary account of the poverty of the East End of London, *The People of the Abyss* (1903), alternately sees the inhabitants as social victims and as dregs, the evolutionarily unfit; *The Iron Heel* (1907) is a distopic vision of the future of Chicago under a totalitarian dictatorship. The underlying contradictions of London's time emerge here with a commitment to competitive individualism and also a fear of centralized power. Even the socialism of the time stressed the efficiency of nationalization and centralization, and yet London could only conceive this as the result of individual initiative. This is illustrated in *The Dream of Debs* (1914) or the posthumously completed *The Assassination Bureau* (1963), where socialist millionaires use force and violence to bring about universal peace and justice.

The underlying despair, most clearly visible in London's account of his alcoholism, *John Barleycorn* (1913), where an inner 'white logic' argues against all purpose or meaning, seems to have underpinned most of his life, and his death was at least partially caused by his own indulgence in drink and drugs.

Dr David Corker

London's stories appeared originally in such volumes as *The Son of the Wolf* (1900), *Children of the Frost* (1902), *South Sea Tales* (1911), and *The Scarlet Plague* (1915). Other novels include: *Before Adam* (1907); *The Valley of the Moon* (1913). See also: Dale Walker and James E. Sisson III, *The Fiction of Jack London: A Chronological Bibliography* (1972); Charmian London, *The Book of Jack London* (1921); Joan London, *Jack London and his Times* (1939); Irving Stone, *Sailor on Horseback* (1938); Earle Lubor, *Jack London* (1974).

James I. McClintock, *White Logic* (1976) is a critical study of the stories.

278

LOOS, Adolf 1870–1933

Austrian architect and journalist

Adolf Loos spent his formative years in the Vienna of the 1890s – the same environment that fostered Otto Wagner and the members of the Wiener Sezession group – among them Gustav Klimt, Josef Hoffmann and Joseph Olbrich. It was a decade of artistic and intellectual ferment producing, in addition to the painters, architects and designers, avant-garde musicians and the prototype psychoanalyst, Sigmund Freud*.

Loos was taught building and architecture in several provincial schools. The years 1893–6 were spent in the United States where, among other stimuli, he saw the Chicago World's Fair of 1893. He returned to Vienna in 1896 and began work as a journalist writing in a strikingly satirical style about fashion, design and architecture. It is as an architectural critic that Loos has influenced the architectural Modern Movement and his reputation is founded largely on two major essays – *Ornament und Verbrechen* ('Ornament and Crime') of 1908 and *Architektur* ('Architecture') of 1910. The former is a highly opinionated piece of writing, using anthropological evidence to back up the idea, put forward by Loos, that civilized man avoids decoration and that this level of civilization should also be reflected in his architectural environment. In the article Loos sharply attacks protagonists of the florid Art Nouveau style, among them Eckmann and Olbrich, and suggests, as an alternative, that a return to Classicism is the correct path for architectural development. There is a strong traditionalist lurking behind most of Loos's words and classical detailing enters much of his architectural work. *Ornament and Crime* was reprinted in the French periodical *L'Esprit nouveau* in 1920 and had a tremendous impact upon avant-garde architects there at that time. It paved the way for Loos's own arrival in Paris in 1923.

Loos fell out with the Sezession group in 1898 supposedly because Hoffmann would not let him design an interior for the Sezession building, and he spent the next ten years producing a number of interior designs in Vienna. In 1898 he designed some shop fittings for Goldmann and Salatch for which he employed a rectilinear wooden framework. In 1899 he produced a design for the *Café Museum* and in 1904–6 he altered and extended a villa at Montreux for a Viennese client in which he made use of luxury materials like marble, resembling Hoffmann's use of the same material in his Palais Stoclet in Brussels.

The architectural construction with which Loos is most frequently associated and which completes his connection with the unornamented white buildings of the International Modern Movement is the Steiner House of 1910. It is the first example of the modern square box with a very simple, regular plan, a symmetrical façade and a total absence of applied decoration.

Loos's reputation as a Modern architect stems largely from the way he was received in Parisian society in the 1920s, by which time Art Nouveau had lost all of its impact and the mechanistic model for architecture was the norm in the work of individuals like Le Corbusier* and Mallet-Stevens.

Penny Sparke

Many of his writings can be found in A. Loos, *Sämtliche Schriften*, vol. 1 (1962); A. Loos, *Trotzdem* (1930). See also: L. Musitz and Kunstler, *Adolf Loos* (1966); and Reyner Banham, *Theory and Design in the First Machine Age* (1960).

279

LORCA, Federico García 1898–1936

Spanish poet, dramatist

Born in Fuente Vaqueros, Granada, Lorca achieved mythic status as a symbolic sacrificial victim of fascism with his murder in 1936. His work, status and worth have been buried under layers of interpretation and exegesis; his versatility and difficulty have attracted every sort of criticism – the reason for his murder (his homosexuality, his politics, his notoriety?) being a good example of this.

Lorca was a mercurial figure in whose enigmatic work several different elements can be identified. Central to all was the theatrical, sometimes histrionic but always dramatic nature of his life and work. He wrote many experimental plays from folk tragedies to surrealist farces, from puppet plays to almost naturalistic dramas and can be considered Spain's foremost twentieth-century playwright: he incorporated children's songs and games, surrealist devices, symbolic scene settings in his main plays from *Mariana Pineda* (1925) to *When five years pass* (*Así que pasen cinco años*, 1931), *The Public* (*El público*, 1933) to the celebrated trilogy *Blood Wedding* (*Bodas de sangre*, 1933), *Yerma* (1934) and *Bernarda Alba* (*La casa de Bernarda Alba*, 1936). He was at the height of his skill as a ceaselessly inventive dramatist when he was killed. His poetry could also be anecdotal and dramatic (with events and characters); even self-dramatic as in the posthumously published *Poet in New York* (1940). A narrative thread links his famous *Gypsy Ballads* (*Romancero gitano*, 1928), binding the brilliant images together. Lorca loved declaiming his verse aloud.

Lorca was also a painter (he exhibited in Barcelona in 1927) and was an early friend of Salvador Dalí*. His naive, colourist and whimsical paintings underline the power of his poetic imagery by drawing attention to their visual, plastic and sensual basis. For Lorca the image was at the origin of all language; the image was a transposition of the senses, the poet being the 'teacher of the five body senses'. This points to the emotionally vivid way his writing deals with the external world.

A friend of Manuel de Falla, Lorca was also a proficient musician; he collected folk-songs and possessed an acute ear for rhythm and sound, which, allied with visual acuity, underscores all his writing. He often incorporated lullabies, popular songs, cante jondo, into his work.

Lorca's receptivity to the aural, visual and dramatic was the mainspring of his art. Although he began a formal education (Law at Granada University) he never graduated. He was a humorous, provocative and deliberately childish anti-intellectual (he avoided self-analysis, explanation, definitions of poetry), though his critical effort in his generation's revival of Góngora is revealing. Lorca had a strong sense of craft and tradition but always experimented.

By 1927 (with Book of Poems, Poem of the Cante jondo) he was already considered as a major poet. But his famous Romancero gitano (1928) brought him the kind of instant popularity usually denied to modern poets. In these updatings of medieval ballads (romances) Lorca used the gypsy (the romantic outcast, primitive, still tied to elemental forces) as a myth on which to bind his often difficult and private but always sensual images in poems dealing with fundamental passions (sex, death, violence, pain). The following year Lorca left Spain (for the first time) for New York (part failed love affair, part escape from popularity) where the extreme culture shock produced Lorca's most difficult poems (Poeta en Nueva York). He hated Anglo-Saxon culture, but found sympathy with the blacks and Walt Whitman. It is from these explosive, private and surrealistic poems that Lorca started out on another burst of creativity. He founded a student drama group (La barraca) to bring theatre back to the people in the villages (he was always a populist). In 1935 he published his moving and beautifully controlled Lament for Ignacio Sánchez Mejías (Llanto por I.S.M.), a bullfighter friend killed, and his last collection heralding yet another direction, the Diván del Tamarit (1936).

His sudden violent death seemed to many to be the death of a certain kind of carefree artist-child; a quality that most witnesses to Lorca's life selected as essential to his personality (his charm, spontaneity, his mimetic qualities). As a poet it is the literally enchanting way in which Lorca makes the reader participate in the work, combining seductivity with a pressure to communicate. Lorca's identification with the gypsy as persecuted outcast, with the sterile mother, with doomed passionate lovers, with passion, death and violence, could all be metaphors of his own life, but that would be to psychologize his gift, his fertility, what he called the duende (the magical, dionysiacal source of art, close to 'blood', 'death' and found in music, dance and oral poetry).

Jason Wilson

The bibliography on Lorca is vast and is listed in his Obras completas (Madrid 1963). The following translations will help: Poet in New York, trans. Ben Belitt (1955); J. L. Gili, Lorca (1960); Three Tragedies (1961); Five Plays: Comedies and Tragicomedies (1963). See also: M. Durán (ed.), Lorca. A Collection of Critical Essays (1962); C. B. Morris, A Generation of Spanish Poets 1920–1936 (1969); R. M. Nadal, El público. Amor, teatro y caballo en la obra de F.G.L. (1971); I. Gibson, The Death of Lorca (1973); Mildred Adams, García Lorca: Playwright and Poet (1977).

280
LORENZ, Konrad Zacharias 1903–

Austrian ethologist

Konrad Lorenz's father was an eminent surgeon who invented a method of curing a congenital hip disorder, for which he was proposed for (but did not receive) the Nobel Prize. Konrad Lorenz graduated in medicine at Vienna University, but was already more interested in animal behaviour (ethology). He did his best work at the family home in Altenberg during the 1930s. His first major academic post was a chair of philosophy at Königsberg which he held for a year until conscripted. After being a prisoner of war in Russia until 1948 he worked mainly at Buldern. In 1956, together with his geese, he moved to Seewiesen where he stayed until retiring back to Altenberg in 1973, in which year he shared the Nobel Prize with Niko Tinbergen* and Karl von Frisch.

Although Darwin, among others, had made important observations of animal behaviour, Lorenz is aptly referred to as 'the father of ethology' because it was he (and Tinbergen) who first formulated many of the problems of ethology and who, both directly and through his many students, inspired much subsequent work. His naturalistic approach is apparent from the descriptions of jackdaws, geese and other animals in his ever-popular King Solomon's Ring (Er redete mit dem Vieh, den Vögeln und den Fischen, 1949; trans. 1952). Lorenz recognized that behaviour, just like anatomy, is organized into units, such as distinct sequences of movements. He called these units 'fixed action patterns' and studied their function and evolution by comparing them in different species. His 'theory of instincts' explained how fixed action patterns are 'released' in response to stimuli ('releasers') or sometimes occur spontaneously.

Lorenz has tended to dichotomize animal behaviour into the innate and the learned. This has been strongly criticized because 'innate' behaviour is demonstrably dependent on the environment during its development, though in different ways from learning. In his *Evolution and Modification of Behaviour* (1965), Lorenz said that he meant the dichotomy to apply to the animal's 'sources of information' about its environment, not to development. Lorenz also stressed that learning is adaptive and so cannot be independent of the genes (i.e. there must be 'innate teaching mechanisms').

After 1960 Lorenz increasingly concentrated on human behaviour. Much human behaviour, he argues, is the product of evolution ('phylogenetically acquired'). For example, in *On Aggression* (*Die sogenannte Böse*, 1963), he argued that aggression is 'instinctive' in humans and in many other animals; aggression will appear spontaneously in humans unless 'redirected' to some less destructive pursuit. The subsequent controversy was exacerbated by his bold, assertive literary style which makes him liable to misrepresentation. In *Civilized Man's Eight Deadly Sins* (1974), in addition to rehearsing the themes of environmentalism, Lorenz repeated his fear that civilization causes genetic deterioration. (He had previously written on this in a paper of 1940 replete with now retracted Nazi jargon; a mistranslation has led to Lorenz's being falsely accused of racism.) His fear that civilization is dysgenic may have been aroused by his father's work on congenital disorders (cf. Monod).

In addition Lorenz has been interested in the consequences of evolutionary theory for epistemology; early in his life he identified his idea of 'innate' with Kant's *a priori*. *Behind the Mirror* (*Die Rückseite des Spiegels*, 1973) further explores this theme.

Mark Ridley

Lorenz's other writings include: *Man Meets Dog* (*So kam der Mensch auf den Hund*, 1950); *Darwin hat recht gesehen* ('Darwin Has Seen Correctly', 1964); *Motivation of Human and Animal Behaviour* (*Antriebe tierischen und menschlichen Verhaltens Gesammelte Abhandlungen*, 1968); his collected papers, *Studies in Animal and Human Behaviour* (2 vols, London 1970 and 1971); *Vergleichende Verhaltensforschung* ('Comparative Ethology', 1978). See also: *Konrad Lorenz: The Man and His Ideas* (1975), ed. R. I. Evans; A. Nisbett, *Konrad Lorenz* (1976), a biography.

281

LOSEY, Joseph Walton 1909–

US film director

Born in La Crosse, Wisconsin, into a middle-class family of declining wealth and influence, Joseph Losey abandoned his medical studies at Dartmouth College on the eve of the Depression and the New Deal in order to pursue an interest in the theatre. In a classical reaction against an upbringing in which culture and liberalism were offset by snobbery and prejudice, he worked throughout the 1930s almost exclusively on Leftist plays or such agit-prop ventures as 'The Living Newspaper'.

In Hollywood, from 1948 to 1951, Losey made five feature films, which included a charming fantasy designed as a call to peace (*The Boy with Green Hair*, 1948), a powerful but conventional indictment of racial intolerance (*The Lawless*, 1948 – *The Dividing Line* in UK), and a classic thriller in the *film noir* mode (*The Prowler*, 1951). It was during this period, troubled by a sense of uselessness and by the anomaly of his position in Hollywood that Losey joined the Communist Party. As a result, he was obliged to go into exile, in anticipation of being blacklisted for 'un-American activities'.

In England, from 1954 until *The Servant* brought him world-wide recognition in 1963, there ensued a long and difficult period in which Losey was forced to work on subjects which held little interest for him, over which he did not exercise control, and to which he was initially prevented by the blacklist from signing his name. The result was the birth of what has been called Losey's baroque style, evident in the symbolic role played by explosive camera movements and Goya's painting of a bull in characterizing the tyrannical father in *Time Without Pity* (1957), or in the systematic use of mirror images and serpenting camera movements to suggest the ebb and flow of a marital relationship in *Eve* (1962).

Although frustration led to some over-elaboration while Losey was re-establishing his reputation, this 'baroque' style was brought under perfect control from *The Servant* onwards. Essentially it derives from two complementary factors at the root of all Losey's work. First, a theatrical conception of character – prerehearsal before filming begins enables the actors to work in depth, while the pursuing camera allows them to develop characterization in continuity – and second, an acute awareness of the role played by settings as reflectors or elucidators of behaviour.

First with the animator John Hubley in America, then the artist Richard MacDonald in England, Losey established a method of 'pre-designing' his films: with the aid of sketches, details of setting, lighting and movement were pre-planned so that the filmed images would yield *only*, and *precisely*, the impression required by the director's conception. In *The Prowler*, for example, a policeman enviously eyes the spacious archways and elegant white walls of a rich man's Spanish-style house to which he is summoned to investigate reports of a prowler; but as he becomes sexually involved with the lady of the house and contemplates murder for gain, one begins to see the house itself somewhat differently, as a cheap and shoddy imitation, a snare for consumers of the American dream. An even more striking example occurs in *Blind Date* (1959), where the same room looks entirely different when viewed first through the eyes of a young man in love, then again when he is beginning to suffer disillusionment.

It is this exactness of perception which made masterpieces of later Losey films like *The Servant, Accident* (1967) and *The Go-Between* (1971), all three superbly scripted by Harold Pinter*. Here, the roles played (respectively) by the town house foundering into decadence as the master is taken over by his servant, by the dreaming spires and Oxford lawns where the academics are faced with their own inadequacies, by the country mansion bathed in endless summer which tempts a boy to venture disastrously out of his social depth, are absolutely crucial to the barbed analysis of a lingeringly moribund English social system.

The Servant, cold, calculating and glitteringly witty, was generally hailed as the insight of an outsider casting an acidly dispassionate eye on an alien society. But the warmth, the nostalgia even, that infuses *Accident, Secret Ceremony* (1968), *The Go-Between* and much of *Mr Klein* (1976) suggests that in these films Losey is also coming to terms with his own background, one of wealth and privilege remarkably similar to the Middle Western family whose past grandeurs and present decadence are chronicled with a bittersweet mixture of malice and regret in Orson Welles's* *The Magnificent Ambersons*.

Tom Milne

Other films include: *M* (1951); *The Sleeping Tiger* (1954); *The Gypsy and the Gentleman* (1957); *The Damned* (1962); *King and Country* (1964); *Modesty Blaise* (1966); *Boom* (1968); *Figures in a Landscape* (1970); *The Assassination of Trotsky* (1972); *A Doll's House* (1973); *The Romantic Englishwoman* (1975); *Les Routes du Sud* (1978); *Don Giovanni* (1979). See: Tom Milne (ed.), *Losey on Losey* (1967); James Leahy, *The Cinema of Joseph Losey* (1967); Michel Ciment (ed.), *Le Livre de Losey* (1979).

282
LOWELL, Amy 1874–1925

US poet

T. S. Eliot* called her the 'demon saleswoman of poetry'; D. H. Lawrence* felt that she was 'much nicer, finer, bigger' as a person than as a poet; Ezra Pound* held her responsible for turning the fertile Imagist movement into that much feebler phenomenon 'Amygism'. The verdicts of these three major figures have

not helped Amy Lowell's reputation. She is remembered today chiefly for her personal eccentricities: the Manila cigars, the nocturnal work schedule, the bed of many pillows. And if she is read at all, it tends to be in anthologies, where she looks one of the least impressive of the Imagists. Yet Amy Lowell was a more complex person, and a very different kind of poet, than is popularly imagined. The poet who could help Robert Frost* as well as write a book on French Symbolism, and who used long narrative modes as well as miniaturist ones, was more than the narrow and bullying self-promoter that she is sometimes said to have been. Though a follower rather than a leader, she played an active and influential part in the development of Modernist poetry.

Amy Lowell grew up in Brookline, a well-to-do suburb of Boston, and spent most of her life in her parents' house 'Sevenels' (its garden was a source for many of her poems). Educated privately, she left school at seventeen determining to teach herself. A rigorous reading course followed, and a lifelong admiration for Keats – about whom she was later to write a two-volume biography – Tennyson, and Walter Scott. These Romantic influences were evident in her first, undistinguished collection *A Dome of Many Coloured Glass* (1912), published when she was in her late thirties. The lukewarm reviews might have deterred a less ambitious writer, but when the following year she discovered the poetry of H. D. and others in Harriet Monroe's magazine *Poetry*, Amy Lowell became convinced that she was part of a wider movement (as she put it, 'Why I, too, am an Imagiste'). The conviction led her to London, where she met Pound, Richard Aldington and their colleagues, and within two years, much to Pound's displeasure, she had put together the first of her three Imagist anthologies. She continued to champion Imagism and *vers libre* until her death – notably in her critical study *Tendencies in Modern American Poetry* (1917).

Though a zealous promoter of Imagism, Amy Lowell was not by nature a poet of terseness and 'essentiality'. True, her second collection *Sword Blades and Poppy Seed* (1914) had a new power and conciseness; and later, in *Fir-Flower Tablets* (1921), she collaborated with Florence Ayscough in translations of Chinese poetry (an attempt to compete with Pound's *Cathay*). But her instinct was towards looser forms: 'the long flowing cadence of oratorical prose', or as she put it in a more self-deprecating moment 'whirling afflatus'. Collections like *Men, Women and Ghosts* (1916) and *Legends* (1921) contain many ballads and long narratives. *Can Grande's Castle* (1918) is a sustained experiment in what she called 'polyphonic prose'. *A Critical Fable* (1922) provides an extended satirical assessment of her poetic contemporaries. Only in what is perhaps her best collection, *Pictures of the Floating World* (1919), did she properly come to grips with miniaturist forms. The central image of 'Middle Age', for example, is not picturesque, but disturbing and authentic:

Like black ice
Scrolled over with unintelligible patterns by an ignorant skater
Is the dulled surface of my heart.

In this and a handful of other poems ('Patterns', 'In a Garden', 'The Basket', 'Sisters'), Amy Lowell seems a genuine talent rather than a mere camp follower. Her own prediction – 'She'll be rated by time as more rather than less' – may seem unduly genial, for even as a publicist she made mistakes, allowing personal rivalries to obscure her critical judgment (how else could she have preferred John Gould Fletcher to Ezra Pound?). But she did much to overcome popular resistance to modern poetry, had a shrewd eye for the healthy and new, and fought her battles on a surprisingly broad front.

Blake Morrison

The standard edition of the poems is *The Complete Poetical Works of Amy Lowell* (1955). See also: F. C. Flint, *Amy Lowell* (1969); Jean Gould, *Amy: The World of Amy Lowell and the Imagist Movement* (1975).

283
LOWELL, Robert 1917–77
US poet

The scion of an old Boston family, Lowell was descended from the poet James Russell Lowell and related to the Imagist ('Amygist') Amy Lowell*. After entering Harvard, he left to study under John Crowe Ransom* at Kenyon College, Ohio, where he also came under the influence of the poet Allen Tate. The move was a symbolic one, a reaction against the suffocating civilization of money he had inherited in New England which he sought to correct with the classicism and decorum of the Southern tradition. While growing up, as he himself said, as 'Northern, disembodied, a Platonist, a puritan', he grew to despise the values of his forefathers. In 1943 Lowell served five months in prison for refusing military service, and during the 1960s was an active spokesman in both the Civil Rights Movement and in the campaign against the war in Vietnam.

His work shows a three-part movement, as the critic Thomas Parkinson puts it, 'from Roman Catholicism to general Christian piety to a kind of agnostic existentialism'. He in fact entered the Catholic Church in 1940 and seceded from it in 1950. *Land of Unlikeness* (1944), *Lord Weary's Castle* (1946) and *The Mills of the Kavanaughs* (1951) contain studied poems, sometimes clotted with allusiveness and rigid with metaphor, burdened with his sense of the war and a profound alienation from traditional Christian consolations. His principal subject, as he himself glossed it, was 'struggle, light and darkness, the flux of experience'. Another chief theme he found in his personal antagonism towards Boston as a city representative of commercialism. He associated the notions of dread and death and materialism as sterile misconceptions of spirituality, engrossed himself in the works of Hawthorne, Melville, Bunyan, Hooker, and Jonathan Edwards, and accordingly took the stance of an anti-Calvinist. In an Introduction to *Land of Unlikeness*, Allen Tate pin-pointed the concern with a 'memory of the spiritual dignity of man now sacrificed to the mere secularization and a craving for mechanical order'. A number of the early poems are in a sense spoiled by being forced towards a position of religious affirmation. Though some end with strident, rhetorical appeals for divine intercession in the affairs of mankind, however, perhaps most of them succeed in expressing Lowell's keen apprehension of religious vacuity, desolation, and determinism. We must allow in the early work for two strains: the spirit of violence and doom which he loathed in Calvinism, and the sense of grace he perceived as a possibility of his Catholicism. The best-known of the early works is 'The Quaker Graveyard in Nantucket', a powerfully achieved elegy for his cousin Warren Winslow who was killed at sea.

After losing his faith, it was eight years before Lowell brought out another volume, *Life Studies* (1959). A sequence which Stephen Spender* has cruelly but pertinently called Lowell's 'Family Album', *Life Studies* has likewise been inappositely labelled 'Confessional' verse, although the volume was assuredly a new departure towards loose verse forms detailing the poet's feelings of dispossession. The prevailing mood is one of pathos: Lowell defines himself through an ironic inspection of his memories and impressions of childhood and close kin. He discovers both destitution, sometimes comic and ineffectual, and new dignity. Subdued, conversational, and yet strictly controlled in form despite their apparent looseness, the poems can be affectionate and indulgent, as in the close of 'My Last Afternoon with Uncle Devereux Winslow', or directly satirical, as in the portrait of his father 'Commander Lowell'. More emphatically personal is 'Man and Wife', though perhaps the most important and exciting poem is 'Skunk Hour', which moves from satire, through sardonicism, to what Lowell himself called 'affirmation, an ambiguous one'. Throughout *Life Studies*, in fact, there runs an ambiguous statement of personal integrity; the affirmation of human affections ironically characterizes the remainder of Lowell's work.

For the Union Dead (1964) is in many ways more painful than *Life Studies*: a volume of post-Christian poems largely concerned with the failure of personal relationships, its tone is self-condemning. Although the poet is no less morally alert, the poems seem to lack morale and a substitute for the Christian sanction which suffused the earlier work.

Near the Ocean (1967) contains a number of translations, but precedes them with a group of fine poems about the ambiguous moral order Lowell has ascertained. They combine wistfulness with a sense of theological disease; their uncanny poise of tone is undercut by a terrifyingly severe indictment of a land which has lost spiritual values, as in 'Waking Early Sunday Morning' where the earth is figured as 'a ghost/orbiting forever lost/in our monotonous sublime'. The tenor of the poems veers between bitterness at Man's estate and a growing faith in existential consolation.

History (1973) consists of serried blank-verse sonnets. The volume reworks, expands, and puts into chronological order an earlier volume called *Notebook* (1969) and is presumably modelled on *Les Trophées* (by José-Maria de Heredia), a sequence which, just like Lowell's, attempts to chart and evoke the foci of succeeding civilizations, from Greece through Rome and the Renaissance to the landscapes and impressions of its own times. Lowell found the period from 1967 to 1972, during which he seems to have written mainly unrhymed sonnets, a time of happy reversion to his ideal of 'formal, difficult' poetry.

The Dolphin (1973) represents perhaps the happiest marriage possible between the studied, formal, and evasive mode that he indulged for so long in *Notebook* and *History* and a treatment of personal experience that he had cultivated earlier. Exploring a symbol of succour, lovingness, and constancy, *The Dolphin* makes available the best devices that may be recovered from the Symbolists, raising personal emotion to a level of suggestiveness and immutability.

Day by Day (1977) represents a wilful regression to free-verse, 'a way of writing I once thought heartless'. Although these last verses continue Lowell's serial autobiography, they lack the proven fierce rhetoric and syntax of his earlier decades. The prevailing mood is elegiac, rehearsing old friendships and mismanaged love, and indeed the rue and melancholy of certain poems about lost relationships often have an intense poignancy. The finest poems continue to illustrate Lowell's porcelain sensitivity. Lowell clearly regretted leaving behind the grand and formal manner. His last poems demonstrate contemplation and achieved art, though the evidence of fresh insight is disconcertingly weak. Tender-hearted, enduring without demanding, several poems do still touch to magic moments, whimsies, a sense of transience, and the pathos and incorrigibility of the poet's own life.

Dr John Haffenden

Other volumes: *Phaedra* (1961); *Imitations* (1961); *The Old Glory* (1965); *Prometheus Bound* (1969); *For Lizzie and Harriet* (1973). See also: John Crick, *Robert Lowell* (1974); Hugh B. Staples, *Robert Lowell: The First Twenty Years* (1962); Jonathan Price, *Critics on Robert Lowell* (1974); Patrick Cosgrave, *The Public Poetry of Robert Lowell* (1970); and Alan Williamson, *Pity the Monsters: The Political Vision of Robert Lowell* (1974).

284

LUKÁCS, Georg 1885–1971

Hungarian philosopher and literary critic

Gyorgy Szegedy von Lukács, considered by many to be the foremost Marxist thinker of our age, was born in Budapest of a wealthy Jewish family. His father was a self-made banker ennobled by the Hapsburg crown. The Lukácses (originally Löwingers) were thoroughly German in their culture, and their son, who once said he could hardly philosophize in Hungarian, wrote most of his books in German. After a training in law Lukács, eager to learn philosophy and social science, departed for Berlin in 1906, and again in 1909, when he attended the lectures of Georg Simmel*. During this period he began his long and distinguished career as a literary critic, contributing to *West*, a journal strongly opposed to the conventional nationalism of the Magyar establishment while receptive to modernist attitudes in art. From 1912 to 1915 he lived in Heidelberg, continuing his philosophical studies under Heinrich Rickert, a leading neo-Kantian with a stark anti-naturalist bias. There he became acquainted with the charismatic Stefan George circle, made friends with Emil Lask and the Marxist utopian Ernst Bloch*, impressed Max Weber* as an intense, near Tolstoyan youth, and wrote his most influential piece of literary essayism, *The Theory of the Novel* (1916, trans. 1971). Soon after the outbreak of the First World War he returned to Budapest. Dreading a German victory, he was filled with equal dismay at the prospect of the triumph of Western capitalism and its utilitarian values; nor, having sympathized with the anarcho-syndicalism of Georges Sorel since his schooldays, could he at first welcome the October Revolution. None the less, within a week of its foundation in 1918, he joined the Hungarian Communist Party, and served as commissar for public education in the short-lived coalition government headed by the communist Béla Kun, fleeing to Austria after its overthrow by right-wing forces in the summer of 1919. For the next decade he settled in Vienna, devoting himself to the survival of communism in the West, editing an ultra-leftist journal and remaining largely oblivious of such Vienna-based developments as psychoanalysis and logical positivism. Instead his overwhelming concern at the time was the philosophical understanding of political revolution. Between 1919 and 1922 he wrote eight essays that together make up *History and Class Consciousness* (*Geschichte und Klassenbe-*

wusstsein, 1923, trans. 1971), his major contribution to Marxist theory.

In 1931, after a year at the Marx-Engels-Lenin Institute in Moscow, Lukács moved to Berlin, where he started writing Marxist literary criticism, engaging in a two-front polemic – against avant-garde formalism on the one hand, and Stalinist propaganda literature on the other – that was to continue for the rest of his life. Forced to return to Moscow by the rise of Hitler*, he was admitted as a researcher to the Institute of Philosophy of the Soviet Academy of Sciences, where, in addition to some remarkable studies of the European novel, he produced a study of the early thought of Hegel. During the years of the popular front policy (1935–9) his prestige in the Soviet Union was considerable; yet this did not protect him from harassment by Stalinist* hard-liners, nor from a spell of imprisonment in 1941. At the end of the Second World War he returned to Budapest, where he was appointed a professor at the university and sat in the national assembly, despite continuing attacks on his publications. Wisely he refrained from any significant political activities while Stalin* lived, preferring to busy himself with the completion of his Marxist history of modern philosophy, *The Destruction of Reason* (1954). Following the thaw, however, he lent his authority to the restless meetings of the Petőfi Circle, an ideological prelude to the Uprising of 1956. Appointed Minister of Culture in the Nagy government, Lukács was duly deported to a Romanian spa following the Russian invasion. Although he was soon allowed to return to Hungary, he was not readmitted to the Party until 1967. The important works of his last years were the lengthy, though unfinished, summas: *Die Eigenart des Aesthetischen* ('The Peculiarity of Aesthetics', 1963) and *Zur Ontologie des gesellschaftlichen Seins* ('The Ontology of Social Existence', 1971–3).

Although it is possible to divide Lukács's output into literary criticism and his aesthetics and social theory, the one continuous throughout his career, the other only intermittent, the two are peculiarly mortgaged to each other. As a thinker this was both his strength and his weakness. In so far as the point of *History and Class Consciousness* is the elucidation of the purpose and meaning of the social world, this Marxist *opus magnum* may be said to descend from the existential preoccupations of Lukács's early, pre-Marxist literary criticism (see below). Technically speaking, its theme is the spelling out of the genuine sense of Marxism. In Lukács's view orthodox Marxism does not consist in any allegiance to specific tenets, but in its faithfulness to a method: the dialectic. Method as dialectic means not so much a set of rules, but a way of thinking based on the awareness that true thought at once grasps the world and changes it. In this Lukács was emphasizing the Hegelian roots of Marxism, for Hegel had argued that true reason does not fully understand reality until

it realizes that the very act of understanding also belongs to reality, that proper thought is itself a function of the world, which it not only mirrors, but *is*. This uniting of the cognitive and the normative is reflected in the way that Lukács's dialectic works as *praxis*, as opposed to contemplation. Above all dialectical thought implies a sense of *totality*: it requires viewing the social universe as a dynamic, directional whole, existing and acting beyond any given set of mere facts. Facts, indeed, are viewed as 'Momente', partial aspects of the ever-changing whole. For this reason Lukács's 'totality' is pre-eminently characterized by the future, a future both foreseen and created. However, to be concrete, totality needs 'mediations', directional links connecting it with particular phenomena. Without mediations it would be an abstract ideal, and not the concrete historical movement in its substance. Moreover totality as praxis is self-activated: its nature is that of a *subject*. Again, like Hegel's *Geist*, totality must be an 'identical subject-object', both an objective reality and the subject that knows it, and in so doing also knows itself as an active part of it.

Thus, in praxis, knowledge is action, and action knowledge. The subject of this totality, however, must be a collective one, namely a social class, because only a social class can both penetrate social reality and change it. But of the social classes there is only one possible candidate: the proletariat. Only the proletariat can know itself both as a subject and an object, because only workers, realizing that their labour is simultaneously a commodity and their own life, can experience an objective reality stemming, as a source of collective effort, from debased human activity. The worker's very wretchedness forbids him to 'know' the world in any contemplative fashion, and this compels him to self-consciousness *as an object*. Furthermore, the proletariat is a revolutionary class and therefore only it can call on totality as the meaning of future history. (The bourgeoisie is disqualified because it is incapable of dialectical knowledge: rather its thought is characteristically contemplative, detached. The habit of bourgeois rationalism is *reification*, a term Lukács borrows from Simmel and equates with one of the senses Marx adopted for *alienation*; human attributes are mistaken for things and thing-like abstractions, which prohibits the praxis of totality.)

History and Class Consciousness was written to provide a historico-philosophical justification of revolutionary socialism as it emerged in Russia in 1917. Disillusioned by the failure of proletarian uprisings outside Russia, Lukács had turned away from his erstwhile Luxemburgism* (i.e. the cult of spontaneous revolution and workers' councils) towards a Leninist* stress on the rule of the revolutionary party as the vanguard of the masses. Notwithstanding this, the book was condemned by the Comintern in 1924, and ten years later Lukács himself repudiated it. In regard to classical

Marxism as codified by Engels and Lenin, several core tenets of *History and Class Consciousness* were heretical. Having described totality as a subject in history, Lukács ruthlessly ruled out Engels's notion of a dialectic of nature. Similarly no room was allowed for Lenin's 'reflection' theory of knowledge. Again, he bluntly stated that the decisive difference between Marxist and bourgeois thinking is not the primacy of economic causes in historical explanation, but the viewpoint of totality. Indeed, he went as far as to say that historical materialism should be subjected to a critique analogous to that which Marx had performed on bourgeois economics.

In his early, pre-Marxist literary criticism Lukács had placed himself as far as possible from aestheticism and the idea of 'art for art's sake', making his own Arnold's dictum about literature as a 'criticism of life'. He firmly opposed tendentious literary formulae on the grounds that the political meaning of literature should organically emerge from its artistic qualities instead of being simply juxtaposed to them. Even the early *Soul and Form* (1911, trans. 1974), with its near-existentialist response to the meaning of tragedy, regarded literary works as moral gestures, in which an author attempts to give form to his 'soul', and thus define a basic attitude towards life. Similarly *The Theory of the Novel* is concerned with the ethical values of literature, conceived historically. Whereas the ancient epic presented human life in thorough meaningfulness, its heroes always organically linked to their communities, the novel is seen as an essentially bourgeois form representing a desperate bid on the part of the author to recapture a sense of existence amidst a meaningless world. Accordingly the novel's hero is characterized as a solitary seeker, in constant opposition to his social environment. He is prone to abstract idealism, as in *Don Quixote*, or to romantic disillusionment, as in Flaubert's *Éducation Sentimentale*: only in utopian novels like Goethe's *Wilhelm Meister*, or in fleeting glimpses of a natural harmony outside society, as in Tolstoy, can he find happiness or peace of mind. Novelists are the 'negative mystics' of 'godless epochs'.

During the 1930s Lukács broadened and refined the concept of *critical realism*, a staple category of official Marxist aesthetics in the USSR. In particular it came to denote a subtle version of historical consciousness on the part of bourgeois novelists, past and present. Flaubert, Dostoevsky, Balzac and Mann* are among those writers Lukács describes as transcending the class-bias of the bourgeois mind, albeit unwittingly. *The Historical Novel* (written 1938, published in 1955, trans. 1962), perhaps his finest modulation of realism into historico-stylistic terms, cogently relates the birth of historical fiction in Walter Scott to the changes in attitude towards history that attended the French Revolution. In addition Balzac is interpreted as the first major novelist to succeed in depicting 'the present as history', so achieving a higher level of 'realism', paradoxically through his romantically melodramatic characterization.

The fulcrum of Lukácsian realism is the idea of characters as *types*, a concept which he inherited from the poetics of the Enlightenment as well as from classical Marxism, and which he radically historicized. These types are defined by their breadth of characterization, by their self-awareness in times of turmoil, and, most importantly, by their historical representativeness, or the way they are enhanced above the mere average of their age and social class. In other words a realist hero need not be heroic; but what he must convey is an intimation of the historical process as a *totality*. Thus while a handful of 'socialist realists' like the later Gorky* and Sholokhov* are admired for achieving a sense of historical perspective without descending to trivial moralizing, bourgeois naturalism, modernism and Stalinist 'revolutionary romanticism' are each rejected for being 'departures from realism'. In this respect at least Lukács broke with his earlier criticism: instead of envisaging literature as a negative mysticism, he now praised certain selected parts of it for its realistic power of rendering the historical saga of mankind.

The underlying concern with the Hegelian idea of totality survived into Lukács's old age. The great *Aesthetics* is comprised of four main conceptual elements: totality; the primacy of content over form; reflection as mimesis; and the idea of the wholeness of man. While the first two derive from Hegel, the role of reflection comes from Engels and Lenin's theory of knowledge (with which he at last became reconciled) skilfully combined with Aristotle's mimetic theory of art; and the 'whole man' theme incorporates the lofty ethico-aesthetical ideals of Weimar classicism. Above all art embodies man's self-awareness: 'art is the self-consciousness of humanity', and so, if it fulfils its ideal, it cannot help but be historically-minded. In being outrightly anthropomorphic art differs from science; in being resolutely inner-worldly it differs from religion; and by its comprehensiveness of vision, by dropping the normative focus on positive paradigms, it is marked off from ethics. By 'overflowing into ethics', however, art as an inner-worldly anthropomorphism endowed with cognitive powers and productive of a cathartic effect acts at an equal distance from disinterested contemplation and practical life; and so prepares man for higher forms of existence. In short, aesthetic knowledge is a necessary mediator between individuality and universality – but only universality in the sense that it is synonymous with 'totality'.

Taking his work as a whole, Lukács strove to restore the rich philosophical heritage of Marxism; and to the extent that it is no longer possible to take at face value Marx's dictum about 'standing Hegel on his feet' he was successful. By stressing Lenin's emphasis on the subjective factor in history as a conquest extending the limits of classical Marxism he laid bare the prophetic and eschatological drive in Marxist thought, together with its lasting pursuit of a logic of history hinging on class conflict and redemptive revolutions. Because of this he has been much criticized for unabashed historicism; but a greater sin was perhaps his inflation of dialectics at the expense of historical materialism in its awareness of social determinisms – an inflation that entailed the identification of science *as such* with 'bourgeois ideology'. Because his dialectics method, which as praxis engulfs history, is self-grounded and submits to no real criteria of objective truth, Lukács the fierce anti-irrationalist can never be entirely free from the taunt that he was himself irrational. He has cast a long shadow on Western Marxism, dooming it to be far more speculative than empirical in content. Thus, for example, the 'critical theory' of the Frankfurt School (*vide* Horkheimer, Adorno) amounts to *History and Class Consciousness* minus the faith in revolutions. Often a first-rate literary critic, his search for a total meaning sometimes led him to stray from the discipline of critical reason. It is perhaps of some relevance that Thomas Mann, in *The Magic Mountain*, portrayed Lukács as Naphta, an intelligent Jesuit in dire need of authority.

J. G. Merquior

Lukács's *Collected Works*, in seventeen volumes, are being published by Luchterhand in West Germany (from 1962). Other translations include *The Young Hegel* (1975); *Studies in European Socialism* (1964); *Goethe and his Age* (1968); *Essays on Thomas Mann* (1964); *The Meaning of Contemporary Realism* (1963); and *The Ontology of Social Being, I, Hegel* and *II, Marx* (1978). See: G. H. R. Parkinson (ed.), *Georg Lukács: The Man, his Work and his Ideas* (1970); I. Meszaros, *Lukács' Concept of Dialectic* (1972); chapters in M. Merleau-Ponty, *The Adventures of the Dialectic* (1973); L. Colletti, *Il Marxismo e Hegel*, (1969); F. Jameson, *Marxism and Form* (1971); S. Avineri (ed.), *Varieties of Marxism* (1977); L. Kolakowski, *Main Currents of Marxism*, vol. III (1978).

285
LUXEMBURG, Rosa 1871–1919

Polish-German revolutionary

Rosa Luxemburg was born of liberal Jewish parents in 1871 in Zamosc, Poland. In 1874 the family moved to Warsaw where the sensitive and intelligent young Rosa was to be drawn into the socialist movement. By 1887 she had made contact with the Revolutionary Socialist Party *Proletariat*. Two years later, however, her activity was discovered by the police and she was forced

abroad. For the next nine years she was to live her life amongst revolutionary exiles in neutral Switzerland.

In 1890 she enrolled at the University of Zürich. Her main interest was classical and Marxist political economy. In the same year she met Leo Jögiches who was to be her lover and close comrade for many years. Very soon she became deeply involved in the polemics and politics of the East European emigration. It was in Zürich that she met the leading Russian Marxist George Plekhanov for whom she had, characteristically, a healthy, and iconoclastic disrespect.

In this period she developed her own clear view on the controversial Polish question. Basing herself upon the method of Marx, although rejecting his political conclusions, she came to oppose the traditional slogan of an independent Poland. Her economic studies of tsarist Russia convinced her that a viable Polish economy made no sense outside of a Russian context. Her political sensibilities led her to conclude that nationalist slogans could only divide the working class in their united struggle against autocracy. Ultimately she believed that only socialism could solve and eradicate national oppression to which, of course, she remained fully opposed. Lenin's* opposition to Luxemburg on this question, and his subsequent uncritical canonization, has meant that her views have, since the 1920s, been either virtually ignored or generally misrepresented.

In 1897 she completed her doctorate entitled 'The Industrial Development of Poland'. It remains a seminal work and has influenced much later research. Luxemburg's reputation had by this time attracted the attention of the leading European Marxist Karl Kautsky. Upon his insistence she moved to Germany in 1898, marrying Gustav Lübeck to obtain German citizenship.

Until the outbreak of the First World War and the collapse of the Second International in 1914 she was to be at the centre of every single major issue within the German and international socialist movement. Invariably she stood on the left on most questions. Scrupulously orthodox at one level, particularly in her opposition to Eduard Bernstein's revisionist challenge to Marxism, at another, she was to show all the originality and independence of thought which both impressed her admirers, including Lenin, and frightened her opponents. This period can be viewed, retrospectively, as part of a preparation for the great trials which she had to face between 1914 and her murder by counter-revolution in 1919.

She established her reputation in a series of major polemics, notably *Social Reform or Revolution* (1899, trans. 1937), *Organizational Questions in Russian Social Democracy* (1903–4, trans. as *Leninism or Marxism*, 1961), and *The Mass Strike, the Political Party and the Trade Unions* (1906, trans. 1925). In all these works she aimed to defend the necessity of working-class revolution against the triple dangers, as she saw it, of revisionism, organizational fetishism and bureaucracy in the Marxist movement. Unlike many of her German and European comrades she was concerned to apply the radical political lessons of the 1905 Russian Revolution to the West. Her emphasis on working-class self-emancipation, particularly through the use of the mass strike, inevitably brought her into conflict with the leadership of German Social Democracy, including Kautsky. The ground was being prepared for her subsequent split from them after 1914.

Luxemburg's other important work in the pre-war period addressed itself to the problem of capitalism's continued stability and the approaching war danger. *The Accumulation of Capital* (1912, trans. 1951) argued that the imminent tendency to crisis had been temporarily offset by the expansion of capitalism into the non-capitalist and non-industrial areas of the world. Although she has been criticized by later Marxists for her simple underconsumptionist theory of crisis, and her misreading of Marx's reproduction schemes, the work still stands as one of the most original contributions to be made to Marxist political economy since Marx himself.

The year 1914 marked a new phase in her life. German Social Democracy supported its own government in war. Luxemburg now became the focal point of the opposition. With Karl Liebknecht and Franz Mehring (the biographer of Marx), she sought to regroup the fragments. This was made difficult by her arrest and imprisonment in February 1915. In April she succeeded in smuggling out of prison her famous *Juniusbrochure* (*The Junius Pamphlet*, trans. 1971) in which she analysed the causes of the war, and the strategy that should be adopted by socialists. Released in December, she continued her anti-war activity but was re-arrested in July 1916. She was to remain in prison for over two years. She welcomed the February and October revolutions in Russia in 1917. Whilst much has been made of her criticisms of early Bolshevik policies relating to the peasantry, nationalities and the Constituent Assembly, her correspondence reveals that her real fear was that the European workers, particularly the Germans, would remain inactive, leaving the Bolsheviks isolated.

In November 1918 she was released. The German Revolution was already underway. Its two great weaknesses, absence of organization (Luxemburg's group, the *Spartacusbund*, was still only in embryonic form), and, the openly hostile attitude of traditional Social Democracy, proved fatal. Reaction mobilized; counter-revolution went on the offensive. In the Civil War which followed thousands died. One of them was Rosa Luxemburg, murdered on 15 January 1919.

Luxemburg's legacy to Marxism has reflected the fate of Marxism itself. Nazism in Germany burned her works. Stalinism* ignored and distorted them. Apart from one early but excellent biography by Frölich

(published in 1939), we have had to await the recent revival of political debate within Marxism for a new appraisal and appreciation of her life and thought.

Michael Cox

See: Dick Howard (ed.), *Selected Political Writings of Rosa Luxemburg* (1971); Paul Frölich, *Rosa Luxemburg: Her Life and Work* (1939); Carl E. Schorske, *German Social Democracy, 1905–17* (1955); Peter Nettl, *Rosa Luxemburg* (2 vols, 1966); Ken Tarbuck (ed.), *The Accumulation of Capital: or What the Epigoni Have Done With Marxist Theory. An Anti-Critique* (1972).

286
LU XUN (Zhou Shuren) 1881–1936

Chinese writer

Lu Xun (pen-name of Zhou Shuren) was born to a privileged scholar-gentry family in Shaoxing. While still a boy he experienced the bitterness of a precipitous decline in familial wealth and prestige when his grandfather, holder of the most advanced degrees the civil service examination system could offer, was deprived of his offices after he had been caught accepting bribes from the families of junior candidates. Then, in his teens, Lu Xun saw his father, an opium smoker and general failure, die spitting blood. After a classical education at home he went to Nanking, where in 1901 he was a member of the first and only graduating class of the School of Mines and Railroads attached to the Jiangnan Army Academy. He was subsequently sent to Japan as a government-sponsored student. There he attended the Kōbun College in Tokyo (1902–4), where he was taught Japanese and the rudiments of science, and then the medical school at Sendai. His motives for wanting to be a doctor were twofold: he had been deeply disillusioned by the failure of traditional Chinese medicine to cure his father (who had even been prescribed ink); and he was aware that the rapid modernization of Japan was associated with the introduction of Western medicine. Like Japan, China was being subjected to an onslaught of Western influences, and Lu Xun saw that the Confucian tradition was wholly inadequate for the new challenge.

During his second year at Sendai a slide of a Chinese prisoner about to be executed was shown at the end of a class. What struck Lu Xun were the uncaring expressions on the faces of the Chinese bystanders. It was at that point that he decided that his countrymen's spiritual sickness was a far more pressing concern than their physical health. The treatment he came to propose was a difficult one: it amounted to nothing less than the remoulding of the Chinese personality, and in particular the remoulding of his own scholar-gentry class. Quitting his studies, he dedicated his life to literature. He also turned rebel to his own class, asserting that the scholar-gentry blamed China's backwardness on the 'inherited superstitions' of her common people as a ploy designed to absolve their own irresponsibility. The way to cope with Western culture, he reasoned, was neither to shun it by praising the glories of Chinese antiquity, nor to embrace it whole-heartedly, but rather to learn to look out on it, so that China might take her place as one civilization among many. His writings, which were mainly devoted to this end, may be divided into three groups: his translations, his stories, and his essays, or *zawen*.

During the early part of his stay in Japan, when he still thought that China might solve her problem through the adoption of Western science, Lu Xun translated two of Jules Verne's novels into Chinese; but after leaving Sendai to devote himself to writing he deliberately sought out literature from weak and oppressed countries, for example the stories of Leonid Andreyev and Vsevolod Garshin. It was not until after he had gone back to China (in 1909, becoming a science teacher at the Zhejiang Normal School in Hangzhou) that he began writing his own fiction. His first short story, 'Remembrances of the Past' (*Huaijiu*), was composed in classical Chinese on the eve of the Republican Revolution of 1911. In it a strict, hypocritical and slow-witted Confucian teacher is contrasted by the narrator with a pair of warm, honest and quick-witted family servants. It was not however until six years after the Republic was established, and six years after he had accepted a sinecure with the Ministry of Education, that he joined ranks with the cultural revolution then afoot in Peking and Shanghai, with the publication of 'Diary of a Madman' (*Kuangren riji*, 1918). This was the first *literary* short story to be written in the vernacular; previously only commercial fiction writers had switched from classical Chinese, a purely written language spoken by no one. Borrowing both title and form from Gogol, Lu Xun used them to voice his radical and unflattering view of Chinese society. The sixth entry of the 'Diary' reads:

Pitch black, don't know if it's day or night.
The Zhao family's dog has started barking again.
Fierce as a lion, timid as a rabbit, and crafty as a fox. . . .

The dog clearly referred to the Chinese character as Lu Xun envisaged it: a lion before inferiors, a rabbit before superiors, and a fox when the other's social status was uncertain. Like the madman in his story, Lu Xun saw Chinese society as a cannibalistic feast in which the strong devour the weak, the educated the unlettered, and the old the young. Those not directly involved merely stand around, like the bystanders in the slide that had left such a lasting impression upon him.

In all Lu Xun wrote only twenty-five vernacular stories, collected in 'Outcry' (*Nahan*, 1923) and 'Wandering' (*Panghuang*, 1926). In each of them the oppressed, be they women, children or members of the working classes, are illiterate, and hence innocent of Confucianism. Formally, with only one exception, the stories were each strongly influenced by foreign models. The exception – 'The True Story of Ah Q' (*Ah Q Zhengzhuan*) – is the most famous. In this rambling tale, first published serially in a newspaper, Lu Xun employs the diction and structure of traditional popular fiction in an attempt to sum up the weaknesses of the Chinese people in the person of the vagabond ne'er-do-well Ah Q. Of all Ah Q's defects the most serious is his inability to face up to the here and now of reality. Instead he escapes, either into a past where his ancestors are rich and powerful, or into a future peopled by his as yet unborn children; and when temporal evasion is impossible, Ah Q simply rationalizes failure into success, transforming each set-back into a 'psychological victory'. Such was the impact of the story that 'Ah Q-ism' and 'psychological victory' passed immediately into everyday conversation. Chinese scholars who boasted complacently about China's history while disdaining the Johnny-come-lately accomplishments of the West were now dismissed as victims of 'Ah Q mentality'.

In addition, and in a few deft strokes, 'The True Story of Ah Q' also exposed the Republican Revolution for what it was, a superficial and deceptive change in the form of government that left the fabric of Chinese society virtually intact: the common people remained outside the effective political structure. Beginning in 1925 personal and political events conspired to radicalize Lu Xun still further, so that he gradually moved away from fiction toward a more direct form of criticism, the political essay. The personal events centred mainly on Xu Guangping, a student twenty years his junior who had attended his classes at the Women's Normal College in Peking, and who subsequently began writing to him in 1925. Soon after initiating the correspondence (preserved in 'Letters from Two Places', *Liangdi shu*, 1933) she became leader of a student movement organized to oppose appointments made by the Ministry of Education. Siding with the students, Lu Xun was temporarily dismissed from his own post at the ministry. Then, in 1926, the police fired into a crowd of people demonstrating against China's weakness in the face of foreign aggrandizement, killing forty-seven of them, including another of his students. This drew forth some of Lu Xun's most vitriolic compositions, for which he earned a place on an arrest list of fifty 'radicals'. After a period of hiding he was forced to flee Peking, accompanied by Xu Guangping. Together they found teaching posts in Canton, where in April 1927 they witnessed at first hand Chiang Kai-shek's bloody purge of communists from the Guomindang – a party Lu Xun had previously held out some hope for. Now he turned to communism as the only solution to China's problems. At the same time he moved, with Xu Guangping (who now became his wife) to Shanghai, the most cosmopolitan and revolutionary city in China. There he was to spend the last nine years of his life.

In Shanghai he devoted prodigious energies to cultivating younger writers, fostering the 'woodcut movement' (of the Eighteen Society, whose slogan was 'out of the salon and into the streets'), translating, founding short-lived publishing houses, lecturing, and campaigning for the simplification and eventual elimination of Chinese ideographs (to be replaced by an alphabetic system). At the same time he composed score upon score of zawen, directed mainly at the Guomindang and its rightist sympathizers. No contemporary was able to match him in this essay form, either in clarity of thought or in brilliance of style. Constituting the bulk of his creative work during the last decade of his life, the incisiveness of Lu Xun's satire ensured the survival of his zawen, so that they became valued by critics in the later People's Republic above his other writings, as contributing more to both literature and revolution. Praised by Mao Tse-tung* as 'a hero without parallel in our history', Lu Xun the iconoclast became himself an idol.

Yet Lu Xun's status as a national hero of Chinese Communism is perhaps deceptive. Above and beyond being a great writer he was an internationalist. His translations (which continued throughout his Shanghai period, until his death from tuberculosis, when he was working on the second part of Gogol's *Dead Souls*) were outstanding because Lu Xun himself set great store by them. He continually urged his fellow-writers to spend more time rendering foreign works into Chinese, for, as he argued, translations make a larger contribution than shoddy original work. In the burgeoning of left-wing literature in the wake of the 1927 purges he translated several important pieces of Soviet criticism expressly to raise the prevailing level of discourse. In addition he also argued for a higher level of self-criticism among writers. In 1931, noting that no contemporary left-wing writer actually came from peasant or worker stock, he said that the best they could do was to produce novels of exposure, against their own classes. Because he scorned those who pretended to know how peasants thought and felt, he was sometimes attacked by the left as well as the right. He was therefore a more isolated figure, and his politics more critical, than his posthumous reputation in China suggests. Passionate in his concern for social justice and in his vision of China as a member of a world community of nations, Lu Xun has, even in translation – left a rich legacy to share with his fellow men.

Professor William Lyell

Lu Xun's complete writings (10 vols, 1956–8) and complete translations (10 vols, 1959) have been published in Peking. Recommended translations: *Ah Q and Others: Selected Stories of Lusin* (Wang Chi-chen, 1941); *Selected Works of Lu Hsün* (Yang Hsien-yi and Gladys Yang, 4 vols, 1956–60); *A Brief History of Chinese Fiction* (also the Yangs, 1959); *Silent China: Selected Writings of Lu Xun* (Gladys Yang, 1973). See also: William A. Lyell, *Lu Hsün's Vision of Reality* (1976); Merle Goldman (ed.), *Modern Chinese Literature in the May Fourth Era* (1977); Lin Yü-Sheng, *The Crisis of Chinese Consciousness – Radical Anti-traditionalism in the May Fourth Era* (1979); V. I. Semanov, *Lu Hsün and his Predecessors* (trans. 1980).

M

287

McCARTHY, Mary 1912–

US novelist

After the unhappy childhood in Seattle, Washington, which she describes in *Memories of a Catholic Girlhood* (1957), Mary McCarthy escaped east to Vassar College, where she was deeply influenced by Vassar's simultaneous encouragement and crippling of intellectual seriousness in its women undergraduates. 'Arresting performance in politics, fashion, or art is often taken by the Vassar mind to be synonymous with accomplishment.' This substitution of an outer display of self for the infinitely more difficult struggle to act upon an achieved knowledge became the mark of Mary McCarthy's modern demon, a type most famously realized in Henry Mulcahy, the villain of *Groves of Academe* (1952). By pretending he has been fired for having been a Communist, Mulcahy calls the liberal bluff of ultra-progressive Jocelyn College and gets re-hired. 'He's loyal to himself, objectively, as if he were another person . . . he's foregone his subjectivity and hypostatized himself as an object.'

The popularity of *The Group* (1963) owed much to McCarthy's satiric ventriloquism of a group of Vassar graduates who blatantly lack McCarthy's own intelligence and authority. In all her novels, the promising, intelligent heroines tend to fail, turn into a self-parody, or get killed off. Many of McCarthy's sharpest satiric jibes are, however, rewrites of her own past. In *The Group*, up-to-date iconoclastic Kay Strong marries a would-be radical writer immediately after graduation, as McCarthy did. However, while Kay struggles to make Harald appreciate her 'Russel Wright cocktail shaker in the shape of a skyscraper' and eventually kills herself, McCarthy got work writing for the *New Republic*, the *Nation* and *Partisan Review*, and got divorced in 1936 – rather like Margaret Sargeant, the almost nameless divorcee heroine of the linked stories in McCarthy's brilliant first book, *The Company She Keeps* (1942). Margaret is on her way to Reno when she has a one-night stand, including a humiliating morning after, with 'The Man in the Brooks Brothers Shirt'. At the complacently Stalinist* magazine *The Liberal*, Margaret is branded a Trotskyite*, the same fate that befell McCarthy, according to 'My

Confession' (1951), her attack on the witch-hunting of her notorious namesake, Senator Joseph McCarthy.

From 1938 to 1946, McCarthy was married to the critic and man of letters Edmund Wilson*, whom she divorced to marry Bowden Broadwater. Since 1961, when she married diplomat James West, she has spent most of her time in Paris, though she has been one of the most effective critics of the American involvement in Vietnam. Her fame rests mainly on her satires of liberal intellectuals, particularly in *The Groves of Academe*, now the classic novel of the American liberal arts college, and *A Charmed Life* (1955), her dissection of an intellectual summer colony. McCarthy's readers are held by the attitudes she satirizes, rather than the meagre or arbitrary action. She is less a novelist than an intellectual satirist, like Thomas Love Peacock, or a writer of *contes philosophiques*, like Voltaire.

As a critic, McCarthy regrets the 'snubbing' rejection of the 'novel of ideas' by 'pure' novelists, symbolized for her by Henry James. For McCarthy, as for Tolstoy, the novelist she respects most, the 'idea' at the heart of the novel is actually a moral imperative, a way of being in the world. Yet in McCarthy's world of self-perpetuating oligarchies – the college, the writers' colony, the socially determined 'group', even the aesthetes and liberals trapped in an airplane in *Cannibals and Missionaries* (1979) – it is almost impossible to act honestly.

McCarthy feels that the decline of descriptive language has weakened the novel. In past fiction, as in the historic past which she celebrates in *Venice Observed* (1956) and *The Stones of Florence* (1959), the outer appearance yields inner truths: for this reason McCarthy sees aesthetic experiences as part of moral development, like Peter Levi's quixotic admiration for Borromini in *Birds of America* (1971). Yet the loss of a morally reliable world is fodder for McCarthy's satire. As in nineteenth-century fiction, her vindictively accurate catalogues – especially of clothing and décor – hold the key to character, but for McCarthy they ironically display an alienation from nature and the body.

The development of twentieth-century fiction owes little to Mary McCarthy, though her critics do seem irritated to have to admit that formally unfashionable McCarthy has probably written the most incisive intellectual satire of her generation. It may well be, however, that McCarthy's satire is ultimately not vicious enough. Unlike most satirists, she makes her own moral stance clear; she doesn't share the anarchic energy behind much contemporary 'black comedy'. McCarthy writes in a calm, strongly cadenced prose, more effective in sentence units than in paragraphs or chapters. Her habit of letting her readers know she knows what's right works better in her essays (*On the Contrary*, 1962; *The Writing on the Wall*, 1970) than it does in her fiction. She values honesty, self-knowledge, unself-conscious pursuit of the good, and 'aidôs', the mixture of 'care or ruth' briefly evoked in *The Groves of Academe*. 'The concept doesn't exist for us', so McCarthy mockingly traces the consequences of its loss.

Helen McNeil

See: Elizabeth Niebuhr, 'The Art of Fiction XXVII', *Paris Review*, 27 (1962); Elizabeth Hardwick, 'Mary McCarthy' in *A View of My Own* (1963); Norman Mailer, 'The Case against McCarthy' in *Cannibals and Christians* (1966); Barbara McKenzie, *Mary McCarthy* (1966); Doris Grumbach, *The Company She Kept* (1967); Irwin Stock, *Mary McCarthy*, University of Minnesota Pamphlets on American Writers No. 72 (1968).

288

MACDIARMID, Hugh (Christopher Murray Grieve) 1892–1978

Scottish poet

Hugh MacDiarmid was born Christopher Murray Grieve in the little Scottish Border town of Langholm on 11 August 1892, the son of a rural postman. The family lived in the post office building beneath the local library and young Grieve had access to a collection of some 12,000 books which he claimed to have read by the age of fourteen. He attended Langholm Academy, then went to Edinburgh to study at the university and train as a schoolteacher at Broughton Junior Students' Centre, but when his father died in 1911 he abandoned all idea of a steady career. As he explained in *Lucky Poet* (1943): 'I was very early determined that I would not "work for money", and that whatever I might have to do to earn my living, I would never devote more of my time and my energies to remunerative work than I did to voluntary and gainless activities.'

In the First World War, Grieve served with the Royal Army Medical Corps and was invalided home from Salonika suffering from cerebral malaria. In 1918 he married Margaret Skinner and the couple moved to Montrose where Grieve became chief reporter of the weekly *Montrose Review*, the father of two children, a Labour member of the Town Council, a Justice of the Peace; and also a founder of the Scottish Centre of P.E.N., the National Party of Scotland, and two magazines. The first of these, *Northern Numbers*, was a fairly conventional Georgian publication to which Grieve contributed poems in English. As editor of the *Scottish Chapbook*, though, Grieve introduced his readers in 1922 to the work of 'Hugh MacDiarmid'. The first MacDiarmid lyric, 'The Watergaw', was a memory of his dead father and brought a new intellectual element to Scots poetry, for the poet had combined the strength of oral Scots with the range of Scots words preserved in Jamieson's *Etymological Dictionary of the Scottish Language*. The result was variously termed 'Lallans' (Lowland Scots), 'synthetic Scots' and 'aggrandized Scots'; whatever the label there was no doubt that MacDiarmid had shaken the Scots language to its linguistic roots and that the heather was about to be set on fire.

MacDiarmid's early lyrics were published in *Sangschaw* (1925) and *Penny Wheep* (1926), and spectacularly broke with the Burns tradition. MacDiarmid replaced Burns's Standard Habbie Stanza (which had been *de rigueur* in Scots poetry since the eighteenth century) with concise and sensuous quatrains that packed a philosophical punch; his characteristic method was to isolate a particular image, then seek out its cosmic implications. Although he used the slogan 'Dunbar – Not Burns!' in the 1920s, MacDiarmid was not confined to Scottish precedents. He was fully aware of the developments in European poetry and alive to the linguistic innovations contained in two key works published in 1922 (the *annus mirabilis* of modernism): Eliot's* *The Waste Land* and Joyce's* *Ulysses*. In 1926 he made his own supreme contribution to the century's literature with his long poem *A Drunk Man Looks at the Thistle* (1926).

With this masterpiece MacDiarmid virtually remade Scotland in his own image. The narrative was, basically, a functional vehicle for MacDiarmid's views. A drunk man, during his unsteady odyssey to the bed of his beloved Jean (a folk equivalent of Homer's Penelope), stumbles on a hillside and there, by the light of the full moon, considers the thistle as a rugged symbol of Scotland's past and potential. As the alcoholic spirit wears off it is replaced by a deep psychological spirituality and the drunk man's sobriety is penetratingly expressed in verse of great dignity. Scotland is no longer treated as a country with defeatist obsessions but a nation with a glorious future:

> The thistle rises and forever will,
> Getherin' the generations under't.
> This is the monument o' a' they were,
> And a' they hoped and wondered.

Although MacDiarmid had immortalized modern Scotland in the verse published in the 1920s, he was to find himself a prophet without honour in his own country. In 1929 he had gone to London to edit *Vox*, a radio magazine, which collapsed after three months. The poet almost collapsed with it. He left his wife in

London while he worked as a publicity officer in Liverpool; after a disastrous year there he returned to London to be divorced in 1932. He then married a Cornish girl, Valda Trevlyn, and, with their baby Michael, the family moved to an abandoned cottage on the Shetland island of Whalsay in 1933. Economically impoverished, MacDiarmid was still poetically and politically active. His *First Hymn to Lenin and Other Poems* (1931) had initiated the political poetry of the 1930s and during that decade MacDiarmid, who joined the Communist Party in 1934, moved from Scots to a deliberately didactic poetry in English. His island exile also inspired him to introduce geological data into poems like 'On a Raised Beach' from *Stony Limits and Other Poems* (1934).

When he did leave Whalsay, at the age of forty-nine, it was to do a war job: first as a fitter on Clydeside, then as a deckhand on a Norwegian ship. When the war ended he was again technically unemployed though his poetic output was prolific and his creative energies were directed to the epic and erudite English poetry subsequently collected under titles like *In Memoriam James Joyce* (1955) and *The Kind of Poetry I Want* (1961). Widely recognized as the poetic equal (and perhaps superior) of Dunbar and Burns he was far from settling down as a mellow Grand Old Man. In 1951 he obtained a derelict, rent-free cottage in Biggar, Lanarkshire, and remained there for the rest of his life (with frequent trips all over the world). His political opinions continued to give offence: he had been expelled from the National Party in 1933 for his communism and expelled from the Communist Party in 1938 for his nationalism. In 1957 he encountered great hostility by rejoining the Communist Party in the wake of the Soviet suppression of the 1956 Hungarian Rising.

MacDiarmid created modern Scots poetry and attracted dozens of disciples so that the contemporary Scottish poet has a bilingual choice to make between Scots and English (and a further choice between conventional English and the highly cerebral English favoured by the mature MacDiarmid). He was a great creative artist who also delighted in polemics (his hobby, as listed in *Who's Who*, was 'Anglophobia'). Yet there were two sides to the man, a private Chris Grieve and a public Hugh MacDiarmid. This contrast startled all who knew him and could observe his ability to shift from a cosy chat to a shatteringly incisive discourse.

Alan Bold

MacDiarmid's poetry is contained in *Complete Poems 1920–1976* (2 vols, 1978) and his memoirs and opinions are gathered in *Lucky Poet* (1943) and *The Company I've Kept* (1966). See also: Kenneth Buthlay, *Hugh MacDiarmid* (1964) and Duncan Glen, *Hugh MacDiarmid and the Scottish Renaissance* (1964).

289
MACKINTOSH, Charles Rennie 1868–1928

Scottish architect and designer

Standing half-way between the English Arts and Crafts Movement and European Art Nouveau, Mackintosh is a unique figure, part of both the nineteenth and the twentieth centuries. He combines, in his designs for architecture, interiors and furniture, extreme decoration with extreme functionalism, evolving an aesthetic idiom which is very much his own.

Born in Glasgow in 1868, Mackintosh's first love was for two dimensions and he spent much time up until 1900 and again in the last decade of his life with decorative graphic work – pencil sketches and watercolours – producing designs, in the early period, which are reminiscent of Aubrey Beardsley and the Dutch symbolist painter, Jan Toorop. Simplified stylizations of natural forms, particularly flowers and their stems, appear in these designs and recur throughout his career. Mackintosh's architectural training was broad and in the same year as he was articled to the Glasgow architect John Hutchins (1884) he signed on as an evening student at the Glasgow School of Art to study painting and drawing. He moved in 1889 to the firm Honeyman and Keppie as a draughtsman but left temporarily in 1891 to travel to Italy on the scholarship he had won. It was at Honeyman and Keppie that he met another draughtsman, Herbert McNair, who was to introduce him to two sisters, Margaret and Frances MacDonald. The group soon became known as 'The Four' publishing their graphic designs in periodicals at home and abroad.

In the late 1890s Mackintosh began designing furniture for various tearooms in Glasgow with simple, stylized pieces of furniture. He is best known for the high-backed ladder chairs and white painted chairs with an abstracted rose motif. The interiors were total environments with the same shapes and motifs echoed throughout. In 1898 Mackintosh started work on his design for a new building for the Glasgow School of Art – his best known piece of architectural work. The form of the building, completed in 1909, is dictated entirely by its internal function and plan and the large, unembellished windows look forward to the Modern Movement.

Other architectural projects of the following decade reflect the same progressive attitude combined with attention to detail and a smattering of controlled decoration. In 1899 Mackintosh designed Windyhill and, in 1902, Hill House. His reputation abroad grew when a design for a room was exhibited at the 1902 Turin exhibition and in the same year he was commissioned to design a music room in Vienna. Links with the Vienna Sezession group were strong, particularly with Josef Hoffmann.

After 1910 Mackintosh's work declined rapidly and in 1914 he moved with his wife, Margaret MacDonald, whom he married in 1900, to Suffolk and subsequently to the South of France where he returned to watercolours for the last five years of his life. Although Mackintosh's designs are few in number they are striking in their originality and have influenced many designers who came after him both in England and in Europe.

Penny Sparke

See: T. Howarth, *Charles Rennie Mackintosh and the Modern Movement* (1952) and R. Macleod, *Charles Rennie Mackintosh* (1968).

290
McLUHAN, Herbert Marshall 1911–

Canadian culturologist

Born in Alberta, Canada, McLuhan studied at Manitoba University but took his PhD in Thomas Nashe at Cambridge University. He has since taught in American and Canadian universities (Catholic institutions or branches of them), and works from his Centre for Culture and Technology, University of Toronto. He became a Catholic in 1937 and this sense of the universe as a purposeful system of incarnate energies impregnates his vision. His main value lies in his exploration of the interfaces set up between traditional genre studies, and his methods lie nearer to those of Alfred Korzybski and Roland Barthes* than to the separatism of sociology, literary criticism or pure semantics. In fact his excellent literary criticism repeatedly refers to the cultural and technological context of writing – Mallarmé and Joyce* in relation to newsprint, Tennyson to optics, Coleridge to 'radial' thinking, Pope to print technology, and so on. These approaches stem partly from Cambridge attitudes towards literary studies, and partly from the teachings of H. A. Innis, of which he writes in the introduction to a 1964 edition of the latter's *The Bias of Communication*. Innis belongs to the Chicago University school of the 1920s which included, in its field of teaching and reference, Robert Ezra Park*, Max Weber*, John Dewey* and Thorstein Veblen*. From Park, Innis learned 'how to identify the control mechanisms by which a heterogeneous community yet manages to arrange its affairs with some degree of uniformity', and how technological devices 'have necessarily modified the structure and functions of society'. McLuhan developed these assumptions into a radical investigation of how 'the extensions of man' change both the external and the internal environments (the concept of an internal environment draws on the work of the Canadian experimental psychologist Hans Selye, whose *Stress* and

The Stress of Life appeared in 1950 and 1956). In 1953 McLuhan founded, with the distinguished anthropologist Edmund S. Carpenter, the journal *Explorations*, a major vehicle for environmental and cultural studies. The selection in *Explorations in Communication* (1960) indicate the distinction of its contributors, who included Northrop Frye, Siegfried Giedion, Fernand Léger*, David Riesman, Robert Graves* and Gilbert Seldes. The semantic category of these studies is indicated in the introduction which speaks of exploring 'the grammars of such languages as print, the newspaper format and television', 'revolutions in the packaging and distribution of ideas and feelings', the 'switch from linear to cluster configuration' in order to understand the 'almost total subliminal universe' of the modern form of 'preliterate man' living within the circuitry of electric media in 'the global village'. The new outlook is 'tribal'. The danger is not merely illiteracy but mediocrity, a society anti-individualistic in its repudiation of the previous print-media culture which still lingers on in a predominantly visual, tactile, oral and aural environment. (Although *Explorations* ended in 1959, an abbreviated version appeared as a supplement to the University of Toronto *Graduate* magazine through the 1970s.)

The warnings implicit in *Explorations* are explicit in *The Mechanical Bride* (1951), a brilliant analysis of advertising and propaganda methods subtitled 'Folklore of Industrial Man' (McLuhan has always been concerned to expose contemporary mythology), and designed to show how the media of magazines, newspapers and films control consumption and self-definition in the capitalist state. In fact, the State emerges as a malign work of art (a concept partly derived from Jakob Burckhardt's analysis of Machiavelli). The mechanization of choice moulds human life caught in 'a radical separation between business and society, between action and feeling, office and home, between men and women'. McLuhan believes that these divisions cannot be healed until their fullest extent is perceived. Popular culture, therefore, must be studied to understand the full effect of the media. The historical implications of changes caused by the shift from script to print to electric technology – the major media transition – is documented in *The Gutenberg Galaxy* (1962) from a large variety of texts, selected to elucidate changes towards 'social change which may lead to a genuine increase of human autonomy'. McLuhan's principle is: 'If a technology is not understood either from within or from without a culture, and if it gives new stress or ascendancy to one or another of our senses, the ratio among all our senses is altered. . . . The result is a break in the ratio among the senses, a kind of loss of identity.' William Blake on the 'perceptive organs' and James Joyce's multilingual *Finnegans Wake*, as a spatial involvement of the whole body-mind system, are presented with a wide range of social, psychological and scientific analysis in 'a mosaic pattern of perception and observation', 'the mode of simultaneous awareness' which is the basis of a culture, its practical and observable 'tribal or collective consciousness'. Media hypnosis is to be restricted by understanding the means and arts of communication. The artist functions primarily in this 'new clairvoyance' of the state's design, a prophetic necessity since 'the new electric galaxy of events has already moved deeply into the Gutenberg galaxy', causing 'trauma and tension to every living person'.

Understanding Media (1964), which gained McLuhan international fame and a cult status in America, examines the grammars of communication technology, encouraging the student of 'integral patterns' to 'live mythically and in depth' in order to comprehend 'the medium is the message' – that is, how the grammars of environment afford major clues to present and future. 'The machine turned Nature into an art form', and our own 'proliferating technologies have created a whole series of new environments', with the arts functioning as 'anti-environments' or 'counter-environments': 'art as radar acts as "an early alarm system" ', 'the function of indispensable perceptual training rather than the role of a privileged diet for the elite'. McLuhan's political and religious attitudes appear in his presentation of 'the revulsion of our times against imposed patterns' and of 'a faith that concerns the ultimate harmony of all beings'. Without social awareness in depth, patterns will be dictated: 'electric technology is within the gates'. One instrument of resistance, which entered the popular jargon of the 1960s, is to recognize 'hot' media – 'low in participation' – from 'cool' or requiring 'completion by the audience', which is therefore actively engaged rather than passively manipulated.

After 1964, McLuhan found himself in demand to analyse, predict and advise. His aphoristic ability to harness slogan or advert methods to penetrating social analysis of surprising sources found favour with the business world (as much as it was suspiciously loathed by the academic fraternity) and his *Dew-Line Newsletter* supplied the information culture controllers needed. In spite of this ambivalence in political action, he continued to function as an early warning system. *The Medium is the Message* (1967, with the designer Quentin Fiore) is a print and picture collage of media criticism composed with considerable wit and humour, a probe (a favourite term of action in his writings) into 'the environment as a processor of information', and therefore as a virulent propaganda system. *War and Peace in the Global Village* (1968, with Fiore) is 'an inventory of some of the current spastic situations that could be eliminated by more feedforward'. At this stage, McLuhan had come to believe that technologies are 'self-amputations' rather than the extensions of the body. 'Mosaic vision' is still necessary to combat 'corporate

decision-making for creating a total service environment on this planet'. *Counter Blast* (1969), acknowledging the methods of Wyndham Lewis's* *Blast* (1914) and incorporating design and typography techniques partly explored in *Explorations 8* (reissued in 1967 with the Joycean subtitle, *Verbi-Voco-Visual Explorations*), probes book, film, videotape, etc. as shapes of our consciousness, and therefore as the form of contemporary myth in which human energies are incarnated (another of his recurrent terms): 'The electronic age is the age of ecology. . . . The Age of Implosion in education spells the end of "subjects" and substitutes instead the structural study of the making and learning process. Software replaces hardware. . . . In the Age of Information, the moving of information is by many times the largest business in the world.' Much of the history and theory of these later works is contained in one of McLuhan's most substantial books, *Through the Vanishing Point* (1968, with Harley Parker), a challenge to perception restricted to the 'rear view mirror' point of view by analysing the history of space design in the arts, including the origins, images and effects of perspective and 'multi-level space' – necessary, since 'civilization is founded upon the isolation and domination of society by the visual sense'. *From Cliché to Archetype* (1970, with Wilfred Watson) is a fascinating discourse on language through such categories as 'Author as Cliché (Book as Probe)', 'Cliché as Breakdown' and 'The One and the Mini'. The range of examples is, once again, extraordinary, and the vivacity of McLuhan's perceptions unmatched. *Culture is Our Business* (1970) returns to his old obsession, American advertising as mythology – 'a world of festivity and celebration' which indicates 'a flip in American society from hardware to software' and how 'advertizing provides the corporate *meaning* for the experience of the private owner ... complex social events and "meanings" minus the experience of the commodities in question'. McLuhan's warning now extends to criticism of the USA's war in Vietnam as part of 'the electric infamy environment'.

Needless to say, his beliefs, techniques and conclusions have aroused both controversy and downright hatred. (The best criticism of McLuhan's work is Sidney Finkelstein's *Sense and Nonsense of McLuhan*, 1968.) But he himself has separated his personal intentions from his emphatic style, particularly in an excellent interview in *Playboy* magazine (No. 64, 1969): 'I'm making explorations . . . my books constitute the *process* rather than the completed product of discovery; my purpose is to employ facts as tentative probes, as means of insight, of pattern recognition, rather than to use them in the traditional and sterile sense of classified data, categories, containers. I want to map new terrain rather than chart old landmarks. But I've never presented such explorations as revealed truth. As an investigator, I have no fixed point of view, no commitment to any theory – my own or anyone else's.'

Eric Mottram

See: Gerald E. Stearn (ed.), *McLuhan Hot and Cool* (1968); Harry S. Crosby and George R. Bond (eds), *The McLuhan Explosion* (1968); Donald F. Theall, *The Medium is the Rear View Mirror: Understanding McLuhan* (1971).

291

MAGRITTE, René-François-Ghislain 1898–1967

Belgian artist

The Belgian surrealist painter René Magritte may be said to have cultivated a career of minimal incident, electing to spend most of his life in a neat house in the suburbs of Brussels with his wife and a succession of pet Pomeranian dogs. Out of this unimpeachably respectable existence – typified by Magritte's perennial bowler hat and businessman's suit – came forth some of the most disquieting images in modern painting.

Magritte's premise is that 'the world is a defiance of common sense'. Our everyday surroundings are fraught with mystery – a mystery as potent as it is, in essence, banal. Where other Surrealists go to great lengths to document complex dream versions of reality, Magritte worked from the things around him in an unruffled, deadpan style, pursuing a few fundamental ideas in the manner of a speculative philosopher. Painting was for him a medium in which to explore intellectual puzzles, and his work as a whole represents a kind of elegant treatise on certain problems of consciousness.

In particular, Magritte was fascinated by questions of perception and conception, the ways in which our sightings of phenomena and our images thereof are oddly disjunct. *Familiar Objects* (1927–8) portrays five men with blank stares, each with a different object suspended before his eyes – a lemon, a sponge, a pitcher, a knotted ribbon, a sea-shell in which may be discerned the form of a naked female body. Are these to be interpreted as obsessional delusions? It may be that Magritte is simply dramatizing the hypothesis that at any given moment our perception of a material object turns into a mental concept, the object proper being emptied of its corporeality: we unconsciously seek to project this phantom form from conceptual space back into the external world.

In thus addressing himself to the gap between the mental and the material, Magritte established that 'there is little relation between an object and that which represents it'. Our conventional sign-systems, whether verbal or pictorial, are inadequate to the task of truly isolating what is singular in the object, since 'whatever its manifest nature may be, every object is mysterious'. Magritte often went about a picture by asking himself in what way a given object might be represented so as to demonstrate this intrinsic mystery. Each object, he thought, possesses just one property or aspect which will, if exposed, illuminate its singularity. Rejecting the usual Surrealist practice of arbitrary association, Magritte purported to calculate *exactly* the one correct answer to 'the problem of the object'. 'He has a thirst for precise mysteries,' commented his friend Louis Scutenaire.

Magritte's calculations led to the invention of a whole set of devices to defamiliarize the object and so force the spectator to witness it under the bright light of visual surprise. In *Homesickness* (1941), a recumbent lion poses next to a gentleman with wings leaning against a parapet, lost in thought. Neither protagonist appears concerned about the bizarreness of the arrangement. In *The Heart of the Matter* (1928), Magritte offers an enigmatic collocation in the manner of De Chirico*, evoking a lingering sense of profundity shorn of explanation: a burly woman with a cloth over her face stands beside a tuba and a closed suitcase. A clue to this image derives from one of the few details in Magritte's bland biography: one night his mother was drowned and her body recovered from the local river with her nightgown wrapped round her head. But the tuba and the suitcase remain a perfect mystery.

Elsewhere the artist tampers with the rules of physical plausibility. In *The Listening-Room* (1952), he shows us an apple so huge as to occupy all the space in a room. He paints a sky built of solid azure cubes, a petrified lightning-flash, a granite bird on the wing, a cloud slumped to the ground, a door key which bursts into flames. In *Not to be reproduced* (1937), a man with his back to us stands before a mirror in which he is reflected not full-face, but *still* with his back to us. Hybrid forms – a chair with a tail, a mountain shaped like an eagle, a carrot turning into a bottle, a cigar-fish (or fish-cigar!) – enact propositions about the compatibility of alien entities. All this is done with a perfectly cool sense of logic. Thus the creature depicted in *Collective Invention* (1935) is an anti-mermaid – a woman's lower body with the upper body and head of a fish. It is a typical example of Magritte's system: he has taken the proposition *mermaid* and scrupulously reversed its terms. In so doing he has not created something counter-mythical, but rather something *doubly* unreal. Nevertheless the soberly academic paintwork encourages the feeling that this chimera is somehow 'a matter of fact'.

These paradoxical images, with their deliberately unhelpful titles, have done much to imprint a certain image of Surrealism upon the popular consciousness. While Magritte has had an influence on the visual arts, notably on painters in the orbit of Pop Art such as Oldenburg*, Dine and Johns*, his deepest impact has been in the field of commercial art. An American television network adopted as its emblem Magritte's image of an eye with the iris composed of a section of sky with clouds (*The False Mirror*, 1929); the publicity brochure of an international airline exploits his image of a soaring cut-out bird superimposed on a seascape (*The Large Family*, 1947). The repertoire of Magrittian devices of surprise is regularly exploited in magazine ads across the globe. Their inventor, who himself once worked for an advertising agency, designing illustrations for a furrier's catalogue, might have been amused by this further paradox of an idiosyncratic approach to the 'problem of the object' being made into a 'collective invention' – though it must be said that the products Magritte advertised in his paintings are rather less congenial than those promoted by commercial pastiche.

Roger Cardinal

By Magritte: *Manifestes et autres écrits* ('Manifestos and other texts', 1972). On Magritte: P. Nougé, *René Magritte ou Les Images défendues* ('René Magritte or The Forbidden Images', 1943); P. Waldberg, *René Magritte* (1965); D. Sylvester, *Magritte* (1969); S. Gablik, *Magritte* (1970; A. M. Hammacher, *Magritte* (1974); H. Torczyner, *Magritte: Ideas and Images* (1977).

292
MAILER, Norman 1923–

US novelist

Born in New Jersey, his family moved to Brooklyn, New York, when he was four. He graduated from Harvard in 1943 and married for the first time in 1944, shortly before being drafted into the army to serve in Leyte, Luzon and Japan. In his long and uneven career as a novelist, commentator on the American political scene, poet and film writer/producer, the central theme of his work has always been to relate the large-scale economic, political and institutional events of the national to the inner spiritual condition, the lifestyles and the choices of individuals, in their sexual bodily existences.

In his first novel, the highly successful *The Naked and the Dead* (1948), the army is an organism which feeds off the repressed and channelled energies of those it has swallowed. The soldiers' thoughts are predominantly about sex and money, and yet these seemingly private realms are the very sources of the competitive masculine energy which will ensure that they conform, out-perform each other, and excel in courage or control of others. Even the general, Cummings, finds the battle won in his absence, so that we see that his personal weight and authority derive from the army and not from his will. The ambiguous hero-figure, Hearst, is a liberal whose beliefs in high-mindedness and detachment are impotent to intervene in the situation, to control it, or to prevent his death.

Mailer's second novel, *Barbary Shore* (1951), similarly translates the struggle between Marxist and capitalist ideologies into personal terms, as the again ex-communist, McLeod, tries to atone for his own bloody past yet to reaffirm his own relationship to ideals of justice and progress. His adversary, the FBI agent Hollingsworth, is, by contrast, an adolescent figure who keeps his role at a distance from his personality, and thereby grants to authority an empty zombie.

Clarifying his ideas under the influence of Wilhelm Reich's* psychology with its equation of political and sexual repression, and various existentialist ideas, Mailer produced a volume of fragments and essays, *Advertisements for Myself* (1959), with its key essay 'The White Negro', an attempt to define authentic behaviour without involving morality or sanctions. This line of speculation was continued in *Cannibals and Christians* (1966) in the essay 'Metaphysics of the Belly', where he explores the idea that the soul can die, indeed that it lives only by those of our acts which nourish it, and that, having died, only empty forms of spirits exist. Even the way we eat, digest and excrete are indicative of our acceptance or avoidance, the guilt, fear or courage with which we face our lives. The clearest fictional expression of these ideas is his *American Dream* (1965) in which the hero, Rojack, war-hero, television personality, ex-Senator and academic, finally rejects the swollen image from which he derives his status, by killing his wife. The divorce of his true and false selves started in the war, when, by shirking the challenge in the eyes of those he was killing, he chose to identify himself with an image of bravery and success. He and his father-in-law, Kelly, become materially successful by identifying with and allowing themselves to be used by those institutionalized forces which run the country. This is seen as a form of black magic, selling one's soul in return for material power, and, in the process, becoming larger than life, bloated with non-human, social power.

The other side of the coin is explored in *Marilyn* (1973), a rather weak account of Marilyn Monroe's tragic attempts to come to terms with the enormous power she wielded as the nation's sex-queen, tapping the energy from the fusion of personal beauty and generalized desires.

Much of Mailer's critique of American society stems from his belief that the leaders in particular, and the population at large, refuse to perceive these collective energies even though they identify with them and consume them via the media. This refusal to see he calls 'the plague' or 'totalitarianism', and is re-created in a concentrated form in *Why are We in Vietnam?* (1967), in which the hip-talk of a bear-hunting disc-jockey embodies all the psychoses and aggressions pent up in the American psyche. *A Fire On the Moon* (1970), on the other hand, laments the effect of this blindness in totally depriving the moon-shot of any human significance or poetry, making it into a piece of technological common sense.

At one point in the Kennedy* administration, Mailer thought that decisive leadership could awaken the nation to the struggle for the possession of its own souls, and he cast Kennedy in that role in *The Presidential Papers* (1963), but Kennedy's death and the Vietnam war placed Mailer on the side of the protesters, and in *The Armies of the Night* (1968) he champions the power of those marching on the Pentagon to outflank the embedded military mind by acting in a spontaneous and natural way. His own image in these later books, however, is that of a muddled and puzzled participant, somehow left behind the march of events in a way reminiscent of Henry Adams in *The Education of Henry Adams* (1918). The white magic which his hero Rojack managed to perform by acting decisively and courage to exorcize his cowardice has seemingly no obvious political counterpart, and hence Mailer's vision has seemed weaker in the 1970s.

Dr David Corker

Mailer's other works include: *The Deer Park* (1955); *Deaths for the Ladies* (1962); poems, *The Idol and the Octopus* (1968); *Miami and the Siege of Chicago* (1968); *The Prisoner of Sex* (1971); *On the Fight of the Century* (1971); and a film script, *Maidstone: A Mystery* (1971). A complete bibliography to 1970 can be found in *Norman Mailer: The Man and His Work* (1971), ed. Robert Lucid. See also: Donald L. Kaufman, *Norman Mailer: the Countdown* (1969); Richard Poirier, *Mailer* (1972).

293

MALCOLM X (Malcolm Little/El Hajj Malik El-Shabazz) 1925–65

US racial leader

Malcolm Little was born in Omaha, Nebraska, the son of a West Indian mother and black American father. His father, a Baptist minister and follower of Marcus Garvey, moved the family to Lansing, Michigan, when Malcolm was very small. His father's black nationalist beliefs were very unpopular in this overwhelmingly white community; the family home was burned and his father murdered. Malcolm, however, moved relatively easily among whites. It was not until he visited an older half-sister in Boston in 1940 that he discovered the sub-culture of black ghetto life. He was never the same again. After finishing the eighth grade, he left school and Michigan behind and moved to Boston. He quickly acquired a fascination for street life and became immersed in a world of 'hustling' – drugs, night life, theft and prostitution. He operated in Harlem during most of the Second World War, but in 1945 he returned to Boston, was soon arrested for burglary and sentenced to prison. He was not yet twenty-one years old.

Malcolm Little's first reaction to prison was blind rage. His anger began to take focus, however, when members of his family in Detroit began writing to him about their discovery of the 'natural religion of the black man'. From them he learned of the teachings of Elijah Muhammad* and the small black religious sect known as the Nation of Islam. Muhammad taught a version of history in which black Americans had a central and dominant role. The racial degradation which Malcolm had experienced was explained as being the work of the white devil (all whites in Western civilization). Malcolm now came to realize that his lifestyle and those of black Americans had been inhibited by self-hate and shame over their blackness. Complete rejection and withdrawal from whites was the answer, and this could only be accomplished by adhering rigidly to the Nation of Islam's programme of disciplined personal behaviour. Malcolm Little now had an explanation for his anger and a programme of redemption.

He was released from prison in 1952 and joined his family in Detroit where he applied formally for admission into the Nation and threw himself into the activities of the local mosque. He went to Chicago where Elijah Muhammad personally trained him as a Muslim minister and gave him the name Malcolm X. In 1953 he was sent East and quickly developed a reputation as a dynamic speaker who attracted new converts to the teachings of Muhammad. Malcolm X built a growing base of support in New York and founded the Nation's newspaper, *Muhammad Speaks*. As America's news media responded to the spreading Civil Rights Movement in the late 1950s, it also became more interested in other phenomena in black America. Malcolm saw this as an opportunity to put more blacks in touch with the saving teachings of Elijah Muhammad. His charismatic personality drew large crowds, and his message of hatred and rejection served as a stinging antithesis to the sermons of love and forgiveness being popularized by Martin Luther King, Jr*. He was soon the best known black Muslim – more widely quoted and sought after than Elijah Muhammad. This popularity began to arouse jealousy in other Muslim leaders, however, and when Malcolm X sought to make the Nation of Islam more responsive and active in organizing among black communities, Elijah Muhammad consistently held him back. Distance appeared between prophet and minister. Finally, after an intemperate response to John F. Kennedy's* assassination in November 1963, Malcolm X was ordered to be 'silent' in public, and by March 1964 pressure on him had reached the point that he knew he could no longer function nor was he wanted in the Nation of Islam. This was a shattering blow, for he always maintained that he owed his very salvation as a human being to the message and guidance of Elijah Muhammad.

Malcolm struggled to find a new perspective on his religious beliefs and his commitment to mass action by blacks. He made a pilgrimage to Mecca, meeting many leaders of the African and Arab nations and never escaping the international spotlight. His exposure to orthodox Islam deepened his spiritual devotion, but drew him away from the doctrinal and social narrowness of the 'Black Muslims'. He returned to the US more open to the possibility of reconciliation with whites (but only by maintaining separate groups) and committed to non-sectarian mass action. He formed the Organization of Afro-American Unity and had just begun to project a new mission for himself when he was assassinated by three members of the Nation of Islam at a public meeting in New York on 21 February 1965. Malcolm left his wife (whom he married in 1958), four children, and a vacuum in the black struggle for dignity and opportunity in America. He had an asset that no other black leader of the time had: he was from the masses, had suffered their plight, and had conquered the depths. After encountering Malcolm X's mass appeal other black leaders were forced to deal with some hard racial truths in America regarding their integrationist goals. He forced them to recognize the validity of a growing demand for 'black power'.

Professor Lester C. Lamon

See: Malcolm X (with Alex Haley), *The Autobiography of Malcolm X* (1964); C. Eric Lincoln, *The Black Muslims in America* (1961); and John Henrik Clarke, *Malcolm X: The Man and His Times* (1969).

294

MALEVICH, Kazimir 1878–1935

Russian artist

Initiator of Suprematism (a radical 'hard-edged' abstractionism in painting), and generally one of the pioneers in twentieth-century art, Malevich developed his talents and theories slowly, not reaching the climax of his evolution until his late thirties. In this he resembles Kandinsky* – the other internationally famous abstract innovator in modern Russian art – though in almost every other respect their ideas and careers make an instructive contrast.

Born near Kiev of humble parents (many of the leaders of the Russian 'modern movement' were provincials), he lived successively in Kursk, from 1902 in Moscow (where he managed to get some art education), in Vitebsk (from 1919) where he joined the art college headed by Chagall* – whom he quickly superseded – and finally (from 1922) in Petrograd/ Leningrad. His earliest surviving works, from the first decade of the century, have Art Nouveau elements; after *c.* 1908 his style evolves rapidly through several well-defined stages. Heavily-outlined, powerful, lumbering peasant figures characterize a primitivistic phase in which curvilinear rhythms dominate the canvas; subsequent developments take him close (though not derivatively so) to Italian Futurist methods, to geometricized figures reminiscent of Léger*, to a Cubist dissection of the object: always his bold colour sense plays a primary role in the organization of the composition. By *c.* 1913 the 'alogism' that was to form a main plank of his aesthetic theory is discernible in works (e.g. the famous *Englishman in Moscow*) that outstrip any Western European analogues in their antirational daring and fragmentation.

Malevich was close to other representatives of the second (post-Symbolist) phase of modernism: notably to the literary Futurists, who similarly developed the concept of *sdvig* (dislocation) as a prime element of their aesthetic. He illustrated various Futurist books, and designs for the Futurist opera *Victory over the Sun* (1915) opened the path to Suprematism. Suprematist paintings were first shown late in 1915, and caused a furore within the avant-garde (notably a violent quarrel with Tatlin*). Unlike Kandinsky's – though with no less spiritual verve – his abstractionism 'liberated' the painting from any connection with representationalism, creating a universe of free-floating, geometrically simple monochrome shapes against a white background suggestive only of limitless space. Though a vigorous controversialist, his aim was not *épatage*, but a breakthrough on behalf of the autonomy and cognitive status of art, informed by an intense awareness of beauty as an independent category.

From *c.* 1920 painting occupied him less, and he devoted himself more and more to educational endeavours, to writing and – with his disciples (notably El Lissitzky) at *Unovis* – to devising ideal architectural models (*planity*), whose lack of functionalism emphasizes how remote his concerns were from the post-Revolutionary Constructivists, on whom his innovations nevertheless had an impact. In 1927 he travelled to Germany with a substantial exhibition of his works; these remained in the West and are the source of the major public collection at the Stedelijk Museum, Amsterdam. His short book of the same year, *The Non-Objective World*, was influential at the Bauhaus and beyond. However, the atmosphere in the USSR was already turning against his approach to art, and his last years (though he remained a focus for modernist endeavours in Leningrad) were passed in obscurity. The paintings and drawings of this period, largely inaccessible, and sometimes unjustly impugned as a 'sellout', are extremely interesting: Suprematist elements are combined with a pervasive cross motif in a 'classicizing' return to recognizable subject-matter, notably the transcendentally-simplified human figure.

When Malevich died and was buried in his Suprematist-decorated coffin, the anti-modernist reaction in the USSR (even indeed outside it) was in full swing. For years his heritage was publicly ignored; only since the 1960s has Soviet scholarship begun tentatively to explore it, and a small proportion of the works to emerge from museum store-rooms. It lived on, however, not only through the force of his example on his many followers, but as a crucial formative element in much modern design, and above all as one of the noblest modern expressions of an anti-utilitarian, anti-romantic justification of the autonomy and spiritual purpose of art.

Robin Milner-Gulland

Apart from *The Non-Objective World*, Malevich's voluminous writings are little known; they have recently however been appearing in English (*Essays in Art*, ed. T. Andersen, Copenhagen 1968 onwards). See also: C. Gray, *The Russian Experiment in Art* (1971); S. Compton, *The World Backwards: Russian Futurist Books 1912–16* (1978); T. Andersen, *Malevich* (Stedelijk Museum, Amsterdam 1970).

295
MALINOWSKI, Bronislaw Kaspar 1884–1942

Polish/British anthropologist

Bronislaw Malinowski, one of the most influential scholars in modern British social anthropology, was born in Cracow in 1884 and died in New Haven, Connecticut, in 1942. He obtained his PhD at Cracow University in 1908 in physics and mathematics, but illness prevented him from pursuing these subjects. While convalescent he turned to the study of anthropology, notably Frazer's *Golden Bough*, and, after studying at Leipzig, he came to London as a post-graduate student at the London School of Economics. His publications on the Australian Aborigines (1913) and the Mailu of New Guinea (1915) earned him a DSc degree in 1916, but a major breakthrough in his career had already occurred in 1914, when, with the support of Professor C. G. Seligman, he attended the meeting of the British Association for the Advancement of Science in Australia. He then undertook fieldwork in New Guinea for much of the next four years. It was his fieldwork in the Trobriand Islands which was decisive in shaping his approach to what he conceived, in effect, as a new discipline, social anthropology.

Malinowski was closely linked with the LSE from 1920 to 1938. He was appointed Lecturer in Social Anthropology for 1922–3, becoming Reader in 1924 and Professor of Anthropology in 1927. By 1938 his health was not good and he went to the USA for a sabbatical year. Following the outbreak of the Second World War he became a visiting professor at Yale until 1942, when he was appointed to a permanent professorship, an appointment cut short by his death. In the relatively short period of intense academic work between the wars Malinowski, more than any other individual in Britain, changed the leading ideas and fieldwork strategies of his subject away from preoccupations with comparative ethnology and cultural evolution towards the study of contemporary non-western societies. His influence was notable in three main areas: fieldwork, theory and methods of teaching.

Malinowski's fieldwork was characterized by its depth, care for detail, a balance of quality against quantity, and a concern for the apparently inconsequential imponderabilia of life – collected as far as possible in the vernacular. This gave his ethnography a richness unusual for his time, which enabled him to demonstrate the close contextual (i.e. functional) interrelationship of many aspects of social behaviour. He was not, of course, the first functionalist in British anthropology, but in his hands functionalism became an analytical tool at several levels of abstraction. First, the function of an institution was seen in terms of its effects on other institutions, from which principles of social organization could be induced. Second, the study of function included 'an analysis of the effects of an institution on the maintenance of specific relationships and the achievement of specific ends as defined by the members of a particular community' (Kaberry, in Firth, 1957). Third, Malinowski saw function 'as the part played by an institution in promoting social cohesion and the persistence of a given way of life or culture in a given environment' (Kaberry, *ibid.*). Thus his insistence on the need for prolonged and detailed fieldwork was the concomitant of his championing of the functionalist theory. In a series of books on aspects of his Trobriand fieldwork published between 1922 and 1935 these concepts were elaborated and refined. Concurrently he was developing a theory of needs which he defined as follows: 'By need, then, I understand the system of conditions in the human organism, in the cultural setting, and in the relation of both to the natural environment, which are sufficient and necessary for the survival of group and organism. A need, therefore, is the limiting set of facts. Habits and their motivations, the learned responses and the foundations of organization, must be so arranged as to allow the basic needs to be satisfied' (*A Scientific Theory of Culture*, 1944).

Malinowski's seminars at the LSE have acquired an honoured place in the history of anthropology, partly because they attracted many able students who subsequently attained positions of importance in the discipline and developed many of his ideas. The seminars were notable for their scope, rigour, polemical character and wit. Indeed, the manuscript of *Coral Gardens and their Magic* (1935) was there subjected to page-by-page scrutiny. Many of his students have testified to the stimulation, sense of inspired leadership and strong affection which Malinowski gave them. Not surprisingly, there were elements of messianic dedication in his teaching and research which stamped the character of social anthropology for many years after his death. His writings retain an important place in anthropological literature and show no sign of being consigned to 'history'. On the other hand, his work has inevitably generated much criticism, aspects of which must be mentioned briefly.

The functional concept is self-evidently limited in analytical value. Moreover, despite his debt to Durkheim*, Malinowski used it more for the study of culture than of society. His empiricism led him to this position. But to give the study of culture the central place in anthropological theory was, in the eyes of many scholars, to preclude an effective comparative study of social institutions regardless of their particular empirical character. Similarly, these theoretical constraints limited his studies of economics, magic and religion.

Malinowski's work, because it was so clearly directed against accepted prevailing attitudes within anthropology, bears plainly the marks of his time. But if one discounts these, there is still an enormous amount of ethnographic information and analysis in his writings worthy of careful study. As a fieldworker he remains a major exemplar, and as an analyst his insights can still stimulate. Certainly an understanding of his career is necessary in order to appreciate the present character and interests of British social anthropology.

Peter Gathercole

Other major works include: *Argonauts of the Western Pacific* (1922); *Crime and Custom in Savage Society* (1926); *Sex and Repression in Savage Society* (1927); *The Sexual Life of Savages in North-Western Melanesia* (1929). See also: R. Firth (ed.), *Man and Culture: An Evaluation of the Work of Malinowski* (essays, 1957); M. W. Young, *The Ethnography of Malinowski: the Trobriand Islands 1915–18* (1979).

296
MALRAUX, André 1901–76

French novelist, essayist and political activitist

Malraux was born and educated in Paris, but his early years are not well documented. In the early 1920s, his interest in archaeology took him to the Far East, where he also came into contact with revolutionary politics – in Laos, for example, as well as in China. After his return to France in 1927, he became involved with anti-fascist activities; 1936 saw him in Spain, as a member of the International Brigade, fighting for the Republican cause. After escaping from imprisonment in the Second World War, he joined the Resistance, and in due course became a tank commander. In the post-war world his political activities were bound up with the career of General de Gaulle – as a minister in de Gaulle's 1945–6 administration, as an active member of the Gaullist RPF (*Rassemblement du peuple français*), and again as a minister (of Culture) after de Gaulle's return to power in 1958.

In a sense, the whole of Malraux's work – whether as novelist or philosopher of art, autobiographer or political figure – is a single expression of his reflection upon his experience of life. His novels, for example, are closely linked to the political and social reality of which he had direct knowledge, with the exception of his first work, *Lunes de papier* ('Paper moons', 1920, described by the author himself as *farfelu* – hare-brained). The words 'hero', 'action', 'History' recur constantly in discussions of Malraux's work, and not without reason, whether in *La Tentation de l'Occident* ('Temptation of the West', 1926), carrying events and the action they demand on to the metaphysical plane, *The Conquerors* (*Les Conquérants*, 1928, trans. 1929), set in Canton at the time of the general strike of 1925, *The Royal Way* (*La Voie royale*, 1930, trans. 1935), showing Perken in his search for temples lost in the depths of the jungles of Asia, *Man's Estate* (*La Condition humaine*, 1933, trans. 1948), Malraux's most famous novel (for which he was awarded the Prix Goncourt), portraying the revolutionary events in Shanghai in 1927, *Days of Contempt* (*Le Temps du mépris*, 1935, trans. 1936), *Days of Hope* (*L'Espoir*, 1937, trans. 1938), arising directly out of his activity in the Spanish Republican cause, or *The Walnut Trees of Altenburg* (*Les Noyers de l'Altenburg*, 1943, trans. 1952). Faced with the need to participate in events related to major conflicts, but in a world where human existence has no obvious justification, characters seek to give meaning to their life, not only through their action and the sense of community which comes from acting together for a cause (often revolutionary), but also through their death, or rather, perhaps, the manner of their dying.

In the post-war world, his writing is represented by two major works: in *Voices of Silence* (*Les Voix du silence*, 1951, trans. 1953), Malraux's reflection turns from action to art for evidence that man may transcend his contingency through artistic creation; whilst the *Antimemoirs* (*Antimémoires*, 2 vols, 1967 and 1974, trans. 1968) are a meditation upon the experience of a lifetime, and more particularly upon Malraux's significant encounters with some of the major world figures.

Malraux's importance is considerable, not only for any lasting value his writing might have, but also – and more especially – for the impact of his work upon the rising generation of the 1930s. It might indeed be held that *Man's Estate*, along with Céline's* *Journey to the End of the Night*, is a key work in the decade preceding the Second World War.

Keith Gore

See: D. Boak, *André Malraux* (1968); P. Galante, *Malraux* (1971); C. Jenkins, *André Malraux* (1972); J. Lacouture, *André Malraux, une vie dans le siècle* (1973); A. Madsen, *Malraux* (1977).

297

MANDELSTAM, Osip Emilievich 1891–1938

Russian poet

Mandelstam was born in Warsaw, but grew up in a Jewish family in St Petersburg. He spent much of the period from 1907 to 1910 as a student in Western Europe. His first volume of poems, *Stone* (*Kamen*), appeared in 1913. After the Revolution he remained in Russia, and in 1919 began to live with Nadezhda Yakovlevna Khazina, with whom he was formally married some years later. From this time until his death he lived in many different places, suffering increasing hardship as he was progressively excluded from serious literary work. In 1934 his authorship of satirical verses about Stalin* brought him three years of exile in the town of Voronezh. Shortly after his return, he was again arrested and sent to a labour camp. By now he was a very ill man; he is reported to have died in a transit camp near Vladivostok.

One may see the primary poetic impulse in Mandelstam as the struggle against chaos. His earliest poems show clearly the influence of the poet Fyodor Tiutchev, who saw day as a golden cover thrown over the chaos of night, and almost all his writing – in this respect very much the product of St Petersburg – speaks of the fragility of human culture. This note becomes more intense in his later, more tragic work.

In opposition to chaos, his first book, with its significant title of *Stone*, celebrates the ordering impulse which is seen in civilization, and particularly in great works of architecture. In this stress on the positive, building spirit, Mandelstam is at one with the Acmeist school, who praised the real, physical world as against the other-worldly longings of the Symbolists. In his view Acmeism was the 'nostalgia for world culture' and his conception of poetry was one of *recognition*; the poets of all ages echoed one another, the poetic word was an enduring living force. He wrote some remarkable essays on the poetry of the past and present, notably his *Conversation about Dante* (*Razgovor o Dante*, written in 1933, published in Moscow in 1967). Far more than most Russian poets he saw the civilization of the Mediterranean as the summit of human achievement; a recurrent notion in his writing is that

'Hellenism' succeeded in domesticating chaos and providing an area of human warmth for life in the world. This he saw as the continuing task of the poet, particularly in the barbarian modern age.

In keeping with these beliefs, Mandelstam's poems often refer explicitly to poets and artists of earlier centuries: Bach, Racine, Ovid, Petrarch and many others. The verse of the first two books also shows a striking ability to create harmonious and rich verbal constructs – the sound of the verse embodies the beliefs. But it would be wrong to imagine him, even in his earlier work, as a simple classicist; even in *Stone*, and much more so in the aptly named *Tristia* (1922), the dominant note is one of loss. Happiness lies in recognition and recovery, but this is generally denied to the modern poet. A characteristic poem in this respect is one written in 1920 and beginning, 'I have forgotten the word I wanted to say.' Mandelstam tended to write clusters of poems in which images and themes recur, and in the group to which this poem belongs the central motifs are the swallow (a brief visitor to the dark North), Psyche, Persephone and the underworld of shades, all of them expressing fragility, negativity and emptiness. The formal order of the poem only emphasizes by contrast the real disarray that lies at the heart of it.

The feeling of loss, which was clearly provoked in part by Mandelstam's understanding of the Revolution, is even more apparent in the small body of poems written between 1921 and 1925 and published in 1928 – almost his last published poetry. In such magnificent pieces as 'The Slate-Pencil Ode' ('Grifelnaya Oda') and 'January 1st 1924', he expresses a tragic vision of his age, likened to an animal with a broken backbone. These are fragmentary, broken odes (comparable in their way to T. S. Eliot's* work of the same period), poems of great and often puzzling richness whose main theme is the difficulty or impossibility of writing odes in the great tradition which stretches back through the eighteenth-century poet Derzhavin to Pindar.

After 1925 the difficulty of writing forced Mandelstam into a period of poetic silence which was only broken in the 1930s and particularly in the 'Notebooks' written in Voronezh between 1935 and 1937. Here all the bridges are down; the poems are more intensely tragic than anything that he had written before. They are a strange mixture of clarity and obscurity. Mandelstam now sees his destiny very clearly and many of the poems express a lucid courage and even acceptance, but at the same time the fear of chaos and cruelty and the poet's inner turmoil often force the writing into a jagged, elliptical and hermetic form which contrasts sharply with the first two books. This is particularly true of the menacing and defiant 'Verses about the Unknown Soldier' ('Stikhi o neizvestnom soldate'), the oblique result of an unavailing attempt to write an ode in praise of Stalin.

Officially the importance of Mandelstam's poetry is

only very grudgingly recognized in the Soviet Union, but for many readers both there and in the West his reputation has now eclipsed even that of Pasternak*. To a certain extent this is perhaps an elite cult which feeds on Mandelstam's difficulty, but it seems beyond doubt that he is one of the three or four great Russian poets of this century.

Peter France

Mandelstam's collected works have been published in Russian, edited by G. P. Struve and B. A. Filippov, 3 vols, New York 1964–71. Translations include *Selected Poems* (trans. C. Brown and W. S. Merwin, 1973); *Poems* (trans. J. Greene, 1977); *The Prose of Osip Mandelstam* (trans. C. Brown, 1965); *Selected Essays* (trans. S. Monas, 1977). The best general study of Mandelstam is C. Brown, *Mandelstam* (1973). See also the two volumes of memoirs by Mandelstam's widow, N. Mandelstam, *Hope against Hope* (trans. M. Hayward, 1971) and *Hope Abandoned* (trans. M. Hayward, 1974).

298
MANN, Luis Heinrich 1871–1950

German writer

The eldest son of a prosperous Hanseatic merchant, and brother of Thomas Mann*, Heinrich Mann was born in Lübeck in the same year as Bismarck's creation, the second German Empire, which was to furnish the subject-matter and concern of the novels and essays of his maturity. He was intended to follow his father into the family firm, and at the age of thirteen was sent, as part of his preparation for this, to visit trading relatives in St Petersburg. But the journal the boy kept of the journey shows rather the precocious talent of the born writer, and an early gift for drawing. Sharing his generation's sense of being late-comers to the achievements of the nineteenth-century bourgeois protestant ethic, Heinrich struggled to free himself from his inheritance until his father recognized the inevitable, and made a will dissolving the family firm and enabling Heinrich and Thomas to live the life of literary *rentiers* in the last years of the century. Heinrich never returned to Lübeck. Ill-health, a love affair with a failed opera-singer, a deep attachment to his actress-sister Carla and no fixed abode all went to make up a typical literary life-style of the time.

Fontane, the Naturalists, and above all Heine, were the writers he first admired. But he soon turned to the differentiated psychology of Hermann Bahr and Paul Bourget, who left their mark on his first, tentative novel *In Einer Familie* (1894). Bourget's pessimistic conservatism, adapted to German affairs, can also be traced in his brief editorship of *Das zwanzigste Jahrhundert,*

Blätter für deutsche Art und Wohlfahrt (1895–6), a journal devoted to the monarchist, militarist, anti-democratic and anti-semitic views of the threatened petty bourgeoisie. This is a curious episode, less of a false start than in retrospect it might seem. It represented a first attempt to put *l'art pour l'art* attitudes behind him and engage critically with his society. It gave way to a programmatic realization that what Germany lacked was a tradition of the social novel as a means to social self-knowledge. Suddenly discovering his talent as a satirical novelist while in Italy, he set about making good this lack. His first novel of any stature, *In the Land of Cockaigne* (*Im Schlaraffenland*, trans. 1929), appeared in 1900. It tells the tale of the rise and fall of an unscrupulous young man on the make – the model is Maupassant's *Bel Ami*. All the figures, from the kept women to the bought newspaper editors, are the creatures of the grand capitalist J. J. Turkheimer. Three characteristics show themselves in this novel which were to become Mann's hallmark: the theme of power (and the intellectual's relationship to it); the impersonal 'dramatic' presentation, with a cast of thousands; and the set-piece of a theatrical performance as the touchstone of social values – in this case the radical chic of an expensive audience getting its thrills from a dire Naturalist drama about the Plight of the Workers, a brilliant parody on elements from Hauptmann's *Die Weber* and Zola's *La Bête humaine*. There is as yet no unspoken moral basis for this satire on capitalism abounding beyond a worldly anti-bourgeois fastidiousness. His next novels, the trilogy *Die Göttinnen oder die drei Romane der Herzogin von Assy* (1903, 'The Goddesses or the Three Novels of the Duchess von Assy'), are symptomatic of his ambivalence. On the one hand he is overtly critical of decadent aestheticism; but on the other, Mann's intense, florid prose, and the extravagance of his heroine's life-styles indicate that he is as much fascinated by as critical of the current Nietzschean vitalism. But from now on the criticism prevails, not only of the compensatory psychology of decadence (*Pippo Spano*, 1905), but also of the compensatory psychology of power (*Small Town Tyrant, Professor Unrat oder das Ende eines Tyrannen*, 1905, trans. 1944). Concurrently with these Mann wrote his major essay *Flaubert und George Sand* (1905), a subtle study of the socially alienated artist. The degree of both criticism and identification in this essay marks a stage in his development towards the sense of social commitment for which his later work is known.

A real signal came with his rhetorical manifesto *Geist und Tat* ('Mind and Action', 1910), which exhorted German intellectuals to abandon their remote and acquiescent attitude towards the institutions of power, and to look to the French style, where a politically responsible public could demand (and get) a political responsibility from its writers. The man of letters is understood as the public conscience of his country.

Increasingly, he came to define his position as that of the French republican democrat. The two novels he was at work on are in tune with this declaration. *The Little Town* (*Die kleine Stadt*, 1909, trans. 1931) is a happy return to the Italy of Mascagni and Puccini and memories of Garibaldi: a stagnant Italian town is brought to comic, democratic life by the upheavals and self-knowledge provoked by the disturbing visit of an operatic troupe. The satirical, negative counterpart to this Utopian idyll is the famous novel for which he had been gathering material since 1907: *The Man of Straw* (*Der Untertan*, 1918, trans. 1947). The scene is the ugly little German town of Netzig in the 1890s, the tale the rise of the characteristic figure of the period, the hollow bully Dietrich Hessling, whose aggressive posturings are modelled on those of his histrionic master Kaiser Wilhelm II. To tell 'the inner history of the period' is its purpose, and Mann's old insight into the psychology of compensatory aggressiveness out of impotence is developed to interpret a whole generation: his own generation of sons, the empty-handed inheritors of an older generation's achievement. Role-playing, performance, is now endemic to the entire society, from monarch to subject: 'Theatre, and not even good theatre' – the tawdry pretentiousness of Wagner's theatre. The defeat of the old liberal tradition of 1848 forms the novel's climax – and, given that the book was finished in 1914, a prophetic one.

The First World War was the occasion of a fundamental estrangement, private and public, between the two brothers. Thomas Mann's response to the outbreak had been the traumatic discovery, in his own terms, of Germany and patriotism. Heinrich, with his French republican allegiance, came out with a major essay, *Zola* (1915); the passionate rhetoric of Zola accusing the French Second Empire on behalf of the wronged Dreyfus acts as a figure for Mann's own opposition to Germany's initiation of the war. His denunciation of Zola's time-serving literary contemporaries stung Thomas into a complex self-justification, in *Betrachtungen eines Unpolitischen* (1918). The classic dispute between Heinrich's Utopian republicanism and his brother's sceptical conservatism was not resolved until 1922 when the two Manns reunited in a sustained defence of the vulnerable Weimar republic.

The years that followed were the years of Heinrich's greatest fame and political activity, from his funeral speech at the grave of the assassinated Kurt Eisner in 1919 to his turning away from Germany, in *Bekenntnis zum Übernationalen* ('Commitment to the International Idea', 1932), to Coudenhouve-Kalergi's hope for a united Europe. The rich harvest of political essays is the work of this decade for which he will be remembered (*Macht und Mensch*, 'Power and Humanity', 1919; *Diktatur der Vernunft*, 'Dictatorship of Reason', 1923: *Sieben Jahre*, 'Seven Years', 1929). The works of the imagination are frailer. *The Chief* (*Der Kopf*, 1925, trans.

1925), set in high government places, was intended to be the social novel of the Republic as *Der Untertan* had been for the Empire; but caught in the daily battle of criticizing and sustaining the Republic in reality, he could not find a suitable form to present it in fiction.

An energetic advocate of all good liberal causes, he moved further left in his views as the National Socialists took hold of Germany. Dismissed as President of the Literary Section of the Prussian Academy of Arts in 1933 (he had been appointed in 1931), he crossed into France only days before the burning of the Reichstag. As the father of the German intellectual left he became chairman of the *Schutzverband deutscher Schriftsteller*, writing for the many German journals-in-exile, moving progressively nearer the Communist position, which attacked not so much Nazism as a German phenomenon but Fascism as the instrument of international capitalism. Exile stimulated his imagination as well, and these years saw two of his finest novels: *King Wren* (*Die Jugend des Königs Henri Quatre*, 1935, trans. 1937) and *Henri IV King of France* (*Die Vollendung des Königs Henri Quatre*, 1938, trans. 1938), an image in historical terms of the power-struggles and hopes of his own time.

In 1940, with the invasion of France, he fled again, to the USA by way of Spain. His last years were spent in straitened circumstances in California, writing unproduced film scripts and the novels *Der Atem* ('Breath', 1949) and *Empfang bei der Welt* ('The World Receives', 1956). The major work of this last, and saddest period of his life (his second wife Nelly Kröger killed herself) was his autobiography, the historical, impersonal account of a life in his time: *Ein Zeitalter wird besichtigt* ('An Age is Viewed', 1945). He died as preparations were being made to welcome him back to the new German Democratic Republic.

Heinrich Mann was a prolific and uneven novelist. Apart from *Der Untertan* and *Henri Quatre* there is still no consensus on what constitutes the canon of his major works, and his reputation has fluctuated since his death almost as much as when he was alive. Always regarded as an established classic in the DDR, postwar Western Germany of the *Wirtsschaftswunder* seemed ready to forget him, at least until the recent revival of the old wish for social responsibility in the novel restored his stock, and led to a wider recognition of his pre-war importance.

Joyce Crick

Other works include: novels: *The Poor* (*Die Armen*, 1917, trans. 1917); *Kobes* ('Kobes', 1925); drama: *Schauspielerin* ('The Actress', 1911); *Die grosse Liebe* ('Great Love', 1912); *Madame Legros* (1913); essays: *Das öffentliche Leben* ('Public Life', 1932); *Der Sinn dieser Emigration* ('The Meaning of this Emigration', 1934); *Es kommt der Tag* ('The Day will Come') (1936); biography: Klause Schröter, *Heinrich Mann*

(Hamburg 1967). See: David Roberts, *Artistic Consciousness and Political Conscience: The Novels of Heinrich Mann* (1971).

299

MANN, Thomas 1875–1955

German novelist

Son of a prosperous north German grain merchant and a mother of partly Brazilian origins, Thomas, younger brother of Heinrich Mann*, was born in Lübeck. He began writing early and was fortunate enough, on leaving school, to be able to devote most of his time to it. In 1893 Mann left Lübeck for Munich which became his home for the next forty years. His marriage to Katia Pringsheim in 1905 resulted in six children, a number of whom were to become distinguished in their turn as writers or scholars. In 1929 Mann was awarded the Nobel Prize; in 1933 the rise of Nazism forced him and his family into exile, first in Switzerland, then in the USA where he was held in high honour, his home in Pacific Palisades, California, becoming something of a place of pilgrimage. After the war he returned to Switzerland and settled there for the remainder of his life.

At the age of only twenty-six, Mann achieved immediate success with his first novel, *Buddenbrooks* (1901, trans. 1924). This surprisingly mature work is the history of four generations of a family of grain merchants from prosperity and full integration into the Hanseatic community in which they live to final alienation and decline. The single-minded vitality of the Buddenbrook clan is able, in its great days, to assimilate and control its rogue members with their dangerous traits of fecklessness or lethargy: but these elements are gradually reinforced by a more powerful and complex strain – that of the imagination with its tendency to question and even subvert the stolid self-assurance of the practical life. In proportion as imagination, art and the probing intellect assert their claims, the Buddenbrook hold on life diminishes until, in the musically gifted but physically feeble Hanno, the last of the line, it disappears altogether.

The tendency, supported by Mann's reading of Schopenhauer, to view the imagination as a force essentially hostile to the crude vitality of life is one which fuels much of Mann's earlier fiction, notably the novellas *Tonio Kröger* and *Tristan* (1903), both in their different ways studies in the predicament of the writer. In Mann's possibly most famous work, *Death in Venice* (*Der Tod in Venedig*, 1911; trans. in *Three Tales*, 1929), the protagonist, Gustav von Aschenbach, is a mature and renowned writer who has subjugated the moral dubieties of the imagination to the demands of a classicizing art of intransigent ethical and aesthetic rigour. But Aschenbach's (in Nietzsche's term) Apolline solutions are undermined and finally obliterated: on a journey to Venice he encounters the Polish boy Tadzio whose almost perfect beauty, though seeming at first a confirmation of Aschenbach's classical ideals, gradually tempts him into sensual indulgence, Dionysian disintegration and finally death. *Death in Venice*, then, is concerned with the essential paradox of the artistic endeavour: the ethical and aesthetic realms which Aschenbach has thought to reconcile with one another prove in the end to be warring elements: and the story itself, which is constructed with consummate artistry, thus implicitly calls its own very virtuosity in question.

The Magic Mountain (*Der Zauberberg*, 1922, trans. 1927) was originally conceived as a comic pendant to *Death in Venice*, but grew to a novel of considerable length. It is, ironically, a *Bildungsroman*: ironically because its, hero, the innocent young Hans Castorp, is educated to life not, like the traditional hero of the German novel of education, via life itself, but in the hermetically sealed environment of a Swiss tuberculosis sanatorium whose entire *raison d'être* is disease and death. Does disease heighten the sensibilities, ennoble the personality? Hans Castorp is at first romantically disposed to think so, but finds himself disenchanted by the relentlessly trivial preoccupations of most of the sanatorium's denizens. More deeply demanding are the claims on his consciousness of a small number of characters who act as educators or at least as perpetrators of particular, exclusive viewpoints: Hans Castorp's cousin Joachim, devoted to a Prussian ethics of duty; Settembrini, an Italian rationalist and humanist; Naphta, a Jew turned Jesuit turned Marxist, advocate of a reviving terror; Dr Krokowski, adherent of psychoanalysis; Claudia Chauchat, bearer to Hans Castorp of the darkly irresistible attractions of Eros in a diseased body; and Mynheer Peeperkorn, the aged and tragically impotent apostle of vitalism. Hans Castorp, representative of Germany, pays respectful heed to all these mentors, but does not unequivocally decide for any of them. History, in the shape of the First World War, erupts into his timeless dream and precipitates him on to the fields of Flanders: perhaps, the narrator reflects in the book's final sentence, Love will rise from this universal carnage. Both here and in his earlier vision in the chapter entitled 'Snow', Hans Castorp rejects the enticing darknesses of experience in favour of health and life: but it is possible to feel that Castorp's options remain somewhat abstract, unrealized and in context unrealizable against the author's obvious enthralment by the forces of decay.

In addition to other preoccupations, *The Magic Mountain* is much concerned with the problem of Time, and in particular with the disjunction between consciousness and chronology. Mann's next major work, the tetralogy *Joseph and his Brothers* (*Joseph und seine Brüder*, 1933–43, trans. 1934–44), extends this theme further to probe the relationship between time and myth and to investigate the patterns formed by a mythic appropriation of history – many of the characters in the first volume, *The Tales of Jacob* (*Die Geschichten Jakobs*), are prone to see themselves as types in whom time-bound particularization is of far less importance than their mythical status. But Joseph, the story of whose rejection by his brothers, slavery and rise to favour and administrative genius in Egypt is the subject of the other three volumes, is of a more modern, sophisticated turn of mind: unabashed by his knowledge of his place in the scheme of things, he adapts this knowledge to his own ironic purposes, seeing myth in terms of psychology and highly conscious of the fact that he is 'in a story'. The young Joseph, handsome, gifted, egoistic and something of a rogue, undergoes a long process of education in which he is twice cast into the pit and twice resurrected to become finally adviser to Pharaoh and provider during the great famine; as in Genesis, he is ultimately reconciled with his father and brothers. Like *The Magic Mountain*, the Joseph tetralogy is a kind of *Bildungsroman* depicting the progress both of its protagonist and also, as Mann himself indicated, of the human race as a whole to arrive at a point where myth becomes fruitfully integrated into history and egoism gives place to responsibility.

The writing of the Joseph tetralogy was almost exactly contemporaneous with the rise and fall of the Hitler* regime and it was part of Mann's intention to oppose to the crude racist mythologizing of the Nazis a treatment of myth which should be light, lucent and ultimately humanistic. In *Doktor Faustus* (1947, trans. 1948), however, the light mood disappears to make room for Mann's fullest treatment of the suspect and demonic nature of the imagination. The devil grants to Mann's Faust, the composer Adrian Leverkühn, the traditional twenty-four years of heightened existence, at the end of which he shall succumb, via the syphilis he has already contracted, to the hell that awaits him. Leverkühn's creativity shall be intensified and he shall find, in his music, the true passion which, according to this highly sophisticated devil, can, at this late stage of men's culture, inhere only in ambiguity and irony. But a clause is attached to the pact – the eschewal of love. Hence, Leverkühn's genius, the devil goes on to say, will be that of sickness, a type of genius which life loves far more than the plodding progress of health. But Leverkühn's story is transmitted to the reader via a narrator for whom the composer's genius, however great its fascinations, is essentially suspect: the scholar Serenus Zeitblom, a representative of the humanistic tradition submerged and silenced during the Nazi era. Zeitblom writes his account of Leverkühn's life during the last two years of the war, ending as the Allied troops are marching into Germany: and he develops during the time of that narration from a bumbling, slightly absurd figure into a figure of moving dignity as he laments the fate of his country. Above all, Zeit-

blom is a *decent* man; and although Mann attempts no crude equation between Leverkühn's career and the course of Nazism, he does, by setting the decent against the damned, limited order against creative chaos, achieve the effect of a dialogue between the forces at work in the German – and, indeed, the human – psyche. Mann reverts here to his early theme of the contrast between the man of imagination and the man of the practical life – but the contrast here is far more subtly differentiated and has a far greater resonance.

In *Confessions of Felix Krull* (*Bekenntnisse des Felix Krull*, begun 1911, resumed 1951, published 1954, trans. 1955), however, the man of imagination makes his last and most light-hearted appearance. The long line of Mann's artist figures, stretching from Hanno Buddenbrook and Tonio Kröger via no less a figure than Goethe (in *Lotte in Weimar*, 1940) to Leverkühn, culminates in Felix Krull, the artist as illusionist. Blessed with a combination of extreme good looks, quick wits and a flawless acting technique, Krull in effect makes his life his material, rising from obscure beginnings to the pleasures of assumed aristocracy and justifying his roguery with a paradoxical evaluation of himself as a practitioner of high moral self-discipline. In comic form, the novel is concerned with the moral dubiety of the aesthetic enterprise. But Mann only completed the first half of this parodistic exercise in the picaresque: completion in the traditional pattern would have had to involve Krull in some form of remorse and penitence – as it is, he leaves us in the full flush of triumph.

And this, perhaps, has its own appropriateness. Mann's ultimate stance is that of the humanist, concerned to explore those forces by which the health of life is threatened. Yet many readers have felt that the health of life fails to engage the full weight of Mann's creative interest, but is merely implicitly posited somewhere outside the text, theoretically deferred to but never imaginatively realized. Other serious disagreements have arisen: is Mann's famous irony an expression of balance and mature judgment or does it too often function as a means of evading the issues involved? Does his frequent play with paradox result in revealing perceptions or only in a kind of higher glibness? Are his novels over-schematized? These are problems which will continue to be discussed: but discussed in the context of the realization that Mann's commanding stature as a novelist – his range, creative energy and sustained technical mastery – can hardly be seriously questioned.

Corbet Stewart

See: *Gesammelte Werke* (12 vols, 1960). Other translations include: *The Holy Sinner* (1951); *The Black Swan* (1954); *Stories of Three Decades* (1936). See also: E. Heller, *The Ironic German* (1958); R. Gray, *The German Tradition in Literature* (1965); T. J. Reed,

Thomas Mann: the Uses of Tradition (1974); T. E. Apter, *Thomas Mann: the Devil's Advocate* (1978).

300
MANNHEIM, Karl 1893–1947

German sociologist

Karl Mannheim, a founder of the sociology of knowledge (*Wissenssoziologie*), was born in Budapest, studied at the universities of Budapest, Berlin, Paris and Freiburg, had academic posts at Heidelberg, Frankfurt, the London School of Economics and the University of London, and died in London. His biography, which is one of intellectual and geographical migration, falls into three main phases: Hungarian (to 1920), German (1920–33), British (1933–47). Among the most important early intellectual influences upon Mannheim are the Hungarians Georg Lukács*, Béla Zalay, Bernhard Alexander, Geza Revesz, and the Germans Georg Simmel*, Edmund Husserl*, Heinrich Rickert and Emil Lask. Mannheim was also strongly influenced by the writings of Karl Marx, Max Weber*, Alfred Weber, Max Scheler and Georg Dilthey. Through these and other writers, German historicism, Marxism, phenomenology, sociology and – much later – Anglo-Saxon pragmatism became decisive influences upon his work.

The writings of Karl Mannheim's Hungarian phase – primarily on literary and philosophical themes – remain largely untranslated. His essay *Lélek és Cultura* ('Soul and Culture', 1918) – which shows the influence of Georg Simmel's philosophical ideas – is a notable and interesting exception. It demonstrates Mannheim's first, tentative attempts to go beyond the German idealist view of history and society. In the German phase, Mannheim's most productive, he gradually turns from philosophy to sociology although he never abandons philosophical questions and concerns himself particularly with the investigation of the possible social roots of culture and knowledge. Many of his essays on methodological, epistemological and substantive aspects of the new sociology of knowledge – as theory of the existentiality of thought – have become sociological classics. In this period, Mannheim writes on the interpretation of *Weltanschauung*, on the structural analysis of epistemology, on historicism, on the ideological and sociological interpretation of intellectual phenomena, on conservative thought, on the problem of generations, on competition as a cultural phenomenon, and on the nature of economic ambition. Two early essays (1922–4) posthumously published and translated as *Structures of Knowledge* (1980) and particularly Mannheim's most influential work, *Ideology and Utopia* (*Ideologie und Utopie*, 1929, trans. 1936), were also written during this period. All these writings testify to Mannheim's ambitious attempts to prepare the ground for and carry out a comprehensive sociological analysis of the structures of knowledge. In *Ideology and Utopia*, he tries to show that all mental structures with the exception of the knowledge of the natural sciences are context-dependent and therefore different in distinct social and historical settings. The sociology of knowledge, as developed here by Mannheim, though founded upon the analysis of ideology, abandons its original Marxist formulation, according to which ideology is 'necessarily false consciousness'. Mannheim reformulates the problem of ideology and distinguishes between two conceptions of ideology: (1) the 'particular conception', in which the total mental structure of an asserting subject is *not* yet called into question or seen as determined by its social and historical location; and (2) the 'total conception', in which the subject's entire categorical apparatus is related to, and derived from, the social and historical situation. The sociology of knowledge, as an exponent of the total conception of ideology, is thus concerned with the ways in which objects present themselves to the subject according to the differences in their social location. Mannheim argues that this reformulation of the concept of ideology has created a thoroughly new situation, analogous to a transformation of quantity into quality; as soon as suspicion of ideology is asserted about one's own situation, i.e. with the emergence of the 'general-total conception of ideology', the simple theory of ideology develops into the sociology of knowledge, and the whole noological structure is seen as 'ideological', as determined by the social and historical location of individuals and groups. As a sociologically oriented history of ideas, the sociology of knowledge makes the existentiality of thought its research focus, and investigates the specific expressions of this existentiality together with the different structures of consciousness which are its result. The sociology of knowledge thus relates the entire thought structure of the asserting subject in two ways to the social and historical situations: (1) by attempting to show when and to what extent the structures of social location participate in the production of mental and intellectual phenomena; and (2) by inquiring if and in what sense thought is concretely influenced by 'social existence'.

Ideology and Utopia and its related essays on the sociology of knowledge became the centre of attention of a vigorous intellectual dispute in Germany towards the end of the Weimar Republic, in part because of the, as many critics argued, 'relativistic' implications of Mannheim's argument. (Mannheim, however, never accepted this charge of relativism but claimed that, on the contrary, his brand of 'relationism' prepared the ground for a new comprehensive 'perspective' capable of transcending heretofore fragmented and partial social and political perspectives; the 'socially unattached' intelligentsia, he maintained, had an instrumental role in developing such a synthetizing perspective.) The sociology of knowledge dispute was concerned with the most important epistemological and methodological issues confronting German sociology and, though involving a considerable range of theoretical and philosophical traditions, centred eventually on the relationship between Marxism and the sociology of knowledge, with Marxists and Critical Theorists alike often linking the latter's sudden popularity to a neutralization and betrayal of Marxism.

Mannheim's British phase was in some ways foreshadowed by the more pragmatic and practical orientation already evident in his writings prior to his emigration from Germany, in particular *Die Gegenwartsaufgaben der Soziologie* ('Present Tasks of Sociology', 1932). The comprehensive analysis of the structure of modern society must, Mannheim argues, be the task of applied sociology, especially through democratic social planning, in which education must occupy a central role. These new emphases in Mannheim's thought developed and matured rapidly, under the influence of Anglo-Saxon pragmatism, after he settled in Great Britain. Three books are of particular importance here: *Man and Society in an Age of Reconstruction* (*Mensch und Gesellschaft im Zeitalter des Umbaus* (1935, trans. 1940), *Diagnosis of Our Time* (1943), and the posthumously published essays *Freedom, Power and Democratic Planning* (1959). During this period, reflecting Mannheim's intellectual and practical concerns, he founded Routledge & Kegan Paul's 'International Library of Sociology and Social Reconstruction'.

The original themes of the sociology of knowledge were formulated in Germany during a period of major social crisis, and may be seen, as Mannheim himself saw them, as the product of one of the greatest social dissolutions and transformations, accompanied by the highest form of self-consciousness and self-criticism. The renewed interest in the problems posed by the sociology of knowledge today, often accompanied by a fascination with Weimar Germany's experience of political, social and cultural achievements and dissolutions, perhaps reflects the experience of a similar crisis in our own period and may therefore be said to owe more to the course of events than to the course of analytical progress.

Professor Volker Meja and Professor Nico Stehr

Other translations: *Essays on the Sociology of Knowledge* (1952); *Essays on Sociology and Social Psychology* (1953); *Essays on the Sociology of Culture* (1956); *Systematic Sociology: An Introduction to the Study of Society* (1957); *An Introduction to the Sociology of Education* (with W. A. C. Stewart, 1962). See also: David Kettler, *Marxismus und Kultur: Mannheim und Lukács in den ungarischen Revolutionen 1918/19* (1967); Gunter W. Remmling, *The Sociology of Karl Mannheim* (1975); A. P. Simonds, *Karl Mannheim's Sociology of Knowledge* (1978).

301

MANSFIELD, Katherine 1888–1923

New Zealander writer

Some may feel that Katherine Mansfield's reputation has been unduly enhanced by the growth, during recent years, of militant feminism and the very large claims advanced for women writers in so far as they represent a distinctly feminine point of view. Her private life has also captured the popular imagination and commendable attempts have been made to correct the view of her created by over-zealous friends and associates.

She was born in New Zealand and grew up in Wellington and the surrounding countryside. As a music student she went to England and attended Queen's College, London. A return to her own country proved so unsuccessful that she was allowed to go back to London, where she began to write short stories. An impulsively early marriage in 1909 was a disaster, but in 1911 she met the critic John Middleton Murry* and the two began a partnership which lasted until her death. The Great War brought the shattering blow of her brother's death on the Western Front, a contributory factor in causing her to turn for inspiration to the New Zealand of her childhood. She died in France from a gradual deterioration of the lungs, exacerbated by the bizarre treatment she received under the supervision of the mystic Gurdjieff*.

Mansfield's work shows the strong influence of Chekhov in its brilliant awareness of suppressed impulses and its remarkable sensitivity to even the most trivial of sounds and touches of light and colour. In stories such as 'Pictures', the account of an elderly singer's efforts to find work as a film extra, 'The Little Governess', in which an innocent English girl in Munich loses her job after fleeing from a would-be seducer, and 'Je ne parle pas français', where the author describes her affair with the poet Francis Carco, she displays an unrivalled ability to portray sympathetically characters who at first seem merely irritating or absurd. Her women and children especially show her as a creative artist of apparently inexhaustible resource.

She was responsible for deepening and extending the technical reach of the short story as following the direction indicated by Chekhov. Her handling of dialogue is boldly impressionistic and owes much, in its frequent renderings of the actual timbre and pitch of words and phrases, to her years as a music student. She is wholly unromantic in her treatment of events, showing herself conscious alike of haphazard cruelty, menace, violence and deception. Her exceptional talent formed itself very early, and her first collection, *In a German Pension* (1911), though she later rejected it, displays range fully and maturely. The longest of her works is *Prelude* (1918), a meticulously constructed novella based on her New Zealand experiences.

Mansfield's influence can be felt most obviously in American women writers such as Flannery O'Connor, Eudora Welty and Carson McCullers, all of whom, with varying success, reproduced her impressionistic technique and her sense of lurking evil. She did not change the nature of the short story single-handed, but it can be said that her mastery of the form inspired a loosening up and a broadening of aim and scope which make her among the finest practitioners of the genre.

Jonathan Keates

Other collections: *The Garden Party* (1922); *The Dove's Nest* (1923); and *Something Childish* (1924). See also: John Middleton Murry, *Katherine Mansfield and Other Literary Studies* (1959); Jeffrey Meyers, *Katherine Mansfield: A Biography* (1978); Anthony Alpers, *The Life of Katherine Mansfield* (1980).

302
MAO TSE-TUNG (also Mao Zedong) 1893–1976

Chinese Communist leader

Universally accepted as the most influential twentieth-century Communist leader outside the main stream of European Marxism, Mao Tse-tung was born in one of the central inland provinces of China of a successful peasant family. He became one of the founders of the Chinese Communist Party in 1920 after having completed his education at a much older age than his peers. By profession a schoolmaster who graduated from the First Hunan Normal School and who never studied at a university, either in China or abroad, he quickly became absorbed in underground revolutionary organization, being active in both the Kuomintang or Nationalist Party as well as the new Communist Party of China in the 1920s. After establishing in the field his own distinctive style of revolutionary base area, he was accepted in 1935 as one of the five senior leaders in the Party, and in 1943 he became its Chairman, a post which he held for the rest of his life. It was he who proclaimed the new People's Republic of China in 1949, and his was the thrust behind China's swift abandonment of the Soviet Russian model. The Hundred Flowers Movement (1957), the Great Leap Forward (1958), the People's Communes (1958) and the Great Proletarian Cultural Revolution (1966–70) were all stamped with Mao's originality and intellectual daring. Only after his death did the feeling become articulated in China that, while Mao had been essential for the success of the Chinese Communist Party in taking power and in establishing its own characteristic path of development, the prolonged social and political turbulence, and economic disruption, which accompanied

his more dramatic policies from the late 1950s onwards, were counter-productive in terms of results for the Chinese people.

In his youth Mao was influenced by such Western heroes as Napoleon, Lincoln, Washington, Garibaldi and Peter the Great, along with the Meiji reformers of Japan and their contemporaries in China who had preached reform. He was especially excited by the two Cantonese radicals of the late nineteenth century, Liang Chi-chao and Kang Yu-wei. Mao was already twenty-five when he was first attracted to Marxism, and only at the age of twenty-seven did he begin to call himself a Marxist. That was the same year in which he attended the first inaugural Congress of the Chinese Communist Party. He had already determined upon a revolutionary career for the sake of modernizing China, when he discovered this ideal tool for his goal. 'Communism,' he once told a sentimental scholar, 'is not love; Communism is a hammer which we use to destroy the enemy.' It was the October Revolution of 1917 in Russia which had most effect on him.

Because of his late introduction to Marxism and his lack of a university education, he struck his colleagues in those early days as a barrack-room or backwoods philosopher. Djilas, the Yugoslav Marxist, complained that 'his Marxism is simplified'. But Mao might have taken this as a compliment, because one of his enduring concerns was to render the new philosophy intelligible to ordinary people as well as to scholars, and to localize it so that the Chinese peasant could understand it as well as the European factory worker. He tried to restate the fundamentals of Marxism in universal categories applicable to various stages of history and all kinds of revolutionary situation.

What endeared him to Third World radicals was his emphasis on the peasants, who had been neglected by the European Marxists. He saw no reason why the revolutionary energy which he detected in the peasants of his own province, downtrodden by useless tradition and exploited by greedy landlords and warlords, should not be tapped, especially in a country where capitalist development had hardly begun and there were very few Chinese proletarians, strictly defined.

Another thing which distinguished him from his colleagues in the Chinese Communist movement was his studied rejection of Russian or Comintern leadership in the Chinese revolution. He insisted that the problems of Chinese society should be analysed in their own right and not merely covered with Russian labels. During the 1940s when the possibility of the Party coming to power first dawned, Mao elaborated the necessity for China to follow out its capitalist phase before introducing socialism. But after 1949 he found himself caught up, like his colleagues, in a determination to pursue the two goals of individual emancipation from semi-feudal traditions on the one hand, and socialism on the other hand, in parallel.

No one doubted Mao's ideals. He was constantly concerned for the elevation of the underprivileged, for the interests of the poor peasants *vis-à-vis* the rich peasants, for the emancipation of women and the better treatment of children. 'It is to the advantage of despots,' he wrote, 'to keep people ignorant; it is to our advantage to make them intelligent.' But he lacked the practical administrative gifts to see these ideals put into practice. He was good at drafting blue-prints, but for their implementation he depended on others who lacked his insights. Partly because of this, but also because of an underlying sense of personal insecurity derived from his upbringing, he never trusted his colleagues in the Chinese leadership. Much of their common energy during the twenty-seven years in which Mao 'ruled' China was expended in wasteful infighting and political manoeuvring within his 'cabinet'.

One of the outstanding Maoist innovations was to stress above all else the power of revolutionary will, of subjectivist voluntarism in human affairs, what Professor Stuart Schram calls 'the infinite capacity of subjective forces to change objective reality'. Mao thus considered the question of class status as something depending upon the subjective attitude of the person in question: it was possible for the Chinese bourgeoisie to be transformed under proletarian and peasant leadership, so that they could eventually become admitted to the exclusive club of 'the people' on good behaviour and after remoulding. Within the theatre of Marxist-Leninist dialectics, Mao stressed the law of the unity of opposites, or universality of contradiction, a Hegelian concept which found echoes in the Chinese intellectual tradition. Contradictions could be either antagonistic or non-antagonistic. Other Chinese ideas which permeate his writing are the ideas of compromise and of the middle path, a very Confucian notion. Mao was particularly fond of identifying first the revolutionary fighters, then their chief enemies, and finally declaring that the challenge was to organize the middle ground between in one's own favour, even if this meant temporarily allying in a 'united front' with distasteful bedfellows. He was also fond of quantifying this formulation, to give encouragement to the inevitably small number of revolutionaries in any society.

In the end most of the works of Mao come down to somewhat immature philosophical treatises, a good deal of description of the individual campaigns in the Chinese revolutionary struggle, plus constant commands to his readers to act thoughtfully and rationally in their day-to-day lives, to 'be resourceful, to look at all sides of a problem, to test ideas by experiment, and to work hard for the sake of the common good' (Schram). This was the Samuel Smiles element in Maoism, of near-Victorian admonition to become a better person, which was so necessary in the situation of twentieth-century China, still excessively influenced by scholastic traditions from the Chinese past.

Mao's writings were published in five volumes of selected works, all of which have been translated into many languages and distributed around the world. A famous selection of some of his more interesting passages was put together in Peking in the 1960s and became known as the 'Little Red Book' of *Quotations of Chairman Mao*, originally edited by the Chinese army under defence minister Lin Piao. This pocket book quickly became a world best seller. Another compendium of Mao's unofficial writings and talks was put together, also by Lin Piao, under the title *Long Live Mao Tse-tung Thought*.

Mao was no mean poet, over and above his many other roles, and although his poems do not translate easily they have been admired by Chinese and foreign critics alike.

Military affairs is another area of human life in which Mao gained something of a reputation, particularly in the Third World during the 1960s. He never had any formal military training, but in the fighting which surrounded his attempts to establish Communist bases in the interior of China, and the efforts of the Chinese government of that day to suppress them, he had perforce to outline strategy and tactics if not actually to take command. What he did in the 1920s and 1930s when he was frequently in the thick of guerilla war was to codify the traditional wisdom, as sharpened in practice among his own men, for dealing with a superior and better armed enemy. One of his notable contributions was the philosophy that a successful guerilla army was one which could not only forge good relations with the civilian peasantry in the area, but even develop a capacity to lose itself among them. If the peasantry supported the guerillas, then the enemy forces would never learn enough information about them. Mao's gloss on this was to insist that political work was equally important to military work, and under his guidance the Chinese Red Army went very far towards becoming a populist force, even helping the civilian inhabitants over their hurdles of voluntary reform of their own society. Mao also elaborated the ideas of luring the enemy deep into one's own territory, stretching it and attacking it piece by piece. But military critics like Jacques Guillermaz, the French military attaché in China during some of that time, felt that Mao's military ideas were not strictly original nor were they crucial in gaining the ultimate Communist victory. The People's Liberation Army continued to praise his military virtues all the same, and this reached absurd heights during the Cultural Revolution under the defence minister, Lin Piao – who later betrayed Mao but who earlier tried to place him on a ridiculously high pedestal.

In the end Mao's Communism turned out to be an extremely sophisticated blend of pragmatism and revolutionary fervour. Most of his followers were unable to resolve these contradictory forces satisfactorily within themselves. Chinese politics after Mao's death showed the continuing difficulty of absorbing such highly different approaches to the problems of the day. Nevertheless, despite his waning popularity at the end of his career, Mao had the distinction of governing the affairs of a quarter of mankind for a quarter of a century, a lot which does not fall to many men. Nor was his governance a passive one seeking stability: he turned his back on such goals and preferred to preside over rapid social, economic, cultural and political change in his motherland. One could almost say that he invented the Chinese state as we know it in the second half of this century, and by his sturdy will and political skills he changed the lives of 900 million peasants so that they found themselves working, not for landlords or for themselves, but for a collective entity roughly representing either their own village or the considerably larger structure which was called the People's Commune. Mao was not so successful in industry, which he never understood as well as he did agriculture, and he also failed to convert the country's intellectuals, its artists and writers and teachers, to the same high ideals for which he himself stood. Nevertheless, modern China as it is today is unthinkable without the lifework of Mao Tse-tung, and there are many people in other countries, especially in Africa, Asia and Latin America – but also in Europe and North America – who attribute to his example and teaching the impulse which moved them to seek social change in their own societies. Mao was the last giant Marxist of our era, but he was also the first non-European. Whereas Marxism by the 1950s had become in the international view tainted by the blatant nationalism and brutality of Stalin*, notably in his expansion into Eastern Europe, Mao came out openly differing from both Stalin and Lenin*, and the Third World experienced something of a renewed faith in the Communist programme. Mao's influence was thus world-wide, although he himself left China only twice in his life, both times to visit the Soviet Union only late in his career.

Dick Wilson

Mao's writings are mostly collected together in *Selected Works of Mao Tse-tung* (Peking), vols I–III (1965), vol. IV (1961), and vol. V (1977). Useful collections or excerpts from his writings and talks are: Stuart Schram, *The Political Thought of Mao Tse-tung* (1969); Jerome Chen, *Mao* (1969); *Mao Tse-tung Unrehearsed*, ed. Stuart Schram (1974). See also *Poems* (Peking 1976). Biographies: Stuart Schram, *Mao Tse-tung* (1967); Dick Wilson, *Mao: The People's Emperor* (1979). See also *Mao Tse-tung in the Scales of History*, ed. Dick Wilson (1977).

303
MARCUSE, Herbert 1898–1979

German/US social philosopher

Regarded as the official ideologue of the 1968 'campus revolutions', Herbert Marcuse was born into a prominent and prosperous Berlin Jewish family, and educated at the crack Augusta Gymnasium and at the Universities of Berlin and Freiberg. In 1934, after the establishment of the National Socialist regime in Germany, he took refuge in the USA, becoming a citizen in 1940. There he first joined Max Horkheimer* and Theodor Adorno* in the former Frankfurt Institute for Social Research, re-established at Columbia. Further appointments followed at Harvard, Brandeis and – beyond the normal mandatory retiring age – in the University of California at San Diego. In the later war years and for some time after Marcuse worked for the Office of Intelligence Research, originally the OSS. (Those of his New Left admirers who know that in this capacity he prepared reports for the CIA would presumably think to flatter him by suggesting that he was a saboteur!) An unsuccessful attempt was once made to prevent San Diego giving him another one-year contract, on the grounds that in his vastly popular lectures he was – like Socrates – 'corrupting the youth'.

Marcuse's protracted graduate studies were on Hegel, the results eventually appearing as *Reason and Revolution* (1941). His own philosophy, and his picture of the history of philosophy, have remained always profoundly Hegelian. Nothing much, for instance, is seen to have been done in the Middle Ages; and nothing of value to have been written first in English. There is also the same high love of abstractions. The meaning of these is never spelt out and precisified in terms of concrete particulars, nor is the truth of the propositions in which they are embraced to be tested by reference to crude and stubborn fact. Consider, for instance, a typical Hegelian revelation from *Reason and Revolution*: 'For what does the unity of identity and contradiction mean in the context of social forms and forces? In its ontological terms, it means that the state of negativity is not a distortion of a thing's true essence, but its very essence itself.' A second constant theme is the claim to be in some sense truly Marxist, even if Marx himself was not. Thus almost immediately after quoting Marx as saying in *Capital* that 'capitalist production begets, with the inexorability of a law of Nature, its own negation', Marcuse contends: 'it would be a distortion of the entire significance of Marxian theory to argue from the inexorable necessity that governs the development of capitalism to a similar necessity in the matter of transformation to socialism.' Other pretenders to the Marxist name have described Marcuse as a belated Young Hegelian, exposed therefore to the full force of the Founding Fathers' polemic against *The German Ideology*.

In his second book, *Eros and Civilization* (1955), Marcuse comes to terms with Freud*. Characteristically what appeals is the late Freud of the metaphysical theory rather than the earlier therapist. Equally characteristically Marcuse appears to accept it all, including Thanatos the Death Instinct, without demanding any evidential credentials. Most importantly, perhaps, he attempts to distinguish what has to be repressed for the sake of any civilization at all from the restraints required by a single society.

Third comes the much less read *Soviet Marxism* (1958), and fourth his most popular and presumably most influential *One-Dimensional Man* (1964). Here he contends that modern society – but mainly, it would seem, those societies normally recognized as most liberal – is intolerably repressive; the one small hope of improvement lying in some revolutionary elite which may, as Rousseau might have said, force the unenlightened to be free. Indeed the repression alleged is so total that it becomes impossible for Marcuse to account for the publication, much less the reception, of his own book: 'Technical progress, extended to a whole system of domination and co-ordination, creates forms of life (and of power) which appear to reconcile the forces opposing the system and to defeat or refute all protest in the name of the historical prospects of freedom from toil and domination.' It is in the same book that Marcuse develops the bizarre thesis that the business of analytic philosophy is to make people incapable of rational criticism of the social environment: 'logic', in the words of Horkheimer and Adorno, 'has its foundation in the reality of domination'. Since logic of its very nature can forbid only incoherence and self-contradiction, Marcuse is here in effect warring against rationality under the false colours of reason.

In *An Essay on Liberation* (1969), and in his contribution to *A Critique of Pure Tolerance* (1969), Marcuse, under the similarly inept banner of freedom, seeks to pick out those various forces, including the alienated students, which might co-operate to establish the absolutism of a revolutionary elite. The title of his essay, contributed to *A Critique of Pure Tolerance* – 'Repressive Tolerance' – irresistibly recalls slogans issued by the hyper-totalitarian Ministry of Truth in Orwell's* nightmare *1984*.

As the self-stymieing nature of much of Marcuse's work becomes apparent, his future reputation looks increasingly insecure. Kolakowski*, in the definitive *Main Currents of Marxism*, wrote of him: 'There is probably no other philosopher in our day who deserves as completely as Marcuse to be called the "ideologist of obscurantism".'

Professor Antony Flew

See: Alasdair MacIntyre, *Marcuse* (1970).

304

MARINETTI, Filippo Tommaso 1876–1944

Italian writer

Marinetti was born to a wealthy lawyer living in Egypt. He studied briefly in Paris and made the city his cultural home, soon writing for and editing literary periodicals which attempted to introduce French Symbolist poetry to Italy. His own poetry, of which there was much, was in French until 1912, Symbolist, but with a violent idealist-anarchistic character. In 1909 he published the 'Futurist Manifesto' in *Le Figaro*. It exalted the machines, the violence and the competition of the modern world, and demanded that art abandon conventional subjects and styles, and glorify the present.

The Manifesto was generally interpreted as an iconoclastic tirade in favour of modernism. In fact it went much further, as other manifestos by Marinetti himself and by the painters Boccioni and Carrà and the 'musician' Russolo showed. Futurism wanted art not to *signify* life – least of all 'arty' life – but to *be* life. Conversely, it saw everything in social life as having meaning, as being a language, even food, clothes and gait, and sought to exploit the expressive power of every conceivable medium. War was the perfect aesthetic event.

Marinetti was probably more consciously aware of the impact of what he was proposing than most of the Futurist artists (with the exception of Boccioni). Art was to be part of the competition of modern life rather than an alternative to it. He held 'serate' – soirées – in theatres where Futurist poetry and music and politics were declaimed. He travelled frenetically, promoting Futurism, organizing exhibitions of painting, paying for the publication of books, and cajoling one artist after another into audacious innovation. By 1914 he was vigorously agitating for Italy's entry into the Great War.

He was a staunch supporter of Fascism – one of the first; indeed Mussolini* borrowed much from Futurism – though personally too anarchist to accept corporativism, and too intelligent to stomach the party's imperialist xenophobia. But he never ceased to look after the interests of the Futurist movement, and so tried to keep it in the good graces of the regime.

He made an art of the literary manifesto, bringing to it lyricism, rhetoric and a concise, punchy clarity of diction. He pioneered visual poetry, in which syntax all but disappears, and in which the graphic element of calligraphy and typography played as important a role in the expression as the meaning of the words themselves, mingling writing with drawing and abstract shapes. The influence of these innovations, from Apollinaire* to the concrete poets and beyond, is incalculable. Marinetti wrote a large number of books which mixed memoir and political and artistic polemic, as well as novels, one of which brought him prosecution for obscenity. His prose style was sharp and simple, but degenerated into empty verbosity later in life. His plays and theoretical writings on the theatre were enormously influential: he proclaimed the abolition of polite, highbrow theatre, which was to be fused with music hall and vaudeville; he destroyed the barrier between stage and audience; he pioneered very short ('synthetic') plays – in one of which only the actors' legs and feet were visible. He wrote abstract aural pieces for radio in the 1930s, and helped make a futurist film.

Marinetti's credit has been low in academic circles because of his fascist associations. Among artists, however, he has had so profound an influence that scarcely any artist in any field can have entirely escaped it. The whole twentieth-century avant-garde owes much of its general audacity and willingness to ignore the past, as well as a number of its detailed innovations, to Marinetti personally and to his Futurist movement. His personal creative works, however, only have real stature for their formal qualities and for their energy. Marinetti does not express profound feelings and thoughts; he can be brash and frivolous. For this reason, though his importance to culture of this century will grow ever more apparent, his works will always have a limited emotional appeal.

Christopher Wagstaff

Some major works: *Mafarka le futuriste* (Paris 1909); *La Ville charnelle* (Paris 1908); *Zang Tumb tuuum* (Milan 1914); *Les Mots en liberté futuristes* (Milan 1919); *L'alcova d'acciaio* (Milan 1921). Contained in collections and anthologies are his theatrical writings: *Teatro*, ed. G. Calendoli (Rome 1960); and theoretical writings: *Teoria e invenzione futurista*, ed. L. De Maria (Milan 1968); *Selected Writings*, ed. R. W. Flint (New York/London 1972). For his visual poetry, see *Tavole parolibere futuriste*, ed. Caruso and Martini (Naples 1977).

MÁRQUEZ, Gabriel García, *see* GARCÍA MÁRQUEZ, Gabriel

305
MATISSE, Henri 1869–1954

French painter, sculptor, print-maker, illustrator and designer

Henri Matisse was born at Le Cateau Cambrésius in France. As a student he first studied law, then in 1890 turned seriously to painting. For a while he attended classes at the École des Beaux Arts in Paris under the tuition of the Symbolist painter Gustave Moreau.

Later Matisse was to use elements from the work of several contemporary artists in order to formulate an original and vibrant style of his own that rapidly became influential as far afield as Moscow and New York. The teachings of Moreau resulted in Matisse taking an imaginative rather than a naturalistic look at the world. At the same time the primitivism of both Puvis de Chavannes and of Gauguin interested him deeply. Besides these concerns he also appreciated the search for simplicity of structure undertaken by Cézanne. In addition Matisse continually endeavoured to increase the brilliance of colour in his painting. For these experiments he found Paul Signac's theories based on Seurat's colour perceptions vital.

By 1905 Matisse's art had become sufficiently developed to attract a number of followers including Derain, Vlaminck, Rouault* and Marquet. The art critic Louis Vauxcelles, when reviewing the Parisian exhibition at the Salon d'Automne in that year referred to a number of paintings there as those of wild beasts, Les Fauves. This term (Fauvism) remained to designate the work produced by Matisse and his group during the next few years. Their revolutionary style, until the Cubists became more influential, was considered the most avant-garde in Europe.

Besides drawing and painting in the brilliant sunlight of southern France, Matisse visited Spain, Morocco and Italy between 1907 and 1913. These journeys, viewing other cultures and periods besides his own, confirmed for Matisse that rules in art had no existence outside individuals. His aesthetic belief was akin to that of the philosopher Henri Bergson*. Each work of art should be the result of artistic intuition which is expressed through that work. Matisse's painting and sculpture in fact became an equivalent of his own individual sensibility's response to the visual world. It was not therefore a naturalistic representation of objects as seen by the artist. He practised essentially what was to become known as French Expressionism. This should not be confused with its more pessimistic counterpart, German Expressionism.

Except for one haunting grey war year in 1915, Matisse's constant theme was the joy of life. He felt this as a glorious pantheism, 'a nearly religious feeling' that he had towards man and nature. Mostly naked people, dancing and making music, perhaps relaxing in sunlit landscapes or richly coloured interiors, were his commonest subjects.

Using a dynamically flowing line to control the forms and single colours to give shape a brilliancy, in his mature work Matisse dispensed with tonal variations to suggest the three-dimensionality of an object. This in turn emphasized the flat surface of the canvas and reduced spatial recession.

Matisse's desire to synthesize his imaginative identifications with his subject-matter in the art work led to progressive simplification. In the series of reliefs known as *The Backs* the last one is almost a complete abstraction. The single standing nude female becomes a powerful unity of strength and serenity.

This idea of serenity was important to Matisse. He aimed to avoid depressing subject-matter. In his writings he proposes that his art should be an appeasing influence on tired working people, a mental soother that should 'like a good armchair rest the weary from fatigue'.

In the years immediately before his death whilst sick and bedridden Matisse continued to produce his art. By tearing and cutting brightly coloured paper into large shapes he was able to form compositions by giving the pieces to assistants to assemble under his instruction. When attached to walls these shapes seem to float reflectively or energetically in space, reanimating the themes from former years when Matisse painted the murals for the Barnes Foundation at Merion in the USA in the early 1930s, and from 1945 to 1951 decorated the Chapel of the Rosary at Vence not far from his last home. As a superb designer, whether illustrating with etchings Mallarmé's poetry and working on a small scale or producing larger designs for sets to Diaghilev's* ballet *Le Rossignol*, Matisse, through his unification of the sensual and imaginative, informed his best work with a vibrant lyricism and delightful harmony.

Pat Turner

Important works include: *Woman with the Hat* (1905); *Joy of Life* (1905–6); *Le Luxe II* (1907–8); *Harmony in Blue* (1908); *Dance* (1909–10); *Lady in Blue* (1937). Book illustration: mainly in the 1940s and mostly of poetry including Baudelaire's *Les Fleurs du Mal* and James Joyce's *Ulysses*. See also: 'Notes d'un Peintre' published in *La grande revue*, December 1908. About Matisse: A. Barr, *Matisse, his Art and his Public* (1951); W. Liebermann, *Matisse, 50 Years of his Graphic Work* (1956).

306
MAUGHAM, William Somerset 1874–1965

English novelist

No modern writer's fame has ebbed so swiftly as that of William Somerset Maugham. Scarcely had he died than his former associates began to lay bare the framework of a private life he had most successfully concealed during his lifetime. His homosexuality, his callous treatment of his wife, his skilful distortions of his early life, his failure adequately to confront his extraordinary success, were all descanted upon and his stature was thus reduced with remarkable speed. Much of what he had written was now denounced as stale, second-hand and pompous: his tendencies to cliché and carelessness were condemned; it became obvious, through the flood of revelations and hastily compiled memoirs, that his stories, far from being based on personal experience, as it was claimed, were founded on the adventures and gossip of his friends; and works like *The Razor's Edge* (1944) and *The Summing-Up* (1938) seemed like the unbearably portentous disclosures of a mediocre mind.

Some of what he had to say about himself was true. Brought up largely by his uncle, a clergyman, in Kent, he was sent to King's School, Canterbury, and, after a spell at Heidelberg learning German, he became a doctor. Writing, rather than medicine, began to claim him, and after the publication of *Liza of Lambeth* (1898) he went to live in Paris, where a series of attempts at playwriting for the London stage culminated in the success of *Lady Frederick* (1907). After this he began on a more or less uninterrupted celebrity and prosperity, and was able to gratify his lifelong urge to travel, visiting China, Malaya and the Pacific islands, all of which form vivid backgrounds to his excellent short stories. At his villa at Cap Ferrat he embodied, for an admiring English and American public, the ideal of a successful writer.

Nearly all his novels were filmed and several became best-sellers. Of enduring interest are *Of Human Bondage* (1915), an attempt to rival Lawrence's* *Sons and Lovers* and Compton Mackenzie's *Sinister Street*, and *Cakes and Ale* (1930), a magnificent *roman à clef* based on the literary establishment of the 1920s and the figures of Thomas Hardy and Hugh Walpole. Altogether less successful is *The Razor's Edge*, encompassing themes far too profound for Maugham's essentially shallow mind.

His truest application of talent lies in the various collections of short stories. He admired Maupassant and the admiration bore good fruit. As a story-teller he has few rivals in economy of detail and sense of gathering speed, and his ability to communicate atmosphere and location in a few telling lines is an enviable skill. If he is likely to survive, it must surely be in this genre, and not in his grandly designed novels.

Jonathan Keates

Other works include: *The Moon and Sixpence* (novel, 1919); *A Writer's Notebook* (autobiographical, 1949). See also: Robert Larin Calder, *W. Somerset Maugham and the Quest for Freedom* (1972); Antony Curtis, *The Pattern of Maugham* (1974); Frederic Raphael, *Somerset Maugham and His World* (1976).

307
MAURIAC, François 1885–1970

French writer

The youngest of five children, Mauriac was born in Bordeaux on 11 October 1885. His early years were spent either there or on family properties in the *landes*, the area of pine forests and vineyards to the south of the city which was to provide him with the settings for so many of his works. He was educated first by the Marist fathers in Bordeaux at the Collège Grand-Lebrun and, after his baccalauréat, at the university. In 1907 he went to Paris and in 1908 registered at the École des Chartes which he subsequently left within a year. Having arrived in the capital, however, he was, in spite of his deep attachment to his native region, to spend most of the rest of his life there. In 1913 Mauriac married; his first child, the novelist and critic Claude Mauriac, was born the following year. During the First World War Mauriac, unfit for active service, worked for the International Red Cross but was repatriated from Salonika in 1917.

Already his reputation as a novelist was growing but the publication of *Le Baiser au lépreux* (1922) and *Genitrix* (1924) (both in *A Kiss for the Leper*, 1950) brought him instant success on a large scale. During the two decades between the wars Mauriac's output was high by any standards with a number of novels, especially *Thérèse* (*Thérèse Desqueyroux*, 1927, trans. 1947), *The Knot of Vipers* (*Le Nœud de vipères*, 1932, trans. 1951), and *The Frontenac Mystery* (*Le Mystère Frontenac*, 1933, trans. 1951), guaranteeing his status as an international writer. In 1934 he was elected to the French Academy.

Although he had contributed articles to papers like *Le Gaulois* or *Sept* during these years Mauriac became much more active as a journalist after the outbreak of the Spanish Civil War, writing regularly for *Temps présent* and *Le Figaro*. His open commitment to politics continued to grow. During the Occupation he wrote *The Black Note Book* (*Le Cahier noir*, 1943, trans. 1944) under the pseudonym of Forez and after 1944 he embarked on the many hundreds of articles subsequently to be known as the *Bloc-notes* which appeared in *La Table ronde*, *Le Figaro* and *L'Express*. An ardent supporter of De Gaulle, whom he first met in 1944, he was frequently attacked by the left for his conservative views, but he became an increasingly influential Catholic intellectual and voice of conscience for many. He resumed novel writing, though with less success than before, and wrote his last play, *Le Feu sur la Terre* ('Fire on the Earth', 1951), and a number of essays: in 1952 he was awarded the Nobel Prize for Literature. During the last twenty years of his life he remained as prolific as ever, producing in particular several volumes of personal and political memoirs. His last complete novel

Maltaverne (*Un Adolescent d'autrefois*, trans. 1970) appeared in 1969.

Despite his full and varied career Mauriac will be best remembered for his novels and especially for those written during the 1920s and 1930s. Without exception they are characterized by a satirical portrayal of the middle-class society of the Bordeaux region, by a deep-rooted and anguished conflict between sin and purity (prompting Gide* in 1928 to accuse Mauriac of serving both God and Mammon), by an evocation of the natural world he had known as a child and by the use of it as a source for an elaborate symbolic representation of the human conflicts with which his novels deal. His interest in the depiction of human psychology at a time when the influence in France of Dostoevsky and Freud* was strong is illustrated too by a number of essays both on other writers and on the art of novel writing. More than this, however, whether we define Mauriac as a 'Catholic novelist' or, as he preferred, a 'Catholic who also wrote novels', it is the influence of his own religious conviction which provides his analyses of human problems with an extra dimension and which even in an increasingly anti-religious age ensures that his work will remain of interest and value for many.

Professor J. E. Flower

See *Œuvres complètes* (1950–6) and a 2-volume *Œuvres romanesques* (1965). The complete plays and novels are being published in the Pléiade series edited by Jacques Petit. See also: N. Cormeau, *L'Art de François Mauriac* (1951); J. de Fabrègues, *Mauriac* (1971); A. Séailles, *Mauriac* (1972); M. Alyn et al., *Mauriac* (1977). In English: M. Moloney, *François Mauriac* (1958); C. Jenkins, *Mauriac* (1965); J. E. Flower, *Intention and Achievement* (1969); J. Lacouture, *François Mauriac* (1980).

308
MAUSS, Marcel 1872–1950

French sociologist and anthropologist

Mauss has often been called the *alter ego* of the prominent French sociologist, Émile Durkheim*. He was Durkheim's nephew and like him was born in Épinal within a rabbinic family. At the University of Bordeaux he worked under his uncle and did brilliantly in his *agrégation*. He went to Paris and studied ancient languages and then anthropology, though he was never a field-worker. In 1901 he was made director of studies at the École Pratique des Hautes Études in the history of religions of non-civilized peoples. He was later made joint director of the newly founded Institut d'Ethnologie of the University of Paris in 1925, and was also professor at the Collège de France (1931–9). In 1940 he retired and sadly witnessed the harassment of Jewish colleagues by the Germans, although he himself remained physically unmolested. Whilst possessing great erudition – 'Mauss knows everything,' his students said of him – he never acquired the highest of academic attainments. When he was young he was constantly under pressure to help his uncle and fervently researched ethnology for the *Année sociologique*, edited by Durkheim, and which was so influential among French academics.

After 1917 when Durkheim died, Mauss became his literary executor and always looked upon himself as possessing the mantle of his uncle. His efforts to revive the *Année sociologique* produced limited success. Although he published no book, he exerted through teaching and articles considerable influence over sociologists and anthropologists in the 1920s and 1930s, in particular G. Gurvitch, R. Bastide, G. Bataille, B. Malinowski*, A. R. Radcliffe-Brown*, E. E. Evans-Pritchard*, R. Needham, Mary Douglas, L. Warner, and above all Claude Lévi-Strauss*.

Much of Mauss's work up to the time of the First World War was done in collaboration with other Durkheimians, especially H. Hubert, and, in the morphological study on the Eskimos (1906), he was assisted by H. Beuchat (trans. as *Seasonal Variations of the Eskimo: A Study in Social Morphology*, 1979). In this monograph Mauss demonstrated that social life in its many forms was dependent on a material substratum, but at the same time, it was not the sole determinant of social life. It is impossible for society to maintain a constantly high level of activity and therefore social life passes through stages of activity (or hyperactivity) and recuperation. Two such clear phases exist in Eskimo life. In the summer the Eskimo hunt caribou, live in tents, and are dispersed over a wide geographical area. In the winter they are sustained by fish, dwell in longhouses or igloos, and live in high social density. During this period they are subject to continuous religious exaltation (often in the *kashim* or communal house), when myths and legends are recounted, coupled with dancing and magical ceremonies. By contrast, little religious activity occurs in the summer period beyond rites of passage. Rules relating to sex, property and family life also vary with the seasons. Mauss noted that the break between the two phases is not always clear-cut but the bi-phasal rhythm is of extreme methodological importance.

Biological and technological factors influence social behaviour but so do social factors and this position is to be seen in Mauss's rejection of 'natural' behaviour. In a concern for dovetailing psychology with sociology he sought to show that psychology was dependent on or limited by cultural variables. In 'Techniques of the Body' (1935) he demonstrated that virtually no behaviour in sexual, physical or mental spheres is determined in form by innate drives or mental predispositions. Basic human activities have to be learnt and their manner is determined by social norms, which are inevitably relative.

It is generally accepted that Mauss's most influential work was his essay, *The Gift: Forms and Functions of Exchange in Archaic Societies* (1925, trans. 1954), which has turned out to be the forerunner of what is now known as exchange theory. Mauss attempted to derive from ethnographical data and early literature principles whereby a gift has to be repaid. What is given does not consist exclusively of a physical present, of wealth, of real and personal property. It may contain courtesies, entertainment, ritual, women, children, dances, military assistance, the recognition of status. In primitive societies at least, a gift has to be repaid since the recipient stands under an obligation so to do. Failure to respond brings with it social censure. Thus, the elements of the gift-exchange process are related to individuals and groups as much as to the objects themselves; and not only is wealth thereby circulated but so are social relationships. In work, a form of exchange, a man may be said to give something of himself and therefore wages and nothing more are not a satisfactory response. Part of the abhorrence of charity is that the gift is not intended to be repaid. Few if any gifts are spontaneous and disinterested; and generosity is never free from self-interest. Even religious thought is partially based on gift-exchange between an individual and his god. This is an important element in sacrifice – a subject to which in collaboration with Hubert he made a significant contribution. Like Durkheim, Mauss saw that contract is not an amoral social mechanism, but is based on an implied morality: 'Gift-exchange fails to conform to the principles of so-called natural economy or utilitarianism.'

The gift was a perfect example of what Mauss called a total social phenomenon, since it involved legal, economic, moral, religious, aesthetic and other dimensions. He held that it was total social facts rather than institutions that should be the chief subject-matter of sociology. The discipline has to study the concrete and the whole – the facts to be examined are to be total social facts. And Mauss laid perhaps greater emphasis on facts than did Durkheim. Thus, it is necessary to look at entire social systems and to describe their functions. Here one recalls such American functionalists as Parsons* and Merton. Nevertheless, unlike them, Mauss lays emphasis upon the historical dimension. Lévi-Strauss held that Mauss's approach to sociology, especially the notion of a total social fact, inaugurated a new era for the social sciences. This era Lévi-Strauss himself developed in seeing social systems as interactions between groups which reveal a hidden structure. His interpretation of Mauss has been questioned by Victor Karady.

Although Mauss was trained in philosophy, he was much less philosophical in his writing than Durkheim. Both were influenced by Neo-Kantianism. Mauss was also critical of the alleged extremisms of Durkheim in excluding psychology as part of an explanation of social phenomena, in his near metaphysical concept of society and in his theory of effervescence. In rejecting sociologism, Mauss saw that the task of the social sciences was a study of the entire man and that biology, psychology and sociology could all make contributions within limits. Again, unlike Durkheim, Mauss was openly committed to socialism, evident not least in *The Gift*. Although Mauss said the sociological study of primitive religions was what interested him most, he did not share Durkheim's concern for religion in the present and the future.

Dr W. S. F. Pickering

The majority of Mauss's works appear in *M. Mauss. Sociologie et anthropologie*, ed. G. Gurvitch, with an introduction by C. Lévi-Strauss (3rd edition 1966) and *M. Mauss. Oeuvres*, ed. V. Karady (3 vols, 1968–9). Other translations: *Primitive Classification* (1963); *Sacrifice, Its Nature and Function* (1964); *A General Theory of Magic* (1972); *Sociology and Psychology: Essays* (1979).

309

MAYAKOVSKY, Vladimir Vladimirovich
1893–1930

Russian poet

The son of a forestry official, Mayakovsky grew up in Georgia, but came to Moscow after his father's death in 1906. He quickly became involved in revolutionary politics and was given an eleven-month spell of solitary imprisonment while still in his teens. For a time he was an art student, but from 1912 onwards he devoted himself principally to poetry. He was a leading figure in the Russian Futurist movement and took part in their provocative public appearances. After the October Revolution, he immediately threw himself into the struggle on the side of the Bolsheviks and during the Civil War period worked prodigiously hard on propaganda posters. In the 1920s his modernist and functionalist position, represented by the journal *Lef*, came under attack from other factions in the Soviet literary arena and gradually he became more isolated. However, he continued to serve the revolutionary cause, producing long and short poems, plays and all sorts of propagandist work, giving frequent public readings of his poetry and travelling abroad quite extensively. In 1930, under the strain of literary harassment and an unhappy love affair, he shot himself.

Mayakovsky's work is dominated by his own self-image, from the early tragedy *Vladimir Mayakovsky* (1913) to the unfinished testament to posterity *At the Top of my Voice* (1930). As a Futurist, and later as a Soviet poet, he sets himself, the rebel, against the forces of comfort and conformity, represented in turn by the pre-revolutionary bourgeoisie and the new bourgeoisie of the 1920s. His constant enemy is *byt* – an untranslatable Russian word evoking the stifling inertia of ordinary life – as satirized for instance in his best play, *The Bedbug* (*Klop*, 1929). Particularly in his long poems, *A Cloud in Trousers* (*Oblako v shtanakh*, 1915), *The Backbone-Flute* (*Fleita-Pozvonochnik*, 1916), *Man* (*Chelovek*, 1918) and *About That* (*Pro Eto*, 1923), Mayakovsky expresses his own pain, his non-acceptance of the world as it is and his demand that it be transformed. His own suffering – often caused by love – is seen as standing for that of the oppressed people of the world and one of his characteristic themes is that of self-sacrifice, often expressed through Christian analogies (e.g. Golgotha). Although in many of his public pronouncements and poems he adopts a hard, even brutal tone, one should not overlook his thirst for love and tenderness, which is seen for instance in such recurrent images as those of water, of animals and of lips – thus in *A Cloud in Trousers*:

> But you cannot turn yourself inside out like me
> and become nothing but lips!

As a Futurist, Mayakovsky was close to those who believed in the 'self-sufficient word', though he himself never went very far in the direction of 'pure' poetry. Later, as a poet of the Revolution, he took up a more functionalist position and in his article 'How Verse is Made', rather in the manner of Edgar Allan Poe, he analyses one of his own poems, showing how all its formal features are designed to affect and persuade an audience. Mocking theories of inspiration, he stresses the importance of skill (*masterstvo*) and gives advice on the best ways of developing it. This does not imply following set patterns however, since in his view poetic impact (and thence value) depended above all on novelty. He often expressed a provocative and not entirely sincere contempt for the art of the past.

In fact, both before and after the Revolution, Mayakovsky is remarkable as a worker in words. He was a significant and influential innovator in Russian verse, placing a new importance on rich and unexpected rhymes to bind together lines where the number of syllables varies greatly. His poetry is essentially for the ear (he was a formidable performer) and rhythm plays a primordial role in it; this is emphasized on the printed page by his 'ladder' layout, in which lines are divided into smaller sense-units. His work is also remarkable for its metaphorical inventiveness and for its striking combinations of very different registers of language, colloquial, technical, noble and grotesque. His best poems are not dense and highly structured short lyrics but large, loose-textured and varied compositions in which the reader/listener is carried forward by the daring and vigour of the speaking voice.

Although much abused in his lifetime, Mayakovsky has come since his death to be officially regarded as the great poet of Soviet Russia. His actual popularity has probably never matched his official standing, and for many poetry lovers he has been eclipsed by Pasternak* or Mandelstam* – or on a more popular level Esenin. He has not had any significant disciples (although his influence may be detected in much recent poetry), and he appears fifty years after his death as a magnificent and isolated figure who led a dramatic life and left a splendid body of poetry.

Peter France

His works are available in numerous Russian editions and in the following translations: *The Bedbug and Selected Poetry* (trans. M. Hayward and G. Reavey, 1961); *Mayakovsky* (trans. and ed. H. Marshall, 1965); *Wi the Haill Voice* (trans. into Scottish by E. Morgan, 1972); *Complete Plays* (trans. Guy Daniels, 1971); *How are Verses Made?* (trans. G. M. Hyde, 1970). On Mayakovsky: E. J. Brown, *Mayakovsky, a Poet in the Revolution* (1973); W. Woroszylski, *The Life of Mayakovsky* (trans. B. Jaborski, 1972); R. Jakobson, 'On a Generation that Squandered its Poets', in E. J. Brown (ed.), *Major Soviet Writers* (1973).

310
MEAD, Margaret 1901–78

American anthropologist

Born into a New England academic family, Margaret Mead took a BA at Barnard College and higher degrees in anthropology at Columbia University. Here she was greatly influenced by her teachers, Franz Boas*, the father of modern American anthropology, and Ruth Benedict, whose interest in the relationship between 'culture' and 'personality' was to provide the central scientific preoccupation of Margaret Mead's career.

In 1925 Mead carried out her first field-study, in Samoa, becoming one of the first women to do anthropological field-research, and one of the few American anthropologists of her generation to work outside the Americas. She took into the field a problem posed by Boas: whether adolescence was a culturally specific experience, which happened to occur in modern Western societies, or (as the Western folk-view had it) whether adolescence was the symptom of profound biological changes which inevitably manifested themselves in disruptive behaviour. The relaxed, sexually free, responsible Samoan maidens were presented to the American public, in *Coming of Age in Samoa* (1928), as the resolution of that particular argument, and the book became a best-seller.

Her next study, of early childhood in Manus (*Growing up in New Guinea*, 1931), was less explicitly directed

towards the testing of a hypothesis, but her description of how another culture raised its children was directly relevant to educational debates then in progress in the United States – particularly since the Manus employed the free-and-easy techniques in favour in avant-garde European kindergartens. The real problem suggested by the book was left unexplored, namely the contrast between the expressive and indulged Manus infants and the driven adults they were later to become.

The theme of these early works remained the leitmotif of Mead's work. 'Human nature' is plastic, cultural conditioning and environment are more vital than biological factors in determining what kinds of people are found in different societies. Perhaps the most radical version of this argument is to be found in her *Sex and Temperament in Three Primitive Societies* (1935), in which the contrasting male and female types in three New Guinea societies were analysed to show that there is nothing natural or universal about particular 'masculine' or 'feminine' role expectations. Scepticism was aroused at the time by the fortunate coincidence that her field-work happened to occur among three societies which formed such a perfect contrast for her purposes, but if the impressionistic descriptions cannot be accepted without reservations, the broad lines of her reports, and the conclusion drawn, have proved reasonably acceptable.

During the Second World War Mead was active in a team which made 'national culture' studies of allies and enemies for the US government, and even after the war she produced significant academic studies, notably her *Continuities in Cultural Evolution* (1964). She also remained for the greater part of her professional life on the staff of the American Museum of Natural History. None the less she increasingly devoted herself to public or popular activities, which she saw as an essential product of her anthropological studies. As she wrote in her autobiography, *Blackberry Winter* (1972): 'I have spent most of my life studying the lives of other peoples, faraway peoples, so that Americans might better understand themselves.' The point of view she propagated was liberal and optimistic, and perhaps characteristically American in its emphasis on cultural malleability, providing a sort of academic blessing for the melting-pot. An intelligent, sophisticated and religious person, she escaped the intellectual vulgarization which her popularizing role might have implied, retaining a sense of the complexity of social issues, and an openness to new ideas. *Margaret Mead: The Complete Bibliography 1925–1975* (ed. Joan Gordon, 1976) lists over 1,400 items, bearing witness to a passion for communication which was rewarded by the attention and interest of millions both inside and outside the social sciences.

Professor Adam Kuper

311

MEINECKE, Friedrich 1862–1954

German historian

Meinecke was born into a cultivated Prussian family of civil servants and protestant ministers before the foundation of the German Reich whose intellectual origins he was to chart. He lived long enough to witness, if not to understand, its destruction. During an exemplary academic career he held chairs of history at the universities of Strasbourg, Freiburg and Berlin, and edited the influential *Historische Zeitschrift* until replaced by the Nazis in 1935. He was made Rektor of the Free University of Berlin in 1948.

Meinecke's three most significant works, *Cosmopolitanism and the National State* (*Weltbürgertum und Nationalstaat*, 1907, trans. 1970), *Machiavellism: the Doctrine of Raison d'État and its Place in Modern History* (*Die Idee der Staatsräson in der neueren Geschichte*, 1924, trans. 1957), and *Historism: the Rise of a New Historical Outlook* (*Die Entstehung des Historismus*, 1936, trans. 1972), are studies in the history of ideas, of which, together with Dilthey and Troeltsch, he is regarded as a founder. His characteristic stance is one of attentive sympathy for the particularity of his subject, and he prefers to apprehend ideas as they are realized and modified by outstanding individuals. The emphasis is placed less on those phenomena, economic and social, which determine ideas and values, than on history as the realm of freedom and self-fulfilment. The emergence and survival of an entity Meinecke regards, particularly in his earlier works, as sufficient indication of its value: 'even the apparent immorality of the state's power-political egoism can . . . be ethically justified. For what springs from the deepest individual nature of a being cannot be unethical' (*Cosmopolitanism*).

The optimism underlying such statements was put to the test by the events of 1918 and, later, by the rise of Nazism. Under the pressure of political reality Meinecke came to see the relationship of power to morality as more problematic. In *Machiavellism* he criticizes Hegelianism for the tendency to 'sanction and authorize factual developments', and in *Historism*, which argues persuasively against the received view of historicism as a specifically German phenomenon, he again points to the dangers of moral relativism. His attachment to the ideas of individual identity and development, which he regards as the essence of historicism, nevertheless remains, but without his earlier confidence in the immanent value of humanity and its diverse manifestations to support it. By now Meinecke had come to see the realms of culture and politics, of spirit and matter, as distinct. The inadequacies of such a conception are most evident in *The German Catastrophe* (*Die Deutsche Katastrophe*, 1946, trans. 1950), which substitutes chance for historical explanation and averts its gaze from the links between German culture and the origins of Nazism.

In the elegance, clarity and impartial empathy of his best work Meinecke is a remarkable exponent of the historicist tradition. Although he may appear now as a victim of the crisis of that tradition, and as a figure epitomizing the ambiguous relationship of much German thought to a European 'mainstream', his individual contribution to intellectual history has nevertheless received belated recognition outside Germany since his death: it is notable that the translations into English and French of his major works are all of them posthumous.

Roger S. Huss

Other works include: *The Age of German Liberation, 1795–1815* (*Das Zeitalter der deutschen Erhebung, 1795–1815*, 1906, trans. 1977); *Ein schaffender Spiegel* (1948); and the autobiographical *Erlebtes, 1862–1901* (1941) and *Strassburg, Freiburg, Berlin 1901–1919. Erinnerungen* (1949). See also: G. G. Iggers, *The German Conception of History* (1968); R. A. Pois, *Friedrich Meinecke and German Politics in the 20th Century* (1972).

312

MERLEAU-PONTY, Maurice 1908–61

French philosopher

Merleau-Ponty was born in Rochefort-sur-mer. After completing his secondary education, he studied philosophy at the École Normale Supérieure in Paris, achieving the *agrégation* in 1930. From 1931 to 1944 he taught philosophy, with a brief spell in the army from 1939 to 1940. In 1945, he was appointed to a post at the Université de Lyon, where he became professor in 1948. In 1949, he returned to Paris to take up the chair of Child Psychology and Pedagogy at the Sorbonne, and, in 1952, was elected to a chair at the Collège de France. His first books, *The Structure of Behaviour* (*La Structure du comportement*, 1942, trans. 1963) and the *Phenomenology of Perception* (*Phénoménologie de la perception*, 1945, trans. 1962), were the product of work in philosophy and psychology on which he had been engaged throughout the 1930s. At that time, the intellectual atmosphere in France was receiving a new stimulus from the work of the German philosophers, Hegel, Husserl* and Heidegger*, which challenged the dominant trend of French academic philosophy. Although all three were to shape Merleau-Ponty's thought, the phenomenology of Husserl was to prove particularly influential. Merleau-Ponty spent some time before the war consulting Husserl's unpublished manuscripts at the Husserl Archives in Louvain, and considered himself to be a phenomenologist, following in the footsteps of Husserl. He has been criticized for misinterpreting or misrepresenting Husserl, but it is clear that he felt he was being faithful to Husserl's most fundamental intentions. Seeking a method which would enable him to avoid the philosophical difficulties of both rationalism and empiricism, and more specifically, the problems raised by dualism, he stressed the need to return to our original experience of the world, to investigate the genesis of that understanding of the world which we normally take for granted, and to take as the central theme of philosophy the construction of sense and meaning and the constitution of knowledge. His work has been described as a philosophy of ambiguity, because of his interest in indeterminate categories of experience, such as the 'probable' or the 'ambiguous'; his interest in categories or concepts which do not have too precise a meaning is part of his critical attitude towards the claims of rationalism.

Although Merleau-Ponty's reputation in France has suffered as a result of the trend away from phenomenology in the direction of structuralism, he is acknowledged as a major exponent of phenomenology. With the translation of his major works, his influence is slowly beginning to make itself felt outside France. His work has proved of interest to many non-philosophers as well, notably in the field of aesthetics. Another aspect of his thought to attract considerable attention has been his analysis of the role of the body and its significance for philosophical reflection.

In 1945, after the Liberation, he collaborated with Sartre* and a number of other intellectuals in the founding of the review *Les Temps modernes*. He is sometimes thought of as an Existentialist, but in fact there were significant philosophical and political differences between himself and Sartre, and his association with the review came to an end in 1952. The disagreement became public in 1955 with the publication of his book *Adventures of the Dialectic* (*Les Aventures de la dialectique*, trans. 1973) which included a lengthy critique of Sartre. While he had been sympathetic to Marxism in the 1940s, Merleau-Ponty now became increasingly disillusioned and moved definitively away from the intellectual left wing. At the time of his death he had returned to philosophy and was making notes for a work (posthumously published in 1964 under the title *Le Visible et l'invisible*, trans. *The Visible and the Invisible*, 1968) which is more Heideggerian than Husserlian in inspiration.

Margaret Whitford

Other works: *Humanism and Terror* (*Humanisme et terreur*, 1947, trans. 1969); *Sense and Non-Sense* (*Sens et non-sens*, 1948, trans. 1964); *In Praise of Philosophy* (*Éloge de la philosophie*, 1953, trans. 1963); *Signs* (*Signes*, 1960, trans. 1964); *The Prose of the World* (*La Prose du monde*, 1969, trans. 1974). Translation of collected essays and articles: *The Primacy of Perception and Other Essays* (1964); *Phenomenology, language and*

sociology (1974). See also: Colin Smith, *Contemporary French philosophy* (1964); Albert Rabil Jr, *Merleau-Ponty: Existentialist of the Social World* (1967).

313
MERTON, Thomas 1915–68

US monk

Merton was born at Prades in the French Pyrenees. Both his parents were artists: his mother, an American, died when he was six; his father, a New Zealander, when he was sixteen. He was brought up by his mother's family in Maryland, New York and Bermuda, and educated at the Lycée Ingres, Montauban, France, Oakham School, Rutland, England, and at the universities of Cambridge (England) and Columbia, where he wrote a thesis on William Blake. For a while he was a card-carrying member of the Communist Party, but resigned long before his conversion to Roman Catholicism in 1938. After two years teaching English at the Franciscan university (St Bonaventure's) in New York, he entered the strict Cistercian (Trappist) Abbey of Gethsemani, Kentucky, in 1941, taking the name Louis in religion. He was ordained priest in 1949, and served as the Abbey's novice-master from 1955 to 1965. In the latter year he was allowed to withdraw from the communal life and live in a hermitage within the monastic enclosure. In 1968 he was invited to attend a conference of Asian Benedictine and Cistercian religious (men and women) in Bangkok, where he was killed by the malfunction of an electric fan.

Merton achieved international fame with his exuberant autobiography, *The Seven Storey Mountain* (1948), and was a prolific and beguiling – if somewhat florid – writer on monasticism and monastic renewal until the day of his death. He deplored the involvement of many modern monastic orders in education and social work. To him, monks should be marginal people, withdrawn from the world for the sole and all-absorbing purpose of looking for God. Monastic communities should be structured and administered to provide a disciplined framework in which to pursue this end. While he cherished the communal aspects of monastic life, he argued – controversially – that in maturity monks should be allowed to live in total solitude.

If Merton had lived in the Middle Ages he would no doubt have founded his own Order, in the manner of Bernard of Clairvaux, the founder of his own. Instead, in searching for monastic renewal he looked beyond the mainstream of the Western monastic tradition to the Desert and Greek Fathers – Origen, Clement, Cassian, Diadochus of Photike – and latterly outside it, to the methods of practices of Asia. He was particularly drawn to Zen Buddhism as a means of 'being' in the world. He was convinced that communication in depth, across the lines that had hitherto divided religious and monastic traditions, was not only possible but desirable. His work gave fibre to the fashionable craze for Eastern religion and ethics of the 1960s, and is being continued both in theory and practice, pre-eminently by Aelred Graham and Bede Griffiths.

Timothy O'Sullivan

Principal works: N. Burton, P. Hart and J. Laughlin (eds), *The Asian Journal of Thomas Merton* (1973); *Collected Poems* (1977); P. Hart (ed.), *The Monastic Journey* (1977); *Mystics and Zen Masters* (1969); *Seeds of Contemplation* (1949); *The Silent Life* (1957); *The Waters of Siloe* (1949). See T. P. McDonnell (ed.), *A Thomas Merton Reader* (rev. edn, 1975); G. Woodcock, *Thomas Merton, Monk and Poet* (1978).

314
MESSIAEN, Olivier 1908–

French composer

One of the most gifted French composers of any age, Messiaen attended the Paris Conservatoire from 1919 to 1930, where his teachers included Paul Dukas (composition), Marcel Dupré (organ) and Maurice Emmanuel (history of music). In 1931 he took up the post of organist at the Église de la Sainte Trinité in Paris, a position he still holds today. Together with Jolivet and others he formed in 1936 the group 'La Jeune France', dedicated to restoring a sense of seriousness to French music, then dominated by the anti-romantic aesthetic of the composers of 'Les Six'. During the war he was interned by the Germans in Stalag VIII, where he performed for the first time his apocalyptic *Quatuor pour la fin du temps* (1941) before the entire assembly of prisoners in icy conditions. Upon his release, he resumed teaching duties in Paris, becoming in 1947 Professor of Analysis, Aesthetics and Rhythm at the Conservatoire. His radical experiments with musical language in the early 1950s attracted to his classes some of the outstanding young composers of the day, including Boulez* and Stockhausen*. After the death of his first wife in 1959, he married his former pupil Yvonne Loriod, for whom he had written many of his piano works. In 1966 he became Professor of Composition at the Conservatoire, and since then he has also travelled and taught extensively throughout the world.

Any discussion of Messiaen's music must take as its starting point a consideration of his artistic personality, which offers an intensely private and individual response to the traditional concerns of Christianity, nature and human love. The astonishing power and commitment of his work derived in some measure from his unquestioning acceptance of the diverse influences of his childhood, whilst its attraction resides in the integration of a radical reappraisal of the elements of musical language with an aesthetic which derived unashamedly from Wagner and the French Symbolist writers.

Many of these features are present in the early works of the late 1920s and 1930s. If the titles of the piano *Preludes* (1928) reflected an obvious Debussyism* (*les sons impalpables du rêve*, *un reflet dans le vent*, and so on), those of the subsequent organ pieces – which stand in the line of Franck and Alain – show a more characteristic commitment to sacred subjects: *Le Banquet céleste* (1928), *L'Ascension* (1933) (which also exists in an orchestral version), *La Nativité du Seigneur* (1935) and *Les Corps glorieux* (1939). In the 1940s this line was extended by *Visions de l'Amen* (1943, for two pianos), *Vingt regards sur l'enfant Jésus* (1944, for piano), and *Trois petites liturgies de la Présence Divine* (1944, for women's choir and orchestra). The fact that these pieces mainly comprise a number of short descriptive movements points to his lifelong preference for episodic forms, with simple but sharp internal contrasts, rather than for the integrated, developing forms of the Austro-German tradition. The imaginative stimulus to using sacred texts in this way, Messiaen suggests, arose out of his childhood delight in the fantastic elements in Shakespeare (Ariel, Puck); in manhood he creates comparably fantastic tableaux illustrative of the 'truths' of Catholic dogma, whose range embraces the extremes of peace and violence, reverence and penitence.

In the 1930s, he had also composed two song cycles for Wagnerian voice to his own surrealistic texts (he derived his literary bent from his mother, who was a writer). These celebrated his marriage (*Poèmes pour Mi*, 1936) and the birth of a child (*Chants de terre et de ciel*, 1938). In the 1940s he pursued the themes of secular love in three works devoted to the Tristan and Isolde myth: *Harawi* (1945, for voice and piano), *Turangalila-Symphony* (1948, for orchestra), and *Cinq rechants* (1949, for twelve solo voices). These works represent the summation of the first part of his life. In the Symphony especially, the remarkable new eroticism is projected on one hand through a glittering rhythmic brilliance, and on the other hand, through a spaciousness in its repose that had already been adumbrated by the timeless contemplations of the early organ music.

In all these works, there had been several technical innovations: still working within a tonal framework, he had devised a number of pitch modes ('of limited transposition') characterized by internal symmetries which he used in various combinations; in response to the disassociation of pitch and rhythm functions in the *Rite of Spring* of Stravinsky*, he approached purely rhythmic thought from several standpoints: he derived small cells from a Hindu treatise (Sharngadeva), employed Greek rhythms based on more conventional ideas of the poetic foot, used prime numbers to determine larger proportions, and built multi-levelled rhythmic structures out of rhythmic canons and ostinati. Increasingly he came to prefer the 'free, unequal durations' he found in nature to what he considered to be the artificial metric regularity of traditional music.

These concerns came to a head in a number of experimental, and highly influential, keyboard pieces: the *Modes de valeurs et d'intensités, Neumes rythmiques* and *Cantejodjaya* of 1949; the *Île de feu I* and *II* of 1950; and the *Livre d'orgue* of 1951. These works, in part or in whole, reflected the obsessive contemporary desire for a high degree of ordering in all the simply identifiable musical dimensions – a desire to a certain extent fostered by post-war analyses of the music of Webern*. In pitch terms, although Messiaen used the twelve-tone scale modally more often than serially, he here developed mechanistic permutational patterns in a spirit he viewed as redolent of the Middle Ages. In rhythmic terms, he measured note-lengths as additions of durational values, which he then permutated according to 'interversion' procedures. Comparable methods were applied to dynamic values and to different modes of articulation. Although twelve-tone, these means embodied nothing of the organic processes found in the music of the school of Schoenberg*, and, indeed, were both in conception and practice crude to a degree. Nevertheless, from a historical point of view, they undoubtedly ushered in a new phase of European music, and their fruits are, to a certain extent, still with us today.

Immediately after these works, however, there was a dramatic change. For personal reasons he turned to a contemplation of nature – something he knew well from his boyhood in Grenoble – in which he saw, if not a solace, then certainly a refuge from the world. His principal concern was to transcribe the melodies, rhythms and timbres of birdsongs for conventional instruments, and to intersperse the results with musical passages descriptive of the birds' natural habitats. In this he considered he was extending the nature music of Wagner and Debussy. Whilst there had been elements of birdsong in his earlier works, now three pieces were entirely given over to it: the *Réveil des oiseaux* (1953, for piano and orchestra) which like the later *Chronochromie* (1960, for orchestra) includes an elaborate dawn chorus; *Oiseaux exotiques* (1956, for piano and orchestra), a fantasy combining birdsong from all over the world; and *Catalogue d'oiseaux* (1956–8, for piano).

The works since 1960 have shown once again a profusion of concerns: there is the consolidation of nature imagery (*Chronochromie, La Fauvette des jardins*, 1970, for piano, and *Des canyons aux étoiles*, 1971, for orchestra); a return to sacred subjects (*Couleurs de la Cité Céleste*, 1963, for piano and small orchestra, *Et expecto resurrectionem mortuorum*, 1964, for orchestra, *La Transfiguration de notre Seigneur Jésus Christ*, 1963–9, for choir, seven

soloists and orchestra, and *Méditations sur le mystère de la Sainte Trinité*, 1969, for organ); and an extension of his interest in exotica (*Sept Haikai*, 1962, for piano and orchestra, which includes an imitation of Sho, the Japanese mouth organ). In these works, Messiaen's life-long concern with musical colour achieves a new prominence, especially in the selection and juxtaposition of chords and textures. The sonorities are more brittle, and rely particularly on the 'mysterious' resonances of greatly expanded percussion sections. And it would be surprising if all these features do not achieve a new synthesis in the work he is currently preparing for the Paris Opera House, *St Francis of Assisi*.

Whilst the elements of the Messiaen legacy are in themselves clear enough – and none has been more influential than his concern with the formation of musical language, as testified by his idiosyncratic *Technique de mon langage musical* ('Technique of my Musical Language', 1942) – it is the power of his innate gifts that has led even those whose aesthetic and musical attitudes are quite other than his into recognizing him as one of the extraordinary figures of our time.

Christopher Wintle

Most of Messiaen's works are published either by Durand or Leduc (Paris). See: Robert Sherlaw Johnson, *Messiaen* (1975); Claude Samuel, *Conversations with Olivier Messiaen* (1976).

315
MEYERHOLD, Vsevolod (Vsevolod Emilievich Meierkhold) 1874–1940

Russian theatre director

When Constructivism evolved in Russia, reaching its fullest fruition in the early 1920s, the theatre director Vsevolod Meyerhold was amongst its most active protagonists and exponents. Constructivism in Russia intended to make of any creative work a committed political device that fulfilled an agitational role. Furthermore it aspired to adopt forms and processes of evolving the work that were appropriate to this task. The elimination of the isolation of the art-work from the exigencies of daily life was one such principle, and Meyerhold, despite the *fin-de-siècle* flavour of his early productions, became committed after the Revolution to a theatre without stage lighting, employing sets that were an apparatus for the actors and not at all evocative of another time or place. Real soldiers, actual lorries and machine guns, farming equipment, and newsreel film were all incorporated into his agitational productions. The most celebrated of them were *The Magnanimous Cuckold* (by Crommelynck, set by Popova) and *The Death of Tarelkin* (by Sukhovo-Kobylin, set by Stepanova). The whole appearance of his productions was declamatory and vigorously anti-illusionistic, an ensemble over which Meyerhold, as director, was the totally dominant figure. His actors were permitted only minimal initiative and were called upon to perform athletic feats according to a precise system of movements devised by Meyerhold and called *biomechanics*: Meyerhold's stage began to resemble both a cabaret and a circus but with a pungent and politically committed aspect that in the most literal way was to involve the audience. Meyerhold also became involved with the organization of mass plays in the open air. For these and other projects he employed Constructivist designers and worked closely with writers sharing his commitment to the Revolution.

Dr John Milner

See: Edward Braun, *Meyerhold on Theatre* (1969); J. M. Symons, *Meyerhold's Theatre of the Grotesque* (1973).

316
MIES VAN DER ROHE, Ludwig 1886–1969

German/US architect

Mies van der Rohe and Le Corbusier* are the most important architects of what has been called the Heroic period of Modern Architecture, the period between the wars when the theories and style of the new architecture were first demonstrated. The double challenge that the architects of this time took upon themselves was to derive a form of building which could exploit the new manufacturing technology, which could make use of machine produced parts, and more importantly to create an undecorated architecture, an intention first suggested by Adolf Loos's* essay *Decoration and Crime* published in 1908. Through this latter ambition the pioneer architects identified themselves with the urgency of modernism, the desire to break once and for all with the irrelevancies and encumbrances of the past. Although recent reassessment has often been directed towards finding parallels between the works of this period and the more distant past, notably the comparison by Colin Rowe of the villas of Le Corbusier and Palladio, and although a more detailed analysis of Mies might show an unbroken line from the German neo-classicism of Schinkel, received through Behrens with whom he worked at a formative time, the spirit of the early modern movement was obsessively, to borrow Moholy-Nagy's phrase, the New Vision.

In his later work Le Corbusier displayed a huge and varied talent, whereas Mies held to the same aims, the desire for clarity and purity, expressed through a strict rectilinear geometry and careful detailing, throughout his long career. These qualities were characteristics of all his mature works, from first to last, and this consistency of effort and inspiration explains why his in-

fluence is so pervasive, and why he can be considered above all others as the father of steel and glass architecture. The prophetic nature of his abilities can be judged by the models of the glass tower blocks, done between 1919 and 1921.

Mies's mature style found its first clear expression in the design of the German Pavilion for the 1929 International Exhibition in Barcelona. In this small one-storey building can be found the essence of what was to inform the rest of his life's work, demonstrated with complete authority. The characteristics of the style were the building placed upon a pedestal, the use of opulent materials, treated as pure clear-cut rectilinear horizontal and vertical surfaces, spaces within and without treated as overlapping and interlocking, transparent external walls, and a separation of the structure from the walls, using non-load-bearing partitions around a regular placing of load-bearing columns, allowing for a free composition of the plan. This approach allowed him to compose the plan unrestricted by the demands of support and gravity, as a painter might compose an abstract painting. The similarity between the plan of the Barcelona Pavilion and the contemporaneous Dutch de Stijl school is notable. It has been pointed out elsewhere that this freedom of the plan was achieved at the cost of a much more rigid, stratified section than is usual with traditional load-bearing wall buildings.

For the Pavilion, Mies designed a chair, a stool and a glass-topped table, examples of which were carefully placed within the buildings to further structure and enhance the clear geometrical organization of the space. The deep transparency of the building conveys a sense of space that flows through and beyond the Pavilion, as if this were some local organization within a universal continuous system, which was capable of consistently organizing the placing of furniture and the relationship of one building to another. Thus from this one building he was able to realize a total vision that would allow him confidently to tackle any scale of work, from the layout of a large campus to the design of other exquisite single transparent pavilions.

Apart from the few pieces of furniture, the Barcelona Pavilion only contained a statue by Georg Kolbe placed on a pedestal in a pool. As with all his best work, the beauty of the composition is best appreciated when empty, devoid of the random casualness of everyday life.

The ideal of continuous space which he was to serve in later buildings, notably in Crown Hall on the Illinois Institute of Technology campus, by stopping the internal partitions short of the ceiling, allows for no clear demarcation of one space from another, and explains why clearly defined doors and isolated windows, the ancient items that mark one space from another, and inside from outside, are an anathema to Mies.

His career divided between the work in Germany,

which he left in 1937, and the work of the rest of his life in America. Apart from the Barcelona Pavilion his major achievements include the organization of the Weissenhof exhibition in 1927 at which the major architects of the new style, including Le Corbusier, Gropius*, J. J. P. Oud and Hans Scharoun, at his invitation contributed buildings to a master plan by Mies, producing a unique assemblage of seminal buildings of the Modern Movement, the Turgendhat house in Brno, Czechoslovakia, in 1930, and the model house for the 1931 Berlin Building Exhibition. These latter two buildings were adaptations of the style of the Barcelona Pavilion to the requirements of a dwelling.

In 1930 he was appointed Director of the famous design school, the Bauhaus, on Gropius's recommendation, and remained so until, by his own decision, the school was closed in 1933. His cool courage at this time in the face of considerable harassment by the Fascists was unwavering. He left for America in 1937.

Soon after arriving he was appointed Director of Architecture at what was to become the Illinois Institute of Technology, consequently coming to live in Chicago, the city where he was to remain for the rest of his life, and which was to come to contain the greatest concentration of his buildings. In the 1940s and 1950s there developed a deep empathy between his work and the work of the native American architects.

In his inaugural address at IIT he gave a rare and illuminating insight into his philosophy. Education, he asserted, consisted of leading the student from materials, through function, to creative work. He then, with great passion, expounded the virtues and beauty of primitive building methods. In this was an echo of neo-classicism, of the belief that the Greek temples were a refined development from the first primitive hut, from Adam's first house in Paradise.

He was a man of few public utterances, unlike Le Corbusier, who was to the end a tireless polemicist. His two most famous typically sparse statements were 'less is more' and 'God is in the details'. These two, however, when read against his buildings are as revealing as all the volumes produced by Le Corbusier.

There is an interesting divergence in the work in America of the two newly resident pioneer architects and past directors of the Bauhaus, Mies and Gropius. Gropius after the Second World War, working with Konrad Wasehumann, undertook to develop a system for mass producing housing, called the General Panel house. Mies started at about the same time the design of a house for a close friend, Dr Edith Farnsworth. The house was to take six years to reach completion. Two more opposed uses of the new techniques and materials of building would be difficult to imagine. In retrospect the seeds of difference are evident in the work done by the pioneers of pre-war Europe, but the early enthusiasm still allows the work to be read as a concerted effort. Mies's differences with much of other Modernist

orthodoxy began to become clearer in the post-war period. The early edict that form follows function, he gently and firmly inverted, stating that as the function of building was liable to change during its lifetime, then the only permanent quality is beauty. This problem of the subservience of the function to the beauty of the building he resolved in many of his schemes by dropping the necessarily enclosed offices and rooms beneath the pedestal, upon which he then placed the familiar beautiful transparent uncluttered pavilion. This he did with the design for the Bacardi Company in Santiago, which was not built, and with his final building, the National Art Gallery in Berlin. Similarly truth to materials with Mies became love of materials; thus it was love and not truth that informed how he was to treat particular parts of his buildings.

The site for the Farnsworth House was wooded and rural. He produced his most refined example of the steel and glass transparent structure placed upon a pedestal, albeit the latter was a cantilevered slab. As an object to be looked at and from, the house is the clearest expression of a beautifully made object which relates through its transparency the architecture and its setting. The building allowed him to realize the quality suggested by the drawings for the unbuilt Resor House of 1938, which was his first commission in America. The comment still applies that the beauty depends to a large degree on a sense of emptiness. Once marked by occupancy the nature of transparency becomes something quite different from an agent of an open continuous system. When occupied it is more likely to provoke extremes of privatization in at least two ways: first, not having a dark depth into which to withdraw, to avoid the eyes that see all too well, the window walls are liable to be obscured with total curtaining, or as an alternative one needs to own or at least to control the landscape into which the structure is placed.

The designs for court houses that he experimented with throughout his life were less than urban solutions to this paradox.

In 1940 Mies undertook his largest commission, the overall design of the IIT campus in south Chicago and the design of the individual buildings. This was to be the best opportunity to express the idea of a universal building, of the subservience of function to the form. The buildings were designed with the same skeletal steel structure holding to the same set of dimensions into which the variety of uses, chapel, offices, design studios, were then fitted. The overall plan can be seen as an abstract composition, as with the Barcelona plan, but it lacked the dynamics of interpenetration of the earlier plan, seeming to move towards a more regular, symmetrical organization. Many have seen a spirit of Renaissance planning in the final plan, but it might be that it falls rather uneasily between the continuous, interlocking spaces of the earlier work, and the Renaissance genius of place, the concern for focus and forming of particular spaces.

His work included several tower blocks, some for flats, some for offices, and although they are all distinguished by an unequalled clarity of resolution, they are rather more expected than his glass and steel pavilions. Probably the most famous tower is the Seagram Building in Park Avenue, New York, completed in 1958. The building was set back from the line of the avenue, allowing for the setting out of a plaza, the building and the plaza being related by a clear symmetry. The plaza undoubtedly provided an open public space but more importantly it acted as a pedestal, a device that allowed the finely detailed, symmetrical tower to be viewed, at the cost of breaking the line and identity of the avenue.

His influence as an educator was enormous, his most faithful and successful ex-students being perhaps Skidmore Owings and Merrill.

The final building was the National Gallery in Berlin, completed after his death, in 1969. Thus Mies's mature work is begun and finished by two steel and glass pavilions, placed on pedestals, both commissioned by a German government. Their dissimilarities show a move from asymmetry to symmetry and paradoxically, because of his life-long neo-classical interest in universal solutions, a lessening of concern for context. Their similarities and the consistency of his life's work are striking, and a monument to his unwavering genius.

Fred Scott

See: Peter Blake, *Mies van der Rohe* (1966); Philip Johnson, *Mies van der Rohe* (Museum of Modern Art, New York, 1953).

317

MILLER, Arthur 1915–

US playwright

After Eugene O'Neill*, Arthur Miller is the most talented and significant playwright America has produced. His theories of drama are provocative; his plays rich and varied.

Miller was the son of a prosperous manufacturer hit hard by the Depression; and one of the ironically creative results of that terrible period in American history was the compassion that it bred in Arthur Miller ('The icebox was empty and the man was sitting there with his mouth open', *The Price*, 1968). It made him realize how adverse circumstances could diminish man's self-respect and dignity; it made him especially critical of men who by their own acts diminished themselves and other people; it made him cherish those individuals who sought above all to preserve their integrity. 'I am Willy Loman,' says the hero of *Death of a Salesman*

(1949); 'Give me my name,' says John Proctor in *The Crucible*, 1953. The Depression contributed importantly to Miller's sense that the duty of the dramatist is to deal with the moral problems of the day. As a democrat and American he feels that he has a contribution to make to both the theory and practice of the drama. 'The Common man is as apt a subject for tragedy in its highest sense as kings were,' he has written, and has gone on to define tragedy as 'the consequence of a man's total compulsion to evaluate himself justly' (*Tragedy and the Common Man*, 1949). His 'Introduction' to *Collected Plays* (1957), his essays 'On Social Plays' (1955) and on 'The Family in Modern Drama' (1956) are of profound merit and illuminate the reading and viewing of his plays.

His first successful play, *All My Sons* (1947), was a reproach to the capitalist ethic which led manufacturer Joe Keller to market faulty aircraft parts and thus cause the death of a number of pilots, including one of his sons; his second and greatest play, *Death of a Salesman*, lovingly chronicled the last days of Willy Loman, an insignificant man in terms of his career, but a significant human being, who fights to the last against unsympathetic employers, an unhelpful wife, self-centred sons and his own weakness in order to salvage something worthwhile from his life. Willy Loman is, to Arthur Miller, a tragic hero. But Miller's plays are not merely about human potential and its abuse; they are about families. Miller is a moralist who believes that self-realization can only come through helping others; man is a social and caring animal and must show himself as such in his most immediate context, the family unit. But while Miller believes in man's potential for good and happiness he also finds evil and misery wherever he looks. The Lomans live together yet barely understand each other; the great love in the family of immigrant Italians proves a jealous and destructive emotion (*A View From the Bridge*, 1955). Even in the play in which the protagonists are able to articulate precisely how they felt about each other as children, adolescents and adults – *The Price* – there is no real coming together of the brothers Victor and Walter Franz. The play begins with the Victrola playing Gallagher and Shean; it ends with the sound of the laughing record. Miller seems finally to despair of answering the questions he has asked in play after play. 'How may a man make of the outside world a home?' ('The Family in Modern Drama') and how may a man make a nominal home a real one? His most recently published play, *The Creation of the World and Other Business* (1973), indicates his despair – it depicts God as an inept old man, dependent on Satan for breathing life into creation.

Miller is often compared with Ibsen – he adapted *An Enemy of The People* (1950) – and there is something of Ibsen's fatalism in Miller's *The Crucible*, which used the Salem witch trials to point out the true nature of

McCarthyism and implied the continuity of evil and persecution. Two plays which deal with the Second World War, *Incident at Vichy* (1965) and *After the Fall* (1964), also sound a note of pessimism as the protagonists attempt to evade the responsibility for chaos which is truly theirs. Rare indeed is Leduc in *Vichy*, who admits: 'Each man has his Jew: it is the other', and John Proctor in *The Crucible*, who manages finally to be true to himself, his family, his society and his God.

Sensitivity, humour, an effective use of Jewish grammatical inversion – 'Attention, attention must be paid' to Willy Loman – a strong sense of dramatic confrontation and an ability to exploit such scenes to the full characterize Miller's work as a playwright. If nothing is too commonplace to be tragic, nothing is too private to publish, as is evident in the self-critical portrait Miller painted of his relationship with his second wife, Marilyn Monroe, in *After the Fall*. His novel *Focus* (1945), about a non-Jew who looks Jewish and feels he discharges a moral debt by pretending to be Jewish, and his short story/screenplay *The Misfits* (1961) suggest that Miller could have been effective as a novelist, had he so chosen. But he is committed to 'the fated mission of the drama', for 'within the dramatic form [lies] the ultimate possibility of raising the truth-consciousness of mankind to a level of such intensity as to transform those who observe it' ('The Family in Modern Drama').

Dr Ann Massa

See: Dennis Welland, *Arthur Miller* (1961); Edward Murray, *Structure, Character and Theme in the Plays of Arthur Miller* (1966); Leonard Moss, *Arthur Miller* (1967); Robert Martin (ed.), *The Theatre Essays of Arthur Miller* (1978).

318
MILLER, Henry 1891–1980

US novelist

Born and brought up in New York City of German immigrant parents, Miller never completed his college education at City College, New York, but married unhappily and drifted from one job to another before deciding to be a writer. Moving to Paris in 1930 provided a breakthrough and the books he wrote there formed the basis for his reputation. Attacked by Kate Millett* and other feminists as a chauvinistic egotist, exalting his sexual prowess at the expense of women degraded to mere sex objects, his novels, in fact, are fictional autobiography and record his own spiritual growth and the struggles and trials of those around him.

Tropic of Cancer (1934) is an account of his life in Paris, and is a combination of a Bohemian idyll of the rootless, penniless artist existing outside, and over against, bourgeois conventionality, and a Whitmanesque hymn to the power of unfettered experience to liberate the artist into a prophet and visionary for a potentially perfect humanity. Sexuality becomes the means of revealing both our collective, cultural heritage with its often pernicious demands, guilts and shames, and the essence of the individual's accommodation to reality. The fact that desire is created by another and the response to one's own feelings means that here is a way of grasping the intersubjectivity of our experience.

In his next two novels, *Black Spring* (1938) and *Tropic of Capricorn* (1939), Miller continued to use the events of his own life in Paris and New York as metaphors for the human comedy. In order to reach the possibility of love, be believes we must pass through the 'Land of Fuck' in order to emerge from our privacy, self-importance and narcissism, to encounter and accept others, to risk losing our pride and complacency and to go beyond our 'ego-hood'. Without such openness and risk-taking, sex is merely destructive or sterile, as many of Miller's characters demonstrate.

Reflecting on the earlier stages of his life, Miller continued his personal odyssey in the Rosy Crucifixion Trilogy: *Sexus* (1945), *Plexus* (1949) and *Nexus* (1960), but with a lessening of intensity, probably related to his growing certainty of the truth of his views and his determination to preach them in such volumes of essays as *The World of Sex* (1940), *The Wisdom of the Heart* (1941), and *Stand Still like the Hummingbird* (1962).

His criticism of America and the modern world, its conformity, repression, violence and insanity, expressed through the championing of artists and eccentrics, as in *The Air-Conditioned Nightmare* (1945), has created for him a wide following, and many writers from Huxley*, Orwell* and Durrell to Mailer* and the Beat poets have paid tribute to his liberation of explicit sexual material for use in the novel, and his honesty in exploring the fantasy-rich chaos underlying the surface normality of the West.

Dr David Corker

Other works by Miller include: *The Colossus of Maroussi* (1941); essays: *The Cosmological Eye* (1939); *Sunday After the War* (1944); *Big Sur and the Oranges of Hieronymus Bosch* (1957); *Books in My Life* (1952); and *The Nightmare Notebook* (1975). Letters: *Lawrence Durrell and Henry Miller* (1963); *Letters to Anais Nin* (1965). See also: Alfred Perles, *My Friend, Henry Miller* (1956); Jory Martin, *Always Merry and Bright* (1978). Critical studies: Sydney Omarr, *Henry Miller: His World of Urania* (1960); William A. Gordon, *The Mind and Art of Henry Miller* (1967).

319
MILLETT, Kate (Katherine Murray) 1934–

US feminist

Born in St Paul, Minnesota, Kate Millett was the daughter of an insurance saleswoman and a contractor who left the family when she was fourteen. In her early years she went to parochial school, and then just across the Mississippi River to the University of Minnesota in Minneapolis for college. Although she subsequently attended St Hilda's College, Oxford, and Columbia University for her PhD, it was rebellion against an Irish Catholic upbringing in the American Midwest that she believes was formative in her life. Before she wrote *Sexual Politics* (1970), the book that established her as a Women's Movement 'theoretician', Kate Millett was successful as a sculptor, exhibiting in the Judson Gallery in Greenwich Village and in the Miniami Gallery in Tokyo. From 1961 to 1963 she was resident in Japan, where she met her future husband, the Japanese sculptor Fumio Yoshimura. Subsequently they shared a Bowery loft apartment, saying of their relationship that they were 'friends and lovers'.

Whereas, of the two leading American feminist theorists, Betty Friedan* essentially advocated economic independence and social and political leadership for women, a reformist position, Millett articulated a theory of patriarchy and conceptualized the gender and sexual oppression of women in terms that demanded a sex role revolution with radical changes of personal and family lifestyles. The clash between these two women was for a long time epitomized in their differing attitudes towards lesbianism. Having identified sexuality *per se* as the root of masculinist domination of women, Millett consistently sought to affirm lesbianism as part of her programme for the recognition of woman's freedom of sexual expression in general. Friedan, on the other hand, had opposed it – at least up until the National Women's Conference, sponsored by the Federal Government and held at Houston in November 1977. There she announced: 'I've had trouble with this issue. But we must help women who are lesbians in their own civil rights.' Friedan's and the Convention's acceptance of lesbian practice as one of their public policy proposals was seen by most commentators as a vindication of Millett's position.

Intellectually important, *Sexual Politics* was an instant best seller. Its central ideas are that all power relationships are rooted in gender, that men belong to a 'caste of virility' and exercise what they, women and society as well, believe to be a birthright power over women in every arena of human life. Patriarchy (male power) is the dominant mode of Western culture, and women are the victims of submission to it in the family, religion, politics, technology, education, economics, and psychology. 'Patriarchy,' she says, 'decrees that the status of both child and mother is primarily or ultimately dependent on the male.'

Patriarchy also sets woman against woman ('whore and matron . . . career woman and housewife') in the confines of seeking status and security through men. Women, Millett says, are separated and subordinated by men's control of institutions, production and access to information. While men invent and manufacture technologically advanced machines, women are not allowed to have the power of knowledge of their design and production, though they may be allowed to operate them. The central institution of male hegemony however is the nuclear family. The significant symbol for it is sexual intercourse with the man 'taking' the woman. This leads Millett to document, in a somewhat scattered way, what has come to be called sexism. She provides its historical context, together with four literary examples: the works of D. H. Lawrence*, Henry Miller* and Norman Mailer* exhibiting sexual politics, and Jean Genet* through his male homosexual queen illustrating an empathetic possibility with the oppression of women.

While *Sexual Politics* remains Millett's most widely read book, for her it represents an early triumph rather than the summation of her feminist activities. Specifically she says she has endeavoured to free herself of its laboured and academic prose. Having grasped the theory, she has since moved towards understanding its implications. *Three Lives* (1971) is a film that candidly reveals the actual lives of three women expressed in their own voices. An equivalent technique informs *The Prostitution Papers* (1971), a book that is divided into four voices, or chapters: two prostitutes, a woman lawyer who specializes in defending prostitutes, and the author's. While Millett did not invent the vocal reproductive form, her use of it is particularly intense, allowing her subjects to pour out the life and observation of prostitution without any apparent editorial interference. In *Flying* (1974) the mode is extended into her own autobiography. Abolishing privacy, a scrupulous transparency is implied as, in a succession of self-revealing details, she describes her relations with lesbian lovers and the subsequent creativity generated through relationships. *Sita* (1977), styled by one critic as a 'ticker-tape account', is even more explicit in its picture of the demise of a love affair, to the point where even her admirers have wondered in print whether the public wants to know quite so many moments in the life of Kate Millett.

Despite the egocentric indulgence, however, Millett's later books are a valid expression of a new kind of feminism, in their detailing of the suffering and stigmas in a woman's life. That intense and experientially expressed feminism will probably continue to exist alongside the more pragmatic programme proposed by feminists such as Friedan. It will remain an option for some, and Millett will continue to have a divided commitment between writing and action. In constant demand as a speaker and organizer on campuses and cities throughout the United States on behalf of the Women's Movement, she has been involved in many demonstrations, including the seizure, in 1970, of the Statue of Liberty to celebrate the House of Representatives' passage of the Equal Rights Amendment. Outside America she is the best known American feminist, perhaps because of a Marxist dimension in her writings. In 1979 she was expelled from Iran by the Khomeini government, having gone there to support Iranian women against the suppression of their rights. She is sure to be in the forefront, outspoken, volatile, insightful, and therefore, publicly both despised and revered in her centrality to the international women's revolution in the twentieth century.

Gayle Graham Yates

320
MIRÓ, Jóan 1893–

Spanish painter

Jóan Miró was born in Barcelona. Though his father was a prosperous goldsmith in that town Miró's antecedents were farmers and the landscape and peasant traditions of rural Catalonia were an important part of his early artistic and emotional life. In his late teens he studied at the local art school and in 1919, fully committed to being a painter, he made his way to Paris.

After a relatively short time there he made contact with the leading personalities of French art and almost immediately found himself at the centre of the Surrealist movement. By 1922 he had met, through André Masson, the poet Louis Aragon and the 'pope of Surrealism', André Breton*, and later, in 1927, he became a close neighbour of the painters Max Ernst*, Hans Arp* and René Magritte*. But despite this ideological barrage Miró, who returned to his native countryside every summer, retained a measure of independence. In works like *Self Portrait* (bought by Picasso*) and *The Farm* (bought by Hemingway*) he continued to preserve the identities of well-loved domestic objects realistically intact inside a decorative Cubist structure, but with *The Ploughed Field* (1923/4) reality becomes more scrambled until in *Harlequin's Carnival* (1925–5) human figures, animals, plants, etc., were completely replaced by clusters of new symbols, so laying the foundation of his particular personal style. Between 1925 and 1927 he experimented with the sources of creativity by working spontaneously in self-induced states of hallucination and impaired consciousness producing paintings, like *The Birth of the World* (1925), which departed further and further from the appearance of the common-sense world.

He married in 1929 and since then, with the exception of an unsettled period during the Spanish Civil War and the 1939–45 conflict, he has worked in Paris and Spain in a relatively consistent style over a wide variety of media. His paintings have been exhibited world wide, especially in America where he had his first one-man show in New York as early as 1930, and his vast output also includes designs for the theatre (for Massine and Diaghilev*), sculpture, ceramics and murals, notably in the Guggenheim Museum, for Harvard University and in 1957 for the UNICEF building in Paris.

Though linked historically with the Surrealists, and though he himself distrusts the term 'abstract', his particular use of signs and symbols is an important contribution to the development of non-figurative painting. While other pioneers more inclined to theory, like Kandinsky* or Mondrian*, compared non-representational art to music or mathematics, Miró, no doubt prompted by his interest in poetry and involvement with the mainly literary preoccupations of the Surrealists, instinctively chose the equally fruitful analogy of poetic language. But he also placed as much stress on the essentially visual aspects of painting such as colour, line, composition, etc., which the academic, illustrative artists such as Magritte or Dali* tended to neglect.

He cultivated this attitude to form from the start and the works in his first one-man exhibition of 1919 show that he was fully conversant with the latest pictorial advances made by Matisse* and Picasso and had learned to use bright colour, simplifications and perspective distortions. But this sophistication was not complete. In his landscapes and still-lives depictions of vegetables, animals, fruit, foliage and utensils were highly detailed and unschematic and this almost naive particularization carried through into the hieroglyphs which populate the later works. The groups of symbols in *Catalan Landscape* (1923–4) for instance can be given precise collective and individual interpretations. When placed against lushly painted backgrounds, suggesting interiors or landscapes, they conjure a typically strange non-naturalistic world, entered by the imagination rather than the senses, from which the laws of physical anatomy and gravity are missing. But they are not anarchic daubs. They are formally sound and they relate to a valid if fugitive variety of human experience.

It is precisely in this combination of opposites, combining freedom and control, an excess of form with an excess of content, introspective depth with an original system of public signs which accounts for Miró's continuing reputation. His influence in the 1940s is understandable. The Abstract Expressionists, particularly Pollock*, Gorky, and Rothko*, derived forms directly from Miró's earlier work, but it is a more unexpected tribute to the balance he achieves that he was just as admired in the 1960s when ideas of meaning, expression and psychology were out of favour.

David Sweet

See: Clement Greenberg, *Joan Miró* (1949); Jacques Dupin, *Joan Miró; Life and Work* (1962); Roland Penrose, *Miró* (1970).

321

MISHIMA YUKIO 1925–70

Japanese writer

Mishima Yukio is the most versatile, and some consider the best, modern Japanese writer. He committed suicide by *harakiri* after calling on Japan's Self-Defence Forces to rise up against the values of the country's post-war democracy. Some right-wing nationalists regard him as their hero, but in his lifetime politics mattered less to him than the desire to 'conquer the world' by his pen.

Mishima Yukio is the pen-name of Hiraoka Kimitake. In his childhood he was much influenced by his grandmother, a strong-willed and aristocratic woman who kept him apart from other children. The dark romanticism of his imagination is already obvious in his early poems and stories. 'A Forest in Full Bloom' ('Hanazakari no Mori', 1944), his first published story, was written at the age of sixteen. Set in a romantic past, it identifies the author as having a privileged destiny. Its theme is the longing for an absolute ideal of beauty, and the consummation of that longing in death.

The war made a deep impression on Mishima. He later described the period 1944–5 as 'a rare time when my own personal nihilism and the nihilism of the age and the society corresponded perfectly'. He was rejected as unfit for active military service, but exulted in the idea of a glorious death on the battlefield. He found himself completely at odds with the left-wing, egalitarian mood of the post-war years in Japan.

He graduated in law from Tokyo University and was a civil servant for a short time. In 1949 his first major work, *Confessions of a Mask* (*Kamen no kokuhaku*, 1949, trans. 1958), was acclaimed by the critics as a masterpiece. It is an autobiographical novel which describes the author's discovery of his own latent homosexuality, and the 'masquerade of reality' he constructs in order to come to terms with the world outside. The book displays a strong streak of narcissism, and explores a private world of sado-masochistic images – especially that of St Sebastian pierced with arrows – to which Mishima often returned in his later writings.

Over the next twenty-one years Mishima produced an astounding quantity of poetry, drama, essays and fiction, including forty novels and eighteen plays. *Forbidden Colours* (*Kinjiki*, part I 1951, part II 1953, trans. 1968) depicts the mentality and milieu of homosexuals in Tokyo. *The Sound of Waves* (*Shiosai*, 1954, trans. 1956) – the only straightforward love story Mishima ever wrote – brought him great popular success. Many people regard *The Temple of the Golden Pavilion* (*Kinkakuji*, 1956, trans. 1959) as his best novel. It is about a young Zen Buddhist monk perversely obsessed with the beauty of the temple (one of Japan's finest architectural treasures) who finally burns it to the ground. Its theme is characteristic: the sense of an insurmountable barrier between the self and others (the young monk here suffers from a ridiculous stutter) which is only assuaged by an act of wilful destruction. But Mishima also observed contemporary Japanese society with a keen eye. *After the Banquet* (*Utage no Ato*, 1960, trans. 1963), for example, is a vivid satire on the world of politics and patronage.

In 1966 Mishima produced the first part of *The Sea of Fertility*, the tetralogy which he intended to be his crowning achievement. The four successive novels, *Spring Snow* (*Haru no yuki*, 1966, trans. 1972), *Runaway Horses* (*Honma*, 1968, trans. 1973), *The Temple of Dawn* (*Akatsuki no tera*, 1969, trans. 1973) and *The Decay of the Angel* (*Tennin gosui*, 1970, trans. 1974), embrace the whole sweep of Japan's twentieth-century history. The central figures in each book are connected by a cycle of reincarnation. But in the final book the awaited sign fails to appear to confirm the thread of destiny, and the whole logic of the narrative is put in question. Mishima wrote this conclusion after making detailed plans for his own death, and it is a clear statement of his lifelong obsession with the impossible quest for some transcendent truth.

Mishima Yukio had an extraordinary zest for life, and thirst for every kind of human experience. In his late twenties he began a rigorous programme of body-building and martial arts, including *kendo* (swordsmanship) and *karate*. This played an essential part in his personal philosophy of the 'unity of thought and action', a concept with its antecedents in Zen. It also gave him the stamina to keep up a regular routine of writing through every night. At the age of thirty-three Mishima had an arranged marriage, which was successful. He later became the father of two children.

His romantic concern with the role of the Emperor and with *bushido*, the way of the warrior, recurs often in his writing. In 1965 he acted the central role in a film version of his own short story, 'Patriotism', about a young officer who commits *harakiri* at the time of the abortive military uprising in 1936. In 1968 Mishima founded the Shield Society, a 'private army' of one hundred unarmed youths who trained with the Self-Defence Forces. Four of the group's members were with him at the military headquarters in Tokyo where he made his appeal for a return to pre-war nationalist ideals, and one of them died with him.

Mishima's suicide profoundly affected the Japanese people, but had no direct political consequences. His action was widely condemned within Japan, and it prejudiced some critics' assessment of his literary achievement. There is an artificial and morbid strain in some of his work. But he portrayed Japanese life and society in a multitude of aspects with skill and assurance. He used his sure command of classical language and tradition to effect in his modern *Noh* plays and throughout his novels. The novels are untypical of much Japanese fiction in being consistently well-structured, and this makes them accessible to Western readers. Kawabata Yasunari* described Mishima as 'a writer with the kind of exceptional talent which appears only once every two or three hundred years in Japan's history'.

William Horsley

Mishima's other novels include: *Thirst for Love* (*Ai no kawaki*, 1950, trans. 1969); *The Sailor Who Fell from Grace with the Sea* (*Gogo no Eiko*, 1963, trans. 1966). His plays include: *Five Modern Noh Plays* (*Kindai Nogakushu*, 1956, trans. 1957); *Madame de Sade* (*Sado koshaku fujin*, 1965, trans. 1968); 'My Friend Hitler' (*Waga tomo Hittora*, 1968). See also: Henry Scott Stokes, *The Life and Death of Yukio Mishima* (1975); and John Nathan, *Mishima, A Biography* (1974).

322

MODIGLIANI, Amadeo 1884–1920

Italian artist

Modigliani was born in Livorno, Italy. In 1898 after a severe attack of typhus he was forced to abandon his academic studies in classics. From this point in his life his health was always bad with a tendency to tuberculosis from which he eventually died; it was this affliction which helped to earn him the title of 'peintre maudit'. As he showed great promise as a painter his parents sent him to study under Guglielmo Micheli, a pupil of the Macchiaoli painter Giovanni Fattori.

After a serious relapse in 1900 Modigliani travelled throughout Italy attending briefly courses at the academies in Rome, Florence and Venice. During this period he was particularly influenced by the new developments of the Sezession and Art Nouveau artists. It was above all the sculpture of Elie Nadelman which, along with his reading of Ruskin on the Italian Primitives and D'Annunzio's* ideas on aestheticism, led to Modigliani's first elegant attempts at carving in stone. From the beginning of his career his main concern was with the expressive possibilities that might be found in the human face and figure.

In 1906, dissatisfied with the parochial nature of contemporary Italian art, Modigliani moved to Paris

where, financed by his mother, he entered the Académie Colarossi and began to work seriously as both painter and sculptor. He quickly befriended leading avant-garde painters like Vlaminck, Utrillo and Picasso* and critics like André Salmon. His poor health and nervous disposition led him at this time to excesses of narcotics and alcohol which contributed as much to the linear tensions and dissonant colours of his art as to his untimely death.

In 1908 Modigliani showed five works at the Salon des Indépendants. The most important in terms of his future development was probably *Le Juive* of 1907 which shows a range of influences encompassing those of Cézanne, Gauguin, Picasso and Matisse*. His sculpture of this period shows the influence of African tribal art as well as that of his close acquaintance Brancusi*. Both media interacted upon one another positively and from 1910 to 1913 Modigliani's sculpture noticeably shows how far his interests in either were complementary. He attempted to discover formal values by largely disregarding naturalistic modelling and instead developing a synthetic resolution of planes. In this he was of course in step with the experiments of other Parisian artists. To this community of interest he brought a sinuous and rhythmic framework of line bounding his planes and bringing unity to the whole. In his painting these concerns are seen in the use of colour constructively rather than mimetically. Zones of colour bounded by a free and varied line create a simple harmony reminiscent of African and other primitive styles. Before 1914 one of the greatest influences on his work was the large Cézanne exhibition at the Galérie Bernheim. In particular he admired Cézanne's *Young Man with Red Waistcoat* which first showed him how far the painter can use his subject to expressively distort a human image in the service of a lyrical vision. By 1914 both his painting and sculpture can be said to have reached their maturity and the rest of his brief career was dedicated to the perfection and refinement of this personal style. The *Portrait of Paul Guillaume* (1916) is a typical example of his work at its best. The tendency to expressive distortion coupled with the peculiar mixture of refinement and primitiveness, in some respects a formula initiated by Degas, are resolved in a remote almost hieratic image. Despite Guillaume's casual pose and the picture's disregard for a smooth finish, the final image is one of mask-like detachment and even emptiness.

The physical facts of Modigliani's life in Paris during the war and until his death in 1920, described very evocatively in his daughter's critical biography of 1959, are of illness and poverty. He cared little for money and even during the harsh years of the war he was to be found selling his drawings in cafés for trifling sums. This life-style and dedication to art were virtually lost after the war and Modigliani's personal reputation rests partly on his aristocratic disdain for worldly success and his image of doomed martyr. It should perhaps be mentioned that for some time after his death he received very little acclaim in his native country.

In many respects the varied critical response to Modigliani's work reflects the stylistic uncertainties typical of all early twentieth-century art. His drawing, usually executed swiftly and with little pentimenti, has received praise as psychologically astute and formally terse and subtle. On the other hand critics as diverse as Wyndham Lewis* and Anthony Blunt have accused his work of being expressively shallow and inventively weak. These are ultimately questions the spectator must decide for himself by comparing his oeuvre with those of other figurative artists of the period struggling with the possibilities offered by recent experimentation in pictorial expression. There can be no doubt, however, that the later series of nudes, often depicting his mistress Jeanne Hebuterne (e.g. *Reclining Nude*, 1919), represent a unique and powerful contribution to the work of the Paris School. This power stems from a severity of line and richness of colour-matching which directly express his haughty, elegant and possibly nostalgic personality. He exerted virtually no influence on his contemporaries but, in the same way as Rouault*, showed those working in Paris how an expressionist tendency could enrich purely formal interests. He was not an intellectual nor a didactic artist and his work never veered towards neo-classicism or urbane cubism as did that of so many of his colleagues in Paris after 1914.

Richard Humphreys

By Modigliani: *Note e ricordi* (1945). See: J. T. Soby, *Modigliani* (1951); F. Russoli, *Modigliani* (1958, trans. 1959); J. Modigliani, *Modigliani: Man and Myth* (*Modigliani senza leggenda*, 1959, trans. 1959).

323
MONDRIAN, Piet 1872–1944

Dutch artist

Piet Mondrian, born in the small country town of Amersfoort into a strictly Calvinist family, became an early painter of Pure Abstraction. Of all the Abstract painters he might be considered the most widely influential and significant. In the early 1880s he studied at the Amsterdam Academy following a traditional Dutch landscape style of dark, almost monochromatic forms against light skies. An awareness of the work of the Dutch Symbolists added to Mondrian's painting the violently twisted and decorative line of Art Nouveau. By 1907–8 he had rejected dark tones for the brilliant colours of the Fauves and fine lines for the broad brushwork of the Post-Impressionists. In *The Red Mill* (1910–

11) there is considerable simplicity of shape coupled with strong strokes of vivid red.

During 1909 Mondrian became absorbed in Theosophy, the quasi-religious movement that held the central notion that a great 'New Spiritual Epoch' was at hand. During this era the metaphysical realities which in the past had only been available to a few privileged souls in the form of sacred mysteries would be appreciated by increasing numbers of people as their sensibilities became more refined. Like Kandinsky*, Mondrian believed that the artist, as seer, could through his art help produce this new state of being.

In 1911 Mondrian arrived in Paris and from a welter of artistic influences meeting in this foremost centre of the art world he chose Cubism as the most relevant. For him the unemotional scaffolding of Analytical Cubism structure pointed the way to increasing simplification of form. The famous tree and also church series were then carried out, whereby Mondrian severely reduced and gradually abstracted the linear structure of both organic and architectural subjects.

After meeting a fellow theosophist, Dr M. H. J. Schoenmaekers, in 1915 Mondrian formed an artistic group in Holland with his compatriot Theo von Doesberg. Much influenced by Schoenmaekers's neo-Platonic ideas on the relationship of beauty and mathematical proportion they produced a magazine called *De Stijl* and wrote the theory of Neo-Plasticism. This proposed that art had to hold an equal balance between two oppositions, the artist's desire for 'direct creation of universal beauty' and 'the aesthetic expression' of himself. These polarizations they saw as objective and subjective, the one that thinks and the one that experiences, and they wished to marry the two. Ultimately for Mondrian this form resolved itself into the basic opposition of vertical and horizontal, made more dynamic by the use of pure primary colours in solid blocks.

During the 1920s and 1930s, living in an all-white studio in Paris, Mondrian worked simultaneously over long periods on a number of canvases, intuiting the correct balance for his grid forms and colours. The steady progression of this period was from a work such as *Composition Grey Red Yellow and Blue* of around 1920 to *Composition Red Yellow and Blue* of 1937–42. The former is composed of large rectangles of the four colours interlocking and separated only by a narrow line. The latter replaces grey with a white ground that sparkles between the now important and heavier black line grid. Only four rectangles of colour exist in the work. The greater restraint at the same time gives an increased dynamic intensity of contrast.

At the request of Ben Nicholson*, who visited him in Paris, Mondrian went to England in 1938, and then moved to New York in 1940. Fascinated by the rhythms of urban life, of American jazz and the incessant energies of the 'Big City' he painted his celebratory and perhaps most dynamic work, *Broadway Boogie Woogie* (1942–3). In it the now small multiple blocks of bright colour seem to chase each other down the tracks of the grids and pre-empt with their dazzling colour and tonal oppositions the Op Art movement of the 1960s.

Pat Turner

See: Essays: *Plastic Art and Pure Plastic Art 1937 and Other Essays* (1945) and *Circle*, ed. Nicholson and Gabo (1937). See also: Michael Seuphor, *Mondrian* (1957); Frank Elgar, *Mondrian* (trans. 1968); H. L. C. Jaffé, *Mondrian* (1970).

324

MONOD, Jacques 1910–76

French molecular biologist

Monod's background was prosperous and cultivated. On the side of his father, a gifted painter, the family was Huguenot; his mother, an American of Scottish origin, was a talented musician. Monod himself hesitated in the 1930s between science and music: a competent cellist, he was also attracted to a career as a conductor. Indeed, this particular ambition, although unrealized, seems singularly appropriate in retrospect: the many virtuoso lectures he gave, particularly when international recognition of his scientific work had placed him firmly in the public arena, were, whether delivered in his patrician French or hardly less urbane English, remarkably assured performances, assertions of control over intellectual interests of great diversity, held together in apparent harmony. He trained as a biologist in Paris, teaching zoology there before the war, and in America (he was Rockefeller Fellow at the California Institute of Technology in 1936). In 1945, after distinguishing himself during the German occupation in the Resistance (his membership of the Communist Party, which he left over the Lysenko affair, dated from this period), he joined the Institut Pasteur. In 1965 his work there on the replication mechanism of genetic material and the processes by which cells synthesize protein led to his being awarded (together with François Jacob and André Lwoff) the Nobel Prize for Medicine and Physiology (its award to French researchers after a gap of thirty-four years was a much fêted boost for the country's scientific prestige). Monod subsequently withdrew from research; in 1967 a chair of molecular biology was created for him at the Collège de France, and in 1971 he returned to the Institut Pasteur as its Director. He had been critical of the decline in the Institut's fortunes and now presided over a controversial period of reorganization and financial recovery.

While Monod's contribution to science is clearly es-tablished, his broader cultural contribution, which must be essentially a function of his *Chance and Necessity, An Essay on the Natural Philosophy of Modern Biology* (*Le Hasard et la Nécessité*, 1970, trans. 1971), is more doubtful. Monod argues that while modern science and the postulate of objectivity upon which it depends are the foundation of the world we know, men still persist in beliefs about that world which betray an obsolete anthropocentrism. The exercise in *haute vulgarisation* which constitutes the book's centre is basically an unexceptional restatement of neo-Darwinian orthodoxy (it is random microscopic mutations which are the source of the variations on which natural selection operates), supported by considerable technical detail, in which the dominant terminology is drawn from information theory and cybernetics. Chance is at the very origin of life and therefore, he argues, life can have no general purpose; from this standpoint he dismisses the philosophy of Teilhard de Chardin*, dialectical materialism and almost all other explanations of reality as 'animisms', equally misguided. Monod's favourite stance is one of rigorous and unflinching rationality (with mock modesty he claims to be 'a captive of logic, and poor in global intuitions'), yet the ethic of objectivity and the 'authentic' life proposed in his conclusion belong rather to the realms of rhetoric. For many critics (among them Piaget*, Althusser* and Barthes*) Monod's authority is doubtful outside the area of his technical expertise, but *Chance and Necessity*, it can be argued, owes part of the interest it generates precisely to the ambitious scope which makes it vulnerable. This scientifically based statement of atheistic humanism, which takes its title from Democritus, carries an epigraph from Camus*, and is shot through with echoes of Pascal, has the qualities and faults of a specifically French literary-philosophical tradition.

Roger S. Huss

See: *Beyond Chance and Necessity: a Critical Enquiry into Professor Jacques Monod's 'Chance and Necessity'* (contributors: D. Bohm, T. Dobzhansky, A. Koestler, J. Lewis), ed. J. Lewis (1974).

325

MONTALE, Eugenio 1896–

Italian poet and short-story writer

Born at Genoa, Montale spent his childhood along the Riviera coast whose rocky landfalls deeply influenced his early imagery. He also felt the impact of certain fellow-Ligurian poets such as Ceccardo and Sbarbaro whose general outlook he shared. In his youth he abandoned his academic studies to train as a singer, but his singing career was itself cut short when he was conscripted into the army in 1917. After the war his interests led him more towards literature than music and his first volume of verse, *Ossi di seppia*, was published in 1925 by Gobetti whose liberal and anti-fascist views he greatly admired. In 1927 he moved to Florence where he first worked for the publisher Bemporad but was soon appointed Director of the Gabinetto Vieusseux. He was dismissed from the same post ten years later, in 1938, for failing to join the Fascist Party.

In 1939 he published his second collection, *Le occasioni*, contuining somewhat more personal, lyrical experiences. This was followed by a third in 1943, *Finisterre*, although he later incorporated this collection into a larger volume, *La bufera e altro*, in 1956. Both volumes deal allusively with political as well as personal problems and the former is partly a comment on the tensions arising during the war. In 1947 the poet moved to Milan where he became editor of the *Corriere della sera*, and it was in its columns that he first published the short stories making up *Farfalla di Dinard* (1956). This was followed by *Fuori di casa* in 1969 in which he reveals his wry anglophilia, especially his admiration for the eccentric figure of the dandy. A first volume of criticism, *Auto da fè*, appeared in 1966 and a second, more comprehensive one, *Sulla poesia*, in 1976.

In his old age the poet has unexpectedly turned out to be a prolific writer of verse in contrast with his earlier, more limited production. But his really major works are nevertheless those published in the hermetic era, even though his hermetic style, unlike Ungaretti's*, is based on the 'objective correlative' rather than the 'analogy'. His first collection, *Ossi di seppia*, establishes the poet's basic mythology, his belief that mankind can be divided up into Nature's 'fits and misfits', whom he refers to in a non-religious sense as the elect and the damned. Esterina in *Falsetto* is the archetype of the elect who experiences certain Boutrouxesque 'liberations' and sails through life as a thoroughly integrated character. Arsenio, by contrast, represents the alienated personality, but he is oddly a kind of man-talisman with the power to save other souls through acts of self-sacrifice. Such a vicarious religion of 'redemption', however, is still to be understood in a secular sense, and the aim is to integrate characters into an ethico-cultural sphere which Montale describes as a state of 'cordialità' or emotive wisdom. As a self-confessed Nestorian heretic, he tells us that he is more interested in the human than the divine aspects of Christianity and regards God as the Great Irrelevance. His gods and goddesses are instead those who appear to have been destined on earth to help the rest of us with the problems of living.

In *Le occasioni* he attempts to work out this mythology in terms of his own life, and for this purpose he introduces a nebulous female character called Clizia whose function is to integrate him into his previously postulated cultural sphere of 'cordialità'. She has elements of 'stilnovismo' about her and is even perhaps a combination of Dante's Beatrice and Petrarch's Laura. Nevertheless she ultimately fails in her task, because the poet himself is ineluctably one of the damned.

La bufera complicates the previously established mythology by introducing a veiled polemic against Fascism, although the centre of gravity of the collection still remains the problem of the individual in the starkness of his contingency rather than the poet's concern with social developments. Socially and metaphysically speaking, therefore, Montale's basic stance is that of the anti-hero, whose alternating and largely contemplative dialectic between static memorial poses and dramatic forms of recollection provides the main tension in his poetry. His imagery in all his collections is largely one of memorial 'absence', highlighting his attempts to bridge the gulf opened up by death or separation, and his constant aim is to re-establish points of human contact with others. This form of 'pious' recollection represents the limit of his humanism, the anti-hero's consolidation of man against the cosmos; and in the process only a minimal role is attributed to our corporate social efforts.

The poetry of Montale's old age is less hermetic than his earlier verse, and is accordingly more overt and conceptual in its implications. It is partly an ironic commentary on his previous stance as an anti-hero, since even his anti-d'Annunzian (see D'Annunzio*) posture does at times acquire certain heroic dimensions. Largely, however, its aim is to conceptualize his basic philosophy after its earlier hermetic presentation, and this can at times become a form of mocking self-parody. What saves this later type of verse is its witty urbanity, together with the touching humanity of the *Xenia* sequences, in which the previous metaphysical dialogue between the poet and Clizia is replaced by a more down-to-earth, domestic dialogue with his dead wife.

Montale was nominated a Senator for life in 1967 and has received honorary doctorates from a number of universities, including Cambridge. He won the Nobel Prize for Literature in 1975.

Professor Frederic J. Jones

Other poetic works: *Satura* (1971); *Diario del '71 e del '72* (1973); *Quaderno di quattro anni* (1977); *Tutte le poesie* (1977). Translations of his poetry into English: *Poems*, trans. G. Kay (1964); *New Poems*, trans. G. Singh (1976). See also *Eugenio Montale Selected Poems* in the Penguin edition (1969), also trans. G. Kay. Works about Montale: G. Nascimbeni, *Eugenio Montale* (1969), a biography; M. Forti, *Eugenio Montale* (1973); G. Singh, *Eugenio Montale, a Critical Study of his Poetry, Prose and Criticism* (1973); F. J. Jones, *La poesia italiana contemporanea* (1975); Almansi-Merry, *Eugenio Montale* (in English, 1977).

326

MOORE, George Edward 1873–1958

British philosopher

G. E. Moore was born in London into a comfortable middle-class family, and was educated at Dulwich and Trinity College, Cambridge, where he completed the Moral Science Tripos in 1896. Two years later he was elected to a six-year fellowship at Trinity. When his fellowship expired in 1904, Moore was saved by a private income from the urgency of seeking another position, but he returned to Cambridge to lecture in 1911, and became Professor of Mental Philosophy and Logic in 1925. Moore died in the university city where he had spent so much of his quiet and uneventful life.

Moore's name is often coupled with that of his friend and colleague at Trinity, Bertrand Russell*, and the two men probably deserve to be called the co-founders of the modern analytic tradition in philosophy. While Russell's *Principia Mathematica* was a towering landmark in the history of Logic, Moore's *Principia Ethica* (1903) has probably been even more influential in the sphere of moral philosophy. The book swiftly achieved an enormous reputation, particularly among the Bloomsbury Group (Keynes* called it 'better than Plato'); and its effect on theoretical ethics endures even today.

On the book's title page is a quotation from Bishop Butler: 'Everything is what it is and not another thing'; and Moore applies this apparent truism with devastating force to the concept of goodness, the subject of the work. Moore's startling claim is that all the many attempts throughout the history of philosophy to analyse or define goodness are doomed to failure, since goodness is indefinable: '*Good*, if we mean by it that quality which we assert to belong to a thing, when we say that the thing is good, is incapable of definition' (Chapter 1, paragraph 10). The attempt to define goodness in terms of something else Moore called the 'naturalistic fallacy'; goodness, he claims, is *sui generis*; it is a purely ethical quality which cannot be equated with any 'natural', non-ethical property (e.g. the property of being pleasurable). According to Moore, Jeremy Bentham and J. S. Mill, the chief exponents of the dominant utilitarian tradition in Ethics, are guilty of just this fallacy, by equating 'good' with some such property as 'being conducive to the general happiness'. Both Moore's specific criticism of Bentham and Mill, and his general onslaught against 'naturalistic' accounts of goodness have been immensely influential. The debate on whether ethical naturalism is necessarily fallacious, or can somehow be salvaged from Moore's strictures is still not concluded.

If the utilitarian, and other 'naturalistic' definitions of 'good' are to be rejected, how does Moore answer the fundamental question of Ethics, 'What is good?'

His solution is that goodness is a simple, unique unanalysable property which just has to be recognized intuitively: no reason can be given why something is good in itself. This account gave a powerful impetus to the Intuitionist approach to Ethics which flourished during the inter-war years (though for Moore himself the role of intuition was strictly limited: he insisted that the rightness or wrongness of particular acts was a matter for careful calculation).

There is also a more general dimension to the influence of *Principia Ethica*. From the beginning, Moore makes it clear that his enterprise is not a piece of arcane theorizing about the 'nature of goodness', but a painstaking and precise investigation of 'the predicate *good*'. This characteristic stance, which appears increasingly in the essays and articles Moore published later in his career (e.g. the famous 'Is Existence a Predicate?', 1936), is what makes it appropriate to call Moore a founder of the 'analytic tradition': precise linguistic analysis becomes the chief weapon and distinctive activity of philosophy. The main area in which Moore exercised his formidable analytic powers was not specialized or technical philosophical jargon, but rather ordinary language; and nowhere does this emerge more clearly than in his paper 'A Defence of Common Sense' (1923). Here Moore presents powerful arguments to show that some of our ordinary beliefs (e.g. in the existence of an external world) are so certain and deeply entrenched that any philosophical attempt to undermine them must be self-defeating.

The position taken here by Moore is often seen as influencing the development, much later, of the so-called 'Ordinary Language' school (cf. J. L. Austin*) of philosophy. Whether this counts to Moore's credit is debatable; for the exaggerated reverence accorded by some ordinary language philosophers to everyday speech led rapidly to a dreary and barren conception of philosophical enquiry. In fairness to Moore, however, he himself never argued that our ordinary beliefs and expressions must necessarily be the sole repositories of truth. The issue, in any case, is a minor one when set against the greatness of Moore's philosophical achievement. The pioneering contribution he made to linguistic analysis in general, and ethical analysis in particular, firmly secures him his place as one of the architects of twentieth-century philosophy.

Dr John Cottingham

See also: *Ethics* (1912). Moore's *Philosophical Papers* (published posthumously 1959) include 'A Defence of Common Sense' and 'Is Existence a Predicate?'. Useful introductions to Moore's work may be found in *English Philosophy Since 1900* by G. Warnock, and *Ethics Since 1900* by M. Warnock. Standard critical works are: A. J. Ayer, *Russell and Moore: The Analytic Heritage* (1971); and A. R. White, *G. E. Moore* (1958).

327
MOORE, Henry 1898–

British sculptor

The most celebrated sculptor of the twentieth century underwent an orthodox training at Leeds School of Art and then at the Royal College of Art in London. But from an early stage his sources of inspiration were extra-curricular. Roger Fry's* *Vision and Design* led him to Paris to experience the work of Cézanne; and at the British Museum he was deeply impressed by the sculpture of 'primitive' civilizations in pre-Columbian America, the Near East and Archaic Greece. It became clear to him, as he wrote in 1941, that 'the realistic ideal of physical beauty in art . . . was only a digression from the main world tradition of sculpture, whilst, for instance, our equally European Romanesque and Early Gothic are in the main line.' But a tour of Italy ensured that the Renaissance tradition also left its mark on Moore's work – as many of his Reclining Figures testify.

Moore's sculpture of the 1920s and 1930s is extremely diverse. Passing references to Picasso* and Hans Arp* are to be found, and to Mexican and African statuary; Moore's experiments with various media culminated in the late 1930s in a series of 'stringed figures', in which parallel threads of string or wire are set against the flowing curves of the sculptured mass. Several of his 'heads' and 'helmets' carry a surrealist flavour, and in 1936 Moore was a contributor to the International Surrealist Exhibition. But he never saw himself as a Surrealist; and although he was closely associated with Ben Nicholson* and Barbara Hepworth* in the same decade, Moore did not campaign on behalf of any specific attitude or theory. He has, however, always been an articulate analyst of his own work, and in 1937 he seems to have seen his role clearly. Brancusi* has made us shape-conscious, he wrote, by his simple, polished forms, which cast off the superficial excrescences that had overgrown European sculpture since the Middle Ages. But this 'one-cylindered' approach might no longer be necessary: 'We can now begin to open out, to relate and combine together several forms of varied sizes, sections and directions into one organic whole.' Moore's figures followed this course with mounting boldness, splitting into two, three, or four components. Bronze became his favourite medium, and he undertook an increasing number of large sculptures for exterior locations, where they might become an element of city architecture, or (preferably) of natural landscape. Some of Moore's later works are so 'open' that the spectator is able, and indeed encouraged, to walk through them.

Moore advised that 'the sensitive observer must learn to feel shape simply as shape'; many of his own designs have been furnished by the uncomplicated forms of bones and pebbles. But it is the human figure which, above all, has occupied Moore's imagination. As an official War Artist he depicted groups of men and women huddled in air-raid shelters, their faceless immobility suggesting an eternal capacity to endure. In both sculpture and drawing he developed the subtle potentialities of forms to suggest emotional states or qualities, in particular those of maternal or sexual attraction, which animate Moore's 'archetypal' themes of the reclining woman and the mother with child. The power of his *Sheep Piece* (1971–2) lies not only in the physical conformation of the two massive structures, but also in the psychological overtones of warmth and protectiveness which their relationship suggests.

Moore's international reputation was established after the Second World War through major exhibitions in New York, Venice, São Paulo, Toronto, Florence and Zürich. His eightieth birthday was marked in London by an exhibition in Kensington Gardens, largely of recent work, which displayed an undiminished grandeur and vitality.

Patrick Conner

A selection of Moore's writings can be found in *Henry Moore On Sculpture* (1966), ed. Philip James. See also: Herbert Read, *Henry Moore: A Study of his Life and Work* (1965); John Russell, *Henry Moore* (1973); Alan G. Wilkinson, *The Drawings of Henry Moore* (Tate Gallery catalogue, 1977); David Finn, *Henry Moore: Sculpture and Environment* (1977); and *Henry Moore 2: Sculpture and Drawings* (4 vols, 1957–77), eds David Sylvester and Alan Bowness.

328
MOORE, Marianne Craig 1887–1972

US poet

For her last two decades, Marianne Moore was considered 'the greatest living woman poet' in America, a neat little niche which has, on the whole, constrained the understanding of her poetic accomplishment. Sometimes considered eccentric, limited, 'whimsical' (i.e. what one might assume a woman poet to be), Moore has also been placed, wrongly, as a disciple of the Imagist movement. In fact, her deliberate complex poems develop far older traditions of emblem poetry and moral wit, formed according to her own version of modernism: collage-like overlays of the ordinary, the bizarre, and the quoted fragment which are expressed by a syllabic but strongly cadenced metre organized into stanzaic units of sense.

Marianne Moore lived a relatively quiet life, devoted to her mother and brother. After childhood in Carlisle, Pennsylvania, Moore moved to New Jersey and then (with her mother) to New York, where her almost sixty-year 'sojourn in the whale' ended with her being treasured as a kind of cosmopolitan regional poet. At Bryn Mawr College, Moore majored in biology (1905–9), which may partly account for the moral value her poetry puts on precise natural description. At Bryn Mawr, Moore's strong ethical sense was certainly sharpened by the blue-stocking's proud intellectual isolation. In her 'serial' poem 'Marriage', Moore rejected the institution which required 'all one's criminal ingenuity/to avoid!' 'Eve: beautiful woman' is 'the central flaw' in the 'crystal-fine experiment' of pure Adamic existence, too powerful for Moore: 'each fresh wave of consciousness/is poison.'

Many of Moore's early poems, which appeared from 1915 in the little magazines *Poetry*, the *Egoist* and *Others*, assume both an inner enemy in the poem's object of satire, and an outer enemy in a hostile or absent audience. Although Moore's poetry never needs recourse to *persona* to veil the writer's presence in the poem, it displaces her articulate anger by coolly addressing emblematic animals or modes of behaviour. 'You crush all the particles down/into close conformity,' she writes in 'To a Steamroller' (1915), attacking the materialist's destructive attempts to achieve 'impersonal judgment'. In the much-anthologized 'Poetry' her audience's philistinism is taken for granted. 'I, too, dislike it,' she begins, and then pretends to be 'Reading it . . . with a perfect contempt for it' until she discovers its capacity for the 'genuine'.

With the publication of *Poems* (1921) and *Observations* (1924) Moore established herself as an important American poet, a position confirmed by the *Selected Poems* of 1935. Scofield Thayer, editor of the long-established arts magazine the *Dial*, accepted many of Moore's poems and reviews, and from 1925 to 1929, when the magazine ceased publication, Moore did most of the *Dial*'s editing and wrote many articles for it. As an editor Moore intelligently publicized the modern movement, even if her tendency to tinker with work and censor it gave offence to James Joyce* and Hart Crane*, among others. In her perceptive 1931 essay on Pound's* *Draft of XXX Cantos* Moore took Pound to task for not distinguishing 'between Calvin the theologian and Calvin the man of letters'. Moore defended Calvin because, like the Prophets, Blake, Sir Thomas Browne or the natural historians and Elizabethan explorers she prefers to quote, his writing forms a traditional Protestant version of experience which Moore, uniquely of the modernists, was prepared to accept and use.

If Pound's Imagist poetic was a flight from abstraction, Moore's poetry used the material world as a means to describe abstractions. She was interested in exotic or mythical animals as borderline cases of the real, not escapes from it. 'The Jerboa', 'The Plumed Basilisk', 'The Frigate Pelican', 'Sea Unicorns and Land Unicorns', 'The Pangolin', 'The Arctic Ox' all tend towards essence because our habit hasn't blunted their 'natural' capacity for imposed meaning. 'The Jerboa', subtitled 'Too Much', with his 'shining silver house/of sand' is an emblem of humility, almost Blakean in its radiance.

The Romantic and modern terror at the gap between subject and object does not exist in Moore's poetry, where everything is already related. The mind's meditative play merges with the object, a deliberate wit which is expressed formally by Moore's stanzas. The first stanza is 'expedient' following the necessity of the subject, the rest turn the arbitrary pattern of the first into an order, the same within each poem, different from poem to poem. Moore's playing upon a curiously malleable 'real' recalls Wallace Stevens*, who wrote admiringly that for Moore 'Reality is not the thing, but the aspect of the thing'. At first reading Moore's poem 'He "Digesteth Harde Yron" ' 'has an extraordinarily factual appearance. But it is, after all, an abstraction.' Xenophon's 'camel-sparrow', who, Lyly asserted, ate iron, 'was and is/a symbol of justice', according to historian Bernard Laufer, not merely a stupid bird. Moore assembles her emblem through facets which compact into a kind of quiddity or *gestalt* without ever stabilizing visually.

> . . . he
> whose comic duckling head on its
> great neck revolves with compass-needle nervousness
> when he stands guard. . . .

'He' is equidistant from the encyclopedia ostrich and the meaning he dramatizes, a meaning which shifts from justice to the heroic solicitude in the course of Moore's interlocked stanzas. For a parallel to this imputed natural value one must look back in American poetry to Edward Taylor's 'Upon a Spider Catching a Fly' or forward to Elizabeth Bishop's* 'The Man-Moth'. Moore was not, however, a puritan. She takes too much pleasure in assigning her meanings, and she doesn't believe in original sin. In 'In the Days of Prismatic Color' Eve's gift is rather to make obliqueness ambivalent so that now 'Truth is no Apollo/Belvedere, no formal thing', however much one may long for that inaccurate ideal.

After the Second World War Moore felt more sure of her audience, and permitted her ethical views direct expression. In 'The Arctic Ox (or Goat)', the title poem of a 1964 collection, one quotation suffices. The poem ends with hortatory wit: if we can't use the wool which the musk ox generously produces, 'I think that we deserve to freeze.' From 1945 to 1953 Moore translated the *Fables* of La Fontaine. Since Moore undertook translating long after her style was fixed, and she paraphrases rather than imitates, the *Fables* are interesting mainly as Moore's homage to a kindred spirit (though she is actually more like Molière). Moore's *Collected*

Poems (1951) and her mistitled *Complete Poems* (1967, 1968) edit and omit many important earlier poems. 'Omissions are not accidents,' says Moore's one-line Preface to the *Complete Poems*. In the end Moore's belief in values such as 'Humility, Concentration, and Gusto' (the title of a 1948 lecture) and her hard-won power to show 'Feeling and Precision' operating together to reveal truth seemed certainties so alien to her society that it became easier to simply call her eccentric. Perhaps now her readers will find it easier to accept a modernism which isn't based upon despair.

Helen McNeil

See: Jean Garrigue, *Marianne Moore* (a University of Minnesota pamphlet, 1965); *Marianne Moore*, ed. Charles Tomlinson (1969); Laurence Stapleton, *Marianne Moore: The Poet's Advance* (1978), reviewed at length by Helen Vendler in the *New Yorker* (16 October 1978).

329
MORI ŌGAI (Mori, Rintarō) 1862–1922

Japanese writer, translator, critic and army doctor

Mori Ōgai was born in Tsuwano, a castle-town in the south-west of Japan, to a medical family of low samurai status. His early education was of the usual Confucian mould, concentrating on the study of Chinese philosophical works, but in 1872 the family moved to Tokyo and after several years spent studying German and preparing for entry to the university, Ōgai gained admittance to the medical department of Tokyo University in 1877. Illness before his final exams prevented him from graduating well enough to secure a government scholarship to study abroad and so in 1881 he joined the army as a doctor. He spent the next three years on research into army hygiene and on the administration of army medicine, still hopeful, however, that he might yet be given a chance to travel abroad. The chance came in 1884 when he was dispatched to Germany for four years of study under some of the leading medical researchers in Europe. His mastery of German and the ease with which he managed to fit into German society ensured that his years abroad were more rewarding than those of his contemporary and fellow-writer Natsume Sōseki* and that he gained a rare acquaintance with the cultural traditions that had inspired Japan's modernization. In addition to his medical research, he took pains to familiarize himself with German philosophical and literary writing, and gave thought to the problems posed by Japan's scientific backwardness and the process of cultural borrowing Japan was going through at the time.

Upon his return to Japan in 1888 Ōgai set out with missionary zeal to pass on what he had learnt and to ensure that medical and literary opinion did not lag behind their European counterparts. In the medical field he founded two journals and incurred the displeasure of his army superiors by arguing for the rapid modernization of medicine in Japan. He also founded a literary journal, published a number of translations of prose, poetry and drama, mainly from the German, and in the early 1890s published three novellas all closely based on his experiences in Germany. Amongst these was *The Dancing Girl* (*Maihime*, 1890, trans. 1975), which deals with an ill-fated amour between a Japanese studying abroad and a German girl, and touches upon such issues as the freedom that awaits Japanese out of the bounds of their own country and the difficulty for educated young Japanese of achieving anything without yielding to the authority of unenlightened tradition or compromising their hard-won individualism. In the field of literary criticism Ōgai echoed the German critics of the 1880s in rejecting the naturalism of Zola and warned against the confusion of the factual with the artistic; these points were somewhat premature for the Japanese literary establishment, for naturalism did not take root in Japan until the first decade of the twentieth century, but they do bespeak Ōgai's concern to keep debate in Japan abreast with that in Europe.

After service in the Sino – Japanese and Russo – Japanese wars and the publication of his comprehensive textbook on hygiene, Ōgai was in 1907 promoted to the rank of Surgeon General, a position he retained until his retirement in 1916. He had continued his work as a translator of literary works throughout these years but in 1909 he turned to creative literary activity again. In that year he wrote *Vita Sexualis* (trans. 1972), which is an autobiographical work with a fictional veneer and traces his developing sexual awareness from childhood until early adulthood; it was partly a serious study of sexuality, in which Ōgai had a medical interest, and partly a challenge, with its scientific and reflective qualities, to the self-indulgent sexuality of naturalist fiction in Japan, but it was nevertheless banned shortly after its publication.

In 1912 Ōgai turned away from the present as a source of artistic inspiration and took to the writing of history. The immediate cause of this was the suicide in that year, shortly after the death of the Emperor Meiji, of General Nogi, the hero of the battle for Port Arthur who had been personally known to Ōgai. This anachronistic manifestation of *junshi*, the loyal suicide of a retainer wishing to follow his master in death, prompted Ōgai to write a short piece entitled *Okitsu Yagoemon no Isho* ('The Testament of Okitsu Yagoemon') which deals with a similar set of circumstances from the seventeenth century and is based largely on fact. Ōgai expresses no definite attitude towards *junshi* in this work and his purpose seems rather to have been to explore the psychology and social attitudes latent in such expressions of feudal loyalty. By this time Ōgai was aware that Japan's modernization had brought in its train problems of individual morality and adaptation that he had not foreseen, and in this work and those that followed it he endeavoured to examine the authoritarian world of pre-1868 Japan and the traditions that were proving to have such a strong hold on modern Japan.

Ōgai's greatest literary monument is the series of historical novels and biographies he wrote in the last ten years of his life, in which he eschewed fictionality and the present and sought to understand the weight of Japan's past. But he also brought to literary and intellectual debate and to the advancement of medical science in Japan a rationalism which he gained from an understanding of the cultural traditions that were shaping the modernization of Japan during his lifetime, and his role as an interpreter of these to his countrymen was a considerable one.

Dr P. F. Kornicki

Other translations: *The Wild Geese* (Tokyo 1959); and *The Incident at Sakai and Other Stories* and *Saiki Kōi and Other Stories*, both ed. D. Dilworth and J. T. Rimer (1977). See: J. T. Rimer, *Mori Ōgai* (1975); and R. J. Bowring, *Mori Ōgai and the Modernization of Japanese Culture* (1979).

330
MORRIS, Robert 1931–

US artist

Along with Donald Judd, Sol Lewitt and Carl Andre, Morris is considered primarily to be a Minimal sculptor producing roughly human-sized works which stand on the floor, hang from the ceiling or project from a wall.

Born in Kansas City, Morris studied engineering, then worked in film and theatre whilst, in his studio in San Francisco, producing paintings strongly influenced by Abstract Expressionism. In New York in 1961 he made his first two sculptures. These resulted from his direct consciousness of space, movement and time, derived from his performance work and in relation to this knowledge of construction. One of these sculptures was *Box with the Sound of its Own Making*, a nine-inch wooden box which completely enclosed a tape loop recording of the noises produced during the making of the box. This work encapsulates much of Morris's artistic thought. The insistence upon forcing the viewer's awareness on to basic artistic processes of making is a device to remove him from art conventions controlled by taste and expression. At the same time the non-referential character of the work concentrates the spectator's attention upon the physical character of the

art object and the viewer's own physical relationship with it.

Morris's sculpture is simple and geometric in form except where the materials are soft and draped as they are in his felt pieces of 1967–70. The form takes up space in the environment. In addition, the volume of space surrounding the work and bounded by the walls of the room is considered as an integral part of the work. Viewer, sculpture and environment are in a tripartite physical relationship mutually presenting similarities and differences.

The sound of Morris's making, which is inherent in all his works, even the silent ones, suggests the man trapped in the box, determined by the event in which he is involved, by its existence, the process and the duration. There is however for the audience a differentiation of human determination from work to work. In some the viewer is controlled by the sculpture, as he is if he walks through Morris's long grey narrowing tunnel; in others the involvement means doing something to the work such as rolling it. Viewer and object in relationship are both partially determined by the other but the human has a degree of choice, for example as to the pace of movement, which gives him his humanity over and above that of being an object.

These simple works paradoxically because of their restraint focus consciousness on physical human processes which are in fact extremely complex and at times mysterious. Morris's insistence on the physical contains links with phenomenological philosophy which gives primacy to sense experience as the source of knowledge and attempts to bracket out already held values in order to consider the world anew. In his sculpture by exploring the lack of freedom of the individual because of his involvement with objects, as well as the spectrum of choices for action produced by objects, Morris causes his audiences to realize more fully the overabundance of objects in a consumer society.

Pat Turner

Other important works: *I-Box* (1962); Untitled 1967/8 (fibreglass suspended from ceiling); Untitled 1968 (9 open identical aluminium boxes equally spaced); *Continuous Project Continued Daily* (1969). An important series of articles by Morris appeared in *Art Forum* from 1968. See also two exhibition catalogues, of the Whitney Museum (1970) and the Tate Gallery (1971).

331
MUHAMMAD, Elijah 1897–1975

US racial and religious leader

Born into a large, impoverished family on a tenant

farm in Georgia, Elijah Poole was the son of former slaves. After receiving only a minimum of schooling, he left home at sixteen and worked at a variety of unskilled jobs. In 1919 Poole married Clara Evans and in 1923 joined the tide of black migration from the South. He moved to Detroit where he worked for a time at an automobile plant, and, like his father, also did some Baptist preaching. In 1930 Poole met Wallace D. Fard, a mysterious clothing pedlar who claimed to come from Mecca with the mission of awakening the Black Nation to their true and unique greatness within Islam. Under the influence of Fard, usually referred to as 'the Prophet', Elijah Poole's life took on focus and purpose. He was given the name Elijah Karriem, and when he soon became the Prophet's chief assistant, his name was changed to Elijah Muhammad in order to denote his higher status.

When Fard disappeared in 1933, he left some 8,000 black followers (mostly in Detroit) organized as the Nation of Islam. Elijah Muhammad was Fard's logical successor, and he also assumed the mantle of 'Prophet'. Muhammad organized additional 'temples' of followers in Chicago, Milwaukee, and Washington DC, but factional disputes and numerous attempts by outside groups to infiltrate the Nation hindered its growth. By 1942, in fact, membership had declined to less than 1,000. During these years of struggle, however, Muhammad had refined a programme of theological and moral precepts which would become the basis for a mass movement among black Americans in the years after the Second World War. He saw himself as a part of the long tradition of black nationalism in the US and declared that he intended to finish up 'what those before started'. Maintaining that Allah, in the person of Prophet Fard, had explained to him the true story of creation and assured him of the ultimate victory of the coloured peoples of the world, Elijah Muhammad told his black followers that they had been cheated and oppressed by the devil (represented by all whites). Muhammad explained, however, that black Americans had been chosen by Allah to redeem the promise of victory for other oppressed peoples. Before becoming capable of fulfilling this special redemptive role, black Americans were told that they must adhere to a rigid discipline of social and psychological reform. Elijah Muhammad viewed the poverty and degradation of the black masses as the result of persecution by the white devil, but he insisted that they could be saved only by themselves. On the one hand, he elaborated a complex regimen of behaviour partly influenced by orthodox Islam, and yet on the other hand, he borrowed heavily from the values of white middle-class America. Cleanliness, modesty, fidelity, thrift and self-denial were the cornerstones of Elijah Muhammad's social teachings.

The teachings of Elijah Muhammad struck an increasingly reponsive chord during the 1950s and 1960s.

As the civil rights campaigns grew in momentum, black Americans steadily gained in self-confidence and at the same time gave vent to a growing sense of group indignation at their oppressions. Elijah Muhammad's strategy during these years was to achieve a higher profile for his followers and his message. His most prominent minister was Malcolm X*, a former convict of keen intelligence and powerful personality. Largely through the work of Malcolm X, membership grew and considerable public attention descended upon Muhammad's Nation of Islam. His followers came to be known popularly as 'Black Muslims', and both whites and black civil rights leaders voiced fears of Muhammad's influence. Muslims were denounced as black racists and apostles of hate. And yet they grew in public stature throughout the 1960s, benefiting from the publicity attendant to the conversion of heavyweight boxing champion Muhammad Ali (Cassius Clay) and surviving a damaging split when Malcolm X left the sect (and subsequently was assassinated a year later) in 1964. As membership grew, so did the financial resources of the organization and the personal power of Elijah Muhammad. The Muslims opened a variety of small businesses and built up a multi-million dollar headquarters in Chicago, complete with elegant homes for Muhammad and the families of most of his eight children.

As the heat of the 1960s passed and as Elijah Muhammad's reputation increased, he became less strident in his denunciation of whites. Membership stabilized and the urgency of the movement declined. Nevertheless, at the time of Elijah Muhammad's death in 1975 there were over seventy-six mosques in the US and an estimated 200,000 members. At Elijah Muhammad's direction, his son, Wallace Muhammad, became the new leader of the Nation of Islam.

Professor Lester C. Lamon

See: C. Eric Lincoln, *The Black Muslims in America* (1961); E. U. Essien-Udom, *Black Nationalism: A Search For an Identity in America* (1962); and Louis Lomax, *When the Word Is Given* (1964).

332
MUNCH, Edvard 1863–1944

Norwegian painter

The naturalistic description of appearances in painting reached its culmination in Impressionism. Munch was a leading figure in transcending this, creating an art of the archetypal and symbolic. Born in provincial Norway, he became, through his assimilation of French art and especially that of Gauguin, one of Europe's principal artists at the turn of the century. The undulating lines of contemporary Art Nouveau, normally essentially decorative, provided him with a vehicle for pro-found psychological revelations. His principal themes were sex, love, loneliness, illness and death.

Many of his paintings originated in emotionally painful memories, for example his earliest masterpiece *The Sick Child* (1885–6) recalling the death of a sister. The intensity of this painting was largely achieved through prolonged scratching away of layers of paint, the novelty of which method caused contemporaries to condemn it as 'unfinished'. The pain of loss is ac-companied by the pain of isolation, as in *The Death Chamber* (*c.* 1894–5), where members of the bereaved family stand stiffly, each wrapped in his own incom-municable thoughts. In Munch's work, individuals are isolated not only from each other but also from nature, including their own nature, which becomes a threat-ening 'other'. Nature, furthermore, is symbolically equated with Woman. Munch was profoundly mis-trustful of sexual love, sensing union with a woman as a kind of death, as can be seen most obviously in *The Vampire* (1894), but also in his many versions of *The Kiss*. This was not simply misogyny – see, for example, his sympathetic treatment of a young girl's anxiety in *Puberty* (1894) – but something much deeper: the fear of the destruction of the creative ego through its (des-perately desired) union with natural forces. The flow-ing lines in many of his landscapes are the same as those of the hair in his ambivalently sexual *Madonna* (1893–4). In *The Scream* (1893), probably his most fa-mous painting, the form of the screaming creature in the foreground is echoed in the forms of the landscape beyond and the swirling blood-red sky above: anxiety is raised to a cosmic level.

Despite his emphasis, however, on the more painful aspects of life, Munch was aiming at a broad synthesis of all fundamental aspects of human experience, bal-ancing the dark against the light. In 1902 he exhibited, under the title of *The Frieze of Life,* a series of pictures which between them were intended to show 'life in all its fulness, its variety, its joys and its sorrows'. Close parallels exist between his art and the drama of Strind-berg, of whom he painted several portraits, and Ibsen, for whose *Ghosts* he designed the décor in Max Reinhardt's* 1906 production. Like them, he raised contemporary themes, acutely observed, to a more uni-versal plane, infused with a partly tragic, partly mys-tical vision.

In 1908–9, Munch underwent a nervous breakdown. With certain notable exceptions, his work after that date seldom achieved the dramatic intensity of his early work nor was it any longer revolutionary in art-historical terms. He had already, however, by then had the profoundest influence on European art, having be-come famous in Germany during the 1890s, somewhat helped by a fortunate art-world scandal. Technically, his paintings and graphic work, especially his wood-cuts, directly influenced such German Expressionists

as Nolde* and Kirchner*. But in a deeper sense, too, it could be claimed that he was the single most im-portant spiritual precursor of Expressionism. He com-bined the traditional mysticism and anxiety of Northern art with a specifically modern awareness of the predicament of the individual cut adrift from the restrictions, and the securities, of a socially sanctioned system of values.

Gray Watson

See: J. P. Hodin, *Edvard Munch: Norway's Genius* (1945); Hannah B. Muller, *Edvard Munch: A Bibliography* (1951); Otto Benesch, *Edvard Munch* (1960); Werner Timm, *The Graphic Art of Edvard Munch* (1969); Reinhold Heller, *Edvard Munch's 'The Scream'* (1972); John Boulton Smith, *Munch* (1977).

333
MURDOCH, Jean Iris 1919–

Anglo-Irish writer

Dublin-born novelist, philosopher and literary critic. One of the most prolific of England's post-war novelists – nineteen novels by the end of the 1970s – she has been the most consistently inventive, intellectually serious, and continually entertaining of the impressive little group of novelists who first emerged in the early 1950s (her *Under the Net* appeared in 1954, along with William Golding's* *Lord of the Flies* and Kingsley Amis's* *Lucky Jim*: a year after John Wain's *Hurry On Down*). In an important sequence of critical essays she has outlined her case for the 'liberal' school of fiction (a case which appears to have originated with her but is reinforced by the parallel arguments of her husband, the critic John Bayley, in his *The Characters of Love: A Study in the Literature of Personality*, 1960). She argues that the best fiction-makers – the preferred list includes Shakespeare, Jane Austen, George Eliot, Tolstoy – pre-sent a sense of 'the absurd irreducible uniqueness of people and of their relations with each other'. Modern fiction, in the era of imagism, surrealism, and Eliot*-Poundean* classicism, enclosed people into a restric-tive dryness, or boundedness, of personality and action. But life is neither static nor determined, it is messy and accident-prone, and people are at their fullest when allowed freedom to ride life's *divers et ondoyant* currents (as W. J. Harvey describes them in his related polemic *Character and the Novel*, 1965). It was by regis-tering this freedom and granting it to their people, by creating and advocating 'a community of free beings', that the liberal nineteenth-century novelists (products of an age of Liberalism) achieved their greatness. They also achieved virtue: 'The artist is indeed the analogue of the good man, and in a special sense he *is* the good man: the lover who, nothing himself, lets other things be through him.' That Iris Murdoch's ideas about the importance of freedom in novels owe a great deal to Sartrean* existentialism is clear from her *Sartre: Romantic Rationalist* (1953). Her interest in virtue – a goodness outside the monodic determinisms and consolations of either Marxism or Christianity – has been pursued not only in her novels but in her more straightforward philosophical reflections, *The Sovereignty of Good* (1970) and *The Fire and the Sun: Why Plato Banished the Artists* (1977).

Iris Murdoch has argued that Sartre's 'breath-taking argument' for the novel (and it is essentially her own) fails of fruition in his own fiction. And a similar gap between a noble theory and an actual fictional praxis is observable in her own novels. Repeatedly they press at the issue of freedom from the imprisoning nets of political and religious beliefs (*Under the Net* was not accidentally her first title). They keep asserting the importance of respecting 'the otherness of the other person' (John Bayley's phrase), particularly in love relationships. They endorse the right to their own 'utter particularity' of dozens of rebarbatively weird people. They take joy in the 'messy contingency', the surprising accidentalism of life (*An Accidental Man* is, again not accidentally, one of her fiction's titles, 1971). And yet her fictional world reads, cumulatively at least, as one tightly bounded by the narrow circle of upper-middle-class landowners, clerics, intellectuals, Fellows of Oxford colleges and these people's children, lovers, students and friends, which customarily composes it. There is freedom, but only within this exclusive talkative bourgeois world and the kinds of sexual groupings and regroupings it allows. Even *The Red and the Green* (1965), Iris Murdoch's rare political-historical novel, about Dublin's 1916 Easter Rising, quickly lapses into what most of her novels welcome, and most of her regular readers recognize, as the repeated sexual gothic of an 'Iris Murdoch' plot. (There is a devastatingly amusing parody of it in Michael Frayn's *The Tin Men*, 1965: 'I can't imagine,' exclaims a clever-dick exponent of the Murdoch way in novels, 'what you were thinking of writing a novel about if not sexual relationships.') 'Real people are destructive of myth,' she has said, 'contingency is destructive of fantasy and opens the way for imagination.' Richly engaging Iris Murdoch's novels usually are; none the less her imagination is continually collapsing into fantasy; just as her sense of what constitutes the contingent has established a recognizable mythology of English life that is all her own.

Valentine Cunningham

See: 'Against Dryness: A Polemical Sketch' (1961), reprinted in *The Novel Today: Contemporary Writers On Modern Fiction*, ed. Malcolm Bradbury (1977); A. S. Byatt, *Degrees of Freedom* (1965; Miss Byatt's bibliography lists the critical essays to 1965).

334
MURRY, John Middleton 1889–1957

English literary critic

Born to ambitious lower middle-class Londoners, Murry became a scholar of Christ's Hospital (1901) and of Brasenose College, Oxford (1908). But he preferred the bohemian life of Paris in the vacations to the tired civilization of Oxford and its promise of academic security. Under the shadow of Bergsonian* philosophy, Fauvism and Post-Impressionism, he began a risky lifetime's career of editing and reviewing by founding the magazine *Rhythm* (1911). In doing so he developed an exceptional 'nose' for the significant trends in modernist art, as well as submitting to such vital influences on his life as were provided by D. H. Lawrence* and Katherine Mansfield*, whom he eventually married.

Murry's endless absorption in self-analysis, the turbulence of his private life, and his vacillating character made him the butt of parody and satire to many contemporaries. Yet these were but the obverse of his merits as a critic – namely his capacity to enter vicariously into the lives and sufferings of authors, and to interpret them to the world. Hence his first important book, *Dostoevsky: A Critical Study* (1916). This was followed by work as editor of the *Athenaeum*, and as a reviewer for the *Times Literary Supplement*.

The year 1922 saw the publication of two of his most important books: *The Problem of Style* (the Clark lectures) and *Countries of the Mind*, a volume of essays which shows the breadth of his literary sympathies, as well as his ability to reveal the buried lives of the authors studied and (characteristically) of himself at the same time.

Soon after Katherine's death in 1923, Murry discovered 'God' – at least in the sense of a certainty that he was not, after all, alone in an empty universe. From this moment, despite the increasing desperation of his emotional life, his critical work took a new turn. *Keats and Shakespeare* (1925), *The Life of Jesus* (1926) and *God* (1929) really form connected studies of souls whom he saw as having preceded him through a 'vale of soul-making' into a spiritual state of completer humanity. Other seekers were later to be added to the pantheon: Lawrence (a much-flawed example) in *Son of Woman* (1931), Blake in *William Blake* (1933), Katherine herself, and even in the end *Jonathan Swift* (1954).

Despite the appearance of extreme heterogeneity in Murry's writings, the underlying project is clear: to explore the power of the imagination as it restlessly crosses the frontiers of poetry, philosophy, theology. This exploration is always a self-exploration also, and it came to expression not only in books, but in action: the editorship of *Peace News*, the founding of Community Farm, an involvement in many aspects of 'alternative politics', before and after the 1939–45 war.

Murry's sort of criticism is out of favour today. The lone entrepreneur has been largely superseded by the academic, the spiritual biographer by the student of a self-sufficient 'text', the human sympathizer by the structuralist or Marxist 'scientist' of literature. But while Murry loses favour with the critical establishment, he continues to stand for the things the general reader is interested in, and especially for the belief that reading great works is a way of meeting people who challenge the dull assumptions on which ordinary life is mostly conducted. For Murry, literature shows us how to live by putting us in the company of our spiritual superiors and exemplars. This is why his work will remain valuable, and even come into its own again, at least among those who are in pursuit of, as Murry put it, their own 'completion'.

Brian Wicker

Murry published sixty titles, covering (apart from those already mentioned) such topics as: *Aspects of Literature* (1920); *Things to Come* (1928); *Between Two Worlds* (autobiography, 1935); *The Defence of Democracy* (1939); *John Clare and Other Studies* (1950); *Love, Freedom and Society* (1957). A complete list is included in the standard biography by F. A. Lea (1959). Other biographical material is available in his widow's memoir, *To Keep Faith* (1959). See also: Rayner Heppenstall, *John Middleton Murry: A Study in Excellent Normality* (1934).

335
MUSIL, Robert 1880–1942

Austrian novelist

Robert Musil was born in Klagenfurt into a family of civil servants, academics and officers. His father, a civil service engineer and university professor, was ennobled in 1917, shortly before the fall of the Hapsburg monarchy. Musil's career shows both his attachment to conservative family traditions and his efforts to break free from encirclement by stifling authority and family expectations. He was sent to a military academy to be trained as an officer, but left to study mechanical engineering in Brünn and in 1902 he became an instructor at the technical university of Stuttgart (Germany). He developed a remarkable breadth of talent spanning the sciences and arts. In 1903 he took up philosophy and experimental psychology, as well as mathematics and physics at Berlin University, where he gained a doctoral degree in 1908 with a dissertation on the positivist philosopher Ernst Mach, whose theory of cognition strongly influenced Musil's perception of the crisis of individuality in the age of mass society. He stayed in Berlin until 1910, when he returned to Austria to work first as a librarian and then as editor of a

literary-political magazine (*Die Neue Rundschau*). He became an officer in the First World War, edited a newspaper for soldiers, worked in the press service of the Austrian ministry for foreign affairs and then as a civil servant in the war ministry. From 1923 onwards he lived as a freelance writer, constantly plagued by financial worries. In 1938, after the incorporation of Austria into the German Reich, he emigrated to Switzerland where he died in intellectual and social isolation.

Musil's first novel, *Young Törless (Die Verwirrungen des Zöglings Törless*, 1906, trans. 1955), is a sensitive fictional transposition of the author's experiences as a student at the senior army cadet school at Weisskirchen. In retrospect, i.e. after the rise and fall of fascism in central and southern Europe, this novel came to be seen as a subtle portrayal of the psychological predeterminations of fascist character traits slumbering beneath the smooth façade of conservative bourgeois respectability, correctness and patriotism, a reading which Musil himself supported. Influenced by Dostoevsky, Nietzsche and Mach, Musil rejected the naturalist mode of writing. He is therefore not interested in giving a faithful account of a boarding-school milieu pervaded by the sergeant-major mentality of the masters and the parade-ground command tone of their language. Musil's primary concern is with Törless's mind and his reflection of experience. For Törless reality is at one time a rationally ordered, causally connected set of alien and distinct entities, which at other times lose their distinctness, from a diffuse merger and assume a close and intimate familiarity. At such times Törless feels drawn into a kind of mystical union with people and objects, his identity dissolving in a contradictory complexity of de-individualizing emotions. Musil's description of Törless is clearly influenced by Mach's theory of cognition which conceives man as a disjointed ensemble of experiential moments, capable of a multiplicity of moral and amoral stances. Within the experiments in group dynamics, led by his fellow student cadets, Beineberg and Reiting, with Basini as their chief victim, Törless is a participant observer, identifying both with the persecutors and the victim. He becomes involved in a plot of blackmail, devious manipulation, cynical subjugation and dictatorial exploitation in which the victim responds with subaltern submission and servility. The interpersonal relations amongst the cadets in *Young Törless* do indeed reveal traits of the 'authoritarian personality' (see Adorno*) and a type of group dynamics, complete with aspects of mass psychology, which became all too familiar in the subsequent age of fascist dictatorships. Törless, far from opposing the callous schemes of the ringleaders in the plot, uses it to explore the confusions and uncertainties of his own morality, of the borderlines between the rational and the irrational. He finally has to leave the institution because he raises uncanny questions about the irrationality of the apparently rational which are felt to threaten the condescending paternalism and the positivist categories of truth operated by the school-masters. The tale about boys in their period of puberty becomes a visionary narrative about the seductions of authoritarian society and positivist rationality at the turn of the century, with the conservative intellectual fascinated by irrationalism, mass manipulation and cold connivance in experiments in human enslavement.

Musil's subsequent development can be plotted in a number of essays ('Politisches Bekenntnis eines jungen Mannes', 1913; 'Geist und Erfahrung', 1921; 'Die Nation als Ideal und Wirklichkeit', 1921; 'Das hilflose Europa', 1922; 'Der deutsche Mensch als Symptom', 1923), short stories and novellas (e.g. 'Drei Frauen' and the stories edited in 1936 under the title *Nachlass zu Lebzeiten*) and plays (*Die Schwärmer*, 1921, and *Vinzenz und die Freundin bedeutender Männer*, 1923). All these works may be regarded as preliminary studies to one of the most voluminous and complex novels of the twentieth century: The Man without Qualities (*Der Mann ohne Eigenschaften*, 3 vols, the first portion of which was published in 1931, the second in 1933, the rest posthumously in 1943 and 1952, trans. 1953–60). This major work, an intricately wrought pattern of fiction and thought, of powerful similes and philosophical abstraction, of detailed character portrayal and sweetly tentative sententiousness, has remained a giant torso.

The setting is 'Kakania', a country whose name was fashioned by Musil from the two 'k's in the official designation of Austria before the First World War, when it was 'kaiserly-kingly'. That Austria is not only a crucible of nations and races, of currents of thought traditional and modern, feudal and bourgeois, it is also used as a paradigm to describe and reflect the fundamental shifts in the socio-political fabric and in mental attitudes which occurred in twentieth-century European society as it grew out of and took over from that of the nineteenth century. In other words, the novel is an attempt to trace a world in transition, a world of traditional values and institutions, of aristocratic and popular culture pervaded by feudal stratification and order being undermined and exploded by the mathematical spirit of capitalist technology and profiteering rationality, by the cash nexus as the quantifying leveller of all qualities and the foundation of a democracy of clashing egoisms. Qualities of character once considered the inalienable hallmarks of personality formation, the distinctness of individuality, the uniqueness of personal demeanour are revealed as clichéed stances, as conformist practices following the shibboleths of a bygone age. They now serve as ready-made costumes which society has on offer in a variety of measurements, all calculated to make the individual useful and usable within the macro-social mechanism of a struggle of all against all and of the martial hegemony of states and superstates. This is the scenario

in which Ulrich, Musil's protagonist and alter ego, strikes his pose as a 'man without qualities', that is one who has an abundance of qualities but is committed to none of them. He is alienated by a society in a state of anomie, with its legal and moral consensus eroded, about to sweep away the feudal veneer of the old order to reveal the bleak pattern of a lacerated social cohesion being reforged by the relentless forces of global technology and technocracy. Ulrich is out of tune with the old aristocratic conservatism, but loves its idealist commitment to high culture. He is equally out of tune with the profiteering spirit of finance capital, which negates cultural values, but he admires its energy in reshaping nature and society. Unable to take sides, disgusted by the limitation of the real, he seeks refuge in a realm of pure spirit, of the infinity of the possible, in a utopian idyll where he can merge in mystical union with a kindred soul (his sister Agathe).

As a bourgeois in well-heeled retirement at the comparatively young age of thirty-two Ulrich experiences society and politics as a comic and fatal charade, as a world provoking cynicism, satire and withdrawal. Yet Musil is too complex and intellectually sophisticated to allow Ulrich's escape into a utopian idyll appear as a simple reaffirmation of pure mysticism and irrationality. The journey into the idyll of pure thought, pure feeling is part of Musil's pathology of the critical bourgeois intellectual's position in the history of contemporary society. This history is seen as one of warring ideologies hell-bent on dressing up the world of economic necessity as a realm of ideas, and economic prosperity as freedom and happiness. In *The Man without Qualities* Musil is attempting to restate the need for a world transcending material necessity. While large sections of humanity are still far from affluent, this kind of concern remains the privilege of a class living in luxury. But Ulrich's groping for a utopia of the possible is not so much a denial of the necessity for modern technology to become universally accessible; but more a protest against the reduction of man to conformism with programmes of social convention and mass-produced images. If the novel is agonizingly left fragmentary, then so are the issues of contemporary history which it reflects.

Wilfried van der Will

Musil's collected works are available in a critical edition, ed. Adolf Frise (9 vols, 1978). See also *Tagebücher* (2 vols, 1976). About Musil: Karl Dinklage (ed.), *Robert Musil. Leben, Werk, Wirkung* (1960); Burton Pike, *Robert Musil: An Introduction to his Work* (1962, trans. 1972); Wilfried Berghahn, *Robert Musil*, Rowohlt monographien (1963, trans. 1978). See also *Musil Forum*, a bi-annual journal (from 1975).

336

MUSSOLINI, Benito 1883–1945

Italian politician

Benito Mussolini was born in the Romagna and he was executed by Italian partisans on 23 April 1945. He was a qualified schoolteacher (his subject was French) but from an early stage he made his living as a journalist and propagandist. At this time he was a Socialist and after periods in exile in Switzerland and Austria he became editor of *Avanti!*, the Socialist journal. He became alienated from Socialism due to his demand that Italy participate in the First World War. In the aftermath of Italy's defeat at Caporetto in 1917 and the disintegration of Italian political life that ensued, Mussolini decided to form his own political party.

His supporters were revolutionary war veterans and determined anti-Bolsheviks who formed groups which amalgamated in March 1919 to constitute the Fascist party. By October 1922 their *Duce* had managed to become Prime Minister. His meteoric rise was partly the result of the crises of previous years but mostly because he threatened to seize power unless given it legally. And, indeed, his Fascist squads were ready to fight their way to the capital, which allowed his coup to be named 'the March on Rome'.

Mussolini was certain that his success in politics would depend on his possessing total control of Italian affairs. He not only sanctioned the assassination of the Socialist leader Matteotti in order to intimidate all opposition, but he ruthlessly imposed his own policies. By 1925 he was able to pronounce himself Italian dictator and to hold eight other ministries besides. In 1929 he came to an agreement with the Roman Catholic Church which ensured that it would not criticize his misdeeds.

The source of Mussolini's power was not traditional and it gave the world something new to think about. It was based on a readiness to use violence combined with a skilful charismatic approach, a combination of warlord and populist. He took personal responsibility for Italy's fortunes and, when the symbolic trains ran on time, he could also reap the credit. His followers, of whom many were non-Italian, saw him as the man who could transform backwardness through progress, a notion that could, however, only be fostered through dynamic foreign policies. Despite Fascist claims that Mussolini was 'always right', domestic successes were few.

After an early excursion into Greek waters, Mussolini decided in 1935 to colonize Ethiopia. He rejoiced in the gravest acts of barbarism which included the burning alive of a generation of intellectuals and other prisoners. The highpoint of his foreign ambitions came at Munich in 1938 where he, and one of his admirers, Adolf Hitler*, could prove that they were able to dictate to the great democracies as well as to their own people. Italian participation in the Second World War, which was part of this demonstration, failed nevertheless to produce anything but a series of humiliating disasters. Mussolini naturally suffered from this and when the Allies invaded Sicily he was overthrown. Following the Nazi invasion of Italy, however, he was freed in order to found the new Fascist Republic of Salo.

Mussolini's ideas were far cleverer than Hitler's although they lacked the Nazi leader's distinctiveness. Mussolini was more conventional, too, since the problems he identified were the traditional ones of Europe. Hitler's, on the other hand, tended to be ones which most people saw as specifically German. It was, as a consequence, easier for non-Italians to sympathize with Mussolini. He was, for example, always concerned to find the correct place for organized labour in society, even in Salo, something that Hitler tended to think unproblematical. Similarly it comes as no surprise to find that until 1938 the appeal of the Nazis' racial politics escaped the *Duce* although he later keenly assisted in the extermination of the Jews of Europe.

The intellectual background of Italian Fascism may readily be sought in a reaction against the dominant ideologies of the era, liberalism, Socialism and, perhaps, Catholicism. Action was more important than doctrine or debate. Fascism's relation to nationalism, however, was something that caused difficulties. In seeking a new aggressive form of nationalism, which was not defined like Nazism in racial terms, Mussolini's growing reliance on Hitler led to his own patriotism being doubted. And as Hitler's armies began to suffer defeat, even the Fascists of Italy began to question the wisdom of being sacrificed for Germany. Mussolini's political ideas depended on dynamism. Contraction and failure destroyed the fiction he had managed to purvey. It is, even so, a remarkable fact that twenty-two years of Fascist rule in Italy were ended only by the Allies' invasion and not by any widespread anti-Fascist revolt amongst the Italian people.

Dr Anthony Glees

See, in translation: *My Autobiography* (1928); *The Political and Social Doctrine of Fascism* (1949). About Mussolini: G. Ciano, *Diaries 1939–43* (1946); Edward Tannenbaum, *Fascism in Italy 1922–45* (1973); Dennis Mack Smith, *Mussolini's Roman Empire* (1978).

N

337
NABOKOV, Vladimir Vladimirovich 1899–1977

Russian/US novelist

Nabokov was a writer (primarily a novelist) who wrote in two languages (Russian and English), had two literary careers (as an émigré under the pen-name of Sirin and as a major American author), and whose art is preoccupied with worlds within and beyond other worlds. Born in St Petersburg, the son of a well-known liberal politician, he left Russia with his family after the Revolution of 1917. After taking a degree in French and Russian at Cambridge, he settled in Berlin, where he became a prominent and distinguished member of the Russian émigré literary world (the name Sirin is an obscure homage to the Russian publishing house which brought out Andrey Bely's modernistic novel *Petersburg*, much admired by Nabokov). His first novel, *Mashenka*, was published in Russian in 1926 and translated into German two years later (English *Mary*, 1970). Its theme of exile, loss, and erotic yearning, as well as its comic and parodistic elements, and its self-conscious illusionism, foreshadow later and greater works, especially those which hold up distorting mirrors to a distorted reality, like *Despair* (1936/1966), *Invitation to a Beheading* (1935/1960), and *Bend Sinister* (1947). The erotic strain in *Mashenka* foreshadows *Lolita* (1955), while the element of fictitious biography is developed in *Glory* (1932/1971) and *The Defence* (1930/1964) as well as two novels which, with *Lolita*, may be considered his crowning achievement, *The Gift* (1937/1963) and *Pale Fire* (1962), the former a sophisticated revaluation (by means of parody) of the Russian literary tradition, the other a novel lying hidden among the references and cross-references of a misleadingly erudite commentary to a limpid and lengthy pastiche poem in the manner of Robert Frost* (with more than a dash of Wallace Stevens*). The writings and rewritings of biography/autobiography, doubtless an artistic transformation of personal insecurity, also lie behind Nabokov's first novel in English, *The Real Life of Sebastian Knight* (1941).

Nabokov, who married in 1925 and had one son, Dimitri, in 1934, continued to live and work in Berlin, where his father had been assassinated by right-wing extremists in 1922, until history (a nightmare from which, like Joyce's* Stephen Dedalus, he could not awake) forced him to move to Paris, and thence, in 1939, to the USA. His peregrinations are recorded, very subjectively, in his 'real' autobiography, *Speak, Memory*, but his full bitterness at the horrific turn of historic events is evoked (always by way of parody and mockery, never direct commentary) in *Invitation to a Beheading*, a Kafkaesque work uninfluenced by Kafka*, and *Bend Sinister*, a kind of carnivalesque *1984* in which European totalitarianism is grotesquely garbed in the banalities of American comic strip. In America, in addition to a fairly obscure academic career, Nabokov enjoyed some small repute as a lepidopterist, until his life was transformed by the overnight notoriety of a novel which 'respectable' publishers would not handle, *Lolita*, now recognizably one of the seminal works of contemporary American fiction. Suddenly the émigré academic (not unlike his own creation, *Pnin*, 1957) became a best-seller. He moved with his wife to Montreux, and continued to live there in a hotel until his death, publishing regularly.

Lolita has been considered variously as a story of true love and as forming part of the 'literature of exhaustion', and there is no doubt that part of its fascination lies in its power of appealing at different levels. The love of the obscure émigré, Humbert Humbert, for the nymphet Lolita (both household words since Nabokov) is both text and pretext in a symbolic journey in the American tradition (and loaded with Americana past and present), part flight, part quest, where innocent desire plays a deadly game with retributive lust, the latter being embodied in the character of one Clare Quilty, C. Q. the pursuer, the avenging angel or the devil in disguise. Quilty is (like Emerald in *Pale Fire*) simply, on another level, the novelist playing chess with his protagonist, or the mechanism of 'plot' with its ineluctable ending. On the moral plane, he is an emanation of Humbert's guilty conscience, and when Humbert kills him in a mock-Hollywood shoot-up, Humbert is a lost soul. 'Decadent' as the subject-matter of *Lolita* may be, the centre of attention in the novel is not morbid psychology but the creative potentialities of language itself: Nabokov's wit plays over a wide range of narrative modes and devices, exploring in particular the tensions of memory and desire, the quasi-erotic longing for a symbolic order.

The exceptional awareness of the limits of literary conventions, born of Nabokov's peculiarly 'extraterritorial' (to use George Steiner's term) situation, has led critics to emphasize his kinship with such writers as Borges*, Robbe-Grillet*, and Pynchon*, at the expense of his Russianness and the direct relationship of his art to such writers as Pushkin and Chekhov via Bely. Nevertheless, just as Nabokov influenced American fiction, so it influenced him: his work became more labyrinthine and mannerist, while remaining beneath the surface profoundly personal, even plangent. The crazed commentator of *Pale Fire* is a sadomasochistic double of the scholarly Nabokov, who edited and translated – very brilliantly – Pushkin's *Eugene Onegin* (1964); the family chronicle of *Ada* (1969), strikingly combining motifs from American and Russian culture, is a kaleidoscope of statelessness as well as an exercise in translation; while the strangely brief *Transparent Things* (1972) and *Look at the Harlequins* (1974) are respectively the fictionalized epilogue and the index-cum-bibliography to Nabokov's life's work, as if death might coincide, by a higher authorial logic, with 'the end' on the page. Although occasionally hinting at new stylistic departures, these late works are nostalgic and solipsistic, suggesting that the mandarin stance Nabokov assiduously cultivated in his later years preyed, in the end, on his talent.

G. M. Hyde

Critical studies of Nabokov include: Page Stegner, *Escape into Aesthetics* (1966); L. S. Dembo (ed.), *Nabokov: The Man and his Works* (1967); Andrew Field, *Nabokov: His Life in Art* (1967); Karl Proffer, *Keys to Lolita* (1968); Julian Moynahan, *Vladimir Nabokov* (1971); Alfred Appel, *Nabokov's Dark Cinema* (1974); John O. Stark, *The Literature of Exhaustion* (1974); H. Grabes, *Fictitious Biographies* (1977); G. M. Hyde, *Vladimir Nabokov: America's Russian Novelist* (1977).

338
NADER, Ralph 1934–

US social reformer

Ralph Nader represents the consumer movement in the United States and a form of social activism reaching far beyond consumer affairs. With the publication in 1966 of his book, *Unsafe at Any Speed*, attacking the safety record of the General Motors' automobile, Corvair, Nader first came to wide public attention. Subsequent revelations of General Motors' surveillance of Nader helped launch his public career as a social critic and activist.

During the late 1960s and early 1970s, Nader and his assistants conducted a number of highly visible investigations of government agencies. These carefully documented studies of the failure of government agencies to protect the health, safety and economic well-being of the people provided the impetus for adminis-

trative and legislative reform. Relying heavily upon student volunteers and media exposure, Nader became, without public office or official position, one of the most politically influential persons in the United States.

While continuing the investigation of government and business, Nader in the mid-1970s turned increasingly to more permanent organizations. These groups specializing in litigation before the courts, lobbying before Congress or continuous examination of particular industries or government agencies became the foundation of Nader's activities.

The range of Nader's interests has been broad, ranging from meat and poultry inspection and automobile safety to nuclear energy. Through all of Nader's activities, however, run two themes: that power must be accountable and that individual citizens have the responsibility to ensure that accountability.

Nader's activities emphasized a number of principles to render accountable large concentrations of power. First, where possible, Nader has sought to break up concentrations of power. He championed the consumer co-operative movement and the rigorous enforcement of laws designed to limit the size of business enterprises. In part his long opposition to nuclear energy rests not only on safety concerns but also upon its centralizing effect upon social organization.

Second, Nader has sought to control the exercise of power by both business and government. In areas affecting public health and safety Nader has been a consistent advocate of effective government regulation. The Coal Mine Health and Safety Act, the National Highway Traffic Safety Act, the Occupational Health and Safety Act, the Meat and Poultry Inspection Act represent only some of Nader's successful legislative activities. Nader has worked for more open government. An early supporter of strengthened open government laws such as the United States Freedom of Information Act, Nader through his organizations has become one of the most effective protectors of citizen access to government information. These reforms sought to enable those affected by decisions to understand and influence those decisions.

Third, Nader has stressed the personal responsibility of those persons who work in large organizations. On the principle that evil is committed by persons and not organizations, Nader has pursued reform of the federal civil service to make government officials personally accountable for their decisions. In some areas, Nader has established the precedent that a civil servant may be subject to discipline on the basis of a citizen complaint to a body independent of the civil servant's agency. Nader has also successfully provided protection through legislation to government employees who expose corruption, wrong doing, waste, or inefficiency within government agencies and has sought to provide similar protections for employees of private industry.

Perhaps what makes Nader most unique is the tradition of individual citizen activism he has nurtured. Nader believes in the responsibility of the individual. Crucial to all reform is the ability of citizens to gain access to information regarding government and business, to participate in decisions, and to hold accountable those who exercise power over them. The responsibility of each citizen is to participate in public affairs. It is this vision of individual responsibility and of the role of the individual in social change that may be Nader's most significant legacy.

Professor Robert G. Vaughn

339
NAGEL, Ernest 1901–

US philosopher

Ernest Nagel was born at Nove Mesto, Czechoslovakia, moved to the United States in 1911, and was naturalized in 1919. He attended City College, New York, and obtained an MA in Mathematics and a PhD in Philosophy at Columbia University where he spent his academic career as Professor of Philosophy.

Nagel is most renowned as a teacher and expositor. These gifts were evident in his *An Introduction to Logic* (1934), written with his former teacher, M. R. Cohen, which is a lucid, lively, traditionally oriented introduction to logic. Its greatest merit is its extensive introduction to scientific method which made it a standard text for many years. In *Godel's Proof* (1958), written with J. R. Newman, Nagel succeeds in conveying the content and significance of Godel's* important theorems in a manner which made them accessible to non-logicians. It remains the best elementary exposition of Godel's results.

Nagel, who is a naturalist and logical empiricist, displays in his work the influence of Dewey*, Peirce, Russell* and the Vienna Circle (especially Schlick*) whose meetings he attended briefly. His *The Structure of Science* (1961) is a refined and rich account of the scientific enterprise from that perspective. A central theme in this work is the unity of science; the methods of all sciences are essentially those of the physical sciences. Particular attention is given to explanation which for Nagel, as for the logical positivists, is deductive in form. For instance, in giving a causal explanation of the occurrence of an event at some time in a system, one derives a statement asserting the occurrence of that event from statements specifying the state of the system at an earlier time and the laws governing the system. Explanations in biology in which the behaviour of a system is explained by citing goals or purposes of the system appear at first glance not to be deductive in form. According to Nagel these explanations can be translated into causal explanations of the

deductive type. This general line of argument is extended more controversially to all social sciences; social sciences are capable in principle of discovering general laws which can be used in deductive explanations and in so far as satisfactory explanations have been produced, they are deductive in form. While, according to Nagel, there are more practical difficulties in gathering the requisite data and in achieving value neutrality in the social sciences than in the physical sciences, progress in the former is to be attained by emulating the latter.

The doctrine of the unity of science is a consequence of Nagel's naturalism which he characterizes as the general assumption that spatio-temporally located material bodies are the only agents of causal change. All events, including mental events, are to be explained by reference to such bodies. There can, therefore, be no immaterial spirits. The limited ontology of naturalism generates difficulties in accounting for the ground of the truth of logical and mathematical statements. Nagel has explored these in his *Logic Without Metaphysics* (1956). For instance, the naturalist is committed to rejecting the thesis that arithmetical statements are truths about a realm of non-empirical objects, the numbers. Nagel objects to the view of Mill that such statements are contingent generalizations about physical objects on the grounds that true arithmetical statements are necessarily true. He articulates, somewhat vaguely, the view that mathematical and logical statements are to be understood through the role they play in inquiry and discourse. Their necessity is said to arise in virtue of their exclusive authority in any system of discourse.

W. H. Newton-Smith

Nagel's other works include: *The Logic of Measurement* (1930); *Principles of Probability* (1939); *Sovereign Reason* (1954); *Teleology Revisited* (1979). See also *Philosophy, Science and Method: in Honour of Ernest Nagel* (1969).

340
NAMIER, Sir Lewis Bernstein 1888–1960

British historian

Namier was born of Jewish ancestry in Russian Poland; educated at Lausanne University, the London School of Economics, and at Balliol College, Oxford; and took British nationality in 1913. He had a varied career as businessman, journalist, civil servant, Political Secretary to the Jewish Agency in London, and professor at Manchester University. His long-standing ambitions were to write a history of Europe during the nineteenth century and a history of Great Britain during the age of the American Revolution. Neither were fully realized, yet he created a new technique in historical research which even in his lifetime was known as Namierism.

Namier's main interest in European history was the growth of nationalism, especially in eastern Europe. His work took the form of short essays, collected in *Skyscrapers* (1931), *In the Margin of History* (1939), *Conflicts* (1942), *1848: The Revolution of the Intellectuals* (1946) and *Vanished Supremacies* (1958). They are marked by brilliant generalizations and acute insight rather than detailed research. His account of the origins of the Second World War, *Diplomatic Prelude, 1938–1939* (1948), though now outdated, was a pioneer work in this field. Namier's foreign birth and knowledge of languages made him eminently suitable to be the historian of Europe, but it was his work on British history that made his name widely known.

The publication of *The Structure of Politics at the Accession of George III* (1929) is a memorable event in British historiography. In 1930 came its successor, *England in the Age of the American Revolution*, the first volume of a work which was never completed. Namier spent the last years of his life as editor of the late eighteenth-century section of *The History of Parliament*, which he intended as the culmination of his work on British history but which he also left unfinished.

Namier's method was based on the study of biographies of Members of Parliament and the way they worked together, and was illuminated by careful research and psychological insight. It proved applicable to other periods of history, though there were many problems it could not solve. Because of his dislike of abstract political theory and his belief that much of human behaviour is senseless and irrational, Namier was accused by his critics of 'taking the mind out of history'. He believed in a psychoanalytical interpretation of character which sometimes led him into errors. Other interpretations of the eighteenth century have been developed since Namier's death, but his importance as a historian is not in the answers he gave but in the problems he raised and the techniques he developed for solving them.

John Brooke

Other works: *Facing East* (1947); *Europe in Decay* (1950); *Avenues of History* (1952); *Personalities and Powers* (1955); *Crossroads of Power* (1962); *Charles Townshend* (1964), completed by John Brooke. See also: Sir Herbert Butterfield, *George III and the Historians* (1958); Lucy S. Sutherland, 'Sir Lewis Namier', in *Proceedings of the British Academy* (1962); John Brooke, 'Namier and Namierism', in *Studies in the Philosophy of History*, ed. George H. Nadel (1965); Julia Namier, *Lewis Namier* (1971).

341
NATSUME SŌSEKI (Natsume Kinnosuke)
1867–1916

Japanese novelist

Sōseki was born into an established Tokyo family of townsman origins, but his birth was unwelcome to his parents for there were already five other children and the family fortunes were in decline. He spent the first ten, unsettled, years of his life mostly away from home and when his adoptive parents divorced in 1876 he returned to his real parents; this unhappy spell has widely been taken to be the source of the feelings of insecurity and alienation experienced by Sōseki in later years. In 1893 he graduated from the English literature department of Tokyo University with a rare facility for English, and after several years of teaching he was in 1900 sent to England for two years of study by the Ministry of Education. The years were painful for Sōseki, who lacked the funding, prearranged course of study and social contacts that had made Mori Ōgai's* years in Germany so fruitful; Sōseki seems to have suffered something akin to a nervous breakdown in London and was reported by Japanese visitors to have gone mad. On his return to Japan he lectured for four years at Tokyo University and then in 1907 resigned his position and contracted to write a novel a year for serialization in the Asahi newspaper.

Sōseki's literary début was marked by the publication in 1905 of *I am a Cat* (*Wagahai wa Neko de aru*, trans. 1961) and the number of imitations that appeared bears witness to its popularity. The narrator is a cat and his observations mainly concern the humans he comes into contact with; the device is perhaps an obvious one but Sōseki uses it to satirize the pretensions of the educated middle class in Japan and in this he showed his abiding concern for what he felt to be the problems of his generation – the new creeds of individualism and self-help and the exposure of Japan to all facets of Western civilization. Satire at the expense of the pretentious had a part to play in *Botchan* (1906, trans. 1972) too, in which the narrator-hero epitomizes the old-fashioned virtues that are commendable but inadequate for survival in the complex and westernized society Japan had become.

In 1908 Sōseki started on his first trilogy of novels with the publication of *Sanshirō* (trans. 1977), in which the eponymous young hero personifies the naive optimism of youth that in the other works of the trilogy gives place to disillusionment and a sense of malaise. *And Then* (*Sore Kara*, 1909, trans. 1978) introduced the qualities of reflection and intellectual pondering which are the hallmarks of the remainder of Sōseki's oeuvre along with triangular romantic situations and the guilt that follows the selfish exercise of individualism. The trilogy is completed by *Mon* (1910; trans. 1972) which depicts the consequences of the betrayal of a friendship in the interests of personal romantic success. These themes are pursued more relentlessly and with some narratorial ingenuity in Sōseki's last works, *The Wanderer* (*Kōjin*, 1912–13, trans. 1967), *The Heart* (*Kokoro*, 1914, trans. 1957), the autobiographical *Grass on the Wayside* (*Michikusa*, 1915, trans. 1970), and his unfinished *Light and Darkness* (*Meian*, 1916, trans. 1971).

Sōseki's following has been immense and the hagiography is growing constantly. His appeal lies in his attempt to grasp the truths facing his generation rather than the superficial and circumscribed truths favoured by his contemporaries, the Naturalists, and particularly in his exploration of the psychological consequences of the rapid modernization of Japan.

Dr P. F. Kornicki

See: Beongcheon Yu, *Natsume Sōseki* (1969); S. Matsui, *Natsume Sōseki as a Critic of English Literature* (1975); also H. Hibbett, 'Natsume Sōseki and the Psychological Novel', in D. Shively (ed.), *Tradition and Modernization in Japanese Culture* (1971).

342
NERUDA, Pablo (Neftalí Reyes) 1904–73

Chilean poet

Parral, central Chile, where Neruda was born and brought up by his train-guard father (his mother died early on), is the source of much of his basic imagery – a wet, misty, forested area (rain, river, sea – all natural elements). He adopted the pseudonym Neruda (from a nineteenth-century Czech writer) for fear of ridicule from his 'humble' companions. Neruda always saw himself as a natural, born poet. He linked poetry with the vitalistic elements and natural energies, although the myth of facility and spontaneity has camouflaged the careful craftsman behind the exuberant images. From the start Neruda assumed the role of bard.

Neruda was a very successful poet. His second book, *Twenty Love Poems* (*Veinte poemas de amor y una canción desesperada*, 1924), became one of the best known collections in Spanish. These poems deal with Neruda's move from his provincial roots to the capital Santiago in terms of two contrasting love affairs in a dense and moody language based on symbols and images taken from nature. The poet's *persona* is that of a melancholic anarchist at odds with the world.

But popularity was a trap and Neruda sought a diplomatic post (rather than train as a schoolteacher) to enrich his experience. From 1927 to 1943 he lived outside Chile, in the Far East (Rangoon, Colombo, Java), Spain and Mexico. This was the central (and best?) phase collected in the three volumes of his *Resi-*

dence on Earth (*Residencia en la tierra*, 1925–47). The first two *Residencias* (1925–35) are magnificent crisis poems dealing with Neruda's confusion and loneliness as a foreigner 'abandoned' abroad in terms of the breakdown of his literary and Romantic *persona*.

The borrowed surrealistic devices are moulded into his vision in hermetic poems working out shifting and obsessive emotional knots almost as therapy. But it was the Spanish Civil War, and his friend Lorca's* murder, that shocked Neruda out of his private spiritual anguish. His *Spain in my Heart* (*España en el corazón*, 1937) reflects this change of responsibility in a more conscious, controlled poetry, based on anger, indignation. His years in Spain confirmed his reputation as one of the foremost poets of his age.

Neruda was not converted to Marxism but found in it an answer to his own dark emotions: it was an ordering and granting of purpose to his life. Neruda's best political poems barely differ from his earlier ones with the same luxuriant, sensual language, a 'daylight' poetry of visual, tactile things. The year 1943 was crucial in the development of Neruda's Latin American consciousness: from a visit to Machu-picchu (the Inca fort) he began elaborating his dream of writing an epic combining his commitment to his 'pueblo' (people) with a poetic re-vision of Latin American history. Paralleling this, in 1945 he was elected senator and began a long career in politics that ended with being a presidential nomination (1970, standing down for his friend Allende). Political persecution and exile (1947) pushed him to complete the *Canto general* (1950), a poetical, political history of his continent. He aimed to create a new sense of identity based on his belief in his role and identity with his land and people where the poet interprets the silent masses. In 1951, with Picasso*, he won the Lenin peace prize.

This change towards an earthy simplicity – a constant in his poetry – led to his *Elemental Odes* (*Odas elementales*, 1954) celebrating tomatoes and fallen chestnuts and so forth. From here to his death Neruda was to combine all his phases, using long or short lines with a Protean freedom; the best books being: *Estravagario* (1958); *Memorial de Isla Negra* (1964); the posthumous *La rosa separada* (1973) and *El mar y las campanas* (1973).

Through this diversity Neruda remained a Romantic poet, the *registro sensible* (sensitive register); his best poems are always personal (great erotic and nature poems). Neruda exploited the sensuality of words, the body of the world. He was an amazingly popular public reader and he enjoyed this prestige. He moved through many relationships and places, but his best biography is his poetry (see Monegal). In his personal response to experience Neruda avoided introspection, self-analysis, philosophizing in favour of a poetry of love for the world, objects, women and physical sensations.

From 1970 to 1973 Neruda was Allende's ambassador in Paris. In 1971 he won the Nobel Prize for Literature. He died soon after his friend Allende fell. As a sensitive witness to his age, Neruda condensed in his work the history of Chile and of his continent; what unites his work and makes it Nerudian are the basic responses to nature and the self learned in Parral and childhood, the need to establish a poetic identity with his own working-class roots and his craftsmanship. Neruda was a poet who sought a responsible social function that fused his personal anguish (the misery of being isolated and unloved) with the need to forge a new myth (based on solidarity) as a way to deal with the individual's death. He was both innovative, modern and anachronistic, prolonging the Romantic/symbolist tradition.

Jason Wilson

The three-volumed *Obras completas* (1973) is the basic text; see his *Confieso que he vivido. Memorias* (1974, trans. as *Memoirs*, 1978). See also: N. Tarn (ed.), *Selected Poems* (1970); B. Belitt, *Five Decades. A Selection (1925–1970)* (1974); R. Pring Mill, *Pablo Neruda. A Basic Anthology* (1975). Criticism: G. Brotherston, *Latin American Poetry* (1975); in Spanish, E. R. Monegal, *El viajero inmóvil. Introducción a Pablo Neruda* (1966); A. Flores (ed.), *Aproximaciones a Pablo Neruda* (1973).

343
NICHOLSON, Ben 1894–

British artist

Born into a family of extravert artists, Ben Nicholson studied for a brief period at the Slade School of Art, but then moved rapidly away from the mainstream of Edwardian painting. During the 1920s, during which he worked closely with his first wife Winifred Dacre, his still-lifes became increasingly more schematic, employing the pared-down profile of a bottle, a glass or a guitar, and sometimes scraps of newspaper or lettering. He travelled frequently on the Continent, where he was inspired by the work of Cézanne, Picasso* and Braque*, and in the following decade by Mondrian*.

In the mid-1930s Nicholson's work became abstract to a more radical and controversial degree. He experimented with rarefied colour and, significantly, with carved surfaces; in 1934 his first white reliefs were exhibited in London. In the same year he married the sculptor Barbara Hepworth*. Well aware of the close relationship of his own painting to other forms of art, he became in the mid-1930s an active member of 'Unit One', a group of British painters, architects and sculpturs which spread the concept of a 'modern movement' in Britain. With Naum Gabo* and the architect Leslie Martin, moreover, he edited *Circle – International Survey of Constructive Art* (1937); among the contributors were

Mondrian and Le Corbusier*, and *Circle* firmly identified the work of Ben and Winifred Nicholson, Henry Moore* and Hepworth with the School of Paris and with an 'international modern' style.

Nicholson's art was not restricted to austere geometrical forms; he has remained fascinated by the outlines of household utensils, the coastal curves and rooftops of Cornwall (where he lived during the 1940s and most of the 1950s), and the contours of the lakes and hills of Switzerland. In his view abstraction represents not a withdrawal of the artist from 'reality', but a means of bringing art back into everyday life, and a liberation of form and colour. The constant features of his work are delicacy, precision and a readiness to explore new textures and configurations. Towards the end of the 1950s he began to increase the scale of his productions, a development which led in the 1960s to his 'relief projects' for free-standing walls. Nicholson has enjoyed international recognition since the 1950s; a major retrospective exhibition of his work toured the United States in 1978–9.

Patrick Conner

The artist's statements and reminiscences are collected in *Ben Nicholson*, a *Studio International* special issue, ed. Maurice de Saumarez (London and New York 1969). Exhibition catalogues: Tate Gallery, 1969; and *Ben Nicholson: Fifty Years of his Art*, Albright-Knox Art Gallery, Buffalo, N.Y., 1978. See also Herbert Read, *Ben Nicholson, Paintings, Reliefs, Drawings* (vol. I, 1948; vol. II, 1956), and *Ben Nicholson, Drawings, Paintings and Reliefs 1911–68* (1969).

344
NIEBUHR, Reinhold 1892–1971

US theologian and social moralist

Niebuhr was ordained to the ministry of the American Evangelical Church in 1914 and from 1915 to 1928 he was minister of the Bethel Evangelical Church in industrial Detroit, an experience which was strongly to colour his thinking and activities for the remainder of his life and career. On the one hand, he viewed at close quarters the impersonalism, self-interest, callousness and cupidity of American business and industrial life; on the other, he experienced with dismay the hopeless inadequacy to deal with this of the mild and moralistic idealism of contemporary American theology, especially that determined by the utopian and progressivist Social Gospel, which had been heavily influenced by turn-of-the-century European liberal protestantism.

Called to be Professor of Applied Christianity in Union Theological Seminary in New York City in 1928, he became one of the most important figures within American protestantism in the following forty years. It was widely alleged that Niebuhr was heavily influenced early in his career by the new neo-orthodox theology associated with Barth* and Emil Brunner, and there is truth in this allegation. Certainly, much of his effort was directed from the beginning towards resuscitating the Christian doctrine of sin, and of original sin, and it is perhaps unfair that Niebuhr's work has been interpreted almost exclusively as devoted to this topic, for there is much in it besides. He taught that the essence of sin is pride, the pride of man in his human accomplishments which is forever in danger of being absolutized. This sin is to be characterized as *original*, for there is nothing in the human dimension which is untouched by it – industrial advance, creative culture, the impressive products of religion. In his earlier days Niebuhr was impressed and influenced by Marxism, and his sharpest words seemed to be reserved for American big business and the products of 'the American Dream', built as these were on what he regarded as an excessive American adulation for and pursuit of individualistic, capitalistic freedom, unrestrained and unhampered by state control and interference. But as his thought developed, he became increasingly critical also of the pretensions of (leftwing) revolutionaries, who were tempted by their pride to absolutize *their* achievements in a godless direction. Also, his profound researches on the Christian doctrines of sin and grace impelled him to judge that the Marxist analysis of the human predicament, as grounded in economic and social factors alone, was superficial and unacceptable. In other words, his increasingly theo-centric theology reflected his disillusionment with merely human panaceas.

Influenced as he was by the Barthian protest in Europe, and although firm parallels can be drawn between Barth's work and his own, certain clear divergences developed as Niebuhr's thought developed. He became extremely critical of the marked 'churchy' tone of Barthian neo-orthodoxy, and came to deplore the tendency of such theology to be inward-looking, designed to alter and determine the thought of those within the Christian community, to the detriment of going out into the world with the intention of engaging and challenging and changing the thought of those in factory, board-room and market-place. And indeed, Niebuhr himself was no mere academic theoretician, but during his career actively involved himself in political, social and international affairs, both off and on academic campuses. Again, it is vital to recall that his heavy stress on sin was but the other side of the coin of *human freedom*, for which he had a high respect. Indeed, sin is a *misuse* of freedom; man sins *in* freedom. This view made him very critical of Barth's tendency so to exalt the sovereignty and freedom of God that man's dignified and responsible freedom is undercut. Third, Niebuhr was (unlike the Barthians) anything

but a Christian exclusivist; he spoke of a 'hidden Christ' operating in the human dimension as a whole, and never denied the possibility of grace to those who live and strive outside the Christian circle. Accordingly, he spoke of those 'indeterminate possibilities' which belong to mankind as such, striving for human betterment and a more just society. It is most unfortunate that this aspect of Niebuhr's optimism is not better known than it is, in order at least to offset the unjust stereotype of him as a thinker whose principal topic was human sinfulness and limitation.

Possibly the phrase which most readily springs to mind at the mention of Niebuhr's name is 'Christian realism', a theme which further distinguishes him from neo-orthodox Barthians. For Niebuhr taught that Christians must not shrink from going out into the world in order to engage in social and political predicaments of great complexity and even danger. But if they do, they must avoid political and ethical naivety like the plague. They must not fail to recognize that social reality is an area of power, and that therefore there may be occasions when power must be balanced with power. For these reasons, Niebuhr himself did not hesitate to attack the pacifists of the 1930s. He deplored their naive and quietistic refusal to dirty their hands with 'militarism', because they did not see that a power-movement like German National Socialism could, in the circumstances, only be countered and destroyed by superior power. Likewise, in the context of American political life, he did not on occasion shrink from advocating the use of power within the state in order that the weak and defenceless be defended and justice upheld. Although he personally abhorred violence, his Christian realism led to a refusal to absolutize pacifist forms of non-resistance.

Although Niebuhr objected to being called a 'theologian', and although he has been stereotyped as a social moralist and political activist, it would be gravely mistaken to interpret his thought outside of that Christian faith which insists that the moral ambiguities of history cannot be finally eliminated in space and time, and that the consummation of world affairs is only to be looked for in the final judgment and reconciliation of God.

Professor James Richmond

Niebuhr's works include: *Does Civilization Need Religion?* (1928); *Moral Man and Immoral Society* (1932); *The Nature and Destiny of Man* (2 vols, 1941–3); *Christian Realism and Political Problems* (1954). See: C. W. Kegley and R. W. Bretall, *Reinhold Niebuhr, Social and Political Thought* (1956); G. Harland, *The Thought of Reinhold Niebuhr* (1960); John C. Bennett, 'Reinhold Niebuhr', in A. W. and E. Hastings (eds), *Theologians of our Time* (1966).

345

NIEMEYER, Oscar 1907–

Brazilian architect

In 1930 Niemeyer began his architectural studies at the National School of Fine Art in Rio de Janeiro and in 1934 joined the office of the influential Lucio Costa who at that time was responsible for much of the restoration of Brazil's historic buildings. Costa, who tried to dissuade Niemeyer because of the limited amount of work he could offer such a promising young man, became one of the two major influences in his life. The other was the important European Le Corbusier*, who paid a brief visit to Brazil in 1929 and returned for a spell of three months in 1936 to work on his plans for the campus of the University of Rio de Janeiro and a new building for the Ministry of Education. Niemeyer worked directly under Le Corbusier and as a result of this fruitful and exciting experience produced his designs for the Athletic Centre in Rio and the Aeronautical Training Centre at São José dos Campos. Like Le Corbusier he saw architecture as a fine art and continued to associate with painters and sculptors, believing that a successful environment can only be achieved if all those concerned with the total design are closely involved with the project right from the start and like Le Corbusier in this respect he was something of an elitist.

In 1939 he built the Brazilian Pavilion for the New York World Fair in conjunction with Lucio Costa with whom he was later to be associated on a far grander scale in his most dramatic contribution to modern design at Brasilia.

The dominant style in Brazilian architectural history is the extremely flamboyant and richly decorative Portuguese Baroque which came to a full colonial flowering in a country which offered an equally rich and exotic natural environment for its undoubted excesses. A somewhat mundane functionalism followed, but after the Second World War Brazil became one of the leading countries in the development of the ideas of the Congrès Internationaux d'Architecture Moderne (CIAM) culminating in 1957 with the concept of Brasilia.

Brasilia was conceived as a bureaucratically controlled city of superblocks and functional zoning. Luca Costa drew up the Utopian plans and Niemeyer was appointed Architectural Adviser to Nova Cap, the organization instituted to create the brave new capital. Later he was made Chief Architect.

Though we may have second thoughts as to the wisdom of the scheme, bearing in mind the bleak living conditions of the majority of Brazilians at the time and bearing in mind that Brazilian political systems are far from democratic, it can be argued in Niemeyer's defence that he did see the project as an architectural challenge and did approach each individual building with care and attention to functional rightness.

He designed the Hotel in 1958 and later the same year the President's Palace. He built the Law Courts and the Cathedral and the whole scheme was based on a policy of rapid urbanization. Despite the urgency, Niemeyer's forms have a grace and refinement and his solutions to the varying problems set by the diverse requirements are novel and wholly satisfying. The result is a kind of super-modern Baroque reduced to a crisp geometric formal arrangement which well answers the needs required of it.

Niemeyer's first really personal contribution to modern architecture was the Church of St Francis which he built at Pampulha outside Belo Horizonte in 1942 and, though not without its critics, it has a rightness and simplicity of form well suited to its modest scale.

The house he built for himself outside Rio de Janeiro in 1953 reflects his understanding of Le Corbusier's civilized thoughts on how to live well and it seems that it is at this scale that Niemeyer is at his best and not in the vast impersonal scale of Brasilia. Like Le Corbusier he is often tempted to overreach himself.

John Furse

See: *The Work of Oscar Niemeyer*, Foreword by Lucio Costa (1950); Charles Jencks, *Modern Movements in Architecture* (1973).

346

NOLAND, Kenneth 1924–

US painter

Kenneth Noland was born in Asheville, North Carolina. After war service in the US Air Force he studied art at Black Mountain College which, though dominated by the Bauhaus purism of Josef Albers*, also attracted various talents of the American avant-garde including John Cage*, Buckminster Fuller* and Merce Cunningham. He took further advantage of the GI Bill to study for a year in Paris, returning to settle in Washington DC in 1949.

In Washington he taught painting and drawing mainly at Catholic University and over a period met and became friendly with Clement Greenberg, David Smith* and the painter, Morris Louis. At this time Noland's work was heavily influenced by Klee* and Mondrian*, but in 1953, after a visit to New York with Louis where they saw in Helen Frankenthaler's studio her *Mountains and Sea* (1952), it moved in a new direction. The significance of this painting was technical. It was made not by applying opaque pigment to a prepared ground with a brush or knife but by pouring thin water-based paint directly on to absorbent canvas. This meant that instead of being just the filling in, of drawn decorative or geometric shapes colour was granted a new freedom directly to form, with the paint, looser, almost natural elements. Noland's use of this innovation clearly shows, combined with geometric structures which recall his studentship under Ilya Bolotowsky at Black Mountain, in his first mature works of 1958. In these, like *Ex-Nihilo* (1958) and later *That* (1958/9) and *Virginia Site* (1959), he used simple target-like configurations with distinct rings of different colours interspersed with areas of plain canvas, surrounded by a loose halo of thinner paint.

In 1959, when he exhibited these paintings, he met Jules Oliski and Frank Stella*, making up the triumvirate of 'colour painters' whose presence dominated the New York galleries and the art magazines for most of the following decade, supported first by Greenberg and then another critic, Michael Fried, who saw in them the culmination of the Modernist tradition of abstract art. Since then he has been internationally exhibited and collected and has had regular one-man shows in New York. The devices used in the paintings changed; from circles to chevrons then to horizontal bands, such as the 22 ft long *Via Blues* (1967). In 1971 he made a set of works which returned to the mottled surfaces of the stain technique, e.g. *Sutter's Mill*, and in the last four years he has experimented with irregularly shaped canvases. Since 1966 he has also made metal sculpture.

Noland's paintings, though really quite simple and often very beautiful, were the subject of intense concept-laden contemporary promotion which has tended to distort their real value. What will remain of his reputation in the future is therefore hard to calculate.

David Sweet

See: Kenworth Moffett, *Kenneth Noland* (1977). Articles for critical background: Clement Greenberg, 'Louis and Noland', in *Art International*, vol. IV, no. 5 (1960); and Michael Fried, 'Art and Objecthood', in *Artforum*, vol. V, no. 10 (1967.

347
NOLDE, Emil 1867–1956

German painter

Born into a German peasant family in an area then Danish, and now Polish, Emil Hansen (he took the name of his village, Nolde, only in 1902) was trained as a wood carver in Flensburg; then, after periods in Munich and Berlin, he taught technical drawing for six years in St Gall. At the age of thirty-one he committed himself to painting, studying in Munich, in Paris at the Académie Julian, and in Copenhagen, where he met his wife. From 1900 he divided his time between the island of Alsen and Berlin. His work gradually evolved from the heightened Impressionism characteristic of Sezession art, and in 1906 he found himself lionized by Kirchner* and the wild and rebellious young artists of *Die Brücke* in Dresden. In 1910 he quarrelled bitterly and publicly with the Sezession president, Max Liebermann. But meanwhile, in 1909, he had completed his first fully mature work, *The Last Supper*, and this was soon followed by a nine-part altarpiece, *The Life of Christ* (both are now at the Nolde Foundation at Sëebull). In 1913–14 he took part in a government expedition to the South Seas, which confirmed him in his primitivistic tendencies.

His character as a painter was now formed, and he developed little over the next twenty years, gradually withdrawing to the house he built near the North Sea. His splendidly immediate watercolours, of flowers and dramatic skies, date mostly from this period. In 1920 Nolde had joined the Nazi party, attracted by its nationalist and racial tenets, but in 1937 he was singled out for special condemnation in the Degenerate Art campaign. 'All the ideals of my life,' he wrote in 1942, 'are turned into disgust.' Isolated in his house at Sëebull, the old man believed he had actually been forbidden to paint, but embarked secretly on a series of tiny watercolours, self-exploratory and automatist in character, the *Ungemalte Bilder* or 'Unpainted Pictures', which many regard as his testament. After the war he was one of the few great survivors left in West Germany, and – perhaps undeservedly – enjoyed a martyr's homage.

Nolde's contribution to twentieth-century art lies above all in his uniquely powerful colour, and in his creation of perhaps the only fully convincing religious paintings of our time. 'Expressionism' was a label he always rejected, but in some respects his art epitomizes all that we mean by it; an art that appeals to the guts rather than the intellect, and where intensity is sought above all other values. Its primitivism was authentic, but it also comes out of a complex historical synthesis; in the 1900s he met Munch* and Ensor, looked at Grünewald and medieval art, read Nietzsche, and linked all this to his experience in Paris of Daumier, Van Gogh and Gauguin.

The 1909 *Last Supper* owes much to Rembrandt's *Conspiracy* but goes further towards the primitive; the mask-like heads are his inheritance from Ensor, but here they no longer embody hypocrisy. In Nolde the mask regains the meaning it had in the Dionysiac theatre – the god that speaks through man at moments of extreme emotion – and *Excited People* (1913, Sëebull) seems almost an illustration to Nietzschean ideas. Nolde always opposed himself to the element of negation in the modernist aesthetic (and implicit in Cubism): 'Instead of disintegration I sought after cohesion, instead of the break-up of forms I wanted concentration, and in place of taste and technique I searched for deepened expression, broad planes, and healthy strong colours.' He also spoke of an art made up of 'magically illuminated areas of planes', and in *Christ Among the Children* (1910) we watch the sequence of a blue Christ turning away from the sombre apostles, to become identified with the yellow abandoned rhythms of the children. Often Nolde borders on vulgarity, but his magnificently frank sensuality – as in the *Candle Dancers* (1912) – gives him a full-bloodedness rare in our time. In describing him as 'a demon of the lower depths' his contemporary Paul Klee* was contrasting him with his own more butterfly-like sensibility, yet at the same time affirming his value. 'Metaphysical or unworldly abstractionists often forget that Nolde exists. I do not.'

Timothy Hyman

Most of Nolde's major works are in the Nolde Foundation at Sëebull, who also publish his writings and other material. See: Peter Selz, *Emil Nolde*, Museum of Modern Art, New York 1963; Werner Haftmann, *Emil Nolde* (1959).

348
NOZICK, Robert 1938–

US social philosopher

Born in Brooklyn, educated at schools in New York City and in the universities of Columbia and Princeton, Robert Nozick held a Fulbright Scholarship in Oxford before his first appointment at Harvard in 1965. His *Anarchy, State and Utopia* (1974) won a National Book Award in 1975, and was widely hailed as heralding the emergence of a brilliant new philosophical super-star.

Although its flow is sometimes interrupted by indulgences in superfluous symbolism, the verbal parts are consistently fresh, luminous and vital. The book is perhaps best described as a general offensive against the prevailing tendencies towards a state-imposed uniformity of condition; tendencies epitomized and, hopefully, rationalized in the main life's work of Nozick's respected older colleague John Rawls*. In *A Theory of Justice* Rawls assumed: that all the wealth produced or to be produced in any society must be available for distribution, free of any legitimate prior claims, at the absolute discretion of the sovereign collective; and that all individual talents, and the fruits of their exercise, are to be regarded as collective assets. Curiously Rawls neither recognized these assumptions as totally socialist, nor considered them reasonably questionable.

Nozick, by contrast, argues for a conservative alternative: that everyone has a right to keep both whatever he has, unless it has been unjustly gained, and whatever he may in the future by the free exercise of his own talents and energies acquire. In a typically radical argument Nozick asks us to consider a situation in which half a population is born two-eyed and the other half eyeless. Suppose that eye transplant operations were possible. Would justice require that the state take all the second eyes by force for transplanting into the sockets of the eyeless? But now if we allow that everyone has a basic right to their bodily parts, how can we possibly maintain that everything produced by the exercise of any of those parts must be treated as a collective asset, as public property? With the same vigorously swinging libertarian radicalism Nozick also argues: that income taxes are morally equivalent to forced labour; that the position of a citizen subject to, and supposedly part of, an unlimited Rousseauian democracy can be no better than that of a slave; that the protagonists of a Rawlsian, or any other, programme of approved distribution will have to forbid all capitalist acts, even between consenting adults; and – just by the way – that in the USA today everyone ought to be a vegetarian.

Professor Antony Flew

O

349

O'CASEY, Sean 1884–1964

Irish playwright

Born into the Dublin working class at a time when conditions in the city were perhaps the most barbarous in Europe, O'Casey might seem on first reflection to be a classic proletarian artist. However, both his background and his career are more complex than any such formulation.

O'Casey's family had roots in both the Catholic masses and in the tiny Protestant minority. Brought up in an atmosphere of missionary Protestantism and poverty, he quickly turned his back on all religious affiliations. His plays, however, not only reflect sectarian tensions (e.g. *The Plough and the Stars*, 1926), their language utilizes the rhythms and images of Victorian hymnology and pious rhetoric – usually to bitterly ironic effect. The occasional satires directly at sectarian folly in the early plays grow, none too painlessly, into the theme of *The Bishop's Bonfire* (1955).

Educated on the Bible, Shakespeare, and visits to Dublin's conventional Victorian theatre – Boucicault and music hall for the most part – it was O'Casey's lot to find on his entry to the theatre in the Abbey an admirably independent company but one dominated by self-consciously aristocratic ambitions. O'Casey's relationship with W. B. Yeats* was never easy, and the latter's rejection of *The Silver Tassie* (1928) virtually sent O'Casey into English exile. His relationship with Lady Gregory, on the other hand, was deeply felt on both sides, and assisted his maturing as a writer.

O'Casey's politics evidence a further area of uneasy dislocation. A left-winger from the outset, he regarded the 1916 rebellion as a bourgeois adventure in nationalism; the antagonism which greeted *The Plough and the Stars* in part stems from the Irish public's inability to assess its political origins, and in part reveals their resentment of O'Casey's personal detachment. In the 1930s he constantly announced himself to be an orthodox communist, though his exile in England lends an air of unreality to many of his later pronouncements.

The plays are usually seen as falling into two groups. The first – *The Shadow of a Gunman* (1923), *Juno and the Paycock* (1924), and *The Plough and the Stars* – are ostensibly naturalistic dramas of working-class life during the Irish troubles; the Shakespeare of *1 Henry IV* is a

powerful influence here. *The Silver Tassie* is a transitional work employing expressionist techniques in Act 2 depicting the Great War. From the 1930s onwards there is a greater concentration on formal organization together with a more determined political purpose – *The Star Turns Red* (1940) is important here. The late plays have a caustic celebratory quality, as in the near-unstageable but brilliant *Cock a Doodle Dandy* (1949).

O'Casey's reputation has fallen now. His language, in its gutsy lushness, appears sentimental, while his political concerns can appear remote. He is nevertheless a natural man of the theatre, whose appetite for life often allowed him to swallow some rather undercooked moments in dramatic construction. His six volumes of autobiographies (1939–56, collected in *Mirror in My House*, 1956), written in the third person, shed much light on Irish conditions and attitudes. In an age where literature has overshadowed theatre, and where the seminar room dominates both, O'Casey's talents require a sympathetic hearing.

W. J. McCormack

Other plays include: *Within the Gates* (1934); *Red Roses for Me* (1946); and *Behind the Green Curtains* (publ. 1961). See: David Krause, *Sean O'Casey: The Man and His Work* (1962); R. Ayling and M. J. Durkan, *Sean O'Casey, a Bibliography* (1978); C. Desmond Greaves, *Sean O'Casey, Politics and Art* (1979).

350

ODETS, Clifford 1906–63

US dramatist, screenwriter and director

Clifford Odets was born into a wealthy, middle-class, Jewish family which moved from Philadelphia to the Bronx when he was aged six. Leaving school at fifteen, he acted with several small theatre companies, becoming a founder-member of the influential Group Theatre, set up in 1931 by Harold Clurman, Cheryl Crawford and Lee Strasberg to revitalize the social meaning of drama, using and exploiting Stanislavskyan* techniques. A poor actor, Odets turned to writing, and *Waiting for Lefty* was first performed in 1935. He was by then a member of the Communist Party, and his commitment to left-wing politics is nowhere more in evidence. A 'proletarian morality tale', *Lefty* is radical in both content and dramatic method. Set at a highly-charged union meeting, where a proposed strike is under discussion, actors planted in the audience make it a part of the action, and the theatrical performance a truly group experience. Like Brecht*, Odets used a number of 'alienation' techniques to present a series of flashbacks within the framework of the strike meeting. But while Brecht's plays of the 1930s are often coldly analytical, *Lefty* appeals to raw emotions. In his production notes Odets advised: 'Do not hesitate to use music wherever possible. It is very valuable in emotionally stirring an audience.' These techniques also indicate the long-standing influence of the cinema on Odets's theatrical work.

Lefty, and plays like *Till the Day I Die* (1935), dealing with the struggle of the German Communists, led to Odets being labelled a proletarian writer. But he was more often concerned with the spiritual decay of the middle classes, notably in *Awake and Sing!* (1935). This has resulted in frequent comparisons with Chekhov, with whom he shared an ear for dialogue, and an ability to portray that peculiar kind of self-absorption which leads to self-destruction. Clearest examples of this are *Golden Boy* (1937), *The Big Knife* (1949), and *The Country Girl* (1950; retitled *Winter Journey* in Britain).

Odets was soon courted by Hollywood, and wrote his first screenplay, *The General Dies at Dawn*, in 1936. He continued to write for Group Theatre, but after the company folded in 1941, his stage-work became increasingly sporadic, and less overtly political. (Odets's testimony before the House Committee on Un-American Activities in 1952 lost him many admirers.) His plays became more obviously personal, concerned with the tortured individual rather than class conflicts. The earlier, ideologically-committed pieces are often criticized for their naivety, but they have a passion and an integrity which is lacking in much of the later work. The central character in *The Big Knife* gives up a promising career in boxing to become a successful Hollywood actor, selling his soul to the studio; the play ends with his suicide. Odets repeatedly returned to this theme of lost opportunities and forsaken principles, and it is easily related to his own transition from committed playwright to, ultimately, screenwriter on an Elvis Presley* pot-boiler.

The major achievement of Odets's later work is its vivid characterization; this is particularly true of *The Country Girl*, his most frequently revived play. But Odets's most important contribution to twentieth-century drama remain the Group Theatre productions, and especially *Waiting for Lefty*. He here brought something new, in form and content, to the American stage, and was a major influence on the development of a political theatre in Britain in the late 1930s.

Paul Nicholls

Other plays: *Paradise Lost* (1935); *Rocket to the Moon*

(1938); *The Silent Partner* (1938); *Night Music* (1940); *Clash by Night* (1941); *The Russian People* (an adaptation, 1942); and *The Flowering Peach* (1954). His screenplays include: *None But the Lonely Heart* (1944); *Deadline at Dawn* (1946); and adaptations of his own plays. In 1960 he also directed *The Story on Page One*. About Odets: R. Baird Shuman, *Clifford Odets* (1962); and E. Murray, *Clifford Odets* (1968). See also Harold Clurman, *The Fervent Years* (1945).

351
OLDENBURG, Claes 1929–

US artist

'Everything I do is completely original – I made it up when I was a little kid.' Born in Stockholm, Oldenburg was brought up in Chicago from 1936. Slightly an outsider, he created an imaginary island, Neubern, a coherent parallel reality worked out in minute detail, which contained the germs of most of his later work.

After interdisciplinary studies at Yale, he worked as a crime reporter while attending night classes at the Art Institute of Chicago. Arriving in New York in 1956, it was the life of the slums that inspired his exhibition/environment *The Street* (1960). Next year he set up *The Store*, in which were exhibited parodies of clothes, food and other objects, for example *Blue Shirt, Striped Tie* and *Slice of Yellow Pie* (both 1961). The splashed paintwork on this pseudo-merchandise was a recognition of Abstract Expressionism, then the dominant style in avant-garde painting. But Oldenburg's involvement with vulgar, everyday reality was in deliberate opposition to abstract art's hermeticism. Inspired by Kaprow's idea that Pollock's* actions were more significant than the finished product, he staged several Happenings at The Store and later elsewhere.

An important exponent of Happenings, Oldenburg became, with Warhol*, one of the principal figures of American Pop Art. Invited to exhibit uptown, he continued to make parodies of consumer goods, but glossier and more commercial-looking than before, and without the splashes. He played with textures, creating a hard, geometrical *Bedroom Ensemble* (1963) and, by contrast, 'soft machines', for example the *Soft Typewriter* (1963) and *Soft Dormeyer Mixer* (1965). He also played with scale, as in the *Floorburger (Giant Hamburger)* (1962) and *Giant Pool Balls* (1967). The interest in scale led on to designs for colossal monuments, very few of which, unfortunately, have been executed. One that has been is the *Lipstick Monument* (1969) for Yale University, a gigantic tube of lipstick rising from a tank's caterpillar tracks. Unrealized proposals include a *Teddy Bear* (1965), at least the size of the surrounding buildings, for Central Park, New York, and a *Ball* (1967) for the River Thames, London, like a vast lavatory cistern, rising and falling with the tide.

Throughout these excursions into theatre and urban design, Oldenburg's approach remains essentially that of a painter. He needed to expand beyond painting's traditional confines because of his desire to be fully involved with the real world, to touch and be touched. The tactility in his work is therapeutic both for himself and for society, especially American society. As an immigrant, he has been fascinated by everything typically American and in his creative-destructive *alter ego*, Ray Gun, he has semi-ironically fused himself with American maleness. He celebrates the democratic aspiration to freedom but, through his humour, undermines the repressions of a culture still both puritan and phallic, proposing instead a more complete, childlike, tactile freedom, related to Freud's* concept of 'polymorphous perversity'. Satirical and mystical, realistic and fantastic, personal and public, Oldenburg's complex art aims at a synthesis completely human.

Gray Watson

Books by Oldenburg: *Injun and Other Histories* (1966); *Notes* (1968); *Notes in Hand* (1971); *Raw Notes* (1973); *Photo Log* (1976). See: Barbara Rose, *Claes Oldenburg* (1970); Ellen H. Johnson, *Claes Oldenburg* (1971); Lawrence Alloway, *American Pop Art* (1974); Paul Carroll, *Proposals for Monuments and Buildings 1965–1969* (1969).

352

OLSON, Charles 1910–70

US poet

Educated at the Universities of Wesleyan, Yale and Harvard, Olson taught at Clark and Harvard, and also worked for the Office of War Information and for the Democratic National Committee. He took a legendary step in his career when he went to teach at Black Mountain College, North Carolina, from 1948 until its demise in 1956. Famed as a radical community which, according to its chronicler Martin Duberman, prefigured later manifestations of a 'counter-culture', Black Mountain College at some time hosted such talents as John Cage*, Merce Cunningham, Buckminster Fuller*, Josef Albers*, Paul Goodman*, Robert Rauschenberg*, and Robert Creeley, although its educational programme was far less cogent than popular history and sentimental association purport. As College Rector, Olson fully impressed the community with his charismatic personality and sometimes obscurantist cultural interests. The *Black Mountain Review* (1954–7; reprinted in 3 vols, 1969) earned Olson and his dubious affiliates the label of a so-called 'Black Mountain School of Poetry', although the interests and

achievements of the group were too diverse to give meaning to the title: 'Literary history', Robert Creeley remarked, for example, 'defines us in a sense we neither had time nor interest to consider.' It is important, therefore, to assess Olson's poetry and prose writings less for their influence than for their intrinsic worth.

While Olson belongs in a poetic tradition with Ezra Pound* and William Carlos Williams*, he departs from them in the dimensions of his vision of a cosmology and a history immediate to each individual and active in everyday experience. His manifesto, 'Projective Verse' (*Poetry New York*, 1950), concerns the nature of perception, and seeks to obliterate the customary distinctions between subject and object. Reality is unfinished business in which the perceiver – the poet – is a necessary part, an object, of the total world experience. Olson's metaphysic, which derives in good part from A. N. Whitehead*, regards a geographical location as a part of a man's body (quite like Williams's observation that 'A thing known passes out of the mind into the senses'), and as having 'cells which can decant/ total experience'. As a theory of poetics, 'Projective Verse' is perhaps ultimately unavailing. Its central credo, however, which holds that individuals partake of a corporate existence necessarily including the inanimate, is also extolled in *Call Me Ishmael* (1967). Ostensibly a critique of *Moby Dick*, Olson's little study foreshadows the radical concerns of his own poetic achievements in expounding the central importance, not of personality and egocentricity, but of space and time.

These concerns eventually obtained in Olson's major work, *The Maximus Poems* (3 vols: 1960, 1968, 1975), which may be regarded in three aspects: (1) individuals and heroes as seen under a new dispensation as parts of a process; (2) the historicity of prehistory, whereby even myth is seen as a fact of experience; (3) history and myth as available to and continuous with each individual experience. Olson's miscellaneous poems, collected in *Archeologist of Morning* (1970), contain some of his most accomplished work and pursue like concerns to the epic. Few could deny that Olson's writings, both verse and prose, are vexatious, cryptic, self-indulgent, and too often obfuscatory, but they do pursue a co-ordinated purpose and meaning, even if the skeins are tangled.

A major subject of *The Maximus Poems* is history, which Olson regards as a study, not of discrete dates and outstanding individuals, but of energya and total experience. Any particular historical occasion subsumes all places and times. The concept has an aesthetic dimension in that history provides the information necessary for poetry. By the same token, Olson takes what he regards as the traditional notion of the hero – a study in character and personality – and frees it from considerations of chronology and a spurious type of psychology. What a hero symbolizes is urgent with temporal, geographical, and cultural implications of an order beyond that of the individual biography.

Whatever subject-matter he thought important Olson haphazardly incorporated in the poem. The design hampers the reader's comprehension by dismissing logic and plot, but helps Olson to express his urgent sense of interpenetrating time, place, person and concept. He endeavours to reintegrate the steps of the historical process, an effort which leads to a challenging examination of history and prehistory, and indeed devolves into a full consideration of myth and cosmology. He seeks to locate the precise times and places of discoveries in the New World, a search concentrated in the city of Gloucester, Massachusetts, which he elects as representative of historical America. But Olson also ventures to establish a continuity from man's earliest times, a continuity in which cultural diffusion and artistic expression run parallel. Numerous sections of *Maximus* further the task of reintegration by welding a mass of semantic and cultural topics. The reason why Olson co-opts such a variety of times and places is evidently assertive: he pursues, to borrow phrases from Lévi-Strauss*, an ideological analysis through an almost arbitrary breakdown of temporal realities. The effect can be to 'consecrate either the worst forms of prejudice or the most hollow abstractions', and indeed Olson must to some extent be held liable on both counts. While he himself insists on attaining a state of mind which is metaphysical, his procedure represents for the reader an aesthetic programme – at best, a poetic realization – rather than a dogmatic enlightenment on historical form. The poet attempts to represent the collective consciousness of his race, and arrogates to that end diverse myths; it soon becomes clear that he is not treating them with due respect, but is creating his own composite version. In the last analysis he assumes to himself god and hero and historical function as the proper capacity of the subjective poet: 'The whole living thing of creation is that moment when you know what you feel or do.' Olson takes it upon himself, learnedly if perversely, to be the image of man – Maximus – and so to body forth history and natural history.

Dr John Haffenden

Other works: *A Bibliography on America for Ed Dorn* (1964); *Proprioception* (1965); *Reading at Berkeley* (1966); *Selected Writings*, ed. Robert Creeley (1966); *Human Universe and Other Essays*, ed. Donald Hall (1967); *Pleistocene Man* (1968); *Causal Mythology* (1969); 'The Art of Poetry XII', *Paris Review*, 48, 1970; *The Special View of History*, ed. Ann Charters (1970); *Poetry and Truth* (1971); and *Additional Prose*, ed. George F. Butterick (1974). See also: Ann Charters, *Olson/Melville, A Study in Affinity* (1968); M. L. Rosenthal, *The New Poets: American and British Poetry since World War II* (1967); and Martin

Duberman, *Black Mountain, An Exploration in Community* (1972).

353
O'NEILL, Eugene Gladstone 1888–1953

US dramatist

To all intents and purposes modern American drama began with Eugene O'Neill. The son of a famous actor father, he began writing in a tuberculosis sanatorium where he had spent six months in 1912. His first produced play, *Bound East for Cardiff*, staged by the Provincetown Players in the Wharf Theatre in 1916, marked a sharp break with a theatre which for the most part had simply exchanged the melodrama of action for a melodrama of character, in replacing the sentimentalities of nineteenth-century popular art with a naturalism which O'Neill rejected as the mere 'holding of the family Kodak up to ill-nature'. He wished to transcend 'the banality of surfaces' and in his early sea plays he offered tone poems, lyric portraits of marginal characters straining to make sense of a life whose dominant mood was one of loss and whose central need was for a sense of belonging.

In part this sense of alienation was a product of social divisiveness, a division between the classes, which he dramatized in *The Hairy Ape* (1922), and between races, which he presented in *All God's Chillun* (1924). But this merely concealed a more fundamental sense of abandonment.

Accused of pessimism, he insisted that he was concerned with the tragic spirit, for 'to me, the tragic alone has that significant beauty which is truth. It is the meaning of life – and the hope.' And tragedy, for him, emerged essentially from the gulf between human aspirations and their consistently denied fulfilment – transcendence deriving from the greatness of the dream and the persistence with which it is pursued. But the same gulf which could generate tragedy could equally create a fierce undertow of absurdity and in fact it is this rather than any sense of tragic transcendence which really typifies his work.

For the transfiguring Apollonian vision, the dream designed to aestheticize life and give it the shape which in reality it lacked, devolved all too often into simple self-deception. More often than not his plays are not about a glorious struggle against fate, an heroic pursuit of the unattainable. They are concerned with the desperate illusions which are the acknowledgment of defeat. It is difficult, indeed, to think of any of his plays which adequately expressed this potential. In *Beyond the Horizon* (1920) the visions are wilfully abandoned, as fate intervenes to deflect the aspiring mind into simple irony. *The Emperor Jones* (1920) is an account of the collapse of illusion and character alike. *Anna Christie*

(1921) pitches wilful sentimentalities against determinism. Yank, in *The Hairy Ape*, is ironically transfigured but his vision is hopelessly naive and self-destructive in a way which has very little to do with the tragic. Even *Desire Under the Elms* (1924) and *Mourning Becomes Electra* (1931) offer psycho-pathology in the place of tragic fatalism.

But his talent lay elsewhere. He was a determined experimenter. In *The Emperor Jones*, for example, he mobilized the *mise en scène*, making it an active element in a play which concerned itself with the deconstruction of character and language. Brilliantly original, it dramatized a personal and racial reversion to archetype. In *The Great God Brown* (1926) he used masks to dramatize the public and private selves of his characters and in *Strange Interlude* (1928) breathed life into the dramatic aside, seeing this as an apt symbol of the conscious and unconscious self.

Few of his plays were without flaws. His enthusiasms were seldom less than total, whether it be for such devices as those identified above or for the work and ideas of Schopenhauer, Nietzsche, Strindberg, Freud* and Jung*. Their mark is clear on his work. Too often, indeed, character became a function of idea and subject deferred to method. But he was a writer of genuine originality and energy. His range was phenomenal and in his last plays, plays written as he wrestled with disease, he created some of the most powerful works of modern drama.

The Iceman Cometh (1939) is set in Harry Hope's New York bar. In many ways we are apparently offered an absurdist vision. A group of individuals are suspended in a timeless void, cut off from past and future. Their vulnerability, the irony of their situation, seems simply exacerbated by action. Thus they pass the time sitting motionless, using drink to deny the consciousness which is the source of their pain. Virtually all of them are betrayers. They have failed the causes which they have served, the people they have loved, the world which in their youth they had perceived as opportunity but which now they regard as a lost cause. Their drunkenness, their retreat into self, into unreality, is a protection against knowledge of that imperfection. And yet there is a crucial connection between their imperfection and the compassion which is equally generated by despair and which becomes a primary value.

The Iceman Cometh was, O'Neill suggested, a denial of any other experience of faith in his work and it was so primarily through his acceptance of that progression identified by Albert Camus* when he asserted that 'The end of the movement of absurdity, of rebellion, etc. . . . is compassion . . . that is to say, in the last analysis, love.' Certainly his dedication to his greatest play, *Long Day's Journey into Night* (1939–41), speaks of a 'faith in love' inspired by his marriage to Carlotta, which enables him to face his dead in a play written 'with deep pity and understanding and forgiveness'. It is a play which re-creates his own painful family experiences. Set in 1912, the year of his own attempted suicide, it is an attempt to understand himself and those to whom he was irrevocably tied by fate and by love. It is the finest and most powerful play to have come out of America.

C. W. E. Bigsby

See *The Plays of Eugene O'Neill* (3 vols, 1951). The principal biographies are by Arthur and Barbara Gelb (1974) and by Louis Sheaffer (Boston 1968).

354

ORTEGA y GASSET, José 1883–1955

Spanish philosopher and essayist

Ortega studied philosophy at Madrid University and from 1905 to 1907 in Leipzig, Berlin and Marburg. He was appointed professor of metaphysics in Madrid in 1910, a post he occupied until 1936 drawing large audiences with his eloquent and dramatic accounts of philosophy. In 1902 he began a steady flow of articles, reviews and books which continued almost throughout his life and constitutes the eleven volumes of his *Complete Works*. In 1923 he founded the *Revista de Occidente*, Spain's leading cultural and philosophical periodical. He left the country during the Civil War, but returned in 1945 to continue his writing and teaching amidst the asphyxiating anti-intellectualism of Franco's Spain, viewed with hostility by Catholic fanatics and with suspicion by the authorities.

He is remembered in Spain primarily as an elitist social theorist and as a critic of philosophical rationalism. Like many Spanish intellectuals, he commented freely on a vast range of topics – history, art, literature, music, painting, sociology, women, sport, education, psychology – and soon acquired a gigantic intellectual standing among the semi-educated reading public of the day who were awed by what more exacting readers are inclined to dismiss as his dilettantism, rhetoric and frequent theoretical vulgarities. In his early sociopolitical works, *Invertebrate Spain* (1921, *España invertebrada*, trans. 1937), *The Dehumanization of Art* (1925, *La deshumanización del arte*, trans. 1956), and *The Revolt of the Masses* (1929, *La rebelión de las masas*, trans. 1932), all heavily influenced by German right-wing theories, he argued that culture and civilization are intrinsically opposed to democracy. The modern age is unique in its rejection of the elitist concept of society. Instead of obediently receiving their values, models and goals from an aristocracy of 'superior' men, the 'mass man' is now presuming to impose his own values of conformism, intolerance and vulgarity as ruling social principles. Ortega's most famous work in this vein is his short essay *The Dehumanization of Art* which is a provocative defence of modern art, literature and music on the grounds that it is anti-egalitarian and unde-mocratic. Ortega claims that the intention of 'difficult' artists like Mallarmé, Stravinsky*, Picasso*, Joyce* or Pirandello* is deliberately to humiliate and exclude the masses from cultural life which is always an elite activity. 'Mass men', Ortega claims, are always 'realists' in art and literature, since they appreciate the arts only to the extent that the latter reflect their everyday existence. In *The Revolt of the Masses* he strikes a contemporary note by appealing for European unity in defence of a common Western culture against the barbarism of socialists and similar mediocrities.

Ortega is extremely thin on detail. Nowhere does he explain how the elite will be chosen (he merely claims it is an elite of 'excellence', not money) and virtually his only definition of the superior man is the utterly circular argument that he freely wills his own goals while the masses passively obey norms 'set by others'. However, his hatred of mass politics and tastes is at the heart of his copiously developed critique of rationalism. In such books as *The Modern Theme* (1923, *El tema de nuestro tiempo*, trans. 1931, which includes 'The Decline of Revolutions'), *History as System* (1935, *Historia como sistema*, trans. 1961), 'Ideas and Beliefs' (1940, *Ideas y creencias*), he argues the need to 'subject reason to life'. Utopian rationalism (i.e. 'thought abstracted from the abundant and splendid stream of life') is typical of the revolutionary's tendency to develop the critical faculty at the expense of the 'biological' continuity of life. We must learn to reason 'historically', i.e. to confine our intellectualizing to the limits set by the time and place we live in: 'We must seek out our circumstances . . . in their limitation and specificity . . . the reabsorption of circumstance is the real destiny of man. . . . I am myself and my circumstances' – a statement which has been hailed as a great Spanish contribution to existentialism.

Such arguments might be taken as a straightforward defence of historicism: the world and human consciousness evolve at a set rate and rationalism should not attempt to alter the outcome. Nevertheless, Ortega did not identify himself with the conservative or ultra-right political movements of his day. He always considered himself a liberal, and viewed Nazism and militarism with the same patrician contempt as socialism and other 'mass' manifestations. This liberal, individualist thrust in his thought exonerates him from the charge of reaction and fascism, but lays him open to the accusation of confusion and inconsistency. Just as the 'superior' man is self-willing, so must we all 'possess a set of convictions about the world which must be truly ours' (*Man and Crisis*, *En Torno a Galileo* 1933, trans. 1959), for 'it is false to talk of human nature . . . man must not only make himself but is free by compulsion' (*History as System*). Thus man must apparently think for himself and seek personal authenticity,

but such thinking should not run against the prevailing ideological currents of his day, or, as Ortega puts it, he must be 'abreast of his times' (*a la altura de los tiempos*). This may be a useful appeal for the modernization of Spanish thought, but it sounds very much like the subjection of human reason to the dictates of fashion.

Ortega is now out of favour in Spain, his thought having once been favourably viewed by the founders of the Fascist Party. Apart from a few American and Continental Cold War warriors, and a number of cautious liberal opponents to Franco, Ortega has had few supporters in the last thirty years. But *The Dehumanization of Art* remains a provocative explanation of modernism which continues to stimulate readers.

Dr John Butt

Ortega's complete works, in eleven volumes, have been published by *Revista de Occidente* (1946–69). See P. Garagorri, *Introducción a Ortega* (1970).

355
ORTON, Joe 1933–67

English playwright

Joe Orton was the first modern English playwright to transfer the clown's phallic fun from the stage to the page. A prankster, Orton wanted to goose his audience and take it for a tumble. His unique style of wit and stage mayhem tested the values of English society and often scandalized it. 'I know that my voice is better than anyone else,' he once wrote to his agent. 'It is vulgar and offensive to middle-class susceptibilities.' Always the outsider (a working-class lad who was both an unrepentant homosexual and a former prisoner who had done time for comically defacing public library books), Orton's anger was never co-opted by his meteoric success. Instead, it made his laughter more dangerous. 'Cleanse my heart,' Orton wrote in an unpublished novel during the ten years of his literary apprenticeship. 'Teach me to rage correctly.' On stage, he found the proper outlet for his hostility. He reinvented the farce genre to marry terror and elation.

Orton was born John Orton in Leicester. He was the first of four children. His mother was a factory worker and char. His father was a gardener. Asthmatic and underprivileged as a child, Orton didn't pass his 11-plus; and, by the time he was fourteen, this quintessential master of modern English could neither spell nor speak properly. He conceived the idea of being an actor and going to RADA, even before he'd had an amateur role. But he persevered; and in 1951 he was accepted. While at RADA, where he did well, Orton met Kenneth Halliwell who was, at twenty-five, eight years older and much more sophisticated. Halliwell, who killed Orton with a hammer in 1967 and then took his own life, became Orton's mentor. They lived together, and, after brief stints in repertory, set out to become writers. The writing was Halliwell's idea. Their novels, with such titles as *The Mechanical Womb* and *The Last Days of Sodom*, were comic novels in the Firbankian* mode, a writer they both idolized. By 1957, Orton and Halliwell were writing separately but with equal failure. Orton's frustration, an anger at both his own public invisibility and the inadequacy of his writing, fed fantasies of disruption. He set out his battle plan long before he had the talent to achieve it. 'To be destructive,' he wrote in *The Vision of Gombold Proval* (1961), 'words had to be irrefutable . . . if you could lock the enemy into a room somewhere, you could get a kind of seismic disturbance.'

The comic defacements of library books they thought middle-brow were salvoes that misfired. Orton rewrote blurbs on the jacket and collaged covers. In 1962, when they were arrested, Orton and Halliwell finally made the newspapers; but also earned six months in jail. After jail, Orton's laughter finally found its target. 'Being in the nick brought detachment to my writing. I wasn't involved any more.'

Between 1963 when his first play was accepted and 1967 when he died, Orton became a playwright of international reputation. His oeuvre was small but his impact was large. By 1967 the term 'Ortonesque' had worked its way into the English vocabulary, a shorthand adjective for scenes of macabre outrageousness. Orton wrote three first-class full-length plays: *Entertaining Mr Sloane* (1964), *Loot* (1966) and *What the Butler Saw* (1967), as well as four one-act plays. Two films were made from his plays, and *Loot* was voted the *Evening Standard*'s Best Play of 1966. Orton's plays had often scandalized audiences (he fanned the flames by damning himself in print under the pseudonym Edna Welthorpe) but his wit made the outrage scintillating. Orton's laughter bore out Nietzsche's dictum that 'He who writes in blood and aphorisms does not want to be read, he wants to be learned by heart.' Orton brought the epigram back to the contemporary stage to illuminate a violent world. 'It's life that defeats the Christian Church, she's always been well-equipped to deal with death' (*The Erpingham Camp*, 1965). 'All classes are criminal today. We live in an age of equality' (*Funeral Games*, 1966). Orton's laughter created a 'panic'. His stage gargoyles tried to frighten their audience into new life.

Unlike Harold Pinter*, whose work Orton began by imitating and ended by parodying, Orton created images of action, not entropy. 'The whole trouble with Western civilization,' Orton wrote in his diary, 'is the lack of anything worth concealing.' In Orton's world there is no uncertainty and no secrets. Reality is outrageous enough without mystifying it. People say what they mean – but the truth does not help them. 'How dare you involve me in a situation for which no memo has been issued,' says the corrupt Detective Truscott in *Loot*. All Orton's characters speak a language of reason and live a life of chaos.

Orton found a way of extending the boundaries of farce beyond the bedroom; and in his masterpiece, *What the Butler Saw*, he turns the genre itself into vision of life. Orton fed his characters into the fun machine and made them bleed. 'As I understood it, farce originally was very close to tragedy and differed only in the treatment of its themes like rape, bastardy, prostitution,' Orton said. He returned comedy to its aggressive roots, a hard-edged attack on society to show it the flimsiness of reason and the thin carapace of normality. A master craftsman and an instinctive anarch, Orton produced out of his dark fantasies that rarest of theatrical by-products: joy.

John Lahr

See: *The Complete Plays* (1977); *Up Against It* (unproduced film script for the Beatles, 1979); *Head to Toe* (novel, 1971). See also John Lahr, *Prick Up Your Ears: The Biography of Joe Orton* (1978).

356
ORWELL, George 1903–50

English essayist and novelist

Orwell's real name was Eric Blair and he was born in India, the son of an official in the Opium Service, and was brought to England by his mother at the age of three. He gained a scholarship to St Cyprian's, a fashionable Preparatory School where Cyril Connolly* was among his contemporaries. His family were of what he called 'the lower-upper middle class', that is the 'upper-middle class without money'. He was crammed for a scholarship to Eton, but did little work there, already being something of an odd man out and against the system. His most brilliant contemporaries went on to Cambridge, but he entered the Burma police, a very unprestigious part of the Imperial Civil Service. He endured it for five years, but resigned in 1927, having come to hate the social pretentiousness of the British in Burma and their indifference to Burmese culture. All this comes out in his first published novel, some say his best pre-war novel, *Burmese Days* (1935).

Burmese Days is often taken to be socialist because it is anti-imperialist. But between 1927 and 1934 Orwell often called himself, when other young writers asked 'Where do you stand?', simply 'a Tory anarchist'. He was firstly an individualist who resented one man or one culture imposing its values on another; and though he was familiar with socialist arguments about economic exploitation, he did not fully agree with them until 1935 and 1936. Immediately after his return from Burma he tried to write novels, which have not survived, and published a few essays, poems and book reviews. Searching for material and wondering whether English working men suffered like the Burmans, he began spasmodic but intense spells of living among tramps. He taught some poorly paid jobs in awful private schools and knew poverty. He ran out of money while spending a year and a half writing in Paris, worked as a dishwasher, and lived in a Parisian slum, all of which experience led to his first and characteristic published book, *Down and Out in Paris and London* (1933). Victor Gollancz published it and had great faith in Orwell as a writer, especially as a novelist, though political differences finally led to a rupture. He suggested the theme of *The Road to Wigan Pier* (1937) to Orwell, who wrote it as a brilliant account of how the unemployed live, adding an eccentric but provocative section announcing both his conversion to socialism and the indifference to freedom of most socialist intellectuals.

He went to Spain to fight, not to write, but *Homage to Catalonia* (1938) resulted. It sold badly at the time but is now seen both as a classic and an honest description of war, and as one of the shrewdest of polemics against the Stalinist* attempt to dominate both the Spanish Republic and the whole international Left. For a brief period until 1939 he was militantly anti-war, close to pacifism, a member of the Independent Labour Party, often mistakenly called – like his new publisher Frederic Warburg – Trotskyite*, because they were strongly Left-wing, egalitarian and both anti-Labour Party and anti-Communist. Gollancz continued to publish his novels, *A Clergyman's Daughter* (1935), *Keep the Aspidistra Flying* (1936) and *Coming Up For Air* (1939). Only the latter, written in the middle-brow tradition of Dickens and H. G. Wells*, came up to the now extraordinarily high standard of his documentaries and his essays. The war had a great influence on him. He saw the need to defend even a shoddy and hypocritical democracy against Fascism, but thought, as in *The Lion and the Unicorn* (1941), that a socialist revolution was taking place in the ranks of the British army. He rescued patriotism from its identification with nationalism, trying to show that its roots were radical as much as Conservative. Being tubercular, he was not accepted for military service and wasted two years in the BBC's Far Eastern Service before becoming Literary Editor of *Tribune*, a wholly congenial post with Aneurin Bevan as the Editor. He was an 'English Socialist' of the kind of Michael Foot and Bevan: libertarian, egalitarian, but quite untheoretical, almost anti-theoretical. Early in the war he conceived a grand design for a three-volume novel of social analysis and warning which would deal with the decay of the old order, the betrayal of the revolution and what an English totalitarianism would be like if it ever came to power. This design never came to be, but the pre-war novels have some such connection with his masterpiece *Animal Farm* (1945) and his most famous work, *1984* (1949). *Animal Farm* is a story of the good revolution of the animals betrayed by the (Stalinist) pigs. It is not a parable of the impossibility of revolution; and *1984* is *not* a *prophecy* of what will happen but a satiric warning of what could happen if power is pursued for its own sake – despite some right-wing American critics reading him in a contrary sense. His values remained those of a left-wing socialist until his early death from tuberculosis, only his hope of seeing 'the Republic' emerge in our times declined.

There is so much more in Orwell than his books. Some critics plausibly see his genius as an essayist. 'A Hanging' and 'Shooting an Elephant' are both ambiguously short-story or personal recollections, but both didactic or moral writing of great stature. His *Tribune* 'As I Please' column virtually invented mixed column journalism, polemical and discursive. Rich humour is found in nearly all his essays, as when he would mock the fierce readers of *Tribune* by describing the mating habits of a common toad or the virtues of a sixpenny Woolworth's rose, all of which would form part of the good life, even in the classless society.

He wrote major essays on censorship, plain language, the social beliefs of boys' magazines, and on pornography and violence: he believed passionately in liberty, but also in condemning the bad both morally and aesthetically. Literary criticism would be the less without his seminal essays on Dickens, Swift and in 'Inside the Whale' on the failings of the intellectuals in the 1930s. The *Collected Essays, Journalism and Letters* (4 vols, 1968), edited by his second wife and widow, Sonia Orwell, together with Ian Angus, though not in fact 'complete', for the first time enabled the remarkable range of his essay writing to be appreciated. Unfortunately by 1968 many distinguished critics had committed themselves to positions based on little more than reading his books. Almost certainly he is the greatest English polemical writer since Swift, and a master of simple prose, someone whose style has had more influence than any over his contemporaries: plain, easy, colloquial, yet precise and capable of great variations between the formal, the informal, the leisurely and the excited. He always distinguished between good writers and bad men; he insisted against the Left that Pound* and Eliot* were great writers, though he condemned them as moralists. Those who admire Orwell's plain speaking against Communism may need reminding that his values became and remained Socialist through and through.

He wrote well on national character and is rightly seen, for his style, his common-sense philosophy, his simple way of living and love of the countryside, and his somewhat eccentric preoccupations with little things as well as great moral issues, as essentially an

English writer. Above all else, he said of himself he was 'a political writer', with a hatred of 'totalitarianism' and a love of 'democratic Socialism'. But in the phrase 'political writer', the integrity of each word is of equal value.

Professor Bernard Crick

See: Richard Rees, *George Orwell: Fugitive from the Camp of Victory* (1962); George Woodcock, *The Crystal Spirit* (1966); William Steinhoff, *George Orwell and the Origins of 1984* (1975); *George Orwell: The Critical Heritage*, ed. Jeffrey Meyers (1976); Bernard Crick, *George Orwell: A Life* (1980).

357
OSBORNE, John James 1929–

British actor, dramatist and screenwriter

Born in London, John Osborne was educated at Belmont College, Devon, where he was 'unhappy for most of the time'. He left school at seventeen, and after a brief foray into journalism found various jobs in theatres, making his acting début in *No Room at the Inn* at Sheffield in 1948. He had been writing drama as early as 1946, and *The Devil Inside Him* (written in collaboration with Stella Linden) was staged in 1950, after which he pursued the dual career of actor and playwright. In 1956 Osborne joined the newly-formed English Stage Company at the Royal Court, and in their opening season they produced his *Look Back in Anger*, for which he won the *Evening Standard* Award for Most Promising Playwright. This play also gained for Osborne the reputation of being an 'angry young man', and of having brought 'realism' to the British stage. Neither of these labels has helped Osborne in his subsequent career. He followed the success of *Look Back in Anger* with *The Entertainer* (1957), in which he developed the elements of music hall present in the earlier work, and *Luther* (1961), a piece in the tradition of Brecht's* *Galileo*. In 1964 he matched his achievement in the theatre by winning an Oscar for his screen adaptation of Fielding's *Tom Jones*. Several of his plays have also become feature films, notably *Look Back in Anger* (1958) and *The Entertainer* (1960). Osborne's most controversial work for the stage remains *Inadmissible Evidence* (1965); hailed by some as a masterpiece, others have seen it as misogynistic and reactionary. The writer's own estimation of the piece may be gauged from his having personally directed a prestigious revival in 1979. During the 1960s and 1970s Osborne continued to write prolifically for the theatre, and for television, which he had dismissed in 1961 as being run by 'dim, untalented little bigots'. His work during this period found scant critical favour, and neither aimed for nor achieved popular success. Osborne became increasing-

ly concerned with publicly defending his plays against critical attack. During the 1960s he also revived his acting career, with a notable appearance in David Mercer's television play *The Parachute* (1967), and occasional feature films. He has been married five times.

'There aren't any good, brave causes left.' Whether you agreed with them or not, these words, spoken by Jimmy Porter in *Look Back in Anger*, articulated a mood widespread in the Britain of the mid-1950s. Yet the phrase now has a hollow ring, particularly in view of the subsequent appearance on the political scene of movements such as CND and the New Left. *Look Back in Anger* is the story of the breakdown of a less-than-typical marriage; its central character is the prototype for what have been termed Osborne's 'individuals-in-a-mess', and is one of the most fascinating and infuriating figures in the modern theatre. But he is no radical, and was surely never intended as such; nor is the play itself a work of 'realism' (the opening minutes are in fact a classic piece of stage naturalism). That these facts went largely unnoticed in 1956 may in part explain the disappointment felt by Osborne's earliest admirers over much of his later writing.

Osborne has never been afraid to experiment in his drama: in 1959 he wrote a musical comedy, *The World of Paul Slickey*, and in 1972 successfully adapted *The Picture of Dorian Gray* for the stage. Ronald Hayman has called him 'technically promiscuous', and certainly much of his work since *Look Back in Anger* has been highly stylized. In *Inadmissible Evidence*, three different clients in a solicitor's office are played by the same actress, suggesting the mental fatigue and confusion of Mailand better than any amount of dialogue. *A Sense of Detachment* (1972) is Osborne's most experimental work to date, and, although highly entertaining, the play's technical inventiveness often appears to be its sole *raison d'être*. Osborne also tends to rely heavily on monologue; at his best (in *Luther*, for example) he is brilliant; in some of the later plays, however, he is merely tedious. For over two decades it has been impossible to ignore the name of John Osborne, as he has consistently proved himself a writer of immense gifts. Unfortunately, he has yet fully to utilize those gifts, and produce the major work of which he is capable. Only by doing so will he finally remove from around his neck the albatross which is the reputation of *Look Back in Anger*.

Paul Nicholls

Osborne's other published stage plays are: *Epitaph for George Dillon* (1955, with Anthony Creighton); *The Blood of the Bambergs* (1962); *Under Plain Cover* (1962); *A Patriot for Me* (1965); *A Bond Honoured* (1966, from Lope de Vega's *La Fianza Satisfecha*); *Time Present* (1968); *The Hotel in Amsterdam* (1968); *Hedda Gabler* (1970, an adaptation of Ibsen); *West of Suez* (1971); *A Place Calling Itself Rome* (1972); *The End of Me Old*

Cigar (1975); and *Watch It Come Down* (1975). His work for television includes: *A Subject of Scandal and Concern* (1960); *The Right Prospectus* (1971); *Very Like a Whale* (1971); *The Gift of Friendship* (1971); *Jill and Jack* (1974); *You're Not Watching Me Mummy* (1978); and *Try a Little Tenderness* (1978). See also: S. Trussler, *The Plays of John Osborne* (1969); R. Hayman, *British Theatre since 1955* (1979).

358

OUSPENSKY, Peter Demianovich 1878–1947

Russian occult philosopher

Ouspensky was born in Moscow into a markedly intellectual and artistic family. His father was an army officer who had a passionate interest in the arts and in mathematics which was inherited by Ouspensky himself. Even as a child he showed a decided taste for literature, especially for poetry, and for painting. During his teens he developed a strong interest in the natural sciences and in psychology, subjects which he studied at Moscow University. His outstanding ability as a mathematical philosopher became clear with the publication of his first book, *The Fourth Dimension* (*Chetvertoe Izmierenie*, 1909) and he might well have opted for an academic career had it not been for an all-absorbing interest of a somewhat different kind which made him resolve to embark on a career as a writer and journalist. Largely as a result of reading books on theosophy, Ouspensky became convinced that the knowledge afforded by the sciences and the possibilities that they offered for extending that knowledge would give at best a very partial account of the nature of man, of the world in which he lives and of the universe of which that world forms a part. Motivated by the conviction that some deeper and higher form of knowledge must exist somewhere, he set out in 1913 on an extended journey to Egypt, India and Ceylon to look for some source of this real knowledge. An account of some of his experiences and of his reflections upon them is to be found in his book *A New Model of the Universe* (1931).

The outbreak of war in 1914 caused him to return to Russia, by way of England, and in Moscow in 1915 he found the source he had been looking for in the person of G. I. Gurdjieff*, whose pupil he became and remained until 1924. The Russian Revolution of 1917 forced him to leave the country and for some while he joined Gurdjieff in the Caucasus, but moved on to Constantinople in 1919. Here he lived in very straitened circumstances, giving lessons in English and mathematics, until in 1921 the publication of an English translation of his book *Tertium Organum* in America led to his coming to England, where he settled for the remainder of his life, except for the war years 1940–5, which he spent in America.

Ouspensky's books *In Search of the Miraculous* (1949), *The Psychology of Man's Possible Evolution* (1950) and *The Fourth Way* (1957) give a remarkably full account of what it was that he learned from Gurdjieff. The two main strands, which are intertwined, concern on the one hand the psychology and the possible development of individual man and on the other the organization of the universe and the place of mankind within it, the two being inter-related on the oft repeated Hermetic principle: 'As above, so below', that is to say that laws and relations which obtain on the scale of the universe, the macrocosm, will be found to obtain on the scale of individual man, the microcosm, and below. There exist real possibilities for the individual to evolve psychologically into a state of consciousness far higher than that in which he spends the whole of his ordinary life. Even during his waking hours, a man is always in a subjective state which is scarcely to be distinguished from sleep. Many characteristics serve to prevent him from waking from this state of sleep, chief among them man's ignorance of his own state, so that self-study is a prerequisite for any possibility of change. Only by this means can a man learn, for instance, that he is the continual prey of negative emotions and negative imaginings which cut him off from reality; that he is not, as he fondly imagines, a single, unified personality but a mass of diverse and often contradictory 'I's, each of which insists on having his own way for a brief moment and is then displaced by another; that individual man, as we know him, is a rather badly running machine in which mental, emotional, instinctual and motor activity tend to interfere with each other a good deal of the time. A change from this state of affairs can come about for the individual only with the help of knowledge and guidance coming from those who have themselves progressed to a higher state of consciousness. Ouspensky formulates two laws which operate on all levels and all scales: the Law of Three, or the triad, and the Law of Seven, or the octave, which account for the progression of all natural processes and indicate the conditions in which any change can take place. One instance of the Law of Seven is what Ouspensky terms 'The Ray of Creation', a formulation of the structure of the universe which shows, among other things, the situation of the Earth and of mankind in relation to all other worlds.

These and many other ideas formed the basis of a system of extremely practical psychological exercises to the exposition of which Ouspensky devoted himself during the 1920s and 1930s in England and in America during the war years. He did this by means of lectures and by the conducting of classes, and through the efforts of his many pupils, among the best known of whom were Maurice Nicoll and Kenneth Walker. Ouspensky's impact on the life of his time was very considerable, not only through his published work but also through the formation of countless 'groups' of people who were involved in 'the Work', as it was most often called.

Dennis Fry

See also: *Symbolism of the Tarot: the Philosophy of Occultism in Pictures and Numbers* (trans. A. L. Pogossky, St Petersburg 1913, New York 1976); *Talks with a Devil* (*Razgovory sd'iavolot*, Petrograd 1916, trans. Katya Petroff, London 1972); *Strange Life of Ivan Osokin* (New York 1947, London 1948).

359
OWEN, Wilfred 1893–1918

British poet

Brought up in the back streets of Birkenhead and Shrewsbury, where his father was Assistant Superintendent of the Railways, Wilfred Owen first became aware of his poetic calling at the age of ten or eleven. The dominant presence of his childhood was his devout and adoring mother, who hoped he might eventually enter the Church. It was as a result of her influence that, having failed to win a scholarship to London University, he accepted an unpaid post as lay assistant to the Vicar of Dunsden, Oxfordshire, in return for board, lodging, and coaching towards a second attempt at a university scholarship. Fifteen months in the vicarage convinced him that his belief in evangelical religion was less strong than his allegiance to poetry, and he left in 1913 to teach English in France, first at a Berlitz School, and subsequently as a private tutor. For more than a year after the outbreak of war he could not decide whether or not to join up, but in September 1915 returned to England and enlisted in the Artists' Rifles. Plunged into the battle of the Somme in January 1917, he was involved in heavy fighting and, in May, was found to be suffering from neurasthenia, or shell-shock, and invalided back by stages to Craiglockhart War Hospital, near Edinburgh. There he met Siegfried Sassoon and, largely as a result of the older man's encouragement and practical criticism, abandoned the sub-Keatsian luxuriance of his early style in favour of the disciplined sensuality, the passionate intelligence characteristic of the poems written during the fourteen months that remained to him. Sassoon's influence is discernible in the shock-tactics,

and especially in the explosive colloquialisms, of such of Owen's first 'war poems' as 'The Dead-Beat' and 'Dulce et Decorum Est', but he soon found his own more meditative and resonant voice.

The ten months following his discharge from Craiglockhart in November 1917 were the most creative of his life. He was based in Scarborough and Ripon and spent a succession of leaves in London, where he was introduced to a wider circle of literary acquaintance that included Arnold Bennett*, H. G. Wells*, Robert Ross, Osbert Sitwell, and Charles Scott Moncrieff. The last three and certain of Owen's other friends were homosexual, and the extent to which he came to acknowledge and indulge his own latent homosexual tendencies at this time is a matter of speculation. What is certain, however, is that he wrote more eloquently than other poets of the tragedy of young men killed in battle because he felt that tragedy more acutely.

He was being considered for a home posting when Sassoon returned wounded to England, and Owen decided that his duty as a poet lay in taking his friend's place as a witness to the suffering of the troops. He crossed to France in September 1918, was awarded the Military Cross some weeks later, and seven days before the Armistice was killed.

He lived to see only five of his poems in print, but the selections edited by Sassoon (1920) and Edmund Blunden (1931) were a potent influence on the left-wing poets of the 1930s, who hailed him as hero and martyr for his stand against 'the old men' responsible for the conduct of the war, against whose successors they were themselves in revolt. Owen's use of pararhyme (*escaped/scooped*, *groined/ground*) was widely emulated; the fragmentary Preface to his poems became one of the most famous of literary manifestos; and the compassion, learnt among the poor at Dunsden, expressed in his poems from the Western Front, reached an international audience as the basis of Benjamin Britten's* *War Requiem* (1962).

Jon Stallworthy

See C. Day Lewis (ed.), *The Collected Poems of Wilfred Owen* (1963) and Harold Owen and John Bell (eds), *Wilfred Owen: Collected Letters* (1967). About Owen: D. S. R. Welland, *Wilfred Owen: A Critical Study* (1960, revised 1978); Harold Owen, *Journey from Obscurity* (3 vols, 1963, 1964, 1965); Jon Stallworthy, *Wilfred Owen: A Biography* (1974); and Dominic Hibberd, *Wilfred Owen* (1975).

P

360

PARETO, Vilfredo 1848–1923

Italian sociologist and economist

As the son of an Italian aristocrat exiled for Mazzinian sympathies, Pareto spent his earliest years in France. After his family returned home he completed his education at the Polytechnic Institute in Turin, graduating in mathematics and physics. He worked first as a railway engineer and then as manager of an iron-mining concern. Living in Florence, he was drawn into contemporary debates over free trade, which he favoured as a means of promoting the further development of newly unified Italy. His contributions elicited interest from Léon Walras, Professor of Political Economy at the University of Lausanne. To this chair Pareto himself succeeded in 1893. From the turn of the century onwards he lived largely as a recluse, suffering particularly from disillusionment with the inefficiency and corruption that characterized liberal politics in the new Italy. Only with Mussolini's* accession to power in October 1922 did Pareto re-emerge into public life, accepting appointment as Senator within the Fascist regime. By the time of his death in the following August he was already having second thoughts about the wisdom of such association with the Duce.

Pareto's main works as an economist were the *Cours d'économie politique* ('Course of Political Economy', 1896–7) and the *Manuale di economia politica* ('Manual of Political Economy', 1906). Here his most notable contribution was to lend to the study of such topics as income distribution a more rigorous mathematical foundation than was then usual. This proved symptomatic of a more general positivist aim to make the laws of society come as close as possible, in generality and predictive power, to those which he had studied earlier in physics. Pareto saw that, at least in the abstract, economics dealt with a relatively tidy sphere of broadly logical behaviour devoted to the maximization of material gain. But clearly there were grave difficulties in applying economic theory to the real world, where it came into conflict with a more richly diverse set of motivations, many non-rational in nature. It is for his sociological studies of these phenomena that Pareto is best remembered. With Weber* and Durkheim* he ranks as a founding father of twentieth-century academic sociology; in particular he contributed important ideas to the psychological dimension of social studies.

In *Les Systèmes socialistes* ('Socialist Systems', 1902) Pareto accepted that class struggles were a reality. But he dissented from the Marxist view that proletarian victory would bring them to an end. One elite would merely be replaced by another, claiming to speak in the proletariat's name. Pareto stressed that, because of differential natural ability, some such 'circulation of elites' was inescapable. The few wielding real power could do so only so long as they proved more capable than any competitors at the task of manipulating the rest of society. Such control was most successful when practised by those who understood the nature and scope of non-rational motivation. This was the linkage which Pareto sought to explore in *Mind and Society* (*Trattato di sociologia generale*, 1916–23, trans. 1963). Despite strained vocabulary and turgid prose, this ambitious attempt to construct a general framework of laws about behaviour became Pareto's most renowned work. Its investigation of the interaction between rational and non-rational conduct centred around a model involving a threefold categorization. We must distinguish between 'sentiments' (characteristics of the mind that are permanent but not directly observable), 'residues' (observable actions that relate to such sentiments and take the form of conduct which is, at least partly, non-rational), and 'derivations' (rhetorical structures which rationalize the residues). Pareto suggested that, though all these factors were constantly acting upon one another, sentiments were clearly the strongest of the three. He concluded that the chief element in an elite's retention of power was an ability to exploit derivations as a means of putting a rational veneer upon its authority. Thus he erected the framework for a doctrine of power and propagandist manipulation divorced from any consideration beyond that of oligarchical self-preservation.

In earlier times Pareto's assertions about the inevitability of elite domination would have seemed quite simply platitudinous. But in the twentieth century, so full of rhetoric about egalitarian democratic fulfilment, his ideas have had an altogether more abrasive effect.

Professor Michael Biddiss

Other works: *Fatti e Teorie* ('Facts and Theories', 1920); *Trasformazione della Democrazia* (1921). For an excellent selection and commentary, see S. E. Finer (ed.), *Vilfredo Pareto: Sociological Writings* (1966). See also: G. C. Homans and C. P. Curtis, *An Introduction to Pareto* (1934); T. Parsons, *The Structure of Social Action*, vol. 1 (1968); J. H. Meisel (ed.), *Pareto and Mosca* (1965); R. Aron, *Main Currents in Sociological Thought*, vol. 2 (1968); and C. Wright Mills, *The Power Elite* (1956)

361
PARK, Robert Ezra 1864–1944

US sociologist

Robert E. Park was born in Harleyville, Pennsylvania. While still young his family moved to Minnesota and it was in the American Midwest that Park grew up, attending the Universities of Minnesota and Michigan. Between 1882 and 1898 he worked as a journalist in several large cities including New York and Chicago, developing a sensitivity to the dynamics of urban life which was to prove fruitful in his later sociological writings. Park's influential concept of the modern city as a 'social laboratory' is inconceivable without the work of these years. Indeed the distinctive style of Park's approach to sociology results from the unique fusion of a professional background in what would later be called 'feature journalism' with the insights of European sociological theory, creatively assimilated in a quest to understand the nature of social life and the human personality.

In 1899 Park moved to Harvard where he took his MA after studying philosophy with Josiah Royce and William James. He then went to Germany where he worked with the philosopher Windelband and the sociologist Simmel*, taking his PhD at Heidelberg in 1904 with a dissertation entitled *Masse and Publicum*. On his return to America Park taught as an assistant in philosophy at Harvard for a year before taking up a post as secretary to the Congo Reform Association, an organization devoted to publicizing the facts about Belgian misrule in the Congo. Through the influence of the American Negro leader Booker T. Washington he became interested in the problems of race relations, a field to which he was to devote several of his most important papers, and on which he exercised a seminal influence. In 1914, already fifty, Park joined the department of sociology at the University of Chicago where he remained until he retired in 1929. During this time he wrote, with Ernest W. Burgess, his most influential work, the *Introduction to the Science of Sociology* (1921). This book was to introduce generations of American students to the great European sociologists but it was no mere survey of other men's ideas. Park built upon previous achievements an original approach to sociology as 'the science of collective behaviour'. Patterns of interaction rather than institutional struc-

tures or supposed 'laws' of development were his prime focus and though the influence of Simmel, in particular, is strong, Park's treatment of these patterns under the four typical forms of competition, conflict, accommodation and assimilation represents an important new contribution to sociology. The theoretical framework developed in the *Introduction* proved valuable in structuring Park's empirical work in such fields as racial conflict, the influence of the press and the social patterns of city life. After his retirement Park resumed his travels, visiting Brazil, South Africa, India and Malaya. He taught in Hawaii and at Yenching University in Peking before moving, in 1936, to Fisk University, a Negro institution in Nashville, Tennessee.

Through his own work and that of such students as Louis Wirth, E. Franklin Frazier and R. D. MacKenzie, Park was a formative influence on the development of empirical sociology in the USA. Indeed, perhaps his most valuable influence was in turning American sociology from the sterile quest for laws of history to the investigation of patterns of interaction prevalent in the world about us. Topics such as the 'marginality' of a man who moves in several social spheres and is not completely at home in any, the problematic relationship between geographical and social proximity, and the development of personality in a social environment largely fixed by custom and tradition are vividly treated in his work in a way that unites theoretical insight into their typical features with a journalistic eye for the unique and particular. This combination made Park's work a tempting model for a rising generation of sociologists few of whom were able to draw upon a similar range of worldly experience. For this reason many of Park's concepts tended to be somewhat mechanically applied in the investigations of his less talented followers and, as a result, his reputation as a theorist has suffered in comparison with that of such contemporaries as George Herbert Mead and younger men like Talcott Parsons*.

David J. Levy

Park's other works include: *The Immigrant Press and its Control* (1922); and *Collected Papers*, ed. Everett C. Hughes (3 vols, 1950–5). See also: *Robert E. Park: On Social Control and Collective Behavior*, ed. Ralph H. Turner (1967); Pitirim Sorokin, *Contemporary Sociological Theories* (1928).

362
PARKER, Charles Christopher, Jr (Bird) 1920–55

US jazz alto saxophonist, composer

Charlie Parker embodied the popular stereotype of the jazz musician as an inspired, self-destructive genius. From a man whose personal and professional life was a chaos of narcotics, alcohol and abused personal relationships flowed an endless stream of inventive and passionate improvisation performed with astounding virtuosity. Whereas early jazz and swing had been multiracial and intimately linked with light-hearted entertainment, bebop, the music of Parker, was predominantly for black people, played by black people (at first), and it was serious. Although it grew out of swing, it deliberately broke with tradition, and this break was significant for black Americans.

Parker was a self-taught musician who, at the age of nineteen, was playing alto saxophone with the Jay McShann band. He soon dropped out and went to live in New York, taking on casual jobs, and sitting in with the bands that played in the clubs of 52nd Street, where the new style of Parker, Dizzy Gillespie (trumpet), Thelonius Monk (piano) and Kenny Clarke (drums) was being worked out. Clarke was moving the accents from the first and third beats of the bar to the second and fourth. Gillespie and Parker were developing the melodic and harmonic aspects of the music, at first independently of each other.

Their music avoided the simple harmonies of earlier jazz, added chords to the sequences of the tunes they played, and filled out major and minor triads with the higher intervals. In their melodic improvisations they tended to make great use of these higher intervals, and of alterations to the standard intervals – the characteristic sound of Bird and Diz has lowered fifths and ninths, often accented at the end of a phrase on the second quaver of the first beat in the bar (the name 'bebop' is in imitation of this). Their phrases were not tailored to the conventional two- and four-bar lengths, and would cross the junctions between the sections of the song that they were playing, making it quite difficult for non-musicians listening to follow the solo. This obscurity was partly offset by the fact that Parker often chose either the chord sequence of *I Got Rhythm* or of the twelve-bar blues – naturally with added harmonies.

Slam Slam's Blues (1945) has Parker and Gillespie standing out from the other, more conventional, swing players for the rhythm, phrasing and harmonic structure of their solos. In 1943 Parker and Gillespie were in the Earl Hines and then the Billy Eckstine big bands, and in 1945 recorded together in sessions that have become classic. Parker's erratic behaviour led to a break with Gillespie (who rarely played with him after that), and Miles Davis* joined the Parker quintet for a series of recordings for the Savoy and Dial labels.

Three types of Parker solo can be mentioned here: very fast quaver runs, spiced with triplets, syncopation and great variety of accent on *Ko Ko* (1945); blues such as the slowish *Parker's Mood* (1948) where rhythmic variety and melodic agility are combined with intense emotional expression; and ballads (*Embraceable You*, 1947) where Parker embroiders on the melody with

flurries of semi- and demi-semiquavers through added passing chords.

Parker's health and constitution began to give way under the strain of heroin, alcohol and disordered living, and his usefulness as a musician suffered when he could not be counted on to turn up for engagements. He went through a number of marriages (the first at the age of fifteen), and was hospitalized. He recorded with strings (*Just Friends*, 1949), toured with various organizations and bands, and played in a justly famous concert in Toronto in 1953. He became more and more down and out, and finally died while watching television in the apartment of a friend.

Parker's unedifying life fuels the legend of the artist sacrificing himself to his art, and that of the black man oppressed by the American system. But the music he played is not a matter of legend. It laid the basis of the language of jazz improvisation for the next twenty years, turned jazz towards the cult of the solo improviser, and offered an example of supreme cultural achievement to two generations of black Americans.

Christopher Wagstaff

Parker's recordings have been reissued on LP records by Savoy, Spotlite, Verve, and many other labels. Transcribed solos can be found in *Charlie Parker Omnibook* (1978). See: Robert Reisner, *Bird: The Legend of Charlie Parker* (1962); Ross Russell, *Bird Lives* (1972); Leonard Feather, *Inside Bebop* (1949, republished as *Inside Jazz*).

363
PARSONS, Talcott 1902–79

US sociologist

Against the highly empiricist background of American sociology, Parsons stands out as an 'incurable theorist', to use his own self-characterization. After an undergraduate degree in biology and graduate studies in economics at the London School of Economics, he did a doctorate in sociology at Heidelberg. In 1927 he joined the Harvard economics department and four years later transferred to the newly formed sociology department at Harvard. He stayed there until his retirement in 1973 and served as Department Chairman from 1944 to 1956. A great deal of his influence comes from having taught more than a dozen of the best known contemporary American sociologists, including Kingsley Davis, Marion Levy and Harold Garfinkel.

The central concern of Parson's first book, *The Structure of Social Action* (1937), is the problem of order – why society is not characterized by a Hobbesian war of all against all. He maintains that a satisfactory solution to this problem is possible only if men are seen as striving to achieve a shared system of ends and guided by common norms. The importance of a shared normative structure, he argues, was converged on by Alfred Marshall, Pareto*, Durkheim* and Max Weber*. His analysis proved extremely influential, partly because it was the first major English-language exposition of Durkheim and Weber.

Parsons's subsequent work is remarkable for the wide range of substantive issues and theoretical topics covered. His interests have ranged from the Nazis to school classrooms to developing his own conceptions of power and influence. One of his more influential analyses tackles the place of professionals in modern society. It is unsatisfactory, he argues, to characterize businessmen as self-interested and professionals as altruistic for they both play major roles in the same economy. Instead of seeing them in motivational terms, he argues for classifying them in terms of how they relate to others in their work. This he does in terms of a set of pattern-variables which are neutrality–affectivity, universalism–particularism, specificity–diffuseness and performance–quality. By this approach business men and professionals fit together easily for both are doing the same type of activity in their occupational roles. Both relate to others neutrally (without emotion), universalistically (in terms of objective criteria), for specific purposes and in terms of the performance they expect of the other.

Parsons has developed his own variety of structural-functionalism which focuses on four functional dimensions or problems. As any system in order to survive has to solve four functional problems – adaptation, goal-attainment, integration and latency (pattern maintenance and tension management) – a system can be analysed in terms of these functional dimensions. For a society, the economy focuses on adaptation, the polity on goal-attainment, the stratification system on integration and socializing institutions like the family and school on latency. This classification also provides the basis of Parsons's human action schema. Cultural systems, personality systems, and social systems varying in size from two-person groups to societies can all be analysed in terms of the functional dimensions. In his *Societies: Evolutionary and Comparative Perspectives* (1966) and *The System of Modern Societies* (1971) he combines the four functional dimensions with an evolutionary perspective. This provides a view of human history as the gradually evolving differentiation of sub-systems of a society each focusing on a particular functional problem.

Many sociologists in the 1940s and 1950s related their research to his ideas and used concepts from his work for he is the leading non-Marxist sociologist of his generation. In the 1960s, his view of society as based on normative consensus and geared to the solution of four functional problems came under increasing attack. Many argued his approach could not deal with change and conflict. Now this reaction is viewed as too

simplistic and the ways of dealing with these topics in his framework are being explored.

Dr K. S. Menzies

Other works include: *The Social System* (1951); *Economy and Society*, with N. Smelser (1956); *Sociological Theory and Modern Society* (1967); and *The American University*, with G. Platt (1973). Critical evaluations of his ideas can be found in H. Bershady, *Ideology and Social Knowledge* (1973); M. Black (ed.), *The Social Theories of Talcott Parsons* (1961); K. Menzies, *Talcott Parsons and the Social Image of Man* (1977); and G. Rocher, *Talcott Parsons and American Sociology* (1975).

364
PASOLINI, Pier Paolo 1922–75

Italian film-maker, writer

The brutal murder of Pier Paolo Pasolini on a piece of waste ground on the outskirts of Rome on 2 November 1975 brought to a hideous end the most spectacular artistic career in Italy since the Second World War. Known outside Italy mainly as a film-maker, Pasolini was also a novelist, poet, essayist and journalist and a public figure of some notoriety. His early novels – *Ragazzi di vita* (1955) and *Una vita violenta* (1959) – established him as a linguistic innovator. His poetry – *Le ceneri di Gramsci* (1957), *La religione del mio tempo* (1961) – managed to combine public content with a highly distinctive speaking voice, in sharp contrast to the prevailing poetic tradition in which a largely private content was expressed from a somewhat impersonal stance.

He began his film career as a script writer for a number of generally undistinguished films about the Roman underworld. The first film he directed himself, *Accattone* (1961), also had an underworld and sub-proletarian setting (as indeed do his novels), but its treatment was very remote from the kind of 'low-life picturesque' favoured by his contemporaries. With *The Gospel According to Matthew* (1964) he took a further step away from the debased heritage of neo-realism, but laid himself open to a different misconstruction – this time as 'Catholic-Marxist'. In fact he was neither (though he was both religious and politically left-wing) and the appellation only makes sense to the extent that Catholicism and Marxism are the two great rival orthodoxies in Italy whose influence it is impossible to escape. Pasolini, however, was a heretic in relation to both, constantly and self-consciously at odds with every form of either Marxist or Catholic orthodoxy. His political heterodoxy was most clearly revealed in 1968, when he published a poem 'Dear students, I hate you', which was instantly read as an attack on student radicalism and a defence of the riot police. It re-emerged around 1973 when he took up position against the campaign to liberalize the abortion law. It was also in the course of this debate that Pasolini 'came out' on the question of his own homosexuality. Meanwhile, his religiosity became increasingly pagan. While never losing his respect for what he called the 'sacrale' (sacredness), he came to locate this sacredness further and further away from the world of organized religion, particularly as organized by the Vatican and Christian Democracy. What he did retain, however, was a sentimental attachment to the religion of the poor, to be defended against lay intellectuals and prelates alike.

Pasolini's later films, beginning with *Oedipus Rex* (1967), are distinguished by an overt fascination with primitivism and by an underlying structure through which he sets out to affirm values antithetical to those of modern capitalist society. The values he opposes are those of technology, capitalism, patriarchy, heterosexual monogamy, conformity and repression. Against those negative but all too real features of the modern world Pasolini sets up various imaginary alternatives. Most of his films are set in the past – in the Middle Ages or in prehistory. When set in the present – as with *Theorem* (1968) or *Salò* (1975) – they show bourgeois society as a network of corruption and repression from which only a few innocents can escape. In all the films there is a search for lost innocence, which is always regressive, coupled with a recognition that recovery of this innocence is difficult if not impossible. Knowledge always comes too late, and takes the form of a knowledge of being already guilty.

Stylistically, these films are chiefly remarkable for the role they ascribe to the image. Whereas most films consist of a series of shots whose meaning is established either through contrast or continuity with other shots composing the narrative, in Pasolini's films narrative continuity is weak and each shot stands on its own, evocative of a meaning which is not always decipherable in narrative terms. The result is to enhance the imaginary character of the films, since not only is the intellectual content predicated on a negation of contemporary reality, but the presentation of it is hallucinatory and dream-like. Whereas in his essays Pasolini is explicit in his denunciation of the modern world, but unable to envisage any realistic alternative, the films do offer an alternative – but only to the extent that the world they portray is avowedly imaginary. That this imaginary journey might bring one closer to a psychic 'real' that ordinary reality denies is a dialectical possibility not to be dismissed.

Geoffrey Nowell-Smith

Other films include: *Uccellacci e uccellini* (1966); *The Decameron* (1970); *The Arabian Nights* (1974). Books include: a volume of essays, *Empirismo eretico* (1972); a collection of journalism, *Scritti corsari* (1975); and his last work *La Divina Mimesi* (1975). See: Oswald

Stack, *Pasolini on Pasolini* (1969); P. Willemen (ed.), *Pier Paolo Pasolini* (1977); Enzo Siciliano, *Vita di Pasolini* (1978).

365
PASTERNAK, Boris Leonidovich 1890–1960

Russian poet and novelist

Boris Pasternak grew up in a highly cultivated Moscow environment; his father Leonid was an important painter and his mother a former concert pianist. Much influenced by Scriabin, Pasternak at first wanted to become a composer; it was only in 1912, after some months as a philosophy student in Germany, that he committed himself to poetry. After the Revolution he remained in Russia, and in 1922 published his best-known book of poems, *My Sister Life* (*Sestra moya – zhizn*, 1922). This was followed soon afterwards by *Themes and Variations* (*Temy i variatsii*, 1923). In the 1920s Pasternak occupied a somewhat isolated position in the Soviet literary world; he was a poet of great prestige, but many regarded him as at best a lukewarm friend to the new regime. Various writings of this period show his attempt to come to terms with the Revolution, both long poems such as *Lofty Malady* (*Vysokaya bolezn*, 1924) and *Lieutenant Schmidt* (1926–7) and the volume of lyric poetry *Second Birth* (*Vtoroe rozhdenie*, 1932), which also reflects the break-up of his first marriage and his love for the woman who was to become his second wife.

From early on Pasternak had also been writing prose and he came to place more and more emphasis on it as a means of doing justice to his own experience and that of his country. In 1931 he published the autobiographical *Safe Conduct* (*Okhrannaya gramota*) and in the 1930s he began work on his novel *Dr Zhivago*. This was the great work of his last two decades, though he also produced several remarkable sequences of verse and a large number of memorable translations, in particular of Shakespeare. *Dr Zhivago* was rejected by the journal *Novy Mir* in 1956, but at the end of the following year it was published in Italy and in 1958 Pasternak was awarded the Nobel Prize for literature. This gave rise to a violent campaign of denunciation in the Soviet Union; Pasternak was expelled from the Writers' Union and forced to decline the prize in order to remain in his native country. Greatly shaken by this experience, he died near Moscow in 1960.

For most non-Russian readers, Pasternak is above all the author of *Dr Zhivago*, and this is as he would have wanted it. For many Russian readers, however, his finest work is to be found in his early collections, particularly *My Sister Life*. In the pre-Revolutionary period he had been associated with the Futurist movement and his early poems show a verbal inventiveness (and sometimes obscurity) which matches that of

Mayakovsky*. But Pasternak was not interested in verbal experiment for its own sake. His conception of poetry was essentially expressive; in his words, 'focused upon a reality that has been displaced by feeling, art is a record of this displacement'. In his poems figures of speech, sound orchestration and rhythm all serve to render the vivid feeling of life. One of the dominant themes is renewal or transfiguration, often conveyed through images of weather, wind, rain and storm. The starting point is personal experience – *My Sister Life* is constructed round a love affair – but Pasternak characteristically brings together the great and the small, the universe and the detail. He later interpreted the excited consciousness of *My Sister Life* as reflecting the heightened vitality of the year of revolutions, though it is worth noting that the poems which compose it were written between February and October 1917.

My Sister Life brought Pasternak an outstanding reputation, but he later turned against the 'frills and fancies' of his early verse, aiming for what he once described as an 'unheard-of simplicity'. This is opposed rather to official jargon than to obscure poetry; what he was interested in was a realistic art that would 'contain' the world (Chekhov and Chopin were models), and this did not necessarily involve writing poems of banal accessibility. Even so, his late poems are certainly easier for the average reader. At their best (and above all in the poems which make up the final chapter of *Dr Zhivago*) they show the same concern for life as the early work, together with an increased emphasis on ethical and historical questions. All of this is well seen in one of Pasternak's most famous poems, 'Hamlet'. At times, however, and particularly in his last collection *When the Weather Clears* (*Kogda razgulyaetsa*, 1956–9), there is something of a decline into banality.

Dr Zhivago (trans. Max Hayward and Manya Harari, 1958), although hailed by some Western reviewers as a novel in the Tolstoyan tradition, is very much a poet's novel, a highly personal view of the destiny of modern Russia as experienced by a young doctor-poet to whom Pasternak attributes some of his own best poems. Many of the themes of the early collections are present in the novel, together with their author's intense awareness of the life of the world. The book is permeated by a symbolism which is accentuated by the poems of the final chapter; it expresses Pasternak's faith in traditional ethical and religious values and his hope for a future in which the best features of the Revolution (seen here largely in negative terms) and of the old intellectual tradition would be reconciled. One may feel that the novelist is too close to his hero and does not always avoid a certain sentimental idealizing, but it can hardly be denied that *Dr Zhivago* is a major novel of this century. At the same time, it should not be allowed to overshadow the marvellous achievement of the early poems.

In the Soviet Union, Pasternak is still officially denied his proper place, but for younger generations he has remained a poet and novelist of the first importance, and an emblematic figure of the freedom and power of poetry.

Peter France

Pasternak's works, with the exception of *Dr Zhivago*, are in the three-volume Russian edition by G. P. Struve and B. A. Filippov (Michigan 1961). Other translations include: *Fifty Poems* (trans. Lydia Pasternak Slater, 1963); *Poems* (trans. E. M. Kayden, 1959); *The Poetry of Boris Pasternak* (trans. G. Reavey, 1959); *Collected Prose*, ed. C. Barnes (1977). On Pasternak see: H. Gifford, *Pasternak* (1977); D. Davie and A. Livingstone (eds), *Pasternak: Modern Judgments* (1969); V. Erlich (ed.), *Pasternak: a Collection of Critical Essays* (1978).

366
PAVESE, Cesare 1908–50

Italian novelist and poet

Pavese began his career with *Lavorare stanca* ('Work makes you tired', 1936), poems which owe much to Walt Whitman, and are unlike those written by the leading Italian poets of the time, Ungaretti* and Montale*. Pavese's initial ideal of objectivity and immediacy in 'story-poems' soon gave way to subjectivity and abstruseness, and he turned to prose, but *Lavorare stanca* remains, in Pavese's phrase, the 'great monolith' in which he set out, once and for all, the themes he was to treat with growing complexity and subtlety in his narrative fiction, which is set mostly in Turin and the Piedmontese hills, Le Langhe. His concerns are with the question of whether human relationships constitute restrictions within (or in spite of) which peace can be found, as in *The Political Prisoner* (*Il carcere*, 1947, trans. 1955), in which prison becomes a sustained metaphor of the protagonist's predicament, or the means to fulfilment and complete humanity. Pavese explores the tension between the demands of individual integrity and those made by social roles most deeply in 'A Woman Alone' ('Tra donne sole', in *La bella estate*, 1949, trans. 1953).

Influenced by Jung* and Frazer, Pavese attempted, not entirely successfully, to elaborate an anti-supernatural theory of myth, with childhood experience, outside time, as the formative period, after which experience repeats itself to become myth. *Dialogues with Leukothea* (*Dialoghi con Leucò*, 1947, trans. 1965) represents his most systematic attempt to formulate his views on the subject, but he works out his ideas more successfully in his fictions than in his more theoretical works. Probably his most satisfying novel is his last,

The Moon and the Bonfires (*La luna e i falò*, 1950, trans. 1952), in which the protagonist compares the world he knew as a boy with that of his return to it after an absence of twenty years, realizing finally that freedom and maturity lie in the willing and understanding acceptance of one's destiny. The novel also offers a penetrating analysis of the tensions inherent in post-war Italian society.

The influence on him of Melville, Dos Passos* and other American novelists has led critics to regard Pavese as a neo-realist; but since his technique depends on the creation of rhythms and patterns of events, and his richly allusive style demands to be read and reread as one reads poetry, he is perhaps best considered as a post-modernist.

Towards the end of his life, Pavese returned to poetry with *Verrà la morte e avrà i tuoi occhi* ('Death will come and have your eyes', 1951), which some have seen as the finest modern Italian cycle of love lyrics.

Professor Brian Moloney

Pavese's other books include: *Paesi tuoi* (1941); *Prima che il gallo canti* (1949); *Il diavolo sulle colline* (in *La bella estate*, 1949); and *Il mestiere di vivere (diario 1936–1950)* (1952). See: D. Lajolo, *Il vizio assurdo* (1960); G.-P. Biasin, *The Smile of the Gods: A Thematic Study of Pavese's World* (1969); and A. Guidacci, *Il mito Pavese* (1967).

367

PEAKE, Mervyn Laurence 1911–68

English novelist and artist

Mervyn Peake was born the son of a missionary doctor in Kuling, China. He attended Tientsin Grammar School and, on his family's return to England, Eltham College in Kent; subsequently he trained at the Croydon School of Art, and 1929–33 at the Royal Academy Schools. For much of his life he practised as a painter and illustrator, as well as writing poetry and plays, but his reputation as a major figure is based on the three Titus novels: *Titus Groan* (1946), *Gormenghast* (1950), and *Titus Alone* (1959; revised edition edited by Langdon Jones, 1970).

Peake is the most accomplished Fantastic Realist in modern English literature, having more stylistically in common with Dickens than with any of his British contemporaries. The world of Gormenghast and its inhabitants is the exaggerated one of dreams and nightmares. Where Dickens was eccentric, Peake is entirely grotesque. His only rival in scale is Tolkien* whose work, if better known to the public, lacks the inexhaustible invention and depth of Peake's. Perhaps his nearest contemporary parallels were not writers at all but the Fantastic Realist painters of Vienna: Fuchs,

Brauer, Hutter. Like theirs, his work is surreal in its conceptions and yet rendered with a meticulous technique and a concern for detail that is almost pathological in its intensity. It induces in the reader to an exceptional degree that 'subtle attitude of awed listening' which was H. P. Lovecraft's test for success in fantasy. Peake's own outlook he described in a radio talk, 1947: 'As I see it, or as I want to see it, the marvels of the visible world are not things in themselves but revelations to stir the imagination – to conduct us to amazing climates of the mind, which climates it is for the artist to translate into paint or into words ... whether he can assimilate and build from it an original work of art depends largely on how deeply he is obsessed by his work.'

The books are concerned with growth and the search for liberation in the early life of Titus Groan, the seventy-seventh Earl, with whose birth in the ancient precincts of Gormenghast Castle the novel opens. The narrative of the first two novels is long and complex. The third and much shorter volume was not properly finished because of the progress of the author's Parkinson's Disease. None the less *Titus Alone* in its revised version is an extraordinary book. After the incestuous density of its predecessors, the space and speed of the third is one of fiction's great dislocating events. The mind, coffered into the elaborate chambers of Gormenghast, is suddenly reeling across phantasmagorical landscapes and through settlements which belong if anywhere to the future. This transposition from the archaic to the futuristic, without passing through a reality in any way contiguous to our own, confirms the autonomy of Peake's creation and heightens the sense of wonder. If it is possible to put Gormenghast into a frame of mind reminiscent of the late eighteenth century's preoccupation with the Middle Ages (for this reason Peake is sometimes referred to as a gothic novelist), this is no longer tenable once the author's own mind begins to panic. Peake's illness has introduced an urgent rhythm that is quite unexpected. The trilogy is hereby turned into more than a brilliantly contrived other-world. It has become the strangest kind of autobiography and an emotionally powerful work of art.

Peake is a virtuoso prose writer in the baroque style. His syntax is never experimental but his use of words is muscular and flamboyant, his images are outlandish and transferred to the reader with a lurid three-dimensional tactility. This power of incision is the consequence of a technically spectacular writer being perfectly focused upon his vision and therefore having the capacity to trace it in all its paralogical ramifications. One only has to read the work of an imitator such as John Barth to be reminded of how exceptional Peake's performance is. Since Peake, the novels of García Márquez* have come closest to giving an equivalent sensual enchantment and imaginative satisfaction of the intellect. Although a writer of short stories, Borges* too has much in common with him. Peake's acclaim was posthumous and there is still no commendable biography or study of his work.

Duncan Fallowell

Also by Mervyn Peake: *Mr Pye* (1953); *Boy in Darkness* (a novella in *Sometime, Never*, 1956); *Selected Poems* (1972); *Writings and Drawings of Mervyn Peake* (1974); *Peake's Progress*, ed. Maeve Gilmore (1979). See also: Maeve Gilmore, *A World Away: a Memoir of Mervyn Peake* (1970); John Batchelor, *Mervyn Peake: a Biographical and Critical Exploration* (1974); John Watney, *Mervyn Peake* (1976).

368
PESSOA, Fernando António Nogueira 1888–1935

Portuguese poet

The son of a music critic who died when the future poet was five years old, Fernando Pessoa left his native Lisbon for South Africa when his widowed mother married by proxy the Portuguese consul in Durban. After completing an English education at Durban High School, Pessoa returned to Lisbon permanently in 1905. He began a course of study at the university, but soon abandoned it, and after the failure of a printing press which he attempted to set up, he found employment as commercial correspondent to various firms in Lisbon. The modest income from this employment, and the limited demands it made upon his time, enabled him to devote himself to literature, above all poetry, and to the study of philosophy, metaphysics, theosophy, occultism and astrology, all grist to his poetic mill. In philosophy, it was Schopenhauer's idea of the terror of existence which most affected this deeply introspective and contemplative young man; in literature, it was above all the French symbolists and post-symbolists, though the influence of Shakespeare and of the nineteenth-century English poets was also far from negligible. Indeed, nearly all his early poems, up to 1909, were written in English.

Having heralded, in a series of articles published in 1912 in the Oporto literary journal *A Águia*, an imminent renaissance in Portuguese poetry, to be characterized by a quest for the transcendental, he proceeded himself to play a leading part in that movement, publishing between 1914 and 1916 poems of striking, not to say startling, originality, which were on the one hand extremely esoteric (notably *Paùis*, 'Quagmires') and on the other strident, tumultuous, and clearly owing much to Walt Whitman (*Ode Triunfal*, 'Triumphal Ode'; *Ode Marítima*, 'Seafaring Ode'). Although there was real depth and suggestive power in these compositions, Pessoa seems already to have felt that they had

been published, and perhaps written, for the wrong reasons – to disconcert, to shock and to mystify the staid Lisbon *bourgeoisie* as exaggerated statements of the new literary movement. In January 1915, in a letter to Armando Cortes-Rodrigues, a fellow-poet, we find him explicitly repudiating all poetry of an insincere and exhibitionist kind, and speaking of the fundamental seriousness of his poetic mission, which, as he saw it, was to probe the mystery of existence and to explore problems of identity and of man's relationship with the universe.

Convinced that 'make-believe is self-knowledge', and that the best way to be objective about oneself is to 'depersonalize' oneself (a conscious play on words, for his family name means 'person'), Pessoa devised a way of exploring his own many-sided personality and at the same time of expressing man's metaphysical doubts and fears. Early in 1914, he had 'created' three other poets, Alberto Caeiro, Ricardo Reis, and Álvaro de Campos, whom he called his heteronyms, and from then onwards he frequently wrote in their names as well as in his own – about a third of his poetic output is 'heteronymic'. In this, Pessoa compared himself with a dramatist who creates characters and attributes to them attitudes and utterances with which he does not necessarily agree. At all events, whether he wrote in their names or in his own, Pessoa expressed the same fundamental metaphysical preoccupations, but was able to express them in widely differing ways, from widely differing viewpoints. Of the heteronyms, it is Campos who is at once the most human and the most speculative; the other two, though well differentiated, suffer from a certain rigidity and finality in their attitudes. All three write almost exclusively in free verse, whereas Pessoa nearly always uses regular verse in his 'orthonymic' poetry.

His poetry has been criticized for a certain lack of human warmth. The poet himself put his finger on this when he complained in one of his English sonnets that he was 'estranged by consciousness from sentiment'. Indeed, it could be said that the strongest emotions expressed in his verse relate to one form or another of intellectual frustration. Within his self-imposed limitations, however, he has produced some of the most memorable and haunting evocations there have ever been of man's doomed attempts to make sense of himself and of his surroundings.

Though he published two slender volumes of English verse in 1918 and 1921, the only volume of Portuguese poems published in his lifetime was a symbolist-occultist interpretation of episodes in Portuguese history, entitled *Mensagem* ('Message', 1934). The poems published in his lifetime in such short-lived periodicals as *Renascença, Orpheu, Exílio, Centauro, Athena, Contemporânea* and *Presença* amount to only a small proportion of his poetic works. At the time of his death, he was known and admired only in Portugal. Since then, with the systematic publication of his writings both verse and prose, he has won international renown as an early existentialist poet of great distinction and originality. Selections from his poetry have been translated into all the major European languages.

Professor Peter Rickard

The poetic works have been published in nine volumes (Lisbon 1942–69), and in one volume, including his English poems (Rio de Janeiro, 2nd edition, 1965). Of his prose writings the most important are: *Páginas íntimas e de auto-interpretação* ('Self-analysis'), ed. J. do Prado Coelho and G. R. Lind (1966); *Páginas de estética e teoria e crítica literárias* ('Aesthetics, Literary Theory and Criticism'), ed. G. R. Lind and J. do Prado Coelho (1966); and *Textos filosóficos* ('Philosophy'), ed. A. de Pina Coelho, 2 vols (1968). The standard biography, *Vida e obra de Fernando Pessoa. Historia duma geração* by J. G. Simões (2 vols, Lisbon, 1950), needs correction in the light of *Fernando Pessoa, Notas a uma biografia romanceada* by E. Freitas da Costa (Lisbon, 1951). See also J. do Prado Coelho, *Diversidade e unidade em Fernando Pessoa* (1963).

369
PIAGET, Jean 1896–

Swiss psychologist, philosopher and biologist

Jean Piaget was born in Neuchâtel, Switzerland. His father was a Professor of Medieval Literature and one of his grandparents was English. He was a precocious youngster. Between seven and ten he interested himself in the study of birds, fossils and natural history. By fifteen he had become an authority on molluscs and had published a number of articles on this topic. On their strength he was offered a post as Curator of the important mollusc collection at the Natural History Museum at Geneva. One can imagine the consternation of the Museum Director when he found he was only dealing with a schoolboy.

At the University of Neuchâtel he took his doctor's degree in zoology. He next studied psychology in Zürich, read Freud* and attended Jung's* lectures. A year later in 1919 he left for Paris where he spent two further years studying abnormal psychology, logic and the philosophy of science at the Sorbonne. Piaget did some work in elementary schools in Paris where he engaged children in conversations modelled on psychoanalytical questioning, with the aim of discovering something about the thought processes underlying their answers. Piaget was then appointed Director of Studies at the Institut J.-J. Rousseau, Geneva (1921); Assistant Director (1929); Co-Director (1932). His other appointments include: Professor of Philosophy, University of Neuchâtel (1925); Professor of the History of Scientific Thought, University of Geneva (1929); Professor of Experimental Psychology and Director of the Psychological Laboratory, Geneva (1940); Professor of Child Psychology at the Sorbonne and Director of the Centre International d'Epistémologie Génétique, Geneva (1955). He was at one time associated with UNESCO as its Assistant Director General.

Piaget's main contribution to knowledge has been to open up to experimental investigation the whole subject of concept formation. As a result of suggestive questioning and making the subject handle concrete materials such as building blocks and toys, he showed how the child learned to employ simple classifications and serial ordering, upon which the more complex hypothetico-deductive reasoning of the adolescent and adult is based. His experiments have dealt with such topics as logic, mathematics, space, time, chance, morality, play and language. His work is of interest from a number of different points of view. From that of the psychologist, a knowledge of the normal process of concept formation in the individual is likely to help in the understanding of the thought of the abnormal adult. In the educational field it is of considerable importance to realize at what levels it is possible to acquire certain abstract concepts. Much of our teaching may be thwarted if we teach certain subjects before the child is ripe for them. From the point of view of the philosopher of science, the origin of concepts which have been so widely used in science is clearly important. Piaget has shown that the space, time and causality of physics are adult conceptions, and that the conceptual apparatus by means of which the child orders the world around him is of a much more naive variety than had previously been suspected.

Apart from attempting to provide a philosophical foundation for his empirical findings, to which study he has given the name of *genetic epistemology*, he has also developed a sociological theory based on the notion of social exchange between individuals. His work in moral psychology suggests that at least in our society there exist in the child two levels of morality. At an early stage the child follows the voice of authority, whilst at adolescence, equity and justice begin to play a dominant role. In the biological field, Piaget has carried out studies concerned with evolutionary adaptation. One may mention his work on a specific kind of snail inhabiting the Alpine lakes, in which he showed that the shape of their shells was related to the harshness of their environment. He attempted to explain this phenomenon by constructing an evolutionary theory, which he took as a *tertium quid* between Lamarckianism and Neo-Darwinianism.

Piaget has written at least fifty books and numerous articles. This has led to some repetition and to a certain looseness and prolixity of expression in his writings. He has been criticized by psychologists for being too philosophical and by philosophers for being too psychological. Perhaps this is the fate of any creative thinker whose work straddles different disciplines. It would, however, be difficult to deny Piaget a place among the great thinkers of this century. He has carried out a Copernican revolution in our study of child thought, and he has shown how adult thought has its roots in it.

Dr Wolfe Mays

Translations of Piaget's work include: *The Language and Thought of the Child* (1924); *Judgment and Reasoning in the Child* (1924); *The Child's Conception of Causality* (1927); *The Moral Judgment of the Child* (1932); *The Child's Concept of Number* (with Alice Szeminska, 1952); *The Origin of Intelligence in the Child* (1953); *The Child's Construction of Reality* (1955); *The Child's Conception of Space* (with Bärbel Inhelder, 1956); *Play, Dream and Imitation in Childhood* (1962); *The Mechanisms of Perception* (1969); *The Child's Conception of Time* (1969); *Biology and Knowledge* (1971); *Structuralism* (1971); *Insights and Illusions of Philosophy* (1972); *The Principles of Genetic Epistemology* (1972). See also Howard E. Gruber and J. Jacques Vonèche (eds), *The Essential Piaget* (1977). About Piaget: Margaret Boden, *Piaget* (1979); Peter Bryant, *Perception and Understanding in Young Children* (1974); J. H. Flavell, *The Developmental Psychology of Piaget* (1963); H. G. Furth, *Piaget and Knowledge* (1969); T. Mischel (ed.), *Cognitive Development and Epistemology* (1971); Brian Rotman, *Jean Piaget: Psychologist of the Real* (1977); James Russell, *The Acquisition of Knowledge* (1978).

370

PICASSO, Pablo (Ruiz y) 1881–1973

Spanish/French artist

Pablo Picasso was born into a comfortable middle-class family in Málaga, Spain, in 1881. His father was a curator of a museum and teacher of painting. From an early age Picasso had shown remarkable talent which his father made every effort to foster. By 1895 the family had moved to Barcelona where Picasso's professional life began, centred around the café of 'El Quatre Gats'. It was in Barcelona that Picasso saw Symbolist works including those of the Englishman Burne-Jones, whose sad-eyed processions carried the same inward melancholy as the Continental Symbolists. Picasso's own Symbolist 'Blue' period with its subject-matter of old age, poverty and lonely clowns maintained this mood of psychological depression, but in its contemporaneity of subject-matter came closer to the poetry of Jules Laforgue.

For the first time in 1900 Picasso left Spain, visited France and decided in 1904 to settle in Paris. From then on he holidayed frequently in his native land until 1934 when he became a permanent exile. France then became his second mother country and promoted his talent to such an extent that he became a living legend as the greatest twentieth-century artistic genius of the Western world, comparable with such masters as Velázquez and Manet, both of whom influenced him deeply.

It is perhaps useful to consider the vast oeuvre of Picasso in phases. The early 'Blue' period gave way to a happier 'Pink' period in Paris, whilst Picasso was living with Fernande Olivier. It was, for this restless man, a brief time of relative tranquillity when his work reflected a classic serenity. This was soon to be shattered.

During 1906 and 1907 Picasso painted the awkward and primitive *Demoiselles D'Avignon*, undoubtedly one of the key works of the first half of the twentieth century, when he was only twenty-five years of age. This painting set in motion the movement that later became known as Cubism, without which it is doubtful whether Pure Abstraction such as that of Mondrian* and Malevich* would have occurred when and in the way that it did.

Picasso's concern with primitivism as a way of seeing afresh, of connecting again with the vital creative forces of artistic endeavour that he felt had been lost to the Renaissance tradition produced the *Demoiselles*, a bold and dramatically direct statement. Five figures of nude women squat or stand showing progressive distortions and flattenings of form from left to right of the work. Space is diminished and colour limited. Picasso had become aware of African tribal carvings and early Iberian sculpture in the Trocadéro Museum in Paris. He had also seen much of the work of Gauguin with its primitive South Sea island subjects. He well knew also Cézanne's painting with its floating colour orchestrations of the structure of space and object. Both these artists had shown regularly at Paris exhibitions in the years immediately preceding 1907.

Georges Braque* was introduced to Picasso at this time, saw the *Demoiselles* and understood its revolutionary significance. He himself had studied Cézanne thoroughly. Together the two painters went on 'roped together like rock climbers' to work out Cubist form which had as its central tenet the breaking of singlepoint perspective. Both Braque and Picasso felt that perspective had become 'a stranglehold on art', stultifying it with irrelevant rules. It was possible to remember an object from another view whilst seeing it in front of the eyes. Perception became multidimensional if you included existing concepts. They realized that this could form a new reality for art.

During the early analytical stage of Cubism from 1907 until 1912 objects were painted as though viewed from many angles. Simple, often rectangular, hence the name Cubist, facets of these various views were then painted flat, overlapping and parallel to the picture surface, emphasizing that surface and shutting out distance. Bright colour was abandoned to avoid an emotional impact and to focus on the restructuring of space–object relationships. Only later did rich and at times brittle colour appear during the synthetic Cubist period (1912–15). At this time also decorative patterns were used and actual paper cut-outs or pieces of objects stuck on to the canvas surface to form *papier collé* or collage. This latter technique was in part to emphasize the flatness or two-dimensionality of the canvas and therefore the autonomy of the work of art as an object in its own right denying its role as an illusion of natural appearances. However, it was also to make concrete for the viewer the reality the artist was dealing with. Both Picasso and Braque had felt around 1912 that their myriads of small facets had become too abstract. For this reason they also added words or parts of words to the paintings, labels for the objects in fact.

The First World War separated the two artists, for Braque, as a Frenchman, had to enlist. They did not see each other again. During the war Picasso met Diaghilev*, master of the Ballets Russes, and worked on sets for the ballet *Parade*. He also loved and married one of the dancers, Olga. As a result of his marriage he produced many portraits and statuesque half-figures of full and fruitful women and children. These take on once more a Classical figurative appearance, at times parodying that style. A return to Classical form was common throughout Europe after the war in many of the arts. However, in Picasso's case it was not long lasting; Dada and Surrealist ideas provided more exciting material to work with.

André Breton*, the poet leader of the Surrealist movement, knew Picasso and admired his work. Picasso in turn took an interest in Breton's writings and the Surrealist journal he edited called *La Révolution Surréaliste*. 1925 was the year of the first large Surrealist exhibition and it was also the date of Picasso's painting *The Three Dancers* with both Surrealist and Expressionist influences. In it Picasso utilizes again, as he had done for a year or two previously, Cubist flattening of form and lack of depth in space. Three figures, with a fourth death's head, entwine in a primitive dance of conflicting passions. The Surrealist element in the work which gives the left-hand figure its violent contortions derives from Freudian* concerns with the erotic. The woman, both symbolically and expressively sexual, is linked with the man and the death's head on the right. Between the two and across the linked hands is a cruciform figure suggesting pain and suffering. Picasso had taken the traditional archetypal theme of love and death and added to it several personal significances connected not only with his own marital difficulties but also with the past love affair of a friend who had committed suicide.

Throughout the 1930s Picasso's work carried this double level of interpretation, the universal and the particular, with much use of visual metaphor. A hand could also look like a bird's wing and so suggest the qualities of touch as well as of vision. There is no doubt that Picasso was very physical in his approach to his art. He enjoyed sculpting and was strongly aware of volumetric form. It was this very acute consciousness that made him more especially able to visualize forms as expressive shapes.

At the time of the Spanish Civil War in 1936 Picasso had acquired facility with a great range of expressive subject-matter and formal devices. His experiments with themes of young maidens carried off by bulls or horses, of man desiring and woman enticing, of crucifixion and fear meant that for the greatest theme of his life, *Guernica*, he had a vivid repertoire on which to draw.

The war itself was a shock to Europe. For the first time the political far left confronted and fought fascism. The outrage of bombing one of Spain's small and defenceless towns with no warning meant a deepening of Picasso's commitment to communism and the total absorption of his dynamic personality in the theme of war. Again the archetypal themes of weeping women, of animals and savagely torn bodies were given a new and personal significance by Picasso's physical and emotional identification with his subject-matter.

The forms in *Guernica* and other works of the period became sharply jagged, hard in colour and texture, twisted and wrenched apart with the tensions of pain and grief. Yet at the same time a classically rhythmic structure underlies the drawing and composition. The twentieth-century element remains as the degree of distortion set in Cubist space.

Faced soon with the isolation, deprivation and hardship of Paris during the Second World War, Picasso sculpted and painted with whatever materials he could assemble. The works were bleak, gaunt and at times fragile. The *Charnel House* of 1944 competes with *Guernica* as a great visual document of protest against human suffering.

After the war, the joyous release gave rise to works of warmth, wit and invention. Picasso's sculptural interests turned more to pottery which he carried out at Vallauris in the Mediterranean South. By Françoise Gilot he produced more children and life was perhaps supremely zestful. However, although great themes were not lacking, a more literal look at war as in the painting *Massacre in Korea* of 1951 did not produce works to compare with *Guernica*.

The creativity of this period that commands the greatest respect is more personal and self-revealing. Drawings of old age and youth where Picasso sees himself as less than heroically hiding behind a mask to gaze on the beauty of his young beloved move the viewer at the deepest levels.

Intermittently also, Picasso explored, after the war, paintings of earlier artists. Variations on Velázquez's

Las Meninas are works of a high order in their own right. As interpretations of the enclosed social milieu of court life and its infantas they must frequently have reminded Picasso of his own. He had from youth been encouraged as a prince among painters. During his mature life the world press followed him as routinely as any member of royalty.

In many senses for Picasso, as for Matisse*, intuition and expression were one, but as a Spaniard he responded most strongly to themes of the greatest dramatic content which meant ultimately to tragedy.

Pat Turner

See: Christian Zervos, *Pablo Picasso* (*catalogue raisonné*, 23 vols, 1932–71); Alfred H. Barr (ed.), *Picasso: Fifty Years of His Art* (1946); H. Jaffé, *Picasso* (1964); J. Berger, *Picasso: Success and Failure* (1965); John Golding, *Cubism* (1965); J. Crespinelle, *Picasso and His Women* (trans. 1969); Timothy Hilton, *Picasso* (1975).

371
PINTER, Harold 1930–

British dramatist

Pinter's early background was Jewish Hackney, East London. After wartime evacuation he attended Hackney Downs Grammar School, then the Royal Academy of Dramatic Art for two disenchanting terms. In 1948–9 Pinter twice stood trial for refusing National Service and was fined as a conscientious objector. *Poetry London* published two poems (1950). After a spell at the Central School of Speech and Drama Pinter began his acting career in earnest by touring Ireland with Anew McMaster's repertory company. Between 1951 and 1957 Pinter acted, wrote poetry, married (one son), did odd jobs, and wrote an unpublished novel, *The Dwarfs*. Since 1957, though occasionally acting and frequently directing, Pinter has written for all media, including celebrated screenplays for Joseph Losey*, and published a *Proust Screenplay* (1978). In 1973 Pinter joined the National Theatre as associate director.

Nearly all Pinter's plays remove a wall from a domestic interior and reveal existences in process. Truth of character relationship is uncertain, unverifiable and remains unexplored by dramatic exposition. Evasion of communication exacerbates the menace of intruders – agents or victims of psychological and physical domination and dispossession. Pinter's foremost stylistic is obtrusive idiomatic naturalism heightened, almost expressionistically, by an hallucinatory atmosphere which is duplicated by patterns of structural augmentation evoking alternate laughter and apprehensive silence in the audience. The plays are powerful emotional experiences not intellectual blueprints of modern thought. Comedy is a means not an end. The complic-

ity of laughter qualifies the audience's final recognition of a state of being: the failure or betrayal of friendship and love.

In the first plays, *The Room* (1957), *The Dumb Waiter* (1957), *The Birthday Party* (1958) and *A Slight Ache* (1959), a mundane setting is entered by something bizarre which brings blindness, betrayal and death. An incapacitated and alien bearer of identity, a blind Negro, enters the room of an elderly housewife's subservient existence with a silently dominating husband who eventually kicks the Negro to death, precipitating his wife's blindness. The two men waiting argumentatively beside the dumb waiter of a café basement for instructions are neither workmen nor lodgers but hired gunmen. The order is that one kill the other. The birthday party is given by two strangers for the seedy bullying lodger of a seaside boarding house. Hysteria and final breakdown follow celebration and the strangers abduct the lodger. A slight ache anticipates the blindness that occurs with the admission of a voiceless tramp matchseller to a seemingly complacent middle-class household. In all, physical disability symbolizes moral deficiency.

The year 1960 saw the first performance of four plays. *A Night Out* studies naturalistically the shifting pattern of domination from mother to son, son to prostitute, the son failing to grasp the one possibility of friendship in an otherwise jeering world. *The Caretaker* is Pinter's masterpiece of intuitive psychological insight into three damaged lives: a tramp, an ex-mental patient and his brother, warped by 'normality'. The need for mutual 'caretaking' is betrayed by alternating self-assertion, aggression, domination and rejection. In spite of critical insistence on allegorical interpretation (fostered by the symbolism of the earlier plays), the exhausting realism of *The Caretaker* established Pinter's popular reputation. *The Dwarfs*, a strained reworking from the earlier novel, are creatures of a paranoid imagination breaking down at the betrayal of friendships. In *Night School* and, later, *Tea Party* (1965), Pinter saw the danger of capitulating to mannerism which, he felt, would amount to betrayal of his characters.

A developed sense of dramatic form produced two virtuoso pieces, *The Collection* (1961) and *The Lover* (1963), concerned, respectively, with verification of the truth or otherwise of an adulterous betrayal, and the almost algebraic inversion of a pattern of erotic domination. It was as if Pinter were practising for a large-scale formal assault on the mind and senses which is *The Homecoming* (1965), a modern *King Lear*. Shakespeare explores a pagan world bereft of Christ's grace, Pinter a womanless family abandoned to animality and suburban barbarism, unredeemed by human love, tainted and tainting all.

The script of *The Basement* (1967) dates back to 1963 and both characters and structure belong to the earlier period. Sexual rivalry as an expression of combative egoism leads to a circular pattern of intrusion, betrayal and expropriation. In 1969 Pinter turned startlingly to the extremes of Beckettian* austerity and attenuation in *Landscape* and *Silence*. But with *Old Times* (1971) and *No Man's Land* (1975) it could be seen that the primary concern was with double betrayal, by fallibility and disclosure, of memory, that both appropriates and rejects – in thought, image or embodied intruder, the past marooning the present, leaving Pinter's characters stranded by time as well as in place.

Pinter's most recent work, *Betrayal* (1978), focuses through retrospective time sequence on the illusory nature of assumed mutuality in love and friendship. Love can only be betrayed if it is real. The origin of all betrayals lies in fostering initial illusion. The characters are incapable of consummating true betrayal. Beneath the patterned, desultory surface there is the intensity of the later Shakespeare sonnets.

Pinter's plays, particularly the earlier, are often discussed in terms of Theatre of the Absurd, Black Comedy, or Comedy of Menace. Acknowledged admiration for Kafka* and Beckett might appear to support this, but the most powerful and least discussed artistic influences are the multifarious traditions of comedy absorbed through years of acting. Pinter's style and power are copied but rarely followed. The young Joe Orton* is a conspicuous example. The plays of Harold Pinter bear witness to truth and their essential 'influence' is witnessed daily.

Ronald Knowles

Other works: *Revue Sketches* in *A Slight Ache and Other Plays* (1961); *Night* (1969); *Five Screenplays* (1971); *Monologue* (1973); *Poems and Prose* (1978); *The Hothouse* (written 1958, first performed 1980). See also: J. R. Brown, *Theatre Language* (1972); Martin Esslin, *Pinter. A Study of His Plays* (3rd edition, 1977).

372
PIRANDELLO, Luigi 1867–1936

Italian poet, short-story writer, novelist and dramatist

The Sicilian Pirandello was educated at the Universities of Rome and Bonn, where he wrote a doctoral thesis on his native dialect. That he wrote verse (*Mal giocondo*, 1889; *Pasqua di Gea*, 1891) was more an indication of the prestige of poetry than a recognition of his true gifts. In Rome in 1893, Pirandello was induced by a fellow Sicilian, Luigi Capuana, to write prose. His first novel, *The Outcast* (*L'esclusa*, 1908, written in 1894, trans. 1925), deals with a woman wrongly suspected of adultery, cast off by her husband, and forced by social pressures to become what she was thought to be. The themes of Pirandello's early fiction are the contrast

between appearance and reality, form and life, the tragedies of a society which values appearance and formality. Until 1910–12, Pirandello wrote novels and short stories – sketches of peasant and middle-class life, coloured by his conviction that external reality is unknowable and that we are irremediably alone. He is capable of humour, as in *The Jar* (*La giara*, short story 1909, play 1925, trans. 1928), but for the most part his laughter is either sardonic or compassionate, as he explains in the essay *L'umorismo* (1908).

Although in his first fiction Pirandello seemed the natural heir of the Sicilian naturalists, Verga and Capuana, he soon turned to the exploration of ideas. The first full formulation of his attitude to life comes in the novel *The Late Mattia Pascal* (*Il fu Mattia Pascal*, 1904, trans. 1923). The phrase 'relativity of personality' is often used to describe his belief that personality is a subjective phenomenon. Deriving from Alfred Binet and Henri Bergson*, Pirandello's attitude is philosophically unsound, but expressed with lucidity and emotional conviction.

His ear for the spoken language led him naturally to cast his tales in dramatic form, with lively dialogue. He wrote his first play, *The Vice* (*La morsa*, trans. 1928) in 1908, and he was several times invited to write for the theatre. In 1916, he wrote nine plays in a year, of which the best known is *Right you are, if you think so!* (*Così è, se vi pare!*, 1918, trans. 1960). In this group of plays, the ideas at stake are recognizably Pirandellian, but his techniques are conventional. Contacts with avant-garde theatre groups between 1915 and 1920 helped him to clarify his ideas. He learned from Craig the importance of harmonizing all elements on the stage, and from Bragaglia the use of lighting to clarify the action. From 1920 onwards, his stage directions became much more detailed and precise, his sets less realistic, often illustrating symbolically the different levels of reality at which the action takes place.

Pirandello's 'total theatre' has its origin in the story *A Character in Distress* (*Tragedia di un personaggio*, 1911, trans. 1938), which led to the play *Six Characters in Search of an Author* (*Sei personaggi in cerca d'autore*, 1921, trans. 1923). This is often regarded as the first in a 'trilogy' which is crucial for our understanding of his contribution to the theatre, the others being *Each in his own way* (*Ciascuno a suo modo*, 1924, trans. 1924) and *Tonight we improvise* (*Questa sera si recita a soggetto*, 1930, trans. 1932). He stresses that the theatre is illusion, but that it is superior to life since it has, or rather, *is* form, 'form that moves', and so has a stability missing in life, which is all flux. His plays therefore have a polemical thrust and are not concerned with pointing to an alternative set of values other than in the realm of abstract ideas. His situations are contrived, so exceptional that they can never constitute the basis of another norm. As Raymond Williams writes: 'It is, really, a mystification of demystification, since the experience . . . depends on a theatrical special case.' *Henry IV* (*Enrico IV*, 1922, trans. 1923) remains Pirandello's most performed play, because it is the most imbued with deep feeling. Henry's tragedy is that the mask of madness, which he has consciously chosen to wear, is at the end of the play forced on him by the pressures of emotions outside his control. In his depiction of the loss of identity and the reduction of personality to a social role, Pirandello achieved his greatest success.

Professor Brian Moloney

Pirandello's other works include: the novel *The Old and the Young* (*I vecchi e i giovani*, 1913, trans. 1928); and the plays *Naked* (*Vestire gli ignudi*, 1923, trans. 1924) and *The Man with a Flower in his Mouth* (*L'uomo dal fiore in bocca*, 1926, trans. 1928). See: G. Giudice, *Luigi Pirandello* (1963); A. L. De Castris, *Storia di Pirandello* (1966); R. Williams, *Modern Tragedy* (1966).

373
PLANCK, Max Karl 1858–1947

German physicist

Max Planck was born in Kiel where his father was Professor of Constitutional Law. Educated at the Maximilian-Gymnasium in Munich, he studied mathematics and physics at the Universities of Munich and Berlin, obtaining his doctorate in physics from Munich in 1879 for a thesis on the second law of thermodynamics. He then taught physics at Munich until he was appointed to a special chair in mathematical physics at Kiel in 1885. In 1889 he moved to a professorship at Berlin made vacant by the death of Gustav Kirchhoff. He was President of the Kaiser-Wilhelm Institut (1930–5) which after the Second World War was renamed the Max-Planck Institut.

In his early years Planck made significant contributions to physics, particularly to the understanding of heat and physical chemistry. His work at the time received little attention. Between 1894 and 1900 Planck worked on thermodynamics, statistical mechanics and electro-magnetic theory. By applying his work in these areas in novel ways to the problem of black-body radiation, Planck was led in 1900 to the discovery of the quantum, a discovery which was to revolutionize physics. A black-body (approximated by a piece of soot) is a perfect absorber of radiation which when heated emits all types of radiation. At the end of the last century no law had been discovered which would correctly predict the distribution of radiation given off by a black-body. The Rayleigh-Jeans law (1900) worked for high but not for low temperature. Wilhelm Wien's formula (1883), on the other hand, gave correct predictions for low but not high temperatures. Planck, who at a previous stage had had doubts about the atomic theory of matter, now assumed that for his purposes the radiating matter could be thought of as composed of discrete vibrating electrons. Prior to Planck it had been assumed that energy was given off continuously by radiating electrons. Working on the entirely novel assumption that the energy was in fact given off in discrete bundles, Planck arrived at his radiation law which correctly predicts the distribution of radiation from a black-body for all temperatures. In Planck's theory the energy, E of an electron vibrating with frequency, v, is given by the equation: $E = nhv$. h is a constant now known as Planck's constant whose value he calculated to be 6.55×10^{-27} erg-seconds. The discrete, quantized character of energy is revealed through the fact that n can only take as values 0, 1, 2, . . . For this work Planck was awarded the Nobel Prize in 1919.

Planck was subsequently exercised by the problem of reconciling the emission of radiation in discrete bundles with the application to the radiation once emitted of Maxwell's field equations which appeared to require treating it as continuous. It was left to Einstein* to show how to extend the quantum treatment to all radiation. The discovery of other areas requiring a quantum approach led to the development of Quantum mechanics by Schrödinger* and Heisenberg*. The crucial role played in that theory by Planck's constant led to the realization that it is one of the most fundamental of all physical constants. Planck's work was crucial to the discovery of Quantum mechanics which represents the most fundamental transformations in physics since Newton.

Planck was cultured, musically talented and politically conservative. He wrote extensively on the state of physics and on the philosophy of science, vigorously attacking the early positivists who regarded physical objects as complexes of sensations. Planck was a realist holding it to be a cardinal principle of science that there is a real external world existing independently of our cognition which is not directly knowable and which is governed by immutable laws, to be discovered not created by the scientist. A firm believer in causality, he sought to refute the indeterministic construal of Quantum mechanics by attempting unconvincingly to distinguish between what he called the 'world picture of physics' and the 'sense world'. The world picture of physics was, he held, rigorously deterministic. Any indeterminism indicated by Quantum mechanics reflected only uncertainly in the correlation of items from these two worlds. His determinism did not extend to human action, for he maintained that the individual ego acting in its own living present is not subject to causation. A religious man, who held that there was no real opposition between science and religion, he argued for the existence of God by appeal to a version of the argument by design. Notwithstanding his strong belief in the success and importance of physics, he had a somewhat cynical view of institutionalized science deriving from his feelings early in his career that certain vested interests had stood in the way of the recognition of his work. Writing in his *Scientific Autobiography* (1949), he remarked that new truths triumph not by convincing opponents and making them see the light but rather because the opponents eventually die.

W. H. Newton-Smith

Planck's work include: *Treatise on Thermodynamics* (*Vorlesungen über Thermodynamik*, 1897); *Theory of Heat Radiation* (*Vorlesungen über die Theorie der Wärmestrahlung* 1923); *Introduction to Theoretical Physics* (1932); *Where is Science Going?* (1933); *The Philosophy of Physics* (1936); *The Universe in the Light of Modern Physics* (1937).

374
PLATH, Sylvia 1932–63

US poet

Sylvia Plath's suicide launched a tragic myth which was largely validated by the dramatic, intensely imaged, and highly personal poems of her posthumous *Ariel* (1965). Today, Plath's life and writings are still often seen through the distorting glass of opinions about the myth of poet as female victim and rebel. In the women's movement, Plath has functioned both as an image of heroic development towards a female poetic and as a contemporary avatar of a much older type, the suicide-prone Romantic poet, sensitive to the point of madness, persecuted by family and society. While such uses of Plath involve misreadings of her total accomplishment, the ways in which a writer can be used inevitably become part of that writer's historic role. And Plath is one of the few recent poets to have had an undoubted social, as well as literary, impact.

Part of the 'personal' reading of Plath has a genuine basis in her text. One need not agree with A. Alvarez's aesthetic of death in *The Savage God* (1971) – where he argues that suicide and attempted suicide are, for the writer, existential investigations of extremes – in order to feel that Plath's phenomenal development during her short career owed much to the energies released when she began to incorporate covert, then overt allusions to her private life in her poetry. Like many mythologized poets (Shelley, Byron, Heine) Plath made inner biographical incident and subjective images of herself into part of the poetic armoury with which she faced her audience. In *Ariel* and in some earlier poems, Plath represented herself and threats to herself through a few repeated images: moon, egg, blank-faced corpse, sack of blood. She used several *personae*: the mummy ('All the Dead Dears'), the Jew ('Daddy'), the ritual victim ('The Bee Meeting'), the resurrected corpse ('Lady Lazarus'), the cold nihilist

('Lesbos'). Often, as in 'Tulips', the speaker is assaulted by the physical world, from which she longs to escape ('Fever 103°', 'In Plaster'). Plath's masks are convincing, their dilemmas passionately expressed, but ultimately they are fictions, more about a way of seeing than about the 'real' person seeing it. Plath began and ended as a metaphoric poet, and her literary life was highly professional.

In 'Daddy', probably her most famous poem, Plath moves from mute grief at her lost father (Otto Plath had died when Plath was eight) to rejection of Oedipal obsession with both father and husband. In this poem Plath's story fragments do seem to play a partly extra-literary role in creating sympathy for the author, while the mythic images carry the thematic burden of an archetypal truth.

> If I've killed one man, I've killed two –
> The vampire who said he was you
> And drank my blood for a year,
> Seven years, if you want to know.

The apparently casual revision of 'a year' to 'seven' has been left in the finished text to signal that the mythic vampire is Plath's real husband, English poet Ted Hughes*, whom she had known for seven years. At first the 'daddy' addressed by the poem is an archetypal patriarch, 'Marble-heavy, a bag full of God,/ Ghastly statue.' But he also comes from Germany, like Plath's father, and he is seen 'at the blackboard' like Plath's father, an entomologist who researched into the habits of bees. The poem's pressure towards a psychological resolution forces the private event over into myth, where, as myth, it can be encompassed, if not solved. Plath's father is described as a fascist, Plath as 'a bit of a Jew', biographically incorrect remarks which express the larger truth that 'Every woman loves a fascist', and woman will remain enslaved until the concept of the all-powerful 'daddy', whether father or husband, has been violently rejected: 'Daddy, daddy, you bastard, I'm through.'

Plath's first volume of poems, *The Colossus* (1960), was an impersonal, highly crafted collection of poems whose interpretable ambiguities located it firmly in the era influenced by the criticism of T. S. Eliot* and William Empson*. Plath had obviously been reading the metaphysical poets and Jacobean dramatists, as well as W. B. Yeats* and Emily Dickinson. She further enlarged her vocabulary by writing with a thesaurus at hand. The *Colossus* poems are written in tightly imaged, short lines, and precise stanzas. Plath's small characteristic body of images was already present: the colours white, black, and blood-red. There is a threatening, even Gothic, outer world, as in 'Hardcastle Crags', and lurking, insinuating death, as in 'Two Views of a Cadaver Room'. The poet, when present, is almost bewitched by 'The Disquieting Muses' with heads like darning eggs' brought down on her from the cradle by her witch-like mother: 'And this is the kingdom you bore me to,/Mother, mother.'

When *The Colossus* was published, Plath had already settled in England with Ted Hughes. In the early years of their marriage, Plath and Hughes worked closely together, and some of Hughes's interests are reflected in Plath's use of primitivist animal imagery. Even when she was an undergraduate at Smith College in Massachusetts, Plath had deliberately taken on influences. At first she wanted to become a short-story writer like Frank O'Connor: 'I will imitate until I can feel, I'm using what he can teach.' In the apprentice pieces subsequently collected in *Johnny Panic and the Bible of Dreams* (1977), Plath aimed for the impersonal writerly craft of the 1950s. As she wrote in her diary, 'I justified the mess I made of life by saying I'd give it order, form, beauty, writing about it. The highly formed writing would then reciprocally "give me life" (and prestige to life).'

While Plath's drive for success has dismayed critics who like their tragedy pure, it meant that she strove to understand other writers in order to extend her own range. When Plath read the poetry of Theodore Roethke* in the late 1950s, she adapted his use of Jungian* archetypal image to re-work painful personal loss into poetic knowledge; Roethke's influence is almost palpable in poems like 'Maenad', 'Dark House' and 'The Beast' and in the theme of the lost father. In the summer of 1959 Plath and poet Anne Sexton* visited Robert Lowell's* poetry seminar at Harvard. Plath was deeply impressed by the 'confessional' mode of Lowell's *Life Studies*, even if her own poems do not seek to give the impression of the 'real' poet to the extent that Lowell's do. Also, Plath, unlike Lowell, read history primarily as myth. Now that some – but not all – of the poems written between *The Colossus* and *Ariel* have been collected in *Crossing the Water* (1971) and some others written during the period of *Ariel* have appeared in *Winter Trees* (1971) it is clear that Plath arrived at the rage and recognition of *Ariel* through poems like 'I am Vertical', which embraces the temptations of death and release from the body:

And I shall be useful when I lie down finally:
Then the trees may touch me for once, and the flowers
   have time for me.

Other poems focus on specifically womanly compulsions, expressing loathing and identification: 'Heavy Women', 'The Zoo-Keeper's Wife', and 'Three Women: A Monologue for Three Voices' (1968), a 1962 BBC broadcast.

The Bell Jar (1963), Plath's autobiographical novel, begins the story of Esther Greenwood's breakdown and attempted suicide as a satiric novel of adolescence. Esther, like Plath, has won a literary prize and goes off to New York to be exploited by the women's magazine which has awarded it. Through her episodic adventures, Esther realizes that the radical hostility between men and women can't be got rid of by throwing up, taking a purifying bath, writing a scathing letter, briefly adopting a false identity, or even cynically getting herself deflowered. Destined, as a woman, for the life in the kitchen which was the 'feminine mystique' of the 1950s, Esther feels she can't write unless she has the mysterious 'experience' denied her by the banality of her aspirations. Esther stops writing, sleeping, and washing: 'I could see day after day after day glaring ahead of me like a white, broad, infinitely desolate avenue.' She takes sleeping pills and crawls underground to die. Rescued (like Plath) after her suicide attempt, Esther spends months in a mental institution (quite wittily described). Helped by a friendly woman doctor, Esther sees the 'bell jar' of schizophrenic isolation rise, and she returns to the outside world. She now realizes, among other rejections, that she hates the overbearing mother whom she always tried to please. Although it lacks the metaphoric power of the poems in *Ariel*, *The Bell Jar* is an important novel, since it links its heroine's breakdown to the contradictory social demands of the age, and it does so with a lucid appreciation of complexity.

Helen McNeil

See: Charles Newman (ed.), *The Art of Sylvia Plath: A Symposium* (1970); Margaret D. Uroff, *Sylvia Plath and Ted Hughes* (1979); Judith Kroll, *Chapters in a Mythology: The Poetry of Sylvia Plath* (1976); Gary Lane (ed.), *Sylvia Plath: New Views on the Poetry* (1978).

375

POIRET, Paul 1879–1944

French couturier

Born in Paris, the young Poiret showed great aptitude for painting, drawing, costume design and the performing arts. In an effort to divert these interests his father, a draper, refused to send him to university, apprenticing him instead to an umbrella-maker. But, with scraps of silk from the workshop, Poiret constructed miniature costumes, and was soon selling sketches of these to the fashion establishments he visited in the course of delivering umbrellas. At seventeen, his father finally relenting, he went to work for Jacques Doucet, then the leading designer in Paris. At the Maison Doucet Poiret designed the most famous theatrical costume of the century – the white suit worn by Sarah Bernhardt as the Prince Imperial in *L'Aiglon*.

In 1903 Poiret opened his own salon. The Fauve of fashion, he startled the public with a bright new spectrum of colours. Filling his windows with artistic arrangements of foliage, fabrics and frivolities appropriate to the season as a backdrop to his designs, he invented modern window display. More important perhaps, in those early days of the feminist movement, was his contribution to the modern fashion revolution. His designs – slender, supple tunics tied gently beneath the bust and descending in a simple sheath to the floor, reminiscent of classic Greek and oriental draperies – liberated women from the huge hats, billowing skirts and stiff corsets of the Belle Époque.

To popularize his new fashion look, which prefigured Bakst, Diaghilev* and the Ballets Russes, Poiret commissioned two illustrated books, *Les Robes de Paul Poiret racontées par Paul Iribe* (1908) and *Les Choses de Paul Poiret vues par Georges Lepape* (1911). These established the modern style and tradition of fashion illustration. In 1911 he also established the Martine School of Decorative Arts, in the belief that barriers between fashion and the applied arts should not exist. Under his direction the School created a total design environment, or 'complete lifestyle': curtains, draperies, wall panels and papers, screens, porcelain, tapestries, rugs, embroideries, bedclothes, furniture fabrics and the furniture itself were all linked by the same design motifs and colour themes. The *style Martine*, developed by girls with no formal artistic straining, was a striking and original blend of naivety, naturalism and sophistication similar to, but in no way derivative of, the work of Henri Rousseau and Matisse*.

Poiret was also responsible for creating 'designer fabrics' as we know them today. The fabrics which he commissioned from the painter Raoul Dufy revolutionized the French textile industry, and resulted in the first production of printed satins, velvets and linens. In addition his interest in perfumes led him to create modern promotional packaging. Replacing then prevalent light floral scents with his own more exotic blends, his preparations, sold under the *Rosine* label, were presented in boxes with nightgowns, matching handkerchiefs or luxurious drawstring bags. The perfumes were followed by *Rosine* soaps, toilet-waters and *eaux de cologne*, with a range of day, evening and stage make-up.

A passable actor and director, Poiret was renowned as a patron of the arts and a collector. He delighted in devising elaborate entertainments, among them the 'Bal de la Mille et Deuxième Nuit' (1911), which symbolized the extravagance, exuberance and elegance of his heyday. But his facility for business was no match for his talent: through a series of financial misadventures he was forced to give up his practice in 1929. Poiret 'le Magnifique' died in poverty, his last years clouded by Parkinson's disease.

Kaori O'Connor

By Poiret: *My First Fifty Years* (*En habillant l'Époque*, 1930, trans. 1931); *Revenez-y* (1932). See also: Palmer White, *Poiret* (1973); *Catalogue de l'exposition 'Poiret le Magnifique'* (Musée Jacquemart-André, 1974).

376
POLANSKI, Roman 1933–

Polish film director

For a man whose mother died in Auschwitz and whose wife was murdered, Roman Polanski makes films less graphically violent than might be supposed. He does, however, take a pointedly absurd view of the world which cruelly and implacably separates its subjects into survivors and victims. Polanski's films are essentially heartless – perfect metaphors for the cool but troubled 1960s and early 1970s – kept buoyant by a strong curiosity and wry, bizarre humour.

Polanski was born in Paris to Polish parents who returned to Cracow when he was three. There he fended for himself from an early age after his parents were arrested by the Germans. Films, Polanski has admitted, were an escape. He began acting at the age of fourteen and appeared in the films of Andrej Wajda*, notably *A Generation* and *Innocent Sorcerers*. After art school Polanski attended the Lodz Film School where his short film *Two Men and a Wardrobe* (1958) attracted considerable attention. This fifteen-minute exercise drew far more from the Polish avant-garde, particularly the Theatre of the Absurd, than from the dominant tradition of social realism. Polanski's first feature, *Knife in the Water* (1962), was also made in Poland, after a sojourn in Paris. This cool tale about a *ménage à trois* aboard a yacht develops the jaundiced view of human behaviour apparent in the short film and it introduces the intruder figure that was to become central to many of the later films. At the time *Knife in the Water* was read as about the conflict between the Polish bourgeoisie and rebellious youth, although it now looks more like the product of a fundamentally more conservative and pessimistic universal philosophy.

Polanski's next feature was made two years later at the invitation of a Polish producer working in England. Ostensibly a horror film made for a company specializing mostly in sex products, *Repulsion* (1965) in fact remains one of Polanski's most disturbing films for its treatment of a young woman's sexual obsession and mental disintegration. The presiding influence was Luis Buñuel*, a debt acknowledged in the credits' reference to *Un Chien Andalou*. The fissures of Catherine Deneuve's cracking-up gain concrete form through the use of surreal images, particularly those inside her oppressive, crumbling London mansion block whose very walls split open in the end and turn against her.

Polanski's commercial astuteness enabled him to find financial backers eager for cultural prestige: Hugh Hefner of *Playboy* magazine financed *Macbeth* (1971).

Rosemary's Baby (1968) – the first Hollywood film by a director from behind the Iron Curtain – which turned the occult into a subject for major rather than second features, was produced by William Castle who made his reputation in low-budget exploitation films.

In a sense, Polanski's recurring explorations of sexual tensions, linked to a visceral rather than intellectual surrealism, have made the director attractive to commercial backers.

Money for Polanski's second film in England, an earlier project called *Cul-de-Sac* (1966), was forthcoming after the success of *Repulsion*. The result was a public and critical failure that nevertheless remains Polanski's personal favourite. The themes of intrusion and sexual humiliation find a broader base than before in a black comedy and satire strongly influenced by Beckett* and Pinter*, and reinforced by the use of Jack MacGowran and Donald Pleasance, both known foremost as actors for the respective playwrights. Polanski's next film, *Dance of the Vampires* (1967), affectionately parodied horror films and in it Polanski played a bumbling assistant that echoed his role in an earlier short film about a master–servant relationship, *Le Gros et le maigre* (1963). Sharon Tate, his wife, played one of the leading parts in *Dance of the Vampires*. She was murdered later in Los Angeles by the followers of Charles Manson. Polanski's next film, based on Shakespeare's *Macbeth*, was his bloodiest and also continued the diabolic, supernatural theme of the hugely successful *Rosemary's Baby*; it has been noticed that the only birth in the Polanski canon brings forth the child of Satan.

Polanski's style was given its freest rein in *What?* (1972), a droll and inconsequential piece of humour in which an American innocent abroad finds herself in the middle of a comedy of sex and embarrassment. Polanski again appears in the film, clearly delighted to observe such strange behaviour in rich summer villas. The wry, throwaway humour (which teases at the edges of much of his work) is the same kind that in *Chinatown* (1974) put an unglamorous bandage on the nose of its hero.

Restricted settings, like the villa in *What?*, are made much of by Polanski, who favours long takes and frugal editing to allow the cast as much space as possible and to enhance the atmosphere of the geography. Castles in *Cul-de-Sac* and *Macbeth*, apartments in *Repulsion*, *Rosemary's Baby* and *The Tenant* (1976) are all treated in an expressionistic fashion. The urban paranoia of the last three is also central to *Chinatown*, one of his least personal but most successful works. The script by Robert Towne was the first that Polanski did not have a hand in but its themes of complicity and urban corruption make it central to Polanski's cinema.

From the mid-1970s Polanski has worked in France after fleeing America following a sex scandal. Whether the personal pressures in his life are beginning to take their toll is hard to say. However, *The Tenant* (1976) was a disappointing small-scale return to the territory of *Repulsion*. Polanski's leaving America forced him to give up the direction of *Hurricane*, since when his only picture has been an adaptation of Thomas Hardy's *Tess* (1979) filmed in France. It opened in Paris to a mixed reception.

Chris Petit

See: Ivan Butler, *The Cinema of Roman Polanski* (1970).

377
POLLOCK, Jackson 1912–56

US painter

After the Second World War the centre of avant-garde painting switched from Paris to New York, where a revolutionary new movement, later to be called Abstract Expressionism, emerged. The principal artists of this New York School were Pollock, de Kooning* and Rothko*. It was Pollock who, in de Kooning's words, 'broke the ice'. It was also Pollock who probably departed the furthest – certainly further than de Kooning – from all European antecedents.

Born in Cody, Wyoming, Pollock studied in New York under the Regionalist painter Thomas Hart Benton. The old masters who interested him most were those who stressed vigorous movement; his favourite moderns were Picasso* and Miró*. He became interested in Jung* and it was to a Jungian psychotherapist that he turned for help with his alcoholism. In the 1940s, in search of a personal yet universal mythology, he painted a series of pictures filled with references to archaic symbols, including *Guardians of the Secret* and *Pasiphaë* (both 1943). Deciding that these were too literal, and partly inspired by Surrealist automatism, he sought to convey the workings of his Unconscious more directly through abstract marks, transforming the canvas into an 'all-over' field of energy. In 1947, he began placing the canvas on the floor and throwing or dripping paint on to it, while moving around it. The act of painting became like a ritualistic dance, involving his whole body. Complete trance-like concentration and a total psychic involvement with the picture, as it developed its 'independent life', was essential. When successful, the dense web of swirling lines conveyed a sense of liberated energy and perfectly controlled yet spontaneous movement, as in free-form jazz, which Pollock loved. The 'all-over' quality suggested an endless time–space flux. Physically very large, violent yet (increasingly) lyrical, Pollock's dripped paintings constitute his 'heroic' phase. Among the first were *Gothic* and *Full Fathom Five* (both 1947). Some, like *One* and *Autumn Rhythm* (both 1950), evoke the mood of the natural environment, specifically that of Long Island, while remaining totally abstract. Using such paints as Duco, Dev-o-Lac and (silver) aluminium, Pollock produced extraordinary colour harmonies. Nevertheless, he was a draughtsman even more than a colourist and it was the linear element which predominated. In 1951–2 he restricted himself to black and white; at the same time, strongly figurative motives reappeared. The following year, he painted what many consider his masterpiece, the massive *Blue Poles*. The dark blue poles of the title act as markers of rhythm in a frenzied field of bright, artificial colour, providing the work with its special strength and authority.

Pollock's influence on subsequent art has been immense, though in two essentially contradictory directions. Some, believing his work represents a new beginning in painting, have tackled some of the formal, pictorial problems it raises. For others, his 'action painting' has signalled the end of painting as such, pointing rather to the artist as performer or shaman. Pollock's status as a culture-hero makes it difficult to distinguish what is inherent in his paintings from what is reflected back into them from the legends woven around him. Perhaps the distinction is anyhow a false one. Pollock himself sometimes wondered, not whether he was making good paintings, but whether he was making 'paintings' at all. The ambiguity of his influence may result from the ambiguity, and hence the richness, of his life's work.

Gray Watson

See: Bryan Robertson, *Jackson Pollock* (1960); Francis V. O'Connor, *Jackson Pollock* (1967); I. Tomassoni, *Jackson Pollock* (1968); Bernice Rose, *Jackson Pollock: Works on Paper* (1969); Alberto Busignani, *Pollock* (1971); C. L. Wysuph, *Jackson Pollock: Psychoanalytic Drawings* (1971); B. H. Friedman, *Jackson Pollock: Energy Made Visible* (1973).

378
POPPER, Sir Karl Raimund 1902–

Austrian/British philosopher

Karl Popper was born in Vienna, the son of a well-to-do lawyer. Both Popper's parents were Jewish, but were baptized in the Lutheran Church before he was born. Popper's late teens coincided with the upheaval following the First World War and the collapse of the Austrian Empire. At this time Popper was strongly influenced by socialist thought; for a short time he became a Marxist, but was soon disenchanted. His wide-ranging interests while he was a student at the University of Vienna included philosophy, psychology, music and science; after taking his PhD in 1928 he qualified as a secondary-school teacher in mathematics and physics. In the later 1920s he became involved in the internationally renowned Vienna Circle of philosophers, and he received encouragement from some of its members, notably Herbert Feigl. From the beginning, however, Popper was highly critical of the group's central doctrines, and many of these criticisms appeared in his masterpiece *The Logic of Scientific Discovery* (*Logik der Forschung*, 1934). A year before Hitler* marched into Austria, Popper left Vienna with his wife, and took up a position at the University of New Zealand in Christchurch. Here he perfected his English, and in 1945 published the work which won him recognition in the English-speaking world, the two-volume *The Open Society and its Enemies* (fifth edition 1966). In 1946 he took up residence in England. He taught at the London School of Economics, and was made Professor of Logic and Scientific Method in 1949. He was knighted in 1972, and continued to be philosophically productive – his *Objective Knowledge* appearing in 1972.

The Logic of Scientific Discovery is a powerfully original contribution to our understanding of scientific method. When Popper wrote this book the prevailing account of empirical science was that it used 'inductive methods' – that is, inferences from particular observations and experiments to universal laws. Yet ever since Hume such inductive procedures had faced a serious problem: how can observation of a finite number of particular instances logically justify the scientist's confident belief in general laws which are supposed to hold good for all time? Popper's revolutionary suggestion was that the problem of induction was irrelevant to scientific knowledge. How scientists arrived at their theories was a matter for psychology, not logic. What was important was the *testing* of a scientific theory once proposed. And here Popper argued that strictly logical, deductive reasoning is applicable: scientific theories cannot logically be guaranteed to be true, but they are logically capable of being proven *false*. And it is this – the principle of falsification – that is the essence of the logic of science. Science thus works by a process of *Conjectures and Refutations* (the title of a later book – revised 1972 – in which Popper amplified his position). A scientific theory has the status of a tentative hypothesis which is then matched against observations; if the observations actually made are inconsistent with those predicted by the theory, then the theory is refuted and the way is open for a new conjecture.

One remarkable feature of Popper's book is that, at a time when the verificationism of the Logical Positivists was the ruling doctrine, he had already grasped the fundamental weakness that was to lead to its ultimate downfall (i.e. its inability to specify a logic for the verification of scientific law). In place of verifiability Popper's slogan was falsifiability; though, unlike the Positivists, Popper never offered his principle as a criterion of meaningfulness. Instead he suggested it as a principle of demarcation, which separated genuine science from pseudo-science. The mark of a true scientific theorist was the willingness to 'stick one's neck out': theories which did not take the risk of empirical falsification were not entitled to claim scientific status.

It would be hard to overestimate Popper's influence on the methodology of science. It is probably correct to say that the bulk of scientists practising today would accept the Popperian model of the status of scientific theories. On the philosophical front, two problems with Popper's approach are worth noting. First, it is not at all clear that the problem of induction can be disposed of as neatly as Popper supposed. Second, the work of Thomas Kuhn* has demonstrated the extent to which entrenched scientific theories are immunized against the possibility of falsification. But even Popper's strongest critics would admit that the contemporary scene in the Philosophy of Science would be unrecognizable without the foundations which he laid.

There is a close link between Popper's seminal work on scientific methodology and the important contribution to political theory and sociology which he went on to produce. The scientific attitude, as defined by Popper, was one of 'critical rationalism' – the preparedness to submit one's ideas to criticism and modification. This approach, Popper proceeded to argue, was applicable not just in science, but throughout social life, and was the hallmark of what he called the 'open society'. The open society is a highly individualistic one, characterized by free critical thinking; it is a society where individuals are confronted with responsibility for their personal decisions. The closed society, by contrast, embodies the 'organic' view of the state: it is in effect a throw-back to 'tribalism', where the identity of individuals is submerged within a harmonious whole. This distinction leads to the main thesis of *The Open Society and its Enemies*: totalitarianism, with its closed society, is not, in essence, a new movement, but is a form of reactionary primitivism – an attempt to resist the increasing expansion of the critical powers of individual man.

Popper's targets, the theorists of the closed society, are Plato, Hegel and Marx. His attack on Plato upset many scholars, but Popper is undoubtedly correct in arguing that the concept of justice in Plato's *Republic* is a collectivist one in which individuality is subordinated to the good of the state. Popper's most violent strictures are reserved for Hegel for his totalitarian glorification of the state, his 'bombastic and hysterical Platonism'. The triumph of Popper's book, however, is his systematic and devastating attack on all aspects of Marxist theory. In particular, Popper attacks Marx as an economic 'historicist'. The argument ties up with the companion work to *The Open Society*, *The Poverty of Historicism* (1957); historicism is there defined as 'an approach to the social sciences which assumes that historical prediction is their principal aim, and which assumes that this aim is attainable by discovering the "rhythms" or the "patterns", the "laws" or the "trends" that underlie the evolution of history'. Popper's position is that even in the natural sciences complete deterministic prediction is impossible; and his arguments against the possibility of determinism in the social sphere provide a powerful challenge to any sociological theory with serious predictive aspirations.

In his later book, *Objective Knowledge* (1972), Popper returned to his fundamental preoccupation – the development of human knowledge. Popper now saw his earlier notion of science proceeding by a constant process of conjecture and refutation as a special case of evolution by natural selection: the continuous production of tentative conjectures and 'the constant building up of selective pressures on these conjectures [by criticizing them]'. The evolution of knowledge is, in effect, a continuation of the 'problem-solving' activities in which all organisms are engaged. In developing this position, Popper introduced an important conceptual category which he labels 'World 3'. Most philosophers have habitually distinguished between the objective world of physical things and the subjective world of human experience; to these two categories (which he labels Worlds 1 and 2 respectively) Popper now adds a third, independent world of philosophical and scientific knowledge, of 'problems, theories and critical arguments'. This world, though the product of human activity, has a real and autonomous existence whose repercussions on us are as great or greater than those of our physical environment. Popper has made great claims for the explanatory power of this notion of a man-made yet autonomous Third World. In particular, he has proposed that the thorny problem of the emergence of self-consciousness can be solved by analysing it in terms of an interaction between the self and the objects of World 3. Though this is certainly a fascinating approach, it has yet to be satisfactorily developed; and it is not at present clear whether it will turn out to be as philosophically fruitful as Popper confidently predicts.

If his latest ideas have met with some scepticism among the philosophical establishment, this is nothing new to Popper, who has always been something of a rebel. In his early career he was a lone critic of the orthodoxy of the Logical Positivists; in later life he has consistently condemned the dominant 'linguistic' approach to philosophy as a retreat from the 'great problems' into trivial scholasticism. Whatever the truth of this judgment, there can be no doubt about Popper's own extraordinary contribution to the 'great problems'. To categorize or neatly label this contribution is impossible, for Popper's thought ranges so widely and illuminates so many different aspects of philosophy. He is one of the truly original and creative thinkers of the century.

Dr John Cottingham

Perhaps the most stimulating introduction to Popper's work is to be found in his own intellectual autobiography, *Unended Quest* (London 1976, originally *Autobiography of Karl Popper*, Chicago 1974); see also: Thomas Kuhn, *The Structure of Scientific Revolutions* (1962); I. Lakatos and A. Musgrove (eds), *Criticism and the Growth of Knowledge* (1970); R. Bambrough (ed.), *Plato, Popper and Society* (1967); Brian Magee, *Popper* (1973).

379

PORTER, Katherine Anne 1894–1980

US writer

Among the wealth of American short-story writers in the twentieth century Katherine Anne Porter still holds her own as one of the most outstanding. Her reputation rests on three slender volumes of published stories, though by her own account she has written and destroyed others 'literally by the trunkful' since her childhood.

Miss Porter was born at Indian Creek, Texas, a great-great-great-grand-daughter of Daniel Boone. She was educated at Southern convent schools, and (she says) read widely in English and translated classics and, later, in modern writers. She began writing in her childhood and, supporting herself by literary journalism, lived during what she calls her 'growing years' completely outside literary centres and fashions. She made no attempt to publish anything until she was thirty but, by the late 1920s, her stories had attracted critical acclaim in the literary magazines. In 1930 she brought together six of them in a limited edition under the title of one of her best stories, *Flowering Judas*. After a visit to Europe, she published a novelette, *Hacienda* (1934), and an enlarged edition of *Flowering Judas* (1935). A second novelette, *Noon Wine*, appeared in 1937. In 1939, *Pale Horse, Pale Rider* (*Noon Wine, Old Mortality* and the title story) was published, in 1941 a novelette *No Safe Harbor*, and in 1944 *The Leaning Tower and Other Stories*. After that she worked on a study of Cotton Mather and on a novel, which appeared in 1962 under the title of *Ship of Fools*.

Miss Porter's very best stories remain in the mind in surprising detail and can be read again and again for their beauty of form and depth of subtle implication. Outstanding among these is 'Flowering Judas'. It embodies her chief virtues: a style clear and restrained, never overloaded yet carrying a weight of suggestion which enriches and deepens the story; a form which is thoroughly organic, complex in detail yet simple and inevitable in its completion; and a moral theme of power and subtlety conveyed through a symbolism which is among the most artistically skilful in modern writing.

In her symbolism, which is neither obscure nor over-emphasized, she uses both the accepted great myths of religion and folk-lore and the smaller symbolic meanings which attach themselves to words and actions. It is perhaps, above all, by her management of this latter technique that her stories achieve their memorable force.

Speaking of her small output during her writing life Miss Porter once said that it was all she was 'able to achieve in the way of order and form and statement in a period of grotesque dislocations in a whole society'. This gives some idea both of her concern with the world and of her sense of what a story should be.

Geoffrey Moore

See: Harry John Mooney, Jr, *The Fiction and Criticism of Katherine Anne Porter* (1957); Ray B. West, Jr, *Katherine Anne Porter* (1963); William L. Nance, *Katherine Anne Porter and the Art of Rejection* (1963); George Hendrick, *Katherine Anne Porter* (1965).

380

POULENC, Francis 1899–1963

French composer

Poulenc's early career was determined not so much by his formal studies with Charles Koechlin (which took place in 1921–4, after he established himself as a composer) as by his association with Jean Cocteau* and with fellow-members of the group known as Les Six. Poulenc came to the attention of this circle in 1917 with his precocious and absurd *Rapsodie nègre* for voice and chamber ensemble, a work showing those qualities of cool wit and sophistication which were to mark much of his output. He followed Cocteau's demands for economy and crispness in many of the works which immediately followed the *Rapsodie*, but the musical influence of Satie* was gradually superseded by that of Stravinsky*: the early wind sonatas, for two clarinets (1918), clarinet and bassoon (1922), and brass trio (1922), show this quite clearly. Inevitably his talent was noticed by Diaghilev*, for whom he wrote *Les Biches* (1923), a suave and seductive picture of high society life.

Les Biches proved Poulenc's almost Stravinskyan ability to take alien kinds of music, whether from history or from the dance band, and make them his own. He applied this skill with capricious delight in many of his subsequent larger works, creating in his *Concert champêtre* for harpsichord and orchestra (1927–8), for instance, a knowing backwards glance at eighteenth-century elegance. The Concerto in G minor for organ, strings and timpani (1938) looks back through Liszt to Bach, and to a grand rhetoric which is nonchalantly coupled with music of café-style triviality. More exuberant pastiches are to be found in the Concerto for two pianos and orchestra (1932) and in the Piano Concerto (1949), which is rather rare among Poulenc's post-war works in its outgoing vivacity.

His cultivation of a more serious manner can be dated to 1936, in which year he returned to a devout Catholicism. A simple inward piety is expressed in the sacred pieces which followed, including the *Litanies à la Vierge Noire* for women's or children's voices and organ (1936), the Mass in G major for unaccompanied choir (1937) and various motets, while the larger religious works for soprano, choir and orchestra, a *Stabat mater* (1950) and a *Gloria* (1959), are in a colourful and dramatic style which shows Poulenc's continuing debt to Stravinsky. He did not, however, follow that master in taking up serialism, but instead pursued his own very French style, tuneful and diatonic, bringing it to a peak of refinement in his late sonatas for flute (1956), clarinet (1962), and oboe (1962).

Poulenc's later works also include three operas of very different character: *Les Mamelles de Tirésias* (1944), a typically witty setting of Apollinaire's* play; *Dialogues des Carmélites* (1953–5), where the convent location of Bernanos's libretto gave him the opportunity for an operatic exposure of his religious manner; and *La Voix humaine* (1958), a soprano monologue of fleeting mood set to words by Cocteau. The last of these in particular shows the sensitivity to language which made Poulenc the most versatile and distinguished contributor to the repertory of French song since Fauré. Specially noteworthy are his song cycles to poems by Apollinaire (*Le Bestiaire*, 1919; *Banalités*, 1940; *Calligrammes*, 1948), Eluard (*Tel Jour, telle nuit*, 1936–7; *Le Fraîcheur et le feu*, 1950; *Le Travail du peintre*, 1956), Cocteau (*Cocardes*, 1919), and Carème (*La courte paille*, 1960). Many of these were written for the baritone Pierre Bernac, with whom from 1935 he appeared often in recitals.

Paul Griffiths

Other works: *Aubade* for piano and small orchestra (1929); *Suite française* for ten instruments or piano (1935); *Sextet* for piano and wind (1932–9); *Les Animaux modèles*, ballet (1940); Violin Sonata (1942–3, revised 1949); *Figure humaine* for chorus (1943); *L'histoire de Babar* for narrator and piano (1940–5); *Sinfonietta* (1947); Cello Sonata (1948); Sonata for two pianos (1952–3); many solo piano pieces. Writings: *Emmanuel Chabrier* (1961); *Moi et mes amis* (1963); *Correspondance, 1915–1963*, ed. Hélène de Wendel (1967); *Journal de mes mélodies* (1964). About Poulenc: Henri Hell, *Francis Poulenc* (1958, trans. 1959); Jean Roy, *Francis Poulenc* (1964).

381
POUND, Ezra Loomis 1885–1972

US poet

Born in Idaho, in the American north-west, of Quaker parents, Ezra Pound moved East as a child when his father became an assayer at the US Mint in Philadelphia. He studied at Hamilton College, the University of Pennsylvania, where he met William Carlos Williams* and the imagist poet Hilda Doolittle. A year of postgraduate study in Romance languages led to a small scholarship to travel and study in Europe. In Italy he published his first book of verse, *A Lume Spento*, in 1908. In England from 1909, he taught a course at the Regent Street Polytechnic which he turned into a collection of lively and original essays on *The Spirit of Romance* (1910; revised 1953), but his life in London is now better remembered for his spirited involvement in contemporary literary movements. Together with F. S. Flint, he promulgated the aesthetics of imagism, that crucial reaction against the metaphysical speculation and heavily declarative syntax of Victorian public verse. Advocating 'direct treatment of the "thing", whether subjective or objective', the pure imagist poet described objects or emotions in non-literary language, leaving explicit analysis, where necessary, to the reader.

While in London, Pound also promoted individual careers. Though W. B. Yeats's* generous testimony to Pound's helpful advice probably overstates the effect the young American could have had on his late work, there is no doubt that Pound arranged for the publication of Joyce's* *Portrait of the Artist as a Young Man* and some of Eliot's* early short poems, and Pound's midwifery at the delivery of *The Waste Land* is a matter of record.

His own poems written during this period, published in various collections like *Exultations* (1909), *Canzoni* (1911) and *Ripostes* (1912), show an increasing economy of expression, and they also reflect his interest in classical and medieval subjects. It may be because the theory of imagism discourages the presence of 'subjects' that he began to turn increasingly to translation, a device by which an author can transmit ideas without overt editorial comment. Pound's version of poems by the Chinese Li Po, taken from Japanese transliterations and English prose translations by Ernest Fenollosa, was published as *Cathay* in 1915. Like his translation of the Old English *The Seafarer* (published in *Ripostes*) and his 'Homage to Sextus Propertius') in *Quia Pauper Amavi*, 1919), *Cathay* contained a number of mistakes – some intentional, some inspired, and others just wrong – yet the effect of these works is of astonishing insights into the sensibilities of three entirely different cultures.

As Pound began to have more and more to say –

about the war and its causes in the economics of Europe and America – imagism began to look increasingly mannered and miniaturist to him. It was at this point that he began work on a much more ambitious project for his poetry. Originally conceived as a Browning-esque dramatic monologue about the ironies of attempting to educate America in the European past, the first three *Cantos* (published in *Quia Pauper Amavi*) were later revised so as to give prominence to a reworking, in 'Seafarer' metre, of what Pound took to be the oldest kernel of the Odyssey story, the epic hero's visit to the underworld. Just as Odysseus had to beat back the beguiling shades of his comrades and relations (including his own mother) so as to get, from Teiresias, the facts he needed to pilot himself and his crew back to Ithaca, so Pound had to raid the past selectively in order to guide his culture back 'home' to the integral society from which he thought it had departed. The *Cantos*, which finally comprised well over a hundred separate, though related, poems, were to occupy him for the rest of his long life.

Despairing of the revolution in taste and politics which he had once hoped to further in England, Pound left London in 1920. Together with his English wife, the artist Dorothy Shakespear, he lived for a while in Paris, before settling in Rapallo, Italy, four years later. His departure from the city in which his chief interests had been formed, and his poetry much firmed, was signalled in *Hugh Selwyn Mauberley* (1920), for many critics still his most admired work. An allusive, multi-faceted satire on English life and letters, *Mauberley* is also a kind of exorcism, like Eliot's 'Prufrock' and Wallace Stevens's* 'The Comedian as the Letter C', of an aspect of the author as dilettante that he felt he had outgrown.

In Italy Pound formed an alliance with the American violinist, Olga Rudge. Their daughter, Mary, born in 1925, was fostered by a peasant family in the Tyrol. But Dorothy also remained in Rapallo, and their son, Omar, was born there in 1926. By 1930 Pound had completed the first thirty *Cantos*, and he continued to produce essays on literature and economics, incorporating his ideas and discoveries into *Cantos* XXXI to LXXI. His attraction to Italian fascism, as his short book *Jefferson and/or Mussolini* (1935) makes clear, was based on his analogy between the remaking of the Italian economy under Mussolini* and the work of Jefferson, Madison and Martin Van Buren in establishing the American Republic. His infamous broadcasts from Rome under the sponsorship of the fascist regime began in 1940 and continued until after the United States was at war with Italy. As he saw it, Pound never attacked the basic American principles of government, but supported the Constitution against its perversion by more recent American administrations. In 1943 he was indicted for treason by a Washington, DC, grand jury, and in 1945, near the end of the

European war, was imprisoned in a US Army 'disciplinary training centre' north of Pisa. Returned to the United States later that year to stand trial, he was found to be 'suffering from a paranoid state' and unfit to advise counsel. He was subsequently committed to St Elizabeth's Hospital, outside Washington, for treatment.

In St Elizabeth's he continued to read and write, completing his translations from Confucius first made into Italian (finally published in English as *The Unwobbling Pivot and The Great Digest*, 1947) and *Cantos* LXXIV–LXXXIV, begun in Pisa. The *Pisan Cantos* (1948) are thought, even by critics normally hostile to Pound, to be especially sensitive evocations of his mental state as he reflected on his public and private life in his captivity. For them he was awarded, amidst considerable controversy, the prestigious American Bollingen Prize for poetry in 1949. In 1956 he completed and published the next ten *Cantos* as *Section: Rock Drill*. In 1958 his indictment for treason was quashed, and he was released from St Elizabeth's to join his daughter Mary and her husband in Italy. In 1959 *Cantos* XCVI–CIX appeared as *Thrones*, and ten years later, *Drafts and Fragments of Cantos C–CXVII*. He died in 1972.

Ezra Pound's life and work invite the adjective 'modern' not least in their perennial difficulty. Though most of his translations and shorter poems have found an uneasy place in contemporary critical esteem, the *Cantos* have yet to be accommodated in the school and university courses that now govern the sense of a 'tradition' in English and American literature. This must be due in part to their wide range of reference to Greek, Latin, Provençal, early American, and Chinese history, as well as his recollections (mainly in the *Pisan Cantos* and later) to the author's many friends and antagonists, both illustrious and obscure. Again, the *Cantos* do not tell a story, or pause – except occasionally – for moments of lyric repose, but dive restlessly into various versions of the past to find whole chunks of letters, laws, books on economics, and (more rarely) works of literature, with which to confront the wayward present. Though these documents are sometimes cited with inviting economy and almost always 'rhymed' with great subtlety, readers accustomed to the self-sufficient literary object, the 'words on the page', have been deterred by the pressure outwards into non-literary materials beyond the poet's aesthetic frame. One answer to this problem is that Pound was always more of a translator and a maker of syllabi than he was a poet in the conventional sense of the term, and that a major satisfaction of the *Cantos* is predicated in a subsequent reading of the documents towards which they gesture. But the reader is not expected to have got there before the poet, and the guilt or pique apparently felt by some critics at not having anticipated Pound's cultural 'set' is probably misplaced.

Not just the form, but also the contents of the *Cantos*, have given offence. Regular readers of poetry can accept the denunciation of usury in the much-anthologized *Canto* XLV as being in some general sense against nature, but Pound's more specific and contemporary advocacy, elsewhere in the *Cantos*, of the state control of credit has been criticized as too cranky, or at any rate too unliterary, a subject for poetry. Cranky it certainly was not; the economic theories of Douglas, Gesell, Alexander Del Mar and Christopher Hollis, whatever their differences, had in common a search for alternatives to monetarism, an attempt to put money back into the community and to get unemployed men and facilities back to work, without committing the taxpayer to ever-increasing charges for interest. The last decade has not rendered this issue any less relevant than it was in the 1930s. Whether Pound managed to make poetry out of the topic depends partly on the success with which he worked it in with other themes. In the *Cantos*, at least, it was always part of his larger subject, or what might be called his one idea: that every contrivance of the human imagination, from a metaphor to a political system, may be either derived from, or imposed upon, nature. Telling the difference is the one essential discrimination, the necessary moral discipline. This idea did not originate with Pound, but it connects his earliest imagism with the most specific topics in the *Cantos*. 'Banker's Credit' is suspect, therefore, because it does not reflect the 'natural' wealth of a country's material and human resources.

But Pound's anti-semitism remains beyond accommodation. Though restricted largely to his broadcasts and other polemical pieces, and though derived ultimately from the rhetoric of the American Populists, whose economics Pound shared, his use of Jews as a shorthand for usurers showed a failure of sympathy and foresight that cannot be brushed aside by his admirers. It is hard to deny, furthermore, that elements of the paranoia and hectic self-righteousness that have accompanied the more serious forms of anti-semitism are present in Pound's work, even when he is not treating of the economy.

Ultimately Pound's reputation must rest on his life's work, the *Cantos*. He finally came to see them as a failure, because though begun as an epic on the model of *The Divine Comedy* they never get their hero (in this case, the poet himself) home to Paradise at the end. But the *Cantos* are a classic 'made new': an address to the times adducing ancient sources of a better future. In this respect they resemble millennial projections, and should put the reader in mind of that other great, unfinished apocalypse, *Piers Plowman*. Both poems keep interrupting their progress towards the empyrean to cite contemporary abuses, especially by those institutions (for Langland the monasteries, for Pound the banks) considered by the authors to be most capable of reforming the fallen society, and therefore most culp-

able in failing to do so. The *Cantos* are a great synthesis, a great excursion in an open field of reference.

Stephen Fender

For the complete *Cantos* (except nos LXXII and LXXIII) see *The Cantos of Ezra Pound* (1972). See also: *Selected Poems* (1975); and *Ezra Pound, Selected Prose 1909–1965*, ed. William Cookson (1973). The standard biography is Noel Stock, *The Life of Ezra Pound* (1970). See also: Hugh Kenner, *The Poetry of Ezra Pound* (1971); and *Paideuma*, a journal devoted to Pound studies (quarterly, from the University of Maine at Orono).

382
POWELL, Anthony 1905–

British novelist

Anthony Powell was educated at Eton and Balliol College, Oxford. Before and after the war, during which he served in the Intelligence Corps and as a Liaison Officer, he worked in publishing and literary journalism. Powell's early work, such as *From a View to a Death* (1933), is often compared to Evelyn Waugh's*.

Powell's substantial achievement is *A Dance to the Music of Time*, a sequence of twelve novels published between 1951 and 1975. All have the same narrator, Nick Jenkins, whose public career generally seems to parallel Powell's own. The limitations of a single standpoint are overcome by allowing Jenkins to be a willing ear to the anecdotes of others, to assess, if necessary, conflicting evidence about an event at which he was not present. Jenkins's unobtrusive sense of self plausibly makes him the recipient of the ravings and meanderings of more egotistical characters. The limited social world in which he moves – upper- and middle-class (except for the intrusion of military service) – also makes credible Jenkins's ability to follow the careers and fortunes of many of the several hundred characters who appear in the novels. Another kind of unity is provided by Powell's graceful, speculative style which contains – without deadening – the idiomatic, often eccentric actions and speech of his figures.

The first novel, *A Question of Upbringing* (1951), opens with a scene which evokes for Jenkins a Poussin picture in which people move 'hand in hand in intricate measure: stepping slowly, methodically, sometimes a trifle awkwardly, in evolutions that take recognizable shape.' The last novel, *Hearing Secret Harmonies* (1975), closes with a passing reference to the same scene. In between is an extraordinary feat of recollection. The arrangement of events is usually chronological although Powell allows excursions into earlier periods, for example at the beginning of *The Kindly Ones* (1962) where Jenkins recalls his childhood near Aldershot (his father was a soldier) on the eve of the First World War. This also illustrates Powell's attitude towards public events, referred to only on the rare moments when they impinge on his characters' lives or, in the final three books which cover as great a spread of time as the first nine, to establish the period. His people are generally inward-looking. The war, which is covered by the trilogy, *The Valley of Bones* (1964), *The Soldier's Art* (1966) and *The Military Philosophers* (1968), is seen sometimes as a masquerade, sometimes as a dull if grotesque bureaucratic exercise in which the individual struggles with paper or other intractable individuals and the enemy is almost unmentioned. The incursions of death, for instance during the air-raid in *The Soldier's Art*, are the more effective for being understated.

Jenkins's social world expands during the first half of the sequence and contracts through mortality in the second. Most of the new figures introduced during the six final novels – Pamela Flitton ('It was Death she liked'), the novelist X. Trapnel, the necrophile though not dislikable Russell Gwinnett – have a macabre aspect. The individual characters are rarely types, although Powell uses some of them as yardsticks for generalization: the industrialist Sir Magnus Donners exemplifies the mysterious banality of power, the painter Barnby is used as a mouthpiece for comments about womanizing. Besides the frequent reappearances of such characters and the narrator's well-disposed and tolerant curiosity towards them, another link between the novels is provided by Jenkins's preoccupation with art. Musicians, painters, writers emerge; Jenkins himself works on a book about Robert Burton ('melancholy' well describes the tone of the three final books). The chief antithesis among many in the sequence is between the will to power and the intrinsically less energetic drive to create. The embodiment of the latter is the story-teller; the former is most amply suggested by Widmerpool who progresses jerkily from business success to military rank to politics to a peerage. An ogrish figure to the reader, his pretensions are undermined by sexual humiliation. On a solitary run at school he is the first character named. Member of a sinister 1960s commune in the final novel, he collapses and dies (shouting 'I'm leading, I'm leading now') on another run and his death closes the account. All that is retrieved from the closing débâcle is a Modigliani* drawing, salvaged 'a little crumpled' from a bonfire of Widmerpool's effects by Bithel, one of the most pathetically comic figures in *The Music of Time*. The ordering of social confusion through art, mediated through Nick Jenkins the novelist, and the partial survival of that art are Powell's final aims.

Philip Gooden

The other novels of *The Music of Time* are: *A Buyer's Market* (1952); *The Acceptance World* (1955); *At Lady Molly's* (1957); *Cassanova's Chinese Restaurant* (1960);

Books Do Furnish a Room (1971); *Temporary Kings* (1973). See also Bernard Bergonzi, *The Situation of the Novel* (1970).

383
PRESLEY, Elvis Aaron 1935–77

US popular singer

Although the invention of rock 'n' roll is generally accredited to Bill Haley, it was Elvis Presley who transformed a new musical vogue into a social phenomenon. The son of a poor farm worker from South Tupelo, Mississippi, Presley's dangerous good looks and wonderfully expressive voice made him the first and most charismatic media icon in the post-war development of an independent youth culture based on music.

In 1954 he recorded for Sun Records, Memphis, a song called *That's All Right Mama*. Though not a national success at the time, it defines the sources of rock 'n' roll: a white country singer records a black song and for the first time, instead of eliminating black emotion and physicality, retains them in a new synthesis of country music and the blues. Colonel Tom Parker became Presley's manager soon after, and in 1955 they signed a contract with RCA Records. Most of his classic rock 'n' roll numbers were recorded the following year: *Heartbreak Hotel*, *Blue Suede Shoes*, *Tutti Frutti*, *Lawdy Miss Clawdy*, *Shake Rattle and Roll*, *Hound Dog*, etc. Presley's impact, conveyed by his records and stage appearances with their swaggering content of sex and insubordination, was amplified through films, and hysteria climaxed in 1957 with the film *Jailhouse Rock*, which many cinema managers banned when it became associated with teenage rioting.

At the end of 1957 Presley was drafted into the army and when he returned to civilian life it was without anarchic overtones. Hereafter he was simply the world's most famous pop singer. Only at his death, the victim of obesity and drugs, did he again touch the deepest emotions of the public.

Presley was not a composer, he did not direct his own career, and his only articulation was in performance. At its height his music was blamed for the rise of 'juvenile delinquency', a period catch-phrase which referred only to the negative aspect of a spectacular outburst of energy among young people. Positively, he was the inspirational figurehead in the origination of a new cultural group, with its own financial resources, between the traditional categories of childhood and adulthood – that of youth.

Duncan Fallowell

Alan Harbinson, *The Life and Death of Elvis Presley* (1977).

384
PROKOFIEV, Sergei Sergeievich 1891–1953

Russian composer and pianist

Born in the village of Sontsovka, the son of an agricultural engineer who managed a large estate in the Ukrainian steppe, Prokofiev was musically precocious to an unusual degree. By 1902, when he received his first formal tuition in music from the composer Rheinhold Glière, he was already the composer of two operas and numerous short piano pieces. On Alexander Glazunov's advice, he entered the St Petersburg Conservatory in 1904, where he spent a stormy and unhappy ten years. At a time of increasing political tension, the Conservatory provided a less than ideal environment for the unruly student, and his classes with Rimsky-Korsakov, Lyadov, Winkler and Cherepnin made less impact on his development than his contact with progressive artistic groups in St Petersburg – the 'World of Art' and the Evenings of Contemporary Music. At the height of the Scriabin cult, and in the heyday of the literary Symbolists, he was encouraged to evolve a novel style of his own, and some of his most iconoclastic and aggressive music dates from the immediately pre-war years – works like the First and Second Piano Concertos (1912 and 1913), and the piano *Sarcasms* (1912–14). The highly charged Romanticism of late Scriabin and early Strauss* also influenced him for a time, and by contrast with his piano music, his early songs, symphonic poems, and the opera *Maddalena* (1911–13) are intense and strongly atmospheric works.

His career as a St Petersburg 'enfant terrible' took a new turn in the summer of 1914, when, on a trip to London, he attended the season of Diaghilev's* Ballets Russes, the heady glamour of which he found irresistible. For the first, and perhaps the only time in his career, he found the direct influence of another composer inescapable: the impact of Stravinsky's* ballets, in particular *The Rite of Spring*, is evident in many of his large works of the following years, from the ballet *The Buffoon* (1915) to the Second Symphony (1925). The occasion also marked the beginning of Prokofiev's own involvement with the Ballets Russes, which was to last until Diaghilev's death in 1929.

The first of Prokofiev's works to gain international recognition, the 'Classical' Symphony – deliberately close to Haydn in style, but with 'something new' as well – was written in the summer of 1917, as political events in Russia were reaching a crisis. With the Revolution and the ensuing civil war, it seemed to Prokofiev that his own country might, for the foreseeable future, have graver concerns than for new music. In May 1918 he left for the United States, where his reception was initially encouraging: the music of Stravinsky and the performances of Rachmaninov had set

an artistic fashion for all things Russian. He was soon disillusioned, however, by both the commercialism of concert promoters and the basic conservatism of audiences, and it was increasingly in Western Europe, particularly in Paris, that he found a more receptive audience for his music. Yet it was in these artistically and financially difficult first years abroad that some of his most characteristic and popular works were written. The music for *The Buffoon*, revised in 1920, the Third Piano Concerto (1921), the opera *Love of Three Oranges* (1919), and the Fifth Piano Sonata (1923, rev. 1953) are flights of energetic fancy, clear, incisive, and often humorous; Prokofiev's music was never more dynamic nor more whimsically imaginative.

By the end of the 1920s, the time of the opera *The Fiery Angel* (1923, rev. 1926–7) and the ballet *The Prodigal Son* (1929), Prokofiev was at the height of his composing career in the West. As a pianist, too, he was in demand throughout Europe and in North and South America. But in 1929, with the death of Diaghilev and his spirit of artistic adventure, and with the repercussions of the Wall Street collapse in Europe, the market for new music received a severe blow. Between 1932 and 1936 he received only two commissions – the Sonata for Two Violins (1932) and the Second Violin Concerto (1935) – from Western Europe. Over the same period he received seven Soviet commissions, including those for *Lieutenant Kije* (orchestral suite, 1934), *Romeo and Juliet* (ballet, 1936), and *Peter and the Wolf* (symphonic tale, 1936) – three of his best known and finest scores. He had renewed contact with the Soviet Union during a concert tour in 1927. After some years of apparent indecision he returned there permanently in the spring of 1936.

Prokofiev's first Soviet works – works in which he was very conscious of the need for a much wider popular appeal – are the result not merely of a process of simplification in his idiom; his musical style underwent a change of emphasis. The Romanticism of his youth, never entirely absent from his works, re-emerged: in his Second Violin Concerto, *Romeo and Juliet* and *Alexander Nevsky* (cantata, 1939) it takes the form of a more serene lyricism and textural warmth. The earlier whimsy with which he juxtaposed dynamic ideas was resolved in the clarity and breadth of his later musical structures: his later symphonies and sonatas have a typically Russian 'epic' feel to them. The sardonic humour of *Love of Three Oranges* was replaced by the elegant wit of *The Duenna* (opera, 1940–1) and *Cinderella* (ballet, 1944) – though, sadly, after *Cinderella*, in the face of the Second World War and the Communist Party's strictures on the arts which both preceded and followed it, Prokofiev's music was rarely frivolous in content. The characteristic works of his later years – the Fifth and Seventh Symphonies (1944 and 1952), the operas *Semyon Kotko* (1939) and *War and Peace* (1943, rev. 1946–52), the music for Eisenstein's* *Ivan the Ter-*

rible (1944–8) – are 'heroic' and traditional works, serious in intent.

After 1938 Prokofiev's contact with Western Europe ceased; he gave no further concerts abroad. In 1941 he suffered the first of a series of heart attacks. His last concert appearance, as the conductor of his Fifth Symphony, was in 1945. After a bad fall that year his health deteriorated. His prodigious rate of composition slowed down in his last years, and he died of a brain haemorrhage on 5 March 1953, the same day as Stalin* died.

The scope of Prokofiev's career, and the contradictions it embodies, are in most respects a product of the times in which he lived. Cut off from the roots of his own Russian traditions by the Revolution in 1917, he had to attempt to rediscover them in 1936, but by then he was a product of the sophisticated 1920s in the West. Yet, as a Russian, and because of his uncompromising personality, he had found it difficult to meet the West on its own musical ground, and in any case his efforts were pre-empted by Stravinsky. Outside Russia, his music, and especially the dynamic nature of his earlier piano music, has become a familiar element in contemporary concert programmes, but his overall influence has been indirect. His return to Russia had a significant impact on the course of Soviet music, however, and the flavour of Prokofiev's melodies, rhythms and turns of cadence characterized much of the music of Khachaturyan, Kabalevsky and even Shostakovitch* in the 1940s and 1950s. In the longer term, he has become a Soviet classic.

Rita McAlister

Other works include: operas: *The Gambler* (1917, rev. 1927–8); *The Story of a Real Man* (1948); ballets: *Le Pas d'Acier* (1926); *The Tale of a Stone Flower* (1948–53); symphonies: no. 3 (1928); no. 4 (1930); no. 6 (1947); concertos: for piano: no. 4 for left hand only (1931); no. 5 (1932); for violin: no. 1 (1917); Sinfonia Concerto for Cello and Orchestra (1950–2); *Cantata for the Twentieth Anniversary of the October Revolution* (1937); and nine sonatas for piano (1909–47). See: *Sergei Prokofiev: Autobiography, Articles, Reminiscences*, ed. S. Shlifstein (1956, trans. 1960); *Prokofiev by Prokofiev* (1979); Israel V. Nestyev, *Prokofiev* (trans. 1961); Victor Seroff, *Prokofiev: a Soviet Tragedy* (1968); Claude Samuel, *Prokofiev* (trans. 1971).

385
PROUST, Marcel 1871–1922

French novelist

Marcel Proust was born into an upper-middle-class family of strong scientific and artistic interests that marked both the subject-matter of his future writing and the metaphors through which he was to convey his picture of the mind. His father was an eminent physician, conversant with French psychology of the day, and his mother, with whom he had the more intense relationship, a cultured and witty woman. The letters exchanged between mother and son show the ambivalent intimacy that may have been responsible for his susceptible and unhappy adult relationships, which were homosexual.

Of contemporary influences, that which most affected him during his education at the Lycée Condorcet and the École des Sciences Politiques (where he took degrees in law and philosophy) was perhaps Henri Bergson's*, but to speak of this one only would be an absurdly narrow assessment of a catholic taste that had absorbed not only the finest writings of the nineteenth century in France and England but the classics of world literature, music and painting. Both direct references and metaphors in his writing show what he owed to Baudelaire, Nerval, George Eliot; to the Bible, and the Italian Renaissance; to French medieval epic, and to hundreds of other works of art. As one critic says, 'he sucked so much nourishment into his own great plant that his successors had to grow roots in other ground' (J. Cocking; see bibliography).

There has been a widely held picture of the young Proust as a dilettante; this in spite of the publication of a collection of short stories, 'portraits', and poems in his twenties (*Les Plaisirs et les jours, Pleasures and Regrets*, 1896, trans. 1950); the translation and annotation of some Ruskin in his thirties; and the discovery in the 1950s of an early unfinished novel, *Jean Santeuil* (1952, trans. 1955). Nevertheless, it is still true that, although Proust was clearly brilliant, he published nothing of major artistic importance until *Remembrance of Things Past* (the inept English title for *À la Recherche du temps perdu*, 1913–27, trans. 1922–31). His previous sketches, and longer essays or fiction, show that he already had all his themes, many of his characters, a gift for imagery, and wit; but he was still groping towards a structure for these, and still often lacked complete stylistic control. It does seem that he may have had a sudden inspiration, round about 1909, comparable to that he describes for the hero of his novel, even if it was only how to use insights long held. The result was *Remembrance of Things Past*, the greatest twentieth-century French novel so far, and considered by some to be the greatest twentieth-century European novel.

Its influence has been huge: its unprecedentedly bold use of a subjective first-person narrator, its stress on the relativity of perception, its radical departures from linear chronology, and its ostentatious patterning by image, association and coincidence have profoundly marked the novel both inside and outside France. Even French novelists of the 1930s and 1940s like Malraux* and Sartre*, seeming to depart from Proust with novels exploring political decisions and the biological solidarity of the human species, still show their debt to Proust's psychological perceptions and his methods of creating fluid or volte-face character. More recently, the French *nouveau roman* (see Robbe-Grillet*, Sarraute*, Butor*) has taken up the lessons of *Remembrance of Things Past*, and woven them into a game more elaborate than anything since Gide's* *The Counterfeiters* (which is, incidentally, often wrongly credited with many of Proust's narrative innovations). And in general, modern preoccupations with the interpretation of chaotic material, or with the meaning of language, had already reached perhaps their most adult expression and their most satisfactory explanation in *Remembrance of Things Past*.

Proust's novel is not an easy one; Roger Shattuck claims that it is the least read of the modern classics, and it is true that to read it with enjoyment, one must discard all habits of short cutting. One of Proust's earliest critics, Léon Pierre-Quint, recommended that readers should start with twenty pages a day for the first week, then, slowly working up, increase this by five pages a day. Yet, like all great novels, it is its peculiar balance between simplicity and complexity that makes *Remembrance of Things Past* rewarding. The plot, for instance, can be seen as a bare and satisfying one – an odyssey of kinds. The nameless narrator, whom critics usually call Marcel, grows up longing to be a great artist, and filled with attractive but illusory notions about travel, the aristocracy, and love. He superficially fulfils his worldly ambitions, going to places he had wanted to visit, achieving outstanding social successes, and entering close relationships with three of the women he desires; but he finds that none of these experiences brings him the excitements he had hoped for, and that love can be agonizing. Above all, though his evaluation of art deepens and brings him a certain wisdom, he cannot, himself, create. Finally – in the last 200 pages of the total 3,000 – he reaches a nadir of discouragement. Nature no longer moves him; he cannot even believe in art. Then – an ending presented as quasi-miraculous – a series of physical sensations brings back to him a flood of involuntary memories, which make him both realize the richness of his own life, and, by suggesting to him the continuity of his personality – which he had mainly experienced as disparate and contradictory – give him the faith to create his work of art: a book about his life. He is approaching death, but, after this illumination, he retreats from the world with a new appreciation of ecstasy and sadness to write his work with what strength he still has.

Within this uncluttered framework, Proust plays dazzling variations on certain conceptions of time, personality, love and art – some his own, some clearly in a nineteenth-century lineage, some coinciding startlingly with those of other great contemporary thinkers whom he could not have read, like Freud*. Those suggestions of Proust's which have disturbed the largest number of critics are the ones about love. Proust illustrates over hundreds of pages his own assertions that love is almost always unreciprocal and that we attribute to the loved one qualities and faults which issue merely from our own imaginations. We fall in love less with the beauty, kindness or intelligence of the beloved than as a result of our belief that he or she represents a world into which we wish to penetrate but from which we feel excluded. These ideas are stated baldly in *Remembrance of Things Past*, but it is still surprising that they should have seemed so controversial, since most of them had already been mooted, in one form or another, by Mme de la Fayette, Racine, Constant, Stendhal, and Flaubert. Other insights of Proust's have been greeted with equally strong reactions; for instance, the fact that a large number of his characters prove bisexual has not made critics realize how heterosexually biased the novel had been before him, but has, instead, provoked numerous accusations of partiality on Proust's part and affirmations of the critics' own orthodox sexuality.

More acceptable has been Proust's depiction of the power of involuntary memory, which he shows as able to break down habit – the great blunter of perception – and to restore our freshest impressions of years ago, both sensory responses and intimate hopes and fears of the time. And, although few critics have tackled his style in detail, all now accord him the praise of being one of the greatest prose stylists. Proust is a master of the short, maxim-like sentence, and of the deliberately dissonant repetition, but he is more famous for the long sinuous sentences that re-create the multilayered quality of both physical sensations and inner associations; for the metaphors and similes which have the gift of seeming simultaneously an accurate commentary and joyously extravagant; and for his handling of the generalizations about human nature that appear on almost every page, and that are couched in physical and figurative terms that make them more integrated with the fictional narrative than in many other great novels.

What, finally, also makes *Remembrance of Things Past* a work of genius is its comedy. The same early critic who recommended a gradually increasing daily quota of Proust was honest enough to admit that it was only on his second reading that he realized how amusing the novel was; the first time he was too overwhelmed by the prose-poetry and the generalizations to notice the entertainment. Proust has at his command an unusually wide range of comic talents: he is able to write, with equal success, in a vein of relaxed whimsy or one of burlesque caricature. He follows the nineteenth-century movement away from divisions of genre, rarely strictly separating darker topics from amusing ones, and often, at the gravest moments, slipping in some light-hearted aside; he also takes much further than did Flaubert, Balzac or Stendhal the exploitation of tics of speech for comic effect. There is, too, a less frequently commented-on tradition of French literature into which Proust falls: the earthy one. He treats gross subjects with such delicate irony that many commentators have been able to overlook them, and to judge the work over-refined, or 'art for art's sake'; in fact, there are physically farcical episodes, scatological diatribes, and much play on love of food. Among Proust's finest comic passages are literary parody, deliberately bathetic combinations of phrases, and embroidery on an already comic reference after an interval of pages or even chapters; and one of his most frequent sources of comedy is snobbery, which he sees everywhere: in love and even in sadism (the sadist is trying to penetrate into the circle of the glamorously wicked).

Proust's novel has been said to be rarefied, masturbatory, merely toying with political issues – this in spite of a profound thoughtfulness in its treatment of the Dreyfus Affair and anti-semitism, the First World War, the possibilities of class-mobility, and the mutual fascinations whereby the aristocracy and working classes maintain each other in rigid stereotypes. Devoted Proustians would, however, doubtless maintain that the greatest reward of reading him is the changes he effects in one's own perception of sense-impressions.

Dr Alison Finch

Other works include By Way of Sainte-Beuve (Contre Sainte-Beuve, 1954, trans. 1958). Publication of Proust's complete Correspondance, ed. Philip Kolb, began in 1970. See: G. D. Painter, Marcel Proust: A Biography (2 vols, 1959 and 1965). See also: Samuel Beckett, Proust (1931); J. Cocking, Proust (1956); G. Poulet, L'Espace proustien (1963); V. Graham, The Imagery of Proust (1966); G. Brée, The World of Marcel Proust (1967); J. H. P. Richard, Proust et le monde sensible (1974); R. Shattuck, Proust (1974); M. Bowie, Proust, Jealousy, Knowledge (1978).

386
PUDOVKIN, Vsevolod Illarionovich 1893–1953

Russian film director

Born into a family of peasant extraction in Penza, Pudovkin studied physics and chemistry at the University of Moscow. Mobilized during the First World War, he joined the Russian artillery and, after being wounded in 1915, spent three years in a POW camp before escaping. On his return to Moscow he worked as an industrial chemist until 1920. Then, at the age of twenty-seven, inspired by D. W. Griffith's* Intolerance, he enrolled at the State Cinema School where he worked under Vladimir Gardin before moving to join the workshop of Lev Kuleshov, six years his junior. In this period Pudovkin took part in the writing, direction, acting and set-design for a number of films, notably Kuleshov's The Extraordinary Adventures of Mr West in the Land of the Bolsheviks (1924) and Death Ray (1925).

In 1925 Pudovkin joined Mezhrabpom-Russ to direct a popularizing account of Pavlov, Mechanics of the Brain, and a short comedy, Chess Fever (1926). These led at once to his first internationally famous work, Mother (1926), an adaptation of Gorky's* novel commemorating the political enlightenment of a revolutionary's mother during the unsuccessful revolution of 1905. Like other Soviet directors, Pudovkin produced probably his best, and certainly his most celebrated, work by 1930. Just as Mother parallels Eisenstein's* Battleship Potemkin (1925) in its return to 1905, so Pudovkin's The End of St Petersburg (1927) complements Eisenstein's October (1927) in its account of the successful revolution of 1917. Storm over Asia (1928), his last major film of the silent era, told the story of a Mongolian hunter in his struggles against the British Occupation Forces during the Civil War. At the end of the 1920s Pudovkin returned to acting, taking the starring role in Otsep's A Living Corpse, as well as parts in Kuleshov's The Gay Canary and Kozintsev's and Trauberg's The New Babylon (all 1929).

The 1930s were a depressed period for Pudovkin, as for other Soviet directors. After the failure of Life is Very Good (1930), unsuccessfully revised as The Story of a Simple Case (1932), Pudovkin completed Deserter (1933), on the struggles within German Communism, a film exemplifying the call for the experimental use of sound, particularly sound-image counterpoint, announced in Pudovkin's, Eisenstein's, and Alexandrov's 1928 manifesto. The year in which he received the Order of Lenin, 1925, also saw the death of his established scenarist, Nathan Zharki, in a road accident which also injured Pudovkin. Illness subsequently kept him away from the studios, maintaining his involvement at the level of theoretical work and teaching at the Higher Cinema Institute. In the later 1930s Pudovkin's talents were channelled into the genre of patriotic historical dramas produced by the Soviet propaganda machine to combat the rise of Fascism. Victory (1938) deals with a popular revolt against the Polish occupation of Moscow in the seventeenth century; Minin and Pojarsky (1939) celebrates the partnership between the Novgorod butcher and the Moscow prince which liberated the homeland from the Poles in 1612.

Pudovkin entered the 1940s by co-directing, with documentarist Esther Schub, the anniversary feature Twenty Years of Cinema (1940) before returning to historical drama with Suvorov (1940), a study of the later years of the eighteenth-century general of the same name. His wartime work consisted of newsreel and documentary work, together with a version of the great popular patriotic theatrical success of the day,

Simonov's story of the partisans, *In the Name of the Fatherland*. Pudovkin did not long survive the post-war freeze. *Admiral Nakhimov* (1946), devoted to the memory of the Commander of the Black Sea Squadron in the Crimean War, was severely criticized (along with Eisenstein's *Ivan the Terrible*, Part 2) by the Central Committee of the Party, and released the following year in a revised version. This was followed by *Zhukovsky* (1950), a simplified biography of the nineteenth-century aerodynamicist, collaboration with Yutkevitch on the reworking of Ptouchko's drama of homecoming from war, *Three Returns* (1948), and the rural love story *The Return of Vasily Bortnikov* (1953). Pudovkin died of a heart attack, on the Baltic, in the same year.

Pudovkin's influence stems from his trilogy of crises of conscience – *Mother*, *The End of St Petersburg*, and *Storm over Asia* – and from his theoretical treatises *Film Technique* (1926) and *Film Acting* (1934). Certainly, Pudovkin cannot easily be assimilated to the highly associative and disjunctive montage aesthetic explored by Eisenstein and Vertov*, a distinction encapsulated by Eisenstein when he described Pudovkin's use of editing as being designed to provide 'linkage', his own to cause 'collision'. Instead we have, in Georges Sadoul's words, a series of 'romanesque films marked by an approach at once lyrical, psychological, and social, showing the evolution of characters who are individualistic yet selected for their value as social types'.

Philip Drummond

See: *Izbrannyiye Statyi* ('Selected Texts', 1955); *Film Technique and Film Acting* (1958); Barthélémy Amengual, *V. I. Poudovkine* (1968); Luda and Jean Schnitzer, *Vsevolod Poudovkine* (1966); Jay Leyda, *Kino: A History of the Russian and Soviet Film* (2nd edn, 1973).

387
PYNCHON, Thomas 1937–

US novelist

Born in Long Island, New York, Pynchon graduated in engineering at Cornell University and has produced to date three novels and a handful of short stories and articles. He has evaded all personal publicity, submitting no interviews or correspondence, so that his work stands very much by itself.

Pynchon's first novel, *V* (1963), creates a world constituted by a bewildering variety of groups and individuals, all searching for truths to live by and emerging with an utterly fantastic variety of life-styles; these range from the systematic sexual exploitation and extermination of an African people to the exaltation of plastic surgery or dentistry to the status of a religion. Of the central characters, Benny Profane sees himself as a *schlemiel*, at the mercy of the material world, and

hence excused effort or involvement, while Stencil, searching for 'V', the object of his grandfather's quest, which is simultaneously a place, a person and a truth, treats himself as a character in a work of fiction, and hence refers to himself in the third person. References to 'V' abound in the book, but their very multiplicity undermines the quest as a whole, especially when their common element emerges as a desire to fuse with the mineral world, to become inert, stable and immortal.

The Crying of Lot 49 (1966) takes the heroine Oedipa Maas into a twilight zone between paranoia and the revelation of an alternative postal communication system, Trystero, which seems to offer a way of transcending alienation and of genuinely being in touch with others across space and time. The more information she gains, however, the more the plot thickens in a baroque fashion, and the closer it gets to an obsessive and insane need for there to be a parallel realm of meaning and truth to the obvious everyday world. In *Gravity's Rainbow* (1973), however, this quotidian reality has been entirely swallowed up in the nightmare of the Second World War. The hero of the book is Tyrone Slothrop who, subjected to Pavlovian conditioning in childhood, finds himself sexually aroused by the future firing of a V2 rocket, and drawn to its place of impact. This inversion of causal sequence finds many echoes in the book and picks up the earlier themes of erotic submission to the world of matter and technology. Instead of 'gravity's rainbow', a natural parabola of excitation and release, of life and death, science seeks a continuous increase of energy and power, abetted by the multinational companies which profit by war. War is the logical outcome as the greatest possible centralization of power, squandering of energy, growth of knowledge and mobilization of individuals' energy through the eroticization of violence and submission by sado-masochistic conditioning.

Pynchon's vision is thus an entropic one in which the accumulation and dissemination of information and the geometrical increase in usable and used energy create a situation in which there is no central organizing agency or truth. At the same time, this is also a moral insight into the ways we have brought this upon ourselves by seeking to be the victims or passive objects of forces we identify as being outside ourselves. Our inner neuroses and paranoia create the history we ostensibly seek to avoid.

Dr David Corker

Pynchon's other works include some short stories: 'Low Lands' (*New World Writing*, 16, 1960); 'Entropy' (*Kenyon Review*, 22:2, 1960); and 'Under the Rose' (*Noble Savage*, 3, May 1961). See also: *Mindful Pleasures: Essays on Thomas Pynchon*, ed. George Levine and David Laverenz (1976); and *Pynchon*, ed. Edward Mendelson in The Twentieth Century Views series (1978).

Q

QUENEAU, Raymond 1903–76

French writer

Born in Le Havre, Queneau studied philosophy at the Sorbonne from 1920 to 1925. He participated in the Surrealist movement between 1924 and 1929, but thereafter, while still remaining close to contemporary intellectual developments, he generally avoided doctrines and schools. With *Le Chiendent* (*The Bark-Tree*, 1933, trans. 1968), his first novel and possibly his best, he reached literary maturity. Here the formative influences – Joyce*, Flaubert, Hegel, silent cinema, comic strips – are perfectly harmonized, and the primary – and recurrent – themes of illusion and reality, time, history, perception and identity and the quest for knowledge are elaborated in Queneau's favourite setting of suburban Paris. More novels followed, some autobiographically-based, as well as a number of important essays and critical articles, most now republished in *Le Voyage en Grèce* ('The Journey to Greece', 1973), and several translations. In 1938 Queneau began his long association with the Paris publishing house of Gallimard; he became secretary-general in 1941 and, in 1945, director of Gallimard's *Encyclopédie de la Pléiade*. After the war he further developed his range of activities, producing poetry, short stories, more novels, songs (for Zizi Jeanmaire) and film scripts (for Buñuel* and René Clément) and exhibiting his paintings. His literary reputation grew with the popularity of *Exercices de style* (*Exercises in Style*, 1947, trans. 1958) – ninety-nine stylistic variations on one simple anecdote – and after his election to the Académie Goncourt in 1951; it was further consolidated in 1959 by the commercial success of *Zazie dans le métro* (*Zazie*, trans. 1960), the comic adventures of an anarchic child unleashed on the adult world. In 1960 he joined the Ouvroir de Littérature Potentielle, an experimental group which enabled him to combine literary work with his life-long fascination with mathematics.

While he acknowledged the arbitrariness and inevitable imperfection of language, Queneau was ever preoccupied with enriching the possibilities of literary discourse – annexing the syntax and vocabulary of spoken French, borrowing from other languages, adding his own inventions. His treatment of the French language does, however, fall short of the revolution implied in the polemics of *Bâtons, chiffres et lettres* ('Strokes, Figures and Letters', 1950). Queneau sought to break down barriers not merely between linguistic codes but also between literary kinds: he claimed to see no essential differences between the novel and poetry, and in much of his work in both genres he applied the formal rigour whose absence he had eventually found intolerable in Surrealist writing. The assimilation of the culture of the past, through simple quotation and more complex patterns of allusion, and his adaptation of devices from other artistic genres, notably film, theatre and music, are also essential features of his technique. But his achievement extends beyond the merely technical, for he succeeded in creating a complete imaginative universe – one in which the problems of existence are examined with a discretion and a humour which challenge received ideas and never allow of definitive solutions. Queneau himself is perhaps best approached with similar open-mindedness for he resists any simple categorization. Just as he belongs to no school, so he engenders none (despite his influence on Boris Vian and the *nouveau roman*); and the various attempts made to isolate individual aspects of his work fail, by definition, to do justice to this writer's rich variety.

Dr Chris Shorley

Other major works: *Pierrot mon ami* (*Pierrot*, 1942, trans. 1950); *Le Dimanche de la vie* (*The Sunday of Life*, 1952, trans. 1976); and *Les Fleurs bleues* (*Between Blue and Blue*, 1965, trans. 1967), all novels; *L'Instant fatal* (*The Fatal Moment*, 1948); *Chêne et chien* ('Oak and Dog', 1937); and *Le Chien à la mandoline* (*The Dog with the Mandolin*, 1965), verse. On Queneau: Jean Queval, *Raymond Queneau* (1971); Jacques Guicharnaud, *Raymond Queneau* (1965). See also Martin Esslin's essay 'Raymond Queneau, b. 1903' in *The Novelist as Philosopher*, ed. John Cruickshank (1962).

QUINE, Willard Van Orman 1908–

US philosopher

'To be is to be the value of a variable' ('On What There Is') is one of those aphoristic quotations which haunt philosophy examination papers, and it epitomizes Quine's philosophy. Questions of ontology, ontological commitment and reference are never far from the centre of attention in his writings and his thought on such questions is coloured by viewing philosophical problems through the spectacles of formal logic.

Quine has spent most of his academic life at Harvard University, where he is Edgar Pierce Professor of Philosophy. Born in Akron, Ohio, he graduated from Oberlin College in 1930, having majored in mathematics. He went on to write a doctoral thesis on logic under A. N. Whitehead* at Harvard, and has taught there since 1936. Before this he also visited Vienna and studied mathematical logic at Warsaw and Prague. In Prague he met Rudolf Carnap* who had a formative influence on his philosophy, although this influence is tempered by the other sources to which Quine traces his philosophical ancestry, namely the American pragmatists John Dewey* and Charles Saunders Peirce.

Epistemology, which Quine conceives as concern with the foundations of science, would be a label that could be attached to all of his philosophy even though this appears to fall into two distinct categories: formal studies in logic and the foundations of mathematics, on the one hand, and works on language and the philosophy of logic, on the other. The motivation behind Russell* and Whitehead's studies in the foundations of mathematics was epistemological. A reduction of mathematics to logic would both explain and justify the privileged status accorded to mathematical theorems by showing them to be of the same character as self-evident logical truths. The work of Cantor and Dedekind on the nature of numbers had already shown that numbers can be defined in terms of sets, or collections of objects, but Russell's paradox indicates that some care is needed to formulate a contradiction-free theory of sets. The final step in reducing number theory to logic would thus be to show that logic can provide a theory of sets. Quine contributed to this programme, developing his own system (New Foundations) of set theory. This system has perplexed philosophers and mathematicians since its conception in that the considerations motivating its construction are largely pragmatic – it is designed to avoid Russell's paradox while preserving as much as possible of Frege's original system, so eliminating the complications introduced in *Principia Mathematica* (see Russell). Quine's system does not rest on prior intuitions as to what sets exist, and in consequence is not readily compared with the other systems of set theory now commonly used by mathematicians. Indeed, many unsuccessful attempts have been made to prove New Foundations inconsistent.

Just because of the unobviousness of its postulates, New Foundations cannot claim to be successful as an epistemological underpinning for mathematics. Conceptual clarification is gained by the reduction of mathematics to set theory, but epistemological guarantees are not supplied. In a later work, *Set Theory and its Logic*

(1963), Quine sets out in detail the view that logic stops where ontological commitments begin and that ontological commitments begin in mathematics just where sets have to be admitted as the values of variables open to quantification.

In the minds of Russell and other logical empiricists, this reductive programme in mathematics was paralleled by a programme for giving natural science an epistemological foundation in sense experience. This programme was most nearly completed by Carnap in his *Logische Aufbau der Welt*. Initially attracted by the project of the *Aufbau*, Quine soon, with Carnap, realized that it could not be completed; the sentences of scientific theories cannot be translated into sentences about sense data. His reaction to the failure of these two reductive programmes was, however, much more radical than Carnap's.

In his famous 'Two Dogmas of Empiricism' (*Philosophical Review*, 1951), Quine attacked the conception which underwrites the reductive programmes – the idea that each meaningful sentence must either have its own, determinate empirical content, or be true in virtue of the meanings of the words it contains. In his view the Vienna Circle did not take the verification theory of meaning seriously enough. Combining Peirce's claim that the meaning of a sentence turns purely on what would count as evidence for its truth with Duhem's view that theoretical sentences have their evidence not as single sentences, but only as parts of theories, the conclusion should be that a theory as a whole (or even the totality of beliefs generally held by a community) is the unit of empirical significance. The resulting picture, which many have found seductive, is of a system of beliefs as a field of force on which experience impinges at the periphery to effect distortions of the field, modifying not just individual beliefs but also the interconnections between beliefs, i.e. modifying the structure of the whole field. Some beliefs, those near the periphery, are more susceptible to modification in the light of experience than others, those nearer the centre, but this is only a matter of degree; there is no distinction in kind between mathematical statements, lying near the centre, and statements about trees which lie near the periphery. Empirical content attaches only to the whole system of beliefs, and how it is distributed over the sentences expressing individual beliefs is not a question admitting a unique answer.

The consequences of this denial that one can talk of *the* empirical content of a sentence are far reaching and their development occupies the bulk of Quine's subsequent philosophy. He sees two direct consequences: (i) there is no uniquely correct way of translating one language into another, since any translation preserving the empirical content of the whole is 'correct' (the thesis of the indeterminacy of translation); (ii) the want of a plausible alternative lends support to Dewey's naturalistic approach to language and epistemology.

For Dewey, meaning is primarily a property of behaviour; there can be no likeness or distinctness of meaning beyond what is implicit in people's dispositions to overt behaviour. Pursuit of this approach gives rise to the idea of radical translation.

The hypothetical radical translator is a field linguist, who is also a convinced behaviourist psychologist of the B. F. Skinner* variety and so sees language acquisition as the acquisition of dispositions to specific verbal responses on receipt of certain physical stimuli. He is confronted with a tribe of natives who have had no contact with the outside world and is to attempt a translation of their language. He starts correlating utterances with situations, guessing at what gestures signify assent and dissent. He then tries to establish, for some of these utterances, the conditions under which assent and dissent occur, so establishing their 'stimulus meaning' (the physical stimuli which trigger assent and dissent responses). This provides him with data on which to construct his 'analytical hypotheses' as to the logical structure of the native utterances and hence to propose a theoretical picture of their language. It is this idea which has been taken up by one of Quine's associates, Donald Davidson, who claims that reflection on radical translation is the route to insight on the nature of language. This claim has been a centre of debate for philosophical logicians in Britain and America for the last ten years.

Dr Mary Tiles

The system New Foundations appeared originally in 'New Foundations for Mathematical Logic', *American Mathematical Monthly*, 1937; an extended version is contained in the collection *From a Logical Point of View* (1953), which also contains 'Two Dogmas of Empiricism' and 'On What There Is'. Other works include: *Word and Object* (1960); *Ontological Relativity and Other Essays* (1969); and *Philosophy of Logic* (1970). Detailed responses to *Word and Object* are contained in D. Davidson and J. Hintikka (eds), *Words and Objections: Essays on the Work of W. V. Quine* (1969).

R

390
RADCLIFFE-BROWN, Alfred Reginald 1881–1955

British anthropologist

Brought up in genteel poverty in Birmingham, where he attended the King Edward School, A. R. Brown (later Radcliffe-Brown) was sent to Cambridge by an elder brother. He read Moral Sciences, taking a first, and went on to be W. H. Rivers's* first pupil in anthropology. He carried out field-studies in the Andaman Islands (1906–8) and Australia (1910–12), but in contrast to his famous anthropological contemporaries Boas* and Malinowski*, his central contribution was to be theoretical rather than ethnographic. Shortly after completing an initial ethnological account of the Andamanese Radcliffe-Brown was converted to Durkheim's* view of the sociological enterprise, and parallel with Durkheim's nephew Mauss* he devoted his life to the application of Durkheimian sociology to the findings of modern ethnography. His *The Andaman Islanders* (1922) is largely concerned with demonstrating that ceremony and ritual are to be understood as ways of maintaining the sentiments on which socially required behaviour depends. The actual Andaman ethnographic materials cited were taken largely from the reports of an earlier observer. Similarly his Australian studies relied heavily on the ethnographic reports of others, but brought to these a powerful analytic mind, rigorously defining the synchronic relations among institutions. His essays on Australian social organization remain central texts in the debate on these complex systems.

In 1921 Radcliffe-Brown was appointed to a foundation chair in social anthropology in Cape Town, subsequently holding chairs in the discipline in Sydney, Chicago, and from 1937 until his retirement in 1946, in Oxford. In these universities he was the central figure in the establishment of what amounted to a new discipline, so marked was the break with the ethnological tradition. Much of Radcliffe-Brown's writings in the latter part of his career consists of essays and lectures aiming at a definition and defence of the new science. Consequently a certain repetitiveness and contentiousness is often apparent, and the more specific essays and analyses have lasted best. In particular, Radcliffe-Brown's development of his views on kinship have proved important. He insisted on the systematic nature of kinship organization, the parts of the systems to be understood in their interrelationships.

While the Durkheimian influence was central, Radcliffe-Brown remained an evolutionist in the tradition of Herbert Spencer. Societies were like organisms, and could be studied by the methods of the natural sciences. Like organisms, they evolved in the direction of increasing diversity and complexity. 'Culture' was a product of a set of social relations. Social relations, social structure, provided the primary reality with which an anthropologist dealt. The anthropologist's aim was to uncover the normal form of such a system of relationships, and by comparison with similar sets to establish general laws of social relationships. An enduring value of this formulation is that it clears the decks for a rigorous study of the internal relationships characterizing a set of social facts, reducing the temptation to make a precipitate escape into psychological, biological or historical reductionism. Because he insisted that the parts of such systems of social relations contributed to the maintenance of the system as a whole, Radcliffe-Brown was often called a functionalist. This led to a confusion with Malinowski's ideas, which he deplored, but even among some who call themselves functionalists he has gone out of fashion because of his positivist insistence that systems of social relations can be directly observed, that their forms can be established empirically. Although still a controversial figure, it is difficult to think of another theoretical writer to set beside him in British sociology and social anthropology in the past half-century.

Professor Adam Kuper

The Social Anthropology of Radcliffe-Brown, ed. Adam Kuper (1977), is the most extensive collection of Radcliffe-Brown's shorter studies and essays, while *A Natural Science of Society* (1957) is a series of posthumously published lectures. See also Adam Kuper, *Anthropologists and Anthropology* (1975).

391
RANSOM, John Crowe 1888–1974

US poet

John Crowe Ransom's reputation is justifiably high despite the smallness of his output. Although he continued to produce influential criticism to the end of his life, his reputation as a poet rests mainly on three books published between 1919 and 1927.

He was born in Pulaski, Tennessee, the son of a Methodist minister, and went both to school and university (Vanderbilt) in Nashville. Following his graduation, he was awarded a Rhodes Scholarship and read Greats at Christ Church (1910–13). This taste of Oxford life in the mellow early-Georgian period underlines his Southern sense of tradition. Like some latter-day Augustan, he found himself, as he said in his essay on 'Lycidas' published in 1938, 'in manners, aristocratic; in religion, ritualistic; in art, traditional'. This statement of what Ransom felt to be the outstanding qualities of the Anglo (Southern) American tradition is not greatly different from his fellow (Northern) American, T. S. Eliot's* 'royalist in politics, classicist in literature, and Anglo-Catholic in religion'. However, in the application of their principles and the manner in which they arrived at them, there is a great difference between the two poets. Whereas Eliot moved into 'Modernistic' areas far away from the Calvinist–Unitarian–Transcendentalist heritage of New England, Ransom continued without any feeling of anachronism in the way of the old South. The results may be seen in their work. However curious his diction or mythical his South, there is in Ransom's verse a sense of rootedness. In Eliot's one feels the strain of a great creative achievement; like his friend and fellow countryman, Ezra Pound*, he manufactured a style out of cultural fragments based on his own personal and highly idiosyncratic reading.

From 1914 to 1937, Ransom taught at Vanderbilt University and became one of the founders of the *Fugitive*, a magazine which flourished in the 1920s and was devoted to what was best in the Southern tradition. The last thing the Fugitives wished to preserve (if they are to be believed) was the nineteenth-century image of a magnolia-and-crinoline South, with ideas of chivalry derived from Sir Walter Scott. It was from this – partly, at least – that they were fugitives; they were also fugitives from northern industrialism and carpetbagging. Ransom, his pupil Allen Tate, Donald Davidson, and, later, Robert Penn Warren and Cleanth Brooks, applied themselves to the idea of the South as they knew it in the 1920s. In the process they produced a number of excellent poems and essays – and such vigorous manifestos on Southern culture as *I'll Take My Stand* (1930). In 1937, Ransom became a Professor of English at Kenyon College, Ohio, where he remained, teaching, writing criticism, and editing the *Kenyon Review* until his retirement in 1959.

Ransom's reputation as a poet rests on *Chills and Fever* (1924) and *Two Gentlemen in Bonds* (1927), since *Poems About God* (1919) has long since been unobtainable and Ransom never reprinted any poems from it in subsequent collections. *Grace After Meat* (1924) was

an English selection from the first two volumes. Ransom's style ranges from the fragile evocation of 'Vision by Sweetwater' to the subtle polemic of 'Antique Harvesters'. Yet a similar tone is common to both; it is the note of irony. Robert Penn Warren, who has written more helpfully and knowledgeably about Ransom than most critics, devotes an essay to this feature of Ransom's work, arguing that it goes back beyond 'romantic irony' to 'Socratic irony'. By comparing the facts of a situation with the ideal of what it might be, Ransom is able to make comments which are both sharp and wise. His poems are precise, finely wrought, often archaic in diction, tough-minded, and strangely haunting. He is hardly ever precious or sentimental, despite the odd flavour of his language, which, for all its quaint and courtly elegance, gives the impression of being natural to the man.

In the field of criticism Ransom became known as a 'formalist' – that is, a critic who devotes more attention to the form and style of a poem than to its 'content'. His criticism is actually much deeper than this, however. In *God Without Thunder* (1930) he attacked both the values of science and liberalism in religion. Art, with its emphasis on aesthetic forms, he maintained, checks the impulses of Rousseau's 'natural' man, whereas science moves towards the ever greater satisfaction of his material desires. His idea of a critic was that he should be 'ontological', concerned with the very being of a poem, not investigating 'meaning' and 'form' as if they were separate entities, but accepting them as they exist, in the fusion of their poetic life. It is a theme similar to that propounded by Archibald MacLeish in his dictum that 'A poem should not mean but be' or by Wallace Stevens* in his arresting 'A poem must defeat the intelligence almost successfully'. Through the study of literature as an art, Ransom believed, the reader might come close to 'the world's body', which was in danger of being reduced to 'types and forms' by science. Despite this (one is almost inclined to say) Ransom, like his fellow 'New Critics', believed firmly in the value of close textual reading. But perhaps these two beliefs are not totally irreconcilable.

Geoffrey Moore

See: Robert Penn Warren, 'John Crowe Ransom: A Study in Irony', *Virginia Quarterly Review*, XI (1935); Cleanth Brooks, *Modern Poetry and the Tradition* (1939); Yvor Winters, 'John Crowe Ransom and Thunder Without God', in *The Anatomy of Nonsense* (1943); Allen Tate (ed.), 'Homage to John Crowe Ransom: Essays on His Work as Poet and Critic', *Sewanee Review*, LVI (1948); J. L. Stewart, *John Crowe Ransom* (1962).

392
RAUSCHENBERG, Robert 1925–

US artist

Rauschenberg's art does not operate within fixed limits. Heterogeneous and open-ended, it straddles boundaries both between different domains of art and between these and the outside world. The categories into which it is sometimes put, proto-Pop, neo-Dada, junk, etc., merely characterize it by certain of its aspects and do little justice to its richness and complexity.

Born and educated in Texas, Rauschenberg studied painting in Kansas and Paris before enrolling at Black Mountain College, North Carolina, under Albers*, primarily for the discipline which Albers offered. On leaving, Rauschenberg produced a series of White Paintings, which he described as 'hypersensitive', registering as they did the colours and shadows of passers-by: these have been compared with Cage's* – slightly later – silent piece *4'33"*. Then came a series of Black Paintings with strongly textured surfaces. There are close parallels between these monochrome works and those of Yves Klein*. In 1953 Rauschenberg turned to red, which for him was the most difficult colour. The climax of the red series was *Charlene* (1954), in which appear photographs, newsprint, fabrics, a flattened parcel and even a functional light bulb, along with the paint. This led directly to his Combine Paintings and Free-standing Combines, operating somewhere between painting and sculpture. If the physical substantiality of paint was already stressed in the monochrome works, in the Combines it is just one substance among several others. As Rauschenberg put it: 'A pair of socks is not less suitable to make a painting with than wood, nails, turpentine, oil and fabric.' Each component of his extended 'palette' brings with it associations specific to its background. Paint brings the tradition of painting and most specifically (since it is usually splashed on) that of de Kooning*; photographs, when included, conjure up various associations depending on their subject-matter, as well as suggesting a pin-up board; while the other objects, usually categorized as junk, far from being reduced simply to elements within a formal composition, are given a new lease of life and new meanings by being placed in this non-utilitarian context. Particularly successful Combine Paintings are *Bed* (1955), containing a real pillow, sheet and patchwork quilt, the sinister *Canyon* (1959), containing a flattened oil drum and stuffed eagle, and *Trophy I* (1959), dedicated to the dancer Merce Cunningham, with whose troupe Rauschenberg, like Cage, was closely associated. The most striking Free-standing Combine is probably *Monogram* (1959), whose main motif is a stuffed angora goat encircled by a rubber tyre. In 1959–60, Rauschenberg made *Thirty-Four Drawings for Dante's Inferno*, the only time he directly illustrated a text. During the 1960s his paintings mainly consisted of silkscreened images, a notable example being *Estate* (1963). In these, as in his Combines, Rauschenberg creates a specifically urban poetry, largely from the detritus of technological, industrial civilization. An involvement with technology's active side came in 1966 when he co-founded EAT (Experiments in Art and Technology), evidence of his refusal to accept the confines of a specialist professon.

The triumph of Abstract Expressionism in avant-garde art circles had, by the mid-1950s, led to an impasse. Rauschenberg's art was, with that of Jasper Johns*, the principal means by which this was overcome. By abandoning art's ivory-tower isolation and proposing all aspects of the modern world as in principle equally worthy of artistic attention, Rauschenberg not only paved the way for Pop Art but, more widely, helped create an inclusive, outward-looking aesthetic to which nearly all subsequent art is deeply indebted.

Gray Watson

The main study of Rauschenberg is Andrew Forge, *Robert Rauschenberg* (1969). See also: 'The Artist Speaks: Rauschenberg' in *Art in America* (May 1966); Dore Ashton, *The Unknown Shore* (1962); Calvin Tomkins, *The Bride and the Bachelors* (1965).

393
RAVEL, Joseph Maurice 1875–1937

French composer

Of mixed Swiss-Basque parentage, Ravel was born in the Basque region of France but grew up in Paris. In 1889 he entered the Paris Conservatoire, where he remained until 1904, studying composition with Fauré and others. During this period he came to know Satie*, whose influence is to be felt in his earliest published work, the *Meneut antique* for piano (1895). He was also one of the 'apaches', a group of self-styled outlaw artists which also included the poet Tristan Klingsor and the pianist Ricardo Viñes: Klingsor supplied the text for one of his great vocal works, *Shéhérazade* for soprano and orchestra (1903), and Viñes gave the first performance of most of his earlier piano works, including the *Pavane pour une infante défunte* (1899, orchestrated 1910) and *Jeux d'eau* (1901).

Between 1901 and 1905 Ravel entered four times the competition for the Prix de Rome; the failure of the judges to award him the prize, despite the fact that he was already a mature and proven composer, caused a public scandal. There was also heated debate at this time about his debt to Debussy* and Debussy's to him. Undoubtedly *Shéhérazade* owes something to the composer of *Pelléas et Mélisande*, though the work has a languid opulence which is quite foreign to Debussy's style; equally, the similarities between *Jeux d'eau* and some of Debussy's more brilliant preludes can be attributed to a shared appreciation of Liszt rather than to direct imitation.

In any event, Ravel was swiftly drawing away from the ambit of the older composer. In 1907 he produced two major Spanish works, the orchestral *Rapsodie espagnole* and the one-act comic opera *L'heure espagnole*, which, while contributing to a favoured genre among French composers, strike a quite individual note. The composer's distinctive quirky gaiety is to the fore, and for all their gusto the scores show too his high regard for technical precision, for an exact matching of means to effect and for the creation of perfect musical objects. He was to return to the Spanish motif again at the end of his career in the orchestral *Boléro* (1928) and in *Don Quichotte à Dulcinée* (1932), a set of three songs for voice and piano or orchestra.

Spain was not the only country Ravel visited in his music. He was often stimulated by the prospect of applying his skills to conventional musical genres: the Viennese waltz in *Valses nobles et sentimentales* for piano (1911, orchestrated 1912) and in the dark orchestral fantasy *La Valse* (1919–20), the Baroque suite in *La Tombeau de Couperin* for piano (1917, orchestrated 1919), gypsy violin playing in *Tzigane* for violin and piano or orchestra (1924) and jazz in the Piano Concerto in G major (1931). By using such disguises he was able to distance himself from his creation, and this tendency led him gradually to abandon the harmonic lushness and the rich colour washes of his earlier output. His ballet or 'choreographic symphony' *Daphnis et Chloé* (1909–11), commissioned by Diaghilev*, marked the end of his impressionist period, a sustained wander through the idyllic Grecian landscape that Debussy had discovered in his *Prélude à 'L'après-midi d'un faune'*.

Daphnis was followed by a number of works in which Ravel appears to have been testing new possibilities, composing more slowly and circumspectly than hitherto. In the *Trois Poèmes de Stéphane Mallarmé* (1913), a refined and rarefied score for soprano and nonet, he reacted, though at some distance, to the experience of *Pierrot lunaire*: there are tinges of atonality, and the instrumentation is modelled on Schoenberg's*. The Piano Trio of 1914 has middle movements more exactingly patterned on a Malayan verse form (the pantoum) and on the passacaglia, presaging the full-blown neo-classicism of *Le Tombeau de Couperin*. Then, in his Sonata for violin and cello (1920–2), Ravel produced an acerbic response to the bitonality and the neo-classical imitations of Stravinsky*.

Contemporary with this last work was the best known of Ravel's orchestrations, his version of Mussorgsky's *Pictures from an Exhibition*. He was a masterly orchestrator, developing his technique from that of Rimsky-Korsakov and creating scores of crystal clarity in which every detail tells. Apart from the Mussorgsky, he also orchestrated music by Debussy, Satie, Schumann and others as well as a great many of his own piano compositions. His scoring suggests a willingness to take pains with the tiniest detail, a fascination with perfecting musical objects which is also apparent in the substance of many of his works: *Boléro*, based on the continued redecoration of one idea, is only the most blatant example.

Another facet of this concern with the small is exposed in those works in which Ravel entered the world of childhood with penetrating insight, notably *Ma Mère l'oye* for piano duet (1908, orchestrated 1911), based on Pérrault's fairy-tales, and the opera *L'enfant et les sortilèges* (1920–5) to a libretto by Colette in which a child is hounded by the animals and household objects he has abused.

Ravel never married, nor did he accept any official position. He appeared only rarely as a pianist or conductor: he had originally intended the G major concerto for himself, but did not in the event play it (the contemporary left-hand concerto, a searching shadow of its exuberant companion, was composed specially for Paul Wittgenstein). Vaughan Williams* was one of his private composition pupils; those influenced by his music make up a larger group, embracing Milhaud, Roussel, Poulenc* and even Boulez*.

Paul Griffiths

Other works: String Quartet in F (1902–3); Sonatine for piano (1905); *Miroirs* for piano (1905); Introduction and Allegro for harp and sextet (1906); *Cinq Mélodies populaires grecques* for voice and piano (1904–6); *Histoires naturelles* for voice and piano (1906); *Gaspard de la nuit* for piano (1908); *Deux Mélodies hébraïques* for voice and piano or orchestra (1914); *Trois Chansons* for chorus (1915); *Chants populaires* for voice and piano (1910–17); *Ronsard à son âme* for voice and piano or orchestra (1924); *Chansons madécasses* for voice and trio (1925–7); Violin Sonata (1923–7). About Ravel: Vladimir Jankélévitch, *Ravel* (1959); Rollo H. Myers, *Ravel* (1960); H. H. Stuckenschmidt, *Maurice Ravel* (1968); Arbie Orenstein, *Ravel* (1975); Roger Nichols, *Ravel* (1977).

394
RAWLS, John 1921–

US philosopher

The publication in 1971 of *A Theory of Justice* by the Harvard philosopher, John Rawls, met with an acclaim unprecedented in contemporary philosophy, and rapidly generated a vast corpus of critical books and articles. The reason for Rawls's extraordinary influence was twofold. First, in place of the 'analytic' or 'linguistic' approach to ethics, which had dominated the subject since the war, Rawls reverted to the older tradition of 'normative ethics' – the attempt to construct principles setting the standard for human conduct. Second, Rawls's mammoth book (nearly six hundred pages long) provided the first major attempt, since Kant, to elaborate a non-utilitarian system of ethics.

Rawls's theory of justice may be called a 'hypothetical choice' theory. Its central idea is that we can arrive at just principles for use in society by considering what principles *would* be adopted by free and rational beings in a hypothetical 'original position' where they are not allowed to know what personal circumstances they will actually face in real life. This constraint (called by Rawls 'the veil of ignorance') is crucial in securing fairness: if I cannot know whether I am to be black or white, male or female, intelligent or stupid, weak or strong, then, according to Rawls, I am bound to select principles which do not favour one particular group at the expense of another. The two principles of justice Rawls argues must be selected in the 'original position' are the principle of liberty (there is to be the maximum liberty compatible with a like liberty for all); and the controversial 'difference principle' (inequalities are to be permitted only if they benefit the least advantaged members of society).

An inevitable reaction has followed the initial enthusiasm for Rawls's work. Intense academic analysis has cast logical doubt on the validity of Rawls's derivation of his principles of justice; it also appears doubtful whether the outcome of Rawls's system, on its most natural interpretation, is really counter-utilitarian. Nevertheless, for the rest of this century at least, the problems of justice and fairness in society will almost certainly tend to be discussed within the frame of reference laid down by Rawls.

Dr John Cottingham

A Theory of Justice (1971); N. Daniels (ed.), *Reading Rawls* (1975); Brian Barry, *The Liberal Theory of Justice* (1973); Robert Nozick, *Anarchy, State and Utopia* (1974).

395
RAY, Man 1890–1976

US artist

Man Ray probably did more than anyone else to integrate the traditions of photography and avant-garde painting. Growing up in New York, where his family had moved from Philadelphia when he was seven, he first encountered modern art in the gallery of the photographer Stieglitz. In 1913 came the Armory Show, where Duchamp's* *Nude Descending a Staircase* enjoyed a *succès de scandale*. Ray's sensibility was in many ways

very close to that of Duchamp and when they met soon afterwards, they became lifelong friends. Like Duchamp's, Ray's *oeuvre* is unified not by a consistent stylistic development but rather by a witty and enquiring intelligence. Like Duchamp, too, Ray was quick to appreciate the central cultural importance of the machine and to incorporate it, with highly ambiguous connotations, into his painting. A work of 1920 includes cogwheels interlocking so tightly that they are unable to turn, and the word 'Dancer' which can also be read 'Danger'. Duchamp and Ray were the leading figures in the short-lived New York Dada movement and in 1921 Ray followed Duchamp back to Paris, where he was introduced to the circle of writers and intellectuals who, believing that Dada was now outliving its usefulness, were evolving the doctrines of Surrealism. Ray created several powerfully sinister Surrealist objects, including *Gift* (1921), a flat-iron to which is attached a row of tin-tacks, and *Indestructible Object*, originally called *Object to be Destroyed* (1923), a metronome to which was clipped a photograph of an eye. He collaborated with the Surrealist poet Paul Eluard to produce a book of love poetry, *Facile* (1935), in which his photographs were integrated with Eluard's verse in a visually superb combination.

Photography brought Ray into the most fashionable circles in France, somewhat in contrast to his more revolutionary Surrealist connections. His film *The Mystery of the Château of Dice* (1926) was made during a house-party at the home of the Vicomte de Noailles, whose distinguished guests provided the cast. Ray produced fashion photography of the highest order as well as portraits of many of the leading artistic and cultural figures of the age. Perhaps his most original contributions in the photographic field were the inventions of new technical processes, arrived at in suitably Dada style by chance accidents. Most famous of these was the 'Rayograph', produced by placing objects directly on to sensitized paper, thus obviating even the need for a camera. He also exploited the phenomenon of 'solarization', some of his most remarkable solarized photographs being published in his album *The Age of Light* (1934).

In 1940 Ray escaped from occupied France and went to live in Hollywood, almost immediately meeting his bride-to-be, Juliet. In 1951 he returned with her to Paris, his spiritual home. With his love of girls and fast cars and his ability to mix in widely differing circles, Ray was gifted with exceptional charm as well as talent and originality. Despite several excursions into the sinister, the principal quality in his work is a commitment to freedom, individuality and happiness.

Gray Watson

Man Ray's other books include: *Électricité: 10 Rayographes* (1931); *La Photographie n'est pas l'Art* (1937); *Man Ray* (1944); *Revolving Doors* (1972). His other films were: *The Return to Reason* (1923); *Emak Bakia* (1926); *L'Étoile de Mer* (1928). On Ray: Louis Aragon, Jean Arp *et al.*, *Man Ray: Sixty Years of Liberties* (1971); Roland Penrose, *Man Ray* (1975); Arturo Schwarz, *Man Ray* (1977).

396
RAY, Satyajit 1921–

Indian film director

The most distinguished film-maker to emerge from India, Satyajit Ray is also the one who most successfully bridges the gulf between Eastern and Western cinemas. Coming from a cultured middle-class background, Ray completed his studies of music and the arts at Santineketan, to whose founder he devoted the documentary *Rabindranath Tagore* (1961). With a keen critical interest in film (Hollywood, Jean Renoir*, the Italian neo-realists) but no prior professional experience, he embarked in the mid-1950s on what was to become one of the cinema's major trilogies: *The Song of the Road* (1955), *The Unvanquished* (1956) and *The World of Apu* (1959). Working in a minority language, Bengali, and in face of the indifference of the bulk of the Indian film industry, Ray succeeded in part thanks to the international acclaim which greeted his work from the very beginning.

Subsequently his subjects, mostly taken from existing Bengali stories, have ranged widely. *The Music Room* (1958) and *The Goddess* (1960) were both depictions of an upper-class society in decline, brought down by pride and superstition. The early 1960s saw several delicate studies of the difficulties faced by Indian women in rural and urban societies: *Two Daughters* (adapted from Tagore* stories, 1961), *The Big City* (1963) and *Charulata* (1964). *Days and Nights in the Forest* (1970), a brilliantly realized portrayal of four young town dwellers out of their depths in the country just outside Calcutta, opened a fresh decade of achievement, marked by a number of films on the irreconcilable tensions created by the decline of traditional values in Calcutta: *The Adversary* (1970), *Company Ltd* (1971) and *The Middleman* (1975). Though Ray used colour as early as *Kanchanjungha*, made in 1962, most of his work has been photographed in black and white, with the camera in the hands of only two photographers, Subrata Mitra and Soumendu Roy, but colour was used for two recent oblique studies of the impact of world events on Indian rural societies, *Distant Thunder* (1973) on the famine caused by the Second World War and *The Chess Players* (1977), which depicts the annexation by the British of an Indian State. This latter film is a departure too in being made in Urdu for the mass Hindi market.

Ray is a complete film author, responsible for the direction, script and (since 1961) the music of all his films, and working closely with a constant team of actors and technicians whom he has trained himself. Though he remains essentially true to his Indian, or more precisely Bengali, origins, Ray must also be seen as the greatest heir to the humanist tradition of Western film-making which uses a basically realistic film style and finds its European peak in the work of Renoir and the neo-realists. Though he describes himself as a commercial director, Ray's work derives from a moral impulse. His statement in 1958 that 'working in Bengali, we are obliged morally and artistically to make films that have their roots in the soil of our province' sets out a programme to which he has kept faithfully ever since.

Dr Roy Armes

Other films: *The Philosopher's Stone* (1957); *Expedition* (1962); *The Coward and the Holy Man* (1965); *The Hero* (1966); *The Zoo* (1967); *The Adventures of Goopy and Bagha* (1968); *The Inner Eye* (documentary, 1974); *Golden Fortress* (1974); *Bala* (documentary, 1976). See: Satyajit Ray, *Our Films, Their Films* (New Delhi 1976); also Marie Seton, *Portrait of a Director – Satyajit Ray* (1971); and Robin Wood, *The Apu Trilogy* (1972).

397
REICH, Wilhelm 1897–1957

Austro-US psychoanalyst

Wilhelm Reich, psychoanalyst, Marxist and prophet of the sexual revolution, was the elder son of a prosperous Jewish, but unreligious, farmer. Born in Galicia and brought up in Bukowina, he was an Austrian citizen, even though these two provinces ceased to be part of Austria after the collapse of the Hapsburg empire in 1918. When he was fourteen his mother committed suicide, his father died three years later, and in 1916 he joined the Austrian army, seeing active service in Italy. At the end of the war Reich went to Vienna, an impoverished twenty-one-year-old war veteran, both his parents dead and his childhood home, which he never revisited, cut from him by the new frontiers drawn by the Treaty of Versailles. After a brief flirtation with the law Reich became a medical student and, aged only twenty-two, a practising psychologist and member of the Vienna Psychoanalytical Society. In 1927 he published the first version of his most famous book, *The Function of the Orgasm*, sought psychoanalytical treatment with Freud* who refused, and spent some months in a sanatorium for the tuberculous. In 1928 he joined the Austrian Communist Party, and was a co-founder of the Socialist Society for Sex Consultation and Sexological Research, which aimed to make sexual and psychological counselling available to the working classes. In 1929 his *Dialectical Materialism and Psychoanalysis* was published in Moscow, and in 1930 he moved to Berlin, which in view of his Austrian citizenship was not such a foolhardy act as it sounds. There he again founded an association working for the sexual liberation of the masses.

Although by no means the only psychoanalyst concerned to reconcile Freud and Marx, nor the only Marxist to be interested in Freud, Reich's political activities got him into trouble with both camps. In 1933 he was expelled from the German Communist Party, which thought he was diverting into sexual-hygiene campaigns energies that were, in view of the rise of Hitler*, urgently required for direct political action, and in 1934 he was dropped by the International Psychoanalytical Association, which hoped, vainly as it turned out, to weather the storm of fascism by remaining academic and apolitical. In the same year Reich published *The Mass Psychology of Fascism* in Denmark and *Character Analysis* in Vienna, and emigrated, first to Denmark, then to Norway, and finally, in 1938, to the United States, where he remained until his death in 1957 of a heart disease in the psychiatric wing of the Lewisburg Penitentiary, where he was serving a two-year sentence for contempt of court: he had refused to admit the competence of the courts to adjudicate on matters of scientific fact and, in particular, on whether the 'orgone accumulators' he had invented really were capable of curing physical and mental illnesses. The line of thought which led him to make such a claim is accepted by his disciples as evidence that he was, as he himself thought, a persecuted saviour of mankind who had successfully broken out of the 'intellectual framework of . . . the civilization of the last 5,000 years', but is regarded by the more sceptical as evidence that from 1934 onwards Reich was a crank and perhaps a little mad.

The year 1934 is in any case the turning point in Reich's life and thought. His writings before that were, and still are, taken seriously by those most competent to judge them. His view, expressed in *The Function of the Orgasm*, that damning up of libido is the fundamental cause of all neurosis and that, given the ubiquity of neurosis, full orgastic capacity is a rarity, has become almost a commonplace among psychoanalysts, as has also the idea, expressed in *Character Analysis*, that the aim of psychoanalytical treatment is to challenge and dissolve the character armour which neurotics construct to repress their native spontaneity. Similarly, his idea that the cause of sexual repression is the bourgeois authoritarian family, in which the fathers repress the sexual spontaneity of their wives and children, and that the masses only accept social repression because they are sexually repressed is still around in Marxist circles. But there is something crude, unscholarly, provincial and ranting about even his earlier writings which is an embarrassment to those who are sympath-

etically disposed to them. Indeed Reich himself came to feel that his writings on orgasm were liable to misconstruction and vulgarization and to fear that they would be used to unleash 'a free-for-all fucking epidemic'. The 1960s slogan Make Love Not War was a posthumous tribute to his ideas to which he would have given only qualified blessing.

After 1934, however, Reich's ideas took the turn which isolated him from both his Freudian and his Marxist roots, and led him into territory where only a few have been able to follow him. After a short period in which he sought to dissolve character armour by physical means, assuming, surely correctly, that character is reflected in posture and muscle tone and that compelling patients to relax would facilitate release of whatever had been repressed, he embarked on a search for the physical basis of libido and persuaded himself that he had found it. There was, he claimed, a substance, orgone energy, which was 'visible, measurable and applicable' and 'universally present and demonstrable visually, thermically, electroscopically and by means of Geiger-Müller counters'. The activities of this substance were responsible, he declared, not only for sexual excitement and discharge but also for everything that the religious designate as love. By discovering it Reich had, he believed, broken down all boundaries between science and religion and taken a step forward in human consciousness comparable to that taken by Jesus Christ, who was in Reich's opinion the archetypal genital character. Furthermore, this orgone energy could be stored in accumulators or 'orgone boxes' and used to cure physical and mental illnesses. No one else has ever succeeded in seeing orgone energy and in 1954 the US Federal Food and Drug Administration sued Reich for renting a fraudulent therapeutic device, thereby initiating the train of events which ended with his death in the psychiatric wing of a prison, but none the less 'legally sane and competent' – an ironic end to the life of a man who was both a victim and a hero of the catastrophes of our times.

Dr Charles Rycroft

Translations of Reich's work include *Character Analysis* (1949); *The Function of Orgasm* (1942); *The Sexual Revolution* (4th revised edition 1969); *Selected Writings*, ed. Mary Boyd Higgins (1960). *The Encyclopedia of Philosophy* gives a full bibliography. About Reich: Paul A. Robinson, *The Freudian Left* (1969); Ilse Ollendorf Reich, *Wilhelm Reich: A Personal Biography* (1969); Charles Rycroft, *Reich* (1971); Leo Raditsa, *Some Sense about Reich* (1978).

398
REINHARDT, Ad 1913–67

US painter

In 1935 Reinhardt graduated from Columbia University, where he had studied with Meyer Schapiro, and simultaneously attended the American Artists School (with Carl Holty and Frances Criss) and the National Academy of Design (with Karl Anderson). Holty encouraged him to join the American Abstract Artists group and he did so in 1937. In the same year he joined the Artists Union and was hired by Burgoyne Diller on the Federal Art Project as an 'Artist, Class 1, Grade 4' in the Easel Division.

After hovering indecisively between different styles, in the early 1940s an individual manner prevailed. It was a hard-won victory; for Reinhardt cerebration ranked as highly as 'pure' feeling, and any change in stance had to be justified and defended intellectually. He joked about the distinction between his late 1930s 'late-classical-mannerist-post-cubist, geometric abstractions' and his post-1940 'rococo-semi-surrealist fragmentation' and 'all-over-baroque-geometric-expressionist patterns'. But Reinhardt's jokes were always serious, as his cartoons demonstrate. He was aligning himself with non-gestural New York painting in a quest for a serene, stable, cool art inspired by studies of Chinese and Japanese culture and Islamic decoration, with Alfred Salmony at the New York Institute of the Fine Arts (1945–51). His 1940s paintings, lately reconsidered by critics, have been compared to Oriental scrolls or Persian carpets, achieving an effect of deliquescence, a loss of spatial bearings. He called his late 1940s work 'archaic colour-brick-brushwork impressionism and black-and-white constructivist calligraphies'. Styles followed thick and fast until in 1953 the first of the 'early-classical, hieratic, red, blue, black monochrome square crossbeam symmetries' was created. His reputation rests on these pictures and the theories which support them.

The most mysterious of his works are the black-on-black paintings of 1960 to 1966, symmetrical in format with a horizontal band bisecting a vertical of equal size, both trisecting the sides of the canvas, painted in extremely close-toned colours. His political vigilance and artistic militancy had been concentrated into a one-man campaign for purity. 'Fine art can only be defined as exclusive, negative, absolute and timeless,' he wrote in 1957, and though he saw his late works as a critique of the religiosity creeping into the thought of the masters of Abstract Expressionism, the strings of negatives by which art is defined in his essays indicate a mystical approach akin to Zen or St John of the Cross's 'Dark Night of the Soul'. Reinhardt's influence was on a younger generation of artists working on 'minimal' structures. Regarded as an entire career, however, his achievement may finally prove closer in quality to that of Rothko* or Newman than he himself would have accepted. In his lifetime Reinhardt was attacked fiercely. Even supporters lost faith when he agreed to a retrospective exhibition at the Jewish Museum in New York. There are more pressing problems than those of art politics, however. Reinhardt's nihilism and the sheer presence of the paintings remain at loggerheads. The last word remains with the artist: 'I'm just making the last paintings which any artist can make.'

Stuart Morgan

Art as Art, ed. Barbara Rose (1975), is a selection of Reinhardt's writings. See: Lucy Lippard, *Ad Reinhardt: Paintings*, a catalogue for the Jewish Museum exhibition (1967); *Ad Reinhardt: Art Comics and Satires* (Truman Gallery catalogue, 1976); Thomas Hess, *The Art Comics and Satires of Ad Reinhardt* (1975).

399
REINHARDT, Max 1873–1943

Austrian/German theatre producer and director

Max Reinhardt was foremost among the theatrical innovators who, at the turn of this century, created the concept of the director as the principal artistic force in the theatre. Born near Vienna as the son of a Jewish merchant – his original family name was Goldmann – Reinhardt was already, as a boy, deeply imbued with the enthusiasm for the theatre which plays so large a part in the life of Vienna, a city in which the spirit of an old tradition of *commedia dell'arte* and flamboyantly spectacular baroque machine opera was still alive and in which a splendid national theatre, the *Burgtheater*, provided excellent performances of the classics at nominal prices.

At the age of nineteen Reinhardt obtained his first engagement as a character actor (while still in his teens he particularly excelled in old men's parts). Otto Brahm, the director of the Berlin Deutsches Theater, the cradle of German naturalism, brought him to Berlin in 1894, when he was twenty-one. For seven years he was a leading member of the company of that most famous of German theatres, but became gradually dissatisfied with the lack of colour, the excessive emphasis on the sordid side of life, inherent in the naturalistic style prevalent there. To escape from the depressing monotony and greyness of this work he induced a number of his fellow-actors to join him in a group which gave late-night cabaret performances and soon attained fame under the title *Schall und Rauch* ('Sound and Smoke'). This group developed into a full-scale company which also presented full-length plays, the *Kleines*

Theater (1902), under Reinhardt's leadership. Here he began to cultivate a post-naturalistic repertoire, based on neo-romantics like Wilde, Hofmannsthal and Schnitzler, as well as the early expressionism of Strindberg and Wedekind. So successful was this work that in 1905 Reinhardt was offered the directorship of the Deutsches Theater as successor to Brahm.

Reinhardt's approach was basically theatrical. For him the actor was the centre of the dramatic experience and the stage a place of magic. The rapid development of technology had given him the chance of achieving hitherto undreamt-of effects on the stage through the use of hydraulics, revolving platforms and, above all, electric lighting which could be dimmed and faded at will and thus make the director a veritable painter in light. Reinhardt was one of the first theatrical practitioners to realize the full potential of this new technology: he abandoned painted backdrops and went in for solidly built, three-dimensional scenery, which, when revolved, could make the audience actually see the characters on the stage moving from indoors to outdoors, or walking through the narrow streets of Venice, crossing bridges over canals, while the sun was rising or going down. To achieve these effects Reinhardt evolved the concept of the director as the presiding intelligence over a whole team of artists and technicians, the guiding spirit who conceives the basic plan of the play: its total meaning, its prevailing colour scheme, its spatial dimensionality, the mood of its lighting, and then initiates and co-ordinates the work of the specialists – the set and costume designers, the lighting engineer, the musical director, the creator of masks and properties and other artists and technicians. But, above all, in Reinhardt's new concept, the director was the guiding spirit and co-ordinator of the actors whom he had to mould into a coherent whole, where the work of each enhances that of all the others. Reinhardt's work with actors was immensely inspiring and spectacularly successful. Having himself been a superb actor, he could show each of his actors how he could best use his own potential.

In the Deutsches Theater Reinhardt at first concentrated on the classical repertoire which he imbued with the full force of his new stage magic. Among his first major successes were productions of Shakespeare's *A Midsummer Night's Dream*, *The Winter's Tale*, *Romeo and Juliet*, *Twelfth Night*, Kleist's *Kaethchen von Heilbronn* and Schiller's *Brigands*.

But Reinhardt's ambitions went beyond the traditional proscenium arch theatre; he wanted to create a complex of theatres to meet all possible stylistic demands: an intimate theatre for plays requiring the subtlest psychological nuance; and, at the other end of the spectrum, a large open arena holding thousands of spectators to accommodate performances requiring large crowds of extras. The first step towards realizing this programme was the building of a small theatre

adjoining the Deutsches Theater, the *Kammerspiele* (Chamber Theatre), which was opened in 1906. Here the stage was barely raised above the level of the auditorium so that the four hundred spectators could get the feeling of being in the same room with the characters in plays by Ibsen and Strindberg. To realize the second part of his plan Reinhardt began to convert a big circus building in Berlin, the Zirkus Schumann, into an immense theatre with an open arena stage, the *Grosses Schauspielhaus* (Large Spectacle House), which, after many delays caused by the First World War was finally opened in November 1919.

In the meantime, however, Reinhardt had broken out of the conventional theatre building altogether. To exploit the full and at that time still sensationally novel impact of the new theatrical magic, he created a series of spectacles which almost totally dispensed with speech and largely relied on visual imagery alone. These were his famous *Pantomimen* (mime plays, rather than pantomimes in the English sense of the word), of which the most spectacular, which established him as a world celebrity, was *The Miracle*, staged in December 1911 at Olympia, the great London exhibition centre. He transformed the vast hall into the interior of a Gothic cathedral, where thousands of spectators could see the fortunes of a medieval nun, who leaves her convent for a life of sensual love only to find, on her repentant return many years later, that the Madonna herself has taken her place there to spare her shame and punishment. So successful was this spectacle that Reinhardt was asked to re-stage it in Vienna (1912), Berlin (1914) and New York and other major American cities (1924).

After the First World War Reinhardt wanted to return to his native Austria. In 1920 he staged, on the Cathedral square of Salzburg (where he had spent one of his early seasons as a young actor) Hofmannsthal's adaptation of the old English morality play, *Everyman*. This production marked a further stage in Reinhardt's movement away from the traditional theatre space: here he used the backdrop of the façade of the baroque church, as well as the whole town itself; the voices calling for Everyman in the hour of his death came from all the church spires of the city and even from the distant castle high on the hill above it, and as night fell and Everyman went to his death, all the church bells of Salzburg began to toll. This production not only became a classic which was repeated annually for several decades, but it also initiated the first of the great international music and drama festivals, which have since then become so important an annual feature throughout the world. Reinhardt was, without doubt, the creator of this concept, the inventor of the modern festival idea.

Throughout the 1920s and early 1930s Reinhardt presided over a vast theatrical empire in Berlin, Vienna (where he had acquired the Theater in der Josefstadt) and Salzburg, where he resided as a grand seigneur in a castle built by one of the archbishops of the city, Leopoldskron. In addition he staged spectacular open-air productions in places as diverse as a square in Venice, the garden of an Oxford College or the Boboli gardens in Florence.

After Hitler* came to power in Germany, Reinhardt had to leave Berlin and, while continuing to run his theatrical enterprises in Austria, spent an increasing amount of time in the United States. He opened a theatre academy in Hollywood and directed a film version of *A Midsummer Night's Dream* for Warner Brothers in which he showed his brilliance with actors by making James Cagney as Bottom and Mickey Rooney as Puck give the best performances of their lives (1935).

After Hitler's occupation of Austria in 1938 Reinhardt moved to the United States. He repeatedly tried to achieve a success on Broadway, but failed in each instance.

Martin Esslin

Reinhardt's own writings are published in *Schriften* (1974). There is a Max Reinhardt research centre (Max Reinhardt Forschungsstaette) in Salzburg and a Reinhardt Archive at the New York State University at Binghamton, N.Y.

400

RENOIR, Jean 1894–1979

French film director

The most influential of all French film directors, Jean Renoir was the second son of the Impressionist painter Auguste Renoir, whose impact on him was crucial (see his book of memoirs, *Renoir, My Father*, 1962). Throughout his life Jean Renoir remained open to the influence of landscape, outside events and the personalities of others, and many of his films are examples of true collaborative effort. For years he was uncertain about his career, serving as a cavalry officer and pilot in the First World War and working for years in ceramics. Only at the age of thirty did he turn to film-making, inspired principally by Erich von Stroheim's *Foolish Wives*. His first films were made for his own production company, with his wife as star. From his very first film, *La Fille de l'eau* (1924), the characteristic themes of landscape and love, and an intermixing of varied styles were apparent. His major silent film, an adaptation of Zola's *Nana* (1926) was commercially unsuccessful and his later silent films were commercial ventures.

In the 1930s, which were the years of his greatest successes, he achieved notable impact with *La Chienne* (1931) and *Boudu sauvé des eaux* (1932), both starring the anarchic Michel Simon. *Toni* (1935) was a major

departure. Shot on location with little known players, it shows a deepening social concern and in many ways anticipates post-war Italian neo-realism. In 1936, with Jacques Prévert, he made *Le Crime de Monsieur Lange*, in which the social optimism of the Popular Front is most apparent, and subsequently took his political commitment a stage further by making *La Vie est à nous* (1936) for the French Communist Party. But Renoir was not a man to be confined within one style or ideological approach and his work far transcends the limitation of the cinematic 'poetic realism' of the period. Subsequent films include a delicately observed adaptation from Maupassant, *Une Partie de campagne* (1936), a passionate denunciation of war, the highly successful *La grande illusion* (1937), a patriotic epic *La Marseillaise* (1938) and a further adaptation of Zola, *La Bête humaine* (1938). His masterpiece is *La Règle du jeu* (1939) which, beneath surface frivolity, shows a disintegrating society on its way to self-destruction.

Renoir spent the 1940s in exile in Hollywood where he made a number of notable films, among them *The Southerner* (1945), despite the alien atmosphere of the studios. After a visit to India to make *The River* (1950), he returned to Europe to direct a number of colourful meditations on art and life, among them *Le Carrosse d'or* (1953) and *French Cancan* (1955). In his later years he explored new methods of production and his last film, *Le petit théâtre de Jean Renoir* (1970) was shot for television.

The impact of Renoir's work and personality has been enormous. Apart from the inspiration given by his great series of works in the 1930s, he has personally influenced a large number of young film-makers at a crucial moment of their careers: Luchino Visconti* in the late 1930s, Satyajit Ray* while in India in 1950, and above all the group of would-be film-makers gathered around André Bazin and the magazine *Cahiers du cinéma* in the late 1950s – Truffaut*, Godard*, Rivette, Rohmer among them.

Dr Roy Armes

Renoir's other films are: *Sur un air de charleston* (1927); *La petite marchande d'allumettes* (1928); *Marquitta* (1927); *Tire au flanc* (1928); *Le Tournoi dans la cité* (1929); *Le Bled* (1929); *On purge bébé* (1931); *La Nuit du carrefour* (1932); *Chotard et cie* (1933); *Madame Bovary* (1934); *Swamp Water* (1941); *This Land is Mine* (1943); *The Diary of a Chambermaid* (1946); *The Woman on the Beach* (1948); *Elena et les hommes* (1956); *Le Testament du Docteur Cordelier* (1961); *Le Déjeuner sur l'herbe* (1959); *Le Caporal épinglé* (1962). Books by Renoir, as well as his book on his father, are: *The Notebooks of Captain Georges* (a novel, 1966), and *My Life and My Films* (1974). See also: André Bazin, *Jean Renoir* (1974); Leo Braudy, *Jean Renoir – The World of His Films* (1972); Raymond Durgnat, *Jean Renoir*, (1975).

401

RESNAIS, Alain 1922–

French film director

A delicate child, Alain Resnais was educated at home by his mother, developing a lifelong love of literature and music. Subsequently he studied first acting, and then film editing at the IDHEC (French Film School). While still in his teens he made a number of short amateur films and, later, two feature-length dramas (now lost) and a number of studies of painters, all in sixteen millimetre format. The success of one of the latter led directly to the beginning of his professional career, with three documentaries on *Van Gogh* (1948), *Gauguin* (1950) and Picasso's* *Guernica* (1950). In the next nine years, while planning a breakthrough into feature film making, he was commissioned to direct five documentaries on a wide variety of subjects: colonization (*Les Statues meurent aussi*, 1950–3), the Nazi concentration camps (*Nuit et brouillard*, 1955), the French National Library (*Toute la mémoire du monde*, 1956), industrial safety (*Le Mystère de l'atelier 15*, 1957), and the manufacture of polystyrene (*Le Chant du styrène*, 1958). With these unlikely subjects he developed the techniques which he would use in his early features: a disregard for the synchronization of image and sound and instead a separation and new fusion of the elements of image, music and text (the latter often by a well-known literary figure, such as Paul Eluard or Raymond Queneau*).

Resnais's début as a feature film maker came in 1959 with *Hiroshima mon amour*, from a script by Marguerite Duras*. In the 1960s he followed this same pattern of work on four further features, collaborating with Alain Robbe-Grillet* on *L'Année dernière à Marienbad* (1961), Jean Cayrol on *Muriel* (1963), Jorge Semprun on *La Guerra est finie* (1966), and Jacques Sternberg on *Je t'aime, je t'aime* (1968). All five films are marked by the use of novel formal structures: the interplay of past and present in *Hiroshima*, the refusal of chronology in *Marienbad* and its opposite, the strict chronology of *Muriel*, the flash forward shots of anticipation in *La Guerre est finie* and the almost aleatory interweaving of levels of time and reality in *Je t'aime*. When he resumed his directing career in 1974, with *Stavisky* (from a script by Semprun) and then, in 1977, with *Providence* (shot in English from a text by David Mercer), the same technical assurance was apparent, but also a certain shallowness beneath the immaculate surface.

Resnais's reputation, based on his work between 1955 and 1963, is secure, but he remains a paradoxical figure, ten years older than the New Wave directors with whom his name was once erroneously linked: a one-time amateur film-maker whose work denies improvisatory freedom; an intellectual film-maker whose stated preferences are for Hitchcock*, the comic strips and pulp fiction serials; a creator of revolutionary filmic structures whose working methods seem to cry out for the controlled atmosphere of the traditional studio. His direct impact is undeniable – all four of his first writers went on to direct features – and elsewhere in modern cinema one finds a more diffuse influence as powerful but hidden as the mainsprings of his own creative imagination.

Dr Roy Armes

All Resnais's professional films are mentioned above. See: Roy Armes, *The Cinema of Alain Resnais* (1968); John Ward, *Alain Resnais or the Theme of Time* (1968); James Monaco, *Alain Resnais* (1978).

402

RICHARDS, Ivor Armstrong 1893–1979

English poet and critic

English poet, critic, mountaineer and teacher, whose pioneering work on the reader's response to literature not only helped establish with great *éclat* the study of English literature at Cambridge University, England, after the First World War, but also (through the tremendous influence of his lectures, his writings and his pupils – who included William Empson* and F. R. Leavis*) gave twentieth-century western literary criticism its most long-lived critical tool, the practice of Practical Criticism. Richards was a great educator, in England, in pre-revolutionary China, and at Harvard. He believed in the power of literature to educate for living. Literature in the service of the 'good of man' remained a central concern, even after he had ceased putting so bluntly the utilitarian view of literature's 'value' that he developed early in *Principles of Literary Criticism* (1924).

Obviously, to be of greatest value literature must be read well, so Richards's pedagogic insistence on the ethically heuristic process of reading soon turned into a concern with hermeneutics in theory and practice. In an influential succession of books beginning with his most famous *Principles of Literary Criticism* and his *Practical Criticism* (1929), and going on unflaggingly into *Interpretation in Teaching* (1938), *How to Read a Page: A Course in Effective Reading* (1942), and beyond, he tackled, as a teacher, the problems of teaching, and learning, how to interpret literary texts. His stance was always complex – not least because in an impressively long working life his thinking never stood still. He turned his classrooms, for instance, into laboratories for testing reader-responses and was taken to have provided a scientifically rigorized, materialistic criticism; and yet he also loved mountains, yielded readily to Coleridge's influence (see his *Coleridge on Imagination*, 1934), grew to admire Plato very strongly (he did a 'simplified' version of *The Republic*, 1942), and had suspicions of the post-Gutenberg machine-age as strong as anything more regularly associated with Dr and Mrs F. R. Leavis. Again, he was an élitist, interested in educating the literary responses of 'meditative people' (i.e. 'those who most matter'), and yet he devoted a large part of his life's energies to advocating the pedagogic virtues of the simplified form of English (*Basic English*) that he developed with C. K. Ogden, his early Cambridge ally (co-author with him of *The Meaning of Meaning*, 1923), and to devising sets of basic language manuals (including the *Through Pictures* and the *Workbook* series). But the contradictions did converge in his kept-up humanism, his belief in the imaginative products of man, the language user, as humane instruments, and in the necessity of teachers educating readers into this humaneness ('teachers able to help humanity to remain humane'). In particular Richards's success in making Practical Criticism stick, in granting a method and a vocabulary to several generations of readers (*stock response, private poem, storehouse of recorded values, scientific* as against *emotive language*: all these standard pieces of critical rhetoric originate with him), was rooted in his persuasion that good readings of literature could be a kind of post-religious salvation in the chaos of modern unbelief. Literature, he argued, did not at any period persuade one actually to believe things – it consisted not of statements requiring assent, only of *pseudo-statements* – but it did provide initiation and experience in necessary kinds of human feeling.

At first Richards believed strongly that readings could be wrong, but gradually, under the attractions of the Platonic dialogue and of Niels Bohr's* Principle of Complementarity (see *Complementarities: Uncollected Essays*, edited by John Paul Russo, 1976), he came to prefer the view of readers as involved in an endless debate about the meaning of a poem's pseudo-statements in which no one would be wrong, or feel wronged. Literary criticism – it was Richards's finest, if most arguable humanitarian notion – would thus provide a valid defence against, a salutary siphoning away of, the disagreements that lead mankind to war. And it is perhaps not least among the ironies attaching to Richards's labours that the lifelong arguments that led to this position – the insistence on the *pseudo-statement*, on the *words on the page*, on the poem as polysemic, multivalent, densely layered, and richly ambivalent – should have encouraged others, particularly the structuralist and post-structuralist ('deconstructionist') progeny of the so-called New Critics, in their retreat from the humane view, which Richards himself retained, of literature having to do Arnoldianly with life, of its being connected significantly with more than just the mind (a mind viewed solipsistically, surrealistically) of a mere player with language. Much in Richards's practice has given succour to this modernist critical retreat from real contexts

– his casual way with history, his Cambridge scorn for Oxford philology, his concentration on reading single, discrete poems or pages, his lifelong interest in the processes going on in the reader's mind and, as it were, in the mind of the text. But his equally convinced faith in the relevance of literature to man in his 'loneliness' and 'ignorance', within 'the inconceivable immensity of the universe', exposes the belittling and denuding of texts entailed by their being more fashionably locked up entirely into themselves.

Valentine Cunningham

Other works include: *The Foundation of Aesthetics* (with C. K. Ogden and James Wood, 1922); *Science and Poetry* (1926; reissued as *Poetries and Sciences* 1970); *Mencius on the Mind* (1932); *Basic Rules of Reason* (1933); *Basics in Teaching: East and West* (1935); *The Philosophy of Rhetoric* (1936); *Basic English and Its Uses* (1943); *Words on Paper: First Steps in Reading* (with Christine M. Gibson, 1943); *Speculative Instruments* (essays, 1955); *Why so, Socrates? A Dramatic Version of Plato's Dialogues: Euthyphro, Apology, Crito, Phaedo* (1964); *So Much Nearer: Essays Towards a World English* (1968); *Design for Escape: World Education Through Modern Media* (essays, 1968); *Internal Colloquies: Poems and Plays* (1971); *Poetries: Their Media and Ends* (essays, 1973); See: *I. A. Richards: Essays in His Honor*, ed. R. Brower, H. Vendler, J. Hollander (1973); Cyrus Hamlin, 'I. A. Richards (1893–1979): Grand Master of Interpretations', in *University of Toronto Quarterly*, Spring 1980.

403
RIEFENSTAHL, Leni (Helene Bertha Amalie)
1902–

German film director and photographer

Born in Berlin, Leni Riefenstahl was the daughter of a rich plumbing and heating engineer. Against her father's wishes she decided at an early age to be a dancer, and was trained at the Berlin Russian Ballet School. After touring Europe for three years in various companies, she rejected Max Reinhardt's* plans for her to have a part in Arnold Fanck's film *The Holy Mountain* (*Die heilige Berg*, 1925), one of many 'mountain films' attracting large audiences in Germany throughout the 1920s and 1930s. Over the next few years she appeared in a number of similar ventures, including the highly successful *Storms over Mont Blanc* (*Stürme über dem Mont Blanc*, 1930), experience which not only developed her considerable acting ability, but also exposed her to the complexities of location photography. It was against this background that, with the help of Bela Balazs, she directed her first film, *The Blue Light* (*Das blaue Licht*, 1932), which she also produced, wrote and starred in. This won the Gold Medal at the Venice Film Festival immediately establishing Riefenstahl as a remarkably talented woman in a male-dominanted industry. Idolized in Germany, the Nazis quickly recognized a compatibility between her style and theirs: Hitler* himself commissioned Riefenstahl to make *Sieg des Glaubens* ('Victory of Belief', 1933), a short documentary of the Nürnberg party congress brilliantly capturing the spirit of the Nazi movement, and the near deification of its leader. This was the decisive stage of her career: protected by her friendship with Hitler even from the interference of Goebbels, she enjoyed a unique advantage over other chroniclers of the Reich; but when the Reich itself collapsed, her career went with it. Although she repudiated everything to do with Nazism in 1952, she was unable to resume life as a director, and only completed one film after the war, *Tiefland* (1954), a project begun in 1940, but abandoned then due to one of her recurrent breakdowns in health. Her natural talent however was not to be daunted. She re-emerged at the end of the 1960s as a photographer, producing two acclaimed studies of remote African tribal life, *The Last of the Nuba* (1969) and *The People of Kau* (1976). At the age of seventy-five she began deep-sea diving and underwater photography, which led to the equally remarkable *Coral Gardens* (1978).

There is now little disagreement that, whatever their politics, Riefenstahl's films represent a rare cinematic achievement. *Triumph of the Will* (*Triumph des Willens*, 1935) is a record of the 1934 Nürnberg party congress. From the first sight of Hitler's plane emerging from the clouds, to the pace of the triumphal drive through Nürnberg, to the Führer's appearance in one long shot amongst the rows of immaculate uniformed soldiers, walking amongst so many beetles to pay homage to the dead in the gigantic stadium, her genius here lies in her ability to create a mounting tension surrounding an event the outcome of which is never in doubt. This was followed by *Day of Freedom* (*Tag der Freiheit*, 1935), about the Wehrmacht, intended to redress the fancied slight of their exclusion from *Triumph of the Will*. Her masterpiece, however, was *Olympia* (*Olympische Spiele*, 1936), an epic documentary of the Munich Games in two parts, recording athletes and sports as an evocation of human physical beauty at rest or in motion. The first part, the lyrical *Festival of the Nationals* (*Fest der Völker*), includes a mystical, languid eurhythmic display expressing the sensual aspects of physical exercise, followed by a sequence on contemporary Berlin and, inevitably, Hitler, juxtaposed with footage on Greece filmed by Willy Zielke. Part Two, *Festival of Beauty* (*Fest der Schönheit*), depicts the Olympic Village, and the main events. Apart from its brilliant photography and accompanying score by Herbert Windt, the film was a feat of organization. Riefenstahl employed thirty cameramen in special pits, on rails and hoists, often with equipment that had been specifically manufactured for her requirements. It took six months just to train the photographers of the diving sequences. But the work owes its coherence to the eighteen months' solitary editing by Riefenstahl once the Games were over, reducing 400,000 metres of film to 6,151. Of the many awards given to *Olympia*, perhaps the least expected were the diploma and Gold Medal presented to Riefenstahl by the Olympic Committee in 1948, the time when she was suffering most heavily for her Nazi associations.

Olympia was followed by *Berchtesgaden über Salzberg* ('Berchtesgarden near Salzburg', 1938), a short documentary on Hitler's mountain retreat, and in 1944 a terse, gloomy portrait of the sculptor Arno Breker.

Michael Pick

See: Glenn B. Infield, *Leni Riefenstahl: The Fallen Film Goddess* (1976); also David Stewart Hull, *Film in the Third Reich* (1969).

404
RILKE, Rainer Maria 1875–1926

Austrian poet

Born, like Kafka*, into the German-speaking minority in Prague, Rilke suffered in his early years from enforced oscillation between extremes; from the smothering influence of his posturing, religiose mother to the rigours of a Prussian-style military academy; from the aridity of two terms at a business school in Linz to the adoption, back in Prague, of a pose of *fin-de-siècle* aestheticism. His studies, which, being subjugated to his early efflorescence as a writer, were somewhat perfunctory, took him from the universities of Prague to Munich and thence to Berlin. In Munich he had met and fallen under the influence of the remarkable Russian intellectual Lou Andreas-Salomé (who had been loved by Nietzsche and was later to become one of the early pupils of Freud*). In 1899 and 1900 Rilke, who became for a while her lover, accompanied her on two journeys to Russia. On his return he joined an artists' colony in Worpswede in north Germany, where he met and married the sculptress Clara Westhoff, a pupil of Rodin. But the claims of marriage, or indeed of any demanding emotional relationship, were always, for Rilke, irreconcilable with his poetic vocation, and the couple, after the birth of a daughter, agreed to separate. Soon afterwards, in August 1902, Rilke moved to Paris.

Throughout his life, Rilke was a restless traveller and a detailed biography would therefore have to consist in large part of a conscientious account of his itineraries. Three places, however, may be singled out as the significant *loci* of his life: Russia, Paris and the Canton Valais of Switzerland. In later life Rilke himself was to point to the contrasting influences on his own sensibility of Russia and Paris. From the former he gained a sense of the inexorable and intransigent vastness of experience. In *Das Stundenbuch* ('The Book of Hours', 1899–1903, published 1905), the work most directly influenced by the Russian journeys, a humble Russian monk addresses to God utterances which can only ironically be described as prayers: for God here, far from representing the God of Christianity (which Rilke had vehemently repudiated in his Tuscan Diary of 1898), is a figure of fluctuating significance, sometimes creator, sometimes created by the speaker, now entreated, now despised, the origin and the goal of ceaseless proliferations of metaphor. The *Stundenbuch* is an abundant and a fluent work, but in its very fluency Rilke saw signs of danger: Paris, and in particular the example of Rodin, was to provide the necessary antidote. *Das Buch der Bilder* ('The Book of Images', 1902) and, more radically, *Neue Gedichte* ('New Poems', published 1907 and 1908) are concerned essentially with the tension between perception and experience: but experience not, as in the *Stundenbuch*, on a cosmic scale, but in the form of isolated minutiae, objects or beings whose elusive significance both attracts and challenges the poet's 'shaping spirit'. The element of challenge is more intensely dramatized in the novel *The Notebook of Malte Laurids Brigge* (*Die Aufzeichnungen des Malte Laurids Brigge*, 1910, trans. 1930). The eponymous hero of this work, a young Danish poet living in Paris, is possessed of (and by) an acute and painful power of empathy; immediate perceptions, childhood memories and recollections from history and myth crowd in upon him, but Malte's sensibility is too passive for him to be able to master creatively the overwhelming multiplicity of experience. Ironically then, *Malte Laurids Brigge* is a work of art constructed out of the agonies of artistic insufficiency.

The claims of experience *vis-à-vis* the individual consciousness: this, essentially, is the theme of Rilke's two major cycles, *Duino Elegies* (*Duineser Elegien*, trans. 1939) and *Sonnets to Orpheus* (*Die Sonette an Orpheus*, trans. 1936), both completed in Muzot in the Canton Valais of Switzerland in 1922. The *Elegies*, begun at Duino, a castle on the Adriatic, in 1912, took Rilke ten years to complete and were regarded by him as his major achievement, They are a series of ten poetic meditations on a number of interrelated problems, the chief of which is that of the creative sensibility (and, by extension, the human sensibility as a whole) in a transient world; its awareness, in the light of inevitable death, of the disparate and fragmentary nature of human achievement and the impermanence of love; its consciousness of, but inability to emulate, figures which, through their all-consuming singleness of aim, achieve a kind of existential integrity – the hero, the saint, the child, the animal. Chief of these figures, and the poet's ultimate point of reference, are the terrible

and unapproachable Angels, beings of infinite beauty and cosmic energy, whose sublime indifference to man is an implicit rejection of him. The *Elegies* move from lamentation over man's alienation to a triumphant climax in which the transformatory powers of man are celebrated: his ability to overcome alienation by translating outer experience into 'Weltinnenraum' (world-inner-space), a realm of inner sensibility in which time, and hence transience, is overcome by being transformed into space – the infinite space of the creative imagination which can overcome even death. Orpheus, the tutelary deity of the *Sonnets*, is the singer-god who, in gentler, more conciliatory form, possesses the undivided consciousness of the Elegiac Angels and in particular their ability to move unconcernedly between the realms of the living and the dead. Polarities are reconciled not in any static synthesis, but rather in a sort of mobility of spirit which can comprehend and even emulate the fluid and the fixed, productive dynamism and significant stasis:

Zu der stillen Erde sag: ich rinne.
Zu dem raschen Wasser sprich: ich bin.
(Say to the still earth: I flow/Say to the rapid water: I am.)

Rilke's work, it is perhaps fair to say, is important not so much for any particular 'Weltanschauung' which may be extracted from it as for the unmistakable tone and range of utterance. Although Rilke was the most cosmopolitan of German-speaking poets (his later work contains several cycles of poems in French) and although he assimilated influences from many sources, these heterogeneous elements are transmuted by an intensely individual poetic voice. It is a voice which has not pleased all his readers and he has been blamed by some critics for such faults as over-preciosity or a somewhat ethereal brand of sentimentality. But Rilke's range is considerably wider than his detractors admit, and extends from the most subtly delicate lyricism to the most piercing angularity of Modernism. Rilke is a master at dissolving the fixed forms of the external world and reshaping them into new ones; at infusing everyday objects with new and vivid significance; at finding verbal correlatives for the most elusive and evanescent emotions. His poetic sensibility was at once extraordinarily fine and intensely ambitious; or, to put it another way, he had on the one hand the artist's desire for form and, on the other, an acute and anxious awareness of a vastness of experience which no formal impulse could subjugate. It is his expression of the tension between these extremes and his total dedication to its resolution that places Rilke firmly in the mainstream of modern poetry.

Corbet Stewart

The standard edition of Rilke's works is *Sämtliche*

Werke, ed. Ernst Zinn (6 vols, 1955–66). Other translations include: *Selected Works, Vol. I: Prose*, trans. G. Craig Houston (1954); *Vol. II: Poetry*, trans. J. B. Leishman (1960); *Selected Letters of Rainer Maria Rilke 1902–1926*, trans. R. F. C. Hull (1947). See also: E. M. Butler, *Rainer Maria Rilke* (1941); H. E. Holthusen, *Rainer Maria Rilke: A Study of his Later Poetry*, trans. J. P. Stern (1952); Frank Wood, *Rainer Maria Rilke: The Ring of Forms* (1958); H. F. Peters, *Rainer Maria Rilke: Masks and the Man* (1960); E. C. Mason, *Rilke* (1963).

405
RIVERS, William Halse Rivers 1864–1922

British anthropologist

W. H. R. Rivers was born at Luton near Chatham, Kent, the son of a clergyman and the nephew of James Hunt, the flamboyant founder and president of the Anthropological Society of London (1863). He studied at Tonbridge School and entered St Bartholomew's Hospital in 1882, graduating as a doctor in medicine in 1888. After further studies in Jena and Heidelberg he was appointed to a lectureship in Physiological and Experimental Psychology at Cambridge in 1893. In 1898–9 Rivers took part in the Cambridge Expedition to the Torres Strait under the leadership of A. C. Haddon. Further journeys included a visit to the Todas in southern India (1902), and extensive travelling through Melanesia (1908 and 1914). During the First World War he worked as a psychiatrist at Maghull Military Hospital, which specialized in the treatment of shell-shock. When he died unexpectedly of a strangulated hernia he was President-in-Charge of the Royal Anthropological Institute and a Fellow of the Royal Society.

Rivers's most decisive contributions were made in social anthropology, though he never held a university position in that field. He was a shy man with an awkward stammer who allowed his fellowship at St John's (Cambridge) to safeguard him from the meandrous avenues of self-promotion, avenues which led lesser men to greater fame. Even now all but one of his books are out of print. In the available *Kinship and Social Organization* (1914) Rivers described the *genealogical method* for recording kinship material, a method which is still standard practice among anthropologists. Convinced that kinship terminologies provide evidence of former marriage regulations and are strictly correlated to attitudinal systems, he achieved in these matters a level of analytical sophistication rarely attained since: his concern in establishing a genealogy of possible marriage systems has even been confused by later anthropologists with inadequate descriptions of definite marriage systems.

In his Introduction to *The Todas* (1906), and in *Anthropological Research outside America* (1913), Rivers provided the first rigorous theorization for ethnographic field-work method. Although, despite his travels, he never personally practised the field-work he advocated, his techniques were vindicated by his pupil John Layard and by Malinowski*, in eastern and northern Melanesia respectively; it is through their works that Rivers's influence, seldom directly credited, has been most effective.

Towards the end of his career Rivers was himself influenced by the German Historical School of Anthropology (of which P. W. Schmidt was the most prominent figure), and by the historical speculations of his friend Sir G. Elliot Smith. This led him to make some first-rate investigations on regressive aspects in culture, in particular the 'disappearance of useful arts' in some societies. But his achievements in this particular domain were again undervalued, this time largely because of the dominant place achieved by the Functionalist School in the years immediately following his death.

A. R. Radcliffe-Brown* was Rivers's first student in social anthropology, and there can be no doubt of the last imprint left on the pupil's anthropological style. It was, however, left to other pupils to develop Rivers's proficiency in kinship studies, among them W. E. Armstrong, Brenda Z. Seligman and John Layard; and while Malinowski was never formally under Rivers's tutelage, it is indicative that Malinowski deliberately chose to match his work with the Cambridge recluse.

Such reputation as Rivers enjoyed during his life came to him also from his studies in neurophysiology and psychology. He provided a controversial distinction between *protopathic* and *epicritic* nerve sensitivity, concepts elaborated in an investigation with and on Henry Head (nervous terminations recovered sensitivity after a nerve had been severed in Head's arm), as well as pioneering work on perception of colour and shape in different societies. He also participated in the then current debate on the group-mind, focusing his attention on the effects of *suggestion*, which he traced in the manifestations of alcoholic intoxication; while *Instinct and the Unconscious* (1920) and *Conflict and Dream* (1923) proposed a neat compromise between Freud's* metapsychology and Hughlings Jackson's hierarchical theory of the nervous system.

Dr Paul Jorion

Other works include: *The History of Melanesian Society* (2 vols, 1914) and *Psychology and Ethnology* (1926). See also: R. Slobodin, *W. H. R. Rivers* (1978).

406

ROBBE-GRILLET, Alain 1922–

French novelist and film-maker

There seems little obvious connection between Robbe-Grillet's early life and his subsequent career as the best known and most radical figure in the group known as the *nouveau roman*. He grew up in Brittany, studied agriculture, and worked as an agricultural scientist in various parts of the world before becoming a full-time writer.

His first novel, *Un Régicide*, was completed in 1949, and, although it was provisionally accepted for publication at the time, it eventually appeared only in 1978. It was the publication of his second novel, *The Erasers* (*Les Gommes*, 1953), which began his career as a writer of critical notoriety. The French, who thrive on literary scandals, were, with a few notable exceptions, appalled first by what they saw as a pointless, detailed description of a dehumanized world, then by the apparent lack of novelistic coherence in his books, and most recently (since the late 1960s) by the blatantly sado-erotic aspect of his work.

Robbe-Grillet grew up reading Kafka*, Faulkner*, Raymond Roussel and Queneau* but without realizing that they did not represent the mainstream of conventional fiction, so that his own challenge to traditional novel forms can to some extent be seen as unwitting or involuntary. However, once he was aware of his subversive position, he merely continued to develop and refine it. His creative work has always been accompanied by an explicit interest in theoretical questions, and he has published numerous essays and interviews on the novel. Although his preoccupations in this field have gradually changed over the years (partly in response to changes in the preoccupations of French literary theorists such as Roland Barthes*), the underlying concern which unites both his theory and his practice is the problematic nature of interpretation.

In the early years Robbe-Grillet gained a reputation as the champion of *chosisme*, the flat, meticulous description of the physical world – a tomato slice or the layout of a banana plantation. The implication is that the world can be described but not interpreted. The attacks on plot and character in the early essays (collected in *Towards a New Novel*, *Pour un Nouveau Roman*, 1963) were based on the fact that they constitute false interpretative models for fundamentally meaningless experience: life cannot be read as narrative, nor people as characters. The detectives who appear intermittently throughout Robbe-Grillet's work illustrate (sometimes very comically) the impossibility of interpreting or making sense of the factual evidence they are confronted with. Wallas, the hero of *The Erasers*, becomes so disorientated that he ends up by accidentally committing the crime he is supposed to be investigating.

The jealous husband whom we are invited to imagine as the source of the apparently narratorless *Jealousy* (*La Jalousie*, 1957) is in a similar position to the detective's, for he is tantalized by an inability to interpret appearances. There are signs that his wife is having an affair with a friend but he proves incapable of reading them as straightforward indications of her adultery, and in his feelings with the external world he is forced to choose between pure factual observation on the one hand and obsessive, unbridled imagination on the other.

With the appearance of *In the Labyrinth* (*Dans le labyrinthe*, 1959) it became clear that we can no longer even count on the unambiguous presence of the physical world in Robbe-Grillet's novels. The world represented in these later novels is self-contradictory and inconsistent. Characters change names, plots go round in circles, descriptions of reality prove to be descriptions of paintings or theatrical performances, or vice versa. The policeman-narrator in *Souvenirs du Triangle d'Or* (1978) simply invents his reports. It is not only impossible to give meaning to the world but also to represent it. Writing is severed from reality: it does not mediate perception or experience, but constructs them.

For this reason we can no longer talk of realism in the traditional sense of the word. The real world is one thing, the written world of Robbe-Grillet's novels another. Or so it seems, until we are pushed one step further and see that what we take to be the real world is also just a set of constructions and myths which happen to be popularly shared. It might be possible to speak of a new kind of realism in Robbe-Grillet's fiction, consisting in the representation of these collective views or the current mythology about the world. The exaggeratedly stereotyped setting and plot of *The House of Assignation* (*La Maison de rendez-vous*, 1965) in a world of prostitution, vice and drug-smuggling in Hong Kong, or those of *Project for a Revolution in New York* (*Projet pour une révolution à New York*, 1970) in a world of revolutionary conspiracy and subway violence in New York exemplify very well the new forms of this realism. Realism in Robbe-Grillet consists in drawing attention to our contemporary mythology and not necessarily in distinguishing between reality and invention, in making a coherent narrative, or in avoiding contradictions.

The sado-eroticism which has increasingly invaded the novels since *The House of Assignation* is in one sense simply an extension of this representation of popular mythology and culture. But it could also be read as a metaphor for the writing that represents these myths. For recent French literary theory insists that language, and writing in particular, is not simply an abstract grammatical system, but has an intractable corporeal existence. In this and in the other aspects of his work, Robbe-Grillet has played an important part in the reexamination of the relationship between reality and representation, world and word which has dominated French thinking over the last twenty-five years.

Robbe-Grillet has also had a career, if a less prestigious one, as a film-maker. His first venture was a script for a film made in collaboration with Alain Resnais*, *Last Year at Marienbad (L'Année dernière à Marienbad*, 1961). Since then he has made a number of experimental films with limited distribution under his own direction which explore in cinematic terms many of the same themes and problems found in his novels.

Ann Jefferson

Robbe-Grillet's other novels are: *The Voyeur (Le Voyeur*, 1955) and *Topology of a Phantom City (Topologie d'une cité fantôme*, 1976). The link between the films and the novels is exemplified in the publication of what Robbe-Grillet calls *ciné-romans*, discursive and fairly fluent versions of his film scripts: *L'Année dernière à Marienbad* (1961); *L'Immortelle* (1963); and *Glissements progressifs du plaisir* (1974). Other film titles include: *Trans-Europe-Express* (1967); *L'Homme qui ment* (1968); and *L'Éden et après* (1970). See also: Stephen Heath, *The Nouveau Roman* (1972); Ann Jefferson, *The Nouveau Roman and the Poetics of Fiction* (1980).

407
ROETHKE, Theodore 1908–63

US poet

Born in Saginaw, Michigan, Roethke attended the University of Michigan and the University of Harvard, and subsequently taught English at Lafayette College, Pennsylvania (where he also coached tennis), Pennsylvania State College, and Bennington College, Vermont, before becoming Professor of English at the University of Washington from 1948 until his death. He published his first volume of poetry, *Open House*, in 1941, and later books won him numerous awards including the Pulitzer Prize in 1964, the Bollingen Prize in Poetry, and the National Book Award.

Burdened by a fierce sense of inadequacy in the adult world, of an emotional and spiritual insufficiency, Roethke turned for succour and understanding in his early verse – particularly his second volume, *The Lost Son and Other Poems* (1948) – to the world of his childhood, imaging his quest for moral growth and enlightenment in a sensitive response to the mystery of plant life. He in fact remained fixed for inspiration throughout his life on memories of his father's greenhouse, which he called 'my symbol for the whole of life, a womb, a heaven-on-earth'. His major themes are a sense of psychological dislocation and loss of mature identity, a feeling of selflessness and awe before the organic life of flora and fauna, and (in numerous poems) an apprehension of emotional and spiritual transcendence overcoming existential anguish. Although some poems show a certain derivativeness from literary models such as W. B. Yeats*, perhaps the majority manifest fully compensating qualities of sensory tact and achieved lyricism of an extremely high order. Much of his work is powerfully original, at once frightening in its radical imperatives and illuminating. The sequence entitled 'The Lost Son' evokes the primary forces of life in a spirit both of regressiveness and of courageous emotional enquiry. Scrutinizing the specific vegetal scenes of his boyhood, the poem wins through to a feeling of quiescence by a process of dark querulousness: 'After the dark night' Roethke himself commented, 'the morning brings with it the suggestion of a renewing light, the coming of "Papa" . . . the papa on earth and heaven are blended.' 'Open Letter' and Roethke's other essays collected by Ralph J. Mills (*On the Poet and His Craft: Selected Prose of Theodore Roethke*, 1965) provide succinct and shrewdly self-aware snippets of information about his own poetry and the stages of his writing.

With a similarly deft combination of lyrical power and profound psychological inquisition, *Praise to the End!* (1948) furthers the poet's obsession with what he called 'the dark world'. Shifting from negative moods to tactile assurance, the title poem attains momentary rest in intimate association with natural life: 'sublimation carried to its ultimate end', Roethke wrote in one of his letters (see *Selected Letters of Theodore Roethke*, ed. Ralph J. Mills, 1968).

Roethke's growth in technical accomplishment and the ever deeper exploration of his themes are genuinely all of a piece. From several fine longer sequences and individual poems, 'Meditations of an Old Woman' (*Words for the Wind*, 1958) deserves special mention: the poem impersonates and probes the valedictory thoughts of the character as she wavers through periods of alienation, pain and confusion, before reaching a tender close in which the woman finds herself at peace with Nature, with the onset of death, and with herself.

Roethke's gift is consummately sustained in this last volume, *The Far Field* (1964), which was posthumously published. Among a number of notable poems in the book, the title poem merits its place as the final expression of the poet's sublime art of marrying his intuitions of the fecundity and indeed the mysticism of life with his own lambent style, in the face of the morbid fears and emotional breakdowns from which Roethke found no respite in his personal life. It is not at all surprising that his poetry exercised a compelling appeal for younger poets such as Sylvia Plath*; her early work collected in *The Colossus* (1960) shows the marked influence of Roethke's work and the colour of his mind.

Dr John Haffenden

See: *The Collected Poems of Theodore Roethke* (1966). See

also: Karl Malkoff, *Theodore Roethke: An Introduction to the Poetry* (1966); Rosemary Sullivan, *The Garden Master: Style and Identity in the Poetry of Theodore Roethke* (1975); and Jenijoy La Belle, *The Echoing Wood of Theodore Roethke* (1976).

408

ROGERS, Carl Ranson 1902–

US psychologist

Born in Oak Park, Illinois, Carl Rogers describes his background as one marked by close family ties, a very strict and uncompromising religious and ethical atmosphere and what amounted to a worship of hard work. Having spent two years at Union Theological Seminary, he then spent two further years at the new Institute for Child Guidance where he received an orthodox Freudian* training prior to taking up a position as child psychologist in the Child Study Department of the Society for the Prevention of Cruelty to Children, in Rochester, New York State. He spent twelve years there during which he published *Clinical Treatment of the Problem Child* (1939) before joining Ohio State University. After five years there, he spent further periods of time at the Universities of Chicago and Wisconsin before becoming a Resident Fellow at the Center for Studies of the Person, La Jolla, California.

Rogers has been called the Dean of the Encounter movement in view of his pioneering work in relation to the development of counselling and reality-oriented psychotherapy. The appearance of *Counselling and Psychotherapy* (1942) and *Client-Centered Therapy: Its Current Practice, Implications and Theory* (1951) quickly laid the foundations of a therapeutic movement which is optimistic in philosophy, anti-elitist in posture and which challenges the rigid orthodoxy of both classical Freudianism and mid-West puritanism. Reacting against the formal therapist–patient scenario, with the therapist endowed with knowledge, technical skills and experience and the patient endowed only with his problems, Rogers re-framed the therapeutic encounter, postulating an equality between 'counsellor' and 'client', discarding much of the complex theory and jargon of psychoanalysis and emphasizing three cardinal qualities in the counsellor. The first, *empathy*, he defined as sensitive listening, an ability to enter the world and the experience of the other person; the second, *genuineness*, is defined as congruence or realness and refers to the lack of façade, professional detachment or distance on the part of the counsellor, while the third quality is *caring*, or prizing, whereby the counsellor possesses unconditional positive regard for the person who is the client. In the encounter, the crucial therapeutic activity is not treatment, interpretation, revelation, or advice but listening. The two basic beliefs that underpin Rogerian psychotherapy are that the person has a basically positive direction or, in the language of Rogers, possesses an instinctual self-actualizing tendency, and experience for the individual is the highest authority. These two beliefs, endorsed throughout the encounter movement, also underpin the remarkable plethora of so-called 'fringe' and unorthodox therapies which have flowered since the Second World War in the United States, a development which explains why Rogers is seen as one of the founders, along with Abraham Maslow and Fritz Perls, of the 'new' psychotherapies.

Most Rogerian work is done within the so-called Encounter group (*Encounter Groups*, 1977), whose optimum size ranges between six and ten members. A counsellor or facilitator encourages participants to express their true and immediate feelings about their selves and each other and the aim of therapy is the facilitation of 'growth', a key word in this form of psychotherapy. Encounter approaches have been used not merely in psychiatry and clinical psychology but in business, education, probation and penal settings, and even in areas of political and racial conflict. Indeed, Rogers, particularly in his later writings, such as *On Becoming a Person* (1961) and *Carl Rogers on Personal Power* (1978) classifies his theories more in terms of a philosophy of living suitable for people in various walks of life rather than as a therapy for people who are sick and suffering.

Rogerian psychotherapy is an optimistic creed which posits the possibility of self-perfection for all and which rejects the notion of man as a flawed, forked animal battling with conflicting passions and impulses. It has flowered particularly in North America and it has played a key role in the gradual movement there away from the notion of formal and expensive psychoanalysis for the relatively rich and few to a populist and widely available therapy available to the masses. In so far as Rogers's ideas have been tested, there is some support for his views on the importance of empathy, genuineness and caring, but the aims of client-centred therapy are difficult to evaluate in more specific terms and the applicability of such theories to the treatment of more severely ill psychiatric and other medical patients remains to be established.

As one of the founders of the Association of Humanistic Psychology, Rogers takes a profoundly anti-behaviourist stance and his most recent writings have tended towards endorsement of the 'experiential' at the expense of the 'rational' in man. While he disavows any responsibility for the more extreme movements within the field of encounter and growth, his rejection of expertise in favour of immediacy has given the movement an intellectual respectability. While his own practice has stayed close to mainstream group and individual psychotherapy, his followers have taken encounter ideas and developed them in therapeutic packages which involve marathon groups, gestalt theories, body massage, meditation and such physical activities as dance and jogging.

Anthony W. Clare

See: C. B. Traux and R. R. Carkhuff, *Toward Effective Counselling in Psychotherapy: Training and Practice* (1967); M. A. Lieberman, I. D. Yalom and M. B. Miles, *Encounter Groups: First Facts* (1973).

409
ROLLAND, Romain 1866–1944

French writer

After a provincial childhood, Rolland entered the Lycée Louis-le-Grand in Paris in 1880; six years later, he moved to the École Normale Supérieure, and, in 1889, was successful in the competitive *agrégation* in history. A period at the École Française in Rome was followed, in 1895, by the publication of his doctoral thesis, *Histoire de l'opéra en Europe* ('History of the opera in Europe'). At the same time, he became a teacher of history at the École Normale Supérieure, and (from 1900) of the history of music at the Sorbonne.

His love of music lasted throughout his life, and led to biographies of Beethoven (1903) and Handel (1910), as well as to seven volumes on *Beethoven the Creator (Beethoven, les grandes époques créatrices, 1928–43, trans. 1929), Souvenirs sur Richard Strauss* ('Memories of Richard Strauss', 1948), etc.

Music is also present in his best known novel, *John Christopher (Jean-Christophe, 1904–12, trans. 1910), a ten-volume roman-fleuve* which takes the form of a fictional biography of a German composer. His other novels are less successful, as is his theatre, to which his general approach is clear from the title of his *Le Théâtre du peuple* ('People's theatre', 1903). Rolland's ambition was to write popular theatre, but his series of plays collected under the title of *Théâtre de la révolution* ('Theatre of the Revolution', 1898–1900), like his *Tragédies de la foi* ('Tragedies of Faith', 1897–9), foundered on the rock of dramatic theory: the mistaken idea that the people could appreciate only simple dramas, presented in the broadest terms.

There can be no doubt that Rolland was a man firmly rooted in the nineteenth century. His youthful loss of religious faith, closely linked in time to his discovery of music (particularly that of Beethoven), led him towards an idealism of a German type, which was confirmed during his years in Rome by his contacts with Malwida von Meysenburg. His philosophical interests ranged from Spinoza, through Goethe, and on to Nietzsche; his humanism, influenced partly by Tolstoy, led him to friendship with Charles Péguy (in whose *Cahiers de la Quinzaine* he published *John Christopher*), as well as with personalities as diverse as Gor-

ky*, Tagore* and Gandhi*. All of these relationships were evidence of his belief in humanity and his internationalism, together with the pacifism it implied. Such views led him on occasion into controversy, particularly after the outbreak of the First World War, which found him in Switzerland. At a time when many authors considered that their patriotism could be proved only by outright jingoism, Rolland published *Above the Battlefield (Au-dessus de la mêlée, 1915, trans. 1916), an appeal to men of goodwill on both sides of the conflict to abandon fanatical patriotism in favour of a reasoned search for an end to conflict. It earned for him the Nobel Peace Prize, but also expressions of hatred and accusations of cowardice from the more nationalistic of his fellow-countrymen. His *Salut à la révolution russe* ('Salute to the Russian Revolution', 1917) was similarly misinterpreted, providing further evidence of the difficulty involved in any attempt to combine the ideals of internationalism, revolution, non-violence, and even romantic mysticism.

Keith Gore

Other works by Rolland – novels *Colas Breugnon* (1919); *Clérambault* (1920); *Pierre et Luce* (1920); *The Soul Enchanted (L)âme enchantée*, 7 vols, 1922–33, trans. 1927–35); musical studies – *Musiciens d'autrefois* (1908); *musiciens d'aujourd'hui* (1908); *Voyage musical au pays du passé* (1920); biographies – *Vie de Michel-Ange* (1908); *Vie de Tolstoï* (1911); *Mahatma Gandhi* (1924); *Vie de Ramakrishna* (1929); *Vie de Vivekananda* (2 vols, 1930); *Péguy* (2 vols, 1944). See: J.-B. Barrère, *Romain Rolland par lui-même* (1955), and *Romain Rolland, l'âme et l'art* (1966); J. Robichez, *Romain Rolland* (1961).

410
ROLLING STONES, The 1962–

British rock 'n' roll band

Mick Jagger (b. 1943), Keith Richard (b. 1943), Brian Jones (1944–69), Charlie Watts (b. 1941) and Bill Wyman (b. 1941) formed their musical taste on the growing number of urban black American rhythm and blues players whose work was becoming known in England in the late 1950s. This strident strutting music of heavily rhythmic guitar, harsh harmonica wails and raw vocal style offered intense emotional excitement along with a subversive challenge to white sexual and social conventions. The Rolling Stones' emergence in the 1960s as 'The Greatest Rock 'n' Roll Band In The World' was on the development and exploitation of these roots.

Their early performance repertoire and recordings consisted of material derived directly from artists like Muddy Waters, Bo Diddley, Howlin' Wolf, Jimmy Reed, Slim Harpo and Chuck Berry. This deliberate embracing of transatlantic idiom and myth was re-created and given thrilling freshness through Jagger's extraordinary voice. Early in 1962 he had bitten off the tip of his tongue in a gym mishap, which radically altered his delivery and lent extra lasciviousness to the sexual ambiguities of songs like 'I'm A King Bee' and 'Walking the Dog' (both on *The Rolling Stones*, 1964). In the still highly repressed climate of late-Tory, post-Profumo Britain, the erotic rhythmic assertiveness and unabashed suggestiveness of lyric constituted a threat to the bourgeois citadel. This was augmented by a public posture of cynicism and defiance, carefully orchestrated by Andrew Loog Oldham, the group's manager. Deliberately shunning The Beatles'* whimsical charm, and refusing the popular music form of consolatory romantic love, The Stones marketed a mood of aggressive anger which caught a genuine feel of the times, despite being initially channelled through rural and urban Negro frustration;

With their fourth and fifth LPs (*Aftermath*, 1966, and *Big Hits (High Tide And Green Grass)*), 1966), Jagger and Richard largely turned their backs on borrowed material in favour of their own compositions. Songs like 'Satisfaction', 'Paint it Black', 'Get Off Of My Cloud' and '19th Nervous Breakdown' relocated the target of a ferocious resentment firmly within experience of drugs and capitalist media neurosis. Elements of nihilism and sado-masochism were central to the group's work in the 1960s, and were to endure in its productions. Another central element was trans-sexualism. Jagger's stage act as a non-musician had always been provocatively athletic, partly from childhood agilities acquired from his physical education instructor father, partly from imitation of James Brown. Through androgynous make-up and gesture, and sexually cajoling voice distortion, he questioned the supposed rigid divide between male and female in a manner broad enough to include self-mockery. Overt transvestism, later to be copied *ad nauseam* in the rock world, was broached with Jerry Schatzberg's publicity photograph for the single 'Have You Seen Your Mother, Baby, Standing in the Shadow?', 1966. Apocalyptic, primeval atmospheres of bacchanalian violence were projected through a version of rhythm and blues deliberately jagged, hard and flashy, with some tracks (such as 'Jumpin' Jack Flash', on *Through The Past Darkly*, 1969) partially recorded on cassette to achieve this effect.

The vast youth following for this symbolic desecration of public order produced hysterical establishment reaction. Systematic harassment of the group by media and police culminated in the arrest of Jagger and Richard, and their sentencing to imprisonment on petty drugs offences. The convictions were quashed on appeal, not without some atypical assistance from a *Times* leader ('Who Breaks A Butterfly On A Wheel?', 1 July 1967), which drew a parallel with the hounding of Stephen Ward in the Profumo affair, and suggested

that the case was 'a symbol of the conflict between the sound traditional values of Britain and the new hedonism'. Further cannabis charges against Brian Jones were partially responsible for his leaving the group in 1969 and his apparent suicide that year in the swimming pool of his Sussex house, where A. A. Milne had written *Winnie the Pooh*.

Late 1960s political ferment was superficially reflected in *Beggars Banquet* (1968) with 'Factory Girl', 'Salt of the Earth' and notably with 'Street Fighting Man', taken by many as an invitation to storm the barricades, but in fact proposing rock 'n' roll as a substitute area for revolutionary action. The invitation to ecstatic participation which was a feature of music festivals of the period gave serious encouragement to a vague diabolism in the group's work. Brian Jones's fascination with the Dionysiac musical rituals of the Moroccan Bou Jeloud (*Joujouka*, 1972) was registered in *Their Satanic Majesties Request* (1967), and developed specifically in 'Sympathy for the Devil' (on *Beggars Banquet*), the number Jagger was singing at the Altamont Speedway, California, in 1969, while below him Hell's Angels bodyguards stabbed to death a young black. This sacrificial death flowed with seeming inevitability from the demand for adulatory homage exerted by gods, devils and stars alike. It nullified the optimism of the Woodstock generation. Lucifer resurfaces in 'Midnight Rambler' (on *Let It Bleed*, 1969), with Jagger incorporating words from the confession of the Boston Strangler. Nevertheless, *Let It Bleed* presents a synthesis of the Stones' musical excellence across a range of rock, blues and country styles.

In the 1970s their politics of delinquency became increasingly dominated by camp theatricality and international drug-culture chic, purveyed through lavishly staged shows and some powerful recordings.

John Porter

Other LPs include: *The Rolling Stones No. 2* (1965); *Out Of Our Heads* (1965); *Between the Buttons* (1967); *Get Yer Ya Yas Out* (1970); *Sticky Fingers* (1971); *Exile on Main Street* (1972); *Goats Head Soup* (1973); *It's Only Rock 'n' Roll* (1974); *Black and Blue* (1976); *Some Girls* (1978); See: David Dalton, *The Rolling Stones* (1972); Roy Carr, *The Rolling Stones* (1976); *The 'Rolling Stone' Rock 'n' Roll Reader*, ed. Ben Fong-Torres (1974).

411
ROMAINS, Jules (pseudonym of Louis Farigoule)
1885–1972

French poet, novelist and playwright

Jules Romains received his education in Paris, first at the Lycée Condorcet, then at the École Normale Supérieure, where he successfully sat the *agrégation* in philosophy in 1909. He was a teacher until the end of the First World War, when he decided to devote himself to his literary career. He was elected to the Académie Française in 1946.

The philosophical part of his upbringing shows itself in his devotion to *Unanimisme*, a notion not far removed from utopian socialist visions of the 1840s, in that it was related to L'Abbaye, a kind of poetic collective, based on the interdependence of those who made it up. For Romains, the individual exists side by side with the group in society; the two entities are not in opposition, but complement each other: the individual exists in his own right, but also as a part of a wider unit (or units) in which he is united with other men. His collection of poetry, *La Vie unanime* ('Unanimist life', 1908) was published by L'Abbaye.

Other volumes of verse followed during the next thirty years, but he owes his reputation mainly to his activity in other areas. As early as 1906, he published *Le Bourg régénéré, conte de la vie unanime* ('The regenerated town, a tale of unanimist life', 1906); other works of fiction include the famous *Les Copains* ('The pals', 1913), the practical-joking adventures of a group of friends, and the three volumes collectively entitled *The Body's Rapture* (*Psyché*, 1921–9). His fictional monument, however, is made up of the twenty-seven volumes of *Men of Good Will* (*Les Hommes de bonne volonté*, 1932–47, trans. 1933–48, 10 vols). Here, he attempts a portrait of his century from 1908 to 1933 in the form of a single novel, rather than in a succession of interlocking or episodic volumes.

The immediacy of the undertaking has now diminished, and it may be that his best chance of remaining in the public memory will prove to be through his theatre. Three of his plays deserve particular mention, two of them centred on the character of a distinguished, but vain and ageing geographer: *Monsieur le Trouhadec saisi par la débauche* ('Monsieur le Trouhadec possessed by debauchery', 1923), and *Le Mariage de Monsieur le Trouhadec* ('Monsieur le Trouhadec's marriage', 1925). His most famous piece for the theatre remains *Doctor Knock* (*Knock, ou le triomphe de la médicine*, 1923, trans. 1925): it could be described in terms of negative *Unanimisme* in that it portrays a whole society united in its subjection to the charlatanism of Dr Knock. The play is often described in terms of totalitarianism because of its analysis of the way in which Knock succeeds in achieving complete domination over a community. But it may equally be held that the community itself exploits Knock as a means of arriving at a state of psychological dependence. Perhaps the play's lasting success derives from this ambiguity: Knock, after all, is not the first charlatan to have been portrayed in the French theatre.

Keith Gore

See: M. Berry, *Jules Romains: sa vie, son oeuvre* (1953); A. Bourin, *Connaissance de Jules Romains* (1961); A. Cuisenier, *Jules Romains et l'unanimisme* (1935); A. Figueras, *Jules Romains* (1952).

412

ROSSELLINI, Roberto 1906–77

Italian film-maker

The collapse of fascism brought about by the Resistance and by Allied invasion (1943–5) led to an extraordinary regeneration of the Italian cinema. While the germs of the new cinema were already developing during the last years of fascism (see, notably, Visconti's* *Ossessione*, 1942) the sudden explosion that took place in 1945 was quite unexpected. One film in particular served to draw world-wide attention to the new cinema. This was *Rome Open City*, made by Roberto Rossellini in the last months of the war and depicting the city of Rome under German occupation a year previously. *Rome Open City* was followed by *Paisà* (1946), an episode film recounting the progress of the Allied liberators up the peninsula, and by *Germany Year Zero* (1947), the story of a small boy in devastated post-war Berlin. Rossellini's work of this period, together with that of De Sica, De Santis, Visconti and others, served to define the characteristics of the movement that came to be known as 'neo-realism' – a concern with contemporary 'social' subjects, using real locations and non-professional actors and aiming to reach the truth of a situation by the most immediate and unvarnished approach possible. It very soon emerged, however, that the unity of the neo-realist movement was very contingent and in particular dependent on the political unity of the anti-fascist alliance forged during the Resistance. When this political unity was threatened, with the onset of the cold war, the majority of neo-realist filmmakers opted for the socialist-communist left and the claims of 'national-popular' culture, but Rossellini took his own path, which was closer to that of Christian Democracy and the American alliance. Between 1949 and 1954 he made a number of films with Ingrid Bergman which were aimed to international markets and imbued with religious spirituality, and which were widely regarded in Italy as a betrayal of what neorealism stood for. They were, however, vigorously defended in France by André Bazin and other writers of *Cahiers du Cinéma* and were highly influential on the French New Wave directors of the 1960s, such as Truffaut*, Godard* and Rivette. Bazin argued that the attentive, observational style displayed in Rossellini's films, particularly *Journey to Italy* (1953), was in fact the true neo-realism and in a famous metaphor described Rossellini as someone who crossed rivers on the stepping-stones provided by nature rather than by constructing an artificial bridge of bricks.

In the early 1960s Rossellini further refined his observational style by his discovery of the potential of the Pancinor or 'zoom' lens, which permits continuous variation of the camera's visual field. He also turned his attention increasingly to the production of special effects (somewhat incongruously for someone whose reputation was based on his scrupulous realism). The new techniques he developed proved particularly applicable to the television screen, and almost all his work from the mid 1960s onwards was made for television. After *The Rise to the Power of Louis XIV*, made for French television in 1966, he embarked on a series of productions of his own covering major events in the development of world civilization, in both material and intellectual aspects. He returned to the cinema and to the problems of post-war Italy with *Anno Uno* (1974), a film about the Christian Democrat leader Alcide De Gasperi, but the most successful works of his later years are probably the telefilms on *Blaise Pascal* (1971) and *Descartes* (1974).

Overall, Rossellini's work is characterized by a vacillation between observation and didacticism and between simplicity and grandiosity. In some films he is content to show; in others he insists on demonstrating. Sometimes his vision is naive; at others it passes through false naivety to a pretentious intellectual vacuity. A charlatan of genius, his greatest contribution to the cinema lay in his ability to combine simple direct observation with an eager didactic intent. His aim was to let reality communicate itself through the cinema, but when this didn't happen spontaneously he was always prepared to help it on a little bit.

Geoffrey Nowell-Smith

Other major films include: *Francesco, Giullare di Dio* (1950); *Europa '51* (1952); *India* (1958); *Viva l'Italia* (1960); *Acts of the Apostles* (1968); *The Age of the Medici* (1972). See J. L. Guarner, *Roberto Rossellini* (Madrid 1973).

413
ROTHKO, Mark 1903–70

US artist

There were two principal streams in New York Abstract Expressionism: the gestural painting of Pollock* and de Kooning*, and colour-field painting, of which Rothko was probably the foremost representative.

Many of his paintings in the 1930s were of isolated human beings in cities. Early in the 1940s, inspired by Surrealist automatism and by his interest in Classical mythology, he began to paint biomorphic images, as in *The Omen of the Eagle* (1942), where he hoped to evoke 'the spirit of Myth, which is generic to all myths of all times. It involves a pantheism in which man,

bird, beast and tree . . . merge into a single tragic idea.' The backgrounds of these paintings were thinly washed, suggesting an atmosphere suffused with a magic light. Increasingly, these washed backgrounds ousted the semi-figurative elements, in accordance with his desire to create a general and universal symbolic image. This he finally achieved by 1950, from which time on he consistently used an arrangement of soft-edged rectangles, placed vertically above each other. Nearly all his paintings from then until his death are in this format, the most usual variant being a vertical canvas with two or three horizontal rectangles. Because the image is symmetrical one is not encouraged to see it in relational terms, as one would with Mondrian*, but on the contrary as holistic, an effect increased by the fact that the rectangles seem to fill the whole canvas. Rothko's paintings are usually extremely large, not because he wished to create a public art but, on the contrary, because he believed that the large scale made them more intimate. As he said: 'To paint a small picture is to place yourself *outside* your experience as a stereopticon view or with a reducing glass. However you paint the large picture, you are *in* it. It isn't something you command.' Rothko's scale is architectural, in that rather than a space being created within the painting, the painting, or group of paintings, modifies the real space of its environment. The mood generated is essentially contemplative and mystical. Although he greatly admired Matisse*, Rothko's use of colour was never sensuous or hedonistic. Rather it was a vehicle for transcendence of this world. The paintings made at the very end of his life were entirely grey and black. In 1970 he committed suicide. There is about his art something perhaps passive, certainly tragic and, above all, profoundly moving.

Gray Watson

See: Diane Waldman, *Mark Rothko* (1978); also the catalogue to his exhibition at the Museum of Modern Art, New York (1961).

414
ROUAULT, Georges 1871–1958

French painter

Rouault was born in Paris of a poor family and received his first tuition in drawing from his grandfather, Alexandre Champdavoine, at the age of ten. At fourteen he became an apprentice in stained-glass decoration with the firm of Tamoni & Hirsch. He trained for five years during which time he was engaged mostly in the restoration of medieval windows. In 1890 he became a student at the École des Beaux-Arts where, after studying for two years under Élie Delaunay, he entered the studio of the symbolist painter Gustave Moreau. He soon became the master's favourite pupil. Moreau's predilection for mystical subject-matter and style stimulated Rouault's already strong preference for religious and hieratic painting. During the 1890s he also came under the influence of the neo-Catholic writer Léon Bloy. Bloy later introduced him to the scholastic philosopher, Jacques Maritain, who wrote an essay on Rouault in 1924, by which time he was acquiring an international reputation.

Rouault's first entries for the Prix de Rome, *Samson tournant la meule* (1893) and *Le Christ Mort pleuré par les Saintes Femmes* (1895, were unsuccessful and this led to a psychological crisis at the end of the decade. In 1898 he held the job of curator at the Musée Moreau for a brief period. His first exhibits at the Salon d'Automne between 1903 and 1908, having lost their explicitly religious aspects and discovered some of the recent developments in art, were to associate him in the public's mind with the Fauve painters, such as Matisse* and Vlaminck, whose work his resembled in fierceness of form and colour though not in spirit. The series of clowns and whores shown in 1905 caused a particular sensation on account of their almost barbaric portrayal of misery and degradation. In 1910 he received wide acclaim as a result of his first one-man show at the Galérie Druet. His fame was further advanced in 1913 when the major Parisian dealer, Ambrose Vollard, bought the entire contents of his studio. (In fact in 1947, upon the dealer's death, a large number of these canvases were returned to Rouault who burned over 300 of them.) In 1952 he was given a major retrospective in Paris and upon his death six years later he was honoured by a state funeral. During his life he became an important, if often reclusive, representative of the modernist Catholic institution. His output was large and varied and includes oil paintings, gouaches, water colours, tapestries, enamels and graphics executed with considerable versatility. In 1929 he designed the sets and costumes for Diaghilev's* ballet *Le Fils Prodigue*.

Rouault's art is characterized by two major themes, one formal and the other iconographic. The deep luminosity of his colours, very often sombre reds and blues, and the thick, almost primitive dark lines which enclose and highlight them, reveal an obvious debt to his experience in working on stained-glass. His deep concern for the continuing health of an expressive religious art ran parallel to this adoption of certain modern aspects of style. The colour and line are thus Fauvist in one sense but highly traditional in another. Where his art is not straightforwardly religious in content it dwells upon the outcasts of society whom Picasso* had introduced into his work of the 'Blue' period. Clowns, acrobats and prostitutes are portrayed with an expressionist intensity more typical of German and Scandinavian artists than of French ones – although Rouault balanced this content with scathing

portraits of the more successful members of society, like advocates and judges, who are antithetically opposed to the potentially redeemed failures. His work has, thus, in its imagery of revealed despair and evil, a kinship with that of the nineteenth-century satirist Daumier. His art, very largely drawn out of the literary inspiration of writers like Bloy and Péguy, is a visual equivalent for that area of French literary culture which combines an interest in modern form with essentially conservative intellectual concepts. Jacques Maritain once described Bloy as 'Job on the dunghill of modern civilization', and this description would no doubt have suited Rouault. Man was, in this apocalyptic version of catholicism, a fallen creature facing a terrifying Old Testament deity. Of his own work Rouault once wrote that it was 'A cry in the night! A stifled sob! A laughter that chokes itself!'

In 1916 Rouault stopped painting and began to work on a series of graphic works, the most important of which were fifty-seven plates collectively entitled *Miserere et Guerre*. These were commissioned by Vollard. The original composition was transferred by photomechanical process on to the copper plate which Rouault would then work over with a variety of engraving tools. The luminosity and strength of the finished plates are, as in the oil paintings, founded on deep colours bounded by thick expressive lines. In many respects these works echo the late canvases and prints of Rembrandt, an artist, along with Daumier, who exerted a great influence on Rouault's mature style. This can also be seen in his other major print series of the same period, *Réincarnations du Père Ubu*, *Le Cirque* and *Paysages Légendaires*.

In 1929 Rouault began painting again. Although at first he struggled with his old medium he gradually overcame these problems and went on to produce a succession of masterpieces which, during the 1940s, became solely religious in content. In 1938 he was given a major exhibition of his graphic work at the Museum of Modern Art in New York and in 1945 a retrospective by the same gallery which included the large windows he had executed for the church at Assy.

Rouault was in many respects a painter apart in France. The urbanity and intellectualism common to the mainstream of the Paris school were quite at odds with the expressionist conscience he represented. He opposed an enlightenment vision of man perfected and free with his own of man fallen and bestial. His art was explicitly dogmatic and was executed from a traditional stance of the artist as scourge rather than as comforter. His contemporary, Matisse, using a related pictorial vocabulary, was aiming at an art which would function as a 'calmant cérébral'. He wished to transcend ethical issues by ignoring or denying the religious sense of the fatality of the self's relationship with the world. He has written, 'We must learn how to discover joy in the sky, in the trees and the flowers. How to draw happiness from ourselves, from a full working day and the light it can cast into the midst around us.' Rouault believed that this missed the religious truth of 'la condition humaine'.

Richard Humphreys

Rouault's two publications are: *Souvenirs intimes* (1926) and *Correspondance de Rouault et de Suarès* (1960). See: L. Venturi, *Georges Rouault* (1948); J. T. Soby, *Georges Rouault* (1945); P. Courthion, *Rouault* (1962).

415
RUSSELL, Bertrand Arthur William, Earl
1872–1970

British philosopher

Russell was born into an aristocratic family; his grandfather, Lord John Russell, had twice been prime minister. Orphaned at the age of three, the will of his freethinking parents was set aside with the result that he and his older brother (upon whose death in 1931 he succeeded to the earldom) were given a strict and puritanical upbringing by their paternal grandmother. When Russell entered Cambridge in 1890, he had been, apart from a period spent preparing for scholarship examinations, educated entirely at home by governesses and tutors. He entered Cambridge with a passionate interest in mathematics which he claimed (*Autobiography*, vol. I, 1967) had been at one time all that prevented a suicidal outcome to his adolescent loneliness and despair.

Russell sought in mathematics the certainty and perfection of object he had lost when he abandoned his early religious beliefs, and was gradually disillusioned by the teaching at Cambridge, where, 'The "proofs" that were offered of mathematical theorems were an insult to the logical intelligence' (*My Philosophical Development*, 1959). His final undergraduate year was devoted entirely to philosophy and he absorbed the prevailing Hegelian idealism of the time. Study of the *Greater Logic*, however, led Russell to the conclusion that 'all [Hegel] says about mathematics is muddleheaded nonsense' (P. A. Schilpp, ed., *The Philosophy of Bertrand Russell*, 1944) and in 1898 he was ripe to follow his friend G. E. Moore* in revolt against idealism.

Moore persuaded Russell in the name of common sense to accept the existence of fact independent of experience, while Russell reinforced the rebellion by exposing the logical nerve of the argument by which the English Hegelian, F. H. Bradley, had sought to establish the impossibility of knowledge of anything which did not involve knowledge of everything. Russell saw in Bradley's argument the same mistake about relations which he previously discerned in Leibniz (in *A Critical Exposition of the Philosophy of Leibniz*, 1900),

the belief that every relation requires foundation in the intrinsic properties of the objects related; these intrinsic properties turn out on deeper investigation to be properties of the whole which the objects compose. The critique of Bradley provided the foundation for the subsequent development of Russell's techniques of analysis: understanding of a complex can be achieved by an account of how its simple parts form a whole.

While the revolt against idealism was mounted in the name of common sense, there remained much in Russell's thinking not sanctioned by common sense. Maintaining that for a word to mean something it must stand for some kind of object, Russell was led to a belief that numerals, predicate-expressions, even the definite article must stand for non-material entities of some kind. This crude Platonism was eroded over the following decades by the successive development of logical techniques which enabled Russell to distinguish between the apparent logical form of a sentence and the true form of the proposition it expressed. The principle, that for something to be meaningful it must stand for something, could then be applied only to the true logical form.

The soil in which these techniques germinated was the philosophy of mathematics. In 1900 Russell attended a conference in Paris where he encountered the work of the Italian mathematician, Giuseppe Peano. Impressed by the rigour, and aided by the advances, in Peano's work, Russell wrote a treatise (*The Principles of Mathematics*, 1903) which, while heavy with Platonic commitment, was able to eliminate numbers as metaphysical entities in favour of similarity classes, i.e. of classes all members of which can be placed in one–one correspondence with each other. This was the first step in what became a highly influential programme (see Carnap*) for 'logical construction', the principle of which emerged in 1918 under the slogan, 'Whenever possible logical constructions are to be substituted for inferences to unknown entities' (*Mysticism and Logic*, 1917).

Because he regarded *class* as a logical notion, the *Principles* was Russell's first defence of the 'logicist thesis': 'that all pure mathematics follows from purely logical premises and uses only concepts definable in logical terms' (*My Philosophical Development*). Russell soon discovered he had been anticipated by sixteen years in the work of the German mathematician, Gottlob Frege, but it was Russell who uncovered a problem with the notion of class which threatened the logicist programme for mathematics. Known as 'Russell's Paradox', it points out that the class of all classes not belonging to themselves can neither belong nor fail to belong to itself. The paradox turned out to be one of a family of similar difficulties and could not be ignored. Frege was eventually led to abandon logicism, but Russell pressed on.

Between 1900 and 1910, Russell collaborated with

his friend and former teacher at Cambridge, A. N. Whitehead*, on an improved presentation of the logicist position, the three-volume *Principia Mathematica* (1913). During this period Russell was frustrated by his inability to find a satisfactory solution to the problems surrounding his paradox. Progress on another front suggested a way of eliminating classes in the same spirit as numbers had been eliminated. The progress consisted in a logical representation of sentences involving definite descriptions. Known since as 'Russell's theory of descriptions', it obviated the problems caused by descriptive expressions which purport to refer to what in fact does not exist. However, to apply a similar idea to classes in such a way as to avoid all the paradoxes ('the ramified theory of types') invalidated vital parts of mathematics and Russell was forced to resort to what many regarded as an *ad hoc* principle, the axiom of reducibility.

Principia and its problems stimulated important mathematical and philosophical work in the three decades after its publication. Among the philosophical work was that of Russell's pupil, Ludwig Wittgenstein*, who acknowledged, in his *Tractatus*, the importance of the distinction between apparent and true logical form which had emerged with the theory of descriptions. Wittgenstein's principles of 'atomicity' and 'extension' in turn clarified further for Russell the aim and nature of analysis. Between them these principles suggest the world consists of 'atomic facts' which can be described by propositions, the truth of each of which is independent of every other atomic proposition and from which one can infer all other true propositions.

Wittgenstein's development of this idea avoided confronting questions about how human beings know or could know the world so conceived. Russell's development was alive to such epistemological questions from the start. Even before he had assimilated the influence of Wittgenstein, the theory of descriptions had suggested the outline of a sophisticated version of Hume's empiricism. Russell founded his empiricism on the principle, 'Every proposition which we can understand must be composed wholly of constituents with which we are acquainted' (*Mysticism and Logic*) and developed some of Whitehead's techniques for eliminating, by means of logical constructions, such theoretical ideas in science as points, instants and particles, with which we could not claim acquaintance (*Our Knowledge of the External World*, 1914).

Logical atomism required a purification of the notion of acquaintance. Russell wanted the constituents of atomic propositions to be known by acquaintance, but for the propositions to retain their logical independence, this acquaintance had to be based on pure experience without taint of inference. To claim to be acquainted with a particular man involves inferences based on more immediate sensory experience, hence men and other material objects are notions requiring elimination by means of logical constructions. Russell even attempted (in *The Analysis of Mind*, 1921) to replace the knowing subject by a construction. He was the first to acknowledge the limitations in his analyses and the shortcomings of his logical constructions. In his last major philosophic work (*Human Knowledge, its Scope and Limits*, 1948), he explored the extent to which what we accept as knowledge can be founded on the data of immediate experience by means of nondeductive inference.

It is difficult to gauge Russell's influence. Important though *Principia* was, it did not set the style of subsequent mathematical foundations. Mathematicians concurred with the view expressed by Gödel* in 1944 that compared to Frege the logical precision of *Principia* represented 'a considerable step backward'. In philosophy the influence of Russell's epistemological theories has waned with growing doubts about the intelligibility of the immediate personal experience which Russell required for the foundation of knowledge. Where Russell's influence is still strong, it is probably so complete and pervasive it is hard to detect. Russell set new goals and problems for philosophic inquiry and demonstrated a new way of pursuing them. Anglo-American philosophy nowadays pays much lip service to the name of Frege, but the conduct of analytical philosophy remains a most sincere, if often unconscious, tribute to Russell.

Part of the explanation for the pervasiveness of Russell's influence lies in his skill as a popularizer and in the charm and accessibility of many of his important works. Addressing an audience of philosophers in 1966, Quine* testified, 'I think many of us were drawn to our profession by Russell's books.' Russell's influence, moreover, extended well beyond academic philosophy. Involved directly in many social and political issues he wrote passionately about most of them. His pamphleteering on behalf of pacifism and against conscription during 1914–18 earned him at first a fine, then loss of his Cambridge lectureship, refusal of a passport, and finally six months in prison. His pacifism cost him many friends on the right, but he was not afraid to alienate his friends on the left when, after a visit to Russia, he published a prophetic attack on the communist regime in *The Practice and Theory of Bolshevism* (1920). He stood unsuccessfully for parliament as a woman suffrage candidate in 1907 and again as a Labour candidate in 1923. Interest in the education of his children led him to establish with his second wife (he was married four times) a progressive school, Beacon Hill. He lectured extensively in the United States, both on tour and in university posts. His unconventional ideas, particularly about sexual morality (see *Marriage and Morals*, 1926), led to a civil lawsuit in 1940 which successfully blocked his appointment at City College, New York.

He was awarded the O. M. in 1949 and the Nobel Prize for Literature in 1950. During the last fifteen years of his life, he tried to impress upon the world the threat to human survival posed by nuclear arms. He helped to found the Campaign for Nuclear Disarmament in 1958 and was sent to prison for a second time (two months reduced to seven days) in 1961 for civil disobedience activity with the Committee of 100.

Dr J. E. Tiles

Other works: *The Problems of Philosophy* (1912); *An Introduction to Mathematical Philosophy* (1919); *The Analysis of Matter* (1927); *An Inquiry into Meaning and Truth* (1940); *A History of Western Philosophy* (1945). Collections of Russell's articles and essays: *Philosophical Essays* (1910); *Logic and Knowledge*, ed. Robert C. Marsh (1956); *Basic Writing of Bertrand Russell, 1903–1959*, ed. R. E. Egner and L. E. Dennon (1961); *Essays in Analysis*, ed. Douglas Lackey (1973). For Russell's life, see his three-volume *Autobiography* (1967–1969) and R. W. Clark, *The Life of Bertrand Russell* (1975). Critical studies: F. P. Ramsey, *The Foundations of Mathematics* (1931); D. F. Pears, *Bertrand Russell and the British Tradition in Philosophy* (1967); A. J. Ayer, *Russell and Moore: The Analytical Heritage* (1971).

416
RUTHERFORD, Ernest 1871–1937

British physicist

Most Nobel prize-winning scientists are remembered for a single contribution. Rutherford, in keeping with the great enthusiasm and energy he brought to his work, is known for at least three major advances of modern physics.

Born and educated in New Zealand, with notable encouragement at Canterbury College, he sought further training in J. J. Thomson's Cavendish Laboratory, at Cambridge University, in order to escape the colony's limited opportunities. His arrival, in 1895, came shortly before the discovery of X-rays and radioactivity, and he soon became the dominant figure in the latter field, even more so than Henri Becquerel or Pierre and Marie Curie.

Rutherford early detected that the radiation from uranium was not uniform, and labelled the weakly penetrating rays 'alpha' and those able to pass through thin sheets of foil 'beta'. (The far more penetrating gamma radiation was discovered by Paul Villard in 1900.) He next examined thorium, which also was known to be radioactive, and found a gaseous emission which he called 'emanation'. The emanation itself rendered everything it touched radioactive, and Rutherford recognized that an 'active deposit' was being laid

down. This active deposit, in turn, changed into a series of other radioactive products, each with a characteristic period or 'half-life', and for those capable of determination, specific chemical properties.

The source of the enormous quantities of energy emitted in these reactions and the mechanism of the phenomenon itself were major puzzles early in this century; their solution helped overturn the Victorian attitude that the edifice of scientific knowledge was largely complete. In 1902–3, Rutherford and a chemical colleague, Frederick Soddy, advanced an iconoclastic interpretation of radioactivity. Alchemy had long been exorcized from 'scientific chemistry', but these young men in effect reintroduced transmutation. Radioactivity, they maintained, was a spontaneous disintegration of an unstable atom into another atom, which might itself be unstable, with the simultaneous emission of radiation. It was primarily for this work that Rutherford was awarded the Nobel Prize (in chemistry!) in 1908. But the transistory nature of many radioactive bodies presented a problem, for could substances which were not permanent be considered elements? And if they were elements, could so many fit into the limited number of boxes of the periodic table of elements? These were resolved in the affirmative a decade later by Soddy and Kasimir Fajans.

Rutherford subsequently devoted ever more attention to the alpha rays. Betas had been identified as electrons by Becquerel in 1900, and by 1903 Rutherford had shown alphas to be particles, but confirmation that they were charged helium atoms eluded him until 1908. In his experiments he had noticed that alphas often were deflected from their paths, a fact he considered impressive in view of their great velocities and relatively large mass. More precise measurements under his sponsorship led him to challenge the prevailing picture of the atom as a sphere of positive electrification, with negative electrons embedded here and there in it. To account for the large-angle deflections suffered by some alphas when striking atoms in a target, Rutherford proposed that the atom's mass was concentrated in a sphere at least ten thousand times smaller than hitherto accepted, and the electrons were seen as orbiting this core. The 'nuclear model of the atom' proved extremely valuable when Niels Bohr* added quantum conditions to the orbits and was able to explain much data that had been collected. Not only was the atom no longer considered stable and uniform throughout, but it was now irrevocably tied to the modern concepts of quantum physics.

Of Rutherford's three major contributions, the transformation theory was in radioactivity, the nuclear model may be placed in atomic physics since it gave a new structure to the atom, and the last was in nuclear physics: indeed, it was the origin of this subject. The alpha particle, as indicated above, was known to be an energetic particle ejected from many radioactive elements. Why not, Rutherford reasoned, use it as a projectile to disrupt nuclei and learn something about their structure, much as he already had used it to investigate atomic structure? In experiments begun during the First World War and published in 1919, he bombarded nitrogen with alphas, caused a rearrangement of the nuclear constituents, and produced oxygen and protons. Thus his 1902–3 work on radioactivity with Soddy had involved spontaneous, or uncontrollable, nuclear transformations, while the 1919 research showed that nuclear changes could deliberately be made to occur, although the means were 'natural', i.e. the projectiles came from naturally decaying radioelements. This set the stage for deliberate transformations by articficial means, namely the accelerating machines that began to proliferate in the 1930s, as more copious beams of more energetic projectiles were needed to bombard the heavier elements. The first successful machine transmutation was achieved, appropriately enough, in Rutherford's laboratory by John Cockcroft and E. T. S. Walton, in 1932, and a spin-off benefit of their work was the earliest confirmation of Albert Einstein's* famous $E = mc^2$ equation of 1905, stating the equivalence of mass and energy.

Rutherford held professorships at McGill University, Manchester University, and Cambridge University, where he succeeded his old teacher J. J. Thomson. He was also active in numerous professional organizations, serving for example as president of both the Royal Society and the British Association for the Advancement of Science. Many honours came to him, including the Order of Merit, knighthood, being raised to the peerage as Baron Rutherford of Nelson, the Copley and Rumford Medals of the Royal Society, and several honorary degrees. He was widely regarded as the greatest experimental physicist since Michael Faraday. But, like Faraday, he has strong claims to theoretical advances as well, for though his work was not highly mathematical, his contributions clearly consist not just of experimental discoveries but ideas and interpretations. Rutherford was notable also as a highly successful laboratory director, training a generation of physicists to fill many of the chairs in the British Commonwealth, and imparting superior research skills that earned these students the highest honours in science. In this connection, he was a key figure in the transition from 'little science' to 'Big Science', the evolution from a sealing-wax and string economy of science to a science characterized by large apparatus, research teams, and generous funding. Although he died before nuclear fission was discovered, Rutherford stands firmly as a major link in the scientific chain leading to nuclear weapons and nuclear reactors. Indeed, many of his students worked on the applications of nuclear energy which their 'Prof' did so much to reveal.

Professor Lawrence Badash

Most of Rutherford's scientific articles are gathered in *The Collected Papers of Lord Rutherford of Nelson* (3 vols, 1962, 1963, 1965). A bibliography of all his books, and almost everything written about him appears following his entry by Lawrence Badash in the *Dictionary of Scientific Biography* (1975), vol. 12. See also: A. S. Eve, *Rutherford* (1939); E. N. da C. Andrade, *Rutherford and the Nature of the Atom* (1964); and Norman Feather, *Lord Rutherford* (1940, revised 1973).

417
RYLE, Gilbert 1900–76

British philosopher

Ryle was educated at Brighton College and Queen's College, Oxford, where he took firsts in 'Mods', 'Greats' and 'P.P.E.'. At the age of twenty-four he became a lecturer at Christ Church, and was to remain an Oxford don all his life. In 1945 he was appointed Waynflete Professor of Metaphysics at the university, and from 1947 to 1971 he edited the important philosophical journal *Mind*. During the post-war expansion of university education, Ryle's academic prestige was in many ways unrivalled, and he exercised a unique influence on the way philosophy was taught and practised in Britain.

Ryle produced many influential articles, but his most famous philosophical contribution is his book *The Concept of Mind* (1949). This exemplifies Ryle's unique philosophical style – witty, discursive, and, depending on your taste, delightfully or irksomely rich in examples ('By feelings I refer to the sorts of things which people often describe as thrills, twinges, pangs, throbs, wrenches, itches, prickings, chills, glows, loads, qualms, hankerings, curdlings, sinkings, tensions, gnawings and shocks'). The book's purpose is to demolish a widely prevailing account of the human mind which Ryle dubs 'Descartes's myth': 'What has physical existence is composed of matter . . . what has mental existence consists of consciousness. . . . There is thus a total opposition between mind and matter. . . . Such in outline is the Official Theory. I shall often refer to it with deliberate abusiveness as the dogma of the ghost in the machine.' To construe the mind as a mysterious ghostly entity distinct from the body is, according to Ryle, a kind of logical error – a 'category mistake'. Mental states, claims Ryle, are not occult private events occurring in the 'mind', but are simply dispositions to behave in a certain way: 'To talk of someone's mind is . . . to talk of the person's abilities, liabilities and inclinations to do certain sorts of things.'

Ryle's position here can be seen as a sophisticated philosophical articulation of the behaviourist approach to psychology which has been dominant for much of this century. But as an account of mental phenomena, it conspicuously fails to do justice to the undeniable existence within each of us of thoughts and feelings which are often not manifested in any overt behaviour. In spite of this difficulty, to which Ryle was never to offer a satisfactory answer, his book has had a pervasive and continuing influence, which has more to do with method than content. For *The Concept of Mind* articulates a particular view of philosophy: the job of the philosopher is seen not as theory-construction or system-building, but as the task of clarifying concepts ('determining their logical geography', as Ryle put it) and removing conceptual confusion. Ryle is thus entitled to be seen, along with Austin* and, in his later period, Wittgenstein*, as a prime exponent of the method of conceptual analysis which to this day dominates so much of the philosophy of the English-speaking tradition.

Dr John Cottingham

See also: *Dilemmas* (a collection of essays, 1954); *Plato's Progress* (1966). A valuable collection of critical articles on Ryle is *Ryle*, ed. O. Wood (1970).

S

418

SALINGER, Jerome David 1919–

US writer

J. D. Salinger was born in New York City of a Jewish father and Christian mother. He graduated from Valley Forge Military Academy, then studied at New York University and Ursinus College. He never received a degree but did attend Whit Burnett's short-story writing class at Columbia. During the Second World War he took part in the D-Day landings and five campaigns. His war experiences may have had a marked effect upon his attitude towards man, as he has chosen to live in seclusion with his family in New Hampshire, granting only one interview and avoiding all contact with the public. This lifestyle, combined with lengthy gaps between appearances in print, has given Salinger an aura of mystery.

He has been one of the most popular American authors and remains an important fiction writer of the post-war period. His major work is the novel of adolescent rebellion, *The Catcher in the Rye* (1951). Holden Caulfield, the protagonist, is a twentieth-century alienated youth trying to find what he considers honesty in a materialistic and superficial post-war America. Speaking in an adolescent vernacular with a strongly black humorous tinge, he finds that the word 'phony' describes most of what he sees. One can find in this novel the major themes of Salinger's best work: the inability of man to live without love; the need for acceptance of people's shortcomings, this acceptance possibly proving to be a sign of wisdom; and the importance of children, who can provide the key to a return to emotional stability.

The movement towards emotional stability and a reintegration with human society also occurs in Salinger's best short story, 'For Esmé – with Love and Squalor' (1950). Through the influence of two children the protagonist is able to achieve a sense of peace with himself despite the horrors of war. Esmé in particular permits Sergeant X to overcome the squalor of his situation. This 'squalor' would be explored again the following year in terms of twentieth-century society in *Catcher*.

Peace is not, however, granted to Seymour ('Seemore'), the poet-sage of the Glass family, whose suicide is described in 'A Perfect Day for Bananafish' (1948).

Chronicling the Glass family has become Salinger's primary literary effort, and a number of the stories collected in *Nine Stories* (1953) contain various family members. Salinger's interest in Zen Buddhism is reflected in Seymour's influence upon various of the younger Glasses, who have been both aided and hindered in their development by Seymour's stress upon universal love, looking beyond externals to what lies beneath, and intense introspection. Seymour's suicide has not lessened the validity of his teachings for the younger Glasses and, one suspects, for Salinger himself.

The style in later works concerning the Glass family like 'Franny' (1955), 'Zooey' (1957), 'Raise High the Roofbeam, Carpenters' (1955), and 'Seymour: An Introduction' (1959) is, with the exception of 'Franny', verbose, lacking in focus and, unlike *Catcher*, not particularly humorous. Salinger places a heavy hand upon the narrative, which mars the effectiveness of the tales. There is a self-indulgence in 'Zooey', 'Roofbeam', and 'Seymour' which tends to blunt appreciation of Salinger's ideas.

Dr E. A. Abramson

Other collections of Salinger's work include: *Franny and Zooey* (1961); *Raise High the Roofbeam, Carpenters; and Seymour: An Introduction* (1963). See also: Frederick L. Gwynn and Joseph L. Blotner, *The Fiction of J. D. Salinger* (1958); William F. Belcher and James W. Lee (eds), *J. D. Salinger and the Critics* (1962); Warren French, *J. D. Salinger* (1963); and Malcolm M. Marsden (ed.), *If You Really Want To Know: A Catcher Casebook* (1963).

419

SANDBURG, Carl 1878–1967

US writer

Carl Sandburg was more than a writer; he was an institution. As a novelist, a biographer, a dramatist, a writer of children's stories, a folk-singer and a collector of folk-songs, he celebrated, throughout his long life, the men, ideas, ways and speech of the Middle West where he was born. His birthplace was Galesburg, Illinois, and he came of a family of Swedish immigrants. When he was thirteen, he left school to work as a labourer and, for the next seven years, travelled in Kansas, Nebraska and Colorado. In 1898, he went back to Galesburg with the trade of house-painter, enlisted in the Sixth Illinois Infantry, and was sent to the Spanish-American War. After eight months' service, however, he returned once more to Galesburg, and, between the ages of twenty and twenty-four, worked his way through the local college. In 1902, he left again on his wanderings, ending up in 1910 in Milwaukee as secretary to the mayor.

In the meantime he had married the sister of Steichen the photographer and published a pamphlet with the title *In Restless Ecstasy* (1904). In 1913, at the age of thirty-five, he moved to Chicago and began a career as a journalist and poet. As a result of the publication of 'Chicago' and other poems in the newly-founded magazine *Poetry*, he was awarded a literary prize (1914). More solid success, however, came with the appearance of *Chicago Poems* (1916), capped by *Cornhuskers* (1918). At the end of the war he went to Stockholm as a foreign correspondent, but returned to join the Chicago *Daily News* as an editorial writer. After the publication of *Smoke and Steel* (1920), Sandburg began to tour the country as a lecturer and folk-singer. Another book of poems, *Slabs of the Sunburnt West*, came out in 1922, and, in the same year, a children's book, *Rootabaga Stories*.

In 1926, Sandburg brought out the first two volumes of his monumental biography of Lincoln, *Abraham Lincoln: The Prairie Years*, and, in 1927, *The American Songbag*, a collection of folk-songs. In 1928 he published *Good Morning, America* and was Phi Beta Kappa poet at Harvard. His biography, *Mary Lincoln: Wife and Widow*, was published in 1932, and a year later he retired from the *Chicago Daily News* to work full-time on his biography of Lincoln. He was then fifty-four. If he had retired from journalism, however, he had not retired from professional life. In 1936, in the middle of the Depression years, after a period as lecturer at the University of Hawaii, he brought out his most ambitious, and perhaps his best book of poems, *The People, Yes* (1936). *Abraham Lincoln: The War Years* (4 vols) appeared on the eve of the Second World War, after which time Sandburg published a novel, *Remembrance Rock* (1948), and an autobiography, *Always the Young Strangers* (1953). In his old age Sandburg was still giving lectures and singing folk-songs in his own highly individual way all over America.

Sandburg is often compared with Whitman, but the resemblance – except in some of the early poems like 'Chicago' – is scarcely more than superficial. Whitman was far more of a 'literary' man than Sandburg. He may have talked about going among the people but his composition was of the study. Not the rhythms of speech or folk-song, but the rhythms of the Bible were Whitman's interest. The antithesis and parallelism in Whitman's verse are based on literary example; the free rhythms of Sandburg spring direct from talk and verbal story-telling. To this degree, he is an heir of Mark Twain and the 'tall-tale' tellers of the West. Indeed, many modern tall-tales may be found in *The People, Yes*. The faith that Sandburg had in Lincoln as the greatest representative of the democratic spirit of America comes from the folk-faith in Lincoln that he encountered in his early prairie wanderings. Finally, where Whitman used the egocentric 'I' as a symbolic device, and, like other questioners and askers of his time, probed his own soul in relation to the universe, Sandburg was a political and social recorder. This, however, is no mean feat. As a representative of the spirit of the Middle West and of his time, Sandburg is unique.

Geoffrey Moore

See: Harry Golden, *Carl Sandburg* (1961); Richard Crowder, *Carl Sandburg* (1963); Gay Wilson Allen, *Carl Sandburg* (1972); Lucas Longo, *Carl Sandburg: Poet and Historian* (1972).

420

SANTAYANA, George 1863–1952

Spanish/US philosopher and critic

Born in Madrid of Spanish parents, Santayana was taken by his mother to Boston at the age of eight. He was educated at Harvard, a pupil of William James and Josiah Royce, and he himself taught philosophy there until 1911 when he resigned his professorship. He lived first in England, which he had visited in 1896, and then briefly in France before in the 1920s he settled permanently to a life of strenuous contemplation in Rome, the city where, in the words of his splendid autobiography *Persons and Places* (3 vols, 1944–53), 'nature and art were most beautiful, and mankind least distorted from their complete character'. In his last years he was cared for by the sisters of a Catholic nursing home.

The Sense of Beauty (1896), Santayana's first book apart from a volume of verse published two years earlier, adopts a naturalistic approach to aesthetics and argues that the object of beauty is in effect endowed with the observer's reaction to it; beauty may be defined as 'pleasure objectified'. The sub-title of *The Life of Reason* (5 vols, 1905–6), the major work of this early period, was 'The Phases of Human Progress'. Here Santayana again presents a naturalistic interpretation of consciousness and analyses the role of reason in human life and the extent to which consciousness is capable of ordering disparate impulses into a harmonious whole. As in *Interpretations of Poetry and Religion* (1900), he views the religious impulse as essentially a poetic truth, so that religion may be described as 'poetry intervening in life', a point of view unfairly summarized in the quip that for Santayana there is no God and Mary is his mother.

His philosophical writings in the 1920s and 1930s both reinforce and refine these earlier statements. *Scepticism and Animal Faith* (1923) acts as an introduction to the arguments advanced in *The Realms of Being* (4 vols, 1927–40) where Santayana attempts to combine his radical scepticism with a theory of universal 'essences', modes of being which do not exist but which are nevertheless real. Belief in the realm of matter, which is anterior to the other realms of essence, truth and spirit, depends upon an act of 'animal faith', an instinctive belief, since matter may be apprehended only through its exemplification of essences.

It has sometimes been claimed that Santayana was neither an American nor a philosopher. He never adopted American nationality yet he spent forty years in that country and announced: 'It is as an American writer that I must be counted, if I am counted at all.' In his identification of the 'genteel tradition' in American life and thought Santayana was probably unfair to some of the Transcendentalists whose doctrines together with those of Calvinism he regarded as the sources of much that was antipathetic to him in American life. The phrase passed into common usage and was taken up by later and even more iconoclastic critics. In *The Last Puritan: A Memoir in the Form of a Novel* (1936) Santayana examines in fictional form the effects of this tradition in the 'absolutist conscience' of his hero Oliver Alden. Philosophical stances are embodied in some of the characters but the book is first and foremost an eminently readable novel which depicts a tradition in decay with a wry and ironic compassion.

The fact that Santayana in his work combined philosophical and literary activities has to some extent ensured that he has not received the attention he deserves either as a philosopher or as a critic. His special gift was for metaphor rather than for linguistic analysis, and his avoidance of the specialized concerns which have occupied philosophy during this century caused him to be viewed as the last humanist. While it is true that his entire writing, in poetry, fiction, essay and philosophy, may be interpreted as an extended meditation upon the human condition, his epistemology and ontology are now beginning to receive serious analysis.

Howell Daniels

Santayana's other works include: *Three Philosophical Poets: Lucretius, Dante, and Goethe* (1910); *Character and Opinion in the United States* (1920); *Soliloquies in England and Later Soliloquies* (1922); *Dialogues in Limbo* (1926, rev. 1948); *Dominations and Powers* (1951). See also: James Ballowe (ed.), *George Santayana's America* (1967); Douglas Wilson (ed.), *The Genteel Tradition* (1967); R. C. Lyon (ed.), *Santayana on America* (1968); Daniel Cory (ed.), *The Letters of George Santayana* (1955). About Santayana: Paul A. Schilpp (ed.), *The*

Philosophy of George Santayana (1940); Daniel Cory, *Santayana: the Later Years: A Portrait with Letters* (1963); Newton P. Stallknecht, *George Santayana* (1971); Timothy L. S. Sprigge, *Santayana: An Examination of His Philosophy* (1974); Lois Hughson, *Thresholds of Reality: George Santayana and Modernist Poetics* (1977).

421
SAPIR, Edward 1884–1939

US anthropological linguist

Undoubtedly among the most brilliant and original contributors to the discipline, Sapir came somewhat fortuitously to linguistics. Transplanted to the US from his native Lauenburg (Pomerania) at the age of five, he won a scholarship to Columbia, graduated with distinction in 1904, and immediately embarked on a Master's degree which seemed to point him firmly to a career as a Germanist. Still at Columbia, he met and came under the influence of the distinguished anthropologist Franz Boas*, who had pioneered work on the cultures and languages of the American Indians. Fired by Boas's erudition and the richness of his concept of linguistic structure, Sapir changed completely the direction of his research, first leaving to do field-work among the Wishram Indians of Washington State and then undertaking a grammatical analysis of the Takelma language, for which he gained his doctorate in 1909. Within a few years, seizing the opportunities offered by an initially nomadic professional career (Berkeley 1907–8, Pennsylvania 1908–10, Ottawa 1910–25), he had widened his knowledge to include Yana, Paiute, Nootka and several of the Athabaskan group of languages. His first major appointment was as Chief of the Division of Anthropology in the Geological Survey of the Canadian National Museum; from there, he went to a chair in Chicago (1925–31) where he carried out some of his best known work on the Navaho and Hupa, and finally to Yale where he became mentor to a glittering group of research students, among them Mary Haas, Morris Swadesh and Benjamin Lee Whorf*. He died at Yale, after a series of heart attacks.

Sapir was a prolific and far-ranging writer, although by no means all his output reached print: at his death he left a mass of *inedita*, only a small part of which has been published, and sketches for a major work on the *Psychology of Culture*. *Language* (1921) was his only book. Otherwise, Sapir's professional writings consist of crisp accounts of the phonology and grammar of Amerindian languages, monograph collections of texts, anthropological studies, and a handful of articles of wider theoretical import. He also composed poetry and wrote on music and literary criticism and, towards the end of his life, on Talmudic scholarship.

When Sapir began his field-work with the Wishram, foundations for the study of Amerindian languages had been laid by several cultural anthropologists – principally Boas – but extant linguistic material had been assembled less for its own sake than as part of a wider investigation of culture. It was fragmentary and gave little idea of relationships. Sapir aimed to redress the balance. He focused clearly on language, while retaining the research methods of an anthropologist (intensive work with an informant followed by a period 'in the field'), and developed as the need arose new techniques of linguistic analysis. He refined traditional concepts of typology and classification, applying his ideas not only to Amerindian languages but also to problems in the Indo-European and Semitic groups, notably the position of Tocharian.

Among linguists and non-specialists alike, Sapir is best remembered for his work on the interdependence of language and thought. Though sceptical about any deterministic relation of language and culture, his fieldwork convinced him that: 'Language and our thoughtgrooves are inextricably interrelated, are, in a sense, one and the same' (*Language*). He gave strong encouragement and material assistance to Whorf, who had arrived independently at similar ideas, whence the now almost universal label 'Sapir–Whorf hypothesis'. In its strongest form (one to which neither scholar would probably have subscribed) it claims that linguistic structure so conditions thought patterns as to *determine* perception of the outside world. In a weaker version – that language predisposes a particular world view – the theory now has many adherents and an impressive body of supporting evidence, though its interpretation remains inevitably controversial. In more narrowly linguistic circles, Sapir is quoted for his 'psychological' view of the phoneme (he believed that native speakers have an intuitive awareness of the pertinent soundunits of their language as much as of words), and for his theory of linguistic 'drift', an attempt to see, beyond the 'mechanistic' concept of language, change as a series of blind sound laws, a much longer-term coherence and directionality in the evolution. In the late 1970s, and in only slightly different guise, these are still live issues. Important as these technical questions are, Sapir's influence has been much more fundamental and pervasive – it amounts almost to an attitude of mind in linguistic research; for the mentalism/mechanism debate was essentially a struggle of the titans, Sapir versus Leonard Bloomfield (1887–1949). If Bloomfield gained the ascendant from the 1930s to the late 1950s, linguistics has now returned to an orientation much more in tune with that of Sapir.

Dr John N. Green

See: *Selected Writings of Edward Sapir in Language, Culture and Personality*, ed. D. G. Mandelbaum (1949); *Navaho Texts*, ed. Harry Hoijer (1942); *Phonology and Morphology of the Navaho Language*, ed. Harry Hoijer (1967). The best critical appreciation of Sapir in the context of twentieth-century American linguistics is that of Georges Mounin, in *La Linguistique du XXe siècle* (Paris 1972). See also J. M. Penn, *Linguistic Relativity versus Innate Ideas* (1972).

422
SARRAUTE, Nathalie 1902–

French novelist

Nathalie Sarraute was born in Russia of Russian parents, and although she spent part of her childhood in Paris, French for her, as for a number of other major post-war writers in France, is not her mother tongue. After obtaining a degree in English at the Sorbonne, she spent a year at Oxford University and another at Berlin University. In 1922 she began studying law at the Faculté de Droit in Paris where she met her future husband. For ten years she practised as a lawyer. Three daughters were born between 1927 and 1933.

During the 1930s her earliest serious efforts at writing took the form of short prose pieces which, after being rejected by a number of prestigious publishers, eventually appeared in 1939 under the title *Tropismes* – a key term in her work. As she was Jewish, she had to go into hiding during the Occupation, and she survived by taking a pseudonym and posing as governess to her own children.

It was only after the war that her writing career began in earnest, and at that stage it seemed to fit into the existentialist atmosphere that dominated those years. She published a number of essays in *Les Temps modernes*, edited by Sartre*, who also wrote a preface to her first novel, *Portrait of a Man Unknown* (*Portrait d'un inconnu*, 1948). Her second novel, *Martereau*, appeared in 1953. Her essays attacking the continuation of traditional forms of the novel and proposing new lines of development were published in book form (as *The Age of Suspicion*, *L'Ère du soupçon*) in 1956 and attracted the attention of Alain Robbe-Grillet* who shared her impatience with so-called conventional fiction. It was this collaboration which consolidated the existence of the *nouveau roman*, a term coined in 1957 and used to describe the novels of Sarraute, Robbe-Grillet, Butor*, Claude Simon and a number of others. The earlier novels are now read as part of this movement. Other novels followed: *The Planetarium* (*Le Planétarium*, 1959), *The Golden Fruits* (*Les Fruits d'or*, 1963) which established Nathalie Sarraute among the prizeminded French as a major literary figure by winning the Prix International de Littérature, *Between Life and Death* (*Entre la vie et la mort*, 1968), *Do You Hear Them?* (*Vous les entendez?*, 1972), and *Fools Say* (*Disent les imbéciles*, 1976).

Although the polemical essays attacking character and plot in particular assured her of a central place in the *nouveau roman*, Nathalie Sarraute seems to have found her association with her fellow-writers in this group increasingly uncomfortable during the 1960s when a shift in emphasis from representational values to those of pure writing took place.

She has always regarded the representation of psychological reality as the central feature of her work, and her own particular view of it is summed up in the term 'tropisms'. The anonymous characters in her novels, whatever their overt preoccupations and behaviour, are all ultimately subject to the 'tropism', to the 'terrible desire to establish contact' (a phrase borrowed from Katherine Mansfield*), a longing for contact with the other and a concomitant fear of rejection. The underlying action of her novels consists in a ceaseless mutual probing and testing between the characters, which goes on behind the pretext or mask of purely social behaviour: buying a chair, telling anecdotes, discussing a book, admiring a piece of sculpture.

Although passion and desire in these novels are as intense and as extreme as in Dostoevsky (who might be granted the status of influence), Sarraute's is a world of talk. All contact, betrayal or violence take place behind and by means of talk whose potentially destructive effects are adumbrated through what Sarraute calls a 'sous-conversation' of imagery, rather than through conventional psychological analysis. This emphasis on dialogue in the novel has a parallel which Sarraute herself has drawn with the works of two English novelists, Henry Green* and Ivy Compton-Burnett, who would both be better regarded as co-researchers than as direct influences in this area of fiction.

However one evaluates Sarraute's contribution to our understanding of human psychology, it is primarily her attitude towards language which marks her as modern and constitutes her achievement. In her works language is shown to have lost its authority, its power to speak the truth, its ability to describe and its capacity to express. In Sarraute's world, to speak is necessarily to speak in platitudes and clichés. Attempts to describe reality only succeed in obscuring it, just as self-expression can only result in inauthenticity. The utterance of truths becomes nothing more than a form of tyranny. The function of the novels is to make us aware of the treacherous nature of language, and to create a sense of the reality of the tropism by indirect means rather than through the dangers of direct or conventional representation.

Ann Jefferson

L'Usage de la parole (1980) is Sarraute's most recent novel. She has also written radio plays: *Silence* (*Le Silence*, staged at the Théâtre de France in Paris by Jean-Louis Barrault (1967); *The Lie* (*Le Mensonge*,

1967); *Isma* (1970); *C'est Beau* (1973) and *Elle est là* (1978). See also: Stephen Heath, *The Nouveau Roman* (1972); Ann Jefferson, *The Nouveau Roman and the Poetics of Fiction* (1980).

423

SARTRE, Jean-Paul 1905–80

French philosopher, novelist, playwright, essayist, left-wing militant

A traditional French educational background prepared Sartre well for a characteristic middle-class career. After the *lycée*, he went to the École Normale Supérieure, where he studied philosophy. He failed his first attempt at the *agrégation* completely, but tried it again the following year (1929) and came out first in that competitive examination. From this point, the road ahead was clear for a successful future as a teacher, first in a *lycée* and then in the university. And, indeed, following his military service, he was appointed to a teaching post in Le Havre in 1931; his teaching career subsequently took him to Laon, and then to Paris, where it eventually came to an end in 1944: his period of notoriety had begun.

We may believe Sartre when, in his autobiography, *Words* (*Les Mots*, 1963, trans. 1964), he tells us that he began writing in his earliest years. His first published text dates from 1923, when he was still only seventeen, but it was not until 1936, with the publication of two pieces of work, that he gave some solid indication of his future development. The first, *Imagination: a Psychological Critique* (*L'Imagination*, 1936, trans. 1962), is a revised version of a study of theories of the imagination from the time of Descartes on, first undertaken as a student in 1926, and includes an account of Husserl's* views, with which Sartre had come into contact in the year 1933–4, when he had lived and studied in Berlin. The second text, *The Transcendence of the Ego: an Existentialist Theory of Consciousness* (*La Transcendance de l'Ego: esquisse d'une description phénoménologique*, 1936, trans. 1957), together with an article published in 1939 under the title 'Intentionality: a fundamental idea of Husserl's phenomenology' ('Une idée fondamentale de la phénoménologie de Husserl: l'intentionnalité', trans. 1970), was written during his stay in Berlin. All three are of importance, not only as evidence of Sartre's early interest in the imagination and his dissatisfaction with deterministic views of individual psychology, but also as a reminder that, contrary to what seems often to be believed, his philosophical existence did not begin only in 1943, with the publication of *Being and Nothingness: an Essay in Phenomenological Ontology* (*L'Être et le néant, essai de phénoménologie ontologique*, 1943, trans. 1956).

Indeed, the importance of Sartre's intellectual activity during the 1930s cannot be exaggerated. Publication dates give a false sense of chronology: the fact of the matter is that a whole series of works was being elaborated concurrently in the pre-war years: apart from those already mentioned, Sartre was also working on his *Sketch for a Theory of the Emotions* (*Esquisse d'une théorie des émotions*, 1936, trans. 1962, and *The Emotions, Outline of a Theory*, 1948), the stories collected in 1939 under the title *Le Mur* (1939, trans. as *Intimacy and Other Stories*, 1949, and *The Wall and Other Stories*, 1948), *The Diary of Antoine Roquentin* (*La Nausée*, 1938, trans. 1949, and as *Nausea*, 1949), in progress since 1931, *Psychology of the Imagination* (*L'Imaginaire, psychologie phénoménologique de l'imagination*, 1940, trans. 1949), the second part of *Imagination. Being and Nothingness* itself was the result of his philosophical reflections since the encounter with the thought of Husserl in 1933, and began to take form in 1939. By the time it appeared in print, it was already in one sense a work attached to Sartre's past rather than to his present: the notion of commitment, which began to assume importance for him in 1940, had brought about a change of emphasis in his thinking.

A change of emphasis, but not a revolution, in that his literary, aesthetic, and moral preoccupations remained strong, continuing to produce tension with that part of him which aspired towards a direct involvement in the affairs of the day. *The Diary of Antoine Roquentin*, quite apart from its considerable qualities as a novel, provides clear evidence why this should be so. To the extent that the starting-point for Roquentin's diary is an anxiety to do with the nature of being and existence, the novel clearly has metaphysical resonances; Roquentin perceives the problem, however, largely in terms of his immediate environment. The awareness of his own contingency through the insistence with which the material world forces itself upon his attention is linked to the absence of relationships between him and his fellow-men. This has the advantage of making it possible for him to view the inhabitants of Bouville from a privileged, detached standpoint, and to take a highly critical view of their behaviour and of the 'values' by which they live. On the other hand, his observation of them as manifestations, amongst others, of the phenomenon of Existence, does nothing to relieve his anxiety: he can be no less contingent than they. It is not, therefore, surprising that he should seek an escape from an obsession with his contingency in a direction that removes him even further from other men: a work of literature, independent of the material world, having its being in the non-real universe of the imaginary, will both distance him from his fellows and place him in a situation superior to them.

The procedure is consistent with Sartre's views on the imagination and the imaginary, but it is Sartrean in other respects as well. Roquentin shares Sartre's romantic view of the privileged situation of the artist, as well as the notion that salvation may be achieved through the production of works of art: and it may well be that this one idea, more than any other, prevented Sartre, until relatively recent times, from understanding that commitment implies necessarily the abandoning of any kind of individual privilege. In addition, Roquentin illustrates the curious link between Sartre's aesthetic and moral views which will be evident in many of his characters. The work of art is absolute and non-contingent because it is imaginary; but it is the product of the imagination of the artist, who is relative and contingent. It may therefore be a source of salvation for the artist, as Roquentin sees, in that he, as a contingent existent, must transcend himself in the act of creating the non-contingent art-object. As Roquentin equally clearly sees, however, such a form of salvation may apply only to the past; it is neither a justification for the future self (which does not exist), nor a guide for living.

Others are not so clear-sighted: they, too, will seek to create an image – an image of themselves, which will therefore exist *outside* them, but which at the same time will *be* them, and with which they will attempt to coincide. The most obvious examples are those bourgeois in *The Diary of Antoine Roquentin* who actually pay painters to fix the image on canvas, in what Sartre elsewhere calls 'portraits officiels', whose function is to 'defend man against himself'. The attempt is understandable: our existence is not justified, we have no prior definition, we create ourselves through our acts, and can be known as a complete entity only when the series of acts is complete – namely, at death. The resulting anguish is what may lead us to anticipate that moment by the creation of a self-image which, since we shall see it as definitive, will at the same time dictate our future conduct. The procedure is characteristic of the 'bad faith' (*mauvaise foi*) displayed by so many of Sartre's characters, attempting to persuade themselves that they have succeeded in the impossible task of bringing about a coincidence between the real and the ideal.

The theme is exploited throughout a large part of Sartre's career – most notably in his theatre, always concerned with action (an ambiguous term, in that the 'action' we see in a play is imaginary, and so unreal), and with his characters' attempts to escape the consequences of the need to act. The fact should not surprise us: the evidence of the autobiography is that, despite his efforts in other directions, Sartre himself remained attached to his role as a writer at least until the 1950s.

In the meantime, his growing reputation placed him in the forefront of French intellectual life, and made him a figure of international consequence. Along with a group of more or less like-minded intellectuals and artists (amongst them Simone de Beauvoir*, with whom he had enjoyed a close relationship since 1929, and who would continue to participate closely in his varied activities), he had emerged as a significant force in the first post-war generation. The Existentialist vogue of the years immediately following the liberation of Paris, combined with his own intense activity, meant that his name was constantly before the public. It was not simply a matter of publishing novels or writing plays, but also of taking part in a great debate about the nature of Existentialism, attacked on the left as a manifestation of a bourgeois culture in the process of decomposition, and on the right as a form of mental illness. Sartre was, of course, more concerned about the attacks from the left than about the reactions of the right, and many of the articles he produced for his monthly revue, *Les Temps modernes*, which began publication in October 1945, were an attempt to present his views on contemporary issues as well as on his situation as a writer (see, for example, his *Présentation* in the first number, in which he defines his editorial line and gives his views on committed literature).

His controversial position in public life led inevitably to tension between himself and those around him. As early as June 1946, Raymond Aron* left *Les Temps modernes*; a few months later a quarrel with Camus* kept them apart for a year. The final break with Aron (along with Arthur Koestler*) came at the end of 1947, and with Camus in 1952. At the same time, he was involved in the ideological differences of the post-war world, and in 1948 was a leading figure in the creation of a new – but not long-lived – political party, the Rassemblement Démocratique Révolutionnaire (RDR). The 1950s, corresponding with the point at which he finally realized that the fact of being a writer gave him no particularly privileged position, see him more and more heavily engaged in the affairs of the day, the more so in that the Algerian war emerged as a conflict which demanded commitment. The list of the events on which he took a stand between that time and his death is very long – whether by writing, interview, public declaration, or direct participation. He made pronouncements on major political and international issues, stood up for what he saw as oppressed minorities, gave his moral or material backing to struggling or harassed left-wing publications. Eventually his activity was severely restricted by the deterioration of his eyesight to a state of near-blindness.

Even before the onset of physical infirmity, however, it was clear to Sartre himself that he had never been, and was not, the kind of intellectual he would wish to be in the contemporary world – a man ready and able to put his gifts at the service of the people instead of using them as a means of perpetuating a bourgeois culture. It is true that, in this respect, he was not necessarily his own best friend. During the 1950s, he published his study of Jean Genet*, as well as three plays; the 1960s saw the appearance of his autobiography, his adaptation of the *Trojan Women*, and a number of studies of painters; his three large volumes on Flaubert followed in 1971–2. All of this work is of a kind one might well expect from an intellectual of

Sartre's background. And, indeed, the same might be said of his *Critique de la raison dialectique* ('Critique of dialectical reason', 1960), intended as a bridge-building operation between Existentialism and Marxism, but given relatively little attention, partly, no doubt, because many have been daunted by its 750 closely printed pages. It is not, of course, the case that such work prevented Sartre from continuing on his more obviously political course; on the contrary, as his bibliography makes clear. Nevertheless, it is a fact that, by the age of fifty, he had become a victim of his own reputation: whatever his own wishes in the matter, his public image was already firmly fixed. The problem is well illustrated by the award to him, in 1964, of the Nobel Prize for Literature. Sartre wished to refuse the prize, both because he believed that the writer should not allow himself to be transformed into an institution, and because he had no desire for the bourgeois respectability bestowed by the Swedish Academy. But he discovered that potential recipients are not consulted as to whether or not they are prepared to accept the prize; what is more, they may not refuse it. Despite his resistance, Sartre *is* the Nobel prizewinner for 1964.

For a man who worked so energetically and so productively, Sartre left a surprising amount of work incomplete. Apart from some fragments, the Ethics promised at the end of *Being and Nothingness* did not see the light of day; the same is true of the final volume of his *Roads to Freedom* (*Les Chemins de la liberté*, 3 vols, Paris 1945–9, trans. 1947–50). The second part of the *Critique de la raison dialectique* was not written, and the fourth and final volume of the study of Flaubert was abandoned. This is not necessarily evidence of failure, but rather of the fact that changing circumstances may, for example, deprive long-term projects of their *raison d'être*. Failures there have been, most notably in the area of bridge-building between Existentialism and Marxism: for the Sartre of the 1940s and 1950s, such an operation was unrealizable both because of the resistances of Communist orthodoxy and Party suspicion of the bourgeois intellectual, and because of his own inability to free himself from many of the middle-class, liberal, idealist and romantic assumptions of his earlier years. After 1968 – too late – he saw that the intellectual should put himself at the disposal of the proletariat whose interests he wishes to promote, while avoiding the imposition of his own categories or habits of thought. Nevertheless, his achievement was great – as an intellectual influence in the whole of the period since 1945, and, curiously, as a moral example whose honesty and self-questioning have, with time, been recognized even by those who were his enemies.

Keith Gore

Other works include: Plays – *The Flies* (*Les Mouches*, 1943, trans. 1946); *No Exit* (*Huis clos*, 1945, trans. 1946); *The Victors* (*Morts sans sépulture*, 1946, trans.

1949, as *Men Without Shadows* in UK); *The Respectful Prostitute* (*La Putain respecteuse*, 1946, trans. 1949); *Dirty Hands* (*Les Mains sales*, 1948, trans. 1949, as *Crime Passionnel* in UK); *Lucifer and the Lord* (*Le Diable et le bon Dieu*, 1951, trans. 1953, as *The Devil and the Good Lord* in USA, 1960); *Kean* (1956, trans. 1956); *Loser Wins* (*Les Séquestrés d'Altona*, 1959, trans. 1960, as *The Condemned of Altona* in USA, 1961); 'Existential Psychoanalysis' – *Baudelaire* (1947, trans. 1950); *Saint Genet, Actor and Martyr* (*Saint Genet, comédien et martyr*, 1952, trans. 1953); *L'Idiot de la famille: Gustave Flaubert de 1821 à 1857* ('The Idiot of the Family: Gustave Flaubert 1821–1857', 3 vols, 1971–2). The most important of Sartre's periodical and occasional writings are collected in *Situations* (10 vols, Paris 1947–76). See also: *Un Théâtre de situation* (1973), ed. M. Contat and M. Rybalka, who also produced the indispensable *The Writings of Jean-Paul Sartre: a Bibliographical Life* (*Les Écrits de Sartre: chronologie, bibliographie commentée*, 1970, trans. 2 vols, 1974). On Sartre: Francis Jeanson, *Le Problème moral et la pensée de Sartre* (1947, rev. 1965) and *Sartre par lui-même* (1954); R. Laing and D. Cooper, *Reason and Violence: a Decade of Sartre's Philosophy 1950–60* (1964); A. Manser, *Sartre, a Philosophic Study* (1966); I. Murdoch, *Sartre: Romantic Rationalist* (1953).

424

SATIE, Erik 1866–1925

French composer

Now recognized to be one of the major influences on experimental music this century, Satie was born in the Normandy port of Honfleur of part-Scottish ancestry and brought up in a sheltered environment coloured by the friendship of an eccentric seafaring uncle. He received his first musical training from the local organist, a pupil of the Niedermeyer school of church music, and as a result developed a life-long interest in plainsong and the ritual of the Catholic Church. After an unsuccessful stay at the Paris Conservatoire he took up the life of a bohemian and was employed as second pianist at the famous 'Chat Noir' cabaret in Montmartre where he was to be exposed to the influences of the music-hall song and the infectious rhythms of the American cakewalk and early ragtime. Already writing short piano pieces in a rather austere modal style (*Sarabandes*, 1887, and *Gymnopédies*, 1888) he was to become involved with the mystic sect of the Rosicrucians headed by Sâr Peladan who asked him to contribute pieces of incidental music for the 'Rose-Croix' productions (*Upsud, Le Fils de l'Étoiles, Messe des Pauvres*, 1892–5). His mentor's increasing interest in the music and aesthetic of Wagner compelled him to dissociate himself from the sect and Paris life as a

whole and he took lodgings in the shabby southern suburb of Arceuil-Cachan where he remained for the rest of his life. Satie's tendency towards introversion and moodiness deprived him of many worthwhile friendships; however, his early meeting with Debussy* caused him to cement a life-long relationship which, though fraught with constant misunderstandings on Satie's part, was to prove a major contribution to the musical output of both young composers.

At the turn of the century French musical life was dominated by the influence of Wagner and César Franck with the result that leading composers of this period like D'Indy, Debussy and Dukas were writing romantic orchestral and operatic works of massive proportions; Satie, in contrast, had only produced a handful of café songs and piano miniatures while enduring a life of total self-sufficiency and utter poverty. A decision at the age of forty to improve his own musical education by enrolling for a three-year course in counterpoint at the Schola Cantorum run by D'Indy showed him to be a man of continuing intellectual curiosity and humility. On gaining his diploma in 1908 he felt disillusioned by the fact that his new works were contrived and lacked the intuitive simplicity of his earlier ones: as a result he composed very little until the appearance of the suite for orchestra or piano entitled *En Habit de Cheval* (1911). Despite this personal crisis, performances of his music were becoming more regular and with the encouragement of his friends and teachers he was spurred on to write and publish more works. The piano suite *Sports et Divertissements* (1914) is indicative of his mature style with its twenty thumbnail sketches of recreational pursuits painstakingly drawn in the most expert musical calligraphy and smattered with examples of the composer's laconic scenic descriptions.

The coming of the Great War, coupled with the onslaught of Cubism and Dada on the sensibilities of the Parisian artistic milieu, occasioned a meeting between the composer and Jean Cocteau*. This, together with a commission in 1916 from Diaghilev*, resulted in the first Cubist 'Ballet Realiste' called *Parade* with choreography by Massine and sets designed by Picasso*. At last Erik Satie's reputation as France's foremost avant-garde composer was established and during the remaining years of his life he was to produce two further experimental ballets as well as *Socrate*, a symphonic drama for orchestra and voices (1919), which represented a return to the classical proportions and economy of means and expression in his first piano compositions.

Satie's great contribution lies not only in his development of musical statements which are unique in construction, but also in his inspired aesthetic sense which endeavours to extend the listener's realm of aural perception. Most of his mature works are short and convey an elongated time sense using modal harmonies, repeated rhythmic patterns, aphoristic melodic shapes and a minimum of dynamic variation. Major composers who have openly acknowledged their debt to Satie number Ravel*, Debussy, Stravinsky* and some members of 'Les Six' who continued to write collaborative works for Diaghilev after his death. In the US Aaron Copland* and Virgil Thomson cite the ballet *Relâche* (1924) with its special film score for René Char's 'Entracte Cinématographique' as a seminal influence in their own works; Varèse* compares some of the Rosicrucian music to early experiments in electronic music and 'process composers' such as Steve Reich and Terry Riley have derived inspiration from Satie's use of a minimum of melodic material. The greatest influence of the post-war period has been in the works of John Cage* and contemporaries where the concept of 'Musique d'Ameublement' (Wallpaper Music) has formed a basis for their mixed-media events and 'Happenings'.

Michael Alexander

See: Pierre-Daniel Templier, *Erik Satie* (1932, trans. 1969); Rollo Myers, *Erik Satie* (1948); Roger Shattuck, *The Banquet Years* (rev. edn 1968); James Harding, *Erik Satie* (1971) and *The Ox on the Roof* (1976).

425
de SAUSSURE, Mongin-Ferdinand 1857–1913

Swiss linguist

By virtue of one book, *Course in General Linguistics* (*Cours de linguistique générale*, 1916, trans. 1959), edited posthumously from students' lecture-notes, Saussure is commonly acknowledged as the father of modern linguistics and of the 'structuralist' movement.

Ferdinand de Saussure was the son of a prominent Genevese Huguenot family which had emigrated from Lorraine during the French wars of religion in the late sixteenth century. Ferdinand displayed a bent for language study in childhood and, after a false start reading science at Geneva University, went to study philology at Leipzig and Berlin. At twenty-one Saussure published his *Mémoire sur le système primitif des voyelles dans les langues indo-européennes* ('Memoir on the original system of vowels in the Indo-European languages'), a monograph which has been described as 'the most splendid work of comparative philology ever written'; its chief theoretical conclusion, propounded by Saussure purely on the basis of logical analysis, was corroborated almost fifty years later from archaeological evidence.

Saussure lectured at the École Pratique des Hautes Études, Paris, from 1881 to 1891, before returning to a chair at Geneva, where he remained until his death.

His life was uneventful; after publishing his doctoral dissertation in 1881 he wrote only some short notes and reviews, and his publications, like the bulk of his teaching, were concerned exclusively with the established discipline of Indo-European philology. Saussure resisted requests to expound his ideas on the theoretical foundations of linguistics, and finally lectured on the subject only because a colleague teaching general linguistics happened to retire in the middle of a session.

Saussure's *Course* can be seen as part of a shift from the nineteenth-century emphasis on the historical approach as the key to understanding cultural phenomena to the twentieth-century emphasis on the sociological approach. For the ordinary (non-scholarly) speaker, Saussure said, his language has no history; if we wish to describe a language as a vehicle of communication, we need to explain not how its various components came to have their present form but how they relate to one another as a system now. Saussure called this kind of non-historical description 'synchronic' as opposed to 'diachronic'. In a synchronic '*état de langue*', what matter are not the individual components but the system of relationships between them. To understand the 'value' of the English word *sheep* we need to know that it contrasts with another word *mutton*; French *mouton* enters into no such contrast, so the 'value' of *mouton* is rather different from the 'value' of *sheep*. The units of sound called 'phonemes' are likewise defined by their contrasts with other phonemes. Saussure compares language to chess, in which the past history of a game is irrelevant to the situation reached at a given point, and the potential of any piece depends crucially on its relationships with other pieces, but not on its intrinsic properties: we could agree to replace the white queen by a lump of chalk without affecting the state of play.

It is oddly difficult to say how far Saussure has influenced subsequent thought. The idea that what matters in a system of meanings are the contrasts between elements rather than the elements themselves is axiomatic in contemporary linguistics; but this idea was already implicit in the work of Franz Boas*, independently of Saussure. The related notion that the realms of thought and speech-sound are devoid of inherent structure, being articulated only by various languages which bring them into different arbitrary relationships with one another, was abandoned by later linguists such as Roman Jakobson* (without this rejection being presented explicitly as a repudiation of Saussure). Saussure's Durkheimian* view of language-structure as inhering in society as an organism, rather than in its individual members, has been largely ignored by subsequent linguists (and the relationship between Saussure's and Durkheim's thought has itself become a controversial question). Finally, recent work on language variation and change has suggested that Saussure's sharp distinction between synchrony and diachrony cannot be maintained, and that (contrary to Saussure's assumption) language changes may themselves be systematic in nature.

Within linguistics, Saussure has become something of a cult figure whom many regard as a master but few read closely enough to appreciate how little they agree with him. Saussure's lasting influence has been primarily on the 'structuralist' movement, currently represented, for example, by Claude Lévi-Strauss*, which takes its paradigm of enquiry from linguistics but applies it chiefly to other subjects.

Geoffrey Sampson

See: E. F. K. Koerner, *Ferdinand de Saussure* (1973); Jonathan Culler, *Saussure* (Glasgow 1976).

426

SCHLICK, Moritz 1882–1936

Austrian philosopher

Moritz Schlick was born in Berlin of prosperous parents. He studied at the University of Berlin where he did research in physics under Max Planck* obtaining his doctorate in 1904 for a thesis on the reflection of light in a non-homogeneous medium. After teaching at the University of Rostock from 1911 to 1917 he was appointed Professor at the University of Kiel in 1921 and moved as Professor to the University of Vienna in 1922. He remained there until his death in 1936 when he was fatally wounded on his way to lecture at the university by a deranged student making his second attempt on Schlick's life.

Schlick's background in science played a major role in his philosophical activities. He was one of the first philosophers to understand the physical content and philosophical significance of Einstein's* Special and General Theories of Relativity. His early work, *Space and Time in Contemporary Physics* (*Raum und Zeit in der gegenwärtigen Physik*, 1917), provided a lucid nontechnical introduction to relativity theory in which the verificationism characteristic of his mature philosophical position can be discerned. He argued that Einstein's work provided decisive reasons for rejecting the Kantian enterprise of attempting to discover synthetic truths about the structure of space and time through *a priori* investigations. In his *General Theory of Knowledge* (*Allgemeine Erkenntnislehre*, 1918) he broadens his Kantian critique arguing that in no sphere of knowledge are there *synthetic a priori* judgments. At this stage Schlick held that there was a genuine controversy between realism and idealism which could be resolved philosophically in favour of what he called critical realism. The critical realist does not seek a certain base for knowledge in the Cartesian tradition but rather takes the individual sciences to provide knowledge of

reality and limits himself to weeding out contradictions in science and to understanding the significance of scientific achievements. Schlick attempted to resolve the traditional mind–body problem through identifying brain process with mental processes. In this work, as in his latter writings, the influence of Hume, Mach, Poincaré, Russell* and Hilbert are evident.

Hans Hahn (mathematician), Phillip Frank (physicist) and Otto Neurath (economist), who had been meeting informally to discuss the philosophy of science, were responsible for Schlick's appointment in Vienna. Schlick became the leader of this group holding a weekly seminar whose participants included (besides the above) Friedrich Waismann, Herbert Feigl, Kurt Gödel*, Rudolf Carnap*. The group, known as the Vienna Circle, developed and propagated Logical Positivism. Schlick's influence derives from his own work after coming to Vienna and through his organization of the Vienna Circle, which met regularly until his death.

Stimulated by these meetings and by his reading of Wittgenstein's* *Tractatus Logico-Philosophicus*, which arguably he misinterpreted, Schlick re-examined his philosophical position. He ceased to see philosophy as a means for acquiring knowledge. Philosophy became the activity of revealing the meaning of propositions. With the exception of analytic statements which are true in virtue of their meaning and say nothing about the world, the meaning of empirical assertions is to be displayed by showing what would verify their truth. This doctrine was enshrined in his notorious verification principle (the central tenet of logical positivism) that the meaning of a sentence is the method of its verification. Henceforth metaphysics as traditionally conceived was to be dismissed. Logical analysis of the meaning of an assertion of a metaphysician would reveal three possibilities. The assertion might be analytically true and hence it would say nothing about the world. It might be a verifiable and hence meaningful empirical assertion, the investigation of the truth of which would be a matter for science. Or, more likely, it would be a meaningless concatenation of signs. Returning to the realist–idealist controversy, Schlick now argued that this represents a pseudo-problem, for the assertion of the realist that there is a transcendental reality and the denial of that assertion by the idealist are both meaningless in virtue of being unverifiable. Schlick applied his style of analysis to a wide range of concepts. For instance, he sought to remove metaphysical elements from the conception of causality by reducing causality to a matter of mere regularity in a manner reminiscent of Hume. He also discussed concepts specific to individual sciences arguing against vitalism in biology and displaying the variation in the sense in which the concept of space is used in different sciences.

Unlike other members of the Circle, Schlick took the

scope of science to include ethics and in his lively and provocative *Problems of Ethics* (*Fragen der Ethik*, 1930) argued that theoretical ethics is a factual science whose cardinal principle is the empirical law that men act so as to maximize their own pleasure. To say that an act is good is to say that society holds the act to be pleasure increasing. Thus, the determination of the good is a factual matter. For one sensitive as Schlick was to the importance of ascertaining the meaning of expressions, his analysis of ethical concepts is surprisingly crude.

Schlick was instrumental to the development and propagation of the doctrines of Logical Positivism. Often caricatured and generally rejected, the school as such has waned as much through a growing realization of the simplistic character of their conception of science as through an awareness of the philosophical problems in the verification principle. The logical positivists aspired to have philosophy take science seriously; to maintain the highest standards of rigour and clarity; to concern itself with meaning. Its influence can be seen in these continuing trends in contemporary philosophy.

W. H. Newton-Smith

All Schlick's papers published between 1909 and his death are among those included in *Philosophical Papers*, vols I and II (1979); these volumes also include biographical sketches and a bibliography.

427
SCHOENBERG, Arnold Franz Walter 1874–1951

Austrian composer

It is reported that during army service in the First World War, Arnold Schoenberg was asked by an officer if he was that controversial composer of the same name; to which he replied, 'Somebody had to be, and nobody else wanted the job, so I took it on myself.' The answer neatly sums up his sense of the inevitability of his creative mission, and the belief that his personal wishes had little to do with it: he was in many ways an unwilling revolutionary, driven by the need for continual clarification of his emotional and artistic concerns.

The son of a free-thinking Jewish shoemaker, Schoenberg was born in Vienna and began composing at the age of nine. He was virtually self-taught, beyond some lessons from the slightly older Alexander von Zemlinsky; his real training derived from the practical experience of playing classical chamber music, conducting workers' choirs, and making hack arrangements and orchestrations of other composers' works. By the turn of the century he had already composed two major pieces, the string sextet *Verklärte Nacht* and the vast romantic cantata *Gurrelieder*. After an unhappy period as musical director of a cabaret in Berlin (1901–

2) he returned to Vienna, where he gained the support of Mahler and began teaching composition privately – his earliest pupils included Alban Berg* and Anton Webern*. In 1908 a personal and artistic crisis turned Schoenberg's music sharply in the direction of extreme, *Angst*-ridden subjectivity, made possible by an equally sudden and extreme transformation of its language. In such works as the *Five Pieces for Orchestra* (Op. 16, 1909) and the monodrama *Erwartung* (Op. 17, not performed until 1924) he drew near to the aesthetic ideals of the Expressionist painters, and began himself to paint in intervals when he felt composition impossible.

Failure to secure either adequate means of living or an audience for his music in Vienna led him to move back to Berlin in 1911 – via Munich, where he established contact with Kandinsky* and became associated with the Blaue Reiter group. In Berlin he was befriended by Busoni*, acquired more pupils and gained performances from London to St Petersburg, but this good fortune was cut short by the outbreak of war. He served for a time in the Austrian infantry, and in the immediate post-war years addressed himself to the problem of picking up the cultural pieces in a shattered and inflation-torn Vienna. His *Verein für musikalische Privataufführungen* (Society for Private Musical Performances, 1918–22) drew its performing talent from Schoenberg's ever-widening circle of pupils and admirers, presented a wide range of contemporary music in thoroughly rehearsed and repeated performances, and became the model for many later and larger Modern Music organizations in Europe and America. This activity coincided with a creative blockage, only cleared as Schoenberg developed the 'method of composition with 12 notes related only to one another' which first made its appearance in the *Serenade* (Op. 24) and piano pieces (Opp. 23, 25) composed 1921–3.

In 1925 Schoenberg returned to Berlin for the third time, as director of the Composition Masterclass at the Prussian Academy of Arts, in succession to Busoni. This period of comparative eminence (he once described it as 'the time when everybody made believe he understood Einstein's* theories and Schoenberg's music') saw the production of such large-scale works as the *Variations for Orchestra* (Op. 31, 1926–8) and the opera *Moses und Aron* (1930–2) but came to an end with the rise of Nazism: in 1933, he was dismissed from his post as part of Hitler's* campaign to 'break the Jewish stranglehold on Western Music'. In the same year he emigrated to the USA. After a short period teaching in New York and Boston, he moved to California and taught first at the University of Southern California (1935–6) and then at the University of California in Los Angeles (1936–44). Compelled to resign from the latter post on a tiny pension at the age of seventy, Schoenberg spent his last years teaching, writing and composing, frequently in precarious health. He died in

Brentwood Park, Hollywood: it is said that his last words were 'Harmony! Harmony! Harmony!'

By temperament a romantic, but intellectually committed to classical ideals of structural proportion and consistency, Schoenberg in many respects resembled his first musical hero, Brahms. His creative path was guided by instinct first, only secondarily by the desire for a rational explanation of what instinct had produced. His earliest characteristic music synthesized and built upon the achievements of Brahms and Wagner, from whom he derived two distinct but interdependent concepts: that of 'the unity of musical space', whereby the constituent elements of a composition – melody, accompaniment, harmony, rhythm – should be intimately related expressions of the same idea in different dimensions; and the principle of 'developing variation', which tended ever away from exact repetition of ideas towards their perpetual transformation as a major structural impulse. The dazzlingly quick mind and passionate urge for maximum communication which he brought to the development of these two concepts makes such a fundamentally traditional score as the String Quartet No. 1 (Op. 7, 1905) already daunting in the sheer volume of musical information which the listener must assimilate.

The emotionally and intellectually supercharged style of this and other works of the early 1900s exploded after 1908 into the music of Schoenberg's 'Expressionist' phase, where he strove to represent extreme states of mind and feeling more or less directly, without any intervening decorum of form. His ideal, he said, was a music 'without architecture, without structure. Only an ever-changing, unbroken succession of colours, rhythms and moods.' The works of this period are accordingly characterized by an unprecedented degree of harmonic ambiguity, asymmetry of melody and phrase-lengths, wide and dissonant melodic intervals, abrupt contrasts in register, texture, stasis and dynamism. All twelve notes of the chromatic scale occur with extreme frequency and consequently the harmonic language shifts away from any kind of diatonic hierarchy towards a state of total chromaticism – an 'emancipation of dissonance' which does not, however, prevent the covert and allusive operation of tonal functions and so belies the popular misnomer, 'atonality', which posterity has happily foisted on it.

In fact, Schoenberg was concerned almost at once to reintroduce principles of 'architecture' into his music, aware that the supremely intuitive, quasi-improvisational achievement of *Erwartung* was by definition unrepeatable, and that his linguistic revolution had for the moment put traditional means of large-scale organization beyond his grasp. Most of his works for the next decade were vocal, the text helping to determine the progress of the form. At the same time he began to concentrate on intensive development of the constituent tones of principal thematic ideas, and

cultivated a wide range of canonic and other 'ancient' contrapuntal devices to provide structural backbone. All these tendencies are found in *Pierrot Lunaire* (Op. 21, 1912) for instrumental ensemble and *Sprechstimme* (half-sung recitation), an ironic cycle of rondel-settings with elements of Expressionist cabaret which has remained one of his best-known scores; and they reached a new intensity, and an impasse, in the unfinished oratorio *Die Jakobsleiter* (*Jacob's Ladder*, 1917–22), a fragment of a gigantic project that brought his musical, philosophical and religious dilemmas into sharp focus.

To employ a psychological metaphor: the 'Expressionist' works had brought a host of previously inadmissible musical 'traumas' into the open, harbingers of chaos and disruption which nineteenth-century tradition and theory had rigorously suppressed. Schoenberg's struggle was to accept and assimilate these 'negative' forces into the existing scheme of musical discourse, to objectify them in an enlarged musical language which he could consciously apply in further works. His solution was the development of the '12-note method'. A fixed series of all the notes of the chromatic scale, derived from the initial melodic and harmonic ideas for a piece, becomes the kernel, the essence, the germinating cell of that piece's unique tonal properties. The series is developed continually through transposition, inversion, retrograde motion, in whole or in part, in melodic lines and in chords, to provide an inexhaustible and self-consistent source of invention which Schoenberg then deploys on the largest scale through a revivification of classical forms. The works of the 1920s, such as the Wind Quintet (Op. 26, 1924) and String Quartet No. 3 (Op. 30, 1927), are imbued with an almost neo-classical spirit while retaining something of the raw immediacy of the Expressionist vision.

In the 1930s Schoenberg continued to refine and develop the method, enlarging its melodic vocabulary and relaxing some of his original 'rules' for 12-note composition to effect an accommodation with an intermittent sense of traditional tonality. He even composed some diatonically based works of his own, averring that there was 'still a lot of good music to be written in C major'. Tonal and serial resources enriched each other in the 1940s in a series of works where the old Expressionist urgency is recaptured within a sure structural control: the String Trio (Op. 45, 1946) and the 'ghetto' cantata *A Survivor from Warsaw* (Op. 46, 1947) are the peak of this development. His last works were vocal, to his own texts: he left unfinished the first of a series of *Modern Psalms* dealing with the predicament of Man (principally, but not exclusively, Jewish Man) in the Atomic Age.

During his lifetime and for twenty years after it, Schoenberg's music was generally more talked about than listened to. But his influence has been immense. Not only was he the mentor, inspirer and incarnate artistic conscience of three generations of pupils, many of whom (e.g. Berg, Webern, Wellesz, Eisler*, Gerhard, Skalkottas, Cage*) became important figures in their own right; but his compositional methods have been adopted and extended by countless others. Perhaps none of them has been driven to forge the 12-note method out of his own experience by a similarly compelling need: but the basic techniques of the method are so fruitfully simple, so easily adapted to multifarious ends, that it has itself become the cornerstone of most succeeding innovations, an integral part of our century's musical thought. Unfortunately, it has also engendered in many quarters a stress on technique and abstract formal criteria at the expense of music's expressive content, the 'idea', the 'representation of a *vision*' which for Schoenberg was music's paramount *raison d'être*. Only in recent years has the balance begun to be redressed, in the study of his own works, away from what he called 'how it is done' towards 'what it *is!*'

Schoenberg was a pithy and ironic writer whose pungent style was influenced by his friend Karl Kraus*. In addition to the texts and libretti of many of his works he wrote poetry, a play, some stories and a vast number of essays and aphorisms on musical and other topics, as well as several pedagogical works. The most celebrated of these last, *Theory of Harmony* (*Harmonielehre*, 1911, rev. 1922, trans. 1978), is an idiosyncratic but often massively illuminating study of traditional harmonic principles up to the threshold of his own radical departure from them. The paradox is characteristic. He may yet be seen, not as modern music's *monstre sacré*, the composer audiences most like to hate, but as the last great custodian of the ethical (as opposed to aesthetic) values of musical Romanticism, and their chief deliverer into the modern world.

Malcolm MacDonald

Other works include: operas – *Die glückliche Hand* (1913); *Von heute auf Morgen* (1929); *Kol Nidre*, for chorus and orchestra (1938); *Das Buch der hängenden Gärten* (song cycle, 1908–9); *Ode to Napoleon*, for reciter and piano quintet (1942); *Pelleas und Melisande* (symphonic poem, 1902–3); two Chamber Symphonies (1906 and 1938); *Suite in G* for strings (1934); *Theme and Variations* for wind band (1943); concertos for Piano (1942), Violin (1935–6), Cello (1932–3), and String Quartet (1933); five String Quartets (1897, 1905, 1908, 1927, 1936); *Phantasy* for violin and piano (1949). Writings: *Style and Idea* (1950, rev. 1975); *Selected Letters* (1964), ed. E. Stein. See: J. Rufer, *The Works of Arnold Schoenberg* (trans. 1962); C. Rosen, *Schoenberg* (1975); M. MacDonald, *Schoenberg* (1976); H. H. Stuckenschmidt, *Schoenberg: his Life, World and Work* (trans. 1977).

428
SCHRÖDINGER, Erwin 1887–1961

Austrian physicist

Educated in Vienna, Schrödinger succeeded, shortly after his war service, to the chair, earlier held by Einstein*, at Zürich. He was already expert in the frontiers of relativity theory, statistical mechanics, and the old quantum theory, but his great discovery, the invention of wave mechanics, came five years later, late in 1925, when he was thirty-seven. He subsequently taught at Berlin, Oxford, and Graz, and spent the last seventeen years of his career at the Dublin Institute for Advanced Studies.

Under the influence of his earlier teacher Franz Exner, of a lifelong preoccupation with the problem of reconciling free will and determinism, and of a famous 1924 paper by Niels Bohr* and others, Schrödinger had first toyed with the idea of solving the problems of the old quantum theory by turning energy-momentum conservation into a purely statistical law. But the experimental results came out against this and Schrödinger turned instead to the ideas which had recently been proposed by Louis de Broglie. De Broglie had conceived electrons as classical particles with which waves were, nevertheless, somehow associated and which allowed periodic particle motions only when they interfered with themselves constructively rather than destructively. Surprisingly, this rather makeshift theory of de Broglie's had yielded the correct relativistic energy levels of the hydrogen atom.

Schrödinger's idea was to construct a fully consistent wave theory of electrons, which would yield the successes of de Broglie's theory and which would stand in the identical relation to Newtonian particle mechanics that wave optics (and ultimately Maxwell's equations for the electromagnetic field) stood to Newton's particle theory of light. The theory, wave mechanics, which Schrödinger obtained more or less by a trial and error process, with various wave equations guessed by analogy, failed to fulfil all Schrödinger's intentions, but nevertheless became the theory which physicists still believe, but with a different interpretation. For the problem of recovering particle-like behaviour from the new theory proved much more refractory than Schrödinger had anticipated. Schrödinger's equation did not allow localized particle-like wave packets to remain localized, and to treat several particles by his equation he had to consider waves in an abstract higher dimensional space rather than in ordinary physical space. Max Born then proposed that Schrödinger's waves be reinterpreted as merely statistical descriptions of the behaviour of particles. But it was later realized (though only rigorously proved some forty years later) that a mere statistical ignorance interpretation of the Schrödinger wave-function is mathematically untenable. Therefore it became standard theoretical practice, which remains with us today, to treat Schrödinger's waves as physically real up to the point at which the system interacts with a measuring apparatus, and as expressing our statistical ignorance immediately after that interaction. Schrödinger was one of the first to point out the inconsistency of this procedure, through his famous cat paradox, in which a cat ends up in a state in which, according to the theory, it is neither dead nor alive and only becomes definitely the one or the other when we ourselves examine it. The difficulty is that the mathematical theory we have inherited from Schrödinger is deterministic, whereas the interpretation we now graft on to it is indeterministic: the conflict between these two aspects has never been satisfactorily resolved, but the theory works.

It was soon discovered by Schrödinger himself that an apparently rival quantum theory, Heisenberg's* matrix mechanics, which had been invented shortly before Schrödinger's wave mechanics, was in fact mathematically equivalent, at a deep level, to Schrödinger's own theory. Heisenberg's approach proved to give a profounder insight into what had to be done to the theory of light in order to generate the particle properties of photons. Schrödinger's idea had been simply to couple his equation with Maxwell's equations in order to provide a unified classical continuum theory of light and matter. Though such a theory gave a beautifully visualizable classical account of the emission and absorption of radiation by atoms (and attempts have been made to revive this theory recently, by Jaynes, under the name of 'neo-classical radiation theory') it has never proved possible to account successfully for the particle properties of both matter and radiation within such a view. The orthodox modern theory of radiation is quite different, and owes more to Heisenberg and Dirac than to Schrödinger.

Schrödinger continued in later life to draw attention to the unsatisfactory character of the quantum theory of which he had been the joint inventor. In other work he helped to clarify the foundations of general relativity and of thermodynamics and statistical mechanics. His 1944 book *What is Life?* was a brilliant popular exposition of the state of molecular biology and its relations to the law of entropy increase. In an epilogue Schrödinger defended the mystical view that our minds are part of the mind of the deity, as one possible way to reconcile the inexorability of God's laws with human freedom.

Jon Dorling

Schrödinger's more popular works include: *Science and the Human Temperament* (1935); *Science and Humanism* (1951); *Nature and the Greeks* (1954); *Mind and Matter* (1958); *My View of the World* (1964); See also: L. Wessels, 'Schrödinger's route to wave mechanics',

Studies in History and Philosophy of Science (1979); W. T. Scott, *Erwin Schrödinger, an Introduction to his Writings* (1967); Schrödinger, *Papers on Wave Mechanics* (1928); A. d'Abro, *The Rise of the New Physics* (1951).

429

SEFERIS, George (George Seferiadis) 1900–71

Greek poet and critic

Seferis was born in Smyrna and educated in Athens and Paris. The defeat of Greece by Turkey in 1922 and the consequent expulsion of the Greek population of Asia Minor meant that Seferis ever after felt himself an exile. The loss of his homeland was compounded by voluntary exile: Seferis was a member of the Greek diplomatic service throughout his working life, serving in Britain, Albania and Lebanon, and with the Greek government-in-exile in Egypt during the Second World War. He ended his career as Greek Ambassador in London in 1962, and the following year he was awarded the Nobel Prize for Literature.

Seferis was the leading member of the Greek 'Generation of 1930', which comprised a large group of writers determined to renew Greek poetry and fiction by both delving into the Greek tradition and keeping abreast of contemporary developments abroad.

Seferis's first great poem was *Mythistorema* (1935), which is seen as a turning point in Greek literature. Here Seferis broke away from the patriotic themes, folksy diction and traditional versification which characterized much of earlier Greek poetry: in free verse and in a language firmly based in contemporary educated urban speech, the poet develops the symbol of the voyage, which was so congenial to him: the exile, a latter-day Odysseus with his companions, chronicles his attempts to return home. The influence of T. S. Eliot* is clear not only in Seferis's use of the 'mythical method', but also in his depiction of the Greek landscape as a waste land that is both painful and very dear to him. His tone of voice is characterized by the use of the first person plural, which indicates that he is speaking for the whole of Greece, even the whole of European humanity, lost between two world wars.

In three collections aptly entitled *Imerologio katastromatos* (*Logbook A* 1940; *B*, 1944; *C*, 1955), the poet charts his wandering progress, sending 'bottles in the sea' from the various places in which he has chosen (or has been obliged) to stay, both in Greece and abroad. Like *Mythistorema*, these poems reflect Seferis's tragic view of life, with their insistence on the themes of parting and loss; although against all this Seferis sets a constant plea for human justice to counteract the injustice of fate.

In *Kichli* (*Thrush*, 1947) there is a change. This is another long poem based on the Odysseus theme, but here the voyager seems to arrive finally at his destination, even if the reader interprets this as being death. In this highly obscure poem Seferis explores more metaphysical themes than in his earlier poetry: a religious (if not strictly Christian) vision pervades this poem, which should be seen together with *Logbook C*, where he is inspired by the medieval and Orthodox riches of Cyprus.

In his collected essays, Seferis, again influenced by Eliot, seeks to establish what is of most value in the modern Greek literary tradition. Both his poetry and his essays have made him the most influential figure both among his contemporaries and among later generations of Greek writers.

Peter Mackridge

Poems: *Collected Poems 1924–1955*, trans. Edmund Keeley and Philip Sherrard (1969); *Three Secret Poems*, trans. Walter Kaiser (1969). Essays: *On the Greek Style*, trans. Rex Warner and T. D. Frangopoulos (1967). Journal: *A Poet's Journal: Days of 1945–1951*, trans. Athan Anagnostopoulos (1974).

430
SEXTON, Anne Harvey 1928–74

US poet

From the internal evidence of her poems it would seem that Anne Sexton spent her life in a state of traumatic shock by clinging tenaciously to the belief that death was the only certainty in a disturbingly chaotic world. Her early life, however, was apparently normal enough. She was born in Newton, Massachusetts, and like Sylvia Plath* grew up in Wellesley, Massachusetts. After attending Garland Junior College she married Alfred M. Sexton in 1948 and had two daughters, Linda and Joyce. At the beginning of the 1950s she worked as a fashion model in Boston and then began to write poetry under the influence of W. D. Snodgrass and Robert Lowell*. It was at Lowell's poetry class at Boston University that she first met Sylvia Plath, in 1958.

The two young women got on well and Anne Sexton has described their somewhat morbid relationship in her essay 'The barfly ought to sing' in *The Art of Sylvia Plath* (ed. Charles Newman, 1970). After listening to Lowell's views on poetry Sexton and Plath would go to drink martinis at the Ritz: 'Often, very often, Sylvia and I would talk at length about our first suicides. . . . We talked death with burned-up intensity, both of us drawn to it like moths to an electric light bulb. Sucking on it!' Sylvia Plath's last poems were influenced by Anne Sexton's work and they in turn influenced Sexton's subsequent development.

Anne Sexton's first collection, *To Bedlam and Part*

Way Back (1960), established her as a determinedly confessional poet. She related her experiences of mental breakdown, attempted suicide and hospitalization in highly organized verse characterized by staccato rhythms and sharp, brittle rhymes. She described herself as 'I, who chose two times/to kill myself' ('The Double Image') and made powerful images from her clinical environment, as in 'Lullaby':

> My sleeping pill is white.
> It is a splendid pearl;
> it floats me out of myself.

From 1961 to 1963 she was a scholar at Radcliffe and during this period her second collection *All My Pretty Ones* (1962) appeared. In this she intensified the personal nature of her poetry, dwelling on the loss of her parents (both of whom died in 1959) and confronting such painful subjects as 'The Abortion' with its final image of 'this baby that I bleed'.

In 1967 she won the Pulitzer Prize in poetry for *Live or Die* (1966); in 1969 she gained a Guggenheim Award and published her *Love Poems* (1969). In fact while her private agony haunted her verse she was winning great public acclaim as a writer. She lectured in creative writing at Boston University from 1969 until 1972 when she was made a professor after the publication of *Transformations* (1971). Perhaps affected by criticisms of self-indulgence she attempted, in that volume, to objectify her poetry and reflect the external world rather than endless internal conflict.

Anne Sexton was not completely at ease with impersonal subjects. When, in *The Book of Folly* (1972), she explored what she took to be the American political nightmare the result – in, for example, 'The Firebombers' – suggested parody rather than passion:

> We are America.
> We are the coffin fillers.
> We are the grocers of death.
> We pack them in crates like cauliflowers.

More typically the book included 'The Jesus Papers', a sequence that displayed her tormented obsession with religion. The last two collections she prepared for publication reworked the Keatsian theme of being 'half in love with easeful death': *The Death Notebooks* (1974) she hoped 'when it comes to my death let it be slow/let it be pantomime, this last peep show'; in *The Awful Rowing Toward God* (1975) her style shifted from tight forms to an almost abandoned freedom as she conducted a dialogue with a flawed deity. She died on 4 October 1974, the year of her divorce. A posthumous collection *45 Mercy Street* (1976), edited by her daughter Linda, showed that at the end of her life she was distressed by the breakdown of her marriage, for she wrote in

'Divorce' that 'I have killed our lives together,/axed off each head'.

Alan Bold

See also: *Selected Poems* (1964); Cameron Northouse and Thomas P. Walsh, *Sylvia Plath and Anne Sexton: A Reference Guide* (1974).

431
SHAH, Idries 1924–

Afghan writer

Sayed Idries Shah was born at Simla in India, into a family directly descended from Mohammed, and from many of the great Sufi masters of Central Asia, notably Afghanistan, the family home. Having studied the Moslem heritage in the company of Sufis, Shah has written many books based on their teaching, and he is generally recognized as the leading disseminator of Eastern wisdom in the West. Between *The Sufis* (New York 1964) and *Learning How to Learn* (London 1978) his collections of mostly ancient parables and anecdotes have had a huge circulation throughout the world. Those who study with him are recommended to familiarize themselves with these entertaining but oddly pointed stories, as a result of which the student is expected to lose his complacent satisfaction with much that had previously been taken for granted.

Retaining a strong sense of spiritual values, Shah's concern has been to reveal the essentials which underlie all cultures, the hidden factors responsible for the behaviour of individuals, alone and in relationship with others in different environments and circumstances; and the links between these factors. While it is difficult to summarize an enterprise that does not, like most contemporary didactic Western teaching, summarize itself, certain themes recur. In particular Shah discounts the attention given in the West to the appearances and superficialities of culture – often reflecting what is merely habit or fashion – and suggests such attention would be more appropriately applied to the study of the springs of culture, to the unconscious and mixed motives of people, and to the even more mysterious motivations of groups of people. Again, he disagrees with the practice of piecemeal cultural analysis, maintaining that a culture, like an individual, is indivisible, and cannot therefore be studied objectively if some aspects of it are deliberately excluded, or others disproportionately promoted. To do this obscures overall patterns. For example, Shah has observed how, both on personal and on community levels, immediate disasters prove in the long term to be blessings, and vice versa, yet the available evidence for this has had little impact on reactions to events as they occur.

Through his own wide experience, as a reader and as a traveller, through his books, and through the Institute for Cultural Research, which he established in London in 1966, Shah has endeavoured to create the conditions for the objective study he advocates. His exact status remains indefinable. Disclaiming the identity of a guru, and disclaiming any intention to found a cult or a sect, he also rejects the academic cap. An Eastern Orientalist, he is perhaps best seen as an embodiment of the tradition in which the contemplative and intuitive aspects of the mind are regarded as being most productive when working together.

Michael Rubinstein

Shah's other books include: *Caravan of Dreams* (1968); *The Way of the Sufi* (1968); *Tales of the Dervishes* (1967); *Thinkers of the East* (1971); *Wisdom of the Idiots* (1970); *The Magic Monastery* (1972); *The Dermis Probe* (1970); *The Exploits of the Incomparable Mulla Nasrudin* (1966); *The Pleasantries of the Incredible Mulla Nasrudin* (1968); *The Subtleties of the Inimitable Mulla Nasrudin* (1973).

432
SHAW, George Bernard 1856–1950

Irish writer

'I am a typical Irishman,' Shaw told G. K. Chesterton*, 'my family came from Yorkshire.' He was born in Dublin on 26 July 1856, the third and last child of George Carr Shaw, a redundant Civil Servant turned grain merchant, and his wife Lucinda Elizabeth, a lapsed Protestant who tampered with the occult. They were an unattractive couple and they achieved a miserable marriage that began in Synge Street – 'an awful little kennel' Shaw later described it. They did not physically ill-treat their son: they ignored him. If he had failed to come home from one of the genteel day schools to which he was sent, he did not think that either of them would have noticed.

Mrs Shaw despised her husband who was a failed teetotaller, and she seems to have felt that their son was tainted by a similar ineffectualness. She looked down on all men: except one, 'a mesmeric conductor and daringly original teacher of Music' called George John Vandeleur Lee. The impact of this man on the Shaw household was revolutionary. Having discovered Mrs Shaw to be a fine mezzo-soprano, he trained her voice, made her the right-hand woman of his Amateur Musical Society and invited the Shaws to share both his smart house in Dublin and his seaside cottage at Dalkey. He banished family prayers, reduced Mr Shaw to nullity and filled the house with music. The ménage-à-trois was all the more remarkable in the strict caste society of Ireland since Lee was Catholic and the Shaws Protestant. But in 1873, in rather dubious circumstances, Lee suddenly left Dublin for London. A fortnight later, on her twenty-first wedding anniversary, Mrs Shaw followed him. Though she was to bring both her daughters to live with her, she left 'Sonny' (as he had been called) in lodging with her husband. It was then, turning deprivation to advantage, that Shaw taught himself music from textbooks and the piano. After leaving school in 1871 he had become a junior clerk in 'a highly exclusive gentlemanly estate office', Uniacke Townshend & Co. Early in 1876 he resigned and, one of his sisters having died, went to take her room in his mother's home in London.

These first twenty years in Ireland had left Shaw bereft of all passions except two: the passion of laughter and a passion for reform. His early experiences were to control to an extraordinary degree the range and tone of his work. The art of paradox, which turned tragedy on its head and fulfilled a moral obligation to optimism, became his 'criticism of life'. Believing that he had inherited from his father the tendency to an obsession, he transferred it from drink to work, making himself, as he said, into a writing-machine. For professional purposes he dropped the name George (so uncomfortably shared by Lee and his father) and created a public being, G.B.S., a 'pantomime ostrich' which was modelled on the example of Lee whom he depicted as a phenomenon too impersonal to attact affection, but whose mercurial personality had won him the admiration, so much sought after by Sonny, of Mrs Shaw.

Shaw's progress in London at setting himself up as 'a professional man of genius' was dismayingly slow, and over the first nine years he calculated that he had earned less than ten pounds. 'I did not throw myself into the struggle for life: I threw my mother into it. I was not a staff to my father's old age: I hung on to his coat tails.' In this period he wrote five novels that were rejected by every publisher, though four of them eventually achieved publication in socialist magazines.

In 1884 Shaw joined the Fabian Society which, up to the First World War, often by means of permeating the Tories and Liberals with its socialist ideas, chiefly expressed the opinions of Shaw and Sidney Webb*. The Fabian Society became Shaw's new family and his socialist reforms a means of changing society so that no child should have to go through the sort of upbringing he had endured. Believing himself to be unlovable, he made out of Collectivism a weapon against individualist romantic propaganda. Shaw's socialism was composed of the abolition of private property plus the introduction of equality of income. To this, as a refinement to democracy, aimed at achieving efficiency and real adult suffrage, he proposed adding the Coupled Vote – every valid vote going to a man-and-woman. Shaw's socialism, which invades many of his plays and much of his journalism, found its outlet in numerous Fabian Tracts (of which he made a selection in *Essays in Fabian Socialism*), in *The Intelligent Woman's Guide to Socialism and Capitalism* (1928) and *Everybody's*

Political What's What (1944). Shaw also spent a great deal of time speaking at street corners and working on committees, but eventually concluded that William Morris was right and that it had not been practical for socialists to enter the circus of party politics. Shaw believed that the Labour Party, so far from being a force for socialism against capitalism, was a trade union party dedicated to fighting the employer's federations in a new class war. A measure of his disenchantment with British politics may be seen from his enthusiasm for Soviet Russia which he visited in 1931 and advertised on his return as an experimental Fabian colony.

Shaw was known as a journalist and critic long before he became famous as a playwright. His art reviews in *Our Corner* and the *World* (1885–9), though mainly anonymous, made him well-known among his colleagues; while his celebrated musical criticism, first as 'Corno di Bassetto' in the *Star* (1888–90) and then as 'G.B.S.' in the *World* (1890–4), extended his fame. From 1895 to 1898 he contributed theatre criticism to the *Saturday Review*, making outrageous use of Shakespeare (whose politics, he claimed, 'would hardly impress the Thames Conservancy Board') to promote his campaign for a revolution on the late-Victorian stage. According to his successor Max Beerbohm*, he had become 'the most brilliant and remarkable journalist in London'.

But most critics agreed that he would have made a 'better Bishop than a playwright'. Almost all of them acknowledged that he could produce entertaining prose extravaganzas (*Arms and the Man*, *You Never Can Tell*), but they were based not on human emotions but piles of bluebooks, tracts, social statistics (*Widowers' Houses*, *Mrs Warren's Profession*). Sometimes these compositions, amalgams of lecture and farce, the critics conceded, were almost as good as plays.

Success did not finally come until, during the Vedrenne–Barker management at the Court Theatre, the special furniture hired for a royal command performance of *John Bull's Other Island* on 11 March 1905 crashed beneath the King who was laughing too hard and flung Shaw's reputation high into the air. Despite his efforts to do so ('I am not in the popular entertainment business'), Shaw never fully recovered his unpopularity. *Fanny's First Play* ran for 622 performances in London (1912–13), and the number of revivals of *Pygmalion* (1913) and *Saint Joan* (1923) established him as a box-office success throughout the world.

But under the sparkle and to one side of the sermonizing lay an ingenious Shavian theme. He believed that he had inherited from his parents incompatible qualities that he must reconcile within himself. In *The Quintessence of Ibsenism* (1891) he had stressed the importance of efficiency over aspiration, but in later writings such as *Candida* (1894) and *The Perfect Wagnerite* (1898) he tried to expand this pragmatism so that it might serve not just a social but a religious purpose. From this process emerged his concept of the Life Force which is not a symbol of power but a unit of synthesis. With this new religion came new drama in which, as a series of parables, Shaw rewrote past history and tried to navigate a course for the future. The synthesis of *Man and Superman* (1903) was a fantasy, and when in *John Bull's Other Island* (1904) and *Major Barbara* (1905) he tried to apply it to actual life he found that he could not reconcile all the separated elements. Like a conjuror with too many objects revolving in the air, he had to dispense with something and, in *Back to Methuselah* (1924), it was the body that he eliminated. In later years Shaw lusted after a non-physical consummation – 'all life and no matter' – between earth and heaven. That man would have to change out of all recognition or be superseded by another species did not cause him to despair, for he had increasingly turned his attention away from the individual and the body as a vehicle of emotion. At times, like Ellie Dunn at the end of *Heartbreak House* (1919), he appears 'radiant at the prospect' of the human species being scrapped, and the Life Force taking another mate.

Shaw did not stop short at rewriting the past: he re-enacted it. Many of his affairs with women were three-cornered, often with the wife of some socialist friend. Shaw flirted, but never made love to anyone's wife. He acted his own version of Lee in other people's households – a sort of Sunday husband. In these relationships he was seeking a second childhood in which he received all the attention he had been denied. His liaisons became part of his theatrical life, the excitement producing an ejaculation of words from which plays were born. In 1898 he married Charlotte Payne Townshend, 'my green-eyed millionairess', who came from the same family as the Dublin estate agents. At Charlotte's request it was a *mariage blanc*. In their fashion they loved each other and when Charlotte died in 1943 Shaw was grief-stricken. Her death had been a great loss to him, he admitted; then at the last moment he turned it into a Shavian joke – 'a great financial loss'.

Michael Holroyd

The most complete edition of Shaw's work was the Standard Edition in 36 volumes published under the imprint of Constable between 1931 and 1951. His authorized publisher today is the Bodley Head which between 1970 and 1974 brought out his *Collected Plays and their Prefaces* in 7 volumes and so far 2 volumes of a 4-volume edition of his *Collected Letters* (1965, 1972), ed. Dan H. Laurence, who is also preparing the definitive bibliography. Among the many biographies, those by St John Ervine (1956) and Hesketh Pearson (1942, revised 1961) may be recommended. See also: Eric Bentley, *Shaw* (1946, revised 1957); Martin Meisel, *Shaw and the Nineteenth*

Century Theatre (1963); J. M. Wisenthal, *The Marriage of Contraries* (1974); Alfred Turco Jr, *Shaw's Moral Vision* (1976); *The Genius of Shaw*, ed. Michael Holroyd (1979). *Bernard Shaw and Mrs Patrick Campbell: Their Correspondence*, ed. Alan Dent (1952); *Ellen Terry and Bernard Shaw – A Correspondence*, ed. Christopher St John (1931).

433

SHOLOKHOV, Mikhail Aleksandrovich 1905–

Russian novelist

Mikhail Sholokhov's novel *And Quiet Flows the Don* (*Tikhiy Don*) has been unique in the acclaim which it has received from public and critics in both the Soviet Union and the West. Grigory, the main hero of the novel, is a figure with whom many can feel sympathy; however little a contemporary reader might seem to have in common with a Cossack struggling through the horrors of the Russian civil war, he presents with anguished sharpness the bitter choice confronting those who were attracted by the ideal of Communism and at the same time repelled by the barbarity and ruthlessness of Bolshevik practice.

In 1925 Sholokhov embarked on the formidable task of explaining the role of the Cossaks in the revolution. The Russians traditionally regarded them as willing servants of the tsars in suppressing any stirrings of dissent, but in 1917 the Cossacks refused to side with the right-wing parties. Fear that they might lose their prosperous landholdings made them reluctant to identify completely with the Red cause and Grigory found himself involved in a hopeless rebellion against Soviet power in the central Don area. All the complex political dilemmas of the Cossacks are reflected in his waverings and heart-searchings. Sholokhov has given a remarkably accurate account of the war, which he witnessed in his homeland, and has placed his hero at the centre of conflicts of class and local allegiances which threaten to destroy his personality.

Although *Tikhiy Don* depicts faithfully the shattering of the old Cossack traditions in the years from 1912 to 1922, the work rests its main reputation on its success as imaginative fiction. In contrast to those who were brutalized by the endless carnage Grigory becomes increasingly sensitive and noble, but his development seems valid thanks to Sholokhov's abundant use of concrete detail. He is shown throughout the novel in ever-changing relationships with all too human members of his village and his openly declared attachment with Aksin'ya breaks even the free conventions of Cossack society

The author found great difficulty in finishing the novel, but eventually in 1940 published the last part in which Grigory is driven to final surrender to Bolshevik power. By this time Sholokhov had been given official recognition as a leading Soviet writer and did not suffer for his refusal to provide a trite ending at a time when literature was expected to serve as an arm of propaganda for official optimism. Instead the more orthodox critics tried to explain that the tragedy of Grigory must be set agains the triumph of the new era which was dawning. Oceans of ink have been spent on this classic Soviet novel; with the less artificial climate which came in after Stalin's* death there has been general recognition that as a reaction away from the 'anti-psychologism' of the early 1920s Sholokhov was returning to the traditions of the nineteenth-century – on which he had principally been nurtured after leaving school at the age of thirteen – and that Grigory's downfall followed the classical recipe for a tragic hero who is destroyed not by his weaknesses but by his positive qualities.

None of Sholokhov's other works can approach *Tikhiy Don* for literary merit, though *Virgin Soil Upturned* (*Podnyataya tselina*) has been successful with Soviet readers, and the first part in particular contains some striking scenes on the collectivization of agriculture. As a young man Sholokhov had considerable difficulty in getting his work published without heavy cutting and distortion – and indeed the 1953 edition of *Tikhiy Don* was shamelessly bowdlerized throughout. Rumours were started that he had plagiarized the novel and these have been persistently revived, though no hard evidence ever seems to have been produced to support them.

Sholokhov has not felt kindly disposed towards many members of the Moscow intelligentsia and has lived the greater part of his life at Vyoshenskaya on the middle course of the Don near the village where he was born. Showered with honours by the State and the recipient of the Nobel Prize for Literature in 1965 he has generally taken a hard line against any dissident voices in literature and furthered the cause of conservative careerists aspiring to positions of power in the literary hierarchy. Most Russians acknowledge his achievement as the leading writer on the civil war, though many would attack his role in public life.

Professor A. B. Murphy

Tikhiy Don in four 'books', was published over twelve years, from 1928 to 1940. It was translated in two volumes, *And Quiet Flows the Don* (1934) and *The Don Flows Home to the Sea* (1940); but an English translation of the entire text *And Quiet Flows the Don*, has been issued in Moscow (1960). *Podnyataya tselina* (1932–60) has been similarly dismembered into *Virgin Soil Upturned* (1959) and *Harvest on the Don* (1961). Sholokhov's other work includes *Tales from the Don* (*Donskiye rasskazy*, 1926, trans. 1961). See also: D. H. Stewart, *Mikhail Sholokhov – a Critical Introduction* (1967); L. Yakimenko, *Sholokhov: A Critical Appreciation* (trans. 1973); and A. B. Murphy, M. Duncan, V. Swoboda and V. P. Butt, 'A Commentary on *Tikhiy Don*' (in *New Zealand Slavonic Review*, from 1975).

434

SHOSTAKOVITCH, Dmitri Dmitrievitch 1906–75

Russian composer

Shostakovitch was born in St Petersburg and took piano lessons from the age of nine. It soon became clear that he had exceptional talent and in 1919 he was enrolled at the Conservatoire in that city (by this time renamed Petrograd). He was obliged to support his family by playing for silent films but nevertheless completed his course with a First Symphony (1925) so well received that it immediately became part of the repertoire, first in Russia and then abroad, a position it has maintained to the present.

It revealed the composer as open to much of the exploratory music being written in the West at the time – Hindemith's* and Berg's* in particular – as well as reflecting the conflicting Russian traditions: symphonic in the manner of Tchaikovsky and more Russophile after the example of the Five, the famous nineteenth-century group of composers, amongst whom Rimsky-Korsakov had been prominent. The latter's son-in-law, M. Steinberg, had been Shostakovitch's composition teacher.

Shostakovitch graduated as a pianist as well as composer and after leaving the Conservatoire won a prize at a recital contest in Warsaw and gave concerts throughout Russia. Composition remained of paramount importance to him, however, although he continued to give recitals, principally involving his own music, throughout his career.

In the late 1920s Shostakovitch's musical modernism continued in the Second and Third Symphony, the ballets *The Golden Age* (1930) and *The Bolt* (1931), and the operas *The Nose* (1930) and *Lady Macbeth of Mtensk* (1934). Two current tendencies were present in Soviet music at the time – the 'proletarian' which insisted that music should be widely comprehensible and the 'modernistic' which asserted that revolution in art should accompany revolution in society. Both tendencies had their associations and both were wound up in the early 1930s as the ideas of Socialist Realism were formulated.

Shostakovitch inclined towards the modernistic tendency but there are clear signs of stylistic crisis in his Fourth Symphony (withdrawn during rehearsal in 1936). An unwieldy and discursive structure supports a language that is not fully coherent and this problem, together with an article 'Chaos instead of Music', which appeared in *Pravda* in 1936, concerning his opera

Lady Macbeth of Mtensk, forced on him a retrenchment and reconsideration.

Starting with the Fifth Symphony (1937) his style becomes clearer and more traditional but equally more personal. Long-range tonal organization deriving from classical practice is allied with a detailed concentration on motif usually expressed in traditional forms. He turned to chamber music at this time beginning his series of string quartets and producing two definitive works in piano chamber music – the Piano Quintet (1940) and the Piano Trio (1944). Both won Stalin* prizes as did the Seventh Symphony (1941), the *Leningrad* composed and premiered under conditions of great privation during the German siege of that city. This work became the musical symbol of the Russian resistance when performed in concerts in the USA and unoccupied Europe.

At the end of the war Shostakovitch failed to produce a victory symphony: instead his Ninth, perhaps from fear of comparison with Beethoven's, was a *jeu d'esprit* that revealed nothing of the horrors of the previous years. This failure possibly contributed towards a government intervention in music in 1948 as the state's duty to have concern for all aspects of cultural life was reasserted. Between then and 1953 Shostakovitch produced two types of work – the public, e.g. film scores, which won him Stalin Prizes and the title People's Artist, and the private, including the First Violin Concerto (1948) and the song cycle *From Jewish Folk Poetry*. Neither of the latter was released until 1953; at the same time the Tenth Symphony was performed.

Although still within a traditional idiom these works reveal a widening of the language and a willingness to experiment a little with structure and with the success of these pieces Shostakovitch's final period was set. He turned increasingly towards the more personal medium of the string quartet and produced many fine works in this genre: 7 and 8 (both from 1960), 12 (1968) and 13 (1970) and 15 (1974) are particularly remarkable pieces. Those dating from the late 1960s reveal an interest in twelve-note technique (cf. Schoenberg*), always used within a diatonic context as a deepening of the expressive power of the music.

More public music from this period utilized the virtuosity of Russian performers, e.g. Oistrakh in the two Violin Concertos (the Second dating from 1967), und Rostropovitch in two Cello Concertos (1958 and 1967), or, alternatively, involved text in an exposition of the composer's increasing obsession with death.

In their various ways the Thirteenth and Fourteenth Symphonies (1962 and 1969) and *Suite to Poems by Michelangelo* (1974) make explicit a despair left implicit in the brooding chamber music of the time and, although honours continued to be showered on him both at home and abroad, the music of his last works is largely powerfully depressive, the more so for being contained within clearly defined structures.

In the context of European music Shostakovitch was a conservative, like Britten*, whose music he admired. But Schoenberg had said there was much good music still to be written in C major and Shostakovitch undoubtedly contributed much to this quantity. In the field of Russian music he was the first internationally acclaimed musical talent to emerge from the Soviet Union and was its most prominent representative throughout his career. Because of the interventionist nature of its government his career may also function as a touchstone for relationships between music and society: a relationship that, in Shostakovitch's case, was not always of the happiest.

Malcolm Barry

Other works include: two Piano Concertos (1933 and 1957); *24 Preludes and Fugues* for piano (1951); and the choral work *The Execution of Stepan Razin* (1964). See : D. Rabinovich, *Dmitri Shostakovitch* (1959); N. Kay, *Shostakovitch* (1971); R. Blokker with R. Dearling, *The Music of Shostakovitch* (1979); *Testimony: the Memoirs of Shostakovitch*, ed. S. Volkov (1979). See also: Boris Schwarz, *Music and Musical Life in Soviet Russia 1917–70* (1972).

435
SIBELIUS, Jean 1865–1957

Finnish composer

Jean Sibelius is Finland's greatest composer and a master of the symphony. His music bears witness to an all-consuming love of the nordic landscape and a preoccupation with its mythology, and more particularly, the repository of myth enshrined in the Finnish national epic, the *Kalevala*. Born in Hämeenlinna in Finland, he was christened Johan Julius Christian but subsequently Gallicized it, on discovering a set of visiting cards used by a sea-faring uncle who had adopted this form of the name. He showed an early talent for the violin and little interest in the law studies to which his family had set him. After some years in Helsinki as a pupil of Martin Wegelius, with whom he studied composition, he went abroad to Berlin in 1889 and the following year to Vienna, where he became a pupil of Goldmark. Up to this time his output comprised chamber music as opportunities to compose for the orchestra had been few. Helsinki did not possess a permanent symphony orchestra until 1888.

The *Kullervo Symphony*, an ambitious seventy-minute, five-movement work for soloists, male chorus and orchestra, put him on the map in 1892, and together with *En Saga* (1893), *Karelia* (1893) and the *Four Legends* (1895) established him as the leading figure in Finnish music. His popularity abroad began to grow a decade later with such works as *Finlandia* (1900) and *Valse triste*

(1903). The 1890s show him developing as a nationalist composer, working within the Romantic musical tradition and responding positively to the influence of Tchaikovsky. His student works also show the influence of the Viennese classics and, of course, Grieg. After the Second Symphony (1902) and the Violin Concerto (1903, revised 1905), he moved away from the climate of post-Romanticism towards a more austere and classical language. His instinctive feeling for the Viennese classics strengthened, and works such as *Pohjola's Daughter* (1906) and the Third Symphony (1904–7) show a classicism at variance with the spirit of their time. In 1907 Mahler visited Helsinki and their oft-quoted exchange on the nature of the symphony reveals the difference of emphasis in their approach to the form. Sibelius said he admired 'its severity and style, and the profound logic that created an inner connection between all the motifs', to which Mahler replied, 'No, for me the symphony must be like the world: it must embrace everything.'

Championed by conductors, such as his countryman Robert Kajanus, Hans Richter, Sir Henry Wood and others, as well as such important critics as Rosa Newmarch and Ernest Newman, Sibelius's music gradually won acceptance both in England and America. In 1899 he had acquired the German publisher, Breitkopf and Härtel, and made numerous visits to both Germany and Italy. Busoni* was among the figures who championed his music; he conducted both the Second Symphony and *Pohjola's Daughter* in Berlin. In 1909 Sibelius was operated on for a throat tumour, which may account for the greater austerity and depth of his Fourth Symphony (1911), as well as the greater seriousness and concentration of such scores as *The Bard* and *Luonnotar*.

With the outbreak of the First World War in 1914 he was cut off from his German royalties. He composed during this period a large number of light instrumental pieces in the hope of repeating the great success of *Valse triste*, the rights to which he had sold on derisory terms. From the war years comes the Fifth Symphony (1915), which he twice revised and which reached its definitive form only in 1919. The voyage from the climate of Slav romanticism that had fostered the First Symphony (1899) into the wholly isolated and profoundly original world of the Sixth (1923) and Seventh (1924), at a time when the mainstream of music was moving in other directions, was one of courageous spiritual discovery. Like all great artists, Sibelius's approach to the symphony is never the same. From the vantage point of the Fourth, it would be impossible to foretell the shape and character of the Fifth. Likewise, the Sixth is wholly unpredictable a phenomenon when viewed from the achievement of its predecessor, and in terms of the musical climate of the 1920s. There is no set of prescriptive rules for any Sibelius symphony: each differs from the other and from the genre as a whole. The Seventh's one movement is completely original in form, subtle in its handling of tempi, individual in its treatment of key and wholly organic in growth.

Tapiola (1926), in which his lifework culminated, united the symphonic process with his lifelong preoccupation with nature and myth. The sheer stature of the seven symphonies overshadowed Sibelius's achievement in the field of the tone-poem. This genre occupied him throughout his creative life and his contribution to its literature is no less important than that of Liszt and Richard Strauss*. Incidental music for the stage also constitutes an important part of his output and culminated in the ambitious and imaginative score he composed for the 1926 production of *The Tempest*. This saw the end of his creative career though it is almost certain that an Eighth Symphony was composed and subsequently destroyed. After the 1920s, Sibelius gave up conducting and travelling and retired to the isolation of his home in Järvenpää, some miles outside Helsinki.

Robert Layton

See: Cecil Gray, *Sibelius: The Symphonies* (1931); Gerald Abraham (ed.), *Sibelius: A Symposium* (1947); Robert Layton, *Sibelius* (1965) and *Sibelius and his World* (1970); Erik Tawaststhaerna, *Sibelius* (1968, trans. 1976); see also F. Blum, *Jean Sibelius: An International Bibliography on the Occasion of the Centennial Celebration* (1965).

436

SILONE, Ignazio (Secondo Tranquilli) 1900–78

Italian writer

Ignazio Silone came from humble farming origins in the Abruzzi mountains. His family, with the exception of one brother, were killed in an earthquake when he was fifteen. He identified intensely with the sufferings of the peasantry, and through his activism on their behalf soon reached the position of leader of the Youth Movement of the Italian Socialist Party. By 1926 he was leader of the clandestine organization of the Communist Party under the fascist dictatorship, but eventually left the party in disgust over the policies of Stalin*. In *Emergency Exit* (*Uscita di sicurezza*, 1965, trans. 1968) he explains that his membership of the party was a matter of choosing to live and work with those men who were struggling for justice and humanity. It was not an ideological choice but a moral one. He discovered, however, that in choosing his companions he was getting caught up in their theoretical and factional struggles, and was losing sight of the needs of the Italian peasantry. This caused a conflict in Silone which was the central event of his life as man and as writer.

His first novel, *Fontamara* (1930, trans. 1934), was an attempt to carry on in some way, from exile in Switzerland, the work he could no longer do in the clandestine party in Italy. It tells of a village in which the peasants are abused by the local bourgeoisie and by the fascist state. It traces the development of a clear-sighted political conscience in one villager, who sacrifices himself in order that the other villagers might achieve a similar consciousness. The next novel, *Bread and Wine* (*Pane e vino*, 1937, trans. 1937), tells how a young communist on the run from the fascists learns to know and love the peasants in whose name he became a communist, and how he falls out with the party over its Stalinism. Faced with the impossibility of defeating fascism alone, and his inability to work within the organized party, he concludes that the answer is to develop his own humanity: moral conscience based on love for his fellow men.

Silone's principles are by now closer to those of Christ than those of Marx. Indeed, one of his later books, a play, *The Story of a Humble Christian* (*L'avventura di un povero cristiano*, 1968, trans. 1970), is based on the life of another Abruzzese, Pietro da Morrone, a saintly man elected Pope Celestine V, who abdicated because the papal crown imposed on him intolerable conflicts with his principles.

Silone re-entered politics at the end of the war, as one of the leaders of the Socialist Party (PSIUP) and as editor of *Avanti!*, Italy's most widely read newspaper at that moment, but he withdrew again in 1948. He later edited the monthly *Tempo Presente* from 1956 to 1968. One of his artistically most accomplished novels, *A Handful of Blackberries* (*Una manciata di more*, 1952, trans. 1954), examines the repressive role of the Communist Party bureaucracy in Italy in the aftermath of the war, and again portrays a man choosing between the party and the suffering human beings with whom he feels a bond.

Two things have conspired to produce a situation in which Silone has been far more widely appreciated abroad than in Italy. First, his novels are not written in the precious style that the Italian literary establishment values. Second, he admits to both Christian and Socialist ideals, making himself something of an embarrassment in both camps. Only recently has the respect accorded him in Europe and the US (for which there are ideological explanations) led the Italians to question their neglect of him.

All Silone's writings are attempts to understand himself and to make contact, through that understanding, with other people. In all of them there is an element of the thriller, with the characters working and living in hiding of some sort, and they are all political works, dealing with the central issues of what a man is to do in the here and now. But most of all, they are exami-

nations of conscience sparked off by close human contacts. For Silone writing was at once a political act and an offer of companionship.

Christopher Wagstaff

Other important works: *The Seed Beneath the Snow* (*Il seme sotto la neve*, 1940, trans. 1942); *The Secret of Luca* (*Il segreto di Luca*, 1956, trans. 1958); *La volpe e le camelie* ('The Fox and the Camellias', 1960). See: R. W. B. Lewis, *The Picaresque Saint* (1959); Luce D'Eramo, *L'opera di Ignazio Silone* (1971).

437
SIMMEL, Georg 1858–1918

German philosopher and sociologist

Born in the very heart of Berlin, Simmel stayed in that thriving commercial and cultural centre until 1914. Quite an urbane 'Berliner' – and 'The Metropolis and Mental Life' ('Die Grosstädte und das Geistesleben', 1903) is perhaps the most genial essay on modern urban culture ever written – Simmel became a symbol of intellectual modernity in a milieu stifled by Wilhelmian pomp, Prussian bureaucracy, and professorial rigidities, yet pulsating with intellectual and political counter-currents. Through prolific writings, virtuoso lecturing, and cultivated salons hosted with his wife Gertrud, herself an accomplished philosophical writer, Simmel became a magnet for Berlin's intellectual elite in the two decades preceding the First World War.

Simmel's parents stemmed from the Jewish community of Wroclaw (Breslau). Before they married and moved to Berlin his mother converted to Protestantism, his father, while travelling in Paris on business, to Catholicism. Georg, the youngest of seven offspring, was baptized in his mother's faith. Often described as Jewish in intellectual style and physical mannerisms Simmel rarely expressed any affinity with his ancestral traditions, though he did once confess to the Jewish philosopher Martin Buber*, 'We really are a remarkable people.' Despite his Protestant affiliation, expressed anti-Semitism was a factor in keeping him from a regular academic post for nearly all of his career.

The academic establishment also frowned on Simmel's apparent dilettantism. A person of wide-ranging aesthetic as well as philosophic interests, Simmel studied piano and violin and wrote on the history of music, befriended Germany's leading poets Rainer Maria Rilke* and Stefan George, corresponded with the French sculptor Auguste Rodin, and published memorable essays on the theatre and on Michelangelo and Rembrandt. His scholarly work was often reproached for its 'aestheticism'.

When Simmel was sixteen his father died; his guardian, the musical publisher Julius Friedländer who founded the famed 'Edition Peters', bequeathed him fortune enough to live comfortably despite the fragility of his academic status. The combination of religious and academic marginality with independent means fortified Simmel's disposition to pursue work noted for its individuality and earned him the reputation of a 'brilliant gadfly'.

After studying history, psychology, anthropology and philosophy at the University of Berlin, where his mentors included such luminaries as Mommsen, Treitschke, Droysen, Grimm, Lazarus and Bastian, Simmel established himself as a philosopher with a dissertation on Kant (1881) and a few years later began to offer courses on ethics, epistemology, and aesthetics as an unsalaried lecturer at his alma mater. His two major early works were *The Problems of the Philosophy of History* (*Die Probleme der Geschichtsphilosophie*, 1892, revised 1905 and 1907, trans. 1977) and *Einleitung in die Moralwissenschaft* ('Introduction to the Science of Ethics', 2 vols, 1892–3). Both works reflect his longstanding concern to adapt the formulations of Kant to the problems of contemporary philosophy. His *Kant: Sechzehn Vorlesungen* ('Lectures on Kant', 1904) remains a fresh and distinctive interpretation of that philosopher; characteristically, he observed that the book was 'not only one by Simmel about Kant, but also by Kant about Simmel'.

Simmel's most profound work was *The Philosophy of Money* (*Philosophie des Geldes*, 1900, enlarged 1907, trans. 1978). It begins with a tightly argued formulation of a 'relativistic' metaphysics and epistemology, and goes on to develop a speculative interpretation of the effects of a money economy on modern culture. These effects include an accentuation of man's capacity for rational calculation and an enormous expansion of the domain of human freedom, and at the same time a pervasive moral deracination and the manufacture of cultural products which are alienated from the absorptive capacities of human consumers. In his later years, under the impact of Bergson*, but with renewed interest in Goethe, Schopenhauer, and Nietzsche as well, his chief project was to articulate a philosophy of life. In *Lebensanschauung: Vier Metaphysische Kapitel* ('View of Life: Four Metaphysical Chapters', 1918; chapter 1 trans. in D. N. Levine, 1971) he argued that an essential characteristic of human life is the propensity both to create novel forms and then to attack those forms as obstructions to the life process, and that death should be regarded not as the termination of life but as an integral dimension of life itself.

In Germany Simmel was known chiefly as a neo-Kantian, a philosopher of culture or a philosopher of life and as such his influence on the major German thinkers of this century – including Ernst Cassirer, Edmund Husserl*, Max Weber*, Max Scheler, Alfred Schutz, Albert Schweitzer, Ernst Bloch*, Georg Lukács* and Max Horkheimer* – has been amply documented. Outside Germany, however, he was and is known chiefly for his work as a seminal sociologist, indeed one of the pantheon of founding fathers of modern sociology along with Émile Durkheim* and Max Weber.

Simmel began to lecture on sociological topics in 1887 and published his first sociological monograph, *Über soziale Differenzierung* ('On Social Differentiation'), in 1890. In that work and again in 'Das Problem der Soziologie' ('The Problem of Sociology', 1894) Simmel staked out a programme for sociology he would follow the rest of his life: one which conceived sociology as an abstract discipline devoted to analysing the diverse forms of social interaction, forms such as exchange, conflict, super- and subordination, secrecy and honour. For this view of the field he is often labelled a 'formal sociologist'. His major work in this vein was published in *Soziologie: Untersuchungen über die Formen der Vergesellschaftung* ('Sociology: Studies of the Forms of Association', 1908), a work which continues to stimulate sociological investigators. Especially well known are its discussion of the ways social conflict produces group cohesion, its analysis of the effect of group size on modes of interaction, and its depiction of social types like 'the stranger', 'the poor', 'the mediator' and 'the renegade'. Its most striking features include the attempt to apply the Kantian notion of *a priori* categories to the domain of social interaction, and the direction of sociological attention to the phenomenology of everyday interaction. Simmel's delineation of what persons experience in sociable gatherings, when exchanging letters, or in relationships coloured by jealousy or gratitude has helped inspire scholars to create what is known now as the 'sociology of everyday life'.

Simmel's sociological writings won him immediate attention in other countries and were promptly translated into several foreign languages. His impact was greatest in the United States, thanks largely to the efforts of sociologists Albion Small and Robert Park* at the University of Chicago. He was also a major influence on German sociology in the 1920s.

Despite this record of achievement and the constant support of leading German academics like Weber, Rickert and Husserl, Simmel was consistently denied a regular appointment in the German university system. Only in 1914, four years before his death, did one materialize at the University of Strasbourg. He lectured there for but one semester when the outbreak of war closed down the lecture halls. The war fired his German nationalism: Simmel lapsed into uncharacteristic sentimentality about its energizing potential and publicly abetted the German war effort. Yet the civilized philosopher in him was not wholly subdued. In the *Berliner Tageblatt* of 7 March 1915 he dared to publish a luminous article on 'The Idea of Europe', in which he scorned 'the blindness and criminal frivolity of a handful of Europeans' for sparking off a war which entailed 'the suicidal destruction of existing European values', and tried to discern some way in which the idea of Europe might yet survive as a 'locus of spiritual values which the contemporary cultured man reveres'.

Professor Donald N. Levine

Other works: *Kant and Goethe* (1906); *The Sociology of Religion* (*Die Religion*, 1906, trans. 1959); *Schopenhauer und Nietzsche* (1907); *Hauptprobleme der Philosophie* (1910); *Philosophische Kultur* (1911); *Goethe* (1913); *Fundamental Problems of Sociology* (*Grundfragen der Soziologie*, 1917, trans. 1950); *Der Krieg und die geistigen Entscheidungen* (1917); *Zur Philosophie der Kunst* (1922). Anthologies: K. H. Wolff, *The Sociology of Georg Simmel* (1950); D. N. Levine, *Georg Simmel on Individuality and Social Forms* (1971); P. Lawrence, *Georg Simmel: Sociologist and European* (1976). On Simmel: N. Spykman, *The Social Theory of Georg Simmel* (1925); R. Weingartner, *Experience and Culture: The Philosophy of Georg Simmel* (1962); D. N. Levine *et al.*, 'Simmel's Influence on American Sociology' in *American Journal of Sociology*, 81 (January and March 1976); L. Coser, 'Georg Simmel' in *Masters of Sociological Thought* (1977).

438
SIRK, Douglas 1900–

German/US film director

It was only in the 1970s that the genius of Douglas Sirk was recognized. Even in his last years at Universal, when films like *All That Heaven Allows* (1955) and *Imitation of Life* (1959) were huge commercial successes, his mastery was ignored. His work, however, is important not only in itself as the richest body of melodrama to emerge from Hollywood, but also in terms of the complex aesthetic and stylistic questions it raises.

Sirk himself is the locus of many contradictions. Of all the German émigré population in Hollywood, Sirk was arguably the one most fascinated and stimulated by American culture. Yet he brought to Hollywood a breathtaking knowledge of European avant-garde theatre of the 1920s, painting, poetry and music.

Hans Detlef Sierck was born in Hamburg of Danish parents. After spending his early childhood in Skagen, he returned to Hamburg. His university education was wide-reaching: law in Munich, philosophy in Jena, and finally art history in Hamburg, where he studied under Erwin Panovsky. His mastery of lighting, composition and set-design undoubtedly owes much to this period. Another important formative experience was in Munich in 1919, when he witnessed the short-lived Bavarian Soviet, the only revolution to be masterminded and led by poets and intellectuals.

He entered the theatre in 1920, as a second-line *dramaturg* at the Deutsches Schauspielhaus, Hamburg. From 1923 to 1929, he was artistic director at the Schauspielhaus, Bremen, followed by seven years as *Direktor* at the Altes Theater, Leipzig. He proved an extremely gifted theatrical director, already demonstrating his ability to transform and to transcend awkward material. His knowledge of the structure of classical drama stemming from his productions of Molière, Shakespeare, Büchner and others, was to prove invaluable in enabling him to shape the intractable material with which he was confronted in Hollywood.

In 1934, his production of Shakespeare's *Twelfth Night* at the Berlin Volksbühne led to an invitation to join UFA, the leading German film studio. In spite of his left-wing reputation and the political controversy surrounding his period at Leipzig, Sierck was allowed considerable freedom at UFA. In his early films there (like *April, April*, 1935), he immediately displayed his extraordinary ability to transform recalcitrant material into something substantial and outstanding. His second feature, *Das Mädchen vom Moorhof* (1935), already filmed by Victor Sjöström, revealed many of what were to become Sirkian trademarks: the use of mirror shots, the dismantling of suspense and the theme of the exposure of hypocrisy.

His decision to make *Schlussakkord* (1936) was a landmark in his career, for in choosing an atrociously mawkish story on which he would make a full-blooded assault, he was breaking away from literary values to pursue the purely cinematic. He also made other major melodramas in Germany in 1937: *Zu Neuen Ufern*, which transformed Swedish actress Zarah Leander into a star, and *La Habanera*. In these tough, anti-colonialist films, he showed a mastery of the medium that was to be apparent in his later Hollywood masterpieces, *Written on the Wind* (1956) and *The Tarnished Angels* (1957).

In December 1937, Douglas Sirk (as he became known) left Germany for Hollywood, via Paris and Holland. After a difficult period at Columbia under the idiosyncratic Harry Cohn, and a happier period alfalfa farming, he signed with Universal in 1950. As 'house director', he had little control over the choice of projects, but could at least restructure material, shoot and edit as he wished. Only when maverick producer Albert Zugsmith spent a brief period at Universal was Sirk able to pursue two projects of his own choice: *The Tarnished Angels*, an adaptation of William Faulkner's* novel of the Depression, *Pylon*, and *Written on the Wind*. To understand Sirk, it is instructive to compare these two masterpieces with the films he made with producer Ross Hunter, like *All That Heaven Allows* and *Imitation of Life*. All four are brilliant films, yet in those produced by Hunter, Sirk somehow triumphs over the material: in those produced by Zugsmith, he has the freedom to express his personal vision of America. Ross Hunter imposed on Sirk 'happy endings' which were at variance with Sirk's leanings towards themes of despair and disintegration, and which result in irony. In *The Tarnished Angels* and *Written on the Wind*, Sirk could follow through his vision of men and women driven to extremes in a society on the point of collapse. Both films deal with breakdown and with failure. In the latter, images of infirmity, of alcoholism, of sexual frustration and of fear of sterility abound. Throughout his work, images of illness recur, with individual illness representing social breakdown. Problems of vision also predominate, as characters suffer from blindness, or fail to see themselves, or others, clearly. Sirk's use of mirrors throughout his films also underlines this theme, suggestive too of the surfaces within which the characters are trapped.

Sirk believed that criticism and comment in art should be distanced, and that melodrama was the ideal genre at that particular historical conjecture to express his views on American society. He respected the rules of the genre, and used it to expose mercilessly the hypocrisy and deceit of Eisenhowerian America. His films shatter the complacency of American society in the 1950s, revealing the possibility of imminent collapse.

He was arguably the greatest stylist in Hollywood in the 1950s. In *Imitation of Life*, his last Hollywood film and one of Universal's most successful films commercially, he again succeeded in transcending a dreadful story through brilliant use of lighting, composition, camerawork and music. Sirk left Hollywood in 1958, leaving *Imitation of Life* as his farewell gesture. He returned to Europe, directing theatre in Germany, and teaching film at the Munich Film School. The influence of his work on a new generation of directors, ranging from Rainer Werner Fassbinder to Bernardo Bertolucci, has been increasingly evident during the 1970s.

Linda Miles

See: Jon Halliday, *Sirk on Sirk* (1971).

439
SISSON, Charles Hubert 1914–

English writer

C. H. Sisson was born in Bristol. His was a lower-middle-class family residing in a working-class neighbourhood. By dint of hard work and wide reading, Sisson made his way by scholarships through Bristol University and on to studies on the Continent, in a Germany already mobilizing under the Nazis and in a crumbling Third Republic in France. He returned to England, entered the Civil Service, was sent to India during the war, and on his return ascended in the Civil Service to high administrative rank before retiring in 1973.

His earliest literary work was translations: of stories by Supervielle, poems by Heine, etc. He also contributed, from his twenty-first year, to the *New English Weekly*, developing there, with remarkable consistency, his political and literary thought. Once described as a 'political agnostic', Sisson is certainly a man wary of distorting orthodoxies of left or right. He had a mild flirtation in his university years with the Left, but the English Left, dominated by public school figures, he found a thin and unrealistic movement. In 1978 he wrote, 'The book of all others which confirmed my alienation from the more hopeful leftism of the day was the *Speculations* of T. E. Hulme. To read that book as I read it was to say good-bye for ever to the sentiments of liberalism, if not to its practice, which is something quite different.'

Sisson's political analysis was first tested at length in *The Spirit of British Administration* (1959), widely regarded as a *locus classicus* in considerations of this aspect of British life. Sisson employed a comparative method to draw practical conclusions. His prose, marked by a witty severity, bears close affinities with that of the masters of seventeenth-century writing he most admires, pre-eminently Swift.

The unsentimental and realistic politics he learned from administrative experience as well as from his wide reading in English, French, German and Latin, and which he expressed in his essays and prose books, has its counterpart in his poetics. It was a reading of Ezra Pound* that opened his ears to the rhythms of modern verse, and his affinities with the modernists are close. With Eliot* he has the most intimate and ambivalent relationship. Sisson was as disenchanted with the modish poets of his generation as they – no doubt – were with him. His critical volume *English Poetry 1910–1950* (1971) draws an uncommonly clear map of the first half of the century and with a deft critical particularism achieves convincing and surprising reassessments of established and neglected writers. Outstanding are the advocacies of Edward Thomas, Isaac Rosenberg and Ezra Pound.

Several collections of poems preceded the publication of *In the Trojan Ditch: Collected Poems and Selected Translations* (1974), the book which established Sisson as a leading poet much as *The Avoidance of Literature: Collected Essays* (1978), which incorporates material from the full range of Sisson's critical and analytical work, revealed the breadth of his prose achievement over four decades.

Translation was his ideal apprenticeship and, in later years, his discipline. He has translated Virgil, Horace, Lucretius, Catullus, La Fontaine, Dante and many other writers, and their effect on his verse is marked. The early poems found Heine and honed their edges against his poems. Virgil's influence on the mature and major poems – 'In Insula Avalonia' and 'The Usk', for example – is notable. Sisson found the right poet at the right time. Catullus took him through a difficult transition; and Dante took him to his most recent tones.

Though Sisson can – and has – written with extraordinary skill in conventional rhymed forms, he trusts more to the unexpected rhythms of free verse, establishing a norm and varying it as the poem develops. Yet this suggests too conscious an artifice: Sisson is not an artificer. He has learned to reject whatever 'appears with the face of familiarity', to save prose meanings for prose and to use poetry to discover what he does not know. He is the least literary of modern poets, 'nearest to my own language in sleep': the poet of the transition between sleep and waking, when the contents of the mind are in a fluid state and combine in unexpected yet sometimes momentous ways. It is a memory of Henry Vaughan, the experience of a visit to the Usk river, and several decades of theological study and debate with himself, that produced 'The Usk', a poem Donald Davie characterized as 'one of the great poems of our time' – persuasive in rhythm and in the fusion of diverse experience into a troubled and troubling whole. It included the lines:

> Lies on my tongue. Get up and bolt the door
> For I am coming not to be believed
> The messenger of anything I say.
> So I am come, stand in the cold tonight
> The servant of the grain upon my tongue,
> Beware, I am the man, and let me in.

Michael Schmidt

Anchises (1976) followed on from the collected poems. A new collection, *Exactions*, and a chronological *Collected Poems* are projected.

440
SITWELL, Dame Edith 1887–1964

British poet

Edith Louisa Sitwell, the eldest child of Sir George and Lady Ida Sitwell, was born 7 September 1887 in Scarborough. She, and her brothers Osbert and Sacheverell, were raised in the family home at Renishaw Hall, Derbyshire, and Edith endured the claustrophobia of a private education and the active dislike of her parents who were suspicious of her introspective nature. One governess, Helen Rootham, was exceptional in encouraging Edith's imaginative tendencies and introducing her to the poetry of Rimbaud. She left home, at the age of twenty-six, in 1913 and for some months took an office job in London. She was, as she observed, 'the poor member of a rich family'.

Edith's hypersensitivity was outraged by the outbreak of the First World War and her cultural values were expressed in her annual poetry anthology *Wheels* (1916–21). It included work by all three Sitwells (thus inviting charges of nepotism); by Aldous Huxley*; and by Wilfred Owen*, to whose memory the 1919 edition was dedicated. Edith, who emphasized her resemblance to Elizabeth I, gained a reputation as an eccentric aristocratic aesthete whose weird appearance was a substitute for real poetic talent. However, the poems in *Façade* (1922) revealed a genuine talent for linguistic invention and sophisticated wit; these 'patterns of sound' (as Miss Sitwell called them) suggested a sumptuous verbal texture by sacrificing conventional narrative in favour of an elaborate system of internal rhymes, assonances and dissonances.

In June 1923 *Façade*, set to music by William Walton, was given its first public performance at the Aeolian Hall in London and was angrily received by an audience who thought their legs were being pulled. As Miss Sitwell wrote in her autobiography *Taken Care Of* (1965): 'Never, I should think, was a larger and more imposing shower of brickbats hurled at any new work.' This sensation made Miss Sitwell fair game for sustained abuse in the popular press and she became a figure of fun. Noël Coward* parodied her as the absurd Miss Hernia Whittlebot and she was enough of an institution to be cruelly caricatured in Wyndham Lewis's* *The Apes of God* (1930) where she appears as Lady Harriet, an 'old harpy' who listens to 'the little brassy tinkle of her verses for the grown-up nursery'.

Miss Sitwell was not, though, willing to be the fashionable scapegoat for the satirists and her poem *Gold Coast Customs* (1929) renounced the playful experimentation of her early work in favour of a more substantial exploration of the breakdown of privileged society. She then wrote no more poetry for a decade and turned to prose books including a major critical reassessment of *Alexander Pope* (1930), a study of *English Eccentrics* (1933) and a look at *Aspects of Modern Poetry* (1934). After her long poetic silence she published *Street Songs* (1942) which consolidated her position as a serious poet. Her new poems were passionate comments on the injustice of war and were informed with a religious sense of torment. 'Still Falls the Rain' described the raids of 1940 as a modern crucifixion; *The Shadow of Cain* (1947) was an indignant reaction to the dropping of the atomic bomb on Hiroshima. At last she was regarded as a major modern English poet and not as a footnote to what F. R. Leavis* called 'the history of publicity'.

As she grew old with dignity honours were heaped on Miss Sitwell. In 1954, the year she was received into the Roman Catholic Church, she was made a Dame of the British Empire; in 1950 she became Vice President of the Royal Society of Literature; and in 1963 she was made a Companion of Literature. She succeeded as a poet in spite of her early penchant for self-dramatization and her public feuds with other writers obscured the magnanimity she showed by encouraging younger writers like Dylan Thomas*.

Alan Bold

Edith Sitwell's poetry is contained in *Collected Poems* (1957) and her career is surveyed in *Edith Sitwell: Fire of the Mind* (1976), an annotated anthology by her friends Elizabeth Salter and Allanah Harper.

441
SKINNER, Burrhus Frederic 1904–

US psychologist

Born at Susquehanna, Pennsylvania, and educated at Hamilton College, New York, and at Harvard, Skinner became a fellow of Harvard in 1931; he was Professor of Psychology at Harvard from 1947 to 1975. His *Behavior of Organisms* appeared in 1938, and *Science and Human Behavior* in 1953. Skinner's most famous book is the utopian novel *Walden Two* (1948); the definitive statement of his philosophical and scientific outlook is *Beyond Freedom and Dignity* (1971).

Most of Skinner's work as an experimental psychologist has been concerned with behaviour modification in animals. The following is a stock example: 'We study the height at which a pigeon's head is normally held, and select some line on the height scale which is reached only infrequently. Keeping our eye on the scale we begin to open the food tray very quickly whenever the head rises above the line. The result is invariable: we observe an immediate change in the frequency with which the head crosses the line' (*Science and Human Behavior*). In this standard Skinnerian experiment, the food is termed the *reinforcer*; presenting the food whenever the desired response is produced is called *reinforcement*; the resulting change in the frequency with which the head is lifted is the process of *operant conditioning*.

Skinner's meticulous and painstaking research has shown how such procedures can be extended to produce remarkably complex behavioural responses. But Skinner's major importance lies not in his experimental results, impressive though they are, nor in the theory of conditioned response (which was first systematized by Sechenov and Pavlov), but in his insistence that it is proper, and indeed desirable, to apply the methods and procedures of behavioural psychology to the human domain. Skinner pioneered such ideas as the teaching machine and programmed learning; his inventions include mechanical baby-tenders, and the 'Skinner box' – a controlled environment for monitoring behavioural changes. Yet even this, for Skinner, is merely a beginning. While other behavioural psychologists have adopted the techniques of conditioning to effect cures of specific mental disorders (cf. John Broadus Watson*), Skinner seeks, via the same means,

to recondition society itself. 'What would you do,' asks the hero of *Walden Two*, 'if you found yourself in possession of an effective science of behavior? Suppose you found it possible to control the behavior of men as you wished. What would you do?' Skinner's answer, made explicit in *Walden Two*, is that he would design a new society – a society in which stability, harmony and satisfaction would be, in the literal sense, behaviourally engineered. The methods which Skinner advocates for this end are much simpler than the eugenics and hypnotherapy envisaged in Huxley's* *Brave New World*. Skinner's 'technology of behaviour' would rely largely on reinforcement, especially 'positive' rather than 'negative' reinforcement (in plain English, a system of rewards, rather than coercion or punishment). 'We can achieve a sort of control under which the controlled, though they are following a code much more scrupulously than was ever the case under the old system, now *feel free*. That's the source of the tremendous power of positive reinforcement.'

The vision of a controlled society is hardly unfamiliar in this century. What is remarkable, not to say disturbing, is Skinner's enthusiasm for it. It needs to be asked, in particular, what place remains, in Skinner's scheme of things, for individual freedom and responsibility. Skinner's answer is quite uncompromising. In *Beyond Freedom and Dignity*, he proposes that we should abandon completely the notion of 'autonomous man' – the free, responsible agent who is the author of his actions. 'As a science of behavior adopts the strategy of physics and biology, the autonomous agent to which behavior has traditionally been attributed is replaced by the environment – the environment in which the species evolved and in which the behavior of the individual is shaped and maintained.' Autonomous man is simply 'a device used to explain what we cannot explain any other way. His abolition has been long overdue.'

To support his case, Skinner defends a radical form of philosophical behaviourism. Good science, claims Skinner, has no place for appeal to internal mental states. To explain someone's conduct by reference to an inner feeling is as unhelpful as the ancient view that a falling body accelerates because it feels more jubilant as it finds itself nearer home. 'Young people refuse to get jobs not because they feel alienated, but because of defective social environments.'

Of the many criticisms that could be levelled against Skinner's approach, two may be mentioned here. First, the rejection of explanations appealing to inner mental states is too glib. Attributing jubilation to stones is unhelpful precisely because it is *anthropomorphic*: we are ascribing to stones person-like properties which they do not in fact possess. Yet this hardly shows that it is inappropriate to invoke such properties when we come to deal with an *anthropos*, a person; people, as we all know from direct personal experience, quite simply *do* possess feelings.

Second, and more generally, Skinner's version of a 'scientific' approach to society is flawed by a fundamental contradiction. Freedom and autonomy, he claims, are a sham; all human behaviour is environmentally determined. Yet on the other hand, we are told that 'the intentional design of a culture and control of human behavior is essential' (*Beyond Freedom and Dignity*). Intentional design and control *by whom*? Clearly, in Skinner's scheme of things there are, after all, autonomous agents – the behavioural technocrats and planners. These godlike creatures apparently stand outside the deterministic nexus that binds the rest of us: they take free and rational decisions about how our culture is to be designed. The upshot is that Skinner's insistence on a planned society presupposes the existence – at least for a minority – of the very autonomy that his deterministic behaviourism rules out.

Despite its contradictions and lack of philosophical sophistication, Skinner's message retains a firm hold on much contemporary thought. 'When a science of behavior has been achieved, there's no alternative to a planned society.' This slogan from *Walden Two* is likely to remain relevant for the foreseeable future, even if a little reflection shows that it is better construed as a sombre warning than as the cheerful blueprint for progress which Skinner intended.

Dr John Cottingham

Skinner writes with admirable clarity and forcefulness, and the writings mentioned are the best introduction to his ideas.

442
SMITH, David Roland 1906–65

US sculptor

Smith's art training consisted of a year at Ohio University, two weeks at Notre Dame University and about five years as a painting student at the Art Students' League in New York under John Sloan and Jan Matulka, 'the guy I'd rather give more credit than anyone else'. Other formative influences were a vacation spent on a Studebaker plant at South Bend, Indiana, an evening class in poetry in Washington DC and, around 1930, meetings with the informal 'group' of artist friends of John D. Graham (Stuart Davis, William de Kooning*, Jean Xceron and Arshile Gorky). From 1935 to 1936 he travelled to Greece, the USSR, London and Paris with his first wife Dorothy Dehner.

As a man, Smith was stubborn, passionate, vulnerable and boundlessly ambitious. As an artist, he spent thirty years refining techniques for drawing in welded steel. Beginning with coral constructions made in the Virgin Islands in 1931, Smith moved slowly from painting to sculpture, evolving hybrids from early modern forms, yet retaining a concern with figuration. His output includes incidental virtuoso performances such as the *Medals for Dishonor*, a group of satirical anti-war plaques shown in 1940, or the nearly unbelievable production of twenty-six large sculptures in thirty days in 1962 at Spoleto, Italy. Yet the main pressure is from uncertain experiments with Constructivism through an assured command of Surrealist imagery in the 1940s to the abstract, Cubist language of the late 1950s and 1960s.

Critics have stressed Smith's formal concerns at the expense of personal identity. Throughout his career he dramatized his relationships and states of mind. Works such as *Pillar of Sunday*, a comment on his mother's Methodist beliefs, *Home of the Welder*, a complex domestic scene, and *Becca*, dedicated to one of his daughters, speak of celebration and dread of women. Both of Smith's marriages ended in divorce. Drawings return obsessively to images of women courting and defying destructive masculine forces. The battle of the sexes – 'who shall have the mastery', in Chaucer's terms – is fundamental to Smith's thinking. 'I only make girl sculptures,' he told Frank O'Hara in a TV interview, 'I don't make boy sculptures at all.' Nevertheless, Smith thrived on male companionship. *Blackburn – Song of an Irish Blacksmith*, a tribute to a workmate, is a rhapsody on male values and routines.

Apparent shifts of intention between early and late Smith sculptures can be resolved in various ways. One metaphor is outstanding. Smith's father had been an inventor. Smith himself collected antique cannons and dreamed of a 'sculpture train', a mobile exhibition of his work to be drawn through the towns of America. His love – hate relationship with modern techniques and artefacts was the overriding 'influence' on Smith, greater even than Cubism. Disciples demonstrate exactly the paradox of factory worker versus blacksmith – Alain Kirili emphasizing the latter, Antony Caro and his St Martins 'school' the former. There is a point in American art history when extravert 1930s politics undergoes a sea-change. With the evolution of the New York School in the early 1940s artistic decision-making may or may not have inherited the role which 'public' activities had previously occupied. In Smith's case his entire career can be regarded as a struggle for hard-won freedom, his early political fervour by no means diminished, but rather enhanced by the unprecedented clarity and expressive power of the late *Zigs* and *Cubi*.

Stuart Morgan

See: Rosalind Krauss, *Terminal Iron Works* (1971); Garnett McCoy (ed.), *David Smith* (1973); Paul Cummings, *David Smith: The Drawings* (Whitney Museum of American Art, 1979).

443

SMITHSON, Robert 1938–73

US sculptor and critic

Smithson was born in Rutherford, New Jersey, where his family doctor was William Carlos Williams*. In 1954 he won a scholarship to attend the Art Students' League in New York and did so on a half-day basis until 1956. Leaving the army after six months of service he hitch-hiked around the United States and Mexico for two years. After exhibiting paintings and assemblages (1959–62) he retired from art for two years, marrying Nancy Holt in 1963. In 1965 he re-emerged as a sculptor and a year later his essay 'Entropy and the New Monuments' was published in *Artforum*, the first of a set of reflections on contemporary art, some couched in fictional form, written in a depressive Romantic style reminiscent of De Quincey or Poe. Four one-man exhibitions at the Dwan Gallery (1966–70) led Smithson to a concept of large, outdoor projects resulting in *Asphalt Rundown* (1969), *Partially Buried Woodshed* (1970), *Spiral Jetty* (1970) and *Broken Circle – Spiral Hill* (1971). The two-year period from 1971 to 1973 was one of frustration; proposals for projects were repeatedly rejected. Finally a mining company in Creede, Colorado, accepted a plan for a tailings pond. Before starting work on this Smithson travelled to Texas and staked out the plan of the *Amarillo Ramp*. On 20 July 1973 he was photographing the site from the air when his plane crashed, killing the pilot, the photographer and Smithson himself.

Gradually the oversimplified approach to Smithson as a minimalist, a conceptual artist or an earthwork sculptor are being replaced; in a sense he was all of these, as well as a painter in a late Abstract Expressionist manner and an industrial designer *manqué*. The view of Smithson as a theorist whose art was thrown up tangentially by his writings is disproved by gigantic finished works such as the *Spiral Jetty*, a 1,500-feet long path of boulders twisting out into the pink crystalline waters of the Great Salt Lake, possibly the greatest American sculpture of the 1970s. Lucy Lippard's contention that he was 'for many years virtually the only artist to consider the ways in which art could *affect* life' minimizes the ambiguity of his political stance and the endless frustrations he had to face. Smithson was and remains a misfit. If the personality he cultivated in his lifetime was that of the bored pedant, speeding in movie theatres on 42nd street, evolving literary conceits commensurate with a passion for science fiction, crystallography, horror films and strip mining, he was also a dedicated polemicist, infuriating opponents with the flamboyance of his prose and the hectic, near-nonsensical splendour of his imagination. As his 'non-sites', metal containers holding rock from mapped, documented sites, his earthworks – the first, *Tar Pool and Gravel Pit*, was proposed in 1966 – and the late experiments with industrial design succeeded each other logically, with the writings as theoretical support, he explored variations of the dialectic he sought between art and life, 'site' and 'non-site', order and chaos. Equal only to Robert Morris* as a theorist, his major achievements may have been to break the back of a second generation of Greenberg-inspired formalist criticism and to disentangle late 1960s art from its Duchampian* assumptions. His influence, strongly felt by senior post-minimalists (Eva Hesse, Mel Bochner, Sol LeWitt), has increased in the late 1970s with the upsurge of 'phenomenological', semi-architectural sculpture (Alice Aycock, Mary Miss, Richard Fleischner, George Trakas).

Stuart Morgan

Smithson's writings are anthologized in Nancy Holt (ed.), *The Writings of Robert Smithson* (1979). See: *Robert Smithson Drawings* (New York Cultural Center catalogue, 1974); Lawrence Alloway, 'Robert Smithson's Development', *Artforum*, November 1973; John Coplans, 'The Amarillo Ramp', *Artforum*, April 1974; Nancy Holt and Liza Béar, 'Robert Smithson's Amarillo Ramp', *Avalanche*, Summer/Fall 1973. See also: the special Robert Smithson issue of *Arts Magazine* (May 1978).

444

SOLZHENITSYN, Aleksandr Isayevich 1918–

Russian writer

Solzhenitsyn was born in Kislovodsk. His father, a Moscow University student, served as an artillery officer until the summer of 1918, when he was accidentally killed six months before Solzhenitsyn was born. In 1924 his mother, a shorthand typist, moved to Rostov-on-Don where Solzhenitsyn received his first schooling. On leaving school in 1936 he hoped to be a writer but, being unable to pursue his writer's vocation in Rostov, he took a degree course in mathematics and physics at Rostov University supplemented by a two-year correspondence course in literature. He married N. A. Reshetovskaya in 1940 and was appointed a physics teacher at Morozovka in the Rostov region. Called up in October 1941, he was commissioned as an artillery officer the following year, fought at Kursk in 1943 and participated in the advance towards Germany. In February 1945, during the battle for Koenigsberg, he was arrested for having made disrespectful references to Stalin* in private correspondence and was returned to Moscow for investigation and sentencing to eight years' imprisonment followed by 'perpetual exile'. In July 1946 he was transferred from parquet-laying work in a block of apartments on Lenin Prospekt to the 'Sharashka' at Marfino, ten miles north of Sheremet'yevo airport (Mavrino of *The First Circle*, *V kruge pervom*, 1968), where his scientific training was used to promote research into listening devices. He was later transferred to a Siberian labour camp, the setting of his first published work *One Day in the Life of Ivan Denisovich* (*Odin den' Ivana Denisovicha*, 1962), from which he was released in 1953. The first thing he learned after his release was news of Stalin's death. Serious recurrence of cancer obliged him to enter the Tashkent clinic which forms the setting for *Cancer Ward* (*Rakovy korpus*, 1969) where he eventually recovered. He was not released from 'perpetual exile' until 1956 and then chose to live in Torfoprodukt, near Vladimir, the scene of *Matryona's Place* (*Matryonin dvor*, 1963). While living there he was visited by Reshetovskaya, who had previously divorced him, and they decided to remarry and settle in Ryazan. His literary fame and notoriety date from this point.

The publication of *One Day in the Life of Ivan Denisovich* in Tvardovsky's journal *Novy Mir* in 1962 became a political event of the first magnitude. This masterpiece of twentieth-century prison literature was the first work published in the Soviet Union to give an explicit picture of life in Stalin's slave-labour camps. Although Solzhenitsyn became famous almost overnight and was publicly praised by Khrushchev, his outspoken criticism of Stalinism and the Soviet establishment soon proved too much for the Soviet authorities and by 1966 he had ceased to find official outlets for his work. His plays *Candle in the Wind* (*Svecha na vetru*, 1968) and *The Lovegirl and the Innocent* (*Olen' i shalashovka*, 1969), as well as his novels *The First Circle* and *Cancer Ward*, were all prohibited, notwithstanding his frequent appeals to the Union of Soviet Writers. When he was awarded the Nobel Prize for Literature in 1970 a campaign of vilification was launched against him, his *August 1914* (1971) had to be published abroad like his earlier novels, and his role as spokesman of Soviet dissidence began gradually to assume as great an importance as his role as writer. This fact received endorsement with his decision to release for publication abroad in 1973 Parts I and II of *The Gulag Archipelago*, his carefully documented exposure of the Soviet slave-labour camp system. The attacks on him and his associates increased in ferocity until, in February 1974, he was arrested, stripped, interrogated and then summarily exiled to the West. He took up residence in Zürich, where he was later joined by his second wife (formerly Natalya Svetlova) and their three sons.

His residence in the West has been marked by a vociferous opposition to Western life and policies that has been almost as uncompromising as was his opposition to the authorities in the Soviet Union. He has reputedly continued to work on the two remaining 'knots' (as he has called them) of his trilogy about the Russian participation in the First World War and the causes of the revolution of 1917 (provisionally entitled *October 1916* and *March 1917*, though other volumes are planned to follow). Those works which he has actually published, however, have been primarily documentary, e.g. the completion of *The Gulag Archipelago* and his study of Lenin, *Lenin in Zürich* (1975), or of largely autobiographical interest, such as *The Oak and the Calf* (*Bodalsya telyonok s dubom*, 1979). Since taking up residence in the USA on an estate near Cavendish in Vermont, his name has been associated with several stormy jeremiads against the West as well as against Communism. The most noteworthy of these was his speech at Harvard on being made an honorary Doctor of Letters in June 1978, when he denounced the West for its abrogation of Christian responsibilities and its spiritual bankruptcy, comparing it unfavourably with the spiritual intensity achieved by the Russian people.

It can now be seen that Solzhenitsyn belongs to a very respectable tradition of denunciatory literature which has its beginnings in Russian literature with the eighteenth century and the critical realism of much nineteenth-century writing. It is equally clear that the spirit of denunciation has tended – at least for the time being – to overwhelm the literary element in his work. The harsh but memorable portrayal of the prisoners in *One Day* and *The First Circle*, the profound, often symbolic, analysis of the institutional forms and attitudes which gave rise to such *gulag* worlds, and the compressed power of the writing made his first works into outstanding examples of a literature combining denunciation of the Soviet system with universal literary values. His studies of the sickness pervading Soviet society in such brilliant pictures of enclosed, intimately observed worlds as those of *Cancer Ward*, the finest of his novels, or his little masterpiece *Matryona's Place* demonstrate his remarkable authority as a writer who can characterize as well as castigate, create in microcosm as well as macrocosm, whose range of treatment is matched by an equivalent understanding of the depths of emotion and thought involved in human relationships. With the appearance of *August 1914* doubts about his imaginative range and his ability to handle panoramic events – on a scale matching Leo Tolstoy's achievement, with which Solzhenitsyn has inevitably invited comparison – may have seemed justified, but the ten-volume projected epic, if it matures, will very likely dispel any such apprehensions. For, by contemporary standards, Solzhenitsyn's literary work, like his thinking, has been of a size and scale virtually without parallel and he has assumed the responsibility for such size as if it were his birthright.

His birthright was the October Revolution and the Soviet Union which sprang from it. His life has been contemporaneous with its history. His commitment to Christianity derived from the bitterest personal experience, but his dislike of the Communist system, like his criticism of the West, appears to be based on sincere, if vague, concepts of justice and responsibility which have their source in the human conscience. He has been keen to assert that 'Justice exists so long as there exists at least a few people who can feel it'; or 'A writer's tasks . . . concern the secrets of the human heart and conscience, of the conflict between life and death, the overcoming of spiritual sorrow and those laws extending throughout all humanity which were born in the immemorial depths of the millennia and will cease only when the sun is extinguished'; or a writer is both 'a humble apprentice beneath God's heaven' and (as his character Volodin declares in *The First Circle*) 'the writer is a teacher of the people . . . a great writer is, so to speak, a second government. That is why no regime anywhere has ever loved its great writers, only its minor ones.' Solzhenitsyn has qualities of that kind of greatness in him. So long as he remains true to his most striking dictum: 'One word of truth shall outweigh the whole world', he will remain among the most significant moral authorities of the twentieth century.

Professor Richard Freeborn

Other works: *For the Good of the Cause* (1964); *Short Stories and Prose Poems* (1970); *A Lenten Letter to Pimen Patriarch of all Russia* (1972); *'One word of truth . . .' The Nobel Speech on Literature 1970* (1972); *From under the Rubble* (1975), a collection of essays on Russian cultural and political problems (with others). See also: G. Lukács, *Solzhenitsyn* (1970); J. B. Dunlop *et al.*, *Aleksandr Solzhenitsyn: Critical Essays* (1973); L. Labedz, *Solzhenitsyn – a Documentary Record* (1973); C. Moody, *Solzhenitsyn* (1973); K. Feuer, ed., *Solzhenitsyn: a Collection of Critical Essays* (1976).

445

SOUTINE, Chaim 1894–1943

Russian painter

Born in a Jewish ghetto in the small village of Smilivitchi near Minsk in Russian Lithuania, Soutine's early life was one of extreme poverty and, even after his arrival in Paris in 1913 where he studied at the École des Beaux Arts, he continued to live in the most wretched circumstances. He also drank heavily. His studies, though important, were not the major influence on his work. This is to be found in the art galleries of France and Holland where his lasting admiration for the great realists – in particular Rembrandt, Chardin and Courbet – was formed. Strangely, the seemingly obvious affinity for Van Gogh was vehemently denied. Ironically this liking for the past was partly responsible for the undoubted decline in quality after his discovery by the American art collector Alfred C.

Barnes in 1923. Barnes bought a large number of paintings and Soutine's way of life changed literally overnight. He couldn't cope. He became increasingly ashamed of the early work and went to great lengths to destroy as much of it as he could lay his hands on. Quite simply he felt it to be far too crude and uncontrolled to compare in any way with what he saw as the real art of the museums. He particularly disliked the series of landscapes painted at Ceret in Provence between 1919 and 1922 which in retrospect seem to be by far the most meaningful works of his entire oeuvre. Full of impulsive, often exaggerated gesture, the paint surges across the surface of the canvas drawing immediate attention to the underlying energy of the subject. The picture-plane is of prime importance and the brush strokes themselves as essential to our understanding of the pictorial space as the motif itself. Here we can clearly see the impact Soutine was to have on the later American Abstract Expressionists and in particular on Willem de Kooning*.

The choice of subject-matter was unremarkable, though the series of still-lives worked between 1922 and 1926 which include the Rembrandt pastiches of the carcasses of beef show a morbid liking for the dead animal which hints at an almost primitive sympathy for a way of life which was becoming increasingly foreign to him. Soutine undoubtedly lost his way and certainly lost the richly expressive urgency of the early years, but in so doing drew attention to the fundamental truth of his vision.

John Furse

M. Wheeler, *Soutine* (The Museum of Modern Art, New York 1950); *Chaim Soutine*, Exhibition Catalogue with introduction by David Sylvester (The Arts Council, London 1963).

446

SOYINKA, Wole 1934–

Nigerian writer

Poet, playwright, novelist, polemicist and critic, producer, actor and academic, Wole Soyinka represents to many the conscience of Nigerian Independence. Just as the plays on which his reputation chiefly rests combine the techniques of Yoruba folk opera and ritual masquerade with Brechtian* and Absurdist devices, so has his creative philosophy absorbed the ideas of Nietzsche, Existentialism, Old World mystery traditions and the New Left into the world view of Yoruba religion, a world view which in his work becomes self-aware and self-critical.

Born in 1934 in Abeokuta, Soyinka studied at Ibadan and Leeds. In the early 1950s he was associated with the Royal Court theatre in London, and it was there that he was first staged in 1959. Soon his plays were performed in the capitals of three continents, and within a few years he had come to be regarded as the brightest star in the rising constellation of African university wits, and one of the most promising dramatic poets writing in the English language. By 1967 he had published seven plays, a novel and a volume of poetry (*Idanre*, 1965). He has won numerous awards, among them the John Whiting prize, shared with Tom Stoppard*, in 1966, prizes at the Dakar Festival of Negro Arts for *The Road* in 1965 and for *Kongi's Harvest* in 1966, and the Jock Campbell prize awarded by the *New Statesman* in 1969. His prophetic and militant voice has never been a comfortable one. Satire and invective mark his challenges of the social and political forces which stultify human growth. His masque *A Dance of the Forests* (1963), performed by his own theatre group at the Nigerian Independence Celebrations of 1960, created a furore; at the same time he attracted opprobrium for his iconoclastic attacks on the Negritude movement ('A tiger does not proclaim his tigritude, he pounces'). During the Nigerian civil war his critical voice was silenced by a two-year term of detention on unspecified charges, most of it served in solitary confinement. Soyinka's journal of his ordeal, *The Man Died* (1972), combines direct indictment with searching self-observation. Predictably it was received with almost unrelieved hostility, and Soyinka spent the following years abroad as 'a sort of itinerant lecturer'. He has held academic positions in Ibadan, Lagos, Cambridge, Sheffield and Ife where he is now professor, and has served as co-editor of *Black Orpheus* and *Transition*. His professional career in Nigeria has been stormy with public defiance of confining structures. Lately he has been active in urging the adoption of Swahili as the lingua franca of Africa.

Soyinka is often described as pre-eminently a satirist. But his work exhibits a no less consistent preoccupation with ontology and mythopoeia. The early essay 'The Fourth Stage' (in D. W. Jefferson, ed., *The Morality of Art*, 1969) and his recent work *Myth Literature and the African World* (1976) reflect difficult working through to a philosophical stance which is religiously rooted rather than analytically derived. Ogun, traditionally the god of the forge, of iron and of war, is the archetype with whom Soyinka's imagination interacts. In 'The Fourth Stage' he transfuses the traditional myth with elements derived from the Aeschylean Prometheus of Nietzsche's *Birth of Tragedy*: Ogun emerges as a god of radical creativity. In *The Road* (1965) he is confronted as the mystery of psychological, social and technological breakdown and breakthrough; in the poem *Idanre* his myth is enlarged to encompass rebellion; finally in *Madmen and Specialists* (1971) the archetype disappears into that human energy to which Nietzsche gave the name of Socrates, 'The type of theoretical man who finds an infinite delight in whatever exists', and in

whom Apollonian contemplation and Dionysian ecstasies have been merged and transmuted into 'cool paradoxical thought and fiery affects'. Lately the god has reappeared as the inspiring force behind African liberation in *Ogun Abibiman* (1976), an epic praise poem based on the life of the Zulu king Shaka.

His two novels show the growth of his commitments. *The Interpreters* (1965), a work of complex and difficult texture, deals with the creative search for 'new laws of living' by a group of young Nigerian intellectuals. The psychological possibilities they embody are tested in encounters calling for flexibility, compassion and social responsibility, and are found wanting. The end of this as of many other works leaves the reader poised at the edge of an abyss, with 'only a choice of drowning'. *The Interpreters* ends on these words; *Season of Anomy* (1973) ends on 'In the forests, life began to stir.' It is an allegory of political change in which the psychological distress of the individual is of significance only in so far as it fuels the collective commitment. For Soyinka, abandoning the subjective 'tragic vision' was a wrong choice. The dilemma, worked through in the poetry of the same period, is confronted in 'Joseph' –

> a time of evil cries
> Renunciation of the saintly vision
> Summons instant hands of truth to tear
> All painted masks, that poison stains thereon
> May join and trace the hidden undertows
> In sewers of intrigue
>
> (*A Shuttle in the Crypt*, 1972)

Like the deity he celebrates, Wole Soyinka has consistently given his genius and his energies to bridging 'labours through the night of transition'. He will undoubtedly continue to challenge the inhumanities of unreflective men wherever he perceives them.

Annemarie Heywood

See: Gerald Moore, *Wole Soyinka* (1971); and E. D. Jones, *Wole Soyinka* (1973).

447
SPENDER, Stephen Harold 1909–

English poet and critic

Stephen Spender was born in London, the second son of a Liberal journalist. He was educated at University College School in Frognal, and at University College, Oxford. It was here that he met the poet W. H. Auden*, whose first printed book of verse was produced by Spender on a hand-press in 1928. His other Oxford friends included the poets Louis MacNeice and Bernard Spencer; but the verse he wrote at Oxford was strongly influenced by Auden's ideas and style, the curt, elliptical 'scientific' style of Auden's early work. Even then, however, his poems contained a romantic, dithyrambic element – adversely commented on by F. R. Leavis*, in *Scrutiny*, at the time. The poems beginning 'Oh young men oh young comrades' and 'Your body is stars whose million glitter there' are good examples of this.

The first important collection, *Poems* (1933), has in it most of Spender's best poetry. At once, when it was published, he became part of a journalist's imaginary trinity of Oxford left-wing poets; Auden and Cecil Day Lewis were the other two. The poems concern human relationships and have social commitment; two of the most successful are about the poor children of London and the unemployed (in the 1930s Spender was briefly a member of the Communist Party). The best verse is taut in structure; and rhyme, although it occurs, is rare, and seldom more than assonance (shoulder/poor) or half-rhyme (stop/gap). The poems that are direct rhetorical outbursts, although they are genuine and generous expressions of emotion, do not wear so well. Unlike Auden, from whom in the early days he took his vocabulary and some of his subject-matter, Spender was never very interested in form.

Other poems of the 1930s (for example, 'Polar Exploration' and 'An Elementary School Classroom In A Slum', spiritually indebted to Auden and W. B. Yeats*, respectively) are successful; but mixing of the metaphors in some can be disastrous ('Alas for the sad standards/In the eyes of the Old Masters/Sprouting through glaze of their pictures!'). The obsession with the self almost never, in Spender, produces good poetry. The poems about the Spanish Civil War avoid this fault but are tokens, well-meaning gestures, rather than exciting in themselves. The poems of 'Love and Separation' (as they are titled in the *Collected Poems*, 1954), written in 1937–9, have more truck with rhyme, handled rather gingerly: and 'Song' is one of Spender's most effective poems – a hybrid of ballad, nursery rhyme and Auden love lyric, but triumphantly successful. Too many of Spender's poems, however, are like dreams told to a stranger; they mean a lot to him but infinitely less to the reader. It is significant that the best piece in the latest book, *The Generous Days* (1971), is straight observation, a description of the appearance and attitude to art of an American art student of an anarchist kind.

Spender, although he first achieved fame as a poet, has also written books of criticism, a verse play that was performed by the Group Theatre (*Trial of a Judge*, 1938), short stories, a novel, and an autobiography (*World Within World*, 1951). He edited the magazine *Horizon* with Cyril Connolly* in 1939–41 and *Encounter* with Melvin J. Lasky in the post-war period (1953–66). Sections of a *Journal* have appeared in the *London Magazine* in the last few years. Spender's later role, in fact, has been that of a man of letters and a cultural

ambassador. He was awarded the CBE in 1962. From 1970 until very recently he occupied the Chair of English at University College, London.

Gavin Ewart

Criticism: *The Destructive Element* (1934); *The Creative Element* (1953); *The Struggle of the Modern* (1963). Fiction: *The Burning Cactus* (short stories, 1936); *The Backward Sun* (novel, 1940).

448
SPENGLER, Oswald 1880–1936

German historian

Spengler came from a middle-class north German family of moderate means. After a brief period as a secondary school teacher in Hamburg (his specialities were Mathematics and Natural Science), he left the profession for ever, settling in Munich and living modestly on the income from an inheritance and the proceeds of articles and reviews. The subjects of his doctoral thesis (Heraclitus) and of his qualifying thesis for the teaching profession ('The development of the organ of sight in the chief stages of animal life') were an unlikely prelude to historical activity, but they are consistent with the speculative cast of his writing and with its constant exploitation of biology as a source of metaphor. Neither in practice nor temperamentally was he ever part of the German historical establishment, and ill-health was probably merely a contributory factor in his refusal of chairs of history at Göttingen and Leipzig after *The Decline of the West* had made him a public figure.

The Decline of the West (*Der Untergang des Abendlandes*), on which Spengler's reputation is based, appeared in two volumes, *Form and Actuality* (*Gestalt und Wirklichkeit*, Munich 1918, trans. 1926) and *Perspectives of World-History* (*Welthistorische Perspektiven*, 1922, trans. 1928). Its success in Germany (in particular the success of its first volume) owed much to an understandable but not strictly warranted confusion in readers' minds between Germany's military defeat and the more far-reaching and gradual decline evoked by Spengler. Although in the 1920s Spengler was to address himself specifically, if with limited success, to the German political situation, what he offers in *The Decline* is both a philosophy of history and, as a corollary, a prediction of the future course of Western civilization as a whole. Spengler's view of history is cyclical and organic, and has little room for causality: cultures move through the 'age-phases of the individual man'; plant-like, they realize the possibilities contained within them and, having fulfilled themselves, die. Spengler particularly stresses the specificity of cultures (concerning himself chiefly with the two he describes as Classical and as Western or 'Faustian'), which express their individual 'soul' in a succession of forms (economic, social, artistic) and remain impenetrable to other cultures – an extreme development of the historicist idea of individuality. Yet it is a paradox of the work that Spengler's whole method is a comparative one which asserts parallelisms between separate cultures in spite of their discontinuity: Democritus and Leibniz, Archimedes and Helmholtz are thus, to use Spengler's term 'contemporaries', appearing at the same stage in Classical and Western culture respectively.

The dominant tone of *The Decline* is elegiac, both because Western Culture is presented as potentially absent (already well engaged in its final phase, it will pass through the tyranny of Caesarism before it subsides for ever), and because Spengler's attitude towards cultures which have *already* disappeared affirms their inaccessibility while striving to overcome it imaginatively (in this respect there are some surprising similarities with Lévi-Strauss's* *Tristes Tropiques*). Spengler pursues this paradoxical ambition by the ingenious detection of symbolic correspondences *within* cultures (which allows him to intuit them as comprehensible totalities), by the use of biological analogy to characterize *all* cultures, by the deployment of parallels ('homologies') *between* cultures, and, more generally, by the setting of these cultures against the permanence of an indifferent cosmic back-drop which establishes them as ephemeral if significant incidents in a common pathos.

The ethical relativism professed by Spengler and the importance he attributes to the state place *The Decline* within the historicist tradition, but, drawing freely upon Nietzsche (with Goethe, an important influence), he also smuggles an aristocratic ethic into history. This preference no doubt lay behind his subsequent hostility to Hitler* (a 'heroic tenor' rather than a 'hero') and National Socialism, to which the nationalism, the opposition to parliamentary democracy and the corporate conception of the state evidenced in his political writing might otherwise have been expected to draw him.

Spengler's reputation never regained its high point of the early 1920s and his conception of history, which was never an orthodoxy, is now largely discredited, but *The Decline* can still provide intellectual excitement (see, for example, his chapter, 'The Meaning of Numbers') and, in its solemnly resonant celebration of transience, moments of aesthetic pleasure.

Roger S. Huss

Other works include: *Man and Technics: A Contribution to a Philosophy of Life* (*Der Mensch und die Technik: Beitrag zu einer Philosophie des Lebens*, 1931, trans. 1932); *The Hour of Decision: Germany and World-Historical Evolution* (*Jahre der Entscheidung: Deutschland und die weltgeschichtliche Entwicklung*, 1933, trans. 1934);

Politische Schriften (1932). On Spengler see: H. Stuart Hughes, *Oswald Spengler: A Critical Estimate* (1952); R. G. Collingwood, Oswald Spengler and the Theory of Historical Cycles' in *Antiquity: a Quarterly Review of Archaeology*, I, September 1927; Theodor W. Adorno, 'Spengler nach dem Untergang' in *Der Monat*, May 1950.

449

SPOCK, Benjamin McLane 1903–

US paediatrician and author

Son of a corporation lawyer, Benjamin Spock grew up in a puritanical but devoted New England family. After graduating from Yale, he went on to study at Yale Medical School and qualified as a doctor in 1929 at the College of Physicians and Surgeons, Columbia University. He served residencies in paediatrics and psychiatry, and as part of his psychiatric training underwent five years in psychoanalysis. Between 1933 and 1947 Spock practised paediatrics in New York City during which period he also taught paediatrics at Cornell Medical College and acted as consultant in Paediatric Psychiatry to New York City Health Department.

After a period of wartime service in the US Naval Reserve as a lieutenant commander Spock moved to Minnesota to join the staff of the Mayo Clinic and later became Associate Professor of Psychiatry with the Mayo Foundation, University of Minnesota. From there he became professor of child development at the University of Pittsburg (1951–5), and occupied the same post at Western Reserve University from 1955 until he retired in 1967.

It was during this period of service in the Naval Reserve that Spock wrote the bulk of what was to become his major work. First published as *The Commonsense Book of Baby and Child Care* (1946) and later simply as *Baby and Child Care*, the book known to two generations of parents as 'Dr Spock' now has worldwide sales which currently exceed 28,000,000.

Keynote of *Baby and Child Care* was reassurance – 'Trust yourself. . . . Don't be afraid to trust your own common sense.' It was unique in offering to the ordinary parent a detailed guide to the child's physical, social and emotional development and well-being, couched in non-technical terms. Its appeal was further strengthened by Spock's highly distinctive conversational approach, a style he perfected when reading the manuscript aloud to his wife Jane, who also collaborated on research and the enormously detailed index.

Before the appearance of *Baby and Child Care*, child-care experts had tended towards the inflexible and prescriptive, especially in the areas of feeding and toilet training. *Baby and Child Care* succeeded in popularizing the growing feeling among psychoanalysts, educators and paediatricians that greater understanding and flexibility were essential in the care of young children.

In subsequent editions Spock made it clear that this had indeed been his intention but also expressed concern at the swing towards a child-centred culture and the over-permissiveness which he felt typified American child-rearing through the 1950s and 1960s. In the 1979 edition Spock attempts to eliminate the sexist bias of which he has been accused by feminists; for the first time the child is referred to as 'she' and he acknowledges the changes in parental roles – 'Now I recognize that the father's responsibility is as great as the mother's.'

A member of SANE (Committee for a Sane Nuclear Policy) since 1962, Spock became increasingly involved in the American peace movement, until in 1968 he, with other opponents of American involvement in Vietnam, was tried for conspiring to 'counsel, aid and abet' violations of the conscription law. He was found guilty but later acquitted, and continued to be active in the peace movement. His later writings reflect his increasing concern with the wider problems of society. *Decent and Indecent – Our Personal and Political Behaviour* (1969) is dedicated to 'the young people, black and white, who are being clubbed, jailed and even killed for showing us the way to justice'.

Helen Waites

Other works include: *A Baby's First Year* (with J. Reinhart and W. Miller, 1954); *Feeding Your Baby and Child* (with M. Lowenberg, 1955); *Caring for Your Disabled Child* (with M. Lerringo, 1965); *Dr Spock on Vietnam* (with Mitchell Zimmerman, 1968). See Jessica Mitford, *The Trial of Dr Spock* (1969).

450
STALIN, Joseph 1879–1953

Russian political leader

Joseph Vissarionovich Dzhugashvili – Stalin – was born at Gori in Tiflis province. A Georgian by nationality, he was the son of a shoemaker. In 1893 Stalin completed his studies at the ecclesiastical school in Gori. He entered the Tiflis Orthodox Seminary, which at that time was a hotbed of revolutionary ideas – populist, nationalist as well as Marxist. In 1897 Stalin became involved in Marxist circles there. In 1898 he officially joined the Tiflis Russian Social Democratic and Labour party organization. Until his first arrest in March 1902 he was active in revolutionary politics. Over the next few years, but like thousands of the same generation, he was to be imprisoned and deported several times. Despite the mythology surrounding Stalin's early political years, it is clear that his overall role was only minor and his influence mainly provincial. He spoke no foreign languages. Unlike other Russian Marxists he had no experience of the European labour movement. As a Marxist theoretician he was irrelevant. He was above all an organization man whose roots were entirely Russian. It was for this reason alone that Lenin* valued him. Stalin's one claim to early intellectual credibility, *Marxism and the National and Colonial Question* (1913, trans. 1936), was even written under Lenin's direction.

After the February Revolution in 1917, Stalin returned to Petrograd. For a short period and with Kamenev and Muranov, he led the Bolshevik Party. He declared himself in favour of lending critical support to the Provisional Government and of a Bolshevik – Menshevik unification. For fifteen days he opposed Lenin's 'April Theses' which called for a revolutionary transfer of power to the newly formed Soviets. His role during the October Revolution was marginal. The view, again fostered by Stalin in power, that he was Lenin's right-hand man and closest collaborator during the uprising is a complete distortion. Ironically, this description fits Trotsky* far better.

During the Civil War Stalin, like many Bolsheviks, had military tasks thrust upon him. In this period his conflict with Trotsky, the main organizer of the Red Army, began to assume serious proportions. His ill-will towards military 'specialists' of any kind and his refusal to obey orders during the Polish campaign were first shots in a long battle. In these conflicts Lenin consistently supported Trotsky.

Stalin's real role, however, was at the centre of the Party machine. With Sverdlov he kept the Party running during the repression of the Bolsheviks in July and August 1917; he was co-director of *Pravda*; one of the seven members of the Politburo, which was set up in October to prepare the insurrection, but never met; and he was Commissar for nationalities. He was one of the four members of the 'small cabinet' of the Central Committee set up after October (Lenin, Trotsky, Sverdlov, Stalin). In 1919 Stalin was appointed Commissar for the Peasants' and Workers' Inspectorate (Rabkrin) and made one of the five established members of the first Politburo (Kamenev, Krestinsky, Lenin, Stalin, Trotsky); in April 1920 he became a member of the Orgburo. In April 1922 he was appointed as the Party's General Secretary. In the space of five years his organizational capacity and personal ambition at the centre of the merging party bureaucracy had led to an unbelievable accumulation of administrative posts.

In 1922 Lenin fell ill. In the course of the same year Stalin began to oppose Lenin on several fronts – on the foreign trade monopoly; on the Constitution of the USSR; on the Georgian nationality question; and on Lenin's increasing opposition to Stalin's power. In his Testament in 1922–3 Lenin finally called for Stalin's removal. Lenin's last heart attack in January 1923 probably saved Stalin.

With Lenin incapacitated (he died in January 1924), the oppositional tendencies divided and with his own control over the machine, Stalin's rise to power was assured. The receding prospects of world revolution, the political and social exhaustion inside Russia after the Civil War, and the general demoralization which pervaded the Party, all worked in Stalin's favour. The Left Opposition led by Trotsky, whatever the correctness of their views, were doomed to defeat. History was rapidly turning against a revolutionary programme.

Stalin's general strategy corresponded with the needs and aspirations of the growing party bureaucracy. Socialism in one country, the campaign against egalitarianism, forced industrialization and collectivization and the whole conservative-nationalist retrenchment of the 1930s all related to their interests. The purges and destruction of the Old Bolshevik Party between 1936 and 1939 led to their final consolidation as a group.

Stalin's policy after 1929 was dictated by two considerations. One, was to ensure his own position and the second was rapid economic growth at any cost. The logic of this inevitably led to increasing repression, economic wastage and the extension of the forced labour camp system. Industrialization was thus purchased at enormous social and political cost.

The Second World War at first threw Stalin into disarray. It is clear that the Pact with Hitler* (1939–41) had lulled the USSR into a false sense of security. Furthermore the purges of the Red Army in 1937 had left the country dangerously exposed. All of these weaknesses were rapidly revealed in the early months of the war. However, Nazi racist savagery, the enormous sacrifice made by the Soviet people, and Allied military aid, finally helped turn the course of the war. Stalin, who had, in large part, prepared the ground for early Soviet setbacks, received much of the subsequent personal acclaim.

The post-war years saw no relief for the Soviet people. Sacrifice was still the order of the day. Repression in all spheres of life intensified – estimates of the total number of victims of Stalin's purges, policies and persecutions run as high as 17,000,000. The Cold War was functional for Stalin in so far as it provided the necessary justification for his harsh internal policies and his personal power. He died on 5 March 1953, revered, feared, but not loved; the USSR a world power, but clearly at variance with the socialist ideal.

Michael Cox

See: Boris Souvarine, *Stalin: A Critical Study of Bolshevism* (1939); Leon Trotsky, *Stalin: An Appraisal of the Man and His Influence* (2nd edn 1946); Isaac Deutscher, *Stalin: A Political Biography* (2nd edn 1966); Robert Conquest, *The Great Terror* (1968); Leonard Schapiro, *The Communist Party of the Soviet Union* (2nd edn 1970).

451

STANISLAVSKY, Konstantin (Konstantin Sergeyevich Alexeyev) 1863–1938

Russian theatre director and actor

Stanislavsky was the stage-name of the son of a wealthy Moscow industrialist. He was, from an early age, fascinated by the theatre, and although, upon completion of his formal education, he joined the family business, Stanislavsky devoted much of his energy to amateur acting and directing. In 1888 he founded the Society of Art and Literature. In 1897 he met Vladimir Nemirovich-Danchenko, a successful playwright and teacher, and found they shared a profound disillusion with the state of contemporary Russian theatre. Out of their meeting came the establishment, in 1898, of the Moscow Art Theatre. The 'realism' of this new company made it an immediate success, with major productions of Gorky*, Maeterlink, Shakespeare, and, most important of all, Chekhov. From 1906 they frequently toured abroad. Although taking much of the directing upon himself, Stanislavsky also continued his own career as a performer, becoming one of Russia's leading actors, and the consummate interpreter of Chekhov. But Stanislavsky himself became increasingly dissatisfied with his own performances, and in 1906 attempted, for the first time, an analysis of acting techniques. From this he developed, over a period of years, a system of training actors which has become known as the 'Stanislavskyan Method'.

Following the October Revolution, Stanislavsky continued to live and work in the USSR, making a major tour of Western Europe and the United States in 1922–4. During the 1920s he came in for considerable criticism at home, where he was accused of catering for bourgeois tastes. But, although producing several revolutionary dramas, he refused to give in to pressure, and was, during the 1930s, welcomed into the fold of official 'socialist realism'. In fact, the situation developed in which the methods of the bourgeois Stanislavsky were supported in opposition to those of the Marxist Bertolt Brecht*. Stanislavsky spent his last years writing, and died in the city of his birth.

The essence of Stanislavsky's system is a rejection of the 'theatrical' in favour of the 'creative'. He recognized that much acting, including his own, was merely imitative, a series of stage-tricks slavishly repeated. In the work of a great actor, on the other hand, he saw an 'inner-truth', a sincerity which made a performance a 'reality' both for the actor and his audience. He wrote that, 'Nothing should take place . . . on the stage without having first gone through the filter of the artistic feeling for truth.' Acting, instead of being a conscious 'trick', should become a habit, a natural process. If someone 'acts' a role, rather than 'experiencing' it, his performance is a lie, and therefore, in Stanislavsky's terms, non-creative. He found that through total relaxation, attained by intensive physical and psychological exercises, it was possible to 'summon up' a performance at will, but always as a new experience, rather than a mechanical process. He called this the re-creation of 'the life of the human spirit'.

It is a popular misconception that Stanislavsky's system demands that an actor be 'taken-over' by his part. On the contrary, it calls for a high degree of control, over voice, physical movement, and the emotions. Stanislavsky often quoted the Italian actor Tommaso Salvini (1828–1916): 'An actor lives, weeps and laughs on the stage, and while weeping or laughing, he observes his laughter and tears.' It is impossible to over-estimate the effect of Stanislavsky's ideas on the subsequent training of actors, especially in the United States, where Lee Strasberg, at the Actors Studio in New York, changed the whole face of American acting with his own idiosyncratic interpretation of 'the Method'.

Paul Nicholls

See: *My Life in Art* (1924, his only book to be published in the USSR during his lifetime); *An Actor Prepares* (1936); *Building a Character* (1949); and *Creating a Role* (1961). See also: David Magarshack, *Stanislavsky: A Life* (1950) and *Stanislavsky on the Art of the Stage* (1950); R. Williams, *Drama in Performance* (1954); S. Moore, *The Stanislavski System* (1965).

452
STEIN, Gertrude 1874–1946

US writer

Born in Allegheny, Pennsylvania, and brought up in Vienna, Paris and California, Gertrude Stein's background combined European culture with an interest in contemporary American theories of education. Later, while at Radcliffe College, she attended Harvard lectures and read psychology under William James. During a brief career as a medical student she studied brain anatomy at Johns Hopkins University, publishing two articles in *Psychological Review*, in 1896 and 1898.

She was first to recognize the aesthetic implications of James's pragmatism. Observation based upon inductively gathered data was to stimulate her interest in things being 'the same but different'. James taught her to exclude nothing in the search for evidence, but also to simplify by discerning patterns. After she became a writer she believed that her repetitive speech

in 'word portraits' would reveal the 'bottom nature' of people.

By 1902 she felt that medicine was 'not interesting' and joined her brother Leo in Paris. They settled at 27 rue de Fleurus, which became a clearing house for modernism for nearly thirty years. Many friends, among them Sherwood Anderson* and Hemingway*, would also be writers in exile who, as she would put it in *transition* in 1928, found America very Victorian and, like one's parents' home, a comfortable place to grow up in but not a good place to work. The years between 1907 and 1910 (before Leo was replaced by Alice Toklas) were formative for Gertrude, who tended to sit silently while Leo held forth about aesthetics, Freudian* psychoanalysis or his own painting. She was, however, busy observing people, thinking about language, pictures, the nature of time and being.

In 1905 at the Salon d'Automne Gertrude and Leo had bought Matisse's* painting *Woman with a Hat*. Thereafter their controversial art collection grew, as did their group of friends, which included, besides Matisse himself, Braque* and the young Picasso*, who painted Gertrude's portrait in 1905–6. During sittings she composed parts of *The Making of Americans* (not published until 1925), a long 'history' in which she attempted to describe every known human type.

By 1914 she had accomplished what she considered to be a major literary innovation. Cubism, as developed between 1908 and 1912 by Braque and Picasso, inspired Stein's 'composition' of objects, not in space but in time. She abandoned the traditional chronological story sequence and instead incorporated her knowledge of James's philosophy with Cubist attitudes and with Bergson's* notion of *durée*, denying the traditional view of an objective static world and re-creating it perceptually as a world in continuous flux. 'In composition,' she said, 'one thing is as important as another thing.'

Through analysis of dream life Freud had discovered the continuous present tense of the unconscious; Stein sought to elucidate the continuous present tense of conscious experience through art. In a 1934 lecture she stated: 'The business of art . . . is to live in the actual present, that is the complete actual present, and to completely express that complete actual present.' The continuous present tense, in which the structure or compositional mode corresponds to the structure of dynamic events, was her attempt to suspend time within a narrative form by demonstrating all aspects of her subject, just as Cézanne and the Cubists presented the aspects of a mass from many perspectives at once in their paintings. During many experiments between 1903 (in *Q.E.D.* later published as *Things as They Are*) and 1914 (in the prose 'still lifes' of *Tender Buttons*) Stein produced *Three Lives* (1909), of which the most important is 'Melanctha'. Here her theory of 'immediate history' and an interest in American syntax lead to her 'direct description'. She wanted to write 'the thing itself' and exploit values of words other than their accepted denotative meanings. 'A noun is the name of anything, why after a thing is named write about it,' she said in 'Poetry and Grammar', another lecture. In her efforts to join art to life she also sought a distinction between cause and effect. As she wrote of herself in *The Autobiography of Alice B. Toklas* (in fact a self-study, told 'through' Miss Toklas, who had become Gertrude's companion), 'She knows that beauty, music, decoration, the result of emotion should never be the cause ... of emotion.... They should consist of an exact reproduction of either an outer or an inner reality.'

When she was fifty-six, Stein decided that she and Miss Toklas must become publishers. *Lucy Church Amiably* (1930) initiated Plain Editions. A good example of her 'landscapes', almost nothing happens in this novel 'that looks like an engraving' and reproduced her delight in the countryside near her home at Belignin. Other Plain Editions included *How to Write* (1931), and the prose portraits *Matisse, Picasso and Gertrude Stein* (1933). But it was not until the publication of *The Autobiography of Alice B. Toklas* that she gained some of *la gloire* and the sales she craved. Following a successful lecture tour in America, Bennett Cerf of Random House offered to take over all the unsold Plain Editions stock and publish one book of Gertrude Stein's a year. Her reputation was further enhanced by the successful production of her friend Virgil Thomson's opera *Four Saints in Three Acts*, in 1934, for which Stein had written the libretto in 1927. The performance, in Hartford, Conn., was followed by a second American lecture tour. But the triumph was shortlived. In 1935 *transition* – whose editor Eugene Jolas had valued Stein, along with her innovative opposite James Joyce*, as the symbolic figure of his 'Revolution of the Word' – issued *The Testimony Against Gertrude Stein*, in refutation of *The Autobiography*. Its contributors, who included many of her former friends, said that she had no understanding of the times. Thus Braque claimed she misunderstood Cubism, seeing it 'in terms of personalities'; Matisse that she represented the epoch without taste and without relation to reality; Tristan Tzara* that she was a megalomaniac.

Since then Stein's work has evinced more ridicule and antagonism than appreciation. Many critics cannot accept her gargantuan egotism ('Think of the Bible and Homer, think of Shakespeare and think of me') which blinds them to her moral and physical courage, particularly during the two World Wars. Her frequently tedious repetition and apparent naivety often discourage perception of her ability to integrate subject and technique. The search for 'meaning' prevents many readers from experiencing Gertrude Stein's real contribution to Modernist literature: her concern to reveal all reality through the sounds and rhythms of language and her joyful immersion in the present.

Alison Armstrong

Stein's many writings include: *Portrait of Mabel Dodge* (1912); *Geography and Plays* (1922); *A Book Concluding with As a Wife has a Cow* (1926); *Lectures in America* (1935); *Paris France* (1940); *What are Masterpieces* (1940); *Brewsie and Willie* (1946). See also: Robert Bartlett Haas (ed.), *A Primer for the Gradual Understanding of Gertrude Stein* (3 vols, 1971–4). About Stein: Elizabeth Sprigge, *Gertrude Stein: Her Life and Works* (1957); John Malcolm Brinnen, *The Third Rose* (1959); Robert Bridgman, *Gertrude Stein in Pieces* (1970); Janet Hobhouse, *Everybody Who Was Anybody* (1975).

453

STEINBECK, John (Ernst) 1902–68

US novelist

John Steinbeck has always been popular with both European and American readers. As a serious novelist, however, he seems to have been more highly regarded outside his own country. Whereas the French included him in their honourable roll of 'les cinq grands' modern American novelists, it is almost *de rigueur* for American critics to dismiss his achievement with some such adjective as 'sentimental' or 'primitive'. It is true that there is more than a streak of sentimentality in Steinbeck, and that his work, in general, showed a falling-off after *The Grapes of Wrath* (1939). He wrote some good things after that, however, and the sharpness of American critical comment makes one suspect an animus which has more to do with the sociology of his novels than with their literary merit.

There is a tendency, in other words, to criticize Steinbeck's treatment of social issues for being oversimplified and his characters for being grotesques. On both counts, the allegations are not without some justification. It is doubtful, however, whether it is valid criticism of a novel to say that *paisanos* never in real life lived like the characters of *Tortilla Flat* (1935), nor Oklahoma dirt-farmers like the Joads. The criterion is surely whether, given the terms within which he is working, the novelist's work as a whole has life and substance, and presents a convincing picture of human existence.

Steinbeck's best work – which is probably to be found in his short stories – does carry this kind of conviction. *The Red Pony* (1949) has that peculiar mixture of sympathy and savagery, an awareness of life's fundamentals, which all Steinbeck's best work has. When he attempts the larger canvas, however, his vision tends to become warped by the very sympathy which makes his shorter work so satisfying. This is true of *In Dubious Battle* (1936) and *The Grapes of Wrath* where fierce loyalties forced him nearer to propaganda than is healthy for a novelist. In quite another type of novel, *Of Mice and Men* (1937), not only the type of character chosen but also the manner in which the (simple-minded) protagonist is treated is more simple (and sentimental) than the highest standards require. Similarly, the near-whimsicality of *Tortilla Flat* turns into the gamey indulgence of *Cannery Row* (1945), without touching that norm of human conduct which, if Steinbeck only knew it, was his *forte*. Yet another attempt, *East of Eden* (1952) was too large, too rambling, and too melodramatic for success, although, as one is always forced to recognize with Steinbeck's work, it is full of excellent things.

The quality of the *farouche* in Steinbeck spills over into his writings. Unlike Hemingway*, he cannot seem to keep it in check for the sake of artistic perfection. Technically, there is some similarity between the two writers. Both, by selecting the minutiae of a given situation, render its inner emotion through a series of apparently objective notations. So far as their preoccupations are concerned, however, they seem to be working on different co-ordinates. Hemingway was always a conscious artist. Steinbeck comes near to achieving that kind of perfection only when, by a happy accident, his feeling for a simple human situation fuses with his talent for selecting significant detail. It is this quality which he so triumphantly achieves in *The Red Pony* and which could perhaps be called, after the French, 'poetic realism'. Here Steinbeck's 'primitivism' is subordinated to his humanity.

The so-called 'primitivism' of Steinbeck's view of life has been referred to his background. Born in 1902 in Salinas, California, he knew at first hand both the richness of nature and the poverty of man in 'The Long Valley'. From 1919 to 1925 he went to Stanford University, supporting himself by working as a labourer and 'sampling' courses that interested him. In 1925 he worked his way to New York on a cattle boat, as others had worked their way to Europe. Having written pieces for university magazines, his purpose was to make his living as a writer. After a short time as a reporter, however, he went back to California, and worked at whatever jobs he could get while writing his early novels.

The first to appear was *Cup of Gold*, an account, in fictional form, of the life of the buccaneer, Sir Henry Morgan. His early stories, all based on a Californian valley, were published in 1932 under the title of *The Pastures of Heaven*, a title taken from the Spanish and chosen with some ironical intention. *To a God Unknown*, in the following year, foreshadowed that feeling for the land, its nature and its rhythms, which was to be so strong a motif in Steinbeck's later work. During the twenty-seven years from *Tortilla Flat* to the award of the Nobel Prize in 1962, Steinbeck was a highly controversial figure, never lacking courage to attack the problems of the moment nor to present the joys and tribulations of people about whom only an act of self-abnegation would force the average novelist to write.

Steinbeck was always fascinated by biology. One remembers the land-turtle crawling across the Western highway at the beginning of *The Grapes of Wrath* and the comment that this implies on the 'Okies' who are to make their pilgrimage to California. Men may or may not have souls, he seems to be saying; this is something which cannot be measured or tested. What one *can* perceive, however, is that they are as subject to natural laws as the animals. This biological interest in human existence no doubt accounts for whatever simplification of human motive critics have found in Steinbeck's work. Yet despite this he never, as a narrower author might, gives the impression of being clinical, precisely because of the love and care he has for the simple people about whom he writes. He has an unembarrassed ability to speak out. He does not try to be clever or sophisticated. At his best he strikes a note of affirmation and this, coupled with his talent for selective detail, makes some of his characters and scenes stay in the mind long after the precise details of the novel or story have faded. Whether or not that makes him a great novelist is another matter. What is indisputable, however, is that he was a highly talented and serious one.

Geoffrey Moore

See: E. W. Tedlock Jr and C. V. Wicker, *Steinbeck and his Critics: A Record of Twenty-Five Years* (1957); Peter Lisca, *The Wide World of John Steinbeck* (1958); Warren French, *John Steinbeck* (1961); and F. W. Watt, *Steinbeck* (1962).

454
STEINER, Rudolf 1861–1925

Austrian founder of anthroposophy

Rudolf Steiner was born in Karljevec and spent his youth in the small villages of Lower Austria, where his father was a railway official. His interest in science and philosophy led him to Vienna, where he took his degree in mathematics, physics and chemistry. Invited to edit the scientific writings of Goethe, he moved to Weimar and there met many leading intellectuals, including Heinrich von Treitschke, Hermann Grimm and Ernst Haeckel. But the Weimar years (1889–96) were a lonely period for Steiner, as he sought a bridge between the prevailing scientific philosophy of objective enquiry based on clarity of observation and thought and his inner life which since childhood had revealed the reality of a spiritual world to him. Could the objectivity and rigour of science be applied to the study of that world? It was this question which led to his doctoral dissertation published in revised form as *Truth and*

Science in 1892 and to his standard work in philosophy *The Philosophy of Freedom*, first published in 1894 (both trans. 1964, one vol.). The sub-title of the *Philosophy* reveals its intention: 'Results of the Observation of the Soul according to the Scientific Method.' In this work, which provided the basis for his later research into spiritual questions, Steiner argued against the Kantian idea of the essential limitation of human knowledge, maintaining that human thinking if properly developed was capable of uniting material phenomena with their spiritual archetypes. For Steiner the world of appearances and essences was not only knowable but could be brought together on the stage of human consciousness.

In 1897, having published some ninety-five titles, Steiner left Weimar for Berlin, where he edited an avant-garde literary magazine and taught at a Workers' Training Institute. Convinced that Western culture stood in urgent need of a new and conscious spiritual understanding, for the next two decades, through numerous articles, lectures and books, he discussed the nature of the human soul and spirit, the possibilities of inner development through meditation, the spiritual history of mankind and the earth, and the realities of reincarnation and karma. Works of this period include *Theosophy* (1904, trans. 1975), *Knowledge of the Higher Worlds and Its Attainment* (1909, trans. 1965) and *Occult Science: an Outline* (1910, trans. 1970). At the same time a greater realization of the central significance of the Christ-being for human evolution led to many lectures and studies on different aspects of Christology. It was at the end of his time in Berlin that his connections with the Theosophical Society weakened, and that he began to talk more of his own Anthroposophy, meaning less a wisdom of man than a new awareness of man's humanity. In 1912 he created the Anthroposophical Society, and in 1913 began work on its main centre, the Goetheanum in Dornach, Switzerland. This wooden, twin-domed structure burned down in 1922, leading to the present concrete building and the refounding of the Anthroposophical Society and the 'High School for Spiritual Science' in 1923–4.

From 1910 on Steiner also turned his attention to a renewal of the arts, in particular speech, drama, painting and movement. The First World War interrupted much of this work, but also generated many practical questions from teachers, farmers, doctors, priests, therapists and others, and gave Steiner an impetus towards many new initiatives which have since flourished not only in Europe but in many other parts of the world. There are now close on 200 Waldorf or Steiner schools, aiming to give normal children a complete education for individual freedom and responsibility, as well as a number of homes and villages for the handicapped. A medical and therapeutic movement in hospitals, clinics and therapy centres has also been developed, and even a new kind of agriculture,

bio-dynamic farming, grew out of Steiner's talks to farmers in 1924. His work with priests led to a movement for religious renewal, the Christian Community, while his many artistic and architectural indications have given many artists and architects a new relation to colour and form.

Steiner did not live to see more than the beginnings of these initiatives, but died in Dornach in 1925. His life and work present us with a challenge and a puzzle. He was neither a mystic nor a scientist in the ordinary sense, but attempted to develop a science of the spirit capable of illuminating questions of life.

Christopher Schaefer

A complete list of Steiner's works is published by the Rudolf Steiner Press, London. See also: A. P. Shepherd, *Scientist of the Invisible* (1954); J. Hemleben, *Rudolf Steiner: A Documentary Biography* (1975); J. Davy (ed.), *Work Arising* (1975).

455

STELLA, Frank Philip 1936–

US painter

Born in Malden, Massachusetts, Stella attended Phillips Academy, Andover, where he studied under Patrick Morgan and met Carl Andre and Hollis Frampton. In 1954 he entered Princeton, where he was taught by William Seitz and Stephen Greene. Fellow students were Walter Darby Bannard and Michael Fried. After leaving Princeton Stella worked as a house painter before beginning his Black series. In these his great influence was Jasper Johns*, whose one-man exhibition at the Castelli Gallery Stella saw in 1958. 'The thing that struck me,' he said, 'was the way he stuck to the motif.' In this, his first major series of twenty-three paintings (Winter 1958–February 1960), he opted for neutral stability rather than emotional flux. Using dollar-a-gallon commercial black enamel he painted even, unruled symmetrical 'stripes' which followed the shape of the canvas and left 'pinstripes' of white showing between them. In a lecture at the Pratt Institute in 1960 Stella spoke of finding a new solution to problems of balancing the parts in a painting. Lean, sombre, hypnotic, his Black series adapted the all-over technique of Pollock*. Abstract Expressionism had foundered in the late 1950s. The shift in sensibility effected by Stella – paralleled in sculpture by Andre and Don Judd and in film by Hollis Frampton – was towards symmetry, reticence and iconicity. In the Black paintings, as Stella himself explained, he 'forced illusionistic space out of the painting at a constant rate of using a regulation pattern'. In the Aluminum series which followed Stella found a radical solution to the problem of space 'left over' between the modular bands; the space was simply cut away, following a suggestion of Darby Bannard.

Stella was investigating the viability of shape, in Michael Fried's phrase. In his *Three American Painters* catalogue of 1966 Fried continued, 'I mean its power to hold, to stamp itself out, and IN – as verisimilitude and narrative and symbolism used to impress themselves – compelling conviction. Stella's undertaking in these paintings is therapeutic: to restore shape to health.' Fried, like other formalist critics of the time, was quick to take up Stella's cause, using as an appropriate critical tool a dogmatically applied version of Clement Greenberg's argument that modernist painting would thrive only by purification and separation from the other arts. That purification and separation, he believed, would only take place when painting acknowledged its limitations. That a canvas *was* a flat canvas, sculpted into a given shape, that that shape could interact with the shapes depicted within the canvas. . . . Stella's approach seemed a proper, logical, even dutiful extension of Greenberg. One of his triumphs as an artist, however, has been to outpace his critics, to provide them with the unexpected and, like any great artist, to renew criticism and adumbrate new critical forms by means of his work. Operating in series, Stella has explored squares, mazes and concentricity, perimeters and polygons and notched Vs. The series are carefully named and defined in William Rubin's monograph. In 1966 Stella's progress was complicated by the introduction of irregular configurations. From now on his path would parallel that of Ellsworth Kelly and Kenneth Noland*, and the main issue of his painting would be the juxtaposition of uninflected areas of colour. With the Protractor series in 1967, Stella returned to scholarly interests from his Princeton days – Arabic design and Hiberno-Saxon illustration. In these huge, almost architectural, paintings the eye is sent hurrying around curved contours in such a joyous, even luxurious way that it is impossible to ignore the strong emotional impact of Stella's art, which formalist critics seemed intent on forgetting. With the Polish Village series (1970–3) painted wooden reliefs were notched and superimposed, while the Brazilian series (1974–5) was made in aluminium and steel. The Exotic Bird series which began in 1976 took the scribbly application of colour and the buffing effects a stage further, fixing 'found' shapes like drawing curves over the loose surface. Loose, relaxed, humorous, they signalled another departure in a distinguished, self-conscious career, both inside and outside the avant-garde.

Stuart Morgan

See: William Rubin, *Frank Stella* (New York, Museum of Modern Art, 1970); Brenda Richardson, *Frank Stella: The Black Paintings* (Baltimore Museum of Art, 1976); Philip Leider, *Stella Since 1970* (Fort Worth Art Museum, 1978).

456
STEVENS, Wallace 1879–1955

US poet

Now ranked, with Eliot*, Pound* and W. B. Yeats*, as one of the outstanding English language poets of the twentieth century, it is only since his death that Wallace Stevens's technical mastery and seriousness have gradually assured him a reputation. There were perhaps two main reasons for this: first, his peculiar difficulty, arising from a conjunction of simple declarative grammar with extreme allusiveness of style; and, second, the unfashionableness of his poetic manner. In an age which demanded the bareness of later Yeats and the acerbity of early Eliot, Stevens's highly polished surfaces were impenetrable to all but the most persevering of readers. In particular some critics claimed that his poetry lacked 'the urgency of human passion'. However, just as over the years most readers of poetry have grown familiar with Eliot's elliptical style, his personal references and highly subjective choice of literary allusions, so they have acclimatized themselves to Stevens. He is, in some respects, indeed, easier for the 'unliterary' person – that ideal intelligent reader for whom even Eliot craved – since his difficulties are intrinsic and do not depend on reference to a body of literature which may or may not be known. Stevens's chief fault is a tendency towards whimsicality and aestheticism, but he is no more a mere player with words than Eliot is a mere paster-together of quotations. A meditative poet of the highest order, Stevens masked his seriousness with flippancy and bravura – mannerisms that were part of his literary *persona*.

Stevens was born in Reading, Pennsylvania, the son of Garret Barckalow Stevens and Mary Catherine Zeller Stevens. The Zeller family was Dutch and, according to Stevens's own account, went to America for religious reasons. After studying law at Harvard, where he was attracted to the teaching of Santayana*, Stevens attended the New York University Law School. During the period between 1904, when he was admitted to the Bar, and 1916, when he became a member of the Hartford Accident and Indemnity Company, he practised both law and poetry in New York. He was associated with a Greenwich Village group of whom the leader was Alfred Kreymborg, and his poems were published in small magazines, among them Harriet Monroe's *Poetry*. It was not until he was forty-four that *Harmonium*, his first book, appeared. A second edition, revised and enlarged, was published in 1931, followed in 1935 by *Ideas of Order*. *Owl's Clover*, which he excluded from his *Collected Poems* (1954), came out in 1936, and was followed by *The Man with the Blue Guitar* (1937), *Parts of a World* and *Notes Toward a Supreme Fiction* (both 1942). *Esthétique du Mal* (1945), *Transport to Summer* (1947), *A Primitive Like an Orb* (1948), *Auroras* *of Autumn* (1950) complete the poetic canon, although since his death in 1955 Samuel French Morse has published plays and poems, either unprinted in book form or allowed to go out of print, in *Opus Posthumous* (1957). This book also contains Stevens's aphoristic 'Adagia' and other prose complementary to *The Necessary Angel: Essays on Reality and the Imagination* (1951).

A corporation lawyer in Hartford for nearly forty years of his life, Stevens negotiated the world of business with that mixture of diffidence and authority which is also part of the success of his poems. Behind what at first sight might seem like a charming example of Connecticut rococo, there stands the solidity of a Dutch barn, a toughness of mind scarcely equalled among poets of our time.

The surely savoured ambivalence of his situation reveals itself in the title of his first book. And the titles of the poems: 'Le Monocle de Mon Oncle', 'The Paltry Nude Starts on a Spring Voyage', 'The Worms at Heaven's Gate', 'Tea at the Palaz of Hoon' – what are we to make of them? Some have acute, if oblique, relevance; others are comments on the irony of the human situation as Stevens saw it. Stevens's poetic manner varies from the extravagent rhetoric of 'The Comedian as the Letter C' to the subtle sobriety of 'Esthétique du Mal'. Two main themes run through the bulk of his poetry: first, the matter of belief in the modern world, and second, the philosophical problem of appearance and reality. The 'belief' poems are central. From 'Sunday Morning' to 'Notes Toward a Supreme Fiction', Stevens was engaged by the problem of the religious man in a world whose religion he cannot accept. The woman in 'Sunday Morning' asks why she should 'give her bounty to the dead'. She feels that the things of this world are all that we know, in contrast to the myths of an afterlife which men in their hunger have fabricated for themselves. And yet, even despite her acceptance that 'divinity must live within herself', she still feels the need for some 'imperishable bliss'. The answer that Stevens gives is a stoical one: that 'Death is the mother of beauty.' The awful fact of death, the knowledge that it is really the end of existence, and that there is nothing beyond, enable us to savour the bitter-sweetness of the human situation. Stevens mocks the vision of paradise which we have created after our own image. There was a man called Jesus, but his tomb is no 'porch of spirits', only a grave. We are alone on this earth. No benign spirit watches over us. We have the world in our time, and that should be enough.

But it is not enough. If the reasoner is religious by nature, as Stevens was, age and maturity will yearly increase the necessity for belief in someone or something greater than man. Stevens found it in poetry, the 'supreme fiction'. As he said in a memorandum to Henry Church in 1940: 'The major poetic idea in the work is and always has been the idea of God. One of the visible movements of the modern imagination is the movement away from the idea of God. The poetry that created the idea of God will either adapt it to our different intelligence, or create a substitute for it, or make it unnecessary.' 'Notes Toward a Supreme Fiction' deals with the basic philosophical and spiritual imperatives towards which Stevens had steadily been moving all his life. The imagination, in its attempt to abstract truth, brings up the idea of man, 'major man' – not the exceptional man, but the best in every man. Change, which we deplore as bringing death and destruction, is the source of vital freshness in life and its many forms. The flow of reality is that which brings us our moments of perfection, of happiness and love. The 'order' that Stevens seeks must be flexible, organic, partaking of the freshness of transformation. We must celebrate the world by a constant and amazed delight in the unexpectedness of each moment, a more difficult rigour than to follow ceremony in the form of traditional beliefs. This is the poet's way, and every man can be a poet, not necessarily by writing poems but by living with sensibility and wholeness.

'Notes Toward a Supreme Fiction' comprises an aggregate of ideas and feelings, expressed with such mutational amplitude, with such controlled jugglery of parenthetical impressions, that half a dozen lines of simultaneous commentary would be needed to do it justice. Yet, being supplied, they would, of course, do no justice at all, for it is the essence of Stevens's art that 'poetry is the subject of the poem' and that it 'must defeat the intelligence almost successfully'. Consistenly, and with great courage, Stevens tackled what he saw to be the main problem of our time. Because he did it in poetry, and poetry which is very difficult, his art has not been sufficiently recognized. But by doing it this way, which was the only way he could – for he was a poet and not a philosopher – he could in a sense take his speculation further. His poetry begins where most other poetry leaves us, in a state of heightened awareness. Through the aesthetic experience he explored the possibility of a new epistemology, pushing the boundaries of poetic communication to a new limit. There is only one other modern American poet who is comparable with him in seriousness and range, and that is T. S. Eliot.

Geoffrey Moore

Recommended critical books are Frank Kermode, *Wallace Stevens* (1060); Ashley Brown and Robert Haller, *The Achievement of Wallace Stevens* (1962); Marie Boroff, *Wallace Stevens, A Collection of Critical Essays* (1963); R. H. Pearce and J. H. Miller, *The Act of the Mind* (1965); Helen Vendler, *On Extended Wings* (1969); and A. Walton Litz, *Introspective Voyager* (1972).

457

STOCKHAUSEN, Karlheinz 1928–

German composer

Karlheinz Stockhausen's formative years were spent in one of the most extreme eras of recent history. Nazi Germany was not only highly emotional, it was also highly philistine and anti-intellectual. It is therefore not surprising that, after some works written in requirement for the examination of the Cologne High School for Music, and fired by Messiaen's* latest, highly revolutionary pieces (he went to study with him a year later), he should have made a clean and complete break with 'the past', and with *Kreuzspiel* (1951) composed one of the first totally serial works in Europe. At the same time as this highly intellectual (though also metaphysically conceived) work and similar ones that followed, he was exploring the technology of electronic music, information theory, phonetics and other scientific disciplines. This can be seen in the new music periodical *Die Reihe* which he edited and to which he contributed theory and analysis. In particular a whole volume was devoted to Webern*, acknowledging his position of father-figure of the new movement.

In order to escape a certain atomism characteristic of the early works, Stockhausen began, with *Kontra-Punkte* (1953) for ten instruments (the title itself is indicative of the change away from pointillism) and the *Klavierstücke* (1952–61), to think in what he called Gruppen, groups or complexes of sounds tending to some central character. All sounds were no longer equally important, no longer organized on an equal footing; some were ornamental to others. Such masterpieces as *Zeitmasze* (1956) for five woodwinds, *Gruppen* (1957) for three orchestras and *Gesang der Jünglinge* (electronic music, 1956) also belong to this phase. They combine extremely strong structures with a liberated imagination such that created an explosion in the musical world of the late 1950s.

It was one of Stockhausen's strengths that he was able, in the 1960s, to continue exploiting serial ideas even though his music became much more 'open'. Pieces had variable forms (*Momente*, 1964; *Plus Minus*, 1963; *Mikrophonie I*, 1964; *Solo*, 1966), and a collection of highly characterized little sections often with individual titles became more important than the logic of the piece as a whole. Stockhausen saw this as a concentration on the 'Now' – living for the moment. Moment Form was his name for it.

A crucial aspect of many of these works, and some of their predecessors, is in the principle of mediation between two extremes – as it were from black to white with several stages of grey in between. All these steps would then be equally covered in some serially constructed order. For instance, *Kontakte* for tape, piano and percussion uses six degrees of change (from big to small) in the spatial location of the quadrophonic sound, in the volume of the sound, in the texture, in the register, in the speed and in the instrument family. (Six dimensions!) These changes occur within one 'moment'. The moments are then themselves serialized into six types, and so a typical Stockhausen hierarchy is built up.

The next development was a refinement in two directions. First, in works like *Prozession* (1967) for Stockhausen's own group of four players, *Kurzwellen* (1968), *Spiral* (1968), *Pole für 2* (1969–70), *Expo für 3* (1969–70), the score is reduced to indications as to which parameters (loudness, register, size of event) should increase and which should decrease – certainly a reduction to essentials. Players take material from each other or from a short-wave radio and treat it improvisationally according to the instructions.

The second sort of refinement was the reduction of instructions to the players to short verbal texts, *Aus den sieben Tagen* (1968), and *Für Kommende Zeiten* (1968–70). This again had the aim of getting to the heart of the matter, in this case of developing musicians' intuition and ability to communicate with each other on the deepest levels. To escape from the dehumanizing tyrannies of complex rigid notation, technical performing problems, shallow self-consciousness and over-intellectualism one text – *It* for ensemble – goes:

> think NOTHING
> wait until it is absolutely still within you
> when you have attained this
> begin to play
>
> as soon as you start to think, stop
> and try to reattain
> the state of NON-THINKING
> then continue playing

This text clearly demonstrates the renewal of spiritual life for which Stockhausen craves. It is a theme which runs through all his works, all his thinking. Even in the more carefully structured works of the 1970s such as *Mantra* (1970) for two pianos and ringmodulators and *Inori* (1974) for Mime and orchestra, the theme is fundamental. *Mantra* is a reflection of divine order (the many within the One) and *Inori* is concerned, in the part of the mime, with different international gestures of prayer, outward gestures directing the spirit inward to the music and to the divinity. Many of the products of the 1970s have a visual, and indeed visionary, aspect, often resulting from dreams. The extraordinary individuality of works such as *Trans* for orchestra (1971), *Musik im Bauch* for six percussionists and musical boxes (1975), *Sirius*, electronic music with trumpet, soprano, bass clarinet and bass (1977), and *Jahreslauf* for Japanese Gagaku orchestra and dancers (1977) – all of them 'choreographed', 'dressed' and 'lit' by the composer – testify to Stockhausen's unquestioning acceptance of his 'received' visions, and to his faith in their value. These works seem to be the legacy of no known tradition; Stockhausen himself confesses to an only partial understanding of their meaning. He has become something of a guru for a wider audience (many of them young) than has ever been possible before. Passages like the last 'region' of the two-hour electronic and concrete work for tape *Hymnen* (1967) and the Tibetan-monk-inspired work *Stimmung* (1978) for six voices have had a profound impact on the spirituality of our time, reaching far beyond the normal modern music audience. As he said, 'What I'm trying to do, as far as I'm aware of it, is to produce models that herald the stage after destruction. I'm trying to go beyond collage, heterogeneity and pluralism, and to find unity; to produce music that brings us to the essential ONE. And that is going to be badly needed during the time of shocks and disasters that is going to come' (Interview in *Music and Musicians*, London, May 1971). Few composers would wish to be so articulate, but few would deny the importance of the mission.

Jonathan Harvey

Other important works by Stockhausen are: *Carré* (1960); *Punkte* (1952, revised 1962); *Mixtur* (1964); *Telemusik* (1966) and *Licht* (1977 to the present). His key writings can be found in the four volumes of his *Texte* (from 1963). About Stockhausen: Karl H. Wörner, *Stockhausen: Life and Work*, trans. Bill Hopkins (1973); Jonathan Cott, *Stockhausen: Conversations with the Composer* (1974); Jonathan Harvey, *The Music of Stockhausen, An Introduction* (1975); and Robin Maconie, *The Works of Karlheinz Stockhausen* (1976).

STONES, The Rolling *see* ROLLING STONES, The

458
STOPES, Marie Carmichael 1880–1958

British pioneer of birth control clinics, palaeobotanist

Marie Stopes was born in Edinburgh to Charlotte Carmichael and Henry Stopes. Her mother was an enthusiast of the Rational Dress Society and the first woman in Scotland to take a university certificate. Her father was a brewer whose major interest in life was archaeology. Between them they taught their daughter nothing positive about human sexuality. Marie Stopes was to become one of the most famous women of her time as a result of her passionate belief that the human race would improve through the selective use of birth control.

After an inauspicious academic start with no formal education until twelve Stopes won a science scholarship and at the age of nineteen enrolled in the science faculty at University College, London. After two years of study she won her degree in botany and geology and gained the Gilchrist Scholarship which took her to Munich to study the cellular structure of ovules and ova of cycad specimens. It was here that her long and platonic relationship with an assistant professor included her first kiss which she described as 'quite horrid'. In Munich she won a doctorate after the university rules had been changed on her behalf. In 1904 she became the first woman on the scientific staff of Manchester University. She won a DSc in London in 1905, becoming the youngest Doctor of Science in Britain.

Stopes married a Canadian geneticist Dr R. R. Gates in 1911 and, still a virgin, left him in 1914. Since lawyers seemed unable to advise her on her marital plight, characteristically she undertook the task of reading all the books on sex in three languages in the British Museum. In 1917 the marriage was annulled on grounds of non-consummation.

Although her reputation as a fossil botanist was unrivalled it was unlikely that this would provide the fame of which she had dreamt since her earlier years. The path to fame was started by the publication in 1918 of her book *Married Love*. In this Stopes sought to tell the world what she had discovered from her hours in the British Museum – that it was possible to combine a happy marriage with perfect sexual experience at the same time as avoiding unwanted pregnancies. Stopes was at the time thirty-eight, a virgin, and unmarried.

In 1918 she married H. V. Roe, a wealthy manufacturer and aviator. Her dream of establishing birth control clinics was cemented by his financial position. In 1920 she opened the Mother's Clinic for Constructive Birth Control in Holloway – the first birth control clinic in the British Empire. She favoured the use of trained nurses in her clinic, feeling that women would respond to them more readily than to doctors.

There was intense rivalry and disagreement among the various pioneering birth control campaigners – a situation which increased in bitterness for the rest of Stopes's life. The Malthusian League was a major early rival. Their clinic in Walworth, south London, favoured the Dutch cap while Stopes invented her own cervical cap which she trademarked the Pro-race cap.

As well as rivalries within the movement Stopes, editing her own periodical, the *Birth Control News*, was constantly involved in, and continued to arouse, intense public and religious debate. As part of this, in 1922 she issued a writ for libel against a Dr Halliday Sutherland who as a Catholic medical doctor contended that birth control education was nothing but a cruel experiment on the poor who were unable to resist. Sutherland's appeal went to the House of Lords where he was supported by a vote of four to one. Fame together with public sympathy and admiration belonged to Stopes. The Catholic Church became her bitter enemy. The result of the happenings of all these years took their toll of Marie Stopes. She became increasingly idiosyncratic and difficult to deal with. In 1924 she fulfilled another dream and gave birth to a much-wanted child, whose birth announcement *The Times* refused to print. Over the following years she continued her fight for birth control and applied herself increasingly to her literary interests by writing poetry, plays and more books. Despite her insistence that she would live to 120, one of the century's most extraordinary women died in 1958 alone and unloved.

Her dream of free contraceptive advice for all who ask has become a reality, in Britain, as part of the care offered by the NHS. The clinic which she founded and ran until her death continues to operate.

Janice Bumstead

Other books include: *Ancient Plants* (1910); *Love Letters of a Japanese* (1911); *Wise Parenthood* (1918); *A Letter to Working Mothers; on How to have Healthy Children and Avoid Weakening Pregnancies* (1919); *Radiant Motherhood* (1920); *The First Five Thousand* (1925); *Mother England* (1929); *Love Songs for Young Lovers* (1939); *Joy and Verity* (1952). See also: H. V. Stopes-Roe, with Ian Scott, *Marie Stopes and Birth Control* (1974); R. Hall, *Marie Stopes* (1977).

459
STOPPARD, Tom 1937–

British playwright

The *ex cathedra* opinions of dramatists on drama are generally to be treated with wariness, but two of the more uncompromisingly sensible have come from Tom Stoppard. The first, derived from his early experience as a critic, is that the audience owes the playwright absolutely *nothing*. The second is that the theatre ought to be in the hands of people who understand show business.

From these two dicta there arises what he himself identifies as a consuming fear of being boring. To avoid this he often fills his plays with contrasting elements: at one moment, metaphysical discussion, at another song-and-dance. Of his major plays, *Jumpers* (1972) and *Travesties* (1974) end with popular tunes ('Sentimental Journey' and 'My Blue Heaven' respectively) and their success may well have something to do with the fact that they send their audience home humming. Other playrights have attempted to use music in the same way, but their efforts have usually come across as forced and programmatic. With Stoppard they seem spontaneous outgrowths of the exuberant dialogue and construction, which in turn are an expression of the writer's humanity. Other playwrights may treat of the human condition, social or metaphysical, with more

obvious earnestness. He is almost alone in making the audience feel, through the actual texture of his work, that the condition is really worth bothering about – or, in plainer terms, that life might actually be worth living.

Stoppard has divided his plays, in interviews, into 'nuts-and-bolts comedies' and seriously intended works. But this is misleading; the differences are more of scale than of kind. The obsessively neat patterning and verbal leap-frogging of *The Real Inspector Hound* (1968) parallel those in *Rosencrantz and Guildenstern are Dead* (1967), *Jumpers* and *Travesties*. The hugely successful farce *Dirty Linen* (1976) may be slight but it deals with personal responsibility in public situations, as do the overtly political *Professional Foul* (television, 1976), *Every Good Boy Deserves Favour* (music by André Previn, 1977) and *Night and Day* (1978).

EGBDF deals with the persecution of dissidents in Soviet Russia, *Professional Foul* with state terror in Stoppard's native Czechoslovakia (which he left at the age of two). These later plays have prompted critics to welcome (or deplore) Stoppard's increasing 'seriousness'. But there is nothing in them that could not be foreseen from *Jumpers*. This, the best comedy written in English since the war, is in essence a plea against intellectual bullying; and the introduction of a pugnacious (and electorally victorious) Radical-Liberal Party, represented on stage by a trendy and omnicompetent University Vice-Chancellor, is a clear indication of the ease with which this can extend to physical bullying. The nicest (though still dangerously self-absorbed) character on stage is the Professor of Ethics, trying to justify his belief in a moral force which he chooses, rather to his own embarrassment, to call God. In declaring that morality goes deeper than politics, and crucially influences it, Stoppard has written a political play that makes most others of the species look dangerously naive. *Travesties*, formally less satisfying, takes the argument a step further by examining the motives that make men into politicians, or for that matter artists: to each his own ego-trip. The play lines up Joyce*, Lenin*, the Dadaist Tristan Tzara*; if the author's sympathies are obviously with the first, the artist, rather than with the two disparate (and highly plausible) philistines, this rarely upsets the comic balance.

Presiding over the whole, remembering it and usually getting it wrong, is the minor consular official Henry Carr, one of Stoppard's immortal onlooker figures (like Rosencrantz, Guildenstern, George of *Jumpers*, the theatre critics of *Inspector Hound* and the timid Moon of the 1966 novel *Lord Malquist and Mr Moon*). These culminate perhaps in the suaver academic philosopher of *Professional Foul* who is finally – and this may mark a decisive breakthrough in Stoppard's work – nudged into action. That he takes it by making exquisite and scrupulous use of the enemy's moral weapons is a sign that Stoppard's symmetrical sense remains as safe and satisfying as ever. He is an inveterate punster, and his awareness of jargon as a political weapon sometimes recalls Orwell*. But he believes too in the saving power of wit; indeed he exemplifies it.

Robert Cushman

Other plays include: *Enter a Free Man* (1968); *If You're Glad I'll be Frank* (radio, 1966); *Albert's Bridge* (radio, 1967); *After Magritte* (1970); *Dogg's Our Pet* (1971); *Artist Descending a Staircase* (radio, 1972); *New-Found-Land* (1976); *Dogg's Hamlet* and *Cahoot's Macbeth* (1979). See: Ronald Hayman, *Tom Stoppard* (1977).

460

STRACHEY, Giles Lytton 1880–1932

British biographer and essayist

After an oppressive childhood in London, much undermined by ill-health, and an unhappy year at Liverpool University, Lytton Strachey went up to Trinity College, Cambridge, in 1899. Cambridge altered the whole tenor of his life. As a member of a secret society known as the 'Apostles', he was brought into contact with older men such as Desmond MacCarthy, G. E. Moore* and Bertrand Russell* and, among his contemporaries, Maynard Keynes* and Leonard Woolf. Extracting from Moore's *Principia Ethica* the equation that personal relationships plus aesthetic sensibility equalled the good life, Strachey took the nineteenth-century cult of homosexuality and turned it into a weapon of twentieth-century revolt. As a member of the Bloomsbury Group that developed in London from the Cambridge Apostles and included E. M. Forster*, Roger Fry* and Virginia Woolf*, he proclaimed a fierce antagonism to the dogmas of Christianity and the worldly religion of success.

It was not until 1918, when his polemic *Eminent Victorians* was published, that he became well-known. The war (in which he had been a conscientious objector) acted as a catalyst in the writing of these four biographical essays, altering Strachey's original concept of the book so that its theme became the ironic sifting of those Victorian pretensions that seemed to have led civilization into a holocaust. Its impact was tremendous. The world was weary of big guns and big phrases, and Strachey's witty polemic was specially appealing to the jaded palate of the younger generation. His four subjects were treated with the acuteness of caricature. In 'Cardinal Manning' he attacked the Church; in 'Dr Arnold' he ridiculed the tribal deity of the public schools; in 'The End of General Gordon' his target was imperialism and power politics; and in 'Florence Nightingale' he exposed the false basis of

that humanitarianism with which the Victorian Age had salved its conscience.

Three years later he produced his classic life of *Queen Victoria* which was to become a model for future biographers. From the anarchism of *Eminent Victorians* he reverted to his natural romanticism and produced a perfectly constructed biography that playfully enhanced the legend of the little old lady on the throne – a whimsical, teasing, half-admiring, half-mocking view that found in Victoria a quaintly impressive symbol of a quaintly impressive age. With his Mandarin style, so exactly suited to anecdote, he gave us by means of carefully plotted chapter-stories, a life of miraculous compactness that was a work, not of polemics, but of art.

Then, in 1928, came his last biography *Elizabeth and Essex*, subtitled 'A Tragic History'. This story of the love-affair between Queen Elizabeth and the Earl of Essex was quite unlike Strachey's previous books. An experiment in biographical technique, it was constructed along the lines of a five-act Elizabethan play. Wherever possible, Strachey treats his readers as onlookers, and the visual scenes are neatly framed by entrances and exits. The other great influence on him was that of Freud* whose theories concerning father – daughter relationships he used to describe Elizabeth's underlying attitude to Essex's death. Between the lines of the book may be read something of Strachey's own homosexual love-affair with the handsome Old Etonian, Roger Senhouse. He imagined Elizabeth's feeling for Essex as being similar to his own for Senhouse. Though the book was frowned upon by academic historians, this dual involvement gave it an extraordinary tension and design.

Strachey's battles as a polemicist are mostly won, but his influence persists as the man who revolutionized modern biography. In his private life, he set an example of forbearance in human relationships. For the last sixteen years of his life he lived with the painter (Dora) Carrington and her husband Ralph Partridge in a *ménage-à-trois* that involved other men and women whose amatory gyrations produced a tragi-comedy of intensely felt emotions.

On 21 January 1932 Strachey died from cancer of the stomach. 'If this is dying,' he said just before the end, 'then I don't think much of it.'

Michael Holroyd

Other works: Strachey's first book was a volume of literary criticism, *Landmarks in French Literature* (1912); in 1948, as part of his Collected Works, most of his essays were regrouped by James Strachey and published as *Biographical Essays* and *Literary Essays*. A selection of all these essays, with some hitherto uncollected additions, entitled *The Shorter Strachey*, ed. Michael Holroyd and Paul Levy, appeared in his centenary year 1980. A pornographic *jeu d'esprit*,

Ermyntrude and Esmerelda, came out in 1968; in 1971 his autobiographical writings were edited by Michael Holroyd in a volume called *Lytton Strachey by Himself*, and the following year there appeared *The Really Interesting Question and Other Papers*, ed. Paul Levy, that contained some of his Apostles' speeches. About Strachey: Michael Holroyd, *Lytton Strachey, A Critical Biography* (1968, revised 1971).

461
STRAUSS, Richard George 1864–1949

German composer and conductor

Strauss was born in Munich, a true Bavarian. His father was Germany's foremost horn-player and his mother was of the Pschorr Brewery family. Richard was brought up comfortably and first showed signs of unusual talent when he composed a Christmas song at the age of four. He entered the Munich Ludwigs-gymnasium in 1874, went to Munich University in 1882 and thence to the Academy of Music in 1894. By the time he was sixteen he had mastered every aspect of composition, and in 1885 was given his first musical post as assistant to Hans von Bülow in Meiningen. After only a month, Strauss was left in charge of the Ducal Orchestra, where he learned the repertoire by having to play it. Between 1886 and 1889 he was third conductor at the Munich Court Theatre where he suffered under two seniors, both jealous because of the demand for Strauss to conduct his own works elsewhere. In 1887 his *Aus Italien* branded him avant-garde in Munich itself. In 1889 he became a musical asistant at Bayreuth and conductor of the Weimar Court Theatre where his revolutionary tone-poem *Don Juan* was first heard. In 1894 his first opera *Guntram* was a failure (it was too Wagnerian in concept) but he married the prima donna, Pauline de Ahna, daughter of a general and his former pupil. From then on she ruled Strauss and his life with iron discipline.

Further tone-poems added lustre to his reputation for variety and instrumental skill, and in 1896 he returned to Munich as principal conductor. In 1897 his only child, Franz, was born and in the following year the family moved to Berlin where Strauss became principal conductor at the Court Opera, a post he retained until 1918. So far his output, apart from considerable conducting engagements, was in two forms: Songs (*Lieder*) and the Tone-Poems.

In 1901 he redeemed the failure of *Guntram* with *Feuersnot* (Dresden), a light and indelicate opera produced as a tilt against the Munichers. In 1903 Strauss received his PhD degree from Heidelberg as token of their esteem, an honour which he always cherished and wrote into every signature. The first important opera *Salome* (Dresden 1905) was to his own libretto from a German translation of Oscar Wilde's play. This fascinatingly barbarous score scandalized the Kaiser and Kaiserin and was censored by the Church in Vienna. But it soon brought Strauss sufficient royalties to enable him to build his ideal house in Garmisch at the foot of the Bavarian Alps. Next came *Elektra* (Dresden 1909), another morbid one-act opera, this time to a libretto by the brilliant Austrian poet, Hugo von Hofmannsthal. At this point Strauss may be seen as leader of European music, verging on the emergent achievements of the Second Viennese School of composition (Schoenberg*, Berg* and Webern*). Had he pushed his thoughts beyond *Elektra* into complete atonality, Strauss would have aligned himself with them. But instead he quickly succumbed to a charmingly romantic libretto by Hofmannsthal who did not want to lose such a collaborator. This was, in avant-garde terms, a retrograde step, for the opera was *Der Rosenkavalier* (Dresden 1911). It made a fortune for both Strauss and Hofmannsthal, and immediately Strauss made or authorized many popular arrangements of its melodies. Hofmannsthal's next libretto was a complex one: a new translation of Molière *Le Bourgeois Gentilhomme* (as a play with incidental music) followed by the one-act opera *Ariadne auf Naxos* (Stuttgart 1912). In this cumbersome form the hybrid work was scarcely viable and only after much recrimination between its two creators was the opera prefaced by a sung prologue to make an evening's entertainment (Vienna 1916) and the play was abandoned. But in between the two versions of *Ariadne*, Strauss and Hofmannsthal embarked upon their most ambitious project, a huge fairy-tale moral, very complex in its story and making heavy demands upon producer and theatrical effects. This was *The Woman without a Shadow* (*Die Frau ohne Schatten*, Vienna 1919). Before it had been half finished, the First World War intervened.

Strauss lost his entire fortune, banked in London, and had to postpone his intention to give up conducting altogether in 1914, when he was fifty years old, so as to devote his full time to composing. In 1915 he completed a vast symphony that told a day's adventure in the Alps (*Eine Alpensinfonie*, 'Alpine Symphony', 1915) but this was – had to be – the last composition conceived in massive terms.

In 1919 Strauss became co-director of the Vienna Opera with Franz Schalk (they did not get on), and began to work on a bourgeois comedy as an opera to his own libretto. *Intermezzo* (Dresden 1924) was conceived in a series of almost filmic scenes, scored in a new and economic manner; but the two former collaborators again worked on *Die aegyptische Helena* (*The Egyptian Helen*, Dresden 1928), a less than satisfactory opera, and the partnership culminated with *Arabella* which attempted to be a later Viennese story in the *Rosenkavalier* vein. Hofmannsthal completed a difficult scene the day before his sudden death in 1929, leaving

Strauss to finish composing, and to supervise the production (Dresden 1933) – a task which Hofmannsthal had always insisted upon undertaking.

In the same year Strauss returned to Bayreuth to conduct Wagner's *Parsifal* in the emergency of Arturo Toscanini's withdrawal on political grounds. This put him unintentionally into Nazi favour and helped to secure him the (unwanted) post of Head of the German Chamber of Music (Reichsmusikkammer) in 1934. Strauss was at a loss for an operatic partner until he found Stefan Zweig* and his adaptation of Ben Jonson's *Epicoene*. Called *The Silent Woman* (*Die schweigsame Frau*, Dresden, 1935), the libretto suited Strauss admirably, and he quickly composed the complex, jovial score. But Zweig was Jewish and the Nazis were in full power in 1935. After four performances the opera was proscribed and because of a politically tactless letter between Strauss and Zweig which the authorities intercepted, the composer was stripped of his office, reputation and all performances of his works in the Reich for a year.

Now unable to work any longer with Zweig, Strauss was recommended to a scholarly but extremely dull man called Joseph Gregor, whose three synopses (which all had their origins in previous ideas by Hofmannsthal or Zweig) were found to be acceptable. These operas, *Friedenstag*, *Daphne* and *Die Liebe der Danae*, were composed and were moderately successful between 1940 and 1946. By then the Second World War had begun and Strauss was again financially handicapped by lost royalties. He began to compose in an altogether fresh and economic manner as exemplified in the intellectual opera *Capriccio* (Munich 1942), and by several fragrant orchestral works of chamber proportions. He was mortified by the destruction of the principal German and Austrian opera houses in which his masterpieces had first been presented, and his *Metamorphosen for 23 Solo Strings* expresses his grief in music.

Strauss's Jewish daughter-in-law and his two half-Jewish grandsons came under his protection in Garmisch, and in order to secure their immunity Strauss was forced to abide by detestable political actions in order to save them – which he did. At the end of the war he was a sick man, almost penniless, and disgusted at the vanquished regime. Sir Thomas Beecham organized a Strauss Festival in London in 1947, where he was fêted and made to feel most welcome. He died in 1949, with his final composition *The Four Last Songs* (*Vier letzte Lieder*, London 1950) a perfect epitaph.

Strauss's composing career bridges sixty years, from *Don Juan* in 1889 to the *Four Last Songs* in 1948. This included contemporary romanticism, through a period of almost atonality (and certainly abrasiveness) and back to lush romanticism at a time when the so-called leading composers were treading harsher paths. A fervent admirer of Mozart, Strauss had an unparalleled skill with orchestral sound, a 'lifelong love-affair with the soprano voice' and the instant ability to create a theme to highlight words, then to get as much out of that theme as he possibly could. As a first-rate conductor he came to minimize his gestures to a flicker, yet got enormous results thereby; and this practical ability not only earned him a great deal of money but it put him constantly among working musicians, new works by others and the standard repertoire.

Alan Jefferson

Ballets: *The Legend of Joseph* (*Josephslegende*, Paris 1914); *Whipped Cream* (*Schlagobers*, Vienna 1924). Other tone poems: *Death and Transfiguration* (*Tod und Verklärung*, 1890); *Thus Spake Zarathustra* (*Also sprach Zarathustra*, 1896); *Don Quixote* (1898); *A Hero's Life* (*Ein Heldenleben*, 1899). Concertos: Violin (1882); Horn No. 1 (1885); Horn No. 2 (1943); Piano (1890); Oboe (1946); *Duet Concertino* for Clarinet, Bassoon and Strings with Harp (1948). Chamber music: Two Suites for 13 Winds (1882, 1884); Two Sonatinas for 16 Winds (1944, 1946). 197 Songs for voice and piano; 16 Songs for voice and orchestra (1868–1950). About Strauss: *Strauss – Hofmannsthal Correspondence* (1952, trans. 1961); Norman Del Mar, *Richard Strauss, A Critical Commentary on his Life and Works* (1962, 1969, 1972); E. Krause, *Richard Strauss, Gestalt und Werk* (1956, *Richard Strauss, The Man and his Work*, 1964); *Richard Strauss. Correspondance. Fragments de Journal*, ed. R. Rolland (1951, *Strauss – Rolland Correspondence*, 1968); A. Jefferson, *Richard Strauss* (1973).

462

STRAVINSKY, Igor Fedorovich 1882–1971

Russian composer

Born into a prosperous middle-class family, Stravinsky was a late starter as a composer. His father was a bass singer at the Maryinsky Theatre in St Petersburg, and Stravinsky had the Russian theatre, particularly ballet, in his blood. He attended St Petersburg University (1901–5), allegedly studying criminal law and legal philosophy, in fact developing his musicianship. It was not until 1902, with the death of his father, that he began to study composition, privately, with Rimsky-Korsakov. A close relationship thereafter developed between the young Stravinsky and this master, until the latter's death in 1908.

Stravinsky was twenty-eight when he was abruptly launched into international fame, which never left him, by *The Firebird* – the first of the glittering series of Russian ballets prompted and staged by his compatriot Diaghilev*. But some of the works written prior to that date are of key importance, his 'gradus ad Parnassum'. Starting with some derivative piano pieces, such as the *Scherzo* (1902) and the *Sonata in F sharp minor* (1903–4), his apprenticeship ends with the *Symphony in E flat* (1905–7). Three orchestral works follow which are of genuine artistic importance: the short fantasy *Fireworks* (1908), the *Scherzo Fantastique* (1907–8), and the lost *Chant Funèbre* (1908) in memory of Rimsky-Korsakov. The *Scherzo*, for instance, even allowing for the sense of orchestral colour handed down from his teacher, the scherzando element of Mendelssohn, and a dash of Wagner and Tchaikovsky, still contains music which is recognizably Stravinsky's own. And it was after hearing a performance of this work, together with *Fireworks*, in early 1909, that Diaghilev invited Stravinsky to be associated with his new Ballets Russes.

Until 1913, when he moved to Switzerland, Stravinsky lived with his wife Catherine at Oustilug, a small village about a hundred miles south of Brest-Litovsk. His family included two sons, Theodore and Soulima, and two daughters, Ludmilla and Milena. The outbreak of war in 1914 cut him off from Russia, and he did not return there until 1962, when an official visit brought him back to the city renamed Leningrad. But in 1920, after spending the years of the First World War in Switzerland, he settled in France. It was there, as he said, particularly in Paris that 'the pulse of the world was throbbing most strongly'. In 1934 he became a French citizen; the following year he published his memoirs – in French. He remained in France until 1939, when he emigrated to America, following several visits to, and commissions from, that country. That was a year of triple bereavement for the composer, when his elder daughter Ludmilla, his wife Catherine, and his mother all died. Soon after his arrival in America he was joined by Vera de Bosset, who became his second wife in March 1940. The couple settled in Los Angeles. Here they stayed until September 1969, when, largely for medical reasons, they moved to New York. There Stravinsky died in 1971, at the age of eighty-nine.

His output falls into three phases, Russian, neo-classical and serial. The first phase consists primarily of works written for the stage, of which there were nine: *The Firebird* (1910), *Petrushka* (1911), *The Rite of Spring* (1913), *The Nightingale* (1914), *Renard* (1916), *The Soldier's Tale* (1919), *Pulcinella* (1920), *Mavra* (1922), *The Wedding* (1923). The last of these was also the last to be written for Diaghilev, who produced all but one (*The Soldier's Tale*). Other works of this phase include some important songs, chiefly *Three Japanese Lyrics* (1913) – wrongly claimed by many as showing the influence of Schoenberg*, whose *Pierrot Lunaire* had been heard by Stravinsky shortly before – *Pribaoutki* (short nonsense songs, 1914, for which no translation is possible), and the *Three Stories for Children* (1915–17); the cantata *The King of the Stars* (1912), which is a vision of the Last Judgment by the Symbolist poet Balmont; and the *chant funèbre* in memory of Debussy*, called *Symphonies of Wind Instruments* (1920). It is as-sumed that this work contains similarities of scoring to the earlier piece written for Rimsky-Korsakov, unless and until that is discovered.

Stravinsky's second phase, which terminates with the opera *The Rake's Progress* (1948–51), is usually, and correctly, described as neo-classical. In the case of this composer, neo-classicism was not simply a retreat into the past, nor a form of academic pastiche, nor merely a series of quotations of other composers' ideas; rather it was a re-thinking, and a re-application of aesthetic principles of the classical period. Stravinsky's curiosity was insatiable, and it is interesting that as he moved forward and progressed, so his musical sources extended further into the past. Machaut and Gesualdo came to replace Bach and Beethoven. The majority of his neo-classical works are for the concert hall rather than the stage, and they culminate in the two great orchestral works, the *Symphony in C* (1940) and the *Symphony in Three Movements* (1945), first heard in Chicago and New York respectively. Indeed, after the Russian works of the first phase, the interest in Stravinsky's new compositions was stronger in America than it was in Europe – which was one factor in his deciding to emigrate to that country.

To this second phase belong some of Stravinsky's best-known and most performed works. Concert works include the *Symphony of Psalms* (1930), the Violin Concerto (1931), *Duo Concertant* (1932), and the *Mass* (1948); stage works include *Oedipus Rex* (1927), *Apollo* (1928), *Persephone* (1934), *Orpheus* (1947). It will immediately be obvious that these titles show a marked predilection for classical Greek ideals. The exception is *The Card Party* (1936), though this is imbued, from first note to last, with the vocabulary of classic dancing, and the classic tradition of the theatre. The same may be said for the ballet based on arrangements of Tchaikovsky's music, *The Fairy's Kiss* (1928).

In his third phase Stravinsky exploits the possibilities of serialism, following the example of Webern*. Beginning hesitantly with the *Cantata* (1952), and the *Canticum Sacrum* (1956), which mark the transition, Stravinsky's characteristic style gradually reveals itself as being chiefly appropriate for vocal, religious music in this last stage of his life. Representative works are *Threni* (1958), *A Sermon, A Narrative and A Prayer* (1961), *Abraham and Isaac* (1963), and *Requiem Canticles* (1966), which was his last important work. It should be heard together with the *Introitus* in memory of T. S. Eliot* (1965), which contains the opening words of the Requiem. Other works of this phase include, for the stage, *Agon* (1957) and *The Flood* (1962), and, for the concert hall, *Movements* for piano and orchestra (1959) and *Variations* (1964) in memory of Aldous Huxley*. One of the chief fruits of his exploration into the possibilities of the serial method is his discovery of a new form of choral polyphony, based on canon. The creative impulse behind this was religious. He was a man of profound faith; as he says in *The Poetics of Music* (1947), quite explicitly, his creative work is the product of his conscience and his faith; indeed the Russian Orthodox Church gave him just that spiritual *ordonnance* on which his life rested. Since choral, polyphonic music is traditionally the music of the church, it was through choral music that Stravinsky realized his religious nature. Moreover serialism, as a principle of composition, is as remote as it could be from subjective emotion; and in this respect Stravinsky saw his new polyphony as most truly reflecting the spiritual aspiration of the universal church.

Stravinsky is the most representative of twentieth-century composers. His career began when, in the wake of Wagner, Western music had forsaken a single, common language. The period between the wars witnesses a polarization, between the Austro-German school on the one hand, whose representative was Schoenberg, and the Franco-Russian school on the other, of whom the most prominent was Stravinsky. The final period of his life witnessed his bringing together these two streams, so long divided. In this sense his work may be seen as reuniting and revitalizing twentieth-century music.

He has exercised a mesmeric hold over successive generations of European musicians, who no sooner would become acquainted with a particular aspect of his style, and maybe reproduce it themselves, than they would be disconcerted to see that its creator had moved off into some fresh territory. With each successive phase Stravinsky altered the face of Western music. He was incapable of repeating himself. Born outside the Austro-German tradition, he was not subject to the ardent yet limiting nationalism of the Second Viennese School, which claimed so many casualties in the first half of the twentieth century; at the same time he had the liveliest curiosity about everything that affected the *materia musica*, and about all aspects of music, from that of his contemporaries right back to the pre-classical period.

The Russian works of Stravinsky's first phase have a chief identifying characteristic – the development of rhythm, and metre, as an entity in itself. The nineteenth century, the age of Romanticism, had singled out harmony as the most important factor in musical composition; it was regarded as the parent of melody, the source of music's structures; rhythm was taken to be of subsidiary importance. *The Rite of Spring* abruptly changed that. Rhythm, as a separate structural element, was now emancipated – a fact which many later composers have recognized as a turning-point in the evolution of Western music, notably Messiaen* and Elliott Carter*.

The neo-classicism of Stravinsky's second phase has frequently been criticized, even dismissed as irrelevant and reactionary, by the more radical avant-garde, particularly in Europe. Pierre Boulez* may be taken as representative of this shade of opinion. But the criticism is usually based on a misunderstanding of Stravinsky's creative purpose, which was one of order, and the revitalizing of tradition. This feature is indeed a prominent one in works of all three phases, not least in his serial works. It was a view he shared with Webern. But whereas the latter interpreted the twelve-note laws of his teacher Schoenberg within the strict confines of the Viennese tradition, Stravinsky saw in Webern's technique the suggestion of something much broader; an entirely new concept of order, and fresh possibilities for the enrichment of the melodic/harmonic tradition of Western music as a whole. He discovered new areas of tonality beyond the limits of the major and minor keys. The range of the tonal spectrum appeared enormous, extending from, at the one end, primary chords and keys, to, at the other end, the most abstruse chromatic relationships. Serialism seemed to Stravinsky the means whereby this new resource, hitherto untapped, could be exploited. He said in 1958, which was the year of the *Threni* and *Movements*, 'My recent works are composed on the – my – tonal system' (in *Conversations*, see below).

This fresh and latest discovery was to prove just as far-reaching and radical as his exploitation of rhythm in the works of his first phase. It is even now being taken up by Western composers – the last to be influenced by Stravinsky – and clearly indicates the direction that music will take in the remaining years of the twentieth century.

Francis Routh

Stravinsky's music is published by Boosey and Hawkes, B. Schott's Sohne, and J. and W. Chester Ltd. See: *Chroniques de ma vie* (1935), trans. as *Chronicles of My Life* (London 1936) and *An Autobiography* (1936). With Robert Craft: *Conversations with Igor Stravinsky* (1959); *Memories and Commentaries* (1960); *Expositions and Developments* (1962); *Dialogues and a Diary* (1963); *Themes and Episodes* (1966); *Retrospectives and Conclusions* (1969). By Robert Craft: *The Chronicle of a Friendship* (1972); *Prejudices in Disguise* (1074); *Stravinsky in Pictures and Documents* (1978). See also: N. Nabokov, *Igor Stravinsky* (1964); Francis Routh, *Stravinsky* (1975); R. Vlad, *Stravinsky* (Rome 1958, trans. 1960, 3rd edn 1978).

463

SUTHERLAND, Graham 1903–80

British artist

Sutherland's early work follows the strong tradition of English 'romantic' artists who have imposed their own intense, even surreal, vision on the countryside of Britain; the basis of all his paintings, according to Sutherland, is 'a sudden and personal encounter with some part of nature'. In 1921 he abandoned an apprentice-ship as a railway engineer to study at the Goldsmiths' College School of Art in London, and by 1930 he had gained a certain reputation for his intimate etchings inspired by the work of Samuel Palmer.

In 1931 Sutherland turned his attention to painting, but his distinctive, often sombre studies of hills, rocks and trees date from his first visit to Pembrokeshire in 1934. Soon afterwards he added lithography to his repertoire: in this medium he was able to exploit the idiosyncratic use of strong colour which characterizes many of his works from this time onwards. As an official war artist he extended his range with powerful depictions of quarries and foundries, twisted girders and bomb-shattered masonry.

His post-war style is generally sharper and more forceful than that of the pre-war landscapes. In the late 1940s and early 1950s he executed a succession of sculptured 'Forms' derived from plants or from semi-human trunks and limbs. Many of his later pictures are based on insects, birds and animals, some of them hybrid or imaginary, often with beak, claws or pincers fiercely conspicuous. Hostile-looking vegetable and thorn shapes form another recurrent theme.

Sutherland's portrait of Somerset Maugham* (1949) inaugurated his somewhat unexpected career as a por-traitist. His subjects are typically strong, elderly per-sonalities, closely observed. He executed several religious paintings for churches, of which the first was a pain-racked *Crucifixion* for St Matthew's, Northamp-ton. His work became widely known in Europe and North America through a series of retrospective exhi-bitions in the 1950s; in Britain official approval took the form of commissions for portraits of Churchill and Adenauer, for commemorative paintings to be pre-sented to visiting dignitaries, and (most notably) for the huge tapestry, 'Christ in Glory in the Tetramorph', behind the altar of the new Coventry Cathedral.

Patrick Conner

See: Douglas Cooper, *The Work of Graham Sutherland* (1961); Francesco Arcangeli, *Graham Sutherland* (Milan 1973); and *Graham Sutherland. The Complete Graphic Work*, compiled and introduced by Roberto Tassi (1978).

464
SUZUKI, Daisetsu Teitaro 1870–1966

Japanese Buddhist philosopher

Since he was the son of Ryōjun Suzuki, a medical doctor and Confucian scholar whose family religion was Rinzai Zen, and Masu, who was an adherent of a mystic and unorthodox belief connected with the

Shin sect (Jōdo Shinshū, or True Pure Land Sect), it is not a coincidence that Daisetsu Suzuki grew to be-come the greatest exponent in this century of Zen and Shin, the two representative schools of Buddhist thought in Japan.

In his early twenties, while he was a student at Tokyo Imperial University, Suzuki dedicated himself to Zen meditation in Kamakura. At twenty-seven, he joined Paul Carus of La Salle, Illinois, to assist in translating Chinese Buddhist texts into English. While working on the editorial staff of the Open Court Pub-lishing Company, he produced translations, including the *Discourse on the Awakening of Faith in the Mahayana* (1900). When he came to Europe in 1908, he was invited by the Swedenborg Society to translate *Heaven and Hell* into Japanese. After fourteen years abroad, he returned home to become a lecturer in English at Gakushū-in School, where he was later promoted to a professorship, and at Tokyo Imperial University. At forty-one he married an American, Beatrice Erskine Lane, and in 1921 moved to Kyoto to take the chair of Buddhist philosophy at Otani University. There he began publishing the *Eastern Buddhist*, which is still today one of the leading Buddhist journals in English in the world. The rest of his life was dedicated to writing, translating and lecturing both at home and abroad. In 1936 Suzuki came to London to lecture on Zen at the First Convention of the World Congress of Faiths and also gave lectures on Zen at Oxford, Cam-bridge, Durham, Edinburgh and London Universities. At the age of ninety-five he resumed editorship of the new series of the *Eastern Buddhist* and died in July that year.

Suzuki's contributions to world spiritual culture are incalculable. The phenomenal popularity of Zen in the West after the Second World War is the direct result of his efforts. He was the first to write seriously about Zen in English, and he kept up his zeal and energy in introducing Zen to the West until his last days. It is also from his works that many Westerners have come to know about Shin teaching which centres around Amida Buddha and emphasizes absolute trust in his power.

Suzuki's activity was not motivated by conventional religious fervour or mere evangelism. He really under-stood both Eastern and Western thought and endeav-oured to make people of the East and West understand and appreciate each other's spiritual heritage. His Japanese translations of English works include Eman-uel Swedenborg's *Heaven and Hell* (Tokyo 1910), *The Divine Love and the Divine Wisdom* (Tokyo 1914) and *The Divine Providence* (Tokyo 1915). *Mysticism, Christian and Buddhist* (New York 1957, etc.) clearly shows his insight into world spiritual culture. His greatest contribution, however, lay in popularizing Buddhist concepts in the West. It is through his lucid explanation that one easily learns of the state called 'satori', where there is no subject – object confrontation and where one attains 'absolute freedom, even from God' (*Essays in Zen Buddhism, First Series*, 1927).

Dr Hisao Inagaki

Suzuki's other works include: *Outlines of Mahayana Buddhism* (1907); *Essays in Zen Buddhism, Second Series* (1933), *Third Series* (1934); *Studies in the Lankavatara Sutra* (1930); *The Lankavatara Sutra* (a translation from the original Sanskrit, 1932); *An Index to the Lankavatara Sutra* (Kyoto 1933); *An Introduction to Zen Buddhism* (Kyoto 1934); *Manual of Zen Buddhism* (Kyoto 1935); *Zen Buddhism and its Influence on Japanese Culture* (Kyoto 1938); *The Essence of Buddhism* (1947); *The Zen Doctrine of No-Mind* (1949); *A Miscellany on the Shin Teaching of Buddhism* (Kyoto 1949); *Studies in Zen* (1955); and *Shin Buddhism* (1970).

465

SVEVO, Italo (pseudonym of Aron Schmitz, known as Ettore) 1861–1928

Italian writer

Born an Austrian Jew, brought up speaking Triestine dialect, educated partly in Germany at a College of Commerce, and having his cultural roots in continental Europe rather than in peninsular – not to say culturally insular – Italy, Svevo is best seen as Italy's first Modernist.

In 1880, Svevo took an uncongenial job in a bank, remaining there until 1899, when he joined his father-in-law's firm to manufacture a famous underwater anti-fouling compound which he was occupied in selling to the navies of England, France, Germany and Italy in the period just before and after the 1914–18 war. (His perceptive comments on England in the post-war period are to be found in the essays *Londra dopo la guerra* written for the Triestine newspaper La Nazione in 1920.) The modest international acclaim which came to Svevo in the 1920s was the result of activity on his behalf by James Joyce*, who greatly admired him and had given him English lessons in Trieste.

Svevo's first novel, *A Life* (*Una vita*, 1892, trans. 1963), deals with the suicide of a bank clerk whose conviction of his own intellectual superiority masks a personality divided between dreams of self-assertion on the one hand and of love and harmony on the other. *Una vita* sets off the Schopenhauerian ideal of renunciation against the Nietzschean concept of the will: Nitti is a provincial caricature of the Superman. In this respect, *Una vita* can be compared to Thomas Mann's* *Buddenbrooks* (1901).

The apparent simplicity of structure of *As a Man Grows Older* (*Senilità*, 1898, trans. 1932) conceals both structural and psychological complexity. Emilio Bren-

tani, an unsuccessful author who has led a sheltered life, decides at the age of thirty-five to embark on a facile love affair. His self-deception and egoism lead to failure in love, undermine his one deep friendship (with the sculptor Balli) and contribute to the death of his neglected sister, Amelia. When reality becomes a subjective fiction, chaos ensues, and community is impossible. Brentani's adventure falls into two parts, which echo each other, separated by a central stasis. This, together with a shifting point of view, and increasingly subtle techniques of irony, draws the reader irresistibly into the self-contained world of the narrative.

This ability to involve the reader into the unfolding action is also a feature of Svevo's last finished novel, *The Confessions of Zeno* (*La coscienza di Zeno*, 1923, trans. 1930), the memoirs of a middle-aged neurotic, written mostly before, but partly after, an unsuccessful and interrupted course of psychoanalysis. It is the first major European novel to make thoroughgoing use of Freudian* techniques for the purpose of narrative strategy. Since Zeno is an unreliable narrator, whose humour and optimism are engaging despite his vices and his habit of evading the truth of any issue, the reader has a particularly dynamic relationship with him. *La coscienza* is a comic masterpiece, but Zeno's humour is retrospective, never completely erasing the memory of tears shed and pain endured. The action is set in the period ending in 1915, when Italy declared war: the chronology reminds one of that of Thomas Mann's *The Magic Mountain* (1924) and Musil's* *Man without Qualities* (1930). It is, therefore, both a study in egoism and a radical critique of European civilization, drawing freely on that flow of ideas which has become the mainstream of our culture – Hegel, Schopenhauer and Nietzsche, Darwin, Marx and Freud.

The sequel to *La coscienza* – *Further Confessions of Zeno* (including *Le confessioni del vegliardo*, *Umbertino*, *Il mio ozio* and *Un contratto*, 1928, trans. 1969) – remains unfinished, as do a number of short stories. Svevo also wrote several plays, but had little talent for the theatre.

Professor Brian Moloney

Svevo's other works include: the tales *A Hoax* (*Una burla riuscita*, 1926–8, trans. 1929) and *The Nice Old Man and the Pretty Girl* (*La novella del buon vecchio e della bella fanciulla*, 1926–8, trans. 1930). See: P. N. Furbank, *Italo Svevo. The Man and the Writer* (1966); B. Moloney, *Italo Svevo: a Critical Introduction* (1974).

466

SZASZ, Thomas Stephen 1920–

US psychiatrist

Born in Budapest, Hungary, Thomas S. Szasz emigrated to the United States and graduated in medicine at the University of Cincinnati in 1944. Following an internship at Boston City Hospital, and postgraduate training in medicine at Cincinnati General Hospital, he studied psychiatry at the University of Chicago from 1946 to 1948. Between 1949 and 1951 he was a research assistant at the Chicago Institute of Psychoanalysis and a member of its staff until 1956. In 1956 he was appointed professor of psychiatry at the State University of New York, Upstate Medical Center in Syracuse, N.Y., a post he has held since that time.

Professor Szasz's background in psychiatry is that of orthodox psychoanalysis. Indeed, he has written a number of papers on the subject, one in particular, 'The Concept of Transference' (*International Journal of Psychoanalysis*, 1963), being regarded as a classic. However, it is for his celebrated insistence that mental illness is a myth that Szasz has attracted world-wide attention. He argues that the notion of mental illness derives its support from such conditions as syphilis of the brain and states of delirium in which individuals may manifest certain disorders of thinking and behaviour. However, in Szasz's view, these are more correctly termed diseases of the brain rather than mental diseases. The vast majority of what are termed mental illnesses do not manifest any underlying physiological or chemical abnormality and in Szasz's view do not qualify as diseases but are better classified as 'problems of living' (*The Myth of Mental Illness*, 1961).

Mistaking the metaphor for fact, which Szasz believes is what orthodox doctors and psychiatrists continually do, is not a harmless mistake in his view. Rather he sees the medical conceptualization of mental illness as a deliberate policy by the medical profession to obscure and indeed deny the ethical dilemmas of life and to transform them into medical and technicalized problems susceptible to 'professional solutions' (*Ideology and Insanity*, 1973). From such a philosophical base, Szasz has conducted a fierce polemical campaign against orthodox psychiatry and has compared psychiatrists and psychoanalysts to medieval inquisitors searching for the signs and symptoms of non-existent illnesses, and to totalitarian thought-police, implementing socially approved methods of behaviour under the guise of therapy (*The Manufacture of Madness*, 1971).

Szasz's name is often bracketed with that of R. D. Laing* with both being seen as seminal thinkers in the anti-psychiatric movement. However, Szasz has emphatically stated his opposition to Laing whom he accuses of merely inverting not only the logic but also the vocabulary of psychiatry and appropriating them to serve his own idiosyncratic theoretical principles and therapeutic methods. The psychiatrists have borrowed the disease model from medicine and, on the strength of it, declare psychiatry to be a branch of medicine whereas in fact it is a speciality based on the combination of a medical metaphor and the police power of the state. The anti-psychiatrists have borrowed the model of exploitation – of colonialism, foreign invasion and plunder – from the Old Left and, on the strength of it, declare anti-psychiatry to be a branch of the New Left, i.e. a movement based on the combination of a martial metaphor and 'the persuasive power of apocalyptic promises and prophecies' (*Schizophrenia: The Sacred Symbol of Psychiatry*, 1979).

Szasz's views, despite his adoption by the left as a champion of radical anti-psychiatric opinion, are actually sturdily right-wing and individualistic. His insistence that mental illness is a myth leads him to oppose the role of the psychiatrist in court and the notion of mental illness as an excusing condition in certain criminal situations. Instead of seeing the schizophrenic individual as a patient needing treatment, Szasz regards him as a person disrespectful of the rights of others. The grandiose or paranoid individual, likewise, is seen as boastful and self-centred.

Szasz is also an uncompromising opponent of socialized medicine. Indeed, the only psychiatry that can be practised with dignity, in his view, is that in which a fee passes between the patient and the therapist, i.e. so-called 'contractual' psychiatry (*The Ethics of Psychoanalysis*, 1965). All other forms of psychiatry are coercive and paternalistic and maintain the individual patient in a submissive and passive position relative to the therapist.

Szasz has continued to publicize his views in a steady output of books and journal articles. There is general support for his view that many life problems are in danger of being medicalized into disorders requiring medical diagnosis and treatment. However, there is considerable argument concerning his views of the more serious psychological disorders such as schizophrenia, manic-depressive psychosis and the more crippling neurotic conditions.

Anthony W. Clare

Other works: *Law, Liberty and Psychiatry* (1963); *The Second Sin* (1974); *Ceremonial Chemistry* (1974); *Psychiatric Slavery* (1976); *Heresies* (1976); *Karl Kraus and the Soul-Doctors* (1977); *The Myth of Psychotherapy* (1979); *The Theology of Medicine* (1979).

T

467

TAGORE, Rabindranath 1861–1941

Bengali writer

A poet, novelist, dramatist, essayist, composer, painter and educationalist, Rabindranath Tagore was a modern-day Renaissance man, who dominated the cultural life of Bengal for the first half of this century. He was the seventh, and the youngest, son of Debendranath Tagore, a wealthy Brahmin landlord of Calcutta, who was a founder of the Brahmo Samaj, a reformist Hindu movement which emphasizes monotheism. He was tutored at home, and became proficient in Bengali, Sanskrit and English. At sixteen he was sent to England to study law, a subject that failed to interest him. After his marriage at twenty-three he left Calcutta to manage the family estate at Silaidaha. He did so for seventeen years, and then moved to Santiniketan (Abode of Peace), the family retreat near Bolpur, about a hundred miles north of Calcutta. Here he founded an experimental school for boys which blossomed into an international university, Visvabharati, twenty years later.

He began writing verses when he was in his teens, and published his first volume of poems at eighteen. Later, he was to find the running of the family estate artistically rewarding. The close contact with the enchanting Bengali landscape fired his poetic imagination, while the insight that he gained into peasant life served him well in his works of fiction. In the 1890s his considerable output of poetry was complemented by drama (*Chitrangada* and *Malini*) and fiction (*Chitra*). The sadness caused him by the deaths of his wife and two children, between 1902 and 1907, was to be reflected in the mellowed sharpness of his later work.

His poetic genius found its most accomplished achievement in *Gitanjali* ('Song Offerings'), which appeared in Bengali in 1910. The English translation published two years later, and praised by, among others, Ezra Pound* and W. B. Yeats*, won him the Nobel Prize for Literature in 1913. This, and the knighthood that came in 1915, made him an international celebrity. In his lecture tours of America, Europe, Japan and South-East Asia he stressed the need for blending the ancient heritage of the East with the material achievements of the West. His catholic humanism is well captured in *The Religion of Man* (1931), where he regards love as the key to human fulfilment and freedom, and the surplus energy that finds expression in creative art as the most outstanding characteristic of human nature.

Although he did not participate actively in the freedom struggle of his countrymen, he was not apolitical. He renounced his knighthood in protest against the Amritsar massacre, committed by imperial Britain, in 1919. India honoured him in 1947 by adopting *Jan Gan Man* ('Mind of the People'), one of his songs, as the national anthem, as did Bangladesh, a quarter of a century later, with its adoption of his *Sonar Bangla* ('Golden Bengal').

He left a deep mark on the arts of Bengal, and thus of India and Bangladesh. By releasing Bengali prose from the traditional form of classical Sanskrit he made literary Bengali accessible to the masses; and by introducing new types of metres he enriched Bengali poetry. His song-poems remain as popular with the Bengali elite as they do with the peasants. He also introduced the forms of short story and opera to Indian literature and theatre. By combining the classical Indian arts with the folk traditions, and encouraging a creative interchange between eastern and western artistic forms, at Visvabharati he blazed a new path in education.

Dilip Hiro

Fifty of Tagore's 160 books have been translated into English, often by himself. See: *The Collected Poems and Plays* (1936); *Hungry Stones and Other Stories* (1916); *Stories from Tagore* (1918); *My Reminiscences* (autobiography, 1917); *Sadhana: The Realization of Life* (essays, 1913); *Thought Relics* (essays, 1921); *The Religion of Man* (essays, 1931); and the novels *The Home and the World* (1919) and *Gora* (1924). *A Tagore Reader* (1961) is the best anthology. About Tagore: E. Rhys, *Rabindranath Tagore* (1915); E. J. Thompson, *Rabindranath Tagore: His Life and Work* (1921); S. Sen, *Political Philosophy of Tagore* (1929); and H. R. Kripalani, *Rabindranath Tagore: A Biography* (1962).

468

TANGE KENZO 1913–

Japanese architect

Tange's work is both national and international in

flavour. Born on the island of Shikoko in the south of Japan, he began his architectural training in the Department of Architecture at the University of Tokyo in 1938 and after a short break continued his studies there from 1942 to 1945. He worked initially with two leading Japanese architects, Kunio Mayekawa and Junzo Sakakura, both of whom had worked in the Paris office of the influential European Le Corbusier* and who had become the pioneers in post-war Japan of the international style sparked off by his Marseilles Unité begun in 1947 and completed in 1952. Often referred to as 'Brutalist', it is tough and uncompromising and built of exposed concrete.

Tange is an academic and has continued to teach at the University of Tokyo where he became Professor of Architecture. His many writings on the theory of architecture include the well-known 1966 paper on 'Function, Structure and Symbol' in which he outlined his belief that between 1920 and 1960 there was a period of functionalism based on the complexities of form, whereas since 1960 architects have been concerned with structures based on systems of communication.

His most important contribution to Japanese cultural life is his 1949 competition-winning design for the Peace Centre at Hiroshima, a city completely devastated by the first American atomic bomb four years earlier. The Peace Centre is one of the world's great symbols and Tange's design (made in collaboration with Takashi Asada and Sachio Otani) is based on a co-ordinated arrangement of three basic elements: a Community Centre, the Memorial Museum which houses the documentation of the bombing and its effects, and a Peace Plaza. It was Tange's first large-scale scheme and it established him as one of the most important international architects of the post-war years.

His thinking on the larger urban scale made him a major influence in CIAM (Congrès Internationaux d'Architecture Moderne) and in 1961 he founded his famous URTER (Urbanists and Architects Team) based on the early Bauhaus thinking of the German Walter Gropius* who was later instrumental in forming the Architects' Collaborative in America.

Twenty-five young architects, including his own students at the University, jointly involved themselves in all aspects of specific projects, focusing particularly on the environmental needs of human beings rather than on any abstract problems of architectural style.

A student of ancient Japanese vernacular building, Tange is well aware of the tradition he has inherited and his concern with a vision of an integrated balance between the new technology and the needs of ordinary people has rightly earned him the professional esteem in which he is held.

John Furse

Kenzo Tange and Udo Kulterman, *Kenzo Tange* (Zürich 1970). See also: Charles Jencks, *Modern Movements in Architecture* (1973).

469

TANIZAKI JUNICHIRŌ 1886–1965

Japanese novelist

Tanizaki was born to a declining townsman family in Tokyo and his schooling was not without its difficulties and uncertainties as a result of his father's constant business failures, but in 1908 he managed to enter the Japanese literature department of Tokyo University. He was already inclined towards a literary career but he had little taste for the Naturalist type of fiction that dominated Japanese letters at the time and he preferred the exotic and decadent writings of Nagai Kafū, who later helped to establish Tanizaki as a novelist in the public eye. In 1910 he was forced to withdraw from the university for non-payment of fees and he then set out on a lifetime of literary activity by helping to found a new literary magazine.

Amongst the pieces he published in the magazine was 'Shisei' (1910, 'The Tattoo') in which a tattooer inscribes a giant spider on the back of a beautiful woman. When the tattoo is complete she is more imperious and confident and looks upon the tattooer as the first of the many men she will subjugate with the help of the tattoo. The element of the grotesque in this short piece is more characteristic of his early works, but the piece also contains the germs of a theme that runs through much of his oeuvre, and that is the abasement of the male before the female, often with incestuous or masochistic connotations. Other lasting characteristics of his work that appear in 'Shisei' and such early works as *Fumiko no Ashi* (1919, 'Fumiko's Feet') are his foot-fetishism and notorious lavatorial obsession.

During these years Tanizaki was a thrall of the West and its exotic attractions and held Japan in contempt. However, he began to alter his opinion and recognize the value of the Japanese tradition after the great earthquake of 1923, which devastated much of the Tokyo–Yokohama area, and after his subsequent move to Kansai, the area of Japan that centres on Osaka and Kyoto and is a repository of traditional culture. This shift came to the fore in *Some Prefer Nettles* (*Tade Kuu Mushi*, 1929, trans. 1955), in which the hero is fascinated by Western visions of feminine beauty but is at last drawn to the traditional charms of a Kyoto woman.

For much of the war Tanizaki worked on *The Makioka Sisters* (*Sasameyuki*, 1943–8, trans. 1958), a major work which seeks to recapture and preserve the atmosphere of Kansai before the war and the passing of the old ways, and which depicts in the troubled circumstances of one family both the confusion of the traditional and the modern in contemporary Japan and the difficulties of maintaining a balance between the two. In *Shōshō Shigemoto no Haha* ('The Mother of Captain Shigemoto', 1950) Tanizaki once again took up the theme of an idealized, remote and dominant female figure and combined this with incestuous undertones and imagery associated with the eleventh-century classic, *The Tale of Genji*, which he translated into modern Japanese several times during the last thirty years of his life.

In later years Tanizaki came to recognize the inevitability of westernization and the dilution of the Japanese tradition. In *The Key* (*Kagi*, 1956, trans. 1961) and *The Diary of a Mad Old Man* (*Fūten Rōjin Nikki*, 1962, trans. 1965) he put aside his interest in the well-worked but ever popular theme of the tension between tradition and modernity in Japan and turned to the subject of sexual desire in the aged, which he treated with some humour and structural experimentation.

Tanizaki has sometimes been seen as a writer to whom aesthetic considerations were more important than ideas. Ethereal notions of beauty do indeed have a part to play in many of his works. But it belittles his work to pass over his interests in tradition and the effects of beauty on the behaviour of men, or to place undue emphasis on the obsessions that feature in his writings.

Dr P. F. Kornicki

H. Hibbett (ed.), *Seven Japanese Tales* (1963), is a collection of Tanizaki's shorter works, including 'The Tattooer'. See also: D. Keene, *Landscapes and Portraits – Appreciations of Japanese Culture* (1971); and J. T. Rimer, *Modern Japanese Fiction and its Traditions* (1978).

470

TATLIN, Vladimir Evgrafovich 1885–1953

Russian artist

Tatlin was amongst the most original and influential creative talents to emerge in Russia during the years of upheaval and trauma between the beginnings of the First World War and the tribulations of the early years of the Russian Revolution. The son of an engineer, he became first a sailor and only subsequently turned his attentions to creative work, practising initially as a painter and emerging from the circle of daring Russian artists associated with Larionov and Goncharova. Rapidly Tatlin became aware of adventurous innovations in Russian art circles where a new primitivism was emerging; in addition he increasingly learnt of Parisian art and of Cubist painting in particular. After association with Russian group activities, amongst them the *World of Art*, *The Donkey's Tail* and *The Union of Youth*,

Tatlin left Russia to visit Berlin and Paris, a journey which confirmed the impression that Cubism had upon him to such a degree that on returning to Russia he began to construct Cubist still-life reliefs from diverse materials (1913). This led to an increasingly refined and brilliant investigation of construction according to the qualities of particular material elements: his constructions arose from a harmonizing of the demands of different materials. The constructor no longer imposed forms upon his materials, but instead became an explorer of their inherent properties. The results of these investigations, displayed at the exhibitions *Tramway V* and *0.10* in 1915, posed a definition of creative activity that appeared to rely upon material rather than aesthetic criteria and which was in sharp contrast even to the geometrical abstraction in painting simultaneously evolved by Malevich* in Russia. After the Bolshevik Revolution, Tatlin was an active figure in the reorganization of the artistic life, and increasingly his principle of material construction appeared to chime in with attempts to define a theory of creative work appropriate to Marxist society. Rodchenko and other Russian Constructivists owed much to Tatlin in their work, adopting a politically committed stance that was specifically against individual artistic activity. Tatlin remained aloof from this group, although his proposed *Monument to the Third International* (1918) is a pioneer work in its commitment to the incorporation of elements of Communist ideology and activity into the work itself.

Later in his career Tatlin returned to stage design but also evolved an extraordinary project, *Letatlin* (1929–33), a glider designed to be the ideal transport of the new society.

Tatlin's work shows irregular brilliance rather than continuity; his investigation was too vigorous and far reaching for stylistic considerations to be paramount. The element of utopianism in his work revealed an intellect of great originality: his works, many regrettably lost, reveal a craftsman of extraordinary succinctness, as well as a literate man with close connections with contemporary Russian writers. A leading organizer of the Russian art world, first in Moscow (1918–19) and subsequently in Petrograd (Leningrad) in 1920–5 and Kiev (1925–7), Tatlin's influence was widespread and pervasive. In later years (1933–52) he returned to theatrical design and to the study of gliders.

Dr John Milner

See: C. Gray, *The Great Experiment: Russian Art 1863–1923* (1962); T. Andersen, *Vladimir Tatlin* (1968); John Milner, *Russian Revolutionary Art* (1979).

471

TAWNEY, Richard Henry 1880–1962

British economic historian

In so far as egalitarian ideas form part of the culture of British society, we can discern the influence of men like R. H. Tawney, distinguished economic historian, social philosopher, and passionate enemy of privilege. He was born in Calcutta in 1880, the son of an Oriental scholar in the Indian Educational Service. After his family returned to England, he trod the well-travelled path from Rugby School to Balliol College, Oxford. There were many in Oxford at the turn of the century who helped inculcate in Tawney and others what has been called the 'politics of conscience'. He did not remain content, however, with charitable attempts to better the life of the urban poor. A two-year period in the East End of London helped deepen further his indignation at the extent of social inequality in Britain. The most formative experience of his early life, though, was his work as first tutor and perennial inspiration of the Workers' Educational Association (WEA). This organization grew out of an attempt to prise open the gates of the ancient universities to give to working people educational opportunities monopolized by elites. This objective was never realized, but none the less Tawney was instrumental in the emergence of a movement in adult education in which his egalitarian Anglicanism found its most complete expression. This we can see in the moving *Commonplace Book* (1972) which he kept while travelling between WEA classes in the Potteries and Lancashire before the First World War.

The same set of moral commitments that made Tawney a pioneer in adult education led him in 1914 to join the British Army as a private soldier. His two-year period of service in the Manchester Regiment was abruptly ended on the first day of the Battle of the Somme when he was severely wounded. On his return to England, he recuperated at the home of the Bishop of Oxford, Charles Gore. He joined other prominent Anglicans, such as William Temple, later Archbishop of Canterbury, in an attempt to formulate more clearly the social message of the Church of England and to alter its form to meet the challenge of war and its aftermath. He took up a Fellowship at his old college, Balliol, at the end of the war, and returned to work on the ethical and historical problems which were to occupy him for the rest of his life.

The academic distinction between moral philosophy and history, which many take for granted today, was one which made no sense to Tawney. Largely through his teaching for the WEA and after 1921 at the London School of Economics, his life-long academic home, he developed a concept of economic history of significant influence today. In his view, the subject entailed the retrieval of the resistance of groups and individuals in the past to the imposition on them of capitalist thought and behaviour. It is apparent, therefore, why conservative historians lament his influence and why liberal and socialist historians celebrate it. In his first book, *The Agrarian Problem in the Sixteenth Century* (1912), written to provide his WEA classes with a suitable textbook, he examined patterns of agricultural development, protest and litigation which surrounded the movement to enclose land in Tudor England. A decade later he developed the arguments which were to emerge in his best known book, *Religion and the Rise of Capitalism* (1926). This famous study showed how alien to the tradition of the Reformation was the assumption that religious thought had no bearing on economic behaviour. Tawney captured in unforgettable Miltonic prose the clash within religious opinion that preceded the abnegation of the social responsibility of the Church, and suggested that 'religious indifferentism' was but a phase in the history of Christian thought which could and ought to be ended.

No one who read Tawney could miss the present-mindedness of his history. Indeed it was that very quality which made his work so attractive to a generation of students. He taught them that the study of economic history could raise fundamental questions concerning human behaviour and moral values. The same desire to speak to major social issues and to avoid the desiccation of academic specialism can be seen in his more speculative essays in social philosophy, *The Acquisitive Society* (1919) and *Equality* (1931).

The unifying theme of his work on educational policy for the Labour Party over forty years, his published and professional writing, and his teaching was a belief in equality that stemmed from his Anglican convictions. To appreciate the full extent of his influence, we must set his contributions in the contexts of the history of the socially committed wing of the Church of England and of the history of that part of the British Labour Movement which came to socialism through a belief that capitalism was sin.

Dr J. M. Winter

Other works: *Land and Labour in China* (1932); *The Attack and Other Papers* (1953); *Business and Politics under James I* (1958); *The Radical Tradition* (1964); *History and Society* (1978); *The American Labour Movement and Other Essays* (1979). See also: R. Terrill, *R. H. Tawney and his Times* (1973); J. M. Winter, *Socialism and the Challenge of War* (1974).

472

TEILHARD DE CHARDIN, Pierre 1881–1955

French theologian and scientist

Teilhard de Chardin's family were substantial landowners in the Auvergne, near Clermont-Ferrand. Until shortly before Pierre's birth they had been *légitimistes* (supporters of the Bourbon pretender, who looked to Rome for political as well as religious guidance) and were deeply involved in affairs of church and state during his childhood. Teilhard entered the novitiate of the Society of Jesus at Aix-en-Provence in 1899 where, during twelve years of intensive training in philosophy and theology, he pursued a childhood interest in geology. After ordination, in 1911, he was allowed to carry on with his un-priestly studies in Paris: geology at the Institut Catholique; palaeontology at the Museum of Natural History. His research was interrupted by service as a stretcher-bearer during the First World War but continued afterwards, especially on extensive journeys in China in the 1920s and 1930s and in central and southern Africa in the early 1950s. His last years were spent in the USA, lecturing and publishing scientific papers. Permission to publish books which combined his scientific and theological ideas – the distinctive essence of his work – was withheld during Teilhard's lifetime.

Teilhard attempted to relate Christian tradition, especially on evolution, to twentieth-century scientific understanding of nature. His ideas are most comprehensively expressed in *The Phenomenon of Man* (*La Phénomène humain*, 1955, trans. 1959) which has been much criticized for its optimism. Here, the universe is seen as an evolutionary process, always moving towards greater complexity; with it has gone a movement towards higher levels of consciousness. The process has been marked by a few dramatic leaps upwards, notably the emergence of life on earth, and the development of rational self-consciousness in man. As a result of the latter, evolution is no longer subject to the laws of nature alone: man has a hand in directing it. In the fulfilment of this process, all things will be gathered up in God.

Teilhard's philosophical theology is rooted in this fulfilment, and is most fully worked out in *Le Milieu divin* (1957, trans. 1960), a devotional and highly personal work begun in the 1930s. For Teilhard, all matter has a sacramental quality. As a consequence of the Incarnation the universe is in a process of 'Christification'.

The huge range of Teilhard's ideas and methods is both his strength and his weakness. As a synthesist of many disciplines he is vulnerable in an age of specialists. The fact that so little of his work was published during his lifetime meant that he did not have the benefit of comment and criticism by his contemporaries, although some of them – Sir Julian Huxley, for example – recognized that he was on the 'same quest' as Teilhard, 'pursuing parallel roads ever since we were young men'. On the other hand Teilhard's range has caused his work to serve as a bridge between different schools of philosophy, whether Christian, Hu-

manist or agnostic. More generally, he has become something of a hero for environmentalists.

Timothy O'Sullivan

Other translations: *Letters from a Traveller* (1962); *The Future of Man* (1964); *Hymn of the Universe* (1965). See: C. Cuenot, *Pierre Teilhard de Chardin* (trans. 1965); A. Hanson (ed.), *Teilhard Reassessed* (1970.

473

THOM, René 1923–

French mathematician

René Fréderic Thom was born in 1923 at Montbéliard (Doubs), and educated at the Lycée Saint-Louis and at the École Normale Supérieure in Paris. After taking his doctorate he was Maître de Conférences at Grenoble and Strasbourg, before taking a chair in the Faculty of Sciences at Strasbourg in 1957. Since 1964 he has been be a Professor at the Institut des Hautes Études Scientifiques at Bures-sur-Yvette. Thom was awarded the Fields Medal in 1958, the equivalent of a Nobel Prize in mathematics. He became a member of the Académie des Sciences in 1976.

Thom's most influential work has been his 'Catastrophe Theory', an attempt to explain why certain surprises occur in systems which are known to be fully predictable. The key to understanding Thom's problem is the idea of a 'continuous' process in which a small change in the controls produces a small change in the effect. For example, as the petrol level in the tank of a car goes down by one millimetre the needle on the dashboard moves a tiny distance towards 'Empty' on the dial. The smaller the movement of the petrol level, the smaller the movement of the needle. There are many situations in which several such continuous processes act simultaneously to produce a composite result. For example, a pain-killer pill may contain x mg of aspirin and y mg of codeine. The net effect of this is that it has a certain potency in quietening a painful tooth, say. We may express such an effect in terms of a number z, the number of pills or part pills needed to reduce the experienced pain of the tooth to zero. It is natural to expect the control variables x and y to control the potency of the pill – as expressed by the number z – *continuously* in the sense described above, namely that small changes in x and y produce only small changes in z. However, there are some situations in the sciences and in technology where the processes are known to be both fully predictable and continuous and yet, when operating simultaneously produce a strange result: every now and then the effect variable (i.e. corresponding to z above) suddenly flips from one value to a different value. It was the occurrence of these situations which Thom set out to study, explain and classify. How does it come about that certain systems turn predictable continuous inputs into evidently predictable, but surprisingly *dis*continuous outputs? Thom showed that if we limit our attention to systems in which there are five or fewer control variables the number of patterns in which these 'flips' can occur is strictly limited too. In fact Thom identified eight basic cases which he named the 'simple minimum', 'fold', 'cusp', 'swallow tail', 'butterfly', 'hyperbolic umbilic', 'elliptic umbilic' and 'parabolic umbilic'.

Thom's theory presented in full in his book *Stabilité structurelle et morphogenèse* (*Structural Stability and Morphogenesis*, 1972, trans. 1976) spread rapidly around the mathematically educated world. Professor Christopher Zeeman acted as Thom's T. H. Huxley. In impact Thom's theory had the characteristics of a cultural phenomenon. The reason for this seems to lie partly in the unique choice of the name 'Catastrophe Theory', partly in the way in which the theory was illustrated with an extraordinary variety of examples chosen from biology, psychology, industrial relations and medicine, as well as the more classical examples in engineering and control theory, and partly because it was a reflection of Thom's depth of insight as a new kind of philosopher-mathematician.

In assessing Thom's theory there are certain tendencies to misconception which have been amplified by the 'cultural phenomenon' mentioned above. First, there is no intrinsic reason why the theory should have been styled a 'catastrophe' theory. It is concerned with sudden flips occurring in continuous systems, but it is quite arbitrary whether one regards such flips as 'up' or 'down'. In a less deeply pessimistic age it might have seemed natural to call Thom's theory a 'breakthrough' theory or a 'take off' theory. Second, many of the more exotic examples which have been given of Thom's theory, e.g. in accounting for the condition of *anorexia nervosa* or the biting behaviour of angry-frightened dogs, are really more like suggestive general analogies than precisely verifiable applications of the mathematics. Third, if the theory seems to give us a certain limited degree of comfort that only a certain finite number of types of catastrophe can occur, this is an aspect whose practical significance is effectively nil. (Thom's classification still allows an infinite variety of catastrophes to occur, and does not, in any case, offer a complete theory of all possible catastrophes.) Fourth, Thom's theory, though a remarkable mathematical triumph, does not do anything to underwrite a generally deterministic model of the universe. The mathematics does not and could not establish the validity of this essentially metaphysical view of things.

Christopher Ormell

See Yung Chen Lu, *Singularity Theory and an*

Introduction to Catastrophe Theory (1976); Christopher Zeeman in *Scientific American*, April 1976.

474

THOMAS, Dylan Marlais 1914–53

Welsh poet

Dylan Marlais Thomas was born on 27 October 1914 at 5 Cwmdonkin Drive in Swansea where his father D. J. Thomas taught English at the Grammar School and harboured unrealized ambitions to be a poet. D. J. gave his son the consciously literary names Dylan (the 'sea son' of the *Mabinogion*) and Marlais (a Welsh river adopted as bardic name by D. J.'s uncle) and encouraged him to read and recite poetry. Dylan stayed in his father's house until he was nineteen, referring to himself as 'the Rimbaud of Cwmdonkin Drive'.

If his home was excessively bookish, Dylan had no inclination for academic pursuits and liked to escape from 'splendidly ugly' Swansea. Near his house was Cwmdonkin Park, where he played and observed such unforgettable figures as 'The Hunchback in the Park'. Even more exciting were the summer holidays spent at Fern Hill dairy farm in north Carmarthenshire, the home of his aunt Ann Jones. Dylan drew on his adolescent experiences in poems like 'After the Funeral' (in memory of Ann Jones who died in 1933) and the ecstatic 'Fern Hill' in which he recalled how he 'was young and easy under the apple boughs'.

Dylan left school in 1931 and spent his time acting with the Swansea Little Theatre, reporting for the *South Wales Daily Post* for fifteen months, and hanging about bars and cafés. He cultivated a romantic poetic persona but it was no sartorial pose; in the three years between leaving school in 1931 and leaving Swansea for London in 1934 he produced more than 200 poems including all the *18 Poems* (1934), most of the *Twenty-five Poems* (1936), early versions of many later poems and ideas that would subsequently be used in works like *Under Milk Wood* (1954). It was the most creative period of his life and, by contrast, he wrote only eight poems in the last seven years of his life.

Thomas's poetry made an immediate and rather sensational impact on the public. His style was an individual mixture of the sensuous elements in poetry (as practised by Keats and G. M. Hopkins) and the linguistic experiments of Joyce* and Eliot*. When 'Light breaks where no sun shines' was published in the *Listener* of 14 March 1934 it provoked a storm of protest from readers who found the imagery obscene. However, Thomas's revitalization of the romantic tradition gained the admiration of Stephen Spender*, Eliot, Edwin Muir and Edith Sitwell*, who described the work *Twenty-five Poems* as 'nothing short of magnificent'. Thomas's early poetry was astonishingly dense in metaphor and treated sexual matters with surrealist manners. In a letter to Pamela Hansford Johnson – with whom he conducted an epistolary affair – he wrote in November 1933 that 'every idea, intuitive or intellectual, can be imaged and translated in terms of the body'.

Thomas had moved to London in 1934 and met Caitlin Macnamara, a twenty-two-year-old dancer who had been dismissed from the chorus line of the London Palladium. The couple spent a holiday together in the Welsh fishing village of Laugharne and returned there after getting married on 12 July 1937 in Cornwall. Despite the great critical success of his poetry and the income derived from wartime film work and post-war broadcasting, Thomas was unable to control his domestic destiny. His drinking was reaching epic proportions and the marriage was punctuated by frequent periods of despair. In 1949 Margaret Taylor, wife of the historian A. J. P. Taylor, obtained for the Thomases the Boat House on the estuary of the river Taf in their beloved Laugharne and for the remaining four years of his life this was home for Dylan and Caitlin and their three children.

The cliffside house had a magnificent view of the bay and in his garden shed, which he called 'the shack', Thomas composed poems like 'Over Sir John's hill', 'Author's Prologue' and 'Poem on his birthday'. Perhaps because he was suspicious of the apparently effortless precocity he had once enjoyed – or perhaps because he could no longer respond so readily to his insights – Thomas evolved an excruciatingly painstaking method of composition. He would retire to his shed in the afternoon after the pubs had closed and endlessly revise his poetry, sometimes making as many as 200 work-sheets for one poem. As a result Thomas's mature poetry became more and more formally intricate so that the finished product contained a complex of cross-association and a delicate embroidery of interweaving internal rhymes. Thomas was still an inspirational poet but the source of his poetry was no longer anatomical but natural; he was also anxious to live up to the Welsh tradition of technical expertise and to become a master of 'my craft or sullen art'.

In 1950 Thomas made, at the invitation of John Malcolm Brinnin, the first of four trips to America. His public performances of poetry delighted American audiences, for Thomas's incomparably rich delivery conformed to their expectations of a bard drunk on the music of words. His private performances as an obstreperous drunk scandalized his hosts who constructed, out of a few indiscreet incidents, a monument to Dylan as an outrageous artistic clown. He was depressed by the malicious gossip that surrounded him in America, exhausted by the demands of extensive reading tours, and dismayed by the alcoholic pace his American admirers imposed on him. Yet he returned in triumph for his third trip in 1953. The previous year

Thomas's *Collected Poems* (1952) had appeared to a crescendo of critical applause and he surpassed that with the New York reception of the stage version of his radio play *Under Milk Wood* (1954). The wit and brilliant linguistic invention of the play were enthusiastically appreciated and Thomas was well on the way to becoming an American institution; Boston University invited him to collaborate with Stravinsky* on an opera on the re-creation of the world.

Thomas had earned substantial sums of money in America but had saved none of it so that life back in Laugharne, the setting of *Under Milk Wood*, became intolerable, and he embarked on his fourth and final visit to the USA to direct an expanded version of his play. His alcoholic decline was by this time complete and he suffered from *delirium tremens* and constant anxiety. When Thomas became uncontrollable his American doctor injected him with morphine; probably the effect of the drug, plus the intake of alcohol, proved fatal. On 4 November 1953 he was taken in a coma to St Vincent's Hospital, New York, and died five days later. The cause of death was diagnosed as 'Insult to the brain'. The poet's body was brought back to Wales to be buried in St Martin's Churchyard, Laugharne. Since then an academic industry has grown up around Thomas and his legend has been exhaustively examined; his poetry remains as the work of a virtuoso who created some of the finest lyrical works of the twentieth century.

Alan Bold

Thomas's poetry has been arranged, in chronological order of composition, in *The Poems* (1971, revised 1974), ed. Daniel Jones; his broadcasts and stories can be sampled in *Quite Early One Morning* (1954) and *A Prospect of the Sea* (1955). See also: John Malcolm Brinnin, *Dylan Thomas in America* (1956); Caitlin Thomas, *Leftover Life to Kill* (1957); Constantine FitzGibbon, *The Life of Dylan Thomas* (1965); and Paul Ferris, *Dylan Thomas* (1977).

475

TILLICH, Paul 1886–1965

German/US Lutheran theologian

Tillich, a contemporary of Karl Barth* and Rudolf Bultmann*, was educated in the universities of Berlin (as were Barth and Bultmann), Tübingen and Halle. Ordained to the Lutheran Ministry, he served as an army chaplain in the First World War. His initial university teaching was done at Marburg, Dresden (the Technische Hochschule) and Leipzig, and in 1929 he was appointed Professor of Philosophy at Frankfurt. Tillich had been from his early days a committed and practising Religious Socialist, and in response to his criticisms of the Nazi regime he was dismissed from his Chair and forced to leave Germany. Through the good offices of Reinhold Niebuhr*, he was invited to join the faculty of Union Theological Seminary in New York City, where he eventually became Professor of Philosophical Theology, a post which he held until 1955, when he was made a University Professor at Harvard. Shortly before his death he moved from Harvard to the Divinity School at the University of Chicago.

Tillich's thought (an amalgam of philosophical ontology, existentialism, depth-psychology and Christian theology) is both difficult and immensely complicated, and almost impossible to summarize succinctly in a short space, but it is arguable that his main life's work is his three-volumed *Systematic Theology* (1951–63) and that the fundamental principle of this is his 'method of correlation', whose influence overflowed into many of his other writings. There are, in his view, two 'poles' of Christian theology – the 'situational' and the 'revelatory' poles. Other styles of theology which obscure the former of these, like Karl Barth's, are harshly criticized on the grounds that their emphasis on the latter is grotesquely distorting. Central to Tillich's thinking is the notion that the basic structure of theology is that of 'question and answer'; man, just because he is essentially the creature of God, continually asks existential questions; systematic theology scrutinizes such questions and gives them technical form; these questions receive the answers formulated by theology from the divine self-manifestation under the guidance of the questions which lie at the heart of human existence itself. No man, in Tillich's view, can receive answers to questions which he has never asked! In his investigation of the 'existential' questions Tillich does not, of course, ignore existentialist philosophy; but he insists that their sources are to be found in human 'culture' in a wide sense – in poetry, drama, novels, films, the plastic arts, therapeutic psychology and sociology. The influence of modern psychoanalysis comes out in *Systematic Theology* II in his study of the process of salvation: included in his analysis of human 'fallenness' (an existential category) are estrangement, suffering, loneliness, doubt, despair, the tendency to suicide, and meaninglessness. Correspondingly, the salvific work of 'Jesus as the Christ' is formulated so that these elements are abolished and replaced by the essential elements of 'the new man'. In his work Tillich is at pains to overcome criticisms that he is a subjectivist or a mere psychologizer or that he is vulnerable to the charges of subjectivism traditionally levelled at existentialism. Hence, he refused to be labelled as an 'existentialist' and preferred the descriptive title 'ontologist'. The background to his investigations, he insisted, is the notion of 'Being'; God is for him 'Being-Itself'; sinful man is estranged from his genuine 'being'; Jesus as the Christ brings 'New Being' to the world.

Another book of Tillich's worthy of mention is his *The Protestant Era* (trans. 1948). Here he gives expression to his scepticism about the viability of that era which was begun by the sixteenth-century Reformation. But he is convinced that the fundamental principle of that Reformation should not and will not die, because of its fundamental importance for all Christian churches – the principle of prophetic protest against every power which claims divine character for itself. The prophetic protest, he insists, is necessary for every church and for every secular movement if it is to avoid disintegration – it has to be expressed in every situation as a contradiction to man's perennial attempts to give absolute validity to his own thinking and acting. This kind of thinking was influential not merely within the American churches, but inspired many of the religiously based protests against American social and foreign policy characteristic of the late 1960s, protests rooted in that pragmatism and activism which have always been characteristic of American religion as a whole.

Tillich's theological system and writings have inevitably evoked much disagreement. More orthodox theologians protested that his theology was grotesquely biased towards the twentieth-century 'situational' pole to the detriment of the 'revelatory' one in Scripture and tradition; others complained that his translation of traditional religious symbols into the abstract terminology of idealism, psychoanalysis and existentialism evacuated the latter of their essential meaning. Be that as it may, his thinking and writing did have an incalculably widespread effect upon the post-war American intelligentsia. Influences upon his thinking have been hinted at above; the fundamental ones were probably the thought of the Romantic German theologian F. D. E. Schleiermacher (1768–1834) and the idealist philosopher F. W. J. von Schelling (1775–1854), who was the subject of his very earliest research.

Professor James Richmond

Other works include: *Love, Power and Justice* (1954); *Morality and Beyond* (1963). See: Wilhelm and Marion Pauch, *Paul Tillich: His Life and Thought* (1977); Alastair M. McLeod, *Tillich* (1973); J. Heywood Thomas, *Tillich: An Appraisal* (1963); Kenneth Hamilton, *The System and the Gospel: A Critique of Paul Tillich* (1963).

476

TINBERGEN, Nikolaas 1907–

Dutch ethologist

Niko Tinbergen was born in The Hague into an exceptionally talented family: his elder brother Jan later won the Nobel Prize for economics and his younger brother Lukas did important biological work before dying young. As well as his biological skills, Niko Tinbergen was a hockey player of international standard. He studied biology at Leiden University and later returned there after a visit to Greenland. During the 1930s he studied many problems in animal behaviour (ethology) with a multiplicity of students and collaborators. In the war he was among many academics imprisoned by the Nazis for denouncing their treatment of the Jews; after his release he briefly joined the Dutch 'underground'. Soon after the war Tinbergen moved to Oxford University, where he remains. In 1973 he shared the Nobel Prize with Konrad Lorenz* and Karl von Frisch, making the Tinbergens the only pair of brothers to have received this prize.

Tinbergen has been an enthusiastic observer and photographer of natural history from an early age and in 1930 collaborated on a book of such observations and photographs of birds, *Het Vogeleiland* ('The Bird Island', 1930). However, it is for the ingenious design of experiments that Tinbergen is particularly famous. During the 1930s he studied many problems of how animals, mainly insects, find out about their environment (for example, navigation, locating food). He met Lorenz in 1936 and used Lorenzian terminology for a while. When imprisoned, Tinbergen wrote two children's books about animals and his important *Social Behaviour in Animals* (1953), which summarizes some of his earlier work. His ethological classic *The Study of Instinct* (1951) has the same structure as modern ethology; he suggested that there are four main areas of ethological inquiry: development, physiological mechanisms, survival value and evolution of behaviour.

By moving to Oxford Tinbergen introduced ethology to the English-speaking world; and, in part stimulated by the many evolutionary biologists at Oxford, Tinbergen's own research changed increasingly to the problem of survival value. He has worked particularly on sea-birds; for example, he discovered (again by simple experiments) a suite of behavioural adaptations in gulls to reduce predation on eggs and young. His work on gulls is described in *The Herring Gull's World* (1953) and in *Signals for Survival* (1969, based on one of his award-winning television films). His autobiographical *Curious Naturalists* (1958) enchantingly relates his work on gulls as well as the earlier work on insects.

Tinbergen's films and popular books have done much to popularize ethology; but unlike many popularizers he has not prognosticated vulgarly on man's predicament. In later years Tinbergen has become more interested in man. He has studied ethologically a kind of autism ('Kanner's syndrome', concerning children who are excessively withdrawn from society) which he interprets as resulting from a conflict between the child's apprehension and its frustrated desire for society. This study illuminated Tinbergen's claim that ethology can contribute methodologically as well as theoretically to the study of man.

Mark Ridley

Tinbergen's other books are: *Eskimoland* (1935); *Inleiding tot de Diersociologie* ('Introduction to Animal Sociology', 1946); *Kleew* (1948); *The Tale of John Stickle* (1954); *Bird Life* (1954); *Animal Behaviour* (1965); *Tracks* (1967); and two volumes of papers, *The Animal in its World* (1972 and 1973).

477

TIPPETT, Sir Michael 1905–

English composer

Michael Tippett received an orthodox musical education, but developed late as a composer. It was only after two periods of study at the Royal College of Music in London (1923–8, 1930–2) that he began to assemble the elements of his personal, mature style. The sinuous rhythms of Tudor polyphony, the exuberant syncopations and inflected harmonies of jazz, Stravinsky's* avoidance of regular accentuation and traditional diatonic progressions, would all contribute to a distinctive energy and vitality. But it was the synthesis between fugue and sonata, between elaborately unified and intensely dramatic formal principles, so powerfully achieved in the music of Beethoven, which fired Tippett's imagination most decisively. His first completely characteristic and successful work, the *Concerto for Double String Orchestra* (1939), belongs to a series of symphonic compositions – three piano sonatas, four string quartets, four symphonies, a piano concerto and a concerto for orchestra – in which the energy of interacting contrapuntal lines often supports only occasional hints of traditional harmonic or modal thinking. And in the later works, for all their reliance on easily detectable thematic and textural recurrences, even that degree of tonal chordal practice may be dispensed with.

Tippett's early teaching and performing activities with amateurs, and his radical political sympathies, led to a permanent adherence to pacifism, for which he was briefly imprisoned in 1943. His oratorio, *A Child of Our Time* (1939–41), is his most politically explicit work, dealing with the murder of a German diplomat by a young Jew in 1938. But it was only when Tippett turned away from such documentary concerns to explore the symbols and themes of Jungian* psychology in his first opera *The Midsummer Marriage* (1946–52) that he released a flow of inspired lyricism whose conviction and formal coherence triumphantly compensate for any obscurities or oddities in either plot or libretto. His three later operas, *King Priam* (1958–61), *The Knot Garden* (1966–70), and *The Ice Break* (1972–6), as well as the choral work *The Vision of St Augustine* (1963–5), all explore human aspirations, stressing the need for individuals to comprehend the psychic as well as social forces within, around and beyond them. By writing his own texts (or choosing appropriate extracts, in the case of *The Vision of St Augustine*) Tippett has revealed an idiosyncratic way with words, but an instinctive sense of the formulations needed to set his elaborate melodic lines in motion. In spite of the more naturalistic aspects of his two later operas, and of the texts set as part of the *Symphony No. 3* (1970–2), it is the exploration of myth and creative energy which remains most crucial. Tippett succeeds in communicating so forcefully because the importunate melodic eloquence and exhilarating superimpositions of his most characteristic textures are controlled by clear formal outlines, with easily perceptible repetitions and variations. Even in the absence of traditional tonal structures, there is a clear distinction between fundamental and ornamental aspects. Tippett's highly original style is also intensely coherent.

Arnold Whittall

See: Tippett's own collections of essays, *Moving into Aquarius* (2nd edition 1974) and *Music of the Angels* (1980). Michael Tippett's music is published by Schott. See also: *Michael Tippett. A Symposium on his Sixtieth Birthday*, ed. Ian Kemp (1965).

478

TOLKIEN, John Ronald Reuel 1892–1973

British writer and philologist

Tolkien was born in Bloemfontein, South Africa, but on his father's death in 1895 his family moved to Birmingham, at first to a cottage at Sarehole Mill outside the town, later into the city itself. He was educated at King Edward School, Birmingham (with a short spell at St Philip's Grammar School), and went to Exeter College, Oxford, as a scholar in 1911, reading Honour Moderations in classics and English language and literature, in which he was awarded a first class. His academic career was interrupted by military service between 1915 and 1918; after leaving the army he rapidly established himself as a distinguished philologist and successful academic, being appointed Reader in English Language at the University of Leeds in 1920 and Professor in 1924. In 1925 he was appointed Rawlinson and Bosworth Professor of Anglo-Saxon at Oxford, where he remained for the rest of his academic life. He became a friend of C. S. Lewis* and was a member of the 'Inklings' circle.

Tolkien's mythical fictions, for which he is now famous, clearly grew from the same root as his professional and personal absorption in language (a talent he showed from an early age, not only becoming proficient in Anglo-Saxon and Gothic as a schoolboy, but also inventing languages at the same age). His imaginary world derived partly from a 'made-up' language, based on Finnish, begun in 1915, which needed a history to explain it (this language eventually became 'Elvish'). He began writing the poems and stories which eventually became *The Silmarillion* as early as 1916. His first published book of fantasy was, however, a children's book, *The Hobbit* (1936). The publishers, Allen & Unwin, expressed interest in a sequel, which finally emerged as a far more serious creation: *The Lord of the Rings*, written between 1939 and 1945, and published as a trilogy in 1954 (*The Fellowship of the Ring* and *The Two Towers*) and 1955 (*The Return of the King*). This, his most important work, achieved at first a respectable *succès d'estime* but went on to become a bestseller on both sides of the Atlantic and, on the face of it surprisingly, to become a 'campus cult' particularly among the 'alternative culture'. It was followed by the publication of slighter pieces, notably *Tree and Leaf* (1964) – a reprint of the well-known lecture 'On Fairy-Stories and the short story 'Leaf by Niggle', both of which illuminate Tolkien's methods and intentions in *The Lord of the Rings*. *The Silmarillion*, a collection of legends and histories narrating the story of his imaginary world 'Middle-Earth' and 'Elvenhome' from its creation down to the end of its 'first Age', was edited by his son Christopher Tolkien and published posthumously in 1977, when it immediately became a best-seller. The cult of Tolkien's books is no longer as widespread as it was in the 1960s, but it still continues (there is a *Tolkien Newsletter* whose members sometimes correspond in Elvish), and the volume of published criticism of Tolkien's fantasy world steadily increases.

Tolkien believed in the making of fantasies as not only a legitimate and vital but a high form of art in which, as he wrote in the lecture 'On Fairy-Stories' (1939), man resembles God in the divinely granted faculty of 'sub-creation' of secondary worlds (as opposed to the primary world created by God). Consistent with this was his habit of referring to his stories as 'discoveries', rather than inventions; and his imaginary Middle-Earth is, unsurprisingly, structured on firmly Christian lines.

Why what began as the spare-time hobby of a professor of Anglo-Saxon should have become so widely popular is an interesting question. On a thematic level, *The Lord of the Rings* fits into a still strong tradition of romantic, pastoralist attacks on the evils of industrialism; and clearly Tolkien's insistence on the need for reverence towards non-human forms of life held a strong and valid appeal to ecologically-minded people alert to the possible horrors of technological progress. Second, it feeds what is clearly a large appetite for myth, for heroism, and for imaginary marvels, while presenting this with a novelist's attention to detail and privileged entry into the characters' consciousness. Tolkien's content may be drawn from a wide variety of Dark Age and medieval sources, but his narrative conventions are the familiar ones of realist fiction. Third, his world has the attraction of completeness; it has its own cosmology, mythology, history, variety of species, languages, scripts, maps, genealogies, and even calendar. This world has also the ambiguous appeal of simplicity: there is hierarchy but no class, love-stories but no passionate sexuality, village life (among the hobbits) but no labour – in other words, a world without the problems which affect human existence, dominated by a satisfactorily simple conflict between Good (the Elves and other 'Free Peoples') and Evil (Morgoth, Sauron and Mordor). Finally, the elegiac mood of Tolkien's writing (*The Lord of the Rings* is set almost at the end of the imaginary era of Middle-Earth, and we are constantly referred back to a vanished past still more remote and wonderful) which increases the same nostalgic appetite for myth and remoteness on which it feeds.

Janet Montefiore

Other works: *Beowulf, the Monsters and the Critics* (1936); *Farmer Giles of Ham* (1949); *Adventures of Tom Bombadil* (1962); *Smith of Wootton Major* (1967). See: Humphrey Carpenter, *J. R. R. Tolkien* (1977); Neil D. Isaacs and Rose A. Zimbardo (eds), *Tolkien and the Critics* (1968); Robert Foster, *Guide to Middle-Earth* (1975). For a dissenting view, see Edmund Wilson, 'Ooh, Those Awful Orcs' in *The Bit Between my Teeth* (1956).

479

TOYNBEE, Arnold Joseph 1889–1975

British historian

Toynbee's family background and marriage (in 1913) to Rosalind Murray, daughter of the classicist Gilbert Murray, seemed to presage an academic career, but in the First World War Toynbee was employed in the Political Intelligence Department of the Foreign Office. He observed the Versailles peace conference at close quarters, and out of his experiences as correspondent on the war between Greece and Turkey came *The Western Question in Greece and Turkey* (1922). Its success led to a professorship in history at the University of London held conjointly with the post of Director of Studies at the British Institute of International Affairs. Work on the yearly volumes of the influential *Survey of International Affairs* and his magnum opus *A Study of History* proceeded simultaneously; the destructive national passions of the 1930s analysed in the *Survey* were transcended in Toynbee's world history by the rise and fall of civilizations.

The first six volumes of *A Study of History* (2 vols, 1934–61) published in the 1930s compared twenty-one civilizations, seven of them extant, and all subject to a rhythm of growth and decay. Toynbee thought that civilizations developed as responses to challenges imposed by their environments, although the nature of these responses was not predetermined. Subsequent growth depended on the creative efforts of an elite whose culture was imitated by the rest of society. But when the creativity of the elite waned, and the majority withdrew their assent to the values of the minority, a loss of social unity and sense of direction followed. This waning of creative power and failure of response Toynbee detected already in Western civilization of the twentieth century, and manifested in such strategies of withdrawal as 'archaism' and 'futurism'. The most likely end to this process of disintegration, as in previous cases, was the formation of a universal state by a dominant coercive minority. But the intermingling of peoples and religions might yet provide the preconditions for the emergence of a new universal religion, on which Toynbee pinned his hopes of ending the secular rhythm of rise and fall.

After a further spell of service in the Foreign Office as Director of the Research Department in the Second World War, Toynbee resumed his work on *A Study of History* and published four more volumes in 1954. These volumes served as appendices to the first six rather than breaking new ground; but it became clear that the chief purpose of history is the distillation of the higher religions. A one-volume abridgment in 1947 gave Toynbee the status almost of a prophet in America, yet Toynbee's aims and methods came increasingly under fire. Apart from factual errors serious criticism has focused on Toynbee's inclination to make history a stalking-horse for religious ideas, and on his penchant for scientific laws. In these ways, as in others, Toynbee's work has more in common with that of the great Victorian polymaths than with that of modern specialist historians, but it has served to articulate twentieth-century doubts and hopes for Western civilization.

Peter Jones

Toynbee's prodigious output included: *Greek Civilization and Character: the Self-revelation of Ancient Greek Society* (1924); *The World and the West* (1953); *An Historian's Approach to Religion* (1956); *East to West: A Journey round the World* (1958); *Acquaintances* (1967). See: M. F. Ashley-Montagu (ed.), *Toynbee and History* (1956); Pieter Geyl, *Debates with Historians* (1958); Roland N. Stromberg, *Arnold J. Toynbee* (1972).

480

TRAKL, Georg 1887–1914

Austrian poet

Georg Trakl was born into a Protestant family in Salzburg, the fourth of six children. He became passionately attached to his youngest sibling, Grete, a child as impulsive and artistically talented as himself, and it is likely that at puberty their relations became incestuous. By his teens Trakl was experimenting with alcohol and drugs, at the same time as he was composing his first poems.

In 1908 he became a pharmacy student in Vienna, pursuing a career in which his main interest seems to have been the fact that it permitted him access to chloroform, veronal and cocaine. Only a sturdy physique helped sustain him in his excesses: one night he collapsed in the snow after a heavy drinking bout and slept there until dawn, whereupon he roused himself to write a prose poem – 'Winter's Night'. The dangerous equation of artistic inspiration and artificially induced states of rapture was in part modelled on the example of Rimbaud, whose 'hallucinated' writings Trakl discovered at this time.

By 1909 Trakl had begun to publish in reviews, and to frequent literary circles. But already symptoms of psychological disturbance were evident: he was subject to acute phobias, had persecution fantasies and spent long hours in brooding isolation. In Innsbruck, however, working as a dispensing chemist to the military garrison, he met the literary editor Ludwig von Ficker, the one man who felt moved to assist him in his troubled search for clarity and form. Even so the publication of his *Gedichte* ('Poems') in 1913 was counterbalanced by Trakl's inability to hold down a steady job and his consequent drifting between Vienna, Innsbruck and Salzburg. A visit to Berlin in 1914 to see Grete, who had all but died of a miscarriage, combined with his drug addiction to accelerate the final slide into psychosis. Ficker offered him half of an award donated by Wittgenstein* (the other beneficiary was Rilke*), but when Trakl reached the bank to collect the money he suddenly dashed away in panic. Then in September 1914 he was mobilized in the medical corps and posted to Galicia. Put in charge of ninety wounded men, he saw one of the soldiers shoot himself, and tried to follow suit. He was committed to a psychiatric hospital in Cracow and diagnosed as a schizophrenic. A month later he killed himself with an overdose of cocaine. Three years later Grete too took her own life.

Trakl's early poetry conjures up a Tyrolean landscape peopled and witnessed by indistinct peasants and a few specific figures such as his sister and an anonymous stranger. Despite evocations of harvesting and golden summer days, the emotional trend is towards darkness and decline, from light to shade: 'The sighing of lovers breathes in the twigs/And over there a mother with child decomposes' ('All Souls' Day'). But as his work develops, such elegiac movement recedes, and his poems come to epitomize a despair insecurely redeemed by occasional dreams of innocence, associated with a few exceptional individuals ('Song of Caspar Hauser', 'Elis'). 'Grodek', his last poem, contains the line: 'All roads lead to black decay.' In its mixture of

whispering neo-Symbolist evocations of spiritual states and rasping Expressionist outbursts (the portrayal of urban decadence in 'The Sultry Suburb' for example), such poetry was of its time. It also tended towards surreal formulae: 'In the next room the sister plays a sonata by Schubert/Very softly her smile sinks into the crumbling well' ('On the way'). To the attested influence of Rimbaud may be added those of Baudelaire, Lenau and Hölderlin, as well as that of the Lutheran Bible.

Rilke's impression of Trakl's poems was that they partook of a space 'as impenetrable as the space within a mirror', and this is their attraction. It is a poetry of auguries which resist facile interpretation, but which in their uncertainty can mesmerize the reader's imagination. But if Trakl's disquiet becomes strangly seductive, the intangibility of the effect is deeply problematical. Mindful of the poet's tragic life, early critics were drawn to the notion that Trakl was essentially an imagist whose style of juxtaposed allusions clothed a somewhat limited range of themes: guilt, solitude, suffering, corruption and the thrill of death. Oblique references to Christian myth, as in the harrowing 'De Profundis', which alludes to a heavenly bridegroom, a bush of thorns and angels, along with hints of rape and murder, seemed to situate the poet's meanings within reasonably recognizable limits. But it then became clear that his idiom of allusion and imagery was highly complex, that his use of words was ambiguous and their connotations uncertain. His lines were seen to rotate around an unspoken core of meaning, impenetrable to others and obscure even to himself. The painstaking accumulation of cross-references across the poems, undertaken to establish a glossary of the poet's associations, revealed for every pattern an inconsistency. Nor could Trakl's intentions be unravelled from his manuscripts, since these too disclosed little evidence of consistency in their alterations. Thus the last line of 'Helian' originally read 'The jovial god opens his golden eyelids', but became 'The silent god lets sink his blue eyelids over him' – an unfathomable volte-face of meaning.

More recently Trakl has been seen less as a neo-Romantic communicant with Nature, more as a modernist manipulator of subtle aesthetic structures. His technique is perhaps one of intricate self-plagiarism, in which each new poem is the product of a play of permutations of old images. (Some critics even speak of 'serial poetics'.) If the meaning of his images cannot be located in a stable complex of associations, then it may be their power derives from the very fact of their shifting: the occasional interlinkings of images and subsequent collapses of coherence may be mimetic of processes central to Trakl's overall vision: 'It is the sweet time of love./In a boat down the blue river/How perfectly image lines up beside image – /And all drifts down in peace and quiet' ('Autumn transfigured').

Drifting, shifting, sinking – these are motions that inform both the writings and the lifestyle. Indeed, the poetry becomes the indirect register of psychological states. Its nominal style – sentences that often consist of noun-phrases bereft of a verb, the use of ellipsis as in apposition or suppression of articles, the dreamlike present tense, the lack of a firm narrative voice, the tendency of abstractions to take concrete form, the compulsive repetition or near-repetition of private commonplaces – indicates a mind caught up in itself, straining to make sense of acutely ambivalent emotions, yet unable to communicate directly with the outer world. In short, the very style of schizoid experience, whereby the world and self are dissociated and where objects appear in frozen isolation as stark metaphors of alienation: 'There is a stubble field into which falls black rain./There is a brown tree which stands alone./There is a hissing wind which whips round empty hovels –/How dismal is this evening' ('De Profundis'). And so the elemental bareness of the poet's landscape looms up as a reflection of a losing struggle to impress meaning and connectedness upon an experience of discontinuity.

Roger Cardinal

See: *Dichtungen und Briefe* ('Poetry and Letters'), ed. Killy and Szklenar (2 vols, 1969). *Selected Poems* (1968) provides a translation of some of Trakl's work. On Trakl: T. J. Casey, *Manshape That Shone* (1964); M. J. Kurrik, *Georg Trakl* (1974).

481
TRILLING, Lionel 1905–75

American critic, teacher and novelist

Born and educated in New York, Trilling based his life-long academic career at Columbia University. As a member of the English Faculty in the early 1930s he and Jacques Barzun established a series of seminars on the social and cultural context of literary ideas. Trilling's work as a teacher cannot be overemphasized. His rise through the professional ranks at Columbia to University Professor in 1970, and various appointments at Harvard, Oxford and elsewhere highlighted his Transatlantic reputation. His critical essays were often based directly on his teaching experience or his lectures.

His first published work appeared in the Jewish magazine, the *Menorah Journal*, edited by Elliot Cohen. His first full-length work, *Matthew Arnold* (1939), was based on his doctorate and was followed, in 1943, by a study of E. M. Forster*. This book was the product of what Trilling termed a lengthy quarrel with American literature and its introductory chapter provided him with a title for his first collection of essays. This,

The Liberal Imagination (1950), aimed to put liberal, or progressive, ideas and assumptions 'under some degree of pressure', whilst in turn assuming 'the inevitable intimate, if not always obvious, connexion between literature and politics'.

Trilling believed that the tendency of liberalism 'to organize the elements of life in a rational way' led to a reduction of ideas and, indeed, humanity. His novel, *The Middle of the Journey* (1947), tackled the overtly political issues confronting liberal intellectuals in America during the 1930s and 1940s. The central character, John Laskell, expresses 'an idea in modulation' – namely that the individual is neither autonomous nor completely conditioned, underlining Trilling's belief that self-hood consists of maintaining a position both within and beyond culture. His reading of Freud* in this context compounded his view of literature as of paramount importance in confronting and expressing this concept.

His essays in *The Opposing Self* (1955) concentrated on the idea of the self as it emerged in the nineteenth century with 'its intense and adverse imagination of the culture in which it [had] its being'. In *Beyond Culture* (1965) he expanded on this in the light of the increasingly obvious existence of 'two cultural environments'. The second, an 'adversary' culture, set up in opposition to the larger culture, ultimately defeats its individualist aims as it becomes a form of minority Establishment. The implications of such a situation extend far beyond the difficulties facing those involved in the teaching of modern literature. Trilling recognized the validity of the opinion that literature and the arts in general have achieved the status of religion. *Sincerity and Authenticity* (1972) concludes with an examination of the extent to which 'the doctrine that madness is health', symptomatic of social alienation, has gained theoretical credence amongst intellectuals. His impassioned and lucid rejection of such trends asserts the overall humanism of his thought.

Criticized variously by some as reactionary, conservative, over-secular or lacking in systematic clarity, Trilling has left a concise and challenging contribution to the study of literature, society and morality.

Susan Allen

Other works include: *Freud and the Crisis of our Culture* (1955), also included in *Beyond Culture*; *A Gathering of Fugitives* (1956); *Mind in the Modern World* (1973); short stories include 'Of This Time, Of That Place'; *The Experience of Literature* (1967) is an anthology. See also: Nathan A. Scott Jr, *Three American Moralists: Mailer, Bellow, Trilling* (1973); Quentin Anderson, Stephen Donadio and Steven Marcus (eds), *Art, Politics and Will: Essays in Honour of Lionel Trilling* (1977).

482
TROTSKY, Leon 1879–1940

Russian revolutionary

Born Lev Davidovich Bronstein into a moderately prosperous Jewish farming family in the southern Ukraine, Trotsky early became active in the Russian workers' movement and embraced Marxism. He was arrested in 1898 for political activity in the town of Nikolayev, imprisoned, and deported to Siberia. Escaping in 1902, he travelled to London where he met Lenin* for the first time and he began, with Lenin's encouragement, to write for the journal *Iskra* and to argue for its political standpoint – the building of a centralized Russian workers' party – in lectures and debates within Russian émigré circles in Europe. From the first he displayed a powerful literary and oratorical talent.

Present in 1903 at the Second Congress of the Russian Social-Democratic Party, at which the historic schism between Bolsheviks and Mensheviks occurred, Trotsky sided with the Mensheviks against Lenin. Though he would soon distance himself from them to stand outside both factions for more than a decade, on this issue he felt, and wrote, that Lenin's theory of organization was undemocratic, aiming to substitute the efforts of a revolutionary elite for the initiative of the workers themselves.

Trotsky returned to Russia in 1905 to play a prominent part in the revolution of that year as a leader of the St Petersburg Soviet of Workers' Deputies. The lessons he drew from this experience included reflections on the nature of workers' democracy and the theory, identified with his name, of permanent revolution: he formulated this now in the argument that the Russian proletariat, contrary to any orthodox Marxist expectation held by Bolsheviks and Mensheviks alike, might embark upon socialist revolution before the workers of the more advanced capitalist countries.

For his part in the work of the Soviet, Trotsky was again imprisoned and condemned to exile in Siberia. In 1907, making another escape whilst under escort into exile, he returned to Europe to settle in Vienna until the First World War. During that conflict, which he spent in Paris and, briefly, New York, his was a leading voice in the revolutionary opposition to the war by the internationalist wing of European socialism.

After the February revolution in 1917, Trotsky again returned to Russia and at once made common cause with Lenin, eventually joining the Bolshevik Party. This had now, following a change of political position by Lenin, adopted a perspective essentially identical with Trotsky's own conception of permanent revolution. Trotsky became one of the Russian revolution's main leaders: brilliant orator, publicist, organizer, political strategist, President of the Petrograd Soviet. He

prepared and led the October insurrection which delivered power into the Bolsheviks' hands. As Commissar of Foreign Affairs in the first Soviet government, he conducted the peace negotiations with Germany at Brest-Litovsk; as Commissar of War, supervised the construction of the Red Army through civil war and hostile foreign intervention; played a key role in the foundation and early congresses of the Communist International. Throughout these post-revolutionary years, he spoke and wrote on all important political issues, domestic and international, as also on literary, cultural and scientific topics.

From 1923 onwards, and especially after Lenin's death, Trotsky bent his efforts towards opposing the increasingly bureaucratic and authoritarian regime in the Communist Party, the rising power of Stalin*, the latter's internal and foreign policies and the doctrine of 'socialism in one country' which he had begun to put forth. In this connection, Trotsky now developed and generalized the theory of permanent revolution. Defeated by Stalin, he was expelled from the Party in 1927, sent into remote exile near the Chinese border, and in 1929 deported from Russia altogether. During the next decade he would inhabit one brief and insecure refuge after another, in Turkey, then France, then Norway, finally Mexico. Isolated, beset by difficulties, bereft by family tragedies, he continued to write, prodigiously: history, autobiography, diagnosis and warning concerning the danger of Nazism, analysis of the nature of Soviet society, defence of the authentic Leninist heritage, as he construed this, against its Stalinist despoliation, argument for the formation of a new revolutionary International. At work on a biography of Stalin, he was murdered in his home by one of Stalin's agents.

As political thinker and writer, Trotsky's importance is threefold. His work is one of the best examples of the creative application of Marxism in the area of political and historical analysis; between the time of Lenin's death and his own, Trotsky was in this respect without peer. His best writing, a clear, compelling and imaginative prose combining objectivity with the deepest commitment, achieved a standard of literary excellence first set by Marx himself and matched since by Marx's followers too rarely. Finally, in what was a dark period for the revolutionary socialist idea, he came to stand – against the currents dominant in the European workers' movement, gradualist and reformist on the one hand, Stalinist, authoritarian, on the other – for a socialism in which proletarian revolution and workers' democracy must sit side by side.

Trotsky's early analysis of the configuration of Russian society, and his prognosis about the character of the revolution that would emerge from it, provide one of the most striking instances to date of a Marxist theoretical projection confirmed in its broad outline by the ensuing course of events. From 1905 onwards, he challenged the prevalent Russian Marxist belief that, in a backward country with a huge peasant majority, revolution could only mean bourgeois revolution, with its issue the extension of capitalist economy and the establishment of bourgeois-democratic political rule. In *Results and Prospects* (St Petersburg 1906) and then *1905* (Dresden 1910), Trotsky argued that, owing to the specific features of Russia's history in which capitalist development was fostered by the state and based largely on foreign capital, the indigenous forces of the Russian bourgeoisie were too weak, and Russian liberalism insufficiently bold, to lead a revolutionary assault against Tsarism. The Russian working class was small but highly concentrated. Like the compact, relatively advanced capitalist sector which had produced it, it was an expression of what Trotsky was later to call the 'law of combined and uneven development': as capitalism from its heartlands projected its consequences over the globe, heedless of traditional and national boundaries, so the features of modes of production that were, in the classical Marxist schema, distinct, would be found fused together within one social reality; so Russia now combined a modern industrial proletariat with pre-capitalist agrarian and political structures. A successful revolution here, Trotsky asserted, would have to be led by this small, militant proletariat, carrying behind it the land-hungry peasants, and because of this it could not remain a bourgeois revolution. The Russian workers once in power would not be able or willing to leave capitalist property relations intact. Establishing the first dictatorship of the proletariat, they would initiate the transition to socialism. But they could not complete this on their own without linking up with successful socialist revolutions in the West. Confined to a backward country, the enterprise would be doomed to defeat.

The main tenets of this conception were part also of the outlook of Bolshevism by the time it led the Russian proletariat to power in 1917. Later, when revolutions to the west had failed, leaving the young Soviet state isolated, Stalin asserted first the possibility, then the reality, of a socialism constructed in Russia alone. In *The Permanent Revolution* (Berlin 1930) and other writings, Trotsky reaffirmed and developed his original conception. He insisted that the fate of Russian socialism still depended on the outcome of the revolutionary process elsewhere. He extended to the analysis of this process in other backward societies the framework first applied in his treatment of Russia; arguing, in anticipation of much subsequent discussion of 'underdevelopment', that such societies could not reproduce the path followed by the first capitalist nations.

The geographical reach of Trotsky's writings on these and related themes was long, covering Britain and China, Germany, France and Spain, the Soviet Union itself. So extensive an output could not be wholly even in strength. Two of its notable achievements, however, were his analyses of fascism and of the character of the Soviet state, historically novel phenomena still to be assimilated within Marxist understanding. With growing urgency Trotsky warned against the Comintern's complacency towards the Nazi threat in Germany. Nazism triumphant, he predicted, would install not just one reactionary variant of capitalist rule amongst others, but a qualitatively distinct form catastrophic for the working class, predicated on the destruction of its organizations and its means of political self-defence through the mass mobilization against it of petty-bourgeois strata. The Soviet Union, he proposed in *The Revolution Betrayed* (Paris 1936), was neither socialist, as Stalin and his apologists claimed, nor some new type of class, or even capitalist, society, as some critics averred. It was a transitional formation in which the chief economic conquest of the October revolution, socialized property relations, was still extant despite the fact that a privileged bureaucracy had fashioned for itself a monopoly of political functions. To advance to socialism the workers would have to overturn this bureaucratic group by a political revolution. On both these issues Trotsky's contribution was original, level-headed and penetrating, and it remains a starting point for contemporary discussion.

Trotsky was one of the great writers of his time. Keenly interested in literary and cultural subjects to which he devoted a significant part of his output and, in particular, the theoretical study *Literature and Revolution* (Moscow 1923), his own literary achievement was considerable. It was built upon a lucid and incisive style and the ability to present ideas, persons, events, in a complex and vivid way. It encompassed pages of cogent political argument, historical and literary interpretation finely integrating abstract theory with concrete perception, sketches of contemporaries acutely observed; an impressive account of the year *1905*, an autobiographical work, *My Life* (Berlin 1930), unusual in the Marxist canon and remarkable by any standards, and an outstanding work of Marxist historiography, *The History of the Russian Revolution* (Berlin 1931). This was his masterpiece, an epic, in which individuals and masses moved against the vast backdrop of Russia's history to transform the destiny of the whole world.

On questions of socialist democracy and organization, Trotsky's record over forty years was neither uniform nor unblemished. He opposed at first the Leninist party concept, representing it in *Our Political Tasks* (Geneva 1904) as an attempt to hold the working class in tutelage. After 1917 he rejected out of hand all such interpretations of it, upheld it consistently against the charge of having begot the crimes of Stalin. His strictures of Lenin he came to see as unjust and mistaken. *Our Political Tasks* spoke in the name of a democratic socialism open to the struggle between different tendencies; *1905* depicted the soviet form, the workers' council, as the very embodiment of this democratic principle, born of direct proletarian action and expressing as directly as possible the diverse voices within the working class. Though he would share in the necessities, the expediencies and the errors of the Bolsheviks in power, Trotsky was later to return to and develop these themes in his struggle against Stalinism, arguing for the right of tendencies inside revolutionary organizations and, beyond, for a united front within which different currents in the workers' movement could openly compete. Taken all in all, across the inconsistencies, Trotsky's final record was clear: for a socialism both revolutionary and democratic in an atmosphere uncongenial to this synthesis, thus in lonely, but for this very reason vital, continuity with the best traditions of Marxism and of Leninism.

There have been obscurantist and ugly responses to Trotsky's intellectual and political achievement, chief of them the prejudice and obloquy he has suffered in widespread quarters, but also a sectarian involution to which some of his would-be disciples have succumbed. His work stands out, however, as an important source and inspiration of contemporary Marxist research, and the Fourth International which he founded has members and supporters in many countries.

Norman Geras

English translations of Trotsky's works directly referred to here, only a fraction of his total output: *The Permanent Revolution and Results and Prospects* (1962); *1905* (1972); *The Revolution Betrayed* (1965); *The Struggle Against Fascism in Germany* (1971); *Literature and Revolution* (1960); *My Life* (1960); *The History of the Russian Revolution* (1965); *Our Political Tasks* (1980). On Trotsky: Isaac Deutscher, *The Prophet Armed, The Prophet Unarmed* and *The Prophet Outcast* (1954, 1959 and 1963); Louis Sinclair, *Leon Trotsky: A Bibliography* (1972); Baruch Knei-Paz, *The Social and Political Thought of Leon Trotsky* (1978); Irving Howe, *Trotsky* (1978); Ernest Mandel, *Trotsky: A Study in the Dynamic of his Thought* (1979).

483

TRUFFAUT, François 1932–

French film director

'I believe in communication and understanding. Things *can* be communicated. You *can* describe what you are feeling. You can talk.'

Such concern with the spoken, or written, word is not normally associated with the cinema, but François Truffaut confesses to a feeling that he belongs more to the nineteenth century, and perhaps to a literary, humanist tradition that has its roots in Rousseau, Goethe and Balzac.

Under the paternal guidance of André Bazin, Truffaut, in his reviewing days for *Cahiers du Cinéma*, was a rigorous proponent of the 'auteur' theory, which credited directors with personal as opposed to collaborative responsibility for their films. The cinema of François Truffaut bears an uncompromising novelist's signature. Where Godard* uses literary references, they are part of his rag-bag of multi-media quotation. Godard is a radical and dramatic essayist – impatient, didactic and innovative. Truffaut is a traditionalist. His films deal with love, friendship, loss; with human relationships. Plots exist in order for characters to interact, not to relate an A–Z narrative. Only the tone and the preoccupations are constant.

Truffaut is unabashed by stylized 'voice-over' commentary. For him the first person confidential tone not only imposes unity on often very disparate material, but more importantly invites emotional complicity from each individual in an audience.

This intense personal involvement has produced over twenty years a unique autobiographical testament. Truffaut's first full-length film, *The Four Hundred Blows* (*Les quatre cent coups*, 1959), was based strongly on his own childhood experience in a reformatory. The hero, Antoine Doinel (always played by the same actor, Jean-Pierre Léaud), has reappeared at various stages of his *éducation sentimentale*, from the *Antoine and Colette* episode in *L'Amour à vingt ans* (1962) through *Stolen Kisses* (*Baisers volés*, 1969), *Bed and Board* (*Domicile conjugale*, 1970), and what is promised to be the last in the sequence, *Love on the Run* (*L'Amour en fuite*, 1979).

Doinel cannot be interpreted simply as Truffaut's fictional *alter ego*. There is an extraordinary sympathy and identification between actor and director, but Doinel/Léaud, despite the passing years, has remained curiously frozen in perpetual adolescence.

Les quatre cent coups was an international success. With his *Cahiers* friends, Godard, Rivette, Rohmer and Chabrol, Truffaut launched the 'Nouvelle Vague'. At a time of depression on shoe-string budgets these young film-makers dragged the cinema out of the studios and into the streets. With portable light-weight cameras, free-wheeling cinéma-vérité techniques, a regular company of actors, writers, composers and technicians, they made a virtue of improvisation.

But Truffaut's films, from the very beginning, reveal a genuine concern with cinematic vocabulary. His second feature *Shoot the Pianist* (*Tirez sur le pianiste*, 1960) adapted 'B' Feature Hollywood gangster motifs into a daringly uninhibited tragi-comic *jeu d'esprit*. 'It was a genuine experiment. . . . If I felt like shooting a particular scene I just did it, and then followed it with another that was completely different.' The film was a commercial flop.

But with *Jules et Jim* (1961), Truffaut's international reputation was confirmed. The romance, humour and pathos of an impossible *ménage à trois* is described with compassionate irony and lyrical charm.

As a reviewer Truffaut has always attacked makers of 'serious subject' films like Stanley Kramer. 'If you have something to say, say it. Don't make a film about it.' With *Fahrenheit 451* (1966), Truffaut demonstrates the truth of the dictum. Based on Ray Bradbury's futuristic fantasy of the destruction of the written word, Truffaut's picture, despite all its emotional commitment, remains stilted and theoretical.

Like his 'Nouvelle Vague' comrades, Truffaut was nurtured on the cinema. At the age of fifteen, he had started his own ciné-club, called Le Cercle Cinémane. 'What first attracted me to the cinema was my love of fiction and what led me to want to make films was my desire to structure a fictional story.' But where Truffaut's preoccupation with style and structure leads him towards imitation (as with his Hitchcock*-influenced 'thrillers' *The Bride Wore Black* (*La Mariée était en noir*, 1967), and *Mississippi Mermaid* (*La Sirène du Mississippi*, 1969)), he can be awkward and remote. Where he pays direct tribute to the cinema, however, as in *Day for Night* (*La Nuit américaine*, 1973) he is assured, affectionate and romantically involved.

Truffaut reveals his supreme artistry when he focuses on the intimate paradoxes of human behaviour. In *The Wild Child* (*L'Enfant sauvage*, 1969) Truffaut himself took the role of Dr Itard, teacher of the Wild Child of Aveyron. The film is quite literally about language and communication, about the relationship between teacher and pupil, director and actor. The deceptively spare almost documentary style is elegantly sensitive to psychological nuance and contains images of breathtaking beauty.

In his best films, Truffaut's presence whether as writer, actor, director (or all three) informs every frame. His insistence on individual values rejects all Bond-age blockbuster formulae. It may mean that his work can be flawed, miniaturist, sometimes casual or even too subjective, but it is never slick or pontificating. With all due modesty, the source of Truffaut's inspiration is always himself. He remains sceptical about patriotism, existential pessimism, politics (he has never voted) and religion. 'My religion is the cinema. I believe in Charlie Chaplin*. . . . I make films to realize my childhood dreams, to make me feel good, and to make others share in that feeling.'

Paul Sidey

Other films include: *Silken Skin* (*La Peau douce*, 1966); *Anne and Muriel* (*Les deux anglaises sur le Continent*, 1972); *The Story of Adèle H* (*L'Histoire d'Adèle H*, 1975). See: François Truffaut, *Hitchcock* (1967); Graham Petrie, *The Cinema of François Truffaut* (1970); Don Allen, *Truffaut* (1974); François Truffaut, *The Films in My Life* (1979).

484
TURING, Alan 1912–54

British logician

Alan Turing was born in London and was educated at Sherborne and King's College, Cambridge. A fellowship at King's College (1935) led to two years (1936–8) working with Alonzo Church at Princeton. During the war Turing worked in the Communications Department at the Foreign Office, and in 1945 he joined the National Physical Laboratory to work on their early computer known as ACE. In 1948 he took the post of Reader at Manchester University, again working on problems associated with computers. He died of poisoning, possibly accidental, in June 1954.

It is astonishing that Turing's famous paper on computable numbers was published in 1937. In it he performed an historic thought experiment: he postulated a computer which could take its instructions from a paper tape containing a sequence of 1s and 0s, could print new sequences of 1s and 0s, which would then, if necessary, join the sequence of instructions. In this way it would modify its own program. Turing showed that any machine which was capable of doing this much was, in a certain sense, the match of any other machine which could do this much. He called a machine of this kind a 'Universal Automaton'. (This is usually called a 'Turing Machine' today.) A small, slow Turing Machine will be capable of doing anything which can be done by a larger, faster Turing Machine, assuming that there are no physical limitations on the storage of the program. Essentially the smaller machine can always be programmed to plod on, and to get there in the end.

The earliest steps in the development of computers were diverse, uncoordinated, and mixed up with interests in tabulation, statistics, ballistics, telecommunications. Yet out of this somewhat confusing mêlée a wise strategic decision emerged: to build general-purpose machines capable of modifying their own programs. The hardware would be as flexible as possible: programs punched on paper tape would supply the specialist features required to meet any specific difficulty. The result was that most of the computers subsequently made embodied a potentially limitless computing facility: there was no knowing what they might be brought to do. This maintained the essentially 'magic' feeling of the machine, and acted as a sustained intellectual stimulus for programmers and analysts. Such machines were, in effect, the Universal Automatons Turing had foreseen in 1937.

It could easily have been otherwise. That it was not was largely due to the efforts of Alan Turing and John Von Neumann*.

Christopher Ormell

Alan Turing's papers were as follows: 'On Computable Numbers. . .' (1937); 'Systems of logic based on ordinals' (1939); 'Computing Machinery and Intelligence' (1950); and 'The Chemical Basis of Morphogenesis' (1952). See also: S. Turing, *Alan M. Turing* (1959).

485

TURNER, Frederick Jackson 1861–1932

US historian and teacher

Turner was born in Portage, Wisconsin, when that state had barely emerged from the frontier, and his thought can be viewed as a vindication of that birth. He attended the state university between 1880 and 1884 and, after a year as a journalist, taught in Madison until he moved to Harvard in 1910. For a year, 1888–9, he ventured east to Johns Hopkins University in Baltimore, then the foremost seminar for historical research in the United States. He was there versed in the stern exigencies of German historical method and irritated by the laconic indifference of easterners to the contribution of the West to American society. The Hopkins seminar, personified by Herbert Baxter Adams, preached the 'germ' theory of Anglo-Saxon constitutional development, whereby the democratic institutions of the United States – best exemplified on the East Coast – had evolved via England from the medieval tribes of Germany. In his decisive 1893 essay, 'The Frontier in American History', Turner accepted the evolutionary perspective (also represented at Baltimore by Woodrow Wilson and Richard T. Ely) but displaced German woods for American forests, rancid-buttered Ostrogoths for frontier Jacksonians. It was, Turner claimed, the sociology of the American frontier that had created the American predilection for democracy, that 'the existence of an area of free land, its continuous recession, and the advance of American settlement westward, explain American development.' For the frontier initially drove the settler back upon the primitive and stripped away his European inheritance, impelled individualistic self-reliance and created the American temperament, coarse but inquisitive, inventive and materialist, exuberant and individual.

This essay was immensely influential, both in breaking the eastern stranglehold on the vision of the American past and, not in creating a myth of the American character, but in fashioning its first plausible sociological explanation. It was the more persuasive, since it appealed to a culture vanishing and regarded with nostalgic affection by Americans. Nothing else matched its influence, though Turner did venture other theses, notably an argument for the historical importance of geographical sections and even a plea for an urban interpretation of American history. But he was essentially an essayist, if he can be deemed a willing writer at all, and only one editor, Albert Bushnell Hart, ever managed to extract a full-length narrative from him. Turner was entranced by research, the accumulation of fascinating if unassimilated note cards, and his writing is notable for long passages of tedious detail, interspersed with paragraphs of lucid – if not always related – insight. He was perhaps most successful and most content as a teacher. At the University of Wisconsin he established one of the best graduate programmes in history at a state university. His students were some of his greatest assets, for they collected his essays, published several posthumous volumes, tidied up and defended the frontier thesis decades past its author's demise and wrote his definitive biography. In Carl Becker, Ray Allen Billington, Avery Craven, Herbert E. Bolton and Frederick Merk, Turner left a legacy wider than his own thought.

Michael O'Brien

Works include: *The Rise of the New West, 1819–1829* (1906); *The Frontier in American History* (1920); *The Significance of Sections in American History* (1932); *The United States, 1830–1850: The Nation and its Sections* (1935). About Turner: R. S. Billington, *Frederick Jackson Turner* (1973); Carl Becker, *Everyman his own Historian* (1935); Wilbur R. Jacobs (ed.), *The Historical World of Frederick Jackson Turner* (1968); Richard Hofstadter, *The Progressive Historians* (1968); R. Hofstadter and S. M. Lipset, *Turner and the Sociology of the Frontier* (1968).

486

TZARA, Tristan (Samuel Rosenstock) 1896–1963

Romanian/French writer

A Romanian by birth, Tzara adopted the French language and in later life French nationality. His career as a cultural terrorist began in 1916 when, in neutral Zürich, he joined other refugees like Hugo Ball, Richard Huelsenbeck and Hans Arp* to mount that brief but savage assault on Western cultural values known as Dada. Tzara was in his element as the ebullient impresario of this most anarchic of movements in the arts, contributing to the recitation of wild multilingual poems at the Cabaret Voltaire, setting up provocative exhibitions of Dada paintings, organizing stage performances at which the Dada group would, by their incoherent proclamations and insults, goad the audience into frenzied protest, and spreading the Dada message of subversion across Europe by way of publications and tireless correspondence with other avant-garde leaders like Apollinaire*, Marinetti*, Haussmann and Breton*.

In 1920 Tzara settled in Paris, joining forces with

André Breton and his *Littérature* group to launch a further series of outrageous spectacles. Eventually, though, bourgeois audiences began to enjoy being insulted and Dada scandal became a cultural commodity like any other. While Breton led the group into the new adventures of Surrealism, Tzara stuck to his individualist path, eventually to join up with the Surrealists again in the early 1930s, when he produced some of his best poetry. Later, Tzara's emergent Marxist concerns led him out of Surrealism: an active member of the Resistance during the Occupation, he entered the French Communist Party in 1947.

Tzara's most prized texts are his Dada manifestos, written to be performed in public and full of rumbustious tomfoolery and astringent wit. His is the language of a sophisticated savage, by turns silly, aggressive, and truculently paradoxical: 'I am writing a manifesto and there's nothing I want, and yet I'm saying certain things, and in principle I am against manifestos, as I am against principles. . . . I won't explain myself because I abhor common sense.'

The poems of the Dada period are characterized by extreme semantic and syntactic incoherence: improvised nonsense statements are interspersed with random slogans or headlines, with puns, invented words and printer's errors tossed into the mixture. The resultant texts exhibit a staccato singularity, a kind of sublime inarticulacy. 'Dada is an anti-nuance cream,' Tzara drily observed.

The remarkable thing is that Tzara persisted in this experiment in linguistic deviancy, maintaining a studied inconsequentiality until, by a mysterious reversal, his style modulated from unreadable gibberish into a seductive and fertile surrealist idiom. *L'Homme approximatif* (1931) is his best-known poem, an extended meditation on mental and elemental impulses in which the obscure play of words gives rise to felicitous lyrical passages with images of stunning beauty: 'sweet utterance at rest within my hand magic freshness/deep down in the cormorant at its breast flying spinning like an astral sign/light when expressed forfeits its petals.'

Essentially Tzara's poetry exemplifies the principle of new insights being generated through the exacerbation of singularity, as he indicated in an early aphorism: 'To concede to each element its identity, its autonomy, is the necessary condition for the creation of new constellations, since each has its place in the group. The thrust of the Word: upright, an image, a unique event, passionate, of dense colour, intensity, in communion with life.' Passing from Dada spontaneity through Surrealist automatic writing, Tzara arrived at a mature style of transparent simplicity in which disparate entities could be held together in a unifying vision.

In retrospect, harmony and contact had been Tzara's goals all along. The 'great destructive negative work' of Dada was a prelude to the renewal of mental perspectives, and the rampant nihilism of the *Dada Manifesto 1918* was counterbalanced by a desire to lay hold of the jostling realities of existence: 'Abolition of logic: DADA . . . abolition of memory: DADA; abolition of archaeology: DADA; abolition of prophets: DADA; abolition of the future: DADA . . . Liberty: *DADA DADA DADA*, the roaring of contorted pains, the interweaving of contraries and of all contradictions, freaks and irrelevancies: LIFE.'

Roger Cardinal

Other works: *Vingt-cinq poèmes* ('Twenty-five poems', 1918); *De nos oiseaux* ('Of our Birds', 1929); *L'Antitête* ('The Anti-head', 1933); *A haute flamme* ('Flame Out Loud', 1955). In course of publication: *Oeuvres complètes* (vol. I, 1975; vol. II, 1977). In English: *Seven Dada Manifestos and Lampisteries* (trans. B. Wright, 1977). On Tzara: René Lacôte, *Tristan Tzara* (1952); Mary Ann Caws, *The Poetry of Dada and Surrealism* (1970).

U

UNAMUNO, Miguel de 1864–1936

Spanish writer

Born in Bilbao into a bourgeois family, Unamuno studied philosophy and letters and became a professor of Greek at Salamanca. Already famous as an essayist in his early thirties, he was made into a European celebrity when his deportation to the Canary Islands by the dictatorship of Primo de Rivera aroused a storm of protest well beyond Spain (1924). Unamuno went to Paris for a while, but soon was chosen as rector of his old university. He died in Salamanca shortly after a characteristic clash with a nationalist general at the beginning of the Spanish Civil War.

Unamuno belonged to the critical '1898' generation, a brilliant group of writers deeply engaged in national soul-searching. His first major work of essayism, *En Torno al Casticismo*, 1895, endeavours to raise the conception of the hispanic above its cheap 'exotic' overtones while at the same time musing over the right way to tackle a national tradition. He sets out to grasp the 'intra-historical' below the merely historical, the inner historicity, that is, of a culture, a task which he starkly distinguished from the contemplative disquisitions of German-like historicism as philological scholarship. The moral of the essay is that Spanish purity (*casticismo*) must be valiantly sought in a renewed contact with modern Europe, not in parochial isolation. For a time, Unamuno's thought tried to reconcile the irrational and instinctive with logic and analysis (e.g. in *Amor y Pedagogía*, 'Love and Pedagogy', 1902), but before long he turned against science and the 'biological values' of modern culture and asserted himself as an uncompromising vitalist in a strong irrationalist sense, not uninfluenced by his reading of Kierkegaard, Nietzsche, William James and Bergson*. All vital values were for him irrational, and everything rational contrary to life.

In 1905, the tricentennial of the first part of *Don Quixote*, Unamuno published his most original book, the *Vida de Don Quijote y Sancho* 'commented' by him. He cast himself in the role not of a Cervantist, but of a Quixotist. For him, the squire Pança is foolish – in fact, more foolish than the knight – and 'Our Lord Don Quixote' is rescued from the comical light of Cervantes's novel in order to impersonate a crusade of faith against reason. Truth is not an object of thought

but a driving force in conduct, a matter of guts, not of intellect. Unamunian 'misologism' reaches its consummation. What the wise, prudent Sanchos of our own world never understand is that we should inveigh against our dead machine civilization just as Don Quixote did against the windmills. Whilst positivism, empiricism and naturalism are condemned out of hand, Don Quixote's passion for a justice beyond law receives praise, as does his strenuous search for glory, his 'hunger for immortality'. In his beautiful interpretation of the cave of Montesinos episode, the hispanic theme comes back in full: like his hero, Unamuno wants to cut his way to the genuine core of tradition through the useless jungle of stale traditionalisms.

His best poetical and fictional output also dates from the first two decades of this century. If his unmusical philosophical poems (*El Cristo de Velásquez*, 1920) are seldom reckoned among his best, his main novels, *Niebla* ('Fog', 1914), *La Tía Tula* ('Aunt Tula', 1921), and novellas (*Tres Novelas Ejemplares y un Prólogo*, 1921) set Spanish story-telling on a new track, deliberately opposed to naturalist models. However, Unamuno was above all a master of the essay, as confirmed by his most accomplished work as a moralist, *The Tragic Sense of Life in Men and in Peoples* (*Del Sentimiento Trágico de la Vida, en los Hombres y los Pueblos*, 1913, trans. 1921). Following Nietzsche, Unamuno holds that there are no philosophies, just philosophers: thought springs from existential attitudes. Now man is eternally resisting his own nature as a finite being. Catholicism, i.e. Christianity, gave this tragic resistance its best rationale in the idea of a God who renders us immortal, thus maximizing our will-power before the unacceptable reality of death. Faith as a tragic sense of life is in a constant fight against despair. It is less a creed than an absurd hope. The 'sweet, redeeming uncertainty', anguish, becomes for Unamuno as for Kierkegaard the truest religious feeling and the basis for the inner leap from extreme denial to extreme assertion. Like its faith, the life of the Christian is bound to be restless: it is an *agon*, for as a Christian he must combat in himself the husband, the father and the citizen (hence the title of his reprise of *Del Sentimiento Trágico*, *La Agonía del Cristianismo*, 1924). The paradigm can be nothing less than Christ's own passion: the Golgotha is the goal. Unamuno's 'dolorismo' is the other face of his agonism.

Modern scholarship on the history of Christian thought has detected a curious Lutheran temper in

531

Unamuno, who nevertheless always extolled Catholicism, even above Christianity. The tragic view of life and the upholding of a faith which is no 'creed' and is born of despair sounds indeed like Luther's own religiosity. Yet unlike Luther's, and unlike the thought of other antirationalist 'philosophers of life' (e.g. Bergson), Unamuno's piety evinces no mystical inclination: his religious outlook is fundamentally ascetic. Spanish catholicism seems to him most authentic precisely because it is highly ascetic and agonistic, whereas Roman catholicism lost its spiritual strength in a facile, erroneous attempt to marry the Gospel to Roman law (in the canon law). At bottom, however, the Unamunian agony is not confessional: it eschews every church, and aims at the perfect solitude of the individual in his yearning for eternity.

Unamuno's essays are couched in a terse style made of humourless fragments bristling with paradoxes: the blunt preaching language of a lonely prophet, of 'the Spanish Carlyle', 'don Miguel', the proud Basque who shook Spain up by the scandal of his burning prose. He was one of Europe's greatest individualists, who wrote that 'the only vital problem is the problem of our individual, personal destiny' – and as such, and in so far as he is much less of a believer than Kierkegaard, perhaps the most typical among proto-existentialists. Yet this fierce anarchic personality loved his country with all his heart, and only a true Spaniard could have written his briefest description of the human condition: 'Life is bullfighting.'

J. G. Merquior

The works of Unamuno have been collected into a modern edition by the publisher Aguilar, Madrid. The best study of his thought is by Julián Marías, *Miguel de Unamuno* (Madrid 1943). See also: Ernst Robert Curtius, *Kritische Essays zur europäischen Literatur* (Bern 1954), and José Luís Aranguren, *Catolicismo y Protestantismo como formas de existencia* (Madrid 1952).

488
UNGARETTI, Giuseppe 1888–1970

Italian poet and critic

Born in Alexandria, Egypt, Ungaretti led a somewhat undisciplined life in his youth, being particularly attracted to a group of young anarchists headed by the Italian novelist Enrico Pea. His intense interest in poetry was awakened during his schooldays by his studies of Petrarch and Leopardi in the Italian and by Baudelaire and Mallarmé in the French tradition. In 1912 he left Egypt for Paris to complete his education at the Sorbonne, and while he was there he took an active part in the avant-garde literary and artistic movements of the time, counting among his friends such figures as Apollinaire*, Max Jacob, Modigliani* and Braque*. When Italy entered the war in 1915 he joined the army as a private and was fortunate enough to make the acquaintance at Udine of the critic Ettore Serra, through whose good offices his first volume of poetry *Il porto sepolto* was published in 1916. This was later incorporated into *Allegria di Naufragi* (1919), although the collection underwent many changes before the definitive edition entitled *Allegria* appeared in 1942. His second volume *Sentimento del tempo* was published in 1933 and marked a significant change in his manner of writing.

During the 1920s and 1930s the poet worked as a journalist in Rome, until in 1936, finally disgusted by the empty bombast of the Fascist regime, he emigrated to Brazil where he was appointed Professor of Italian Literature in the University of São Paulo. His self-imposed exile prompted his third volume of verse, *Il Dolore* (1947), largely concerned with the death of his nine-year-old son, Antonietto, and the disasters which overwhelmed his native Italy during the Second World War. This volume is regarded as a deviation from his main line of inspiration, but it nevertheless marks the climax of his baroque period.

In 1942 the poet returned to Italy and was appointed Professor of Modern Italian Literature at the University of Rome. During the remainder of his life he published a number of other volumes of verse, notable among which are *La terra promessa* (1950) and *Un grido e paesaggi* (1952). These were accompanied by a good deal of prose-writing which included important articles of criticism on his favourite authors as well as works of pure imagination such as *Il deserto e dopo* (1961). The poet died in Milan in 1970 after a short illness.

Culturally Ungaretti belongs to the hermetic movement, although his early style was also influenced to some extent by the French symbolists and the Italian futurists. The hermetic movement's most prominent stylistic feature is its involution of imagery, although this was practised not with obscurantist purposes in mind but because the poets of the school recognized that they were pressing against the limits of expressibility in language and could represent their moods imaginatively and symbolically, but rarely conceptually. Ungaretti's overall outlook is that humanity is orphically suspended between Heaven and Hell, as if hanging by the spider's web of intellect over a Pascalian abyss. His poetry attempts to evoke the terrors of this 'existential' abyss while at the same time seeking comfort from his immediate sense-impressions and from working within the slowly evolving literary tradition. His poetry is thus born at the intersection of the present and the past, with his own experiences in the foreground and the lyric tradition acting as a type of chorus and whispering compelling, atavistic melodies in the wings.

In his view poetry arises through the transformation of the contingent into an aesthetic – not a conceptual – form of absoluteness. In his two-lined poem *Eterno* he emphasizes the Bergsonian* view that our vision of the abyss is the result of a change of register rather than a reality, one which transmutes the flux of the outer world into the serene beauty of the inner one:

> Tra un fiore colto e l'altro donato
> L'inesprimibile nulla.

(Between the flower plucked and the other proffered
The inexpressible void.)

This brief hiatus between outer reality and the inner vision is consequently the break which permits a poem to transcend an immediate situation and become an interpretation of a mood rather than the reproduction of a scene.

Later he associated the 'abyss' with the baroque outlooks of a Michelangelo and a Góngora, and the somewhat impressionistic style of *Allegria* then changes to the discursive style of *Il Dolore*, although the process is mediated by the collection *Sentimento del tempo* in which an attempt is made to recapture in a modern key the thematic and prosodic continuity of the preceding Italian tradition and its sense of maturing through time. As the process gains momentum, there is a diminution of the 'fulminatory' analogy which is the hallmark of the poet's hermetic period; but even in *Il Dolore* the flashing analogical image still makes its appearance in the most unexpected circumstances.

All these momentary insights and human perspectives are contained within a conscious metaphysic of regained innocence summed up in the phrase:

> Cerco un paese
> innocente.
>
> (I seek an innocent
> country.)

The poet believed that after the Fall mankind suffered a catastrophe – its immersion in Time – which it has been trying to rectify ever since. Orphically speaking, therefore, life is destined to come full circle and regain the lost innocence of the Garden of Eden. This is more an innocence regained aesthetically, however, than conceptually; so that our aesthetic triumphs are our pledge of virtue, our testimony of 'redemption', before God. On the individual level 'redemption' is achieved by a form of self-fulfilment, symbolized in the works of Ungaretti's old age by the figure of Aeneas. The latter combines, it seems, a humanist – almost a pagan – piety with a deep sense of Christian pity or charity, and he creates a new Promised Land for that restless nomad, the human being. It is one which evokes a feeling of 'redemption' through a sense of wholeness or memorial fulfilment at the end of life, when the individual finally moves into a higher state of consciousness. This sense of fulfilment is, of course, ultimately merged with the broader pattern of innocence regained implicit in the historical tradition, but the innocence which Ungaretti seeks is one which is culture-saturated, not gratuitously God-given – a vision of an eternalized humanity freed from the bondage of Time.

Professor Frederic J. Jones

Other works: *La guerra* (1919); *Poesie disperse* (1945); *Il povero nella città* (1949); *Il taccuino del vecchio* (1960); *Morte delle stagioni* (1967); *Dialogo* (with Bruna Bianca, 1968); *Tutte le poesie* (1969); *Innocence et mémoire* (1969); *Propos improvisés* (1972); *Lettere a un fenomenologo* (1972); *Vita di un uomo: Saggi e interventi* (1974). English translations: *Life of a Man* (1958), enlarged and reprinted as *Selected Poems of Giuseppe Ungaretti*, trans. and ed. Allen Mandelbaum (1975); *Giuseppe Ungaretti Selected Poems*, trans. and ed. P. Creagh (1969). About Ungaretti: L. Piccioni, *Vita di un poeta Giuseppe Ungaretti* (1970); C. Ossola, *Giuseppe Ungaretti* (1975); F. J. Jones, *Ungaretti Poet and Critic* (1977).

489

UPDIKE, John 1932–

US novelist and poet

John Updike was born in Pennsylvania and educated at Harvard and the Ruskin School of Drawing and Fine Art at Oxford. Critical opinion has always been sharply divided over his literary status, many seeing him as the archetypal *New Yorker* short-story writer, producing mannered, vivid, yet vacuously descriptive prose concerned primarily with the banalities of fornication. However, beneath this exterior dwells a religious writer who has created a series of commonplace characters, especially 'Rabbit' Angstrom of *Rabbit Run* (1960) and *Rabbit Redux* (1971), muddled and incapable of controlling their lives or loves, yet whose very failure or incompetence has its roots in their perceptions of the inevitability of our solitude, frailty and death. This awareness cuts them off from identifying themselves with the roles they are asked to play, plunges their lives into chaos and cuckoldry, due to their paralysing sense of horror and compassion, and yet makes them the embodiment of value in their environments.

Many of these figures are conservatives, like George Caldwell in *The Centaur* (1963), an idealistic teacher fascinated by knowledge, Piet Hanema in *Couples* (1968), who is inwardly pious, and who tries to preserve old-fashioned skills and perfectionism in the building trade, or Thomas Marshfield in *A Month of Sundays* (1975), who is a Christian minister and eschews existentialist, ritualist and humanist revisions of his religion. However, this conservatism is not seen as a defence or protection against experience, nor an ethical straitjacket keeping their actions within the conventional, but rather a refusal to accept the easy solutions of American optimistic pragmatism, and instead to preserve a sense of the mystery out of which we seek to relate to others and our circumstances by words and actions which are always inadequate and misleading. Out of this, Updike creates both comedy and pathos, especially from the essential strangeness of the confrontation with another's body and the meanings it has for us.

Dr David Corker

Other works include: *The Carpentered Hen and Other Tame Creatures* (poems, 1958); *The Poorhouse Fair* (novel, 1959); *Pigeon Feathers and Other Stories* (1962); *Telephone Poles and Other Poems* (1963); *Of the Farm* (novel, 1965); *Mid Point and Other Poems* (1969); *Bech: A Book* (episodic novel, 1970); *Museums and Women and Other Stories* (1972); *Marry Me* (1974); *Buchanan* (play, 1976); *The Coup* (1978). See also: Joyce B. Markle, *Fighters and Lovers: Theme in the Novels of John Updike* (1973); Edward P. Vargo, *Rainstorms and Fire: Ritual in the Novels of John Updike* (1973).

V

VALÉRY, Paul 1871–1945

French poet and thinker

Of mixed Italian and Corsican blood, Valéry was born in Sète, a Mediterranean port which was to inform his whole imaginary world as a poet. Already by the age of nineteen he had written between two and three hundred poems, was engaged in painting and fascinated by music (in particular that of Wagner) and architecture. Then, as a law student at the University of Montpellier, he added mathematics and physics to his interests. Moving to Paris he continued to write poetry until 1892, assiduously frequenting the milieu of the Symbolists, who, with Mallarmé as their focal point, sought to make poetry as pure, abstract and evocative as music. In his late teens Valéry also came under the spell of the aesthetic theories of Edgar Allan Poe, according to which the poet must always be aiming at the effect that he is going to create on the reader. But neither Poe nor the Symbolists offered Valéry a satisfactory account of the world of the emotions, and it became his credo that the intellect should take control. Giving up poetry he decided to devote himself to a rigorous exploration of the way in which 'the closed system that is the mind' functions.

To this end he read widely not only in philosophy but also in the sciences. Believing that it was physicists and mathematicians who held the key to an understanding of consciousness, he endeavoured to discover algebraic formulae which would express the constants and the variables of human reactions. But the main source for his researches was his own self. Abandoning all received ideas, his enquiry focused on the question 'Que peut un homme?' – 'Of what is a man capable?' *Une Soirée avec Monsieur Teste* (1894) presented a dialogue between Valéry and the strange character of Monsieur Teste, a fictional shadow employed to represent the intellect at its most abstract. Using a constant and constantly reflected self-awareness as his method, Teste attempts to transform even the inevitable weaknesses of the flesh and the knowledge of death into what he calls geometrical figures.

In his concern to establish a method of thinking Valéry next turned his attention to Leonardo da Vinci, whom he took as an exemplar of the universal mind. The *Introduction à la méthode de Leonardo da Vinci* (1895)

establishes three stages of thought: a detailed observation of nature and man; the development of mental imagery, including the processes of induction and analogy; and, finally, construction. However, the core of his explorations into human possibilities was the famous *Cahiers* (2 vols, 1973–4), the notebooks to which, from 1894 until the end of his life, Valéry consigned the observations and ideas that he worked on in the early hours of each morning. Beside this formidable and perhaps unique enterprise, Montaigne's labyrinthine testings of himself, or Gide's* fictional projections, seem digressive and self-indulgent. Valéry is not concerned with the contingent, surface individuality, but with what he calls *le moi pur*, later described in mathematical terms as the universal invariant, the pure functioning of the consciousness.

The author himself said that the *Cahiers* represented the best of him. Since they have been readily accessible to the public only since 1973, the full scale and portent of Valéry's activity has yet to be recognized. Before, it was widely accepted that between 1895 and 1912, when he again began to write poetry, there was a 'silence' broken only by one or two brilliant essays (including 'La Conquête allemande' of 1899, which prophesied the rise of German power). But the long poem which eventually emerged, and which immediately established Valéry as a leading poet, can now be seen in relation to a continuous intellectual activity. Working within the constraints of traditional form (which Valéry regarded as a necessary challenge), 'La Jeune Parque' (1917) – like the two collections that followed it, *Album de vers anciens* (1920) and *Charmes* (1922) – couples an intense cult of abstraction with an equally intense, palpitating sensuality. It is this, rather than any technical innovation, that marks Valéry's finest achievements as a poet. With regard to 'La Jeune Parque', he claimed that the prolonged struggles with the combinatory qualities of language, the manipulation of the multiple possibilities of sound and sense inherent in words, were an important aspect of his understanding and mastery of himself. Although he insisted that his prime concern had been to exploit the musicality of verbal patterns, the poem is a profound examination of the working of consciousness in his symbolic human creation ('the young Fate'), its awakenings as she emerges from sleep, the gradual construction of her sense of identity, the physiological awareness of her sexuality and her simultaneous psychological reactions, and her recognition of recurrences and flux within her own being which reflect those of nature and interact with them.

Valéry's standing as a major poet was put beyond doubt with the publication of *Charmes*, which contained one of the most impressive pieces of the twentieth century, 'Le Cimetière Marin'. Like 'La Jeune Parque', this poem springs initially from formal, musical preoccupations, but in this case it is the consciousness of a mature man at the height of his powers which is examined. Inserted into a diamantine Mediterranean setting, he experiences a fusion with nature which takes him to a peak of transcendence; but then, obeying the inevitable cyclical rhythms of nature, he drifts from the midday dazzle into a shadowed sense of mortality, until finally the lifting sea winds coincide with an invigorated acceptance of the limits of the human condition. The same coming-to-terms with the psyche through nature is sought elsewhere in the volume. 'Aurore' enacts the awakening of the poet in a garden at dawn; 'Le Rameur' brings together a rower's movement over water with his passage through time; and 'La Platane' and 'Palme' use trees as symbols of growth, of patience, and of the dual 'earth-rooted' heaven-seeking tendency of man.

Although there is evidence to suggest that Valéry continued to write poetry of a more experimental kind after 1922, he did not publish any. Instead he made his living as a critic and an essayist, the extraordinary breadth of his interests being attested in collected volumes such as *Variétés* (1924) and *Autres Rhumbs* (1927) and *Tel Quel* (1941). In 1925 he was elected to the French Academy, and in 1937 was appointed Professor of Poetics at the Collège de France. As a literary critic he was particularly forward-looking in his insistence on the impossibility of distinguishing between form and content, on taking a poem as an object – a view that has become a central tenet of much modern criticism. But if aesthetics were his profession, his relentless pursuit of his original question – 'Que peut un homme?' – took him into widely different spheres. In this context three works, written in his favoured dialogue form, are of note. In the first, *Eupalinos* (1922), the shades of Socrates and Phaedrus evoke the architect Eupalinos as a model of the thinker-constructor who is obliged to pit himself bodily against intractable matter, and then shape it according to the laws of his own mind. Thus, by constructing out of nature the creator learns how to construct himself. In the companion *L'Ame et la danse* (1922), Valéry discovers in the dancer's art a further aspect of creativity: the capacity of the human being to transcend apparent limitations, to go beyond the self. The third, *L'Idée fixe* (1932), reintroduces Monsieur Teste, and reflects Valéry's attempt to understand the new physics of Planck*, Einstein*, Schrödinger* and Heisenberg*. Numbering several of the leading French physicists of the day among his friends, including Paul Langevin and Louis de Broglie, he hoped that the theories which had so revolutionized man's way of looking at the world would be applied to the complex living organism itself. Thus, Monsieur Teste, using his familiar *tabula rasa* technique, interrogates a doctor on a number of crucial issues in psychotherapy: the function of the senses, of memory, of suggestibility, the differences between group and individual behaviour, how to account for the individual's appetites and repugnances, the nature of dreams, which he finds more interesting for their formal structure than for any apparent symbolism; and throughout sees man as a being turned always to the future with a potential which is always capable of development. Interestingly, at the end of the dialogue, it is Einstein who is introduced as a modern example of the universal thinker idealistically seeking the secrets of the unity of nature.

If, summing up Valéry's varied achievements, one had to pin-point his exemplary importance in the modern world, it would be his role as a *maître à penser*. 'I work for those who come after me,' he said. His method was to formulate those precise, unequivocal questions which are at least capable of precise, unequivocal answers. He teaches, by example, how to think, the what to think being constantly ahead.

Professor Margaret Davies

For the complete works see: *Oeuvres I & II* (1957 and 1960); and, in translation, *The Collected Works of Paul Valéry* (15 vols, 1956–75). See also: J. R. Lawler, *Lecture de Valéry* (1963); J. Robinson, *L'Analyse de l'esprit dans les Cahiers de Paul Valéry* (1963); Emilie Noulet, *Paul Valéry* (1950); W. N. Ince, *The Poetic Theory of Paul Valéry* (1970); Christine Crow, *Paul Valéry: Consciousness and Nature* (1972); C. G. Whiting, *Paul Valéry* (1979).

491
VALLEJO, César 1892–1938

Peruvian poet

Vallejo was a difficult, tortured poet whose reputation rests partly on his 'mythic' status as a lyric poet 'crucified' by the contradictions of his age. It is because his poetry (as opposed to his derivative prose and shrill journalism) acutely embodies the conflicts of the 1920s and 1930s that Vallejo has become a crucial figure in Latin American culture.

Vallejo was born in Santiago de Chuco in Andean Peru, the eleventh and youngest son. His happy, pious childhood ended with the death of his adored mother (1918), an event scarring all his later activity – *mother* is a model word/emotion for home/love/security/meaning that Vallejo transformed into community/Spain/

brotherly-love/hope/future, and her absence is the loveless, alienated world of meaningless adult existence. Early on Vallejo determined to become a poet, an ambition that became a painful struggle throughout his life best seen as a series of *tests* (tested by poverty, by being unjustly imprisoned in Peru, by publishing and not being acclaimed, by leaving Peru for Paris and never returning, etc.). His life/work can be summarized as a series of rejections resulting in a haunting fusion of nostalgia for a lost happiness and a utopian belief in its return, constant in his poems. Vallejo's ambition can be gauged by his displacements from a provincial Andean home to Trujillo (1913–17) the provincial capital, to Lima (1918), and to Paris/Madrid/Moscow (1923–38). Vallejo sought the crucible of his age. His bitter but chosen bohemian life in Paris – on the brink of starvation but refusing to work – meant surviving off friends and sporadic journalism and only makes sense within his ambition.

His choice was not easy; it coincided with the Depression, the growth of fascism, the solidification of Stalinism* – in which he participated passionately, visiting Russia (1928, 1929, 1931), working for the Spanish Communist Party and the Republican cause. As a poet he tried to resolve the gap between the lyric poet and the political activist without extinguishing either.

This exemplary struggle – in the form of a dialogue with himself – resulted in a prolonged silence lasting, apart from a few published poems, to his death in 1938. His self-consciousness of his own inner heterogeneity, coupled with his aim of being immediate, emotional and honest, produced the 'secret' posthumously published poems that today set him above his more facile companions. Only while dying did Vallejo resolve this struggle in his *Spain, take this Cup from me* (*España, aparta de mí este cáliz*) without betraying his lyrical ego or his faith in a new society.

Vallejo's books of poems follow this journey: *The Black Heralds* (*Los heraldos negros*, 1919) was his laboratory where he tried out voices, styles, poses; coming to terms with personal experience through literature. His basic obsessions (key words such as mother, home, pain, bread, anguish) are seeded here. By *Trilce* (a neologism, 1923) his stuttering uncertainty ('I don't know' his *leitmotiv*) was embodied in a critique of poetry; breaking up words, syntax; using puns, playing with typography; fusing experimental techniques to his own world vision in some startling emotional and direct poems. His central posthumous poems, *Human Poems* (*Poemas humanos*), deal, in a language close to colloquial prose, with his ambivalent, gutsy and idiosyncratic attempt to heal the split (first within himself) between the poet and his age, between feeling and expression, public and private, individual and collective; poems eloquent of a drama suffered to its ultimate consequences (and Vallejo's virtual self-destruction). This

is the source of Vallejo as culture-hero, both exemplary and inimitable.

Jason Wilson

The best edition of Vallejo is *Obra poética completa* (1968). For those who read Spanish, the best introduction is A. Flores (ed.), *Approximaciones a César Vallejo* (2 vols, 1971); in English, J. Franco, *César Vallejo: the Dialectics of Poetry and Silence* (1977); and J. Higgins, *César Vallejo: an Anthology of his Poetry* (1970). The following translations: R. Bly, *20 poems* (1962); E. Dorn and G. Brotherston, *Selected Poems* (1975); C. Eshelman and J. R. Barcia, *Complete Posthumous Poems* (1979).

492
VARÈSE, Edgard Victor Achille Charles 1883–1965

French/US composer

Varèse was born in Paris, educated partly there and in Turin (his father was Piedmontese), then entered the Schola Cantorum in Paris in 1904. At the Schola he studied composition and conducting with d'Indy, counterpoint and fugue with Roussel, and Medieval and Renaissance music with Charles Bordes. In 1905 he was admitted to Widor's composition class at the Paris Conservatoire. From 1907 to 1913 Varèse lived in Berlin where he earned his living mainly as a copyist, and met Busoni*, Hofmannsthal, Richard Strauss* and Romain Rolland*. This period also coincided with his first marriage, which ended in divorce. He returned to Paris in 1913 and in 1915 was mobilized, but within the same year he was invalided out of the army. At the end of the year he sailed for New York, where he lived for most of his subsequent life, except for a period in Paris (1928–33), other trips to Europe and stays lasting a few months in New Mexico and Los Angeles. He married again in 1921 and became a US citizen in 1927. Varèse spent a considerable amount of time and energy in activities related to music other than composition. From 1921 to 1927 he helped run the International Composers' Guild, which he founded with Carlos Salzedo. Varèse chose the works for the concerts of new music which the Guild organized. The following year (1928) Varèse founded the Pan American Association of Composers with Henry Cowell and Carlos Chavez. Most of his life Varèse conducted (and actually founded more than one choir), but he never made a career of conducting. He also gave lectures, classes and lessons from time to time, but he seems to have had only three serious students of composition: André Jolivet, Chou Wen-chung and Marc Wilkinson. Varèse never earned much from his compositions and his output was small. At various times he received money from patrons (including the conductor Stokowski), but in 1933 he was refused a Guggenheim grant for research and the same year he applied unsuccessfully to the Bell Telephone Company for a post to research acoustics, film and radio. Varèse also submitted proposals elsewhere for research and technical collaboration but it was not until the 1950s, when he was already in his seventies, that he won practical co-operation and was able to produce his last two major works, *Déserts* and *Le poème électronique*. For *Déserts* he recorded tapes in Philadelphia factories, then worked on these tapes in the studio of French Radio in Paris (1954). And in 1957–8 he worked in the Philips studios at Eindhoven, Holland, on *Le poème électronique*, commissioned for Le Corbusier's* Pavilion for Philips at the Brussels World Fair in 1958.

It is a cliché to say that Varèse was ahead of his time and that he could not realize his intentions fully before the availability of tape and the development of electronic studios after the Second World War. But his works of the 1920s (notably the three pieces for various ensembles – *Hyperprism*, 1922–3, *Octandre*, 1923, and *Intégrales*, 1923–5) are perfectly realized in their medium, even if the instrumentalists are expected to be mechanically precise and brilliant rather than pliant or expressive. Certainly Varèse had a sense of artistic isolation, but it is easy to suspect that he wrote relatively little for personal rather than for strictly musical reasons. He suffered prolonged bouts of depression: *Déserts* is, among many other things, the document of his despair after a period of fourteen years when he completed no work at all. Yet as a man he was popular. He charmed people and seems to have enjoyed the effect he could have on them. In Greenwich Village, New York, as well as in international musical circles, he was known as a generous and hospitable man.

Varèse believed that genius was romantic: a work was only classic after it had been accepted. He told people that he was not a musician but that he worked 'with rhythms, frequencies and intensities'. Yet he was opposed to all systems and despised the 12-note method of Schoenberg*. He admired Debussy* for 'balancing with almost mathematical equilibrium timbres against rhythms and textures – like a fantastic chemist'. Varèse's own music epitomizes an analytic perception of sound, in which not only pitch and duration, but attack, decay, dynamic and timbre are all detached from traditional conceptions like melody, harmony and orchestration, and are made equivalent subjects of compositional or 'artistic' choice. The most precise control of these factors could be achieved by electronic means. Yet it may be argued that all art necessitates compromise, and in works like *Hyperprism*, for nine wind instruments and percussion, or *Ionisation* (1931), for thirteen percussionists, there is no feeling that instruments or instrumentalists are being used as substitutes. Chou Wen-chung has observed that there seems to be a fundamental difference between Varèse's

works for instruments and those which include voices. The atmosphere of picturesque mystery and threatening drama in *Ecuatorial* (1934) for bass voices and ensemble, and in his final work, *Nocturnal* (1961, completed by Chou Wen-chung) for solo soprano, bass voices and orchestra, harks back to the world of Debussy and French symbolism, which is found in *Offrandes* (1921) for soprano and chamber orchestra, and in an even earlier song, 'Un grand sommeil noir' (1906). Most of Varèse's music before 1920 was lost or destroyed; much of it is supposed to have been burnt in a fire in 1918, but Varèse suppressed some works himself. The huge orchestral piece *Amériques* (1920–1, revised mostly by 1929) already shows the essentials of Varèse's musical character. *Intégrales*, for eleven wind instruments and percussion, was the first work to be described as 'spatial'. In 1929, if not earlier, Varèse said that he wanted his music to be projected, literally, in space, like beams of light coming from different sources. He achieved this vision once – in *Le poème électronique*, which was relayed through over 400 speakers placed along the parabolic and hyperbolic curves of the Philips Pavilion at the Brussels World Fair in 1958. Composers like Boulez*, Messiaen*, Stockhausen* and Xenakis have long acknowledged Varèse as one of the seminal influences on developments in music since the Second World War. In 1950 Varèse lectured at the Darmstadt holiday courses, which set the latest fashions in avant-garde music. Of the Darmstadt composers, it was perhaps Luigi Nono whose music related most specifically to Varèse's in its austere and rugged surface, as well as the way attention shifts among different musical elements, so that one in particular (whether rhythm, timbre, and so on) is selected for attention while the others are relatively inactive. In America in the 1950s Varèse became a rediscovered hero. But his individuality – sometimes rebarbative – is likely to deter composers from drawing from his example, and the more recent return to expressive melody and lyrical qualities in new music are far from Varèse's heroic stance. Yet his concept of music as 'organized sound' is likely to prove one of the most significant musical ideas of the twentieth century.

Adrian Jack

Other compositions include: *Arcana* (1926–7) for large orchestra; *Density 21.5* (1936) for solo flute. See: F. Ouellette, *Edgard Varèse* (1966, trans. 1968); Louise Varèse, *Varèse: A Looking-Glass Diary, Volume 1: 1883–1928* (1972). Analysis of Varèse's work has appeared in: *The Score*, no. 19 (Marc Wilkinson, March 1957); *Perspectives of New Music* (Gunther Schuller, Spring 1965; Milton Babbitt, Spring 1966; Chou Wen-chung, Fall 1966; John Strawn, Fall 1978); *Musical Quarterly*, vol. 52, no. 2 (Chou Wen-chung); *Music Review*, XXVIII, no. 4 (Arnold Whittall); *Music and*

Musicians (Adrian Jack, November and December 1975).

493
VAUGHAN WILLIAMS, Ralph 1872–1958

English composer

Vaughan Williams was slow to make an impression as a composer. His first published work, the very successful song 'Linden Lea', did not appear until 1902, and as late as 1908–10 he went to Paris to complete his studies under Ravel*, having been previously the pupil of Parry and Stanford in London and of Bruch in Berlin. However, by the time he went to Paris the main features of his style were already formed. He had for some years been collecting English folk-songs – his volume of *Folksongs from the Eastern Counties* was published in 1908 – and he had made use of this material in such utterly characteristic pastoral impressions as the orchestral *In the Fen Country* (1904). What he learned from Ravel was certainly not technique, for he could never boast anything like Ravel's precise craftsmanship, but confidence to continue along the path already mapped out. The Paris period saw not only his first important chamber work, the String Quartet in G minor (1908), but also his first symphony, *A Sea Symphony* with soloists and chorus (1909), and three other important compositions: the song cycle *On Wenlock Edge* setting Housman for tenor and piano quintet (1909), the inventive overture to *The Wasps* (1909) and the *Fantasia on a Theme of Thomas Tallis* (1910).

This last work was remarkable for its rich interplay of different string groups – two orchestras and a quartet – and also for its use of Tudor music, which Vaughan Williams had come to appreciate as musical editor of the *English Hymnal* (1906). He made a more direct return to the world of Tallis and Byrd in his *Mass in G minor* for unaccompanied chorus (1920–1), but the pervasive influence of Tudor music is to be found in his very distinctive harmonic style, which had its origins also in the folk-music he continued to collect, to arrange, and to use in such works as *A London Symphony* (1913) and *A Pastoral Symphony*, with soprano or tenor soloist (1921).

From this point his style was more or less fixed. He produced occasional surprises, notably in the aggressive and forceful manner of his Fourth Symphony (1931–4), but generally his music is marked by a flowing melodic ease, by his unusual handling of consonant harmony, and by moods of pastoral rambling or religious serenity. After Elgar's* death in 1934 he was regarded as the outstanding British composer of his day and he produced a large quantity of the expected choral music, ranging from festival oratorios to psalms and anthems for the Anglican church. There were also

five more symphonies, among which the *Sinfonia antarctica* for wordless female voices and orchestra (1949–52) was derived from music he had written for the film *Scott of the Antarctic* (1948). In addition, he turned during this later period to the composition of opera, beginning with *The Shepherds of the Delectable Mountains* (1922), a one-act treatment of an episode from Bunyan which was eventually incorporated in his full-length morality *The Pilgrim's Progress* (1906–51). This major testament was found undramatic when it at last reached the stage in 1951, and neither of Vaughan Williams's other big operas, *Hugh the Drover* (1924) and *Sir John in Love* (1924–8, after *The Merry Wives of Windsor*), has proved successful. His setting of Synge's *Riders to the Sea* (1925–32), in which he found a subject better suited to the slow speed of his music's movement, is the most effective of his operas.

Vaughan Williams enjoyed a close friendship with Holst* from 1895 until the latter's death in 1934, and each of them profited from criticism and understanding offered by the other. During his lifetime Vaughan Williams also had a great influence on younger English composers, but since his death he has been probably more realistically estimated as a curious offshoot from the tree of music and not a main branch.

Paul Griffiths

Other works: *The Lark Ascending* for violin and orchestra (1914–20); *Job*, ballet (1930); *Fantasia on 'Greensleeves'* for orchestra (1934); *Five Tudor Portraits* for soloists, choir and orchestra (1935); *The Poisoned Kiss*, play with music (1936); *Dona nobis pacem* for soloists, choir and orchestra (1936); *Serenade to Music* for 16 voices and orchestra (1938); Symphony no. 5 (1938–43); Symphony no. 6 (1944–7); Symphony no. 8 (1953–5); Symphony no. 9 (1956–7). Writings: *National Music* (1934); *Heirs and Rebels* (1959). See: Michael Kennedy, *The Works of Ralph Vaughan Williams* (1964); Ursula Vaughan Williams, *R.V.W.: a Biography of Ralph Vaughan Williams* (1964); Roy Douglas, *Working with R.V.W.* (1972).

494
VEBLEN, Thorstein Bunde 1857–1929

US economist and social critic

Despite his assumption of a guise of scientific detachment and objectivity, Veblen's writings form an excoriating critique of American society between 1870 and 1925 and, more generally, document the triumph of 'imbecile institutions' over reason in human affairs.

Veblen was born on a farm and was brought up in highly insular Norwegian communities in Wisconsin and Minnesota. In 1884 he received his doctorate from Yale, but his agnosticism debarred him from teaching philosophy and it was not until 1892 that he received a fellowship in Economics at the University of Chicago, where he remained until 1906. Subsequently, Veblen taught at Stanford and Missouri and in 1918 moved to New York where for a year he was a contributing editor to the *Dial* and taught at the New School for Social Research until 1924. The last years of his life were spent in isolation and near-poverty in California.

Although he was formally an economist, Veblen was actually a true inter-disciplinary scholar who drew on a wealth of archaeological, anthropological, sociological and linguistic knowledge. His students pointed him out as 'the last man who knows everything' and Einstein* described him as one of the world's great political writers, but despite much acclaim he did not receive an academic rank in any way commensurate with his reputation.

Veblen's departure from both Chicago and Stanford resulted from a combination of his scorn for academic boosterism and his refusal to cover his extramarital affairs with the conventional blanket of secrecy. For most of his life he resolutely avoided formal political commitments, but he twice became a cult-figure of the liberal left and, during the 'Red Scare' of 1919–20, was listed by governmental agencies as a dangerous radical. However, with the economic recovery and boom of the 1920s, Veblen's gleeful warnings of possible economic collapse appeared wrong-headed and irrelevant. Ironically enough, Veblen, the master of incisive irony, died complaining of neglect a few months before the stock market collapse of 1929 ushered in the world depression he had long predicted.

Veblen was a Darwinist in that he felt that both biological and social evolution were characterized by blind, purposeless change or drift. Given this conviction, he rejected the Marxian interpretation of historical development as teleological and hence unscientific and utopian, and charged mainstream economists with dealing in neat abstractions while resolutely avoiding consideration of the real factors impinging on the working of the economy. Economic writings were underpinned by conceptions of such putative 'natural' rights as the right to the indefeasible ownership and use of property. These outdated metaphysical conceptions were inappropriate in an era of machine production and their employment by economists served to legitimate and sanctify the economic dominance of businessmen and financier tycoons – the captains of industry – who, in Veblen's view, actually produced little but waste, corruption and exploitation.

Veblen's first two books, *The Theory of the Leisure Class* (1899) and its more specialized economic coda, *The Theory of Business Enterprise* (1904), provided a mordantly witty empirical documentation of these processes. Economic production in capitalist societies was governed by considerations of profit rather than of the usefulness or serviceability of the goods produced. Such production of fripperies and inessentials catered to the appetite for wasteful, conspicuous consumption produced by individuals' desire to win repute by vainglorious display and emulation of the style of life of those above them. Veblen drew a sharp distinction between socially useful 'industrial' occupations and non-productive, 'pecuniary' occupations. He deplored the permeation of American society by the spirit of business enterprise – expressed in chicanery, fraud, self-aggrandisement and predation – and in *The Higher Learning in America* (1918) castigated this spirit as manifested in the 'businesslike' conduct of American universities.

From 1914 Veblen's writings became more topical and more overtly political. In *Imperial Germany and the Industrial Revolution* (1915) and *An Inquiry into the Nature of Peace* (1917) he analysed the causes and implications of Germany's rapid emergence as an industrial and military giant and attempted to assess the possibility that the world war might end in a settlement conducive to lasting peace. His conclusions were pessimistic and perceptive, indeed he forecast that the newly industrialized, militaristic, dynastic nations of Germany and Japan would join forces and provoke an even greater world conflict. The Bolshevik Revolution in Russia led Veblen to hope that the 'vested interests' might similarly be overthrown in America, and the tone of his later writings became more rancorous as his hopes in this direction were dashed.

In personal encounters Veblen was generally extremely uncommunicative and he resolutely refused to subordinate himself to authority, conventions, personal attachments or dogmatic systems of thought. Almost inadvertently he made disciples, but he established no 'Veblenian' school. The institutional economists, who insisted on studying the real-life working of the economy, came closest to being such. None the less, his influence was far-ranging, and is acknowledged in the works of (among many others) the economist J. K. Galbraith* and the maverick sociologist C. W. Mills. To employ a term which Veblen coined in a different context, his reputation has to some extent suffered 'the penalty of taking the lead' – many of his ideas and concepts have passed into common intellectual parlance and have been borrowed by others with scant, or no, acknowledgment.

Dr John Whitworth

Other works: *The Instinct of Workmanship* (1914); *The Vested Interests and the Common Man* (1919); *The Place of Science in Modern Civilization* (1919); *The Engineers and the Price System* (1921); *Absentee Ownership* (1923); *Essays in our Changing Order* (1934). See: Joseph Dorfman, *Thorstein Veblen and his America* (1934); David Riesman, *Thorstein Veblen* (1953); Douglas F. Dowd, *Thorstein Veblen* (1966); John P. Diggins, *The*

Bard of Savagery (1978); John M. Whitworth, *The Insubordinate Mind* (1981).

495
VELDE, Henri van de 1863–1957

Belgian architect and designer

One of the most influential of Art Nouveau designers and theorists, Van de Velde was outstanding for his versatility and style in many fields: architecture, interior design, furniture, painting, typography, dress and ceramics. Trained as a painter, he achieved recognition in Belgium during the 1890s through his typographical designs for the magazines *Van Nu en Straks*, developing a revolutionary linear abstract style that was to be widely imitated. It was at this time that he conceived a strong admiration for the work of William Morris, whose ideals inspired him to abandon painting for the applied arts. In 1893 he embarked on the self-taught study of architecture. The completion of his own country house, the Villa Bloemenwerf, at Uccle near Brussels, two years later gave him an international reputation. The building exemplified many of his ideas: the straightforward use of materials with the constructional methods revealed, the rejection of historical styles in favour of an unornamented vernacular manner (comparable to buildings by the Arts and Crafts architects in England), and the organization by the architect of every detail within the building, including the furniture, kitchenware and even, in this case, the lady of the house's clothing. This care sprang from his belief that the quality of daily life was to a great extent shaped by the standard of design of ordinary artefacts, and from his determination to make his art socially useful.

'Art,' he declared, 'must conquer the machine.' In common with many other designers and architects working in an increasingly technological culture Van de Velde doubted whether mechanical means of production could be reconciled with the maintenance of artistic individuality and excellence. Morris had been stimulated to return to archaizing designs and handcraftsmanship, but he and his followers, generally sympathetic to socialist ideas, were then faced with the inevitable costliness and inaccessibility of their productions. Van de Velde, a supporter of the Belgian Workers' Party, encountered the same paradox. Although he criticized the English Arts and Crafts movement for the narrowness of its potential market, and wanted to make his work more widely available, most of his architectural designs, both before and after his move to Germany in 1898, were executed for wealthy patrons. These included four rooms for Samuel Bing's Galerie de l'Art Nouveau (1896), the Havana Cigar Store, Haby's Barber's Store and other work in Berlin

around 1900; the Art School at Weimar (1904–11), where he was the first director, the Villa Hohenof (1908), and the Werkbund Theatre in Cologne (1914). In 1917 he moved to Switzerland, and in 1921 to Holland, where he designed the Kröller-Müller Museum, Otterlo (1937–54), another private foundation. In 1925 he returned to Belgium.

In his Berlin designs Van de Velde moved towards a more ponderous manner, with the slow curving forms and elaborately original decoration associated with Art Nouveau. In his later German work he experimented with a sparer functional style, with much use of white in interiors, and, although he was always distinguished by a feeling for consciously decorative elegance, in his final work he approached the spirit of International Modern. Two principles, however, constantly guided his teaching (apart from Weimar, in 1925 he founded the School of Architecture in Brussels, and taught at the University of Ghent between 1926 and 1936) and his designs. First, the importance of line, which, he insisted, must express the internal structure and 'force' of the object of which it is part, and must alone constitute the work's decorative quality; and, second, the need for the artist to invent a wholly original art from his own sensibility, rather than to re-use the language of the past.

Giles Waterfield

Van de Velde's writings include *Jéblaiement d'Art* (1894); *L'Art futur* (1895); *Kunstgewerbliche Laienpredigten* (1902); *Die Renaissance in modernen Kunst* (1901); *Les Formules de la beauté architectonique moderne* (1916); *Story of My Life* (1962). See also: K. E. Osthaus, *Van de Velde, Leben und Schaffen des Kunstlers* (1920); *Henri Van de Velde* (Brussels, Palais des Beaux Arts Catalogue, 1963); A. M. Hammacher, *Die Welt Henry van de Velde* (1967); H. Kreistl and G. Himmelleber, *Die Kurs des deutschen Möbels* (vol. III, 1973).

496
VERTOV, Dziga (Denis Arkadevitch Kaufman) 1896–1954

Russian film director

Born into a Polish family of librarians, Kaufman moved to Petrograd during the First World War. Changing his name to Dziga Vertov (thought by the French film historian Georges Sadoul to signify the notion of 'perpetual motion'), he attended the Institute of Psychoneurology and the University of Moscow, where, anticipating his later interests in sound, he invented a miniature 'laboratory of hearing' based on a gramophone recorder. After the Revolution he was recruited into the newsreel film work of the Committee of Cinematography, where he worked on titling and editing footage from the Revolution and Civil War. He soon took over the *Cine Weekly* series (1918–19), organizing a widespread network of newsreel cameramen, and travelling on the Civil War agit-train 'The October Revolution' with his feature-compilation, *The Anniversary of the Revolution* (1919). In addition to other shorts, he also completed the feature-length *History of the Civil War* (1922).

It was against this background that Vertov emerged as the major champion and theoretician of radical Soviet documentary and newsreel film. His two main subsequent series, *Kino Pravda* (1922–5) and the *Goskino Journal* (1923–5), extended Vertov's formal experiments in montage and in titling, and continued to be supported by polemical and theoretical writing on the cinema. His output in the later 1920s went on to include two films sponsored by interests outside the film industry – *Stride, Soviet* (1926) commissioned by the Moscow Soviet as an informational film for the 1926 election, and *A Sixth of the Earth* (1926), an advertisement of Russia's resources and capabilities on behalf of the trade agency, Gostorg. These were followed by *The Eleventh* (1928), a celebration of the ten years since the Revolution, and *Man with a Movie Camera* (1929), Vertov's feature-length experimental documentary about life in the city and about the practices of film-making.

The hardening of economic and cultural policy in the later 1920s augured badly for Vertov's cinematic radicalism, with its outspoken challenges not only to the cinema of fiction but to the traditional 'neutrality' and 'transparency' of documentary. By the time of the last-named film Vertov was out of favour, and subsequently found few outlets for his work in a period when he was attacked for his formal extravagance and castigated even by Eisenstein*. In the 1930s he was able to complete only three films: *Enthusiasm* (1930), his first sound film, an intricate documentary or 'symphony' as it was sub-titled on the efficiency of the miners of the Don Basin; *Three Songs of Lenin* (1934), a monument composed of a trio of films based on folk-songs from Uzbekistan in Central Asia; and *Lullaby* (1937), a film on the women of the Soviet Union and of Spain. He was subsequently not fully employed, although he spent the period from 1944 until his death in 1954 regularly contributing to the newsreel *Daily News*.

Vertov's importance lies in his radical rethinking of the practices of documentary and newsreel cinema. His work in the aftermath of the Revolution led him to formulate, as his contribution to the Soviet critique of culture, and particularly of cinema, an emphasis upon the importance of documentary as opposed to fictional cinema, a position emphasized by the title of his major newsreel of the 1920s, *Kino Pravda* ('Cinema Truth') and spelt out in contributions to the journal *LEF* by Vertov on behalf of the 'Council of Three' set up in

late 1922 with his wife Elizabeth Svilova, who collaborated on the scripting and editing of much of his work, and his brother, Mikhail Kaufman.

This led to a psycho-social redefinition of the function of cinematography under the rubric of the 'Camera Eye' (and, in parallel, the 'Radio Ear'). This notion entailed a new liberated conception of the function of the camera – which was to function more rather than less freely than the human eye – and of the camera-operator as himself/herself not merely a passive viewer but a liberated participant in the social processes being filmed. The former notion involved Vertov and his collaborators in an extension of the traditional range of the cinematographic process, from candid-camera shooting to complex editing experiments and special effects. The second led him to campaign for an active social application of work with documentary and newsreel film, including an ambitious but abortive attempt, during 1923–4, to establish a mass organization with clubs and correspondents throughout the USSR.

Vertov's virulent rejection of theatrical film (even including Eisenstein's 'acted films in documentary trousers'), together with his remodelling of the documentary mode through exploration of the complex materiality of film language and through visible insistence on the role of the film camera, editor, projection, and audience as agents in the activity of producing film meaning, are most readily seen in Vertov's key work of the 1920s, *Man with a Movie Camera*, a dynamic and bravura homage to the city documentary genre and to the creative work of the camera-operator Kinok.

Vertov's legacy has been complex. First, he strongly influenced the European avant-gardes of the 1920s and 1930s, with his problematic and contradictory mixture of 'realist' and 'formalist' preoccupations; second, the notion of 'Cinema Truth' (*Kino Pravda*) became the key term for the French and American film-makers of the early 1960s working under the translated rubric of 'Cinéma Vérité'; third, the politics of Vertov's work, together with his examinations of ideology at the level of film form prompted Jean-Luc Godard* and his collaborator Jean-Pierre Gorin to rename themselves the Dziga Vertov Group in their attempts to found a new kind of political and social cinema following the May Events of 1968; fourth, the intricacy of Vertov's formalism strongly influenced certain branches of the 1960s and 1970s international avant-gardes, particularly the school of Structural-Materialist film.

Philip Drummond

See: *Statyi, Dnievniki, Zamysly* ('Selected Writings', 1966); *Articles, Journaux, Projets* (1972); N. P. Abramov, *Dziga Vertov* (1965); Luda and Jean Schnitzer, *Dziga Vertov 1896–1954* (1968); Georges Sadoul, *Dziga Vertov* (1971); Stephen Crofts and Olivia Rose, *An Essay Towards 'Man with a Movie Camera'*, in *Screen*, Spring 1977; see also Jay Leyda,

Kino: A History of the Russian and Soviet Film (2nd edn, 1973).

497
VIDAL, Gore 1925–

US novelist and essayist

Gore Vidal was born in 1925. He graduated from Phillips Exeter College in 1943, joined the maritime branch of the Army Transportation Corps and served in the Aleutian Islands (off the coast of Alaska). This experience provided the material for his first novel, *Williwaw* (1946), written at the age of nineteen. The next few years saw a rapid succession of novels, including the *succès de scandale*, *The City and the Pillar* (1948, revised 1965), a matter-of-fact account of homosexual pursuit and disillusion. In the 1950s and early 1960s Vidal also wrote or adapted a number of plays for Broadway and for television. In 1960 he ran for Congress as Democratic-Liberal candidate for a district of New York; he lost but the margin was narrow enough for him to refer to it as 'a victorious defeat'. Linked with the Kennedy dynasty, descended from a political family (his maternal grandfather was an Oklahoman Senator), Vidal has always displayed an ambivalent attitude towards power and politics, as he has to the Hollywood for which he has produced scripts, to America itself. Vidal now lives in Italy and it is hard not to detect resemblances between the narrator of *Burr* (1973) and *1876* (1976), Charlie Schuyler, and his creator in their response to American crassness and greed and cultural parochialism. America is 'the civilization whose absence drove Henry James to Europe' is one of the many agreeable asides in *Two Sisters: A Memoir in the Form of a Novel* (1970). Certainly Vidal distrusts his native literature – 'I always thought that our great novelists were minor provincial writers,' he has stated – and the influences on him have been primarily European and classical. Similarly he derides the arid structural approach of much American academic criticism or the sterility of the French *nouveau roman*. He has frequently announced in his essays and fiction the death of the novel but the lament is tinged with the pleasure of bearing bad news and the knowledge of belonging to a tightening elite that still – just – writes and reads.

Little indication of Vidal's development was given by *Williwaw*, which describes a storm at sea and centres on the fatal rivalry over a prostitute between two seamen. It is written in ' "the national manner". A careful, calculated style, a bit simple-minded but useful in telling this sort of story' (from the author's note). The 'true voice and pitch' which the novelist must discover is partially heard in *The Judgement of Paris* (1952), the account of a self-regarding odyssey made by a young American in Europe, and in the apocalyptic *Messiah* (1954), which describes the growth of a world-wide death-cult. Vidal's elegant, sombre and slightly world-weary voice found its perfect pitch in *Julian* (1964), his account of the apostate Roman emperor who attempted to substitute Hellenism for Christianity. The use of different and sometimes conflicting narrators in this novel showed Vidal's growing preoccupation with the lapses and contradictions of remembered time. *Washington D.C.* (1967) together with *Burr* and *1876* dispose of America's first 200 years in an iconoclastic fashion. In his political trilogy Vidal turns back the carpet on the dirt deposited there by the makers of the American Constitution and others; the corruption of the late 1960s and early 1970s is implicitly prefigured. The author's attitude veers between amused acquiescence in the power-seekers' unchanging natures and anger at the puritanical hypocrisy and electoral gullibility of his native society. None of his earlier works had prepared the ground for *Myra Breckinridge* (1968). The eponymous heroine is a film buff, a diarist and a sex-change who recovers his masculinity and a belief in Christian Science in the parodic happy ending. The book is notable for the clarity of its style and conception, its assault on received sexual notions, its satirical cuts at the flaccid victim, America.

'So at the end, fire' ends *Two Sisters*, a tantalizing and ultimately unrevealing novel. In *Kalki* (1978) Vidal brings the world to a largely unregretted end by means of an epidemic procured by a new messiah. The few survivors cavort in an empty White House, the glittering target of much of Vidal's polemical writing and fiction. In his writing Vidal circles like an urbane bird of prey round a society in decline; the refined mixture of regret, relief and anger is his own.

Philip Gooden

Vidal's other books include: *Myron* (1975); and *Homage to Daniel Shay: Collected Essays 1952–72* (1972). See also: Bernard F. Dick, *The Apostate Angel. A Critical Study of Gore Vidal* (1979).

498
VISCONTI, Luchino 1906–76

Italian film-maker and theatre and opera director

Born into an aristocratic Milanese family in 1906, and brought up with a dilettantish interest in music and horses, Luchino Visconti was drawn to the cinema and to an involvement with left-wing politics when Coco Chanel* introduced him to Jean Renoir* in 1935. After a short while working with Renoir in the France of the Popular Front, he returned to Fascist Italy and made an extraordinary first film, *Ossessione* (1942), which was a direct challenge to the official culture of the period and was widely hailed, on its release after the war, as a precursor of neo-realism. In 1947 he made the mammoth *La terra trema*, an epic about a Sicilian fishing family, loosely inspired by Giovanni Verga's classic novel *I Malavoglia*. If *Ossessione* was a precocious forerunner of neo-realism, *La terra trema* equally precociously outran it. Shot on location, with non-professional actors speaking their own lines in incomprehensible dialect, *La terra trema* emerged, paradoxically, as closer in style to grand opera than to the documentary realism that it originally aspired to. With *Senso* (1954) Visconti attempted a historical spectacular which would be realist in the Marxist or at least Lukácsian* sense of producing a narration that enabled the spectator to grasp the nature of historical reality. Set in the Risorgimento, *Senso* tells a complex story of betrayal and counter-betrayal, in which personal and political are closely but ambiguously intertwined.

The historical process recounted in *Senso* is one of 'passive revolution' (in Gramsci's* phrase) and of muted change achieved by accommodations and compromise. The same process also figures in *The Leopard* (1963), an adaptation of Giuseppe Tomasi di Lampedusa's novel. In both these Risorgimento films the mechanism of the plot works through betrayal, whether sexual or political, while the underlying thematic concern is with the survival or otherwise of class and family groupings in a context of historical change. In *Rocco and his Brothers* (1960) the same mechanisms are returned to a modern setting – the life of a family of Southern immigrants in Milan during the 'economic miracle'. The peasant family is torn apart under the pressure of urban life and its destruction is seen as both tragic and necessary and as the price to be paid if the individuals composing it are to survive. In *Vaghe stelle dell'Orsa* (1965) (known in the US as *Sandra*) a family is also destroyed, but the forces motivating its destruction are more internal. The story of *Vaghe stelle* is that of the Oresteia, and in particular of Electra, the daughter dedicated to avenging her father's death at the hands of her mother and step-father. Again betrayal plays an important role. The daughter Sandra suspects her mother of having betrayed her father, a Jewish scientist, to the Nazis, resulting in his death in Auschwitz. Sandra in turn plays on her brother's (incestuous) love for her and betrays him, leading to his suicide. Sandra, however, survives and there is a sense at the end of the film that a future exists not only for her but for other survivors as well. History continues despite or even because of the family's destruction.

In his later films, however, Visconti shows himself more and more sceptical about history as a progressive development. In *The Damned* (*La caduta degli Dei*, 1969), the story of a German capitalist family destroyed by Nazism, there are no survivors. Nor are there in *Ludwig* (1972), where the mad king is incarcerated by his ministers leaving nothing behind him. Both these films

are set in a recognizable history, whose development is cataclysmically blocked. In *Death in Venice* (1971) and *The Intruder* (*L'innocente*, 1976), on the other hand, there is no history at all. The films are set in their own present, which is our past. They have neither a future of their own nor any connection forward, even implicit, to our present. This cutting off of the past from the present goes along with an increasing interest in deviant sexuality. The protagonists of these late films are the last of their line, and can only live in the present, knowing it to be the end. Significantly, few children are procreated, and none survive. This contrasts sharply with the world of *Rocco* or *La terra trema*, where the break-up of the family leaves behind children who are free to grow and develop. How much this involution of Visconti's concerns connects with his own homosexuality and his approaching death (during the making of *Ludwig* he had a severe stroke from which he never fully recovered) and how much it has to do with political disappointments is hard to determine. Suffice it to say that the later films, for all their splendours, lack the urgent forward-looking drive that characterizes the early ones.

Visconti's film output is not very great – some fourteen features in thirty years – but each of his films is in some way remarkable. Throughout his film-making career he was also busy with theatre and opera productions, in London and Paris as well as in Italy. Among his finest opera productions were Verdi's *Traviata* and *Don Carlo* for Covent Garden. In the theatre he directed Shakespeare, Goldoni, Beaumarchais and Chekhov as well as contemporary plays and (as these names imply) his work in the theatre included a lot of comedy, generally treated in a realistic vein. Although he soon abandoned realism as an aesthetic, he retained a gift for incidental realistic touches, both in theatre and cinema, which help to give substance to productions which would otherwise occasionally seem to be merely spectacular.

Geoffrey Nowell-Smith

Other films: *Bellissima* (1951); *White Nights* (1957); *Lo straniero* (1967; from Camus's *L'Étranger*); *Conversation Piece* (1975). See: Geoffrey Nowell-Smith, *Visconti* (1973); Monica Stirling, *A Screen of Time* (biography, 1979).

499

VOEGELIN, Eric 1901–

German/US political scientist and philosopher of history

Eric Voegelin was born in Cologne but grew up in Vienna where his family moved in 1910. He took his doctorate at the University of Vienna in 1922, serving thereafter as assistant to Hans Kelsen, the philosopher of law whose neo-Kantian outlook strongly influenced Voegelin's early writings on sociology and economics. A fellowship which he held from 1924 to 1927 enabled Voegelin to spend time in the United States, France and England. Many of the influences which were to contribute to his break with neo-Kantian positivism can be traced to these years but it would be a mistake to picture Voegelin's intellectual evolution as a response to purely intellectual influences. Voegelin's distinctive mature position, as seen in *The New Science of Politics* (1952), *Anamnesis* (1966) and the still uncompleted multi-volume study *Order and History* (1956–74), is the fruit of a long meditation on the problem of order in human existence provoked, above all, by the tragic disorder of his own times. He has compared his position to that of Plato who sought to pose the problem of the right order of the *polis* even as the Greek city states were entering a period of definitive decline. Voegelin emigrated to the United States in 1938 to escape the Nazi takeover of Austria and taught subsequently at Harvard, Bennington College, the University of Alabama and Louisiana State University. In 1958 he accepted appointment as Professor of Political Science at the University of Munich but on retirement, in 1966, returned to the United States where he has since been affiliated to the Hoover Institute at Stanford University in California.

Voegelin's approach to the data of history and political science is based upon the insight that each civilization must be understood as a particular response to the problems and mysteries entailed in human existence in a universe whose beginning and end is shrouded in mystery. 'Human society is not merely a fact, or an event, in the external world,' he wrote, '. . . it is as a whole a little world, a cosmion, illuminated with meaning from within by the human beings who continuously create and bear it as the mode and condition of their self realization.' It is through the creation of symbols, of rites, myths and theories, that men make sense of their existence alongside each other and in the unfolding mystery of the process of reality, which we know as the time of history. Political ideas, Voegelin teaches, must be understood as just such a response. Whether he is dealing with the symbolism of revelation in the Bible or that of philosophy among the ancient Greeks, his method is to trace the achieved symbols back to the experiences which engender them. Central to this approach is a philosophy of consciousness developed in creative reaction to the work of Edmund Husserl*. Voegelin treats consciousness as a place of response, 'a ceaseless action of exploring, ordering, articulating, and correcting itself; it is an event in the reality of which it partakes. It is a permanent effort at responsive awareness to the appeal of reality, at bewaring of premature satisfaction, and above all at avoiding the self-destructive phantasy of believing the reality of which it is a part to be an object external to itself that can be mastered by bringing it into the form of a system.' His criticism of such currents of thought as positivism and Marxism is based in the view that they substitute an ideological 'second reality' (the phrase is Robert Musil's*) for the reality of experience, whose truth in turn they deny. Modern ideologies are diagnosed as a fall from the realism concerning man's status in reality achieved in the insights of the classical and Christian thinkers.

Voegelin combines broad and scrupulous scholarship with imaginative interpretation of a high order. In his work the interpretation of the symbols of political society becomes a way of understanding the nature of reality itself, through analysis of the ways in which particular symbols veil or illumine the truth of our experience. This approach is increasingly influential among students of the human sciences, especially in the USA where Voegelin's work has become a matter of intense debate, particularly among Christian and conservative scholars. The forthcoming completion of *Order and History* and the English translation of *Anamnesis* (1978), which contains the core of his philosophy, seem certain to widen the discussion to include others interested in the philosophy of man, for Voegelin's is a work that provokes and inspires even those it cannot compel or convince.

David J. Levy

The four volumes of *Order and History* which have appeared so far are *Israel and Revelation* (1956), *The World of Polis* (1957), *Plato and Aristotle* (1957) and *The Ecumenic Age* (1975); the final volume will be *In Search of Order*. See: *Science, Politics and Gnosticism* (essays, 1968); *From Enlightenment to Revolution* (1975). See also: *Eric Voegelin's Search for Order in History*, ed. Stephen A. McKnight (1978).

500
VONNEGUT Jr, Kurt 1922–

US novelist

Vonnegut's hip, breezy, atraditional style probably accounts for much of his enormous popularity, particularly among young adult readers. However, it is the tension between this light, humorous style and the seriousness of his themes and motifs that draws widespread critical acclaim. In general, each Vonnegut novel asks this question: In a world where technology, power, and greed inevitably produce war, where wealth and prestige have replaced love and kindness, where society's goals have replaced the individual's, where Free Will has become an obsolete notion, is it possible for human beings to have purpose and to live according to meaningful values? The nine novels represent the search for an answer. Vonnegut is variously labelled a science-fiction writer, a fantasist, an absurdist, and a visionary. He is perhaps best understood as a Black Humorist, although Vonnegut prefers to see himself as an 'old fart with his Pall Malls'.

Vonnegut began writing for the *Daily Sun* while he was an undergraduate at Cornell. His formal education, mostly in the sciences and anthropology, was cut short by the Second World War; in 1943 he enlisted in the army. A year later, he was captured by the Germans and sent to a POW camp in Dresden. There he somehow survived the tragic Allied firebombing and this experience obviously changed his view of modern man. Nevertheless, he returned to the United States and worked for the Chicago City News Bureau while attending the University of Chicago. In 1951, after working as a publicist for General Electric for four years, he quit to write full-time. For many years he was able to support himself and his family only by publishing popular stories (many have been reprinted in *Canary in a Cat House*, 1961, and *Welcome to the Monkey House*, 1968), but since the mid-1960s his novels have been financially successful, a fact that seems to embarrass him.

It is no surprise that the first two novels, *Player Piano* (1952) and *Sirens of Titan* (1959), are stylistically more traditional than the later works. *Player Piano* is a re-working of *Brave New World* and *Sirens of Titan* is, at first glance, a somewhat ordinary science-fiction journey through space. However, these two books are seminal in the Vonnegut world. The main characters, Dr Paul Proteus and Malachi Constant, respectively, struggle to find lives worth living. Proteus fights valiantly against a technological, machine-dominated society only to find, in the end, that most people are happy being automatons. Proteus's rebellion fails to save society, but he finds personal satisfaction and, perhaps, salvation in his effort. Constant, in *Sirens of Titan*, is transformed from debauched mogul into a loving, contented and sensitive man. It is no coincidence that he first finds this happiness on Titan; the implication is, of course, that love and peace are difficult in the chaos on Earth. During his journey, Constant discovers that all human evolution occurs in order to rescue a stranded Trafalmadore space traveller. So man has no universal purpose other than this mission and, therefore, mankind has absolutely no Free Will. Even with this discovery, Constant returns to Earth and asserts that human beings should live and love those around them. From these early novels, we learn that it is good, although futile, for the individual to struggle against inhumanity; at the same time, it is necessary for the individual to remain gentle and loving.

The next three novels, *Mother Night* (1962), *Cat's Cradle* (1963), and *God Bless You, Mr Rosewater* (1965), build on the discoveries made in the first two. For many critics, *Slaughterhouse Five* (1969) is Vonnegut's most significant work. Twenty-five years after the fact, the author writes about his Dresden experiences, and it is just this aesthetic distance that makes the novel so powerful. War and death are, of course, classic themes, but Vonnegut approaches these from a new perspective. Billy Pilgrim, survivor of Dresden, finds that he has no control over time, that he comes 'unstuck' and slips in and out from one moment to another. The Trafalmadores (space travellers) suggest cosmic detachment and advise Billy to cope with his chaotic world by enjoying the good moments and ignoring the bad. When catastrophe strikes, simply say, 'So it goes.' Then ignore it. Vonnegut clearly does not believe in this cosmic shrug; he illustrates, by the very act of writing this book, that the horrors of life are too important to ignore. However, one should not collapse into nihilism or withdraw into cosmic detachment under the weight of chaos; instead, one should face the bad (war, atrocities, greed, death, etc.) with grace, compassion and humour. *Slaughterhouse Five* is Vonnegut's testament to these values.

Breakfast of Champions (1973) and *Slapstick* (1976) are both highly personal, eccentric and self-absorbed novels. The fact that both sold well illustrates how many readers have been drawn to the Vonnegut world, even when it becomes a microcosm. The most recent, *Jailbird* (1979), again branches out into a wider world (in this case, American politics); once again, Vonnegut is writing about this crazy modern world with a sense of humour and gentleness.

Gary Thompson

Other works: *Happy Birthday, Wanda June* (1971) and *Between Time and Timbuktu* (1972) are both plays; *Wampeters, Foma, & Granfalloons: Opinions* (1974) is a collection of essays. See also: Jerome Klinkowitz and John Somer, *The Vonnegut Statement* (1973); Stanley Schatt, *Kurt Vonnegut, Jr* (1976); Richard Giannone, *Vonnegut: A Preface to His Novels* (1977); Jerome Klinkowitz and Donald Lawler, *Vonnegut in America* (1977); James Lundquist, *Kurt Vonnegut* (1977).

501

VON NEUMANN, John 1903–57

US mathematician

It is often thought that the electronic computer was invented by mathematicians *mainly* for the benefit of mathematicians. This is far from being the case. In fact it is probably true to say that there was *less* demand from mathematicians for the facilities rendered by the machine in the early years than from physicists, chemists, engineers and technologists.

The electronic computer emerged by degrees from

the electro-magnetic computer during the decade 1935–45, and it was the United States Army which built the first wholly electronic machine (ENIAC) towards the end of the war. It contained about 20,000 thermionic valves. The key idea which opened up the possibility of an efficient automatic computer was the development of switch logic; and this in turn was a natural extension of the idea of Wittgenstein's* Truth Tables. It was not until solid-state devices (initially transistors) were used in the 1950s, however, that the computer became a reliable instrument.

Whilst professional mathematicians as a body showed surprisingly little interest in the early development of computers, there were two mathematician-logicians of exceptional talent who did contribute to the work: Alan Turing* and John Von Neumann. Their unique contribution was a rigorous analysis of the potentialities of the new machine: their long-sighted, semi-philosophical papers provided the theoretical backing without which the development might have easily floundered. Commercial expediency, military security, technical obsolescence, training deficiencies – each of these was a factor which could have brought development to a standstill if it had not been felt that there was a strong theoretical basis for sustained progress.

Von Neumann was a mathematician of wide, all-round interests: an example of a type of generalist mathematician that has become progressively less common as mathematics has become an increasingly formidable labyrinth of complex and highly abstract ideas. He was born in Budapest when the Austro-Hungarian Empire was at its height as a cultural and intellectual power. He was educated at the universities of Berlin, Zürich and Budapest. After teaching for a time at the University of Berlin, he emigrated to America, where (in 1930) he took a chair in mathematical physics at Princeton. Later he moved to the Institute for Advanced Study at Princeton.

At Princeton Von Neumann worked in various areas of mathematics: mathematical logic, set theory, theory of continuous groups, ergodic theory, Quantum theory and operator theory. He was co-author (with Oskar Morgenstern) of a particularly influential and germinal book *The Theory of Games and Economic Behaviour* (1947). For many students of mathematics in the immediate post-war period this book had a profound effect. As the Pythagoreans had shown the surprisingly mathematical character of music, Von Neumann and Morgenstern showed the surprisingly mathematical character of games such as Matching Pennies, Three Boxes, Two Generals: they were also able to show how the concepts needed to analyse games could be applied to economics. (Von Neumann's interest in this area had first evidenced itself nearly twenty years earlier when, in 1928, he read a paper to the Mathematical Society of Göttingen on the mathematical theory of Matching Pennies which he had recently discovered.)

Von Neumann's essay 'The Mathematician' (in *The World of Mathematics*, 1956) expounds his general view of the state of contemporary mathematics. He is not entirely happy with what he sees. He draws a striking contrast between the professional research world of mathematics and that of physics. In the latter the effort of thought, analysis and research is highly concentrated 'on no more than one or two sharply circumscribed fields', whereas the former is essentially diverse, being split into 'a great number of sub-divisions, differing from one another widely in character, style, aims and influence.' He feels that there is a grave danger implicit in this wide dispersal of effort: a risk that advanced work in mathematics will become 'more purely aestheticizing, more and more purely *l'art pour l'art*'.

Von Neumann's own work was never this: he maintained his *mathematical* interest in fields outside mathematics throughout his life: in games, physics, economics, and not least, computers. With Turing he must share much of the credit for the fact that the computer industry developed in a far-sighted, rather than in a narrowly commercial, way: particularly in the decision to build powerful, general-purpose hardware, supplemented by specific-purpose software (programs) to adapt the machine to any particular task required. Of course in the end utility favoured the powerful generalized machine, but this was far from obvious at the beginning, and short-term utility could all too easily have won the day.

Christopher Ormell

See: John Von Neumann, 'The General and Logical Theory of Automata' in *The World of Mathematics*, vol. IV. See also: Leonid Hurwicz, 'The Theory of Economic Behaviour', and S. Vajda, 'The Theory of Games', in *The World of Mathematics*, vol. II.

502
VON STERNBERG, Josef 1894–1969

US film director

Josef Sternberg was born in Vienna in 1894. He moved to New York at the age of seven for three years, then returned to Vienna before settling permanently in the United States in 1908. Leaving school to work for a milliner and then a lace firm, he entered the film industry in 1911 as apprentice to a film-stock handler before moving to a job at the World Film Corporation in 1914. During the war he produced training films and was a Signal Corps photographer. Afterwards he worked as a cutter, writer, editor and assistant director in the United States and in Europe, ennobling his surname by the addition of 'von'.

His Hollywood career took off in the second half of the 1920s, following the prestige of his low-life (and low-budget) drama *The Salvation Hunters* (1925), which led to a contract with MGM, and, via *The Exquisite Sinner* (1925, now lost), to work for Chaplin* on Edna Purviance's comeback picture, *The Sea Gull* (*A Woman of the Sea*, 1926), a film subsequently suppressed by Chaplin. The enormous success of Von Sternberg's *Underworld* (1927), one of the first gangster pictures, marked the beginning of his long relationship with Paramount and led to five films in the next three years, as well as re-editing work on Von Stroheim's *The Wedding March* (1927). The year 1928 saw *The Last Command*, the story of a Tsarist general reduced to the role of a Hollywood extra after the Revolution, *The Drag Net*, now lost, a follow-up to *Underworld*, and a further gangster picture, *The Docks of New York*. In 1929 Von Sternberg made *The Case of Lena Smith*, now lost, dealing with illegitimacy and class-relations in *fin-de-siècle* Vienna, and *Thunderbolt*, a 'gangster fantasy' (Weinberg) exploring the early possibilities of the sound cinema.

In 1930 Von Sternberg went to Europe to produce both English language and German versions of *The Blue Angel* (based on Heinrich Mann's* novel *Professor Unrat*), the story of a schoolmaster who is bewitched and destroyed by a night-club singer. The film introduced Von Sternberg's new discovery, Marlene Dietrich, who then came to Hollywood to provide the cool and often mocking eroticism at the centre of Von Sternberg's love-dramas of the period, commencing with the North African romance *Morocco* (1930) and the spy story *Dishonoured* (1931). In 1931 Von Sternberg punctuated the Dietrich cycle with *An American Tragedy* – replacing the visiting Soviet director Sergei Eisenstein* – before continuing with the 1932 Dietrich vehicles *Shanghai Express* and *Blonde Venus*. After *The Scarlet Empress* (1934), a sumptuous and grotesque account of the rise to power of Catherine the Great, came the last of the Von Sternberg/Dietrich collaborations, the Spanish caprice *The Devil is a Woman* (1935).

Von Sternberg's break with Dietrich and with Paramount led to a mixed bag of projects and associations. *Crime and Punishment* (1935) was followed by his version of an operetta on the life of Elizabeth of Austria, *The King Steps Out* (1936), and the unfinished *I, Claudius* (1937) for Alexander Korda. He moved on to the crime-drama *Sergeant Madden* (1939), followed by his return to oriental intrigue in *The Shanghai Gesture* (1941). After only one completed wartime project, the documentary short *The Town* (1943–4), Von Sternberg's career dwindled in the 1950s with the Cold War comic-strip *Jet Pilot* (1951) and the jewel-smuggling intrigue *Macao* (1952), both of which passed beyond his control. His last film, *The Saga of Anatahan* (1953), his most personal of the period, provides an oneiric account of a group of Japanese sailors who hide on an island for several years beyond the end of the Second World War, caught up in a cobweb of honour and desire with a man and woman from the island.

Von Sternberg is remembered for four main contributions to film history. First, for his totalizing attitude to film authorship, his ambitions in the direction of total creative control sometimes extending beyond mere perfectionism into the realms of sheer autocracy. Second, for his skills in intense pictorial stylization of frequently banal dramatic material through elaborate *mise-en-scène* and virtuoso cinematography. Third, for his contribution, in films like *Underworld*, *The Drag Net*, *The Docks of New York* and *Thunderbolt*, to the early evolution of the crime-film, a contribution later nuanced in such literary adaptations as *An American Tragedy* and *Crime and Punishment*. Finally, and above all, he is remembered for his representations of female eroticism through the figure of Marlene Dietrich in his middle-period Paramount films such as *The Blue Angel*, *Morocco*, *Dishonoured*, *Shanghai Express*, *Blonde Venus*, *The Scarlet Empress* and *The Devil is a Woman*.

Philip Drummond

See: Josef von Sternberg, *Fun in a Chinese Laundry* (1965); Andrew Sarris, *The Films of Josef von Sternberg* (1966); Herman G. Weinberg, *Josef von Sternberg* (1966); John Baxter, *The Cinema of Joseph von Sternberg* (1971).

W

503
WAJDA, Andrzej 1927–

Polish film director

The son of an army officer, Andrzej Wajda spent most of his childhood in the provinces. After the war he studied fine art, then moved on to the newly established film school at Lodz. His student films were unremarkable, but he entered the film industry in the early 1950s.

Wajda was only thirteen when the war broke out, but his first three films show a desire to come to terms with the recent past and form a trilogy of war stories. All were scripted by writers with first-hand experience of the events recounted. *A Generation* (1955) – the title is indicative of Wajda's ambition – was made at a time when notions of 'socialist realism' and 'the positive hero' reigned supreme and is the most conventional of the three in its telling of the political education of a young worker. *Kanal* (1957), a bitter tale of the failure of the Warsaw uprising, established Wajda's reputation abroad, but is surpassed by *Ashes and Diamonds* (1958), a work of enormous subtlety and complexity, set at the moment of the German surrender and benefiting from a dazzling performance by Zbigniew Cybulski. All three films show the richness of Wajda's visual style, which is carried to extremes in his first colour film *Lotna* (1959), an episodic tale built around a horse and set in the period of 1939 when the Polish cavalry found itself confronted with German tanks.

In the 1960s Wajda tried, less successfully, to broaden his style by tackling comedy and epic subjects, only to reach disaster with the unreleased international co-production, *Gates to Paradise* (1967). *Everything for Sale* (1968) was a self-examination prompted by the death of his close friend, the actor Cybulski. A delicate interweaving of fiction and actual events, it remains one of Wajda's major achievements. But despite this success, there is an uncertainty of tone and unevenness of quality in Wajda's subsequent work, as he moves constantly between cinema, the theatre and television. While he has worked on German, British and French co-productions, much of his work is specifically Polish in meaning, as in the series of literary adaptations begun with *The Wedding* (1972). Wajda's finest work of the 1970s is *Man of Marble* (1977) which, like *Everything for Sale*, is a complex reflection on the nature of film-

making, as well as a look back at the Stalinist* era in which the director began his career.

Wajda's early work shows a fusing of the heritage of Italian neo-realism and an indigenous Polish taste for highly wrought visuals, complex symbolism and paroxysms of violence. His name will always be associated with his war trilogy which did much to establish Eastern European film-making as a major force in world cinema. While much of his work is narrowly national in its patterns of meaning, two at least of his later films are self-reflective works of truly European stature.

Roy Armes

Wajda's other films include: *Innocent Sorcerers* (1960); *Samson* (1961); *Siberian Lady Macbeth* (1962); one episode of *Love at Twenty* (1962); *Ashes* (1965); *Roly-Poly* (1968); *Hunting Flies* (1969); *Landscape after Battle* (1970); *The Birch-Wood* (1970); *Pilate and Others* (1972); *The Promised Land* (1975); *The Shadow Line* (1976); *Rough Treatment* (1978); *The Young Ladies of Wilko* (1979). See also: Boleslaw Michatek, *The Cinema of Andrzej Wajda* (1973); Boleslaw Sulik, *A Change of Tack: Making the Shadow Line* (1976).

504
WALEY, Arthur David 1889–1966

British orientalist

A celebrated and prolific translator from Chinese and Japanese literature who succeeded in opening up these areas to the general educated public in a way that had never been done before, Arthur Waley studied classics at Rugby School and at King's College, Cambridge. Waley was his mother's maiden name which he adopted by deed poll in 1914.

At Cambridge, Waley came under the influence of Lowes Dickinson, who had recently travelled to China and Japan; and in the Oriental Print Department of the British Museum, where he worked from 1913 to 1929, his official superior was the poet and Eastern art expert Lawrence Binyon. Waley also almost certainly owed something to the example of Ezra Pound*, whose *Cathay* or poems based on Chinese originals was first published in 1915 and with whom he had an acquaintance about then. After he resigned from the British

Museum, Waley lived off the income he earned from his writings. He never held a full-time post at a university because he preferred not to, but he frequently attended or gave seminars on Chinese poetry at the School of Oriental and African Studies, London University. A Londoner all his adult life, he lived in Bloomsbury and never travelled to the Far East.

Waley's knowledge of Chinese and Japanese was self-taught and from 1918 he published a very large number of books, the main scope of which was literature but which also took in Chinese philosophy and history. Translation from Japanese was, in terms of separate titles, much the smaller part of Waley's *oeuvre*, and he did not really continue with this side of his activities after 1933. On the other hand, his own favourite among his published works is said to have been *The Pillow-book of Sei Shōnagon* (*Makura no Sōshi*, 1928), and undoubtedly his greatest single feat, and not only from the point of view of length, was *The Tale of Genji* (*Genji Monogatari*), brought out in six substantial volumes (1925–33). The two other books from Japanese were *Japanese Poetry: The 'Uta'* (1919) and *The Nō Plays of Japan* (1921).

All these books can be regarded in one way or another as partial translations. That on classical poetry was by intent a rather narrow selection and amounts to some seventy-five smallish pages of actual texts; *Nō Plays* contains translations of nineteen of the dramas and summaries of sixteen more; the *Pillow-book* is another slender work of 160 pages and consists of what Waley regarded as choice excerpts with connecting passages supplied by himself; even *The Tale of Genji* has a chapter of the original unaccountably omitted, though it runs to some eleven hundred pages in the one-volume edition of 1935. Furthermore, all these books have now to some degree been put in the shade by later works by other hands. Yet, Waley's output, even in the circumscribed area of translation from Japanese, has had an enormously beneficial impact on several generations of scholars and students as an introduction to the field; and though he is not above criticism as a translator (he is often accused of misunderstanding the text or embellishing it), the charm, vigour and, in many places, the underlying veracity of his style will continue to appeal. In particular, his translations of Japanese poetry are accurate as well as attractive.

Waley's translations from Chinese, which are too voluminous to mention briefly, have yet to undergo a process of critical sifting and evaluation. No doubt they will, and no doubt much good, hard wheat will be left once the chaff has been blown away. The early *One Hundred and Seventy Chinese Poems* (1918), however, holds a special place in the history of English prosody. Instead of attempting to 'versify' his renderings, in strict metre and rhyme, Waley developed a system of stressed syllables without rhyme, independently, or so he

claimed, of the 'Sprung Rhythm' of Gerard Manley Hopkins (1844–89) whose work was first published in collected form the same year. Consequently, while Waley's example of 'free verse' influenced many of his younger contemporaries, as well as W. B. Yeats*, he has also been the target of those who regret the abandonment of traditional versification.

In answer to his critics Waley contended that as a translator his first loyalty was to the spirit of the originals. His writings were also aimed at the general reader rather than the specialist. In the sense that for many the flavour of Chinese and Japanese literature is the flavour he provided it with, he was almost entirely successful in his endeavour. In C. P. Snow's novel *The Light and the Dark* (1947) a nervous Lewis Eliot, on a risky wartime flight from Bristol to Lisbon, tries to pass the time reading *Genji*, and 'subtle and lovely though it was, I wished it had more narrative power'.

Dr R. H. P. Mason

For a survey of Waley's work see *A Bibliography of Arthur Waley* (1968) by Francis Johns. See also Ivan Morris, *Madly Singing in the Mountains* (1970).

505
WARHOL, Andy (Andrew Warhola) 1928–

US artist, film-maker

Often categorized as a pioneer and leading exponent of Pop Art, Andy Warhol was born of Czech extraction in Philadelphia. He is best known for his paintings and films, but his activities, almost unrivalled in their diversity and volume, have included producing the rock group The Velvet Underground (in the mid-1960s), designing record covers (notably for the Rolling Stones'* album *Sticky Fingers*, with its openable zipper), and writing books (some of them taped conversations, some actually 'written'). From the late 1950s until 1968, when he was near-fatally shot by Valeria Solanis for motives that have never been clearly ascertained, most of his output flowed from the Factory, the idiosyncratic name given to his studio in Manhattan.

Warhol's fame was established by his silkscreen paintings of Campbell's soupcans and other everyday household objects in 1961–2. The popular, commercial images were transferred mechanically from the 'original' photographs to the silkscreen web, and then applied to paper or canvas. A reaction to Abstract Expressionism, they were in almost every respect, when they first appeared, a challenge to normal notions and practices of fine art. To begin with they were exhibited on the West Coast of the United States, not the East. Their subject-matter was drawn provocatively from an area that by definition was segregated from 'serious' artistic endeavour. But more revolutionary still was the idea of using *unchanged* and therefore *unlaboured*, original material, and, further, reproducing this through assistants. This constituted, as Warhol intended it should, the almost total self-effacement of the artist's individuality, although purposely minor infringements (random marks, hand-pressure variations, drips) remained to belie the purity of the endeavour. Paradoxically Warhol's denial of individuality has made him a central personality in contemporary art. This predictable but illogical outcome has naturally attracted suspicion, and Warhol's developments have often raised the consideration: how much is expression and how much is ploy? Given the apparently successful de-individualization of his work, it is difficult to see what prompts its production in the first place. An incorrect summary might suggest that his admirers have mistaken the real target of his aesthetic, which is not the consumer product so much as consumer marketing. On the other hand there can be little doubt that Warhol has significantly contributed to the refashioning of our sensibilities. A Campbell's soupcan is intrinsically neither funny nor sad, nor does it command any other emotional response when set apart from all other objects. The process of de-individualization has not stopped short at the artist, but extends to the viewer. But: are we being ironically rebuked for our willing self-immersion in the surface world of advertisement and brand promotion, or are we being offered a chance to empty out? Both of these, it could be claimed, are legitimate, if not conventional, functions for an artist to pursue.

While Warhol had worked as a commercial illustrator for *Harpers* early in his career, perhaps the more decisive experience was his involvement with a Brechtian theatre collective at the beginning of the 1950s. Interpreting Brecht's* theoretical writings, he composed stage-sets in which drawings of interior objects were pasted or hung on the 'real' artefacts (thus the image of a chair might be attached to the chair which had been used as a model). This was done not as a scenic economy, but as a deliberate re-evaluation of space, of proximity and distanciation.

Not unlike Brecht, Warhol has been concerned to undermine, wherever he can, illusionist representation, treating it as the ideology of truth and humanism which permeates, produces and is produced by Western cultural forms. In his paintings of Jacqueline Kennedy, Elvis Presley*, Suicides and the Electric Chair, all major representational images during the 1960s, he offsets his highly charged subject-matter by a style that is wilfully mundane. These offer a critique of illusionist representation. For examples of non-illusionist representation we must turn back to the soupcans, or to Warhol's films, where he usually jettisons the identificatory processes of character, plot, drama, goal, fictive meaning and psychological truth.

Unavoidably making a film requires 'labour'. Unless the camera is used nothing can be accomplished, and just how it is used involves strategy and decision-making. Warhol's solution to this problem is complex, and perhaps only partial. He has evolved two techniques that, by not denying the procedure and process of film-making itself, allow for no 'effects' except for those which will be immediately recognizable as such. One is the use of a rigid, unmoving camera, sometimes sustained for hours at a time, so that the work seems to approach a zero point of stylelessness. The other is a camera which arbitrarily zooms, focuses, changes angle and depth of field and light intensity and 'sound focus', without apparent purpose. Both these serve, or seem to serve, as a forcing of the audience to the medium itself as a materialist practice. Other techniques, or ploys, include the sudden incorporation of unexposed footage which comes out as a brilliant white on the screen. These cinematographic habits, contrasted to normal 'editing', undermine the audience's status as a cohesive, uncontradictory consumer of an uncontradictory, pre-structured 'knowledge' of the real. This is Warhol's central project in all his work.

Warhol's aim has been to discard the suspension of disbelief which is so necessary for dominant narrative cinema. The epitome of his filmwork is perhaps *Chelsea Girls* (1967), a three-and-a-half-hour doublescreen movie originally arranged so that its seven half-hour reels could be projected in any sequence. Many of the most well-known 'Andy Warhol' films, e.g. *Flesh*, *Trash*, etc., were produced and directed by his colleague Paul Morrissey, and Warhol himself has not been personally involved in his films since 1969, with the important exception of the camerawork for *Women in Revolt* (1972), a study of conflictual sexual disorientations. Most of the 'real' Andy Warhol films have been hidden in a vault, possibly to make the Warhol/Morrissey films more attractive to their audiences, possibly as an annihilation ploy which, of course, produces precisely the opposite effect.

By the mid 1970s Warhol was undertaking commissioned portraits of politicians and wealthy socialites. His later paintings are said to re-incorporate much more the abstract-expressionist hand-involvement, the mark, the scratch, the presence of the producer. But very often, as in the case of the ten *Mao** portraits (1972), each in editions of 250, they are produced in series, and this imposes a blandness that cancels out any suspected eruption of the artist's self. As in the earlier silkscreens, where only minor differences of tonality were noticeable, the emphasis remains on the mechanized and distanciated gesture, and it is for this quality, after a period in which other artists attempted to 'paint psychology', that Warhol is likely to be remembered.

Peter Gidal

Warhol's books include: *Screen Test*, stills from his

films (1966); *The Index Book*, with fold-outs, pop-up soupcans, a record, a balloon, etc. (1967); *From A to B and Back Again* (1975). Among his films are: *Blowjob* (1963); *Empire, Couch, 13 Most Beautiful Women* (1964); *Vinyl, Kitchen, My Hustler, The Shopper* (1965); **** (*Four Stars*, 1966); *Lonesome Cowboys* (1978); and *Fuck* (*Blue Movie*, 1969). His silkscreens, paintings and lithographs are generally identified by their subjects, viz.: Fruit tins, Coca-Cola labels, soupcans (1961); *Marilyn* (Monroe), *Liz* (Taylor), more soupcans (1962); car crashes, lynchings, suicides (1963); Brillo boxes, Kelloggs cornflakes cartons, flowers, *Jackie*, *Elvis* (from 1964); self-portraits, *Marlon Brando* (1965). Most of these and similar subjects were used in succeeding years. Others include: girls, boys, Indians, torsos, transvestites (1974); the Paul Anka T-shirt (1975); Hammer and Sickle (1976). About Andy Warhol: John Coplans, *Andy Warhol* (1971); Peter Gidal, *Andy Warhol: Films and Paintings* (1971); Stephen Koch, *Andy Warhol: Stargazer* (1973).

506

WATSON, James Dewey 1928–

US biologist

In 1947 when J. D. Watson completed his bachelor's degree in biology at the University of Chicago, the science of genetics was well developed but little was known about the nature of the fundamental unit of that science – the gene. Watson's major contribution, in collaboration with the British-born scientist, F. H. C. Crick, was to propose in 1953 a plausible structure for the chemical substance DNA, or deoxyribonucleic acid, and to show how it might account for many of the properties of the gene.

When Watson left Chicago to pursue graduate work at the University of Indiana he was only nineteen years of age. It was his acceptance by Indiana on condition that he study genetics or embryology which turned him from his intended career subject of ornithology.

Following upon his PhD research, Watson came to Europe and worked in Copenhagen and Cambridge, supported first by a Merck post-doctoral fellowship, and subsequently by the National Foundation for Infantile Paralysis. Returned to the United States in 1953 he continued as a research scientist in the California Institute of Technology, then he moved to Harvard where he became the head of the department of biology in 1961. For eight years, beginning in 1968, he also directed the Cold Spring Harbor Laboratory on Long Island.

Watson's genetic research at Indiana concerned the effects of X-ray damage upon bacterial viruses. It was hoped that this approach might yield clues to viral multiplication, a process thought to be virtually ident-

ical with gene duplication. In the event, this indirect approach to the nature of the genetic material proved disappointing. By contrast the direct approach using the techniques of chemistry and physics upon the genetic material looked more promising for unravelling the secrets of the gene. Watson therefore studied the transfer of chemical constituents from infecting virus particles to progeny virus particles using radioactive tracers. Then, fired with enthusiasm after seeing X-ray diffraction pictures shown by the British biophysicist M. H. F. Wilkins, Watson altered his strategy yet again, turning to the study of molecular structure as deduced from X-ray diffraction pictures.

Using data obtained by Rosalind Franklin, Raymond Gosling and Maurice Wilkins at King's College, London, Watson collaborated in Cambridge with Francis H. C. Crick. Having concluded that the genetic material was not a nucleoprotein but simply nucleic acid, they hoped that the structure of this substance would show how the gene works – how it duplicates, changes abruptly when it 'mutates', and expresses itself by giving rise to the heritable characteristics of organisms. Although their first attempt at a chemical structure was a failure, their second, just over a year later, was to be numbered among the most celebrated achievements of twentieth-century science.

A preliminary description of their model was published in *Nature* in the spring of 1953, followed by a second paper on the implications for genetics suggested by the model.

The idea, long discussed, that hereditary traits could be encoded in a specific chemical sequence was here identified with the sequence of 'bases'. Constancy of hereditary transmission, they suggested, was due to the faithful copying of the base sequence; changes or 'mutations' were due to errors in copying. The copying process itself was pictured as involving the opening of the two chains (the double helix) in such a way that new chains could be laid down on each of the originals. The sequence of bases on a new chain was dictated by specific pairing with the bases of the original chain.

Despite modifications to the Watson–Crick model for DNA (deoxyribonucleic acid) its basic principles have been greatly strengthened over the succeeding two decades. Its authors' suggestions regarding its implications for genetics have been followed and confirmed. The chemical sequence of the gene – the genetic code – has been discovered. The mechanism by which this code is expressed, however, proved a far more complex process than Watson and Crick envisaged. Only a broad research programme of biochemistry and structural chemistry sufficed to unravel its mysteries. This triumph in analysis was catalysed by the many theoretical insights which Crick provided between 1956 and 1970. Watson, who was but twenty-five years of age in 1953, received with Crick and Wilkins the Nobel Prize for Medicine in 1962. Three years later, his textbook *The Molecular Biology of the Gene* (1965) appeared. He presented his subject boldly, because he believed the basic concepts provided by the molecular approach were now sound; in short biology had by 1965 as sound a basis as chemistry had enjoyed since 1932 thanks to the Quantum Theory. It was time, he claimed, to re-orient the teaching of biology and give 'the biologist of the future the rigor, the perspective, and the enthusiasm that will be needed to bridge the gap between the single cell and the complexities of higher organisms'.

After many revisions and some hard feeling within the scientific community, Watson published *The Double Helix*, an account of the period of his life spent in Europe which had led to the model for DNA. This very candid, at times corrosive, picture of an ambitious young American research scientist thirsting for the big discovery and winning a share in a Nobel Prize has undermined the public image of the unworldly scientist who solves problems by dedicated industry and accumulated expertise. The Watson in *The Double Helix* appears to view laboratory research with a casual air but professional recognition is for him a very serious matter.

Dr Robert Olby

See: J. Cains, G. Stent, and Watson (eds), *Phage and the Origin of Molecular Biology* (1968); R. Olby, *The Path of the Double Helix* (1974).

507
WATSON, John Broadus 1878–1958

US psychologist

Watson's young days were spent in South Carolina. In 1899 he graduated from Furman University and under the influence of the Furman philosopher, Gordon B. Moore, he moved to Chicago for a PhD in psychology and philosophy. There he came under the influence of John Dewey*, Jacques Loeb, H. H. Donaldson and James Angell. After nine productive years Watson was appointed to a full professorship at Johns Hopkins University, Baltimore. His divorce from Mary Ickes and subsequent marriage to his research collaborator, Rosalie Raynor, led to his enforced resignation in 1920. His academic career closed, he moved into the business world, becoming Vice President of the J. Walter Thompson Company in 1924, and Vice President of William Esty and Company in 1936.

When Watson went to Chicago in 1899 the structural psychology of Wilhelm Wundt had been eclipsed in America by the functional psychology of Angell, William James, and Dewey. This placed emphasis upon mental activity as an adaptive response to the environment. It brought Darwinian ideas into psychology and gave an impetus to the experimental study of animal

behaviour, since the adaptive responses of animals should throw light upon those of man. But functionalism did not reject mentalist terms, nor deny consciousness to animals. Watson studied examples of instinctive behaviour, the migration of terns, and maze-running by the white rat. He became increasingly impatient with the failure of functional psychology to make a clean break with subjectivism. In the winter of 1912–13 Watson gave a series of lectures to Columbia University which he summarized in his famous paper 'Psychology as the Behaviorist Views it' in *Psychological Review* (vol. 20, 1913). Here the main features of his more mature formulation of behaviourism – with the exception of the conditioned reflex – can be found.

As a comparative psychologist studying the instinctive and acquired behaviour of animals, Watson had become increasingly unhappy with the obligation that psychology placed upon him to relate such work to the body of knowledge gained from the study of consciousness in man. When he considered the confusion within psychology, the disagreements over the meanings of terms, the nature of conscious content, and the elements of the mind, he determined to 'throw off the yoke of consciousness' and define psychology as a purely objective experimental branch of natural science in which introspection finds no place, and no line divides man from brute. Each should be placed 'as nearly as possible under the same experimental conditions'. In such a system of psychology when fully worked out, 'given the stimuli the response can be predicted'. The aim of this psychology was the prediction and control of behaviour. Unlike the old structural psychology, therefore, it should be useful to the educator, jurist, business man and physician.

In the programme which Watson sketched out in this paper and more fully in his textbook, *Psychology from the Standpoint of a Behaviorist* (1919), the psychologist's task was to investigate the responses to specific stimuli and to distinguish the acquired from the inborn. As his views matured he came to the following conclusions. There are only three basic inborn emotions, those of rage, fear and love. By 1924 he came to doubt the need for the concept of instinct at all. Instead he listed the baby's reflexes of grasping, kicking, sucking, crying and so forth. Other responses were due to the process of conditioning which begins at birth if not before. Whilst Watson rejected mentalist terms, he regarded speech like any other motor response as a series of muscular contractions, and thought as 'implicit speech'; some weak motor responses still occurred but no sounds were produced.

The concept of the conditioned reflex had been developed by the Russian physiologist I. P. Pavlov. Watson had discussed it in 1915, and in 1924 he made it the major feature of his system. By conditioning, the emotion of fear could be brought out in response to stimuli not normally associated with fear. Thus a white rat, for which the child had no congenital fear, could illicit fear by repeated introduction of a loud sound along with the rat. Such a response could be 'unconditioned' by substituting food for the bang and progressively reducing the distance of the rat from the child.

Although Watson recognized the therapeutic value of psychoanalysis he rejected Freud's* psychosexual theories. From a study of the children of his second marriage he claimed to have demonstrated that no long-term memory of events in early childhood existed, that attachment to the mother could be so weakened by a spell away from home that the son did not rush to his mother's defence when his father attacked her.

Watson's opposition to psychosexual theories was part of his extreme environmentalism, which is seen in his opposition to the claims of the eugenicists, in particular to the results of twin studies, and his confident claims for the potential of conditioning from early childhood. Too much love and attention from the mother generates overdependence of the child upon her. 'Punishment', wrote Watson, 'is a word which ought never to have crept into our language.' Deviant behaviour should be corrected by a process of untraining and retraining using the principles of conditioning. He looked to a future in which society would base its ethics upon the principles of behaviourism. He was not asking people 'to form a colony, go naked and live a communal life', but he was suggesting how the application of behaviourism could 'gradually change this universe'.

The response to behaviourism was not immediate. Watson's influence was felt in psychology both directly, through the work of men like K. S. Lashley, and indirectly through the impact of his writings in the popular press. In the 1930s a new generation of psychologists formulated more sophisticated versions of behaviourism – R. C. Tolman, C. L. Hull and B. F. Skinner*.

Dr Robert Olby

Other books by Watson are: *Animal Education. An Experimental Study on the Psychical Development of the White Rat . . .* (1903); *Behaviour: An Introduction to Comparative Psychology* (1914); *Behaviourism* (1925, 2nd edn 1931); with Rosalie Watson, *Psychological Care of Infant and Child* (1928). His celebrated debate with W. McDougall was published as *The Battle of Behaviorism. An Exposition and an Exposure* (1928). See also: David Cohen, *J. B. Watson, the Founder of Behaviourism: A Biography* (1979).

508
WAUGH, Evelyn Arthur St John 1903–66

British novelist

The son of Arthur Waugh, publisher and literary critic, and younger brother of Alec Waugh, novelist, Evelyn Waugh was educated at Lancing and Hertford College, Oxford. After abortive attempts at schoolmastering and carpentry he turned to literature and in 1928 published a biographical study of D. G. Rossetti. His first novel, *Decline and Fall*, appeared later in the same year. Based loosely on his experiences as preparatory school teacher, it was a racy mixture of burlesque farce and social satire that brought him critical acclaim, a number of journalistic commissions, but little money. Popular success came with *Vile Bodies* (1930), which caught, with seemingly effortless precision, the frenetic social atmosphere of young upper-class London in the 1920s: the Bright Young People, their language, their parties, and their aimlessness. Both in literature and in society Waugh became a fashionable figure, but his happiness was bitterly affected by the break-up, after a few months, of his first marriage. The behaviour of his wife left a scar that is visible in many of his subsequent writings. More immediately, it hastened his reception into the Roman Catholic Church, in September 1930 – an event that Waugh regarded as the most important in his life.

Between then and the Second World War he travelled extensively in Europe, Africa, South America and Mexico. To this period belong: *Labels: A Mediterranean Journal* (1930); *Remote People* (1931); *Ninety-Two Days* (1934); *Waugh in Abyssinia* (1936). These travel books were later abridged into one volume, *When the Going was Good* (1946). The novels of this decade, which draw on the same experiences, are *Black Mischief* (1932), *A Handful of Dust* (1934), perhaps the climax of Waugh's early writings, and *Scoop* (1938).

In the course of the war, during which he served in the Royal Marines and later the Royal Horse Guards, he wrote *Put Out More Flags* (1942) and *Brideshead Revisited* (1945). The second of these, though attacked for its luxuriance and snobbery, was a best-seller in England and in America, bringing Waugh a measure of financial security, and also heralding the deeper concern with religious themes that characterizes his later work. His main achievement during the last period of his life was the trilogy based on his wartime experiences: *Men at Arms* (1952), *Officers and Gentlemen* (1955) and *Unconditional Surrender* (1961). In 1965 these were published in one volume, with some revisions, as *Sword of Honour*. When he died, on Easter Day 1966, he had produced one volume of his autobiography, *A Little Learning* (1964), and was beginning work on the second.

Waugh is primarily a comic novelist, whose books display an anarchic imagination and cast an acute satirical eye on the manners of upper-class society. From the outset he was stimulated by the borderlands where civilization and savagery meet, where the sublime shades into the ridiculous, sanity into lunacy, sadness into hilarity. These oppositions fuelled his sense of the absurd, but also lent substance to his more serious preoccupations. If his work has a central theme, it is the triumph of barbarism in a civilization that has lost touch with the values on which it was founded. Throughout his writings this nostalgia for the values of a happier age finds an image in the country house, beleaguered, encroached upon, or destroyed by the agents of a graceless modern world. His growing disgust with 'the century of the common man' had a political and social complexion which many commentators have found repulsive. In later life Waugh developed an image of eccentric and extreme Toryism which is brilliantly portrayed by him in the opening chapter of his autobiographical novel, *The Ordeal of Gilbert Pinfold* (1957). But he was not a political figure; closer to the heart of both his life and his writings is a romanticism at odds with the conditions of his age and society.

The earlier novels use irony as their characteristic response. In a world of arbitrary cruelties and absurd injustices the novelist observes his creatures with a detachment that shields his own vulnerability. Later, the influence of religion begins to reveal the strain on his irony, making possible the achievement of the war trilogy, in which irony and despair are tempered by a kindling of religious charity that gives to the work an unaccustomed depth of humanity.

To Waugh the question of style was paramount: he looked on writing 'not as an exploration of character, but as an exercise in the use of language'. Hostile to the practices of most modernist writers, he developed a style that was elegant, lucid and precise, in which words were chosen with loving propriety and a strict regard for their etymology. Not surprisingly he was devoted to the works of P. G. Wodehouse*, while another important influence on him was Ronald Firbank*, about whom he wrote one of his best critical essays. Waugh remains, however, a writer who is difficult to identify with any particular school, and he has had no followers of note. He can be seen as an important cross-current to the dominant intellectual and artistic trends of post-war years. To be reactionary was in his view the necessary function of the artist in society. It is not a role that has endeared him to the arbiters of academic critical fashion, but he may yet be read for his humour and lucidity when writers of more importunate relevance and less embarrassing opinions have been forgotten.

Ian Littlewood

Other works: *Edmund Campion* (1935) and *Ronald Knox* (1959), both biographies; *Helena* (1950) is a historical novel; *Scott-King's Modern Europe* (1947), *The Loved One* (1948), *Love Among Ruins* (1953) are short novels. *Work Suspended* (1942) is an unfinished fiction. The *Diaries*, ed. Michael Davie (1976) and *A Little Order*, a selection of his journalism, ed. Donat Gallagher (1977) appeared posthumously. About Waugh: M. Bradbury, *Evelyn Waugh* (1964); Alec Waugh, *My Brother Evelyn and other Profiles* (1967); R. M. Davis (ed.) *et al.*, *Evelyn Waugh: A Checklist* (1972); D. Pryce-Jones (ed.), *Evelyn Waugh and his World* (1973); Christopher Sykes, *Evelyn Waugh, a Biography* (1975). His work is also discussed in Martin Green, *Children of the Sun* (1976).

509
WEBB, Martha Beatrice 1858–1943
WEBB, Sidney James (Lord Passfield) 1859–1947

British social reformers and historians

Martha Beatrice Potter, the daughter of a wealthy railway promoter, described the awakening of her social conscience and her early interest in the problems of London poverty in her distinguished autobiography *My Apprenticeship* (1926), and in the posthumous second volume *Our Partnership* (1948). She drew upon her remarkable *Diary* (microfiche, 1977) to portray the first two decades of her marriage to Sidney James Webb, the talented son of London tradespeople, who gave up his career as a civil servant to devote himself to journalism, social research and political reform.

The Webbs, influenced by Positivist and Utilitarian ideas of public service, did much to shape modern social democracy and the welfare state; but their concept of reform was essentially elitist, for they believed that it was the duty of enlightened intellectuals to reconstruct society in the interests of social efficiency and to the benefit of the poor, the sick and the aged. To this end they put great stress on education and effective public administration. These views are reflected in the policies of the Fabian Society, in which the Webbs and George Bernard Shaw* played a leading role, in their foundation of the London School of Economics in 1895, in their energetic campaign of 1906–11 to reform the archaic Poor Law, and in their launching of the weekly *New Statesman* in 1913.

In 1916, after many years in which the Webbs had sought with limited success to 'permeate' the Liberal and Conservative parties with their reformist policies, they turned to the Labour Party as the favoured means of social reconstruction. After Sidney Webb had helped to devise the party's constitution he drafted its notable 1918 election manifesto called *Labour and the New Social Order*. In 1922 he was elected as MP for Seaham Harbour, holding office in the Labour government of 1924 as President of the Board of Trade and in the government of 1929–31 as Colonial Secretary, but he proved to be an ineffective Cabinet minister. When he was created Lord Passfield in 1924 his wife declined to use the title and continued to be known as Mrs Sidney Webb.

Sidney Webb, a man capable of unremitting work, was a prolific journalist and pamphleteer, writing many of the celebrated Fabian tracts in the heyday of that society; and Beatrice Webb had gifts of imagination and literary style which only too rarely gleamed in their joint work as historians and social theorists. Their first work was *The History of Trade Unionism* (1894), and this was followed by *Industrial Democracy* (1897), *English Local Government* (9 vols, 1906–29), *The Consumers' Co-operative Movement* (1921), *A Constitution for the Socialist Commonwealth of Great Britain* (1921), *The Decay of Capitalist Civilisation* (1923) and *Methods of Social Study* (1932). After the fall of the Labour government in 1931, and affected by the economic depression and the rise of fascism in Europe, the Webbs became convinced that the USSR exemplified Auguste Comte's 'religion of humanity' and *Soviet Communism, A New Civilisation?* (1935) was an extended and for the most part uncritical account of the Stalin* regime. At the instance of Bernard Shaw, who thus sought to commemorate the long partnership of the Webbs, their ashes were interred together in Westminster Abbey.

Professor Norman MacKenzie

See also: M. Cole (ed.), *The Webbs and their Work* (1947); Kitty Muggeridge and Ruth Adams, *Beatrice Webb* (1968); N. and J. MacKenzie, *The First Fabians* (1977); N. MacKenzie (ed.), *The Letters of Sidney and Beatrice Webb* (1978); J. MacKenzie, *A Victorian Courtship* (1979).

510
WEBER, Max 1864–1920

German sociologist

It is now generally recognized that sociology emerged as an important academic discipline not so much through the work of Auguste Comte, who first used the term 'sociology', but rather through the development of three traditions represented by the work of Émile Durkheim* who wrote, it is true, in the tradition of Comte, of Karl Marx, whose work became one of the central intellectual and political facts in European history, and of Max Weber whose range of comparative and historical work approached from the intellectual standpoint of Neo-Kantianism was perhaps more comprehensive than either of the others.

Weber's father was prominent in the National Liberal Party during the Bismarck era. At Heidelberg his original studies were in Law, but, by the time he came

to write his doctoral and habilitation theses, his interest had shifted to Economics and Economic History. His first academic post was as a Professor of Economics in the University of Freiburg, but he moved to Heidelberg after three years in 1896. At Heidelberg he suffered a severe mental breakdown leading to total disablement for four years and to an inability to accept any academic appointment until 1917. His life during this period has been devotedly chronicled in one of the most dignified biographies ever written. The biography was by his wife, Marianne, with whom he is believed to have had an unusual marriage, which, though it may never have been sexually consummated, provided the basis for a remarkable intellectual and moral companionship.

Marianne Weber provided Weber with a home which served as the focus for the intellectual life of some of the greatest intellects of the time in the fields of history, philosophy, economics, politics and literature. He also worked within the *Verein für Sozialpolitik*, an organization concerned with the application of social science findings to politics, and for many years edited and wrote in its journal, the *Archiv für Sozialwissenschaft und Sozialpolitik*. He also participated very actively in German politics, even though the Kantian perspective which he shared with his intellectual companions led him to make a radical dissociation between what he conceived to be the tasks of science and those which he thought appropriate to the politician.

Weber's earliest writing was in economic history. One of his theses dealt with Agrarian Civilization in the Ancient World and another with Trading Companies in the Middle Ages. His contribution in these writings were partly oriented to controversies in German historiography, but he also used these themes for the development of generally applicable sociological concepts and for the understanding of contemporary problems. His association with the *Verein für Sozialpolitik* led him to make investigations of such topics as the condition of agricultural labourers in East Germay and of the Stock Exchange. Informing these studies was a developing interest in studying the role of religious thought in shaping economic behaviour, and the nature of modern bureaucratic organization. Behind this lay a more far-reaching concern amounting to an implicit philosophy of history based upon a conception of the rationalization, secularization and disenchantment of the world. The best known outcome of this concern was Weber's *The Protestant Ethic and the Spirit of Capitalism* (vol. I of *Gesammelte Aufsätze zur Religionssoziologie*, 1920, trans. 1930), in which, stimulated by Ernst Troeltsch, he agreed that it was in Calvinism that the roots of capitalism were to be found, rather than in Judaism, as had been suggested by Sombart. This work was supplemented by comparative studies of Chinese, Indian and Jewish civilization which set out to show the difference which religious thought made to economic behaviour, but which inevitably brought into focus many other structural variables which differentiated these civilizations one from another. Amongst many themes discussed were types of authority and administration, the relations between prophets, priests and administrators, the nature of urban settlements, guild and other occupational organizations and class and status structures. These studies combined with Weber's early studies of ancient and medieval Europe and his study of contemporary issues to provide him with a range of comparative and historical knowledge which has probably had no equal in modern times.

In 1909 the publisher Paul Siebeck invited Weber to edit a new series of books which would replace the by then dated 'Handbook of Political Economy' edited by Gustav Schonberg. Although eventually contributions to this series were published, including those of distinguished authors such as Joseph Schumpeter, Werner Sombart, Robert Michels, Karl Bucher and Alfred Weber, Max Weber grew impatient with the tardiness and the inadequacies of some of his proposed authors, and eventually decided to expand his own contribution on the social structures within which economic systems developed. The original title which Weber gave to his own contribution was 'The Economy and the Arena of De Facto and Normative Powers'. When this was eventually published, together with a new introduction, it was called simply *Economy and Society* (trans. 1967), but it is the original title which specifies Weber's exact intention. He attempts here to outline the basic types of economic action, their organization into alternative types of economic system, and the ways in which such systems operate within a context of legitimating idea systems and structures of power. There are thus book-length sections of the whole volume dealing with the comparative economic systems, the sociology of the world religions, the sociology of law, forms of legitimate authority and administration, and the city, as well as a number of minor themes such as domestic organization, village life and ethnic groups.

Economy and Society constitutes Weber's systematic sociology. No one who reads it could continue to give credence to the view widely held in the English-speaking world after the publication of *The Protestant Ethic and the Spirit of Capitalism* in translation that Weber was a bourgeois idealist anti-Marxist. Nor could it be maintained, as it sometimes is on the basis of Weber's methodological writings, that Weber held purely subjectivist views, believing that history had to be written only from limited value-laden perspectives. What is evident here is an almost brutal realism derived from a reading of history, which took violence and exploitation for granted. No volume in fact could more justifiably claim as its text Marx's assertion that 'All history is the history of class struggles' than Weber's volume on *The City*, which first appeared as

a section of *Economy and Society*. None the less there *are* also normative powers and these Weber treats both in terms of ideological content and in terms of their institutional embodiment in his sections on the Sociology of Religion and the Sociology of Law.

The perspective of *Economy and Society*, and still more the perspective of Weber's early writings, derives from a Kantian approach to history and the social sciences, which was shared ground between Weber and his colleagues who came to visit him. Weber never set out systematically to discuss this approach, nor did he have much to say about Kant. None the less, in the sustained methodological polemics in which he engaged with contemporary authors in the pages of the *Archiv*, Weber's Kantianism is clear. The central Kantian notion which is taken for granted is that of the possibility of sustaining simultaneously a view of the world as consisting of phenomena organized in terms of the categories of space, time and causality, and an alternative view in which man lives in the realm of freedom, confronting the Moral Law, yet free to choose and to make value judgments for which he is responsible. It was from this perspective that Weber wrote about the notion of cause in history, about ideal types contrasted with empirical laws, about the relation between value perspectives and the discovery of causal sequences and about the tension between value freedom and value relevance in social science.

Probably the central idea which Weber has is that of 'relevance for value'. This idea, which he took over from Rickert and modified, suggested that there are a multitude of value starting points from which the manifold of social and cultural facts could be analysed, and it is necessary that every social science investigation should make its value starting points explicit, in order to distinguish these from the value-free investigation of the causal relations between social structures to which they subsequently lead. Unlike Rickert, Weber did not see any way in which an objective basis for value standpoints could be arrived at, and, in his determination to emphasize the responsibility of the individual for his own actions, he leaned towards almost maintaining that the basis of value judgments themselves was arbitrary. Weber himself, however, would argue that to claim that discourse about values is distinct from scientific discourse is by no means to assert that it is irrational.

The second unifying theme in Weber's methodological writings is what might be called an attempt to give an account of the sociological *a priori*. Recognizing that the natural science categories of causation did not apply in the human studies, he sought to give an account of the way in which entities called social relations and groups might be thought of as being constructed, and the way in which they affected individual behaviour. As Weber saw it, social relations could be thought of as arising in meaningful action in which one actor took account of the behaviour of another. Thus the entities, which appear as compelling human behaviour from outside, are seen as human creations, potentially capable of being changed by human beings. This perspective is sometimes called methodological individualism and leads to Weber saying that explanations which are causally adequate should be supplemented by explanations which are adequate on the level of meaning. It is an approach which stands in sharp contrast to Durkheim's assertion that social facts should be treated as things. In these terms Weber went on to develop concepts of social structure which he called ideal types. At first these were types which were very specific and related to his own values. In *Economy and Society*, however, they were more abstract and less relativistic.

Weber has often been contrasted with Karl Marx, and has been said to have 'carried on a lifelong dialogue with the ghost of Karl Marx', or to be the 'bourgeois Marx'. In fact, in most areas, his work is complementary to rather than opposed to Marx. He has the advantage over Marx in not having to come to terms with a Hegelian philosophical vocabulary, and some have argued that restating Marx in a language free of metaphysics would lead to accounts of the mode of production, social relations of production, social classes and the state which are very close to Weber's. It is not true that Weber offered some kind of spiritual determinism which was at an opposite extreme to Marx's materialist determinism. He explicitly denied this. What he did do was to give a structural and methodologically individualist account of the full range of social institutions in history, which included the institutions of production, but also all those other institutions which Marx was inclined to refer to, having the critique of Hegel in mind, as mere ideas, or institutions of the superstructure. Where perhaps Weber did differ from Marx was in his theory of class. He certainly distinguished class from status, as Marx would have done, but he saw class conflict as bargaining going on in any market situation, and going on indefinitely, because he had accepted marginalist economics, whereas Marx, basing himself on the labour theory of value, saw the concept of class as leading, not to bargaining, but to revolution.

At the end of his life Weber was much involved in politics and wrote some quite ephemeral documents, including an account of socialism designed to stop its spread in the army. He also offered himself unsuccessfully as a candidate in the elections in the new Weimar Republic. More interesting from a sociological point of view were his last lectures which have been preserved from student notes and which are published under the title *General Economic History* (*Wirtschaftsgeschichte*, 1924, trans. 1961). On the political level he remained unconvinced that a transition of advanced industrial societies to socialism would mean anything else but the extension of rationalism and bureaucracy to its ultimate point, a prospect which he viewed with horror. To the end he remained a Kantian seeking to the point of despair to find a way in which individuals could remain free of an increasingly reified society.

Professor John Rex

Weber's systematic sociology is set out in his *Economy and Society* (3 vols, 1968). The best introduction to Weber's methodological ideas can be found in *The Methodology of the Social Sciences* (1949), a selection and translation of his essays by Shils and Finch, to be taken with *Roscher and Knies* (1976), trans. Guy Oakes. Other translations include: *The Religion of China* (1953); *Ancient Judaism* (1952); *The Religion of India* (1958) – all from the *Gesammelte Aufsältze zur Religionssoziologie*; *The Agrarian Sociology of Ancient Civilizations* (1974). See also *From Max Weber*, ed. H. Gerth and C. Wright Mills (1946). About Weber: Marianne Weber, *Max Weber* (*Max Weber, Ein Lebensbild*, 1926, trans. 1950); Reinhard Bendix, *Max Weber, An Intellectual Portrait* (1962); Julien Freund, *The Sociology of Max Weber* (*Sociologie de Max Weber*, 1966, trans. 1968).

511
WEBERN, Anton (von) 1883–1945

Austrian composer

Born into the minor Austrian nobility, Webern studied music history with Guido Adler at the University of Vienna, at the same time taking lessons in composition privately with Arnold Schoenberg*, to whom he remained – as did his fellow-student Alban Berg* – a lifelong 'friend and pupil'. In 1906 he was awarded a PhD for an edition of part of the *Choralis Constantinus* by Heinrich Isaac, a Flemish polyphonist of the late fifteenth century.

Although he was to be busy for the rest of his life as a composer, he could never support himself financially by his music. Instead, he made up a living from conducting, private teaching (he never held an official teaching post), and work for his publishers. In the 1930s his music was vilified as 'cultural Bolshevism', and his later years were marked by an extreme withdrawal, which nevertheless saw the development of an important friendship with the poetess Hildegard Jone. In September 1945 he was accidentally shot dead by an American soldier of the Occupation.

Webern's oeuvre is relatively small: apart from a sizeable quantity of early works, a few unpublished later works, and a number of arrangements, there are only thirty-one pieces which bear opus numbers. Over half of these are vocal, his talent being essentially lyrical rather than dramatic. His work divides into three periods: a tonal phase (until *c*. 1907), an experimental 'anti-tonal' and early twelve-tone phase (*c.* 1907–24), and a final phase in which he adopted Schoenberg's twelve-tone serialism. His development as a composer is inseparable from that of his teacher: in his early years especially he could seize upon and extend the radical elements in Schoenberg's music with an intensity irksome to the older man. Unlike his teacher, however, he was a miniaturist by temperament, and few of his pieces last for more than ten minutes. His individuality lay in the extraordinary expressive concentration of his music, and his importance in the fastidiousness with which he refined and developed what he considered to be essentially traditional features of composition.

The works of the first, tonal period show an absorption of, on the one hand, the Classical formal principles of sonata and variation, and, on the other hand, the advanced melody, harmony, textures and instrumentation of composers such as Wagner, Richard Strauss*, Hugo Wolf and Mahler. Whereas the form of the *Passacaglia*, Op. 1, for example, may well have been suggested by the finale to Brahms's Fourth Symphony, the progressive transformation of its themes owes more, perhaps, to the practice of Strauss's tone-poems.

In the second phase, this principle of 'developing variation' gave way to that of 'constant variation'. Traditionally, music had proceeded through the statement, development and repetition of ideas. But now overt repetition was abandoned, leaving merely statement and continual development. This created a style analogous to written prose, and was characteristic of the predominantly negative principles of this phase: nothing was to be too concrete. Directionally-orientated harmony was replaced by 'wandering' harmony and a deliberate annulment of natural tonal hierarchies. The avoidance of familiar formal archetypes led Webern, as it had Schoenberg, to an 'expressionist' reliance on texts to determine the formal outlines of his music, which at this time was predominantly vocal. Indeed, the imaginative world of Webern's music in this period was inseparable from the work of the poets he set: George (Op. 3 and Op. 4), Rilke* (Op. 8), Trakl* (Op. 14), Strindberg (Op. 12) and Kraus* (Op. 13). He also set Goethe (Op. 12), folk texts (Op. 15) and sacred works (Op. 16).

The rootless subjectivity of this music probably derived from the sensitivity of the word-setting in Wagner's music-dramas – indeed, Webern's life-long fastidiousness in the observation of prosody would seem to owe to Wagner's *Sprechgesang* (speech-song, a heightened recitative). In Wagner the significance of the individual words could be enhanced through the inflexions of melody, harmony, rhythm and instrumental colour. Similarly, a wide range of colour is the hallmark of Webern's second phase, particularly in his Mahler-like predilection for unusual combinations of solo instruments, and in the resourcefulness of his ex-

ploitation of individual instrumental effects. The increased intensity of Webern's music, however, lay in his use of frequently angular and wide-leaping lines, and in his dramatic juxtaposition of extreme contrasts in tempo, dynamics, texture and articulation. These features appear most notably in a number of instrumental works written between 1909 and 1914: *Five Pieces for String Quartet* Op. 5; *Six Pieces for Large Orchestra* Op. 6; *Four Pieces for Violin and Piano* Op. 7; and the *Six Bagatelles for String Quartet* Op. 9.

Of such brevity was this music that the publication of Op. 9 was accompanied by an apologia from Schoenberg: 'To express a novel in a gesture, joy in a single breath: such concentration can only be found where self-pity is lacking in equal measure.' In the years after the First World War, therefore, it was partly through an urge to create large structures, and partly through a wish to re-align himself with a musical tradition rooted in Bach and Beethoven, that Webern was led to adopt the twelve-tone system. By fixing the twelve notes of the chromatic scale into a series, which was then unfolded in different versions and transpositions, a new formal classicism could be built out of the previous rootlessness. This neo-classicism also extended into details of melodic structure and textural organization. After three exploratory vocal works (Opp. 17–19) we find that his new, predominantly instrumental music bears Classical titles: *Trio* (Op. 20), *Symphony* (Op. 21), *Quartet* (Opp. 22 and 28), *Concerto* (Op. 24), *Variations* (Opp. 27 and 30) and *Cantata* (Opp. 29 and 31; also *Das Augenlicht*, Op. 26, for chorus and orchestra).

Webern's understanding of the twelve-tone system was arguably more probing – and his use certainly more consistent – than Schoenberg's. Although Schoenberg combined series in a quasi-polyphonic manner, it was Webern who had a deeper grasp of what Milton Babbitt* was to describe as 'combinatoriality'. His earlier procedure of developing small, motivic cells led now to the principle of 'derivation', the division of the chromatic scale into identically constituted cells. Webern also re-introduced – though at a remote level – pitch hierarchies based on the tritone, the diminished seventh or the augmented chord, to govern large-scale musical movement. His scholarly interest in Flemish polyphony had led in the second phase to an extensive exploration of canon, which assumed a greater significance in the twelve-tone works, especially through the exploitation of the harmonic properties of canon-by-inversion.

It was the radicalism of the aesthetic attitudes accompanying these works, however, that was to prove so influential, even though, or perhaps because, they were so deeply rooted in certain nineteenth- and early twentieth-century intellectual currents. Webern's account of music history was historicist and evolutionary: his own music was to be the latest, highest and most inevitable stage in the development of Western (German) music. It would render the need to study earlier theory 'obsolete'. He attempted a Bach-like integration of different *ideas* (polyphony, accompanied melody, etc.) with the newly-conquered twelve-tone *language*. He admired above all everything that led to the greatest possible structural unity, frequently citing Kraus's demands for a moral responsibility towards language, Goethe's work on colour theory and plant metamorphosis, and Bach's purely pedagogic work *The Art of the Fugue*. The latter he described as the 'highest reality', on account of the 'abstract' complexities emanating from a single theme. In such works as the *String Quartet* Op. 28 he aimed at a comparable abstraction, convinced that 'composition with twelve-tone technique has achieved a degree of complete unity that was not even approximately there before'.

These attitudes, far from representing a *volte face* with respect to the preceding Expressionist works, merely redress the imbalance that these in turn had created with respect to his early music. Indeed, most of his later music retains something of the earlier spare, expressive urgency. In the post-1945 era, however, it was principally with abstraction, and less with expression, that Webern's name was associated. With the subsequent international movement towards the extension of the orderable domains of *language*, traditional concern with *idea* in Webern's music was deemed obsolete, and a complete schism with all but the most recent past was effected. Whilst, since its inception, the adequacy of the twelve-tone system as a musical language has always been in dispute, the arguably deleterious effect of this schism on the composition, criticism, teaching and performance of modern music has only more recently been called into question.

Although it seems unlikely that Webern's reputation will ever again stand as high as it did in the 1950s, any revaluation can only emphasize the expressive qualities of some of his later music. Through setting the words of the nature-loving Hildegarde Jone (Opp. 23, 25, 26, 29 and 31), he developed a uniquely tender lyricism which finds its most perfect utterance in the second movement of the *Concerto* Op. 24. It was with such pieces in mind that Stravinsky* remarked: 'Whether there are great, or only new and very individual feelings in his music is a question which I can only answer for myself, but for me Webern *has* a power to move.'

Christopher Wintle

Webern's principal compositions, all of which are mentioned above, are published by Universal Edition, others by Boosey & Hawkes. Source writings include: *The Path to the New Music* (trans. Leo Black, 1963), and *Letters to Hildegarde Jone and Josef Humplik* (trans. Cornelius Cardew, 1967). Important books on Webern include: H. Moldenhauer, *Anton Webern: a Chronicle of his Life and Work* (1978); W. Kolnedar,

Anton Webern (trans. Humphrey Searle, 1961); H. Moldenhauer and D. Irvine (eds), *Anton von Webern: Perspectives* (1966); and *Die Reihe*, vol. 2 (periodical). Other, mainly analytic, articles occur in *Perspectives of New Music, Music Quarterly, Score, Tempo, Music Review*. See also: R. Leibowitz, *Schoenberg and his School* (1949); G. Perle, *Serial Composition and Atonality* (1962).

512

WEIL, Simone 1909–43

French essayist

Simone Weil was born in Paris, where her father worked as a doctor. Like her elder brother André, she showed early signs of a precocious intelligence, fostered by her parents, who, though of Jewish origin, were free-thinking agnostics. André became a brilliant mathematician, an interest shared by Simone, one of her concerns being the problem of abstraction in modern science. She also possessed a facility for languages both ancient and modern. It was from this broad cultural base that her highly original and apposite commentary on the human condition was made.

At sixteen she studied under the philosopher Alain, whose cult of self-mastery and the individual moral will had a life-long influence on her. Other influences were Plato, Spinoza, Pascal, Rousseau, Kant and Descartes, whose Cogito she took as the starting point for her diploma dissertation at the École Normale Supérieure, which she attended from 1928 to 1931.

Simone Weil had a capacity for intense suffering, being prone to debilitating headaches and a conscience so sensitive to inequity that she drove herself inexorably both in her intellectual pursuits and in tearing herself away from them in order to experience the concrete affliction of industrial and agricultural labour. Repelled by the exercise of force, she nevertheless attempted to place herself in the thick of the action in the Spanish Civil War – and again in the French Resistance, this time without success. Her early death in England in 1943 was due to unwillingness to eat more than the rations she thought her compatriots were getting, which exacerbated her tuberculosis; but it undoubtedly also owed much to the exhausting tension of feeling herself to be cut off and ineffectual in the midst of a crisis.

Politically, she allied herself with the left, wishing to take the side of those against whom, she felt, the scales of justice were weighted. She wrote for various left-wing journals and was heavily involved with the trades unions even whilst working as a lycée teacher. She did not assume the conventional identity of either sphere, and attracted the opprobrium of both left and right for her outspoken advocacy of radical change. For the root of her activism was her spiritual insight, which led her to criticize the materialist side of Marx and its Soviet embodiment, as much as the other manifestations of what she apocalyptically called the Great Beast, such as Ancient Rome and Israel. She believed that the Nazis were playing out the blood-stained legacy of exclusivity bequeathed by the very culture they now sought to oppress. Although she embraced the Church in its esoteric aspect, the exoteric collusion of a vengeful Jehovah and Roman bureaucracy repelled her. Seeing as much spiritual validity in the religions of the East as in her own Western inheritance, Weil felt that she, like the Gnostics, must be anathema and therefore could not be baptized.

A sense of cultural heritage features prominently among the needs of the soul outlined in *The Need for Roots* (*L'Enracinement*, 1949, trans. 1952), which she wrote in London shortly before her death, as a programme for the spiritual regeneration of France. The rest of her writing consists of articles, notebooks and other fragments (including poems and an unfinished play), published in various arrangements after her death. She can in turn be mistaken for a Marxist anarchist or a conservative traditionalist, the prophet of tolerance and pacifism or the harbinger of a bleak, strife-torn vision. This has to be seen in the context of her attempt to effect a type of synthesis which is rare in the modern age: following Plato, she held that genuine truths must of necessity be paradoxical in character. We are mesmerized by the cave of illusions in which we live, and to free ourselves from this is almost impossibly difficult.

However, sustained by the few occasions on which she herself experienced the presence of the divine, Simone Weil attests that, as long as we do not rush to fill it with short-term comforts, the void of disillusion can act as a channel for grace. Thus is born a motive for overcoming our alienation from the reality of our condition.

Léonie Caldecott

Other works include: *Gravity and Grace* (*La Pesanteur et la grace*, 1947, trans. 1952); *Waiting on God* (*Attente de Dieu*, 1950, trans. 1951); *Oppression and Liberty* (*Oppression et liberté*, 1955, trans. 1958); *Seventy Letters* (1965); *First and Last Notebooks* (from *Cahiers*, 1956, trans. 1965). *Gateway to God*, ed. David Raper (1974) is an introductory selection of Weil's writings. A. Reynaud, *Simone Weil: Lectures on Philosophy* (*Leçons de philosophie*, 1959, trans. 1978) are reconstituted notes. See also: R. Rees, *Simone Weil: A Sketch for a Portrait* (1966); Simone Pétrement, *Simone Weil: A Life* (trans. 1976).

513
WEILL, Kurt 1900–50

German/US composer

One of the outstanding composers for the theatre in the twentieth century, Weill, a German-born Jew, studied composition with Albert Bing in Dessau and Humperdinck at the Berlin Hochschule. After brief stints as a Repetiteur in Dessau and Kapellmeister in Lüdensheid, Weill returned to Berlin in 1920 as one of six pupils chosen for Ferruccio Busoni's* master class at the Academy of Arts. Weill supplemented his training with counterpoint lessons from Phillip Jarnach, bolstered his income with earnings as chief critic for *Der deutsche Rundfunk*, and broadened his intellectual horizons through membership in Berlin's November Group. In 1933 Weill and his wife, singer-actress Lotte Lenya, both on the Nazis' blacklist, fled to Paris. Two years later they moved to New York, where Weill devoted his energies to the Broadway musical stage until his death in 1950.

Weill assimilated the innovations of the post-Wagnerian generation of German composers (especially Mahler, Reger and Strauss*) in his earliest mature works: String Quartet in B minor (1919), Sonata for Cello and Piano (1920), and Symphony No. 1 (1921). Although all remained unperformed and unpublished during his lifetime, stylistic elements revealed here became firmly entrenched in Weill's musical language: semitonal shifts between successive sonorities, employment of fifth-generated diatonic structures, continual vacillation between major and minor, textures animated by reiterated propulsive rhythmic figures, and the underlying 'romantic' premise that no amount of irony or self-conscious denial could camouflage.

Under Busoni's tutelage until 1924, Weill adopted classic and pre-classic models in composing 'absolute' music characterized by formal concision and clarity of texture. The most successful of these works are the String Quartet No. 1 (Op. 8, 1923) – the first of Weill's compositions accepted for publication, the song cycle *Frauentanz* (Op. 10, 1923), and *Quodlibet* (Op. 9, 1923) – the orchestral suite that Weill extracted from his first theatrical work, the ballet-pantomime *Die Zaubernacht* (1922). *Recordare* (Op. 11, 1923), an *a cappella* setting of the fifth chapter of Jeremiah, *Divertimento* (1922), and *Sinfonia sacra* (1922) perpetuate the religious symbolism so evident in Symphony No. 1, where the chorale idiom had first appeared.

Weill's operatic début, the one-act tragedy *Der Protagonist* (Op. 15, 1926), was the first product of his collaboration with the prolific Expressionist playwright, Georg Kaiser. This stunning score established Weill's reputation as the leading composer for the theatre of his generation and already employed his own technique of 'aesthetic distancing'. Although still tonal, its musical language is rivalled in complexity only by the Violin Concerto (Op. 12, 1925), and its success inspired a companion comic one-act, *Der Zar lässt sich photographieren* ('The Czar has his Photograph Taken', Op. 21, 1928). After the Weill–Brecht* collaboration had ended in 1931 with Brecht denouncing his colleague as a 'phony Richard Strauss', Weill again turned to Kaiser for his last work for the German stage, *Der Silbersee* ('The Silver Lake', 1933).

Although Weill is best known for his collaborations with Bertolt Brecht, the notion (implied by Brecht and echoed in much secondary literature) that Weill was merely a musical amanuensis and that the dramatist was responsible for stylistic shifts in Weill's music is spurious. In fact, Weill had already incorporated modern dance idioms and the instrumentation of jazz, which he called an international folk music, in the cantata *Der neue Orpheus* (Op. 16, 1927), and the one-act film-opera *Royal Palace* (Op. 17, 1927) – almost two years before he initiated the collaboration with Brecht. Weill found in Brecht a librettist whose sociological and theatrical goals were sufficiently similar to his own to yield six works for the stage, three cantatas, and a number of incidental pieces.

By far the most successful was *The Threepenny Opera* (*Die Dreigroschenoper*, 1928), which was translated into eighteen languages for more than 10,000 performances within five years of its premiere. Its unsuccessful imitator, *Happy End* (1929), contains some of Weill's best 'Songs', a genre created by Weill and Brecht from various popular models as the central structural unit of epic opera. The epic style with its aesthetic distance (*Verfremdungseffekt*) and gestic music was first tested in the *Mahagonny Songspiel* (1927) and then expanded to monumental proportions in *Aufstieg und Fall der Stadt Mahagonny* ('Rise and Fall of the City Mahagonny', 1930). Epic features are no less prominent in the *Schuloper, Der Jasager* ('The Yes-Sayer', 1930) and the didactic cantata *Der Lindberghflug* ('Lindbergh's Flight', 1929), both of which enjoyed numerous performances in German schools. The third member of the artistic triumvirate of epic opera, Caspar Neher, wrote the libretto for *Die Bürgschaft* ('The Trust', 1933), which Weill hailed as his return to pure music-making after the Brechtian detour.

The Brecht–Weill partnership was revived briefly in Paris when both suffered the common fate of exile for *Die sieben Todsünden* ('The Seven Deadly Sins', 1933), a ballet with singing staged by Balanchine. During his two-year stay in France, Weill also completed his Symphony No. 2 (1934), *Marie galante* (1934) – a play by Jacques Deval – and the operetta *A Kingdom for a Cow* (1935). Although Brecht repeatedly attempted to renew the association in America, Weill was too successful in his 'second career' to retrace his steps.

With the expressed purpose of continuing his lifelong devotion to musical theatre, Weill hoped to create a genuine American operatic tradition through the popular Broadway medium. To this end he recruited a long list of illustrious dramatists: Paul Green (*Johnny Johnson*, 1936), Maxwell Anderson (*Knickerbocker Holiday*, 1938; *Lost in the Stars*, 1949), Moss Hart (*Lady in The Dark*, 1941), Ogden Nash (*One Touch of Venus*, 1943), Ira Gershwin (*The Firebrand of Florence*, 1945), Alan J. Lerner (*Love Life*, 1948), and Elmer Rice (*Street Scene*, 1947). More than any of his compatriots, Weill was successful in establishing a new identity in his adopted culture. He maintained the craftsmanship and formal invention of his European works, yet depicted Americana in *Street Scene* and the folk opera *Down in the Valley* (1945) as vividly as he had mirrored the milieu of the Weimar Republic in his earlier works. Unfortunately Weill's ultimate goals for American opera were left unfulfilled when he was felled by a coronary while composing a musical version of *Huckleberry Finn*.

Dr Kim H. Kowalke

About Weill: *Über Kurt Weill*, ed. David Drew (1975); Helmut Kotschenreuther, *Kurt Weill* (1962); *Weill – Lenya*, ed. Henry Marx (1976); Gottfried Wagner, *Weill und Brecht: Das musikalische Zeittheater* (1977); Kim H. Kowalke, *Kurt Weill in Europe* (1979).

514
WELLES, George Orson 1915–

US film director

Revered by Modernists such as Jean-Luc Godard*, Welles's work centres on themes remote from Modernist concerns. From his appearance as Death in the early short *The Hearts of Age* (1934) the processes of mortality, corruption and the erosion of innocence haunt his films. Even if the perspectives are altered, the blueprint of classical tragedy, of hubris and nemesis, determines the structure of Welles's dramas, which are played out somewhere between life and legend. Two other traditions also meet in Welles: the ancient art of the storyteller, and the more recent association of the cinema, via Georges Méliès, with the Barnum skills of illusionism. Welles's delight in presenting himself as prestidigitateur is no peripheral eccentricity, but a reason for his exhilarated display of cinematic resources: 'This is the biggest electric train set any boy ever had,' he remarked of the set for *Citizen Kane* (1941).

The son of an inventor and a concert pianist, Orson Welles attended Todd School in Woodstock, Illinois, and there became active in theatre. After directing and acting in plays at the Gate Theatre, Dublin, he returned to America and founded the Mercury Theatre in 1937, and with its company presented a series of radio plays, including the notorious adaptation of H.

G. Wells's* *The War of the Worlds* which panicked many listeners into believing that a Martian invasion was actually taking place. This brought Welles a Hollywood contract that gave him an unusual degree of artistic and financial control, but also fuelled suspicion and dislike. His subsequent career casts light on the contradictions of an industry simultaneously demanding creativity and submission to standardized practices. Like Erich von Stroheim before him, Welles was frequently to discover that studios preferred him to be in front of rather than behind the camera.

His first still-born project was an adaptation of Conrad's* *Heart of Darkness* (later the basis of Coppola's *Apocalypse Now*, 1979). *Citizen Kane* thus became Welles's astonishing début. Many of the stylistic devices of this deservedly famous film – deep-focus compositions, flashback structure, overlapping dialogue, chiaroscuro lighting effects, bizarre camera angles – had a clear lineage, and even the character of Kane himself can be seen as a hybrid of William Randolph Hearst, Fitzgerald's* Gatsby, Howard Hughes and Welles himself; but Welles's massive achievement was to make all these elements entirely pristine as he found expressive use for what had frequently been mere decoration. Described by Borges* as 'a centreless labyrinth', the film is built around a search for the key to the personality of the dead Kane. From a welter of recollections emerges a bleak tale of irremediable loss of innocence, betrayal of hope and love, and the misuse of great power. But because of Welles's exuberant visual style, and the carefully woven web of symmetries and complexity, the impact of *Kane* is anything but bleak.

Following *Kane*, a critical success but relative financial failure, Welles directed *The Magnificent Ambersons* (1942), an elegiac evocation of the decline of a minor aristocratic family at the turn of the century, and his only completed picture in which he does not himself appear. New management at RKO led to its re-editing in Welles's absence and subsequent release in a version 45 minutes shorter than Welles's own. It was not the last time he was to experience such treatment. *Touch of Evil* (1958), a masterpiece of *film noir* which marked his return to Hollywood direction, was shrugged off by Universal without even a trade showing. Ostensibly a banal police story, *Touch of Evil* explores the contradictions between being 'a great detective but a lousy cop' in a meditation on the law that has the maturity to separate principles from their proponents. But, *Kane* apart, it was perhaps only in Shakespeare that Welles could find a physical space large enough for his characters. Three films based on Shakespearian drama (*Macbeth*, 1948, *Othello*, 1952, and *Falstaff*, or *Chimes at Midnight*, 1966), although uneven, project a personal vision without prejudice to the complexity of human nature. The increasing bitterness of his later works finds respite in *Chimes at Midnight*, hailed by some critics as a premature testament and product of a talent that had finally transcended the qualities that gave it birth.

Rejecting Eisenstein's* practice of creating cinematic meaning through the juxtaposition of shots in montage and the isolation of images in close-up, Welles chose to organize his world through intricate camera movements, deep-focus compositions and long takes (the opening, three-minute tracking shot of *Touch of Evil* is a famous example). Such a style democratizes the image, allowing the audience to immerse itself in the dramatic reality of the scene, but the constant camera movement establishes a tension between involvement and distance, between compassion and irony – a tension that is central to Welles's work. Despite his troubled relationships with studio hierarchies, Welles has had enormous influence on both Hollywood and European directors through his demonstration of the expressive powers of cinema, particularly those that derive from large-scale production, and through the magnanimity of his vision. Welles is a hard act to follow, but Francis Coppola, Martin Scorsese and Stanley Kubrick must all be considered at least partial inheritors.

Nigel Algar

Other films include: *The Stranger* (1946); *The Lady from Shanghai* (1948); *The Trial* (1962); *The Immortal Story* (1968); and *F for Fake* (1973). Welles also directed a film version (1955, *Confidential Report* in the UK) of his own novel *Mr Arkadin* (1954). See: André Bazin, *Orson Welles* (rev. 1958, trans. 1978); Joseph McBride, *Orson Welles* (1972).

515
WELLS, Herbert George 1866–1946

British writer

Journalist, novelist, popular historian and sociologist, H. G. Wells was a considerable influence in encouraging the modern mentality which brought scientific scepticism to bear on social, moral and religious questions during the early twentieth century. The logical outcome of the long curve which ran from the Renaissance through the Encyclopedists to T. H. Huxley, a curve sustained by the conviction that man was a rational being, Wells believed that once enlightened education had become universal and scientific techniques widely accepted, half the problems of mankind would be solved.

His beginnings were in complete contradiction to these lofty preoccupations. His father ran a shop in Bromley, Kent, which combined chinaware with cricket accessories, and Wells was born in a small bedroom over the shop. His mother, a simple woman of lower-middle-class origin, reached the height of her ambitions when she became housekeeper to Miss Featherstonhaugh who owned a mansion known as Up Park. It was at Up Park that Wells met some of the characters later to appear in his novel *Tono-Bungay* (1909), 'her leddyship' being drawn as a vivid caricature of his mother's employer.

A scant education led to his becoming a draper's assistant, but the life so appalled him that he quickly ran away. After several false starts he became a chemist's assistant, a post which revealed his lack of Latin. However, he astonished his tutor at Midhurst Grammar School by mastering the greater part of Smith's *Principia* in five hours, and after that nothing could stop his educational advance. At eighteen he won a scholarship to study biology at the Normal School of Science in London, then dominated by T. H. Huxley. The three years he spent there provided the scientific raw material from which he distilled the first wave of his scientific fiction.

Living in near-poverty as a teacher of science, he married his first cousin, Isabel Mary Wells, in 1891: an unfortunate choice which merely increased his financial problems. The *Pall Mall Gazette* printed his first article 'On the Art of Staying at the Seaside', in the same year, and thus began his lifelong habit of emptying his mind on the printed page in journalistic form whenever some urgent question demanded quick expression. Any conflict between his scientific training and his journalistic outpourings, however, was resolved when he wrote his first science-fiction story *The Time Machine* (1895), on the appearance of which W. T. Stead described Wells as 'a man of genius'. Constructing a brilliantly symbolized Time Machine, the Traveller flashes forward to the year 802701 and enters a society divided into two classes, the Morlocks, living and working in caves beneath the earth, and the Eloi, a class of graceful decadent sybarites. 'Man had not remained one species but had differentiated into two distinct animals', the result of the widening of differences between Capital and Labour. *The Time Machine* was a social allegory written with a poetic intensity its author never recaptured. Close on its heel came *The Wonderful Visit* (1895), *The Island of Doctor Moreau* (1896), *The Invisible Man* (1897) and *The War of the Worlds* (1898). Wells knew just how to unlock the imaginative worlds, the latent excitements, buried beneath dull scientific data, but behind the virtuosity lay a deep concern for man and society. There were many comparisons with the work of Jules Verne, but the heroes of Verne's novels were idealized creatures turning invention to their own private account with little concern for the social problems that preoccupied Wells. He saw that he could harness scientific discovery to revolutionize our lives in ways as yet unforeseen. He also realized that science might run off in Frankenstein abandon, gathering more and more power over nature while the ordinary human being had less and less power over himself. He understood his scientific implications to be highly romantic, but each story carried a message, and it was the message that mattered when the drama had exhausted itself. Indeed, his concern for social problems soon drove him to abandon science fiction in favour of his lower-middle-class comedies: *Love and Mr Lewisham* (1900), *Kipps* (1905), and *The History of Mr Polly* (1910). Unlike Dickens, what people did for a living became vital in his books, reflecting the organization of society, its greatest evil, the future always more important than the past or present. However, it was no accident that *Kipps* and *A Modern Utopia* were published in the same year. Wells was simply unable to express all his ideas in fiction. The scientist in him tried to shake off the novelist with *A Modern Utopia*, while the artist clamoured for comic simplicities untroubled by any vestige of science. In *Kipps* and *The History of Mr Polly* Wells drew heavily on his own attempts to climb from lower- to middle-class life, and he became the spokesman for millions of inarticulate people whose frustrations had never achieved such realistic expression in fiction before. Similarly, *Ann Veronica* (1909) crystallized the desire for greater freedom of thousands of young women in the period when the book was written. Here was a middle-class daughter who defied her father, ran off and threw herself into the arms of the man she loved. Wells once again brought to the surface the rational attitude to sexuality latent in the minds of many of his readers. Implicit in these novels his belief in revolutionary progress found modified expression in *A Modern Utopia*, a vision of the future where society was divided into four entirely new classes: the Samurai, a voluntary nobility, the Poietic, the Kinetic, the Dull and the Base.

Attempting to translate theory into practice, Wells had joined the Fabian Society (a London-based group founded in 1883 and dedicated to transforming Great Britain into a socialist state) in 1903. Having created a following among many of the younger members, he quarrelled with the Executive, which included the Webbs* and challenged G. B. Shaw*. Finally he resigned with a burst of that invective which came so readily from his pen. Always impatient, a man who over-reacted to every situation, Wells now abandoned world-making to write what is perhaps his best novel, *Tono-Bungay*. This brought alive an ignorant little man, Uncle Ponderevo, a combination of Whitaker Wright (the financial fraud) and someone in the likeness of all ambitious shopkeepers, to foist on the world a patent medicine, following through its social and psychological consequences with a skill that impressed even Henry James. It was a devastating criticism of unfettered private enterprise in a capitalist society.

However, during the period of the First World War Wells's power as a novelist declined, and it was not until the 1920s that his reputation was restored when he took on the mantle of public educator with *The Outline of History* (1920), a massive survey of world history, and its altogether more successful, 'introduction', *A Short History of the World* (1922). This was a vividly written account that traced the evolution of man from the biological beginnings to his technological incarnation. Already, in several of his novels, he had brought men together as a species, over-ruling national divisions and seeing them in the light of a common destiny. Now he set out to counteract the insidious distortions of national histories with the conception of One World, the outcome of one people and one history. Despite its journalistic shortcomings and lack of precision, it was a remarkable feat which reached an audience of millions. Wells followed it with a number of huge rambling books with all-embracing titles like *The Work, Wealth and Happiness of Mankind* (1932), compendiums of information intended to enlighten the average man.

His later work became repetitious, re-echoing his earlier messages and culminating finally in the despairing *Mind at the End of Its Tether* (1945), which pictured a jaded world 'devoid of recuperative power'. Written during the Second World War, its pessimism can also be attributed to the fact that Wells himself was under sentence of death: doctors told him he would not last another year, and, on 13 August 1946, he duly died aged eighty.

Born into a lower-class background, Wells might have remained a straightforward rebel against society, but it was in a voluntary nobility that he put his trust in the end. Devoted to the ways of science, his brave new worlds were more mystic than scientific. Impatient when people were not driven to action by his plans, they were plans frequently incapable of practical interpretation. A devotee of collectivism, of the group, of the belief that the individual was only a biological device which would decline when it had outlived its use, he stood alone himself against half the world and spectacularly burst out of every group he joined. He was a prophet who expected to be honoured in his own land, a brilliant example of what the ordinary man could become with grave misgivings about the proletariat. As a science-fiction writer he alerted the world to the dangers and benefits of scientific technologies, as a novelist he brought enlightenment and entertainment to a very large audience, as a mass educator he opened areas of knowledge relatively unknown to his readers, as a prophet his predictions were sometimes true, sometimes false. If he never achieved academic respectability, that in his own eyes was a tribute to his powers.

Vincent Brome

Wells's other books include: science fiction: *When the Sleeper Wakes* (1899); *The First Men in the Moon* (1901); novels: *The New Machiavelli* (1911); *Mr Britling Sees It*

Through (1916); non-fiction: *Anticipations* (1901); *New Worlds for Old* (1908); *The Open Conspiracy* (1928); *The Science of Life* (1931, with G. P. Wells); and the immensely readable *Experiment in Autobiography* (1934). About Wells: Geoffrey H. Wells, *H. G. Wells: A Sketch for a Portrait* (1930); Vincent Brome, *H. G. Wells* (1951); J. Kargalitski, *The Life and Thought of H. G. Wells* (trans. from the Russian, 1966).

516
WESKER, Arnold 1932–

British dramatist

Born in the East End of London to a working-class Jewish family, Wesker left school at sixteen, and spent the next ten years in a variety of semi-skilled jobs; he also completed two years' National Service in the RAF. In 1956 he wrote a television play, *The Kitchen*, which was turned down by every company to which he sent it. Undeterred, he went on to write, with more success, a full-length play for the theatre, *Chicken Soup with Barley*, staged at Coventry in 1958, and later transferring to the Royal Court. This was the first in a trilogy of plays – the others are *Roots* (1959) and *I'm Talking about Jerusalem* (1960) – in which Wesker first examined the problems of maintaining, and re-defining, socialist objectives in the context of post-war reality. He may have written with a surer hand since, but the Trilogy contains moments of unsurpassed brilliance. Following the success of *Chicken Soup with Barley*, Wesker revised *The Kitchen* for the stage in 1959. Set in the kitchen of a high-class restaurant, the play illustrates vividly the de-humanizing nature of the modern work-place. 'He works, he eats, I give him money. This is life, isn't it? What is there more?' The very rhythm of the play reveals the inadequacy of Marengo's view of life, even if it supplies no answers to his final question.

'I want to write about people in a way that will somehow give them an insight into an aspect of life which they may not have before. . . . I want to teach.' This was an uncompromising statement of intent made by Wesker in 1958, and one from which he has rarely deviated. In 1961, while in prison for his activities in the anti-nuclear campaign, he became Director of Centre 42, a TUC-sponsored project through which he and other writers and performers sought to make contact with larger audiences. His enthusiasm for the enterprise was based upon a belief in a latent desire amongst working people for greater participation in creative cultural activity: 'There's nothing wrong with football, only there's something wrong with *only* football. There's nothing wrong with rock 'n' rolling, only God preserve me from the girl that can do nothing else' (Ronnie Kahn in *Roots*). Wesker was criticized by some who saw him as neglecting the working-class heritage in order to propagate a bourgeois concept of culture. But while there is some justification in this, Wesker's principled stand against a brutalizing commercial 'culture' demands respect. Dissolved in 1971, Centre 42 was, with all its faults, a sad loss.

Wesker continued, during the 1960s and 1970s, to examine political issues in wholly human terms. In *The Four Seasons* (1965), Adam and Beatrice (or A and B) pass through the seasons of love, experiencing a love and pain which is common to us all. To lose the ability to love is to stop caring, and this lies at the heart of political disillusionment in much of Wesker's work. Death, too, is a universal in the perspective of which human actions must be judged, and Wesker has written poignantly about this most ironic fact of life in *The Friends* (1969) and *Love Letters on Blue Paper* (1977).

Since his initial success, Wesker has been neglected in Britain. He takes risks in his drama, moving from the stifling intimacy of *The Four Seasons* to the epic proportions of *The Journalists* (1975), a controversial dissection of Fleet Street. But he remains one of the major talents of the contemporary theatre, one who recognizes that 'Socialism isn't talking all the time, it's living, it's singing, it's dancing, it's being interested in what goes on around you, it's being concerned about people and the world.'

Paul Nicholls

Wesker's other plays include: *Chips with Everything* (1962); *Their Very Own and Golden City* (1965); *The Old Ones* (1972); *The Wedding Feast* (1974); *The Merchant* (1976, after Shakespeare). Amongst his other publications are: *Fears of Fragmentation* (1970); *Six Sundays in January* (1971); *Journey into Journalism* (1976). See: G. Leeming and S. Trussler, *The Plays of Arnold Wesker* (1971).

517

WHARTON, Edith 1862–1937

US novelist

Few writers have belonged so exclusively to the world described in their novels as Edith Wharton. Born in 1862, Edith Newbold Jones was the child of a rich and influential New York family settled in America since before the Revolution. The values in which she was reared during a dull and over-protected childhood were those typical of a society conscious of European cultural dominance – class, loyalty, respect for money and property and an almost slavish adulation of the old world. At twenty-three she married a socially acceptable Bostonian, Edward Wharton, and the pair spent the next few years travelling in Europe. Successful as the partnership was, Wharton's incipient mental illness produced increasing complications, and his wife's en-

forced solitude drove her to renew an earlier interest in fiction writing.

All her major novels are based on the New York and New England of her early years and are pervaded by an awareness of the rapid social change overtaking America during the closing decades of the century. The society portrayed in *The House of Mirth* (1905), her most successful book, is both rigidly entrenched and nervously aware of its own weakness. Thus the heroine Lily Bart, a genteel orphan riding for a fall in her pursuit of luxury, seems to challenge the assumptions of smart New York as much as she stands in awe of them. Her satirical antetype is offered in Undine Spragg, whose extravagant career of fortune-hunting and excitement-seeking in *The Custom of the Country* (1913) has wider applications, in its glimpses of the flashy, the heartless and the trivial, to the new America as seen by the somewhat embittered Mrs Wharton.

Her favourite theme of the spontaneous defeated by the conventional dominates *Ethan Frome* (1911), a terse, rather Hardyesque tale of an erotic triangle against a New England farming background, and *The Age of Innocence* (1920), arguably her finest achievement, in which the 1870s are lovingly re-created as a setting to a wistful chronicle of love. This novel, and various of her short stories, underline the author's sense of awkwardness in relation to the important shifts in ethics and mores which had taken place simultaneously with her development as a writer. She was both too old to embrace easily a world in which a Lawrence*, an Eliot* or a Scott Fitzgerald* were coming to maturity, and too young to turn her back on its novel significance.

As a writer she enjoyed considerable success, spending most of her later life in France, a country for which she had a truly American fondness. After her death her reputation underwent an inevitable slump, but with the post-war reappraisal of the work of her friend and mentor Henry James her novels were rediscovered and her role as one of the most discriminating of early twentieth-century writers of 'psychological' fiction was duly acknowledged.

James had the clearest influence on her development both in style and aim as a novelist, though she fails to rival him either in penetrative skill or verbal convolution. Like him she learned a great deal from the nineteenth-century French 'realist' school, and certain scenes in *The House of Mirth* read like less crudely sensational versions of Alphonse Daudet or Zola. Much also is owed in her work to English novelists such as Thackeray, whose Becky Sharp is an obvious model for Lily Bart and Undine Spragg, though there is no doubt that Mrs Wharton herself, as novelist and short-story writer, influenced the young Fitzgerald, writing warmly in praise of *The Great Gatsby* on its appearance in 1925. Thus she ranks, in her somewhat subdued, dignified fashion, as a crucial link between the Victorian and modern movements in American fiction.

Jonathan Keates

See: Irving Howe (ed.), *Edith Wharton: A Collection of Critical Essays* (1959); Millicent Bell, *Edith Wharton and Henry James* (1965); Grace Kellogg, *The Two Lives of Edith Wharton: The Woman and Her Work* (1965); Richard W. B. Lewis, *Edith Wharton: A Biography* (1975).

518
WHITE, Patrick Victor Martindale 1912–

Australian novelist

Patrick White was born in Knightsbridge while his parents, members of the Australian squattocracy, were paying one of their periodic visits to Europe. After spending most of his childhood in rural New South Wales he was sent unhappily back to England to finish his schooling at Cheltenham College. After a couple of years' jackerooing† in Australia, he shuttled back again and read modern languages at Cambridge from 1932 to 1935. In the 1930s he tried his hand at plays, poetry including a slim published volume, short stories and novels. In 1939 a first novel, *Happy Valley*, was published in London, followed in 1941 by *The Living and the Dead*, both of them unremarkable works in the modernist *lingua franca*; significantly, the former was set in the snow country of New South Wales and the latter in London. He sees the country and the city as 'like two different races'.

During the Second World War White served as an RAF intelligence officer in North Africa, the Middle East and Greece. Although he found the war 'one long bore', it fed his imagination first with desert landscapes, then with the depths of the Greek way of life and 'the perfection of antiquity'. In 1948 he published his first mature novel, *The Aunt's Story* (London), which remains the most experimental work of this structurally conservative novelist. He then returned to Australia with a Greek friend and they bought a farm at Castle Hill outside Sydney. Suburbia crept up on them, as it does on the Sarsaparilla of his novels, and they moved into the city in 1964. After long aloofness from public life, White became a strong supporter of E. G. Whitlam's Labour government (1972–5). He continues to believe in involvement in public life 'as everything grows rottener and rottener', but his novels eschew political themes.

White's major fiction is primarily concerned with the protestant quest for individual salvation, but the characters through whom he presents this are not Christians, even if the patterning of his books is sometimes accomplished by means of Christian motifs.

Theodora Goodman, heroine of *The Aunt's Story*, resembles many of her successors in her isolation, her social awkwardness, her asexuality and the incommunicability of her vision. The middle section of this tripartite novel is a marvellous rendition of Theodora's inner migration, the coruscating images bringing to life an individual and communal subconscious. She comes to the end of the book mad in the world's terms, but against the clarity of her presumed madness the world is judged.

The Tree of Man (1955) was the first novel White produced after his return to the peculiar vacancy of Australian life. He saw it as his task to 'suggest in this book every possible aspect of life, through the lives of an ordinary man and woman. But at the same time I wanted to discover the ordinary behind the ordinary, the mystery and the poetry.' In this large, slow, almost clumsy novel White offers us a sense of the moments of vision which are vouchsafed to inarticulate, working-class people of no especial glamour or talents. At the same time, he sees larger forces at work imposing their symbolic patterns on a whole community. By this point his vividly metaphorical and epigrammatic style was cutting both ways: creating epiphanies and pillorying the smug materialism of modern urban life.

In *Voss* (1957), his most majestic work, White delves back into Australian history, as into the history of romanticism. The central figure is a stiff, misunderstood, yet charismatic German who leads a doomed expedition into the central deserts. Here for the first time we find a telepathic communication between illuminati, Voss and Laura balancing, even from afar, as Yin and Yang, or self and anima; here, too, is a large symbolic patterning, based upon the events and characters of Christ's Passion, which prefigures *Riders in the Chariot* (1961), a book in which the Biblical parallels were to become undramatic, intrusive.

White is peculiarly eclectic about religious systems and their codes of symbolism. *Riders in the Chariot* draws heavily on Hasidic tradition for its portrayal of the Jewish martyr, Himmelfarb, while its quadripartite design owes much to the Book of Revelation; the twins in *The Solid Mandala* (1966) incorporate a Jungian* dualism; and so on. He sees that, although the religious systems have collapsed and become unavailable, their icons will still serve to image the quest after reality, the moments of vision which make life, even modern life, bearable.

His critics have frequently singled out the acid wit with which the novels lash suburban conformism. Yet his novels claim that a hunger for the truth behind appearances, an access to moments of insight, may be the lot of almost anybody, from the rich old dying lady in *The Eye of the Storm* (1973, the year of White's Nobel Prize for literature) to the ruthless painter, Hurtle Duffield, in *The Vivisector* (1970), a book marked out by fierce self-knowledge, to a proletarian housewife or an idiot. Businessmen are excluded, however: the world of action frequently seems inimical to that of the spirit. Even an active hero like the explorer, Voss, has earned his Australia 'by right of vision', a vision that is asocial, even hateful.

A similar idiosyncrasy of view is to be found in White's two volumes of short stories and in his plays of which *The Season at Sarsaparilla* and *Big Toys* (first produced 1977) are perhaps the best regarded. Rhetorical uncertainty in the plays throws light back on an interesting aspect of the novels: that they are not psychologically penetrating or inquisitive, but seek, in the comic tradition, to portray complex truths by the development of fixed characters, figures in a morality, as it were. The vivacious historical narrative of *A Fringe of Leaves* (1976) brings White closer to conventional story-telling and characterization than ever before.

Chris Wallace-Crabbe

Other works: *The Ploughman and Other Poems* (1935); *The Burnt Ones* (1964) and *The Cockatoos* (1974), both short stories; *Four Plays* (1965); *The Night of the Prowler* (1978), story and film script; *The Twyborn Affair* (novel, 1979). See also: Barry Argyle, *Patrick White* (1967); R. F. Brissenden, *Patrick White* (1966); Patricia A. Morley, *The Mystery of Unity* (1963); and G. A. Wilkes (ed.), *Ten Essays on Patrick White* (1970). Alan Lawson's *Patrick White* (1974) is a substantial bibliography.

†jackeroo: someone from a good background who works as a hand on a grazing estate.

519
WHITEHEAD, Alfred North 1861–1947

British mathematician and philosopher

Born in Kent, the son of an Anglican vicar, Whitehead went to school at Sherborne. In 1880 he entered Trinity College, Cambridge, where, as student, tutor and lecturer, he was to remain for the next thirty years. Although his only university 'subject' throughout this period was mathematics, he acquired extensive knowledge of many fields, including philosophy. After leaving Cambridge for London in 1910, he held various posts in University College, and later the professorship of applied mathematics at Imperial College (1914–24). Then, having reached normal retiring age, he accepted an invitation to start a new career in a new country as professor of philosophy at Harvard, a post he held until 1937. He died in Cambridge, Massachusetts.

Whitehead's early mathematical work culminated in the ten years of collaboration with his former pupil, Bertrand Russell*, that produced *Principia Mathematica* (3 vols, 1910–13). In this they attempted to demonstrate, rigorously and in detail, that logic and pure mathematics are not, as commonly supposed, mutually independent disciplines, but that the characteristic concepts of pure mathematics can be defined in terms of – and its propositions deduced from – those of logic. And while their thesis is far from commanding universal assent, *Principia Mathematica* is, in spite of rivals and reservations, still recognized as one of the major landmarks in the whole field of logic and the foundations of mathematics.

Whitehead's most important philosophical writings came late in his career, starting with *The Principles of Natural Knowledge* (1919), and drew upon an unusually wide range of background knowledge. In particular, he was one of the few thinkers of his time able to discuss relativity on something like equal terms with Einstein*; and in the *Principles* and its successor, *The Concept of Nature* (1920), an essential role is played by ideas borrowed from relativity theory – for example, that of nature as a four-dimensional structure of events, within which there are various different, and equally valid, ways of distinguishing its spatial from its temporal aspects. Whitehead's central problem in these works is one which dates a long way back in empirical philosophy: granted that nature is, as he says, 'that which we observe in perception through the senses', and that the task of science is to describe nature (or the more general features thereof), what is the function of such scientific concepts as those of points, lines, instants, elementary particles, etc., which are not, and could not be, instantiated in sense-perception? Whitehead uses his sophisticated technical apparatus to show how these concepts can be defined in terms of what *is* given in sense-perception – as sets of events progressively diminishing in content towards certain ideals of simplicity – and hence that the theories of exact science are not, as sometimes suggested, about something outside or underlying the world as we perceive it, but are actually descriptions (though of a logically somewhat complex kind) of that world.

In the last phase of his work, from *Science and the Modern World* (1925) onwards, Whitehead advanced from his philosophy of nature to an all-embracing cosmology in which ideas of growth and development became increasingly important. *Every* element of reality, every 'actual entity', whether in the field of biology, physics or psychology, is seen as organically related to its environment, like a plant to the soil in which it grows; it *is* literally a process of self-development or self-creation out of the material provided by its background, and then, the process completed, provides in its turn material for the self-creation of the next generation of actual entities. In his last major work, *Process and Reality* (1929), Whitehead develops this philosophy of organism into a complex system of categories by means of which he attempts to show the essential unity of reality, and present both sides of such time-honoured contrasts as flux and permanence, subjective and objective, God and the world, as mutually indispensable elements within a single totality. Because of its difficulty, and its remoteness in aims and methods from the main body of modern English-language philosophy, this last work received at first somewhat limited attention; but in recent years there has been, in several fields of interest, most notably that of philosophical theology, growing recognition of the relevance and potential value of its characteristic ideas.

Dr T. E. Burke

Other works include: *A Treatise on Universal Algebra* (1898); *The Principle of Relativity* (1922); *Religion in the Making* (1926); *Symbolism* (1927); *Aims and Education* (1929); *Adventures of Ideas* (1933). See: P. A. Schilpp (ed.), *The Philosophy of A. N. Whitehead* (1941), which includes Whitehead's autobiographical notes; and W. Mays, *The Philosophy of Whitehead* (1959).

520
WHORF, Benjamin Lee 1897–1941

US linguist

Benjamin Lee Whorf's is the name most commonly associated with the perennially attractive notion that one's perception and understanding of the world are largely imposed by one's language – so that speakers of different languages in a sense inhabit different worlds. As Whorf put it, 'the grammar . . . of each language is not merely a reproducing instrument for voicing ideas but rather is itself the shaper of ideas. . . . We dissect nature along lines laid down by our native languages.'

Whorf, a descendant of seventeenth-century English emigrants to Massachusetts, was an amateur scholar. He took a degree in chemical engineering at the Massachusetts Institute of Technology, and in his professional career he pioneered the application of this discipline to fire prevention in the chemical industry. Whorf carried out extensive research in linguistics purely as a hobby, and resisted invitations to enter academic life; his engineering career permitted him enough leisure to pursue his studies and to cultivate contacts with the world of academic linguistics at Yale, where the chief influence on his thinking was Edward Sapir*.

Whorf argued his general theoretical notion mainly via detailed studies of the Hopi language of the American south-west. According to Whorf, Hopi is a 'timeless' language; the concept of time as a linear dimension akin to the dimensions of space is not encoded in the structure of Hopi (for instance, Hopi does not extend words for spatial relationships to temporal relationships, as we commonly do in English phrases

such as '*in* the *following* year', '*between* sunrise and sunset'), and correspondingly the Hopi are unaware of time in our sense. The nature of Western physics, Whorf suggests, is heavily influenced by the nature of the European languages spoken by the pioneers of physics; if science had happened to originate among the Hopi rather than in Europe, we could expect modern physics to look very different from what it is.

The extent to which Whorf's thesis is controversial depends on the degree of abstractness of the concepts claimed to be language-relative. When these concepts are fairly concrete there is little debate, e.g. it has been well established that people's ability to remember exact shades of colour depends on the colour-terminology of their language. Whorf recognized that his claim was surprising mainly as it applied to very general ideas such as the basic concepts of physics.

One common line of criticism suggests that the 'Whorf hypothesis' is empty because untestable: what possible evidence could confirm that the exotic features of the Hopi language reflect exotic ways of thinking, rather than merely unusual modes of expressing thoughts which in themselves are much like ours? This objection perhaps stresses the term 'hypothesis' unduly; it may be that we should regard Whorf's idea not as an empirical scientific hypothesis but as a philosophical thesis which can at best be made plausible, never decisively confirmed or refuted.

But another problem is that, even if differences of language are admitted to reflect differences of thought, we are not entitled to assume (as Whorf did assume) that language determines thought rather than vice versa. Indeed, if acceptance of the world view associated with a given language were as 'absolutely obligatory' as Whorf claimed, how is it that physical theories as diverse as, say, those of Newton and Einstein* could have been worked out by speakers of what Whorf himself lumped together as practically one language, 'Standard Average European'? Whorf's point about Hopi physics could be answered by suggesting that, if the Hopi had happened to develop science, then the structure of the Hopi language might have come to be very different from what it is.

Geoffrey Sampson

A selection of Whorf's papers, including most of those concerned with linguistic relativity, is published as *Language, Thought, and Reality*, ed. J. B. Carroll (1956). For a critique, see H. Gipper, *Gibt es ein sprachliches Relativitätsprinzip?* (1972).

521
WIENER, Norbert 1894–1964

US mathematician

A child prodigy, Norbert Wiener was born in Columbia, Missouri, of Russian parentage. His early education was provided by his father Leo Wiener, Professor of Slavonic Languages and Literature at Harvard University. Norbert entered the Graduate School at Harvard, initially to study zoology, at the astonishing age of fifteen – having graduated in mathematics at Tufts College the previous year! In 1913 the young Norbert, still only eighteen, received his Doctorate for a thesis on mathematical logic. The teenage Dr Wiener then travelled to Europe with the aid of a Harvard scholarship. In Cambridge Russell* advised him to concentrate on mathematics – advice which he took, and which shaped his subsequent career. In Göttingen he studied briefly with the master mathematician David Hilbert. Returning to America at the beginning of the First World War, he tried his hand at various occupations before becoming an instructor at the Massachusetts Institute of Technology, in the mathematics department. Wiener remained at the Institute for the rest of his life as full Professor from 1932.

During his career Wiener made significant contributions in various branches of mathematics, including Quantum Theory, Brownian motion and stochastic processes. His reputation and his importance, however, are linked with his work in Cybernetics. It was Wiener who coined the term 'Cybernetics' and, more importantly, put together the concepts which created a new and highly relevant science. His book *Cybernetics* (1948, revised 1961) caught the eye of the public and thereby exerted an influence far beyond the narrow professional circle of university mathematics.

Cybernetics was defined by Wiener as being 'the science of control and communication in the animal and machine'. That a tool or machine can be controlled by its user is a commonplace: that it could be given sensors or antennae to 'feel' its own environment and hence control itself was not – at least in 1948. This is what cybernetics is about: machines and biological processes which regulate themselves automatically, without the intervention of an intelligent agency. Wiener's conception of cybernetics developed out of his preoccupations with control theory, the mathematical analysis of information, and filtering theory (for example, how to get rid of random noise on a telephone line without losing the current message as well). The key impetus was probably some work which he undertook during the Second World War on how to point a gun to fire at a moving object. Cybernetics introduced a new terminology applicable alike to machines, robots, organic processes, biological populations, human groups and institutions. It consisted of words like *stability, information control, input, output, prediction, filtering* and, above all, *feedback*. Negative feedback occurs when a machine dampens its own activity to achieve a certain pre-selected performance. Positive feedback occurs when a machine stimulates its own activity, for example, a microphone picking up its own amplified

output which is then amplified even more, thus producing a high-pitched shriek known as 'hunting'. The sensitivity with which a machine interprets or reacts to its own message poses many deep mathematical problems and it was in this area that Wiener made his specialist contribution.

By isolating the self-regulatory aspects of a machine as being something worthy of separate study, Wiener considerably accelerated the development of the more modern, sophisticated concept of a machine. Before cybernetics emerged, machines were designed for certain conditions, and if the conditions changed, they failed. The *Titanic* sank, the R101 crashed, the tanks of 1917 were virtually invincible, the industrial steam engines took hours to reach full speed and hours to come to rest. Such artefacts lacked flexibility. They were man-made leviathans harnessing vast power, yet subject to little real control. But with the emergence of cybernetics machines were increasingly provided with built-in mechanisms to help them stay 'on course' – for example, the auto-pilot of an aeroplane, the stabilizers on a ferry. Windscreen wipers now parked themselves, central heating held its temperature, rockets balanced on their tails.

The outcome of this revolution is automation; and with the arrival of the microchip, automation is rapidly taking over many a job previously performed by a skilled person. Wiener himself in his book *The Human Use of Human Beings* (1950) was among the first to recognize that, as machines gradually take over their own regulation, the number of tasks requiring minimal human judgment inevitably diminishes. Wiener emphasized the positive side of this: that the extinct jobs were only machine-like jobs after all: that we should re-think human priorities to create more jobs requiring genuinely human judgment. It is a measure of Wiener's percipience that he saw both the problem and the lines on which a solution may be sought so many years ago.

Christopher Ormell

Wiener's other publications include: *God and Golem Inc: A Comment on Certain Points where Cybernetics Impinges on Religion* (1964); and two autobiographical volumes: *Ex-Prodigy* (1953) and *I am a Mathematician* (1956). For details of Wiener's specifically mathematical work, see *The Dictionary of Scientific Biography*, vol. XIV (1976). For a general comment on Wiener's work, see Abraham Kaplan, 'Sociology learns the Language of Mathematics', in *The World of Mathematics* (1956), also the *Bulletin of the American Mathematical Society*, January 1966.

522

WILLIAMS, Tennessee (Thomas Lanier) 1914–

US playwright

Twice a Pulitzer Prize winner, with *A Streetcar Named Desire* (1947) and *Cat on a Hot Tin Roof* (1955), Tennessee Williams is a playwright of great popularity who has utilized his own life and preoccupations to dramatic effect. He grew up, in Mississippi and Missouri, in an often poor household dominated by his mother, a former Southern belle making a difficult adjustment to the twentieth century, and coloured by the disturbing presence of a delicate and extremely neurotic sister. His father was almost always away. Masculinity and femininity, roles and relationships, the Old and New Souths, the individual and society, weak men and strong women, artists and outsiders, violence, maladjustment and alienation: these were the concerns of Williams's life and have become the themes of his plays. These can be read as documents and as analyses, but they also embody a perpetual quest for self-knowledge, on the part of Williams, his surrogates and the rest of his characters.

Williams's first important play, *The Glass Menagerie* (1945), deals movingly with that time of his life when his mother was struggling to keep the home together, his sister was withdrawing from the world and he himself was faced with the necessity, as an artist, of leaving his womenfolk and of working out his own destiny. Nostalgia and hatred for a once halcyon, now debilitating past; reaction against and a desire for the conventional ties of home and family; mixed feelings of guilt and responsibility; a sense of yearning for ecstasy and self-expression – all were equally present in his next play, *A Streetcar Named Desire*, in which Marlon Brando so effectively created the role of Stanley Kowalski, the urban jungle brute, the 'Polack' who marries a genteel girl reared on a now bankrupt plantation and who is confronted, in a clash of cultures, by his wife's sister, Blanche Du Bois. Blanche is one of Williams's finest creations: a woman who feels she is virginal, sensitive and artistic, who in fact is promiscuous, selfish and superficially cultivated, yet who still represents, with pathos and power, whatever virtues may have accrued to civilization. In such later plays as *Summer and Smoke* (1948) and *Sweet Bird of Youth* (1959), Williams continued to represent the Old South as an aging belle and harsh contemporary reality as an aggressive young man. The two rarely come together, except with violence. Stanley rapes Blanche.

Williams admires D. H. Lawrence* a great deal, and in 1951 he wrote a play dedicated to Lawrence, *I Rise in Flames, Cried the Phoenix*. But there is nothing as satisfying as the relationship between Lady Chatterley and her gamekeeper in Williams's plays. In fact, Williams consistently suggests not only that the times are out of joint but seems to subscribe, fatalistically, to a belief in the inevitably unsatisfactory nature of all relationships. Love is rarely returned. In *Cat on a Hot Tin Roof*, Big Mama loves Big Daddy, but the reverse is not true; similarly Maggie and Brick. Gooper and Mae are content with each other, but are unattractive to everybody else. Normality is unacceptable; but abnormality (Brick's homosexuality) offers no alternative.

Although obsessed with the isolation of the artist, with violence between individuals, with heightened sexuality, especially homosexuality, Williams is able to distance himself from his preoccupations. Few of his protagonists are unsympathetic, whether nymphomaniacs like Blanche or virgins like Hannah Jelkes in *The Night of the Iguana* (1961) or shy bachelors like Blanche's suitor Mitch. Only the cruel and perverting Sebastian of *Suddenly Last Summer* (1959) and the monstrous Boss Finley in *Sweet Bird of Youth* are without redeeming features. But only *Night of the Iguana*, Williams's most philosophical play, suggests that the playwright is, on occasion, reconciled to the human condition. Only in that play is there a willingness on the part of all the main characters to admit and accept the limitations of themselves and their universe. Most of Williams's characters are too large for life. To act them requires strength, even flamboyance; but when the casting is right – Anna Magnani as the lusty, remorseful Catholic widow, Serafina, in *The Rose Tattoo* (1950), for instance – the effect is compelling.

Most often Williams works to achieve social realism, though he uses symbols (the glass menagerie, the iguana, Blanche's lampshade), a poeticized language and even neo-expressionism to achieve his ends. *Camino Real* (1953), for example, is a fascinating and ambitious fable of love and death, and mixes the myths of Old World and New – Cassanova and Don Quixote rub shoulders with Kilroy. Williams has experimented with forms other than plays, having published four collections of short stories – *27 Wagons Full of Cotton* (1946), *One Arm* (1948), *Hard Candy* (1956), *Eight Mortal Ladies Possessed* (1975). One of his novels, *The Roman Spring of Mrs Stone* (1950) is not unimpressive. *In the Winter of Cities* (1956) contains Williams's favourites among his poems. His *Memoirs* (1970) are frank; so are the prefaces to his plays and a book by his mother Edwina Dakin Williams (as told to Lucy Freeman), *Remember me to Tom* (1963).

Dr Ann Massa

See: Signi Falk, *Tennessee Williams* (1978); Jac Tharpe (ed.), *Tennessee Williams* (1977); and Richard Leavitt (ed.), *A Tribute to Tennessee Williams* (1978).

523

WILLIAMS, William Carlos 1883–1963

US poet

The son of an Englishman and a Puerto Rican of French and Spanish extraction, Williams studied medicine at the University of Pennsylvania, where he began a lifelong association with the poet Ezra Pound*, and subsequently practised as a doctor in Rutherford, New Jersey, until his retirement in 1951. He also befriended Marianne Moore*, Hilda Doolittle, James Joyce*, W. B. Yeats*, E. E. Cummings*, Charles Demuth*, Marsden Hartley, and many other painters and writers. The American critic Hugh Kenner has asserted that 'American poetry groups itself around twin peaks, Williams and Whitman', while William Empson* has taken the contrary view that Williams 'renounced all the pleasures of the English language, so that he is completely American; and he says only the dullest things'.

Williams is the poet of the particular, the American, the local, and the fact. 'One has to learn', he said, 'what the meaning of the local is, for universal purposes. The local is the only thing that is universal.' Like Pound, he journeyed to Europe and took stock of important movements in the arts, but unlike Pound he rejected Europe in favour of finding the character and reality of his own American environment: 'I couldn't speak like the academy. It had to be modified by the conversation about me.' He learned from such artists as Henri Gaudier-Breszka and Wassily Kandinsky* both that emotions might be derived from the arrangements of surfaces (or words) and that by expressing his environment the poet might marry a sense of place and his imagination. Although he continually produced impressionistic and improvisatory work, Williams's own predilections were Cubist, as demonstrated in a short early poem 'To a Solitary Disciple'. He should in fact be clearly associated with a number of influential art movements, Expressionism, Constructivism and Dadaism, as well as with Cubism. In *Spring and All* (1923), for example, he employed Dadaist jokes, while *A Voyage to Pagany* (1928) illustrates his experiments in improvisation. Like Charles Olson* after him, Williams's abiding concern with the representation of reality, of space and time (motion), led him to draw on the philosophy of A. N. Whitehead* for a theoretical base to his inspiration. In *Science and the Modern World* (1948), for instance, Whitehead stated that 'The objectivist holds that the things experienced and the cognisant subject enter into the common world on equal terms.' Williams strove in his poetry, as Mike Weaver puts it, to see himself as 'a functioning perceiver observing himself in action'. Eschewing traditional theories of poetics, and deploring the monumental example of T. S. Eliot*, he determined as far as possible to avoid abstractions in his own poetry, to dismiss any ideo-logical content, and – taking an important lesson from the movement known as Imagism (in a narrow definition, 'picture-making without content') – to discover the resources of words themselves. It is a premise of his poetry that meaning is a product of form; the arrangements of words and images approximate to reality (the facts and objects of the world about us), and to rearrange words is to discover new meanings. Likewise, according to historians of Imagism, the image itself directly communicates sensation, and to appreciate that notion gives the reader a vantage for understanding Williams's aims and achievements. Williams was briefly associated with a group known as 'Objectivists' (1931), and for that group as for Williams himself the importance of Imagism was as much musical as visual. Williams experimented in his verse with pace, syllabic quantity, and metre, and evolved his own theory of measure: 'Make a musical sequence. . . . Vary the pace as much as you feel impelled to give it a jagged surface.'

Early in life Williams discovered what he termed an 'inner security' from 'a sudden resignation to existence . . . which made everything a unit and at the same time a part of myself'. Accordingly, in surrendering his ego, he determined that words themselves might be readily assimilated to patterns, to ideas, to places and to people, so that the reality of the world should become available to fresh discovery, without pre-existing sentimental or linguistic associations. 'The words,' he wrote in a gnomic but refreshing phrase, 'had come to be leaves, trees, the corners of his house', and again, that 'A poem is a small (or large) machine made of words'. It is relevant to observe, however, that in clinging to real details, Williams was fighting a natural poetic tendency towards the subjective and the romantic, and towards established modes of poetic utterance.

In the American Grain (1925), a study of American history and its heroes, prefigures *Paterson* (1963), an epic in five books which he called an assertion 'of a new and total culture, the lifting of an environment to expression'. The long poem, though jumbled in structure, purposively explores the meaning of life in the city of Paterson, New Jersey, a place in which (typical of the American experience) language is discovered to be in a state of divorce from the real and from the imagination. The city, a male giant, assumes mythic proportions, and is personalized in the figure of Doctor Paterson. The poem studies the locality, its history, its legends, and its present shapelessness of soul, and builds to the possibility that life might be recognized and reintegrated, and that language and imagination might again be equal to the reality of life.

The basic endeavour of Williams's long career in poetry was to discover a foundation for his own identity and the reader's within the immediate environment, on the poet's own understanding that 'poetry is the antithesis of the academy'.

Dr John Haffenden

Other works: *The Autobiography of William Carlos Williams* (1951); *The Collected Earlier Poems of William Carlos Williams* (1951); *The Collected Later Poems of William Carlos Williams* (1963); *The Great American Novel* (1923); *I Wanted to Write a Poem* (1958); *Kora in Hell: Improvisations* (1920); *Pictures from Brueghel and Other Poems* (1962); *Selected Essays* (1954); *The Selected Letters of William Carlos Williams*, ed. John C. Thirlwall (1957). See also: James E. Breslin, *William Carlos Williams, An American Artist* (1970); Walter Scott Peterson, *An Approach to Paterson* (1967); Mike Weaver, *William Carlos Williams, the American Background* (1971).

524
WILSON, Edmund 1895–1972

US man of letters

Son of an eminent lawyer, Edmund Wilson Jr was born and educated in New Jersey. After Princeton and service in France (as hospital orderly) during the First World War, he settled in New York as journalist, editor, and reviewer first for the *New Republic* and later for the *New Yorker*. His range was formidable. He participated as friend or associate with almost every significant literary figure of his age. Last of the great, freelance critics (consciously modelling himself on Saintsbury in England, Croce* in Italy, Taine or Sainte-Beuve in France), he aspired to a metropolitan role that operated no longer from Paris or Vienna or London, but from New York.

Wilson was not preoccupied with the work of other critics, however, nor with theoretical approaches to criticism. The mark of his style, rather, is a critical width and gusto. As scholar, he taught himself Hebrew, Russian, Hungarian. His ever-widening quest took in Haiti, the Zuñi Indians, the Iroquois, the Dead Sea Scrolls. As he himself came to realize (in 'The Author at Sixty'), he became something of an eighteenth- or nineteenth-century figure for whom literature necessarily implied an international community. His task, as he saw it, was to explain the world to America and America to itself. The task was possible, he insisted, because the American and the European intelligentsia spoke a common language. It was an essential task because American achievement might well be the key to the continuity of that internationalism, already exploited (for an English-speaking public) by Eliot* and Pound*.

As a man of letters, he worked in every conceivable genre: as weekly journalist and reviewer (whose authoritative judgments were later collected in *Classics and Commercials*, 1950, chronicling the 1940s; *The Shores of Light*, 1952, chronicling the 1920s and 1930s; and *The Bit Between My Teeth*, 1965, chronicling the 1950s and early 1960s); as poet (*Note-books of Night*, 1942, and *Night Thoughts*, 1961); as playwright (*Five Plays*, 1954); as novelist (*I Thought of Daisy*, 1929); as short-story writer (*Memoirs of Hecate County*, 1946); as essayist and reporter (whose biggest scoop was *The Scrolls from the Dead Sea*, 1955); as literary executor (editing Scott Fitzgerald's* *The Crack-Up*, 1945); as travel-writer in America, Europe and Russia (*The American Jitters*, 1932; *Travels in Two Democracies*, 1936; *Europe without Baedeker*, 1947; *Red, Black, Blond and Olive*, 1956); as autobiographer (*A Piece of My Mind*, 1956; *A Prelude*, 1967; *Upstate*, 1972); and finally as correspondent (*Letters on Literature and Politics 1912–1972*, 1977; *The Nabokov–Wilson Letters 1940–1971*, 1979).

Moving from the privileged literary perception of *Axel's Castle* (1931) to the Communist enthusiasm of *To the Finland Station* (1940), Wilson retreated eventually to the patrician aloofness of his ancestral home at Talcottville in upper New York State. After introducing Proust* and Joyce*, Yeats* and Eliot and Gertrude Stein* to America, he abandoned the symbolist 'decadence' of the 1920s (even visiting the Soviet Union in 1935) for the Marxist ideology of the 1930s. *To the Finland Station* remains one of the best guides to the western sources of Marxism-Leninism. But Wilson turned next to psychological explorations (in *The Wound and the Bow*, 1941) and to his central texts on North American literature and experience: *The Triple Thinkers* (1938); *The Shock of Recognition* (1943); *The American Earthquake* (1958); *Apologies to the Iroquois* (1960); *Patriotic Gore* (1962); *O Canada!* (1965).

Though thoroughly at home in French, English and Russian literatures, Wilson rigorously excluded Spanish and German. In fact, he increasingly enjoyed his role as an opinionated, cantankerous Early American, engaging in quixotic battles with the US Treasury (over unpaid income tax) and with Vladimir Nabokov* (over Russian verse forms and vocabulary). For he remained a tense man who may have resolved his early Marxism and his Americanism, but not his love-hate for contemporary English literature and English men of letters. Nor could he resolve his literary internationalism and political isolationism. Serene in his critical judgments, he felt threatened by contemporary pressures that undermined his national self-esteem. He never truly reconciled himself to Roosevelt's New Deal, let alone the interventions of the Second World War. He loved the Republic, but distanced himself from encroaching democracy. Cornered at last in Talcottville, as recorded in *Upstate*, he faced the ruins of the American dream.

Harold Beaver

See: Sherman Paul, *Edmund Wilson: A Study of Literary Vocation in Our Time* (1965).

525

WINNICOTT, Donald Woods 1896–1971

British paediatrician and psychoanalyst

It was while recovering from a broken collar-bone in the sick room at the Leys School in Cambridge that D. W. Winnicott decided to become a doctor. He studied biology at Jesus College, Cambridge University, and completed his medical studies at St Bartholomew's Hospital, London. In 1923 he was appointed a consultant at Paddington Green Children's Hospital – a post he held for forty years. In addition he became Physician at the Queen's Hospital for Children (until 1933), and Physician-in-charge at the LCC (London County Council) Heart and Rheumatism Clinic for Children. Winnicott calculated that by the time he retired he had seen some 60,000 children and mothers in one clinic or another.

Winnicott's career stands out as one of the most convincing examples of a marriage between theory and practice. During the 1920s he began reading Freud* and was immediately attracted towards psychoanalysis, in particular the new theories of child analysis being developed by Anna Freud and Melanie Klein*. He became Klein's pupil, and later qualified as a psychoanalyst. Just as his teacher had extended classical theory (Oedipal, dwelling upon three-person relationships) by emphasizing two-person (mother and child) relationships, so Winnicott formulated his own conclusions, which were to some extent shaped by his experience as a clinician. Essentially his theory of infant care embraces three facts: (1) a baby needs its mother; (2) the mother enjoys taking care of her baby; and (3) this bond between the two is facilitated and protected by the presence of the father. Talks based on these ideas were broadcast by the BBC in the early 1940s. They also provided the material for two subsequent publications, *The Child and the Family* (1957) and *The Child and the Outside World* (1954). The most salutary aspect of Winnicott's approach was one of tone. In contrast to his theoretical predecessors, who emphasized patterns of trauma in childhood, Winnicott firmly insisted that child-raising can be an exciting and happy experience for all concerned.

Transitional Objects and Transitional Phenomena (1953) contains what is regarded as Winnicott's most original contribution to growth psychology. It concerns the child's first 'not-me' possession. The importance of the object is not what it is – it may be nothing more than a piece of cloth or a handkerchief – but how the child relates to it and uses it. Of particular note is that the object remains with the child at bedtime, as a defence against anxiety. Parents get to know the object's value, and often have to allow it to remain dirty and smelly. It was Winnicott's belief that this first specially loved object, whose pattern of usage appears within the in-

itial year of infancy, enables the child to reach out beyond the mother to the outside world.

Winnicott sustained a dialogue between paediatrics and psychoanalysis across four decades, with a particular interest in the emotional aspects of physical illness. His ability to communicate with both children and their parents was a special gift, reinforced by his awareness of the need to understand young patients within their family and social settings. It was largely through personal example that Winnicott extended the application of what has become a standard medical precept, that care and cure should be synonymous.

Dr David Sturgeon

Other works: *Clinical Notes on Disorders of Childhood* (1931); *Collected Papers: Through Paediatrics to Psycho-Analysis* (1965); *The Maturational Process and the Facilitating Environment* (1965); *Therapeutic Consultations* (1971); *Playing and Reality* (1971).

526

WITTGENSTEIN, Ludwig Josef Johann 1889–1951

Austrian/British philosopher

Ludwig Wittgenstein was born in Vienna, into a large and wealthy family; he was the youngest of five brothers and three sisters, and was educated at home until he was fourteen. He came to England at the age of nineteen to study aeronautics at the University of Manchester, but in 1912 he met Bertrand Russell* and spent five terms studying logic under him at Cambridge. It was during the Great War (he volunteered for service in the Austrian artillery) that he completed the notes for his *Logisch-Philosophische Abhandlung*, a copy of which he sent to Russell from a prison camp in Italy. It was published first in 1921, and then in the following year, together with an English version, under the title *Tractatus Logico-Philosophicus*. The introduction, by Russell, described it as an achievement of 'extraordinary difficulty and importance'. Apart from one short article, it was to be the only work Wittgenstein published in his lifetime.

After completing the *Tractatus* Wittgenstein gave up philosophy; he also gave away a large inherited fortune. He qualified as an elementary schoolteacher, and for several years taught in various remote villages in southern Austria. But in 1929 he returned to Cambridge, submitted the *Tractatus* (already an established classic) as his PhD thesis, and was elected to a research fellowship at Trinity College. During the following decade he became a legendary figure. His 'lectures', given to small groups of devotees, were periods of intense concentration during which Wittgenstein 'thought aloud'; impassioned questions to the students would alternate with agonized silences as the philosopher struggled to achieve a new insight. During this period he wrote the *Philosophische Bemerkungen* ('Remarks', 1964) and the lengthy *Philosophische Grammatik* (1969). He also began work on his most famous book, which was not to be completed until 1948, and was still not fully revised at his death. This was the *Philosophische Untersuchungen*, or *Philosophical Investigations*, which appeared posthumously in 1953.

Wittgenstein was appointed Professor of Philosophy at Cambridge in 1939, but he spent the war years working as a medical orderly in London and Newcastle. He returned to Cambridge in 1945, but found the life of a professor unendurable (he described it to a friend as a 'living death'), and he resigned his post two years later. He lived for a time in Ireland (in total isolation), and visited America; but on his return to England in 1949 it was discovered that he had cancer. He died in Cambridge.

There are three main reasons for the unique fascination of Wittgenstein. The austerity and deep seriousness of his life; his extraordinary writing style, which almost completely avoids 'philosophical argument' as it is traditionally understood; and the curious tension between his earlier work in the *Tractatus* and the later material of the *Investigations*. This last point needs some qualifying. The myth of a near-total split between the 'early' and the 'late' Wittgenstein has now been sharply eroded: a study of some of the more recently published posthumous works has shown a more gentle transition and some elements of continuity. But it remains true that Wittgenstein's later views represent a marked retreat from the position taken in the *Tractatus* on the nature of language and its relation to the world.

The *Tractatus* is essentially a thesis about the limits of language and the limits of philosophy. 'The boundaries of my language mean the boundaries of my world' (Proposition 5.6). The book consists of seven brief propositions, each – save the last – followed by many further propositions (numbered in decimal system) which elucidate and develop what has gone before. An almost obsessive brevity marks the style; the compression does not always make for clarity, and several critics have complained that bald assertion often takes the place of reasoned argument.

The background presupposed by the author is the 'new logic' developed by Russell and the German philosopher Gottlob Frege, which replaced the old Aristotelian system of inference with a new symbolism based on analogies with mathematical functions. Part of Wittgenstein's purpose was to show how the 'truth value' (truth or falsity) of compound propositions depends on, or is a *function* of, the truth value of the elementary propositions out of which they are composed ('the proposition is a truth function of elementary propositions' – Proposition 5). To show this he employed the technique of *truth-tables* (now part of every introduction to logic); and he developed a symbolic notation to express the general form of any truth-function.

Alongside this technical apparatus for dealing with a proposition goes a theory about the relation of language to the world of which the key notion is that of a picture (*Bild*). The 'picture theory of meaning', as it has come to be known, is in one way very straightforward. The world, Wittgenstein asserts, is simply a collection of facts; the most basic kinds of fact are called 'states-of-affairs' or *Sachverhalten*. The proposition (*Sach*) now gets its meaning by being a kind of picture or model of a state-of-affairs. Wittgenstein admits that 'at first sight a proposition – one set out on the printed page for example – does not seem to be a picture of the reality with which it is concerned. But no more does musical notation at first sight seem to be a picture of music, nor our phonetic notation (the alphabet) to be a picture of our speech. Yet these sign languages prove to be pictures, even in the ordinary sense, of what they represent' (Proposition 4.011). In a proposition, Wittgenstein goes on to say, 'one name stands for one thing, another for another thing, and they are combined with one another so that the whole group – like a *tableau vivant* – presents a state of affairs' (4.0311).

At first sight this theory looks innocent enough. Meaningful discourse consists of statements which can be broken down into elementary propositions which correspond (or fail to correspond) with the states-of-affairs they depict. But the austerity of Wittgenstein's conception can soon be seen from the fact that it allows no place for, for example, ethical or aesthetic judgments: these cannot be genuine propositions, since they are not pictures of facts in the world. They are beyond the limits of the sayable. Even logic can assert nothing significant beyond empty tautologies, which 'say nothing', their truth being guaranteed simply by their internal structure (6.1). Indeed the whole of philosophy now becomes strictly unsayable: 'the correct method of philosophy would simply be this: to say nothing except what can be said, i.e. the propositions of natural science – i.e. something which has nothing to do with philosophy – and then, whenever someone wanted to say something metaphysical, to show him that he had failed to give a meaning to certain signs in his propositions' (6.53). The book ends with the famous warning '*Wovon man nicht sprechen kann, darüber muss man schweigen*' – 'What cannot be spoken must be passed over in silence.'

These conclusions anticipate in some important respects the Logical Positivist movement of the 1930s (which rejected as meaningless any proposition which could not be factually verified). A notorious difficulty with this type of philosophical position is that it seems to cut the ground from under its own feet: what is one to make of such philosophical claims as those in the *Tractatus* itself, since on the very theory which the book presents they must be meaningless? Wittgenstein himself admitted that 'anyone who understands me recognizes my propositions as nonsense'; but the nonsense was none the less supposed to be helpful nonsense – like a ladder one climbs up and then throws away (6.54).

For all that, Wittgenstein was convinced that the *Tractatus* represented the final solution to the problems of philosophy. What compelled him to return to the subject, after a gap of some ten years, was not so much the type of difficulty just referred to, as some more technical problems about the logical independence of elementary propositions. More important, Wittgenstein gradually came to see that the way in which language is meaningful is very much more complex than the simple picturing model of the *Tractatus* had suggested. Words, he wrote in the *Philosophische Grammatik*, cannot be understood simply as the names of objects; they have as many different uses as money, which can buy an indefinite range of different kinds of item. Language, he wrote there and elsewhere, is like a toolbag, whose components are as diverse in function as hammer, saw and gluepot.

We have now arrived at one of the key slogans of Wittgenstein's later philosophy: 'The meaning of the word is its use in language' (*Philosophical Investigations* § 43). A detailed examination of the actual working of language in all its variety and complexity was to replace the insistence on a single model to which all meaningful propositions must conform.

The most famous concept Wittgenstein employs in presenting this new view of language is that of the *Sprachspiel* or *language-game*. We understand the meaning of a word by seeing the role it plays in any one of a vast number of language games. The important notions here are multiplicity and diversity. There is no one common essence that explains meaning, any more than there is one common feature shared by all games. In a famous passage Wittgenstein tells us to 'consider the proceedings that we call *games*. I mean board-games, card-games, ball-games, Olympic games. . . . What is common to them all? Don't say *There must be something common or they would not be called games*, but *look and see*.' The conclusion is that there is no one essential feature or set of features, but instead 'a complicated network of similarities overlapping and criss-crossing' (§ 66).

'Overlapping and criss-crossing' is in fact characteristic of the style of the *Investigations*, which makes no pretence to be welded into a set of precisely stated philosophical conclusions. The author describes the book in the preface as 'a number of sketches of landscapes . . . made in the course of . . . long and involved journeyings'. The topic which begins to predominate as the sketches proceed is that of the philosophy of mind, the analysis of mental concepts, and in particular sensations.

Here Wittgenstein makes his most original contribution when he takes on the long-standing philosophical tradition which regards words like 'pain' as names for private sensations. In attacking this view, Wittgenstein manages to avoid the crude Behaviourist position which reduces sensations to their physical manifestations. Instead, his argument turns to the impossibility of what he calls a *private language*: words, to have meaning, must be subject to public rules for their application; so the picture of a man understanding the concept of pain by attending to an inner sensation and then christening it 'pain' is a fundamentally misleading one.

The controversy over the interpretation and validity of the 'private language argument' is still far from over. But as presented by Wittgenstein – as a struggle to free ourselves from a deceptive picture of how sensation words operate – it is characteristic of his later view of philosophy as a 'battle against the bewitchment of our intelligence by means of language' (§ 109). 'What is your aim in philosophy? To show the fly the way out of the fly-bottle' (§ 309).

Wittgenstein's influence has sometimes been destructive of good philosophy. Some philosophers of religion, for example, have recently taken the smug and cosy position that religious discourse can only be understood within its own 'language-game', which is apparently supposed to make it immune from scientific or other outside criticism. Other Wittgensteinians, trading on the idea that philosophy is purely the activity of linguistic clarification, have put forward the obscurantist doctrine that philosophical work on, for example, memory should confine itself to examining how we ordinarily use the word, and need take no account of physiological discoveries about how our brains work.

Wittgenstein himself would probably not have welcomed these developments. He had a horror of disciples, and once observed, 'The only seed I am likely to sow is a certain jargon.' In fact the harvest of Wittgenstein's thought is large, rich and still to be fully digested. Above all, there can be no doubt of his pioneering and lasting contribution to the two issues which have become definitive of so much contemporary philosophy – the nature of language and the function of philosophy itself.

Dr John Cottingham

The best text of the *Tractatus Logico-Philosophicus* presents the original German with an English translation by D. F. Pears and B. F. McGuinness (1961); the *Philosophical Investigations* is translated by G. E. M. Anscombe (1953). The *Blue and Brown Books* (1958) contain useful introductory material to the latter. Other posthumous texts include: *Protractatus* (1971); *Zettel* (1967); and *On Certainty* (1969). On Wittgenstein: E. Anscombe, *An Introduction to Wittgenstein's Tractatus* (1959); N. Malcolm, *Ludwig Wittgenstein, a Memoir* (1958); G. Pitcher (ed.),

Wittgenstein (1971); P. M. S. Hacker, *Insight and Illusion – Wittgenstein on Philosophy and the Metaphysics of Experience* (1972); A. Kenny, *Wittgenstein* (1975).

527

WODEHOUSE, Sir Pelham Grenville 1881–1974

English novelist

When Wodehouse left Dulwich College in 1900 he became a bank clerk. His career was not distinguished. He had an urge to write, and when he gained some success in journalism he left the bank. He had found his vocation. His first successes were his books for boys. For many years such works had been marked by pietism, mawkishness, and an embarrassing sentimentality. Wodehouse, who never preached, wrote with humour, good sense, and understanding of boys at school.

In 1909 he went to New York. For some time the publishers showed little interest in him. When he married Ethel Rowley, a young English widow, in 1914, they had just over a hundred dollars between them. But things changed. His collaboration in musical comedy with Guy Bolton produced plays which delighted audiences in America and England, and for fifty years Wodehouse wrote for the stage. His books, however, were more important, and he had a real triumph when his novel *Something Fresh* (1915) was accepted by the *Saturday Evening Post*. The paper had a vast circulation and an extremely high standard. He wrote twenty-one serials for it, and the English editions were snapped up as quickly as they could be printed.

In the following years he spent most of his time in England. His last visit was in 1939, when Oxford University conferred upon him the honorary degree of Doctor of Letters in recognition of his services to English literature. A little later, in France, the Germans interned him. In 1941 he delivered his broadcasts to neutral America. The reaction to this in England was hysterical and ill-informed. He was a traitor, a disciple of Hitler*, and so on. In fact, the talks were a shrewd criticism of the incompetence of Germans in managing their prisons. In America they were looked on as models of anti-Nazi propaganda.

Before he returned to America in 1947 the animosity of his detractors in England had faded away. The sales of his books, far from falling, increased greatly, and there were many more to come.

He was always modest about his books. They might give readers an hour or so of amusement because of their absurdities and their remoteness from real life, but otherwise they were valueless. He had no message for the world. Intelligent readers will not agree. His characters and their situations arouse laughter not because they are out of this world but because they are plainly within it. He was one of the great writers of the English comic tradition, and for all their lightness his books expose the shortcomings of society and all that is pretentious and unreal.

For many readers the genius of Wodehouse is best revealed in his series of stories about Bertie Wooster, his valet Jeeves and those about Lord Emsworth and Blandings Castle. They are brilliantly written with a continuous felicity of diction and metaphor, and it is in them that the peculiar flavour of the Wodehousian manner can be most fully savoured. It is odd that Bertie, who was in his middle twenties when he was created in 1919, is still of that age, and Emsworth, who in the first story about him was said to have been at Eton in the middle sixties of the last century, is not a day older now. But perhaps it is not so strange. They are of the immortals.

R. B. D. French

See: Richard Usborne, *Wodehouse at Work* (1961), *Wodehouse at Work to the End* (1976), *Sunset at Blandings* (1977); R. B. D. French, *P. G. Wodehouse* (1966); Robert Al Hall, *The Comic style of P. G. Wodehouse* (1976). *Performing Flea*, ed. W. T. Townend (1953), is a collection of letters sent to him by Wodehouse.

528

WOLFE, Thomas Clayton 1900–38

US novelist

Thomas Wolfe, like Theodore Dreiser*, is one of those twentieth-century American leviathians whose work presents a difficult problem in literary evaluation. His writing contains, as Bernard de Voto once said, 'long whirling discharges of words, unabsorbed in the novel, unrelated to the proper business of fiction, badly if not altogether unacceptably written, raw gobs of emotion, aimless and quite meaningless jabber, claptrap, belches, grunts and Tarzan-like screams'. And yet he has great skill in characterization, conveys the 'flavour' of speech or scenes with gusto, is quite a hand at humour and, at times, renders most vividly the emotions of a young man faced with the joys and (particularly) the injustices of this life.

He was born in Asheville, North Carolina, the son of a stone-cutter and a boarding-house keeper, and went first to the University of North Carolina – where the epithet of 'genius' began to be freely applied to him – and later to Harvard, where he became a member of Professor George Pierce Baker's '47' play-writing group. Disappointed with the reception of his plays, he began, while working as an Instructor at the Washington Square College of New York University, the novel which was to become *Look Homeward, Angel*. Before its publication Wolfe went to Europe and, after its initial success, continued writing, either in America or in Europe, the interminable story of his life. Six years later, he brought out *Of Time and the River*, a mammoth work telling of his experiences in New York and Europe. Only two other pieces, *From Death to Morning* (a collection of stories) and *The Story of a Novel*, appeared before his death, of cerebral infection following pneumonia, in 1938. However, he left behind him some millions of words, which, with the benefit of the kind of editing that Maxwell Perkins of Scribner's had given *Look Homeward, Angel*, were published as *The Web and the Rock* (1939), *You Can't Go Home Again* (1940), and *The Hills Beyond* (1941).

In his best pieces, like 'A Portrait of Bascom Hawke', Wolfe achieved that miracle of characterization by which one knows the true writer. And yet one cannot say that he was the complete artist, for the artist has detachment and patience, and ruthlessly prunes out self-pity. Wolfe was never able to do this. He did not lack energy or dedication, but he did lack discipline. He wanted to 'get it all down', just as at Harvard he had wanted to read all the books in all the libraries. And so he let himself go, and the result was often verbosity, repetitiousness and windy rhetoric.

Look Homeward, Angel is the nearest Wolfe came to writing a novel in the accepted sense of the word, mainly perhaps because its tracing of the career of young Eugene Gant from birth to young manhood gives it at least a cyclic form. It is also more 'written', a young man's novel. The later books are collections of impressions, related with energy and an eye for the minutiae of human emotions and behaviour, but seemingly without even the amount of artifice which enabled Hemingway* to convert the reportage of *The Sun Also Rises* into art. But if, in his later work, Wolfe lost whatever sense he had of construction and form, he also lost the orotundity of tone – a sort of backwoods echo of Ecclesiastes and Elizabethan drama – which marred *Look Homeward, Angel*.

Wolfe never seemed to realize that, however vividly he recounted his emotions and experiences, this was not enough. There is little clash of ideas in his novels, little conflict and little resolution. This is the difference between him and Dreiser, who, however ineptly he handled words, at least had something to say about the forces which push and pull people in society. Yet, for all that, there are some magnificent things in Wolfe. If one could establish a new category of novel-writing one might say that his books constitute one long 'story of the heart' – perhaps, even, D. H. Lawrence's* 'one bright book of life'.

Geoffrey Moore

See: Herbert J. Muller, *Thomas Wolfe* (1947); Pamela Hansford Johnson, *Thomas Wolfe: A Critical Study* (1948); A. B. Adams, *Thomas Wolfe, Carolina Student* (1950); Richard Walser (ed.), *The Enigma of Thomas Wolfe* (1953); Louis D. Rubin, *Thomas Wolfe: The Weather of his Youth* (1955); Hugh C. Holman, *Thomas Wolfe* (1960); Richard Walser, *Thomas Wolfe Undergraduate* (1977).

529
WOLFE, Tom 1931–

US essayist and journalist

With the increasing tendency of post-Joycean* fiction to move away from public reality into private exploration, and with the general lack of artistic ambition among journalists, there arose in the 1960s a middle ground in which all the techniques, liberties and high purposes of creative writing were appropriated for the presentation of non-fiction. Tom Wolfe was the most audacious of these new journalists and later confirmed his position as their initiative talent by editing and introducing with a passionate manifesto an anthology under the title *The New Journalism* (1973) which claimed that it represented 'the most important literature being written in America today'.

Inevitably the emphasis turned from the collation and analysis of unadorned facts towards the examination of behaviour and personality in the creation of circumstances, including the personality of the journalist who abdicated his theoretical position as the objective camera in favour of revealing his own prismatic nature. Paradoxically this led to a far higher degree of realism, since the irreverent psyche of the author not only brought the subject more humanly close to the reader but also allowed the reader to place the writing itself in perspective.

On the whole Wolfe's approach to his material is satirical, as is that of his most outrageous protégé, Hunter S. Thompson, whose *Fear and Loathing in Las Vegas* (1971) is new journalism's outstanding book to date (Thompson invented a sub-style for it called 'gonzo journalism' in which the author is the Quixotic hero/victim of events around him, thus eliminating the problem of the wiseacre writer which – along with a too desperate modishness – is the new journalists' greatest pitfall). Wolfe's flair for debunking is made acceptable by the loving care with which he organizes the foibles of social life into a subtle thesis. But his work has demonstrated a growing seriousness and desire to eliminate his own ego from the interplay of events (viz. *The Right Stuff*, 1979).

Reportage was always considered an inferior occupation for a writer, whereas Wolfe is aggressive in his belief that new journalism is the successor to the novel and the short story. What is true is that Wolfe in particular has been able with great success to adapt and pursue the experiments of modern prose fiction in a way that penetrates to a large audience because these experiments are harnessed to a dramatic exterior account of modern life. His conviction is not surprising at a time when the mass media are increasingly seen as a legitimate arena for the forces of art, and it may be compared to the incorporation of Pop Art into the canon of art history. The superficially democratic and sometimes philistine character (viz. *The Painted Word*, 1975) of this writing has seen it published by and large in a new generation of leisure magazines such as *Rolling Stone*, *Esquire* and *Playboy*, and Wolfe himself – a reporter for ten years after taking a PhD in American Studies at Yale, 1957 – has been a contributing editor of *New York Magazine* since 1968.

He designed not only the theory but also the prevailing language of new journalism, overloaded and fast and often slangy, with an obsession for microscopic details justified by his belief in using anything to get the right picture across. Much of the writing is painterly or mannerist. In fact *The Painted Word*, an attack on conceptual art, may easily be turned against him in his tendency to use language as paint. Alternatively he is sometimes capable of handling profound emotional predicaments in a way that the novel always has – by example, inference and embodiment, rather than by exposition: since Wolfe, the brand of a politician's cigarettes, for example, has become significant to his description. Wolfe is at his weakest when polemical (as is Hunter S. Thompson), the arguments being sentimental and glib. His true gift is for the mythologization of modern archetypes by rendering his observations in dynamic cartoon prose. It was a style established in his first book, *The Kandy-Kolored Tangerine-Flake Streamline Baby* (1965), a collection of articles, and since developed in full-length works also.

New journalism has been less successful in the hands of European writers who tend to become too intense in ideology or allegorical in intention, and in Britain the conservatism of the press has consistently mistaken it for self-indulgence or even plain rudeness.

Duncan Fallowell

See also: *The Pump House Gang* (1968); *The Electric Kool-Aid Acid Test* (1968); *Radical Chic and Mau-Mauing the Flak Catchers* (1970); *Mauve Gloves and Madmen, Clutter and Vine* (1976).

530
WOOLF, Adeline Virginia 1882–1941

British novelist

While Virginia Woolf's claim, in 'The Leaning Tower', that English writers tend to be firmly rooted in the middle class might not be altogether true or useful, it is certainly essential to an understanding of her own development. Daughter of Sir Leslie Stephen, critic, man of letters, and editor of *The Dictionary of National Biography*, Virginia grew up in a London household in which distinguished writers and intellectuals were familiar figures, in which books and ideas were everywhere. Denied the formal education which Sir Leslie felt was appropriate for his sons but not his daughters, Virginia was at least given free access to his vast library, whose resources helped compensate for her exclusion from the educational opportunities offered to her two brothers. While she always resented the crippling patriarchal assumptions of life at 22 Hyde Park Gate, its rich intellectual ambience also nourished her and helped shape her early resolve to become a writer.

Liberated by Stephen's death in 1904, Virginia moved with her two brothers and sister, Vanessa, into Gordon Square, and into a new social life built around the Cambridge acquaintances of the Stephen boys. These new friendships, which fashioned the nucleus of the much deplored and admired 'Bloomsbury circle', also brought her a husband in the person of Leonard Woolf, Virginia's 'penniless Jew', who married her in 1911 after his return from Ceylon.

With the solidity of her marriage helping her to deal with the spells of incapacitating and, at times, suicidal depression which constantly assaulted her (until she finally took her life in 1941), Woolf began her novelistic career in 1915 with the publication of *The Voyage Out*. But neither this nor the book to follow, *Night and Day* (1919), is particularly successful or indicative of what was to come. Both are basically pedestrian works, written in the narrative, realist tradition she soon came to realize was an artistic dead-end for her. For Woolf, conventional techniques could produce only conventional fiction; and it was not until the publication of *Jacob's Room* in 1922 that she felt she had finally learned 'how to begin (at 40) to say something in my own voice'. Irrevocably breaking free with *Jacob's Room* from what she calls 'the appalling narrative business of the realist: getting on from lunch to dinner', Woolf devoted the next nineteen years to exploring the different possibilities of that newly discovered voice.

Woolf was not alone, of course, in rejecting traditional techniques. Such rejection accounts for the history of modern art in general and the modern novel in particular. But in many ways Woolf is a more radical innovator than even Conrad*, Ford*, Lawrence*, Joyce*, and Faulkner*. More totally than the others, she cuts herself off from any vestige of narrative energy. It is almost impossible to speak of 'the action' of a Woolf novel. As an artist Woolf was always absorbed with formal rather than substantive concerns, with trying to embody, as she says, 'the exact shapes my brain holds'. While she has frequently been associated with the 'stream of consciousness' novel her writing cannot in fact, be understood by reference to any single label or technique. The astonishingly different forms of each novel – from the minutely detailed street life of

Mrs Dalloway (1925) to the totally artificial, internalized depths of *The Waves* (1931), from the tri-partite structure of *To the Lighthouse* (1927) to the day-long pageant of *Between the Acts* (1942) – suggest the single-minded purpose with which she sought to find fresh ways to express what the experience of living is like.

Woolf's own attempt to create shapes that can make sense out of the fluidity of life is paralleled by the same sort of quest going on inside the novels themselves. If it is possible to generalize about the meaning of the human activity in Woolf's fictional world, we can say that the characters all try, through widely different means, to fashion for themselves from the chaos surrounding them some coherent grasp of their world. Lily's painting in *To the Lighthouse*, Bernard's novel in *The Waves*, Miss LaTrobe's pageant in *Between the Acts*, and Clarissa's party in *Mrs Dalloway*, for example, are all efforts to effect what Woolf herself is seeking in her fiction. The workings of the creative imagination shaping different visions of order is the single great theme in Virginia Woolf's novels.

While Woolf's position as one of the important and original modern novelists seems now to be securely established, it is only recently that such canonization has taken place. During her lifetime and extending until the late 1960s, her critical reputation was extremely uneven, a result of both the inherent difficulties of the fiction itself, as well as her involvement with the notorious Bloomsbury circle of writers, artists and intellectuals. As the term 'Bloomsbury' was for years a highly pejorative designation, Woolf suffered from the same critical opprobrium generally lavished on all manifestations of the phenomenon. Snobbish, sexually effete, morally perverse, politically unaware – the charges brought against Bloomsbury by Sir John Rothenstein, Wyndham Lewis*, and the Leavises*, among others, were also brought against Woolf, and she remained for years the most dismissible of the great modernists.

For reasons that are less literary than cultural, however, the metaphoric significance of 'Bloomsbury' and all its constituent parts – Lytton Strachey*, Clive Bell, E. M. Forster*, Maynard Keynes*, and the rest – has dramatically changed, so that what was once seen as trivial and pernicious is instead hailed as prophetic and socially redemptive. For a culture that is in the process of trying to divest itself of the rigidities of traditional sexual role-playing and masculine constraints, the value the Bloomsberries are seen to place on friendship and art, and their rejection of the use of power in personal relationships, bring them into the cultural mainstream from which they were so long excluded. And at the very centre of this rediscovery stands Woolf herself, the high priestess of Bloomsbury, embodying all the life-giving virtues attributed to it. In its denunciation of masculine oppression, her social criticism, most especially in *A Room of One's Own* (1929)

and *Three Guineas* (1930), is revered by feminists and androgynists alike, and readers now find in her novels an anguished awareness of the plight of the creative woman trapped in a sexist society.

The cultic admiration surrounding Woolf is not altogether edifying. The arguments for her social relevance are grossly distorted, and her feminism is far more complicated than the polemicists of the women's movement make it out to be. Woolf's genuine achievement as a writer, however, should outlast the topical claims made for her. It is above all else in her ability to create the resonant forms of *Mrs Dalloway*, *To the Lighthouse*, *The Waves*, and *Between the Acts* that her reputation will ultimately rest.

Michael Rosenthal

Woolf's other books include: *Orlando* (1928); *Flush* (1933); *The Years* (1937); *Roger Fry: A Biography* (1940). The standard biography is Quentin Bell, *Virginia Woolf* (1972). See also: Avrom Fleishman, *Virginia Woolf: A Critical Reading* (1975); Phyllis Rose, *Woman of Letters* (1978); Michael Rosenthal, *Virginia Woolf* (1979).

531
WRIGHT, Frank Lloyd 1869–1959

US architect

The great American architect died leaving behind the fruits of a working life that spanned some sixty years: years of prolific and original thinking that revolutionized architectural design by introducing a very sophisticated method of composition based on the subtle interplay of geometric forms which link all the elements of a building and its immediate environment into one essentially organic whole.

His initial training was in the School of Engineering at the University of Wisconsin but this formal education seems to have had little obvious lasting effect and was certainly less important to his work than the years of practical experience of long working days on his uncle's farm or the purposeful play induced by his mother's discovery of Froebel learning methods. His love for the land and the expressive possibilities of natural materials dates from this time.

Dissatisfied with the restrictive atmosphere at Wisconsin he moved to Chicago where he formed a close friendly relationship with the architect Louis Sullivan in whose office he eventually worked. Wright never lost his admiration for Sullivan and his faith in an architecture freed from convention based on the supposed great European tradition. As a Mid-West American Wright had no Beaux Arts training and much of the work he did with Sullivan during the six years he spent in Chicago, particularly the designs for private houses, clearly influenced the first buildings he developed as an independent architect – his Prairie houses, designed and built between 1900 and 1909.

Typified by the Willitt's House of 1902, his 'house of the future' is composed of dramatic masses set around an articulate internal spatial arrangement, the geometric form of which is governed by purely functional needs. Embedded in its leafy surroundings it merges into the landscape, giving a sense of safe shelter and durability.

The designs for private houses grow in confidence and daring, culminating in the Robie House built in 1909 on a long narrow site in a wealthy area of Chicago. With its continuous flow of interesting planes and volumes, every component in the design including the fittings combines to give that total unity which Wright called an 'inner order'.

This concentration on housing for a rich minority has brought the obvious criticism that Wright avoided the real social issues of the day, and this is undoubtedly true, though it is equally true that it was their willingness to accept his ideas and to be able to pay for them to be put into practice that consequently influenced the evolution of modern architecture.

The public works are equally impressive. The Larkin Building built in an industrial section of Buffalo in 1904 (and demolished in 1950) was far more than a new architectural form. It was a radical concept of what an office building should be and Wright concentrated on letting as much light as possible into the working area, which was open-plan with a series of galleries running around it and an open vertical court in which the employees could work in uninterrupted space. The most internationally influential of the early works, double-glazing was first used in this building and, most interestingly, the first wall-hung latrines.

The year 1909 saw the end of the productive Prairie House phase, and dogged by personal pressures Wright left for Europe. In his immensely readable *An Autobiography* (1943) he gives an admittedly lurid account of the desperation he felt at the time and also of the tragic seemingly endless story of Taliesin and his attempts to start life afresh in Wisconsin where he had been so happy as a boy.

Taliesin 1 was built with a pioneer spirit of independence and a desire for self-sufficiency. Conceived as an integrated group of buildings and built into the hillside from which it took its form, the living accommodation meandered informally in marked contrast to the earlier Prairie houses. Random gardens and natural vegetation were allowed to flow freely though hinting at ideas to be used later in the Kaufmann House known as Fallingwater.

Wright's concern for an ideal way of life for others was sadly doomed to failure. His Millard House, designed in 1923, is not unlike the box-like form associated with the European architect Le Corbusier* but there was an important difference in the social attitudes of the two men. Unlike Le Corbusier, Wright had no thoughts for mass-production and was still working for a wealthy elite.

World-wide recognition came late to Wright and only in his last twenty years did large commissions come his way.

The Johnson Wax Factory is an office block with walls of brick and glass tubes and an interior with mushroom-like columns giving an air of pure fantasy. The laboratory block with its tree-like Research Tower added later is evidence of Wright's continuing inventiveness and versatility.

But it is his famous Fallingwater that is his masterpiece. Built in 1936 for yet another wealthy client, it is nothing if not dramatic, with its flat terraces poised precariously over the cascading waterfall, the cantilevering made possible by reinforced concrete. As Wright himself wrote: 'This structure might serve to indicate that the sense of shelter – the sense of space where used with sound structural sense – has no limitations as to form except the materials used and the methods by which they are employed for what purpose. The ideas involved here are in no wise changed from those of early work' (*Architectural Forum*, January 1938).

From the beginning Wright's thinking had been concerned with the underlying structure of form and its subsequent meaning and right until the end he stuck to his beliefs. Even the somewhat cumbersome and impractical Guggenheim Museum is not lacking in ingenious solutions.

His influence on others is complex but in terms of the development of the Modern Movement the impact on J. J. P. Oud and the designers of the Dutch De Stijl group is probably the most significant. Wright's designs were published in Holland in 1910 and they were greeted with great enthusiasm for their strictly formal geometric rightness.

Frank Lloyd Wright was a complicated man with a simple approach to life and with the ever-increasing awareness of the need for a unity between the new technology and a fundamental human self-sufficiency there is much still to be learnt from him and the utopian ideals of Taliesin.

John Furse

Vincent Scully Jnr, *Frank Lloyd Wright* (1960); H. A. Brooks, *The Prairie School* (1972).

Y

532
YEATS, John Butler ('Jack') 1871–1957

Irish painter and writer

Jack Yeats was born in London on 29 August 1871. (His only brother was W. B. Yeats*.) J. B. Yeats Senior was a moderately successful portrait painter whose wife came from a west of Ireland merchant family: from them Jack Yeats inherited a vocation and an imaginative *locus*. Some formal training in London quickly led to magazine illustration. The water colours which followed (from 1895 onwards) retain a strong outline sense. From these, by way of illustrations in oil for George Birmingham's *Life in the West of Ireland*, Yeats developed his mature style. Having married Mary Cottenham White in 1894, he moved to Devon. Shortly after the beginning of the new century he returned to Ireland, and in 1903 began to paint consistently in oils.

Though he painted fine landscapes, Yeats's characteristic pictures strategically employ a human figure. He favoured disguised interior settings – tramcars, circuses, theatres, windows provide a solidly human context. Even some early outdoor scenes (e.g. *Before the Start*) carefully provide a social as well as a natural landscape. Often a figure appears virtually to guide the viewer's attention to the picture as a whole. *About to Write a Letter* contains a shy element of self-portraiture in this respect.

During the period 1915–22 Irish political tensions deeply affected Yeats. Whereas his brother moved towards an elegiac celebration of the expiring social order of landlords and governors, Jack Yeats painted *Communicating with Prisoners*, *Bachelor's Walk: In Memory*, etc. The material is explicitly nationalistic; the mood however is elegiac rather than insurgent. Indeed this period reveals profound contradictions in Yeats's art, between narrative assertion and detached observation. The Volunteer soldier in *On Drumcliffe Strand* recalls W. B. Yeats's phrase 'the stone's in the midst of all', as the women turn to scan a face hidden from the viewer. It is not accidental that after the Easter 1916 Rebellion Yeats was seriously ill.

From about 1921 onwards the painting is gradually less affected by the angularity of a training in magazine illustration, though the altered style has more than stylistic implications. Though thematically retrospective, the treatment is exuberant, and the human figures move fluently into the composition. His late years were prolific. Loneliness, a version of the human figure, draws both tragic and comic interpretations of life to it, and the dual perspective is central in Yeats. An important picture of this period is *The Blood of Abel*, in which Yeats prophetically senses the nearness of the European holocaust.

Though the late paintings are often compared with Kokoschka*, there is a direct line of development from the central period of Irish tension. The precise relationships of these paintings – a vivid apprehension of life together with the formalism of an observer – are gradually dissolved. Yeats's prose style in *Sligo* (1930) and *The Amaranthers* (1936) (the best of his 'novels') aspires to the same fluidity. The plays are more problematic.

W. J. McCormack

See: Thomas MacGreevy, *Jack B. Yeats: an Appreciation* (1945); John Berger, *Permanent Red* (1960).

533
YEATS, William Butler 1865–1939

Irish poet and dramatist

W. B. Yeats was born on 13 June 1865, the son of the eccentric but highly articulate John Butler Yeats, who in 1867 gave up a rather half-hearted career as a Dublin lawyer to become an art student in London. In 1863 he had married Susan Pollexfen, the eldest daughter of a Sligo mill-owning family of Cornish descent. Though the marriage itself turned out rather unsatisfactory, the union of the charming and gifted Yeats strain with the brooding introspective Pollexfens was, in J. B. Yeats's phrase, to 'give a tongue to the sea-cliffs' and to provide in W. B. Yeats and in his younger brother, Jack Yeats*, the painter, two artists of world repute. It was with the Pollexfens that W. B. Yeats spent a great deal of his youth, and the effect of the dramatic landscape around Sligo, with its visible reminders of the legendary past, combined with the influence of the Pollexfen family, and in particular his uncle George Pollexfen, to arouse his interest in astrology and Irish mythology, and turned the Sligo countryside into the symbolic landscape of his early poetry. Yet, despite the many shortcomings of J. B. Yeats as a father, he gave to his children an example of dedication to art which encouraged them in their own efforts. Like many fathers of men of genius his considerable talent foreshadowed, though it could not discipline itself to attain, the artistic flowering of the next generation.

Certainly Yeats seems to have learnt little in his formal education, first at the Godolphin School, Hammersmith, and later at the High School, Harcourt Street, Dublin, and the Dublin School of Art.

The Yeats family moved back to Ireland in 1880 and remained in and around Dublin until they returned to London in 1887, moving finally into a house in Bedford Park in 1887. It was in 1889 that Yeats's first substantial major poem, *The Wanderings of Oisin*, was published. This year, 1889, was a significant one for him in other ways: it was at this time that he began to frequent writers and artists who were to be his friends and associates in the Rhymers Club in the 1890s, and it was in this year too that he met and fell in love with Maud Gonne, whose total dedication to the cause of Irish independence and powerful, uncompromising nature were to torture and stimulate Yeats to some of his finest poetry. The year 1896 saw his meeting with another powerful feminine influence on his life, Lady (Augusta) Gregory, who collaborated with him in the collection and publication of Irish folk stories and in his work for the Irish theatre. Both she and J. M. Synge, whom he met in the same year, were inspired by him to write plays of Irish life and in 1904 the Abbey Theatre opened under his management. For the next six years he was engrossed in the job of producer and manager of the theatre. In 1917 he bought a ruined tower, Thoor Ballylee, near Coole Park, Lady Gregory's house in Galway, and the same year married Georgie Hyde-Lees. In 1922 he became a Senator of the Irish Free State and in 1923 was awarded the Nobel Prize for Literature. He died on 28 January 1939 at Cap Martin and was buried in Roquebrune. It was not until 1948 that his body was brought back to Ireland to be buried in the churchyard of Drumcliffe, near Sligo ('under bare Ben Bulben's head'), where his grandfather had been rector.

'I had,' wrote Yeats of himself as he was 'at twenty-three or twenty-four', 'three interests, interest in a form of literature, in a form of philosophy and a belief in nationality.' It was then that a 'sentence seemed to form in my mind. . . . "Hammer your thoughts into unity." ' These preoccupations remained with him for the rest of his life.

At first sight Yeats is a man of seemingly irreconcilable contradictions. One expects of a major writer opinions and a consistent philosophy, a recognizable standpoint in relation to his subject. Yet Yeats is disconcertingly ambiguous in his attitudes: it is the clash between opinions, the tension engendered by ambigu-

ities, that excites him ('Opinion is not worth a rush'). Where many modern writers, such as Eliot*, have resolved their doubts to their own satisfaction by struggling through to a philosophical position which, however subtle and ambiguous, is still a position to which they can give emotional or philosophical assent, Yeats maintains a state of non-commitment. It is the conflict itself that he responds to, the forging of a mythology which can accommodate all opposites ('We make out of the quarrel with others, rhetoric, but of the quarrel with ourselves, poetry'). 'Opinions are accursed' because they harden and embitter the personality, and it is only through the free play of the mind, unfettered by dogma, that the greatness of man can be expressed. It is this ambiguous attitude that characterizes his dealings with, for example, Irish nationalism.

> Have I not seen the loveliest woman born
> Out of the mouth of Plenty's horn,
> Because of her opinionated mind
> Barter that horn and every good
> By quiet natures understood
> For an old bellows full of angry wind?

Perfection of the life and of the work can be attained only by discipline. Thoughts are hammered, not moulded, into unity; the bird on the golden bough can sing of what is past, or passing, or to come because it has itself passed through the purifying fire. The ideal is the dance, the total fusion of body, mind and soul, a Unity of Being symbolized by the whirling movement of the universe, the spinning-off of one spool of life on to the other, the eternal recurrence of the cycles of history.

It is often said that Yeats's 'philosophy' is nothing but elaborate rubbish; but the great purpose of *A Vision* (1937) is to create a myth that can be believed and disbelieved simultaneously. The truth of *A Vision* is an entirely symbolic truth: it is certainly not the truth of philosophy, and not even the truth of religion as it is commonly held by believers. When the so-called 'instructors' appeared 'on the afternoon of October 24th 1917' in response to Mrs Yeats's attempts at automatic writing, they produced such disjointed sentences that Yeats offered to dedicate his life to piecing together their jumbled message. 'No,' was the answer, 'we have come to give you metaphors for poetry.' Poetry for Yeats, as for Mallarmé, and others before him, held the key to existence itself. To give metaphors for poetry was to provide a 'supreme fiction' – supreme *because* fictional. 'Some will ask whether I believe in the actual existence of my circuits of sun and moon. . . . To such a question I can but answer that if sometimes, overwhelmed by miracle as all men must be when in the midst of it, I have taken such periods literally, my reason has soon recovered. . . . They have helped me to hold in a single thought reality and justice.' As with Baudelaire, all Yeats touched he turned into symbol: Ireland, Byzantium, Maud Gonne, the Easter Rising, the Tower, religion, history, magic are all part of the great dance:

> So the Platonic Year
> Whirls out new right and wrong,
> Whirls in the old instead;
> All men are dancers and their tread
> Goes to the barbarous clangour of a gong.

'The fascination of what's difficult', the unending search for a harder and more 'hammered' style, developed partly at the instigation of Ezra Pound*, leads not only to the stark power of Yeats's last poems, but to the 'wild old wicked man' which was the mask which the sensitive youth of the 1890s had by the end of his life assumed, if only perhaps as another 'metaphor for poetry'. His life and his art became increasingly inseparable and both aimed at a powerful, unsentimental vision of things. As the vision of an Ireland that could in reality rival the imagined unity of being, represented to him by the image of Byzantium, receded from his mind, so the ideal country of the imagination became more significant.

Yeats thought of himself and his generation as the 'last Romantics', their theme tradition, their ideal community one in which craftsmanship and artistic creation could flourish, a state without politics; but 'Romantic Ireland' was for Yeats 'dead and gone'; modern society belongs to the politicians. Only in art can man move into a higher reality; only there is it possible that 'things can and cannot be'. Yet for all its rejection of the 'filthy modern tide', for all its prophecies of doom, Yeats's poetry is not ultimately pessimistic. By its firm grasp of the reality of the imagination it has achieved and teaches serenity and freedom.

Since the publication of the *Collected Poems* in 1950 Yeats has found an ever larger audience. Not only has his poetry been increasingly admired, but his prose and his plays – particularly his plays for dancers – have been much more commonly read and acted. Yeats's plays are notable for their very successful use of poetic language in the theatre and for their perhaps rather unexpected power when well performed, but it is in his lyric poetry that he writes with full conviction and mastery, and it is as the writer of some of the finest poems in the language that his work seems certain to survive changes of literary fashion.

Joseph Bain

Yeats's other works include: *Collected Plays* (1952); *Autobiographies* (1956); *Mythologies* (1959); *Essays and Introductions* (1961); *Explorations* (1962); *Memoirs* (1972). See also: *Letters from W. B. Yeats to Dorothy Wellesley* (1940); *The Senate Speeches of W. B. Yeats*, ed. Donald Pearce (1961). The standard biography is Joseph Hone, *W. B. Yeats 1865–1939* (1942). Critical: Louis MacNeice, *The Poetry of W. B. Yeats* (1941); Peter Ure, *Yeats the Playwright* (1963); Richard Ellmann, *Yeats: The Man and the Masks* (1949) and *The Identity of Yeats* (1954); Norman Jeffares, *W. B. Yeats, Man and Poet* (1949); John Unterecker, *A Reader's Guide to W. B. Yeats* (1959); A. G. Stock, *W. B. Yeats, his Poetry and Thought* (1961); Denis Donoghue, *Yeats* (1971); Frank Tuohy, *Yeats* (1976).

534

YEVTUSHENKO, Yevgeny 1933–

Russian writer

Yevtushenko was born in Zima (literally 'Winter'), a remote settlement on the Trans-Siberian Railway, and brought up partly there, partly in Moscow. His surname is that of his mother's family, peasants who were originally exiled to Siberia from the Ukraine after an insurrection; his father by contrast was a Latvian and an intellectual. It would not be too fanciful to find these contrasts in his origins and upbringing reflected in a dichotomy in his personality between the simple and the sophisticated, in his work between the public and the private, the international and the provincially Russian.

He was a precocious versifier, publishing a volume as early as 1949 (*Prospectors of the Future*); *Third Snow* (1955) and particularly the long autobiographical poem *Stantsiya Zima* (trans. as *Zima Junction*, 1956) mark the maturing of his talent. His publications deflected him from his early intention of becoming a professional footballer, and he attended the Moscow Literary Institute (leaving without a diploma). Tremendous popular success began to come his way from the mid-1950s, the period of Soviet 'de-Stalinization'*: it is hard to say whether it was the more intimate aspect of his work, with its fresh spontaneity, or his public voice, touching on the traumas of politics and history (both his grandfathers had disappeared in the Great Terror), that stirred the greater resonances in his contemporaries. It soon became evident that Soviet officialdom had no consistent way of reacting to a loyal subject with a sharply questioning approach, an unquenchable inclination to expand the bounds of the permissible in literature and a wide popular reputation (from *c.* 1962 in the West as well). Khrushchev, while calling him 'ungovernable', evidently came to respect him: he has never been prevented from publishing, though sometimes hampered or censored, and has travelled insatiably.

What of the work itself? The image of the 'Soviet Angry Young Man' dies hard; it was never very appropriate, and by now would be ridiculous. What Yev-tushenko developed early and retains is a voice particularly his own: 'voice' is no mere metaphor, since his work is characteristically rhetorical (presupposing a listener, showing, persuading), and in fact gains much from oral delivery – witness the remarkable phenomenon of the mass poetry-readings of the early 1960s. His rhetoric is most successful not when gran-diloquent, rather (herein lies its originality) when 'con-versational', a confiding dialogue on neither too high-brow nor too simple a level. When his work is re-proached – not unreasonably – for looseness of texture or lack of intellectual polish we should remember that the features occasioning complaint are also integral to his particular talents. He is not naive, however: despite weak moments (usually in the longer poems) he shows a professional's mastery of verbal wit, rhyme, varied diction and dramatic construction.

Controversy has attended Yevtushenko to an extent surely unmatched by any poet of our lifetime. Despite, or because of, his popularity he has been subject to a battery of attacks – literary, moral, political, from a wide variety of standpoints – that vary from the reasoned, to the malicious, to the unanswerable. Through them he has steered a steady course: enjoying life, relishing fame but not being besotted by it, refusing to let anyone twist his arm too far. Though often represented, in the East as in the West, as feather-headedly changeable, he has been perfectly consistent in his stance of 'independently-minded loyalist' (con-demning, for example, the events of 1968 or the expul-sion of Solzhenitsyn* while refusing to become a 'dissident'). His work too has shown a consistency that makes some of it look more substantial and durable than the often fugitive occasions that sparked it off might have led one to suppose.

Yevtushenko and his close colleagues performed an important service when they restored to post-Stalin Russia a sense of artistic community and purpose, a renewed consciousness both of national cultural pride and of belonging to the whole community of modern nations. The movement in English poetry of the 1960s towards popular accessibility and oral effectiveness owes a large debt to him (*Babiy Yar* was *the* poem of the decade, if there was one). His open-heartedness, appreciativeness towards others' achievements, and lack of spite have set a worthwhile example (especially when combined with his sharp and wily intelligence). But above all he has given back respectability to the political dimension of poetry: not in the narrow sense (his humanitarian ethic hardly represents a political programme) but more fundamentally – in an aware-ness that a generation articulates its concerns through poetry, that literature stands at the crossroads of the public and the private.

Robin Milner-Gulland

Translations include: *Selected Poems*, trans. R. Milner-Gulland and P. Levi (1962); and *The Face behind the Face*, trans. A. Boyars and S. Franklin (1979). Yevtushenko's own *Precocious Autobiography* (1963, unpublished in USSR) gives a memorable account of his formative years. See also: Robin Milner-Gulland in *Soviet Leaders*, ed. G. W. Simmonds (1967); P. Blake, 'New Voices in Russian Writing', in *Encounter*, April 1963; and P. Johnson, *Khrushchev and the Arts* (1965).

Z

535
ZADKINE, Osip 1890–

Russian/US sculptor

A thoroughly international figure without strict allegiance to a particular school, Osip Zadkine has remained an active figurative sculptor, inventive and undoubtedly influential, grazing the confines of Cubism, Surrealism and other movements, an individual sculptor preoccupied with the expressive potential of the human figure.

Born at Smolensk in Russia, Zadkine had British relatives on his mother's side and left Russia as a boy to study in England, first at Sunderland (1905) and subsequently in London (1906–8). After his initial introduction to art he established himself in Paris with a studio in the block known as La Ruche (1910) where Chagall* arrived the same year, and which became the focus of a Russian-oriented circle of artists in Paris that maintained close contact with literary innovators, Apollinaire*, Max Jacob, Blaise Cendrars, as well as Picasso*, Delaunay and their Russian wives. By 1912 Zadkine was familiar to the group of sculptors associated with the emergence of Cubism, with Archipenko, Lipchitz and others, and something of their stylizations is evident in the early figures executed by Zadkine in the years in Paris before the outbreak of the First World War. Limbs are hollowed out; heads simplified and bearing an inscribed profile recall directly the conventions of contemporary Cubist painting and the adaptation of Cubist motifs currently undertaken by Laurens and Archipenko in particular. Other works, particularly from the immediately post-war period, echo the differentiated surfaces and rhythmically taut, simplified forms of Brancusi's* sculpture, in particular the series of busts of Mme Pogany.

By the time of the war, Zadkine had exhibited at the Salon des Indépendants and the Salon d'Automne in Paris and at the Neue Sezession in Berlin. His first one-man exhibition followed the war in 1919. Held in Paris it led to increasing recognition first of all in Paris in the early 1920s and subsequently outside France from 1924. Numerous public commissions followed, including a sculpture for Poissy Town Hall in 1932, and large retrospective exhibitions at Brussels (139 sculptures) in 1933 and Manchester in 1935.

Zadkine had been gassed in the First World War and had attempted in works which followed to imbue the dramatic and gestural qualities of his figures with a reflection of his experiences. The immovable placidity of Cubist figures gave way to an atmosphere of dreams and even of nightmares. Zadkine's awareness of the Parisian Surrealists served to emphasize this development. Certain figures have dramatic gestures and expressive silhouettes that recall the cut and welded sculptures of Gargallo and even Picasso. Zadkine's work increasingly took on classicizing references and made of anonymous figures allegories that displayed considerable power. Zadkine fled the Nazi invasion by emigrating to the United States from 1941 to 1945. His *Destroyed City*, erected in Rotterdam in 1953, represents the city re-emergent, an anguished and seemingly damaged figure full, none the less, of urgent vitality. For Zadkine sculpture was rhetorical and monumental, contrasting the anonymity of his figures with the vigour of their symbolism, their significance and even their popularity.

Many large retrospective exhibitions followed in post-war years and many commissions for monumental works, amongst which was the Van Gogh Memorial at Auvers-sur-Oise in 1961.

Dr John Milner

See: Raymond Cogniat, *Zadkine* (1958); Ionel Jianou, *Zadkine* (1964).

536
ZAMYATIN, Yevgeniy Ivanovich 1884–1937

Russian writer

Born into a middle-class background in Lebedyan', Tambov Province, Zamyatin attended the *gimnaziya* at Voronezh and then the Polytethnic Institute at St Petersburg, training as a naval architect. He graduated, despite imprisonment and exile for revolutionary activities on behalf of the Bolsheviks, travelled widely in connection with his work, and published his first short story in 1908. Best known of his early works was *A Provincial Tale* (*Uyezdnoye*, 1913). He continued his dual professions of naval engineering and literature up to 1931, with his mathematical training frequently influencing his literary work. In 1916–17 Zamyatin spent eighteen months in England, supervising the building of ice-breakers at Newcastle-upon-Tyne, and presenting a caustic picture of English life in his stories *The Islanders* (*Ostrovityane*, 1918, trans. 1978) and *A Fisher of Men* (*Lovets chelovekov*, 1922, trans. 1977). Returning to Russia just before the October Revolution, Zamyatin proceeded to question the direction of the revolution, and the future for literature under it, in a series of pungent stories and essays. His futuristic novel *We* (*My*, written 1920, published in English, New York 1924, and in Russian, New York 1952) was denounced as 'a malicious pamphlet on the Soviet government' and has never been published in the Soviet Union. Under increasing attack as an 'inner émigré', culminating in the 'Pil'nyak-Zamyatin affair' of 1929, Zamyatin requested of Stalin*, and was surprisingly granted, permission to emigrate. He settled in Paris in 1931 and died in poverty in 1937, leaving an unfinished novel on the Roman Empire and Attila the Hun, the subject of an earlier play.

We, Zamyatin's only completed novel, depicts an apparently unsuccessful uprising against a totalitarian, glass-enclosed city-state of the distant future. Built on extreme mathematical and collectivist principles, 'The Singe State', having reduced its populace to 'numbers', determines to eradicate all remaining individuality by imposing an operation of 'fantasiectomy', to remove the imagination. *We* is notable for its linguistic and stylistic innovation, combining grotesque and primitivist elements with striking systems of imagery, as well as being a statement of Zamyatin's main philosophical preoccupations: the role of the heretic in the progression of human affairs, the necessity for an endless series of revolutions to combat the stagnation and philistinism of each successive status quo, and the cosmic struggle between energy and entropy. Influenced in its anti-utopianism and promotion of the irrational by Dostoevsky (*The Devils* and *The Notes from Underground*), and in its depiction of the future by H. G. Wells*, *We* can be interpreted as: a prophetic warning against tyranny, a work of science fiction in advance of its time, and a penetrating study of alienation and schizophrenia. Its plot and futuristic detail have been assumed, probably erroneously, to have influenced Huxley's* *Brave New World* (1932), but had an acknowledged impact on Orwell's* *1984* (1949). Parallels can also be drawn with near-contemporary works by Karel Čapek*, and Georg Kaiser, and with Fritz Lang's* film *Metropolis*.

An experimental prose writer and originator of the literary style of 'neo-realism', seen as a dialectical synthesis of Symbolism and Naturalism, Zamyatin was a leading figure of Russian modernism and an important influence on the prose of the 1920s, yet is far better known today in the West than in the Soviet Union, where, unlike most of his disgraced contemporaries, he remains totally unpublished and rarely discussed.

Neil Cornwell

See: *A Soviet Heretic: Essays by Yevgeny Zamyatin* (1970); *The Dragon and Other Stories* (1975); *Mamay*, trans. Neil Cornwell, in *Stand*, vol. 17, no. 4, 1976. About Zamyatin: Alex M. Shane, *The Life and Works of Evgenij Zamjatin* (1968); Christopher Collins, *Evgenji Zamjatin, An Interpretative Study* (1973); E. J. Brown, '*Brave New World*', '*1984*' and '*We*': An Essay on Anti-Utopia (1976).

537
ZWEIG, Stefan 1881–1942

Austrian writer

One of the first writers to employ psychoanalytic concepts in literature, Zweig was born into an affluent upper-middle-class Austro-Jewish family of mill-owners. From an early age he showed intellectual precociousness but he was always introspective, fatalistic and without humour. He graduated from the Vienna *Gymnasium* into the University in 1899, but refused to apply himself as a protest against the narrow and rigid way of life in Austria. He sought 'Freedom' (his keyword) and found it in Berlin in 1901. His first collection of verse had been published in 1900 (*Silver Strings, Silberne Saiten*) and he was already sought after by editors of journals in Berlin and Vienna. Zweig went to Berlin University for a single term and spent most of his time there among the *Bierkeller* 'intellectuals'; it was here that he was overcome by hearing Dostoevsky read aloud for the first time. Although he loathed violence, Zweig was at one with the Russian's concern for human guilt and its expiation, for suffering and anguish of the soul. Zweig was beginning to live this (very Jewish) mental self-torture.

In his desire to improve his intellect so that he might meet and exchange views with the great writers and thinkers of the time, Zweig returned home and obtained his PhD in Vienna in 1904. He had already met the Belgian poet, Emile Verhaeren, whose influence for compassion Zweig eagerly absorbed; and he was already at work on translations of Verhaeren into German – work full of ambitious and idealistic plans for establishing human love and friendship in a pan-European community. Zweig became Verhaeren's disciple, and with his own money was able to travel from country to country as he wished. He met Romain Rolland*, Léon Bazalgette, Rainer Maria Rilke*, Auguste Rodin and (later) Sigmund Freud*. Until 1910, Zweig luxuriated in intellectual rapport with these men and found himself attached to most of them by an emotional longing. He was now fluent in four or five European languages, and Paris became his second home. His visit to India in 1910, to meet Tagore*, brought him into contact with real poverty, and disgusted, he returned hastily to Europe.

Zweig's biographies attracted great attention in these early days of psychoanalysis for, as Zweig once stated, 'My main interest in writing has always been the psychological representation of personalities and their lives.' His novel, *Beware of Pity* (1939), was a best seller and a film was made; but his female characters are especially untrue, for they are created and seen from a man's point of view. His 'critical biographies' also seemed authentic at the time, but they may now be considered less so, more likely symptomatic of Zweig's self-analysis. His biographical characters exhibit complexes and neuroses attuned to the 1920s and 1930s (to Zweig), rather than, for instance, to the times of Erasmus or Queen Elizabeth I or Balzac. Zweig thus discloses his personal fears and instabilities while clearly suffering with every one of his characters.

His association with a married woman, Friderike von Winternitz, had begun with her 'fan-letters' in 1901; and thereafter an extremely complex relationship fluctuated until her determination to possess him – out of sheer admiration – reached marriage in 1914. This somehow compensated for his divorce from all the friends whom the war now made his 'enemies'; but it seems unlikely that it was a complete marriage in the physical sense.

The First World War was a shattering experience for Zweig, who eschewed active service, and worked instead in the Press Bureau and Archives of the Army in Vienna. His assignment to a battle area in 1916 set him angrily against aggressors and war profiteers, and inspired the pacifist play *Jeremiah*, produced in Zürich in 1917. It is an expressionist work constructed in tableaux, with Jeremiah-Zweig welcoming defeat so as to purify the heart and soul, and inspire brotherhood among everybody.

After the war, Zweig, Friderike – and the two daughters by her first marriage – lived together in an isolated house on the Capuchin Mountain in Salzburg. Here he worked in comfort, indulged his passion for silence, order and sometimes succumbed to bursts of emotional imbalance when he was disturbed. He also added to and enjoyed his magnificent art treasures that included Beethoven memorabilia and one of the finest European collections of autographs. He regarded himself merely as caretaker for them all, not their owner. Zweig was a musical amateur and enjoyed the company of musicians who came to Salzburg: Toscanini, Bruno Walter, Ravel* and Bartók* especially.

With the emergence of Fascist dictators, Zweig's morbid fear for the future became more intense. He satisfied his frequent need for 'freedom' by escaping from Salzburg, and its female-orientated household, for the purpose of meetings with old and new personalities such as Gorky* in Russia in 1928. The introduction of a secretary into the Salzburg household set off an unforeseen chain of events: Charlotte (Lotte) Elisabeth Altmann was selected by Friderike. But gradually another involved, one-sided intellectual romance developed until Stefan's and Friderike's marriage was doomed. Zweig now saw Hitler's* persecution of the Jews as a measure instituted directly against himself, and became more and more introspective, often oblivious of the duel over him between the women in his house.

His happy collaboration with Richard Strauss* was cancelled out by the Nazi insult to both of them when it was proscribed because of Zweig's Jewish blood. In 1937 friends began publicly to ignore him, then his books were burned, his house was searched by the police and, in 1938, Austria collapsed before the Nazis. Zweig gave up the unequal struggle and escaped to London with Lotte whom he married at Bath in 1939. But Bath was still too near Hitler and again they fled – in 1941 – to Brazil. Although Zweig was as happy there as he could be anywhere, pessimism overcame reason and he committed suicide with the faithful Lotte at Petropolis in 1942.

The need for freedom, and pity for mankind, tortured Zweig to death. He had lived a comfortable life and escaped the terrible end accorded to others of his race; but the fact that such evil could triumph above the innate good levelled against it was more than he could bear.

Alan Jefferson

Translations of Zweig's work include: *Adepts in Self Portraiture* (*Drei Dichters Ihres Lebens*, 1928, trans. 1928); *Three Masters* (*Drei Meister* – Balzac, Dickens, Dostoevsky – 1920, trans. 1930); *Erasmus* (1934, trans. 1934); *Maria Stuart* (1935, trans. 1935); novels: *Letter from an Unknown Woman* (*Brief eine Unbekannten*, 1922, trans. 1933) and *Beware of Pity* (*Ungeduld des Herzens*, 1939, trans. 1939); autobiography: *The World of Yesterday* (*Die Welt von Gestern*, 1944, trans. 1945). See also: Elizabeth Allday, *Stefan Zweig* (1972).

DATE DUE

GAYLORD			PRINTED IN U.S.A.